International Business

We work with leading authors to develop the strongest educational materials in business, bringing cutting-edge thinking and best learning practice to a global market.

Under a range of well-known imprints, including Financial Times Prentice Hall, we craft high quality print and electronic publications which help readers to understand and apply their content, whether studying or at work.

To find out more about the complete range of our publishing please visit us on the World Wide Web at: www.pearsoneduc.com

International Business

THIRD EDITION

Alan M. Rugman
Indiana University and University of Oxford

Richard M. Hodgetts
Florida International University

An imprint of Pearson Education
Harlow, England • London • New York • Boston • San Francisco • Toronto • Sydney • Singapore • Hong Kong
Tokyo • Seoul • Taipei • New Delhi • Cape Town • Madrid • Mexico City • Amsterdam • Munich • Paris • Milan

Pearson Education Limited

Edinburgh Gate
Harlow
Essex CM20 2JE
England

and Associated Companies throughout the world

Visit us on the World Wide Web at:
www.pearsoneduc.com

First published by McGraw-Hill Inc. 1995
Third edition 2003

ISBN 0 273 67374 2

British Library Cataloguing-in-Publication Data
A catalogue record for this book is available from the British Library.

10 9 8 7 6 5 4 3 2 1
06 05 04 03

Typeset in 10.5/12.5pt Minion by 35
Printed and bound by Rotolito Lombarda, Italy

Contents in Brief

Contents

Chapter 5
International Culture 124

Chapter 6
International Trade 152

Chapter 7
International Finance 179

Chapter 10
Production Strategy 268

Chapter 11
Marketing Strategy 299

Chapter 12
Human Resource Management Strategy 327

Part Five
INTERNATIONAL BUSINESS FRAMEWORKS

List of Cases

Chapter 1

Chapter 2

Chapter 3

Chapter 4

Chapter 5

Chapter 6

Chapter 20

List of Figures and Maps

Figures

Maps

List of Tables

Prefaces

PREFACE TO THE THIRD EDITION

In this Third Edition we re-emphasize the theme of the "triad", i.e. the dominant economies today of the European Union (EU), the United States, and Japan. We have also retained our focus on the strategies of multinational enterprises (MNEs) either based in the triad, or seeking access to triad markets. The MNE is the unit of analysis in this book. The world's 500 largest MNEs continue to dominate international business, and over 430 of them come from the triad. The large MNEs also serve as "flagship firms", i.e. the leaders of localized regional business networks or clusters, in which other MNEs, small and medium-sized businesses, and service organizations also participate.

We emphasize the triad theme in three ways:

1. The data on trade-based international business activity, mainly in Chapters 1–3, have been rewritten and updated. Chapter 1 has been rewritten to explain the role of the triad in international business rather than the simplistic (and incorrect) discussion of "globalization" that pervades many other textbooks. The reality of international business is that MNEs do not have "global" strategies, but that they mainly operate at a "regional" level within and between triad members. It is also important to note that, today, firms and organizations outside the triad need to access at least one of the triad markets in order to build a successful business. We discuss both triad and non-triad MNEs in this book.
2. Of the 100 mini-cases in the book (five in each of the 20 chapters) we have introduced 40 brand new cases and totally revised the remaining 60. There is now a better balance between European, North American, and Asian cases. We concentrate on the strategies of the 500 larger MNEs from the triad, but also include a wealth of new cases from smaller and emerging economies, as discussed below.
3. We have introduced more theory especially in the last two parts of the book. This allows us to analyze more deeply the nature of triad/regional strategies of MNEs, rather than stop at the basic level of internationalization common in other books. In Chapters 1 and 15 we use the "diamond" and "double diamond" frameworks of international competitiveness. We use the global/local framework in Chapter 15 to show that many MNEs need a "local" rather than a "global" strategy. Now, in a rewritten Chapter 20, we analyze the strategy of MNEs, by using three frameworks. This allows us to revise and synthesize the major themes in the book. First is the firm-specific advantage (FSA) and country-specific advantage (CSA) framework to show how firm-level managerial resources are related to mostly exogenous country-specific factors. Second is the "flagship framework" to demonstrate the central role of large MNEs in business networks across the triad. Third is a framework to relate the trade and investment provisions of NAFTA and the FTAA to the deeper political and social integration of the EU.

Overall, the Third Edition has reduced the previous emphasis on US examples and practice in the First Edition in order to build up and consolidate the European and Asian examples and practice introduced in the Second Edition to an equal level.

The Third Edition also has a much greater focus on the emerging economies, China in particular, but also Russia and Poland. We also look at Latin American countries and MNEs, for example, in and from Brazil and Chile. In order to link the activities of MNEs in non-triad economies to the triad theme, we consider MNEs and international business opportunities in the larger non-triad economies. We include relevant cases like Codelco of Chile, Anglogold of South Africa, Brazilian television soaps, Citibank in China, etc. We retain our triad focus on Japan as the leading Asian economy but also consider South Korea, India, Australia, and others in some detail. We also introduce cases on major sports like cricket, which is a huge business in India, Pakistan, and Bangladesh. Indeed, we have added 10 new cases dealing with the service sector, several new cases dealing with the Internet and small business, and also new cases on "themes", especially those of concern to civil society.

Material on culture in Chapters 5, 13, and 14 has been rewritten to reduce the focus on Hofstede's work and to update it with newer approaches. In Chapter 10 on production, there is a greater emphasis on supply chain management and a new case to illustrate this. We have updated material on the WTO and NAFTA and included a discussion of the FTAA. We also explain the B2B (business-to-business) interaction across business networks (in cases like Accor, Nortel, and Michelin) and the role of the Internet (in cases like Amazon.com, CricInfo.com, Skandia, and Dell B2C) much more than in previous editions.

We have also introduced new cases dealing with issues of corporate social responsibility, the civil society and ethics, especially in Chapters 4, 5, 13, and 20. We explore the increased importance of non-governmental organizations (NGOs). In several of the cases we also explain several themes in new cases dealing with APEC, tax havens, global accounting standards, environmental policy, lumber tariffs, and the September 11, 2001 events. We discuss small and medium-sized businesses (SMEs) in more detail in cases like Command Alkon and Mountain Equipment.

Readers and instructors will find this a very student friendly Third Edition of an already popular textbook. It is suitable for community colleges, as well as college students in North America, and for undergraduates in Britain, Europe, and Asia. The upgraded new theoretical material in Parts IV and V now makes it more suitable for MBA students.

We are very grateful for helpful comments from reviewers of the entire manuscript of the Third Edition, namely: Professors Karl Moore of McGill University; Ajeet Mathur of University of Tampere, Finland; David Edelshain of City University Business School, London, and Sony Nwankwo of the University of East London. We would also like to thank those who provided guidance and help with comments on the Second Edition: Brad Brown of the University of Virginia, Hamed El-Said of Manchester University, Ander Hytter of Vaxjo University, Sweden, and Sandy Lindsay of Napier University. We are also very pleased to acknowledge the great dedication and ongoing help and support from Mildred Harris at the Kelley School of Business, Indiana University, and of Helen Rugman.

Over the period December, 2001–March, 2002, a major contribution to Chapters 10–20 was made by Ms Cecilia Brain of Toronto, a former research assistant on the Second Edition of the book who continued working with Professor Rugman as he moved from the University of Toronto to Templeton College, University of Oxford, and now to Indiana University. Cecilia also prepared the index and instructor's manual, and she worked on all of the new cases and all of the tables, bibliography, and other material in the text.

We are also grateful to the team at Pearson Education, Geraldine Lyons, Andrew Taylor, Bridget Allen, Sarah Phillipson, Richard Whitbread, and Simon Lake.

Alan M. Rugman, Indiana and Oxford
Richard Hodgetts, Miami

FROM THE PREFACE TO THE FIRST AND SECOND EDITIONS

Students of international business are fortunate enough to be living in a laboratory where the principles in this book can be used on a daily basis. Virtually every management decision being made today is influenced by global events, and naive thinking about international politics, economics, cultures, exchange rates and foreign competitors can have quick and adverse effects on a firm's bottom line. The objective of this introduction to international business is to provide relevant theoretical and practical insights to management students so that the real world of global business is better understood. We do this in three ways.

First, the text has an extremely strong emphasis on *relevance*. In each of the 20 chapters there are at least five "cases", so the book has a total of over 100 real-world examples of international business issues to provide insight and perspective.

Second, this text incorporates the latest *theoretical* advances in a manner easily comprehensible for university and college students, from BA to MBA level. For example, the text discusses such important material as Michael Porter's "diamond" theory of international competitiveness, the latest work on the theory of multinational enterprises and new research on organizational learning within corporations.

Third, and most important, the text integrates both the practical and theoretical issues through a sustained use of the concepts of *strategic management*. Indeed, this is the first text to have a strategic management focus in the teaching of introductory international business. This unique feature helps students choose from the extraordinarily broad menu of events in the international environment by building confidence in understanding which ones are useful for strategic management analysis at the firm level.

The three elements – relevance, strong theoretical foundation and strategic synthesis – reinforce each other and provide the student with the opportunity to gain deep and lasting insights into the management of international business. In short, this book paints a broad yet detailed picture on the canvas of the global practice of international business.

Listening to the market

Our vision of a practical, thematically integrated text built upon a solid theoretical foundation was further refined through an extensive market research effort. We queried the international business market in several important ways:

1. Hundreds of international business instructors participated in a detailed editorial survey during the formative stages of the project. Our survey revealed many important market trends, including some useful insights about international business professors. In recent years, the international business course has grown in popularity and is now often taught by professors with degrees in areas other than international economics or finance. At many universities, professors of management (especially business strategy and general management) are responsible for the course. We believe that our unique strategic management focus will appeal to traditional economics professors as well as management professors; indeed, international business now combines these approaches.

We also learned that numerous professors with "real-world" experience were finding that older text offerings do not "tell it like it is". In recent years there has been a dramatic increase in the number of international business professors who travel to international meetings and engage in joint international research and dialogue with colleagues from other countries. This book, with its macro-oriented approach, will appeal to this market niche.

2. Our manuscript for the First Edition was subject to a rigorous editorial review process at key stages in its development. We are grateful for the incisive comments and critical suggestions by our colleagues in the profession. In particular, we appreciated assistance from:

   Bharat B. Bhalla, Fairfield University
   Gary N. Dicer, University of Tennessee – Knoxville
   Prem Gandhi, State University of New York – Plattsburgh
   J. Leslie Jankovich, San Jose State University
   Robert A. Kemp, Drake University
   Rose Knotts, University of North Texas
   Michael Kublin, University of New Haven
   Stephen Luxmore, St John Fisher College
   John L. Lyons, Pace University
   David L. Mathison, Loyola Marymount University
   Stanley D. Nollen, Georgetown University
   Moonsong David Oh, California State University – Los Angeles
   Lee E. Preston, University of Maryland
   John Stanbury, Indiana University – Kokomo
   Robert Vichas, Florida Atlantic University

Acknowledgments for the First Edition

The high quality of this book was greatly enhanced by the dedicated secretarial assistance of Amy Ho at the Faculty of Management, University of Toronto. In addition, invaluable research assistance was provided by Samuel He, Bill Mohri, and Bill Gottlieb. Useful comments have been received from Michael Gestrin, Andrew Anderson, Michael Scott and others associated with the Center for International Business at the University of Toronto.

While Professor Rugman served as the Ross Distinguished Visiting Professor of Canada–US Economic and Business Relations at Western Washington University, he received valuable secretarial assistance from Ms Kathleen Finn and useful comments from members of the faculty, especially Robert Spich.

Professor Hodgetts is grateful for the suggestions and continued assistance from Fred Luthans; George Holmes, Professor of Management, University of Nebraska, Lincoln; Gary Dessler and Constance Bates, Management and International Business Department, Florida International University; Jane Gibson, Nova Southeastern University; and Regina Greenwood, Kettering University.

Acknowledgments for the Second Edition

Invaluable research assistance has been provided by Cecilia Brain of the Rotman School of Management, University of Toronto, especially over the three summers of 1997–1999 period when the tables, cases and Instructor's Manual were revised and updated. At Templeton College, University of Oxford, exceptional support has been provided by Denise Edwards.

We are pleased to have worked with members of the Pearson Education team in London, from Publisher Jane Powell to Commissioning Editor Sadie McClelland to Editors Nikki Bowen and Claire Brewer.

DISTINCTIVE FEATURES OF THE THIRD EDITION

This Third Edition of what is now a well-established international business text maintains its unique strategic focus and the use of the triad (North America/European Union/Japan) as a framework within which international business is explored. There is an emphasis on the economic environment facing business and the strategies of multinationals. The real strength of this book lies in its relevance, secured by the use of 100 cases, most of which have been fully revised or replaced. The cases offer a balanced coverage of each of the triad regions. All data have been revised to be fully up to date. Each chapter retains a common pedagogy, which includes Objectives, Active Learning Cases, International Business Strategy in Action, Key Points, Key Terms, Review and Discussion Questions, and Real Cases.

The relevance of the book has been enhanced by the inclusion of 40 brand new cases out of the 100 which form the bedrock of the book. The other 60 cases have been updated and expanded. A list of 100 cases appears after the full Contents list above.

These 100 real-world case examples of actual multinational businesses and their operations and strategies offer balanced coverage of the "triad" regions of North America, Europe, and Japan. This is the only major international business textbook to go beyond an "American" or alternatively "European" perspective, and offer equal treatment of all parts of the triad.

Features of the Third Edition

- Unique triad framework means that each region is given balanced coverage.
- Strategic management approach to international business topics.
- Fully updated tables and figures.
- Forty new cases and the other 60 expanded and updated.
- Updated material and new frameworks to analyze the World Trade Organization, Free Trade Agreement of the Americas, APEC, and other international institutions.
- New material on dot.coms, small business, supply chain management, B2B, ethics, and NGOs etc.
- New and updated material on environmental regulations and corporate "green" strategies.
- Websites of all MNEs and international organizations, which have been added to all the case discussions.
- Expanded coverage of China, Brazil, Chile, Africa, emerging economies, and Asian nations.
- New theoretical material on the firm-specific advantages and country-specific advantages approach.

An instructor's manual is available, which is the best in the field, with over 100 multiple choice questions for each of the 20 chapters, and with extra test banks. In addition to the unique "triad" approach, there are five distinctive features, in particular, that make this book different from competing textbooks.

First, the book examines international business with an integrative framework, using the strategic management viewpoint. The strategic management approach gives the text the integrative theme of "how to manage an international business" and ties the chapters together into a relevant framework.

Second, many of the excessively technical or mechanistic concepts found in other international business textbooks are de-emphasized. For example, we select relevant aspects of foreign exchange rate management, but we leave technical issues, such as the details of "currency swapping" for the purpose of financing international transactions, to a specialized course in international finance. Similarly, absolute and comparative advantage are covered, but these are examined in terms of their relevance to managers of multinationals in formulating and implementing strategy. We have one chapter on international economics, not an entire course. In short, the technical concepts that business majors are learning in their discipline courses are not reinvented in this book; instead, we select analysis that is of relevance to international business students.

Third, each chapter has an opening Active Learning Case that is revisited throughout the chapter. The purpose of this "real life" case is to illustrate how the chapter material is used by multinational enterprises in implementing their strategies. The case also breaks the chapter into subparts and helps to reinforce student learning.

Fourth, there are two Real Cases at the end of each chapter. These cases are drawn from recent newspaper and journal sources and provide the student with an opportunity to apply the chapter concepts to real-world situations. The cases also offer additional information on subjects covered in the chapter.

Fifth, throughout each chapter there are two International Business Strategy in Action boxes. These are drawn from the current literature and provide specific strategy applications of the material being discussed.

Learning Resources

An extensive range of supplementary resources accompany the text to aid student learning and facilitate and enhance teaching. This includes:

For lecturers:

- **Instructor's My Companion Website** provides password-protected electronic versions of the Instructor's Manual and PowerPoint slides as well as a **Syllabus Manager and Testbank of questions.** Available to adopters of the text at ***www.booksites.net/rugman***. Please contact your local sales representative for a password.
- **Instructor's Resource Manual.** This helpful teaching resource (available on-line and in printed format), updated and revised by Cecilia Brain of Toronto University, contains:
  - Chapter objectives, summaries and outlines
  - Suggested class schedules and assignments
  - Answers to review and discussion questions
  - Answers to cases
- **Powerpoint slides.** Full-colour slides including figures, tables and essential elements of the text.
- **Testbank of (approximately) 2000 questions (password protected on-line).**

For students:

- Links to valuable resources on the web
- Interactive multiple-choice questions to help students check understanding and build confidence
- Learning objectives to guide students through the course

Available at ***www.booksites.net/rugman***

For lecturers *and* students:

- Internet learning interactivities entertainingly and informatively challenge and drive home key IB issues
- Video clips to illustrate and extend core IB issues and stimulate discussion

Available at ***www.booksites.net/rugman*** and on:

Student resource CD-ROM

- Contains IB video clips and entertaining, informative and challenging interactivities.
- Further relevant IB hotlinks to topical websites.

A My Companion Website accompanies *International Business* by Rugman and Hodgetts

Visit the ***International Business*** **myPHLIP** Website at ***www.booksites.net/rugman*** to find valuable and customisable teaching and learning material including:

For students

- Internet interactivities that entertainingly and informatively challenge you and drive home key IB issues
- Video clips to illustrate and extend core IB issues and stimulate discussion
- Study material designed to help you improve your results
- Links to valuable resources on the web
- Multiple Choice Questions to help you check your understanding and build confidence
- Search for specific information on the site
- Learning objectives to guide you through your course

For lecturers

- A secure, password protected site with teaching material
- Links to articles and resources on the web
- A syllabus manager that will build and host a course web page
- An electronic, downloadable version of the Instructor's Manual (updated and revised by Ms Cecilia Brain, University of Toronto) including:
  - Chapter objectives, summaries and outlines
  - Suggested class schedules and assignments
  - Answers to review and discussion questions
  - Answers to cases
- Internet interactivities entertainingly and informatively challenge the student and drive home key IB issues
- Video clips to illustrate and extend core IB issues and stimulate discussion (both clips and interactivities created by *Option 6, Inc*. and Professor Roberto Garcia, Indiana University)
- Powerpoint slides of key figures and topics within the text
- The My Companion Website syllabus manager allowing you to create a dynamic, personalised and integrated syllabus online
- Testbank of questions (password protected)

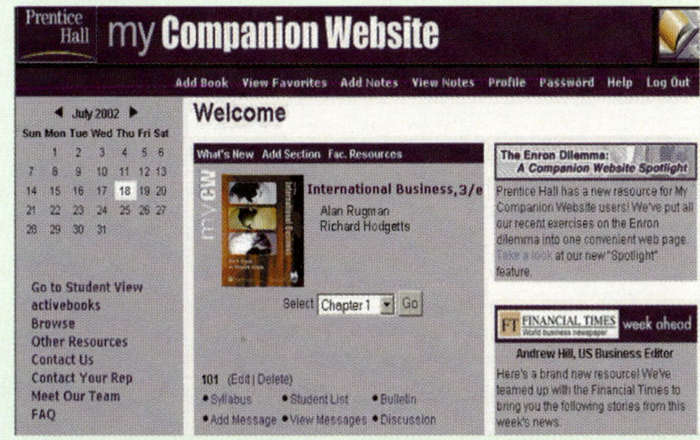

GUIDED TOUR OF THE BOOK

Active Learning case

A real life case that is revisited throughout the chapter to illustrate how the chapter relates to multinational enterprise strategy and activity. It provides a framework of learning for the chapter and comes with thought-provoking questions and weblinks. Answers to the questions appear throughout the chapter in the Active Learning Checks.

Chapter objectives

Outline the core content of the chapter and explain how the chapter fits into the larger structure of the book. A mini-contents list aids navigation throughout the chapter.

Margin notes

Provide easy to understand definitions of key terms highlighted within the text.

International Business Strategy in Action

Drawn from current literature and provide strategy applications for the material under discussion.

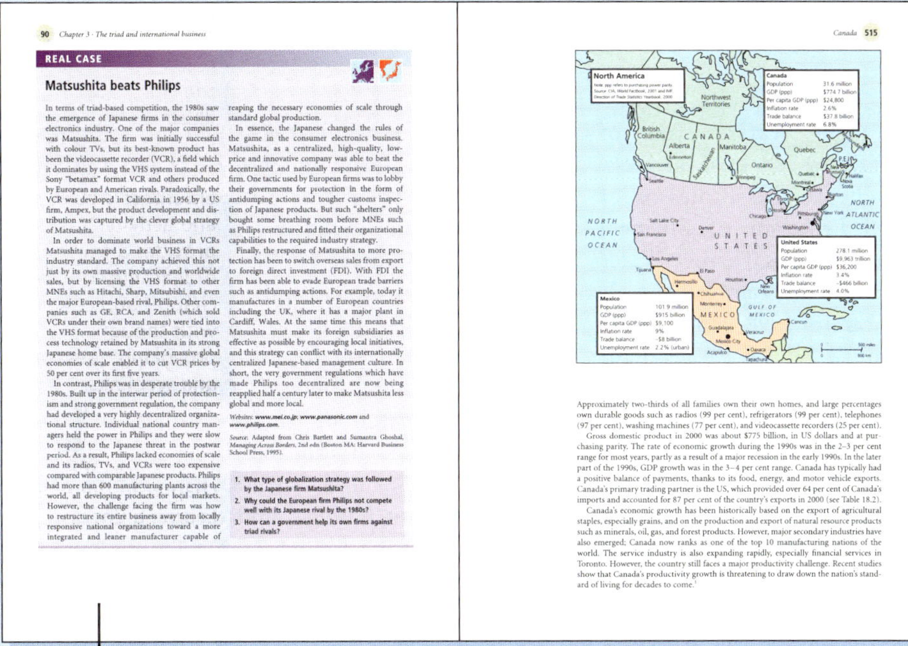

Real cases

Drawn from recent newspaper and journal sources and allow the student to apply the chapter concepts to real-world situations.

Active learning check

Provides answers to the Active Learning case questions throughout the chapter.

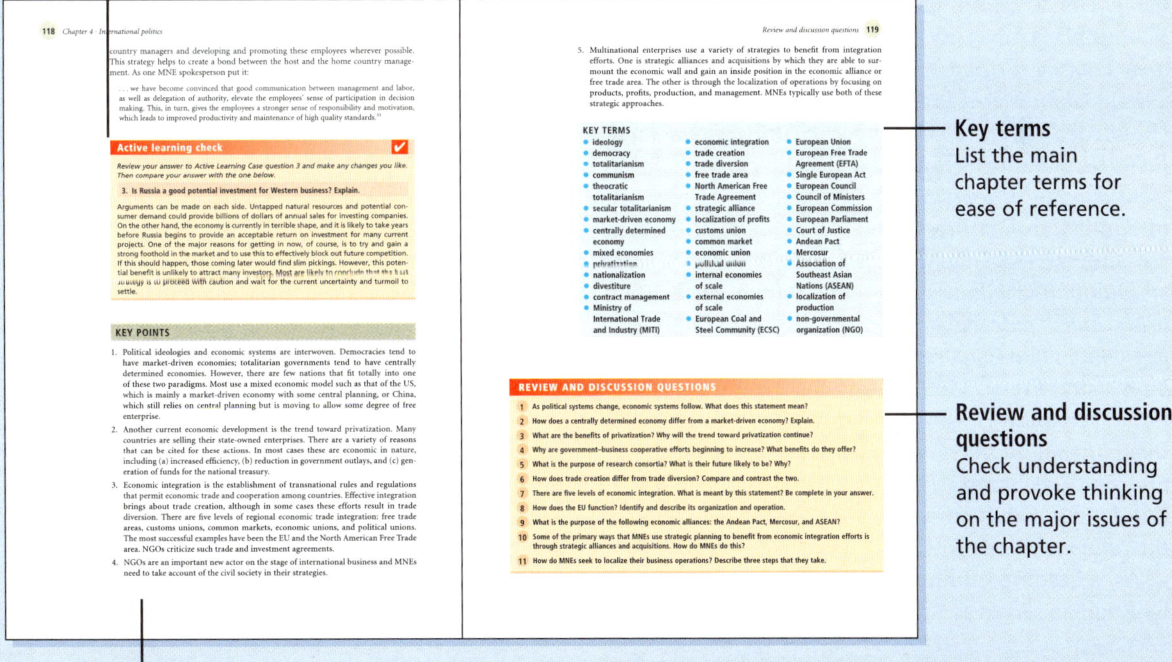

Key terms

List the main chapter terms for ease of reference.

Review and discussion questions

Check understanding and provoke thinking on the major issues of the chapter.

Keypoints

Revisit the main issues covered in the chapter.

About the Authors

Alan M. Rugman is L. Leslie Waters Chair of International Business at the Kelley School of Business, Indiana University, where he is also Professor of International Business and Professor of Business Economics and Public Policy. He was Thames Water Fellow in Strategic Management at Templeton College, University of Oxford, from 1998–2001, where he remains a Fellow. Previously he was Professor of International Business at the University of Toronto 1987–1998, Dalhousie University 1979–1987, and the University of Winnipeg 1970–1978. He has also been a visiting professor at Columbia Business School, London Business School, Harvard University, UCLA, MIT, Warwick Business School, and the University of Paris-La Sorbonne.

Dr Rugman has published over 200 articles dealing with the economic, managerial, and strategic aspects of multinational enterprises and with trade and investment policy. These have appeared in such leading refereed journals as: *American Economic Review, Strategic Management Journal, Journal of International Business Studies, California Management Review* and *The World Economy*. His 30 books include: *Inside the Multinationals* (Columbia University Press, 1981); *Multinationals and Transfer Pricing* (co-author) (St Martin's Press, 1985); *Administered Protection in America* (co-author) (Routledge 1987); *Global Corporate Strategy and Trade Policy* (co-author) (Routledge 1990); *Foreign Investment and North American Free Trade* (ed.) (University of South Carolina Press, 1994); *International Business* (co-author) (McGraw-Hill 1985, 1995); *The Theory of Multinational Enterprises* and *Multinational Enterprises and Trade Policy* (Elgar, 1996); *Environmental Regulations and Corporate Strategy* (co-author) (Oxford University Press, 1999); *Multinationals as Flagship Firms* (co-author) (Oxford University Press, 2000); *International Business* (FT/Prentice Hall, 2000); *The End of Globalization* (Random House, 2000; AMACOM, 2001); and (co-editor) *The Oxford Handbook of International Business* (Oxford University Press, 2001).

As a leading authority in international business, Dr Rugman served as Vice-President of the Academy of International Business in 1989–1990 and was elected a Fellow of the Academy in 1991. He is also a Fellow of the Royal Society of Arts, elected 1998. He has been identified as one of the five most cited scholars in International Business. He has lectured widely across North and South America, the Caribbean, in Western Europe, Australia, and in East Asia.

He has written for the *Financial Times*, Toronto's *Globe and Mail* and *Financial Post*, and many magazines. His research on multinationals, free trade, NAFTA, and globalization has been discussed in the *New York Times, Business Week, US News and World Report, Canadian Business*, and on the television and radio outlets of the BBC, CBC, and numerous other media. He is a member of the TIME Canada Board of Economists.

Born in England in 1945, Dr Rugman became a Canadian citizen in 1973. He earned his BA in economics from Leeds University in 1966, MSc in economic development from London University's School of Oriental and African Studies (SOAS) in 1967, and his PhD in economics from Simon Fraser University in 1974. He was elected to an MA (Oxon) in 1998.

Dr Rugman served as an outside advisor on international competitiveness to two Canadian Prime Ministers over the 1986–1993 period. He was the only academic member of Canada's business International Trade Advisory Committee from 1986–1988 while the United States–Canada Free Trade Agreement was being negotiated. Subsequently he served on the sectoral trade advisory committee for forest products from 1989 to 1993, as NAFTA was negotiated. He has been a consultant to major private sector companies, research institutes and government agencies. These include Exxon/Imperial Oil, Kodak, Royal Bank of Canada, Northern Telecom, and other multinational enterprises. He has also been a consultant to international organizations such as the United Nations (UNCTAD), NAFTA's Commission on Environmental Cooperation, the Organization for Economic Cooperation and Development (OECD), and the Commonwealth Secretariat.

In Memoriam: Richard D. Hodgetts

Richard Hodgetts passed away in November 2001, having battled cancer for several years. Richard worked on the revisions in the period of July–October, 2001. He was as enthusiastic, involved and dedicated as ever to producing clearly written text that is relevant and readable for management students. Richard would have been pleased with the final book.

Alan M. Rugman, Indiana University, March 2002

Richard M. Hodgetts was a Professor of Management in the Department of Management and International Business at Florida International University (FIU). He was born and raised in New York City and earned his BS in management at New York University in 1963, his MBA at Indiana University in 1964, and his PhD at the University of Oklahoma in 1968. He then joined the faculty at the University of Nebraska, Lincoln (1966–1975), where he taught strategic management. After accepting a visiting professorship at Texas Tech University (1975–1976), he joined Florida International University (FIU) in 1976 where he taught international business in both the Executive MBA program and the Graduate Diploma Series program and the strategic management course at the MBA level.

Dr Hodgetts published over 125 articles and research papers in a wide variety of areas including international strategy, international compensation, the development of metrics for world class organizations, and the role of quality in creating sustainable advantage in the 21st century. He was the author or co-author of 50 different books including *International Management*, 5th edition (Irwin/McGraw, forthcoming), which is the best selling international management textbook in the world; *Entrepreneurship*, 4th edition (Dryden, 1999), which is the leading entrepreneurship book in the US market; and a series of quality-focused management books including *Measures of Quality and High Performance: Simple Tools and Lessons from America's Most Successful Firms* (Amacom, 1998). Overall, Richard Hodgetts sold 1 million copies of his textbooks.

Professor Hodgetts also served as a trainer and consultant for a wide variety of organizations and firms including Advanced Micro Systems, AT&T Technologies, Digital Equipment, Eastman Kodak, General Electric, General Motors, Hewlett-Packard, Motorola, Procter & Gamble, Wal-Mart, and the US Federal Reserve System.

Dr Hodgetts was the editor of the *Journal of Leadership Studies* and the book review editor for *Organizational Dynamics*. He was also a member of the review boards of the *Journal of Economics and Business* and the *Journal of Business Research*. Dr Hodgetts wrote a biweekly column titled "Minding Your Business" for the *Ft. Lauderdale Sun Sentinel*. He was also a past member of the Academy of Management Board of Governors (1993–1996) and a member of the Fellows of the Academy since 1983.

In recent years Professor Hodgetts was the recipient of a number of awards including the Outstanding Educator Award, Academy of Management (1999), the John F. Mee, Management Contribution Award, Management History Division, Academy of Management (1998), and the Professorial Excellence Program Award, FIU (1997).

Acknowledgments

We are grateful to the following for permission to reproduce copyright material:

Figures 1.1, 15.1 and 15.2 adapted from *The Competitive Advantage of Nations*, The Free Press, an imprint of Simon & Schuster Adult Publishing Group (Porter, M. E. 1990); Tables 1.1, Appendix 1A, Appendix 1B, Appendix 1D and Figure 3.2 adapted from *Direction of Trade Statistics Yearbook, 2001*, International Monetary Fund (IMF, 2001); Tables 1X, 1XX, 2.1, 2.3, Appendix 2A, Appendix 2B, Appendix 2C, Appendix 2D, Appendix 2E, 9X, 16X, 17.2 and 19X adapted from Fortune, *The Fortune Global 500*, 2001, by permission of Fortune; Tables Appendix 1E, Appendix 1F, 3.1 and 3.2 adapted from *World Investment Report, 2000*, United Nations (United Nations Conference on Trade and Development 2000); Chapter 3 Table from Lagging in Quality in *Wall Street Journal*, 25 May 2001, reproduced with permission of Dow Jones & Co, Inc. via Copyright Clearance Center; Figure 3.1 from *International Direct Investment Statistics Yearbook*, OECD (OECD 1999); Figure 3.3 from *The Quest for Global Dominance*, used by permission of Jossey-Bass, Inc., a subsidiary of John Wiley & Sons, Inc. (Govindarajan, V. and Gupta, A. K. 2001); Tables 3.3 and 16.6, Figure 17.1, Tables 17.4, 17.5 and 18.3 adapted from *Direction Trade Statistics Yearbook, 1996* and *Direction of Trade Statistics Yearbook, 2001*, International Monetary Fund (IMF 1996, 2001); Table 3.4 from *USA Today*, 10 June 1998, by permission of USA Today; Figure 5.1 from "Clustering Countries on Attitudinal Dimensions: A Review and Synthesis" in *Academy of Management Journal*, September, reproduced with permission of Academy of Management via Copyright Clearance Center (Ronen, S. and Shenkar, O. 1985); Table 5.1 adapted from *Ethnologue Languages of the World, 13th Edition*, published and reprinted by permission of SIL International (Grimes, B. F. ed. 1996); Table 5.2 adapted from "Organizational Development and National Culture: Where's the Fit?" in *Academy of Management Review*, January, reproduced with permission of Academy of Management via Copyright Clearance Center (Jaeger, A. M. 1986); Table 5.3 from "The Cultural Relativity of Organizational Practices and Theories" in *Journal of International Business Studies*, Fall, Journal of International Business Studies (Hofstede, G. 1983); Table 5.4 adapted from "Employee Work Attitudes and Management Practice in the United States and Japan: Evidence from a Large Comparative Survey" in *California Management Review*, Vol. 25, No. 1, Fall, by permission of The Regents of the University of California (Lincoln, J. R. 1989); Table 6.1 adapted from http://www.opec.org, by permission of OPEC; Figure 8.1 from *Competitive Strategy*, The Free Press, an imprint of Simon & Schuster Adult Publishing Group (Porter, M. E. 1980); Table 8.1 adapted from "Strategic Planning for a Global Business" in *Columbia Journal of World Business*, Summer, Elsevier Science (Chakravarthy, B. S. and Perlmutter, H. V. 1985); Table 8.2 adapted from *International Dimensions of Management, 2nd Edition*, pub PWS Kent Publishing, reproduced by permission of South-Western College Publishing a division of Thomson Learning (Phatak, A. V. 1989); Figure 8.3 from *Competitive Advantage*, The Free Press, an imprint of Simon & Schuster Adult Publishing Group (Porter, M. E. 1985); Figure 8.5 adapted from *Competitive Advantage*, The Free Press, an imprint of Simon & Schuster Adult Publishing Group (Porter, M. E. 1985); Figure 9.9 from *Matrix Organizations of Complex Businesses*, The Conference Board (Janger, A. R. 1979); Figure 9.10 from "The Multinational Corporation as an Interorganizational Network" in *Academy of Management Review*, October, reproduced with permission of Academy of Management via Copyright Clearance Center (Ghoshal, S. and Bartlett, C. A. 1990); Figure 9.11 adapted from *Comparative and Multinational Management*, John Wiley & Sons, Inc. (Ronen, S. 1986); Figure 10.1 and Table 10.2 from "The New Competitors: They Think in Terms of 'Speed-to-Market'" in *Academy of Management Executive*, May, reproduced with permission of Academy of Management via Copyright Clearance Center (Vesey, J. T. 1991); Table 10.1 adapted from "What America Makes Best" in *Fortune*, Special Issue, Spring/Summer 1991, by permission of Fortune; Figure 10.2 from "Computers and the Coming of the US Keiretsu" in *Harvard Business Review*, July–August, Harvard Business School Publishing Corporation (Ferguson, C. H. 1990); Figure 10.3 from "Japan's Smart Secret Weapon" in *Fortune*, 12 August, by permission of Fortune (Worthy, F. S. 1991); Table 10.3 adapted from "Why Japan Keeps on

Winning" in *Fortune*, 15 July 1991, by permission of Fortune; Chapter 12 Table adapted from "What is a CEO worth?" in *The New York Times*, 17 January 1999, by permission of The New York Times; Figure 12.1 from "Who Manages Multinational Enterprises?" in *Columbia Journal of World Business*, Summer, Elsevier Science (Franko, L. G. 1973); Table 12.1 from "Expatriate Incentives: Beyond Tradition" in *HRfocus*, March, The Institute of Management and Administration (Latta, G. W. 1998); Figure 12.2 from "Compensation of Overseas Personnel" in *Handbook of Human Resource Administration, 2nd Edition*, edited by J. J. Famularo, The McGraw-Hill Companies (Reynolds, C. 1986); Table 12.2 adapted from "The Culture Assimilator: An Approach to Cross-Cultural Training" in *Journal of Applied Psychology*, April, the American Psychological Association and Fred E. Fiedler (Fiedler, F. E., Mitchell, T. and Triandis, H. C. 1971); Table 12.3 adapted from "Cost of Living Index" in *The Economist*, The Economist Newspaper Ltd, London, 7 July 2001; Table 12.4 adapted from "Competition and Change: Mapping the Indiana HRM Recipe Against World-Wide Patterns" in *Journal of World Business*, Vol. 32, No. 3, Elsevier Science (Sparrow, P. R. et al. 1997); Table 13.3 adapted from "Country Risk Ratings" in *Management International Review*, Vol. 26, No. 4, Management International Review (Dichtl, E. and Koeglmayr, H. G. 1986); Table 13.4 adapted from "The Influence of Culture on the Process of Business Negotiations: An Exploratory Study" in *Journal of International Business Studies*, Spring, Journal of International Business Studies (Graham, J. L. 1985); Chapter 14 Table "The Hamburger Standard" from *The Economist*, 3 April 1999, © The Economist Newspaper Ltd, London 3.4.99; Table 15.1 and Figure 17.4 adapted from *International Direct Investment Statistics Yearbook, 2000*, OECD (OECD 2000); Table 15.2 from *United States Countervailing and Antidumping Cases Initiated, 1980–2000*, by permission of US Department of Commerce, International Trade Administration; Figure 15.4 adapted from "The 'Double Diamond' Model of International Competitiveness: The Canadian Experience" in *Management International Review*, Vol. 33, Special Issue No. 2, Management International Review (Rugman, A. M. and D'Cruz, J. R. 1993); Figure 15.5 adapted from *Direction of Trade Statistics Yearbook, 2001*, International Monetary Fund (IMF 2001), *World Development Report, 2000* and *World Development Report, 2001*, The World Bank (World Bank 2000, 2001); Figure 15.6 from "Porter's Diamond Framework in a Mexican Context" in *Management International Review*, Vol. 33, Special Issue No. 2, Management International Review (Hodgetts, R. M. 1993); Figure 15.7 adapted from "Building and Managing the Transnational: the New Organizational Challenge" in *Competition in Global Industries*, edited by M. E. Porter, Harvard Business School Publishing (Bartlett, C. A. 1986) and *Managing Across Borders: The Transnational Solution, 2nd Edition*, Harvard Business School Publishing (Bartlett, C. A. and Ghoshal, S. 1988); Figure 16.2 from "Europe 1992 and Competitive Strategies for North American Firms", reprinted with permission from *Business Horzions* November/December 1991, Copyright 1991 by the Trustees at Indiana University, Kelley School of Business (Rugman, A. M. and Verbeke, A. 1991); Table 16.3 adapted from *The World Competitiveness Report 1989*, IMD, (IMD and World Economic Forum 1989) and *The World Competitiveness Yearbook 2001*, IMD, Switzerland, www.imd.ch (IMD 2001); Table 16.7 from *Nineteenth Annual Report from the Commission to the European Parliament on the Communities Anti-Dumping and Anti-Subsidy Activities (COM(01) 571)*, Office for Official Publications of the European Communities (Commission of the European Communities 2000); Tables 18.1 and 18.2 adapted from *Direction of Trade Statistics Yearbook, 1996* and *Direction of Trade Statistics Yearbook, 2000*, International Monetary Fund (IMF 1996, 2000); Tables 19.2 and 19.3 from Foreign Investment Committee, 31 October 2001, by permission of Foreign Investment Committee, Chile, www.foreigninvestment.cl; Table 19.4 from http://bcb.gov.br, by permission of Banco Central do Brasil; Figures 20.3 and 20.4 adapted from *Multinationals as Flagship Firms: Regional Business Networks*, Oxford University Press (D'Cruz, J. R. and Rugman, A. M. 2000).

Maps: Map 1 adapted from *Direction of Trade Statistics Yearbook, 2001*, International Monetary Fund (IMF 2001); Map 3 adapted from Fortune, *The Fortune Global 500, 2001*, by permission of Fortune; Map 6 adapted from *The Europa World Year Book, 2002*, by permission of Europa Publications, www.europapublications.com; Map 7 adapted from *Labor Force Survey*, 19 September 2001, by permission of Statistics Bureau, Ministry of Public Management, Home Affairs, Posts and Telecommunications, Japan; Map 8 adapted from *Direction of Trade Statistics Yearbook, 2000*, International Monetary Fund (IMF 2000).

Text extracts: "Common barriers for inward foreign direct investment in Japan" box in Chapter 17's "International Business Strategy in Action: Japan and foreign direct investment" from JETRO, *The Survey on Actual Conditions Regarding Access to Japan: Inward Foreign Direct Investment*, 2000.

We are grateful to the Financial Times Limited for permission to reprint the following material:

Table 7.5 Exchange Rates and the Euro, FT.com, © *Financial Times*, 1 October 2001; Table 7.6 Exchange Rates and the Euro, FT.com, © *Financial Times*, 1 October and 2 October 2001; Table 12.X World's Largest Executive Search Agencies, FT.com, © *Financial Times*, 14 May 2001; Table YY World's Largest Executive Search Agencies, 2000, © *Financial Times*, 29 November, 2001; Japanese Car Plants Top Productivity Table, © *Financial Times*, 8 July 2002; Table 20.X Survey of the World's Most Respected Companies, © *Financial Times*, 17 December 2000.

Appendix 19A The 25 Largest Latin American MNEs, 2000, © *Financial Times*, 2001; Appendix 19B The 25 Largest Asia-Pacific MNEs, 2000, © *Financial Times*, 2001; Appendix 19C The Top 25 Largest Eastern European Companies, 2000, © *Financial Times*, 2001; Appendix 19D adapted from The Top 100 Latin American Companies, 2001, © *Financial Times*, 2001; Appendix 19E adapted from The Top 100 Asia-Pacific Companies, 2001, © *Financial Times*, 2001; Appendix 19F adapted from The Top 100 Eastern European Companies, 2001, © *Financial Times*, 2001; Appendix 19G adapted from The Top 100 Middle Eastern Companies, 2001, © *Financial Times*, 2001.

Coke Bottler Boosts East European Presence with Purchase from Parent, © *Financial Times*, 28/29 July 2001, p. 24; Back to Classic Coke, © *Financial Times*, 27 March 2000, p. 20; Survey of the World's Most Respected Companies, © *Financial Times*, 17 December 2001.

In some instances we have been unable to trace the owners of copyright material, and we would appreciate any information that would enable us to do so.

PART ONE

The World of International Business

Chapter 1

Regional and Global Strategy

CONTENTS

OBJECTIVES OF THE CHAPTER

Already in the 21st century we are seeing dramatic developments that are having a profound effect on international business. The political and economic changes that are sweeping China and Russia, for example, are creating new opportunities for multinational firms. At the same time, however, some of the world's economies are slowing down. US growth is currently less than 2 per cent and France, Germany, Italy, Japan, and the UK – the other major economic powers – are doing even more poorly. So while the world of international business offers many opportunities, it also presents challenges and risks. As a result, multinational enterprises must carefully plan and execute their strategies if they hope to succeed.

In this chapter we are going to look at some of the challenges of conducting international business in the 21st century. We will begin by examining trade and foreign direct investment, as well as the emergence of the triad economic blocs of North America, the European Union (EU), and Japan. We will then examine some of the worldwide economic and political changes that are taking place and look at how technology is altering the way international business is conducted. We will also study some of the approaches being used by multinational enterprises both to establish and to maintain their competitive advantage. In the last part of the chapter, the model that we are going to use in our study of international business will be presented.

The specific objectives of this chapter are to:

1. *Define* the terms *international business* and *multinational enterprise.*
2. *Discuss* the two primary ways in which international business occurs: trade and foreign direct investment.
3. *Examine* the impact of the triad on international trade and investment.
4. *Describe* the current state of world economies and the role of government and trade regulations in the conduct of international business.
5. *Discuss* the importance of technology and the role of small and medium-sized enterprises in the international business arena.
6. *Examine* how multinational enterprises use triad/regional strategies to compete effectively in the international marketplace.
7. *Discuss* the determinants of national competitive advantage.
8. *Present* the model that will be used in this text for studying international business.

ACTIVE LEARNING CASE

The Coca-Cola Company goes worldwide with a local strategy

Coca-Cola is the largest selling soft drink in the world, but sales vary by nation. For example, Americans consume almost 30 gallons of Coke annually, in contrast to Europeans who drink less than half this amount and in some countries, such as France, Italy, and Portugal, the average is in the range of 10 gallons. In an effort to increase its European sales, The Coca-Cola Company has been taking a number of steps.

One of these has been to replace local franchisers who have become too complacent with more active, market-driven sellers. In France, for example, Pernod, a Coca-Cola franchisee, was forced to sell some of its operations back to The Coca-Cola Company which, in turn, appointed a new marketing manager for the country. In addition, Coke's price was lowered and advertising was sharply increased. As a result, per capita consumption in France has been going up.

In England, Beecham and Grand Metropolitan used to be The Coca-Cola Company's national bottlers but that has now been turned over to Cadbury Schweppes, most famous for its Schweppes mixers. The latter immediately began a series of marketing programs that resulted in sales tripling within three years.

In Germany the pace has been even faster. Beginning in the early 1990s The Coca-Cola Company identified East Germany as one of its primary targets and began building a distribution network there to both package and sell Coke locally. Meanwhile throughout the entire country the company has taken even bolder steps including the replacement of an inefficient bottling network and the institution of a new, well financed marketing campaign. As a result, Germany is now The Coca-Cola Company's largest and most profitable market in Europe.

But all of this has come at a price. For example, some government agencies and companies have expressed concern about The Coca-Cola Company's overriding emphasis on cost control and market growth and its willingness to push aside those who are unable to meet these goals. As a result, the EU's Competition Directorate has been asked to investigate possible anti-competitiveness tactics. Meanwhile, in the UK, the British Monopolies and Mergers Commission (now the Competition Commission) has investigated The Coca-Cola Company regarding its joint venture with Schweppes; and San Pellegrino, the mineral water company, has filed a complaint with the Commission of the European Communities, contending that The Coca-Cola Company abused its dominant position by giving discounts to Italian retailers who promised to stock only Coke.

Yet none of these actions has stopped The Coca-Cola Company's efforts to establish a strong foothold in Europe. As the EU continues to eliminate all internal tariffs, it will be possible for a chain store with operations in France, Germany, Italy, and the Netherlands to buy soft drinks from the lowest-cost supplier on the Continent and not have to worry about paying import duties for shipping them to the retail stores. So low cost and rapid delivery are going to be key strategic success factors in what is likely to be a major "cola war". The Coca-Cola Company believes that its current strategy puts it in an ideal position to win this battle, although recent developments shed some doubt on whether the company will be as successful as it is forecasting.

On the positive side, Coca-Cola HBC (CCHBC), the world's second-largest Coke bottler, has been strengthening its presence in Eastern Europe through the recent acquisition of its parent group's bottling operations in the Baltic States and Russia. CCHBC is going to pay The Coca-Cola Company $200 million for territories that include the fast-growing markets of Moscow and St Petersburg as well as less developed operations in central and eastern Russia. At the same time, The Coca-Cola Company is investing almost $400 million in Russia and the Baltic in order to bolster sales and market volume is projected to grow 20 per cent annually in this region.

On the other hand, the company has had a number of recent setbacks. Worldwide market growth has been flat and The Coca-Cola Company's effort to develop innovative, non-carbonated products has not proven very successful. The company knows that its future growth is going to depend heavily on its ability to supplement its current product line with new offerings such as calcium-fortified waters, vitamin-enriched drinks, and perhaps coffee and tea offerings. Worst of all perhaps, a few years ago the company began centralizing control and encouraging consolidation among its bottling partners. The Coca-Cola Company believed that, by making all key operating decisions in Atlanta, it could drive up profitability.

Unfortunately, at the same time that it was pushing for this centralized type of operation, regional markets began demanding that the company be more responsive to local needs. In short, The Coca-Cola Company was going global while the market wanted it to go local.

The Coca-Cola Company is now trying to turn things around. In particular, the firm is now implementing three principles that are designed to make it more locally responsive. First, the company is instituting a strategy of "think local, act local" by putting increased decision making in the hands of local managers. Second, the firm is focusing itself as a pure marketing company and pushing its brands on a regional basis and local basis rather than on a worldwide basis. Third, The Coca-Cola Company is now working to become a model citizen by reaching out to local communities and getting involved in civic and charitable activities.

In the past, The Coca-Cola Company succeeded as a multinational because of its understanding and appeal to global commonalities. Today it is trying to hold its market share by better understanding and appealing to local differences.

Websites: **www.coca-cola.com**; **www.cokecce.com**; **www.coca-colahbc.com**; and **www.cadburyschweppes.com**.

Sources: Adapted from Patricia Sellers, "Coke Gets Off Its Can in Europe," *Fortune*, August 13, 1990; Susan E. Kuhn, "Are Foreign Profits Good for Stocks," *Fortune*, November 16, 1992; John Huey, "The World's Best Brand," *Fortune*, May 31, 1993; Howard Banks, "Stomach Share," *Forbes*, November 11, 1996; Patricia Sellers and Wilton Woods, "Where Coke Goes From Here," *Fortune*, October 13, 1997; "Coca-Cola Map: Next Year, The French-Fry Index," *Economist*, December 12, 1997; Dean Foust and Gerry Khermouch, "Repairing the Coke Machine," *Business Week*, March 19, 2001, pp. 86–88; Kerlin Hope, "Coke Bottler Boosts East European Presence with Purchase from Parent," *Financial Times*, July 28/29, 2001, p. 24; and Alan Rugman and Richard Hodgetts, "The End of Global Strategy," *European Management Journal*, August 2001, p. 336.

1. **Why is The Coca-Cola Company making foreign direct investments in Europe?**
2. **How is The Coca-Cola Company improving its factor conditions in Europe?**
3. **How is local rivalry helping to improve The Coca-Cola Company's competitive advantage?**
4. **Is The Coca-Cola Company a multinational enterprise?**

INTRODUCTION

International business The study of transactions taking place across national borders for the purpose of satisfying the needs of individuals and organizations

Multinational enterprises (MNEs) A company headquartered in one country but having operations in other countries

International business is the study of transactions taking place across national borders for the purpose of satisfying the needs of individuals and organizations. These economic transactions consist of trade, as in the case of exporting and importing, and foreign direct investment, as in the case of companies investing funds to up operations in other countries. Over half of all world trade and approximately 80 per cent of all foreign direct investment is made by the 500 largest firms in the world. These companies are called **multinational enterprises (MNEs)** which are firms that are headquartered in one country but have operations in one or more other countries. Who are these firms? Some of them you know by name because you have used their products or seen their advertising. In order of annual revenue, here is a list of those MNEs that grossed more than $100 billion in 2000.

Exxon (US)
Wal-Mart (US)
General Motors (US)
Ford Motor (US)
DaimlerChrysler (Germany)
Royal Dutch/Shell Group (Britain/Netherlands)
British Petroleum (Britain)
General Electric (US)
Mitsubishi (Japan)
Toyota (Japan)
Mitsui (Japan)

Citigroup (US)
Itochu (Japan)
TotalFinaElf (France)
Nippon Telegraph & Telephone (Japan)
Enron (US)

A close look at this list shows that each of these companies comes from one of three geographic locales: the US, the EU, or Japan. We call this the "triad". And of these 16 companies, seven were from the US, four from the EU, and five from Japan. The list helps point up an important fact and one that we will continue to emphasize throughout the book – companies from one of these three geographic locales account for most of the world's international business. The implications of this statement will be explained in greater detail in this next section where a brief overview of the world of international business is provided.

WORLD BUSINESS: A BRIEF OVERVIEW

There are thousands of multinational enterprises that collectively perform a wide range of operations and services.[1] However, if we were to examine what these companies are doing, we would discover that much of their activity could be classified into two major categories: (1) exports and imports and (2) foreign direct investment.

Exports and imports

Exports
Goods and services produced by a firm in one country and then sent to another country

Imports
Goods and services produced in one country and bought in by another country

Exports are goods and services produced by a firm in one country and then sent to another country. For example, many companies in China export clothing and other textile products to the US. **Imports** are goods and services produced in one country and brought in by another country. Japan, for example, is a major importer of petroleum because it must rely on outside suppliers for all of its energy needs. For the UK, the City of London generates exports of financial services that are "invisibles" in the British balance of payments.

In most cases people think of exports and imports as physical goods (clothes, oil, cars) but they also include services such as those provided by international airlines, cruise lines, reservation agencies, and hotels. Indeed, many international business experts now recognize that one of the major US exports is its entertainment and pop culture such as movies, television, and related offerings.

Table 1.1 provides a breakdown of worldwide trade in a recent year. The data show that the EU is the world's single largest exporter, followed by North America and then Asia. The EU is also the largest importer, followed by Asia and North America. If you were to investigate further, you would find that the majority of this export and import activity involves manufactured goods such as industrial machinery, computers, cars, televisions, VCRs, and other electronic goods. However, as will be seen later, an increasing proportion of world trade is in services.

Information on exports and imports is important to the study of international business for two reasons. First, trade is the historical basis of international business and trade activities help us understand MNE practices and strategies. For example, in 2000 the world's largest importers and exporters were the US, Germany, Japan, the UK, and France (see the map of the Top 10 Importers and Exporters in the World and Appendixes 1A and 1B, 2000 data). Note that the world's top importers are also the world's largest exporters. Some of the major products that are traded by these countries include computers, farm machinery, machine tools, automobiles and electronic goods. These

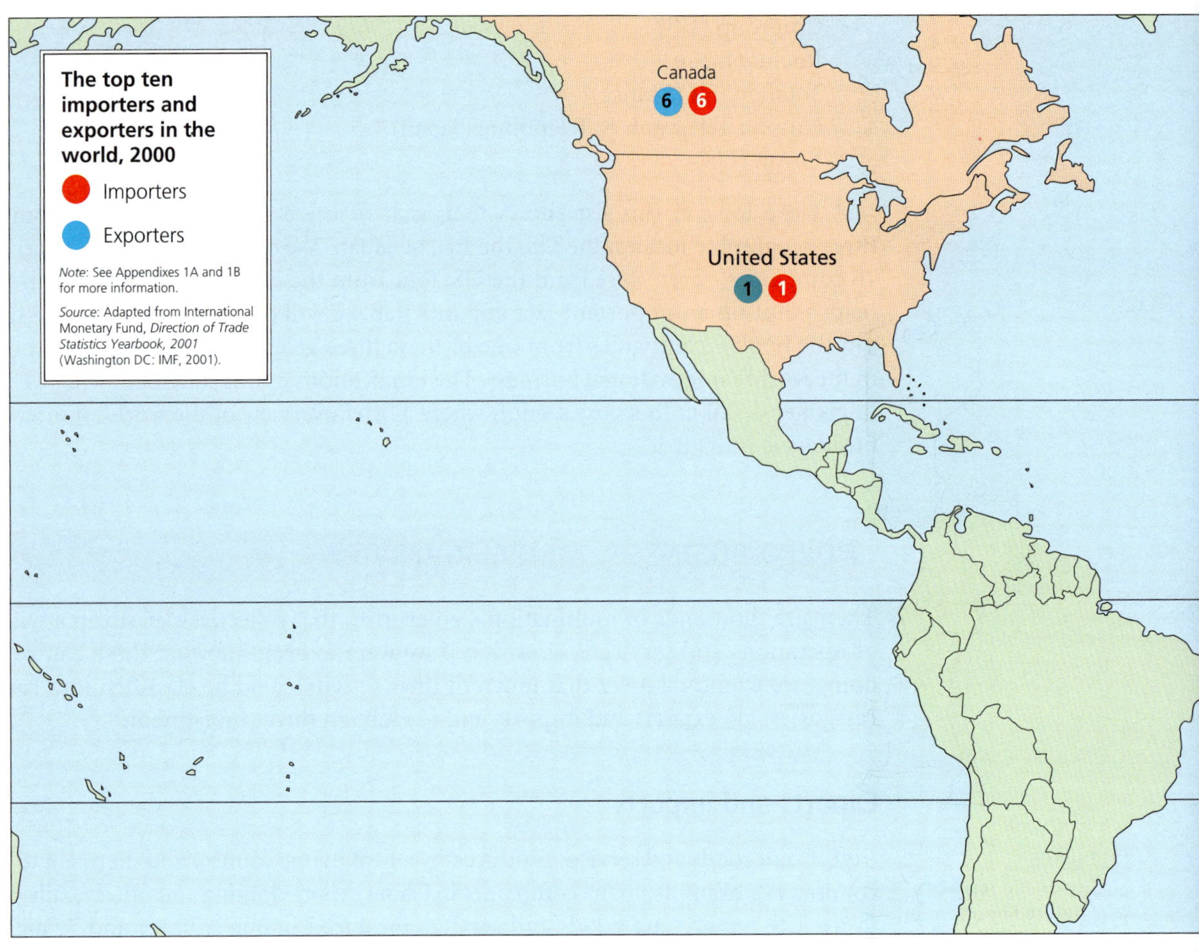

Table 1.1 World trade, 2000

Country/region	*Imports* Billions of US $	*Imports* % of total	*Exports* Billions of US $	*Exports* % of total
North America	1,692.8	25.6	1,213.6	19.1
United States	1,238.2	18.7	771.9	12.1
Canada	262.7	4.0	275.2	4.3
Mexico	191.9	2.9	166.5	2.6
European Union	2,284.9	34.6	2,283.0	35.8
Asia including Japan	1,563.5	23.7	1,742.6	27.4
Japan	377.2	5.7	477.3	7.5
Other Asia	1,186.3	18.0	1,265.3	19.9
All others	1,067.5	16.2	1,129.5	17.7
Total	6,608.7	100.0	6,368.7	100.0

Note: Data for EU include intra-EU trade. Trade data refer to pre-freight and insurance values. Exports are calculated without including freight and insurance while imports include freight and insurance costs.

Source: Adapted from International Monetary Fund, *Direction of Trade Statistics Yearbook, 2001* (Washington DC: IMF, 2001).

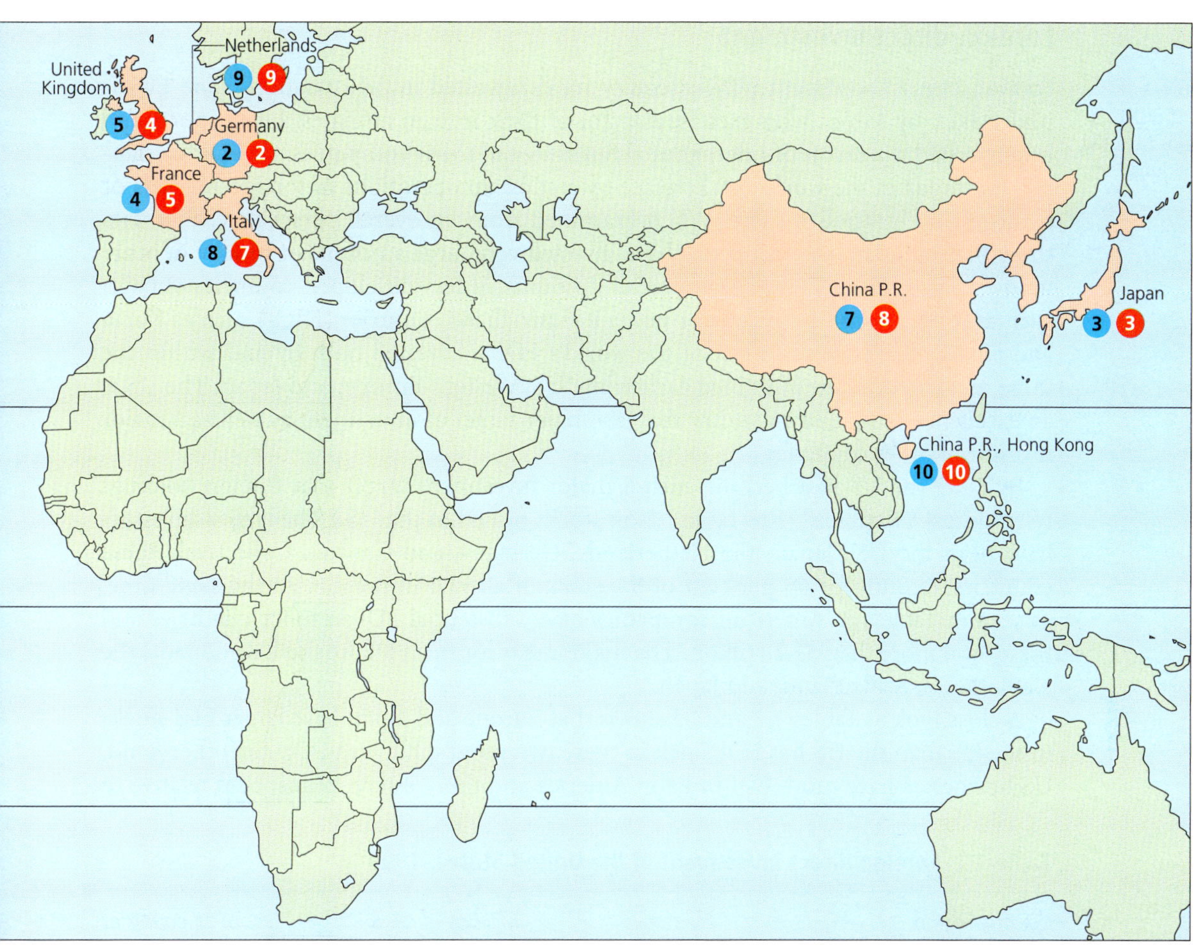

countries sell and buy a large percentage of their goods and services from a small number of countries. (See also Appendixes 1A–1D at the end of the chapter for information on major exporters, importers, and the direction of world trade flows.)

The US trade ties to Canada and Mexico reflect the triad effect, as these three countries are members of the North American Free Trade Agreement (NAFTA). Indeed, nearly 50 per cent of the exports of the US, Canada, and Mexico are to each other.[2] A similar picture of regional trade concentrations appears in the EU, where 60 per cent of all the exports of the 15 member states are with each other.[3] Similarly, Japan has 53 per cent of its trade with its major Asian neighbors.[4]

Information about exports and imports is important for a number of reasons. One is that it helps us better understand the impact of international business on world economies. For example, Japan imports all of its oil. So when the price of oil in the world market rises sharply, we can readily predict that the cost of manufacturing cars in Japan will rise and Japanese auto exports will decline. Conversely, if oil prices decline, we can predict that world imports of Japanese cars are likely to increase. A second reason why exports and imports are important in the study of international business is that they are two of the main drivers of international trade. When worldwide exports and imports begin to slow down, this is a pretty good sign that world economies are going into a slump.

Foreign direct investment

Foreign direct investment (FDI)
Equity funds invested in other nations

Foreign direct investment (FDI) is equity funds invested in other nations. The FDI is undertaken by MNEs who exercise control of their foreign affiliates. Like exports and imports, FDI is a driver of international business and many companies use FDI to establish footholds in the world marketplace by setting up operations in foreign markets or by acquiring businesses there. When examined from an overall perspective, FDI data show that industrialized countries have invested very large amounts of money in other industrialized nations as well as smaller amounts in less developed countries (LDCs) such as those in Eastern Europe or newly industrialized countries (NICs) such as Korea and Singapore. However, most of the world's FDI is invested both by and within the three major groups we identified earlier: the US, Western Europe, and Japan. The US is an excellent example of a country that is a major target of investment as well as a major investor in other countries.

By 1999 the US had become such a major investment target that foreign holdings were almost $1 trillion! (See Table 1.2 on stocks of FDI in the US.) The largest investors have been the UK, Japan, the Netherlands, Germany, and Canada. Collectively these countries account for 66 per cent of the stock of all FDI in the US. At the same time, as seen in Table 1.3, American companies have substantial FDI in other countries and these total more than $1.1 trillion. The major areas for this FDI are the UK, Canada, the Netherlands, Switzerland, and Japan.

A close look at Tables 1.2 and l.3 shows that Europe and Japan have larger FDI stocks in the US than the US has FDI stock in these two geographic areas. On the other hand, US businesses have more FDI in Latin America and the Western hemisphere relative to

Table 1.2 Foreign direct investment in the United States, 1999

Country/region	*Millions of US $*	*% of all countries*
All countries	986,668	100.0
Canada	79,716	8.1
Europe	685,845	69.5
France	77,622	7.9
Germany	111,138	11.3
Luxembourg	54,894	5.6
Netherlands	130,703	13.2
Switzerland	55,280	5.6
United Kingdom	183,145	18.6
Other	73,063	7.4
Latin America and other Western hemisphere	44,591	4.5
Bermuda	13,054	1.3
Mexico	3,612	0.4
Panama	5,896	0.6
United Kingdom Islands – Caribbean	13,883	1.4
Other	8,146	0.8
Africa	1,545	0.2
Middle East	7,087	0.7
Asia and Pacific	167,884	17.0
Australia	10,818	1.1
Japan	148,947	15.1
Other	8,119	0.8

Sources: US Department of Commerce, *Survey of Current Business*, March 2001 and US Bureau of Economic Analysis.

Table 1.3 **Foreign direct investment by the United States, 1999**

Country/region	*Millions of US $*	*% of all countries*
All countries	1,132,622	100.0
Canada	111,707	9.9
Europe	581,791	51.4
France	39,984	3.5
Germany	49,617	4.4
Netherlands	106,436	9.4
Switzerland	51,227	4.5
United Kingdom	213,070	18.8
Other	121,457	10.7
Latin America and other Western hemisphere	223,182	19.7
Bermuda	45,959	4.1
Brazil	35,003	3.1
Mexico	34,265	3.0
Panama	33,429	3.0
Other	74,526	6.6
Africa	15,062	1.3
Middle East	11,137	1.0
Asia and Pacific	185,912	16.4
Australia	33,662	3.0
Japan	47,786	4.2
Other	104,464	9.2
International	3,832	0.3

Sources: US Department of Commerce, *Survey of Current Business*, March 2001 and US Bureau of Economic Analysis.

the Europeans or Japanese. US companies have put much more FDI into the UK and Australia than either of these two nations have FDI in the US.

These recent data reveal two important trends. First, the US is a prime site for FDI by both Japan and countries in Western Europe. Second, US firms have invested most heavily in Western Europe, Latin America and the Caribbean, North America, and Japan. These four regions account for over 95 per cent of the stock of all US FDI. (For more on FDI see Appendixes 1E and 1F at the end of this chapter. We also discuss FDI and the role of MNEs in more detail in Chapter 2.)

Active learning check

Review your answer to Active Learning Case question 1 and make any changes you like. Then compare your answer with the one below.

1. Why is The Coca-Cola Company making foreign direct investments in Europe?

The Coca-Cola Company is making these investments in order to improve its market position. This is being done in three ways. First, the construction of new bottling plants is helping the company produce a low-cost product. Second, marketing expenditures are helping the firm gain the product recognition needed for growth. Third, direct investments in facilities closer to the market are reducing delivery time and eliminating associated expenses.

The triad

Triad
The three major trading and investment blocs in the international arena: the United States, the EU, and Japan

North American Free Trade Agreement (NAFTA)
A regional free trade agreement between Canada, the US and Mexico

As we noted above, a great deal of world trade and FDI is conducted by companies in the US, Western Europe, and Japan. The companies in Western Europe come from nations that are members of the EU and collectively these three areas of the US, EU, and Japan are called the "triad". The **triad** is a group of three major trading and investment blocs in the international arena: the US, the EU, and Japan. Before looking more closely at the impact of the triad on international business, it is important to discuss the countries that are members of this group.

The first of these, the US, has the largest economy in the world with a gross domestic product (GDP) of over $10 trillion! Sometimes when the US is discussed as a member of the triad, Canada and Mexico are included. This is because these three countries implemented the **North American Free Trade Agreement (NAFTA)** in 1994, an international covenant that has resulted in the elimination of many trade and investment barriers between the three. We further discuss NAFTA in Chapter 18. In our discussions of the triad in the book, we will be talking only about the US; if we intend to include Canada and Mexico we will indicate so by referring to them as members of NAFTA. The reason that our triad discussions will include only the US is that the US economy is extremely large when compared with that of Canada and Mexico. As a result, if we were to talk about the 25 largest MNEs in NAFTA we would be discussing American firms only. Canadian or Mexican firms are not big enough to make this list of 25. Simply put, the US economy is so large that this one country constitutes an entire segment of the triad.

The second segment of the triad is the EU. This group of nations, whose history and current developments will be discussed in Chapters 3 and 16, was formed by six countries in the late 1950s. Today there are 15 members of the EU: Austria, Belgium, Denmark, Finland, Germany, Greece, France, Ireland, Italy, Luxembourg, the Netherlands, Portugal, Spain, Sweden, and the UK. In addition, there are more than a dozen countries currently seeking admission to the group (see map, European Union timeline). The collective GDP of the EU is greater than that of the US or Japan and a brief look at some of the economic data in this chapter helps show how important the EU is in the international arena. For example, in terms of imports and exports, as seen back in Table 1.1, the EU accounts for more than 34 per cent of all imports and over 35 per cent of all world exports. Again, this includes 60 per cent intra-EU trade. And in terms of FDI, as seen in Table 1.2, five EU countries (France, Germany, Luxembourg, the Netherlands, and the UK) account for over $550 billion of investment in the US. Quite clearly, the EU is a worldwide economic force.

The third group in the triad is Japan, which like the other two members plays a major role in international business. This is made particularly clear by looking at areas such as importing, exporting, and FDI. As seen in Appendixes 1A and 1B at the end of the chapter, Japan is the world's fifth largest importer and third largest exporter. In addition, it is the largest economy in Asia and of all the countries in the region including Australia, China (and Hong Kong), Malaysia, South Korea, and Taiwan, Japan accounts for 27 per cent of all the imports and 30 per cent of all of the exports! Japan is also a major investor in the other two triad groups. It has more than $400 billion of FDI in the EU, currently one of its favorite investment targets, and over $100 billion in the US.

In examining the current state of world business, the triad merits close attention. Every year countries from these three groups account for more trade and FDI than those of any other economic bloc. As a result, during the 21st century the triad will be of central importance in the study of international business. We will discuss the power of the triad in greater detail in Chapter 3.

TODAY'S GLOBAL ENVIRONMENT

Although the triad continues to dominate the international business arena, the global environment has been changing rapidly in recent years. Today the world economy is quite different from what it was just five years ago. Some of the reasons include an overall slowdown in the triad economies, the introduction of more local and international trade regulation, the impact of technology, and the rise of small and medium-sized multinationals. The following briefly examines each of these.

World economies

Beginning in the early 1990s, the US economy started an unprecedented period of growth. For the next decade, the American economic machine far outperformed all others. The country's GDP rose dramatically and its productivity, which had always been the highest in the world, began to pull away from its nearest competitor, Japan, as the latter slipped into a prolonged economic slump. Germany, the other major economic power, did not do much better than Japan. By the mid-1990s its economy was having problems and by 2002 the country was still fighting to right its economic ship.

Because of its strong economy, during the last decade of the 20th century the US could be counted as a market for exported goods from all regions of the world as well as serving as a major source of FDI. A number of things accounted for the strong US economy. One was the willingness of US businesses to cut their workforces, reorganize their operations, and invest heavily in research and development. By the middle of the 1990s, the US was the most competitive nation in the world and it has held this position well into the millennium. However, as the Clinton administration was coming to an end there were signs that the long period of economic prosperity was beginning to falter. And over the next couple of years the US Federal Reserve found itself having to continually cut the prime rate in an effort to stimulate the American economy. Unfortunately, these efforts did not produce the desired effect and even more importantly, Japan, Germany, and other major economies continued to encounter economic problems. These developments were detailed by the **Organization for Economic Cooperation and Development (OECD)**, a Paris-based intergovernmental organization of the world's most economically advanced nations that provides its members with a forum for examining their economic problems and discussing solutions, when it reported that all three members of the triad were experiencing a decline in their GDP, business investment, and consumer spending.[5] Business firms echoed these findings as they began announcing that they were cutting their workforces. Gateway, the giant US computer maker, announced that it would cut 16 per cent of its workforce and close 19 stores.[6] The announcement came only a few months after the company cut 25 per cent of its workforce and shut operations in Asia and possibly Europe.[7] The company was not alone, many other telecom and dot.com companies went under in the 2000–2002 period, as did Enron, formerly one of the largest companies in the world.[8] Toshiba announced that it was cutting 18,000 jobs;[9] Hitachi reported a $1.2 billion annual loss and said it would eliminate almost 15,000 jobs worldwide;[10] Procter & Gamble announced that it was reducing its workforce by 10–20 per cent;[11] and Daewoo reported that it was laying off 30 per cent of its upper level management staff.[12] Simply put, even firms in the most advanced triad economies were having trouble and everyone was scrambling to stay afloat.[13]

Organization for Economic Cooperation and Development (OECD)
A group of 30 relatively wealthy member countries that facilitates a forum for the discussion of economic, social and governance issues across the world

International trade regulation

Another important international business trend has been the emergence of trade and investment liberalization. Firms in triad countries have prospered in more open markets. Yet, at the same time, triad rivalry has led to some setbacks in trade liberalization. For example, Japan and China have been threatened with trade sanctions by the US unless they allow US firms to sell products and services in their countries. There are also trade conflicts between the EU and the US over bananas, beef hormones, and export subsidies.[14] Many such trade disputes, however, are handled not by countries but by international organizations set up to regulate international commerce. The main one is the World Trade Organization.

World Trade Organization (WTO) An international organization that deals with the rules of trade among member countries. One of its most important functions is to act as a dispute-settlement mechanism

General Agreement on Tariffs and Trade (GATT) A major trade organization that has been established to negotiate trade concessions among member countries

The **World Trade Organization (WTO)** was established on January 1, 1995 and it is now the umbrella organization that governs the international trading system. It is the successor to the **General Agreement on Tariffs and Trade (GATT)**. The GATT was established in 1947. The purpose of the GATT was to liberalize trade and to negotiate trade concessions among member countries. While the early years saw a great deal of progress in reducing tariffs, by the 1980s there was a trend toward protectionism by many countries. At the GATT's eighth round of negotiations in 1986 (called the Uruguay Round because this is where the group met), negotiations dragged on for years before culminating in a number of agreements including reductions on industrial goods and agricultural subsidies, the increased protection of intellectual property rights, and the creation of the World Trade Organization to implement the GATT agreement. Today the World Trade Organization is enforcing the provisions of GATT.

When member nations have a dispute they can turn to the WTO to help resolve it. For example, the US brought a case against the EU charging it with a discriminatory banana import policy and the WTO ruled in its favor. In another case the US requested that Japan be instructed to reorganize its commercial economy so that Kodak could better compete in that market against Fuji, its major rival, but the WTO rejected the claim and ruled in Japan's favor. In recent years the US, the EU, and Japan, in particular, have been using the WTO to help resolve trade disputes and this bodes well for the future of the organization. One of the big issues, however, is China's behavior now that it has joined the WTO.[15] Whether this country will fully comply with WTO rulings now that it is a member or whether it will simply refuse to go along with decisions that are not in its favor is a question many international business observers have asked.[16] However, the important thing to remember about the WTO is that it can enforce its decisions. So countries that refuse to comply can find themselves suffering severe consequences in the form of trade retaliation. Yet, overall, international trade liberalization has arrived and this promises to help stimulate international business transactions and to prevent countries from discriminating against others.

Technology

Another major development that is changing the way MNEs do business is technology. Two areas, in particular, are having a major impact. One is communication technology that has advanced at such a rapid rate that all businesses now use computers and rely on the World Wide Web to both access and send information. In addition, thanks to cellular technology, individuals can now remain in constant contract with both their customers and their home office. Communication technology has advanced so much that the latest technology reports reveal that there now are more than 260 million cellular mobile users in the EU and in the four largest EU countries (France, Germany, Italy, and the UK) over 50 per cent of the population uses the Web![17]

The other major application of technology is for the production of goods and services. Modern factories can now produce goods in a shorter period of time and with fewer defects than ever before thanks to the introduction of "Six Sigma" quality programs (these are discussed further in Chapter 10). These programs are designed to increase quality and to eliminate defects, thus allowing firms to compete in any international market. Six Sigma is a statistical term that means 3.5 errors per million, effectively eliminating performance problems and ensuring that products work as intended.[18] As a result of such programs, Nokia has been able to dominate the international cellular telephone business and Hewlett-Packard has become the world leader in printers. The box "International Business Strategy in Action: Amazon.com" discusses the issues of fast growth of new service businesses.

INTERNATIONAL BUSINESS STRATEGY *IN ACTION*

Amazon.com – one-third of the way there

There are thousands of "global" businesses on the Internet. However, the best known of these may well be Amazon.com. Every day thousands of people go to the company's website to browse and purchase books. A novel that is reviewed on Sunday in the *New York Times Book Review* is likely to get a minimum of 10,000 hits within the next week, as readers check the price, read the comments of others who have read the book and have elected to share their impressions of it, and find out the availability of the offering. An example of the influence of the *Times Book Review* was recently seen when it reviewed *Nickel and Dimed* and gave it a good review. This book had been published earlier in the year and had generated lukewarm sales. As a result, the publisher did not hold out great hope for its sales. However, once the *Times Book Review* said it was worth reading, readers began ordering it. Thousands went to Amazon.com to place an order and within a few hours the current inventory was exhausted. This incident shows not only the impact of the *Times Book Review* but also that of Amazon.com.

Founded in early 1995 by Jeff Bezos, by 2000 Amazon.com ranked 544 on *Fortune*'s list of the 1,000 largest US corporations. That same year the company had sales of $2.7 billion. This is quite an achievement for a five-year-old firm. On the other hand, that year Amazon also reported a loss of $1.4 billion. For every dollar it took in, the company lost 51 cents.

Amazon was initially created to change the way people buy books. The company wanted to offer buyers a virtual store where they could use their computer to place an order that would then be delivered to them by mail. The old days of going to a bookstore was going to be a thing of the past. Amazon was going to bring the bookstore right into the buyer's home via the Internet. In addition to making it easy to buy books, Amazon's prices were lower than those at most bookstores and, despite the addition of shipping costs, it was often less expensive to shop online with Amazon than it was to visit the local bookstore.

From the beginning, Bezos's strategy was to grow as fast as possible. As a result, he began recruiting highly skilled staff to design the e-commerce end of the business, as well as hiring less skilled workers to handle warehouse, distribution, and supply operations. Initially, all of the employees had a common vision regarding what the company wanted to do. However, over the next couple of years this rapid growth resulted in both confusion and internal problems. Among other things, some of the personnel instituted lawsuits against the company for better compensation. And as the firm continued to lose money, its stock price fell sharply. The dot.com crash of 2000 saw investors abandon most of these firms, although Amazon has survived because investors believe that the basic concept of buying books online is a viable one.

Today the biggest problem for Amazon.com is that it is not a global company – it is a US firm. The Internet is really only a tool for business and, in Amazon's case, a way to sell products that are produced by others. And while the company now sells more than just books, it continues to be an American company. One reason is because books tend to sell most heavily in the market where they are published. A college text published in North America, for example, will not sell very much in Europe or Japan. Quite simply, triad and geographic region segment the market – and even within this grouping it can be difficult to sell to other countries. For example, Amazon generates only 10 per cent of its sales outside the US. And while it has customers in Canada, the firm continually confronts a number of problems doing business in this market including how to address Canadian sales taxes and how to deal with the threat by Canadian publishers of having the state-run postal service refuse to deliver "foreign" books. In fact, these problems have created such a headache for Canadian buyers that many of them now order their online books from Canadian suppliers such as Chapters and Borders rather than buy from Amazon. And in Europe, where Amazon operates through foreign subsidiaries, such as Amazon.co.uk, Amazon.fr, Amazon.de, the company offers a totally different stock of books from those marketed in North America and it targets a smaller, more affluent group of customers in this niche. The same marketing strategy is used in Asia. And on both of these continents customers are finding that local book suppliers often do a better job of meeting their needs in terms of both the range of their offerings and the price of their products. In short, Amazon.com is finding that if it wants to be a global competitor it is going to have to formulate a strategy that helps it expand out of the US market and become much more competitive throughout the triad. At the present time, Amazon.com is only one-third of the way there.

Websites: ***www.amazon.com***; ***www.amazon.co.uk***; ***www.amazon.co.jp***; ***www.amazon.fr*** and ***www.amazon.de***.

Sources: Alan M. Rugman, *The End of Globalization* (London: Random House, 2001; New York: Amacom, 2000; Toronto: McGraw Hill Ryerson, 2001); Robert Spector, *Amazon.com Get Big Fast* (New York: Harper Collins, 2000; London: Random House, 2000); and *Fortune*, April 16, 2000, p. F 63.

Small and medium-sized enterprises (SMEs)

Whenever MNEs are discussed, it is common to hear about large firms. In fact, the best known multinationals are companies that have become household words. In the auto industry everyone knows of Honda, General Motors, and Volkswagen. However, there are thousands of **small and medium-sized enterprises (SMEs)**, many of whom are suppliers to these MNEs.[19] Many of these companies have annual sales of less than $5 million, but thanks to innovation, technology, and a well-trained workforce, they are able to compete effectively and they perform functions that multinationals cannot do as efficiently. For example, some SMEs are able to provide their customers with two-day deliveries. In this way, their customers can keep a minimum amount of inventory on hand because the suppliers will replenish the stock every other day. And since these SMEs are small operations that focus heavily on cost control and quality, they are critical to the success of their customers. Result: SMEs are proving to be the backbone of many industries because of their efficiency and flexibility. In this book we will be studying a large number of international business concepts that are used by not just MNEs but also by SMEs. In particular, we discuss the strategies of some SMEs in cases like Command Alkon in Chapter 9 and Mountain Equipment Co-op in Chapter 8.

Small and medium-sized enterprises (SMEs)
The definition of SMEs varies according to the nation. In the US, SMEs are companies with up to 500 employees. In the EU, SMEs have between 11 and 200 employees and sales of under US $40 billion. In Japan, SMEs in industry have up to 300 employees while those in wholesale and retail have up to 150 and 50 employees respectively. Developing countries use the World Bank benchmark of 11 to 150 employees and sales of under US $5 billion

GLOBALIZATION AND STRATEGIC MANAGEMENT

At the end of each chapter in this book we are going to look at some of the ways that MNEs use the ideas that have been presented. In this opening chapter we introduced the world of international business and showed the impact of the triad on international trade and investment. We also noted that the major world economies are beginning to slow down and this, of course, is putting increased pressure on multinational enterprises to maintain growth and profitability. In this section we want to address three areas that are important in understanding how companies are coping with this international environment. First, we are going to look at some of the misconceptions that people have about multinational enterprises and how they formulate their international strategies. Second, we are going to look at some of the criteria that are important to MNEs in achieving strategic competitive advantage. Third, we are going to examine some examples of MNEs that are using concepts that we have introduced in this chapter.

Regional triad strategies

There are a number of misconceptions that people have about the world of international business and it is important to dispel these at the very start of this book. One is the belief that multinationals have far-flung operations and earn most of their revenues overseas. Nestlé is often cited as an example. This company sells over 8,500 products in more than 100 countries and earns more than 95 per cent of its revenues outside of Switzerland. While this is true, Nestlé is an exception to the rule. Most MNEs earn the bulk of their revenues either within their home country or by selling in nearby locales. In fact, recent research reports that:

> More than 85 per cent of all automobiles sold in North America are built in North American factories owned by General Motors, Ford, Daimler-Chrysler, or European or Japanese MNEs; over 90 per cent of the cars produced in the EU are sold there; and more than 93 per cent of all cars registered in Japan are manufactured domestically.
>
> In the specialty chemicals sector over 90 per cent of all paint is made and used regionally by triad based MNEs and the same is true for steel, heavy electrical equipment, energy, and transportation.

> In the services sector, which now employs approximately 70 per cent of the work force in North America, Western Europe, and Japan, these activities are all essentially local or regional.[20]

In order to be successful, MNEs need to create strategies that are regional not worldwide in focus and they need to be responsive to local consumers as opposed to being global in nature and uniform throughout.

Another misunderstanding about MNEs is the belief that they are globally monolithic and excessively powerful in political terms. Actually, the latest research shows that, of the 500 largest MNEs, 198 are headquartered in North America, 156 are in the EU, and 125 are in Japan/Asia. We discuss this further in Chapter 2, Table 2.1. In short, these firms are not spread out around the world but are clustered in the triad. Additionally, these companies are engaged not in global competition but in triad/regional competition; and this rivalry is so strong that it has effectively eliminated the possibility of their either achieving sustainable long-term profits or of building strong, enduring political advantage. In fact, it is now common to find MNEs joining forces with local firms who can help them in their efforts to penetrate local markets. In recent years the **strategic alliance**, a business relationship in which two or more companies work together to achieve a collective advantage, has become extremely popular with MNEs who now realize that they need to develop strategies with a regional or local focus if they hope to succeed.

Strategic alliance
A business relationship in which two or more companies work together to achieve a collective advantage

A third misunderstanding is the belief that MNEs develop homogeneous products for the world market and through their efficient production techniques are able to dominate local markets everywhere. In fact, multinationals have to adapt their products for the local market. For example, there is no worldwide, global car. Rather, there are regionally based auto factories that are supported by local and regional suppliers who provide steel, plastic, paint, seats, tires, radios, and other necessary inputs for producing cars for that geographic region. Additionally, the car designs that are popular in one area of the world are typically rejected by buyers in other geographic areas. The Toyota Camry that dominates the American auto market is a poor seller in Japan and does even poorer in Europe. And the Volkswagen Golf, that does extremely well in Europe, has not made much of an impact in North America. And pharmaceutical firms, which manufacture medicines that are often referred to as "universal products", have to modify their goods to satisfy national and state regulations, thus making centralized production and worldwide distribution economically difficult.

In this book we are going to use examples throughout of what is happening in the international environment and show how an understanding of international business concepts can be useful to companies in addressing these developments. In many cases you will find that things you believed to be true are not. There is a great deal of misinformation about the world of international business. One of these misperceptions is that MNEs are giant corporations that are world dominant. In fact, their success comes most heavily from formulating and implementing strategies on a regional and local basis.

Maintaining economic competitiveness

During the 1980s US businesses saw some of their economic competitiveness eroded by Japanese and European competitors. By the mid-1990s, however, American firms had bounced back strongly and by 2002 the US continued to be the most competitive nation in the world.[21] How did American companies manage to achieve and then maintain this international competitive advantage? One way was by continuing to be innovative. In the computer industry, for example, Intel's research and development (R&D) arm created a continuing flow of new-age computer chips – each more powerful than its predecessor.

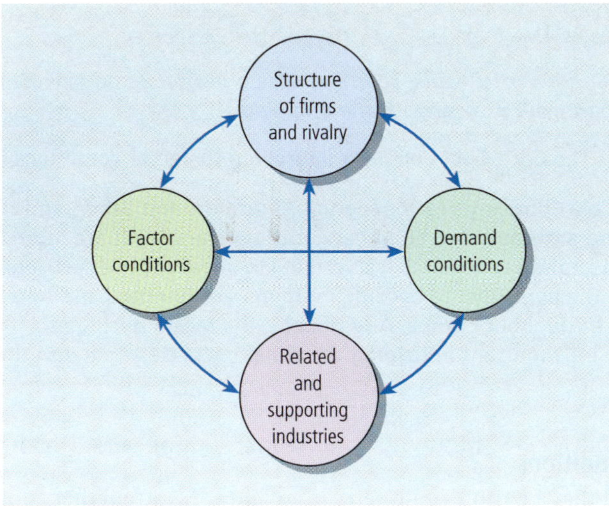

Figure 1.1 Porter's determinants of national competitive advantage

Source: Adapted with the permission of The Free Press, an imprint of Simon & Schuster Adult Publishing Group, from *The Competitive Advantage of Nations* by Michael E. Porter. Copyright © 1990, 1998 by Michael E. Porter, p. 72.

And at the upper end of this market, IBM's R&D prowess helped it capture more and more of the business demand for powerful computers, while at the lower end Dell Computer dominated the field with its high-quality PCs that were sold at rock bottom prices. In other industries as well, from industrial equipment to financial services and from shipping to entertainment, American companies led the way thanks to their ability to innovate. In looking more closely at these developments, a likely question is: Why are some firms able to innovate consistently while others cannot? Michael Porter of Harvard University has provided one of the best answers to this question. After conducting a comprehensive study of 100 industries in 10 countries, Porter found that the success of nations in international competition is determined by four broad attributes that individually and interactively determine national competitive advantage: factor conditions, demand conditions, related and supporting industries, and the environment in which firms compete.[22] The relationships among these determinants are illustrated in Figure 1.1. The following briefly discusses each of these four.

Factor conditions

Factor conditions Land, labor, and capital

According to basic international trade theory, a nation will export those goods that make most use of the factor conditions with which it is relatively well endowed. These **factor conditions** include land, labor, and capital. As a result, if a country has a large, relatively uneducated workforce, it will seek to export goods that are highly labor-intensive. On the other hand, if the workforce is highly educated, the country will seek to produce goods and services that tap the intellectual abilities of these people. However, there is more to international trade theory than merely capitalizing on these basic factors. In order to maintain a competitive position, a country must continually upgrade or adjust its factor conditions. For example, Denmark has two hospitals that specialize in studying and treating diabetes; Denmark also is a world leader in the export of insulin. By creating specialized factors and then working to upgrade them, the country has maintained its premier position in the health-care field. Similarly, the Netherlands, the world's leading exporter of flowers, has created research institutes in the cultivation, packaging, and shipping of flowers. As a result, no one has been able to dislodge that country's foothold in the international flower industry.

Active learning check 

Review your answer to Active Learning Case question 2 and make any changes you like. Then compare your answer with the one below.

2. How is The Coca-Cola Company improving its factor conditions in Europe?

The Coca-Cola Company's factor conditions include land, labor, and capital. The company is using land and capital to build new bottling plants that are more efficient and better suited to meet market demand. It is working to improve the effectiveness of the labor force by getting the personnel to become more market oriented and to sell the product more vigorously throughout Europe. Additionally, the recent decision to "think local, act local" is going to be important in helping the company better tune into the local market.

Demand conditions

Porter states that a nation's competitive advantage is strengthened if there is strong local demand for its goods and services. This demand provides a number of benefits. First, it helps the seller understand what buyers want. Second, if changes become necessary, such as customer desires for a product that is smaller, lighter, or more fuel efficient, the local seller has early warning and can adjust or innovate for the market before more distant competitors can respond. In fact, the more sophisticated the local buyers, the greater the advantage to the local seller. For example, one reason that Japanese firms pioneered small, quiet air-conditioning units is that many Japanese live in small houses and apartments where loud noise can be a problem. Japanese firms also developed units that were powered by energy-saving rotary compressors because customers complained that the price of energy was very high and they wanted a more fuel-efficient unit. As a result, Japanese companies now dominate the world market for small air conditioners. Similarly, Sweden, long concerned with helping the disabled, has spawned a competitive industry that focuses on the special needs of these people, and Denmark's environmental concern has resulted in Danish companies developing highly effective water-pollution control equipment and windmills. In the US, consumers helped to develop a highly efficient fast-food industry, and as the desire for this cuisine spread worldwide, US franchisors like McDonald's and Pizza Hut have been able to tap international demand for their products.

Related and supporting industries

Porter's third major determinant of national competitive advantage is the presence of related and supporting industries that are internationally competitive. When suppliers are located near the producer, these firms often provide lower-cost inputs that are not available to the producer's distant competitors. In addition, suppliers typically know what is happening in the industry environment and are in a position to both forecast and react to these changes. By sharing this information with the producer, they help the producer maintain its competitive position. The Italian shoe industry is an excellent example. Shoe producers interact on a regular basis with leather manufacturers, exchanging information that is useful to each in remaining competitive. This interaction is mutually beneficial to both parties.[23]

Firm strategy, structure, and rivalry

Porter's fourth broad determinant of national advantage is the context in which the firms are created, organized, and managed, as well as the nature of domestic rivalry. No one managerial system is universally appropriate. Nations tend to do well in industries where the management practices favored by the national environment are suited to their industries' sources of competitive advantage. In Italy, for example, successful firms typically are small or medium sized; operate in fragmented industries such as lighting, furniture, footwear, and packaging machines; are managed like extended families; and employ a focus strategy geared toward meeting the needs of small market niches. Germany, in contrast, tends to have hierarchical organizations that emphasize technical or engineering content (optics, chemicals, complicated machinery) that demand precision manufacturing, a careful development process, after-sale service, and a highly disciplined management structure. In Japan, successful firms are often those that require unusual cooperation across functional lines and that demand management of complex assembly operations. Auto production, television manufacturing, and computer assembly are examples of such industries.

National goals are also important. Some countries want rapid results. Others tend to do best in industries where long-term development is valued more. In the US, for example, investors like fast financial returns. So US firms are more likely to invest in new industries such as software and biotechnology where success can come quickly. In Germany and Switzerland, investments are held for long-term appreciation and are rarely traded. These countries are more likely to invest in mature industries where ongoing investment in research and development and new facilities are important but return on investment is only moderate.

Another area of importance is domestic rivalry. Researchers have found that vigorous domestic rivalry and competitive advantage are related. Nations with leading world positions often have a number of strong, local rivals. For example, in Switzerland, the pharmaceutical firms of Hoffman-LaRoche, Ciba-Geigy, and Sandoz help the country to maintain its internationally competitive edge. In Germany, BASF, Hoechst, and Bayer help the country to keep ahead in chemicals.

Active learning check

Review your answer to Active Learning Case question 3 and make any changes you like. Then compare your answer with the one below.

3. How is local rivalry helping to improve The Coca-Cola Company's competitive advantage?

The Coca-Cola Company faces strong competition in Europe. Europeans do not drink as much Coke as Americans do; drinks like coffee and tea are more popular. As a result, The Coca-Cola Company is modifying its strategy to address this market. This includes the building of new bottling plants that can help drive down costs and make the company more price competitive, and new marketing campaigns that are designed to draw customers away from competing products. The Coca-Cola Company is also working to develop non-carbonated drinks and to enter into joint ventures with local partners who understand local tastes and can be useful in helping the company to formulate appropriate strategies.

Porter's determinants as a system

As noted earlier, each of the determinants in Figure 1.1 often depends on the others. For example, even if a country has sophisticated buyers that can provide a company with feedback about how to modify or improve its product (demand conditions), this information will not be useful if the firm lacks personnel with the skills to carry out these functions (factor conditions). Similarly, if suppliers can provide the company with low-cost inputs and fresh ideas for innovation (related and supporting industries) but the firm clearly and easily dominates the industry (firm strategy, structure, and rivalry) and

INTERNATIONAL BUSINESS STRATEGY *IN ACTION*

The Italian tile industry

The Italian ceramic tile industry is an excellent example of how regional manufacturers can gain national, and even international, prominence. The heart of this industry is in Sassuolo near Bologna in northern Italy. Tile has been produced here for over 700 years. So when Italy started rebuilding after World War II, the area began to flourish. Within 15 years the number of local tile companies had increased sevenfold and Sassuolo began to attract engineers and skilled workers.

At first the tile manufacturers had to import raw materials and machinery. There was no white clay in the region, so it was brought in from England. There were no tile equipment manufacturers, so kilns were purchased from Germany, the US, and France; and presses for both forming and glazing tiles were bought overseas. However, the Italian tile producers soon learned how to modify the equipment to better fit their needs, and technicians began leaving the tile companies to set up their own equipment firms. By 1970 companies in the region were exporting tile kilns and presses. At the same time, the local equipment producers were competing fiercely for the business of the tile companies, thus keeping down the cost of making tile; and supporting companies began to establish businesses in the Sassuolo region to offer molds, packaging materials, glazes, and transportation services. Specialized consulting companies soon emerged to give advice to tile producers on plant design, logistics, and commercial, advertising, and fiscal matters. The ceramic tile industry association, Assopiastrelle, started offering services of common interest to the firms: bulk purchasing, foreign market research, and consulting on fiscal and legal matters. A consortium consisting of the University of Bologna, regional agencies, and the ceramic industry association was founded to conduct process research and product analysis.

While these developments occurred, Italian customers continued to give the manufacturers feedback on product quality and ideas for innovative designs and features. This led to intense rivalry in the form of product offerings. At the same time the tile companies began working to improve their equipment and to lower their production costs. One result was a rapid single-fire process for tile making. This system reduced the number of workers by 60 per cent and cut the cycle time by 95 per cent, so more tiles could be made by fewer people. This new equipment was also smaller and lighter than its predecessor and it found an eager international market. The manufacturers also developed a continuous, automated production system to replace the batch process and this, too, drove down costs and increased productivity.

Today the Italian ceramic tile industry is the world leader. In recent years Sassuolo has accounted for 20 per cent of world production and 48 per cent of world exports. As a result, the country's annual trade surplus from this industry alone is now over $1 billion.

Websites: ***www.italiatiles.com*** and ***www.assopiastrelle.it***.

Sources: Adapted from Michael J. Enright and Paolo Tenti, "How the Diamond Works: The Italian Ceramic Tile Industry," *Harvard Business Review*, March–April 1990; ***www.assopiastrelle.it/welcome.html***; ***www.itse.com/exhibitor_pages/467.html***.

does not feel a need to upgrade the quality of its products and services, it will eventually lose this competitive advantage.

Research shows that of the four determinants in Figure 1.1, domestic rivalry and geographic clustering are particularly important. Domestic rivalry promotes improvements in the other three determinants and geographic concentration magnifies the interaction of the four separate influences.[24] The box "International Business Strategy in Action: The Italian tile industry" illustrates how these influences helped Italy develop a premier position in the ceramic tile industry.

Multinationals in action

In each chapter of this book we are going to provide examples of how MNEs are using the ideas that we have been presenting. In this first chapter we have examined the roles of importing, exporting, and FDI in international business, as well as discussing some of the things that MNEs have to do in order to create sustainable competitive advantage.

Here are examples of how three multinationals are using some of these ideas in their operations.

Volkswagen

Volkswagen (VW) is well known in the auto market, although like most MNEs it does much better in its regional market (the EU) than it does in other areas of the triad. The company's four main brands – VW, Audi, Seat, and Skoda – collectively hold 19 per cent of the European auto market and its VW and Audi lines also hold 2.5 per cent of the US market. In the last decade VW's market share in both Europe and America has increased because the company has been doing a number of things well. One is the use of innovative design. The top selling VW brands in the US, for example, all have innovative features such as dashboard instruments like the speedometer and clock that light up in red at night, while those items that the driver touches, such as the radio, are backlit in blue. Commenting on these design features, one auto researcher remarked, "It gives the vehicle some soul, which many of VW's competitors lack horribly."[25] A second factor accounting for VW's success is its commitment to using the most efficient technology in building its cars. VW currently turns out more than 60 models on four main platforms, or chassis components, thus saving itself $1.5 billion a year in manufacturing costs. Yet VW is not counting on the current product line to maintain its competitive advantage. The company is now moving up the line with plans to offer a $35,000 super Passat equipped with an eight-cylinder, W-shaped engine that will deliver super acceleration. On the outside the car will have swooping lines like those found on BMW sedans, while its interior will be a rich mix of walnut and leather. VW intends to position the Passat against the Mercedes S-Class cars which are in the $50,000-plus segment. Quite clearly, the company's future strategy is to become a full-range auto firm with a car for everyone's pocketbook.

Carrefour

Carrefour is the world's second largest retailer (behind Wal-Mart) and the largest in terms of number of stores and geographic coverage. In 2000 Carrefour had almost 9,500 stores spread throughout 22 countries on four continents. What makes the company particularly successful is its ability to create a local strategy for each of its units. Carrefour has a knack for designing its stores to meet local tastes. At least 90 per cent of the goods that it sells in a store cater to the local market because the company believes that each unit should reflect the image of that country.[26] "You have to adapt your food and other products to the local culture", notes the company's chairman and chief executive officer; and this is done in a wide variety of ways.[27] For example, in Catholic Poland, the latest Carrefour hypermarket has a special religion section featuring Bibles, candles, and primers for children who are preparing for their first communion. In China, where many shoppers are superstitious, the company takes care to ensure that vegetables are chopped vertically – not laterally – so as not to bring bad luck to shoppers. And to make sure that it does not stumble badly by getting into countries where it truly does not know how to do business effectively, the company never sets up operations until it has researched the local market for at least one year so that it knows the dos and don'ts of doing business there. As a result, while Wal-Mart has had a wide variety of operating problems in markets such as China, Thailand, and Brazil, Carrefour's efforts in these countries have all worked out well.

Kawasaki and Suzuki

Competition in the international motorcycle marketplace today is greater than ever. Japan is a good example. In this market where Honda and Yamaha are the leaders and

Kawasaki and Suzuki are the next largest competitors, the four firms have consistently led the world market with their technologically innovative sports bikes. The problem for all four, however, is that the high cost of R&D has resulted in very high prices for their bikes. And to make matters worse, international rivals such as Harley Davidson of the US, Triumph of the UK, Ducati of Italy, and BMW of Germany have all been aggressively remodeling their own products, improving the quality and specifications of these machines, setting competitive prices, and stepping up their worldwide marketing efforts. In order to meet these challenges, Kawasaki and Suzuki have now created a strategic alliance.[28] This alliance, the first ever in the Japanese motorcycle industry, breaks the pattern of each company competing fiercely with the other three. In particular, the two firms are going to jointly develop new models and unify their parts procurement and production activities in order to cut costs. They also plan on developing and building off-road motorcycles and high-powered scooters. The alliance could not have come at a better time. Worldwide market demand for motorcycles is poor and both companies have seen declining sales in all three of their market regions: Asia, Europe, and the US. However, the biggest competition is in the large bike market and Kawasaki and Suzuki intend to bypass this niche and focus instead on small bikes and scooters. The two believe that, if they can produce quality products at a competitive price, they can make major inroads in China. In the past this market has proved very difficult for Japanese motorcycle makers because Chinese companies have been able to pirate copies of their machines and then produce them in their own factories, without fear of any government intervention to stop such practices. Under WTO rules this is something that China will have to do in the future or run the risk of severe economic retaliation. The decision by Kawasaki and Suzuki to form a strategic alliance and focus on China may prove to be a very profitable strategic move.

Active learning check

Review your answer to Active Learning Case question 4 and make any changes you like. Then compare your answer with the one below.

4. Is The Coca-Cola Company a multinational enterprise?

The Coca-Cola Company is indeed an MNE. The firm conducts production and distribution activities in nations other than its home country. And in terms of strategy and management orientation, The Coca-Cola Company does three things that illustrate its multinational nature. First, the company modifies its operations to meet local needs. The firm markets on a country-by-country basis. Second, The Coca-Cola Company has international partners who help to run the operation and do not report directly to the company on day-to-day matters. Third, the multinational relies heavily on teamwork by all involved parties and, to a large degree, serves more as a coordinator and cheerleader for the product than as an on-site manager.

THE STUDY OF INTERNATIONAL BUSINESS

As you have seen from the material in this chapter, the world of international business is undergoing a number of major changes. Quite clearly, international business is both an interesting and a challenging area! In this book we are going to study what international business is all about and what MNEs are now doing in order to compete effectively. In this section we examine the current state of the field of international business and then discuss the approach that will be used in this book in studying this field.

Table 1.4 **Comparative differences in the study of international business, 1950–2010**

Topic	*1950–1969*	*1970–1989*	*1990–2010*
Focus of interest	General information	Functional areas of development	Strategic emphasis
Approach to studying international business	Descriptive	Analytical	Integrative
Method of explanation	Heavily historical	Functional	Multidisciplinary
Research emphasis	Interdisciplinary	More quantitative research methods and overseas travel	Quantitative research methods, overseas travel, and international assignment
Enterprise viewpoint	US enterprises	Global enterprises	Multinational enterprises
Countries examined	Industrialized	Industrialized, NICs, and LDCs	Industrialized, NICs, and LDCs
Number of journals	Some	Many	Ever increasing
Journal emphasis	General international topics	Functional	Functional and strategic
Amount of joint research	Some	Much more	Ever increasing

From general to strategic emphasis

The field of modern international business began to develop in the 1950s. At this time there was not a great number of MNEs and most of them were American. World War II had ended less than a decade before and many nations, including Japan and the European countries, were more concerned with rebuilding than with overseas investing. Early international business textbooks were often written by American professors and they offered a general, descriptive approach to the field. There were few international research studies to provide substantive information. International companies that served as teaching examples were often those with international divisions, rather than true MNEs. And professors teaching international business were frequently educated in areas such as economics or general business and relied on an interdisciplinary approach to address the varied needs of the course. (Table 1.4 provides additional comparisons.)

During the 1970s and 1980s the field of international business changed greatly. The economic growth of Europe and Japan, coupled with great strides by newly industrialized countries, resulted in more and more attention being focused on international business. Professors were now becoming much more research oriented and the number of PhD-granting institutions offering at least a minor in international business began to increase. Articles and books by Canadian, European, and Asian professors started to appear and US research sophistication gained markedly. International economics and finance now became primary areas of interest and the general research approach of the 1950s and 1960s was supplanted by more rigorous quantitative and methodological designs. More and more research studies were conducted and the number of journals in the field rose sharply. In the latter part of the 1980s we also saw the beginning of efforts to bring together much of what was happening into a meaningful composite. How could we understand what was going on in the world of international business, when so much seemed to be occurring at the same time? It was becoming evident that many of the developments of the 1970s and 1980s were being studied in too micro a fashion and a more macro approach to the field was needed.

Strategic management
Managerial actions that include strategy formulation, strategy implementation, evaluation, and control and encompass a wide range of activities, including environmental analysis of external and internal conditions and evaluation of organizational strengths and weaknesses

The 1990s saw the emergence of a strategic management focus for drawing together the field of international business. The descriptive ideas of the 1950s and 1960s and the analytical ideas of the 1970s and 1980s were now being combined into an integrative approach. Historical and quantitative research was now being incorporated into models for describing, explaining, and helping predict what was happening in the international business arena. The earlier interdisciplinary and functional approaches were being supplemented by a multidisciplinary approach that drew on information from a wide variety of disciplines that affected international business. New journals in the field were also taking a more strategic management view of developments. This theme of **strategic management**, managerial actions that include strategy formulation, strategy implementation, evaluation, and control, encompasses a wide range of activities, including environmental analysis of external and internal conditions and evaluation of organizational strengths and weaknesses. In this text strategic management will serve as the basis for our overall framework.

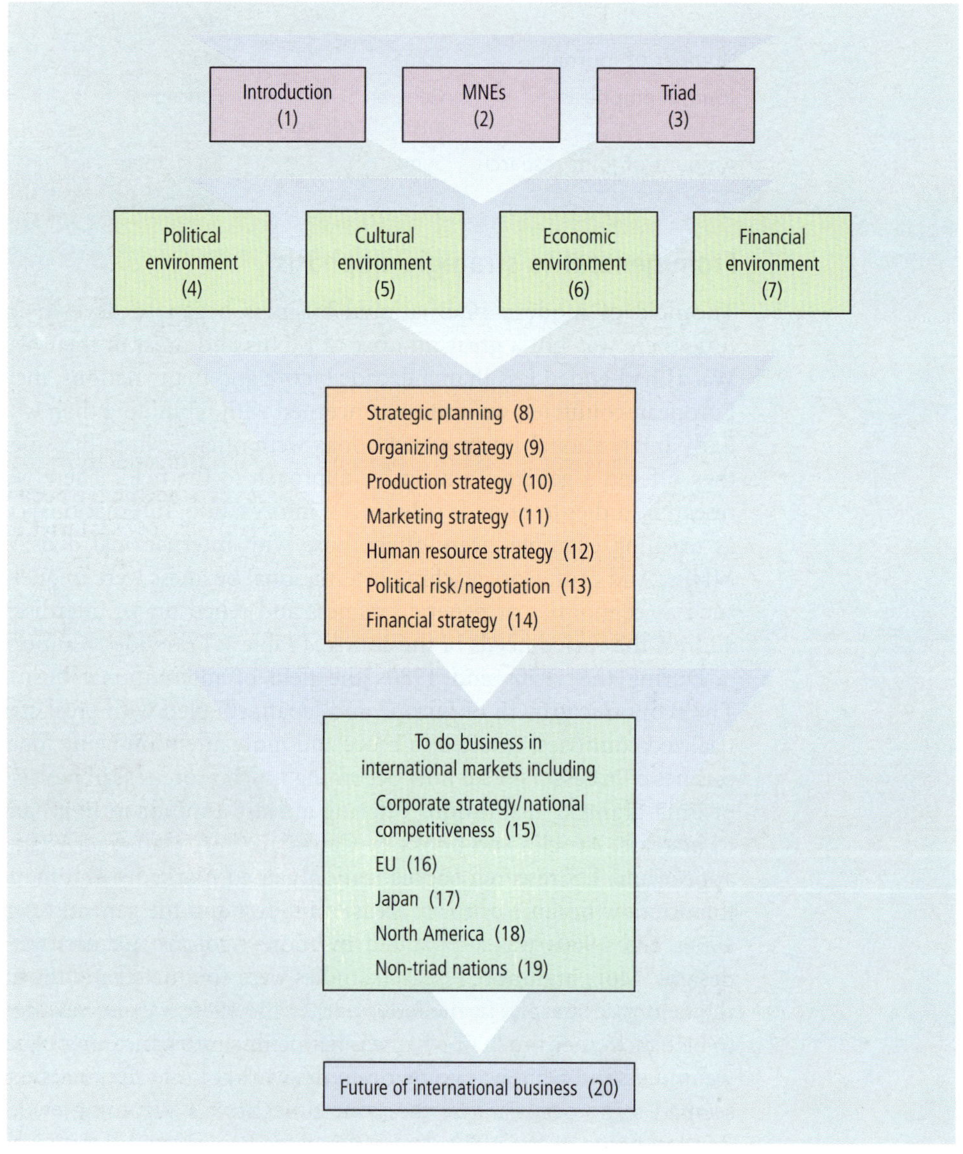

Figure 1.2 **Model for this book**

Framework for this book

This book employs a strategic management approach to the study of international business. In each chapter we will first study international business concepts and then we will examine how MNEs integrate these concepts into their overall strategy.

There are five major parts in this text. Part One is an introduction and encompasses this chapter and Chapters 2 and 3. The focus of attention in this part of the book is on such areas as imports, exports, FDI, the nature of MNEs, and the role and importance of the triad. Part Two examines the environments of international business with particular attention to international politics, culture, trade, and finance. Part Three focuses on international business strategies from a functional standpoint with particular attention to global strategic planning, organizational structures, production strategy, marketing strategy, human resource management strategy, political risk, negotiation strategies, and international financial management and accounting. Part Four looks at the ways in which the information presented thus far in the book is being used by organizations to do business internationally. In this part, specific attention is given to strategic alliances, the flagship framework, and ways of doing business in the EU, Asia, North America, and emerging economies. Part Five provides a look at some of the future challenges in international business.

Figure 1.2 presents an illustration of the model that will be used throughout this book. The current chapter has set the stage for the study of international business. In Chapter 2 we will examine the key actor on this stage: the MNE.

KEY POINTS

1. **International business is the study of transactions taking place across national borders for the purpose of satisfying the needs of individuals and organizations. Two of the most common types of international business activity are export/import and foreign direct investment (FDI). In recent years both have been on the rise. Much of this is a result of large multinational enterprises (MNEs) that are headquartered in triad countries. In particular, triad members account for most of the worldwide trade and FDI.**
2. **At the present time world economies are slowing down and many MNEs are cutting back their work forces in order to more effectively compete in this environment. Small and medium sized enterprises are also finding themselves being challenged. Another important international business development is the emergence of trade regulation. Today the World Trade Organization is the major group responsible for governing the international trading system. A third major development that is changing the way MNEs do business is technology as seen by the changes taking place in both communication and production technologies.**
3. **One way in which these firms are competing is by drawing up strategies that focus on regions and geographic areas, thus ensuring that they are addressing the needs of their local customers. Another way is by continuing to be innovative. A third is by maintaining competitive position by addressing the determinants of national competitive advantage: (a) creating the necessary factor conditions; (b) having strong local demand for the goods and services that are being produced; (c) having related and supporting industries that are internationally competitive; and (d) having a suitable strategy and structure and domestic rivalry that encourages continued innovation.**

KEY TERMS

- international business
- multinational enterprise (MNE)
- exports
- imports
- foreign direct investment (FDI)
- triad
- North American Free Trade Agreement (NAFTA)
- Organization for Economic Cooperation and Development (OECD)
- World Trade Organization (WTO)
- General Agreement on Tariffs and Trade (GATT)
- small and medium-sized enterprises (SMEs)
- strategic alliance
- factor conditions
- strategic management

REVIEW AND DISCUSSION QUESTIONS

1. What is international business all about? In your answer be sure to include a definition of the term.
2. What are the two primary ways in which world trade is conducted?
3. Will foreign direct investment increase or decrease in the current decade? Why?
4. How important are the triad nations in promoting international commerce? Explain.
5. What role does the World Trade Organization play in the international business arena? Is the WTO helpful to international trade or is it a hindrance? Why?
6. Multinational enterprises do not formulate worldwide strategies, but rather regional strategies. What does this statement mean and how does it help us better understand international business?
7. How do the four determinants of national competitive advantage help explain how companies can maintain their economic competitiveness? Be complete in your answer.
8. What are two of the advantages associated with using strategic alliances?

REAL CASE

Big oil gets bigger

Between 1998 and 2001 there were a series of mergers in the oil industry that resulted in a handful of private companies emerging as dominant players. In the US the largest of these was Exxon Mobil, the result of a 1999 merger. In 2000 this company had sales of $210 billion, see table, "Rankings of oil MNEs, 2000" below.

In Europe mergers and acquisitions had created three dominant firms. The largest was BP Amoco which was created by a merger of these two companies in 1998. Since that time the MNE has continued to grow through acquisition as seen by its purchase of both Arco and Burmah Castrol. The company has also been using strategic alliances to advance its position. Its agreement with Solvay, the Belgian chemical group, has provided it with help in staking out a competitive position in the plastics business. Among other things, BP Amoco has acquired Solvay's polypropylene business in exchange for giving Solvay its polymers business. BP Amoco's revenues in 2000 were just short of $150 billion.

The next largest European firm in the oil industry is the Royal Dutch Shell Group whose revenues are now just slightly less than BP Amoco. Unlike most of the other firms in the industry, however, Royal Dutch has opted not to use mergers and acquisitions to increase its size. Instead the company is restructuring and realigning its operations in order to increase overall efficiency and effectiveness.

The third largest European firm in the industry is TotalFinaElf, the result of a merger between Total Fina and Elf in 2000. In that year the merged company had revenues of $105 billion. Among other things, TotalFinaElf is the largest oil producer in Africa and second largest in the Middle East. The company's oil reserves in 1999/2000 grew by 3 per cent and today these reserves are significantly greater

Rankings of oil MNEs, 2000

MNE	*US $ (billion)*
Exxon Mobil	210.4
BP Amoco	148.1
Royal Dutch/Shell	149.5
TotalFinaElf	105.9
Texaco	51.1
Chevron	48.1
ENI	45.1
Repsol YPF	42.3
USX	35.6
Conoco	32.5
SK	31.8
Nippon Mitsubishi Oil	28.0
Tosco	24.5
Phillips Petroleum	21.2

Note: Revenues represent total revenues, including revenues from non-petroleum business.

Source: Adapted from Fortune, *The Fortune Global* 500, 2001.

The largest oil state-owned enterprises, 2000

SOE	*US $ (billion)*
Saudi Aramco	66.0
PDVSA	53.7
Sinopec	45.3
Petrobras	27.0
Statoil	23.6
Indian Oil	22.3

Source: Adapted from Fortune, *The Fortune Global 500*, 2001. Saudi Aramco's revenue was calculated using information from OPEC and EIA and only includes export revenues.

than those of most rivals including both Shell and Exxon Mobil. TotalFinaElf is also the largest producer of liquefied natural gas and holds half of the world's supply of this product.

The next largest companies in the oil industry (fifth and sixth in revenues) are Texaco and Chevron which had revenues in 2000 of $51 and $48 billion respectively. The two are in the process of merging after US and EU regulators approved the deal in 2001.

In 2001, Oklahoma-based Phillips Petroleum acquired Tosco, a major oil refiner. The combined revenues of these two companies in 2000 were just short of $47 billion and this acquisition provides Phillips with a tremendous increase in its refinery capacity as well giving the company a large number of service stations on the west coast of the US.

This pattern of increasing company size through acquisitions has also been used in Asia. In 1999 Nippon Oil bought Mitsubishi Oil, creating Japan's largest oil company. In 2000 Nippon Mitsubishi Oil had revenues of $28 billion.

Why are these oil companies merging? One of the main reasons is that the maturity of existing oil fields is forcing companies to search for new oil deposits in areas that are not easily accessible. Oil exploration in mountainous regions, the frigid Arctic, and ocean depths of more than one mile requires extremely large capital outlays and entails a great deal of risk. In addition, these firms have to invest millions of dollars in research and development and sometimes end up spending years negotiating with governments for the right to drill for oil in the country (or in offshore waters that are controlled by them) and to build refineries and pipelines there. Only large companies with enormous financial resources are able to do this. In addition, state-owned oil MNEs are major competitors, see table, "The largest oil state-owned enterprises, 2000" above. Moreover, if a company has a major oil strike, it has to be able to take advantage of economies of scale in order to bring the oil to market at competitive prices. Again, this development favors large firms. This is why experts in the energy business predict that there will be continual mergers and acquisitions in the industry as the large firms jockey for position and acquire smaller rivals and others in complementary businesses such as chemicals and oil-related products.

Websites: ***www.exxon.com***; ***www.bp.com***; ***www.shell.com***; ***www.totalfinaelf.com***; ***www.chevron.com***; ***www.texaco.com***; ***www.chevrontexaco.com***; ***www.eni.it***; ***www.repsol-ypf.com***; ***www.marathon.com***; ***www.conoco.com***; ***www.sk.com***; ***www.nmoc.co.jp***; ***www.phillips66.com***; ***www.saudiaramco.com***; ***www.pdvsa.com***; ***www.sinopec.com.cn***; ***www.petrobras.com.br***; ***www.statoil.com***; and ***www.iocl.com***.

Sources: Adapted from Fortune, *The Fortune Global 500*, April 16, 2001; Raymond Colitt, "Brazil Seeks Energy Boost," *Financial Times*, June 18, 2001; "In Praise of Big Oil," *Economist*, October 19, 2000; "Hunting the Big One," *Economist*, October 19, 2000; "ChevronTexaco Merger Approved by US Regulator," *BBC.co.uk*, September 7, 2001.

1. **Are companies such as Exxon Mobil, BP Amoco, and Royal Dutch/Shell MNEs? What criteria do they meet that makes them MNEs?**
2. **How important is an understanding of governmental regulation to success in this industry?**
3. **In terms of Porter's determinants of national competitive advantage that are presented in Figure 1.1, which one of these four determinants is most important for these oil companies? Why?**

REAL CASE

Pizza Hut in Russia

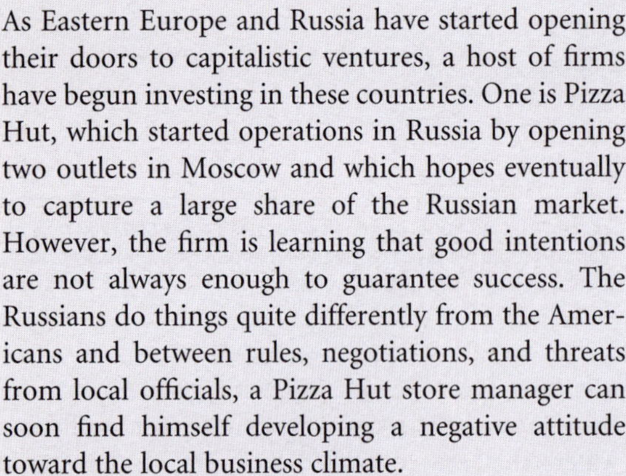

As Eastern Europe and Russia have started opening their doors to capitalistic ventures, a host of firms have begun investing in these countries. One is Pizza Hut, which started operations in Russia by opening two outlets in Moscow and which hopes eventually to capture a large share of the Russian market. However, the firm is learning that good intentions are not always enough to guarantee success. The Russians do things quite differently from the Americans and between rules, negotiations, and threats from local officials, a Pizza Hut store manager can soon find himself developing a negative attitude toward the local business climate.

The two first Moscow units began as joint ventures between PepsiCo, the previous owner of Pizza Hut (in 1997 Pizza Hut became a member of Tricon Global Restaurants), and the city of Moscow. However, this arrangement did not guarantee smooth sailing. For example, one Friday afternoon, soon after the units opened, a local sanitary inspector showed up, announced that the unit had failed to file all the necessary papers, including venereal disease tests for every employee, and wired the doors shut. The manager made a frantic call to local health authorities and was told to see them at 4 p.m. that day. When he arrived, they had left for the weekend. He then made an urgent call to the president of PepsiCo who was bicycling in France. The president called the Russian ambassador to the US and by the next afternoon Pizza Hut in Moscow was back in business.

On the positive side, the restaurant is very popular with customers and the company has managed to keep prices under control by negotiating carefully with local suppliers. Additionally, the manager of the overall operation has found that, by traveling south of Moscow to small farms, he has been able to purchase food of better quality. The farmers were initially unaccustomed to cleaning and boxing their produce carefully before shipping it, but because Pizza Hut pays more for food that is cleaned and prepared, the farmers are now happy to do this.

The company is also learning from experience how to increase operating efficiency. For example, Russian customers prefer US food over their own, so initial attempts to create cuisine with a "Moscow taste" were soon abandoned. The unit manager has also learned that the fastest way to get things done in Russia is often to bypass the system and take matters into one's own hands. For example, when truck drivers are late in picking up supplies, the manager goes out in the street and hires trucks. And there are a few things that the Russians are learning about the way Pizza Hut does business. For example, despite Russian arguments that trained cooks make the best pizzas, the truth is that eager, inexperienced youngsters are usually superior and within a few weeks they are turning out pizzas that trained cooks cannot match. As time goes by it is likely that both sides will continue to learn from each other.

Websites: ***www.pizzahut.com*** and ***www.pepsico.com***.

Sources: Adapted from Allen R. Myerson, "Setting Up an Island in the Soviet Union," *New York Times*, December 30, 1990, Section 3, pp. 1, 6; Lois Therrien, "The Hunger Pangs Let Up a Little," *Business Week*, January 11, 1993, p. 97; and Sunita Wadekar Bhargava, "Gimme a Double Shake and a Lard on White," *Business Week*, March 1, 1993, p. 59; ***www.triconglobal.com***.

1. **Why did Pizza Hut make a direct investment in Russia? Would they not have made more profit by putting these funds into a new, US-based unit?**
2. **How does Pizza Hut use demand conditions to help revise operating strategy?**
3. **How important is an understanding of government regulations to the success of the Moscow operation? Why?**

ENDNOTES

1 United Nations, *World Investment Report 2001* (Geneva: UNCTAD, 2001) stated that there are as many as 60,000 MNEs in the world. But most of them are small companies. The largest 500 MNEs account for over 80 per cent of all the sales of the 30,000 MNEs. We focus on the 500 MNEs in this book.
2 See Alan M. Rugman, *The End of Globalization* (London: Random House, 2000), Chapter 7, pp. 120–137.
3 Rugman (2000) n. 2 above, Chapter 7, pp. 120–129.
4 Rugman (2000) n. 2 above, Chapter 7, pp. 120, 134–136.
5 Joseph Kahn and Edmund L. Andrews, "World's Economy Slows to a Walk in Rare Lockstep," *New York Times*, August 20, 2001, pp. A 1, A 8.
6 Jeff Pruzan, "Nasdaq Falls as Gateway Closes Shops," *FT.com*, January 26, 2001.
7 Scott Morrison and Matthew Leising, "Gateway to Axe Quarter of Workforce," *Financial Times*, August 29, 2001, p. 15.
8 See Andrew Hill, Sheila McNulty, Gwen Robinson, Khozem Merchant and Virginia Marsh, "The Days that Enron Shook the World," *FT.com*, December 23, 2001 and Andrew Hill and Stephen Fidler, "Enron Ties Itself in Knots, Then Falls Over," *FT.com*, January 29, 2002.
9 Alexandra Harney and Ken Hijino, "Toshiba to Axe 18,000 Jobs in Sweeping Restructuring," *Financial Times*, August 28, 200l, p. 1.
10 Michiyo Nakamoto, "Hitachi Slashes 15,000 Jobs and Warns on Profits," *Financial Times*, September 1/2, 2000, p. 1.
11 Emily Nelson, "P&G May Cut 10% to 20% of Work Force," *Wall Street Journal*, March 21, 2001, p. A 3.
12 "Daewoo Motor to Lay Off Managers," *New York Times*, October 26, 2000, p. W1.
13 Gerard Baker, "Growth Slows to Eight-Year Low," *Financial Times*, August 30, 2001, p. 1.
14 Nancy Dunne, "US Sends Top Official to Help Solve Trade Dispute," *FT.com*, November 27, 2001; Frances Williams, "Go-ahead Set for Banana Regime," *FT.com*, October 8, 2001 and Jagdish Bhagwati, "The Unwinnable War," *FT.com*, January 29, 2002.
15 "Edging Closer," *Economist*, June 16, 2001, pp. 71–72 and Rahul Jacob, "HK Reaps Early Reward from Beijing's WTO Move," *FT.com*, November 13, 2001.
16 Dexter Roberts et al., "Will China Follow WTO Rules?" *Business Week*, June 5, 2000, pp. 42–48 and Frances William, "WTO Formally Approves China as a Member," *FT.com*, November 10, 2001.
17 "Western European Telecoms Map," *Financial Times*, June 27, 2001, p. 5.
18 Richard M. Hodgetts, *Measures of Quality and High Performance* (New York: American Management Association, 1998).
19 Also see Paul Ellis and Anthony Pecotich, "Social Factors Influencing Export Initiation in Small and Medium-Sized Enterprises," *Journal of Marketing Research*, February 2001, pp. 119–130.
20 Alan Rugman and Richard Hodgetts, "The End of Global Strategy," *European Management Journal*, August 2001, pp. 333–343.
21 "World Competitiveness Index," *Economist*, May 5, 2001, p. 98.
22 The following section is an abbreviated version of the model and the 10-country empirical analysis of Michael Porter, *The Competitive Advantage of Nations* (New York: Free Press, Macmillan, 1990), especially Chapters 3 and 4.
23 Michael E. Porter, "The Competitive Advantage of Nations," *Harvard Business Review*, March/April 1990, pp. 80–81.
24 Porter, ibid., p. 83.
25 Christine Tierney et al., "Volkswagen," *Business Week*, July 23, 2001, p. 64.
26 Sarah Ellison, "Carrefour and Ahold Find Shoppers Like to Think Local," *Wall Street Journal*, August 31, 2001, p. A 5.
27 Richard Tomlinson, "Who's Afraid of Wal-Mart?" *Fortune*, June 26, 2000, p. 188.
28 David Ibison and Rpohit Jaggi, "Kawasaki Joins Suzuki in Search of an Easier Ride," *Financial Times*, August 30, 2001, p. 15.

ADDITIONAL BIBLIOGRAPHY

Beamish, Paul W. and Calof, Jonathan L. "International Business Education: A Corporate View," *Journal of International Business Studies*, vol. 20, no. 3 (Fall 1989).

Becker, Fred G. "International Business and Governments: Issues and Institutions," *Management International Review*, vol. 32, no. 4 (Fourth Quarter 1992).

Caves, Richard E. "Research on International Business: Problems and Prospects," *Journal of International Business Studies*, vol. 29, no. 1 (First Quarter 1998).

Daniels, John D. "Relevance in International Business Research: A Need for More Linkages," *Journal of International Business Studies*, vol. 22, no. 2 (Second Quarter 1991).

Dunning, John H. "The Study of International Business: A Plea for a More Interdisciplinary Approach," *Journal of International Business Studies*, vol. 20, no. 3 (Fall 1989).

Eden, Lorraine and Lenway, Stefanie, "Introduction to the Symposium Multinationals: The Janus Face of Globalization," *Journal of International Business Studies*, vol. 32, no. 3 (Fall 2001).

Gupta, Anil K. "Converting Global Presence into Global Competitive Advantage," *The Academy of Management Executive*," vol. 15, no. 2 (May 2001).

Hax, Arnoldo C. "Building the Firm of the Future," *Sloan Management Review*, vol. 30, no. 3 (Spring 1989).

Kline, John M. "Trade Competitiveness and Corporate Nationality," *Columbia Journal of World Business*, vol. 24, no. 3 (Fall 1989).

Lecraw, Donald J. "Review of World Investment Report 1992: Transnational Corporations as Engines of Growth," *Journal of International Business Studies*, vol. 24, no. 3 (Third Quarter 1993).

Mulligan, Thomas M. "The Two Cultures in Business Education," *Academy of Management Review*, vol. 12, no. 4 (October 1987).

Nehrt, Lee C. "The Internationalization of the Curriculum," *Journal of International Business Studies*, vol. 18, no. 1 (Spring 1987).

Rugman, Alan M. and Stanbury, William. *Global Perspective: Internationalizing Management Education* (Vancouver BC: Centre for International Business Studies, UBC, 1992).

Rugman, Alan M. and Verbeke, Alain. "Multinational Enterprises and Public Policy," *Journal of International Business Studies*, vol. 29, no. 1 (First Quarter 1998).

Yip, George S., Loewe, Pierre M. and Yoshino, Michael Y. "How to Take Your Company to the Global Market," *Columbia Journal of World Business*, vol. 23, no. 4 (Winter 1988).

APPENDIXES TO CHAPTER 1

Appendix 1A The top 25 importers in the world, 2000

Rank	*Country*	*Value of world imports (in millions of US $)*
1	United States	1,238,200
2	Germany	500,278
3	Japan	377,153
4	United Kingdom	334,967
5	France	331,840
6	Canada	262,721
7	Italy	235,280
8	China P.R.	225,096
9	Netherlands	215,716
10	China P.R., Hong Kong	213,183
11	Mexico	191,904
12	Belgium	172,401
13	Korea	160,479
14	Spain	144,692
15	Taiwan	140,010
16	Singapore	134,630
17	Switzerland	82,542
18	Malaysia	82,195
19	Australia	74,493
20	Austria	72,117
21	Sweden	69,333
22	Brazil	61,875
23	Thailand	56,915
24	Turkey	54,501
25	Ireland	50,640

Note: Imports take into account freight and insurance costs.

Source: Adapted from International Monetary Fund, *Direction of Trade Statistics Yearbook, 2001* (Washington DC: IMF, 2001).

Appendix 1B The top 25 exporters in the world, 2000

Rank	*Country*	*Value of world exports (in millions of US $)*
1	United States	771,991
2	Germany	548,785
3	Japan	477,333
4	France	323,528
5	United Kingdom	282,798
6	Canada	275,183
7	China P.R.	249,195
8	Italy	236,569
9	Netherlands	229,741
10	China P.R., Hong Kong	201,871
11	Belgium	184,565
12	Korea	171,826
13	Mexico	166,455
14	Taiwan	148,122
15	Singapore	137,932
16	Spain	108,850
17	Russia	102,998
18	Malaysia	98,153
19	Sweden	85,159
20	Switzerland	80,526
21	Ireland	76,335
22	Saudi Arabia	74,688
23	Austria	67,455
24	Thailand	65,160
25	Australia	63,615

Note: Exports do not take into account freight and insurance costs.

Source: Adapted from International Monetary Fund, *Direction of Trade Statistics Yearbook, 2001* (Washington DC: IMF, 2001).

Appendix 1C Direction of world trade flows, 1991–2000

	With industrial countries		*With developing countries*		*With other countries n.i.e.**		*Total*	
	Exports	*Imports*	*Exports*	*Imports*	*Exports*	*Imports*	*Exports*	*Imports*
Industrial countries								
1991	1,872.3	1,922.6	614.4	667.2	1.6	1.0	2,488.3	2,592.3
1992	1,963.2	2,009.7	676.0	691.2	1.2	1.1	2,650.0	2,702.6
1993	1,803.6	1,793.7	726.3	708.2	1.1	0.9	2,558.2	2,529.0
1994	2,044.7	2,038.1	809.2	812.7	0.7	1.1	2,914.1	2,902.0
1995	2,416.3	2,398.1	976.8	966.9	1.0	1.3	3,469.8	3,432.0
1996	2,459.1	2,442.2	1,020.5	1,038.1	1.4	1.3	3,564.2	3,553.3
1997	2,507.5	2,483.9	1,077.5	1,107.1	1.5	1.4	3,643.3	3,631.9
1998	2,600.1	2,573.9	992.4	1,105.3	1.2	1.2	3,670.6	3,727.2
1999	2,755.9	2,724.2	988.8	1,210.3	1.9	1.1	3,739.4	3,920.2
2000	2,887.7	2,865.9	1,120.0	1,485.7	2.2	1.4	3,984.3	4,317.0
Developing countries								
1991	583.6	622.7	370.9	366.3	2.1	1.1	984.0	1.006.6
1992	640.4	720.4	429.0	423.6	1.9	2.2	1,102.3	1,162.8
1993	664.6	768.4	470.6	470.0	1.7	1.3	1,160.5	1,261.4
1994	755.8	857.2	569.5	550.4	1.7	1.4	1,358.4	1,432.9
1995	884.2	1,023.1	712.0	691.9	2.2	1.3	1,642.8	1,741.1
1996	954.7	1,084.9	776.3	754.5	2.5	1.9	1,775.6	1,871.4
1997	1,016.9	1,132.4	835.7	804.8	1.8	1.5	1,893.2	1,965.2
1998	1,008.4	1,064.7	735.7	728.5	1.8	1.3	1,773.8	1,814.5
1999	1,114.4	1,071.7	761.1	770.1	1.8	1.3	1,904.8	1,864.9
2000	1,353.9	1,218.3	955.4	983.6	2.5	1.3	1,353.9	2,233.6

* n.i.e. (not included elsewhere) refers to Cuba and North Korea.

Note: Numbers do not add up due to trade to non-identified countries and due to rounding.
Exports are calculated without including freight and insurance while imports include freight and insurance costs.

Source: Adapted from International Monetary Fund, *Direction of Trade Statistics Yearbook, 1996* (Washington DC: IMF, 1996) and International Monetary Fund, *Direction of Trade Statistics Yearbook, 2001* (Washington DC: IMF, 2001).

Appendix 1D World trade flows by major countries and regions, 2000

Countries/regions	*2000 (in billions of US $)*	*% of world*	*Countries/regions*	*2000 (in billions of US $)*	*% of world*
Exports to			**Imports from**		
World	6,368.7	100.0	World	6,608.7	100.0
Industrial Countries	4,024.7	63.2	Industrial Countries	4,370.8	66.1
Developing Countries	2,341.5	36.8	Developing Countries	2,233.6	33.8
Africa	121.4	1.9	Africa	117.6	1.8
Asia	1,265.2	19.9	Asia	1,186.3	18.0
Europe	316.6	5.0	Europe	325.2	4.9
Middle East	266.6	4.2	Middle East	193.5	2.9
Western hemisphere	371.6	5.8	Western hemisphere	410.9	6.2

Note: Numbers might not add up due to rounding.

Source: Adapted from International Monetary Fund, *Direction of Trade Statistics Yearbook, 2001* (Washington DC: IMF, 2001).

Appendix 1E Inward stocks of world foreign direct investment

Country/regions	1990 (in billions of US $)	% of total	1999* (in billions of US $)	% of total
Developed countries	1,380,827	78.4	3,230,800	67.7
North America	507,783	28.8	1,253,555	26.3
United States	394,911	22.4	1,087,289	22.8
Canada	112,872	6.4	166,266	3.5
Western Europe	770,434	43.7	1,757,208	36.8
European Union	723,455	41.1	1,652,322	34.6
Austria	9,884	0.6	23,363	0.5
Belgium/Luxembourg	58,388	3.3	181,184	3.8
Denmark	9,192	0.5	37,830	0.8
Finland	5,132	0.3	16,540	0.3
France	86,508	4.9	181,974	3.8
Germany	111,232	6.3	225,595	4.7
Greece	14,016	0.8	22,948	0.5
Ireland	5,502	0.3	43,969	0.9
Italy	57,985	3.3	107,995	2.3
Netherlands	73,564	4.2	215,234	4.5
Portugal	9,769	0.6	20,513	0.4
Spain	65,916	3.7	112,582	2.4
Sweden	12,461	0.7	68,035	1.4
United Kingdom	203,905	11.6	394,560	8.3
Other Western Europe	46,979	2.7	104,886	2.2
Switzerland	34,245	1.9	73,099	1.5
Norway	12,391	0.7	30,885	0.6
Others	343	0.0	902	0.0
Other developed countries	102,609	5.8	220,037	4.6
Australia and New Zealand	81,549	4.6	151,817	3.2
Japan	9,850	0.6	38,806	0.8
Israel	2,012	0.1	12,366	0.3
South Africa	9,198	0.5	17,048	0.4
Developing countries	377,380	21.4	1,438,484	30.1
Africa	44,104	2.5	93,066	2.0
Asia	211,632	12.0	846,677	17.7
Latin America and the Caribbean	118,300	6.7	485,604	10.2
Developing Europe	1,131	0.1	9,773	0.2
Central and Eastern Europe	2,991	0.2	102,697	2.2
Least developed countries	7,092	0.4	28,602	0.6
Total	1,761,198	100.0	4,771,981	100.0
Addenda:				
Outward stock	1,716,364		4,759,333	
Inward stock	1,761,198		4,771,981	
Difference	−44,834		−12,648	

* 1999 numbers are estimates.

Note: Numbers might not add up due to rounding.
Developing Europe refers to Bosnia and Herzegovina, Croatia, Malta, Slovenia, and TFYR Macedonia.

Source: Adapted from United Nations, *World Investment Report 2000*.

Appendix 1F Outward stocks of world foreign direct investment

Country/regions	1990 (in billions of US $)	% of total	1999* (in billions of US $)	% of total
Developed countries	1,634,099	95.2	4,276,961	89.9
North America	515,350	30.0	1,309,813	27.5
United States	430,521	25.1	1,131,466	23.8
Canada	84,829	4.9	178,347	3.7
Western Europe	866,450	50.5	2,574,926	54.1
European Union	789,401	46.0	2,336,631	49.1
Austria	4,273	0.2	17,522	0.4
Belgium/Luxembourg	40,636	2.4	159,461	3.4
Denmark	7,342	0.4	42,035	0.9
Finland	11,227	0.7	31,803	0.7
France	110,119	6.4	298,012	6.3
Germany	151,581	8.8	420,908	8.8
Greece	853	0.0	783	0.0
Ireland	2,150	0.1	15,096	0.3
Italy	57,261	3.3	168,370	3.5
Netherlands	109,005	6.4	306,396	6.4
Portugal	504	0.0	9,605	0.2
Spain	15,652	0.9	97,553	2.0
Sweden	49,491	2.9	104,985	2.2
United Kingdom	229,307	13.4	664,103	14.0
Other Western Europe	77,049	4.5	238,295	5.0
Switzerland	66,086	3.9	199,452	4.2
Norway	10,888	0.6	38,423	0.8
Others	75	0.0	420	0.0
Other developed countries	252,299	14.7	392,222	8.2
Australia and New Zealand	34,680	2.0	62,453	1.3
Japan	201,440	11.7	292,781	6.2
Israel	1,169	0.1	6,873	0.1
South Africa	15,010	0.9	30,115	0.6
Developing countries	81,907	4.8	468,744	9.8
Africa	12,249	0.7	16,974	0.4
Asia	48,929	2.9	345,206	7.3
Latin America and the Caribbean	20,378	1.2	104,580	2.2
Developing Europe	258	0.0	607	0.0
Central and Eastern Europe	358	0.0	13,628	0.3
Least developed countries	533	0.0	1,653	0.0
Total	1,716,364	100.0	4,759,333	100.0

* 1999 numbers are estimates.

Note: Numbers might not add up due to rounding.
Developing Europe refers to Bosnia and Herzegovina, Croatia, Malta, Slovenia, and TFYR Macedonia.

Source: Adapted from United Nations, *World Investment Report 2000*.

Chapter 2

The Multinational Enterprise

CONTENTS

OBJECTIVES OF THE CHAPTER

Most of the best-known companies in the world are multinational enterprises, and many of their names are easily recognized because their products and services are so popular. This is true for US MNEs, such as General Motors, Exxon, and IBM, but for others as well. Consider, for example, some of the largest industrial multinationals headquartered in the European Union: Unilever (Britain/Netherlands), Fiat (Italy), Nokia (Finland), Volkswagen (Germany), Philips (Netherlands), Peugeot (France), Nestlé (Switzerland), and in Japan: Sony, Fuji, and Toyota. There are also MNEs from non-triad areas such as Samsung (South Korea), Codelco (Chile), Anglogold (South Africa), Nortel Networks (Canada). The primary objective of this chapter is to examine the nature and operations of multinational enterprises; this is the last stage of the internationalization process. In doing so, we will devote particular attention to the characteristics of multinationals and to studying how they manage their operations.

The specific objectives of this chapter are to:

1. *Describe* the characteristics of multinational enterprises.
2. *Explain* the internationalization process.
3. *Explain* why firms become multinational enterprises.
4. *Discuss* the strategic philosophy of these firms.
5. *Examine* select multinational enterprises in action.
6. *Study* some of the ways in which these firms use strategic management.

ACTIVE LEARNING CASE

Disneyland in Europe

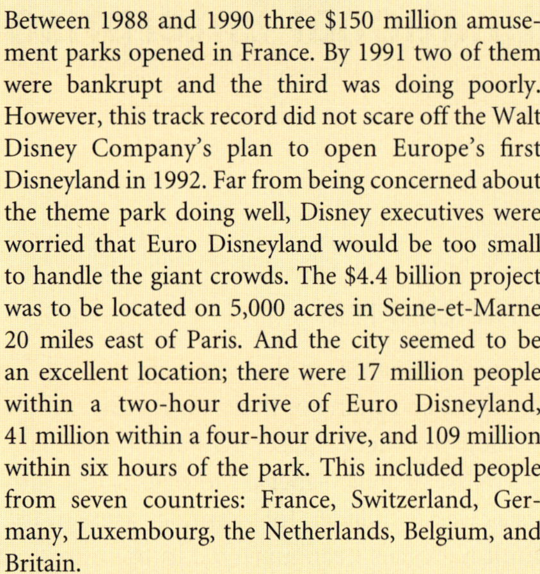

Between 1988 and 1990 three $150 million amusement parks opened in France. By 1991 two of them were bankrupt and the third was doing poorly. However, this track record did not scare off the Walt Disney Company's plan to open Europe's first Disneyland in 1992. Far from being concerned about the theme park doing well, Disney executives were worried that Euro Disneyland would be too small to handle the giant crowds. The $4.4 billion project was to be located on 5,000 acres in Seine-et-Marne 20 miles east of Paris. And the city seemed to be an excellent location; there were 17 million people within a two-hour drive of Euro Disneyland, 41 million within a four-hour drive, and 109 million within six hours of the park. This included people from seven countries: France, Switzerland, Germany, Luxembourg, the Netherlands, Belgium, and Britain.

Disney officials were optimistic about the project. Their US parks, Disneyland and Disneyworld, were extremely successful and Tokyo Disneyland was so popular that on some days it could not accommodate the large number of visitors. Simply put, the company was making a great deal of money from its parks. However, the Tokyo park was franchised to others and Disney management felt that it had given up too much profit with this arrangement. This would not be the case at Euro Disneyland. The company's share of the venture was to be 49 per cent for which it would put up $160 million. Other investors put in $1.2 billion, the French government provided a low interest $900 million loan, banks loaned the business $1.6 billion, and the remaining $400 million was to come from special partnerships formed to buy properties and to lease them back. For its investment and management of the operation, the Walt Disney Company was to receive 10 per cent of Euro Disney's admission fees, 5 per cent of food and merchandise revenues, and 49% of all profits.

The location of the amusement park was thoroughly researched. The number of people who could be attracted to various locations throughout Europe and the amount of money they were likely to spend during a visit to the park were carefully calculated. In the end, France and Spain had proved to offer the best locations. Both countries were well aware of the park's capability for creating jobs and stimulating their economy. As a result, each actively wooed the company. In addition to offering a central location in the heart of Europe, France was prepared to provide considerable financial incentives. Among other things, the French government promised to build a train line to connect the amusement park to the European train system. Thus, after carefully comparing the advantages offered by both countries, France was chosen as the site for the park.

At first things appeared to be off to a roaring start. Unfortunately, by the time the park was ready to open, a number of problems had developed and some of these had a very dampening effect on early operations. One was the concern of some French people that Euro Disney was nothing more than a transplanting of Disneyland into Europe. In their view the park did not fit into the local culture, and some of the French press accused Disney of "cultural imperialism". Others objected to the fact that the French government, as promised in the contract, had expropriated the necessary land and sold it without profit to the Euro Disneyland development people. Signs reading "Don't gnaw away our national wealth" and "Disney go home" began appearing along roadways. These negative feelings may well have accounted for the fact that on opening day only 50,000 visitors showed up, in contrast to the 500,000 that were expected. Soon thereafter, operations at the park came under criticism from both visitors and employees. Many visitors were upset about the high prices. In the case of British tourists, for example, because of the Franc exchange rate, it was cheaper for them to go to Florida than to Euro Disney. In the case of employees, many of them objected to the pay rates and the working conditions. They also raised concerns about a variety of company policies ranging from personal grooming to having to speak English in meetings, even if most people in attendance spoke French. Within the first month 3,000 employees quit. Some of the other operating problems were a result of Disney's previous experiences. In the US, for example, liquor was not sold outside of the hotels or specific areas. The general park was kept alcohol free, including the restaurants, in order to maintain a family atmosphere. In Japan, this policy was accepted and worked very well. However, Europeans were used to having outings with alcoholic beverages. As a result of these types of problems, Euro Disney soon ran into financial problems.

In 1994, after three years of heavy losses, the operation was in such bad shape that some people were predicting that the park would close. However, a variety of developments saved the operation. For one thing, a major investor purchased 24.6 per cent (reducing Disney's share to 39 per cent) of the company, injecting $500 million of much needed cash. Additionally, Disney waived its royalty fees and worked out a new loan repayment plan with the banks, and new shares were issued. These measures allowed Euro Disney to buy time while it restructured its marketing and general policies to fit the European market.

In October 1994, Euro Disney officially changed its name to "Disneyland Paris". This made the park more French and permitted it to capitalize on the romanticism that the word "Paris" conveys. Most importantly, the new name allowed for a new beginning, disassociating the park from the failure of Euro Disney. This was accompanied with measures designed to remedy past failures. The park changed its most offensive labor rules, reduced prices, and began being more culturally conscious. Among other things, alcohol beverages were now allowed to be served just about anywhere.

The company also began making the park more appealing to local visitors by giving it a "European" focus. Disney Tomorrowland, with its dated images of the space age, was jettisoned entirely and replaced by a gleaming brass and wood complex called Discoveryland, which was based on themes of Jules Verne and Leonardo da Vinci. In Disneyland food services were designed to reflect the fable's country of origin: Pinocchio's facility served German food, Cinderella's had French offerings, and at Balla Notte's the cuisine was Italian. The company also shot a 360-degree movie about French culture and showed it in the "Visionarium" exhibit.

These changes were designed to draw more visitors and it seems to have worked. Disneyland Paris reported a slight profit in 1996 and the park has continued to make money since then, although not a great deal (about $50 million annually) given that the operation grosses around $1 billion a year. Nonetheless, Disney has found that the number of visitors continues to increase even in the face of rising prices and the early anti-Disney hostility has all but dissipated. Meanwhile, investors are keeping their fingers crossed, hoping that the worst may now be behind them.

Websites: ***www.disneyinternational.com***; ***www.disneylandparis.com***; and ***www.disney.com***.

Sources: Adapted from Steven Greenhouse, "Playing Disney in the Parisian Fields," *New York Times*, February 17, 1991, Section 3, pp. 1, 6; "Euro Disney Resignation," *New York Times*, January 16, 1993, p. 19; William Heuslein, "Travel," *Forbes*, January 4, 1993, p. 178; Stewart Toy and Paula Dwyer, "Is Disney Headed for the Euro-Trash Heap?," *Business Week*, January 4, 1994, p. 52; Theodore Stanger et al., "Mickey's Trip to Trouble," *Newsweek*, February 4, 1994, pp. 34–39; "International Briefs: Revenue for Euro Disney Up by 17% in Quarter," *New York Times*, January 22, 1998; "Euro Disney Theme Park Cuts Loss, Shares Fall," *Yahoo News: Reuters*, April 22, 1998; Charles Fleming, "Euro Disney to Build Movie Theme Park Outside Paris," *Wall Street Journal*, September 30, 1999, pp. 18, 21; Paulo Prada, "Euro Disney Does Nicely. So Why are Investors Grumpy?" *Wall Street Journal*, September 6, 2000, p. A 20.

1. **What are some of the characteristics of multinational enterprises that are displayed by the Walt Disney Company?**
2. **Why did Disney take an ownership position in the firm rather than simply licensing some other firm to build and operate the park and settling for a royalty on all sales?**
3. **In what way did Euro Disney reflect the strategic philosophy of Walt Disney as a multinational enterprise?**
4. **Did Disney management conduct an external environmental analysis before going forward with Euro Disney? Explain.**

INTRODUCTION

Multinational enterprise (MNE) A company headquartered in one country but having operations in other countries

A **multinational enterprise (MNE)** is a company that is headquartered in one country but has operations in one or more other countries. Sometimes it is difficult to know if a firm is an MNE because multinationals often downplay the fact that they are foreign-held. For example, many people are unaware that Bayer, the drug company, is German-owned; Nestlé, the chocolate manufacturer, is a Swiss company; Northern Telecom is

Canadian; and Ford Motor now owns Jaguar, the British-based auto maker. Similarly, approximately 25 per cent of banks in California are Japanese-owned, but this is often not evident from their names. Simply put, many large MNEs have world holdings far beyond that what is known to the casual observer. Yet these companies have a dramatic impact on the quality of the goods and services being produced around the world. A closer look at the nature of MNEs will make this clear.

THE NATURE OF MULTINATIONAL ENTERPRISES

The United Nations has identified over 60,000 MNEs, but the largest 500 account for 80 per cent of all the world's foreign direct investment.[1] Table 2.1 shows the distribution of the world's largest 500 MNEs. Of these, 430 are from the "triad". There are 185 from the US, 141 from the EU, and 104 from Japan. The fact that 430 of the world's largest 500 MNEs are from the core triad is highly significant. It means that the triad is the basic unit of analysis for MNE strategy. Also, about 80–85 per cent of all the world's top MNEs have been from the triad for the last 20–30 years.[2] Total annual sales of these 500 firms are in excess of $12.5 trillion and they collectively employ over 43 million people.[3] These firms are engaged in a wide variety of operations including autos, chemicals, computers, consumer goods, financial services, industrial equipment, and oil and steel production. Clearly, these large enterprises have a significant impact on international business and the world economy.[4]

The names of the largest triad-based MNEs, as well as those from non-triad countries, are listed in Appendixes 2A–2E. Students should become familiarized with at least some of these MNEs as we proceed through this book. We provide the websites for virtually all of these MNEs as we discuss them in the text, and especially in the cases boxes.

Table 2.1 The world's largest 500 multinational enterprises, 2000

Country	*Number of MNEs*
United States	185
European Union	141
Japan	104
Canada	15
China	12
Switzerland	11
South Korea	11
Australia	7
Brazil	3
Russia	2
Norway	2
Mexico	2
Venezuela	1
South Africa	1
Singapore	1
Malaysia	1
India	1
Total	500

Source: Adapted from Fortune, *The Fortune Global 500*, 2001.

Active learning check 

Review your answer to Active Learning Case question 1 and make any changes you like. Then compare your answer with the one below.

1. What are some of the characteristics of multinational enterprises that are displayed by the Walt Disney Company?

One of the characteristics of a multinational enterprise is that ties of common ownership link affiliated firms. In this case the Walt Disney Company holds a substantial interest in Disneyland Paris, in addition to its ownership of Disneyland and Disneyworld in the US. A second characteristic is that the MNE draws on a common pool of resources. One way Disneyland Paris does this is through the use of trademarks and characters (Mickey Mouse, Goofy, Donald Duck) and the experience of the Disney team in setting up and running similar theme parks in the US. A third characteristic is that MNEs have a common strategy for linking together the affiliates. The Walt Disney Company does this through its overall plan such as the one it used for deciding where to set up Euro Disneyland and how to manage the park.

Characteristics of multinational enterprises

One way of identifying the characteristics of MNEs is by looking at the environment in which they operate. Figure 2.1 shows some of the major forces in this environment. Notice that an MNE has two major areas of concern: the home country of its headquarters and the host countries in which it does business. Stakeholders are not included within these two areas of Figure 2.1 because they can come from anywhere in the world. For example, an investor in Switzerland can purchase stock in Sears Roebuck even though the company does not do business in Switzerland.

One characteristic of MNEs is that their affiliates must be responsive to a number of important environmental forces, including competitors, customers, suppliers, financial institutions, and government (again see Figure 2.1). In some cases the same forces are at work in both the home and host country environments. For example, many of General Motors' competitors in the US market are the same as those in Europe: BMW, Ford, DaimlerChrysler, Honda, and Volkswagen, among others. Similarly, MNEs often use the same suppliers overseas that they employ domestically and it is common to find home country-based suppliers following their MNE customer to other geographic locales in order to provide the same types of services worldwide.

A second characteristic of an MNE is that it draws on a common pool of resources, including assets, patents, trademarks, information, and human resources. Since the affiliates are all part of the same company, they have access to assets that are often not available to outsiders. For example, both Ford and General Motors compete vigorously

Home Country	Stakeholders	**Host Countries**
Competitors		Competitors
Customers		Customers
Domestic affiliates	**Multinational enterprise**	Foreign affiliates
Suppliers		Suppliers
Government		Government
	Banks	

Figure 2.1 **The multinational enterprise and its environment**

in Europe and many of the design and styling changes developed for their European cars have now been introduced in US models. The flow of information and technology between European and US affiliates has led to success in the worldwide market for many MNEs. Similarly, if an affiliate needs expansion funds, an MNE will often help out by working with the affiliate to raise the money. If a loan is needed, the affiliate is likely to find many financial institutions that are willing to provide the money since the MNE will back the loan.

A third characteristic of an MNE is that it links together the affiliates and business partners with a common strategic vision. Simply put, all of the firms with whom the MNE works fit into the company's overall plan of what it wants to do and how it intends to go about implementing this strategy. General Motors (GM) is a good example. The auto giant has announced that it is now going to rely heavily on partnerships to help it grow.[5] GM realizes that no auto maker has all of the resources for achieving leadership in every region of the world or in every product segment. As a result, the company has formed a manufacturing partnership with Toyota to conduct research and development on fuel cell and gas-electric hybrid vehicles. GM also has created an alliance with Fuji Heavy Industries and its Subaru brand that allows GM to benefit from Fuji's strengths in small sport utility vehicles, continuously variable transmissions, and all-wheel-drive systems and, in turn, gives Fuji access to GM's vehicle platforms and other important manufacturing technologies. These types of arrangements are part of GM's new strategic vision – one that is not limited just to building cars. Today the company is looking into ways of providing customers with other auto-related services as seen by its Onstar communications program with wireless phone service that allows drivers to be in constant contact with someone who can give them information and assistance.

Active learning check

Review your answer to Active Learning Case question 2 and make any changes you like. Then compare your answer with the one below.

2. Why did Disney take an ownership position in the firm rather than simply licensing some other firm to build and operate the park and settling for a royalty on all sales?

Disney believed that the theme park was too lucrative a venture to settle for just a royalty on sales. The company felt that it would be giving up too much to simply "take the money and run" when by remaining and managing the operation it could garner a great deal more revenue. Moreover, not only is the revenue potential of the park extremely high, but Disney's initial investment of $160 million was extremely low given the amount of control it maintains and the fees and profits that would be generated should the park prove as highly attractive as company executives were forecasting. Disney also wanted to retain control over its brand name products and services in order to prevent imitation by substandard rivals and this is best done with an ownership position.

The internationalization process

Not all international business is done by MNEs. Indeed, setting up a wholly-owned subsidiary is usually the last stage of doing business abroad, as is shown in Figure 2.2.

Internationalization
The process by which a company enters a foreign market

Figure 2.2 outlines the typical process by which a firm producing a standardized product will seek to involve itself in a foreign market.[6] In this **internationalization** process the firm regards foreign markets as risky due to the fact that, as these markets are unknown to it, the firm faces export marketing costs. To avoid such information costs and risk, its strategy is to go abroad at a slow and cautious pace, often using the services of specialists

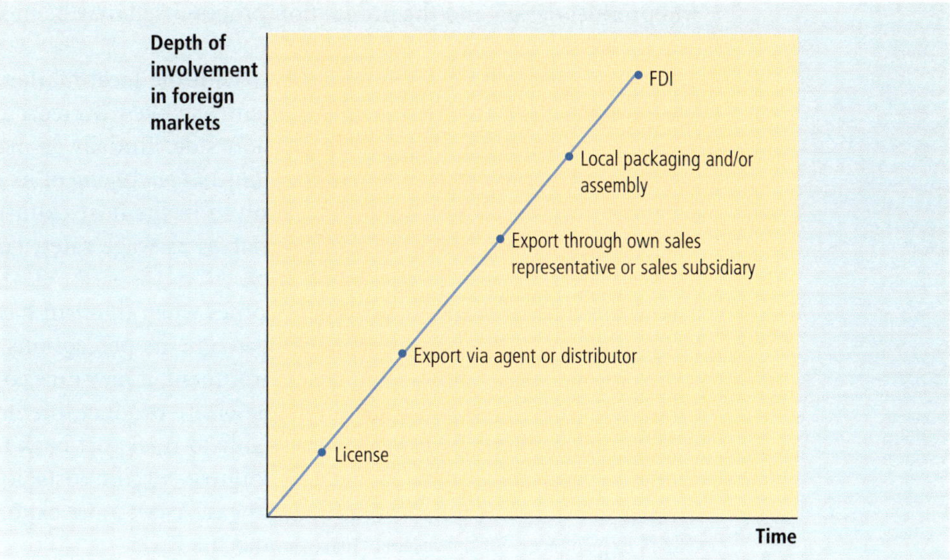

Figure 2.2 **Entry into foreign markets: the internationalization process**

in international trade outside the firm. Over time, familiarity with the foreign environment will reduce the information costs and help to alleviate the perceived risk of foreign involvement.

License
A contractual arrangement in which one firm (the licensor) provides access to some of its patents, trademarks, or technology to another firm in exchange for a fee or royalty

Licensor
A company that provides access to some of its patents, trademarks, or technology to another firm in exchange for a fee or royalty

Licensee
A firm given access to some of the patents, trademarks, or technology of another firm in exchange for a fee or royalty

Initially the firm may seek to avoid the risks of foreign involvement by arranging a licensing deal. A **license** agreement is a contractual arrangement in which one firm, the **licensor**, provides access to some of its patents, trademarks, or technology to another firm, the **licensee**, in exchange for a fee or royalty. This fee often involves a fixed amount upon signing the contract and then a royalty of 2–5 per cent on sales generated by the agreement. A typical licensing contract will run from five to seven years and be renewable at the option of either or both parties. This strategy is most suitable for a standardized product where there is no risk of dissipation of the firm's technological or managerial advantages. Otherwise, licensing will be reserved for a much later stage of entry. Indeed, when it is important for the firm to retain control over its firm-specific advantage in technology (as in internalization theory),[7] licensing will come as the last mode of entry. The firms involved in the process of internationalization, on the other hand, typically are not concerned about losing their firm-specific advantages. Rather, they want to avoid exposure to an uncertain foreign environment. Abstracting from the licensing option (and the more complex problem of joint ventures), the major types of foreign entry for a firm are as follows:

1. The firm sees potential extra sales by *exporting* and uses a *local agent or distributor* to enter a particular market. Often the firm uses exporting as a "vent" for its surplus production and may have no long-run commitment to the international market. If it does well abroad, however, it may then set up its own local sales representative or marketing subsidiary, in the hope of securing a more stable stream of export sales.
2. As exports come to represent a larger share of sales, the firm may increase its capacity to serve the export market. It will set an office for its *sales representative* in a major market, or set up a *sales subsidiary*. This stage marks an important departure for the firm from simply viewing exports as a marginal contributor to sales volume or as a vent for surplus in times of excess capacity. At this stage the firm will often set up a separate *export department* to manage foreign sales and production for such markets

and product design and the production process itself may be modified to tailor products for export markets.
3. After the firm has become more familiar with the local market, some of the uncertainty associated with foreign involvement has been overcome. Now the firm may begin to move on the foreign production side. Initially it may start to use host-country workers to engage in *local assembly and packaging* of its product lines. This is a crucial step, since the firm is now involved in the host-country factor market and must deal with such environmental variables as wage rates, cultural attitudes, and worker expectations in its new labor force.
4. The final stage of foreign involvement comes when the firm has generated sufficient knowledge about the host country to overcome its perceptions of risk. Because it is more familiar with the host-country environment, it may now consider a *foreign direct investment* activity. In this it produces the entire product line in the host nation and sells its output there, or it may even be able to re-export back to the home country. These decisions depend on the relative country-specific costs; for example, if labor is inexpensive in the host nation (as in Southeast Asia), more exporting takes place than if it is expensive (as in Western Europe and the US).

It has become clear that the internationalization process is more complicated than it seems at first glance. Like all generalizations, this schematic path of export commitment relies on simplifications. In reality, the process of foreign entry is sufficiently complicated to depend on a careful weighing of many firm-specific and country-specific factors. A framework to model these firm-specific advantages (FSAs) and country-specific advantages (CSAs) is developed in Chapter 20.

Why firms become multinational enterprises

Companies become MNEs for a number of reasons. One is to *diversify* themselves against the risks and uncertainties of the domestic business cycle. By setting up operations in another country, multinationals can often diminish the negative effects of economic swings in the home country. This is a form of international diversification and it has been widely used by Japanese MNEs, for example, which have found that, while their home economy has been in an economic slump since the 1990s, their US operations have done quite well.

A second reason is to tap the growing world market for goods and services. This is part of the process of growth in an integrated world market, sometimes called "globalization" (i.e. the rapid growth of similar goods and services produced and distributed by MNEs on a worldwide scale). For example, many MNEs have targeted the US because of its large population and high per capita income. It is the world's single largest market in terms of gross domestic product. And since Americans have both a desire for new goods and services and the money to buy them, the US can be an ideal market. MNEs are also targeting China. While per capita gross domestic product is not very high, the country's large population and growing economy make it very attractive to multinationals. In 2001, China entered the World Trade Organization and this acceptance of international rules made China more attractive for MNEs.

Firms also become MNEs in response to increased foreign competition and a desire to protect their home market share. Using a "*follow the competitor*" strategy, a growing number of MNEs now set up operations in the home countries of their major competitors. This approach serves a dual purpose: (1) it takes away business from their competitors by offering customers other choices, and (2) it lets competitors know that, if they attack the MNE's home market, they will face a similar response. This strategy of staking

INTERNATIONAL BUSINESS STRATEGY *IN ACTION*

Italian family firms

In Italy more than 90 per cent of all small and medium-sized companies and some of the largest enterprises are family owned. In the fashion industry, for example, Versace and Missoni are family-held firms. So, too, are Benetton (apparel), Fiat (automobiles), and Pirelli (tires). In addition, Italian families own important manufacturers, as well as having operating control of some of the major banks and transportation companies in the country. For example, the Fiat family's empire grosses more than $7 billion euros annually and employs more than 200,000 people. It does this through the Fiat Group, a conglomerate consisting of over 1,000 firms with holdings in agricultural and construction equipment, automobiles, aviation, commercial vehicles, communications, insurance services, metallurgical products, production systems, and publishing. Most recently the Group has been looking to expand and in June 2001, along with Electricité de France, it bought Montedison, the country's largest agricultural holding company.

Another large family-owned Italian company is Pirelli, which, in recent years, has had annual revenues of around $7.5 million euros and employs around 40,000 people. Most of the firm's revenues are generated from its tire and cable businesses. Recently, along with Benetton, Pirelli has bought a controlling interest in Olivetti, the giant Italian computer and telecommunications corporation. As a result of this acquisition, Pirelli now has a 27 per cent stake in Telecom Italia, a telecommunications, information, and communication technology company with annual revenues of $30 billion euros and a workforce of around 120,000 people. This acquisition has also brought both Benetton and Pirelli into the wireless telecommunications business.

These two examples, Fiat and Pirelli, are typical of the holdings and influence of large Italian families in the country. Through their vast holdings and political power, they have been able to maintain a tight rein on various sectors of the economy. In addition, these family firms are protected against foreign investment by a secretive banking system that is headed by the Milan Bank, Mediobanca. This bank has financed nearly all of the takeover deals in Italy during the last 30 years. The bank also holds board positions on many of the country's conglomerates.

On a macro basis, the Italian business system reflects the twin pressures of local family culture and the increasing demands of international business. Like their larger counterparts, small and medium-sized family businesses are now using their personal and business networks to create MNEs that are branching out into the EU, as well as putting together deals in both North America and Asia.

Websites: ***www.olivetti.com***; ***www.versace.com***; ***www.missoni.it***; ***www.benetton.com***; ***www.fiat.com***; ***www.pirelli.com***; ***www.montedison.it*** and ***www.mediobanca.it***.

Sources: Fred Kapner, "Pirelli Seeks Rumour Probe," *Financial Times*, September 11, 2000, p. 18; Paul Meller, "European Panel Approves Takeover of Montedison," *New York Times*, August 29, 2001, p. W 1; Richard Owen, Clive Mathieson and Caroline Merrell, "Is the Fat Lady About to Sing for Bank Located behind La Scala?" *The Times*, August 4, 2001, p. 43; "Flattering to Deceive," *Economist*, August 2, 2001; ***www.olivetti.com***; Pirelli, annual report 2000; Juliana Ratner, Krishna Guha and Fred Kapner, "Small Stake Won Control of Telecom Italia," *Financial Times*, July 31, 2001.

out global market shares is particularly important when MNEs want to communicate the conditions under which they will retaliate.

A fourth reason why companies become an MNE is to reduce costs. By setting up operations close to the foreign customer, these firms can eliminate transportation expenses, avoid the overhead associated with having middlemen handle the product, respond more accurately and rapidly to customer needs, and take advantage of local resources. This process, known as "*internalization*" of control within the MNE, can help to reduce overall costs.

A fifth reason is to overcome *protective* devices such as tariff and non-tariff barriers by serving a foreign market from within. The EU provides an excellent example. Firms outside the EU are subject to tariffs on goods exported to EU countries. Firms producing the goods within the EU, however, can transport them to any other country in the bloc without paying tariffs. The same is now occurring in North America, thanks to the North American Free Trade Agreement (NAFTA), which has eliminated tariffs between Canada, the US, and Mexico.

A sixth reason for becoming an MNE is to take advantage of technological expertise by manufacturing goods directly (by FDI) rather than allowing others to do it under a license. Although the benefits of a licensing agreement are obvious, in recent years some MNEs have concluded that it is unwise to give another firm access to proprietary information such as patents, trademarks, or technological expertise, and they have allowed current licensing agreements to lapse. This has allowed them to reclaim their exclusive rights and then to manufacture and directly sell the products in overseas markets.

The strategic philosophy of multinational enterprises

Multinational enterprises are different from companies that confine their activities to the domestic market in that MNEs make decisions based on what is best for the overall

company, even if this means transferring jobs to other countries and cutting back the local workforce. In the last decade IBM, ABB, and Sony, for example, have spent considerable sums of money to train and develop local managers to handle overseas operations because the companies are finding that these managers are often much more effective than those sent from the home country. MNEs also hire large numbers of workers in overseas countries. In fact, foreign-owned firms in the US now employ approximately 3 million workers and US multinationals in the EU and Asian blocs account for even more than this number.

As a result there is a great deal of economic interaction in the international arena, giving business firms headquartered in one country a significant impact on the economies of other countries. This is true both when things are going well as well as when they are not. For example, with the recent slowdown of the world economy more and more MNEs are now trimming their workforces. Alcatel, the giant French telecommunications equipment maker, has announced plans to cut 29 per cent of its workforce and to reduce its factories down to a dozen, using outsourcing to handle all other production needs.[8] Philips, the giant Dutch electronics firm, reacting to a severe slowdown in demand for mobile phones and semiconductors, is now eliminating more than 7,000 jobs;[9] and Disney is cutting 4,000 positions, about 3 per cent of its worldwide workforce.[10] These decisions are all based on what is best for the overall company.

This same worldwide approach to operations can be seen in the way MNEs team up to get things done. One example is Airbus, the European consortium that consists of Germany, France, Great Britain, and Spain. Workforces in each of these countries are responsible for designing and building different parts of the aircraft and, as will be seen in the Active Learning Case in Chapter 3, the company has been very successful in recent years. Another example is provided by Mazda's sports car, the MX-5 Miata, which was designed in California, had its prototype created in England, was assembled in Michigan and Mexico using advanced electronic components invented in New Jersey and fabricated in Japan, and was financed from Tokyo and New York. Simply put, MNEs make whatever agreements are in their best interests, even if this means bringing in firms from three or four different countries.

Active learning check

Review your answer to Active Learning Case question 3 and make any changes you like. Then compare your answer with the one below.

3. In what way did Euro Disney reflect the strategic philosophy of Walt Disney as a multinational enterprise?

One way in which Euro Disney reflects the strategic philosophy of the company as an MNE is that Disney is willing to modify the park to meet the preferences of local visitors by catering to their markets. Paris Disneyland is not identical to Disneyland in California. The focus on European roots and culture is now an integral part of the park. In addition, notice how the company used an international approach to funding the project. The monies were not all raised in France. The government helped, but so did banks, private investors, and Disney itself. And when the operation ran into trouble, the company was willing to reconfigure its arrangement and give up some ownership and some revenue in order to get things back on an even keel.

MULTINATIONALS IN ACTION

There are many multinationals that sell a wide variety of good and services. Some are household names such as General Electric and General Motors. Other are not as well known and, in many cases, are SMEs. The following are examples of some MNEs in action.

Cemex SA

Cemex SA is Mexico's largest cement maker. It is also the third largest cement maker in the world and in recent years the company has been much more profitable than its two larger competitors thanks to a series of well-executed strategies. In particular, since the early 1990s Cemex has spent billions of dollars to acquire and fix up smaller cement companies, mainly in Latin America and the Caribbean. Most recently it purchased

Saraburi Cement of Thailand, a move designed to give it a base of operations in Asia.[11] Cemex's basic strategy is to focus on low-income markets where cement is still sold one bag at a time to retail customers and where the economy still needs to build a great many highways, bridges, and harbors.[12]

When Cemex initially embarked on this strategy, many bankers were concerned that the company would still be making most of its money in Mexico, and a devaluation of the peso would severely impact on its international operations. In late 1994 when the Mexican government suddenly devalued its currency, Cemex was generating only 25 per cent of its earnings from overseas operations and the firm was highly leveraged in dollars. However, instead of pulling back, Cemex convinced the bankers that the best strategy was to press forward and buy cement companies in Colombia and Venezuela. The decision was fortuitous. Venezuela soon devalued its own currency, but as its economy went into a tailspin Cemex sent in some of its own executives to straighten out the operation, reorganize the administrative and information systems, integrate the cement and concrete production operations, put in a new distribution system, and cut the workforce. By the end of the year Cemex had doubled the unit's annual cash flow to $200 million. Meanwhile in Mexico, where the firm still generates 50 per cent of its income, a stronger economy has resulted in higher sales and profits. As a result, Cemex is now paying down its debt and expanding operations in Europe and Asia where it is both buying and building plants; and the company estimates that by the end of the first decade of this century annual sales will be in excess of $10 billion and profits will be higher than ever.

Solectron

The Solectron Corporation, headquartered in Milpitas, California, is becoming very well known internationally, although the company's name does not appear on any of its products. This is because Solectron is an outsourcer that generates its revenues by producing goods for other companies.[13] For example, the company recently bought one of Sony's manufacturing plants in Japan. Today Solectron runs that factory and is able to provide the same type of electronic products to Sony at a lower cost than the giant Japanese firm could do itself. Like many electronic companies that design, manufacture, and sell their own products, Sony's return on investment has been shockingly low because of the large amount of capital that is tied up in its factories. In a typical year Sony's return on equity is around 5 per cent. In contrast, Solectron is able to earn a return on equity in the range of 12 per cent. By focusing exclusively on such things as customized electronics technology, state-of-the-art manufacturing, and supply chain assistance, Solectron is able to achieve economies of scale that allow it to produce and deliver goods both quickly and inexpensively. As a result, its customer list is extensive. Large firms such as Cisco Systems, the giant Internet equipment company that books over $20 million a day in web-based sales, rely on Solectron to handle a significant portion of their manufacturing needs. So too do smaller firms such as Handspring Inc., a California-based company that competes in the palm-size organizer market. In Handspring's case, the company realizes that its expertise is in the areas of designing and developing organizers as well as marketing them. As a result, it has turned over the production of these units to Solectron.

Today the cost of building new manufacturing plants is prohibitive for many firms. At the same time, the life cycle of products is becoming increasingly shorter. So if firms are going to reach their profit goals, they are going to have to find new ways to cut their expenses by outsourcing. This is good news for Solectron which is becoming one of the fastest growing MNEs.

BMW

BMW is one of the world's best-known auto firms and for many years it has successfully produced and sold quality cars. As a result, the company has been able to capture and hold a solid share of the middle and upper-middle car market. Most recently, however, BMW has been turning its attention to the lower end of the market. One of its new objectives is to produce a small BMW and sell it at a premium price. This car line, which has been dubbed the 2 Series by the press, is due to hit the market in 2004.[14]

Will BMW be successful in this venture? Some observers are quick to point out that small cars are a tempting but dangerous segment of the market. Profits are often elusive and competition is fierce. One of the big questions that is yet to be answered is how much of a premium buyers will be willing to pay for a small BMW. The company believes that there are customers who will pay a premium for value-added features and high performance. One of the features in the 2 Series will be rear wheel drive, not front wheel drive as is common in most small cars. And while front wheel drive offers better fuel economy, BMW believes that rear wheel drive will provide better handling and give the driver a better feel for the road. In addition, the company intends to give the 2 Series the same distinctive exterior look as its larger cars. As a result of these types of features, BMW feels that it will be able to attract buyers who are willing to pay a premium. In addition, the company is convinced that its name and reputation for quality will help it garner market share. In the past the firm has done exceptionally well and has consistently been one of the most profitable car makers in the world. However, this success has been in the upscale market. Whether the company can make money in the small car market while charging a premium price is going to be an interesting challenge for it.

Levi Strauss

Levi Strauss is one of the few companies that pulled out of China during the mid-1990s because it felt that the government was guilty of pervasive human rights violations. Now the company is back, expanding its manufacturing facilities, and selling its products locally.[15]

The company stopped manufacturing jeans in China after it found evidence of child labor, forced labor, and a military presence at factories that were producing clothing for the firm. The company did not own any of these factories on the mainland; it relied on local subcontractors to perform the manufacturing. However, company guidelines prohibited the suppliers from using child labor, forced labor, or excessive work hours. So when Levi Strauss learned of these violations, the company concluded that its association with the contractors would damage its reputation and it began a phased withdrawal from China.

Now Levi Strauss is coming back into the marketplace and even has plans to start a direct-marketing operation on the mainland. The firm has promised to monitor its new Chinese factories carefully to ensure that they comply with human rights guidelines. At the same time, however, Levi Strauss is glad to be back because, like many other MNEs, the company believes that China is a marketplace of the future. One senior executive in the company put it this way, "You're nowhere in Asia without being in China."

Canon

Canon is one of the world's leading photo and printer firms, but this has not always been true. For many years Canon followed the leaders and worked to improve its technology. However, in recent years the company has taken the lead against firms such as Leica in cameras and Xerox in photocopiers.[16]

Today Canon is in the top three in all of its major business lines; and its original product, cameras, now accounts for less than 10 per cent of sales. However, the firm is the world leader in both single-lens reflexes and compacts, and earns almost one-third of its income from copiers. And to maintain its momentum, Canon has adopted a two-pronged strategy. First, it is seeking to maintain profits by cutting costs in its core business by making suppliers more efficient and by shifting work to factories in Taiwan, in order to reduce the high cost of building some of its products in Japan.

Second, Canon is moving into the digital age by cultivating alliances with companies that know the networking and computer world better than it does. For example, Canon has teamed with Hewlett-Packard, one of its major competitors, to build laser printers. The company is also looking into developing smart printers with personal computer-like abilities including electronic mail; and it is to develop printers that produce high quality photo prints on plain paper. Quite clearly, Canon believes that its future rests with the continued development of innovative products that draw on its core competencies in the optical field.

Table 2.2 reports the geographical expansion between 1970 and 2000 of four of the world's largest MNEs, especially since 1985. The international presence of these MNEs is measured by the number of majority-owned foreign affiliates (subsidiaries) that they have.

Table 2.2 The international expansion of four MNEs

MNE	*Number of majority-owned foreign affiliates*		
	1970	*1985*	*2000*
Ford (US)	65	140	270
Unilever (EU)	94	146	244
Siemens (EU)	84	165	416
Marubeni (Japan)	16	44	170

Source: United Nations, *World Investment Report 2001* (Geneva: United Nations Conference on Trade and Development, 2001).

STRATEGIC MANAGEMENT AND MULTINATIONAL ENTERPRISES

As noted earlier, one of the characteristics of MNE affiliates is that they are linked by a strategic plan. As a result, units that are geographically dispersed and/or have diverse product offerings all work in accord with a strategic vision. The formulation and implementation of strategy will be discussed in detail in Chapter 8. Here we will look at the basic nature of the strategic management process and how select MNEs use strategic planning in managing their far-flung enterprises.

Strategic management of MNEs: an introduction

The strategic management process involves four major functions: strategy formulation, strategy implementation, evaluation, and the control of operations. These functions encompass a wide range of activities, beginning with an environmental analysis of external and internal conditions and an evaluation of organizational strengths and weaknesses. These activities serve as the basis for a well-formulated strategic plan; and by carefully implementing and controlling this plan, the MNE is able to compete effectively in the international arena. Figure 2.3 illustrates the five specific steps in this overall process.

Steps in the strategic management process

Basic mission
The reason that a firm is in existence

Strategic planning typically begins with a review of the company's **basic mission**, which is determined by answering the questions: What is the firm's business? What is its reason for existence? By answering these questions, the company clearly determines the direction in which it wants to go. Shell Oil, BP Amoco, and Texaco, for example, see themselves as being in the energy business, not in the oil business, and this focus helps to direct their long-range thinking. AT&T, Sprint, and MCI view themselves as in the communications business, not in the telephone business. Coca-Cola and PepsiCo see themselves in the food business, not in the soft-drink business.

In recent years a growing number of MNEs have revised their strategic plans because they realized that they had drifted too far away from their basic mission. Unilever, the giant Anglo-Dutch MNE, is a good example. After assessing its operations, the company concluded that it needed to adopt a "back to the core" strategy. As a result, it sold a wide range of peripheral operations, including transport, oil, milling, wallpaper, floor coverings, and turkey breeding. Today Unilever confines its business to consumer products, specialty chemicals, and agribusiness. The firm's strong research and development labs continue to develop new products in each of these areas, thus helping Unilever maintain its worldwide markets.

After determining its mission, an MNE will evaluate the external and internal environment. The goal of external environmental analysis is to identify opportunities and threats that will need to be addressed. Based on opportunity analysis, for example, a number of MNEs have been moving into East Germany. The Deutsche Bank, Germany's largest, has started a network of 250 branches there and Allianz, the giant insurance company, has bought a 50 per cent interest in Staatliche Versicherung, an East German insurance company. BMW has invested there in small startup companies to produce components and tools for its auto manufacturing business, and McDonald's has been opening fast-food restaurants in the region. These companies all see the region as having tremendous financial potential.

However, these expansion decisions were made only after the companies had analyzed the potential pitfalls, and there were many of them. One is that eastern Germans have lived in a centrally planned bureaucracy for almost a half century. Could they adapt to a free-market economy? Would they be able to accept individual responsibility in a country where the state was no longer the major provider? Would they be able to upgrade their inefficient factories and improve the quality of output? Many MNEs believed that, with an influx of capital, the country's economy could be turned around. At the same time, their external environmental analysis showed that it would be necessary to increase worker productivity, improve the local infrastructure, and bring in qualified managers to run the operations until a local cadre could be developed.

The purpose of internal environmental analysis is to evaluate the company's financial and personnel strengths and weaknesses. Examining its financial picture will help the MNE decide what it can afford to do in terms of expansion and capital investment. Examining its financial picture will also help it to identify areas where cost-cutting or divestment is in order. For example, in recent years some major US airlines have sold partial ownership to overseas carriers in order to increase the size of their fleet and better position themselves for competing in the market. By making an evaluation of its personnel, an MNE will be able to determine how well its current workforce can meet the challenges of the future and what types of people will have to be hired or let go.

Internal and external analyses will also help the MNE to identify both long-range goals (typically two to five years) and short-range goals (less than two years). The plan is then broken down into major parts, and each affiliate and department will be assigned goals and responsibilities. This begins the implementation process. Progress is then periodically evaluated and changes are made in the plan. For example, an MNE might realize that it must stop offering a particular good or service because the market is no longer profitable or it might create a new product in order to take advantage of an emerging demand. The box "International Business Strategy in Action: CNN" provides an example of this.

INTERNATIONAL BUSINESS STRATEGY *IN ACTION*

CNN

When United Nations forces liberated Kuwait from the invading Iraqi forces in 1991, people all over the world tuned into the Cable News Network (CNN). In Europe 5.1 million people had access to the CNN channel. By the time hostilities ended, the network had garnered 1.1 million new subscribers. In Japan, broadcasters relied heavily on CNN footage and analysis to provide news from the war. The same was true in the US where the major networks were not as well positioned as CNN to cover the story. Realizing that there was an international demand for global television news, networks in a host of countries began scurrying to enter this new market.

The one that was in the best initial position to take on CNN was the British Broadcasting Company (BBC) and by1997 it had launched a 24-hour local news channel in Britain. This move was a stepping stone to the company's plan of offering up to 18 hours per day of news and entertainment programs worldwide. In this quest, the BBC had some formidable strengths, including the fact that its World Service radio reached 120 million people globally. The company's plan was to use BBC World Service Television and BBC Online News to dominate their respective markets by the turn of the century.

More recently, other competitors have also entered the 24-hour cable news business. One is Rupert Murdoch's Sky News that now offers a 24-hour, London-based news channel to European satellite and cable companies. Another competitor is a group of 10 state-owned European broadcasters operating out of Switzerland, who have pooled their resources to spearhead a 24-hour, multilingual news program called "Euronews". Other European and Japanese competitors have also entered the field, but the biggest competition to CNN is now coming from Fox News Channel, which is part of News Corporation, and MSNBC, which is a joint venture between Microsoft and General Electric's NBC. Both were launched in 1996 and the most recent data show that they are dominating the US market. In the last year Fox News viewership leaped by 62 per cent and MSNBC was up 25 per cent while CNN lost 2 per cent of its audience.

Fox and MSNBC moved into the 24-hour news business when CNN began to look staid. And by dressing up the news with high-decibel talk shows and presenting gossip and entertainment as if it were news, these two channels have been offering stories that appear more exciting and relevant. For example, in the case of CNBC, NBC's business-news channel, one reporter noted that they "have turned coverage of stockmarkets into a breathless motor-racing-style commentary and bred a new variety of devoted business-news junky". CNN, meanwhile, has begun to punch back. Now a division of media giant AOL Time Warner, the company is overhauling both the management team and the structure. It has gathered together the Warner Brothers (WB) network and all the Turner Broadcasting operations, including CNN, into one television-network division. It has also pushed aside some of the old veterans who have been with the company for a long time and installed Jamie Kellner, an entertainment man who helped dream up both the WB network and the Fox channel, and put him in charge of running the division.

CNN's new plan to recapture its hold on the market has two parts. One is an efficiency drive. With 42 foreign bureaus and 1,000 overseas staff, CNN is a costly operation. So the company is going to sharply trim the ranks. The other is to inject new vigor into the mix and presentation of the news. The firm intends to meet the competition by making its own stories more dynamic and hard hitting. Whether or not it will be successful, one thing is clear: A good international business strategy will always attract strong competition and to keep one's position it is necessary to continually evaluate and carefully control operations.

Websites: **www.cnn.com**; **www.bbc.co.uk**; **www.fox.com**; **www.msnbc.com**; **www.microsoft.com**; **www.ge.com**; **www.cnbc.com**; **www.aoltimewarner.com**; **www.corp.aol.com**; **www.warnerbros.com** and **www.turner.com**.

Sources: Adapted from Richard A. Melcher et al., "Everybody Wants to Get into the Act," *Business Week*, March 19, 1991, p. 48; Elizabeth Comte, "The 45th Annual Report on American Industry: Entertainment and Information," *Forbes*, January 4, 1993, p. 143; and "The Network's Not Working," *Economist*, August 4, 2001, p. 58; and **www.scripps.ohiou.edu/cnnbook/press-r.htm**; **www.nando.net/newsroom/ntn/biz/110597/biz11_8118_noframes.html**.

Active learning check

Review your answer to Active Learning Case question 4 and make any changes you like. Then compare your answer with the one below.

4. Did Disney management conduct an external environmental analysis before going forward with Euro Disney? Explain.

The company conducted a thorough external environmental analysis. First, the location of the European population was examined in order to identify how far people would have to travel to visit the park. Second, the company examined the cost of building the park and identified potential sources of funds. Third, the firm determined how the park was to be built and where it would find the necessary contractors. Fourth, the company made a forecast regarding the number of visitors to the park each year, how much they would spend, and what the firm's profit would be on the venture.

However, the company failed in its examination of the cultural preferences of Europeans and the relative competitiveness of its European operation against its North American operation. In particular, Disney failed to take into consideration the effect of exchange rates on the affordability of traveling to France as opposed to Florida to visit its amusement park.

Strategic management in action

There are a variety of ways that MNEs use the strategic management process. In this section we examine how three multinationals have employed a particular segment of the process presented in Figure 2.3 to formulate or implement strategy.

Citibank: analysis of the external and internal environment

Citibank opened its first office in China in 1902 and remained there until 1949 when the communists came to power and seized all private assets. In 1984 Citibank quietly re-established operations in China, and since then it has been carefully formulating objectives and developing a strategic plan for doing business in this giant market. One of the biggest problems for the company is that China's banking environment remains very restrictive. As a result Citibank is now allowed to make local currency loans only to foreign multinationals and their joint venture partners, and the company's investment banking arm, Salomon Smith Barney Securities, can raise capital for Chinese firms only in offshore markets like Hong Kong or New York. Citibank is betting, however, that China's entry into the World Trade Organization (WTO) will eventually change all of this and allow the company to make local currency loans to major Chinese companies such as Legend (personal computers), Haier (consumer appliances) and Konka (electronic goods), and to raise money for these companies on equity and debt markets in Chinese cities like Shanghai and Shenzhen.

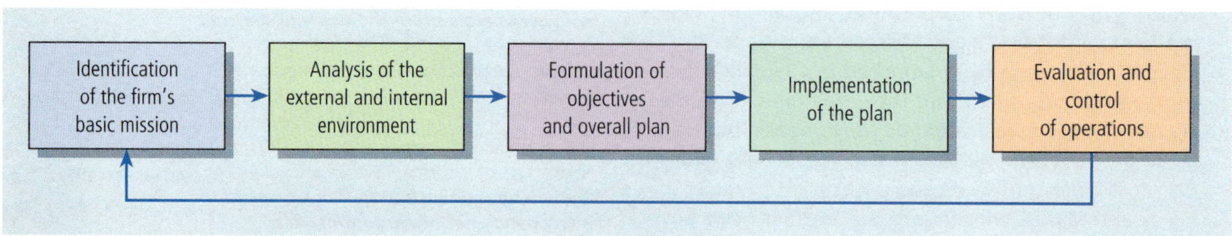

Figure 2.3 **The strategic management process in action**

Citibank is also planning on selling consumer financial services such as credit cards and home mortgages. Under WTO rules these services are supposed to be open to all by 2005 and the company's analysis of the situation leads it to believe that there is a huge pent-up demand for credit cards and other forms of consumer finance.

A third area where the bank is focusing attention is business-to-business (B2B) commerce. As a growing number of Chinese firms conduct commerce over the Internet, net-related financial services are going to mushroom. This is why Citibank has now hooked up with Commerce One, a US-based B2B site, to run its net-based payment systems. Citibank could provide this same service for Chinese exporters.

At the same time, the company realizes that all of these potential opportunities are not going to come to fruition in the near future because of the negative impact this would have on the Chinese economy. Specifically, if Citibank's parent company, Citigroup, were to have unrestricted access to the country's depositors, its superior products and services might well result in Chinese retail customers taking as much as $500 billion in savings out of Chinese banks and depositing it with Citigroup. In turn, this would force the Chinese banks to stop lending money to state-owned enterprises, most of which are operating at a loss. These companies, starved of cash, would then go bankrupt and unemployment would skyrocket. In short, if the government were to move too fast in opening up the banking market, it would sink the economy. Citigroup's analysis of the external and internal environment have shown it that progress in this market will come slowly and, until the government introduces effective state enterprise reform, China's vast consumer financial services market will be largely untapped.[17] In Chapter 20 we discuss other B2B companies such as Air Liquide and Dell.

Zara: implementation of the plan

Zara is the world's fastest-growing fashion retailer. Headquartered in northwestern Spain, the company has expanded rapidly in recent years and by 2001 had over 450 stores in 29 countries stretching from Copenhagen to Tokyo.[18] There are only a handful of Zara units in the US but the company's plans call for a rapid expansion there in the next couple of years.

There are two things that make Zara's implementation of its strategic plan so successful. One is that the company has created a lightning-speed production and distribution system. In an industry where competitors have their goods produced as much as five months in advance of delivery to stores, Zara's turnaround time is a mere three weeks. This means that the company can alter its designs and create new ones as the season moves along, thus allowing it to continually accommodate the changing tastes of its customers. Moreover, because Zara can change designs so quickly, none of its styles last more than four weeks. Coupled with this flexibility is a computerized inventory system that helps the firm minimize warehousing costs. Clothes are sorted in a single distribution center and then shipped out in preprogrammed lots directly to the stores. Twice a week each store receives deliveries that have been triggered by real-time inventory data that are collected through a network of computer handsets that feed information through the Internet into computers at headquarters. This system is so sophisticated and accurate that the company's inventory level is a mere 7 per cent of annual revenues, sharply lower than the 13 per cent of its main competitor.

The other thing that helps account for the firm's success in implementing its plan is the salespeople who act as grass-roots market researchers. Each person has a wireless organizer that is used to enter trends, customer comments, and orders. As a result, if an item does not sell well, it can be off the shelf within weeks. Conversely, if it is successful, company designers can quickly learn this and turn out a new version in a myriad of colors in record time. As an example, when Zara store personnel sold pink men's dress shirts they learned from the customers that they would have preferred a purple one. This information was conveyed to the company's in-house manufacturing team which raced into action. Within two weeks Zara stores were selling purple shirts.

The company implements the same basic strategy worldwide. It does no advertising and the products that it sells in Europe are similar to those in its stores stateside. Inventory control is also given a strong emphasis with all US stores supplied by air from Spain. At the same time, however, Zara does try to create an image that fits local taste. For example, in one of its mid-Manhattan stores the company tore out the entire interior and put in marble-like floors and high-tech lights to create a stunning 10,000-square-foot emporium. Customers, most of whom are in their 20s, are attracted by the feeling of being in an upscale European boutique, even though the prices are sharply lower and are targeted to compete with those at Gap.[19]

Zara has been very effective in implementing its strategic plan as seen by the financial results. In an industry that has been seeing sluggish growth, Zara's sales have been rising by over 20 per cent annually and in one recent year the company netted almost $200 million on sales of $2 billion. As a result the company is now increasing the number of stores in Europe, North America, and Asia, using the same basic approach for implementation that has proven successful thus far.

Nissan: evaluation and control operations

In 1996 Nissan predicted that it would hold 25 per cent of the Japanese auto market by the turn of the century. The company also forecasted continued growth in the US auto market. Soon thereafter, unfortunately, things begin to turn sour. Production efficiency slipped sharply and costs per auto increased to the point where they were much higher than its two major rivals, Toyota and Honda. Nissan also found that it was unable to develop a vehicle with a clear image in the minds of buyers and many of its offerings simply lacked flair. As a result, by 1999 the banks that had been backing Nissan pulled the plug.[20] They had had enough and decided to take their losses rather than hang on and suffer even greater financial setbacks. Fortunately, Renault, the French auto firm, came to the rescue by injecting $6 billion in return for a controlling 36.8 per cent stake.[21]

Since then Nissan has been evaluating and controlling its operations very carefully. The new company president put in charge by Renault has been reducing the size of the workforce and has brought in outside design people to give Nissan's new offerings a more appealing look. The firm is also eliminating marginally profitable models and trying to sharply reduce inventories. If these control efforts can be successfully carried out, the company will again become a major player in both the Japanese and the US auto markets.

These examples of large MNEs sometimes give the misleading impression that MNEs are larger than some countries. This mistake is compounded by the simple listing of the sales of MNEs against the GDP of nations. See Table 2.3. In such a listing GM appears as 23 in the list and it is larger than Denmark. Altogether, there are 15 MNEs in the Top 50 and 52 in the Top 100. There are two problems with this.

First, even the sales of GM at $176.6 billion are tiny in comparison with the size of the US GDP at 8,351 billion. Similarly, the European MNEs are small compared with the EU size (which is not recognized in Table 2.3 – as the individual 15 members are included – but was estimated at $7.9 trillion in 2000). And the largest Japanese MNE, Mitsui, at $118 billion is tiny compared with the GDP of Japan at $4,079 billion.[22]

Second, the measures are biased against the countries. The GDP is a "value-added" concept. It considers the final sales of goods and services. To develop a comparable measure for MNEs requires that only this value added be calculated, not the total sales.

Table 2.3 The Top 100 economies and MNEs, 1999

Rank	*Country/company*	*Billions of US $*	*Rank*	*Country/company*	*Billions of US $*
1	United States	8,351.0	**51**	**IBM**	**87.5**
2	Japan	4,078.9	52	Egypt	87.5
3	Germany	2,079.2	53	Venezuela	87.0
4	France	1,427.2	**54**	**BP Amoco**	**83.6**
5	United Kingdom	1,338.1	**55**	**Citigroup**	**82.0**
6	Italy	1,136.0	**56**	**Volkswagen**	**80.1**
7	China	980.2	**57**	**Nippon Life Insurance**	**78.5**
8	Brazil	742.8	58	Philippines	78.0
9	Canada	591.4	59	Malaysia	77.3
10	Spain	551.6	**60**	**Siemens**	**75.3**
11	India	442.2	**61**	**Allianz**	**74.2**
12	Mexico	428.8	**62**	**Hitachi**	**71.9**
13	Korea, Rep.	397.9	63	Ireland	71.4
14	Netherlands	384.3	64	Chile	71.1
15	Australia	380.8	**65**	**Matsushita Electric Industrial**	**65.6**
16	Russian Federation	332.5			
17	Argentina	277.9	**66**	**Nissho Iwai**	**65.4**
18	Switzerland	273.1	67	Pakistan	64.0
19	Belgium	250.6	**68**	**US Postal Service**	**62.7**
20	Sweden	221.8	**69**	**ING Group**	**62.5**
21	Austria	210.0	**70**	**AT&T**	**62.4**
22	Turkey	186.3	**71**	**Philip Morris**	**61.8**
23	**General Motors**	**176.6**	72	Peru	60.3
24	Denmark	170.3	**73**	**Sony**	**60.1**
25	**Wal-Mart**	**166.8**	**74**	**Deutsche Bank**	**58.6**
26	**Exxon**	**163.9**	**75**	**Boeing**	**58.0**
27	**Ford**	**162.6**	**76**	**Honda**	**57.8**
28	Hong Kong	161.7	**77**	**Dai-Ichi Mutual Life Insurance**	**55.1**
29	**DaimlerChrysler**	**160.0**			
30	Poland	153.1	**78**	**Assicurazioni Generali**	**53.7**
31	Norway	146.4	**79**	**Nissan Motor**	**53.7**
32	South Africa	133.2	80	New Zealand	52.7
33	Greece	124.0	**81**	**E.ON**	**52.2**
34	Finland	122.9	82	Czech Republic	52.0
35	Thailand	121.0	**83**	**Toshiba**	**51.6**
36	Indonesia	119.5	**84**	**Bank of America**	**51.4**
37	**Mitsui**	**118.6**	**85**	**Fiat**	**51.3**
38	**Mitsubishi**	**117.8**	**86**	**Nestlé**	**49.7**
39	**Toyota**	**115.7**	**87**	**SBC Communications**	**49.5**
40	**General Electric**	**111.6**	**88**	**Credit Suisse**	**49.4**
41	Iran	110.5	**89**	**Hewlett-Packard**	**48.3**
42	**Itochu**	**109.1**	**90**	**Fujitsu**	**47.2**
43	Portugal	105.9	91	Bangladesh	47.0
44	**Royal Dutch/Shell Group**	**105.4**	92	Hungary	46.8
			93	**Metro**	**46.7**
45	**Sumitomo**	**95.7**	94	Algeria	46.5
46	Singapore	95.4	**95**	**Sumitomo Life Insurance**	**46.4**
47	Colombia	93.6	**96**	**Tokyo Electric Power**	**45.7**
48	**Nippon Telegraph & Telephone**	**93.6**	**97**	**Kroger**	**45.4**
			98	**TotalFinaElf**	**45.0**
49	**Marubeni**	**91.8**	**99**	**NEC**	**44.8**
50	**AXA**	**87.6**	**100**	**State Farm Insurance**	**44.6**

Source: Adapted from World Bank, *World Development Report 2000/2001* and Fortune, *The Fortune Global 500*, July 24, 2000.

If this is done, then the "size" of the MNEs is reduced by 70–80 per cent. The value added of GM in 2000 was only $46.2 billion, not $176.6 billion. Wal-Mart's value-added measure is $67.7 billion, not $166.8 billion. Similarly, Exxon's value-added measure is $52.6 billion, not $163.9 billion. In fact, only two of the Top 50 are MNEs, Exxon and Wal-Mart. GM, which under comparisons of sales and GDP was the largest MNE, now drops to 53, where even Bangladesh is bigger.[23]

KEY POINTS

1. A multinational enterprise is a company that is headquartered in one country but has operations in two or more countries. There is a series of characteristics that are common to multinational enterprises. These include: (a) affiliated firms that are linked by ties of common ownership, (b) a common pool of resources, and (c) a strategic vision that guides all the affiliates.
2. Multinationals, especially large industrial enterprises, account for a large percentage of world sales and employment. MNEs, large or small, also engage in a wide variety of business activities ranging from manufacturing to retailing to consulting services.
3. The internationalization process is one of going abroad at incremental stages, on the premise that foreign markets are risky. Thus, a typical process is: license, export, sales office, and, finally, FDI.
4. Companies become MNEs for a number of reasons including: (a) a desire to protect themselves from the risks and uncertainties of the domestic business cycle, (b) a growing world market for their goods or services, (c) a response to increased foreign competition, (d) a desire to internalize in order to reduce costs, (e) a desire to overcome tariff barriers, and (f) the chance to take advantage of technological expertise by manufacturing goods directly rather than allowing others to do it under a license agreement.
5. Multinational enterprises have a strategic philosophy that is different from that of home country businesses. In particular, MNEs do not see their company as an extension of its domestic roots. They hire, fire, and transfer personnel to meet global needs, even if this means laying off home country employees. They also combine their talents with those of other MNEs in creating, financing, and managing joint ventures.
6. Successful MNEs rely on the strategic management process, which has five major phases: (a) identification of the firm's basic mission, (b) external and internal environmental analysis, (c) formulation of objectives and overall plans, (d) implementation of these plans, and (e) evaluation and control of operations.

KEY TERMS

- **multinational enterprise (MNE)**
- **internationalization**
- **license**
- **licensor**
- **licensee**
- **basic mission**

REVIEW AND DISCUSSION QUESTIONS

1. **What is a multinational enterprise? Is it likely that the number of MNEs will increase during the next decade? Why?**
2. **What are the three common characteristics of an MNE? Identify and briefly describe each.**
3. **Why do firms become multinational enterprises? Identify and discuss four reasons.**
4. **In what way is the strategic philosophy of an MNE different from that of a domestic firm?**
5. **How successful are the large industrial MNEs? What accounts for this?**
6. **Why has Cemex been so successful internationally? What has it done to win market share?**
7. **What are the five basic steps in the strategic management process? Identify and briefly describe each.**
8. **How has Zara used the strategic management process to help it become a successful multinational?**

REAL CASE

LaFarge: a concrete multinational

Every country needs cement and concrete for construction purposes. But because these materials are extremely heavy, it is very costly to ship them long distances. So cement plants have to be located locally. Typically cement plants are located near limestone deposits and close to large urban areas so that the materials can be easily shipped to their final destination. If the cement has to be shipped any great distance, this is done by boat. For example, Canadian firms export cement to the US by shipping it across the Great Lakes.

In the world cement market, there are thousands of small cement companies. However, there are some very large, multinational enterprises as well. The largest of these is LaFarge, a French MNE that accounts for 10 per cent of the world's cement capacity. In recent years LaFarge's annual revenues have been in excess of $11 billion. In addition to being the world leader in cement and concrete, the company is also a major supplier of aggregates, roofing, and gypsum. In all, the firm offers more than 5,000 services and products ranging from ultra-high performance concrete, ready-mix concrete, and improved roofing materal to plasterboard and insulation systems.

Founded in 1833, LaFarge now has operations in 75 countries and employs almost 85,000 people. The company has 21 per cent of its business in France, another 31 per cent in Western Europe, and 26 per cent in North America with much of the remaining 22 per cent being done in Asia. In Europe it is the industry leader and its recent acquisition of Blue Circle Industries, a UK cement and building company, has helped reinforce its position in this market. In the US LaFarge is the third largest cement producer. Yet Asia is where the company is now putting its focus.

The company is the market leader in both the Philippines and Malaysia and it hopes to significantly increase its presence in China. There are thousands of cement manufacturers in China and they have varying levels of technology. LaFarge hopes to bring its state-of-the-art building technology and experience to China and make it one of the firm's major markets. At present, China is the largest producer of cement, accounting for one-third of the world's production. As the country continues to modernize, however, its need for cement products will increase sharply and those companies that are able to provide high quality, low cost output are going to dominate the industry. Many of the current companies are small and/or inefficient and, in an open market where competitors are allowed to enter unfettered by government regulation and control, companies with modern tools and techniques could radically change the industry and gain large market share in the process. LaFarge wants to be one of these firms.

The company is also slowly entering the Indian market. Its current presence there is small, but the market has great potential and like China many of the cement companies there do not have state-of-the-art equipment. At the same time, there is a very large demand for cement products. At present, India is the fourth largest cement producer in the world. It accounts for approximately 6 per cent of the world's output. So compared with China, it is relatively small, but given that LaFarge can supply only 10 per cent of the world's output, India is a very attractive market. Additionally, there are only 57 companies in the entire industry and many of their factories lack the technology and cement-making skills of LaFarge. So the company is willing to bide its time and slowly build market share here.

Two of LaFarge's biggest assets are its financial strength and its expertise. Most cement plants serve a local market and there is a geographic limit to their coverage. So nations like China and India have to have a great many small cement plants spread throughout the country. In gaining a foothold in these geographic regions it is often easiest to acquire the local producer and then upgrade the facilities by introducing new high-tech equipment, restructuring and streamlining the operations, and doing a better job of marketing to customers. LaFarge has both the capital and the experience to do this. As a result, while local operations are often fairly small, the company's overall operations are huge and its plans for the future call for continued expansion everywhere, especially in Asia.

Websites: **www.lafargecorp.com**; **www.cement.bluecircle.co.uk**; **www.holnam.com** and **www.cemex.com**.

Source: Adapted from **www.lafargecorp.com/lafarge2.nsf**; **www.cemnet.co.uk/news.htm**; **www.cementindia.net/**; "Bagged Cement," *Economist*, July 17, 1999; "The Cemex Way," *Economist*, June 14, 2000.

1. **Why has LaFarge become a multinational enterprise? What are the benefits of this strategy?**
2. **In what way is it clear that LaFarge makes decisions that are best for its overall operations and not just those of its French operation, where the company is headquartered?**
3. **In what way does LaFarge use the strategic management process?**

REAL CASE

Water – the oil of the 21st Century

The water market is a US $400 billion per year market dominated by companies that have the ability to provide infrastructure to treat and distribute water at reasonable prices. Over the years, governments scrambling to find funds to provide water to an ever-increasing population have handed over the management of water provision to private hands. One such case is that of Buenos Aires, the capital of Argentina, where city officials turned to a private water company to update pipes and pumps and to manage the water system. The result was not only an improvement in water quality, but also a decrease in prices that was accompanied by the extension of water services to poorer communities.

Vivendi Water, Ondeo and Thames Water are all aggressively pursuing contracts in Eastern Europe, Asia and Latin America. These companies, all from the EU, are faced with saturated domestic markets under strict government regulations and are thus increasingly relying on foreign markets to maintain profits. Emerging and developing markets provide water MNEs with opportunities to develop water infrastructure in untapped markets. In 2000, an estimated 1 billion people in the world's less-developed economies lacked access to clean drinking water and 3 billion needed improved access to sewage facilities.

Expanding operations to developing nations has not always come without bumps. In 1999, Thames Water and the then Suez Lyonnaise des Eaux (now Ondeo) had to renegotiate their contract for the Jakarta water supply after the Indonesian president was removed from office. They did better than Vivendi Environment, which lost its contract for the water supply in Tucman City, a northern Argentinian city, at about the same time. Because of such political risk, as well as the major capital costs involved, it is common in large projects for a consortium of water companies to be formed. For a Buenos Aires project, Vivendi has partnered with Agbar (of Spain), its main rival Suez Lyonnaise, Anglican Water, Banco de Galicia (an Argentinian bank) and other firms. Let's examine the world's three largest companies in more detail.

(1) Vivendi Water

Vivendi Water was born of the merger between Générale des Eaux and USFilter. Today, the company is the largest water MNE, with 70,000 employees and operations in 100 countries. One of Europe's largest MNEs, Vivendi started out as the water company for Paris. In 1853, Companie Générale des Eaux (CGE) was founded in Paris and was soon supplying water to French cities, including Paris itself. It expanded internationally in the production and distribution of water and by 1880 was in Venice, by 1882 in Constantinople, and by 1883 in Porto. After 100 years, CGE had 8 million water customers in France and was a major international water company. Over the last 50 years, CGE then reinvented itself as a diversified firm, moving into other services such as: waste management; transportation; construction and property; communication and media. By the late 1990s, to reflect its new line of business, it changed its name to Vivendi.

Vivendi grouped itself into three key business areas: utilities (mainly water and electricity); property (office buildings in the business district of Paris and thousands of houses throughout France), and communications (Canal Plus pay TV, mobile phone companies like SFR, Vodafone Air Touch, Cegetel and SGE (Societe Générale d'Entreprises), railways and buses). Vivendi acquired USFilter in 1999, a large producer of water and wastewater treatment equipment. Vivendi also owns Paris Saint-Germain Football Club, B Sky B, and Havas, a media, advertising and publishing empire.

Vivendi moved in 2000 to become a global media, communications, and entertainment MNE by its purchase of Seagram. In contrast, the CEO of Suez, Gesard Mestrallet, failed in ventures with Eon of Germany, Telefonica of Spain, and Air Liquide. In June 2000 Vivendi-Universal was formed with the merger of Vivendi, Canal, and Canadian company Seagram (which owned Universal Studios). After the merger Seagram sold its spirits and wine business and Vivendi divested itself from AOL. The new company is found on the Internet, and in entertainment (including TV, movies, music), publishing, and telecommunications. The company now operates strongly across the triad. Its major strengths are in North America and Europe, but it also has a growing presence in Asia. In Japan it formed a joint venture, Duet, with Sony for music distribution.

(2) Ondeo

Ondeo is the second largest water company in the world. In March 2001, as part of its strategy to be the world's leading water company, Suez Lyonnaise des Eaux (est. 1880) changed the name of its water groups to Ondeo. The Ondeo group is comprised of: Ondeo Nalco – the market leader in water treatment; Ondeo Services – the market leader in water management provision to cities; Ondeo Degremont – the market leader in turnkey engineering; and Ondeo Industrial Solutions – a new division to offer industrial water services. With a presence in 130 countries, sales of US $8.5 billion, and over 60,000 employees, Ondeo holds 28 per cent of the world's water and wastewater market (excluding public sector water monopoly countries such as Canada). Its main rivals in international business are Vivendi Environment, Thames Water (a subsidiary of Germany-owned RWE), and Asurix (a UK company bought by Enron in 1997). Other rivals are large state-owned domestic water companies. Many of these companies are multi-utilities (i.e. in various combinations of gas, electricity, and water management).

(3) Thames Water and RWE

As discussed in a later real case (Chapter 4), Thames Water plc is the largest British water company. In October 2000, Thames Water was acquired by the giant German utility, RWE, for £14 million. The Thames Water senior management team has been left in place to pursue international operations and the Thames Water brand name has been retained by RWE.

As the activities of the core water utility division of Thames Water are still subject to regulation, the company made a early strategic decision to focus its growth on the non-regulated water service business, and on international expansion. It now has major projects in China, Australia, Turkey, Indonesia, the Ukraine, Malaysia, the Philippines, and Thailand. This is a geographic extension of its firm-specific advantage in water production and supply.

In Indonesia, Thames Water has a 25-year contract to supply fresh water to half the population of the capital city, Jakarta. In March 1998 this contract was temporarily rescinded by the new president as he alleged that it was signed with the son of the former President Suharto. Despite being the first Western business to be disrupted by this type of political risk, within a month Thames Water had signed up with the new government of Indonesia.

▶

In an Australian project in Adelaide, Thames Water supplied the technical expertise in collaboration with a French partner. The French did the political lobbying, and their skill in this was reflected by winning the contract shortly after the French government conducted a series of nuclear tests in the Pacific which were strongly opposed by the Australian and New Zealand governments. The political image of Thames Water in Asia was not affected by this association and the British company tends to have "neutral" political risk exposure.

In 1999 Thames Water started moving into the huge US water market. It acquired a New Jersey water utility. In 2001, with the financing of RWE behind it, Thames Water bought America Waterworks, the largest private US private sector water company. Thames Water is now the largest water company in North America.

Thames Water under CEO, Bill Alexander, has developed a portfolio of international operations which build on its core skills, and are closely integrated with its basic British utility business.

Websites: **www.vivendi.com**; **www.ondeo-nalco.com**; **www.thames-water.com**; **www.rwe.com**; **www.seagram.com**; **www.corp.aol.com** and **www.telefonica.es**.

Source: Adapted from Ondeo Nalco, "Nalco Becomes Ondeo Nalco," *News Releases*, March 21, 2001; David Hosein and Paul Rathbone, "Opinion: Water – Unlocking the Floodgate of Value," *Financial Times*, July 16, 2001; Shawn Tully, "Water, Water, Everywhere," *Fortune*, May 15, 2000; Annual Reports of Thames Water plc; Victor Mallet "Suez to Give Water Division New Name," *Financial Times*, March 20, 2001.

1. **Why did Thames Water become a multinational enterprise? Why did Vivendi buy Seagram?**
2. **In general, why do the three major European water companies engage in foreign direct investment to expand their operations to North America and other parts of the world?**
3. **What is the strategic management philosophy of the water MNEs? Does it vary from the French to the British?**

ENDNOTES

1 United Nations, *World Investment Report 2001* (Geneva: United Nations Conference on Trade and Development, 2001).
2 Alan M. Rugman, *The End of Globalization* (London: Random House, 2000), Chapter 7, especially p. 140.
3 *Fortune*, July 24, 2001, p. 234.
4 Alan M. Rugman, *The End of Globalization* (London: Random House, 2000), Chapter 7.
5 Robyn Meredith, "In Policy Shift, G.M. Will Rely On Alliances," *New York Times*, January 18, 2000, pp. C 1, C 14.
6 This figure was first developed in Alan M. Rugman et al., *International Business: Firm and Environment* (New York: McGraw-Hill, 1985), pp. 89–93. It is based on the ideas in Alan M. Rugman, *Inside the Multinationals: The Economics of Internal Markets* (New York: Columbia Press, 1981).
7 Rugman (1981) n. 6 above.
8 Raphael Minder and Daniel Dombey, "Alcatel Cut Plans 'Stun' French," *Financial Times*, June 28, 2001, p. 21.
9 Suzanne Kapner, "Citing U.S. Slowdown, Philips Will Cut 7,000 Jobs," *New York Times*, April 18, 2001, p. W 1.
10 Bill Carter, "Disney Is Cutting 4,000 Jobs Worldwide," *New York Times*, March 28, 2001, pp. C 1, C 13.
11 "The Cemex Way," *Economist*, June 16, 2001, pp. 75–76.
12 Jonathan Friedland, "Mexico's Cemex Wins Bet on Acquisitions," *Wall Street Journal*, April 30, 1998, p. A 14.
13 Peter Landers, "Why Some Sony Gear Is Made in Japan – By Another Company," *Wall Street Journal*, June 14, 2001, pp. A 1, A 10.
14 Scott Miller, "BMW Takes the High Road in Market for Small Cars," *Wall Street Journal*, August 3, 2000, p. A 11.
15 Mark Landler, "Reversing Course, Levi Strauss Will Expand Its Output in China," *New York Times*, April 9, 1998, pp. 1, 5.
16 Edward W. Desmond, "Can Canon Keep Clicking?" *Fortune*, February 2, 1998, pp. 98–104.
17 Neel Chowdhury, "Can Citibank Crack the China Market?" *Fortune*, September 18, 2000, pp. 222–228.
18 Richard Heller, "Galician Beauty," *Forbes*, May 28, 2001, p. 98.
19 William Echikson, "The Mark of Zara," *Business Week*, May 29, 2000, pp. 98, 100.
20 Stephanie Strom, "No. 2 and Not Enjoying the Ride," *New York Times*, May 21, 1998, Section C, pp. 1, 4.
21 Benjamin Fulford, "Renaissance at Nissan," *Forbes*, October 2, 2000, p. 80.
22 Alan M. Rugman, *The End of Globalization* (London: Random House, 2000), pp. 59–60.
23 Martin Wolf, "Countries Still Rule the World," *Financial Times*, February 6, 2002, p. 13.

ADDITIONAL BIBLIOGRAPHY

Beamish, Paul W. and Banks, John C. "Equity Joint Ventures and the Theory of the Multinational Enterprise," *Journal of International Business Studies*, vol. 18, no. 2 (Summer 1987).

Birkinshaw, Julian and Hood, Neil. "Multinational Subsidiary Evolution: Capability and Charter Change in Foreign-Owned Subsidiary Companies," *Academy of Management Review*, vol. 23, no. 4 (October 1998).

Buckley, Peter J. "The Frontiers of International Business Research," *Management International Review*, vol. 31, Special Issue (1991).

Buckley, Peter J. and Casson, Mark C. "Models of the Multinational Enterprise," *Journal of International Business Studies*, vol. 29, no. 1 (First Quarter 1998).

Chernotsky, Harry I. "The American Connection: Motives for Japanese Foreign Direct Investment," *Columbia Journal of World Business*, vol. 22, no. 4 (Winter 1987).

Cho, Kang Rae. "The Role of Product-Specific Factors in Intra-Firm Trade of US Manufacturing Multinational Corporations," *Journal of International Business Studies*, vol. 21, no. 2 (Second Quarter 1990).

Devinney, Timothy M. "Multinationals as Flagship Firms," *Academy of Management Review*, vol. 26, no. 3 (July 2001).

Dunning, John H. *Global Capitalism at Bay?* (London: Routledge, 2001).

Dunning, John H. "The Eclectic Paradigm of International Production: A Restatement and Some Possible Extensions," *Journal of International Business Studies*, vol. 19, no. 1 (Spring 1988).

Hennart, Jean-François. "Can the New Forms of Investment Substitute for the Old Forms?: A Transaction Cost Perspective," *Journal of International Business Studies*, vol. 20, no. 2 (Summer 1989).

Kim, W. Chan and Hwang, Peter. "Global Strategy and Multinationals' Entry Mode Choice," *Journal of International Business Studies*, vol. 23, no. 1 (First Quarter 1992).

Kim, Wi Saeng and Lyn, Esmeralda O. "Foreign Direct Investment Theories, Entry Barriers, and Reverse Investments in US Manufacturing Industries," *Journal of International Business Studies*, vol. 18, no. 2 (Summer 1987).

Kimura, Yui. "Firm-Specific Strategic Advantage and Foreign Direct Investment Behaviour of Firms: The Case of Japanese Semiconductor Firms," *Journal of International Business Studies*, vol. 20, no. 2 (Summer 1989).

Madura, Jeff and Whyte, Ann Marie. "Diversification Benefits of Direct Foreign Investment," *Management International Review*, vol. 30, no. 1 (First Quarter 1990).

Moore, Karl and Lewis, David. "The First Multinationals," *Management International Review*, vol. 38, no. 2 (Second Quarter 1998).

Rugman, Alan M. *Inside the Multinationals: The Economics of Internal Markets* (New York: Columbia University Press, 1981).

Rugman, Alan M. "The Multinational Enterprise," in Ingo Walter (ed.), *Handbook of International Management* (New York: Wiley, 1988), pp. 1–18.

Rugman, Alan M. *The Theory of Multinational Enterprises* (Cheltenham: Elgar, 1996).

Rugman, Alan M. and Verbeke, Alain. "A Note on the Transnational Solution and the Transaction Cost Theory of Multinational Strategic Management," *Journal of International Business Studies*, vol. 23, no. 4 (Fourth Quarter 1992).

Sabi, Manijeh. "An Application of the Theory of Foreign Direct Investment to Multinational Banking in LDCs," *Journal of International Business Studies*, vol. 19, no. 3 (Fall 1988).

Yoshida, Mamoru. "Macro-Micro Analyses of Japanese Manufacturing Investments in the United States," *Management International Review*, vol. 27, no. 4 (Fourth Quarter 1987).

APPENDIXES TO CHAPTER 2

Appendix 2A The 25 largest US MNEs, 2000

Rank	*MNE*	*Industry*	*Sales (in millions of US $)*
1	Exxon Mobil	Petroleum refining	210,392
2	Wal-Mart Stores	General merchandisers	193,295
3	General Motors	Motor vehicles and parts	184,632
4	Ford Motors	Motor vehicles and parts	180,598
5	General Electric	Diversified financials	129,853
6	Citigroup	Diversified financials	111,826
7	Enron	Energy	100,789
8	IBM	Computers, office equipment	88,396
9	AT&T	Telecommunications	65,981
10	Verizon Communications	Telecommunications	64,707
11	US Postal Service	Mail, package, freight delivery	64,540
12	Philip Morris	Tobacco	63,276
13	J. P. Morgan Chase & Co.	Banks: Commercial and savings	60,065
14	Bank of America Corp.	Banks: Commercial and savings	57,747
15	SBC Communications	Telecommunications	51,476
16	Boeing	Aerospace and defense	51,321
17	Texaco	Petroleum refining	51,130
18	Duke Energy	Energy	49,318
19	Kroger	Food and drug stores	49,000
20	Hewlett-Packard	Computers, office equipment	48,782
21	Chevron	Petroleum refining	48,069
22	State Farm Insurance	Insurance: P & C (mutual)	47,863
23	American International Group	Insurance: P & C (stock)	45,972
24	Home Depot	Specialty retailers	45,738
25	Morgan Stanley Dean Witter	Securities	45,413

Source: Adapted from Fortune, *The Fortune Global 500*, 2001.

Appendix 2B The 25 largest European MNEs, 2000

Rank	*MNE*	*Country*	*Industry*	*Sales (in millions of US $)*
1	DaimlerChrysler	Germany	Motor vehicles and parts	150,070
2	Royal Dutch/Shell Group	Britain/Netherlands	Petroleum refining	149,146
3	BP	Britain	Petroleum refining	148,062
4	TotalFinaElf	France	Petroleum refining	105,870
5	AXA	France	Insurance: Life, health (stock)	92,782
6	Volkswagen	Germany	Motor vehicles and parts	78,852
7	Siemens	Germany	Electronics, electrical equipment	74,858
8	ING Group	Netherlands	Insurance: Life, health (stock)	71,196
9	Allianz	Germany	Insurance: P & C (stock)	71,022
10	E.ON	Germany	Trading	68,433
11	Deutsche Bank	Germany	Banks: Commercial and savings	67,133
12	CGNU	Britain	Insurance: Life, health (stock)	61,499
13	Carrefour	France	Food and drug stores	59,888
14	Credit Suisse	Switzerland	Banks: Commercial and savings	59,316
15	BNP Paribas	France	Banks: Commercial and savings	57,612
16	Assicurazioni Generali	Italy	Insurance: Life, health (stock)	53,333
17	FIAT	Italy	Motor vehicles and parts	53,190
18	HSBC Holdings	Britain	Banks: Commercial and savings	48,633
19	Koninklijke Ahold	Netherlands	Food and drug stores	48,492
20	Nestlé	Switzerland	Food consumer products	48,225
21	UBS	Switzerland	Banks: Commercial and savings	47,316
22	ENI	Italy	Petroleum refining	45,139
23	Unilever	Britain/Netherlands	Food consumer products	43,974
24	Fortis	Belgium/Netherlands	Banks: Commercial and savings	43,831
25	ABN Amro Holding	Netherlands	Banks: Commercial and savings	43,390

Source: Adapted from Fortune, *The Fortune Global 500*, 2001.

Appendix 2C The 25 largest Japanese MNEs, 2000

Rank	*MNE*	*Industry*	*Sales (in millions of US $)*
1	Mitsubishi	Trading	126,579
2	Toyota Motor	Motor vehicles and parts	121,416
3	Mitsui	Trading	118,014
4	Itochu	Trading	109,757
5	Nippon Telegraph & Telephone	Telecommunications	103,235
6	Sumitomo	Trading	91,168
7	Marubeni	Trading	85,351
8	Hitachi	Electronics, electrical equipment	76,127
9	Matsushita Electric Industrial	Electronics, electrical equipment	69,475
10	Nippon Life Insurance	Insurance: Life, health (mutual)	68,055
11	Sony	Electronics, electrical equipment	66,158
12	Nissho Iwai	Trading	58,557
13	Honda Motor	Motor vehicles and parts	58,462
14	Nissan Motor	Motor vehicles and parts	55,077
15	Toshiba	Electronics, electrical equipment	53,827
16	Mizuho Holdings	Banks: Commercial and savings	52,069
17	Fujitsu	Computers, office equipment	49,604
18	NEC	Electronics, electrical equipment	48,928
19	Tokyo Electrical Power	Utilities: Gas and electric	47,556
20	Dai-Ichi Mutual Life Insurance	Insurance: Life, health (mutual)	46,436
21	Sumitomo Life Insurance	Insurance: Life, health (mutual)	37,536
22	Mitsubishi Electric	Electronics, electrical equipment	37,349
23	Meiji Life Insurance	Insurance: Life, health (mutual)	29,777
24	Mitsubishi Motors	Motor vehicles and parts	29,636
25	Ito-Yokado	Food and drug stores	28,393

Source: Adapted from Fortune, *The Fortune Global 500*, 2001.

Appendix 2D The largest Canadian MNEs, 2000

Rank	*MNE*	*Industry*	*Sales (in millions of US $)*
1	Nortel Networks	Network and other communications equipment	30,275
2	Onex	Electronics, electrical equipment	16,517
3	Transcanada Pipelines	Energy	16,255
4	CIBC	Banks: Commercial and savings	15,680
5	Royal Bank of Canada	Banks: Commercial and savings	15,452
6	George Weston	Food and drug stores	15,044
7	BCE	Telecommunications	14,859
8	Seagram	Entertainment	14,803
9	TD Bank	Banks: Commercial and savings	13,612
10	Bank of Nova Scotia	Banks: Commercial and savings	12,881
11	Bank of Montreal	Banks: Commercial and savings	12,632
12	Power Corp. of Canada	Insurance: Life, health (stock)	11,383
13	Sun Life Financial Services	Insurance: Life, health (stock)	11,141
14	Canadian Pacific	Energy	10,841
15	Magna International	Motor vehicles and parts	10,513

Source: Adapted from Fortune, *The Fortune Global 500*, 2001.

Appendix 2E The 25 largest third-world MNEs, 2000

Rank	*MNE*	*Country*	*Industry*	*Sales (in millions of US $)*
1	PDVSA	Venezuela	Petroleum refining	53,680
2	Sinopec	China	Petroleum refining	45,346
3	State Power	China	Utilities: Gas and electric	42,549
4	PEMEX	Mexico	Mining, crude-oil production	42,167
5	China National Petroleum	China	Energy	41,684
6	Samsung Electronics	South Korea	Electronics, electrical equipment	38,491
7	Hyundai	South Korea	Trading	36,036
8	Samsung	South Korea	Trading	35,939
9	SK	South Korea	Petroleum refining	31,825
10	Hyundai Motor	South Korea	Motor vehicles and parts	28,755
11	Petrobras	Brazil	Petroleum refining	26,955
12	LG International	South Korea	Trading	23,454
13	Indian Oil	India	Petroleum refining	22,285
14	Industrial and Commercial Bank of China	China	Banks: Commercial and savings	22,070
15	Samsung Life Insurance	South Korea	Insurance: Life, health (stock)	21,227
16	China Telecommunications	China	Telecommunications	20,813
17	LG Electronics	South Korea	Electronics, electrical equipment	20,087
18	Bank of China	China	Banks: Commercial and savings	19,496
19	Petronas	Malaysia	Petroleum refining	19,303
20	Sinochem	China	Trading	18,036
21	Gazprom	Russia	Energy	17,689
22	Korea Electric Power	South Korea	Utilities: Gas and electric	16,543
23	China Mobile Communications	China	Telecommunications	15,045
24	Lukoil	Russia	Mining, crude-oil production	14,416
25	SK Global	South Korea	Trading	14,384

Source: Adapted from Fortune, *The Fortune Global 500*, 2001.

Chapter 3

The Triad and International Business

CONTENTS

OBJECTIVES OF THE CHAPTER

As we noted in Chapter 1, a small number of economies account for a large portion of international investment and international trade. These economies – the US, the EU, and Japan – are referred to collectively as the triad. In this chapter we are going to look more closely at the triad and examine the role and impact of these nations on international business activity. We will also consider their role in both trade and FDI, and look at examples of how each member of the triad pursues target markets in other triad countries. We will also examine some of the economic and political relationships that exist between triad members and how these can impact on the international business community. We will also link to future chapters, such as Chapters 8 and 9, dealing with strategy and structure respectively. In this context, we develop reasons for the need for MNEs to develop regional/triad strategies rather than "global" strategies.

The specific objectives of this chapter are to:

1. *Describe* the major reasons for FDI.
2. *Explain* the role of triad-based MNEs in worldwide FDI and trade.
3. *Relate* select examples of inter-triad MNEs business activity.
4. *Discuss* the economic interrelationships between triad members.

ACTIVE LEARNING CASE

Boeing versus Airbus

In 1970 a European consortium consisting of Germany, France, and Great Britain (Spain later became a member) created Airbus Industrie. The objective of the consortium was to build commercial aircraft with Germany, Great Britain, and Spain taking on the job of constructing the aircraft and France assuming responsibility for assembling it. The logic of the arrangement was fairly straightforward. Given the growth of international travel, there would be a continual need for new commercial aircraft and Airbus wanted to be a major player in this industry.

Until this time, when major air carriers such as American Airlines, Japan Airlines, and Lufthansa needed to replace aging airplanes or increase the size of their fleet, they turned to Boeing or McDonnell Douglas, the two giant American aircraft manufacturers. Cargo carriers such as FedEx and DHL also bought planes from them and, as international air shipments continued to grow rapidly, the annual demand proved to be a boon for Boeing and McDonnell.

The initial challenge for Airbus was to capture some market share and thus establish a toehold in the industry. This, fortunately, was not a problem. The consortium had divided up the responsibility for building the aircraft among its members. In this way, each country was guaranteed some of the work and, in turn, could count on its respective government to provide financial assistance and contracts. In particular, the consortium would have to spend large amounts of money for research and development in order to build competitive, state-of-the-art craft, but by getting support from their respective governments a great deal of the initial risk would be eliminated. This, by the way, was the same approach that had been used in the US and helped account for much of Boeing and McDonnell's success in building large aircraft. For example, much of the funding to build the giant C-5A cargo plane was provided by the US military. Then, by using this same technology, it was possible for Boeing to build its giant passenger aircraft.

Realizing that the consortium would eventually be able to build competitive craft, Boeing and McDonnell lodged complaints with the US government claiming that Airbus was being subsidized by their governments and Washington needed to take steps to protect the US commercial aircraft manufacturing industry. As the governments on both sides met to talk and discuss these issues, Airbus started building planes. It took quite a while, but by 1990 the consortium was not only becoming well established but had back orders for 1,100 planes and by 1997 this number had reached 2,300. In the process Airbus captured over 30 per cent of the world market. One of the major reasons for its success was that it focused on building fuel-efficient craft at competitive prices. Its wide-body, medium-range models, the A300 and A310, for example, were very reliable and the orders started flowing in from a wide number of buyers including large US carriers such as America Airlines and Northwest. During the 1990s the battle in the aircraft market also saw Boeing and McDonnell Douglas merge their operations. McDonnell could not compete effectively in this new, highly competitive market, but when merged with Boeing it could provide the latter with a good chance to prevent Airbus from steamrolling the American aircraft manufacturing industry.

By 2001 Airbus was doing better than ever. Not only had it managed to catch up with Boeing and hold 50 per cent of the overall market, but it was in the throes of making major decisions that could result in its becoming the dominant player in the industry. The company had decided to build a giant, double-decker superjumbo jet. To be known as the A380, this plane will be capable of carrying 555 passengers and the first craft are expected to be delivered in 2006. A host of buyers signed firm orders with the company including Qantas, which ordered 12 of the craft, and Singapore Airlines and Air France which each placed orders for 10. In addition Singapore Air took an option for 15 more. The Singapore deal alone was worth over $8 billion to Airbus, showing how lucrative the market for a superjumbo jet could be. In response, Boeing announced that it was going to build a smaller, faster, longer-range plane that would fly just below the speed of sound. Quite clearly the two competitors were moving in different directions.

Airbus is betting more than $12 billion that airlines will want a superjumbo jet that can carry a large number of passengers on long trips to a given region. Boeing is betting that there is a much larger demand for smaller, faster planes that can take people directly to their destination. In doing so, Boeing has ceded to Airbus a highly profitable jumbo market, wagering that the European group will not earn back its huge investment but rather end up stumbling badly. Boeing's decision to abandon the development of a larger plane (similar to what Airbus is proposing) relied heavily on follow-on studies of the giant 747. The company's engineers concluded that, except in the case of a huge 800-passenger plane, a double-deck design had to be scaled back to a single decker to satisfy technical and safety standards. One reason, according to Boeing engineers, is because a double-deck arrangement is very inefficient. Another is that, in case of evacuation, a two-level airplane can present major problems for those on board.

At this same time Airbus announced that its consortium arrangement was coming to an end and that the company would now be managed as a corporation. Today the Franco–German European Aeronautic Defense and Space Company holds 80 per cent of Airbus, and BAE Systems of Great Britain owns the remaining 20 per cent. This move effectively ended Airbus's life as an organization that operated in the world of business and politics and one in which each partner held a veto, politically motivated committees made many of the important decisions, and when things did not go well state funds could be counted on to prop up the consortium. Now with all of that behind them Airbus is working to streamline its operations and, according to the business partners, shave off about $400 million in annual expenses.

Will Airbus continue to dominate the airways? Its initial challenge is to build the A380 superjumbo. If it can do this and the demand for the huge craft does materialize, Boeing may find itself as a minor player in the industry. On the other hand, while in late 2001 Airbus was recruiting thousands of new workers to help with the project, it was having trouble finding partners to help fund the venture. A number of European suppliers signed up but US and Japanese companies did not. For example, Airbus had offered Japanese manufacturers up to 8 per cent of the work on the A380 in return for funding but had no takers. The company also wanted to get US firms to invest and thus defuse a potential political problem that could result in the American government making it difficult for Airbus to do business in the US. When Airbus first got started, it relied heavily on governmental support. Now that it is very successful, it no longer needs this type of help. However, the American government is unlikely to sit by and let this company dominate the industry while Boeing is forced to take a back seat. In a way, the situation is similar to that in 1970 when Airbus first got started – the main difference is that the two companies now seem to be in opposite positions.

Websites: ***www.boeing.com*** and ***www.airbus.com***.

Sources: Adapted from Steven Greenhouse, "There's No Stopping Europe's Airbus Now," *New York Times*, June 23, 1991, Section 3, pp. 1, 6; Charles Goldsmith, "Airbus Partner Countries Are Seeking Strict Enforcement of 1992 Subsidy Pact," *Wall Street Journal*, June 17, 1997, p. B 9A; Charles Goldsmith, "After Trailing Boeing for Years, Airbus Aims for 50% of the Market," *Wall Street Journal*, March 16, 1998, pp. A 1, 8; Frederic M. Biddle and John Helyar, "Behind Boeing's Woes: Clunky Assembly Line, Price War with Airbus," *Wall Street Journal*, April 24, 1998, pp. A 1, 16; Daniel Michaels, "Giant Jet Gets Orders It Required," *Wall Street Journal*, November 30, 2000, pp. A 17, 19; Stuart F. Brown, "How to Build a Really, Really, Really Big Plane," *Fortune*, March 5, 2001, p. 152; Anne Marie Squeo, "Boeing Plans to Build Smaller, Faster Jet," *Wall Street Journal*, March 30, 2001, p. A 3; Daniel Michaels, "Airbus Signs Up Partners to Help Build Jumbo Jet," *Wall Street Journal*, June 21, 2001, p. A 14; Kevin Done and Gerhard Hegmann, "Airbus to Recruit 6,000 Extra Staff," *Financial Times*, August 2, 2001, p. 17; Mark Odell and Victor Mallet, "Airbus Cuts Back 2003 Production Targets," *Financial Times*, August 8, 2001, p. 15; Daniel Michaels, Zach Coleman, and Guy Chazan, "Airbus Is in Talks with Beijing on Sale of Jets," *Wall Street Journal*, August 21, 2001, p. A 12.

1. **What are three reasons for the Europeans creating the Airbus consortium?**
2. **How will Airbus help the EU compete in the US?**
3. **How will Airbus help the EU compete in Japan?**
4. **In what way did the Airbus consortium use a *keiretsu* approach to building the aircraft? Why do you think it opted for this approach?**

INTRODUCTION

Triad
The three major trading and investment blocs in the international arena: the United States, the EU, and Japan

Over the last decade international business activity has increased dramatically, especially among the **triad** nations. As has already been noted in Chapter 1, foreign direct investment and trade are at an all-time high. At the same time, however, the most active economies in the international arena have remained the same: the US, Japan, and the members of the EU, specially Germany, France, the UK, and Italy. During the current decade, a growing number of other countries will become increasingly prominent on the international business stage. China is moving quickly to establish itself as a major player. Others whom we will be hearing from increasingly will include Australia, Brazil, Canada, India, Mexico, the Netherlands, the Russian Federation, Singapore, South Korea, and Spain to name but 10. Yet despite the increase of international activity by these countries and others in emerging economies, MNEs from the triad will continue to account for most of the world's foreign direct investment and trade. For this reason, every student of international business should be familiar with the triad and be aware of its impact on world commerce.

In Chapter 1 we pointed out that two of the drivers of globalization are foreign direct investment and trade. In this chapter we want to look more closely at these drivers and the role that the triad plays in both. We begin by examining some of the main reasons for foreign direct investment in a triad context.

REASONS FOR FOREIGN DIRECT INVESTMENT

Foreign direct investment (FDI)
Equity funds invested in other nations

Foreign direct investment (FDI) is the ownership and control of foreign assets. In practice, FDI usually involves the ownership, whole or partial, of a company in a foreign country. This is called a foreign subsidiary. This equity investment can take a variety of forms. One is through the purchase of an ongoing company. For example, Solectron, the world's largest contract electronics firm, recently bought C-Mac Industries of Canada in order to acquire C-Mac's expertise in assembling high-end telecommunications and networking systems.[1] Rather than building this business from scratch, Solectron bought its way into the industry through FDI. Another common example of FDI is to set up a new overseas operation as either a joint venture or a totally owned enterprise. For example, Matsushita is now positioning itself to become a major competitor in the European digital industry and has recently entered into a joint venture with British Telecommunications plc for the purpose of developing multimedia wireless services and products.[2] It is important to remember that FDI is different from **portfolio investment**, which entails the purchase of financial securities (especially bonds) in other firms for the purpose of realizing a financial gain when these marketable assets are sold. The objective of FDI is to provide the investing company with the opportunity to actively manage and control a foreign firm's activities, while the objective of portfolio investment is to achieve growth in the value of its financial holdings.[3]

Portfolio investment
The purchase of financial securities in other firms for the purpose of realizing a financial gain when these marketable assets are sold

There are a number of reasons that businesses are interested in taking an ownership position or gain control of foreign assets. The following examines some of the most important of these.

Increase sales and profits

Some of the largest and best-known multinationals earn millions of dollars each year through overseas sales. Table 3.1 shows the triad firms with the largest foreign assets in

Table 3.1 The largest triad-based MNEs, 1999

Ranking foreign assets	*MNE*		*Foreign assets (in millions of US $)*	*Total assets (in millions of US $)*	*Foreign assets as a % of total assets*
1	General Electric	US	141.1	405.2	34.8
2	ExxonMobil Corporation	US	99.4	144.5	68.8
3	Royal Dutch/Shell Group	EU	68.7	113.9	60.3
4	General Motors	US	68.5	274.7	24.9
5	Ford Motor	US	—	273.4	—
6	Toyota Motor	Japan	56.3	154.9	36.3
7	DaimlerChrysler	EU	55.7	175.9	31.7
8	Total Fina	EU	—	77.6	—
9	IBM	US	44.7	87.5	51.1
10	BP	EU	39.3	52.6	74.7
11	Nestlé	Switzerland	33.1	36.8	89.9
12	Volkswagen	EU	—	64.3	—
13	Nippon Mitsubishi Oil	Japan	31.5	35.5	88.7
14	Siemens	EU	—	76.6	—
15	Wal-Mart	US	30.2	50.0	60.4
16	Repsol YPF	EU	29.6	42.1	70.3
17	Diageo	EU	28.0	40.4	69.3
18	Mannesmann	EU	—	57.7	—
19	Suez Lyonnaise des Eaux	EU	—	71.6	—
20	BMW	EU	27.1	39.2	69.1
21	ABB	Switzerland	27.0	30.6	88.2
22	Sony	Japan	—	64.2	—
23	Seagram	Canada	25.6	35.0	73.1
24	Unilever	EU	25.3	28.0	90.4
25	Aventis	EU	—	39.0	—

Note: EU foreign assets data include the assets of MNEs in other member countries, other than their own. Where (—), the MNEs did not provide the data and the *World Investment Report* estimated their ranking by using secondary sources of information or on the basis of foreign to total sales.

Source: Adapted from "The World's Largest TNCs," of the United Nations, *World Investment Report 2000* (New York: United Nations Conference on Trade and Development, 2001).

1999. In the EU, for example, companies in smaller economies need to look outside of their home borders. This helps to explain why 60 per cent of Royal Dutch/Shell's assets and 75 of BP's assets are in foreign markets, including the markets of other EU members. In addition, although Switzerland is not in the EU, nearly 90 per cent of Nestlé's assets are outside Switzerland. The same is true of revenues. Over 50 per cent of Royal Dutch/Shell's sales originate outside its home markets (the Netherlands and the UK) and nearly 70 per cent of BP's sales are from outside the UK.[4] Similarly, in North America, where Canada's economy is only 10 per cent the size of the US, companies like Seagram, which has now been bought by Vivendi, had 73 per cent of its assets in foreign markets, most notably the US.[5]

There are also thousands of smaller firms worldwide that earn the bulk of their revenue from international customers. For an example, see the box "International Business Strategy in Action: Aflac". SMEs also find that with the growth of large multinationals there is often a need for local suppliers and, if they do well, there is a good chance that the MNE will extend the contract and allow them to supply other worldwide locations. So they, too, are interested in FDI because it can help them increase their sales and profits.

INTERNATIONAL BUSINESS STRATEGY *IN ACTION*

Aflac

The insurance industry is dominated by many well-known names: Prudential, Aetna, Northwestern, etc. Prior to 2000, few people in North America had ever heard of Aflac Inc. of Columbus, Georgia. However, the company has been the most successful insurer in Japan, with annual revenues of $9.7 billion and profits well over $650 million in 2000. Aflac is the world's leading seller of cancer insurance, which helps to pay the cost of treating the disease, and it holds 90 per cent of the Japanese market for this coverage. The Japanese subsidiary accounts for over 75 per cent of Aflac's pretax earnings and insures one out of every four Japanese.

The firm began doing business in Japan in 1974. Initially Aflac approached big Japanese insurers as potential joint-venture partners; none of them was interested. Eventually the Ministry of Finance gave the company a license to sell insurance, primarily because no Japanese insurer was in the business so that there would be no competition for local firms.

A key to Aflac's rapid growth and profitability is its system of selling through corporate agencies. The firm has set up in-house subsidiaries in Japanese corporations to handle the sale of its insurance. These subsidiaries would be illegal distributors in the US, but they are very common in Japan. As a result, Aflac eventually ended up with over 40,000 Japanese companies offering its policies to their employees. From Hitachi to Sony, Toyota to Nissan, and Mitsui to Mitsubishi, policyholders throughout the country pay premiums of approximately $21 a month through an automatic payroll deduction plan. Moreover, once they are signed up, few Japanese drop out. In contrast to the US where only 25 per cent of health and accident insurance policyholders remain with the same company for a decade or more, in Japan 75 per cent of Aflac policyholders have been with them for 10 or more years.

Will Aflac be able to continue its success in the market? In many countries such as the US, cancer insurance is declining in popularity because coverage is now provided by basic policies. In Japan, however, the first stage of cancer treatment can cost up to $50,000. Even though the Japanese government is expected to introduce national care insurance, it has made clear that it will not be able to cover the full cost. Furthermore, about four years ago the company began to diversify its product-line. Today over 30 per cent of all sales in Japan are for non-cancer-related insurance. As a result of the costs associated with cancer, Aflac's supplemental coverage remains very popular. The additional success of its new products makes Aflac find the Japanese market to be profitable.

Perhaps the biggest challenge to Aflac's Japanese market share is market deregulation. Aflac has functioned practically as a monopoly in Japan over the last 30 years. In 2001, the Japanese government allowed Nippon Life Insurance and Tokio Marine & Fire to compete in the supplementary insurance market. Aflac need not worry in the short term, since these companies' operating costs are four times its own. In the long run, however, other companies might want to wrestle this profitable market away from Aflac. The company is well aware of this and is expanding its reach by partnering with Dai-Ichi Mutual, Japan's second largest insurance company, to distribute each other's policies. In addition, a joint venture with Communicationware Corporation has seen the development of aflacdirect.com, the first company to provide insurance solely on the Internet.

Aflac has also turned to its domestic market by launching an aggressive marketing campaign featuring a mascot. The Aflac duck, as it has become known, has appeared in a series of television ads screaming Aaaaflaack to oblivious characters. This has had its desired effect and today 95 per cent of Americans recognize the name Aflac.

Websites: **www.aflac.com** and **www.aflac.co.jp**.

Sources: Adapted from Steve Lohr, "Under the Wing of Japan, Inc., a Fledgling Enterprise Soared," *New York Times*, January 15, 1992, pp. A 1, C 5; *Forbes*, January 4, 1993, p. 167; *Fortune*, May 31, 1993, p. 218; ***www.reportgallery.com/aflac/japan.htm***; ***www.oecd.org/publications/figures/money.html*** and Bethany McLean, "Duck and Coverage," *Fortune*, August 13, 2001.

In addition, global markets often offer more lucrative opportunities than do domestic markets. This helps to explain why Coca-Cola and IBM now earn more sales revenue and profits overseas than they do in the US, and why PepsiCo has become Mexico's largest consumer products company. In Japan, it helps to explain why 83 per cent of Nippon Mitsubishi Oil's and over 50 per cent of Toyota's revenues come from overseas sales.[6] It also helps account for the decision by Tesco plc, the British supermarket firm, to expand operations into Eastern Europe and Asia. And the same is true for Wal-Mart, which in recent years has expanded rapidly and now has stores on four continents and appears on the verge of becoming a major competitor in the EU thanks to its FDI in both the UK and Germany.[7]

Enter rapidly growing markets

Some international markets are growing much faster than others, and FDI provides MNEs with the chance to take advantage of these opportunities. A good example is China. Over the past few years the Chinese economy has grown at an annual rate of around 7–8 per cent. This is quite good given that its GDP is in the range of $1 trillion. These data also point to the fact that, if the country continues to move toward a market-driven economy, MNEs are likely to find a huge demand for goods and services that cannot be satisfied by local firms alone. Simply put, China is a market where most multinationals want to have a presence despite the fact that there are many problems in doing business there and virtually no MNE has yet been able to extract an adequate return on its investment.

At the same time, China is not the only emerging market being targeted by multinationals. A growing number of companies are using FDI to gain a foothold in Eastern Europe by acquiring local firms or setting up joint ventures there.

Reduce costs

An MNE can sometimes achieve substantially lower costs by going abroad than by producing at home (see the box "International Business Strategy in Action: Japanese FDI in Scotland"). If labor expenses are high and represent a significant portion of overall costs, an MNE may be well advised to look to other geographic areas where the goods can be produced at a much lower labor price. Surprisingly perhaps, in recent years some Canadian manufacturers have been moving operations across the border to take advantage of lower US labor unit costs.

A second important cost factor is materials. If materials are in short supply or must be conveyed a long distance, it may be less expensive to move production close to the source of supply than to import the materials.

A third critical cost factor is energy. If the domestic cost of energy for making the product is high, the company may be forced to set up operations overseas near sources of cheaper energy.

A fourth important factor is transportation costs. In the recent past Chinese textile firms had gained a major share of the US market. Production costs were so low that, even after adding in transportation expenses, they were able to beat out most competitors. This is no longer true, however. Mexican firms, armed with the latest technology, can now produce high quality, low cost textiles that can be quickly shipped to US customers. And since transportation is but a small percentage of overall costs, the US now buys more textile products from Mexico than from China. On the other hand, in the case of steel, US manufacturers are again finding that their foreign competitors are more efficient and, even when shipping costs are included, they can find local customers for their product. In fact, in 2000 steel imports accounted for approximately 27 per cent of all domestic purchases. In particular, Asian and EU firms accounted for half of all these imports of finished steel products.[8] By continuing to drive down their production costs, international steel makers have been able to remain competitive in the American market.

In recent years many firms have used all four of these reasons to justify moving assembly operations to other countries. For example, low-skill labor costs are much lower in Mexico than in the US, Korea, Hong Kong, Taiwan, or Singapore, so Mexico has become a prime target for the manufacture of labor-intensive products. In fact, some US firms

INTERNATIONAL BUSINESS STRATEGY *IN ACTION*

Japanese FDI in Scotland

American computer MNEs, such as IBM, Honeywell, and NCR, have been active in Scotland since the 1950s. The MNEs were attracted to Scotland because of the availability of low-cost skilled labor and the government's incentives to attract FDI. By the 1990s, Scotland produced one-third of all branded personal computers (PCs) sold in Europe, which represents about 7 per cent of world output. It also accounts for 12 per cent of European production of semiconductors. The foreign-owned electronics sector is quite important in Scotland since it accounts for one-third of all jobs in foreign-owned companies in Scotland. While some EU MNEs have settled in Scotland, the sector is dominated by US and Japanese firms that chose Scotland as an entry port into the EU.

The electronics sector is divided into five sub-sectors: information systems (processing systems, peripherals, support products); semiconductors; telecommunication electronics; consumer electronics (TVs and VCRs); and software and others. Today IBM is the only one of the three information systems producers to remain active in the region. However, 10 other information systems manufacturing companies have settled in Scotland. These companies, which together employ over 6,500 people, include: Compaq (US), Digital (US), Sun Microsystems (US), OKI Electric (Japan), AT&T (US), Apricot (Japan – owned by Mitsubishi Electric), Elonex (UK), Tandem (US), Exabyte (US), and Escom (Germany). Furthermore, two US MNEs, Motorola and Hewlett-Packard, have major telecommunication electronics facilities in Scotland. Together they employ over 3,000 people and completely dominate the telecommunications electronics sub-sector.

While US companies heavily dominate the production of information systems and telecommunications, the production of semiconductors, which today accounts for more than 5,000 jobs in Scotland, is more highly influenced by Japanese MNEs. US MNEs such as Motorola and National Semiconductor established silicon production in Scotland in the 1960s and were followed by Digital and Hughes. Subsequently, Japanese MNEs such as NEC and Fuji Electric chose Scotland as their first European manufacturing location. The initial NEC Scottish facility for the assembly and testing of semiconductor components was upgraded to house the first Japanese wafer fabrication in Europe. There has been a program of continuous investment by NEC to remain competitive in semiconductor manufacturing technology. Fuji Electric started the production of power transistor modules for use in control systems in 1991, the company's first European location. For both NEC and Fuji Electric, it is clear that Scotland provides a low-cost production platform for entry into the EU market.

The Japanese also dominate the consumer electronics sub-sector. MNEs such as Mitsubishi Electronic and Matsushita Panasonic produce color television sets in central Scotland. These companies were initially attracted by the relatively low labor costs, government assistance, and access to the European market. Mitsubishi first located in Scotland in 1979 and now has two plants employing 1,200 people in manufacturing TVs and VCRs. Production of television sets includes 37-inch sets, the largest models in the world. The videocassette recorder plant is Mitsubishi's principal manufacturing facility for sales outside Japan. Matsushita Panasonic opened in 1993 and manufactures flyback transformers for use in television and computer monitors.

The challenges that face the Scottish electronics sector are many. In spite of the continued growth of the sector since the 1950s, the electronics sector failed to develop the higher value-added end of the industry and it now faces a serious competitive threat from lower-cost producers in Southeast Asia, such as Taiwan and Singapore. The sector also failed to develop key supplier linkages or university research infrastructure. The Scottish electronics sector is seeking to transform itself to become more competitive. The creation of the Scottish Electronics Forum may help to foster better linkages with non-business infrastructure. Furthermore, the Alba Centre, a collaborative project between the electronics industry, the public sector and academia, is expected to increase the autonomy of the Scottish industry, while creating key domestic linkages. The centre will include an independent trading house for semiconductor design and an academic centre.

Scotland has key advantages for the industry to develop, one of which is an already existing infrastructure, labor, and access to the EU market. It is in the success of the new steps the Scottish electronics industry is taking that the chance of becoming truly competitive in the world electronics market really lies.

Websites: ***www.ibm.com***; ***www.honeywell.com***; ***www.ncr.com***; ***www.compaq.com***; ***www.sun.com***; ***www.oki.com***; ***www.att.com***; ***www.elonex.co.uk***; ***www.escom.de***; ***www.motorola.com***; ***www.hp.com***; ***www.nec.com***; ***www.neceurope.com***; ***www.fujielectric.co.jp***; ***www.national.com***; ***www.mitsubishielectric.com***; ***www.mei.co.jp***; ***www.panasonic-europe.com*** and ***www.albacentre.com***.

Sources: Alan M. Rugman, "The Five Partners/Flagship Model and the Scottish Electronics Cluster", in Jean-Louis Mucchielli (ed.), *Research in Global Strategic Management*, vol. 6 (Greenwich, CT: JAI Press, 1998), pp. 165–181; ***www.hotecho.org/archive/se20/features/electronics.html***; ***www.hotecho.org/news/news.html***.

Twin factories (Also see *Maquiladoras*) Production operations set up on both sides of the US-Mexican border for the purpose of shipping goods between the two countries

Maquiladoras (Also see *Twin factories*) Production operations set up on both sides of the US-Mexican border in a free trade zone for the purpose of shipping goods between the two countries

have even set up **twin factories**, or ***maquiladoras***, which involve production operations on both sides of the border and the shipment of goods between the two countries. As a result, today US components are shipped into Mexico duty free, assembled by Mexican workers, and then re-exported to the US or other foreign markets under favorable tariff provisions. (This arrangement will be discussed further later in the text.)

Gain a foothold in economic blocs

As we have noted on a number of occasions thus far, there are three major international economic blocs. MNEs that acquire a company in one of these blocs or that enter into an alliance to do business in one of these economic strongholds can obtain a number of benefits including the right to sell their output without having to be burdened by import duties or other restrictions. In the case of NAFTA, for example, the United States–Canada Free Trade Agreement of 1989 was the initial step in fashioning a giant North American market. In January 1994 this agreement was expanded to include Mexico, and in the future Chile will become the fourth member. International MNEs wanting to do business in North America are finding that it is important to gain a foothold in this region through FDI. The same is true in the EU. Over the last decade the membership of this bloc has increased to 15 with the admission of Austria, Finland, and Sweden. Currently, Bulgaria, Cyprus, the Czech Republic, Estonia, Hungary, Latvia, Lithuania, Malta, Poland, Romania, the Slovak Republic and Slovenia are being considered for membership. Turkey has also requested to join the union but has still to meet the required conditions to begin negotiations. Meanwhile in Asia, while Japan continues to be the major economic power, we are likely to see the rise of an "Asian bloc" that includes countries such as Australia, China, India, Indonesia, Malaysia, the Philippines, South Korea, Taiwan, and Thailand. Through the use of trade agreements, these countries are likely to create a bloc that provides a balance to NAFTA and the EU. During the next two decades, it is highly likely that the super economic powers and those in the next economic tier will cooperate to create these blocs in order to stimulate their respective economies and to provide a competitive stance for firms doing business under their umbrella. This means that in Europe we are likely to see most countries including the Russian Federation (but perhaps not Switzerland) becoming members of the EU, while in the Western hemisphere most countries of North and South America join NAFTA. The final result will be three extended triads and any company that wants to do business worldwide will have to have a presence in all three blocs.

Protect domestic markets

Another reason for FDI is to protect one's domestic market. Many MNEs are now entering an international market in order to attack potential competitors and thus prevent them from expanding their operations overseas. These multinationals reason that a competitor is less likely to enter a foreign market when it is busy defending its home market position. Similarly, sometimes an MNE will enter a foreign market in order to bring pressure on a company that has already challenged its own home market. For example, 10 days after Fuji began building its first manufacturing facility in the US, Kodak announced its decision to open a manufacturing plant in Japan.

Sometimes the decision to go international also helps a firm to protect its position with current clients who are going international. For example, when Honda Motors set up operations in Indiana, Nippodenso, a producer of automobile radiators and heaters, established a plant nearby. So did Mitsubishi Bank, the primary bank for Honda. In addition to the extra business it generates, this strategy helps to combat local competitors, such as Indiana manufacturers and banks, who might otherwise gain inroads and perhaps even threaten domestic business should they decide to set up operations in Japan.

Protect foreign markets

Sometimes MNEs will use FDI in order to protect their foreign markets. In the US, for example, from 1981 to 1991 the total number of service stations had declined by over 50 per cent. British Petroleum (BP), which had a substantial investment in this market, realized that in order to protect its investment it would be necessary to make a substantial investment in order to upgrade its stations and increase its market share. The company refines and markets petroleum products and realized that if it could attract a growing number of customers to its service stations, it could profit handsomely by moving its products directly downstream to the final consumer. The company also merged with Amoco, thus assuring itself of a solid market share and, in the process, protecting its investment in this foreign market. Had it not done this, local competitors would inevitably have eroded the firm's position.

Acquire technological and managerial know-how

Still another reason for FDI is to acquire technological and managerial expertise. One way of doing this is to set up operations near those of leading competitors. This is why some US firms have moved some of their research and development facilities to Japan. With this strategy, they find it is easier to monitor the competition and to recruit scientists from local universities and competitive laboratories. Kodak is an excellent example.

The company made the decision to build an 180,000-square-foot research center and it started cultivating leading scientists to help with recruiting. Kodak used all the same approaches that Japanese firms employ in the US: financing research by university scientists and offering scholarships to outstanding young Japanese engineers, some of whom would later join Kodak. In addition, the company hired internationally known scientists to help attract experienced colleagues from leading Japanese companies and to recruit young graduates from the host universities such as the Tokyo Institute of Technology. As a result, Japan is now the center of Kodak's worldwide research efforts in a number of high-technology areas.[9]

Active learning check

Review your answer to Active Learning Case question 1 and make any changes you like. Then compare your answer with the one below.

1. What are three reasons for the Europeans creating the Airbus consortium?

One of the reasons for the Europeans creating the Airbus consortium was to enter a rapidly growing market. As can be seen from the data in the case, billions of dollars will be spent on new aircraft between now and the year 2010. Singapore Airlines alone will be putting out over $8 billion for 25 A380 craft and it is only one of a number of firms that have placed firm orders with Airbus. So there is a huge market for large craft and the Europeans wanted to be in this lucrative market. A second reason for creating the consortium was to help build a stronger EU economy. Airbus provided thousands of jobs and billions of dollars to the member countries and, even with its new arrangement in which it is no longer managed by governments but rather by investors, the company is continuing to provide both jobs and revenues in Europe. A third reason that Airbus was created was to protect the domestic market by making it less reliant on foreign firms such as Boeing. Given that Airbus now holds 50 per cent of the commercial aircraft market, this objective has clearly been attained.

FOREIGN DIRECT INVESTMENT AND TRADE BY TRIAD MEMBERS

As seen thus far, there are many reasons why MNEs make foreign direct investment. In addition, much of this FDI, and trade as well, is made by triad members: the US, the EU, and Japan. The following examines these findings in more depth.

The triad's domination of FDI and trade

Over the past decade the triad has accounted for an extremely large percentage of both FDI *and* world trade. For example, as seen in Figure 3.1, triad countries make billions of dollars of investments in one another. The data in this figure reveal that in 1998 total US FDI was $433.7 billion in the EU and $38.2 billion in Japan. In turn the EU countries and Japan had total investments in the US of $347.1 billion and $109.9 billion, respectively. EU FDI in Japan was $11.5 billion while Japanese FDI in the EU was $38.2 billion. Quite clearly, triad countries are investing large sums of money in each other's operations.

In addition, as seen in Table 3.2, the percentage of global FDI accounted for by triad countries during the last decade has remained around 80 per cent, even though the amount of worldwide FDI has almost tripled.

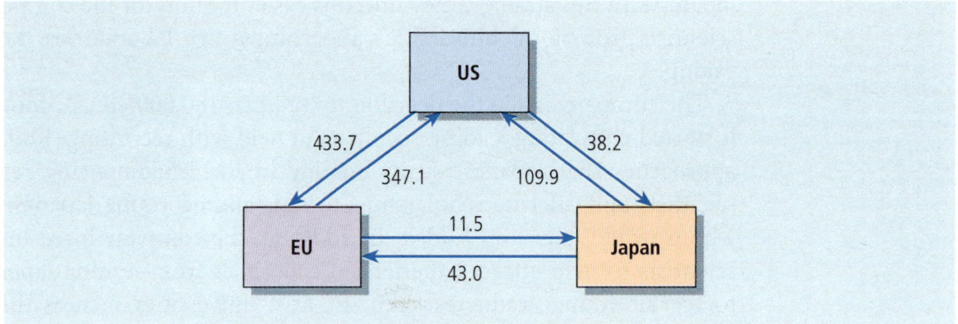

Figure 3.1 FDI in the triad, 1998 (US $ billion)

Note: Data for Japan's outward FDI are 1997 for US and 1996 for EU. More recent data are not available. European Union outward FDI is the sum of outward FDI by: Austria, Finland, France, Germany, Italy, the Netherlands, Portugal, Sweden, and the UK. Data for other EU countries are not available. Except for Portugal and the UK, for which 1998 data are available, the year 1997 was used for EU countries.

Source: From OECD (1999) *International Direct Investment Statistics Yearbook*. Copyright OECD, 1999.

Table 3.2 Ten years of triad FDI

Country/region	*1990 FDI stock (in millions of US $)*	*1990 % world*	*1999 FDI stock (in millions of US $)*	*1999 % world*
US	430,521	25.1	1,131,466	23.7
EU*	789,401	46.0	2,336,631	49.1
Japan	201,440	11.7	292,781	6.1
Triad	1,421,362	82.8	3,760,878	79.0
All others	295,002	17.2	998,455	20.9
World	1,716,364	100.0	4,759,333	100.0

* EU numbers are outward stocks of FDI by every EU member. Thus, intra-EU FDI is included.

Source: Adapted from the United Nations, *World Investment Report 2000* (New York: United Nations Conference on Trade and Development, 2000).

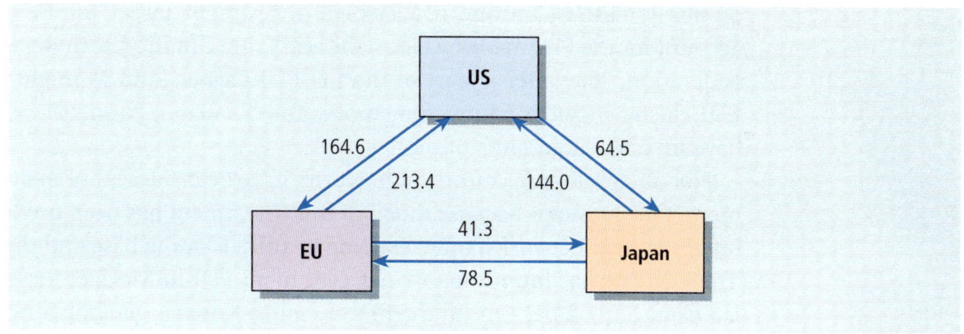

Figure 3.2 **Trade in the triad, 2000 (US $ billion)**

Source: Adapted from International Monetary Fund, *Direction of Trade Statistics Yearbook, 2001* (Washington DC: IMF, 2001).

This dominance by the triad is also seen in the amount of trade done by triad members. Figure 3.2 shows much the same picture for trade patterns in the triad as we saw for FDI; there are very strong two-way trade flows. The EU conducts a large amount of annual trade with Japan and the US, and both Japan and the US do a great deal of trading with both the EU and with each other. Table 3.3 reports the trade of the triad and shows that these three blocs accounted for over 61 per cent of all world imports and over 53 per cent of all world exports in 2000. As a result of such trade (and FDI), it is clear that the triad is the major economic force in the international arena.

Triad FDI clusters

FDI cluster
A group of developing countries usually located in the same geographic region as a triad member and having some form of economic link to this member

While the above data clearly show the importance of the triad in international business, this impact extends well beyond the FDI and trade that take place among its members. Triad countries have also become major investors in poorer nations. The United Nations Centre on Transnational Corporations (UNCTC) reports that triad members accounted for over 40 per cent of the FDI in 25 of the 37 developing countries it studied.[10] Typically, recipients of FDI are part of an **FDI cluster**, which is a group of developing countries that are usually located in the same geographic region as the triad member and have some form of economic link to it. For example, the US tends to be a dominant investor in Latin America and countries such as Mexico, Brazil, and Argentina are part of its FDI cluster.

Table 3.3 **Ten years of triad trade**

	Exports				*Imports*			
Country/region	*1991 (billions of US $)*	*% of total*	*2000 (billions of US $)*	*% of total*	*1991 (billions of US $)*	*% of total*	*2000 (billions of US $)*	*% of total*
United States	421.7	11.7	772.0	11.7	509.3	14.6	1,257.6	19.7
EU*	1,490.3	41.4	2,283.0	34.5	1,580.2	45.3	2,284.9	35.9
Japan	314.8	8.7	477.3	7.2	236.6	6.8	377.2	5.9
Triad	2,226.8	61.9	3,532.3	53.4	2,326.1	66.7	3,919.7	61.5
All others	1,372.0	38.1	3,076.4	46.6	1,158.8	33.3	2,449.0	38.5
Total	3,598.8	100.0	6,608.7	100.0	3,484.9	100.0	6,368.7	100.0

* EU numbers are for exports/imports of every member to/from the rest of the world. Thus, EU exports and import include intra-EU figures.

Source: Adapted from International Monetary Fund, *Direction of Trade Statistics Yearbook, 1996* (Washington DC: IMF, 1996) and International Monetary Fund, *Direction of Trade Statistics Yearbook, 2001* (Washington DC: IMF, 2001).

Similarly, Eastern Europe is a favorite investment target for EU countries and helps account for the FDI made by Germany and France in the Czech Republic and the Russian Federation. The latter is part of the EU FDI cluster. And as might be expected, Japan's FDI cluster includes China, Singapore, and Thailand, countries where Japanese MNEs have invested large sums of money.

Not all developing countries, however, have been successful in attracting triad investment. One reason is because much of this investment has been used by multinationals to build regional networks, often starting near their home base and then working outward. The UNCTC has found that 61 per cent of all FDI in Mexico, for example, comes from US firms and 52 per cent of the FDI in South Korea is generated by Japanese firms. The UNCTC has also found that more than half of all investment into developing countries is going to four nations: Brazil, China, Mexico, and Singapore. And much of this money comes from triad countries that are located in that part of the world. So Brazil and Mexico are recipients of much US FDI and China and Singapore are favorite FDI targets for Japanese firms.

Such investment policies help reinforce our earlier comments about the triad's dominance of regional economic clusters. In the future, triad members may well continue to strengthen their FDI in specific regions, as in Europe, where the EU is a major force in economic development. At the same time, these types of investment strategies by triad members may restrict trade and investment opportunities for some developing countries. This is why it is so important for non-triad countries to be linked to the triad in some way. As will be explained later in the book, by gaining linkage to the triad, a country can benefit by tapping these enormous markets as a supplier to large MNEs or by selling directly to customers in these markets.

THE TRIAD AND REGIONAL BUSINESS STRATEGY

During this first decade of the new century, the triad will continue to dominate the international business scene. In particular, members will pursue market opportunities within their own triad as well as that of the other members. For example, retailing in the US is dominated by Wal-Mart. However, the company is not content to simply sell in its home country or within NAFTA (Canada and Mexico); it has also expanded into both Europe and Asia. In Europe, meanwhile, Tesco is expanding rapidly and pushing into Asia while Carrefour, the French retail giant, has more than 9,000 stores throughout Europe and approximately 100 more in Asia.[11] This pattern of activity is common for triad firms. In fact, one of the best examples is provided by the automobile industry where auto makers are now trying to establish profitable operations in all three triad blocs and are using FDI to help them.

Wal-Mart is not a global business

A more careful analysis shows that "international" expansion does not necessarily mean "global" expansion. For example, Wal-Mart has only 10 per cent of all its stores outside North America. This means that the home triad is still its locus for strategy. It does not have a "global" strategy. This even confuses other professors. For example, an entire chapter in a book on global strategy is directed to learning the "lessons from Wal-Mart's globalization".[12] Yet Wal-Mart is not really a global company. Indeed, in the United Nations *World Investment Report 2001* it is reported that Wal-Mart has one of the lowest scores of any of the 100 largest MNEs. On a transnational index Wal-Mart has a "network spread index" (a measure of actual to possible FDI – of which there were a possible 187 in 1999) of under 5 per cent. Other low scores are for Woodbridge, Mitsubishi, Petróleos

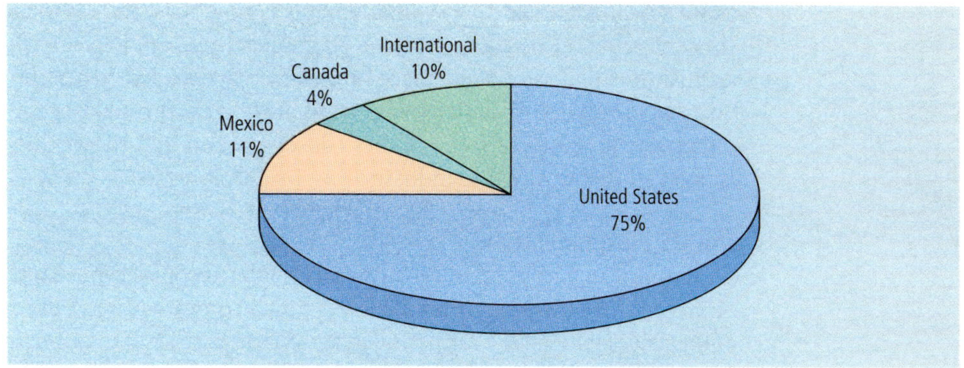

Figure 3.3 Wal-Mart's globalization: global distribution of stores

Source: Vijay Govindarajan and Anil K. Gupta, *The Quest for Global Dominance* (New York: Harcourt, 2001), pp. 52–53. Copyright © 2001. This material is used by permission of Jossey-Bass, Inc., a subsidiary of John Wiley & Sons, Inc.

de Venezuela, Edison, and Nippon Oil. In contrast, many MNEs score over 30 per cent, for example, Shell, Nestlé, Unilever, TotalFina, Aventis, and ABB.

As Figure 3.3 indicates, Wal-Mart is a regional but not a global business. On January 31, Wal-Mart had a total of 3,989 stores. It reported that 1,004 of its stores were "international" and the remaining 2,985 were in the domestic US market. An additional 458 were in Mexico and another 166 in Canada. Thus a total of 3,609 of its stores are in the NAFTA region. Only 380 stores are truly "international", i.e. outside of Wal-Mart's home triad. In other words, Wal-Mart is still a North American business. The locus of its business model strategy and structure is regional and triad-based.

Active learning check 

Review your answer to Active Learning Case question 2 and make any changes you like. Then compare your answer with the one below.

2. How will Airbus help the EU to compete in the US?

Airbus will open up markets in the US by offering alternative aircraft to those being produced by Boeing. These Airbus offerings are not only reliable but fuel-efficient and, as noted in the case, are often provided at very competitive prices. As a result, Airbus has been able to tap a US market that had been previously closed to the EU because no European company could compete with Boeing and McDonnell. Now Airbus has been able to land contracts with US firms such as American Airlines, one of the largest carriers in the world. If the A380 proves successful, it will help Airbus compete ever more effectively in the US.

Triad activity and the automobile industry

The worldwide auto industry, consisting of cars and light trucks, has seen a great deal of consolidation over the last two decades. In fact, there have been so many sales and acquisitions in the industry during this time that it is very difficult to remember all of the deals that have been made. Perhaps the best known has been Daimler-Benz's acquisition of Chrysler to form DaimlerChrysler. However, there have been many others. For example, Ford Motor bought Jaguar and took a controlling interest in Mazda Motors. The company also purchased the auto division of Volvo and, most recently, acquired Rover from BMW. General Motors purchased both Lotus and Saab Auto and now holds 48 per cent of Isuzu.[13] Meanwhile Renault, the French auto maker, decided to move away from trucks and commercial vehicles and toward automobiles. As a result, the firm sold its truck division to Volvo, bought Samsung Motors and gained operating control of Nissan, as we saw in Chapter 2. So while Renault is now focusing on the auto market, Volvo is concentrating on trucks and buses. Of course, these are only a small number of the auto acquisitions that have taken place in the last two decades. In addition, there currently are hosts of joint-venture activities between auto firms throughout the triad. The following discusses the results of some of these developments and shows the large amount of triad activity in this worldwide industry.

The US auto industry

The American auto market for cars and light trucks, in recent years, has been in the range of 16 million units, a number which is down somewhat from the 18 million car market of the mid–late 1980s. Competing in this market are such major firms as General Motors, Ford, DaimlerChrysler, BMW, Saab, Volkswagen, Honda, Toyota, and Nissan.[14] As of the early part of this decade General Motors had approximately 28.3 per cent of this market and Ford held 21.9 per cent. Chrysler had 13.2 per cent. Asian automakers collectively held 32 per cent. Of this, Toyota alone had 10.1 per cent.[15] The remaining 4.6 per cent was held by European car makers such as Daimler, Volkswagen and BMW.[16]

In the case of EU-based auto firms, these companies have been selling cars in the US market for decades and the future promises to see a strong continuation of these efforts. In particular, over the last 10 years German auto makers have started again gaining US market share and more than holding their own against Japanese competition. In particular, BMW, Audi, Mercedes, Porsche, and Volkswagen all saw turnarounds in sales beginning in the mid-1990s. One of the primary reasons accounting for this success was that German producers began building cars that appealed to American buyers. This was in sharp contrast to their earlier strategies where they offered products that were attractive to Europeans, who were far more interested in engineering quality and road handling than were Americans. Now German cars, especially for the luxury market, are sportier and more nimble than their predecessors. They also offer conveniences that US buyers look for in their cars including such mundane things as coffee cup holders. Commenting on this fact, a BMW board member noted that in the past German car makers had traditional disdain for such "petty" offerings and as a result found US buyers responding "by buying the other guys' cars". Now the Mercedes M-Class model being built in Alabama offers no fewer than five cup holders.[17]

European car makers have also found that their Japanese competitors were able to undercut them in two key areas – quality image and price. Many American customers felt that cars such as the Lexus and Infiniti were better products than not just local offerings such as Cadillacs and Lincolns, but BMWs and Mercedes as well. In particular, the Japanese offerings had fewer quality problems and their prices were more competitive. In fact, Japanese firms have continued to lead the way in quality. In one of the most recently released reports on auto quality in North America, J. D. Powers & Associates found that on average auto makers had 147 problems per 100 cars.[18] The number of problems (per 100) for major manufacturers was as follows:

Toyota	115
Honda	133
Nissan	145
General Motors	146
DaimlerChrysler	154
Volkswagen	159
Ford	162

Source: *Wall Street Journal*. Eastern Edition (staff produced copy only) by *Wall Street Journal*. Copyright 2001 by Dow Jones & Co, Inc. Reproduced with permission of Dow Jones & Co, Inc in the format textbook via Copyright Clearance Center.

Toyota and Honda continue to build high quality cars for the US market while the European car makers (and the Americans too!) are farther down the list.

Faced with these challenges, EU manufacturers have made a series of strategic decisions that have tilted the playing field more in their favor. First, they have begun setting up production facilities in the US and thus reduced the cost of transporting their cars. At the same time they have found that, like buyers worldwide, Americans prefer to purchase locally made products rather than imports. This is clearly seen in the case of the BMW 7-series where US demand from the early to the late 1990s tripled, while sales of its other models doubled. Second, German auto makers have sharply cut the time to market. So when one of their cars has become very popular, they can quickly meet the demand. Third, they have begun catering more to US buyers. For example, while European luxury cars are built to be "driving machines", most Americans do not buy these cars because of their superior handling. Rather they are looking for cars that are reliable and comfortable. Fourth, German car makers have continued to stress technical innovation and quality workmanship, two factors that many Americans find particularly attractive when conducting comparison shopping with other luxury cars.

However, not all European auto makers have been highly successful in the US market. Volvo, which sold its car operations to Ford in 1998, and Saab, whose auto business has been acquired by General Motors, are good examples. Both of these car makers have found that, while their worldwide auto sales began increasing in the mid-1990s, their performance in the American market has been stagnant and their market shares are lower than they were 10 years earlier. One reason is because Volvo and Saab were slow to add options such as electric windows and other conveniences that are valued in the US market. A second reason is that they have had trouble producing cars efficiently. Their costs are sharply higher than those of other luxury car makers and, as a result, their selling prices tend to limit market demand. (One of Ford's current objectives is to make Volvo much more cost effective.) A third problem has been that their market niche is dominated by highly competitive firms such as BMW, Mercedes, and Lexus, so they are having difficulty maintaining market share. A fourth problem is their limited model offerings. Finally, there is the challenge of how to change these cars without losing their image in the marketplace. For example, Volvo began offering sportier models, but this strategy was not the right one for a market niche that typically is interested in a family sedan that offers safety and reliability. Similarly, one of the more recent Saab offerings arrived in the US with a hatchback instead of a trunk, a style associated in the US market with inexpensive economy cars. Nevertheless, it appears that both Volvo, as part of Ford's upmarket portfolio of cars, and Saab, as part of GM's, are going to be adopting more international designs and trying to establish themselves as key players in the US premium-car market. Whether this will work or their previous image as manufacturers of family automobiles will prove their undoing is yet to be determined.[19]

The Japanese are also competing very vigorously in the US market. In fact, in recent years Toyota and Honda have both expanded their presence despite the fact that this market is now moving into the maturity phase and it is becoming increasingly more difficult to gain and hold this market share. In particular, the two auto makers have increased their output capacity and are planning additional major expansions.[20] Collectively, they are able to produce approximately 2.5 million cars in the US, giving them a very strong local presence. And through the use of superior engineering and design, they have been able to bring out new models with additional features while keeping their price level. Additionally, as the demand for their autos has increased in recent years, they have been able to respond more quickly to the market and ensure adequate dealer

inventories. Another of Toyota and Honda's recent successes has been their hybrid models that combine a gas engine and an electric motor. Honda's Insight gets combined city/highway mileage of 65 miles per gallon and Toyota's Prius achieves 48 miles per gallon.[21] Moreover, both companies have been focusing attention on the light truck market. Importing these units from Japan has meant paying a 25 per cent tariff, but producing them locally gives the manufacturers a strong competitive position.

In addition, Japanese car makers have found that the downturn in the Asian economy has produced some benefits for their import operations. For example, as the Japanese yen continued to slide against the dollar and fell from 110 to 140, the cost of imports declined, making it more economically feasible to export additional cars to the American market. One of the reasons why the Japanese had begun setting up operations in North America was to deal with the strong yen of the early 1990s which threatened to sharply reduce its ability to sell high-ticket items in competitive worldwide markets. Now that this threat has somewhat subsided, Japanese activity in the US auto market is coming from both overseas as well as domestic production.[22]

Finally, it should be noted that the major competitors in the US market do not produce all of their output in America. The Japanese still import a large percentage of their cars for Japan, and Canada and Mexico have been providing a growing number of cars for this market. Ford and GM, in particular, have long had operations in Canada and in recent years most major worldwide competitors have established operations in Mexico. In fact, DaimlerChrysler recently announced that it is going to invest approximately $2 billion in Mexico over a five-year period.[23] Most of this production is scheduled for the American market.

The EU auto industry

The auto industry in Europe is slightly larger than that of the US. In recent years approximately 16 million vehicles have been manufactured there annually, with Germany, France, Italy, and Belgium accounting for more than half of this production total.[24] Competition in the industry is very strong, and the leading firms, as might be expected, are European, with Volkswagen accounting for one in every five vehicles sold here and Renault, Fiat, and Peugeot rounding out the top four. General Motors and Ford have long had operations in Europe but they are not the lead players, and Japanese manufacturers, Toyota and Honda in particular, are farther back yet. EU-based auto firms know what their local customers want – and they provide it. Other competitors, for all intents and purposes, are "also rans" in this highly competitive market. In an effort to reverse this historical picture, Ford Motor, for example, is now working to rival Mercedes with its new luxury-brand division that includes Jaguar, Volvo, Aston Martin, and Land Rover – all European car names that have been acquired by the company. Ford's current strategy is to take these acquisitions and use them to garner market share. The big challenge, of course, is to overcome the perception that these cars will be not be high quality but rather simply Fords with luxury name brands. The firm's current strategy is to use inexpensive parts in areas where drivers do not care (electronic window motors) but produce unique parts that do matter (transmission). Ford plans to manufacture its brand name cars with one-third standard parts, one-third that will be common among its luxury brands, and the final one-third that will be unique to the specific model.[25] General Motors' recent decision to buy the remaining 50 per cent of Saab is another example of how a US manufacturer intends to take advantage of the luxury car market in the EU.[26] Saab is a well-known European car and with GM's design, styling, and market savvy, it may well become a strong competitor in the upper-level market niche.

Another recent development has been the acquisition or merging of firms. For example, Volkswagen has bought Rolls Royce and VW's Audi unit has acquired Lamborghini.[27] As a result, VW now offers a wide array of car lines in the EU that cover the continuum from lower to higher price levels including Audi, Bentley, Lamborghini, Rolls Royce, Seat, Skoda, and its VW lines including the Beetle and the Passat. Meanwhile, as previously mentioned, Daimler-Benz has merged with Chrysler and DaimlerChrysler is now almost as large as Ford Motor and promises to make the collective firm even more competitive in the EU market.

Triad members are also building or expanding their production facilities.[28] Volkswagen is implementing a multi-billion-dollar investment strategy that involves setting up new operations in Eastern Europe. At the same time Japanese auto producers have substantial vehicle production capability in Europe. As a result, there now is more auto making capacity in Western Europe than in either Japan or the US. This expansion is likely to bring increased competition and put strong pressure on the EU auto makers, some of which are not able to compete with their triad counterparts in terms of quality and price.

Some of the strongest competition may well come from the American auto makers, although they have been having problems of their own. For example, Ford's market share has fallen from 11.6 in 1995 to 8.4 in 2000.[29] Ford has been revamping its strategy and focusing more and more on increased profitability. The old days of producing marginally profitable cars in order to maintain market share are coming to a close. Now the company is concentrating on increased production efficiency by assembling cars worldwide with identical parts. The company has also been stretching its investment dollar by becoming a leader in what is called platform engineering. Designing and tooling a basic set of automotive components such as suspensions, floor pans, and struts can cost $400 million or more. In Europe Ford has managed to pull six different models, ranging from a two-door minicar to a small pickup truck, from one small-car platform.[30] The firm has also installed computer workstations throughout the company. As a result, now that engineers are all wired to the same network, the company is able to integrate engineering, manufacturing, and testing into one system. These developments are designed to prevent the company's European market share from further erosion, while simultaneously increasing the firm's profitability.[31] At the same time, however, Ford's battle in the EU is still uphill and its performance needs to increase sharply.[32]

General Motors is also pushing very hard in the EU marketplace. A good example is the firm's competitive offerings in the small car market. Volkswagen dominates this area with its Golf, the top-selling line that accounts for almost one-third of its sales in Europe. GM is hoping that its Astra, which has consistently run second to the Golf, will help it gain market share. Like Ford, however, it is losing money in Europe and having to take steps to stem these losses.[33] At the same time, Renault is working to mount a competitive challenge in this market.

Some of the Japanese auto makers, meanwhile, have fallen on hard times in Europe. During the early 1990s there was concern that when restrictive import quotas were removed the Japanese would increase their market share sharply. By 1993, for example, they held over 12 per cent of the EU market. However, since then their share has dropped below 11 per cent and many European auto makers feel that the Japanese are going to have a hard time rebuilding share because many buyers find these cars to be bland and uninteresting.[34] Another reason why European auto makers appear unconcerned is that they have sharply increased both the quality and the productivity of their offerings. During the 1980s these firms had a myriad of operational problems. However, as they increased their efficiency, they were able to cut costs and become more price competitive with the Japanese. At the same time, they continued to focus on an area where they have always been leading edge – auto design. By producing stylish and sporty cars that appeal to European buyers, they have found that these cars maintain their resale price, in contrast to many Japanese models that do not. In fact, the strategy used by Japanese luxury car makers has not proven effective in Europe. Many buyers feel that models such as the Lexus and the Infiniti are poor imitations of a Mercedes or other high quality European offerings.

In response to this increased competitiveness, the Japanese are fighting back. They have begun shifting more manufacturing to Europe and tailoring new cars to match local tastes. In particular, they are pumping more and more money into research and development and spiffing up their current offerings. Toyota engineers have introduced a Corolla with over-head lights and tail lights, and they have given the car sturdier brakes and a stiffer suspension than the previous model. At the same time the Japanese are beefing up their dealer networks.[35] If these efforts are successful, the EU car market is going to become even more competitive over the next decade.

The auto industry in Japan

While Japanese cars sell very well in North America and moderately well in Europe, US and EU manufacturers are discovering that they are now able to make inroads in Japan. Firms such as BMW, Mercedes, General Motors, Ford, and DaimlerChrysler all have growing operations in Japan.

One of the biggest problems in this market, unfortunately, has been the recent downturn in the economy.[36] Firms such as Mitsubishi Motors have suffered large annual losses and most Japanese auto makers have been finding that there is less local demand for cars than was expected.[37] As a result, the Japanese auto market in recent years has been encountering slowing demand coupled with a growing number of competitors that are offering a wide array of new products. Some industry analysts believe that this scenario is the same one that will confront auto makers in North America and Europe in the near future: a maturing market and a proliferation of product offerings.[38]

In the case of Japan, the outlook appears even gloomier. The government has increased the consumption tax to 5 per cent from 3 per cent and this has served to dampen new car demand. In order to offset this problem and to compete more effectively, Japanese car makers have begun introducing autos with sporty designs and more environmentally friendly engines, including hybrid cars. In addition, companies such as Nissan have been getting the needed investment and support from Renault who, as noted earlier, now holds operating control of the firm. As a result, things are getting better.[39]

The worldwide auto industry today

The most lucrative markets for cars and light trucks continue to be the US, the EU, and Japan. However, these countries and the auto firms we have been discussing do not tell the entire story. There are other auto manufacturers such as Hyundai, Daewoo, and Kia of Korea, for example, who have worldwide market share and there are a growing number of auto firms that have set up operations in non-triad countries. For example, by the year 2000 over 500,000 passenger cars and more than 1.2 million trucks were being produced in China by either local manufacturers or under joint-venture agreements with auto firms from the triad. GM, Ford, Toyota, and VW all have Chinese partners and are producing cars for this market.[40] One reason for this trend has been well explained by an expert in the area who has recently noted, "China's growing middle class means there is a huge potential for an affordable car."[41] In addition, Canada, Brazil, and Malaysia collectively account for the production of over 6 million vehicles annually. So while the auto market in terms of both production and demand continues to be based heavily in the triad, it is equally important to realize that there is a growing non-triad market that is both producing automotive vehicles and buying them. Yet the triad manufacturers continue to dominate the industry and, as of the turn of the century, six auto firms and their affiliates dominated this market. These companies and their respective market share were the following:

	%
General Motors	24.7
Ford	13.2
Toyota	9.8
Volkswagen	9.1
DaimlerChrysler	8.6
Renault/Nissan	8.4

Active learning check

Review your answer to Active Learning Case question 3 and make any changes you like. Then compare your answer with the one below.

3. How will Airbus help the EU to compete in Japan?

Japanese airlines will continually need to replace and expand their current stock of planes. US aircraft manufacturers had previously satisfied this demand. However, thanks to Airbus the EU now has an industry that can offer Japan a competitive product. Moreover, until Japan creates its own worldwide competitive aircraft industry, Airbus will be able to continue to tap this market potential.

ECONOMIC RELATIONS WITHIN THE TRIAD

As seen in our discussion of the worldwide auto industry, members of the triad compete with each other in their home markets as well as in the markets of the others. Moreover, what happens in one of these markets can affect the situation in another. For example, if Mercedes is very successful with a new model launch in Germany, it is likely that the company will try to sell this car in other worldwide markets both within and outside the EU. Economic conditions also affect triad relations. If the EU economies begin slowing down, auto makers will begin targeting the US and Japanese markets in an effort to offset lower European revenues. Simply put, what happens in one part of the triad can have an impact in the others. The following examines these economic relations by looking at the current state of the major triad economies and some of the recent mergers and acquisitions in the triad.

Triad economies

Beginning in the early 1990s the US economy started the strongest and most sustained period of economic growth in its history. By the time President Clinton's second term of office was drawing to a close, however, the US economy had began to falter and by 2001 the Federal Reserve was continuing to cut the prime rate in an effort to turn things around. At the same time, major American firms were cutting their workforces, most of the dot.com companies had crashed, and individuals who had been loudly advocating that taxpayers be allowed to invest some of their social security contributions into the stock market were no longer being heard. Most companies were reporting lower revenues and earnings and the future forecast was grim.[42]

In Europe things were no better. The German economy was still in poor shape and many firms in France, Italy, and the UK were having problems. With the US economy slowing down, some people wondered how much of an effect this would have on the EU since the US bought almost $200 billion of goods and services annually from the EU. Could the US slowdown throw the EU into a recession?

Yet the big issue continued to be Japan. Beginning in the mid-1990s the Japanese economy started encountering serious problems. One of the major reasons was the large number of bank loans that had been given to businesses that now found themselves unable to repay the loans. This was particularly true in the case of companies that had borrowed large amounts while using their real estate holdings as collateral. In many cases the appraised value of these assets was far higher than the resale value. And when the banks began writing down the loans to reflect the losses, the amount of capital they had available for lending decreased sharply. In turn, this meant that many businesses needing capital for expansion were unable to get it. At the same time, international competition began to increase and markets where Japanese firms once earned healthy profits now generated far lower returns on investment.

Coupled with these developments, in 1998 Asian currencies came under attack as speculators unloaded them in favor of more stable ones. In the process the Japanese yen began to slip precipitously. In the early 1990s the yen stood at 95 to the American dollar, making it one of the strongest currencies in the world. By 1998 the yen had fallen to 145 to the dollar and many Japanese businesses were finding it difficult to purchase goods and equipment in the international marketplace because prices were too high. (More recently the yen has recovered to around 125 to the dollar but the Japanese government has announced that it is thinking about letting the yen weaken more and thus make Japanese goods more attractive to outside buyers.)

Small Japanese businesses, in particular, were finding it difficult to stay afloat because the banks were being hard pressed by stiff new regulatory requirements that the government was mandating to prevent a collapse of the banking system.[43] So rather than lending more money to small firms that were seeking to expand, a growing number of banks moved in the opposite direction and began pushing to collect these loans as they became due. In the process, the banks started pushing many of these firms over the edge. One local analyst for a large credit-research agency estimated that roughly 16 per cent of all bankruptcies were small low-tech suppliers.

Fortunately, not all small and medium-sized companies were facing financial crises that prevented them from expanding operations. Some had sufficient assets to continue to meet the growing demands from their customers for higher quality output at lower prices. However, many firms were finding that they were being squeezed harder to lower their costs because the large Japanese MNEs were under pressure from their own customers to sell products at lower prices. This was particularly true in the personal computer and auto markets, where the multinationals were trying to maintain their profit margins. As a result suppliers from low-cost countries such as China were beginning to make inroads into the Japanese market.

At the same time unemployment began to increase, rising above 4 per cent for the first time in decades. This, in turn, resulted in greater pressure on the yen, and the American and EU governments began considering approaches they could take to help strengthen the Japanese currency and reduce the chances that their own economies would be adversely affected by Asian economic conditions.[44]

These developments show that the triad does not consist of three separate groups but rather three interrelated groups. In particular, the three trade actively with each other and when one of these three begins to slow up this can affect the others. This is why the US and the EU are concerned about Japan's economy and the steps it is taking to correct things. And, of course, both Japan and the EU are concerned about the recent condition of the US economy. Any sustained slowdown could result in problems for their own economies.

Mergers and acquisitions

While all three triad groups are concerned with their economies, this does not mean that trade or FDI between them has declined. As seen in Figure 3.2 the three groups currently do about $700 billion of trade with each other. And as seen in Table 3.2, they also have invested large amounts of money in each other. For example, EU countries have more than $350 billion of FDI in both the US and Japan. So the three groups are closely linked in terms of both trade and FDI.

Moreover, in recent years investors have poured billions of dollars into these economies, betting that they are going to profit handsomely from these investments. American investors, for example, spent more than $7 billion in the first five months of 1998 to purchase Asian properties, most of them in Japan. Table 3.4 provides some examples. Part of this development was a result of the weak Japanese economy. Many companies there had no capital for expansion and were facing declining demand for their goods and services. So they were willing to unload some of their assets as well as take on foreign partners who could provide funds and growth opportunities. At the same time, the impact of Japanese deregulation was beginning to take effect. For a long time both the US and the EU have been encouraging Japan to reduce its protectionist policies and allow greater opportunities for foreign investors. In the early 1990s the government

Table 3.4 Asian acquisitions

Investor	*Company being purchased*	*Purchase price*
Travelers and Salamon Smith Barney	Nikko Securities (25% stake in Japanese operation)	$1.6 billion
Associates First Capital	DIC Finance, 90% stake (Japan)	$995 million
AES	Hanwha Energy power plant (South Korea)	$870 million
Adaptec	Symbios (South Korea)	$775 million
Investment group including George Soros, Enron, and Steel Dynamics	Nakornthal Steel Mill (Thailand)	$650 million
GE Capital	Toho Mutual Life Insurance (Japan) New business, sales network	$594 million
Zions Bancorp	Sumitomo Bank of California	$544 million
Goldman Sachs	Office building/Yamato Mutual Life (Japan)	$455 million
Coca-Cola	Doosan Beverage facility (South Korea)	$441 million
NCR Corporation	NCR Japan, 30% stake	$304 million
American Skiing	Steamboat and Heavenly ski resorts (Japan)	$288 million

Source: Reported in *USA Today*, June 10, 1998, p. 4B.

promised to open up its markets to more foreign goods and even agreed to buy more cars, auto parts, and computer equipment from outside vendors. As the local economy began to falter and the rules and regulations that used to stymie foreign investors began to be withdrawn, the result was a rush by foreign MNEs into this marketplace. This trend has continued to the present as seen by the fact that in 2000 the top 10 merger and acquisition (M&A) firms put together deals worth more than $200 billion. Some of these M&As, however, involved Japanese firms buying or merging with other Japanese firms as in the case of the giant merger between Sanwa Bank, Tokai Bank, and Toyo Trust & Banking, which was valued at over $19 billion and was the largest deal that year. But not all M&As were internal. NTT DoCoMo, the giant Japanese telecommunications company, took a $9.8 billion stake in AT&T Wireless Group.[45]

Similarly, EU firms are very interested in buying American firms and vice versa. Some of the largest acquisitions made by EU companies in the US in recent years include the purchase of ARCO by BP Amoco of the UK for over $27 billion, France Telecom's acquisitions of NTL for $5.5 billion, and Royal Ahold of Belgium's purchase of US Food-service for $3.62 billion. At the same time, US firms have been buying EU companies. Ford Motor put out $2.72 billion to acquire Land Rover from BMW, and Cisco Systems paid $2.15 billion for Pirelli of Italy's fiber-optic operations.[46] So there is still a great deal of FDI being conducted between triad countries.

Additionally, companies throughout the triad are constantly looking for new ideas that will make them more competitive. In particular, American and EU firms are always seeking to emulate Japanese business practices that have proved so successful in the international arena. In the US, for example, the chairman of the Federal Reserve System has expressed the belief that US antitrust practices are out of date and that competitors should be allowed to acquire and merge with each other in order to protect themselves from world competition. This idea has long been popular in Japan where *keiretsus*, or business groups, which consist of a host of companies that are linked together through ownership and/or joint ventures, dominate the local environment and are able to use their combined wealth and connections to dominate world markets.[47] Today many firms including Deere & Company, Ford, IBM, and Harley-Davidson, to name but four, are copying this form of cooperation. Simply put, what happens in one part of the triad often has an effect in other parts.

Active learning check 

Review your answer to Active Learning Case question 4 and make any changes you like. Then compare your answer with the one below.

4. In what way does the Airbus consortium use a *keiretsu* approach to building the aircraft? Why do you think it opted for this approach?

A *keiretsu* is a business group, which often consists of a host of companies that are linked together through ownership and/or joint ventures. In the case of Airbus, notice how Germany, Great Britain, and Spain built the aircraft and France assembled it. This is the same approach used by *keiretsus* that coordinate their operations in such a way that each provides products and services to the group at a very low price. Another reason that the consortium undoubtedly opted for this approach is that each participant benefits because of the money pumped into its economy for doing this work. Under the new organizational arrangement the governmental role in the *keiretsu* disappears but the basic operational approach will remain and the company will still be a *keiretsu* type of organization.

KEY POINTS

1. Foreign direct investment (FDI) is the ownership and control of foreign assets. This usually means the ownership, whole or partial, of a company in a foreign country. Foreigners have invested hundreds of billions of dollars in the US and Americans have similar amounts of FDI invested overseas.
2. There are a number of reasons for FDI. These include increased sales and profits, a chance to enter rapidly growing markets, reduced costs, gaining a foothold in economic unions, protecting domestic markets, protecting foreign markets, and acquiring technological and managerial know-how.
3. While there is a great amount of FDI made every year, most of it (approximately 80 per cent) occurs within or between triad countries. Much of the remaining FDI is in countries that are members of triad-based FDI clusters.
4. The triad nations dominate world trade and investments, and a great deal of this activity takes place both among and within triad countries. For example, the US and Japan do approximately $210 billion of trade annually, the US and the EU account for over $380 billion of trade, and the EU and Japan do $120 billion of business annually. One of the major areas of triad trade is automobiles, which provides an excellent example of the economic interrelationships that exist between triad members.

KEY TERMS

- triad
- foreign direct investment
- portfolio investment
- FDI cluster
- *maquiladoras*
- twin factories
- *keiretsu*

REVIEW AND DISCUSSION QUESTIONS

1. What is FDI all about? Put it in your own words.
2. What are some of the reasons for FDI? Identify and describe four.
3. Why are MNEs interested in investing in Eastern Europe? What conclusions can you draw from Figure 3.1?
4. How much FDI does the EU and Japan have in the US? What conclusions can you reach based on these data?
5. How much FDI does the US and Japan have in the EU? What conclusions can you reach based on these data?
6. How dominant are the triad countries in terms of FDI and world trade? Explain.
7. What is an FDI cluster? Why are certain countries such as Mexico and Venezuela more likely to be in the US cluster than in the EU cluster?
8. Why is the US auto industry likely to be the target of foreign auto makers during this decade?
9. How competitive is the EU auto market likely to become over the next five years? Why?
10. How active are US and EU firms in acquiring companies throughout the world? What accounts for this activity?
11. In what way can a *keiretsu* approach be of value to US and EU companies in becoming more competitive worldwide? Explain.

REAL CASE

Matsushita beats Philips

In terms of triad-based competition, the 1980s saw the emergence of Japanese firms in the consumer electronics industry. One of the major companies was Matsushita. The firm was initially successful with colour TVs, but its best-known product has been the videocassette recorder (VCR), a field which it dominates by using the VHS system instead of the Sony "betamax" format VCR and others produced by European and American rivals. Paradoxically, the VCR was developed in California in 1956 by a US firm, Ampex, but the product development and distribution was captured by the clever global strategy of Matsushita.

In order to dominate world business in VCRs Matsushita managed to make the VHS format the industry standard. The company achieved this not just by its own massive production and worldwide sales, but by licensing the VHS format to other MNEs such as Hitachi, Sharp, Mitsubishi, and even the major European-based rival, Philips. Other companies such as GE, RCA, and Zenith (which sold VCRs under their own brand names) were tied into the VHS format because of the production and process technology retained by Matsushita in its strong Japanese home base. The company's massive global economies of scale enabled it to cut VCR prices by 50 per cent over its first five years.

In contrast, Philips was in desperate trouble by the 1980s. Built up in the interwar period of protectionism and strong government regulation, the company had developed a very highly decentralized organizational structure. Individual national country managers held the power in Philips and they were slow to respond to the Japanese threat in the postwar period. As a result, Philips lacked economies of scale and its radios, TVs, and VCRs were too expensive compared with comparable Japanese products. Philips had more than 600 manufacturing plants across the world, all developing products for local markets. However, the challenge facing the firm was how to restructure its entire business away from locally responsive national organizations toward a more integrated and leaner manufacturer capable of reaping the necessary economies of scale through standard global production.

In essence, the Japanese changed the rules of the game in the consumer electronics business. Matsushita, as a centralized, high-quality, low-price and innovative company was able to beat the decentralized and nationally responsive European firm. One tactic used by European firms was to lobby their governments for protection in the form of antidumping actions and tougher customs inspection of Japanese products. But such "shelters" only bought some breathing room before MNEs such as Philips restructured and fitted their organizational capabilities to the required industry strategy.

Finally, the response of Matsushita to more protection has been to switch overseas sales from export to foreign direct investment (FDI). With FDI the firm has been able to evade European trade barriers such as antidumping actions. For example, today it manufactures in a number of European countries including the UK, where it has a major plant in Cardiff, Wales. At the same time this means that Matsushita must make its foreign subsidiaries as effective as possible by encouraging local initiatives, and this strategy can conflict with its internationally centralized Japanese-based management culture. In short, the very government regulations which have made Philips too decentralized are now being reapplied half a century later to make Matsushita less global and more local.

Websites: **www.mei.co.jp**; **www.panasonic.com** and **www.philips.com**.

Source: Adapted from Chris Bartlett and Sumantra Ghoshal, *Managing Across Borders*, 2nd edn (Boston MA: Harvard Business School Press, 1995).

1. **What type of globalization strategy was followed by the Japanese firm Matsushita?**
2. **Why could the European firm Philips not compete well with its Japanese rival by the 1980s?**
3. **How can a government help its own firms against triad rivals?**

REAL CASE

Codelco, Chile, and the triad

Multinational companies do not have to be privately owned in order to be successful. Codelco is the largest copper producer in the industry. It currently holds 20 per cent of the world's copper reserves and accounts for 16 per cent of the world's annual copper production. Moreover, at current production rates, the company's reserves will last another 70 years.

Codelco's customers are located worldwide, and while copper is a commodity and cost is a critical factor in the sales equation, the company does extremely well. In fact, in recent years it has accounted for 18 per cent of Chile's exports and 4 per cent of its gross domestic product, in addition to providing 8 per cent of the government's total revenues.

Most of Codelco's sales are in Asia (42 per cent) and Europe (30 per cent), with the rest coming from North America (16 per cent) and South America (12 per cent). The company sells a variety of products including Grade A copper cathodes, molybdenum, and refined copper ore, which is shipped by boat to industrial manufacturers and refiners – most of whom are in the triad or are members of NAFTA. And to facilitate its world trade, Chile has concluded a number of free-trade agreements with the EU, Canada, and Mexico and is an associate member of Mercosur. As a result, Codelco is able to surmount many of the common trade barriers that face companies trying to export their products. In addition, the company has five overseas subsidiaries (at least one in each triad market) and more than 20 sales representatives offices around the world.

In addition to owning Codelco, the Chilean government has been very active in working with multinationals and getting them to invest in the local economy. For example, in Santiago, the country's largest city, air pollution is a serious problem because the city is backed up against the Andes and during the winter air pollution is intense. To help reduce this problem, the government sponsored a joint venture led by the Canadian multinational NOVA, along with Chilean and Argentinian partners. The total project involved building a gas pipeline across the mountainous terrain of the high Andes, constructing a processing plant in Santiago, and creating a local gas distribution company. The total cost was more than $1 billion and there was a great deal of opposition by citizen groups who protested the pipeline route. By working with NOVA and setting up extensive community briefings, the government was eventually able to overcome local opposition and the project came to fruition.

Codelco and the Chilean government provide a good example of how smaller economies are now linking themselves to the triad and to other economically advanced countries (such as Canada) and using this strategy both to develop world markets for their exports and to obtain assistance for local FDI.

Website: ***www.codelcochile.com***.

Sources: Bob Galatiuk and Bruce Thomas "Design and Construction of the GasAndes Pipeline Project," in *Proceedings of the 17th International Conference on Offshore Mechanics and Arctic Engineering* (New York: American Society of Mechanical Engineers, 1998); GasAndes, *The Natural Gas Route*, commemorative publication issued for the inauguration of the GasAndes pipeline (Santiago: Gas Andes, 1997); and Warren R. True, "GasAndes Will Flow by Mid Year," *Oil and Gas Journal*, April 21, 1997.

1. **During this current decade, how important will the triad be in the international success of non-triad nations?**
2. **What are some things that non-triad countries can do to stimulate demand for their exports?**
3. **What role can local government play in attracting foreign direct investment to the country?**

ENDNOTES

1 Scott Morrison, "Solectron Buys C-Mac for $2.7 Bn," *Financial Times*, August 10, 2001, p. 19.
2 David Pringle, "Matsushita Looks to Go Digital in Europe," *Wall Street Journal*, May 8, 2000, Section A, p. 39 A.
3 For a discussion of an interesting combination of FDI and portfolio investment, see John Philips and Karen Woolfson, "Franco-German Banking Link-Up Ignore Sceptics," *The European*, April 12–14, 1991, p. 20.
4 United Nations, *World Investment Report 2001* (Geneva: United Nations Conference on Trade and Development, 2001).
5 "EU Clears Vivendi–Seagram Merger," *BBC.co.uk*, October 13, 2000.
6 United Nations (2001) n. 4 above, pp. 90–92.
7 Annual report, 2001.
8 Joseph Kahn, "Bush Moves Against Steel Imports; Trade Tensions Are Likely to Rise," *New York Times*, June 6, 2001, pp. A 1, C 4.
9 Susan Moffat, "Picking Japan's Research Brains," *Fortune*, March 25, 1991, p. 92.
10 "Foreign Investment and the Triad," *Economist*, August 24, 1991, p. 57.
11 Richard Tomlinson, "Who's Afraid of Wal-Mart?" *Fortune*, June 26, 2000, pp. 186–196.
12 Vijay Govindarajan and Anil K. Gupta, *The Quest for Global Dominance* (New York: Harcourt, 2001), pp. 52–53.
13 "Isuzu to Cut 9,700 from Workforce," *Miami Herald*, May 29, 2001, p. 5 A.
14 Kathleen Kerwin and Bill Vlasic, "Manufacturing Autos: Prognosis 1998," *Business Week*, January 12, 1998, pp. 102–103.
15 David Welch, "Finally, Skid Control at GM," *Business Week*, March 25, 2002.
16 Joann Muller, "Ford, GM, and . . . Toyota?", *Business Week*, January 14, 2002.
17 Brandon Mitchener, "German Car Horns are Tooting Again," *Wall Street Journal*, January 7, 1998, p. 18.
18 "Lagging in Quality," *Wall Street Journal*, May 25, 2001, p. 1.
19 For more on this, see Alex Taylor III, "Too Slow for the Fast Lane? Volvo and Saab," *Fortune*, July 21, 1997, pp. 68–72.
20 Nikki Tait and Tim Burt, "US Carmakers Confront a Second Invasion," *Financial Times*, August 24, 2001, p. 15.
21 David Welch and Lorraine Woellert, "The Eco-Car," *Business Week*, August 14, 2000, p. 66.
22 Valerie Reitman, "Japanese Car Makers Plan Major Expansion of American Capacity," *Wall Street Journal*, September 24, 1997, Section A, pp. 1, 12.
23 "DaimlerChrysler in Mexico," *New York Times*, May 24, 2000, p. C 4.
24 Automotive News Data Center and Marketing Systems GmbH, 1999.
25 Scott Miller, "Revving Up Ford's Luxury Marques," *Wall Street Journal*, July 10, 2000, pp. B 1, 4.
26 Gregory L. White, "GM to Buy Remaining 50% Saab Stake in Effort to Expand Luxury-Car Sales," *Wall Street Journal*, January 11, 2000, p. A 10.
27 "VW's Audi Agrees to Buy Lamborghini," *Houston Chronicle*, June 13, 1998, Section C, p. 2.
28 See, for example, John P. Wolkonowicz, "The EC Auto Industry Gears Up for Greater Competition," *Journal of European Business*, November/December 1991, pp. 12–14.
29 Scott Miller, "Enough Already: Ford of Europe Means to Find its Footing," *Wall Street Journal*, August 11, 2000, p. A 12.
30 Alex Taylor III, "The Gentlemen at Ford are Kicking Butt," *Fortune*, June 22, 1998, p. 74.
31 Also see Scott Miller, "Ford Pins Hopes for European Growth on Fiesta," *Wall Street Journal*, August 22, 2001, p. A 12.
32 See, for example, Scott Miller, "Ford Trims Its Capacity in Europe," *Wall Street Journal*, May 15, 2000, pp. A 25, 28.
33 Nikki Tait, "GM Plans Cost Cuts as Europe Losses Mount," *Financial Times*, July 18, 2001, p. 18.
34 David Woodruff and Heidi Dawley, "Japanese Cars Spin Their Wheels on the Continent," *Business Week*, October 13, 1997, p. 50.
35 Ibid.
36 Joji Sakurai, "Japan's Recession Weighs Heavily on Economically Needy Neighbors," *Houston Chronicle*, June 13, 1998, Section C, p. 3.
37 Neil Weinberg, "A Setting Sun?" *Forbes*, April 20, 1998, pp. 118–124.
38 Emily Thornton, "Too Many Cars, Too Few Buyers," *Business Week*, October 20, 1997, p. 56.
39 Christine Tierney, Anna Bawden and Irene M. Kunii, "Who Says It's Iffy Now?" *Business Week*, October 23, 2000, p. 64.
40 Richard McGregor, "VW Chases Private Chinese Market," *Financial Times*, August 24, 2001, p. 19.
41 Karby Leggett, "GM Plans to Make a Compact Car for China's Market," *Wall Street Journal*, September 1, 2000, p. A 8.
42 Andrew Hill and Mary Chung, "Little Cheer in Latest US Jobs Survey," *Financial Times*, August 7, 2001, p. 14.
43 Emily Thornton, "The Other Japan," *Business Week*, February 9, 1998, p. 53.
44 Sheryl WuDunn, "Japan Says Unemployment Has Reached Record High," *Wall Street Journal*, May 30, 1998, Section B, p. 2.
45 Jason Singer and Phred Dvorak, "Can U.S. Keep Lead in Japan's M&A Market?" *Wall Street Journal*, January 24, 2001, p. A 14.
46 Marcus Walker and Anna Wilde Mathews, "As Euro Falls, U.S. Firms Don't Pounce," *Wall Street Journal*, September 18, 2000, p. A 28.
47 For a detailed discussion of *keiretsus*, see George Ming-Hong Lai, "Knowing Who You Are Doing Business With in Japan: A Managerial View of Keiretsu and Keiretsu Business Groups," *Journal of World Business*, vol. 34, no. 4 (1999), pp. 423–448.

ADDITIONAL BIBLIOGRAPHY

Agarwal, Sanjeev and Ramaswami, Sridhar N. "Choice of Foreign Market Entry Mode: Impact of Ownership, Location and Internalization Factors," *Journal of International Business Studies*, vol. 23, no. 1 (First Quarter 1992).

Andersen, Otto. "On the Internationalization Process of Firms: A Critical Analysis," *Journal of International Business Studies*, vol. 24, no. 2 (Second Quarter 1993).

Buckley, Peter J. "Problems and Developments in the Core Theory of International Business," *Journal of International Business Studies*, vol. 21, no. 4 (Fourth Quarter 1990).

Busenitz, Lowell W. "Country Institutional Profiles: Unlocking Entrepreneurial Phenomena," *Academy of Management Journal*, vol. 43, no. 5 (October 2000).

Contractor, Farok J. "Contractual and Cooperative Forms of International Business: Towards a Unified Theory of Modal Choice," *Management International Review*, vol. 30, no. 1 (First Quarter 1990).

Dunning, John H. "The Study of International Business: A Plea for a More Interdisciplinary Approach," *Journal of International Business Studies*, vol. 20, no. 3 (Fall 1989).

Dunning, John H. *Alliance Capitalism and Global Business* (London: Routledge, 1997).

Dunning, John H. "Location and the Multinational Enterprise: A Neglected Factor?" *Journal of International Business Studies*, vol. 29, no. 1 (First Quarter 1998).

Haar, Jerry. "A Comparative Analysis of the Profitability Performance of the Largest US, European and Japanese Multinational Enterprises," *Management International Review*, vol. 29, no. 3 (Third Quarter 1989).

Harrigan, Kathryn Rudie. "Strategic Alliances: Their New Role in Global Competition," *Columbia Journal of World Business*, vol. 22, no. 2 (Summer 1987).

Kim, Wi Saeng and Lyn, Esmeralda O. "FDI Theories and the Performance of Foreign Multinationals Operating in the US," *Journal of International Business Studies*, vol. 21, no. 1 (First Quarter 1990).

Kotabe, Masaaki. "A Comparative Study of US and Japanese Patent Systems," *Journal of International Business Studies*, vol. 23, no. 1 (First Quarter 1992).

Li, Jiatao and Guisinger, Stephen. "The Globalization of Service Multinationals in the 'Triad' Regions: Japan, Western Europe and North America," *Journal of International Business Studies*, vol. 23, no. 4 (Fourth Quarter 1992).

Luo, Yadong. "Toward a Cooperative View of MNC-Host Government Relations: Building Blocks and Performance Implications," *Journal of International Business Studies*, vol. 32, no. 3 (Fall 2001).

Ostry, Sylvia. "Governments & Corporations in a Shrinking World: Trade & Innovation Policies in the United States, Europe & Japan," *Columbia Journal of World Business*, vol. 25, nos. 1, 2 (Spring/Summer 1990).

Parkhe, Arvind. "Interfirm Diversity, Organizational Learning, and Longevity in Global Strategic Alliances," *Journal of International Business Studies*, vol. 22, no. 4 (Fourth Quarter 1991).

Rugman, Alan M. "A New Theory of the Multinational Enterprise: Internationalization Versus Internalization," *Columbia Journal of World Business*, vol. 15, no. 1 (Spring 1980).

Rugman, Alan M. (ed.) *New Theories of the Multinational Enterprise* (London: Croom Helm and New York: St Martin's, 1982).

Rugman, Alan M. "The Comparative Performance of US and European Multinational Enterprises," *Management International Review*, vol. 23, no. 2 (1983).

Rugman, Alan M. and Boyd, Gavin (eds.) *Euro-Pacific Investment and Trade* (Cheltenham: Elgar, 1997).

Rugman, Alan M. and Boyd, Gavin (eds.) *Deepening Integration in the Pacific Economies* (Cheltenham: Elgar, 1999).

Rugman, Alan M. and Verbeke, Alain. "Multinational Corporate Strategy and the Canada–US Free Trade Agreement," *Management International Review*, vol. 30, no. 3 (Third Quarter 1990).

Sullivan, Daniel and Bauerschmidt, Alan. "The Basic Concepts of International Business Strategy: A Review and Reconsideration," *Management International Review*, vol. 31, Special Issue (1991).

Vernon-Wortzel, Heidi and Wortzel, Lawrence H. "Globalizing Strategies for Multinationals from Developing Countries," *Columbia Journal of World Business*, vol. 23, no. 1 (Spring 1988).

Yip, George. *Total Global Strategy* (Englewood Cliffs NJ: Prentice-Hall, 1995).

PART TWO

The Environment of International Business

Chapter 4

International Politics

OBJECTIVES OF THE CHAPTER

Politics and economics are closely linked and often affect each other. A good example is the economic changes that are sweeping Eastern Europe and Asia today. As these countries embrace open markets, their internally driven economies are giving way to market-driven economies. However, this latter development would have been impossible had it not been preceded by the requisite political change as reflected by more democratic governments. The purposes of this chapter are to examine the linkage between political forces and economic change and then to review some of the major forms of economic integration that are being used to create regional trade areas and common markets. In future chapters these topics will be developed in more depth.

The specific objectives of this chapter are to:

1. *Compare* and *contrast* major political and economic systems and to note the linkage between the two systems.
2. *Examine* the primary reasons for the current privatization movement and the economic impact that this movement is having on selected countries.
3. *Describe* the five major levels of economic integration and how each works.
4. *Discuss* how MNEs are using strategic planning to benefit from current worldwide economic integration efforts.
5. *Discuss* the impact of non-governmental organizations (NGOs) on international business.

CONTENTS

ACTIVE LEARNING CASE

How risky is investment in Russia?

When Mikhail Gorbachev began changing the economic policies of the USSR in the late 1980s, many foreign businesspeople viewed this as the beginning of new opportunities. However, by the time Gorbachev resigned in late 1991 no one seemed to know how profitable or risky an investment in Russia might be. The political situation seemed to be one of uncertainty. For example, the new union that was being created was to be called the Commonwealth of Independent States and it was to be a loose economic and political alliance consisting of any of the former Soviet republics that wanted to join. Most of the states did and they signed an agreement that called for open borders and economic cooperation, but no central government. The new political arrangement was therefore in a state of flux.

At the same time the Russians began to implement Western-style economic concepts. The result was devastating. Prices on many goods skyrocketed and people found themselves paying 5 to 10 times as much for these products. At the same time, the value of the ruble sank to around 1 cent and the government-owned foreign exchange bank began denying requests for withdrawals. However, no one dared to close the bank because this would have meant defaulting on nearly $85 billion of foreign debt. Meanwhile, gross national product started to decline precipitously.

In an effort to help the newly formed Russian republic, a number of prominent businesspeople and politicians called for aid in the form of grants, technological assistance, and direct investments. Additionally, the US administration urged that Russia be admitted to full membership in the International Monetary Fund (IMF) and the World Bank. This was soon done and within the next couple of years a growing number of MNEs began to invest. Tetrapak, a Swedish food-packing company, put $60 million into three Russian plants; Ford Motor put $150 million into a car venture and opened over 60 dealerships throughout the country; and PepsiCo and McDonald's started setting up operations.

The severe reforms which accompanied the country's turn toward a free market economy resulted in a number of other dramatic changes including selling over 70 per cent of public companies to private groups, deregulating prices, promoting foreign trade, eliminating central planning, and creating a new banking system. At the same time, these changes brought about a great deal of economic uncertainty and problems for MNEs operating here. For example, many multinationals found that they had to pay protection money to the local mafia. In fact, overall corruption and the lack of a legal structure to protect foreign investments were instrumental in bringing about a near crash of the Russian economy in 1998. The IMF, the World Bank, and the Japanese government had to step in and provide the country with a relief loan. These efforts, however, were stop-gap measures at best.

Today, things have to change sharply and the economy has to be straightened out. In particular, the Russian government must now meet the specific conditions under which the latest IMF loan was negotiated and continue to take steps that will generate economic growth. On the positive side, there are many signs that are cause for optimism. The country has a large middle class and there is a growing small business sector. There has also been a turnaround in industrial output, which during much of the 1990s was declining but in more recent years is now increasing at a 4–8 per cent annual rate. In addition, real gross domestic product is going up and foreign direct investment is on the rise. In the last few years investors have pumped more than $4 billion into Russia including Telia of Sweden and Sonera of Finland which have joined with the Russian conglomerate, TelecomInvest, to create a nationwide mobile phone market. Yet MNEs continue to ask: How risky is investment in Russia?

Websites: **www.ford.com**; **www.imf.org**; **www.worldbank.org**; **www.tetrapak.de**; **www.pepsico.com**; **www.mcdonalds.com**; **www.telia.se**; **www.sonera.fi** and **www.telecominvest.com**.

Sources: Adapted from Paul Hofheinz, "Russia Starts All Over Again," *Fortune*, January 13, 1992; James B. Hayes, "Wanna Make a Deal in Moscow?" *Fortune*, October 22, 1990; Vladimir Kvint, "Siberia: A Warm Place for Investors," *Forbes*, September 16, 1991; Ralph Frasca, "The Russians Are Coming," *Forbes*, February 1, 1993; **www.dfait-aeci.gc.ca/english/NEWS/NEWSLETR/CANEX/960429ae.htm#titleA**; John Thornhill and Robert Chote, "IMF Leads $12.6bn Support Package," *Financial Times*, Tuesday, July 14, 1998; Charles Clover, "Russia Waits on Investor's Judgement," *Financial Times*, Tuesday, July 14, 1998; Martin Walker, "Investing in Russia not for the Weak at Heart," *Europe*, March 1997; Michael J. Mendel and Dean Foust, "How to Reshape the World Financial System," *Business Week*, October 12, 1998, pp. 112–116; Paul Starobin and Olga Kravchenko, *Business Week*, October 16, 2000, pp. 78–84; and Sabrina Tavernise, "Phone Deal Raises Takes in Russia," *New York Times*, August 16, 2001, p. W 1.

1. **What type of economic system now exists in Russia: market-driven, centrally determined, or mixed?**
2. **Would Russia benefit by gaining admission to one of the major economic unions such as the EU? Why?**
3. **Is Russia a good potential investment for Western business? Explain.**

INTRODUCTION: CHANGING POLITICAL SYSTEMS

Over the past two decades there has been a dramatic change in the political systems of many countries. In the Americas both Chile and Nicaragua have seen a return to democracy; and today the former communist countries of Eastern Europe are building, in varying degrees, free-market systems. Meanwhile, in China while the central government is still communist the nation is no longer tightly managed by Beijing. There are a growing number of geographic areas (most of them in the southeastern region) where market-driven companies have blossomed and which lend credence to the contentions of those who hold that China will be a market-driven economy within a few decades. Whether or not this proves true, one thing is certain: political and economic changes are taking place everywhere and this is opening up new opportunities for MNEs.

In particular, the movement toward market-driven economies of countries that were once controlled by the USSR has affected international business. For example, Poland, Hungary, the Czech Republic, Latvia, Lithuania, and Estonia, to name but six, are all creating market-driven economies. Years ago the USSR would not have permitted these satellite nations to abandon the command economy advocated by communist ideology and replace it with a free-market system. Under Mikhail Gorbachev, however, the USSR revised its political and economic thinking – and things have never been the same since.

While this has proved to be good news for the satellite countries, Russia, as seen in this chapter's active learning case, has not been as fortunate. As a result, until MNEs feel that the government is willing to take the steps necessary to ensure that promises are kept and they are able to repatriate their funds, they are going to proceed very cautiously with their investment plans. International politics is a primary concern for these firms. This explains why Cuba has had a great deal of difficulty in attracting foreign capital.

China, on the other hand, realizing that it must walk a fine line between commitment to its current political philosophy and the need to attract outside investments, has been trying very hard to balance both of these concerns. In a recent interview, President Jiang Zemin noted that one of the country's primary economic objectives is to increase gross domestic product at an annual rate of 7 per cent. This is going to require the ongoing development of high technology as well as the initiation of many large-scale projects. During the interview, the president also said that capitalists should be welcomed into the Communist Party, which he chairs. This is radically new thinking and it resulted in an influential Marxist journal criticizing his comments. In response, the government closed the journal![1] So the political situation in China is apparently not changing as quickly as some might think. At the same time, it is obvious that China wants to attract foreign capital in order to ensure that its economic engine continues to function efficiently – and this is going to require a change in the current political ideology. One development in this direction was a recent governmental announcement that the country could no longer ensure the survival of inefficient companies. Firms have to be able to compete with MNEs or face the risk of going under. Additionally, said the government pronouncement, workers would have to accept the fact that they can be laid off, and they would have to be willing to be retrained, if they hope to find employment in this new, competitive job market.[2]

These governmental decrees certainly represent a big change in the way things have been done in China for the last 50 years. The same is true worldwide. International politics and economic integration are altering the way international business is being conducted and those nations that cannot keep up with these developments are going to

Ideology A set of integrated beliefs, theories, and doctrines that helps to direct the actions of a society

Democracy A system of government in which the people, either directly or through their elected officials, decide what is to be done

Totalitarianism A system of government in which one individual or party maintains complete control and either refuses to recognize other parties or suppresses them

Communism A political system in which the government owns all property and makes all decisions regarding production and distribution of goods and services

Theocratic totalitarianism A system of government in which a religious group exercises total power and represses or persecutes non-orthodox factions

Secular totalitarianism A system of government in which the military controls everything and makes decisions which it deems to be in the best interests of the country

Market-driven economy An economy in which goods and services are allocated on the basis of consumer demand

Centrally determined economy An economy in which goods and services are allocated based on a plan formulated by a committee that decides what is to be offered

find themselves falling farther and farther behind. In this chapter we are going to look at the major current economic and political systems and their impact on the world of international business. We begin by examining political ideologies and economics.

Political ideologies and economics

An **ideology** is a set of integrated beliefs, theories, and doctrines that helps to direct the actions of a society. Political ideology is almost always intertwined with economic philosophy. For example, the political ideology of the US is grounded in the Constitution, which guarantees the rights of private property and the freedom of choice. This has helped to lay the foundation for US capitalism. A change in this fundamental ideology would alter the economic environment of the US. The same is true, for example, for China and the former USSR republics. Simply put, the political and economic ideologies of nations help to explain their national economic policies.

Political systems

In the extreme, there are two types of political systems: democracy and totalitarianism. **Democracy** is a system of government in which the people, either directly or through their elected officials, decide what is to be done. Good examples of democratic governments include the US, Canada, England, and Australia. Common features of democratic governments include (1) the right to express opinions freely, (2) election of representatives for limited terms of office, (3) an independent court system that protects individual property and rights, and (4) a relatively non-political bureaucracy and defense infrastructure that ensure the continued operation of the system.

Totalitarianism is a system of government in which one individual or political party maintains complete control and either refuses to recognize other parties or suppresses them. There are a number of types of totalitarianism that currently exist. The best-known is **communism**, in which the government owns all property and makes all decisions regarding production and distribution of goods and services. The best example is Cuba. Another form is **theocratic totalitarianism**, in which a religious group exercises total power and represses or persecutes non-orthodox factions. Iran and some of the sheikdoms of the Middle East are good examples. A third form is **secular totalitarianism**, in which the military controls the government and makes decisions which it deems to be in the best interests of the country. An example is Iraq. Political systems typically create the infrastructure within which the economic system functions and, in order to change the economic system, there has to be a change in the way the country is governed.

Economic systems

There are three basic economic systems: capitalism, socialism, and mixed. However, for the purposes of our analysis it is more helpful to classify these systems in terms of resource allocation (market-driven versus centrally determined) and property ownership (private versus public). In a **market-driven economy** goods and services are allocated on the basis of demand and supply. If consumers express a preference for cellular telephones, more of these products will be offered for sale. If consumers refuse to buy dot-matrix printers, these goods will cease to be offered. The US and EU nations have market-driven economies. In a **centrally determined economy** goods and services are allocated based on a plan formulated by a committee that decides what is to be offered. Cuba and to a large degree China are examples. In these economies people are able to purchase only what the government determines should be sold.

Market-driven economies are characterized by private ownership. Most of the assets of production are in the hands of privately owned companies that compete for market share by offering the best quality goods and services at competitive prices. Centrally determined economies are characterized by public ownership. Most of the assets of production are in the hands of the state and production quotas are set for each organization.

In recent years market-driven economies have become increasingly popular. An example is Russia, which has begun introducing aspects of free enterprise such as allowing people to start their own businesses and to keep any profits that they make.[3] Eastern European countries are another example.

Mixed economies
Economic systems characterized by a combination of market and centrally driven planning

In examining economic systems, it is important to remember that, in a strict sense, most nations of the world have **mixed economies**, characterized by a combination of market- and centrally driven planning. For example, the US, a leading proponent of market-driven economic policies, provides health care and other social services to many of its citizens through government-regulated agencies. So the US has some aspects of centrally driven planning. Other democratic countries with mixed economies include Great Britain, Sweden, and Germany, all of which have even stronger social welfare systems than America. Another example of the role of government in the economy is that of promoting business and ensuring that local firms gain or maintain dominance in certain market areas. The US and EU governments continually pressure the Chinese to open their doors to foreign MNEs and the Chinese government is very active in helping its local firms to do business with the West.

As a result of such developments, there has been a blurring of the differences between market-driven and centrally determined economies. The biggest change has been the willingness of the latter to introduce free-market concepts. At the same time, however, many market-driven economies are making greater use of centrally determined ideas, such as using business–government cooperation to fend off external competitors. An example is the use of political force to limit the ability of overseas firms to do business in their country. In the US, for example, the government is frequently being urged to play a more active role in monitoring foreign business practices. An example of this can be seen in the box "International Business Strategy in Action: Softwood lumber: not-so free trade". On balance, however, we are now seeing a move from central planning to market-driven and mixed economies. The privatization movement that is taking place worldwide provides one prominent example.

INTERNATIONAL BUSINESS STRATEGY *IN ACTION*

Softwood lumber: not-so free trade

In August 2001, the US imposed tariffs of 19.3 per cent on all Canadian softwood lumber. These tariffs are the result of a US Commerce Department ruling that Canada's provincial governments are illegally subsidizing lumber production.

At the core of the dispute are differences in the systems of production in both countries. In the US, most harvested timber comes from private lands and is auctioned off to buyers. In Canada, provincial governments own the land and set cutting fees according to market conditions. US producers argue that government-set cutting fees are below market prices and thus constitute a 35 per cent subsidy to the Canadian industry.

The rift between producers on each side of the border is 20 years old and in 1996 it led to an agreement, the US–Canada Softwood Lumber Agreement (SLA), in which Canada restricted exports to the US to 14.7 billion board-feet. At that time, Canadian producers claimed such a restriction cost them $480 million annually and 11,000 jobs. This agreement was not acceptable to US producers, however, who successfully lobbied their government to impose tariffs on primary and secondary Canadian producers after the expiration of the SLA in 2001.

Canada has called this latest move protectionist. Softwood lumber is one of Canada's most successful industries in the US. In fact, Canadian producers had held a 35 per cent market share prior to the tariff and exports to the US have grown considerably over the last few years, particularly as a result of the lower Canadian dollar. In addition, note the Canadian producers, the latest US claim ignores the extra expenses that Canadian firms have had to pay for road building, replanting, and environmental protection. As a result, the Canadians argue that the tariff is nothing more than a way of protecting the US's inefficient timber industry.

The negative effects of the tariff are now being felt in both countries. American consumers are paying 10 per cent more as a direct result of the tariff, and this has so upset some industry groups that an association of American homebuilders, consumers, and contractors is now lobbying Washington to remove the tariff. Meanwhile in Canada, American firms like Weyerhaeuser, that have bought Canadian competitors in order to increase their own efficiency and market share, now have to pay the tariff, thus reducing their profitability. And within a month of the tariff's enactment, 10,000 industry workers had been laid off, a dozen mills were shuttered, and most of the plants were operating below capacity.

As a result, Canada is now set to battle the US in WTO courts and through NAFTA's dispute settlement panel. In the WTO, Canada intends to argue that the US has erred in its interpretation of the cutting fees as the equivalent of the sale of timber by the government to those companies. In 1994, the NAFTA panel dealt with this dispute, and ordered the US to reimburse Canada $1 billion on collected tariffs. The Canadians are now hoping for a similar success.

Websites: ***www.weyerhaeuser.com***; ***www.dfait-maeci.gc.ca*** and ***www.wto.org***.

Sources: Edward Alden, "Canada to Challenge US Over Import Duties," *Financial Times*, August 21, 2001; Ken Warn, "Timber Duty Escalates US–Canada Trade Dispute," *Financial Times*, August 10, 2001; Ian Jack, "US Hits Value-added Softwood," *Financial Post*, September 5, 2001; "Pettigrew Plans to Lobby Washington on Lumber," *Toronto Star*, September 7, 2001; "Stump War," *Economist*, August 30, 2001; "At Loggerheads," *Economist*, May 22, 2001.

Government control of assets

Privatization
The process of selling government assets to private buyers

Nationalization
A process by which the government takes control of business assets, sometimes with remuneration of the owners and other times without such remuneration

Divestiture
(Also see *Privatization.*)
A process by which a government or business sells assets

Contract management
A process by which an organization (such as the government) transfers operating responsibility of an industry without transferring the legal title and ownership

Over the last decade an increasing number of countries have begun moving toward **privatization**, the process of selling government assets to private buyers. To understand the reasons for, and the economic impact of, this process, it is helpful to examine both the potential benefits of government ownership and the advantages of moving to privatization.

There are six common, and sometimes interdependent, reasons for countries to control business assets, a process known as **nationalization**. These include (1) promoting economic development, for example by coordinating the assets of many businesses into one overall master plan; (2) earning profits for the national treasury; (3) preventing companies from going bankrupt and closing their doors; (4) enhancing programs that are in the national interest; (5) increasing the political or economic control of those in power; and (6) ensuring goods and services to all citizens regardless of their economic status.[4]

The opposite situation, privatization, can take two forms. The most common form is **divestiture**, in which the government sells its assets. The other is **contract management**, in which the government transfers operating responsibility of an industry without transferring the legal title and ownership. The major trend today is toward divestiture.

Some of the primary reasons for privatization include (1) it is more efficient to have the goods and services provided by private business than by government-run companies; (2) a change in the political culture brings about a desire to sell off these assets; (3) the company has been making money and the government feels that there is more to be gained by selling now than by holding on; (4) the purchase price can be used to reduce the national debt; (5) the company is losing money and the government has to assume the losses out of the national treasury; (6) the company needs research and development funds in order to maintain a competitive stance, and it is unwilling to make this investment; and (7) international funding agencies are making assistance to the country conditional on a reduction in the size of the government.[5]

Privatization in action

Many nations have privatization programs.[6] These include countries with moderate per capita gross domestic products, such as Argentina, Brazil, Chile, Mexico, and China, as well as economically advanced nations such as the US, Japan, Germany, and the UK. All feel that their economies can be strengthened through privatization programs.

In the case of Argentina, for example, the government has now ended the nation's phone monopoly and opened up the $10 billion market to outside investors. Previously the two telephone companies that monopolized all long distance and local phone services had their territories firmly established and neither could compete with the other. Now they can, and other telephone companies also have licenses to operate throughout the country. The Argentinian government believes that, as a result of privatization in this industry, competition will increase, phone rates will drop, and service will increase sharply.[7]

In the case of the UK, privatization and deregulation have proven to be a national boon. A few years ago British Telecommunications began downsizing its operations so as to increase its competitiveness and profitability. The firm slashed 100,000 jobs and critics said that privatization and deregulation were hurting the economy. However, just the opposite occurred. Many of the workers who were laid off began finding jobs with small telecommunications firms that were springing up throughout the country. At the same time, there was an influx of large foreign competitors such as AT&T, the giant American telecommunications company, and AB L. M. Ericsson, the Swedish telecom-equipment maker, that have hired thousands of people. As a result, between 1990 and 1999 the number of jobs in the UK's telecommunications industry increased, while prices decreased, and service improved sharply.[8]

Another major group of nations that is turning to privatization is Russia and Eastern European countries. At the grass roots in Russia a market economy is beginning to evolve. Despite the lack of national or local laws to guide them, hundreds of small factories and service businesses are now privatizing themselves and enterprises are pushing ahead with Russian-style versions of leveraged buyouts, employee stock ownership plans, and private spin-offs. Many are also taking their old, outmoded operations and modernizing them. A good example is the Vologda Textile Enterprise company. By significantly reducing its workforce and rebuilding the looms, the firm has found that it can sell all of the textiles that it produces to buyers in the EU.[9]

Government–business cooperation

While governments are privatizing assets, this does not mean that they are distancing themselves from business firms. Both in Japan and in the EU there has been a large amount of business–government cooperation that has been extremely beneficial to the business sector in these countries.

Ministry of International Trade and Industry (MITI)
A Japanese ministry charged with providing information about foreign markets and with encouraging investment in select industries and, in the process, helping to direct the economy

Japan and EU assistance

In Japan, after World War II the Japanese government began formulating plans for regenerating the economy. In this vein, it gave responsibility for implementing the country's trade and industrial policy to the **Ministry of International Trade and Industry (MITI)**. The initial focus of the ministry was on providing protection to Japanese companies and to marketing the products of four major industries: electric power, steel, shipbuilding, and fertilizers. Incentives were created to encourage investment in these industries and to help firms export their products. In recent years MITI's focus has been on targeting less energy-intensive industries for Japanese investment and growth. Prime examples include computers and chemicals, where MITI works cooperatively with

Japanese businesses to help ensure success. In the last decade the focus of MITI has changed from a proactive to a much more cooperative agency; its role today is mainly in funding export markets for Japanese businesses.

Governments in the EU have also been very helpful in promoting businesses. One way has been through the funding of research consortia that have received billions of dollars of research and development (R&D) support from these governments. One of the research programs that has been helped by EU governments is the R&D in Advanced Communications in Europe (RACE for short). Since the late 1980s RACE has received billions of dollars of government money to support research efforts in developing an integrated broadband telecommunications network. Another recipient of government largesse is the European Strategic Program for R&D in Information Technology (ESPRIT II). This consortium has engaged in hundreds of projects dealing with such high-tech areas as information technologies, microelectronics, and computer-integrated manufacturing. Yet perhaps the best-known R&D consortium is EUREKA. This is a pan-European group whose main objective is to create closer cooperation between private companies and research institutes in the field of advanced technologies for the purpose of exploiting commercial opportunities. The projects that are funded bring together companies throughout the EU and involve not just large firms but also small and medium-sized enterprises. Unlike many research consortia, however, EUREKA focuses on projects whose research is now ready to be applied.[10]

The American response

The results of such governmental efforts have not been lost on Washington, which has long recognized the value of an industrial policy that provides benefits similar to those offered by MITI and EUREKA. As long ago as 1990 a special White House panel of experts from industry, academia, and the government released a list of 22 technologies that it deemed as essential to the national defense and economic prosperity of the US. The list included composite materials, flexible computer-integrated manufacturing, and high-definition electronic displays. The list was intended to guide the Critical Technologies Institute, created by Congress in 1990 to conduct long-range strategic planning and to work closely with the private sector in developing important technologies.

Over the last two decades, in particular, the US government has been very active in supporting research consortia to help underwrite some of the costs associated with new technology development. A good example is Sematech, a consortium of 14 semiconductor manufacturing companies, that received $100 million a year in subsidies from the US government to help shore up the chip-making equipment industry. By the mid-1990s these manufacturers were doing so well that the consortium's board voted to end federal funding and the group is now funded entirely by private money.[11] Another consortium that has received government assistance is the National Center for Manufacturing Sciences that has provided a host of important technology breakthroughs including a method for hardening cutting tools by coating them with diamond film. A third has been the Microelectronics & Computer Technology Corporation that has worked on advanced computing, software, and computer-aided design.

In the past US administrations have supported research efforts that promoted industrial competitiveness and technological leadership. This often took one of two paths: (a) the funding of military research that could then be used to create commercially useful products or (b) the direct funding of research efforts by American firms. The big question today is what the technology policy of the Bush administration will be. Whatever the final decision, it is likely to continue the American focus on maintaining a strong, high-tech military and a world-class computer information industry.

Active learning check 

Review your answer to Active Learning Case question 1 and make any changes you like. Then compare your answer with the one below.

1. What type of economic system now exists in Russia: market-driven, centrally determined, or mixed?

At the present time a mixed system exists. The country is moving away from a centrally determined economy, but there is a long way to go. As can be seen from the information in the case, this transition is causing a great deal of economic upheaval. This may even result in a regression toward some of the previously employed, centrally determined decision making. However, the country is not going to go back to the old way of doing things because it has too much committed to its current course of action. In particular, any further IMF loans or assistance from the US, Japan, or the EU will depend on how well the country is holding the line and trying to make its market-driven economy work. So a mixed economic system is going to remain in place and, in fact, this is really the only path the Russians can take in rescuing their economy.

ECONOMIC INTEGRATION

Economic integration
The establishment of transnational rules and regulations that enhance economic trade and cooperation among countries

Economic integration is the establishment of transnational rules and regulations that enhance economic trade and cooperation among countries. At one extreme, economic integration would result in one worldwide free trade market in which all nations had a common currency and could export anything they wanted to any other nation. At the other extreme would be a total lack of economic integration, in which nations were self-sufficient and did not trade with anyone. (The theory of these polar extremes will be discussed in Chapter 6.)

The concept of economic integration is attractive, but there are many implementation problems. In particular, economic integration requires that the participants agree to surrender some of their individual economic power, such as the authority to set tariffs and quotas. For example, if the US and the EU agree to allow free trade of agricultural products, this means that neither side can restrict the other's right to export these commodities to its country. So while free trade may lead to lower prices, those who are unwilling to give up the right to control goods being imported into their country may well be opposed to it.

There are a number of regional economic efforts that have been undertaken over the last 30 years to promote varying degrees of economic integration. The most successful has been the EU although less developed countries (LDCs) have also made integration efforts.

Trade creation and trade diversion

Trade creation
A process in which members of an economic integration group begin to focus their efforts on those goods and services for which they have a comparative advantage and start trading more extensively with each other

Before examining economic integration in more depth, it is important to realize that when countries agree to integrate their economies, this will bring about a shift in business activity. This shift can result in trade creation as well as trade diversion.

Trade creation occurs when members of an economic integration group begin focusing their efforts on those goods and services for which they have a comparative advantage and start trading more extensively with each other. For example, the US and Mexico have an agreement that allows cars to be assembled in Mexico and shipped into the US. As a result, Mexico, a low-cost producer, supplies a large number of vehicles sold in America and both countries prosper as a result.

Trade creation results in efficient, low-cost producers in member countries gaining market share from high-cost member producers, as well as generating increased exports. In fact, a growing number of US companies have moved some of their operations to Mexico or hired Mexican firms to be their supplier because this is a more efficient approach than making the goods in the States. And because efficient regional producers are able to offer lower-price and higher-quality output than their competitors, trade creation results.

Trade diversion occurs when members of an economic integration group decrease their trade with non-member countries in favor of trade with each other. One common reason is that the removal of trade barriers among member countries makes it less expensive to buy from companies within the group, and the continuation of trade barriers with non-member countries makes it more difficult for the latter to compete. Thus trade diversion can lead to the loss of production and exports from more efficient non-member countries to less efficient member countries that are being protected by tariffs or other barriers. Quite obviously, the creation of economic integration groups is beneficial only if trade creation exceeds trade diversion. Otherwise the economic union impedes international trade.

Levels of economic integration

There are five levels of economic integration. These extend from simple economic trade arrangements to full political integration characterized by a single government. The following examines each of these levels beginning with the simplest.

Free trade area

Free trade area
An economic integration arrangement in which barriers to trade (such as tariffs) among member countries are removed

North America Free Trade Agreement (NAFTA)
A regional free trade agreement between Canada, the US, and Mexico

A **free trade area** is an economic integration arrangement in which barriers to trade (such as tariffs) among member countries are removed. Under this arrangement each participant will seek to gain by specializing in the production of those goods and services for which it has a comparative advantage and importing those goods and services for which it has a comparative disadvantage.

One of the best-known free trade arrangements is the **North American Free Trade Agreement (NAFTA)**, a free trade area currently consisting of Canada, the US, and Mexico. The US and Canada created this free trade area with the United States–Canadian Free Trade Agreement of 1989 and the arrangement has now been expanded to include Mexico.[12] While trade diversion can occur under free trade arrangements, NAFTA has generated a great amount of trade creation. In fact, trade between the three members of NAFTA is now in the range of $1 trillion annually![13]

Customs union

Customs union
A form of economic integration in which all tariffs between member countries are eliminated and a common trade policy toward non-member countries is established

A **customs union** is a form of economic integration in which all tariffs between member countries are eliminated and a common trade policy toward non-member countries is established. This policy often results in a uniform external tariff structure. Under this arrangement, a country outside the union will face the same tariff on exports to any member country receiving the goods.

Under a customs union, member countries cede some of the control of their economic policies to the group at large. None of the regional integration groups in existence today has been formed for the purpose of creating a customs union; instead many of them have sought greater integration in the form of a common market or economic union. However, because of the difficulty of attaining this high degree of integration, some countries have effectively *settled* for a customs union. The Andean Pact, which will be discussed shortly, is an example.

Common market

Common market
A form of economic integration characterized by the elimination of trade barriers among member nations, a common external trade policy, and mobility of factors of production among member countries

A **common market** is a form of economic integration characterized by (a) no barriers to trade among member nations, (b) a common external trade policy, and (c) mobility of factors of production among member countries. A common market allows reallocation of production resources such as capital, labor, and technology, based on the theory of comparative advantage. While this may be economically disadvantageous to industries or specific businesses in some member countries, in theory it should lead to efficient delivery of goods and services to all member countries. The best example of a successful common market is the EU although this group has progressed beyond a common market and is now focusing on political integration.

Economic union

Economic union
A form of economic integration characterized by free movement of goods, services, and factors of production among member countries and full integration of economic policies

An **economic union** is a deep form of economic integration and is characterized by free movement of goods, services, and factors of production between member countries and full integration of economic policies. An economic union (1) unifies monetary and fiscal policy among the member nations, (2) has a common currency (or a permanently fixed exchange rate among currencies), and (3) employs the same tax rates and structures for all members. Additionally, most of the national economic policies of the individual countries are ceded to the group at large. While there are no true economic unions in the world, the creation of a single currency, the euro, certainly moves the EU in this direction.

Political union

Political union
An economic union in which there is full economic integration, unification of economic policies, and a single government

A **political union** goes beyond full economic integration, in which all economic policies are unified, and has a single government. This represents total economic integration, and it occurs only when countries give up their national powers to leadership under a single government. One successful example is the US, which combined independent states into a political union. The unification of West and East Germany in 1991 has also created a political union; the two nations now have one government and one set of overall economic policies. And the EU is on its way toward becoming a political union. The European Parliament, for example, is directly elected by citizens of the EU countries and its Council of Ministers, which is the decision-making body of the EU, is made up of government ministers from each EU country.

Economic integration: an overall perspective

Before concluding our discussion of levels of economic integration, four points merit consideration. First, it is not necessary for a country to pursue economic integration by starting with a free trade area and then working up to a common market or an economic union. For example, Great Britain was a member of a free trade area before deciding to leave and enter the EU. Simply stated, countries will choose the appropriate level of economic integration based on their political and economic needs.

Second, economic integration in the form of free trade typically results in a winning situation for all group members, since each member can specialize in those goods and services it makes most efficiently and rely on others in the group to provide the remainder. However, when a bloc of countries imposes a tariff on non-members, this often results in a win–lose situation. Those outside the bloc face tariffs, are thus less competitive with group member companies, and lose market share and revenue within the bloc. Among group members, however, increased competition often results in greater efficiency, lower prices, and increased exports to non-member markets.

Third, and complementary to the above, bloc members often find that their business is able to achieve **internal economies of scale** brought about by lower production costs and other savings within the firm. So while a company in France may have found that its plant was only moderately efficient when producing 1,000 units a week for the French market, it is now highly efficient producing 4,000 units a week for countries throughout the EU. The elimination of tariffs and trade barriers and the opening up of new geographic markets allow the company to increase production efficiency. In addition, since factors of production in a common market are allowed to flow freely across borders, the firm may also achieve **external economies of scale** brought about by access to low cost capital, more highly skilled labor, and superior technology. In short, in-group companies can draw on resources in member countries to help increase efficiency.

Internal economies of scale
Efficiencies brought about by lower production costs and other savings within a firm

External economies of scale
Efficiencies brought about by access to cheaper capital, highly skilled labor, and superior technology

Finally, in the short run, some bloc countries may suffer because other member countries are able to achieve greater increases in efficiency and thus dominate certain industries and markets in the bloc. This may result in an adjustment period that lasts as long as a decade, as these less efficient countries scramble to improve their technology, retrain their workforce, and redirect their economies to markets in the bloc where they can gain and sustain an advantage vis-à-vis other members. In the long run, however, economic integration results in all bloc countries becoming much more efficient and competitive.

Despite the logic of free trade and economic integration, many **non-governmental organizations (NGOs)** criticize MNEs and international institutions. We now discuss these issues. See also the box "International Business Strategy in Action: Non-governmental organizations and political power".

Non-governmental organizations (NGOs)
Non-profit organizations that act to advance diverse social interests (See also Civil Society)

Ethics, environment, MNEs, and the civil society

On December 1999, a coalition of NGOs and labour unions encouraged riots in Seattle and hindered the launch of another round of the WTO. In July 2001, the violent riots in Genoa, at the G7 Summit, were another example of the work of some antiglobalization activists, mainly NGOs, attempting to prevent negotiations by world leaders.

The so-called **civil society** is a loosely organized movement opposed to global business. Demonstrations are composed of environmentalists, anti-poverty campaigners, trade unionists and anti-capitalists that are either part of an NGO or trade union, or are simply individuals that share their views.[14] The lack of a common front across these organizations has meant that, while some protestors are chanting and throwing roses, others are throwing rocks and charging at the police. In fact, these organizations cannot even agree on what exactly needs to be done. The more extremist groups would like to see an end to multinationals and international trade. More moderate demonstrators would like a transformation in the rules of trade with less developed nations, debt-forgiveness, and better labor and environmental standards.[15] Protestors also have different agendas. Trade unionists from developed countries are concerned about the alleged loss of jobs due to globalization, while human rights NGOs are much more concerned with the situation of workers in less industrialized nations. It is important to note that, as with any large-scale social movement, the antiglobalization movement has attracted individuals who are not well informed about the issues at hand.

Civil society
A group of individuals, organizations and institutions that act outside the government and the market to advance a diverse set of interests

The success of the NGOs in criticizing businesses, especially multinational enterprises (MNEs), builds upon less spectacular, but consistent progress in their capture of the environmental agenda of international organizations. The first notable success of environmental NGOs occurred in NAFTA when the Clinton administration in 1993 inserted two side agreements on environment and labor after the first Bush administration had successfully negotiated NAFTA over the 1990–1992 period.

The UNCED Rio Summit reflected the agenda of environmental NGOs, leading to an agreement that sets commitments which governments have been unable to deliver on. The Kyoto Summit in 1997 resulted in the standards for reduction of greenhouse gas emissions, that, again, important economies – most notably the US – would not meet because of the economic and political costs of doing so.

INTERNATIONAL BUSINESS STRATEGY *IN ACTION*

Non-governmental organizations and political power

When the topic of politics in the international business arena is discussed, one is likely to hear about such things as the impact of the government on international trade and the regulation of multinational enterprises (MNEs). In recent years another topic that has been getting increased attention is the role of non-governmental organizations (NGOs) that have been gaining an increasing amount of political power. These NGOs take a number of different forms. The environmental group Greenpeace is the best known, but there are others that have been having notable success, if only because of their nationalist agenda and their willingness to use force, and even violence, to grab headlines. In the 1997–1998 period, for example, some NGOs were extremely effective in defeating the Multilateral Agreement on Investment (MAI). The MAI was designed to make it illegal for signatory states to discriminate against foreign investors and to liberalize rules governing foreign domestic investment between the members of the Organization for Economic Cooperation and Development.

More recently NGOs contributed to riots in Seattle in December 1999 and the violent clashes with the police in Genoa in July 2001. Simply put, NGOs are becoming an important force in understanding international politics and its effect on international business. The NGOs influenced the Clinton administration to add two side agreements to NAFTA; these set up an environmental body in Montreal and a labor standard body in Dallas. In a nutshell, these NGOs managed to work outside the NAFTA agreement to get provisions incorporated into the overall contract. In the process, they showed that NGOs were becoming an important force in the international political arena. In December 1997 at the Kyoto Summit, NGOs were instrumental in getting standards for the reduction of greenhouse gas emissions put into the agreement, even though some of the world's major economic powers, the US being the best example, refused to accept this standard because the technology was not available and the standard could not be met.

These examples show that there is a huge gap between the agendas of some NGOs and the economic reality of global business. And there are hundreds of NGOs, the vast majority of which are special interest groups that want to regulate some aspect of business activity and are seeking government support in achieving their goals. Most of these groups have a nationalist agenda that is politically oriented but this agenda has not been presented to the voters. Unlike the labor movements or the goals of Greenpeace, which have had their agendas directly voted on in elections, most NGOs are reluctant to face the voters because they are concerned that their positions would be rejected by informed voters who would quickly realize that these NGO objectives were unrealistic and extremely costly.

Critics of NGOs contend that the view that these groups have of MNEs as big, bad, and ugly makes for good media coverage. But is it an accurate portrayal? Are their goals realistic or simply an effort to win coverage on the evening national news? Moreover, ask their opponents, why is it necessary to stage riots and other forms of civil disobedience that, in some cases, result in the death of protestors, as happened during the Genoa riots of 2001? If the NGOs have an agenda the electorate needs to know about, why not present the information to them and let people vote on it? These are questions that are going to be the focus of discussion in the near future. In particular, a growing number of governmental personnel, union members, and local citizens are asking why NGOs are unwilling to enter the mainstream of the political process. Additionally, more and more local voters are asking why NGOs feel that their group needs to be an international force in campaigning for issues such as environmental protection when, in the main, most of these matters are local issues. Some are also asking whether the agenda of NGOs is designed to help the worldwide community or whether it is focused more on promoting the needs of the NGO itself. Given their rise in popularity over the last five years, NGOs are likely to be the focus of continuing interest by both international business analysts and local voters.

Websites: ***www.greenpeace.org*** and ***www.oecd.org***.

Sources: James Harding, "Activists Plan Ocean-borne Protests for WTO Meeting," *Financial Times*, September 11, 2001, p. 1; Edward M. Graham, *Fighting the Wrong Enemy: Antiglobal Activists and Multinational Enterprises* (Washington DC: Institute for International Economics, 2000); Alan M. Rugman, *The End of Globalization* (London: Random House, 2000); and Sylvia Ostry, "The Multilateral Trading System," in Alan M. Rugman and Thomas Brewer (eds.), *The Oxford Handbook of International Business* (Oxford: Oxford University Press, 2000), pp. 232–258.

These recent events portray the gulf between the environment agendas of NGOs and the economic drivers of global business. How do we explain the existence of this gulf?[16] Basically, there is a traditional divide between the redistribution and equity concerns of NGOs and the economic and efficiency issues that drive business. Democratic governments in Western economies have incorporated these dual concerns in their political platforms and, at least as part of a broader political package, voters have some say through the electoral process.

Complementary to the undemocratic nature of NGOs, especially in their biased understanding of international trade and investment, is a second failure. This is an intellectual failure of academic theory in which the twin basic paradigms of economics and politics are found wanting as explanations of today's global economy and the nature of foreign direct investment (FDI). In economics, the traditional efficiency-based neoclassical paradigm (with its associated theory of comparative advantages and the overall country gains from free trade) is unsuitable as an explanation of FDI. Despite the efforts by international business writers over the last 30 years to develop a modern theory of the multinational enterprise, most economists are unable to take on board this explanation of the reasons for FDI. As a consequence, the GATT and WTO have developed institutional frameworks to deal with the "shallow" integration of tariff cuts, but have failed to deal with the "deep" integration of FDI.

Related to the out-of-date economics paradigm of free trade is the political science focus on the nation state. Despite minor modifications to nation state paradigms, for example, to incorporate subnational units in decision making, there is a limited buy-in to the alternative International Political Economy (IPE) viewpoint. Indeed, there is another unfortunate parallel between economics and political science in that both sets of work on the role and power of the MNE have failed to change the out-of-date thinking of the majority of academics, despite the abundant evidence of the relevance of MNEs and the global economic and political systems of today. Into this vacuum the NGOs have slipped with their simplistic view of MNEs as big, bad and ugly. Based on prejudice rather than evidence the NGO thinking is now more influential with government in North America and Europe than is the more scientific (and thereby more qualified) work of serious academic scholars working on MNEs.[17]

The issue here is one of process. There is an "administrative heritage" of ideas. Today's media are poorly trained in economics, politics, and international business. Those few who have any training are usually victims of the out-of-date paradigms of traditional economics and political science, which cannot explain FDI and the MNEs. The MBAs of business schools, who are now exposed to the new thinking on MNEs, are in business rather than the media. The professional intermediaries, such as management consultants, have a focus on their business or government clients rather than the media, and their very skills of confidential advice and in-house retraining make them poor advocates in comparison with the NGOs. Finally, the civil service is basically useless in dealing publicly with NGOs as bureaucrats attempt to support and influence ministers rather than entering into the public forum. This institutional failure of academics, consultants, and bureaucrats to prepare a credible case for initiatives such as the Multilateral Agreement on Investment (MAI) and be able to debate it publicly leaves the field open to NGOs.

Yet Graham has exploded the myth that antiglobal activists defeated the MAI.[18] Using careful analysis and "insider" information as a closely involved and well-informed expert on US foreign direct investment policy making, Graham concludes that the draft MAI was a very weak document. In fact, the investment liberalization being negotiated in the MAI was so weak that the US business community stopped supporting it long before antiglobal activists started to protest against it in Paris. There was also a lack of leadership by the US government, as well as tepid support in the EU, and eventually hostility to the MAI by the French government of Lionel Jospin as he was dependent upon left wing "green" support in his political coalition.

Graham discusses environmental issues in trade and investment agreements objectively. He has useful insights on the environmental provisions of NAFTA, especially the important initial Chapter 11 investor-state case on MMT (a gasoline additive). The Canadian Minister of the Environment, Sheila Copps, banned trade and interprovincial trade in MMT, citing it as an environmental and health hazard. The producer of MMT, a US company called Ethyl, used the Chapter 11 provisions to win a settlement from the Canadian government for denial of its business. The Canadian antiglobal activists claimed that this case demonstrated that multinational enterprises (MNEs) could overturn the environmental decisions of host-country governments. The draft text of the MAI had a similar provision to NAFTA Chapter 11, so the antiglobal activists claimed that the MAI was a charter of rights for MNEs to overturn the sovereign domain of governments. They claimed that the MAI was a "NAFTA on steroids".

Graham gives far too much attention to this case which was a purely technical application of Chapter 11 incited by trade lawyers hungry for business, and it has no long-term policy relevance. The Canadian Minister apparently ignored the advice of her bureaucrats in banning the trade in MMT. As soon as trade-related measures are introduced then NAFTA applies. Instead, Copps should have banned the production of MMT, as an environmental hazard, an internal matter subject to Canadian laws. Several subsequent NAFTA Chapter 11 cases have been resolved on technical grounds with no loss of sovereignty to host nations in their environmental policies.

Perhaps what the MMT case really illustrates is the dialogue of the deaf taking place between trade experts and activists. The latter used the MMT case in a general assault on the MAI, and subsequent international trade and investment liberalization initiatives at the WTO and G7 summits. Graham argues that, as a consequence, the environmental NGOs especially have missed the boat. He states that trade negotiators were open and willing to incorporate environmental concerns into the MAI but that violent opposition to it has now closed the window for cooperation between NGOs and governments.

Any more Seattles and Genoas, with the attendant violence, however, will probably alienate the general public from the anticapitalist agenda of the more extreme antiglobal activist. These are a small and over-publicized section of the NGO movement that is apparently opposed to reforming global governance mechanisms; they continue to protest violently against MNEs. Eventually, the most serious NGOs, such as WWF and Oxfam, must disassociate themselves from these violent activists in order to push forward a more sensible cooperative reformist agenda for civil society.

The European Union (EU)

European Coal and Steel Community (ECSC)
A community formed in 1952 by Belgium, France, Italy, Luxembourg, the Netherlands, and West Germany for the purpose of creating a common market that would revitalize the efficiency and competitiveness of the coal and steel industries in those countries

After World War II, Europe needed to be rebuilt and economic cooperation between these countries was paramount. One of the earliest, and most successful, cooperative endeavors was the 1952 creation of the **European Coal and Steel Community (ECSC)** for the purpose of creating a common market that would revitalize the efficiency and competitiveness of these industries. Six countries (Belgium, France, Italy, Luxembourg, the Netherlands, and West Germany) created the ECSC and its success set the stage for the creation of what would eventually become the European Union.

Formation

The foundation of the European Union was laid in 1957 by the Treaty of Rome. The six nations who created the ECSC were the original founders of what was initially called the European Economic Community (EEC) and later the European Community (EC). By

1991 six other nations joined the EC (Great Britain, Denmark, Greece, Ireland, Portugal, and Spain) and by 1995 Austria, Finland, and Sweden were also admitted to the EC which was now renamed the **European Union (EU)**. Today the EU is a major economic group and a growing number of countries have applied for admission.[19] The main provisions of the founding treaty of 1957 were:

European Union (EU)
A treaty-based institutional framework that manages economic and political cooperation among its 15 member states: Austria, Belgium, Denmark, France, Finland, Germany, Greece, Ireland, Italy, Luxembourg, the Netherlands, Portugal, Spain, Sweden, and the UK

1. Formation of a free trade area among the members would be brought about by the gradual elimination of tariffs, quotas, and other trade barriers.
2. Barriers to the movement of labor, capital, and business enterprises would eventually be removed.
3. Common agricultural policies would be adopted.
4. An investment fund to channel capital from the more advanced regions of the bloc to the less advanced regions would be created.
5. A customs union characterized by a uniform tariff schedule applicable to imports from the rest of the world would be created.

Some of the countries that were not members of the initial EEC felt that the objectives of this group went beyond what they were willing to do, but these countries did feel that a free trade agreement would be good for their own economies. As a result, these nations formed the **European Free Trade Association (EFTA)**, whose primary goal was to dismantle trade barriers among its members. Austria, Denmark, Norway, Portugal, Sweden, Switzerland, and the UK were the founding members. In time the distinctions between EFTA and the EC blurred, however, and some of the members (Austria, Denmark, Portugal, Sweden, and the UK) eventually joined the EC. Moreover, in 1992 EFTA signed a treaty that formally gives its members an economic association with the EU. Today EFTA members include Iceland, Liechtenstein, Norway, and Switzerland.

European Free Trade Association (EFTA)
A free trade area currently consisting of Iceland, Liechtenstein, Norway, and Switzerland; past members included the UK (before it joined the EU)

Growth and challenges

Over the years the EU made vigorous headway in pursuit of its objectives. For example, during the 1970s formal barriers to the free flow of labor and capital were gradually dismantled. The **Single European Act (SEA)**, which effectively prevents a country from vetoing any EU decision it deems to be in conflict with its vital interests, was enacted in the 1980s. In the past this veto power had been often used by EU members to protect their respective economic advantages and made it difficult for the group to make decisions. Now veto power is based on a total of 87 votes which are allocated among the 15 members, and 62 votes are needed to pass a proposal.

Single European Act (SEA)
An Act passed by the EU which contains many measures to further integrate the member states, along economic and political dimensions, and which allows the Council of Ministers to pass most proposals by a majority vote, in contrast to the unanimous vote that was needed previously

Other major breakthroughs are occurring in the political and financial areas. With the EC 1992 measures, the EU has transformed itself into a political, economic, and monetary superpower that can speak with one powerful voice about everything from interest rates to defense. In moving in this direction, the EU political leaders negotiated and put into process a method for ratifying two new treaties that would extend the community's powers from their present largely economic role to foreign and security policy and monetary affairs and, eventually, to defense.[20] The effect of such actions may well be the creation of a "United States of Europe."

However, the EU still faces a number of problems. One is disagreement among the members regarding the relationship that should exist between the community and the rest of the world. A second problem is the protection that countries give to their own industries, which is in direct contrast to the spirit of EU rules. A related area is the community's agriculture policies, which provide subsidies and rebates to farmers and have resulted in charges of unfair trade practices. A third problem is the disagreement among the members regarding the amount of protection that poorer countries (Spain, Portugal) should be given before all trade barriers are dismantled.

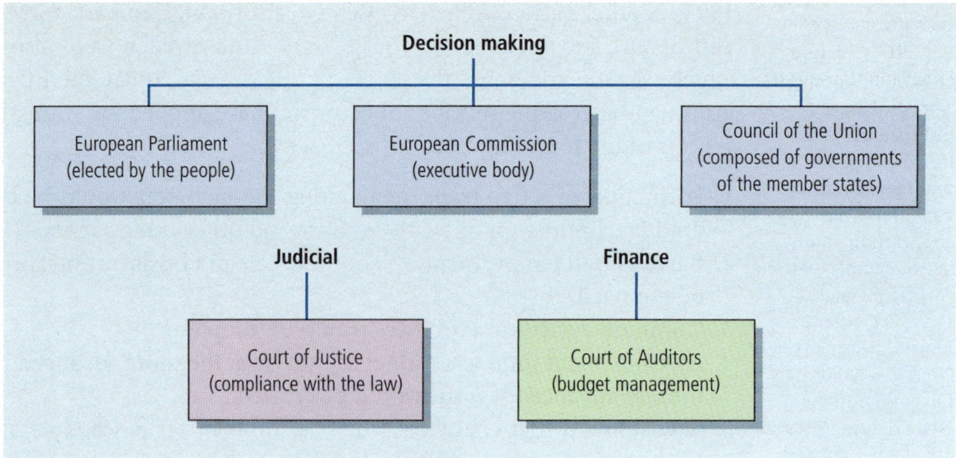

Figure 4.1 **The European Union's institutions**

European Council Composed of the heads of state of each EU member country as well as the president of the European Commission. Meetings of the Council take place at least twice a year and their purpose is to resolve major policy issues and to set policy direction

Council of Ministers The major policy decision-making body of the EU; it consists of one minister from each of the 15 member states and is one of four major institutions of the EU

European Commission A 20-member group chosen by agreement of member governments of the EU; the Commission is the executive branch of the EU

European Parliament A group of 630 members elected directly by voters in each member country of the EU; the Parliament serves as a watchdog on EU expenditures

One of the key goals of EU integration is the free flow of capital, and the recent creation of a single European currency, the euro, will help to bring this about. Closely linked to this goal is the establishment of a central European bank that will regulate the money supply and thus be able to stabilize interest rates throughout the EU. And even if this goal is not fully attained during this decade, the EU is going to be an increasingly powerful economic force in the international arena. A close look at the community's organizational arrangement helps to explain why.

Organization

There are five major institutions that manage the EU: the European Council, the Council of Ministers, the European Commission, the European Parliament, and the Court of Justice. (See Figure 4.1.) A brief description of each of these is set out below.

The **European Council** is composed of the heads of state of each EU member country as well as the president of the European Commission. The Council meets at least twice a year and each head of state is typically accompanied to these meetings by a foreign minister. The purpose of these meetings is to resolve major policy issues and to set policy direction.

The **Council of Ministers** is the major policy decision-making body of the EU. These 15 individuals are the foreign ministers of their respective countries and, with the exception of the budget, they are responsible for final EU decisions.

The **European Commission** has 20 members who are chosen by agreement of the member governments. France, Germany, Italy, Spain, and the UK have two representatives each, and the other members one each. The Commission, the executive branch of the EU, handles a great deal of the technical work associated with preparing decisions and regulations. The group is responsible for drafting legislation for proposal to the Council of Ministers, overseeing the implementation of EU policies, and carrying out studies on key policy issues.

The **European Parliament** currently has 630 members. These individuals are elected directly by the voters in each member country. The Parliament serves as a watchdog on EU expenditures in addition to evaluating other decisions of the Council. More recently, the power of the Parliament has been expanded and this body now has the right to vote on the appointment of commissioners, as well as to veto matters related to the EU budget and single market legislation.

Court of Justice
A court that has one judge appointed from each EU member country; this court serves as the official interpreter of EU law

The **Court of Justice** has one judge appointed from each EU member country; this court serves as the official interpreter of EU law. In most cases this requires the judges to rule on the meaning or application of the Treaty of Rome, based on the actions of member countries, companies, and individuals. Because EU rules are becoming more closely interwoven with national laws in the member countries, in recent years the Court of Justice has been serving increasingly as a court of appeal for national courts on issues that are EU-related.

The future

The EU is a powerful economic union. Empirical studies show that the community has created much more trade than it has diverted from the rest of the world. Moreover, this market has a greater combined gross domestic product than any of the two other major markets: North America, or Japan and industrialized Asia. At the same time it is likely that EU-generated projects will offer major competition to other worldwide industries. For example, Airbus Industries, as seen in Chapter 3, is now a major force in the world aircraft manufacturing industry. Quite clearly, the EU promises tremendous economic gains for member countries.

Other economic alliances

While the EU is the most successful economic union, there are a host of others. The following briefly examines three of these.

Andean Pact

Andean Pact
An economic union consisting of Bolivia, Colombia, Ecuador, Peru, and Venezuela

The **Andean Pact** (sometimes known as Ancom, which stands for Andean common market) is an economic union that was formed in 1969 by Bolivia, Chile, Colombia, Ecuador, and Peru. (Today Venezuela is a member and Chile has withdrawn.) The original objectives of the Ancom countries were to integrate themselves economically, to reduce internal tariffs, to create a common external tariff, and to offer special concessions to the two smallest members, Bolivia and Ecuador. The group also agreed that no foreign direct investment (FDI) would be allowed in sectors such as banking, telecommunications, and retail sales, and that foreign investors in all other sectors would be required to sell at least 51 per cent of their holdings to local investors over a 15-year period. There also are restrictions on annual profit remittance. These regulations have been enforced with a variety of exceptions being allowed. They have also proved to discourage FDI, resulting in Chile leaving the group because it wanted to attract more FDI. The current members of Ancom have had varying degrees of economic success. Overall, however, the group has not been able to achieve tariff-free trade or a common external tariff, and economic development has been far short of expectations. More recently, the group has entered into negotiations with Mercosur to establish a South American free trade area.

Mercosur

Mercosur is a free trade group that was formed by Argentina and Brazil in 1988 to promote economic cooperation. Today the group has been expanded to include Paraguay and Uruguay with Chile and Bolivia as associate members. In all, Mercosur countries have a combined population of over 200 million and a GDP of $1 trillion. In 1995 the members agreed to a five-year program under which they hoped to perfect their free trade area and move toward a full customs union. However, things have not worked out very well in recent years. The group members have been unable to agree on a common agenda and each seems to be striking out in a different direction. For example, Argentina now wants to suspend Mercosur's tariff so that it can abolish important duties on capital equipment while raising those on consumer goods in the hope of boosting economic growth. Meanwhile, Argentina is considering scrapping its membership in the custom union and becoming a free trade area of its own, and Uruguay is hinting at doing the same thing.[21] Summing up the current situation, a Latin American economist who is familiar with the group's current plight wrote in a research study, "Rather than making long lists of unfinished business, what Mercosur needs most is the re-creation of a sense of political understanding and shared interests."[22]

ASEAN

Association of Southeast Asian Nations (ASEAN) An economic union founded in 1967 by Indonesia, Malaysia, the Philippines, Singapore, and Thailand; this economic bloc focuses not on reducing trade barriers among members but, rather, on promoting exports to other nations

The **Association of Southeast Asian Nations (ASEAN)** was founded in 1967 and now includes Brunei, Indonesia, Laos, Malaysia, Myanmar, the Philippines, Singapore, Thailand, and Vietnam. This economic bloc is different from most others in that the primary emphasis is not on reducing trade barriers among the members, although this has been done, but rather on promoting exports to other countries. With the notable exception of Singapore, which has offshore manufacturing assembly plants, the group relies heavily on exports of raw materials. Members have been particularly successful in promoting exports to the Japanese market and to the EU. Until the late 1990s members of ASEAN experienced rapid economic growth, thanks in no small part to the efficiency and productivity of their members as well as to their impressive marketing skills. However, the economic downturn in Asia in recent years has stalled many of these economies, especially Indonesia.

FTAA

The Free Trade Area of the Americas (FTAA) was re-launched in Quebec City in April 2001. All the economies of North, Central, and South America, along with all Caribbean economies (except for Cuba) have agreed to start the FTAA in 2005. It will be built upon the framework of NAFTA, discussed in Chapters 6 and 20 in detail.

Active learning check

Review your answer to Active Learning Case question 2 and make any changes you like. Then compare your answer with the one below.

2. Would Russia benefit by gaining admission to one of the major economic unions such as the EU? Why?

Russia certainly would benefit by gaining admission to an economic union such as the EU. This type of development would make it possible for the country to take advantage of a wide variety of benefits, including free movement of goods and services across borders, trade creation, the possible development of internal economies brought about by the huge market that would then be available for Russian goods, and a strengthening of the nation's currency. Of course, admission to the EU or one of the other major economic unions is unlikely to occur, at least within the next few years. However, it would offer a very big boost to the nation's economy.

ECONOMIC INTEGRATION AND STRATEGIC MANAGEMENT

How can MNEs use strategic management planning to benefit from worldwide economic integration efforts? A number of steps are proving to be particularly helpful. In particular, these include the use of strategic alliances, acquisitions, and the localization of business operations.

Strategic alliances and acquisitions

One of the most common ways of benefiting from economic integration is by creating a strategic alliance, often in the form of a joint venture, with other firms that can provide important forms of assistance. The following examines the use of strategic alliances and acquisitions in the telecommunications and electronics industry and acquisitions in the brewery business.

Telecommunications and electronics

Over the past decade the telecommunications industry has been expanding in terms of both products and geographic coverage. This development represents the convergence of four distinct industries: telephone, mass media (print, broadcast and cable), consumer electronics, and computers. The result has been a growing number of products and services including cellular phones, personal computers, and televisions that are able to receive and interact with each other in both receiving and transmitting information. In addition, the industry has become even more competitive and complex with the advent of wireless networks. In an effort to take advantage of these developments, a number of firms are relying on strategic alliances.[23] A **strategic alliance** is a business relationship in which two or more companies work together to achieve a collective advantage. These alliances can take a number of forms. In some cases companies jointly conduct research or combine their efforts to market a product. In other instances they will license a firm to produce and sell a particular product in a specific market region. In the telecommunications industry strategic alliances have been very important because of the high investment and the need to attain market penetration. A good example is provided by Concert, which is a strategic alliance comprised of AT&T and British Telecommunications. Concert provides voice and data telecom services to multinational corporations and individual users through a network of distributors. This strategic alliance is also interested in increasing its global market presence as seen by its recent decision to buy a 30 per cent stake in Japan Telecom.

Another example of a strategic alliance is provided by Lucent Technologies, which merged its consumer phone unit with that of Philips Electronics NV so that the two could produce a wide range of products from corded and cordless telephones to answering machines and a variety of types of digital cellular phones. This arrangement gave Philips's consumer phone business a strong boost and, at the same time, it helped Lucent, which is very strong in network gear and high-tech chips and software that are used in switches and phones, but which has been having trouble remaining competitive in the face of stiff competition from European suppliers.[24]

Yet another example is that of Microsoft and Sony which teamed up to link personal computers and consumer electronics devices, thus moving closer together on technology standards for digital television and other consumer products. The two firms also endorsed a technology that can connect videocassette recorders, camcorders, personal computers, and other devices. Microsoft's objective in this alliance was to license software from Sony used with the networking technology and use this software with versions of an operating system that it had decided to try to make a standard for non-personal computer (PC) products. The objective of the joint venture was to create a technology that consumers could use to plug a camcorder easily to a PC or television set-top box for sending video mail over the Internet.[25]

Breweries

Not all strategic alliances and joint ventures involve giant multinationals. Many brewers have found, to their regret, that it is difficult to get customers to change brands. This is particularly true in countries such as Germany, England, and the Netherlands, where beer is popular. Customers are often fiercely loyal to local brands, and the only way of tapping into these markets is by purchasing the brewery. Major European brewers have long realized this and have not hesitated to buy operations in other countries. A good example is the purchase of La Cruz del Campo, Spain's largest brewery, by Britain's Guinness. However, the company has a long way to go before it will catch Heineken, which for years has been buying small brewers on the Continent, a strategy now being emulated by large American competitors.

Localization of business operations

MNEs cannot conduct business overseas in the same way that they do at home. Multinationals have to target their offerings carefully to the needs of the regional and local customer. These efforts result in the localization of business operations and typically focus on four areas: products, profits, production, and management.[26]

Products

Localization of products requires the development, manufacturing, and marketing of goods best suited to the needs of the local customer and marketplace. This typically requires modification of products that have sold well in other geographic regions. For example, in North America, buyers use motorcycles primarily for leisure and sports, so they look for high horsepower output and speed. In contrast, South East Asians use motorcycles as a basic means of transportation, so they look for low cost and ease of maintenance; and in Australia, where shepherds use motorcycles to drive sheep, low-speed torque is more important than either high speed or ease of maintenance.[27]

MNEs commonly localize production by investing in research and development, so they can produce the product that fits the specific needs of that market. This is sometimes more difficult than it appears, especially if the MNE has been successful with a product in the home market and is unwilling to change. A good example is provided by the Whirlpool Corporation, which dominated the US market before going to Europe in the late 1980s. The firm believed that the giant $20 billion European appliance market with dozens of marginally profitable companies was on the verge of consolidation and it wanted to be one of the major players. So it bought a majority stake in a struggling appliance operation belonging to NV Philips, the Dutch electronics giant. Then, two years later, it acquired the rest of the operation for $1.1 billion. Whirlpool believed that the European market was highly regionalized because there were so many diverse consumer preferences. For example, the Swedish liked galvanized washers that could withstand salty air; the British washed their clothes more often than many others, so they wanted quieter washing machines, etc. Stoves provided even greater examples of product diversity. However, Whirlpool believed that the market was ready for product consolidation as seen by its support for a "world washer", a single machine that could be sold anywhere on the Continent. As product diversity was reduced, Whirlpool believed, the marginal producers would be driven from the market and its own share would climb. What the company found was that the European market was a lot more competitive than it realized. Sweden's AB Electrolux and Germany's Bosch-Siemens Hausgeraete GmbH proved to be excellent competitors. In particular, they revamped their factories and drove costs down sharply. They also began introducing new products that kept customers coming back. By thus appealing to local tastes, Electrolux and Bosch-Siemens managed to keep Whirlpool's profits to a minimum, while preventing the firm from gaining market share.[28]

Localization of profits

Localization of profits
The reinvestment of earnings in the local market

Localization of profits is the reinvestment of earnings in the local market. MNEs do this by taking their earnings and using them to expand operations, set up new plants and offices, hire more local people, and make the investment more self-sufficient. In the US, for example, Honda started out with an initial investment of $250,000 and has gradually reinvested its US profits. Today the company has almost $2 billion in its motorcycle, auto, and engine manufacturing plants in Ohio. At the same time the company has reinvested almost $200 million in Honda Canada, a manufacturing plant making Honda Civics.

Localization of production

Localization of production
The manufacturing of goods in the host market

Localization of production involves the manufacture of goods in the host market.[29] Many MNEs, upon entering a foreign market, handle this function by exporting from the home country. For a successful relationship, however, this is often only a short-run strategy and is eventually replaced by a local manufacturing base.[30] One strategy for localizing production is to increase the amount of local content in the product by producing more and more of the subunits in the host country. The ultimate step, of course, is to produce the entire product locally. In the case of Honda, for example, the company decided back in the late 1980s to turn its Ohio auto manufacturing facility into a fully integrated, self-reliant entity. The plan involved a number of steps including increasing the plant's production capacity so that it would be able to turn out 500,000 units annually and be able to build these cars with at least 75 per cent domestic content. In the process, Honda localized its production.

The same is true for Toyota. In recent years, the company increased the capacity of its Georgetown, Kentucky plant from 380,000 units annually to 500,000 units and doubled its Corolla production to 200,000 units at its Ontario, Canada facility. It also doubled the production capacity of its Burnaston, England plant and increased auto production in its Thailand factory, while also negotiating with the government to build an engine factory in Tianjin, China.[31]

Another way in which production is localized is by providing added value in operations by modifying the imported product and adapting it to local conditions and tastes. This approach is used when a product requires country-by-country (or regional) changes. In the case of auto manufacturers, for example, this means taking into account the nature of the terrain (unpaved roads require stronger underbody construction), the cost of gasoline (high costs often mean that the market wants smaller, more efficient cars) and which side of the road everyone drives on (right in the US and Latin America; left in the UK and Asia).

Localization of production is often carried out in conjunction with a home country partner, who provides the plant and personnel while the MNE is responsible for the initial product and the technology needed in assembling or modifying the goods. Sometimes, however, the MNE will own the entire operation and depend on local management to help run the organization.

Localization of management

There are a number of ways that MNEs localize management. One is by encouraging home office managers to learn the local culture and become part of the community. Research reveals that companies that staff their subsidiaries with older, mature senior managers from the home country who are fluent in the local language are often more highly productive than are MNEs that staff operations with younger, less experienced managers.[32] A second way of localizing management is by delegating authority to host country managers and developing and promoting these employees wherever possible. This strategy helps to create a bond between the host and the home country management. As one MNE spokesperson put it:

> . . . we have become convinced that good communication between management and labor, as well as delegation of authority, elevate the employees' sense of participation in decision making. This, in turn, gives the employees a stronger sense of responsibility and motivation, which leads to improved productivity and maintenance of high quality standards.[33]

Active learning check

Review your answer to Active Learning Case question 3 and make any changes you like. Then compare your answer with the one below.

3. Is Russia a good potential investment for Western business? Explain.

Arguments can be made on each side. Untapped natural resources and potential consumer demand could provide billions of dollars of annual sales for investing companies. On the other hand, the economy is currently in terrible shape, and it is likely to take years before Russia begins to provide an acceptable return on investment for many current projects. One of the major reasons for getting in now, of course, is to try and gain a strong foothold in the market and to use this to effectively block out future competition. If this should happen, those coming later would find slim pickings. However, this potential benefit is unlikely to attract many investors. Most are likely to conclude that the best strategy is to proceed with caution and wait for the current uncertainty and turmoil to settle.

KEY POINTS

1. Political ideologies and economic systems are interwoven. Democracies tend to have market-driven economies; totalitarian governments tend to have centrally determined economies. However, there are few nations that fit totally into one of these two paradigms. Most use a mixed economic model such as that of the US, which is mainly a market-driven economy with some central planning, or China, which still relies on central planning but is moving to allow some degree of free enterprise.
2. Another current economic development is the trend toward privatization. Many countries are selling their state-owned enterprises. There are a variety of reasons that can be cited for these actions. In most cases these are economic in nature, including (a) increased efficiency, (b) reduction in government outlays, and (c) generation of funds for the national treasury.
3. Economic integration is the establishment of transnational rules and regulations that permit economic trade and cooperation among countries. Effective integration brings about trade creation, although in some cases these efforts result in trade diversion. There are five levels of regional economic trade integration: free trade areas, customs unions, common markets, economic unions, and political unions. The most successful examples have been the EU and the North American Free Trade area. NGOs criticize such trade and investment agreements.
4. NGOs are an important new actor on the stage of international business and MNEs need to take account of the civil society in their strategies.

5. Multinational enterprises use a variety of strategies to benefit from integration efforts. One is strategic alliances and acquisitions by which they are able to surmount the economic wall and gain an inside position in the economic alliance or free trade area. The other is through the localization of operations by focusing on products, profits, production, and management. MNEs typically use both of these strategic approaches.

KEY TERMS

- ideology
- democracy
- totalitarianism
- communism
- theocratic totalitarianism
- secular totalitarianism
- market-driven economy
- centrally determined economy
- mixed economies
- privatization
- nationalization
- divestiture
- contract management
- Ministry of International Trade and Industry (MITI)
- economic integration
- trade creation
- trade diversion
- free trade area
- North American Free Trade Agreement
- strategic alliance
- localization of profits
- customs union
- common market
- economic union
- political union
- internal economies of scale
- external economies of scale
- European Coal and Steel Community (ECSC)
- European Union
- European Free Trade Agreement (EFTA)
- Single European Act
- European Council
- Council of Ministers
- European Commission
- European Parliament
- Court of Justice
- Andean Pact
- Mercosur
- Association of Southeast Asian Nations (ASEAN)
- localization of production
- non-governmental organization (NGO)

REVIEW AND DISCUSSION QUESTIONS

1. As political systems change, economic systems follow. What does this statement mean?
2. How does a centrally determined economy differ from a market-driven economy? Explain.
3. What are the benefits of privatization? Why will the trend toward privatization continue?
4. Why are government–business cooperative efforts beginning to increase? What benefits do they offer?
5. What is the purpose of research consortia? What is their future likely to be? Why?
6. How does trade creation differ from trade diversion? Compare and contrast the two.
7. There are five levels of economic integration. What is meant by this statement? Be complete in your answer.
8. How does the EU function? Identify and describe its organization and operation.
9. What is the purpose of the following economic alliances: the Andean Pact, Mercosur, and ASEAN?
10. Some of the primary ways that MNEs use strategic planning to benefit from economic integration efforts is through strategic alliances and acquisitions. How do MNEs do this?
11. How do MNEs seek to localize their business operations? Describe three steps that they take.

REAL CASE

How environmental regulations can be used as trade barriers

With free trade areas evolving around the globe, many protected industries are now facing unwelcome competition. Free trade agreements generally include a principle of national treatment under which a country must treat all producers, domestic or foreign, equally. However, some seemingly neutral environmental regulations pose a greater burden on foreign producers than on their domestic competitors. Thus, they act as trade barriers under the disguise of environmental regulations.

For example, while environmental groups lobby for newsprint to contain a determined amount of recycled material and domestic producers of newsprint support the regulation, foreign newsprint companies, which have no recycling facilities in the host country, face a competitive disadvantage. This is what has been called a "baptist–bootlegger" coalition. During the US prohibition era, Baptists were opposed to alcoholic consumption on moral grounds, while bootleggers actually benefited from prohibition by the sale of illegal alcoholic beverages. Today, environmental groups and domestic producers often form coalitions to promote their respective interests.

In the newsprint case, the foreign company would have two options if it were to continue to supply material from its home country. It could either open recycling plants in the host country and transport pulp from its country to be processed there so as to meet the environmental regulations or take the recycling material to its home country to be processed. Both alternatives pose significant transportation costs to the foreign producer.

A similar case is presented by the Ontario Beer Can Tax. In the early 1990s the province of Ontario levied a tax of $0.10 on each aluminum beer can. The province argued that these cans were not environmentally friendly and that the tax was designed to encourage the use of refillable glass bottles. US producers of beer and aluminum cans contended that this was a protectionist move, and that the Ontario government was singling out the competition with its beer industry since it had no similar tax for soft drinks and juice cans. Moreover, research studies found that the aluminum can and the glass bottle both affect the environment equally, and 80 per cent of all the cans were being recycled. Additionally, it was found that the larger, heavier glass required more energy to transport than did the lighter aluminum cans.

Sources: Adapted from Alan M. Rugman, John Kirton and Julie Soloway, *Environmental Regulations and Corporate Strategy: A NAFTA Perspective* (Oxford: Oxford University Press, 1999); M. Trebilcock and R. Howse, "Trade Policy and Domestic Health and Safety Standards," *The Regulation of International Trade*, 2nd edn (London: Routledge, 1999); Julie Soloway, "Environmental Trade Barriers in NAFTA: The MMT Fuel Additives Controversy," *Minnesota Journal of Global Trade*, vol. 8, no. 1 (1998); David Vogel and Alan M. Rugman, "Environmentally Related Trade Disputes between the United States and Canada," *American Review of Canadian Studies*, Summer 1997, pp. 271–292.

1. **How can a health and safety regulation become a trade barrier? Provide examples.**
2. **How can different environmental circumstances make one country's regulations inefficient in another country?**
3. **What are some reasons why the government might not be willing to make allowances for different countries?**

REAL CASE

Thames Water goes international

Thames Water plc is the largest British water company. The firm was created in 1989 after Prime Minister Margaret Thatcher privatized the water industry. Today the company supplies the water and sewage services to over 11 million people in the Thames Valley, from the quaint university city of Oxford to one of the world's largest urban agglomerations in London.

While the industry is privatized, the company's water utility division is still subject to regulation by OFWAT, the UK water regulator. This agency sets price controls and regulatory standards over water and sewage services every five years. The logic behind this approach is that it forces British regional water monopolies to make price cuts to the water bills of their customers on a periodic basis. The managerial paradox is that any increases in operating efficiency by a water utility essentially are taxed away every five years. However, in the intervening period there is an incentive for the company to use its economic efficiency improvements to help fund development of its non-regulated commercially based business.

In an effort to take advantage of their competencies in this industry, some water utilities have expanded into electricity and gas. Thames Water, however, has decided against this approach. Instead it has opted for a two-pronged strategy. First, it has kept its focus of operations in the water industry. Today, half of its 12,000 employees are engaged in activities such as the design, engineering, and maintenance of water membrane systems and related water treatment products or in the service and marketing of water-related businesses.

Second, Thames Water has chosen to use its expertise to move into the international arena. Today it has major projects in Australia, Turkey, Indonesia, Malaysia, the Philippines, Thailand, the Ukraine, and the US. Annual revenues in the international market for water are very high and the profit potential is much greater than that in Britain. Additionally, there are not many international competitors.

One of Thames Waters' international clients is Indonesia. The company has a 25-year contract to supply fresh water to half the population of the capital city, Jakarta. In March 1998 this contract was temporarily rescinded by the new president as he alleged that the contract was signed with the son of the former head of government, President Suharto. However, within a month everything had been resolved and things were back to normal. Another Thames Water client is the city of Adelaide in southeast Australia. The firm provides the technical expertise for this project, while its French partner handles the remainder of the contract.

Thames Water is also beginning to make acquisitions in the international arena. One of its initial moves was the purchase of a large US water utility, Etown, in New Jersey for $1 billion. In October 2000 Thames Water was acquired by the massive German multi-utility RWE whose annual revenues are in the range of $60 billion. RWE is a major producer of electricity and natural gas, but the company is relatively inexperienced in the water business. So Thames Water is now the branch of the company that is responsible for RWE's international water business. Drawing upon RWE's capital, Thames recently purchased American Water Works of New Jersey for $4.6 billion in cash and assumed another $3 billion in debt. American Water Works is the largest private water company in the US. It owns 25 water utilities, has operations in 23 states, and serves approximately 10 million customers. RWE has announced that American Water Works' operations will be combined with those of Thames Water so as to achieve economies of scale.

At the present time over 80 per cent of the US water systems are public sector municipal monopolies. As many of these are privatized during this decade, RWE and Thames Water are likely to become major players in the US water market. And as they do, the role of Thames Water will become increasingly more important.

Websites: ***www.thames-water.com***; ***www.ofwat.gov.uk*** and ***www.rwe.com***.

Sources: Annual Reports of Thames Water plc; *Financial Times* and *Wall Street Journal*, September 18, 2001.

1. **How has Thames Water used the UK move toward privatization to help create market opportunities for itself in the international arena?**
2. **How much political risk does a company like Thames Water face when doing business in a country like Indonesia?**
3. **How is Thames Water helping RWE expand its triad operations? Give an example.**

ENDNOTES

1 Craig S. Smith, "Workers of the World, Invest!" *New York Times*, August 19, 2001, Section 3, p. 3.

2 For more on this see Erik Eckholm, "Chinese President Is Optimistic About Relations with the U.S.," *New York Times*, August 10, 2001, pp. A 1, A 8.

3 Paul Starobin and Olga Kravchenko, "Russia's Middle Class," *Business Week*, October 16, 2000, pp. 78–84.

4 R. Molz, "Privatization of Government Enterprise: The Challenge to Management," *Management International Review*, vol. 29, no. 4 (1989), pp. 29–30.

5 Ibid., pp. 32–33.

6 For excellent coverage of privatization, see Dennis J. Gayle and Jonathan N. Goodrich (eds.), *Privatization and Deregulation in Global Perspective* (New York: Quorum Books, 1990).

7 Clifford Krauss, "Argentina to Hasten End of Phone Monopoly," *New York Times*, March 11, 1998, Section C, p. 4.

8 Gautam Naik, "Telecom Deregulation in Britain Delivered a Nice Surprise: Jobs," *Wall Street Journal*, March 5, 1998, pp. A 1, A 6.

9 Michael Wines, "A Factory's Turnaround Reflects a Glimmer in Russia's Economy," *New York Times*, July 2, 2000, pp. A 1, 8.

10 For more on the current state of EUREKA, see Caroline Mothe and Bertrand Quelin, "Creating Competencies Through Collaboration: The Case of EUREKA R&D Consortia," *European Management Journal*, December 2000, pp. 590–604.

11 Alan Goldstein, "Sematech Members Facing Dues Increase; 30% Jump to Make up for Loss of Federal Funding," *Dallas Morning News*, July 27, 1996, p. 2 F.

12 Larry Reibstein et al., "A Mexican Miracle?" *Newsweek*, May 20, 1991, pp. 42–45; and Paul Magnusson et al., "The Mexico Pact: Worth the Price?" *Business Week*, May 27, 1991, pp. 32–35.

13 Alan Rugman and Richard Hodgetts, "The End of Global Strategy," *European Management Journal*, August 2001, p. 334.

14 "Globalization, What on Earth is it About," *BBC.co.uk*, September 14, 2000.

15 "Who are the Prague Protestors," *BBC.co.uk*, September 26, 2000.

16 Alan M. Rugman, *The End of Globalization* (London: Random House, 2001).

17 Sylvia Ostry, "The Multilateral Trading System", in Alan M. Rugman and Thomas Brewer (eds.), *The Oxford Handbook of International Business* (Oxford: Oxford University Press, 2001), pp. 232–258.

18 Edward M. Graham, *Fighting the Wrong Enemy: Antiglobal Activists and Multinational Enterprises* (Washington, DC: Institute for International Economics, 2000).

19 Matthew Kaminski, "Europe's Leaders Set Date for EU Enlargement," *Wall Street Journal*, June 18, 2001, p. A 15.

20 Philip Revzin, "EC Leaders Adopt 2-Year Plan to Forge Political, Monetary Unity in Europe," *Wall Street Journal*, December 17, 1990, p. A 6.

21 For more on some of these problems, see Thomas Catan and Raymond Colitt, "Currency Conflict Puts Strain on Mercosur," *Financial Times*, October 4, 2001, p. 7.

22 "Another Blow to Mercosur," *Economist*, March 31, 2001, p. 34.

23 Sylvia Chan-Olmsted and Mark Jamison, "Rivalry Through Alliances: Competitive Strategy in the Global Telecommunications Market," *European Management Journal*, June 2001, pp. 317–331.

24 John J. Keller, "Lucent, Philips to Produce Phones Jointly," *Wall Street Journal*, June 18, 1997, p. A 3.

25 Don Clark and David Bank, "Microsoft, Sony to Cooperate on PCs, Devices," *Wall Street Journal*, April 8, 1998, p. B 6.

26 Hideo Sugiura, "How Honda Localizes Its Global Strategy," *Sloan Management Review*, Fall 1990, pp. 77–82.

27 Ibid., p. 78.

28 Greg Steinmetz and Carl Quintanilla, "Whirlpool Expected Easy Going in Europe, and It Got a Big Shock," *Wall Street Journal*, April 10, 1998, pp. A 1, A 6.

29 Ferdinand Protzman, "Rewriting the Contract for Germany's Vaunted Workers," *New York Times*, February 13, 1994, Section F, p. 5.

30 "Pepsi Investing $350 Million in China Plants," *New York Times*, January 27, 1994, p. C 3.

31 Brian Bremner et al., "Toyota's Crusade," *Business Week*, April 7, 1997, pp. 104–114.

32 See Robert O. Metzger and Ari Ginsberg, "Lessons from Japanese Global Acquisitions," *Journal of Business Strategy*, May–June 1989, p. 35.

33 Ibid., p. 79.

ADDITIONAL BIBLIOGRAPHY

Busenitz, Lowell W. "Country Institutional Profiles: Unlocking Entrepreneurial Phenomena," *Academy of Management Journal*, vol. 43, no. 5 (October 2000).

Calingaert, Michael. "Government–Business Relations in the European Community," *California Management Review*, vol. 35, no. 2 (Winter 1993).

Dunning, John H. (ed.). *Governments, Globalization and International Business* (Oxford: Oxford University Press, 1997).

Eden, Lorraine. "The Emerging North American Investment Regime," *Transnational Corporations*, vol. 5, no. 3 (December 1996).

Eiteman, David K. "Political Risk and International Marketing," *Columbia Journal of World Business*, vol. 23, no. 4 (Winter 1988).

Geringer, J. Michael. "Strategic Determinant of Partner Selection Criteria in International Joint Ventures," *Journal of International Business Studies*, vol. 22, no. 1 (First Quarter 1991).

Gomes-Casseres, Benjamin. "Firm Ownership Preferences and Host Government Restrictions: An Integrated Approach," *Journal of International Business Studies*, vol. 21, no. 1 (First Quarter 1990).

Goodman, John B. and Loveman, Gary W. "Does Privatization Serve the Public Interest?" *Harvard Business Review*, vol. 69, no. 6 (November/December 1991).

Graham, Edward M. *Fighting the Wrong Enemy: Antiglobal Activists and Multinational Enterprises* (Washington DC: Institute for International Economics, September 2000).

Howell, Llewellyn D. and Chaddick, Brad. "Models of Political Risk for Foreign Investment and Trade: An Assessment of Three Approaches," *Columbia Journal of World Business*, vol. 29, no. 3 (Fall 1994).

Kobrin, Stephen J. "Sovereignty @ Bay: Globalization, Multinational Enterprises, and the International Political System," in Alan M. Rugman and Thomas Brewer (eds.), *The Oxford Handbook of International Business* (Oxford: Oxford University Press, 2000), pp. 181–205.

Lieberman, Ira W. "Privatization: The Theme of the 1990s – An Overview," *Columbia Journal of World Business*, vol. 28, no. 1 (Spring 1993).

Luo, Yadong. "Toward a Cooperative View of MNC-Host Government Relations: Building Blocks and Performance Implications," *Journal of International Business Studies*, vol. 32, no. 3 (Fall 2001).

MacDonald, Kevin R. "Why Privatization Is Not Enough," *Harvard Business Review*, vol. 71, no. 3 (May/June 1993).

Moore, John. "British Privatization – Taking Capitalism to the People," *Harvard Business Review*, vol. 70, no. 1 (January/February 1992).

Ostry, Sylvia. "Governments & Corporations in a Shrinking World: Trade & Innovation Policies in the United States, Europe & Japan," *Columbia Journal of World Business*, vol. 25, nos. 1, 2 (Spring/Summer 1990).

Ostry, Sylvia. "The Multilateral Trading System," in Alan M. Rugman and Thomas Brewer (eds.), The *Oxford Handbook of International Business* (Oxford: Oxford University Press, 2000), pp. 332–358.

Ramamurti, Ravi. "Why Are Developing Countries Privatizing?" *Journal of International Business Studies*, vol. 23, no. 2 (Second Quarter 1992).

Rugman, Alan M. (ed.). *Foreign Investment and NAFTA* (Columbia SC: University of South Carolina Press, 1994).

Rugman, Alan M. "Towards an Investment Agenda for APEC," *Transnational Corporations*, August 1997.

Rugman, Alan and Gestrin, Michael. "US Trade Laws as Barriers to Globalization," *The World Economy*, vol. 14, no. 3 (1991).

Rugman, Alan and Gestrin, Michael. "The Strategic Response of Multinational Enterprises to NAFTA," *Columbia Journal of World Business*, vol. 28, no. 4 (Winter 1993).

Rugman, Alan and Gestrin, Michael. "The Impact of NAFTA Upon North American Investment Patterns," *Transnational Corporations*, vol. 3, no. 1 (February 1994).

Rugman, Alan M. and Verbeke, Alain. "Multinational Corporate Strategy and the Canada–US Free Trade Agreement," *Management International Review*, vol. 30, no. 3 (Summer 1990).

Rugman, Alan M. and Verbeke, Alain. "Multinational Enterprise and National Economic Policy," in Peter J. Buckley and Mark Casson (eds.), *Multinational Enterprises in the World Economy: Essays in Honour of John Dunning* (Aldershot, UK: Edward Elgar, 1992).

Rugman, Alan M. and Verbeke, Alain. "Multinational Enterprises and Public Policy," *Journal of International Business Studies*, vol. 29, no. 1 (1998), pp. 115–136.

Rugman, Alan M., Verbeke, Alain and Luxmore, Stephen. "Corporate Strategy and the Free Trade Agreement: Adjustment by Canadian Multinational Enterprises," *Canadian Journal of Regional Science*, vol. 13, no. 2/3 (Summer/Autumn 1991).

Safarian, A. E. *Multinational Enterprise and Public Policy* (Cheltenham: Elgar, 1993).

Sen, Amartya. *Development as Freedom* (Oxford: Oxford University Press, 1999).

Spar, Debora L. "National Policies and Domestic Politics", in Alan M. Rugman and Thomas Brewer (eds.), *The Oxford Handbook of International Business* (Oxford: Oxford University Press, 2000), pp. 206–231.

Spar, Debora L. "National Policies and Domestic Politics", in Alan M. Rugman and Thomas Brewer (eds.), *The Oxford Handbook of International Business* (Oxford: Oxford University Press, 2000), pp. 206–231.

Spar, Debora L. *Ruling the Waves: Cycles of Discovery, Chaos and Wealth* (New York: Harcourt, 2001).

Trebilcock, Michael and Howse, Robert. *The Regulation of International Trade*, 2nd edn (London: Routledge, 1999).

Whisenand, James D. "Cuba's Legal Structure: How it Affects Foreign Investment and Trade," *Columbia Journal of World Business*, vol. 30, no. 1 (Spring 1995).

Chapter 5

International Culture

CONTENTS

OBJECTIVES OF THE CHAPTER

Across the world people often behave differently, even when faced with similar situations. For example, in the US and the EU most drivers automatically stop at a stop sign, but in many third world countries drivers stop only if there is traffic coming in the other direction. In Mexico, when Presidente Fox gives a speech most Mexicans tune in on television or radio; in the US, when President Bush speaks many Americans switch to a different station and depend on their local newscaster to fill them in on what he said. In France, meetings start on time; in Peru, they often begin late. In Japan, politeness is very important, so people frequently say "yes" when they mean "no". In Australia, most people say what they really mean.

What accounts for these differences? Part of the answer is culture, and culture has a major impact on the way companies do business internationally. In this chapter we will examine the nature of culture, its key elements, and the role that culture plays in the strategic management process of multinational enterprises.

The specific objectives of this chapter are to:

1. *Define* the term *culture*.
2. *Examine* some of the key elements of culture including language, religion, values and attitudes, customs and manners, material goods, aesthetics, and education.
3. *Describe* the four dimensions of culture and some of the most recent research that helps explain the cultural differences among countries and geographic regions of the world.
4. *Discuss* five of the most important culturally related concepts that affect the strategic management decisions of multinational enterprises: management styles, work attitudes, achievement motivation, time, and ethics.

ACTIVE LEARNING CASE

US pop culture

US business may be having trouble selling its hardware – cars, steel, electronic products – in overseas markets, but it is having little trouble selling US software in the form of culture: movies, music, television programming, and home video. Pop culture is so popular that only the sale of aircraft and related equipment accounts for more US exports. And if the definition of pop culture is expanded to include licensed consumer products such as Levi's jeans and Coca-Cola's soft drinks, the US export picture looks even better. For example, the American music industry earns about 70 per cent of its profits outside the US with sales of US television programming to Europe accounting for over $600 million a year. Many people in Europe watch old *Frasier* and *X-Files* programs and now just about everyone watches *Ally McBeal*. One of the most popular films of all time is *Titanic*, which grossed more than $1 billion. There are also record stores everywhere that sell the latest international hits, many of them by such well-known US celebrities as Backstreet Boys, Britney Spears, and Madonna. In fact, US pop culture is so pervasive that it influences the lifestyle of people worldwide.

In an effort to get on the bandwagon, foreign transnationals are now buying into US pop culture. For example, Sony purchased Columbia Pictures and Vivendi bought Seagram for its ownership of Universal Studios; Pioneer Electronics bought 10 per cent of Carolco Pictures, maker of *Rambo*, *Total Recall*, and *Terminator II*; and Japan Victor has invested $100 million in Largo Entertainment, producers of *Die Hard*, *Predator*, and *48 Hours*. In addition, foreign investors are flocking to Disney, and limited partners in film productions such as DreamWorks are also hugely successful in Hollywood.

Despite these developments, a lot of pop culture remains solidly in US hands. A good example is Turner Broadcasting, with CNN in over 100 countries and territories. While the network broadcasts in English, the most popular language in the world, in non-English-speaking nations it is also extremely popular. CNN broadcasting has been able to expand into the international market with the same format used at home. Home Box Office (HBO) is also doing well, with its 2001 hit, *Band of Brothers*, a big international success. Simply put, US pop culture is proving to be a worldwide phenomenon that can transcend national boundaries.

Websites: **www.levi.com**; **www.cocacola.com**; **www.sony.com**; **www.vivendiuniversal.com**; **www.pioneerelectronics.com**; **www.disney.com**; **www.dreamworks.com**; **www.cnn.com** and **www.hbo.com**.

Sources: Adapted from John Huey, "America's Hottest Export: Pop Culture," *Fortune*, December 31, 1990; John Huey, "What Pop Culture Is Telling Us," *Fortune*, June 17, 1991; Christopher Power, "Sweet Sales for Sour Mash-Abroad," *Business Week*, July 1, 1991; Melanie Warner, "TV Exports," *Fortune*, November 25, 1996; Douglas A. Blackmon, "Forget the Stereotype: America Is Becoming a Nation Of Culture," *Wall Street Journal*, September 17, 1998, pp. A 1, A 18.

1. **In what way does pop culture help to overcome language as a cultural barrier?**
2. **How does pop culture help to change country customs and develop universal customs and manners? Give an example.**
3. **How can pop culture in the form of movies, for example, affect the cultural dimensions of a society? Give an example.**
4. **Can pop culture help to encourage achievement motivation in people? How?**

INTRODUCTION

Culture
The acquired knowledge that people use to interpret experience and to generate social behavior

Culture is the acquired knowledge that people use to interpret experience and to generate social behavior.[1] Additionally, culture is shared by members of a group, organization, or society[2] and, as a result, we learn to form the values and attitudes that shape our individual and group behavior.

Culture is learned through both education and experience. And since it is passed from one generation to another, culture is enduring. At the same time it constantly undergoes change as people adapt to new environments. So in just about every country of the world, the current culture is not the same as it was two decades ago.

To be successful in international businesses, managers must understand the cultures of other countries and learn how to adapt to them. In most cases, managers are home-country oriented; they like to do things the way they do in their home market. The challenge they must meet is learning how to broaden their perspective, adapt to other cultures, and make decisions that reflect the needs and desires of those cultures.

Ethnocentrism
The belief that one's way of doing things is superior to that of others

In this process, managers have to fight against **ethnocentrism**, the belief that one's way of doing things is superior to that of others. For example, Nokia must be careful that the way it does business in Finland does not prevent it from adjusting its approach to accommodating US culture and the specific needs of American customers. And Toyota must realize that the way it builds cars in Japan may not work as well in the US or the EU – and adjust its overseas production operations accordingly. Some of the most common types of ethnocentric business behavior include actions such as (1) not adapting a product to a particular market's special needs and (2) filling key positions in overseas units with national managers who have done well in the home market, while overlooking local managers who have performed well. Ethnocentric behavior can be avoided by learning about the culture where one will be doing business. One way of doing this is by understanding the elements of culture.

ELEMENTS OF CULTURE

Culture is a complex, multidimensional subject and, in understanding its nature, we need to examine seven elements: language, religion, values and attitudes, customs and manners, material goods, aesthetics, and education.

Language

Language is critical to culture because it is the primary means used to transmit and interpret information and ideas (see Table 5.1). A knowledge of the local language can help in three ways. First, it permits a clearer understanding of the situation. With direct knowledge of a language, a businessperson does not have to rely on someone else to interpret or explain things. Second, language provides direct access to local people, who are frequently more open in their communications when dealing with someone who speaks their language. Third, an understanding of the local language allows the person to pick up nuances, implied meanings, and other information that is not stated outright.

One of the best examples of the value of language is knowing the meaning of everyday idioms and clichés. For example, one of the authors had a doctoral student who had recently arrived from China. In discussing her course assignments with fellow doctoral students, the student had expressed some concern over a course she would be taking

Table 5.1 Language distribution of the world

Rank	*Language*	*Primary country*	*[Population]*
1	Chinese, Mandarin	China	885,000,000
2	Spanish	Spain	332,000,000
3	English	United Kingdom	322,000,000
4	Bengali	Bangladesh	189,000,000
5	Hindi	India	182,000,000
6	Portuguese	Portugal	170,000,000
7	Russian	Russia	170,000,000
8	Japanese	Japan	125,000,000
9	German	Germany	98,000,000
10	Chinese, Wu	China	77,175,000
11	Javanese	Indonesia, Java, Bali	75,500,800
12	Korean	South Korea	75,000,000
13	French	France	72,000,000
14	Vietnamese	Vietnam	67,662,000
15	Telugu	India	66,350,000
16	Chinese, Yue	China	66,000,000
17	Marathi	India	64,783,000
18	Tamil	India	63,075,000
19	Turkish	Turkey	59,000,000
20	Urdu	Pakistan	58,000,000

Source: Adapted from Barbara F. Grimes (ed.) (1996) *Ethnologue Languages of the World, 13th Edition* (pub Dallas: SIL International).

in multivariate analysis. The American students assured her that, if she studied hard, the course would be "a piece of cake". Confused by the unfamiliar idiom, the student asked her advisor what "a piece of cake" meant. In Chinese, this cliché has no meaning. In fact, many idioms and clichés differ from one country to another and in some cases make either no sense at all or mean something entirely different. For example, in the UK "tabling a proposal" means taking action on the proposal, while in the US it means delaying a decision on the matter.

A knowledge of language is also important because direct translation may be inadequate or misleading. For example, in many countries of the world, the word "aftertaste" does not exist. So a toothpaste advertiser might have trouble explaining how people would feel after brushing their teeth. In other cases, literal translations are inaccurate as seen by the following examples:

> Ford introduced a top-of-the-line automobile, the "Comet", in Mexico under the name "Caliente". The puzzling low sales were finally understood when Ford discovered that "caliente" is slang for a streetwalker.
>
> A major airline promoting its luxury leather seats in Latin America made the mistake of translating the slogan "Fly in leather!" to "Vuela en cuero!" which translates to "Fly naked!" Although the campaign attracted attention, it did not accomplish its main purpose of attracting business travelers.
>
> One laundry detergent company certainly wishes now that it had contacted a few locals before it initiated its promotional campaign in the Middle East. All of the company's advertisements pictured soiled clothes on the left, its box of soap in the middle, and clean clothes on the right. But, because in that area of the world people tend to read from right to left, many potential customers interpreted the message to indicate that the soap actually soiled the clothes.[3]

One of the most common ways of dealing with language barriers is through the use of translators. This is particularly important in the case of written communications, where some people recommend a double translation of the information. First, the material is translated into the second language and then it is translated back to see if the original material and the retranslated material are the same. However, the use of "back-translation" is not perfect. Researchers have found that, even when bilingual experts are employed, there are problems in translation.[4] There is no substitute for being able to speak and write the language fluently.[5]

At the same time, it is important to realize that a growing number of firms have made English their official language for doing business internationally. Matsushita now requires all managers to pass an English competency test in order to be promoted, and Toyota, NEC, Hitachi, Komatsu, and IBM Japan all use the ability to speak English as a criterion in their promotion process.[6] In Europe, as EU nations continue doing more and more business, they need a common language so that they can communicate with one another and to the rest of the world – English has been chosen. Today the European Commission has 11 official languages and a traditionally French-speaking bureaucracy, but English is its working language. One reason may well be because so many people in Western Europe now speak English: 77 per cent of college students, 69 per cent of managers, and 65 per cent of those between the ages of 15 and 24.[7]

Active learning check

Review your answer to Active Learning Case question 1 and make any changes you like. Then compare your answer with the one below.

1. In what way does pop culture help to overcome language as a cultural barrier?

Pop culture helps to overcome language as a cultural barrier in two ways. First, this culture is so popular that everyone worldwide understands it. Language is not necessary for people throughout the world to enjoy Coca-Cola or to appreciate Disneyland theme parks in Japan and France. Second, even if the product or service is presented in English, like a Bruce Springsteen record, young people in Germany, Chile, and Taiwan can understand the music just as well as a teenager in the US or the UK can. Simply put, pop culture often transcends spoken language.

Religion

There are a number of major religions in the world, including Catholic, Protestant, Jewish, Islamic, Hindu, Buddhist, and Confucian. Religions influence lifestyles, beliefs, values, and attitudes, and can have a dramatic effect on the way people in a society act toward each other and toward those in other societies.

Protestant work ethic A belief which holds that people should work hard, be industrious, and save their money

Confucian work ethic A belief that people should work hard at their tasks

Shinto work ethic A belief that people should work hard at their tasks

Religion can also affect the work habits of people. In the US, it is common to hear individuals talk about the **Protestant work ethic**, which holds that people should work hard, be industrious, and save their money. This work ethic helped to develop capitalism in the US because of the importance it assigns to saving and to the reinvestment of capital. However, Americans are not the only people who work hard. In Asian countries where Confucianism is strong, this attitude is known as the **Confucian work ethic**. In Japan, it is called the **Shinto work ethic**. Religious beliefs can influence people's work habits.

Religion also affects work and social customs from the days of the week on which people work to their dietary habits. Even major holidays are often tied to religion. On December 25, Christmas Day, many Americans and Europeans exchange gifts. However, the Dutch exchange gifts on St Nicholas Day (December 6), the Russians do it on Frost Man's Day (January 1), and in many Latin countries, as well as in Latin-oriented communities in the US such as Miami, this activity is often carried out on Wise Men's Day (January 6).

Religion also affects politics and business. For example, when the Ayatollah Khomeini assumed control of Iran, Western businesses soon left the country because of the government's attitude toward them. Over the next decade Iran plunged into a major war with Iraq and the economy weakened significantly. Khomeini's policies also caused trouble with other world governments, most notably the US, whose embassy personnel in Tehran were seized and held hostage by the Iranians. Even today the country's religious beliefs continue to affect its political and economic decisions.

Values and attitudes

Values
Basic convictions that people have regarding what is right and wrong, good and bad, important and unimportant

Attitude
A persistent tendency to feel and behave in a particular way toward some object

Values are basic convictions that people have regarding what is right and wrong, good and bad, important and unimportant.[8] An **attitude** is a persistent tendency to feel and behave in a particular way toward some object. Values influence culture, as seen, for example, by the value Americans now assign to equality in the workplace, resulting in legislation and action against gender and racial discrimination, among others. This value change is also reflected in new attitudes toward dealing with those guilty of such discrimination.

One way of examining value differences among cultures is through the use of value scales. Table 5.2 provides an example. Notice that these 13 value scales are presented in terms of polar lists. The values on the left are markedly different from those on the right.

Table 5.2 **Value scales**

One set of values	*A second set of values*
A view of people as essentially bad	A view of people as essentially good
Avoidance or negative evaluations of individuals	Confirming individuals as human beings
A view of individuals as fixed	Seeing individuals as being in process
Resisting and fearing individual differences	Accepting and utilizing individual differences
Utilizing an individual primarily with reference to his/her job description	Viewing an individual as a whole person
Walling off the expression of feelings	Making possible both appropriate expression and effective use of feelings
Maskmanship and game playing	Authentic behavior
The use of status for maintaining power and personal prestige	The use of status for organizationally relevant purposes
Distrusting people	Trusting people
Avoiding facing others with relevant data	Making appropriate confrontation
Avoidance of risk taking	Willingness to risk
A view of process work as being unproductive	Seeing process work as being essential to effective task accomplishment
A primary emphasis on competition	A much greater emphasis on collaboration

Source: Adapted from *Academy of Management Review*, "Organizational Development and National Culture: Where's the Fit?" by Alfred M. Jaegar. Copyright 1986 by Academy of Management. Reproduced with permission of Academy of Management in the format textbook via Copyright Clearance Center.

In examining country cultures in terms of these values, no country fits entirely on one side or the other. Each is represented by a combination of the two lists. Moreover, in most cases cultures are in a state of transition. For example, in recent years the US has been moving toward the right side of Table 5.2, as seen by legislative and social efforts to provide equality for everyone in the workplace.

The attitudes that emanate from values directly influence international business. For example, Russians believe that McDonald's cuisine is superior to their own (value judgment) and are thus willing to stand in long lines in order to eat at these units (attitude). In Japan, Borden's has found that its products are regarded by customers as superior to those of the competition (value), so it sells Lady Borden ice cream and Borden cheese packaged and labeled in English and consumer demand (attitude) remains high. In France, General Foods sells a chewing gum called Hollywood that has a picture of teenagers riding bicycles on a beach because it has found that customers like the direct association with America (value) and this results in high sales (attitude). Similarly, Swiss chocolate manufacturers know that US customers believe Swiss chocolate products are of high quality (value), so that companies emphasize their Swiss origin and thus generate high sales (attitude). And in Japan, the Levi Strauss company touts its brand name because it knows that the Japanese view Levi's as prestige jeans (value) and buy accordingly (attitude). In short, by being aware of the values and attitudes of the people in the culture, a business firm can effectively position its product.[9]

In other cases there are negative attitudes toward foreign-made goods, causing firms to de-emphasize their origin. For example, while there are many foreign-owned businesses in the US, their names give no indication of their foreign ownership: Firestone Tire & Rubber is owned by Bridgestone, a Japanese firm; Ponds (hand cream) is owned by Unilever, a British/Dutch company; the Celanese Corporation is owned by Hoechst, a German firm; and Standard Oil is owned by British Petroleum.

Customs and manners

Customs
Common or established practices

Manners
Behaviors regarded as appropriate in a particular society

Customs are common or established practices. **Manners** are behaviors that are regarded as appropriate in a particular society. Customs dictate how things are to be done; manners are used in carrying them out.[10] For example, it is customary in many countries for diners to eat a salad first before turning to the main course. In carrying out this custom, they use knives and forks, finish all the food on their plate, and, in many cases, have been taught not to talk with food in their mouth.

At the same time, there are many differences in customs and manners, and visitors often find themselves making social gaffes because this is not the way they do things back home. For example, in Arab countries, it is considered bad manners to attempt to shake hands with a person of higher authority unless this individual makes the first gesture to do so, unlike in the US where a person would not hesitate to offer his or her hand regardless of the person's rank. In Latin countries, it is acceptable to show up late for a party, whereas in England and France promptness is valued. In many Western countries, it is acceptable to talk business when golfing since this is often the underlying reason for the golf match, but in Japan business is never discussed over golf. In the US, it is acceptable for a boss to give a secretary roses to express appreciation for helping to close a big deal; in many Latin countries, such action would be seen as a sign of romantic attachment and therefore inappropriate. When negotiating with Russians and East Europeans, it is common to find them initially making large demands and offering very little in return, but, as the negotiations wind down, they typically will make a large number of concessions. This is in contrast to the German style of making early concessions and trying to get the other party to make early counter-concessions.

Customs also dictate the way companies advertise and market their products.[11] For example, in the US, orange juice is touted as a breakfast drink, but in France, it is sold as a refreshment because the French do not drink orange juice with breakfast. In Japan, Maxwell House coffee is simply called Maxwell because the word "house" is confusing to the customers. In Japan, talc products such as baby powder are sold in the form of powder puff rather than in containers because the Japanese do not like the way loose talc shakes out of a container. Moreover, Americans will often use a talc powder after bathing, but the Japanese feel it makes them dirty again. In Mexico and other Latin countries, soup manufacturers sell cans that are large enough to serve four or five people, while in the US a typical can serves one or two people. This is because families in Latin countries tend to be larger. In the US, men buy diamond rings for their fiancées, but in Germany young women typically buy their own diamond ring; and advertising practices by diamond merchants in the two countries differ significantly. Unless business firms understand the customs and manners of the country, they are likely to have trouble marketing their products.[12]

Material goods

Material goods
Objects made by people

Basic economic infrastructure
The primary economic industries, including transportation, communication, and energy

Social infrastructure
The societal underpinnings of an economy; they consist of the country's health, housing, and educational systems

Financial infrastructure
The monetary system of a country; it consists of the nation's banking, insurance, and financial services

Material goods consist of objects that people make. When studying material goods, we examine how people make things (the technologies that are involved) and who makes them and why (the economics of the situation). In examining this element of a culture, it is helpful to look at the **basic economic infrastructure** such as the country's transportation, communications, and energy capabilities; the **social infrastructure**, which consists of the country's health, housing, and education systems; and the **financial infrastructure**, which provides banking, insurance, and financial services to the population.

A society's technology is also important because it influences the national standard of living and helps to account for the country's values and beliefs. If a country is technologically advanced, its people are less likely to believe that fate plays a major role in their lives and are more likely to believe that they can control what happens to them. Their values are also more likely to be materialistic because they have a higher standard of living.

When doing business in technologically advanced countries, businesses need to have up-to-date products that are either less expensive than current offerings or that provide more benefits. In less technologically advanced nations, these goods may be too advanced because the infrastructure will not support their use or because there is no need for them. For example, one of the current state-of-the-art technology products is wireless cellular telephones. However, the demand for these phones in third world countries is limited because these nations cannot fully benefit from such products. Similarly, while more fuel-efficient, price competitive cars are gaining market share in the US, they have not made major inroads in third world countries because of the limited infrastructure (road and highways) and the small need for new automobiles.

Aesthetics

Aesthetics
The artistic tastes of a culture

Aesthetics relates to the artistic tastes of a culture. For example, the aesthetic values of Canadians are different from those of the Chinese as reflected by the art, literature, music, and artistic tastes of the two peoples. In understanding a culture, we need to study how such differences affect behaviors. For example, opera is much more popular in Europe than in the US. This helps explain why some American opera stars first made their mark in Europe before they achieved successful careers at home. On the other hand, in the area of movie making the US sets international standards, while films produced by Europeans and Asian filmmakers often enjoy only limited success. Movies also help to explain how, in some cases, cultural values are becoming international. The impact of the cinema is felt worldwide and movie stars are international celebrities.[13]

However, there are many aspects of aesthetics that make cultures different. For example, in the US, sex is not used in advertising as much as it is in Europe. An advertisement for the Electrolux vacuum cleaner in America touts its "power", whereas in England advertisements note that "nothing sucks like an Electrolux". Another aesthetically related area is color. In many Western countries, the color black is used for mourning, while white is used for joy or purity. In many Asian countries white is the color for mourning. Quite clearly, aesthetic values influence behavior and we need to understand aesthetic values if we are to appreciate another culture and the way in which businesses must address these values in the international arena.

Education

Education influences many aspects of culture. Literate people read widely and have a much better understanding of what is happening in the world. Additionally, higher rates of literacy usually result in greater economic productivity and technological advances. Education also helps to provide the infrastructure needed for developing managerial talent. As a result, education is a critical factor in understanding culture.

One of the most common gauges of education is formal schooling. In most countries of the world schooling is increasing. This helps to explain why the literacy rate in most countries is on the rise. However, these raw data do not relate the quality of education nor do they provide information regarding how well the supply of graduates meets the demand. On the other hand, the data do offer insights about the overall level of education and, at the university level, the areas of specialization. For example, in Japan and South Korea, there is a very strong emphasis given to engineering and the sciences at the university level; and, in Europe, the number of MBAs has increased sharply in recent years. These data provide insights regarding the market potential of a country, as well as the types of goods and services that are likely to be purchased by people. For example, educationally advanced countries like England, France, and Germany are more likely to be markets for computers and other high-tech equipment than are less educated countries such as Poland, the Czech Republic, and Romania. It is also likely that MNEs doing business in these countries will find it easier to recruit and train local managers in Western Europe than in Eastern Europe.[14]

Active learning check 

Review your answer to Active Learning Case question 2 and make any changes you like. Then compare your answer with the one below.

2. How does pop culture help to change country customs and develop universal customs and manners? Give an example.

Pop culture influences and develops universal customs in a number of ways. One is by changing lifestyles. For example, because of McDonald's, many people around the world now eat fast food as part of their regular diet, and Coca-Cola has changed their drinking habits. Movies and television programs have also introduced what is now a universal language. For example, thanks to *Dirty Harry* movies, the saying, "Make my day", is part of the international lexicon. Levi jeans are another example of a trend that has helped to change the dress habits of people throughout the world.

CULTURAL DIMENSIONS

Language, religion, values and attitudes, customs and manners, material goods, aesthetics, and education are elements of culture that explain behavioral differences among people. In recent years researchers have attempted to develop a composite picture of culture by clustering these differences. This has been done in two ways. Some researchers have looked at cultural dimensions that reflect the similarities and differences among cultures. Others have used these findings to group countries into clusters of nations with similar cultures.

Defining cultural dimensions

Geert Hofstede, a Dutch researcher, has defined four cultural dimensions to help explain how and why people from various cultures behave as they do. His initial findings were gathered over 20 years ago from more than 116,000 questionnaires completed by IBM employees from 70 different countries.[15] This is the largest organizationally based culture study ever conducted, and researchers are continuing to investigate and extend the findings. Hofstede's four cultural dimensions are (1) power distance, (2) uncertainty avoidance, (3) individualism, and (4) masculinity.

Power distance

Power distance A cultural dimension which measures the degree to which less powerful members of organizations and institutions accept the fact that power is not distributed equally

Power distance is the degree to which less powerful members of organizations and institutions accept the fact that power is not distributed equally. People in societies where authority is obeyed without question live in a high power distance culture. Hofstede found that many Latin and Asian countries such as Malaysia, the Philippines, Panama, Guatemala, Venezuela, and Mexico were typified by high power distance. In contrast, the US, Canada, and many European countries such as Denmark, Great Britain, and Austria had moderate to low power distance.

In countries with high power distance, managers make autocratic decisions and the subordinates do as they are told. Often these societies have business structures that are typified by close control of operations and a fairly weak work ethic. Organization structures tend to be tall and managers have relatively few subordinates reporting directly to them. In countries with moderate to low power distance, people put a high value on independence, managers consult with subordinates before making decisions, and there is a fairly strong work ethic. Organization structures tend to be flat and managers directly supervise more subordinates than do their counterparts in high power distance enterprises.

Uncertainty avoidance

Uncertainty avoidance The extent to which people feel threatened by ambiguous situations and have created institutions and beliefs for minimizing or avoiding those uncertainties

Uncertainty avoidance is the extent to which people feel threatened by ambiguous situations and have created institutions and beliefs for minimizing or avoiding these uncertainties. Countries with high uncertainty avoidance try to reduce risk and develop systems and methods for dealing with ambiguity. Hofstede found strong uncertainty avoidance in Greece, Uruguay, Guatemala, Portugal, Japan, and Korea. He found weak uncertainty avoidance in countries like Singapore, Sweden, Great Britain, the US, and Canada.

Countries with high uncertainty avoidance tend to formalize organizational activities and depend heavily on rules and regulations to ensure that people know what they are to do. There is often high anxiety and stress among these people, they are very concerned with security, and decisions are frequently a result of group consensus. Low uncertainty avoidance societies have less structuring of activities and encourage managers to take more risks. People here are less stressed, have more acceptance of dissent and disagreement, and rely heavily on their own initiative and ingenuity in getting things done.

Individualism

Individualism
The tendency of people to look after themselves and their immediate family only

Collectivism
The tendency of people to belong to groups who look after each other in exchange for loyalty

Individualism is the tendency of people to look after themselves and their immediate family only. This dimension is in direct contrast with **collectivism**, the tendency of people to belong to groups that look after each other in exchange for loyalty. Hofstede has found that economically advanced countries tend to place greater emphasis on individualism than do poorer countries. For example, the US, Great Britain, the Netherlands, and Canada have high individualism. In contrast, Ecuador, Guatemala, Pakistan, and Indonesia have low individualism.

Countries with high individualism expect people to be self-sufficient. There is a strong emphasis on individual initiative and achievement. Autonomy and personal financial security are given high value, and people are encouraged to make individual decisions without reliance on group support. In contrast, countries with low individualism place a great deal of importance on group decision making and affiliation. No one wants to be singled out for special attention, even for a job well done. Success is collective and individual praise is embarrassing because it implies that one group member is better than the others. Countries with low individualism emphasize belongingness and draw strength from group affiliation.

Masculinity

Masculinity
The degree to which the dominant values of a society are success, money, and material things

Femininity
The degree to which the dominant values of a society are caring for others and the quality of life

Hofstede defines **masculinity** as the degree to which the dominant values of a society are "success, money, and things". This is in contrast to **femininity**, which he defines as the degree to which the dominant values of a society are "caring for others and the quality of life". He found that countries with high masculinity included Japan, Austria, Venezuela, and Mexico. Countries with low masculinity (or high femininity) included Norway, Sweden, Denmark, and the Netherlands. The US had a moderate to high score on masculinity, as did other Anglo countries.

Countries with high masculinity scores place a great deal of importance on earnings, recognition, advancement, and challenge. Achievement is defined in terms of wealth and recognition. These cultures often tend to favor large-scale enterprises and economic growth is viewed as very important. In school, children are encouraged to be high performers and to think about work careers where they can succeed. Countries with low masculinity scores place great emphasis on a friendly work environment, cooperation, and employment security. Achievement is defined in terms of human contacts and the living environment. There is low stress in the workplace and workers are given a great deal of job freedom.

Integrating the dimensions

These four dimensions describe the overall culture of a society and each culture is unique. At the same time, however, many cultures are *similar* to each other. This can be seen from the information in Table 5.3 where the cultural dimension scores from Hofstede's research for 20 select countries are presented. A close look at these scores shows that some of the nations have similar cultures. For example, the US, the UK and Canada, three Anglo countries, have high individualism, moderately high masculinity, low power distance, and low uncertainty avoidance. In these nations managers expect workers to take the initiative and assume responsibility (high individualism), rely on the use of individual (not group) monetary rewards to motivate their personnel (moderate masculinity), treat their employees as important human resources and not act officiously (low power distance), and keep bureaucracy to a minimum (low uncertainty avoidance). A systematic analysis of Hofstede's data for all of the countries in his survey reveals that most of them fall into a particular cultural cluster. Figure 5.1, based on research by

Table 5.3 **Cultural dimensions for 20 select countries in Hofstede's research**

Country	*Power distance*	*Uncertainty avoidance*	*Individualism*	*Masculinity*
Argentina	49	86	46	56
Australia	36	51	90	61
Brazil	69	76	38	49
Canada	39	48	80	52
Denmark	18	23	74	16
France	68	86	71	43
Germany (F.R.)	35	65	67	66
Indonesia	8	48	14	46
India	77	40	48	56
Israel	13	81	54	47
Japan	54	92	46	95
Mexico	81	82	30	69
Netherlands	38	53	80	14
Panama	95	86	11	44
Spain	57	86	51	42
Sweden	31	29	71	5
Thailand	64	64	20	34
Turkey	66	85	37	45
United Kingdom	35	35	89	66
United States	40	46	91	62

Source: Geert Hofstede, 1983. 'The Cultural Relativity of Organizational Practices and Theories', *Journal of International Business Studies*, Fall, pp. 75–89. Reprinted with permission.

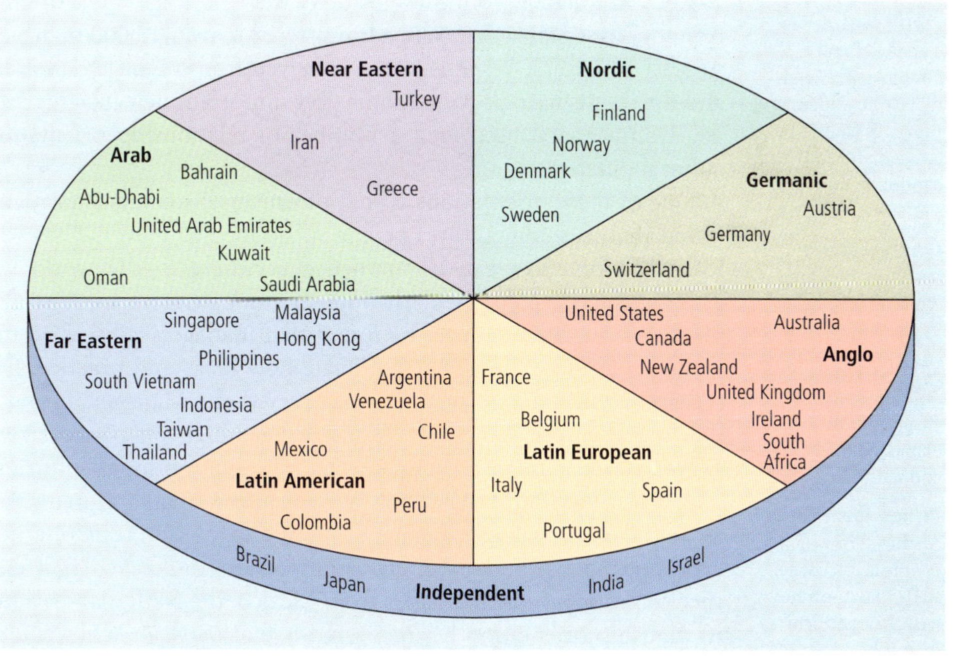

Figure 5.1 **A synthesis of country clusters**

Source: *Academy of Management Journal*, "Clustering Countries on Attitudinal Dimensions: A Review and Synthesis," by Simcha Ronen and Oded Shenkar. Copyright 1985 by Academy of Management. Reproduced with permission of Academy of Management in the format textbook via Copyright Clearance Center.

Simcha Ronen and Oded Shenkar, illustrates this. As you can see, except for four countries (India, Japan, Brazil, and Israel), Ronen and Shenkar were able to place all of Hofstede's nations into one of eight clusters. So Hofstede's research, indeed, has been useful in helping us better understand culture and its importance to international business.

Active learning check 

Review your answer to Active Learning Case question 3 and make any changes you like. Then compare your answer with the one below.

3. How can pop culture in the form of movies, for example, have an effect on the cultural dimensions of a society? Give an example.

Movies influence cultures in that people learn the way things are done in other societies and, in many cases, want to emulate what they see on the screen. For example, to the extent that movies have presented the middle-class lifestyle of Americans, they have helped to increase the drive for materialism among many people and, in the process, increased that society's masculinity score. US movies have also depicted US values of democracy and helped to influence power distance scores. The same can be said for individualism and uncertainty avoidance. Simply put, movies can help to change a country's culture by showing the viewers alternative lifestyles that they may want to pursue.

Recent cultural research

Universalism The belief that ideas and practices can be applied everywhere in the world without modification

Particularism The belief that circumstances dictate how ideas and practices should be applied and something cannot be done the same everywhere

Neutral culture A culture in which emotions are held in check

Emotional culture A culture in which emotions are expressed openly and naturally

Achievement culture A culture in which people are accorded status based on how well they perform their jobs

Ascription culture A culture in which status is attributed based on who or what a person is

In recent years, culture has continued to be a focus of inquiry. In particular, work by another Dutch researcher, Fons Trompenaars, has received a great deal of attention. Trompenaars' work was conducted over a 10-year period and published in the mid-1990s,[16] although he continues to add to these findings.[17] The original data were gathered from questionnaires that were administered to over 15,000 managers from 28 countries. At least 500 usable responses were received from managers in each of these 28 nations and the results have provided some very important new insights into culture. In particular, Trompenaars discovered a number of relationship orientations that help explain cultural differences.

One of these orientations is that of universalism versus particularism. Trompenaars found that in some cultures people subscribed to **universalism** which is the belief that ideas and practices can be applied everywhere in the world without modification. This belief has been particularly popular among American, Australian, German, and UK managers. In other cultures he found that managers subscribed to **particularism** which is the belief that circumstances dictate how ideas and practices should be applied and something cannot be done the same everywhere. Managers from China, Indonesia, and the former Soviet Union, in particular, are high on particularism. Another contrast Trompenaars found was between neutral and emotional cultures. A **neutral culture** is one in which emotions are held in check, as in Japan and many Asian countries as well as, perhaps surprisingly, the UK. An **emotional culture** is one in which emotions are expressed openly and naturally. Trompenaars discovered that emotional cultures are very common among managers from Mexico, the Netherlands, and Switzerland. A third relationship orientation he uncovered is that between achievement and ascription. An **achievement culture** is one in which people are accorded status based on how well they perform their jobs. Trompenaars found this orientation quite dominant in the US and the UK where individual success and accomplishments are applauded. An **ascription culture** is one in which status is attributed based on who or what a person is. For example, an individual who has been with the firm for many years may be listened to because of his or her longevity or because the person is a close friend of the company president. Trompenaars' research reveals that managers in Venezuela, Indonesia, and China, in particular, work in high ascription cultures.

Based on these data, Trompenaars also found that countries could be grouped into clusters. For example, the US and the UK have similar cultures. So too do Asian countries such as Japan, China, Indonesia, and Singapore. The same is true for Latin American countries (Argentina, Mexico, Venezuela, and Brazil), Latin European nations (France, Belgium, Spain, and Italy) and Germanic countries (Austria, Germany, Switzerland, and the former Czechoslovakia).

One thing that is particularly evident from Trompenaars' research is that the way business is done in one part of the world is likely to be different from the way it is done in another. Some American firms that have taken strategies that work well in the US and tried to use them in Japan (an ethnocentric approach) provide a good example. For instance, Office Depot and Office Max have learned that Japanese customers do not like to buy their supplies in large, well-stocked stores that offer discount prices. They prefer small stores where the service is personal – and they are willing to pay higher prices for this convenience. And Spiegel's and Eddie Bauer have learned that they cannot sell the same products in Japan that they do in the US; retail goods have be tailored for the local market.[18]

Internet companies that derive a large portion of their revenues from advertising provide an extreme example of cultural tailoring. Yahoo and MSN, for instance, have different sites for US users, British users, French users, and Japanese users, among others. All sites are written in the country's language and provide country-specific information. This allows these companies to target local advertisers who seek to reach customers in their own markets. See the box "International Business Strategy in Action: A Global Business with a Regional Focus" for another example of a multinational Internet company.

It is clear that culture is an important force in doing business internationally. In this next section we examine the role of culture in strategic management.

INTERNATIONAL BUSINESS STRATEGY *IN ACTION*

CricInfo – a global business with a regional focus

The CricInfo.com website is one of the most widely used in the world. Why? Because cricket is so popular. It is the national sport in India, Pakistan, Sri Lanka, and Bangladesh – over 1 billion people follow the game. Its popularity has turned star players like Indian batsman Sachin Tendulkar into national heroes. Besides the four countries just mentioned, other first class Test Match countries are Australia, England, South Africa, New Zealand, Zimbabwe, and the West Indies. The last, of course, is not a country, but the states of Trinidad, Barbados, Jamaica, and other Caribbean islands, which play together as a federation. Indeed, the West Indies dominated world cricket from the 1970s until the early 1990s, although since then Australia has emerged as the top country. In addition to the team test countries, another 24 nations took part in the Associates Cup in Toronto in July 2001 and three of these qualified for the next World Cup in South Africa in 2002: Holland, Namibia, and Canada. In addition, Kenya will play in the World Cup. So cricket, indeed, is a worldwide popular sport.

CricInfo provides scorecards, statistics, players commentary and "live" commentary on the Internet of games in progress. As a result, the number of users has grown exponentially, making CricInfo.com the third largest sports site on the Internet. It gets up to 200 million hits a month from approximately 15 million users worldwide. The site is now so prosperous that it emerged in 2001 as the lead sponsor for the English Country Championship, the world's oldest competitive cricket league, dating back to Victorian times and the exploits of the legendary founder of modern cricket, Dr W. G. Grace, a Gloucestershire doctor and the sporting equivalent of Babe Ruth in baseball. In contrast, however, cricket attracts far more followers worldwide than does baseball.

CricInfo's annual revenues are US $3 million and it has web pages in 89 countries. The firm's main revenue streams are advertising/sponsorship, e-commerce, content syndication, and licensing deals. Apart from the appeal of its contents, CricInfo is also revolutionizing advertising on the Internet. Using the same URL, a cricket fan in Perth, Australia and a cricket fan in Mumbai, India can receive geographically targeted advertising even if they are following the same game. The multinational nature of the website makes this a necessity.

In partnership with Covigo, a wireless platform provider, a mobile version of CricInfo was launched in 2001 to access the websites of 15 million users through wireless phones. This will allow fans to follow games even when away from computer screens or televisions. Although the firm is still losing money, this is expected to change by 2003 as more advertisers capitalize on the website's ability to reach large numbers of people in key global markets. Among other things, CricInfo shows that the marketing of global sports has to be done with a regional focus.

Websites: **www.cricinfo.com** and **www.covigo.com**.

Sources: "Nigel Cope: Six Success Stories to Watch in the Bombed-out dot.com sector," *Independent*, March 26, 2001; ***www.cricinfo.com***; "The UK's Most Popular Website Goes Mobile," Covigo Press Release, February 20, 2001.

CULTURE AND STRATEGIC MANAGEMENT

Culture influences strategic management in a number of ways from the management style that is used in dealing with international employees to the type of work attitudes that the personnel exhibit to the way in which people manage their time. Culture even helps explain why behaviors that are regarded as unethical in one country are socially acceptable in another. The following examines each of these areas.

Management styles

Mergers and acquisitions (M&As) are proving to be one of the most common ways of gaining an international foothold and/or expanding worldwide operations. When an M&A involves companies from two different cultures, however, this can lead to a misunderstanding of how things should be done or, worse yet, a clash of culture that results in lost effectiveness and morale. As an example of the first, consider the case of the Upjohn Company of Kalamazoo, Michigan which merged with Pharmacia AB of Sweden, which also had operations in Italy. In order to get the merger off to a smooth start, the Americans decided that they and their Swedish and Italian partners should get together as soon as possible, meet each other, discuss their current and future product lines, and begin formulating a comprehensive strategy that could be rolled out beginning the following January. Since the summer was almost upon them and the Americans wanted to get going quickly, they suggested that July and August be set aside for these meetings. Despite their best intentions, however, the US managers failed to realize that their management style, which might be partially described by the cliché "time is money", was unacceptable to their new partners. Why? Because, as the *Wall Street Journal* put it, "Swedes take off the entire month of July for vacation, virtually en masse, and Italians take off August. *Everyone* in Europe knows this, but apparently *hardly anyone* in Kalamazoo, Michigan does."[19] As a result, the summer meetings were not held. Everything had to be rescheduled and the partners eventually had to meet and talk not only about strategy but also about their cultural differences, so that each could better understand the management styles of the other.

Sometimes M&As have a far more significant impact than just misunderstandings that need to be ironed out. In recent years managers in companies that have been acquired by foreign firms have complained that the culture of the acquiring company is radically different from their own. As a result, the management styles of the two groups result in personality clashes, lower morale, and the loss of key personnel. For example, after Daimler-Benz bought Chrysler, it quickly became evident that Daimler intended to run things its own way. Then, in short order, many of the senior-level Americans were either terminated or chose to leave because they did not like the new management style. Included in this group were most of the key auto design people who were responsible for some of Chrysler's biggest market successes in the late 1990s including the PT Cruiser. Today a number of these individuals have now been hired by General Motors, which is hoping that these auto design managers can do the same thing for it that they did for Chrysler. Meanwhile Daimler has decided to delegate more authority to the US managers for North American operations because it now realizes that its German culture approach is not working.

The above example is not unique. Recent research reports that foreign acquisitions account for one-sixth of all M&As in the US[20] and it is likely that this percentage holds for many other countries as well. In addition, researchers have found that in the US following an M&A an average of 20 per cent of the company's top management team will leave within the first year and 70 per cent will be gone within five years.[21] What accounts for these results? Executives who have been involved in foreign acquisitions report that some of the main reasons include differences in management styles, communication problems, the difficulties of developing trust, and the belief that the foreign firm lacks an understanding of how the local company does business. Here are some select comments by senior executives of three US companies that were purchased by foreign firms:

> *Acquired by a Japanese firm*
> They had little insight into American management and culture. Little understanding of US markets. They had problems understanding our marketplace versus theirs on identical product lines. There was greater involvement in daily operations. People were placed into our operation. Their staff attempted to hand down directives with little or no knowledge of how our operation was run. They had a poor attitude toward women in industry.
>
> *Acquired by a Finnish firm*
> The greatest issue was foreign versus US culture as opposed to company culture (i.e., language and how it is interpreted). National cultures were very different. We were open, friendly, quick to decide. The Finnish acquirer was more closed, argumentative, distrustful, and prone to endless discussion. Lack of trust, language differences, distribution channels, work habits, country cultures, and humor were problems. They were bureaucratic, dogmatic, political, and very much into form over substance.
>
> *Acquired by a British firm*
> British, colonial, male only, totally out of step with American meritocracy. British old school tie versus "up-and-at-em" US tigers. US companies were much more aggressive – more risk taking, more delegation, more bias to action. They were bureaucratic, cold, and short-term oriented. Short-term profits became essential. Management was not people oriented. They blamed employees for industry problems and hard times. The management style of the UK parent was basically a parent–child relationship. There was a total absence of understanding of the US company's business and culture and no real interest in learning about them.[22]

These responses are undoubtedly similar to those made by foreign firms acquired by American companies. In short, both the national and the organizational culture of the acquirer influences the way it tries to manage the purchased firm. In the process, the acquirer often tries to use its management style to run things and this creates a clash with the managers in the acquired company who are accustomed to doing things differently. For an example of the European dairy industry's international expansion, see the box "International Business Strategy in Action: Danone and Parmalat – going international, staying local".

INTERNATIONAL BUSINESS STRATEGY *IN ACTION*

Danone and Parmalat – going international, staying local

The dairy industry, in the main, is a local industry. Most dairy products sold at local supermarkets come from processing plants within a 500-mile radius. However, this does not mean that these firms are all small, local operations. On the contrary, there are a small number of very large MNEs in this industry that do business worldwide and target their dairy offerings to local demand. The best known of these is Nestlé, which began operations in 1904 when it opened evaporated milk factories in both Europe and the US. Today the company is the largest dairy company in the world and has operations in 86 countries. There are a couple of other large competitors as well, although they do not compete on as broad a scale.

One of these is Danone, a French MNE whose annual revenues of euros 14.3 billion ($13.2 billon) make it one of the world's 500 largest firms. The company's product line is not as broad as Nestlé's, but it is just as big as the Swiss MNE in the dairy sector. Danone has operations in 120 countries and employs over 86,000 people. However, its primary base is Europe where it generates 24 per cent of its revenues in France and another 35 per cent more throughout the rest of Europe.

Danone was originally a Spanish yogurt producer that merged with the French firm Gervais in 1967. Then in 1973 the company merged with BSN, a glass manufacturer, and adopted the packaging capability of the glass system to the food business. However, the glass business was dropped in the late 1970s and since then Danone has focused on defining its place in the dairy industry and determining how it can better address the cultural demands of its local customers. With the decision to focus most heavily in Europe and to take advantage of the expanding EU, Danone has now set up centralized purchasing and research departments in order to obtain economies of scale in food distribution across the Continent. At the same time the company has been looking to gain a greater presence in other markets including North America and recently took a 40 per cent stake in Stonyfield Farm, an organic yogurt maker based in Londonderry, New Hampshire. While Stonyfield will continue to operate autonomously, this firm's strong customer relations program and its expertise in marketing fast-growing organic products provides Danone the opportunity to further increase its US market share to exploit the strengths of its new acquisition.

And to ensure that it continues to focus on its main business of dairy food, Danone has sold off its grocery business and withdrawn from brewing and packaging. Today the company's efforts are being directed most heavily toward the distribution of French-made dairy products. So in both Europe and its worldwide markets, Danone is working to answer the question: How can we develop and market French-made dairy products that meet the needs of the local market?

The other major global rival to Nestlé is the Italian MNE, Parmalat. Like Danone, Parmalat markets a wide variety of dairy products including milk, yogurt, desserts, butter, and cheese. Yet the company is best known for its development of ultra high temperature pasteurized milk (UHT) that lasts up to six months without refrigeration. By specializing in the production and distribution of UHT milk across Europe, Parmalat was able to cut both production and distribution costs and to increase its profitability. At the same time, and unlike Danone, the company has been more vigorous in its international expansion. In addition to moving into France and Germany in the 1970s, the company began expanding into North and South America soon thereafter. As a result, today Parmalat earns 32 per cent of its revenues in Europe, 31 per cent in North and Central America, and another 29 per cent from South America. Australia and Asia account for the remaining 8 per cent.

Like its two other competitors, Nestlé and Danone, Parmalat carefully targets its products to the local market and seeks to acquire local companies that have established markets. For example, Parmalat has purchased Ault Dairies, one of Canada's largest operations, as well as Beatrice Foods, another major Canadian firm. Today Parmalat is that country's largest dairy firm. Parmalat also has its subsidiaries employ the company's food expertise to exploit their local markets. For example, drawing on its UHT technology, Parmalat's Australian subsidiary has been able to export milk products throughout the Asian market and the company's Argentinian subsidiary, which specializes in UHT milk products, has been able to create export markets in Brazil and Venezuela. In addition, in catering to local tastes the company has developed a wide variety of products such as a dessert called *dulce de leche*, which it now exports to a large number of countries including the US, the UK, Russia, Spain, Uruguay, and Venezuela.

Danone and Parmalat are good examples of companies that sell products that are culturally influenced. In Danone's case, it has chosen to do so by staying primarily in Europe. Parmalat, on the other hand, has been much more active in the larger international arena. Both, however, have been successful because they have been able to blend their expertise with the needs of their specific markets.

Websites: ***www.danone.com***; ***www.parmalat.net*** and ***www.nestle.com***.

Sources: ***www.danone.com; www.parmalat.net***; "A Small Town's Big Cheeses," *Economist*, May 29, 1997; and Nikhil Deogun, "Danone Group Scoops Up 40% Stake in Stonyfield Farm," *Wall Street Journal*, October 4, 2001, p. B 9.

Work attitudes

A second way in which culture influences strategic management is the way it impacts on work attitudes, which are important to MNEs because these attitudes influence both the quality and quantity of employee output.[23] For example, workers in Anglo cultures are taught to believe in the work ethic, but this ethic is not unique to these cultures. As noted earlier, many people around the world believe in hard work – and it shows in their attitudes. In many Asian countries, for example, job attendance is viewed as a major responsibility and *everyone* comes to work *every* day. One researcher, commenting on the Japanese, has noted that 100 per cent work attendance is critical, and "men and women, in whatever role or rank, must make a commitment to the things they do and show it by being there".[24] Another common cultural work attitude among Asians is that they remain on the job for the entire workday, in contrast to people in other areas of the world who believe that, if they can get their work done early, they should be allowed to go home.[25] In Japan, if someone were to do this, it might well be misinterpreted. Here is an example reported by a researcher:

> A student of mine from Japan told me the story of his good friend who worked at . . . a major bank and had been kept exceptionally late at work for a period of months in order to complete a major project. When the project was complete, the section chief sent the staff home early every day for a week. After two days of coming home in the afternoon, his mother, with whom he lived, confronted the young man. "Please," she asked him, "go to a bar, go play *pachinko*, but don't come home so early. The neighbors are stopping me on the sidewalk to ask whether you are having troubles at work, and it is embarrassing to have to explain to everyone".[26]

Another important aspect of work attitude is organizational commitment. Research shows that US factory workers are very committed to their companies; so, too, are Japanese workers. Although many people would have anticipated this finding, they are unlikely to have realized two additional facts: (1) worker commitment among US factory employees is almost as high as that of their counterparts in Japan, and (2) job satisfaction is higher among US factory workers than among Japanese factory workers.[27] These data are presented in Table 5.4 and help to shed light on the similarities of work attitudes in the two countries. It is likely that both Americans and Japanese would be surprised by the results of this research, which involved over 8,300 workers from both countries and is the largest and most detailed body of survey information on US and Japanese factory workers undertaken to date.

International research reveals that work is important to many people. This has been clearly illustrated through research on work goals and what individuals are looking for in their jobs. Table 5.5 reports the importance of a series of work goals among workers in seven different countries. A close look at the table shows that interesting work, on average, is the most important objective. Moreover, the researchers found that this finding is consistent internationally and holds true for different organizational levels, for men and women, and for all age categories.[28] People want interesting work.

Commenting on this research, Itzhak Harpaz has noted that the major findings have a number of practical implications. For example, the emphasis that employees give to interesting work points to the need for challenging, meaningful jobs. Additionally, when the work is interesting and challenging, the personnel are willing to exert greater effort. This has led Harpaz to conclude that "intrinsically motivated employees are concerned with the expressive aspects of work life (i.e., interesting work, autonomy, advancement), not necessarily for the purpose of securing more financial rewards, but because these very rewards are associated with intrinsically motivating jobs".[29]

Table 5.4 Organizational commitment and job satisfaction among US and Japanese factory workers

	United States	*Japanese*
Organizational commitment		
(1 = strongly agree; 5 = strongly disagree)		
Willingness to work harder than is necessary in order for the company to succeed	3.91	3.44
Willingness to take any job in order to continue working for the company	3.12	3.07
Perceived similarity between personal values and those of the company	3.15	2.68
Pride in working for the company	3.70	3.51
Willingness to turn down another job with more pay in order to stay with the company	2.71	2.68
Feeling of very little loyalty to the company	3.45	3.40
Job satisfaction		
Overall satisfaction with the job (0 = not at all; 4 = very)	2.95	2.12
Willingness to recommend this type of work to a friend (0 = no; 2 = yes)	1.52	0.91
Willingness to take this job again, if starting all over (0 = no; 2 = yes)	1.61	0.84
How well the job measures up to the type of work that was desired when starting out this job (0 = not what was wanted; 2 = exactly what was wanted)	1.20	0.43

Source: Adapted from James R. Lincoln, "Employee Work Attitudes and Management Practice in the United States and Japan: Evidence from a Large Comparative Survey," *California Management Review*, Fall 1989, p. 91. © 1989 by The Regents of the University of California. Reprinted from the *California Management Review*, vol. 32, no. 1. By permission of the Regents.

Table 5.5 Average and intra-country ranking of work goals: a seven nation comparison

Work goals	*Belgium*	*Britain*	*Germany*	*Israel*	*Japan*	*Netherlands*	*United States*
Opportunity to learn	5.8*	5.55	4.97	5.83	6.26	5.38	6.16
	7†	8	9	5	7	9	5
Interpersonal relations	6.34	6.33	6.43	6.67	6.39	7.19	6.08
	5	4	4	2	6	3	7
Opportunity for promotion	4.49	4.27	4.48	5.29	3.33	3.31	5.08
	10	11	10	8	11	11	10
Convenient work hours	4.71	6.11	5.71	5.53	5.46	5.59	5.25
	9	5	6	7	8	8	9
Variety	5.96	5.62	5.71	4.89	5.05	6.86	6.10
	6	7	6	11	9	4	6
Interesting work	8.25	8.02	7.26	6.75	6.38	7.59	7.41
	1	1	3	1	2	2	1
Job security	6.80	7.12	7.57	5.22	6.71	5.68	6.30
	3	3	2	10	4	7	3
Match between the people and the work	5.77	5.63	6.09	5.61	7.83	6.17	6.19
	8	6	5	6	1	6	4
Pay	7.13	7.80	7.73	6.60	6.56	5.27	6.82
	2	2	1	3	5	5	2
Working conditions	4.19	4.87	4.39	5.28	4.18	5.03	4.84
	11	9	11	9	10	10	11
Autonomy	6.56	4.69	5.66	6.00	6.89	7.61	5.79
	4	10	8	4	3	1	8

* First row shows average rank on a scale of 1 to 10.
† Second row shows ranking of work goals within each country, with a rank of 1 being *most* important and 11 being *least* important.

Source: Adapted from Itzhak Harpaz, "The Importance of Work Goals: An International Perspective," *Journal of International Business Studies*, vol. 21, no. 1 (First Quarter 1990), p. 81.

Achievement motivation

Achievement motivation
The desire to accomplish objectives and attain success

Another cultural factor, closely linked to work attitudes, is **achievement motivation** as reflected by the desire to accomplish objectives and attain success. How achievement driven are people across the world? Achievement drive in the US and EU countries tends to be high. It is also increasing in Japan, where recent evidence points to a growing number of Japanese who are now embracing what is being called the "era of personal responsibility". No longer are many Japanese looking to their company or the government to ensure their future – they are doing it for themselves. In fact, at the opening of a recent conference on economic change, the vice-chairman of the country's largest business lobby summed up this thinking when he said, "By establishing personal responsibility, we must return dynamism to the economy and revitalize society".[30] At the same time, recent research reveals that achievement drive in places like Eastern Europe is not very high.[31] Industry managers in the former Czechoslovakia, for example, have much lower achievement drive than do American managers. As Eastern Europe makes the transition from a command economy to a market economy, however, this is likely to change. After all, the need for achievement is a learned need, largely determined by the prevailing culture and, if Eastern European countries are going to succeed in the competitive environments of the 21st century, they will have to foster high achievement motivation among their people.

The same is true in China. Research conducted among Chinese managers soon after the country began moving toward a market-driven economy found that most managers placed low value on such things as earnings, promotion, and challenging work – goals that are ranked very important by high achievers. Over the last two decades, however, there has been a change in Chinese culture and achievement drive is increasing. One recent study found that Chinese employees are now much more economically oriented than previously and many workers favor reward systems that give *more* to high performers than to others. So the seeds of achievement motivation drive are taking root in China.[32] This is good news for MNEs and certainly helps explain why a country like Singapore has done so well. Research among second generation Singaporean Chinese businesspeople has found that many of them have the characteristics of high achievers: a willingness to take risks, a desire for autonomy, individualism, a willingness to actively search the environment for opportunities, initiative, and ambition.[33] This may well be one of the reasons why, despite a recent downturn in the South East Asian economy, Singapore has continued to be relatively economically successful.[34]

Active learning check 

Review your answer to Active Learning Case question 4 and make any changes you like. Then compare your answer with the one below.

4. Can pop culture help to encourage achievement motivation in people? How?

Pop culture can help to encourage achievement motivation in two ways. One is through movies and television fare that show a lifestyle that people would like to emulate. A second is by creating a desire in people to copy the famous artists that they see and hear. In both cases individuals would have to work hard to achieve the success, fame, and fortune that others have acquired through their own efforts. To the extent that pop culture convinces people that they, too, can achieve bountiful rewards, the culture serves to build high achievement motivation in people.

Time and the future

Still another element of culture that has an important effect on how MNEs carry out their strategy is the society's view of time. In some European cultures it is important to be on time, while in other cultures tardiness is acceptable behavior. Similarly, in some African cultures time is not a constraint; in fact, lateness is acceptable behavior.[35] As noted earlier in the chapter, the same is true in many Latin cultures of both South America and Europe.

Sometimes a culture's view of time directly influences decision making. For example, Japanese managers are known to take a long time to make up their minds to do something. However, once they have decided on a plan of action, implementation takes place fairly quickly. This is in direct contrast to many Western cultures where decisions to proceed are often made quickly, but commitment is much slower in coming.

Sometimes the culture's view of time influences long-term strategy. For example, foreign MNEs have found that firms in the Far East, especially Japanese companies, are very long-range in their planning efforts and they do not expect to generate a quick return on their investment. These firms are willing to invest today and wait 5 to 10 years to earn an adequate profit. This makes the companies particularly attractive to US firms looking for investors. A good example is Walt Disney, which has raised almost $1 billion from Japanese investors in return for making them limited partners in movies produced by Disney.[36] The financial arrangement is ideal for both sides. Disney gets interest-free capital that it can use to make films; and the investors have future earnings that, if the movies are successful (as are most Disney films), will provide a handsome return on investment.

Ethics

Ethics
A set of moral principles and values that govern behavior

Another area, often overlooked in the examination of culture's effect on strategic management, is that of ethics. **Ethics** is standards of conduct and morality. The way business is done in one country can be different from the way it is done in another because of the accepted standards of moral behavior. For example, in triad nations product piracy and counterfeiting are illegal. However, in many countries in Asia MNEs have found that their patents, copyrights, and trademarks are not respected and the government, at best, is helpless to prevent it and, at worst, does not care. The music business is a good example. The International Federation of Phonographic Industries has estimated that music piracy in China in one recent year cost the industry $620 million and in the worldwide market the total was $5 billion![37] Another common piracy area is film. Within a week of the US release of *Dr Seuss: How the Grinch Stole Christmas* DVD copies were selling on China's streets for about US $1.20 each;[38] and Hollywood hits such as *Gladiator* and *Shanghai Noon* could be purchased on DVD for $2 in movie lobbies, soon after they were first shown in American theatres.[39] One reason for this problem is that China's legal system is riddled with loopholes that make it easy to avoid punishment. In particular, evidence of prior sales is required before a counterfeiter faces criminal liability. As a result, few offenders ever go to prison, and regulators largely ignore those who knowingly assist counterfeiters by providing such things as transportation, storage, and raw materials.[40] Violations of patents, copyrights, and trademarks are simply not regarded as unethical by most Chinese (or Asians, for that matter), the majority of whom do not understand why these forms of intellectual property rights should be protected in the first place. MNEs have to consider this type of cultural thinking as they do business in Asia.

Other ethical issues in the workplace include equal opportunity and freedom from a hostile work environment. These issues have proved very important to MNEs doing business in the US and the EU, in particular, where there are laws guaranteeing the rights of employees – and they are rigidly enforced. In the US, Japanese MNEs have found themselves facing lawsuits from women and minorities who have charged that they are systematically discriminated against in the workplace in terms of equal opportunity; and some of these firms have been hit with sexual harassment lawsuits. For example, the Equal Employment Opportunity Commission charged Mitsubishi with sexual harassment of more than 300 women and the company became a target of picketing and a boycott by the US National Organization for Women and other activist groups. The firm eventually settled the suit, agreeing, among other things, to donate $100,000 to women's causes and to make substantial cash payments to some of those who brought lawsuits of their own.[41]

Nor is this problem confined to Asian firms doing business in the US. Companies in the UK, for example, are finding that discrimination lawsuits brought by employees are becoming more common. In 1994 approximately 4,500 sex and race discrimination lawsuits were filed with employment tribunals in England and Wales. By 2000 this number was in excess of 8,000, an increase of over 75 per cent.[42] In one of these lawsuits, a woman working as an investment banker at Deutsche Bank's London office and earning over $400,000 annually resigned and sued the company for sex discrimination. She won her case before a tribunal and received an out-of-court settlement of over $1.4 million. Most settlements involve much smaller sums, but with the large increase in the number of lawsuits many MNEs in the UK are realizing that they need to take action to ensure that they are not sued. At the same time, the legal system in the UK continues to change, making it easier to sue for bias, raising the amounts that can be awarded, shifting the burden of proof from claimants to defendants, and allowing third parties such as the Equal Opportunities Commission to sue on behalf of individuals. Given this changing environment, a growing number of firms doing business in the UK are now starting to adopt a much more proactive stance regarding discrimination. Examples such as these help illustrate how culture affects ethical standards in a country and, in turn, influences the strategies of MNEs.

KEY POINTS

1. Culture is the acquired knowledge that people use to interpret experience and to generate social behavior. There are two major problems that culture creates for those doing business internationally: understanding the cultures of these other countries and learning how to adapt to these cultures.
2. There are a number of key elements of culture. These elements, working in tandem, can create a complex, multidimensional environment in which outsiders have a great deal of trouble understanding how and why the local people act as they do. Some of the major key elements include language, religion, values and attitudes, customs and manners, material goods, aesthetics, and education.
3. While the elements of culture help to explain behavioral differences between people, in recent years researchers have attempted to develop a composite picture of culture by clustering or grouping nations based on these differences. One way in which this clustering has been done is through the use of cultural dimensions: power distance, uncertainty avoidance, individualism, and masculinity. Figure 5.1 provides an example of how these dimensions can be examined in terms of country clusters.
4. In addition to the cultural dimensions that were uncovered by Hofstede's research among IBM employees in the 1980s, more recent work by Trompenaars has provided additional insights into ways of examining the impact of culture on behavior. In particular, this includes consideration of whether the culture subscribes more to a belief in universalism or particularism, is a neutral or emotional culture, and the importance of achievement and ascription in the accordance of status.

5. MNEs must be particularly concerned with the ways in which local cultures can impact on their operations. Some of these primary considerations include management styles, work attitudes, achievement motivation, the importance of time, and the impact of ethics. Examples of each were discussed in the chapter.

KEY TERMS

- culture
- ethnocentrism
- Protestant work ethic
- Confucian work ethic
- Shinto work ethic
- values
- attitude
- customs
- manners
- material goods
- basic economic infrastructure
- social infrastructure
- financial infrastructure
- aesthetics
- power distance
- uncertainty avoidance
- individualism
- collectivism
- masculinity
- femininity
- universalism
- particularism
- neutral culture
- emotional culture
- achievement culture
- ascription culture
- achievement motivation
- ethics

REVIEW AND DISCUSSION QUESTIONS

1. In your own words, what is meant by the term *culture*?
2. In what way do ethnocentrism and misconceptions about other cultures inhibit those doing business internationally?
3. Why is language so critical in understanding international culture? How can this problem be dealt with effectively?
4. In what way is religion a cultural barrier for those doing business internationally? Give an example.
5. What is a value? What is an attitude? In what way are these elements critical to understanding the behaviors of other cultures?
6. What are customs? What are manners? Why does an MNE need to know about international customs and manners?
7. In what way are material goods an important element in understanding international behavior? Discuss and explain two examples.
8. Why would an MNE be interested in learning about a country's aesthetics? Give an example.
9. Education is important because it influences so many aspects of culture. What does this statement mean? Be complete in your answer.
10. In what way do the following cultural dimensions influence behavior: power distance, uncertainty avoidance, individualism, and masculinity? In your answer, be sure to define these four dimensions.
11. In what way has Trompenaars' research helped us better understand culture and its effect on behavior? Cite two examples.
12. In what way do mergers and acquisitions sometimes cause management style problems for MNEs? Give an example.
13. Why are work attitudes of importance to MNEs? Cite and describe two examples.
14. Why would companies interested in doing business overseas be concerned with the achievement motivation of the personnel in that geographic area?
15. In what way is time a cultural element that is of interest to MNEs in the strategic process?
16. How can ethics present a cultural problem for multinationals? Give two examples.

REAL CASE

Skandia: Swedish Internet insurance for the world

The impact of culture on goods and services can be seen everywhere.

For example, in some countries the primary function of a wristwatch is to tell time. Buyers in many third world countries want an inexpensive, but highly reliable unit. In more advanced economies, however, a wristwatch is often part of a person's dress ensemble. So a businesswoman in the EU is likely to have an everyday watch, another for work, and still a third for social occasions. And the watches that sell well to EU businesswomen are often quite different from those that are popular with their US counterparts.

Culture also has an effect on the way business is done in the financial services and insurance industries. For example, in some countries people place a very high value on savings and frugality. When it comes to insurance, these individuals are interested in life insurance policies that will protect their family in case of their death and they want to invest the remainder of their savings in solid, growth funds or stocks that have good track records. In other countries people are more interested in buying minimum life insurance coverage and are much greater risk takers, more than willing to invest the bulk of their money in high-tech stocks.

In recent years a number of companies have begun to realize that, by using the Internet to sell insurance and financial services, they can tailor-make packages for a wide number of international market niches, thus appealing to all groups from low risk investors to high risk takers. One of the most successful of these firms has been the Skandia Group, a Stockholm-based insurance and financial service company.

Skandia is not new in the insurance business. The firm was founded over 150 years ago and in 1900 it became the first non-British insurance firm to enter the US market. However, Skandia incurred big losses in the San Francisco earthquake of 1906 and even more losses during World War I. As a result, the company's international operations became largely dormant with most of its efforts confined to reinsurance (business accepted from another company in order to diversify the overall risk).

In 1986, however, the Assurance and Financial Services (AFS) Division of Skandia, headed by CEO Jan Carendi, began a big push in the US market and over the next 12 years the division grew by 45 per cent annually. In particular, the company began by offering a unit-linked variable life insurance product to independent insurance brokers – and it did all of this over the Internet. As a result, by 1998 the unit was able to generate sales of $3.5 billion while employing fewer than 2,000 people. Basically, what Skandia did was to purchase mutual funds from other companies, include its own insurance package within it, and then sell the package to customers who now were able to purchase life insurance as part of a retirement savings plan. In the process, Carendi transformed the AFS division from a traditional bricks and mortar insurance company into a "clicks and mortar" virtual organization. He also retrained managers so that they would be more flexible, innovative, and responsive to the consumers. So while customers might not see their insurance agent face-to-face, the products were carefully designed to meet their needs and any questions or concerns were handled via the Internet. Carendi also devised a strategy for ensuring that Skandia's offerings were current and appealing, while also ensuring that profits were carefully managed. An actuarial division was created at Skandia to design new insurance products. A sales and marketing group that would sell directly to consumers was put together. In addition, an investment management group was formed and charged with investing the premiums; and an administrative group was organized for managing customer, accounting, and regulatory paperwork.

At the same time, many of the traditional insurance functions were outsourced, so that AFS could focus its efforts on developing new products and using the Internet to expand operations. In the US, characterized by a strong economy and investors who were willing to buy products tied to high-tech growth, the 1990s proved to be boom times for the firm. However, the dot.com bust of 2001 brought this market to a screeching halt. By July 2001 sales of variable annuities were down 50 per cent from the previous year. To offset this loss of income, AFS is now diversifying into more stable markets like Germany, Japan, and Spain in an effort to recover its earlier profitability levels. At the same time, the company's actuaries are busy creating new, more cautious products for US investors. Yet one thing is clear: Skandia is convinced that there are customers worldwide who will buy insurance and financial services if the package is properly tailored. It's all a matter of understanding what the people in that culture want.

Websites: **www.skandia.com**.

Source: Christopher A. Bartlett, *Skandia AFS*, HBS Case 9-396-412 (Boston MA: Harvard Business School, 1996); "Skandia: Client Focus Brings Spectacular Rewards," *Financial Times*, June 23, 2000; Skandia, *Annual Report*, 2000.

1. **Which one of the elements of culture is of most importance to Skandia? Why?**
2. **In creating new products for the worldwide market, how would the products that sell well in the US be different from those that sell well in Europe? Explain.**
3. **How does this case illustrate the role and importance of the Internet in doing business in a multicultural business environment?**

REAL CASE

Cultural differences in international sports

One of the best examples of the impact of international culture can be found in the area of sports. Today, there is no "global" sport. Rather, professional sports are organized more on a triad than on a global basis. While sports are important to the service sector, they tend to be confined to local regions.

For example, in North America the most popular sports are baseball, football, basketball, and hockey. In particular, the first three of these are deeply embedded in the US culture. In baseball, every American child knows that Babe Ruth was a great home run hitter and that Mark McGuire, Sammy Sosa, and Barry Bonds all broke Ruth's home run record. In football, many people follow both their favorite college team as well as pro team. On a given Saturday during football season, millions of Americans sit in front of their television sets to watch college football and they do the same the next day, when the pros play. Monday Night Football always draws one of the largest audiences of the week; and whether or not they regularly watch football on TV, the Super Bowl, matching the two finalists, will typically attract one of the largest audiences of the year. Basketball is played everywhere in America and at the professional level many teams play to sold-out arenas. Everyone knows the rules of the game and the names of the great players. Even young children know that "Michael" was the greatest player in the history of the game – and no one has to tell them Michael's last name. Hockey is less popular although there is a professional hockey league in the US and Canada and it is big business in the US – especially in the large cities that have franchises such as New York, Chicago, and Miami.

On the other hand, these American sports are not very popular in other geographic areas. For example, professional baseball is played in Canada, which has two teams that are part of Major League Baseball, and one of these teams, the Toronto Blue Jays, won the World Series in both 1992 and 1993. (One of the players was a Canadian, while the rest were all Americans.) And there is a professional baseball league in Japan. But that's about as far as the sport's international grasp extends. And while American football is played in Canada (Canadian Football League) it is not a commercially viable sport in either Europe or Asia. Basketball is played in the Olympics, but just about all of the great athletes who play against the US team are also members of the Professional Basketball Association and they make their living playing basketball in America. They simply suit up for their home country for the Olympics and, when the Games are over, they return to the US to play for their team there. Ice hockey has some popularity in northern European countries such as Russia, Sweden, Finland, Norway, and the UK, but it accounts for but a small fraction of the popularity it enjoys in North America.

In Europe, meanwhile, professional football (soccer) is the major sport. Over 100 countries have football leagues and some Europeans view it as a global sport. Yet even this game is not a truly "global" business, although the top teams do compete in national leagues and qualify for regional and triad competitions. For example, Manchester United won the "triple" of the English football league, the FA Cup, and the European Cup in the 1998–1999 season. It then competed with a Brazilian team for an intercontinental cup in November 1999. In turn, the Brazilian team qualified through its national league and Latin American playoffs. And there is even a World Cup for which teams compete every four years. Participation is based on regional qualifications – basically from Europe, the Americas, Africa, and East Asia, but the nature of the competition is regional, not global. Even the football teams have strong regional brand names, with only a handful (like Manchester United) having a presence in other triad markets. And even in the case of Manchester United, there is no interest in the game in the US.

Cricket and rugby are still other examples of sports that are regional in focus. However, these games are played mainly by British Commonwealth countries and have little or no presence in the other two parts of the triad (Japan and North America).

One sport that does seem to be global in focus is Formula One car racing. Races occur around the world, there is a set of 10 or so international racing teams, and major advertising sponsors are eager to gain global exposure through their sponsorship. Yet, again, Formula One car racing is a regional business. The legacy and the history of the sport are European. Races take place primarily in Europe and most of the teams are European (although they have strategic alliances with US and Japanese producers). In fact, only two of the Formula One races take place in North America (Montreal and Indianapolis). Moreover, the most popular auto race in the US is the Indianapolis 500 and more people see this race than either of the Formula One races held in North America.

Another sport that appears to be global is that of professional tennis. However, the circuit of professional events takes place mostly in Europe. In particular, there are tournaments that are built around "grand slam" events in Australia, France, the UK, and the US. And while the sponsors are MNEs, the organization and delivery of each of these professional events is a local responsibility. The same is true of professional golf which has institutionalized triad rivalry in the form of the Ryder Cup, which is competed for by US and European players every two years. Although a few of the better European players also compete in some of the major US events, such as the Masters, the US Open, and PGA tournaments, the European tour is now a solid rival to the formerly US tour and even manages to attract US players to its events. And to complete the triad emphasis, a new Asian golf tour has now been developed. However, there is no global golf business – instead, it is triad-based and as it develops it becomes even less global and more regional.

What are the implications for managers of this analysis of professional sports? There are two. First, it is important to work closely with the national or local leagues since these sports are regional in focus. Second, it is important to try and gain an extension of the company's brand name into at least one other triad market. However this has to be done through an "export" activity rather than by foreign direct investment. This is because, in the final analysis, sports are local businesses.

Sources: Alan M. Rugman, *The End of Globalization* (London: Random House, 2000).

1. **Why is there not a truly "global" professional sport?**
2. **When athletes compete in the Olympics, such as by participating as a member of the country's basketball team, why is this not an example of a global sport?**
3. **What do MNEs need to know if they want to sponsor professional sports events as a way of promoting their name and their products?**

ENDNOTES

1 Pat Joynt and Malcolm Warner, "Introduction: Cross-Cultural Perspectives," in Pat Joynt and Malcolm (eds.), *Managing Across Cultures: Issues and Perspectives* (London: International Thomson Business Press, 1996), p. 3.

2 For additional insights see Gerry Darlington, "Culture – A Theoretical Review," in Joynt and Malcolm (1996) n. 1 above, pp. 33–55.

3 Reported in Jane Gibson and Richard M. Hodgetts, *Organizational Communication: A Managerial Perspective*, 2nd edn (New York: Harper Collins, 1991), pp. 436–437.

4 John R. Schermerhorn, Jr, "Language Effects in Cross-cultural Management Research: An Empirical Study and a Word of Caution," *National Academy of Management Proceedings*, 1987, pp. 2–5.

5 See "Emirate to Fine Bad Grammar," *BBC.co.uk*, February 12, 2001.

6 Kevin Voigt, "Japanese Firms Want English Competency," *Wall Street Journal*, June 11, 2001, p. B7B.

7 Justin Fox, "The Triumph of English," *Fortune*, September 18, 2000, p. 121.
8 Richard M. Hodgetts and Fred Luthans, *International Management*, 4th edn (Burr Ridge IL: Irwin/McGraw, 2000), p. 111.
9 See "European Court Overturns Tobacco Ban," *BBC.co.uk*, October 5, 2000.
10 See, "Fcuk Slogan not Funny," *BBC.co.uk*, July 5, 2000.
11 Andrew Pollack, "Myths Aside, Japanese Do Look for Bargains," *New York Times*, February 20, 1994, Section E, p. 5.
12 Also, see Cacilie Rohwedder, "Diet Foods Enjoy a U.K. Sales Binge, and the Continents May Join Up Soon," *Wall Street Journal*, January 28, 1994, p. A 5.
13 For a contrast, see Peter Gumbel and Richard Turner, "Fans Like Euro Disney But Its Parent's Goofs Weigh the Park Down," *Wall Street Journal*, March 10, 1994, pp. A 1, A 12.
14 Also, see Allessandra Stanley, "Mission to Moscow: Preaching the Gospel of Business," *New York Times*, February 27, 1994, Section F, p. 4.
15 Geert Hofstede, *Culture's Consequences: International Differences in Work-Related Values* (Beverly Hills CA: Sage Publications, 1980).
16 Fons Trompenaars, *Riding the Waves of Culture* (New York: Irwin, 1994).
17 See for example Fons Trompenaars and Charles Hampden-Turner, *Riding the Waves of Culture: Understanding Diversity in Global Business*, 2nd edn (New York: McGraw-Hill, 1998).
18 Yumiko Ono, "U.S. Superstores Find Japanese Are a Hard Sell," *Wall Street Journal*, February 14, 2000, pp. B 1, 4.
19 Robert Frank and Thomas M. Burton, "Cross-border Merger Results in Headaches for a Drug Company," *Wall Street Journal*, February 4, 1997, p. A 1.
20 Jeffrey A. Krug and Douglas Nigh, "Executive Perceptions in Foreign and Domestic Acquisitions: An Analysis of Foreign Ownership and its Effect on Executive Fate," *Journal of World Business*, vol. 36, no. 1 (2001), p. 85.
21 J. P. Walsh, "Top Management Turnover Following Mergers and Acquisitions," *Strategic Management Journal*, vol. 9 (1988), pp. 173–183.
22 Krug and Nigh (2001) n. 20 above, pp. 88, 89.
23 Ferdinand Protzman, "Rewriting the Contract for Germany's Vaunted Workers," *New York Times*, February 13, 1994, Section F, p. 5.
24 Merry I. White, "Learning and Working in Japan," *Business Horizons*, March–April 1989, p. 47. For more on the work ethic in Japan, see Michael Hirsh, "Families United: The Japanese Work Ethic Is Creating Divided Homes," *Fort Worth Star-Telegram*, January 20, 1991, Section A, p. 15.
25 Linda S. Dillon, "The Occidental Tourist," *Training and Development Journal*, May 1990, p. 76.
26 William Ouchi, *Theory Z: How American Business Can Meet the Japanese Challenge* (Reading MA: Addison-Wesley Publishing, 1981), p. 27.
27 James R. Lincoln, "Employee Work Attitudes and Management Practice in the US and Japan: Evidence from a Large Comparative Survey," *California Management Review*, Fall 1989, pp. 89–106.
28 Itzhak Harpaz, "The Importance of Work Goals: An International Perspective," *Journal of International Business Studies*, vol. 21, no. 1 (1990), pp. 75–93.
29 Ibid., p. 89.
30 Yumiko Ono and Bill Spindle, "Japan's Long Decline Makes One Thing Rise: Individualism," *Wall Street Journal*, December 29, 2000, pp. A 1, 4.
31 Reported in Hodgetts and Luthans (2000) n. 8 above, p. 384.
32 Chao C. Chen, "New Trends in Rewards Allocation Preferences: A Sino-U.S. Comparison," *Academy of Management Journal*, April 1995, p. 425.
33 See for example Jean Lee and Havihn Chan, "Chinese Entrepreneurship: A Study in Singapore," *Journal of Management Development*, vol. 17, no. 2 (1998), p. 139.
34 Erik Guyot, Christina Mungan and Richard Borsuk, "Streamlined Singapore Gives Hong Kong a Run for the Big Money," *Wall Street Journal*, November 19, 1998, p. A 19.
35 Robert Grosse and Duane Kujawa, *International Business: Theory and Managerial Applications* (Homewood IL: Irwin, 1988), p. 308.
36 Lisa Gubernick, "Mickey Mouse's Sharp Pencil," *Forbes*, January 7, 1991, p. 39.
37 Cara Buckley, "Worldwide Music Piracy Costs Industry $5 Billion," *Miami Herald*, October 3, 2000, pp. C 1, 10.
38 Craig S. Smith, "A Tale of Piracy: How the Chinese Stole the Grinch," *New York Times*, December 12, 2000, p. A 3.
39 Craig S. Smith, "Piracy a Concern as the China Trade Opens Up," *New York Times*, October 5, 2000, p. W 1.
40 Richard Behar, "Beijing's Phony War on Fakes," *Fortune*, October 30, 2000, p. 193.
41 See Peter Elstrom and Steven V. Brull, "Mitsubishi's Morass," *Business Week*, June 3, 1996, p. 35 and "Mitsubishi Settles with Women in Sexual Harassment Lawsuit," *New York Times*, August 29, 1997, p. A 9.
42 Suzanne Kapner, "Britain's Legal Barriers Start to Fall," *New York Times*, October 4, 2000, p. W 1.

ADDITIONAL BIBLIOGRAPHY

Abramson, Neil R., Keating, Robert J. and Lane, Henry W. "Cross-national Cognitive Process Differences: A Comparison of Canadian, American and Japanese Managers," *Management International Review*, vol. 36, no. 2 (1996).

Adler, Nancy J. and Graham, John L. "Cross-culture Interaction: The International Comparison Fallacy?" *Journal of International Business Studies*, vol. 20, no. 3 (Fall 1989).

Benito, Gabriel R. G. and Gripsrud, Geir. "The Expansion of Foreign Direct Investments: Discrete Rational Location Choices or a Cultural Learning Process?" *Journal of International Business Studies*, vol. 23, no. 3 (Third Quarter 1992).

Black, J. Stewart and Mendenhall, Mark. "Cross-cultural Training Effectiveness: A Review and a Theoretical Framework for Future Research," *Academy of Management Review*, vol. 15, no. 1 (January 1990).

Cavusgil, S. Tamer and Das, Ajay. "Methodological Issues in Empirical Cross-cultural Research: A Survey of the Management Literature and Framework," *Management International Review*, vol. 37, no. 1 (First Quarter 1997).

Francis, June N. P. "When in Rome? The Effects of Cultural Adaptation on Intercultural Business Negotiations," *Journal of International Business Studies*, vol. 22, no. 3 (Third Quarter 1991).

Gratchev, Mikhail V. "Making the Most of Cultural Differences," *Harvard Business Review*, vol. 79, no. 9 (October 2001)

Ghauri, Pervez. "Negotiating with the Chinese: A Socio-cultural Analysis," *Journal of World Business*, vol. 36, no. 3 (Fall 2001).

Gibson, Cristina B. "Do They Do What They Believe They Can? Group Efficacy and Group Effectiveness Across Tasks and Cultures," *Academy of Management Journal*, vol. 42, no. 2 (April 1999).

Hatch, Mary Jo. "The Dynamics of Organizational Culture," *Academy of Management Review*, vol. 18, no. 4 (October 1993).

Kelley, Lane, Whatley, Arthur and Worthley, Reginald. "Assessing the Effects of Culture on Managerial Attitudes: A Three-Culture Test," *Journal of International Business Studies*, vol. 18, no. 2 (Summer 1987).

Kogut, Bruce and Singh, Harbir. "The Effect of National Culture on the Choice of Entry Mode," *Journal of International Business Studies*, vol. 19, no. 3 (Fall 1988).

Lane, Henry W. and Beamish, Paul W. "Cross-culture Cooperative Behaviour in Joint Ventures in LDCs," *Management International Review*, vol. 30, Special Issue (1990).

Lee, Chol and Green, Robert T. "Cross-cultural Examination of the Fishbein Behavioural Intentions Mode," *Journal of International Business Studies*, vol. 22, no. 2 (Second Quarter 1991).

Lenartowicz, Tomasz and Roth, Kendall. "Does Subculture Within a Country Matter? A Cross-cultural Study of Motivational Domains and Business Performance in Brazil," *Journal of International Business Studies*, vol. 32, no. 2 (Summer 2001).

Li, Ji, Lam, Kevin and Qian, Gongming. "Does Culture Affect Behavior and Performance of Firms? The Case of Joint Ventures in China," *Journal of International Business Studies*, vol. 32, no. 1 (Spring 2001).

Makino, Shige and Neupert, Kent E. "National Culture, Transaction Costs, and the Choice Between Joint Venture and Wholly Owned Subsidiary," *Journal of International Business Studies*, vol. 31, no. 4 (Winter 2000).

Manor, Briarcliff and Vermeulen, Freek. "Learning Through Acquisitions," *Academy of Management Journal*, vol. 44, no. 3 (June 2001).

Ming-Hong Lai, George. "Knowing Who You are Doing Business with in Japan: A Managerial View of Keiretsu and Keiretsu Business Groups," *Journal of World Business*, vol. 34, no. 4 (Winter 1999).

Morosini, Piero, Shane, Scott and Singh, Harbir. "National Cultural Distance and Cross-border Acquisition Performance," *Journal of International Business Studies*, vol. 29, no. 1 (First Quarter 1998).

Morris, Tom and Pavett, Cynthia M. "Management Style and Productivity in Two Cultures," *Journal of International Business Studies*, vol. 23, no. 1 (First Quarter 1992).

Nasif, Ercan G., Al-Daeaj, Hamad, Ebrahimi, Bahman and Thibodeaux, Mary S. "Methodological Problems in Cross-cultural Research: An Updated Review," *Management International Review*, vol. 31, no. 1 (First Quarter 1991).

Parameswaran, Ravi and Yaprak, Attila. "A Cross-national Comparison of Consumer Research Measures," *Journal of International Business Studies*, vol. 18, no. 1 (Spring 1987).

Rosch, Martin and Segler, Kay G. "Communication with Japanese," *Management International Review*, vol. 27, no. 4 (Fourth Quarter 1987).

Schmitt, Bernd H. "Language and Visual Imagery: Issues of Corporate Identity in East Asia," *Columbia Journal of World Business*, vol. 30, no. 4 (Winter 1995).

Selvarajah, Christopher T., Duignan, Patric, Suppiah, Chandraseagran, Lane, Terry and Nuttman, Chris. "In Search of the ASEAN Leader: An Exploratory Study of the Dimensions that Relate to Excellence in Leadership," *Management International Review*, vol. 35, no. 1 (First Quarter 1995).

Sivakumar, K. and Nakata, Cheryl. "The Stampede Toward Hofstede's Framework: Avoiding the Sample Design Pit in Cross-cultural Research," *Journal of International Business Studies*, vol. 32 no. 3 (Fall 2001).

Stening, Bruce W. and Hammer, Mitchell R. "Cultural Baggage and the Adaption of Expatriate American and Japanese Managers," *Management International Review*, vol. 32, no. 1 (First Quarter 1992).

Thomas, Anisya S. and Mueller, Stephen L. "A Case for Comparative Entreprenuership: Assessing the Relevance of Culture," *Journal of International Business Studies*, vol. 31, no. 2 (Summer 2000).

Ueno, Susumu and Sekaran, Uma. "The Influence of Culture on Budget Control Practices in the USA and Japan: An Empirical Study," *Journal of International Business Studies*, vol. 23, no. 4 (Fourth Quarter 1992).

Usunier, Jean-Claude G. "Business Time Perceptions and National Cultures: A Comparative Survey," *Management International Review*, vol. 31, no. 3 (Third Quarter 1991).

Zammuto, Raymond F. and O'Connor, Edward J. "Gaining Advanced Manufacturing Technologies' Benefits: The Roles of Organization Design and Culture," *Academy of Management Review*, vol. 17, no. 4 (October 1992).

Chapter 6

International Trade

CONTENTS

OBJECTIVES OF THE CHAPTER

An understanding of international trade is critical to the study of international business. The primary objective of this chapter is to examine key economic theories that help to explain why nations trade. In addition, the role and importance of a country's barriers to trade will be studied and discussion will be focused on why most nations use trade barriers despite vigorous international efforts to eliminate them.

The specific objectives of this chapter are to:

1. *Define* the term *international trade* and discuss the role of mercantilism in modern international trade.
2. *Contrast* the theory of absolute advantage and the theory of comparative advantage.
3. *Relate* the importance of international product life cycle theory to the study of international economics.
4. *Explain* some of the most commonly used barriers to trade and other economic developments that affect international economics.
5. *Discuss* some of the reasons for the tensions between the theory of free trade and the widespread practice of national barriers to trade.

ACTIVE LEARNING CASE

The decline of the UK world export market

Over the last two decades the UK has continued to experience a decline in its share of the world market for a number of products (see table below). At the beginning of this time period, the Japanese were a growing force in the international arena. In fact, they dominated the 1980s and were able to make substantial gains at the expense of both the UK and the US. As the data reveal, both of these countries lost worldwide market share in such industries as: automotive products, office machines, telecom equipment, machinery and transport equipment, chemicals, and textiles.

In the late 1980s, however, the world economy began to see some major changes. Asia, Korea, Singapore, Taiwan, Thailand, and China began to become much more competitive on the world stage. Korea, for example, started expanding its automotive industry; and China's market share of office machines and telecom equipment rose from zero to about 1.3 per cent of the market in 1990 and to 2.4 per cent by the middle of the decade. Meanwhile, thanks to NAFTA, Mexico and Canada were increasing their market share of automotive products and machinery transport equipment. At the same time the US economy began to turn around and starting in 1992 it began the longest sustained economic growth in its history. Not until well into 2000 did the American juggernaut finally begin slowing up. Much of this success was a result of the pounding it had taken during the 1980s from both Japanese and European firms that were able to offer high quality products at very competitive prices. This resulted in the Americans beginning to radically restructure many of their industries, invest billions in new technology, plant, equipment, and information technology, and introduce Six Sigma programs that allowed them to match the quality offerings of worldwide competitors. As a result of these actions, by the end of the 1990s the US share of the world's export market in areas such as automotive products, machinery and transport equipment, chemicals, and textiles was on the rise. Now the big loser was Japan which saw its export market share decline in many areas of manufacturing including auto products, office machines, machinery, and transport equipment as well as in textiles.

Throughout both of these decades, however, the UK's share of these markets, in most cases, has continued to drop. British businesses are finding that imported goods are often of higher quality and lower price than those manufactured domestically. This is not to say that the UK is at a complete disadvantage with its competitors. For instance, during the mid-1990s its worldwide market share of telecom equipment increased (although, as seen in the table below, it has now fallen back) and by the end of the decade its share of automotive products had gone up. So the country's worldwide export market share is in a state of flux and in the face of growing competition it continues to be a major exporter. Additionally, as a member of the EU the UK is ideally positioned to do business on the Continent and tap the economic potential of such large economies as Germany, France, Italy, and the Netherlands. The construction of new auto plants in England over the last decade and the development of both a high-tech sector and a strong financial services industry point to the likelihood that, while the UK may be losing ground in some markets, it will be gaining ground in

	% UK share of the export market			*% US share of the export market*			*% Japanese share of the export market*		
Exports of:	*1980*	*1990*	*1999*	*1980*	*1990*	*1999*	*1980*	*1990*	*1999*
Automotive products	5.8	4.4	4.8	12.7	10.2	11.5	19.8	20.8	15.0
Office machines and telecom equipment	6.4	6.5	5.7	20.2	17.3	16.3	21.1	22.4	11.9
Machinery and transport equipment	7.6	6.1	5.6	17.0	15.9	16.1	14.5	17.7	12.5
Chemicals	8.7	8.0	6.6	14.9	13.3	13.7	4.7	5.3	5.8
Transportation services	6.5	6.6	6.1	15.3	17.0	15.6	9.8	7.9	7.4
Textiles	5.7	4.2	3.0	6.2	5.8	4.8	9.3	5.6	4.5

others. In fact, when looking at the three countries in the table, in every instance except one (Japan in chemicals), the country's market share in 1999 was less than that in 1980. These data help reinforce an important principle of international trade: specialize in those products where you can achieve an advantage. Over time, of course, competitors may erode this advantage by developing even better offerings for the export market. In this case, it is important to either counterattack and win back this market share or find other markets where the country's skills and resources will allow it to compete effectively. With the emergence of more and more industrial countries in Asia, the increasing competitiveness of Latin America, and the emerging industries in Eastern Europe and the former Soviet Union, as well as the economic growth that is being forecast for the EU during the current decade, UK managers have their work cut out for them.

Sources: Adapted from World Trade Organization, *Annual Report*, 1997; ***www.intracen.org***; World Trade Organization, *International Trade Statistics, 2000.*

1. **How does the process of the UK finding market niches help to illustrate the theory of comparative advantage?**
2. **How does a UK manager wanting to buy domestic products illustrate the importance of consumer taste in international trade?**
3. **In what way could the UK use trade barriers to protect its markets from foreign competitors? Who can be affected by these trade barriers?**

INTRODUCTION

International trade
The branch of economics concerned with the exchange of goods and services with foreign countries

International trade is the branch of economics concerned with the exchange of goods and services with foreign countries. Although this is a complex subject, we will focus on two particular areas: international trade theory and barriers to trade.

Some international economic problems cannot be solved in the short run. Consider the US balance of trade deficit. Its trade with Japan and China heavily affects the overall US imbalance. Moreover, this trade deficit will not be reduced by political measures alone; it will require long-run economic measures that reduce imports and increase exports. Other nations are also learning this lesson – and not just those that have negative trade balances. After all, most countries seem to want a continual favorable trade balance, but this is impossible since a nation with a deficit must be matched by a nation with a surplus.[1]

International trade has become an even more important topic now that so many countries have begun to move from state-run to market-driven economies.[2] Inflation and, in many cases, unemployment are severe problems to these nations. Fortunately, enhanced international trade is one way to address a weak macroeconomy.[3]

International commitment to a free market will bring prosperity to the world economic system. Since the time of Adam Smith in 1790, economists have shown that free trade is efficient and leads to maximum economic welfare. In this chapter we will discuss the economic rationale for free trade and the political impediments to it.

Mercantilism
A trade theory which holds that a government can improve the economic well-being of the country by encouraging exports and stifling imports

INTERNATIONAL TRADE THEORY

In order to understand the topic of international trade, we must be able to answer the question: Why do nations trade? One of the earliest, and simplest, answers to this question was provided by mercantilism, a theory that was quite popular in the 18th century, when gold was the only world currency. **Mercantilism** holds that a government can improve the economic well-being of the country by encouraging exports and stifling imports. The result is a positive balance of trade that leads to wealth (gold) flowing into the country. While most international trade experts believe that mercantilism is a simplistic and erroneous theory, it has had followers.

For example, under President Mitterand in the late 1970s and early 1980s, France sought to revitalize its industrial base by nationalizing key industries and banks and subsidizing exports over imports. By the mid-1980s the French government realized that the strategy was not working and began denationalizing many of its holdings.[4] More recently, China has proven to be a strong adherent of mercantilism as reflected by the fact that it tries to have a positive balance with all of its trading partners.

A more useful explanation of why nations trade is provided by trade theories that focus on specialization of effort. The theories of absolute and comparative advantage are good examples.

Theory of absolute advantage

Theory of absolute advantage
A trade theory which holds that, by specializing in the production of goods which they can produce more efficiently than any others, nations can increase their economic well-being

The **theory of absolute advantage** holds that, by specializing in the production of goods they can produce more efficiently than anyone else, nations can increase their economic well-being. A simple example can illustrate this point. Assume that two nations, North and South, are both able to produce two goods, cloth and grain. Assume further that labor is the only scarce factor of production and thus the only cost of production.

Labor cost (hours) of production for one unit

	Cloth	*Grain*
North	10	20
South	20	10

Because labor is the only cost of production, lower labor-hours per unit of production means lower production costs, and higher productivity per labor-hour. As seen by the data above, North has an absolute advantage in the production of cloth since the cost requires only 10 labor-hours, compared with 20 labor-hours in South. Similarly, South has an absolute advantage in the production of grain, which it produces at a cost of 10 labor-hours, compared with 20 labor-hours in North.

Both countries gain by trade. If they specialize and exchange cloth for grain at a relative price of 1:1, each country can employ its resources to produce a greater amount of goods. North can import one unit of grain in exchange for one unit of cloth, thereby "paying", in effect, only 10 labor-hours for one unit of grain. If North had produced the grain itself, it would have used 20 labor-hours per unit, therefore North gains 10 labor-hours from the trade. In the same way South gains from trade when it imports one unit of cloth in exchange for one unit of grain. The effective cost to South for one unit of cloth is only the 10 labor-hours required to make its one unit of grain.

The theory of absolute advantage, as originally formulated, does not predict the exchange ratio between cloth and grain once trade is opened, nor does it resolve the division of the gains from trade between the two countries. Our example assumed an international price ratio of 1:1, but this ratio (P_{cloth} to P_{grain}) could lie between 2:1 (the pretrade price ratio in South) and 1:2 (the pretrade price ratio in North). To determine the relative price ratio under trade, we would have to know the total resources of each country (total labor-hours available per year), and the demand of each country for both cloth and grain. In this way we could determine the relative gains from trade for each country.

Yet, even this simple model of absolute advantage has several important implications for international trade. First, if a country has an absolute advantage in producing a product, there exists a potential for gains from trade. Second, the more a country is able to specialize in the production of the good it produces most efficiently, the greater its potential gains in national well-being. Third, *within* one country the competitive market does not evenly distribute the gains from trade. This last implication is illustrated by the following example.

Prior to trade, the grain producers in North worked 20 hours; they would produce one unit of grain that could be exchanged for two units of cloth. After trade, the grain producers who remain could exchange one unit of grain for only one unit of cloth. The remaining grain producers are worse off under trade. Cloth producers in North, however, work 10 hours, produce one unit of cloth, and exchange it for one unit of grain, whereas previously they received only a half unit of grain. They are better off. If grain producers in North switch to cloth production, then 20 hours of labor results in production of two units of cloth, which they can exchange for two units of grain. They are better off under international trade. As long as North does not specialize completely in cloth, there will be gainers (cloth producers and grain producers who switched to cloth) and losers (those who continue as grain producers).

Since the nation as a whole benefits from trade, the gainers could compensate the losers, and there would still be a surplus to be distributed in some way. If such compensation did not take place, however, the losers (continuing grain producers) would have an incentive to try to prevent the country from opening itself up to trade. Historically this problem has continued to fuel opposition to a free trade policy that reduces barriers to trade. A good example is Japanese farmers who stand to lose their livelihood if the government opens up Japan to lower-priced agricultural imports.

A more complicated picture of the determinants and effects of trade emerges when one of the trading partners has an absolute advantage in the production of both goods. However, trade under these conditions still brings gains, as David Ricardo first demonstrated in his theory of comparative advantage.

Theory of comparative advantage

Theory of comparative advantage
A trade theory which holds that nations should produce those goods for which they have the greatest relative advantage

The **theory of comparative advantage** holds that nations should produce those goods for which they have the greatest relative advantage. In terms of the previous example of two countries, North and South, and two commodities, cloth and grain, Ricardo's model can be illustrated as follows:

Labor cost (hours) of production for one unit

	Cloth	*Grain*
North	50	100
South	200	200

In this example North has an absolute advantage in the production of *both* cloth and grain, so it would appear at first sight that trade would be unprofitable, or at least that incentives for exchange no longer exist. Yet trade is still advantageous to both nations, provided the *relative* costs of production differ in the two countries.

Before trade, in North one unit of cloth costs (50/100) hours of grain, so one unit of cloth can be exchanged for one-half unit of grain. In North, the price of cloth is half the price of grain. In South, one unit of cloth costs (200/200) hours of grain or one grain unit. In South, the price of cloth equals the price of grain. If North can import more than a half unit of grain for one unit of cloth, it will gain from trade. Similarly, if South can import one unit of cloth for less than one unit of grain, it will also gain from trade. These relative price ratios set the boundaries for trade. Trade is profitable between price ratios (price of cloth to price of grain) of 0.5 and 1. For example, at an international price ratio of two-thirds, North gains from trade. It can import one unit of grain in return for exporting one and a half units of cloth. Because it costs North only 50 hours of labor to produce the unit of cloth, its effective cost under trade for one unit of imported grain is 75 labor-hours. Under pretrade conditions it costs North 100 labor-hours to produce one unit of grain. Similarly, South gains from trade. It imports one unit of cloth in exchange for two-thirds unit of grain. Prior to trade, South spent 200 labor-hours to produce the one unit of cloth. Through trade its effective cost for one unit of cloth is $2/3 \times 200$ or 133 labor-hours – cheaper than the domestic production cost of 200 labor-hours. Assuming free trade between the two nations, North will tend to specialize in the production of cloth and South will tend to specialize in the production of grain.

This example leads to a general principle. There are gains from trade whenever the relative price ratios of two goods differ under international exchange from what they would be under conditions of no trade. Such domestic conditions are often referred to as *autarky*, which is a government policy of being totally self-sufficient. Research shows that free trade is superior to autarky. In particular, free trade provides greater economic output and consumption to the trade partners jointly than they can achieve by working alone. By specializing in the production of certain goods, exporting those products for which they have a comparative advantage, and importing those for which they have a comparative disadvantage, the countries end up better off.

The general conclusions of the theory of comparative advantage are the same as those for the theory of absolute advantage. In addition, the theory of comparative advantage demonstrates that countries jointly benefit from trade (under the assumptions of the model) even if one country has an absolute advantage in the production of *both* goods. Total world efficiency and consumption increase under free trade.

As with the theory of absolute advantage discussed previously, Ricardo's theory of comparative advantage does not answer the question of the distribution of gains between the two countries, nor the distribution of gains and losses between grain producers and cloth producers within each country. No country will lose under free trade, but in theory at least all the gains could accrue to one country and to only one group within that country.

Active learning check

Review your answer to Active Learning Case question 1 and make any changes you like. Then compare your answer with the one below.

1. How does the process of the UK finding market niches help to illustrate the theory of comparative advantage?

The theory of comparative advantage holds that nations should produce those goods for which they have the greatest relative advantage. The finding of market niches helps illustrate this theory because it shows that the UK is picking those areas where it has a relative advantage over the competition and exploiting its strengths in these markets. Given the rise of competitiveness in all areas of worldwide exports, few nations have been able to maintain their market share for very long. So the UK will have to continue to use this approach in order to remain one of the world's major export nations.

Factor endowment theory

Factor endowment theory A trade theory which holds that nations will produce and export products that use large amounts of production factors that they have in abundance and will import products requiring a large amount of production factors that are scarce in their country

Heckscher–Ohlin theory A trade theory that extends the concept of comparative advantage by bringing into consideration the endowment and cost of factors of production and helps to explain why nations with relatively large labor forces will concentrate on producing labor-intensive goods, whereas countries with relatively more capital than labor will specialize in capital-intensive goods

Leontief paradox A finding by Wassily Leontief, a Nobel prize economist, which shows that the US, surprisingly, exports relatively more labor-intensive goods and imports capital-intensive goods

International product life cycle theory (IPLC) A theory of the stages of production of a product with new "know-how"; it is first produced by the parent firm, then by its foreign subsidiaries, and finally anywhere in the world where costs are the lowest; it helps to explain why a product that begins as a nation's export often ends up as an import

In recent years more sophisticated theories have emerged that help to clarify and extend our knowledge of international trade. **Factor endowment theory** holds that countries will produce and export products that use large amounts of production factors that they have in abundance, and they will import products requiring large amounts of production factors that are scarce in their country. This theory is also known as the **Heckscher–Ohlin theory** (after the two economists who first developed it). The theory is useful in extending the concept of comparative advantage by bringing into consideration the endowment and cost of factors of production. The theory also helps to explain why nations with relatively large labor forces, such as China, will concentrate on producing labor-intensive goods, and countries like the Netherlands, which has relatively more capital than labor, will specialize in capital-intensive goods.

However, there are some weaknesses with the factor endowment theory. One weakness is that some countries have minimum wage laws that result in high prices for relatively abundant labor. As a result, the country may find it less expensive to import certain goods than to produce them internally. Another weakness with the theory is that countries like the US actually export relatively more labor-intensive goods and import capital-intensive goods, an outcome that appears surprising. This result, discovered by Wassily Leontief, a Nobel Prize economist, is known as the **Leontief paradox** and has been explained in terms of the quality of labor input rather than just man-hours of work. The US produces and exports technology-intensive products that require highly educated labor. The Leontief paradox shows one of the problems with factor endowment theory and helps us to understand why no single theory can explain the role of economic factors in trade theory. Simply put, the subject is too complex to be explained with just one or two theories.

International product life cycle theory

Another theory that provides insights into international theory is Vernon's **international product life cycle (IPLC) theory**, which addresses the various stages of a good's life cycle. In particular, the theory helps to explain why a product that begins as a nation's export often ends up becoming an import. The theory also focuses on market expansion and technological innovation, concepts that are relatively de-emphasized in comparative advantage theory. IPLC theory has two important tenets: (1) technology is a critical factor in creating and developing new products and (2) market size and structure are important in determining trade patterns.

Product stages

The IPLC has three stages: new product, maturing product, and standardized product. A new product is one that is innovative or unique in some way (see Figure 6.1*a*). Initially, consumption is in the home country, price is inelastic, profits are high, and the company seeks to sell to those willing to pay a premium price. As production increases and outruns local consumption, exporting begins.

As the product enters the mature phase of its life cycle (see Figure 6.1*b*), an increasing percentage of sales are achieved through exporting. At the same time competitors in other advanced countries will be working to develop substitute products so that they can replace the initial good with one of their own. The introduction of these substitutes and the softening of demand for the original product will eventually result in the firm that developed the product now switching its strategy from production to

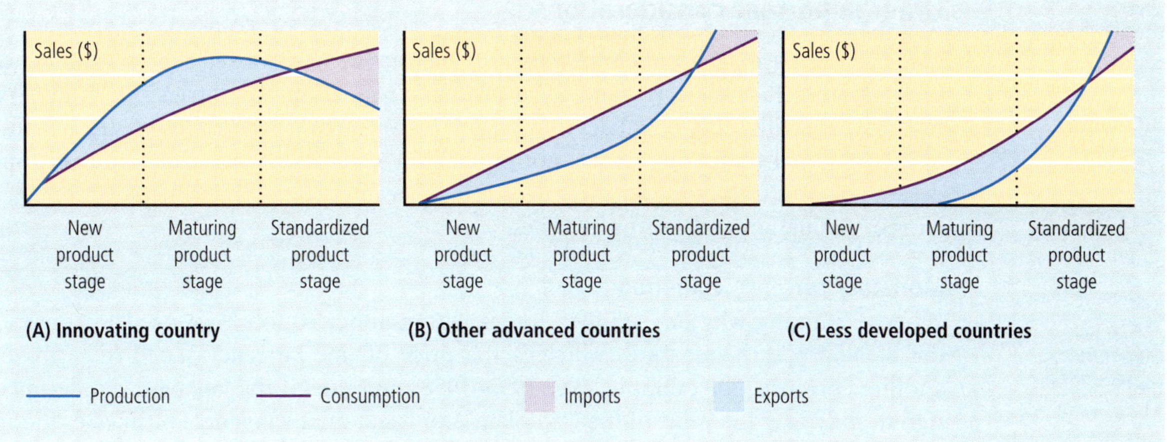

Figure 6.1 The international product life cycle

Source: Raymond Vernon and Louis T. Wells, Jr, *The Manager in the International Economy* (Englewood Cliffs NJ: Prentice-Hall, 1991), p. 85.

market protection. Attention will also be focused on tapping markets in less developed countries.

As the product enters the standardized product stage (see Figure 6.1*c*), the technology becomes widely diffused and available. Production tends to be shifted to low-cost locations, including less developed countries and offshore locations. In many cases the product will end up being viewed as a generic and price will be the sole determinant of demand.

Personal computers and the IPLC

In recent years a number of products have moved through the IPLC and are now in the standardized product stage. Personal computers (PCs) are a good example, although there is a wide variety of PCs and some versions are in the new product and the maturing product phases. For example, the early version of PCs that reached the market in the 1984 to 1991 period were in the standardized product stage by 1995 and sold primarily on the basis of price. Machines that entered the market in the 1996 to 1998 period were in the maturing stage by 1999. PCs with increased memory capability that were in the new product stage in 1999 quickly moved toward maturity, and by 2002 they were being replaced by even better machines.

The next five years are likely to see desktop PCs replaced by laptop and notebook models that are even lighter, faster, more sophisticated, and less expensive than their predecessors. In turn these machines will eventually be replaced by notebooks with advanced Pentium chips, color monitors, long-term battery capability, and diskettes capable of holding billions of bytes. These units are also likely to have telephonic equipment and to serve as a complete communications center from which the international executive can communicate anywhere in the world. These machines will first be manufactured locally and then in foreign markets. Thus PCs will continue to move through an international product life cycle.

The IPLC theory is useful in helping to explain how new technologically innovative products fit into the world trade picture. However, because new innovative products are sometimes rapidly improved, it is important to remember that one or two versions of them may be in the standardized product stage while other versions are in the maturing stage and still others are in the new product phase.

Other important considerations

Many factors beyond those considered in the theories we have looked at greatly influence international trade theory.[5] One is government regulation. Countries often limit or restrict trade with other countries for political reasons. For example, despite the benefits of international trade, the US has not officially traded with North Korea in over four decades or with Cuba for over three decades. Other important factors include monetary currency valuation and consumer tastes.

Monetary currency valuation

Monetary exchange rate The price of one currency stated in terms of another currency

When examining why one country trades with another country, we need to consider the **monetary exchange rate**, which is the price of one currency stated in terms of another currency. For example, over 1995–1998 the value of the Japanese yen declined significantly over the value of the US dollar. As a result, many Japanese businesses found their products becoming much more competitive in the US market. More recently the Japanese government has announced that the yen is again getting too strong and it wants to weaken its value, thus ensuring that Japanese businesses are able to maintain their international competitiveness. Another reason why monetary currency valuation is important is because a foreign firm doing business will report its revenues and profits in home-country currency. So if a British firm sold $10 million of machinery in Canada and the value of the Canadian dollar declined against the Canadian currency, the UK company would report less revenue (in terms of British pounds) than if the Canadian dollar had remained stable or, better yet, increased in value against the pound. In the next chapter we will discuss exchange rates in more detail.

Consumer tastes

International trade is not based solely on price; some people will pay more for a product even though they can buy something similar for less money. This willingness to pay more may be based on prestige, perceived quality, or a host of other physical and psychological reasons. Personal tastes dictate consumer decisions. See the box "International Business Strategy in Action: Nissan: no pain, no gain".

INTERNATIONAL BUSINESS STRATEGY *IN ACTION*

Nissan: no pain, no gain

There are a number of reasons that help explain international trade. One of the most important, although often overlooked, is that of consumer taste. The product has to be "acceptable" to the customer and something that sells well in the home country may not do well overseas. The auto industry provides a good example of this. Cars that sell well in one part of the triad often do poorly elsewhere. Consider BMW and Mercedes, both well known for their high-quality automobiles. In Europe the two firms produce "driving machines" but in the US market consumers are not interested in high performance road handling. They want comfort and luxury in their cars. So BMW and Mercedes have had to modify their interior design and styling and de-emphasize performance factors in order to accommodate local taste.

Another critical factor in the auto industry is price. Over the last decade there has been substantial overcapacity brought about by auto firms building more and more worldwide operations. As a result, any downturn in the worldwide industry today can result in heavy losses because many auto plants are unable to operate above their breakeven point. And this is exactly what happened following the 1997–1998 Asian financial crisis. As many Asian economies began to slow down, auto manufacturers in this region had to downsize quickly in order to stem their losses. Those who could not quickly generate production efficiencies suffered heavy losses. Nissan Motor provides a good example.

Nissan was established in 1933 to manufacture and market the Datsun, a small passenger car, and to sell related automotive components. The firm eventually became Japan's second largest auto maker and the fifth biggest in the world with annual global sales in excess of 2.5 million vehicles. Today Nissan does business in 170 countries selling a wide range of passenger cars as well as commercial vans, buses, and auto-related parts and components. In addition, the company manufactures forklifts, marine equipment (including yachts and boats), aerospace equipment, and textile machinery and an assortment of industrial equipment. However, the bulk of its sales are in auto operations (98 per cent) with industrial machinery and marine equipment (1 per cent) and aerospace equipment and textile equipment (1 per cent) accounting for the remainder. In addition, the firm earns 39 per cent of its revenues in Japan and the remaining 61 per cent from overseas sales. Nissan's primary markets are the triad, with North America accounting for 32 per cent of all sales and Europe bringing in 17 per cent.

When the Asian crisis hit, Nissan began to feel the economic impact almost immediately. And when its sales in North America began to slump because its offerings were not in line with consumer tastes, the company was headed for big trouble. If not for Renault's injection of $6 billion in return for a controlling 36.8 per cent stake, the company might well have gone bankrupt. Today Renault has put in its own CEO to run Nissan. And to cut costs and make the firm viable in the international market, the new CEO has slashed over 20,000 jobs, closed five factories, and sharply reduced inventory. As a result, Nissan is now getting back on its feet.

The Nissan story clearly emphasizes the importance of two international trade theory concepts: product offerings have to be adapted to meet consumer taste and these products must be produced at competitive prices. Failure to do either of these things will leave the firm vulnerable to heavy losses and erosion of market share.

Websites: **www.bmw.com**; **www.daimlerchrysler.com**; **www.nissanmotors.com**; **www.nissan.co.jp** and **www.renault.com**.

Sources: Benjamin Fulford, "Renaissance at Nissan," *Forbes*, October 2, 2000, p. 80; Simon Collinson, "No Pain, No Gain: The Renault–Nissan Shake-up," Case Notes, Warwick Business School, University of Warwick, Coventry, UK, 2001, "Ghost of Nissan," *Financial Times*, November 9, 1999; annual reports, **www.nissan.co.jp**, **www.renault.com**.

Active learning check

Review your answer to Active Learning Case question 2 and make any changes you like. Then compare you answer with the one below.

2. How does a UK manager wanting to buy domestic products illustrate the importance of consumer taste in international trade?

This example shows that people often buy goods based on personal preference, and such characteristics as low price, high quality, or improved productivity are not the only factors influencing the purchase decision. Of course, this "Buy UK" focus will often come into play only when "all other factors are approximately equal". The manager is unlikely to turn down a German-made product that is 10 per cent less expensive in favor of one that is made domestically. So there are limits to the effect of consumer taste on purchase decisions but it is certainly one variable that has proven very important in international trade.

BARRIERS TO TRADE

Why do many countries produce goods and services that could be more cheaply purchased from others? One reason is because of trade barriers, which effectively raise the cost of these goods and make them more expensive to local buyers.

Reasons for trade barriers

One of the most common reasons for the creation of trade barriers is to encourage local production by making it more difficult for foreign firms to compete here. Another reason is to help local firms export and thus build worldwide market share by doing such things as providing them with subsidies in the form of tax breaks and low-interest loans. Some of the other common reasons for trade barriers include:

1. Protect local jobs by shielding home country business from foreign competition.
2. Encourage local production to replace imports.
3. Protect infant industries that are just getting started.
4. Reduce reliance on foreign suppliers.
5. Encourage local and foreign direct investment.
6. Reduce balance of payments problems.
7. Promote export activity.
8. Prevent foreign firms from *dumping*, that is, selling goods below cost in order to achieve market share.
9. Promote political objectives such as refusing to trade with countries that practice apartheid or deny civil liberties to their citizens.

Commonly used barriers

There are a variety of barriers that deter the free flow of international goods and services.[6] The following presents six of the most commonly used barriers.

Price-based barriers

Imported goods and services sometimes have a tariff added to their price. Quite often this is based on the value of the goods. For example, some tobacco products coming into the US carry an ad valorem tariff (see below) of over 100 per cent, thus more than doubling their cost to US consumers. Tariffs raise revenues for the government, discourage imports, and make local goods more attractive.

Quantity limits

Quota
A quantity limit on imported goods

Embargo
A quota set at zero, thus preventing the importation of those products that are involved

Quantity limits, often known as **quotas**, restrict the number of units that can be imported or the market share that is permitted. If the quota is set at zero, as in the case of Cuban cigars from Havana, it is called an **embargo**. If the annual quota is set at 1 million units, no more than this number can be imported during one year; once this quota is reached, all additional imports are turned back. In some cases a quota is established in terms of market share. For example, Canada allows foreign banks to hold no more than 16 per cent of Canadian bank deposits, and the EU limits Japanese auto imports to 10 per cent of the total market.

International price fixing

Cartel
A group of firms that collectively agree to fix prices or quantities sold in an effort to control price

In some cases a host of international firms will fix prices or quantities sold in an effort to control price. This is known as a **cartel**. A well-known example is OPEC (Organization of Petroleum Exporting Countries), which consists of Saudi Arabia, Kuwait, Iran, Iraq, and Venezuela, among others (see Table 6.1). By controlling the supply of oil it provides, the cartel seeks to control the price and profit. This practice is illegal in the US and Europe,[7] but the basic idea of allowing competitors to cooperate for the purpose of meeting international competition is being endorsed more frequently in countries such as the US.[8] For example, US computer firms have now created partnerships for joint research and development efforts.

Non-tariff barriers
Rules, regulations, and bureaucratic red tape that delay or preclude the purchase of foreign goods

Non-tariff barriers

Non-tariff barriers are rules, regulations, and bureaucratic red tape that delay or preclude the purchase of foreign goods. Examples include (1) slow processing of import permits,

Table 6.1 **Members of the Organization of Petroleum Exporting Countries (OPEC), 2001**

Member country	*Quotas (barrels per day)*
Algeria	741,000
Indonesia	1,203,000
Iran	3,406,000
Iraq*	2,719,000
Kuwait	1,861,000
Libya	1,242,000
Nigeria	1,911,000
Qatar	601,000
Saudi Arabia	7,541,000
United Arab Emirates	2,025,000
Venezuela	2,670,000
Total	25,920,000

* Data for Iraq are for 1999 production.

Source: Adapted from ***www.opec.org***

(2) the establishment of quality standards that exclude foreign producers, and (3) a "buy local" policy. These barriers limit imports and protect domestic sales.

Financial limits

Exchange controls
Controls that restrict the flow of currency

There are a number of different financial limits. One of the most common is **exchange controls** that restrict the flow of currency. For example, many Latin American countries will allow exporters to exchange their dollars for local currency, but they place restrictions on access to dollars for purchasing imports. Another common exchange control is the limit of currency that can be taken out of the country; for example, travelers may take up to only $3,000 per person out of the country. A third example is the use of fixed exchange rates that are quite favorable to the country. For example, dollars may be exchanged for local currency on a 1:1 basis, while without exchange controls the rate would be 1:4. These cases are particularly evident where there exists a black market for foreign currency that offers an exchange rate that is much different from the fixed rate.

Foreign investment controls

Foreign investment controls
Limits on foreign direct investment or the transfer or remittance of funds

Foreign investment controls are limits on foreign direct investment or the transfer or remittance of funds. These controls can take a number of different forms, including (1) requiring foreign investors to take a minority ownership position (49 per cent or less); (2) limiting profit remittance, for example, to 15 per cent of accumulated capital per year; and (3) prohibiting royalty payments to parent companies, thus stopping the latter from taking out capital.

These barriers can greatly restrict international trade and investment. However, it must be realized that these barriers are created for what governments believe are very important reasons. A close look at one of these, tariffs, helps to make this clearer.

Tariff
A tax on goods shipped internationally

Import tariff
A tax levied on goods shipped into a country

Tariffs

A **tariff** is a tax on goods that are shipped internationally. The most common is the **import tariff**, which is levied on goods shipped into a country.[9] Less common is the

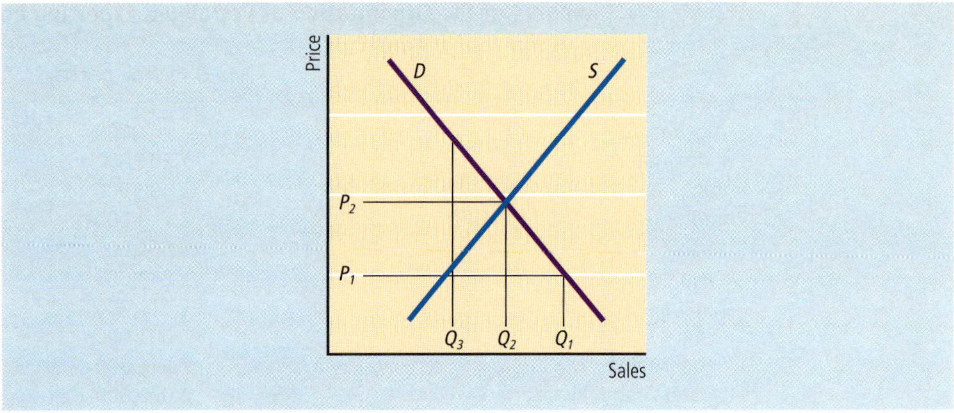

Figure 6.2 **Impacts of a tariff**

Export tariff
A tax levied on goods sent out of a country

Transit tariff
A tax levied on goods passing through a country

Specific duty
A tariff based on the number of items being shipped into a country

Ad valorem duty
A tax which is based on a percentage of the value of imported goods

Compound duty
A tariff consisting of both a specific and an ad valorem duty

export tariff, which is levied on goods that are sent out of the country, or a **transit tariff**, which is levied on goods passing through the country. There are a number of bases on which these taxes are levied. A **specific duty** is a tariff based on units such as $1 for each item shipped into the country. So a manufacturer shipping in 1,000 pairs of shoes would pay a specific duty of $1,000. An **ad valorem duty** is a tariff based on a percentage of the value of the item, so a watch valued at $25 and carrying a 10 per cent duty would have a tariff of $2.50. A **compound duty** is a tariff consisting of both a specific and an ad valorem duty. So a suit of clothes valued at $80 that carries a specific duty of $3 and an ad valorem duty of 5 per cent would have a compound duty of $7.

Governments typically use tariffs to raise revenue and/or to protect local industry. At the same time these taxes decrease demand for the respective product while raising the price to the buyer. This is illustrated in Figure 6.2, which shows what happens when a tariff drives the price of a good from P_1 to P_2 (the world price plus the tariff). As seen in this figure, the quantity demanded declines from Q_1 to Q_2. This price increase allows local producers to sell Q_3Q_2 and thus to take market share away from foreign firms that were exporting Q_3Q_1 into the country. However, as seen in the figure, this is done at the price of charging the consumer more money *and* of reducing the number of buyers who purchase the product. At new price P_2, there are no longer any imports.

There are numerous reasons for using tariffs. One is to protect domestic industries or firms. The US government has used them to prevent foreign companies from selling goods at lower prices in the US than they sell for back home. US auto makers have often accused their overseas rivals of using this tactic. In the case of Japanese car manufacturers, for example, this was a particularly troublesome area when the value of the yen increased sharply in the early 1990s. As a result, argued the US car firms, imported parts and cars had to reflect the increased value of the yen or be subjected to tariffs.[10] Others have made similar arguments. Eastman Kodak, for example, asked the US Commerce Department to impose steep tariffs on the Fuji Photo Film Company. Kodak's argument was partially based on the rising yen. However, it also reflected a concern with **dumping**, which is the selling of imported goods at a price below cost or below that in the home country. In this case Kodak argued that Fuji sold color photographic paper for less than 20 cents a square foot in the US, while charging almost 60 cents a square foot in Japan.[11] For an example of a protectionist tariff, see the box "International Business Strategy in Action: The EU–US courier wars".

Dumping
The selling of imported goods at a price below cost or below that in the home country

INTERNATIONAL BUSINESS STRATEGY *IN ACTION*

The EU–US courier wars

There are many reasons why local businesses encourage their governments to erect barriers to trade. One of the most common is when an industry is not competitive on a worldwide basis and foreign competition could bring about the bankruptcy of local firms. The US steel industry is a good example. The efficiencies of both Western European and Japanese steelmakers have brought new challenges to the American steel industry, which has asked President George W. Bush to protect it from foreign imports.

Sometimes, however, local firms will seek protection from foreign competition even though they are profitable. Why? Because they don't want to give up any of their local market share – and this is what will happen if more entrants are allowed into the industry. A good example is found in the courier wars that are now being fought in the US. The three firms that are involved are FedEx, UPS, and DHL. The first two are American companies that collectively control 80 per cent of the US market. The other is a German company that holds 1 per cent of the market.

FedEx operates out of Memphis, Tennessee where it has a major distribution hub and a large number of aircraft to help meet its commitment of one-day delivery. UPS's airport hub is in Louisville, Kentucky and is complemented by a fleet of 150,000 trucks and 1,700 depots spread across the country. Both firms also do business in Europe, where they are also profitable. Yet, despite their significant size and worldwide market coverage, the two companies have been trying to prevent DHL from building an air fleet business in the US and thus being able to deliver packages and mail just like they do. Moreover, the two giant American firms have been receiving support from the Department of Transportation, which has been lobbied by them to prevent DHL from getting an air license.

One of the arguments put forward by FedEx and UPS is that, while DHL's American subsidiary is 100 per cent US-owned, the parent company is controlled by German owners, including the German post office. This latter arrangement might seem a little strange, but a similar situation exists in Canada. The largest courier service in this country is Purolator, which is owned by the Canadian post office, a Crown monopoly. Yet despite this monopoly, both FedEx and UPS do quite well in Canada. Nevertheless, the two continue to oppose DHL being given the go-ahead to build an air fleet in the US, showing that there are many reasons for barriers to trade including simply wanting to reduce the amount of industry competitiveness in order to increase overall profitability.

Websites: ***www.fedex.com***; ***www.dhl.com***; ***www.ups.com*** and ***www.purolator.com***.

Sources: "A Tricky Business," *Economist*, June 30, 2001, pp. 55–56; "Transportation Labor Urges US Government to Revoke DHL's Air Freight Forward License," *TTD News*, January 30, 2001; Gene G. Marcial, "DHL Could Help Airborne Take Off," *Business Week*, July 9, 2001; Brian O'Reilly, "They've Got Mail," *Fortune*, February 7, 2000.

Another reason for using tariffs is to raise government revenue. Import tariffs, for example, are a major source of revenue for less developed countries. A third reason is to reduce foreign expenditures by citizens in order to improve the country's balance of payments.

Tariffs continue to be one of the most commonly used barriers to trade, despite the fact that they often hurt low-income consumers and have limited, if any, impact on upper-income purchasers. In recent years most industrialized countries have tried to reduce or eliminate the use of these trade barriers and to promote more free trade policies.[12] The US is a good example. (The trade policies of the EU are discussed in Chapter 16 and of Japan in Chapter 17.)

US trade policy

Despite being a highly protectionist nation in its early years, the US has a policy today that generally strives to lower tariffs and trade barriers through the use of multilateral agreements. Since the protectionist disaster of the depression years, the US has sought to minimize the use of tariffs. It supported the General Agreement on Tariffs and Trade (GATT) and the 1994 World Trade Organization which exists to liberalize trade and

Caribbean Basin Initiative
A trade agreement that eliminates tariffs on many imports to the US from the Caribbean and Central American regions

Foreign Sales Corporation Act
Legislation designed to allow US exporters to establish overseas affiliates and not pay taxes on the affiliates' income until the earnings are remitted to the parent company

Trade adjustment assistance
Assistance offered by the US government to US businesses and individuals harmed by competition from imports

investment. Today US tariffs average only 3.7 per cent ad valorem to most countries of the world.[13]

The move away from tariffs does not mean US trade policy is completely open.[14] The US government employs a variety of approaches to promote or discourage international trade. For example, to encourage trade, there is the **North American Free Trade Agreement (NAFTA)**, which eliminates most trade restrictions (such as tariffs) between the US, Canada, and Mexico and extends national treatment to foreign investment, and the **Caribbean Basin Initiative**, which eliminates tariffs on many imports from the Caribbean and Central American regions. Yet the **Trading-with-the-Enemy Act** disallows trade with countries judged to be enemies of the US, including North Korea and Cuba. Also, the US administration has the authority to prevent sales of goods to foreign governments when they are not deemed to be in the best interests of the US. These goods can range from computers to chemicals to materials used for making nuclear weapons.[15]

The US has also used negotiated agreements to limit the type or number of products entering the country. For example, there is a voluntary agreement with Japan that restricts the number of cars imported to the US. At the same time, the US encourages exports through legislation such as the **Foreign Sales Corporation Act**, which allows US exporters to establish overseas affiliates and not to pay taxes on the affiliates' income until the earnings are remitted to the parent company. The government also offers **trade adjustment assistance** to US businesses and individuals who are harmed by competition from imports. This aid takes such forms as loans for retooling and job counseling for those seeking alternative employment.

Active learning check 

Review your answer to Active Learning Case question 3 and make any changes you like. Then compare your answer with the one below.

3. In what way could the UK use trade barriers to protect its markets from foreign competitors? Who can be affected by these trade barriers?

There are a number of steps that the UK could take to protect its markets from foreign competitors. Examples include establishing or increasing ad valorem tariffs, placing quantity limits on various imports, and limiting foreign direct investment. Of course, other countries could retaliate and take similar action against UK-produced goods, so the use of these trade barriers must be selective and should not be undertaken unless efforts at negotiated agreements prove fruitless. As a member of the EU, the UK cannot use such trade barriers against fellow member states.

NON-TARIFF BARRIERS TO TRADE

The economic effects of non-tariff barriers (NTBs) to trade are roughly similar to those of tariffs. They are inefficient distortions that reduce potential gains from trade. There is a wide range of NTBs, as seen in Table 6.2.

Non-tariff barriers have gained prominence in recent years as they have become more visible and more important. And nations are resorting to them more frequently for protection. Sometimes these NTBs are not imposed by countries to interfere deliberately with trade.[16] Rather they arise out of domestic policy and economic management. Examples include tax breaks to reduce regional income disparities or regulations designed to increase local purchasing or employment. These, in turn, result in a type of indirect export subsidy. Other NTBs are more blatant devices that restrict imports or foster exports.

Table 6.2 **Common non-tariff barriers to trade**

Specific limitation	*Customs administrative rules*	*Government participation*	*Import charges*
Quotas (including voluntary)	Valuation systems	Procurement policies	Import deposits
Import licenses	Antidumping rules	Export subsidies and incentives	Supplementary duties
Supplementary incentives	Tariff classifications	Countervailing duties	Import credits
Minimum import limits	Documentation needed	Domestic assistance programs	Variable levies
Embargoes	Fees	Trade-diverting	Border levies
Sectoral bilateral agreements	Disparities in quality and testing standards		
Orderly marketing agreements	Packaging, labeling, and marketing standards		

Quotas

Quotas are the most important NTBs. A quota restricts imports to a particular level.[17] When a quota is imposed, domestic production generally increases and prices rise. As a result, the government usually ends up losing tariff revenues.

Historically the GATT and WTO have prohibited import quotas except on agricultural products, as emergency measures, or when a country has short-run balance of payments problems. Countries have circumvented this regulation most notably for textiles, footwear, and automobiles by negotiating voluntary export restraint agreements that are useful in preventing retaliatory action by the importing country. In general, business would rather be protected by quotas than by tariffs. Under quotas, if future domestic demand is known, businesses can determine their future production levels. Under tariffs, domestic producers must estimate the elasticity of the demand curve for imported products and the future movements in world prices, which is a more difficult challenge.

Buy national restrictions

"Buy national" regulations require national governments to give preference to domestic producers, sometimes to the complete exclusion of foreign firms. In Europe, for example, many of the telephone, telegraph, electricity generation and transmission, airlines, and railroad industries are government-owned and buy from national firms only, thus closing a large market to exporters. On the other hand, countries like the US have a similarly wide range of inefficient "Buy American" regulations at the national and state levels that discriminate against foreign suppliers.

During the 1970s Tokyo round of the GATT negotiations, a mild code to open up government contracts to foreign suppliers was negotiated. Now governments must at least publicize large procurement contracts to make public the winner's bid price or the basis for selecting the winning bid.

Customs valuation

Also during the GATT Tokyo round, considerable progress was made in the area of customs valuation for the payment of duties. In the US, there were nine valuation systems prior to the Tokyo round. Value for duty is now generally based on the invoice cost, and the latitude of customs to reclassify products has been reduced.

Technical barriers

Product and process standards for health, welfare, safety, quality, size, and measurements can create trade barriers by excluding products that do not meet the standards. Testing and certification procedures, such as testing only in the importing country and on-site plant inspections, were (and still are to some extent) cumbersome, time-consuming, and expensive. These costs must be borne by the exporter prior to the foreign sale. National governments have the right and duty to protect their citizens by setting standards to prevent the sale of hazardous products. But such standards can also be used to impede trade. For example, at one point Japan excluded US-made baseball bats from the market because they did not meet the Japanese standard. No product produced outside Japan (even products made by foreign subsidiaries of Japanese MNEs) could bear the certification stamp of the Japanese Industrial Standard (JIS) or the Japanese Agricultural Standard (JAS), and selling in Japan without the JIS or JAS logo was difficult. Similarly, at one time the new regulations for automobile safety in the US required that bumpers be above the height practical for imported subcompact cars, thus creating a technical barrier for these car manufacturers. Today the new code on technical barriers to trade requires consultation between trading partners before a standard that impedes trade is put in place. The code also requires that testing and certification procedures treat imports and domestic goods equally and that the importing country accepts certification testing conducted in the exporting country.

Antidumping legislation, subsidies, and countervailing duties

The GATT and WTO allow importing countries to protect their producers from unfair competition such as "dumping" goods at extremely low prices in an effort to gain market share and to drive out local competition. Importing countries are allowed to impose additional duties on products that have received export subsidies or are "dumped". Before the duties are imposed, however, the country must show that its domestic industry has suffered "material" injury by dumped or subsidized imports. Although products at these artificially low prices provide consumers in the importing country with a "good buy", such competition is thought to be unfair to domestic producers. Domestic producers object to dumping (and also to subsidized imports which can be offset by "countervailing" duties) if the domestic market of the exporting country is closed to them. A good example is the US auto industry, which claims that some Japanese cars are cheaper in the US market than at home, while Japan continues to impede exports of US cars into Japan.

The GATT and WTO have developed a code on countervailing duties and antidumping duties that now expedites the process of determining whether exports have been dumped or subsidized and whether the domestic industry has been injured. This subject is exceedingly complex. Here are some examples (and answers).

If the EU remits value-added taxes on exports by EU producers, is this a subsidy? (No)

If Canada subsidizes production in a specific sector in one of its depressed regions for domestic purposes, are the exports of a subsidized firm subject to countervailing action? (Yes)

If the British government subsidizes the British steel industry and its losses incurred by selling at home and abroad at prices below full cost, are its exports subject to antidumping or to countervailing duties? (Maybe, sometimes)

The problem is complex because of the difficulty in determining what material injury is and how it should be measured. This area is likely to be a point of contention for years to come.

Agricultural products

Trade in agricultural products is highly regulated by quotas and fixed and variable tariffs. And domestic producers are often highly subsidized both directly and by artificially high domestic prices. Agricultural exports are often subsidized as well. And the EU flatly refused to discuss its Common Agricultural Policy (CAP) at the Tokyo round. The CAP sets variable tariffs on imports to maintain high domestic prices by excluding or impeding imports. Moreover, revenues from these tariffs are used to subsidize exports. The CAP infuriates US agricultural producers since it not only reduces their exports to the large European market, but also it reduces world prices and gives them "unfair" competition in third country markets. The US is not without guilt in this area, however, since it also subsidizes the export of many agricultural products.

Export restraints

Over the vigorous objections of countries exporting natural resources, the GATT rounds have moved to tighten the conditions under which exports could be restrained. In general, world tariffs increase with the level of processing (for example, import duties increase as copper is processed from concentrate to blister, to refined copper, to copper wire and bars, to copper pots and pans). This tariff structure makes upgrading of natural resources in the producing country difficult. During the Tokyo round, natural resource-producing countries were largely unsuccessful in their attempts to harmonize tariffs on a sectoral basis in order to increase their ability to upgrade prior to export. However, they did argue successfully for their right to restrict exports to induce further domestic processing.

OTHER ECONOMIC DEVELOPMENTS

In addition to the above, there are other economic developments that warrant consideration. These include countertrade, trade in services, and free trade zones.

Countertrade

Countertrade
Barter trade in which the exporting firm receives payment in products from the importing country

Countertrade is essentially barter trade in which the exporting firm receives payment in terms of products from the importing country. Countertrade forms a major component of East–West trade (for example, Western pipeline products and technology in exchange for Russian natural gas). It is also important in the aircraft industry (for example, the purchase of Boeing 747s by British Airways if Boeing uses Rolls Royce engines) and in defense products (for example, the purchase of US jet fighters by Canada if some of the parts are locally sourced in Canada). Sometimes barter takes the form of a buyback in which the exporter agrees to take products that are locally produced. For example, for years PepsiCo has provided syrup to bottling plants in Russia in return for Stolichnaya vodka, which it then marketed in the West. It has also been estimated that countertrade accounts for between 10 and 20 per cent of total world trade.[18]

Countertrade tends to decrease the efficiency of world trade because it substitutes barter for exchange of goods by the price system. For example, a US exporter of machinery to Indonesia may have to take payment in an "equivalent value" of palm oil or rattan. The exporting firm will then either have to sell these products for which it has no expertise itself or sell them through a broker or other firm. Some party to the trade –

exporter, importer, or consumer – must bear these additional costs. Despite these obvious inefficiencies, countertrade appears likely to continue as an increasingly important factor in the international trade environment of the 21st century.

There is, however, one situation in which countertrade may be beneficial. For example, if a US producer of textile machinery exports to China and agrees to take payment in the form of textile products, importers in the US may perceive a lower risk of variability in product quality and delivery schedules (as a result of US technology and management), and the Chinese may perceive a lower risk of product failure in buying the machinery since the selling firm will not be "paid" unless the machinery performs to specifications.

Trade in services

International trade in services has received relatively little attention from governments or trade economists during trade negotiations. Reliable statistics are seldom collected. However, as high-income countries move toward a service economy, trade in services has grown and become a significant component of the current accounts of many countries.

In 2000 the US exported goods worth $772 billion and imported goods worth $1,224 billion, a deficit of $452 billion on merchandise trade. Also in 2000, the US exported $294 billion and imported $217 billion of services. Its trade surplus in services of $77 billion partly offset its merchandise trade deficit. Finally in 2000, the US had a deficit of $15 billion in the net income receipts from US FDI abroad. Thus the net deficit on these three accounts was $351 billion. Details of the US services and FDI accounts appear in Table 6.3. (The balance of payments account will be explained in Chapter 7.)

Table 6.3 **US balance of current account, 2000**

Items	*Exports (1) (in billions of US $)*	*Imports (2) (in billion of US $)*	*Balance (1)–(2)*
Merchandise trade	772.2	1,224.4	(452.2)
Services	293.5	217.0	76.5
Transfers	14.1	13.6	0.5
TPOT:			
Travel	82.0	64.5	17.5
Passenger fares	20.7	24.2	(3.5)
Other transportation	30.2	41.1	(10.9)
Total	132.9	129.8	3.1
FROS:			
Royalties and license fees	38.0	16.1	21.9
Other private services	107.6	54.7	52.9
US government miscellaneous	0.9	2.9	(2.0)
Total	146.5	73.7	72.8
FDI income	352.9	367.7	(14.8)
Direct investment receipts	149.2	68.0	81.2
Other private receipts	197.4	184.5	12.9
US government receipts	3.8	107.7	(103.9)
Total	1,418.6	1,809.1	(390.5)

Sources: Adapted from US Department of Commerce, *Survey of Current Business*, September 2001 and US Bureau of Economic Analysis.

The flow of services internationally is highly regulated. Internationally traded services such as banking, investment income, insurance, media, transportation, advertising, accounting, travel, and technology licensing are subject to a host of national and international regulations for economic, social, cultural, and political reasons. Trade in services largely falls outside the mandate of the WTO. One of the major trade questions for the next decade will be the regulation of trade in services. Will services be brought into the WTO so that reductions in impediments in service flows can be traded for reductions in barriers to the flow of goods? The US, as the largest exporter and importer of services (and the largest net exporter), supports this proposal. Alternatively, a new organization similar to WTO could be founded to facilitate negotiations on barriers to trade in services and to regulate this trade. The US views this proposal as a poor second-best alternative since it is already relatively open to trade in services and hence has few bargaining chips.

Whatever forum is used, negotiating reductions in barriers to trade in services will be difficult, complex, and lengthy. The barriers are often difficult to list, much less quantify for purposes of negotiation. The issues are often highly charged and not subject to rational analysis. For example, Canada imposes Canadian content requirements on television, radio, and print media to foster a "national cultural identity", to protect its cultural heritage, and to protect the domestic arts, theater, and movie industries. A government that reduced these trade barriers or even agreed to negotiate them would be in trouble with the (protected) Canadian media, as well as with the general public.

Free trade zones

Free trade zone
A designated area where importers can defer payment of customs duty while further processing of products takes place (same as a foreign trade zone)

A **free trade zone** is a designated area where importers can defer payment of customs duty while further processing of products takes place (same as a foreign trade zone). Thus the free trade zone serves as an "offshore assembly plant", employing local workers and using local financing for a tax-exempt commercial activity. The economic activity in a free trade zone takes place in a restricted area such as an industrial park since this land is often being supplied at a subsidized rate by a local host government that is interested in the potential employment benefits of the free trade zone.

To be effective, free trade zones must be strategically located either at or near an international port, on major shipping routes, or with easy access to a major airport. Important factors in the location of a free trade zone include the availability of utilities, banking and telecommunications services, and the availability of a commercial infrastructure.

Over 400 free trade zones exist in the world today, often encompassing entire cities (for example, Hong Kong and Singapore). More than two-thirds are situated in developing countries, and most future growth of these zones is expected to occur there.

The advantages offered by free trade zones are numerous and are mutually beneficial to all the stakeholders. For private firms, free trade zones offer three major attractions. First, the firm pays the customs duty (tariff) only when the goods are ready to market. Second, manufacturing costs are lower in a free trade zone because no taxes are levied. Third, while in the zone, the manufacturer has the opportunity to repackage the goods, grade them, and check for spoilage. Secondary benefits to firms occur in the reduction of insurance premiums (since these are based on duty-free values), the reduction of fines for improperly marked merchandise (since the good can be inspected in a zone prior to customers' scrutiny), and the added protection against theft (resulting from security measures in the bonded warehouses).

On the state and local level, advantages can be realized in terms of commercial services. On a more global level, free trade zones enable domestic importing companies to compete more readily with foreign producers or subsidiaries of MNEs, thereby increasing participation in world trade. Favorable effects are felt on the balance of payments since more economic activity occurs and net capital outflow is reduced. Finally, there is an improved climate for business since a free trade zone reduces bureaucracy with savings to business capital, currently inaccessible because of the delay in paying duties and tariffs. A free trade zone is a step toward free trade and can be an important signal by government to business that the economy is opening up. Opportunity replaces regulation and growth of economic activity should result.

Before the establishment of more free trade zones becomes fully accepted and encouraged, governments must be convinced of their many economic benefits. Free trade zones are a vital necessity if nations are to remain competitive on an international scale. Not only will existing companies benefit from their use, but new industries will be attracted, keeping up the same benefits of world trade.

***Maquiladora* industry**
A free trade zone that has sprung up along the US–Mexican border for the purpose of producing goods and then shipping them between the two countries

The ***maquiladora* industry** along the US–Mexican border is an excellent example of a free trade zone. The low wage rate in Mexico and the North American Free Trade Agreement (NAFTA) of 1994 make the *maquiladora* region both accessible and important to labor-intensive firms in the US and Canada. From only 12 maquiladora plants in 1965, approximately 1,700 existed in 1990. Of these, 55 per cent resulted from US investments. The *maquiladora* industry has been so successful that today only oil earns Mexico more foreign currency.

No Mexican taxes are paid on goods that are processed within the *maquiladoras*. Foreign companies doing such processing can have the benefits of lower wages and land costs than in the US as they increase the value added to their products. In return, Mexico attracts foreign direct investment into permanent plants, creates jobs, and collects taxes on any final products sold to the foreign firms, or within Mexico. Even though the US has several hundred free trade zones of its own, many near seaports or airfields, these lack the low-wage workers of their Mexican counterparts.

Canada does not have free trade zones, but the federal government allows duty drawbacks, which they argue offer many of the advantages of a free trade zone. Unfortunately, these drawbacks, which are repayments of customs duties, apply retroactively and involve enough paperwork to discourage all but the largest or most dedicated organizations. As such, the NAFTA and the lower-wage labor in Mexico have attracted Canadian firms producing labor-intensive products. Free trade zones exist in many other parts of the world than North America, and the advantages of these zones are enjoyed by businesses worldwide.[19]

KEY POINTS

1. **International economics is the branch of economics concerned with the purchase and sale of foreign goods and services. This includes consideration of areas such as international trade, balance of payments, and barriers to trade.**
2. **A number of international trade theories help to explain why nations trade. These include the theory of absolute advantage, the theory of comparative advantage, the factor endowment theory, the Leontief paradox, and the international product life cycle theory. While no one theory offers a complete explanation of why nations trade, they collectively provide important insights into the area. Other key considerations that offer explanations for why nations trade include monetary currency valuation and consumer tastes.**

3. There are a number of barriers to trade. Some of the most common include price-based barriers, quantity limits, international price fixing, non-tariff barriers, financial limits, and foreign investment controls.
4. Although tariffs are often introduced to maintain local jobs and assist infant industries, they are inefficient. This economic inefficiency results in higher prices of imported goods for the consumers. The redistribution of resources from more efficient industry further adds to the cost of a tariff. Such costs do not occur under free trade.
5. Non-tariff barriers (NTBs) provide similar economic inefficiencies to tariffs. Unlike tariffs, however, NTBs are not imposed by nations to interfere deliberately with trade; they arise out of domestic policy. There are several types of NTBs, including quotas, "buy national" restrictions, technical barriers, and export restraints.
6. Countertrade is a form of barter trade in which the exporting firm receives payments in terms of products produced in the importing country. This type of trade is most pronounced in East–West trade, and, although it may be beneficial to the trade partners, it increases the inefficiencies in the world trade system. These economic inefficiencies increase costs and decrease trade volume.
7. Services are an important but somewhat misunderstood component of trade. Despite trade of services in the billions of dollars among high-income countries, the regulation of trade in services has been outside the mandate of GATT. As services increase in importance, future discussion will take place concerning whether an international organization like GATT will carry the mandate to regulate this type of trade.
8. A free trade zone is a designated area where importers can defer payment of customs duty while further processing of products takes place, thus becoming an offshore assembly plant. The majority of these areas exist in developing countries, and they handle approximately 20 per cent of worldwide trade. Free trade zones are advantageous to all because they provide benefits such as increased employment and lower costs to business.

KEY TERMS

- international trade
- mercantilism
- theory of absolute advantage
- theory of comparative advantage
- factor endowment theory
- Heckscher–Ohlin theory
- Leontief paradox
- international product life cycle (IPLC) theory
- monetary exchange rate
- quotas
- embargo
- cartel
- non-tariff barriers
- exchange controls
- foreign investment controls
- tariff
- import tariff
- export tariff
- transit tariff
- specific duty
- ad valorem duty
- compound duty
- dumping
- North American Free Trade Agreement (NAFTA)
- Caribbean Basin Initiative
- Trading-with-the-Enemy Act
- Foreign Sales Corporation Act
- trade adjustment assistance
- countertrade
- free trade zone
- *maquiladora* industry

REVIEW AND DISCUSSION QUESTIONS

1. Why is it difficult to solve international economic problems in the short run?
2. What is the supposed economic benefit of embracing mercantilism as an international trade theory? Are there many disadvantages to the use of this theory?
3. How is the theory of absolute advantage similar to that of comparative advantage? How is it different?
4. In what way does factor endowment theory help to explain why nations trade? How does the Leontief paradox modify this theory?
5. If an innovating country develops a new technologically superior product, how long will it be before the country begins exporting the product? At what point will the country begin importing the product?
6. Of what value is the international product life cycle theory in helping to understand why nations trade?
7. How does each of the following trade barriers work: price-based barriers, quantity limits, international price fixing, non-tariff barriers, financial limits, and foreign investment controls?
8. What are some of the reasons for trade barriers? Identify and describe five.
9. How does the US try to encourage exports? Identify and describe two ways.
10. Non-tariff barriers have become increasingly predominant in recent years. Describe a non-tariff barrier, and list four types, describing how the US does or could use such a device.
11. How does countertrade work? Is it an efficient economic concept?
12. What is a free trade zone? Is it an efficient economic concept?

REAL CASE

Dumping on trade complaints

One of the biggest problems in international trade is the ability of domestic producers to lobby their home governments to erect barriers to trade. In the past, the textile, apparel, and shoe industries were able to obtain protection from cheaper imports through tariffs, quotas, and special measures. Now multilateral trade agreements under the GATT and WTO (and also regional and bilateral agreements such as NAFTA and the emerging Asian Pacific Economic Cooperation forum) outlaw such blatant instruments of protection. However, these agreements have been replaced by more subtle ones.

Prominent as a new type of protectionist device is the use of "unfair trade laws", especially antidumping (AD) and countervailing duty actions (CVD). The economic logic of AD and CVD makes some sense. It is unfair for a foreign producer to "dump" a product in your country below its price in the home country, or below the cost of producing it. Similarly, subsidized foreign products should be offset by a countervailing duty of equivalent effect. The problem, however, lies with the administration of the trade laws, which is subject to political lobbying.

A variety of studies have found that the bureaucrats who administer AD and CVD laws are subject to capture by the home industries, who then use AD and CVD cases as harassment tools against often economically efficient foreign rival producers. For example, Rugman and Anderson (1987) found that the US administration of AD and CVD was used in a biased manner against Canadian producers, especially in resource-based industries such as softwood lumber, fishing, and agriculture. Thus in the Canadian–US Free Trade Agreement of 1989, and again in NAFTA, five-person binational panels of trade law experts were set up to review the decision of the US (and Canadian) trade law agencies.

In a subsequent study, Rugman and Anderson (1997) found that these binational panels were able to remand back (i.e., successfully challenge) the decision of the US agencies twice as often in cases involving Canada as in AD and CVD cases involving the rest of the world. In related work it has been found that the EU is just as bad as the US in that the EU brings in questionable AD measures, especially against Asian countries. Indeed, one of the unresolved problems is how smaller countries can secure access to the protected markets of triad economies such as the US and the EU. In Japan's case there are similar arguments (including those from its triad rivals) that there are entry barriers in place preventing market access.

Websites: ***www.wto.org***.

Sources: Andrew D. M. Anderson, *Seeking Common Ground: Canada–US Trade Dispute Settlement Policies in the Nineties* (Boulder CO: Westview Press, 1995); Alan M. Rugman, *Multinational Enterprises and Trade Policy* (Cheltenham: Elgar, 1996); Alan M. Rugman and Andrew D. M. Anderson, *Administered Protection in America* (London and New York: Routledge, 1987); Alan M. Rugman and Andrew D. M. Anderson, "NAFTA and the Dispute Settlement Mechanisms," *The World Economy*, December, 1997, pp. 935–950; Alan M. Rugman and Michael Gestrin, "EC Anti-Dumping Laws as a Barrier to Trade," *European Management Journal*, vol. 9, no. 4 (December 1991), pp. 475–482.

1. **Why are anti-dumping and countervailing duty measures brought and imposed?**
2. **What is the impact on a firm from a non-triad country if it faces an AD or CVD case in its major market?**
3. **What is the solution to the abusive use of AD and CVD measures by triad economies?**

REAL CASE

APEC: promise and potential

Many politicians and business people say that trade barriers need to be removed in order to promote efficiency and either drive poor performers from the field or force them to revamp their operations and become competitive worldwide. At the same time, however, every country has these barriers and many local industries rely on them for survival. In the US the steel industry is in the doldrums and company inventories are at an all-time high. So steel companies are now petitioning the federal government for protection from both Japanese and Western European steelmakers. In China the government is determined to maintain a positive trade balance by encouraging exports and creating all sorts of trade barriers to discourage imports. At the same time, however, there is growing action toward liberalizing worldwide trade and promoting economic cooperation between countries.

One of the most important groups in this area of international trade and economic cooperation is the Asia-Pacific Economic Community (APEC) that includes Japan, NAFTA (the US, Canada, and Mexico), Australia, Chile, Peru, New Zealand, Russia and a host of Asian economies including China, Hong Kong, Vietnam, Brunei Darussalam, Indonesia, Malaysia, Papua New Guinea, the Philippines, Singapore, South Korea, Taiwan, and Thailand. APEC was founded in Canberra, Australia in 1989 and each year the group now meets in a different country. In 1994 the group met in Indonesia, in 1995 in Osaka, in 1996 in the Philippines, in 1997 in Vancouver, in 1998 in Malaysia, in 1999 in New Zealand, in 2000 in Brunei Darussalam and in 2001 in Shanghai. The fact that government leaders attend these conferences (for example, President Clinton spoke at the 1994 meetings and President George W. Bush in the 2001 meetings regarding their goal of a Pacific free trade area, the need for a uniform investment code, lower regional trade barriers, and copyright protection) lends a great deal of weight to the group's political muscle and has transformed APEC from a largely technical and low-key, shop talk group to a quasi-institution in which member economies are becoming increasingly committed to economic cooperation and trade.

While not a formal international institution like the WTO, APEC now has an emerging consultative process that is helping it overcome such shortcomings as the lack of well-developed procedural rules and the fact that it has no permanent secretariat. The organization has been developing an ongoing trade and investment agenda designed to create free and open trade and investment. In particular, all members have agreed to eliminate tariffs in developed countries by 2010 and in all developing countries by

2020. And in 1995 these countries all agreed to an "action agenda" in which their internal trade barriers would be identified and a voluntary commitment would be made to reduce them. To implement this agenda, APEC members have agreed to trade liberalization measures that are parallel to the main principles of the WTO.

At the 1996 meetings in the Philippines, each member country filed an Individual Action Plan (IAP) and at each subsequent annual meeting these IAPs are reviewed and each member files a formula revealing its own barriers to trade across 13 areas including tariffs, non-tariff barriers, and obstacles to trade in both services and intellectual property. The identification of these trade and investment barriers provides an important benchmark against which future measures for trade and investment liberalization can be negotiated.

Despite the efforts, however, APEC still faces a great many challenges and many observers believe that it has but a small chance to succeed. One of the biggest problems is that APEC has no permanent secretariat and relies on the trade bureaucracy of each year's host nation to advance its agenda. As a result, the 1997 meeting in Vancouver was a great success, but the 1998 meeting in Malaysia saw little progress due to the philosophical difficulty that this country's leader had with free trade.

A second problem is that there are political tensions between some of the members. For example, China and Taiwan are still at loggerheads and there is also political friction between both China and Japan, and China and the Philippines. These types of problems make economic progress difficult.

A third problem is that the inclusion of the NAFTA countries and Chile helps to offset the US–China and US-Japan power struggle to some extent. However, the domestic protectionist influences on the US Congress do not bode well for serious future trade and investment liberalization with the Asian countries, especially China, Japan, and Korea.

At the same time, APEC's potential benefits are enormous. With the WTO in disarray after the Seattle riots, APEC is the best remaining forum for multilateralism. Even slow progress towards tariff cuts and the extension of preferential treatment for developing countries by the newer members will keep multilateralism moving. APEC is also a working group which brings together potential triad rivals, offers China a place in the trade councils of the world, and provides potential economic development bridges to less developed countries.

Website: **www.apec.org**.

Source: Alan M. Rugman, *The End of Globalization* (London: Random House, 2000).

1. **What are three reasons why free trade among the APEC countries would benefit the members?**
2. **What are three reasons why some Asian economies still disapprove of lifting the trade barriers in their respective countries?**
3. **How likely is it that APEC will be successful in its efforts? Why?**

ENDNOTES

1 Asra Q. Nomani and Douglas Lavin, "US and Japan Nearing Accord in Trade Dispute," *Wall Street Journal*, March 10, 1994, p. A 3 and Richard McGregor, "Beans are on the Beijing Menu as Bush Prepares to Talk Trade," *FT.com*, February 21, 2002.

2 Douglas Harbrecht et al., "Tough Talk," *Business Week*, February 20, 1994, pp. 26–28.

3 See, for example, Dana Weschler Linden, "Dreary Days in the Dismal Science," *Forbes*, January 21, 1991, pp. 68–71.

4 Also, see Steven Greenhouse, "French Shift on State-Owned Sector," *New York Times*, April 8, 1991, p. C 2.

5 For additional insights into trade theory, see Nicolas Schmitt, "New International Trade Theories and Europe 1991: Some Results Relevant for EFTA Countries," *Journal of Common Market Studies*, September 1990, pp. 53–74.

6 See Richard W. Stevenson, "East Europe Says Barriers to Trade Hurt Its Economies," *New York Times*, January 25, 1993, pp. A 1, C 8.

7 Lucy Walker, "Sir Leon's Cartel Busters Take to the Road Again," *The European*, April 12–14, 1991, p. 25.

8 Edmund Faltermayer, "Is 'Made in the USA' Fading Away?" *Fortune*, September 24, 1990, p. 73.

9 Edward Alden and Robert Shrimsley, "EU Set to Retaliate if US Imposes Steel Tariffs," *Financial Times*, March 4, 2002.

10 See, for example, Doron P. Levin, "Honda to Hold Base Price on Accord Model," *New York Times*, September 2, 1993, p. C 3.

11 Keith Bradsher, "Kodak Is Seeking Big Tariff on Fuji," *New York Times*, September 1, 1993, pp. A 1, C 2.

12 See, for example, Robert Cohen, "Grumbling over GATT," *New York Times*, July 3, 1993, p. 13.

13 For more on this, see Robert Grosse and Duane Kujawa, *International Business: Theory and Managerial Applications* (Homewood IL: Irwin 1998), p. 233.
14 See, for example, Chris Adams, "Ailing Steel Industry Launches a Battle Against Imports," *Wall Street Journal*, October 1, 1998, p. B 4; and "Steel Vice," *Wall Street Journal*, October 1, 1998, p. A 22.
15 As an example, see Clyde H. Farnsworth, "US Slows Computer for Brazil," *International Herald Tribune*, April 13–14, 1991, p. 5.
16 Claude Barfield, "Nerves of Steel," *Financial Times*, March 1, 2002.
17 Sometimes these are voluntary quotas, as seen in Andrew Pollack, "Japan Takes a Pre-emptive Step on Auto Exports," *New York Times*, January 9, 1993, pp. 17, 26.
18 Dalia Marin, "Tying in International Trade: Evidence on Countertrade," *World Economy*, vol. 13, no. 3 (September 1990), p. 445.
19 Anthony DePalma, "Trade Pact is Spurring Mexican Deals in the US, " *New York Times*, March 17, 1994, pp. C 1, 3.

ADDITIONAL BIBLIOGRAPHY

Anderson, Andrew D. M. *Seeking Common Ground: Canada–US Trade Disputes* (Boulder CO: Westview, 1995).

Baldauf, Artur. "Examining Determinants of Export Performance in Small Open Economies," *Journal of World Business*, vol. 35, no. 1 (Spring 2000).

Brewer, Thomas L. and Young, Stephen. *The Multinational Investment System and Multinational Enterprises* (Oxford: Oxford University Press, 2000).

Brewer, Thomas L. and Young, Stephen. "Multilateral Institutions and Policies: Their Implications for Multinational Business Strategy," in Alan M. Rugman and Thomas L. Brewer (eds.), *The Oxford Handbook of International Business* (Oxford: Oxford University Press, 2001).

Buckley, Peter J. "Government Policy Responses to Strategic Rent Seeking Transnational Corporations," *Transnational Corporations*, vol. 5, no. 2 (August 1996).

Cavusgil, S. Tamer and Sikora, Ed. "How Multinationals Can Counter Gray Market Imports," *Columbia Journal of World Business*, vol. 23, no. 4 (Winter 1988).

Chao, Paul. "Export and Reverse Investment: Strategic Implications for Newly Industrialized Countries," *Journal of International Business Studies*, vol. 20, no. 1 (Spring 1989).

Cho, Kang Rae. "The Role of Product-Specific Factors in Intra-Firm Trade of US Manufacturing Multinational Corporations," *Journal of International Business Studies*, vol. 21, no. 2 (Second Quarter 1990).

Dichtl, Erwin, Koeglmayr, Hans-Georg and Mueller, Stefan. "International Orientation as a Precondition for Export Success," *Journal of International Business Studies*, vol. 21, no. 1 (First Quarter 1990).

Deutsch, Klaus Gunter and Speyer, Bernhard (eds.). *The World Trade Organization Millennium Round* (London: Routledge, 2001).

Dunning, John H. and Mucchielli, Jean-Louis (eds.). *Multinational Firms: The Global-Local Dilemma* (London: Routledge, 2002).

Emmerij, Louis. "Globalization, Regionalization and World Trade," *Columbia Journal of World Business*, vol. 27, no. 2 (Summer 1992).

Green, Robert T. and Kohli, Ajay K. "Export Market Identification: The Role of Economic Size and Socioeconomic Development," *Management International Review*, vol. 31, no. 1 (First Quarter 1991).

Haigh, Robert, W. "Thinking of Exporting? Export Management Companies Could be the Answer," *Columbia Journal of World Business*, vol. 29, no. 4 (Winter 1994).

Han, C. Min and Terpstra, Vern. "Country-of-Origin Effects for Uni-national and Bi-national Products," *Journal of International Business Studies*, vol. 19, no. 2 (Summer 1988).

Hennart, Jean-François. "Some Empirical Dimensions of Countertrade," *Journal of International Business Studies*, vol. 21, no. 2 (Second Quarter 1990).

Koka, Balaji R., Prescott, John E. and Madhavan, Ravindranath. "Contagion Influence on Trade and Investment Policy: A Network Perspective," *Journal of International Business Studies*, vol. 30, no. 1 (Spring 1999).

Markusen, James R. "International Trade Theory and International Business," in Alan M. Rugman and Thomas L. Brewer (eds.), *The Oxford Handbook of International Business* (Oxford: Oxford University Press, 2001).

Miller, Janice S., Hom, Peter W. and R. Gomez-Mejia, Luis. "The High Cost of Low Wages: Does Maquiladora Compensation Reduce Turnover?" *Journal of International Business Studies*, vol. 32, no. 3 (Fall 2001).

Neale, Charles W., Shipley, David D. and Dodds, J. Colin. "The Countertrading Experience of British and Canadian Firms," *Management International Review*, vol. 31, no. 1 (First Quarter 1991).

Ostry, Sylvia. *The Post-Cold War Trading System* (Chicago IL: University of Chicago Press, 1997).

Ostry, Sylvia. "The Multilateral Trading System," in Alan M. Rugman and Thomas L. Brewer (eds.), *The Oxford Handbook of International Business* (Oxford: Oxford University Press, 2001).

Perry, Anne C. "The Evolution of the US International Trade Intermediary in the 1980s: A Dynamic Model," *Journal of International Business Studies*, vol. 21, no. 1 (First Quarter 1990).

Ramstetter, Eric D. "Export Performance and Foreign Affiliate Activity in Japan's Large Machinery Firms," *Transnational Corporations*, vol. 6, no. 3 (December 1997).

Robin, Donald P. and Sawyer, W. Charles. "The Ethics of Antidumping Petitions," *Journal of World Business*, vol. 33, no. 3 (Fall 1998).

Robock, Stefan H. "The Export Myopia of US Multinationals: An Overlooked Opportunity for Creating US Manufacturing Jobs," *Columbia Journal of World Business*, vol. 28, no. 2 (Summer 1993).

Ruggiero, Renato. "Foreign Direct Investment and the Multilateral Trading System," *Transnational Corporations*, vol. 5, no. 1 (April 1996).

Rugman, Alan M. *Multinational Enterprises and Trade Policy* (Cheltenham: Elgar, 1996).

Rugman, Alan M. and Anderson, Andrew. *Administered Protection in America* (London: Croom Helm and New York: Methuen, 1987).

Rugman, Alan M. and Boyd, Gavin (eds.). *The World Trade Organization in the New Global Economy* (Cheltenham: Elgar, 2001).

Rugman, Alan M. and Gestrin, Michael. "US Trade Laws as Barriers to Globalization," in Tamir Agmon and Richard Drobnick (eds.), *Small Firms in Global Competition* (New York: Oxford University Press, 1994).

Rugman, Alan M. and Verbeke, Alain. *Global Corporate Strategy and Trade Policy* (London and New York: Routledge, 1990).

Rugman, Alan M. and Verbeke, Alain. "Strategic Trade Policy is Not Good Strategy," *Hitotsubashi Journal of Commerce and Management*, vol. 25, no. 1 (December 1990).

Rugman, Alan M. and Verbeke, Alain. "Location, Competitiveness, and the Multinational Enterprise," in Alan M. Rugman and Thomas L. Brewer (eds.), *The Oxford Handbook of International Business* (Oxford: Oxford University Press, 2001).

Sampson, Gary P. (ed.). *The Role of the World Trade Organization in Global Governance* (Tokyo, New York, Paris: United Nations University Press, 2001).

Sullivan, Daniel and Bauerschmidt, Alan. "Common Factors Underlying Barriers to Export: A Comparative Study in the European and US Paper Industry," *Management International Review*, vol. 29, no. 2 (Second Quarter 1989).

Chapter 7

International Finance

CONTENTS

OBJECTIVES OF THE CHAPTER

In one way or another, all businesses are affected by international finance. For example, US auto dealers who sell imported VWs and BMWs must adjust their prices as the prices they pay for these cars go up or down because of the euro foreign exchange rate. Similarly, manufacturers who import materials or parts from overseas suppliers are affected by developments such as wage increases paid by suppliers to their own personnel. End users and customers, in the final analysis, are affected because most of these costs are passed on to them. They key exchange rates are the US dollar, the euro and the Japanese yen.

There are many important areas of international finance with which students of international business should be familiar. This chapter focuses on four areas: balance of payments (BOP), the international monetary system, foreign exchange, and the strategic management of international finance.

The specific objectives of this chapter are to:

1. *Describe* the four basic categories that constitute a nation's balance of payments and relate how international transactions are accounted for in this balance.
2. *Relate* the role and functions of the International Monetary Fund.
3. *Explain* why the international debt crisis is going to continue to be a major international finance problem in the new millennium.
4. *Describe* the nature and operations of foreign exchange markets.
5. *Discuss* how exchange rates are determined.
6. *Set forth* international finance strategies that can be used by organizations doing business in the international arena.

ACTIVE LEARNING CASE

Japan's economic challenges

During the 1980s Japan's global trade increased sharply. In the early years of this decade the surplus was around $20 billion annually. By the middle of the decade it has risen to almost $60 billion a year, and by the early 1990s it was over $120 billion. By the end of the decade, however, this surplus had begun to shrink, and by 2000 it was just under $100 billion.

At the same time, however, some things had not changed very much during the decade. One of these was the large trade surplus that Japan continued to run with the US and the EU. In 2000 the US imported over $147 billion of goods and services from Japan while selling approximately $65 billion of goods and services to them. This deficit of $82 billion continued to rankle many members of the US Congress who argued that Japan had to open its door wider to American products. Many politicians in the EU felt the same way. In 2000 Japan had a trade surplus of almost $28 billion with the EU. These two triad groups were not alone.

Many nations have had an ongoing trade deficit with Japan. In 1999 China Hong Kong's trade deficit with Japan was over $20 billion, Taiwan's was more than $16 billion, Korea's was almost $7 billion, and the Philippines' was over $3 billion. At the same time, however, some countries have been consistently running a trade surplus with Japan. China P.R., for example, had a surplus of $22 billion in 2000 and in 1999 the Middle East countries, on a collective basis, also had a surplus of $20 billion.

And while Japan continues to run an overall trade surplus with the rest of the world, there are a number of recent developments that do not bode well for its economy. One is its level of exports that have now begun to decline. The main reason is that most national economies have begun to slow down. So from nearby Asian countries that used to buy large amounts of Japanese exports to the US, which has long been a market for Japanese goods, buyers are not purchasing as much as previously. A second reason is that by 2001 the Japanese yen was around 120 to the US dollar. The Japanese government felt that the yen was too strong and wanted to see it weaken and move into the range of 135–140 yen to the dollar. However, this had not happened, effectively serving to reduce Japanese exports.

Still another reason for Japan's problems is that its economy has continued to remain weak and domestic demand has stayed low. Perhaps worst of all, and closely tied to its internal economic problems, a growing number of Japanese companies have now been transferring their production centers to China and other nearby countries where costs are lower. As a result of such outsourcing, Japan's domestic exports are now likely to decline even further while reimports from these other nations will increase. A good example is provided by automobile production. Over the last five years Japan, Europe, the US, and Taiwan have all invested in China and intend to use their factories in China to produce not only low value-added goods such as clothing and household electric appliances, but also to make high value-added goods such as cars. So, in the future, many of the automobiles that used to be manufactured in Japan and exported throughout Asia will be replaced by Chinese production and Japan may even end up importing cars from China for domestic sale. Quite clearly, the recent downturn in worldwide economies (in particular, the US), coupled with the increasing presence of China in the economic arena, are presenting Japan with new economic challenges.

Sources: "Trade Surplus Nosedives 36% in June," *Taipei Times*, June 24, 2001; "Japan's Trade Balance Shows Signs of Change," *Foreign Press Center Japan*, June 4, 2001; "Japans Trade Surplus Slumps", *BBC.co.uk*, June 20, 2001; IMF, *Direction of Trade Statistics Yearbook*, 2000; "Trading Places," *Economist*, March 25, 1999; and "Big Dents in Japan's Trade Surplus," *BBC.co.uk*, June 21, 2001.

1. **Why is Japan's trade surplus with the US of concern to the US?**
2. **Some countries believe that those with large trade surpluses should reinvest them in poorer countries in order to help these economies. Is Japan in a position to do this?**
3. **If the Japanese economy were to encounter annual inflation of 7 per cent while France's rate was 2 per cent, what would happen to the value of the French franc in comparison with the Japanese yen?**
4. **How could US firms located in Japan profit from an appreciation of the Japanese yen?**

INTRODUCTION

International finance
An area of study concerned with the balance of payments (BOP) and the international monetary system

International finance is an area of study concerned with the balance of payments (BOP) and the international monetary system. A development in one of these areas can affect the other. For example, in recent years a growing number of US firms have established research and development (R&D) centers in Japan.[1] This required a foreign direct investment (FDI), as well as the purchase of foreign exchange (yen) for handling domestic expenses. Have these decisions been successful? In the sense that they are designed to help develop the firm's R&D expertise, the companies report that they have indeed been wise decisions. From a financial standpoint, however, they would get mixed reviews because over the past five years the value of the yen has weakened against the dollar. If the companies were to build these facilities today, the dollar cost would be lower because the yen has weakened. Part of the reason is that the Japanese government has sought to drive down the value of the yen against the dollar in order to stimulate exports and to help jump-start the economy.

The changing value of the US dollar against some of the other major currencies has also affected the cost of some exports and imports.[2] In some cases the US dollar has strengthened. For example from 1998–2001 the dollar has gotten stronger against the British pound and the German mark, while its value against the Hong Kong dollar has remained the same. As a result, a growing number of US multinationals have begun setting up operations overseas, thus shielding themselves against the risk of exporting into a country with a weakening international currency.[3]

This chapter will examine each of the main areas of international finance. While the focus is mainly on the US, the general principles apply to all economies. We begin with the balance of payments because this topic sets the stage for a discussion of the international monetary system and foreign exchange.

BALANCE OF PAYMENTS

Balance of payments (BOP)
The record of all values of all transactions between a country's residents and the rest of the world

One way of measuring a country's economic activity is by looking at its balance of payments. The **balance of payments (BOP)** is the record of the value of all transactions between a country's residents and the rest of the world. There are a wide variety of accounts that determine the BOP, but for purposes of analysis they can be grouped into three broad categories: current account items, capital account items, and reserves.

BOP is a double-entry system, similar to that used in accounting. Every transaction is recorded in terms of both a debit and a credit. Debits record transactions such as the import of a good or service, an increase in assets, or a reduction in liabilities. Credits record the export of a good or service, a decrease in assets, or an increase in liabilities. Using Table 7.1 as a point of reference, the following discussion examines the three broad BOP categories.

Broad BOP categories

International Monetary Fund (IMF)
An agency that seeks to maintain balance-of-payments stability in the international financial system

The **International Monetary Fund (IMF)**, an agency that seeks to maintain balance of payments stability in the international financial system, has developed a standardized BOP system and form of presentation. Table 7.1 presents an abbreviated version of this system. This presentation form is important because it is so widely used. As we see, the table describes each of the three broad BOP categories.

Table 7.1 Balance of payments: IMF presentation

	Debits	*Credits*
I. Current account		
A. Goods, services, and income:		
1. Merchandise	Imports from foreign sources (acquisition of goods).	Exports to foreign destinations (provision of goods).
Trade balance		
2. Shipment and other transportation	Payments to foreigners for freight and insurance on international shipments; for ship repair, stores and supplies; and international passenger fares.	Receipts by residents from foreigners for services provided.
3. Travel	Expenditures by residents (including internal transportation) when traveling in a foreign country.	Receipts by residents for goods and services (including internal transportation) sold to foreign travelers in reporting country.
4. Investment income	Profits of foreign direct investments in reporting country, including reinvested earnings; income paid to foreigners as interest, dividends, etc.	Profits of direct investments by residents in foreign countries, including reinvested earnings; income received by residents from abroad as interest, dividends, etc.
5. Other official	Foreign purchases by government not included elsewhere; personal expenditures of government civilian and military personnel stationed in foreign countries.	Expenditures of foreign governments for goods and services, not included elsewhere; personal expenditures of foreign civilian and military personnel stationed in reporting country.
6. Other private	Payments to foreigners for management fees, royalties, film rentals, construction, etc.	Receipts from foreigners for management fees, royalties, film rentals, construction, etc.
Goods, services, and income balance		
B. Unrequited transfers:		
1. Private	Payments in cash and kind by residents to foreigners without a quid pro quo such as charitable gifts and gifts by migrants to their families.	Receipts in cash and kind by residents from foreigners, individuals or governments without a quid pro quo.
2. Official	Transfers by government of reporting country for pensions, reparations, and grants for economic and military aid.	Transfers received by government from foreigners in the form of goods, services, or cash as gifts or grants. Also tax receipts from non-residents.
Current account balance		
II. Capital account		
C. Capital, excluding reserves:		
1. Direct investment	a. Increased investment in foreign enterprises controlled by residents, including reinvestment of earnings. b. Decreases in investment by residents in domestic enterprises controlled by foreigners.	a. Decreased investment in foreign enterprises controlled by residents. b. Increases in investment in domestic enterprises by foreigners.

Table 7.1 ***(cont'd)***

	Debits	*Credits*
2. Portfolio investment	a. Increases in investment by residents in foreign securities. b. Decreases in investment by foreigners in domestic securities such as bonds and corporate equities.	a. Decreases in investments by residents in foreign securities. b. Increases in investment by foreigners in domestic securities.
3. Other long-term, official	a. Loans to foreigners. b. Redemption or purchase from foreigners of government securities.	a. Foreign loan reductions. b. Sales to foreigners of government securities.
4. Other long-term, private	a. Long-term loans to foreigners by resident banks and private parties. b. Loan repayments by residents to foreign banks or private parties.	a. Long-term loans by foreigners to resident banks or private parties. b. Loan repayments by foreigners to residents.
5. Other short-term, official	a. Short-term loans to foreigners by central government. b. Purchase from foreigners of government securities, decrease in liabilities constituting reserves of foreign authorities.	a. Short-term loans to resident central government by foreigners. b. Foreign sales of short-term resident government securities, increases in liabilities constituting reserves of foreign authorities.
6. Other short-term, private	a. Increases in short-term foreign assets held by residents. b. Decreases in domestic assets held by foreigners, such as bank deposits, currencies, debts to banks, and commercial claims.	a. Decreases in short-term foreign assets held by residents. Increase in foreign liabilities of residents. b. Increase in domestic short-term assets held by foreigners or decrease in short-term domestic liabilities to foreigners.
III. Reserves		
D. Reserves:		
1. Monetary gold 2. Special drawing rights (SDRs) 3. IMF reserve position 4. Foreign exchange assets	Increases in holdings of gold, SDRs, foreign convertible currencies by monetary authorities; decreases in liabilities to IMF or increase in IMF assets position.	Decreases in holdings of gold, SDRs, foreign convertible currencies by monetary authorities; increases in liabilities to IMF or decrease in IMF assets position.
E. Net errors and omissions:	Net understatement of recorded debts or overstatement of recorded credits.	Net understatement of recorded debts or overstatement of recorded credits.
Balances: Balances on merchandise trade	*A-1 credits minus A-1 debts*	
Balance on goods, services, and income	*A-1 through A-6 credits minus A-1 through A-6 debits*	
Balance on current account	*A and B credits minus A and B debits*	

Current account
A balance-of-payments account that consists of merchandise trade, services, and unrequited transfers

Merchandise trade
A balance-of-payments account that reports imports of goods from foreign sources and exports of goods to foreign destinations

Current account

The **current account** consists of merchandise trade, services, and unrequited transfers. (See Table 7.1, parts *A* and *B*.)

Merchandise trade is typically the first part of the current account. It receives more attention than any of the other accounts because this is where the imports and exports of goods are reported, and these are often the largest single component of all international transactions.[4] In this account, sales of goods to foreigners (exports) are reported as credits because they are a source of funds or a claim against the purchasing country. Conversely, purchases of goods from overseas (imports) are recorded as debits because they use funds. This payment can be made by either reducing current claims on foreigners or increasing foreign liabilities.

Merchandise trade transactions can affect a country's BOP in a number of ways. Assume that Nissan Motor of Japan has sold General Motors in the US $600,000 worth of engines and these engines will be paid for from GM's account in a Detroit bank. In this case the imports are a debit to the current account (A-1) and a credit to the "other short-term, private" capital account (C-6b). Here is how the entry would be recorded:

		Debit	*Credit*
A-1	Merchandise imports	$600,000	
C-6b	Increase in domestic short-term assets held by foreigners		$600,000

The result of this purchase is that the US has transferred currency to foreigners and thus reduced its ability to meet other claims.

Services

The services category includes many payments such as freight and insurance on international shipments (A-2); tourist travel (A-3); profits and income from overseas investment (A-4); personal expenditures by government, civilians, and military personnel overseas (A-5); and payments for management fees, royalties, film rental, and construction services (A-6). Purchases of these services are recorded as debits, while sales of these services are similar to exports and are recorded as credits. For example, extending the earlier example of Nissan and GM, assume that the US auto maker must pay $125,000 to Nissan to ship the engines to the US. The transaction would be recorded this way:

		Debit	*Credit*
A-2	Shipment	$125,000	
C-6b	Other short-term private capital		$125,000

GM purchased a Japanese shipping service (a debit to the current account) and paid for this by increasing the domestic short-term assets held by foreigners (a credit to the capital account).

Unrequited transfers

Unrequited transfers A balance-of-payments account that reports transactions which do not involve repayment or performance of any service

Unrequited transfers are transactions that do not involve repayment or the performance of any service. Examples include the American Red Cross sending $10 million in food to refugees in Somalia; the US paying military pensions to residents of the Philippines who served in the US army during World War II; and British workers in Kuwait shipping money home to their families in London. Here is how the American Red Cross transaction would appear in the US BOP:

		Debit	*Credit*
B-1	Unrequited transfers, private	$10 million	
A-1	Merchandise exports		$10 million

Capital account

Capital account items
A balance-of-payments account that involves transactions which involve claims in ownership

Capital account items are transactions that involve claims in ownership. Direct investment (C-1) involves managerial participation in a foreign enterprise along with some degree of control. The US classifies direct investments as those investments that give the investor more than 10 per cent ownership. Portfolio investment (C-2) is investment designed to obtain income or capital gains. For example, if Exxon shipped $20 million of equipment to an overseas subsidiary the entry would be:

		Debit	*Credit*
C-1	Direct investment	$20 million	
A-1	Exports		$20 million

"Other long-term" capital accounts are differentiated based on whether they are government (C-3) or private (C-4) transactions. These transactions have a maturity of over one year and involve either loans or securities. For example, Citibank may have loaned the government of Poland $50 million. "Other short-term" capital accounts are also differentiated based on whether they are governmental (C-5) or private (C-6). Typical short-term government transactions are short-term loans in the securities of other governments. Private transactions often include trade bill acceptances or other short-term claims arising from the financing of trade and movements of money by investors to take advantage of interest differentials among countries.

Reserves

Reserves are used for bringing BOP accounts into balance. There are four major types of reserves available to monetary authorities in meeting BOP deficits (D1 through D4 in Table 7.1). These reserves are analogous to the cash or near-cash assets of a private firm. Given that billions of dollars in transactions are reported in BOP statements, it should come as no surprise that the amount of recorded debits are never equal to the amount of credits. This is why there is an entry in the reserve account for net errors and omissions. If a country's reporting system is weak or there is a large number of clandestine transactions, this discrepancy can be quite large.

US balance of payments

The official presentation of the US BOP is somewhat different from the IMF format presented in Table 7.1. Because the US plays such a dominant role in the world economy, it is important to examine the US system. Table 7.2 presents US international transactions for two recent years.

A number of select entries in Table 7.2 help to highlight the US BOP. Lines 1 and 18 show that exports in 2000 were $390.5 billion less than imports. This trade deficit was greater than that in 1999 when it stood at $275.4 billion, showing that the US continues to have trade deficit problems.

To assess the trade situation accurately, however, we need to examine the data in more depth. This information is provided in Table 7.3. The table shows that US exports are strong in areas such as capital goods, industrial supplies and materials, consumer goods, and auto vehicles, engines, and parts. On the other hand, the US is importing a great deal of capital goods, consumer goods, and industrial supplies and materials.

In the early 1980s US trade deficits were offset by large amounts of income generated by direct investments abroad. Later in the decade massive international borrowing offset these deficits. More recently the situation has improved somewhat, and dollar

Table 7.2 **US international transactions: 1999 and 2000**

Line	(Credits +; debits –)	1999 (in millions of US $)	2000 (in millions of US $)
1	Exports of goods and services and income receipts	1,242,655	1,418,568
2	Exports of goods and services	957,353	1,065,702
3	Goods, balance of payment basis	684,553	772,210
4	Services	272,800	293,492
5	Transfers under US military agency sales contracts	15,920	14,060
6	Travel	74,731	82,042
7	Passenger fares	19,785	20,745
8	Other transportation	26,916	30,185
9	Royalties and license fees	36,420	38,030
10	Other private services	98,143	107,568
11	US government miscellaneous services	885	862
12	Income receipts	285,302	352,866
13	Income receipts on US-owned assets	283,092	350,525
14	Direct investment receipts	123,718	149,240
15	Other private receipts	156,177	197,440
16	US government miscellaneous receipts	3,197	3,845
17	Compensation of employees	2,210	2,341
18	Imports of goods and services and income payments	1,518,106	1,809,099
19	Imports of goods and services	1,219,191	1,441,441
20	Goods, balance of payment basis	1,029,987	1,224,417
21	Services	189,204	217,024
22	Direct defense expenditures	13,334	13,560
23	Travel	58,865	64,537
24	Passenger fares	21,315	24,197
25	Other transportation	34,139	41,058
26	Royalties and license fees	12,613	16,106
27	Other private services	46,117	54,687
28	US government miscellanous services	2,821	2,879
29	Income payments	298,915	367,658
30	Income payments on foreign-owned assets in the US	291,603	360,146
31	Direct investment payments	56,674	68,009
32	Other private payments	139,798	184,465
33	US government payments	95,131	107,672
34	Compensation of employees	7,312	7,512
35	Unilateral current transfers, net	48,913	54,136
40	US-owned assets abroad, (net (increase/financial outflow (–))	437,067	580,952
55	Foreign-owned assets in the US, net (increase/financial inflow (+))	813,744	1,024,218
71	Balance on goods (lines 3 and 20)	(345,434)	(452,207)
72	Balance on services (lines 4 and 21)	83,596	76,468
73	Balance on goods and services (lines 2 and 19)	(261,838)	(375,739)
74	Balance on income (lines 12 and 29)	(13,613)	(14,792)
75	Unilateral current transfers, net (line 35)	(48,913)	(54,136)
76	Balance on current account (lines 1, 18, and 35 or lines 73, 74, and 75)	(324,364)	(444,667)

Sources: US Department of Commerce, *Survey of Current Business*, September 2001 and US Bureau of Economic Analysis.

devaluation has helped to generate stronger demand for US exports, thus partially reducing the annual trade deficit. However, more concerted action will be needed if the US is to continue on this course. One way is to continue to increase US competitiveness in the international market. Another way is to get other countries to reduce their trade barriers and to make international markets more open.

Table 7.3 **US merchandise trade, 1999 and 2000**

	1999 (in millions of US $)	*2000 (in millions of US $)*
Exports	684,553	772,210
Foods, feeds, and beverages	45,532	47,452
Industrial supplies and materials	147,000	171,932
Capital goods, except automotive	310,874	357,034
Automotive vehicles, engines and parts	75,085	80,169
Consumer goods (non-food), except automotive	81,971	90,555
Other goods	35,336	34,775
Adjustments	(11,244)	(9,708)
Imports	1,029,987	1,224,417
Foods, feeds, and beverages	43,579	45,975
Industrial supplies and materials	222,024	299,788
Capital goods, except automotive	295,272	346,663
Automotive vehicles, engines and parts	178,996	195,858
Consumer goods (non-food), except automotive	241,702	281,405
Other goods	43,046	48,333
Adjustments	5,369	6,395

Sources: US Department of Commerce, *Survey of Current Business*, September 2001 and US Bureau of Economic Analysis.

It is important to realize that when a country suffers a persistent balance of trade deficit, the nation will also suffer from a depreciating currency and will find it difficult to borrow in the international capital market.[5] In this case there are only two choices available. One is to borrow from the International Monetary Fund (IMF) and be willing to accept the restrictions that the IMF puts on the country, which are designed to introduce austerity and force the country back onto the right economic track. The other approach is for the country to change its fiscal policy (tariffs and taxes), resort to exchange and trade controls, or devalue its currency. In order to prevent having to undertake austerity steps, the US will have to continue working very hard to control its trade deficit.[6] One way of understanding how this can be done is through knowledge of the international monetary system, the next topic that we consider.

Active learning check

Review your answer to Active Learning Case question 1 and make any changes you like. Then compare your answer with the one below.

1. Why is Japan's trade surplus with the US of concern to the US?

There are a number of reasons why this surplus is of concern to the US. One is that it is the largest single component of international transactions and thus greatly affects America's overall balance of payments. A second is that continuing deficits in this account must be offset by income generated from direct investment abroad, international borrowing, or dollar devaluation. A close analysis of these reasons helps to explain why the US is determined to reduce this surplus sharply and, in the process, strengthen its own economy. So the future is likely to see even greater American pressure on Japan regarding the US annual trade deficits.

INTERNATIONAL MONETARY SYSTEM

International monetary system
The multinational arrangement among the central banks of those countries that belong to the International Monetary Fund

The **international monetary system** is an institutional arrangement among the central banks of the countries that belong to the International Monetary Fund (IMF). This overall monetary system includes a wide variety of institutions, financial instruments, rules, and procedures within which foreign exchange markets function. The objective of this system is to create an international environment that is conducive to the free flow of goods, services, and capital among nations. This system also strives to create a stable foreign exchange market, to guarantee the convertibility of currencies, and to ensure adequate liquidity. The IMF is one of the primary organizations in this system.

International Monetary Fund

International Bank for Reconstruction and Development
(See World Bank.)

World Bank
A multigovernment-owned bank created to promote development projects through the use of low-interest loans

Near the end of World War II there was an international meeting of the major Allied governments to restructure the international monetary system. The group met at Bretton Woods, New Hampshire, in 1944 and agreed to establish a new monetary order. This meeting helped to create the International Monetary Fund (IMF), a multigovernment organization designed to promote exchange rate stability and to facilitate the flow of international currencies. The Bretton Woods agreement also resulted in the formation of the **International Bank for Reconstruction and Development** (now known as the **World Bank**), a multigovernment-owned bank that was created to promote development projects through the use of low-interest loans. The 40 initial participating countries set fixed exchange rates under which each established a par value for its currency, based on gold and the US dollar. Participating countries also funded the IMF and agreed to keep the value of their currency within 1 per cent of the official parity or devalue the currency. If it became necessary to devalue a currency by 10 per cent or more, IMF approval was needed. The overall goals of the IMF were to:

1. Facilitate the balanced growth of international trade.
2. Promote exchange stability and orderly exchange arrangements and discourage competitive currency depreciation.
3. Seek the elimination of exchange restrictions that hinder the growth of world trade.
4. Make financial resources available to members, on a temporary basis and with adequate safeguards, to permit them to correct payment imbalances without resorting to measures destructive to national and international prosperity.

The original IMF framework functioned well for about 15 years. However, by the 1960s problems were beginning to develop. One reason was that the US had been supplying international liquidity through a steady net outflow of dollars for such things as economic aid, private foreign direct investment, and military expenditures. Western European countries were using these dollars to replenish their depleted international reserves. However, as the US began to run large balance of payments deficits, confidence in the dollar began to decline and countries like France started exchanging dollars for gold. The fixed exchange rate system was breaking down and changes were needed. In 1968 the US suspended the sale of gold except to official parties, and in mid-1971 the US closed the gold window completely, refusing to exchange gold for dollars.

Special drawing right (SDR)
A unit of value that has been created by the IMF to replace the dollar as a reserve asset

During the 1970s as the economies of more and more countries strengthened, it became evident that gold and internationally acceptable currencies could not handle the reserve requirements of these nations. In 1970, to help increase international reserves, the IMF created the **special drawing right (SDR)** as a unit of value to replace the dollar as a reserve asset, and today a number of countries peg their currency to the SDR. When first created, the SDR was linked to gold, but since 1974 its value has been based on the daily market exchange rates of a basket of currencies consisting of the US dollar, British pound, French franc, German mark, and Japanese yen (see Table 7.4). Another major

Table 7.4 **World exchange rate arrangements, 2001**

Pegged to a single currency	*Pegged to a currency composite*	*Cooperative arrangements*	*Other managed floating*	*Independently floating*
American Samoa (US $)	Algeria	Austria (euro)	Angola	Afghanistan
Andorra (Spanish peseta and French franc) (1)	Bangladesh	Belgium (euro)	Belarus	Albania
Anguilla (US $)	Botswana	Denmark (euro)	Cambodia	Australia
Antigua and Barbuda (US $)	Burundi	Finland (euro)	Cape Verde Island	Bolivia
Argentina (US $)	Fiji	France (euro)	Chile	Brazil
Aruba (US $)	Hungary	Germany (euro)	China	Canada
Bahamas (US $)	Iceland	Greece (euro)	Colombia	Congo, Dem. Rep.
Bahrain (US $)	Jordan	Ireland (euro)	Dominican Republic	Costa Rica
Belize (US $)	Kuwait	Italy (euro)	Egypt	Croatia
Benin (French franc)	Latvia (3)	Luxembourg (euro)	Guinea	Czech Republic
Bermuda (US $)	Libya (3)	Netherlands (euro)	Honduras	El Salvador
Bhutan (Indian rupee)	Macedonia	Portugal (euro)	Indonesia	Ethiopia
Bosnia–Herzegovina (DM)	Malta	Spain (euro)	Israel	Gambia
Bulgaria (German mark)	Mauritania		Laos	Georgia
Burkina Faso (French franc)	Mauritius		Malaysia	Ghana
Cameroon (French franc)	Morocco		Maldives	Guatemala
Cayman Islands (US $)	Nepal		Nicaragua	Guyana
Central African Rep. (French franc)	Papua New Guinea		Pakistan	Haiti
Chad (French franc)	Rwanda (3)		Poland	India
Comoros (French franc)	Seychelles (3)		São Tomé & Príncipe	Jamaica
Congo (French franc)	Slovakia		Singapore	Japan
Côte d'Ivoire (French franc)	Solomon Island		Slovenia	Kazakhstan
Cuba (US $)	Tonga		Sri Lanka	Kenya
Cyprus (euro)	Vanuatu		Sudan	South Korea
Djibouti (US $)	Western Samoa		Surinam	Kyrgyzstan
Dominica (US $)			Sweden	Lebanon
Ecuador (US $) (2)			Tunisia	Madagascar
Equatorial Guinea (French franc)			Turkey	Malawi
Estonia (German mark)			Uruguay	Mexico
French Polynesia (French franc)			Vietnam	Moldova
Gabon (French franc)				Mongolia
Gibraltar (British pound)				Mozambique
Grenada (US $)				Norway
Guinea-Bissau (French franc)				Paraguay
Hong Kong (US $)				Peru
Iran (US $)				Philippines
Iraq (US $)				Romania
Lesotho (South African rand)				Russia
Liberia (US $)				Sierra Leone
Lithuania (US $)				Somalia
Macao (HK $)				South Africa
Mali (French franc)				Switzerland
Montserrat (US $)				Tanzania
Myanmar (US $)				Thailand
Namibia (South African rand)				Trinidad and Tobago
Netherlands Antilles (US $)				Uganda
New Caledonia (French franc)				Ukraine
Niger (French franc)				United Kingdom
Nigeria (US $)				United States
Oman (US $)				Venezuela
Panama (US $)				Yemen
Qatar (US $)				Zambia
Saudi Arabia (US $)				Zimbabwe
Senegal (French franc)				
St Helena (British Pound)				
St Kitts and Nevis (US $)				
St Lucia (US $)				
St Vincent and the Grenadines (US $)				
Swaziland (South African rand)				
Syria (US $)				
Togo (French franc)				
Turkmenistan (US $)				
United Arab Emirates (US $)				
Wallis and Futuna Islands (French franc)				

Notes: (1) Andorra has two currencies. The Andorran peseta is pegged to the Spanish peseta and the Andorran franc is pegged to the French franc.
(2) Ecuador adopted the US dollar as its national currency on September 15, 2001. (3) Pegged to SDR, an IMF composite.

Source: Adapted from ***http://pacific.commerce.ubc.ca/xr/currency_table.html***.

development was a 1976 IMF amendment that resulted in a managed float system, characterized by flexible exchange rates in which the value of currencies can change. Table 7.4 lists current exchange rate systems.

The managed float system

The managed float system that is used today had its origins in January 1976 when IMF members met in Jamaica and hammered out an agreement. The main elements of the agreement included: (a) floating rates were accepted and IMF members were allowed to enter the foreign exchange market to deal with any unwarranted speculative fluctuations; (b) gold was abandoned as a reserve asset; (c) the amount of contributions made by IMF member countries was increased; and (d) less developed countries were given greater access to these funds.

Major currencies were now allowed to float in relation to each other. As a result, during the 1976–1994 time period, the US dollar, in the main, weakened against the other two major world currencies, the German mark, and the Japanese yen. However, beginning around 1994 the dollar then began to strengthen, especially against the yen, as the Japanese economy sank into an economic malaise. This type of fluctuation of currency values led some to ask whether a floating exchange rate is a good idea or whether there should be a return to fixed rates. There are arguments to be made on each side.

The case for floating exchange rates has two major parts. First, it is argued that a floating exchange rate gives countries autonomy over their own monetary policy. Under a fixed system, the nation's ability to expand or contract its money supply is limited by the need to maintain exchange rate parity. On the other hand, with a floating exchange rate, if a government were faced with unemployment and wanted to increase its money supply to stimulate domestic demand and reduce unemployment, it could do so. Another argument for floating rates is that they would automatically bring about trade balance adjustments. For example, if a nation were importing more than it was exporting and had trouble breaking out of this cycle, the devaluation of its currency in the international market would make its exports cheaper and its imports more expensive. As a result, the exchange rate depreciation would ultimately correct the trade deficit.

On the other side are those who argue for fixed exchange rates. One of their arguments is that these rates force countries to discipline themselves and not expand their money supplies at inflationary rates – something that politicians might do because it was politically expedient. A second argument is that if rates are not allowed to float then speculators cannot buy and sell currencies and cause wild fluctuation in the exchange rates. A third reason is that fixed rates help make business planning easier and reduce the risks associated with exporting, importing, and foreign investment.

Today the argument between fixed and floating rates continues. Each side has its advocates. Certainly it would be impossible to return to the fixed exchange rate system that emerged from the Bretton Woods agreement. However, a different kind of fixed exchange rate system might be more enduring and foster the kind of stability that would facilitate more rapid growth of international trade and investment. For the moment, however, floating exchange rates continue.

The European monetary system

In the discussion of the European Union (EU) in Chapter 4, it was noted that the EU committed itself to establishing a single currency, a commitment that dated back to the Treaty of Maastricht in December 1991. In achieving this single currency goal, the EU's initial objective was to attain convergence between the inflation rates and interest rates of its member states. In particular, the Maastricht Agreement set forth the following convergence criteria: (a) inflation must be no more than 1.5 percentage points above the average of the three lowest inflation rates in Europe; (b) long-term interest rates must be no more than 2 percentage points higher than the average of the three lowest; (c) the exchange rate must have stayed within the narrow band of the EU's exchange rate mechanism for two years without realignment; and (d) the accumulated stock of public debts must not exceed 60 per cent of gross domestic product.[7] The **European Monetary System (EMS)** is a mechanism for attaining this goal. When the EMS was created in 1979 it was given three objectives: (1) to create a zone of monetary stability in Europe by reducing exchange rate volatility and converging national interest rates; (2) to control inflation through the use of monetary discipline; and (3) to coordinate exchange rate policies versus non-EU currencies such as the US dollar and the Japanese yen. Two instruments designed to achieve these objectives are the European currency unit (ecu) and the exchange rate mechanism (ERM).

European Monetary System (EMS)
A system created by some major members of the EU which fixes their currency values in relation to each other (within a band) and floats them together against the rest of the world

The "ecu" is a basket of EU currencies that serves as a unit of account for the European Monetary Union (EMU). The share of each country's currency in the ecu depends on that nation's relative economic weight within the community. For example, 30.1 per cent of the ecu's value was established by the value of the mark in 1989 because that was the estimate of Germany's relative strength and size in the EU economy at that time.

Until 1992 the ERM worked this way: each national currency in the EU was given a "central rate" vis-à-vis the ecu. For example, in 1989 one ecu was equal to 2.05853 German marks, 6.90404 French francs, or 0.739615 British pounds. From these central rates, it was possible to determine the value of a mark against the Italian lira or a pound against the Spanish peseta. Moreover, this central rate could be changed only by a commonly agreed realignment. Prior to 1992, currencies were not allowed to depart by more than 2¼ per cent from their bilateral central rate with other ERM participating currencies. If any of the currencies did reach its outer margin of fluctuation relative to another, the central banks of the two countries were supposed to intervene and keep their currencies within the 2¼ per cent band. In particular, the central bank of the country with the stronger currency was supposed to buy the weaker currency and vice versa. In practice, however, the situation was often left in the hands of the country with the weaker currency.

Supporters of the ERM point to the virtues of fixed rate systems that were discussed in the previous section. However, things have not always worked according to plan. For example, in 1992 speculators began selling the British pound and the Italian lira and buying the mark. Despite efforts by the central banks of both Great Britain and Italy, their currency values fell outside the ERM band. As a result, both nations pulled out of the ERM. This resulted in the EU countries changing the fluctuation band for a time from the initial 2¼ per cent to 15 per cent, although it is now 2¼ per cent again. Since this time there have been speculative pressures that have forced devaluation of the Spanish peseta and the Portuguese escudo. However, the agreement did hold together and in January 1999 all but three of the EU countries accepted the euro as their currency of exchange and in 2002 new euro bank notes and coins reached the general public.

Twelve countries agreed to the exchange rate between their respective currencies and the euro. Table 7.5 provides these data as of 2001. As a result of this agreement, it is now possible for customers to compare prices between countries because everything can be done in a uniform currency. Beginning almost immediately, a number of auto manufacturers, including Daimler-Benz, announced that they would make the euro their currency of reference. In turn, their suppliers will do the same, thus hurrying along the process. Other companies, including Siemens, whose products extend from microchips to power plants, wrote to thousands of companies of their intention to switch their accounting

Table 7.5 **Exchange rates and the euro, 2001**

Country	*Currency*	*Dollar rate*	*Euro rate*
Austria	Schilling	15.1096	13.7603
Belgium	Franc	44.2955	40.3399
Denmark	Krone	8.1207	7.4361
Finland	Markka	6.4931	5.9457
France	Franc	7.1635	6.5596
Germany	Mark	2.1359	1.9558
Greece	Drachma	372.1200	340.7500
Ireland	Punt	0.8601	0.7876
Italy	Lira	2,114.5200	1,936.2700
Luxembourg	Franc	44.0536	40.3399
Netherlands	Guilder	2.4066	2.2037
Portugal	Escudo	218.9390	200.4820
Spain	Peseta	181.7040	166.3860
Sweden	Krona	10.6255	9.7298
United Kingdom	Pound	0.6764	0.6195

Source: Adapted from *FT.com*, October 1, 2001.

systems from national currencies to euros. As a result, it is likely that within a few more years most of the business done in the EU will be in euros and, perhaps, those nations that have not agreed to the common currency, will adopt it.[8] On January 1, 2002, consumers in 12 of the EU member states started using the euro as their domestic currencies. The other three countries – Britain, Denmark, and Sweden – may join the euro in the next few years.

The IMF and the World Bank today

Over the last couple of decades the role of the IMF has declined. Floating exchange rates have resulted in a diminished demand for short-term loans, and no major industrialized country has borrowed money from the IMF for over 20 years. Nations such as Great Britain and the US have financed their deficits by borrowing private money rather than relying on IMF funds. As a result, inspired by the OPEC oil price hikes of 1973 and 1979 and the resulting third world crisis, the IMF has found a new mission for itself.

OPEC price increases of the 1970s resulted in massive flows of funds from major oil importing countries such as Japan and the US to oil producing countries that now sought investment opportunities for these monies. Commercial banks quickly stepped in to recycle these funds by borrowing from OPEC and lending to third world governments in Latin America and Africa. These loans were based on optimistic assessments that proved to be highly inaccurate. A number of reasons accounted for the failure of these third world countries to generate strong economic growth including: (a) rising short-term interest rates worldwide which increased the cost of these debts; (b) poor management of the economies; (c) and a slowdown in the growth rate of the industrialized nations, the main markets for third world products.

As a result, there was a massive debt crisis. Commercial banks held over $1 trillion of bad debts and there was no hope of ever being repaid. Even Mexico, long thought to be highly creditworthy, announced that it could no longer service its $80 billion in international debt without an immediate new loan of $3 billion. Brazil and Argentina, among others, also were unable to make their debt repayments. The international monetary system was on the verge of a major crisis.

This is when the IMF stepped in. Working with several Western governments including the US, Mexico's debt was rescheduled, new loans were made, and an IMF-dictated series of macroeconomic policies were accepted by the Mexican government including tight control over the growth of the money supply and major cuts in government spending. The IMF followed a similar approach in helping other countries. However, there was a problem with the IMF solution. It rested on the economy of these countries turning around and generating sufficient growth to repay the rescheduled debt. By the mid-1980s it was apparent that this was not happening and by 1989 it was evident that the mere rescheduling of debt was not a long-run solution to the problem. In April of that year the IMF endorsed a new approach first proposed by Nicholas Brady, US Secretary of the Treasury.

The Brady Plan rested on the belief that debt reduction was a necessary part of the solution and the IMF and World Bank would have to assume roles in financing it. In essence, the plan called for the IMF, the World Bank, and the Japanese government to each contribute $10 billion to the task of debt reduction. In order to obtain these funds, each debtor nation would have to submit to a set of imposed conditions for macroeconomic policy management and debt repayment. The first application of the plan was the Mexican debt reduction of 1989, which cut that country's debt of $107 billion by about $15 billion.[9]

One result of the IMF's involvement in resolving the third world debt crisis has been the blurring of the line between itself and the World Bank. Under the original Bretton Woods agreement, the IMF was to provide short-term loans and the World Bank was to provide long-term loans. However, the collapse of communism in Eastern Europe and the break-up of the Soviet Union have resulted in a flood of applications for IMF membership from these newly democratic nations, including Russia. These nations are seeking long-term funds for economic growth.

At the same time the World Bank has been moving closer to the IMF. During the 1970s the bank found that many of its loan projects for irrigation, energy, transportation, etc. were not producing the kind of long-term economic gains that had been predicted. On close examination, the bank found that the broad policy environment of the particular country was undermining many of these projects. It was obvious that loan conditions needed to extend beyond the project to the economy at large. So the World Bank devised a new type of loan. In addition to providing funds to support specific projects, the bank now provides loans for the government to use as it sees fit in return for promises on macroeconomic policy. This, of course, is the same thing that the IMF has done in recent years, lending money to debtor nations in return for promises regarding macroeconomic policy.

Today both the IMF and the World Bank are actively involved in their new commitments in Eastern Europe. However, given that both seem to be doing similar jobs, it is quite possible that the two will eventually be merged.

Economic cooperation

No matter what steps are taken to alter the international monetary system, without cooperation among the major economic powers, nothing substantive will happen. In particular, there will have to be greater coordination in the conduct of national policies by the industrialized nations.[10]

> The underlying issue is the extent to which member countries will make exchange rate stability an important part of national policy rather than a residual of domestically oriented policy actions. The freedom in domestic policy making that the present system permits is

both a strength and a weakness of the system. The system allows nations to insulate their domestic price levels from inflation abroad and facilitates the pursuit of sound monetary policies geared more directly to domestic conditions. At the same time, considerable volatility in exchange rates can result when major nations adopt fiscal and monetary policies independently, without serious consideration of the impact of these national policies on the world economy.[11]

It will also be necessary for the developing and industrial countries to resolve their differences regarding the problem of international liquidity. Developing countries, for example, want to see the allocation of SDRs increased on an annual basis with a view to ensuring that their proportion in reserves rises progressively. Industrial countries argue that new SDR allocations could delay needed adjustments that should be made by countries that currently have monetary problems. Each side has arguments in its favor; each has a position it wants to protect.

Finally, it is important to realize that few nations are willing to give up national control over their economic and monetary policies.[12] Yet without some movement in this direction, it is hard to understand how true economic global cooperation will ever be achieved. At present it is virtually impossible for any world monetary organization to rein in the US, Germany, or Japan, to name but three, and to force cooperative policies on them. So for the near future, at least, economic cooperation is likely to be more of an ideal than a reality.

Active learning check

Review your answer to Active Learning Case question 2 and make any changes you like. Then compare your answer with the one below.

2. Some countries believe that those with large trade surpluses should reinvest them in poorer countries in order to help these economies. Is Japan in a position to do this?

Given the latest economic developments, Japan is not in a position to provide very much help to anyone. The country's exports are declining and it is heavily dependent on a number of imports, including oil. In addition, the economy has been in the doldrums for years, domestic demand is low, and with the recent slowing down of the US economy, which Japan depends on to buy much of its exports, it is unlikely that the country will be able to turn things around in the near future. And while Japan continues to run an overall positive trade balance, it has a negative trade balance with China, which is now emerging as a powerful player in the Asian market. Finally, the fact that Japanese businesses are now transferring some of their production sites to other Asian locales means that Japan's exports will decline even more because these businesses can now ship these products to overseas buyers from their new production locales. So Japan needs to focus on righting its economic ship.

Foreign exchange
Any financial instrument that carries out payment from one currency to another

Exchange rate
The amount of one currency that can be obtained for another currency

FOREIGN EXCHANGE

Foreign exchange is any financial instrument that carries out payment from one currency to another. The most common form of conducting foreign exchange payments between banks is the telephone transfer. Between companies it is the draft. By tourists it is the physical exchange of one currency for another. For example, a tourist from Chicago who is visiting Madrid, Spain, will exchange dollars for pesetas. The **exchange rate** is the amount of one currency that can be obtained for another currency. Table 7.6 provides an example. Notice that on October 2, 2001 a Spanish peseta had a value of around six-tenths of one US cent. So for each dollar the tourist exchanged the individual would receive 181.704 pesetas. This exchange rate would also dictate large exchanges of currency, so that a New York bank that wanted to convert $100,000 into Spanish currency on this day would have received 18,170,400 pesetas ($100,000 × 181.704).

For purposes of international business, there are three important areas of foreign exchange that warrant consideration: (1) foreign exchange markets in the US, (2) participants in foreign exchange markets, and (3) determination of exchange rates.

Foreign exchange markets in the US

There are three major ways of conducting foreign exchange in major countries such as the US: between banks, through a broker, and through forward transactions. The interbank market for foreign exchange involves transactions between banks. For example, if an importer wants to buy $100,000 of French francs, the most likely route would be for the individual to ask his or her bank to handle the transaction. If the bank does not trade in foreign exchange, it will contact a large bank, Deutsche Bank, for example, which does, and this bank will sell the francs out of its holdings or enter the interbank market and buy them from other banks.

The brokers' market consists of a small group of foreign exchange brokerage companies that make markets in foreign currencies. These brokers do not take currency positions. They simply match up buyers and sellers and charge a commission for their services. This is in contrast, for example, to Deutsche Bank, which might carry millions of dollars of foreign currencies that it hopes to sell at a profit.

Spot rate
The rate quoted for current foreign currency transactions

Forward rate
The rate quoted for the delivery of foreign currency at a predetermined future date such as 90 days from now

Cross rate
An exchange rate computed from two other rates, such as the relationship between Swiss francs and German marks

There are three types of exchange rates that are important to those dealing in foreign exchange: spot, forward, and cross. A **spot rate** is the rate quoted for current foreign currency transactions. For example, if someone were to buy 100 British pounds for immediate delivery, the individual would pay the spot rate. The **forward rate** is the rate quoted for the delivery of foreign currency at a predetermined future date such as 90 days from now. A **cross rate** is an exchange rate that is computed from two other rates. This rate is of interest to dealers or businesses that are doing business in more than two currencies. For example, suppose that a US firm is doing business with companies in both Switzerland and Germany and that the current value of both currencies as expressed in US dollars is: 2.1359 DM per dollar and SwF 1.619 per dollar. The cross rate would then be:

$$\frac{\text{SwF } 1.619}{\text{DM } 2.1359} = \text{SwF } 0.75799 \text{ per DM}$$

This means that it takes one German mark to equal 0.75799 Swiss francs. The US firm would want to keep track of this relationship because of the impact it can have on the company's cost of goods and profits should the value of either currency increase vis-à-vis that of the other nation.

The forward foreign exchange market is particularly important to MNEs because it lets a customer "lock in" an exchange rate and thus protect against the risk of an unfavorable change in the value of the currency that is needed. This exchange market is very important to firms doing business overseas and dealing in foreign currency.

For example, suppose that a large construction firm in Atlanta, Georgia, orders £500,000 of specially made furniture from a British firm in London with payment due in British pounds within 90 days. As we see in Table 7.6, a British pound on this day was selling for $1.4784 ($1.00/0.67641). So to pay the seller £500,000 today, the construction

Table 7.6 Exchange rates

		Currency per US $	
Country		*Monday*	*Tuesday*
Afghanistan	(Afghani)	4750	4750
Albania	(Lek)	141.35	141.8
Algeria	(Dinar)	75.352	75.433
Andorra	(French Fr)	7.2028	7.1635
Angola	(Readj Kwanza)	24.0775	24.0775
Antigua	(E Carib $)	2.7	2.7
Argentina	(Peso)	0.9999	0.9998
Armenia	(Dram)	554.14	554.14
Aruba	(Florin)	1.79	1.79
Australia	(A $)	2.02634	2.02963
Austria	(Schilling)	15.1096	15.0271
Azerbaijan	(Manat)	4694	4694
Azores	(Port Escudo)	220.141	218.939
Bahamas	(Bahama $)	1	1
Bahrain	(Dinar)	0.377	0.377
Balearic Is	(Sp Peseta)	182.701	181.704
Bangladesh	(Taka)	56.95	56.95
Barbados	(Barb $)	1.99	1.99
Belarus	(Rouble)	1482	1484.5
Belgium	(Belg Fr)	44.2955	44.0536
Belize	(B $)	1.98	1.97
Benin	(CFA Fr)	720.28	716.35
Bermuda	(Bermudan $)	1	1
Bhutan	(Ngultrum)	47.85	47.98
Bolivia	(Boliviano)	6.7435	6.744
Bosnia–Herzegovina	(Marka)	2.1476	2.1359
Botswana	(Pula)	5.9952	5.9952
Brazil	(Real)	2.6705	2.6875
Brunei	(Brunei $)	1.7664	1.7681
Bulgaria	(Lev)	2.1392	2.1264
Burkina Faso	(CFA Fr)	720.28	716.35
Burma	(Kyat)	6.6061	6.6061
Burundi	(Burundi Fr)	847.298	849.101
Cambodia	(Riel)	3835	3835
Cameroon	(CFA Fr)	716.35	716.35
Canada	(Canadian $)	1.5763	1.5763
Canary Is	(Sp Peseta)	181.704	181.704
Cp. Verde	(CV Escudo)	119.75	119.75
Cayman Is	(CI $)	0.82	0.82
Cent. Afr. Rep.	(CFA Fr)	716.35	716.35
Chad	(CFA Fr)	716.35	716.35
Chile	(Chilean Peso)	695.75	695.75
China	(Renminbi)	8.2768	8.2768
Colombia	(Col Peso)	2342.85	2342.85
Comoros	(Fr)	537.112	537.112
Congo	(CFA Fr)	716.35	716.35
Congo (Dem. Rep.)	(Congo Fr)	4.4999	4.4999
Costa Rica	(Colon)	333.98	333.98
Côte d'Ivoire	(CFA Fr)	716.35	716.35
Croatia	(Kuna)	8.2014	8.2014
Cuba	(Cuban Peso)	21	21
Cyprus	(Cyprus £)	0.62714	0.62714
Czech Rep.	(Koruna)	36.8953	36.8953
Denmark	(Danish Krone)	8.1207	8.1207
Djibouti Rep.	(Djib Fr)	172	172
Dominica	(E Carib $)	2.7	2.7
Dominican Rep.	(D Peso)	16.3	16.3
Ecu	(Ecu)	1.09206	1.09206
Ecuador	(US $)	1	1
Egypt	(Egyptian £)	4.2575	4.2575
El Salvador	(Colon)	8.747	8.747
Equat'l Guinea	(CFA Fr)	716.35	716.35
Estonia	(Kroon)	17.0852	17.0852
Ethiopia	(Ethiopian Birr)	8.416	8.416
Euro	(Euro)	1.09206	1.09206
Falkland Is	(Falk £)	0.67641	0.67641
Faroe Is	(Danish Krone)	8.1207	8.1207
Fiji Is	(Fiji $)	2.3123	2.3123
Finland	(Markka)	6.4931	6.4931
France	(Fr)	7.1635	7.1635
Fr. Cty/Africa	(CFA Fr)	716.35	716.35
Fr. Guiana	(Local Fr)	7.1635	7.1635
Fr. Pacific Is	(CFP Fr)	130.209	130.209
Gabon	(CFA Fr)	716.35	716.35
Gambia	(Dalasi)	16.55	16.55
Georgia	(Lari)	2.065	2.065
Germany	(D-Mark)	2.1359	2.1359
Ghana	(Cedi)	7300	7300
Gibraltar	(Gib £)	0.67641	0.67641
Greece	(Drachma)	372.12	372.12
Greenland	(Danish Krone)	8.1207	8.1207
Grenada	(E Carib $)	2.7	2.7
Guadeloupe	(French Fr)	7.1635	7.1635
Guam	(US $)	1	1
Guatemala	(Quetzal)	7.9365	7.9365
Guinea	(Fr)	1960	1960
Guinea-Bissau	(CFA Fr)	716.35	716.35
Guyana	(Guyanese $)	180.5	180.5
Haiti	(Gourde)	25	25
Honduras	(Lempira)	15.61	15.61
Hong Kong	(HK $)	7.7987	7.7987
Hungary	(Forint)	281.2	281.2
Iceland	(Icelandic Krona)	100.04	100.04
India	(Indian Rupee)	47.98	47.98
Indonesia	(Rupiah)	10050	10050
Iran	(Rial) (o)	1750	1750
Iraq	(Iraqi Dinar)	0.311	0.311
Irish Rep.	(Punt)	0.86007	0.86007
Israel	(Shekel)	4.358	4.358
Italy	(Lira)	2114.52	2114.52
Jamaica	(Jamaican $)	45.55	45.55
Japan	(Yen)	120.11	120.11
Jordan	(Jordanian Dinar)	0.7108	0.7108
Kazakhstan	(Tenge)	147.95	147.95
Kenya	(Kenya Shilling)	79.255	79.255
Kiribati	(Australian $)	2.02963	2.02963
Korea North	(Won)	2.2	2.2
Korea South	(Won)	1309.5	1309.5
Kuwait	(Kuwaiti Dinar)	0.3048	0.3048
Kyrgyzstan	(Som)	47.7003	47.7003
Laos	(New Kip)	7600	7600
Latvia	(Lats)	0.6188	0.6188

Table 7.6 *(cont'd)*

Country		Currency per US $ Monday	Tuesday	Country		Currency per US $ Monday	Tuesday
Lebanon	(Lebanese £)	1513.5	1513.5	St Pierre & Miquelon	(F/Fr)	7.1635	7.1635
Lesotho	(Maluti)	9.0225	9.0225	St Vincent	(E Carib $)	2.7	2.7
Liberia	(Liberian $)	1	1	San Marino	(Italian Lira)	2114.52	2114.52
Libya	(Libyan Dinar)	0.6436	0.6436	São Tomé	(Dobra)	8937.2	8937.2
Liechtenstein	(Swiss Fr)	1.619	1.619	Saudi Arabia	(Riyal)	3.7504	3.7504
Lithuania	(Litas)	3.999	3.999	SDR	(SDR)	0.7768	0.7768
Luxembourg	(Lux Fr)	44.0536	44.0536	Senegal	(CFA Fr)	716.35	716.35
Macao	(Pataca)	8.032	8.032	Seychelles	(Rupee)	5.618	5.618
Macedonia	(Denar)	66.7894	66.7894	Sierra Leone	(Leone)	1967	1967
Madagascar	(MG Fr)	6177	6177	Singapore	($)	1.7681	1.7681
Madeira	(Port Escudo)	218.939	218.939	Slovakia	(Koruna)	47.5833	47.5833
Malawi	(Kwacha)	61.48	61.48	Slovenia	(Tolar)	240.43	240.43
Malaysia	(Ringgit)	3.8	3.8	Solomon Is	($)	5.4259	5.4259
Maldive Is	(Rufiya)	11.77	11.77	Somali Rep.	(Shilling)	2620	2620
Mali Rep.	(CFA Fr)	716.35	716.35	South Africa	(Rand)	9.0225	9.0225
Malta	(Maltese Lira)	0.4423	0.4423	Spain	(Peseta)	181.704	181.704
Martinique	(Local Fr)	7.1635	7.1635	Spanish Ports N Africa	(Peseta)	181.704	181.704
Mauritania	(Ouguiya)	256.12	256.12	Sri Lanka	(Rupee)	90.26	90.26
Mauritius	(Maur Rupee)	29.8	29.8	Sudan Rep.	(Dinar)	258.7	258.7
Mexico	(Peso)	9.523	9.523	Surinam	(Guilder)	2178.5	2178.5
Moldova	(Leu)	12.87	12.87	Swaziland	(Lilangeni)	9.0225	9.0225
Monaco	(French Fr)	7.1635	7.1635	Sweden	(Krona)	10.6255	10.6255
Mongolia	(Tugrik)	1100	1100	Switzerland	(Fr)	1.619	1.619
Montserrat	(E Carib $)	2.7	2.7	Syria	(£)	52.675	52.675
Morocco	(Dirham)	11.2785	11.2785	Taiwan	($)	34.55	34.55
Mozambique	(Metical)	21870	21870	Tanzania	(Shilling)	893	893
Namibia	(Dollar)	9.0225	9.0225	Thailand	(Baht)	44.53	44.53
Nauru Is	(Australian $)	2.02963	2.02963	Togo Rep.	(CFA Fr)	716.35	716.35
Nepal	(Nepalese Rupee)	76.208	76.208	Tonga Is	(Pa'anga)	2.02963	2.02963
N'nd Antilles	(A/Guilder)	1.78	1.78	Trinidad/Tobago	($)	6.06	6.06
Netherlands	(Guilder)	2.4066	2.4066	Tunisia	(Dinar)	1.4267	1.4267
New Zealand	(NZ $)	2.46245	2.46245	Turkey	(Lira)	1550000	1550000
Nicaragua	(Gold Cordoba)	13.64	13.64	Turks & Caicos	(US $)	1	1
Niger Rep.	(CFA Fr)	716.35	716.35	Tuvalu	(Australian $)	2.02963	2.02963
Nigeria	(Naira)	112.66	112.66	Uganda	(New Shilling)	1739.5	1739.5
Norway	(Nor. Krone)	8.826	8.826	Ukraine	(Hryvna)	5.3275	5.3275
Oman	(Rial Omani)	0.385	0.385	U A E	(Dirham)	3.6731	3.6731
Pakistan	(Pak. Rupee)	63.15	63.15	United Kingdom	(£)	0.67641	0.67641
Panama	(Balboa)	1	1	United States	(US $)	1	1
Papua New Guinea	(Kina)	3.5595	3.5595	Uruguay	(Peso Uruguayo)	13.76	13.76
Paraguay	(Guarani)	4467.5	4467.5	Uzbekistan	(Sum)	425.99	425.99
Peru	(New Sol)	3.481	3.481	Vanuatu	(Vatu)	148.335	148.335
Philippines	(Peso)	51.4	51.4	Vatican	(Lira)	2114.52	2114.52
Pitcairn Is	(NZ $)	2.46245	2.46245	Venezuela	(Bolivar)	742.805	742.805
Poland	(Zloty)	4.2332	4.2332	Vietnam	(Dong)	15005	15005
Portugal	(Escudo)	218.939	218.939	Virgin Is (British)	(US $)	1	1
Puerto Rico	(US $)	1	1	Virgin Is (US)	(US $)	1	1
Qatar	(Riyal)	3.6408	3.6408	Western Samoa	(Tala)	3.5474	3.5474
Reunion Is de la	(F/Fr)	7.1635	7.1635	Yemen (Rep. of)	(Rial)	169.33	169.33
Romania	(Leu)	30602.5	30602.5	Yugoslavia	(New Dinar)	64.8816	64.8816
Russia	(Rouble)	29.457	29.457	Zambia	(Kwacha)	3805	3805
Rwanda	(Fr)	438	438	Zimbabwe	($)	55.45	55.45
St Christopher	(E Carib $)	2.7	2.7				
St Helena	(£)	0.67641	0.67641				
St Lucia	(E Carib $)	2.7	2.7				

Source: FT.com, October 1, 2001 and October 2, 2001.

company would have to remit a total of $739,200 (£500,000 × 1.4784). If the company waits and pays the bill in 90 days, however, there is an exchange rate risk. If the value of the pound rises vis-à-vis the dollar, the final price will be more than $739,200. Of course, the pound might decline in value, and by waiting 90 days the overall cost will be less than this amount. However, on large amounts most firms will lock in their position. The construction company can do this by purchasing £500,000 today with delivery in 90 days. This is done by purchasing a contract in the forward foreign exchange market. On the date in which the information in Table 7.6 was published, the 90-day rate was $1.4692 per pound and this transaction could be handled through a major bank.

For example, for a fee the Deutsche Bank would sell the company a contract guaranteeing to provide pounds at $1.4692 in 90 days. So the company can purchase this contract and know the price it will be paying, which is $1.4692 × 500,000 or $734,600. In addition, there is typically a fee of 1 per cent on the total value of the transaction, or about $7,346. Thus by locking into an exchange rate today, the firm will end up paying a total of about $741,946 ($734,600 + 7,346). Of course, the pound might decline below $1.4692 by the end of 90 days and the company would have been better off not purchasing the futures contract. On the other hand, the firm is more interested in limiting its exchange rate risk than in making a profit by correctly anticipating the exchange rate of the pound.

The box "International Business Strategy in Action: The Wall Street Crash of 2001" provides an example of how changes in world events can affect MNE performance in international markets.

Participants in foreign exchange markets

There are five major groups that are active participants in foreign exchange markets: traders/brokers, speculators, hedgers, arbitrageurs, and governments.

Traders/brokers

Foreign exchange traders Individuals who buy and sell foreign currency for their employer

Foreign exchange brokers Individuals who work in brokerage firms where they often deal in both spot rate and forward rate transactions

Foreign exchange traders work in commercial banks where they buy and sell foreign currency for their employer. These transactions can be at either the spot rate or the forward rate. This is usually done in response to customer orders, but sometimes the bank will take a position in a currency. Since this can be risky, most banks will keep their exposure to a minimum, focusing primarily on serving clients who need international currency.

Foreign exchange brokers work in brokerage firms where they often deal in both spot rate and forward rate transactions. These individuals typically deal only in foreign exchange transactions, in contrast to banks, which provide this service as just one of many.

Speculators

Speculator In foreign exchange markets, a person who takes an open position

In foreign exchange markets a **speculator** is a participant who takes an open position. This means that the individual either has foreign currency on hand (called a "long position") or has promised to deliver foreign currency in the future and does not have it on hand (called a "short position"). If the speculator is long in a currency, the individual is betting that the price will go up. If the speculator is short in a currency, the individual is betting that the price will go down. For example, if a speculator believes that the British pound will increase in value in the near future, the individual will buy pounds and then sell them when the price rises. Conversely, if the speculator believes that the price is going down, the individual will sell pounds today and replace them at a lower price in the future. Of course, if the market price moves in the opposite direction, the

INTERNATIONAL BUSINESS STRATEGY *IN ACTION*

The Wall Street Crash of 2001

International finance impacts on virtually every business. Companies with overseas operations, for example, are continually concerned with the rise and fall of the currencies in the countries where they operate. Indonesia is a good example as seen by the country's currency crisis of the late 1990s that sent shock waves through the Asian business market. As a result, thousands of firms went bankrupt, the country's currency lost 80 per cent of its value and the stock market plummeted by 60 per cent. In the aftermath, Indonesia was hit with soaring unemployment and inflation led to riots that forced the resignation of the government.

Yet the international financial markets have never suffered anything like the initial effect from the terrorist attacks on the twin towers of New York City's World Trade Center (WTC) on September 11, 2001. In addition to totally demolishing the two buildings as well as several large surrounding structures, the terrorists killed about 3,000 people, many of them Wall Street employees, and rocked the major international financial markets from London to Tokyo. One of the hardest hit groups was the insurers who, based on early estimates, had losses of more than $40 billion. In addition, while the important financial records of businesses in the WTC were located in safe havens such as central computer banks miles away from Ground Zero, the effect of the terrorist actions on a wide number of industries began to quickly surface.

US airlines, already reeling from losses and needing to generate more revenue in order to turn the corner, suddenly found travel dropping sharply. It was clear that Congressional action was needed to ensure the solvency of these carriers. Closely connected to the airlines was the cruise industry that also felt the negative impact. Tourists, many of whom typically flew into their port of departure, cancelled their reservations because they were reluctant to fly. Meanwhile, because of the perceived risks as well as the growing inconvenience associated with newly formulated check-in procedures, tourism went into a nose dive and only recovered in mid 2002. In New York City the mayor urged everyone to go on with their lives as usual, but Broadway announced that a number of shows were being canceled due to lack of ticket sales and most of the remaining shows were not faring very well. Neither out-of-towners nor locals were in a mood for a Broadway evening. This attitude also reflected itself on Wall Street where the stock market began a sharp downturn. Within two weeks of the terrorist act, the New York Stock Exchange's (NYSE) Dow Index had lost 14 per cent of its value. Only during the Great Depression had America seen a turndown this sharp. And for the rest of the world, the financial shock was shared very quickly.

And the NYSE and other major international stock exchanges saw massive sell-offs as investors headed for the sidelines, and companies seeking to raise capital in the international market put their plans on hold. Simply put, as the US economy began to slow down and focus its investment efforts on rebuilding and regenerating its own hard-hit industries, there were going to be less funds available for other things. Even Airbus, which had announced only months before that it was expanding operations and intended to have its new double-decker plane in operation by 2006, was backtracking on its rosy expansion forecasts. The international finance lesson is clear: today's money markets are linked very, very closely. And a catastrophe in one geographic area can have major implications in all of the others. New York City will remain the financial hub of the business world and the effects of the September 2001 crisis will pass. Yet the financial risks that international business firms must assume will not diminish because of the large interdependency that now exists between the major centers of worldwide commerce.

Websites: ***www.nyse.com*** and ***www.airbus.com***.

Sources: *Financial Times*, September 12–30, 2001; October 1–13, 2001 and other supplemental news sources.

speculator can lose a lot of money unless the individual covers the open position and minimizes the loss.

Hedgers

Foreign exchange hedgers Individuals who limit potential losses by locking in guaranteed foreign exchange positions

Foreign exchange hedgers limit their potential losses by locking in guaranteed foreign exchange positions. Many business firms engage in foreign exchange hedging. The Atlanta construction firm, in our earlier example, could have hedged its position by purchasing British pounds in the futures market in order to guarantee that it would be able to buy at $1.4692 a pound. Sellers may fit into any one or more of the categories just discussed above. They may be traders or brokers who feel that $1.4692 is a good price because the pound will fall. Or they may simply be willing to buy the currency today at market price for a client and make their profit from the commission. Or they may be speculators who believe that the price will sink below $1.4692 before they have to deliver the pounds and thus will profit by taking a short position. Or they may be hedgers who have bought the currency at a lower price and want to lock in their profit at $1.4692.

Arbitrageurs

Foreign exchange arbitrageurs Individuals who simultaneously buy and sell currency in two or more foreign markets and profit from the exchange rate differences

Foreign exchange arbitrageurs are individuals who simultaneously buy and sell currency in two or more foreign markets and profit from the exchange rate differences. Arbitrageurs do not incur much risk because the difference in the prices often guarantees a profit. Here is a simple example: Assume that the British pound is being quoted at £1 = $1.47 in New York and £1 = $1.44 in London. By purchasing £1 million in London and selling them in New York, the arbitrageur makes 3 cents per pound, or $30,000 (1,000,000 × 0.03). Of course, there would be expenses associated with carrying out the transaction, and it might not be possible to purchase £1 million at £1 = $1.44 or to sell them at £1 = $1.47 given the forces of supply and demand. However, the transaction does illustrate the basic idea behind arbitrage.

Governments

Although the currencies of most developed countries are allowed to float on the open market, governments will sometimes intervene as buyers or sellers in order to create or maintain a particular price. For example, many countries of the world hold US dollars, so it would not be in their best interests to see the dollar drop sharply. Such a development would reduce the value of their holdings as well as increase the ability of the US to export to them (since imports would now be cheaper given the increased value of their foreign currencies). So governments would intervene to buy dollars in the marketplace in order to shore up the value of the US currency.

Determination of exchange rates

Exchange rates are determined by the activities of the five groups discussed in the previous section. However, there are economic relationships such as purchasing power parity and interest rate parity, as well as other factors that influence exchange rates.

Purchasing power parity (PPP)

Purchasing power parity (PPP) theory An international finance theory which holds that the exchange rate between two currencies will be determined by the relative purchasing power of those currencies

Purchasing power parity (PPP) theory holds that the exchange rate between two currencies will be determined by the relative purchasing power of these currencies. This idea is best illustrated by considering the price of a similar good in two countries, say the US and Germany, and then looking at the effects of inflation. If a particular car in the US costs $22,000 and a similar car in Germany costs 47,000 deutschmarks (DMs), one DM would be worth just under 47 cents (47,000 DM/$22,000 = 2.136 marks per dollar or 46.8 cents per mark), which is where it was in October 2001 (see Table 7.6). But suppose that inflation in the US was 5 per cent in the next year and in Germany it was 10 per cent. The cost of the US car would then rise to $23,100 ($22,000 × 1.05), while the cost of the German car would rise to 51,700 DM (47,000 DM × 1.10). The DM would then, according to the purchasing power parity theory, decline to just under 45 cents (51,700 DM/$23,100 = 2.238 marks per dollar or 44.7 cents per mark).

If the price of all other goods and services in Germany were rising faster than in the US, we would conclude that purchasing power in the US was greater than in Germany.

Moreover, according to the PPP theory, the value of the DM would decline in order to adjust the country's purchasing power parity. Using the automotive example to represent consumer purchases in general in both countries, the DM would drop to 53.15 cents ($23,100/43,461 DM). Simply stated, inflation affects purchasing power, and in order to re-establish parity, foreign currencies will have to increase or decrease in value to reflect these changes.

It is important to realize that the PPP theory is not perfect. Even today there are currencies that are undervalued or overvalued given their purchasing power parity. However, the theory is useful in helping to explain how exchange rates are determined. Interest rate parity also provides insights into this process.

Interest rates

In order to relate interest rates to exchange rates, we must first relate interest rates to inflation. This is done through the **Fisher effect**, which describes the relationship between inflation and interest rates in two countries. There are three key elements in the Fisher effect: (1) the **nominal rate of interest**, which is the interest rate that is being charged to a borrower, called the "money" rate of interest to distinguish it from the "real" rate; (2) the rate of inflation in the country; and (3) the **real interest rate**, which is the difference between the nominal rate and the inflation rate. The Fisher effect holds that, as inflation rises, so will the nominal interest rate because lenders will want to protect the real interest rate. So if bankers in both the US and Germany want to earn a 5 per cent real interest rate and the rate of inflation in Germany is higher than that in the US, then the nominal rate of interest will also be higher in Germany.

Fisher effect An international finance theory which describes the relationship between inflation and interest rates and holds that, as inflation rises, so will the nominal interest rate

Nominal rate of interest The interest rate charged to a borrower; it is called the "money" rate of interest to distinguish it from the "real" rate

Real interest rate The difference between the nominal interest rate and the rate of inflation

International Fisher effect (IFE) An international finance theory which holds that the interest rate differential between two countries is an unbiased predictor of future changes in the spot exchange rate

The link between interest rates and exchange rates is explained by the **international Fisher effect (IFE)**, which holds that the interest rate differential is an unbiased predictor of future changes in the spot exchange rate. Again, using the US and Germany as an example, the IFE holds that if nominal interest rates in Germany are higher than those in the US, the value of the DM will fall by that interest rate differential in the future. This differential is also important in determining forward exchange rates because this rate would be that which neutralizes the difference in interest rates between the two countries. For example, if interest rates in Germany are higher than those in the US, the forward exchange rate for the DM would be lower than the dollar by the interest rate differential. So the yield in dollars on a US investment would be equal to the yield in dollars of a DM investment converted at the forward rate. Thus the forward rate would allow investors to trade currencies for future delivery at no exchange risk and no differential in interest income. If such a differential did exist, traders would then take advantage of this situation and earn income until the difference was eliminated.

Other considerations

Other factors also help to determine exchange rates. One is confidence in the currency. Many people hold dollars because they are convinced that it is a safe haven for their money. Even though the US has run massive trade deficits in recent years, this has not shaken the confidence of many investors. They prefer to have their money in US currency, and this helps to strengthen the demand for US dollars.

Other factors that influence exchange rates are called "technical factors". These consist of such things as the release of national economic statistics, seasonal demands for a currency, the slight strengthening of a currency followed by a prolonged weakness, and the slight weakening of a currency following a sharp run-up in the exchange rate. Although technical factors do not generally result in large exchange rate changes, they do account for some of the movement.

Active learning check

Review your answer to Active Learning Case question 3 and make any changes you like. Then compare your answer with the one below.

3. If the Japanese economy were to encounter annual inflation of 7 per cent while France's rate was 2 per cent, what would happen to the value of the French franc in comparison with the Japanese yen?

Given that prices in Japan would be rising much faster than those in France, the franc would strengthen against the yen. This means that the buying power of French businesses would rise and these companies would be able to purchase more goods and services from Japan than they could have before the yen weakened. In short, the weaker yen would make Japanese goods more attractive to French firms. In addition, other currencies might also strengthen against the yen, depending on the inflation rate in these countries compared with that of Japan.

STRATEGIC MANAGEMENT AND INTERNATIONAL FINANCE

International finance is extremely important in strategic planning by organizations that are doing business in the international arena. These firms do not have to be MNEs; they can be operating locally and simply buying or selling merchandise in the international market.

One of the primary areas of strategic consideration is strategies for dealing with currency exchange rate risk. Another is the financing of international operations.

Strategies for managing currency exchange rate risk

Exchange risk
The probability that a company will be unable to adjust prices and costs to offset changes in the exchange rate

Exchange risk is the probability that a company will be unable to adjust prices and costs to offset changes in the exchange rate. There are a number of reasons that businesses need to develop strategies for managing currency exchange rate risk. One is that it often is impossible to pass along exchange rate increases in the form of higher prices. For example, assume that a giant US computer retailer is purchasing notebook computers from a manufacturer in Taiwan. The cost to the US firm is $500 per unit, the machine retails for $1,000, and all invoices are payable in Taiwan dollars. As we have seen in Table 7.6, a Taiwan dollar is worth 0.0289 US dollars, so for every machine it purchases the retailer must pay 17,301 ($500/0.0289) Taiwan dollars.

Now assume that the US dollar is devalued so that the Taiwan currency is now worth $0.031 US dollars. If the manufacturer continues to charge 17,301 Taiwan dollars, this raises the effective purchase price for the retailer to $536.33 (17,301 × 0.031) per unit and cuts $36.33 off the merchant's profit. The question now becomes: can the company pass this $36.33 increase on to the customer? If not, the company must adjust its strategy.

One step is to negotiate a lower price with the Taiwan supplier and thus share the effects of the devaluation. A second is to pass along the price increase as much as possible and absorb the rest. A third, and complementary, approach is to take steps to minimize exchange risk. The three most common ways of doing this are exchange risk avoidance, exchange risk adaptation, and currency diversification.

Exchange risk avoidance
The elimination of exchange risk by doing business locally

Exchange risk avoidance is the elimination of exchange risk by doing business locally. For the retail firm this means buying notebook computers that are manufactured in the US. In this way, if the dollar is devalued against other currencies, it will not affect the price of labor or materials in the US. The retailer will continue to pay the same price as before the dollar devaluation.

Exchange risk adaptation
The use of hedging to provide protection against exchange rate fluctuations

Exchange risk adaptation is the use of hedging to provide protection against exchange rate fluctuations. One of the most common methods is the purchase of a forward contract, which was explained earlier in the chapter. Another method is to negotiate a fixed dollar price with the other party, such as $500 per unit for a period of 24 months. In this way a change in the exchange rate during this period will not affect unit purchase price.

Currency diversification
The spreading of financial assets across several or more currencies

Currency diversification is the spreading of financial assets across several or more currencies. For example, the computer retailer would be protected, at least initially, against dollar devaluation if it carried enough Taiwan dollars to pay for purchases through the next 12 months. Only after this time period would the dollar devaluation be felt. Moreover, if the company stopped doing business with the Taiwan firm before it had spent all of these local dollars, the retailer would profit from the currency diversification since these dollars would have cost 0.0289 cents and are now worth 0.0310 cents.

Of these three approaches, exchange risk adaptation is most commonly used. The second most popular strategy is currency diversification, but this tends to be more common among large MNEs that have an ongoing need for these currencies.

Financing of operations

Until now our discussion of financial markets has been limited to foreign exchange and the ways in which businesses try to reduce the risks in this market. However, there is another important area that warrants consideration: foreign capital markets. Not all financing is done in the home country. Quite often companies will seek capital on an international basis and borrow or lend money where the rates are most attractive.[13] For an example, see the box "International Business Strategy in Action: Anglogold: going global, raising capital".

As another example, some 200 Canadian companies are cross listed on US stock exchanges. This started in 1883 on the New York Stock Exchange. Similarly, in Canada, US stocks are listed on the Toronto Stock Exchange. By 2001 daily trading volumes for dual listed stocks reached $2 billion.

Borrowing and lending

MNEs that are setting up operations in foreign markets will sometimes borrow money from local banks and institutions there. One reason is that local governments usually subsidize such loans through tax breaks, lower interest rates, and other financial considerations that limit the company's loss potential. For example, many states in the US offer a financial incentive package to companies willing to establish operations in their locale. The states feel that the cost of these packages is more than offset by the jobs and economic strength that the company brings to the community. A second reason for borrowing locally is that MNEs with worldwide operations are able to hedge the risks of holding fluctuating currency by not having all their holdings in one currency. For example, if a company has operations in the UK, France, Germany, and Japan, as well as in the US, the exchange rate of the foreign currencies of these countries will fluctuate vis-à-vis the US dollar. However, the company is unlikely to suffer as a result because its debt obligations on local loans are due in local currency. So if the French franc doubles in value against the dollar, this has no impact on US or French loans that are still due in local currency. The only risk the company runs is that of holding a large percentage of its liquid assets in the currency of a country whose currency becomes devalued. This will decrease the overall assets of the company, although it is unlikely to affect the firm's ability to operate internationally.

INTERNATIONAL BUSINESS STRATEGY *IN ACTION*

Anglogold: going global, raising capital

When it comes to international finance, one of the primary concerns of MNEs is the ability to raise capital through new stock offerings and bank loans. For many years this was a major problem for the Anglo American Corporation of South Africa (AAC), which operated gold mines in that country. During South Africa's apartheid period, trade sanctions, controls on exchange currency, and protectionism all combined to isolate AAC from outside financial markets. Unable to do business in the international arena, AAC focused on expanding its domestic operations by acquiring holdings in a variety of industries including automobiles, newspapers, and vineyards.

As apartheid came to an end, however, there was a gradual liberalization of both trade and investment. And as its opportunity to move into the international arena began to increase, the firm changed its name to Anglogold and began restructuring its operations. Non-core businesses were sold off and the company began focusing heavily on development of its gold and uranium mines. However, its profitability and performance were handicapped by the small size of the South African economy and the fact that the Johannesburg stock market was not very influential in the worldwide financial markets. In addition, the local currency, the Rand, was weak and the company needed to tie its operations to a stronger currency.

In response, Anglogold determined that it needed to link itself to the triad and expand its mining operations worldwide. As a result, the firm incorporated as a UK company and got itself listed on the London Stock Exchange. In 1998 the company was listed on the New York Stock Exchange and today it is also listed on the Paris, Brussels, and Australian stock exchanges (although its primary listing is in London), and the firm now has access to equity capital in the EU and North America, as well as Australia. Most recently the firm's total market capitalization was in the range of $3 billion. Today Anglogold has a workforce of 100,000 and mining operations in North America, South America, Australia, and Africa. As a result of its recent expansion efforts, the company now accounts for 10 per cent of the world's annual gold production and it is able to raise money for expansion operations in a number of worldwide locations.

Websites: ***www.anglogold.com***; ***www.londonstockexchange.com***; ***www.nyse.com*** and ***www.euronext.com***.

Sources: *Anglogold Annual Report, 2000*; "Anglo – Restructuring Like Never Before". *Financial Weekly*, October 23, 1998; "Anglogold Outlines Strategy for Future," *Mining News*, Newark, 1998; Martin Creager, "The Greatest Gold Story Ever Told," *Mining Weekly 4(47)*, December 4–10, 1998; Ernst J. DeJager, "The Transition of Anglogold from a Three-tier Management to a Two-tier Management Company," Dissertation for the Certificate in Management Studies (Templeton College: University of Oxford, 1999); "South Africa's Jumbo Head North," *Economist*, December 10, 1998.

Sometimes an MNE will lend money in the international money market. For example, if Bank of America finds that it can get a higher interest rate in Singapore than in the US, it may deposit some money there. Similarly, if General Motors finds that there are limitations on the amount of profit that it can transfer out of a country, the company may invest in local financial instruments and thus gain interest on funds that would otherwise sit idle.

Eurocurrencies

One of the international money markets that has become extremely important for large MNEs is the Eurocurrency market. **Eurocurrency** is any currency that is banked outside its country of origin. For example, **Eurodollars** are dollars banked outside the US. Similarly there are euro-Swiss francs, euro-German marks, euro-French francs, euro-Japanese yen, and euro-British pounds, to name but five other types of Eurocurrency. The major sources of Eurodollars include (1) companies with excess cash, (2) European banks with foreign currency in excess of their current needs, (3) foreign governments or businesspeople who want to hold dollars outside the US, and (4) reserves of countries such as Japan and some OPEC nations that have large trade surpluses.

Eurocurrency
Any currency banked outside its country of origin

Eurodollars
Dollars banked outside the US

The Eurocurrency market is primarily a Eurodollar market. This market is extremely large (in excess of $4 trillion) and is a wholesale market in which governments, banks, and major corporations conduct transactions. Deposits are primarily short term and consist of savings and time deposits rather than demand deposits. Loans are typically pegged to a certain percentage above the **London Inter-Bank Offered Rate (LIBOR)**, which is the interest rate banks charge one another on Eurocurrency loans.

London Inter-Bank Offered Rate (LIBOR)
The interest rate banks charge one another on Eurocurrency loans

There is also an international bond market that is available to both domestic and foreign investors. This market consists of both foreign bonds and Eurobonds. A **foreign bond** is a bond that is sold outside the borrower's country but which is denominated in the currency of the country where it has been issued. For example, a German corporation floating a bond issue in Spanish pesetas in Spain is floating a foreign bond. A **Eurobond** is a financial instrument that is typically underwritten by a syndicate of banks from different countries and is sold in countries other than the one in which its currency is denominated. For example, a Eurobond to raise $50 million for a Swiss company might be underwritten by a syndicate from five different countries, floated in French francs, and sold in Luxembourg, the Netherlands, Spain, and Italy.

Foreign bond
A bond sold outside the borrower's country

Eurobond
A financial instrument that is typically underwritten by a syndicate of banks from different countries and is sold in countries other than the one in which its currency is denominated

The Eurobond market is centered in Europe, but the bonds are sold worldwide. Some of these bonds offer currency options, which allow the buyer to demand repayment in one of several currencies. This can reduce the exchange risk inherent in a single-currency foreign bond. Corporate Eurobonds have become more popular with investors in recent years because many of them offer a convertibility option that allows the holder to convert the bond into common stock. Another reason that the Eurobond market has become a popular source of funds is that the market is relatively unregulated, so there is little red tape associated with floating an issue. Also, the fact that the issue transcends national boundaries allows the underwriters to create offerings that appeal to a wide geographic segment rather than just a specific national market. Increasingly, US firms are offering non-dollar Eurobonds in an effort to tap available international money sources.

Active learning check 

Review your answer to Active Learning Case question 4 and make any changes you like. Then compare your answer with the one below.

4. How could US firms located in Japan profit from an appreciation of the Japanese yen?

US firms operating in Japan do business in the local currency. So if the value of the yen increased, say, by 10 per cent against the dollar, the value of the company's Japanese assets would increase by a similar percentage as measured in dollars. For example, if an American firm bought land for 100 million yen for a new plant site last year and then sold the land today for 100 million yen, it would still have made a 10 per cent profit when valued in dollars since the yen is worth 10 per cent more than when the initial purchase was made. Moreover, company profits in Japan would result in higher earnings for the MNE when it converts these yen into dollars in computing its annual income. For example, if the subsidiary earned a profit of $1 million before the yen increased in value, the profit would now be $1.1 million. So US firms doing business in Japan could indeed profit from a strengthening of the yen.

KEY POINTS

1. The balance of payments (BOP) is the record of the value of all transactions between a country's residents and the rest of the world. There are three broad BOP categories: current account, capital account, and reserves. The current account consists of merchandise trade, services, and unrequited transfers. Capital account items are transactions that involve claims in ownership. Reserves are funds for bringing BOP accounts into balance.
2. The international monetary system is a market among central banks of the countries that belong to the International Monetary Fund (IMF). The IMF's objectives include the facilitation of balanced growth of international trade, promotion of exchange stability, and the making of financial resources available to the members of the Fund. In recent years the fixed monetary system created by the IMF members in 1944 has been replaced by a managed float system. Currently the IMF faces a number of major problems, including helping third world countries to deal with their international debt crisis and increasing international liquidity.
3. Foreign exchange is any financial instrument that carries out payment from one currency to another. There are three major foreign exchange markets in the US: interbank, brokers, and forward. The five major groups that are active participants in foreign exchange markets are traders/brokers, speculators, hedgers, arbitrageurs, and governments. Exchange rates are determined by the activities of these five groups. The rates are also influenced by purchasing power parity, interest rates, and technical factors such as national economic statistics and seasonal demands.
4. There are a number of international finance strategies that can be of value to firms doing business overseas. Two of the most important are strategies for managing currency exchange rate risk and strategies for financing international operations.

KEY TERMS

- international finance
- balance of payments (BOP)
- International Monetary Fund (IMF)
- current account
- merchandise trade
- unrequited transfers
- capital account items
- international monetary system
- International Bank for Reconstruction and Development
- World Bank
- special drawing right (SDR)
- European monetary system (EMS)
- foreign exchange
- exchange rate
- spot rate
- forward rate
- cross rate
- foreign exchange traders
- foreign exchange brokers
- speculator
- foreign exchange hedgers
- foreign exchange arbitrageurs
- purchasing power parity (PPP) theory
- Fisher effect
- nominal rate of interest
- real interest rate
- international Fisher effect (IFE)
- exchange risk
- exchange risk avoidance
- exchange risk adaptation
- currency diversification
- Eurocurrency
- Eurodollars
- London Inter-Bank Offered Rate (LIBOR)
- foreign bond
- Eurobond

REVIEW AND DISCUSSION QUESTIONS

1 What is meant by the term "balance of payments"?

2 What are the three major accounts in the balance of payments?

3 How would the following transactions be recorded in the IMF balance of payments?
   a. IBM in New York has sold an $8 million mainframe computer to an insurance company in Singapore and has been paid with a check drawn on a Singapore bank.
   b. A private investor in San Francisco has received dividends of $80,000 for stock she holds in a British firm.
   c. The US government has provided $60 million of food and medical supplies for Kurdish refugees in Turkey.
   d. The Walt Disney Company has invested $50 million in a theme park outside Paris, France.

4 What were the original purposes of the International Monetary Fund? How have these purposes changed or been altered?

5 How does the managed float system work? Explain with an illustration.

6 What are two future problems and challenges that will have to be addressed by the international monetary system during the millennium? Describe each.

7 What are the three major foreign exchange markets in the US? Identify and describe how each works.

8 Who are the most active participants in foreign exchange markets? Identify and describe these groups.

9 How are exchange rates determined? In your answer be sure to include a discussion of the purchasing power parity theory.

10 How can a company manage its currency exchange rate risk? Identify and describe three strategies that can be employed.

11 How can a US firm obtain funds in the international money markets? Include in your answer a discussion of Eurocurrencies and Eurobonds.

REAL CASE

HSBC wakes up British banking

What is the world's largest bank? Prior to the merger of Citicorp and Travellers in 1998, it was the Hong Kong and Shanghai Banking Corporation (HSBC). Formed in 1865 by a Scotsman in the then British Colony of Hong Kong, HSBC grew to over 6,500 bank offices in 78 countries by 2001. In the process it became the world's first truly global bank, offering a full range of financial services from retail to corporate banking to insurance and financial management. HSBC built this global business based on its strong Hong Kong base. The bank owns the Hong Kong Bank and most of the Hang Seng Bank, giving it over 40 per cent of the market in the Hong Kong Special Administrative Region of China that was created on July 1, 1997.

Perhaps less well known is that HSBC is also the owner of the former Midland Bank chain in Britain, the Marine Midland banks in the US, and the Hong Kong Bank of Canada. It has also acquired large banks in Latin America including Banco Bamerindus in Brazil. In all these cases HSBC greatly improved the efficiency of the underperforming local banks through better systems and processes. Over recent years, HSBC has implemented a rebanding strategy of all its subsidiaries under the HSBC title and logo. This is meant to build HSBC into a global brand.

Today HSBC is well developed across the triad regions of Asia, Europe, and the Americas. Its diversification strategy has helped to insulate it from the Asian financial crisis of 1997/1998. And its first-mover advantage as a truly global bank will prove hard to match by banks in the still regulated markets of North America and Europe. There is constant pressure in banking to reduce costs through greater scale economies and improved information technology. HSBC is well positioned to continue as an industry leader because of its successful globalization strategy.

In retrospect, one of the world's largest banks came from one of the world's smallest economies.

And it did this despite the regulatory barriers to entry for foreign-owned firms in Europe and North America. As a result the HSBC is an example of a bank using modern management systems and market forces to win out over old fashioned protectionism in a highly regulated worldwide industry.

Perhaps the biggest influence of HSBC and its new efficient banking methods has been on British banking. A further restructuring occurred in British banking in November 1999 when one of the country's four major banks (Lloyds, Barclays, Natwest, and HSBC) was taken over by a much smaller bank. Natwest was acquired by the Royal Bank of Scotland, only one-third the asset size of Natwest, in a drawn out and controversial takeover. Another bank, the Bank of Scotland, first bid for Natwest and the takeover efforts of both the Royal Bank of Scotland and the Bank of Scotland were defended by Natwest Chairman, Sir David Rowland, who is also President of Templeton College, University of Oxford. The takeover was successful because investors were critical of Natwest's old style management and were supportive of the cost-cutting and new information technology methods of the Royal Bank of Scotland. After the acquisition, many Natwest branches were closed, bank buildings were turned into coffee bars, restaurants and hotels, and a leaner, more efficient bank emerged to reclaim its place in British retail banking.

More recently the Bank of Scotland and Halifax, the largest mortgage lender in the country, finalized a merger. This has fast-forwarded Halifax into mainstream banking and greatly increased the Bank of Scotland's scope of operations. It would also allow both banks to streamline their businesses and increase their market focus. These efforts toward restructuring operations and eliminating waste are not going unnoticed by rival banks. Barclays, for example, has now begun closing some of its branches and is introducing a wide array of tools and techniques that are designed to cut costs and increase operational efficiency. It realizes that, to be a successful international operation, it must not only have wide geographic coverage but also be able to offer efficient services. In looking at these recent developments, it is clear that the steps taken by HSBC to modernize its own operations are proving to be a wake up call for British banks as well.

Websites: ***www.hsbc.com***; ***www.citigroup.com***; ***www.bankofscotland.co.uk***; ***www.royalbankscot.co.uk***; ***www.natwest.co.uk*** and ***www.barclays.com***.

Sources: "An Empire at Risk: HSBC," *Economist*, September 7, 1996; S. Kahn, "The Future of Global Banks," *Global Finance*, May 1998, p. 28; and W. Green, "Bland – and Proud of It," *Forbes*, July 14, 1997, p. 94.

1. **If the HSBC were to do business with the People's Republic of China and have substantial holdings of Chinese yuan (renminbi) on hand, what risk might this pose for the bank?**
2. **How could the HSBC manage its currency exchange rate risk?**
3. **As the British retail banks are merged to achieve cost savings and economies, does this increase or decrease the barriers to entry for foreign banks wishing to do business in the EU?**

REAL CASE

World financial crises

Throughout the 1990s, a series of financial crises rocked the world's economy. The first of these was the 1994 Mexico peso crisis. This was followed by the Asian crisis of 1997. Since then there has been the Russian crisis of 1998 and the 1999 Brazilian financial crisis. The following examines the first two of these.

The Mexico peso crisis

In late 1994 Mexico suffered one of the worst financial crises in its history. In less than one month the Mexican peso devalued from 3.45 to the US dollar to 5.57 to the dollar; and by the end of 1995 it was trading at 6.5 to the dollar. This was accompanied by heavy inflation, unemployment, and a severe stock market crash. Some critics claimed that all of this was a result of NAFTA, but this was not so. The crisis was caused by the Mexican government itself which had liberalized trade and financial flows, but had not allowed the peso to float. Moreover, previous governments had kept the peso overvalued. As a result, in less than one year Mexico's foreign reserves were depleted by 75 per cent and the country's current account deficit was equal to 8 per cent of GDP.

Other factors also contributed to the low price of the peso. For instance, as a result of the Zapatista armed rebellion of 1996 in Chiapas, in southern Mexico, both foreign and Mexican investors took tens of millions of dollars out of the country. These developments had far-reaching consequences throughout the region. For example, many investors in other Latin American countries, fearing a similar crash, withdrew their funds from these economies and deposited them in the US for safe keeping.

One unexpected development of the Mexican peso crisis was the devaluation of the Canadian dollar which was sideswiped by the Latin American currency crisis. Thanks to NAFTA, Canada and Mexico had become linked in the international currency markets. At the same time international investors began showing a preference for the US dollar against both the Mexican peso and the Canadian dollar.

Perhaps the most surprising thing about the peso crisis was how quickly the country bounded back. With the help of a $50 billion loan from the US and other countries, a tough economic reform that saw cuts in government spending, and increases in deregulation and privatization, the Mexican economy began to revive. Hardly a year had passed when investors who were running from the region were quickly lured back by short-term interest rates of up to 40 per cent. Additionally, the stock market crash had led to underpriced shares and investors began buying these issues and driving the prices back up. Today the financial crisis of 1995 in Mexico is a thing of the past. The country's economy is healthy and investors are back.

The Asian financial crisis

In the early 1990s, the Asian economies of South Korea, Indonesia, Taiwan, Malaysia, and Japan were being praised as economic miracles. In 1997, these countries faced one of the worst blows to their economies. The Asian crisis began in July 1997, when Thailand stopped pegging its currency to the US dollar. In two months the Thai bath had devaluated by nearly 40 per cent. The effect was two-fold. First, Asian exporters to Thailand faced decreased demand for their product. Second, there was the decrease of investor confidence in the region.

Individual countries in the region faced their own sets of problems. In Malaysia, it was excessive lending to the property sector. Once foreign investment was cut short, overlending, overinvestment, and overproduction led to a downward spiral in the economy. In South Korea, the *chaebols* (large manufacturing conglomerates) that dominated the economy had invested recklessly without regard to profit. In Indonesia, the President Suharto's corruption and lack of accountability led investors to flee the country. In addition, the banking system that the government there had fostered was plagued with bad loans for many unreliable projects. These loans benefited and created wealth for well-positioned individuals – in particular, members of the Suharto family, but they did nothing for the rest of the country.

Some financial observers believe that Western speculators were a major reason for the financial troubles in the region. The trend toward deregulation of the world capital markets and the free flow of capital, it was argued, contributed to the currency panic. Additionally, the relatively good health of these nations prior to 1997 made them attractive to foreign investors and lenders. Unfortunately, many of these loans were short term and were in foreign currency. So while the economy grew, the loans presented no problem. But when trouble looked likely the foreign lenders began calling in their loans. When this happened, the value of the local currencies plummeted and the loans payable in foreign currencies created a debt crisis.

It was initially believed that the Asian economic problem would be contained in that geographic region. However, by mid-1998 the crisis was having an effect on the global economy. The cross-border interconnections of global industries and the resulting interdependence pushed the problem to other regions. Among other things, the crisis led to decreases in the prices of many commodities including oil, metals, grain, pulp, and paper.

Industrial nations came to the aid of these Asian governments. The IMF negotiated billions of dollars in bailouts. Initially, the IMF wanted these governments to decrease their budget deficit and to maintain stable interest rates. By July 1998, however, the IMF was allowing increases in deficits and lower interest rates. This helped ease some of the problems, although there was still a great deal of disagreement regarding what else needed to be done. For example, some observers argued that the government needed to continue to deregulate the country's capital markets, while others blamed the economic disaster on this deregulation.

Sources: "Crisis-ridden Indonesia to Overhaul Ailing Banking Sector," *Boston Globe on Line*, January 27, 1998, **www.boston.com/dailynews/**; Richard Gwyn, "Asian Flu Shows No Sign of Letting Up," *Toronto Star*, July 10, 1998; "A Crisis of Dictatorship," *Washington Post*, Sunday 11, 1998; Raffi Anderian, "Everybody Is Going Down," *Sunday Star*, July 12, 1998; "The Downward Spiral of the Asian Tigers," BBC News, January 8, 1998.

1. **How does a decrease in the value of the Mexican peso affect foreign direct investment?**
2. **How is trade affected by currency devaluations as a result of a financial crisis?**
3. **How are customers in countries undergoing a financial crisis affected by the devaluation of the peso?**

ENDNOTES

1 Susan Moffat, "Picking Japan's Research Brains," *Fortune*, March 25, 1991, pp. 84–96.
2 Jonathan Moore and Moon Ihlwan, "Cheaper Exports? Not So Fast," *Business Week*, February 2, 1998, pp. 48–49.
3 At the same time, there is investment the other way, as seen in Carla Rapoport, "The New US Push into Europe," *Fortune*, January 10, 1994, pp. 73–74.
4 See, for example, Andrew Pollack, "Japan's Trade Surplus Leaps, Putting Pressure on Clinton," *New York Times*, January 23, 1993, pp. 1, 21.
5 See, for example, Marcus Brauchli, "China Is Facing Trade Deficit, Raising Fears," *Wall Street Journal*, December 15, 1993, p. A 11.
6 Also, see Peter Passell, "Big Trade Deficit with Japan: Some Think It's No Problem," *New York Times*, February 15, 1994, pp. A 1, C 2.
7 "From Here to EMU," *Economist*, August 5, 1995, p. 72.
8 Thomas Kamm, "French Labor Unrest, Austerity Budget Renews Doubts About Monetary Union," *Wall Street Journal*, September 21, 1996, p. A 21 and Philip Coggan, "Catch-22 and the Single Currency," *FT.com*, March 2, 2002.
9 Also see Stefan Wagstyl, "Debt Relief Urged for Poorest Seven Former Soviet Countries," *FT.com*, February 19, 2002.
10 For some additional insights, see Edmund Faltermayer, "Does Japan Play Fair?" *Fortune*, September 7, 1992, pp. 38–52.
11 Stefan H. Robock and Kenneth Simmonds, *International Business and Multinational Enterprises*, 4th edn (Homewood IL: Irwin, 1989), p. 108.
12 See, for example, Keith Bradsher, "US Panel Urges Setting Export Target Levels," *New York Times*, February 12, 1993, pp. C 1, 7.
13 For more on this topic, see Bruce G. Resnick, "The Globalization of World Financial Markets," *Business Horizons*, November/December 1990, pp. 34–41.

ADDITIONAL BIBLIOGRAPHY

Aggarwal, Raj and Soenen, Luc A. "Managing Persistent Real Changes in Currency Values: The Role of Multinational Operating Strategies," *Columbia Journal of World Business*, vol. 24, no. 3 (Fall 1989).

Al-Eryani, Mohammad F., Alam, Pervaiz and Akhter, Syed H. "Transfer Pricing Determinants of US Multinationals," *Journal of International Business Studies*, vol. 21, no. 3 (Third Quarter 1990).

Anonymous, "Euro Creates New Possibilities for Money Management," *Harvard Business Review*, vol. 77, no. 1 (January/February 1999).

Berg, David M. and Guisinger, Stephen E. "Capital Flows, Capital Controls, and International Business Risk," in Alan M. Rugman and Thomas Brewer (eds.), *The Oxford Handbook of International Business* (Oxford: Oxford University Press, 2001).

Brewer, H. L. "Components of Investment Risk and Return: The Effects on Common Shareholders from Firm Level International Involvement," *Management International Review*, vol. 29, no. 1 (First Quarter 1989).

Carr, Nicholas G. "Managing in the Euro Zone," *Harvard Business Review*, vol. 77, no. 1 (January/February 1999).

Carstens, Agustin. "Foreign Exchange and Monetary Policy in Mexico," *Columbia Journal of World Business*, vol. 29, no. 2 (Summer 1994).

Choi, Jongmoo Jay. "Diversification, Exchange Risk, and Corporate International Investment," *Journal of International Business Studies*, vol. 20, no. 1 (Spring 1989).

Daly, Donald J. "Porter's Diamond and Exchange Rates," *Management International Review*, vol. 33, no. 2 (Second Quarter 1993).

Damanpour, Faramarz. "Global Banking: Developments in the Market Structure and Activities of Foreign Banks in the United States," *Columbia Journal of World Business*, vol. 26, no. 3 (Fall 1991).

Finnerty, Joseph E., Owers, James and Creran, Francis J. "Foreign Exchange Forecasting and Leading Economic Indicators: The US–Canadian Experience," *Management International Review*, vol. 27, no. 2 (Second Quarter 1987).

George, Abraham M. and Schroth, C. William. "Managing Foreign Exchange for Competitive Advantage," *Sloan Management Review*, vol. 32, no. 2 (Winter 1991).

Hartmann, Mark A. and Khambata, Dara. "Emerging Stock Markets: Investment Strategies of the Future," *Columbia Journal of World Business*, vol. 28, no. 2 (Summer 1993).

Holden, Alfred C. "The Reposition of Ex-Im Bank," *Columbia Journal of World Business*, vol. 31, no. 1 (Spring 1996).

Huczynski, Andrzej. "International Management Behaviour," *European Management Journal*, vol. 19, no. 4 (August 2001).

Kanas, Angelos. "Exchange Rate Economic Exposure when Market Share Matters and Hedging Using Currency Options," *Management International Review*, vol. 36, no. 1 (1996).

Khanna, Ashok. "Equity Investment Projects in Emerging Markets," *Columbia Journal of World Business*, vol. 31, no. 2 (Summer 1996).

Kish, Richard J. and Vasconcellos, Geraldo M. "An Empirical Analysis of Factors Affecting Cross-border Acquisitions: US–Japan," *Management International Review*, vol. 33, no. 3 (Third Quarter 1993).

Kleiman, Gary and Morrissey, Elizabeth R. "African Equity Markets: Testing Latin America's Path," *Columbia Journal of World Business*, vol. 29, no. 2 (Summer 1994).

Kryzanowski, Lawrence and Ursel, Nancy D. "Market Reaction to the Formation of Export Trading Companies by American Banks," *Journal of International Business Studies*, vol. 24, no. 2 (Second Quarter 1993).

Kwok, Chuck C. Y. and Lubecke, Thomas H. "Improving the 'Correctness' of Foreign Exchange Forecasts Through Composite Forecasting," *Management International Review*, vol. 30, no. 4 (Fourth Quarter 1990).

Lee, Kwang Chul and Kwok, Chuck C. Y. "Multinational Corporations vs. Domestic Corporations: International Environmental Factors and Determinants of Capital Structure," *Journal of International Business Studies*, vol. 19, no. 2 (Summer 1988).

Ling-yee, Li. "Effect of Export Financing Resources and Supply-chain Skills on Export Competitive Advantages: Implications for Superior Export Performance," *Journal of World Business*, vol. 36, no. 3 (Fall 2001).

Luehrman, Timothy A. "The Exchange Rate Exposure of a Global Competitor," *Journal of International Business Studies*, vol. 21, no. 2 (Second Quarter 1990).

Luehrman, Timothy A. "Exchange Rate Changes and the Distribution of Industry Value," *Journal of International Business Studies*, vol. 22, no. 4 (Fourth Quarter 1991).

Luehrman, Timothy A. "Financial Engineering at Merck," *Harvard Business Review*, vol. 72, no. 1 (January/February 1994).

Miller, Kent D. and Reuer, Jeffrey J. "Firm Strategy and Economic Exposure to Foreign Exchange Rate Movements," *Journal of International Business Studies*, vol. 29, no. 3 (Fall 1998).

Narayandas, Das. "Prepare Your Company for Global Pricing," *Sloan Management Review*, vol. 42, no. 1 (Fall 2000).

Oxelheim, Lars and Wihlborg, Clas G. "Corporate Strategies in a Turbulent World Economy," *Management International Review*, vol. 31, no. 4 (1991).

Prywes, Menahem. "The Good Work of Financial Crises," *Columbia Journal of World Business*, vol. 27, no. 1 (Spring 1992).

Rada, Juan and Trisoglio, Alex. "Capital Markets and Sustainable Development," *Columbia Journal of World Business*, vol. 27, no. 3, 4 (Fall/Winter 1992).

Spall, Alan. "Beyond the currency question," *Harvard Business Review*, vol. 77, no. 1 (January/February 1999).

Strange, Susan. *Mad Money* (Manchester: Manchester University Press, 1998).

Weisman, Lorenzo. "The Advent of Private Equity in Latin America," *Columbia Journal of World Business*, vol. 31, no. 1 (Spring 1996).

PART THREE

International Business Strategies

CONTENTS

Chapter 8

Multinational Strategy

OBJECTIVES OF THE CHAPTER

Multinational enterprises are businesses that are headquartered in one country, but have operations in other countries. Because of the complexity of this environment, it is particularly important for these MNEs to have well-formulated strategic plans. Large MNEs will do this by conducting a very thorough analysis of their environments and often develop detailed, comprehensive plans for coordinating worldwide activities. These plans will set forth objectives for all major divisions and units and will provide for systematic follow-up and evaluation. Smaller MNEs will use less sophisticated plans. However, all multinationals that conduct strategic planning will use a three-step process: formulation, implementation, and control.

The objectives of this chapter are to:

1. *Define* the term *strategic planning* and discuss the strategic orientations that affect this planning process.
2. *Explain* how strategy is formulated, giving particular emphasis to external and internal environmental assessment.
3. *Describe* how strategy is implemented, with particular attention to location, ownership decisions, and functional area implementation.
4. *Discuss* the ways in which MNEs control and evaluate their strategies.

ACTIVE LEARNING CASE

Vodafone and the triad telecom market

British-based Vodafone is the world's largest mobile phone company. Originally based in the rural town of Newbury, 60 miles along the M4 from its head office in London, over the last decade Vodafone has become a major global corporation through a carefully crafted "triad" strategy. The company began its mobile phone efforts in the UK and the EU and then moved into the US and, most recently, into Japan. By 2001 Vodafone had 83 million worldwide subscribers, giving it 15 per cent of total mobile phone market – and it's not done yet. Among other things, the company intends to spend $10 billion developing its 3G (third generation) network in Europe.

From 1991–1998 Vodafone focused most heavily in Europe where it developed one of the basic ideas that it continues to use in most cases – acquire companies in association with partners. This strategy has given Vodafone access to new markets, while providing it with partners who help it deal with local regulatory environment agencies and provide assistance in addressing the needs of the local market. For example, in the case of Libertel of the Netherlands, Vodafone purchased 70 per cent of the company while Dutch ING, the local partner, held the rest and, in turn, helped Vodafone deal with local challenges and problems.

In addition to its partnership approach, Vodafone has also been very careful to confine its acquisitions to what might be called "safe" countries. Examples include Germany, France, Italy, the US, and Japan, all of which have stable governments and large economies.

In Europe, Vodafone is a major player. Today the company controls Omnitel in Italy and Mannesmann D2 in Germany, and holds a minority (35 per cent) stake in the French SFR organization. Overall, Vodafone has more than 20 million customers in the EU thanks to its acquisition strategy. However, in order to acquire these firms, Vodafone had to divest itself of Orange, the UK's third largest wireless operator. So the company realizes that it cannot rely on acquisitions alone to give it a strong foothold in Europe – EU regulators will not permit it to simply buy up all the competition. Rather, the company's best strategy is to go international, gain market share in all of the major economies, and then link together all of these firms into a worldwide network. And this is precisely what it has done!

In June 1999 Vodafone took a major step in implementing its worldwide strategy when it beat out Bell Atlantic for Airtouch Communications, a California-based firm. As a result of this acquisition, Vodafone Airtouch (VA) was created, giving the overall company a market capitalization of $154 billion and a total of 35 million wireless customers worldwide. Then, soon after the acquisition, VA entered into an agreement with Bell Atlantic (which was soon to merge with GTE) that gave VA a 45 per cent stake in a venture called Verizon Wireless. This decision has proved to be a very good one, as Verizon is now the largest US mobile telephone operator with 28 million subscribers and annual revenues of $14 billion. Commenting on these developments, Chris Gent, the CEO of VA, remarked, "In a market where penetration levels are relatively low but growth looks set to take off, gaining a nationwide footprint with common technology is of paramount importance." This race to maximize footprint with a common technology is the root of every telecom company's international strategy – offer as large as possible "roaming" wireless capability that lends itself to overall lower costs. Perhaps surprising, this roaming technology is more prevalent in Europe than in the US, mostly due to EU-wide cooperation between governmental regulatory authorities regarding common platforms.

Vodafone's next move was in Japan. In late 2001 the company took control of Japan Telecom by investing $2 billion to buy another 21.7 per cent stake in this company and raise its total ownership stake to 66.7 per cent. This decision completed the firm's "triad" strategy. Today Vodafone is a major player in the EU with its holdings in Omnitel, Mannesmann, and SFR. The company is a big force in the US market with its ownership of Airtouch. And in Asia, where the largest market for mobile phones is in Japan, Vodafone holds operating control of Japan Telecom and also owns J-Phone, a large mobile phone operator.

However, the company still faces a number of challenges. In Japan, for example, there are two very powerful competitors. The biggest one is Nippon Telegraph and Telephone's DoCoMo, which had 26 million subscribers in 2001. DoCoMo is three times larger than J-Phone and well ahead of the latter in mobile technology. In addition, DoCoMo recently launched I-mode, a data and entertainment service for mobile phones, as well as introducing a camera phone. To compete with DoCoMo, J-Phone will have to develop new, innovative products that are highly competitive.

The other major competitor is KDDI, the second largest mobile phone company in Japan. In this case, however, J-Phone seems to be holding its own. J-Phone has been capturing nearly 60 per cent of the new subscriber market and is rapidly challenging KDDI for the number 2 spot.

Yet the biggest challenge facing Vodafone will be that of coordinating all of its worldwide holdings so as to maximize shareholder value. In an effort to handle this problem, the company's head office has now abandoned the use of centralized control and opted for a decentralized type of operation. In the US, for example, local partners and operating managers now make many of the major decisions regarding how to do business here. The same is true in Europe. Vodafone is realizing that, in order to manage all of these different units in worldwide markets where regulations and customer preferences are often quite different, the best approach is to create a strategic plan that recognizes and takes advantage of these differences.

Websites: ***www.vodafone.com***; ***www.verison.com***; ***www.omnitelvodafone.it***; ***www.mannesmann.de***; ***www.nttdocomo.com*** and ***www.kddi.com***.

Sources: "Vodafone Moves on Japan Telecom," *Financial Times*, September 17, 2001, p. 20; Vodafone Buying up Japan Telecom," *Toronto Globe and Mail*, September 17, 2001, p. B 9; Michiyo Nakamoto and Thorold Barker, "Vodafone Offer Aims to Cement Takeover," *Financial Times*, September 21, 2001, p. 25; Dan Roberts, "Vodafone Meets Forecasts," *Financial Times*, October 5, 2001, p. 20; Stephen Baker and Kerry Capell, "Wireless Warrior," *Business Week*, May 21, 2001, pp. 56–57; Suzanne Kapner, "Vodafone Set to Lift Stake in Japanese Phone Giant," *New York Times*, September 18, 2001, pp. W 1, 7; Robert A. Guth, "Vodafone is Set to Merge Japan Telecom Co. Units," *Wall Street Journal*, August 27, 2000, p. A 8; and *Vodafone Annual Reports and Accounts*, 1999, 2000.

1. **Given the competitiveness of the environment, how much opportunity exists for Vodafone in the international mobile phone market?**
2. **What type of generic strategy does Vodafone employ? Defend your answer.**
3. **What forms of ownership arrangement is Vodafone using to gain world market share? Explain.**
4. **On what basis would a firm like Vodafone evaluate performance? Identify and describe two examples.**

INTRODUCTION

Strategic planning
The process of evaluating the enterprise's environment and its internal strengths and then identifying long- and short-range activities

Strategic planning is the process of evaluating the enterprise's environment and its internal strengths, identifying long- and short-range objectives, and implementing a plan of action for attaining these goals. Multinational enterprises (MNEs) rely heavily on this process because it provides them with both general direction and specific guidance in carrying out their activities. Without a strategic plan, these businesses would have great difficulty in planning, implementing, and evaluating operations. With strategic planning, however, research shows that many MNEs have been able to make adjustments in their approach to dealing with competitive situations and either redirect their efforts or exploit new areas of opportunity. For example, General Motors has been losing market share in Europe in recent years. As a result, the company is now cutting its European capacity in an effort to stem further losses.[1] Meanwhile Dell Computer has begun to expand its international presence. In 2001 the company became the largest firm in the worldwide PC business with a market share of 13 per cent. Over the next five years Dell intends to double this share, while also expanding into computer services and networking.[2] On a different front, General Electric's strategy is to continue growing in spite of the European Commission's refusal to allow it to merge with Honeywell. Most recently, GE Medical bought Data Critical, a maker of wireless and Internet systems for communicating health-care data; GE Industrial Systems acquired the Lentronics line of multiplexers from Nortel Networks; and GE Capital purchased Heller Financial, a company in the commercial financing, equipment leasing, and real estate finance business.[3] By carefully formulating their strategic plan, these MNEs are finding that they can better cope with the ever-changing challenge of worldwide competition.[4]

STRATEGIC ORIENTATIONS

Ethnocentric predisposition
The tendency of a manager or multinational company to rely on the values and interests of the parent company in formulating and implementing the strategic plan

Before examining the strategic planning process, we must realize that MNEs have strategic predispositions toward doing things in a particular way. This predisposition helps determine the specific decisions the firm will implement. There are four such predispositions: ethnocentric, polycentric, regiocentric, and geocentric. Table 8.1 lists each predisposition and its characteristics.

An MNE with an **ethnocentric predisposition** will rely on the values and interests of the parent company in formulating and implementing the strategic plan. Primary emphasis will be given to profitability and the firm will try to run operations abroad the way they are run at home. Firms trying to sell the same product abroad that they sell at home use this predisposition most commonly.

Table 8.1 **Typical strategic orientations of MNEs**

MNE orientation	*Ethnocentric*	*Polycentric*	*Regiocentric*	*Geocentric*
Company's basic mission	Profitability	Public acceptance (legitimacy)	Both profitability and public acceptance	Both profitability and public acceptance
Type of governance	Top down	Bottom up (each local unit sets objectives)	Mutually negotiated between the region and its subsidiaries	Mutually negotiated at all levels of the organization
Strategy	Global integration	National responsiveness	Regional integration and national responsiveness	Global integration and national responsiveness
Structure	Hierarchical product divisions	Hierarchical area divisions with autonomous national units	Product and regional organization tied together through a matrix structure	A network of organizations (in some cases this includes stockholders and competitors)
Culture technology	Home country Mass production	Host country Batch production	Regional Flexible manufacturing	Global Flexible manufacturing
Marketing strategy	Product development is determined primarily by the needs of the home country customers	Local product development based on local needs	Standardized within the region, but not across regions	Global products with local variations
Profit strategy	Profits are brought back to the home country	Profits are kept in the host country	Profits are redistributed within the region	Redistribution is done on a global basis
Human resource management practices	Overseas operations are managed by people from the home country	Local nationals are used in key management positions	Regional people are developed for key managerial positions anywhere in the region	The best people anywhere in the world are developed for key positions everywhere in the world

Source: Adapted from *Columbia Journal of World Business*, Summer 1985, Balaji S. Chakravarthy and Howard V. Perlmutter, "Strategic Planning for a Global Business", pp. 5–6, Copyright 1985, with permission from Elsevier Science.

Polycentric predisposition
The tendency of a multinational to tailor its strategic plan to meet the needs of the local culture

An MNE with a **polycentric predisposition** will tailor its strategic plan to meet the needs of the local culture. If the firm is doing business in more than one culture, the overall plan will be adapted to reflect these individual needs. The basic mission of a polycentric MNE is to be accepted by the local culture and to blend into the country. Each subsidiary will decide the objectives it will pursue, based on local needs. Profits will be put back into the country in the form of expansion and growth.

Regiocentric predisposition
The tendency of a multinational to use a strategy that addresses both local and regional needs

An MNE with a **regiocentric predisposition** will be interested in obtaining both profit and public acceptance (a combination of the ethnocentric and polycentric approaches) and will use a strategy that allows it to address both local and regional needs. The company will be less focused on a particular country than on a geographic region. For example, an MNE doing business in the EU will be interested in all the member nations.

Geocentric predisposition
The tendency of a multinational to construct its strategic plan with a global view of operations

An MNE with a **geocentric predisposition** will view operations on a global basis. The largest international corporations often use this approach. They will produce global products with local variations and will staff their offices with the best people they can find, regardless of country of origin. Multinationals, in the true meaning of the word, have a geocentric predisposition. However, it is possible for an MNE to have a polycentric or regiocentric predisposition if the company is moderately small or limits operations to specific cultures or geographic regions.

The predisposition of an MNE will greatly influence its strategic planning process. For example, some MNEs are more interested in profit and/or growth than they are in developing a comprehensive corporate strategy that exploits their strengths.[5] Some are more interested in large-scale manufacturing that will allow them to compete on a price basis across the country or region, as opposed to developing a high degree of responsiveness to local demand and tailoring a product to these specific market niches.[6] Some prefer to sell in countries where the cultures are similar to their own so that the same basic marketing orientation can be used throughout the regions.[7] These orientations or predispositions will greatly influence the strategy.[8] For an example of strategic orientations, see the box "International Business Strategy in Action: Arthur Andersen, Accenture and McKinsey".

INTERNATIONAL BUSINESS STRATEGY *IN ACTION*

Arthur Andersen, Accenture, and McKinsey

During the 1990s one of the fastest growing types of global organizations were professional service firms that specialized in areas such as consulting, accounting, publishing, law, public relations, advertising, and so on. And today more and more of these service firms are linking together their worldwide country offices in order to provide seamless service to their multinational clients. Arthur Andersen, Accenture, and McKinsey & Company, three major international consulting companies provide good examples.

Arthur Andersen began in Chicago in 1913 as an accounting firm and by 2001 it had over 85,000 employees in 84 countries. Over these years, its global management and technology consulting group – Andersen Consulting, had complemented the company's audit and accounting services. However, in 1989, as part of a restructuring effort, Arthur Andersen and Andersen Consulting split and became two independent companies. The plan called for each to maintain its individual business and to cooperate under the umbrella of Andersen Worldwide. In 1997, however, Andersen Consulting sought arbitration claiming that Arthur Andersen had breached the agreement by expanding into business consulting in technology integration, strategic business planning, and business transformation. In 2000 the arbitrator ruled in favor of Andersen Consulting but also forced the consulting firm to drop the Andersen name. Today, under the name Accenture – a combination of "accent" and "future" – this company is a leader in global management and technology consulting with over 75,000 employees in 46 countries. And both firms, Arthur Andersen and Accenture, are now free to compete in any market. In addition, interestingly, both have also become major clients to each other.

Another major international consulting firm is McKinsey & Company, which started in Chicago in 1926. Today the firm has 84 offices in 44 countries and generates 60 per cent of its revenue outside the US. McKinsey's core strength is its brand name built on the in-house training and management of its highly skilled people who have been recruited from top business schools. Additionally, the company provides its personnel with continuous learning through team-based project work.

Consulting firms have often been pointed to as recession-proof companies because their services are needed regardless of what happens in the economy. For example, in good times, businesses need consulting assistance to help them deal with things like expansion, mergers, and acquisitions; and in bad times they need help in cutting back operations, trimming the work-force, and refocusing their strategy. The most recent worldwide economic slowdown, however, has led to an unexpected and significant slowdown in consulting as well. In the 1990s, the consulting market was growing by 20 per cent annually, but by 2001 this growth rate had shrunk to 3 per cent. In the process the slowdown has taken its toll on all three MNEs. In the past these global consulting firms focused their efforts on securing long-term relationships with large MNEs and other large organizations, and drawing on their firm-specific advantages and reputation for quality they were able to continually attract new clients. Today, however, all three are in the process of laying off junior staff and recently hired MBAs and looking for innovative ways of getting their costs under control. Some of their critics have wondered aloud why the three are having so many problems. If, indeed, they are experts at helping organizations solve the challenges associated with downturns in the economy, why don't they simply apply some of these solutions to their own current situation? This is a piece of advice that has not been lost on these major consulting firms.

Websites: **www.andersen.com**; **www.accenture.com** and **www.mckinsey.com**.

Sources: Rachel Emma Silverman, "Accenture's Strong Revenue Growth Bucks Industry Slump," *Wall Street Journal*, October 12, 2001, p. B 4; Andersen Worldwide 1996 Annual Report; "Arthur Andersen Legal Link-up Confirmed," *Accountancy*, vol. 121, no. 1256 (April 1998); "DREF, Arthur Andersen Form Partnership," *Industrial Distribution*, vol. 86, no. 9 (September 1997); "Arthur Andersen and Stephen Shortell Form Global Health Care Industry Alliance," *Health Care Strategic Management*, vol. 15, no. 11 (November 1997); "Andersen/Garrigues Merger Is Completed," *International Financial Law Review*, vol. 16, no. 3 (March 1997); "AW Battle Could Take Years," *Accountancy*, vol. 121, no. 1257 (May 1998); C. A. Bartlett, *McKinsey & Company: Managing Knowledge and Learning*, Harvard Business School Case No. 9-396-357, 1996; **www.mckinsey.com**; **www/mckinsey.com/about/feet_on_the_street.htm**; Geoffrey Colvin, "The Consulting Slowdown," *Fortune.com*, August 21, 2001.

STRATEGY FORMULATION

Strategy formulation
The process of evaluating the enterprise's environment and its internal strengths

Strategy formulation is the process of evaluating the enterprise's environment and its internal strengths. This typically begins with consideration of the external arena since the MNE will first be interested in opportunities that can be exploited. Then attention will be directed to the internal environment and the resources the organization has available, or can develop, to take advantage of these opportunities.

External environmental assessment

Competitive intelligence
The gathering of external information on competitors and the competitive environment as part of the decision-making process

The analysis of the external environment involves two activities: information gathering and information assessment. These steps help to answer two key questions: What is going on in the external environment? How will these developments affect our company?[9] One of the most common ways in which this is done is through **competitive intelligence**, which is the use of systematic techniques for obtaining and analyzing public information about competitors.[10] These data are particularly useful in keeping MNEs alert regarding likely moves by the competition.[11]

Information gathering

Information gathering is a critical phase of international strategic planning. Unfortunately, not all firms recognize this early enough. In the case of Harley-Davidson, the large US-based motorcycle manufacturer, it was not until the Japanese began dominating the motorcycle market that Harley realized its problem. A systematic analysis of the competition revealed that the major reason for Japanese success in the US market was the high quality of their products, a result of extremely efficient manufacturing techniques. Today Harley is competitive again. It achieved renewed success because it rethought its basic business, reformulated company strategy, vastly improved product quality, and rededicated itself to the core business: heavyweight motorcycles.

There are a number of ways that MNEs conduct an environmental scan and then forecast the future. Four of the most common methods include (1) asking experts in the industry to discuss industry trends and to make projections about the future; (2) using historical industry trends to forecast future developments; (3) asking knowledgeable managers to write scenarios describing what they foresee for the industry over the next two to three years; and (4) using computers to simulate the industry environment and to generate likely future developments. Of these, expert opinion is the most commonly used.[12] The Japanese and the South Koreans provide excellent examples. Mitsubishi has over 700 employees in New York City whose primary objective is to gather information on American competitors and markets. All large Japanese corporations operating in the US employ similar strategies. The same is true for large South Korean trading firms, who require their branch managers to send back information on market developments. These data are then analyzed and used to help formulate future strategies for the firms.

This information helps MNEs to identify competitor strengths and weaknesses and to target areas for attack. This approach is particularly important when a company is delivering a product or service for many market niches around the world that are too small to be individually profitable. In such situations the MNE has to identify a series of different niches and to attempt to market successfully in each of these geographic areas.[13] The information is also critical to those firms that will be coming under attack.

Information assessment

Having gathered information on the competition and the industry, MNEs will then evaluate the data. One of the most common approaches is to make an overall assessment based on the five forces that determine industry competitiveness – buyers, suppliers, potential new entrants to the industry, the availability of substitute goods and services, and rivalry among the competitors. Figure 8.1 shows the connections among these forces.[14]

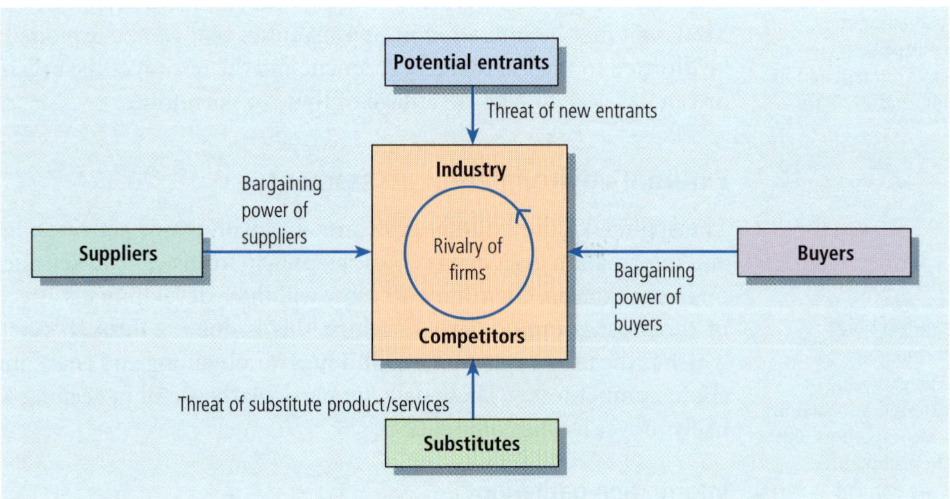

Figure 8.1 The five forces of industry competitiveness

Source: Adapted with the permission of The Free Press, an imprint of Simon & Schuster Adult Publishing Group, from *Competitive Advantage: Creating and Sustaining Superior Performance* by Michael E. Porter. Copyright © 1985, 1998 by Michael E. Porter.

Bargaining power of buyers MNEs will examine the power of their buyers because they will want to predict the likelihood of maintaining these customers. If the firm believes buyers may be moving their business to competitors, the MNE will want to formulate a strategy for countering this move. For example, the company may offer a lower price or increase the amount of service it provides.

Bargaining power of suppliers An MNE will look at the power of the industry's suppliers to see if it can gain a competitive advantage here.[15] For example, if there are a number of suppliers in the industry, the MNE may attempt to play them off against each other in an effort to get a lower price. Or the company may move to eliminate any threat from the suppliers by acquiring one of them, thus guaranteeing itself a ready source of inputs.

New entrants The company will examine the likelihood of new firms entering the industry and will try to determine the impact they might have on the MNE. Two typical ways that international MNEs attempt to reduce the threat of new entrants are by (1) keeping costs low and consumer loyalty high, and (2) encouraging the government to limit foreign business activity through regulation such as duties, tariffs, quotas, and other protective measures.

Threat of substitutes The MNE will look at the availability of substitute goods and services and try to anticipate when such offerings will reach the market. There are a number of steps that the company will take to offset this competitive force, including (1) lowering prices, (2) offering similar products, and (3) increasing services to the customer.

Rivalry The MNE will examine the rivalry that exists between itself and the competition and seek to anticipate future changes in this arrangement.[16] Common strategies for maintaining and/or increasing market strength include (1) offering new goods and services, (2) increasing productivity and thus reducing overall costs, (3) working to differentiate current goods and services from those of the competition, (4) increasing overall quality of goods and services, and (5) targeting specific niches with a well-designed market strategy.

As the MNE examines each of these five forces, it will decide the attractiveness and unattractiveness of each. This will help the company to decide how and where to make strategic changes. Figure 8.2 shows the five forces model applied to the semiconductor industry.

Notice in Figure 8.2 that the suppliers in the semiconductor industry, at the time this analysis was conducted, were not very powerful, so this was an attractive force for the MNE. Buyers did not have many substitute products from which to choose (an attractive development), but there was some backward integration toward purchasing their own sources of supply (an unattractive development). Overall, the attractiveness of buyer power was regarded as inconclusive. The third force, entry barriers, was quite attractive because of the high costs of getting into the industry and the short product life cycles that existed there. It was very difficult for a company to enter this market. The fourth force, substitutes, was unattractive because new products were being developed continually and customer loyalty was somewhat low. The fifth and final force, industry rivalry, was also unattractive because of the high cost of doing business, the cyclical nature of sales, and the difficulty of differentiating one's products from those of the competition.

On an overall basis, however, the industry was classified as attractive. It also appeared that the industry would see consolidation of smaller firms into larger firms that would have greater resources to commit to research and development.

MNEs operating in the semiconductor industry would use this analysis to help them increase the attractiveness of those forces that currently are not highly attractive. For

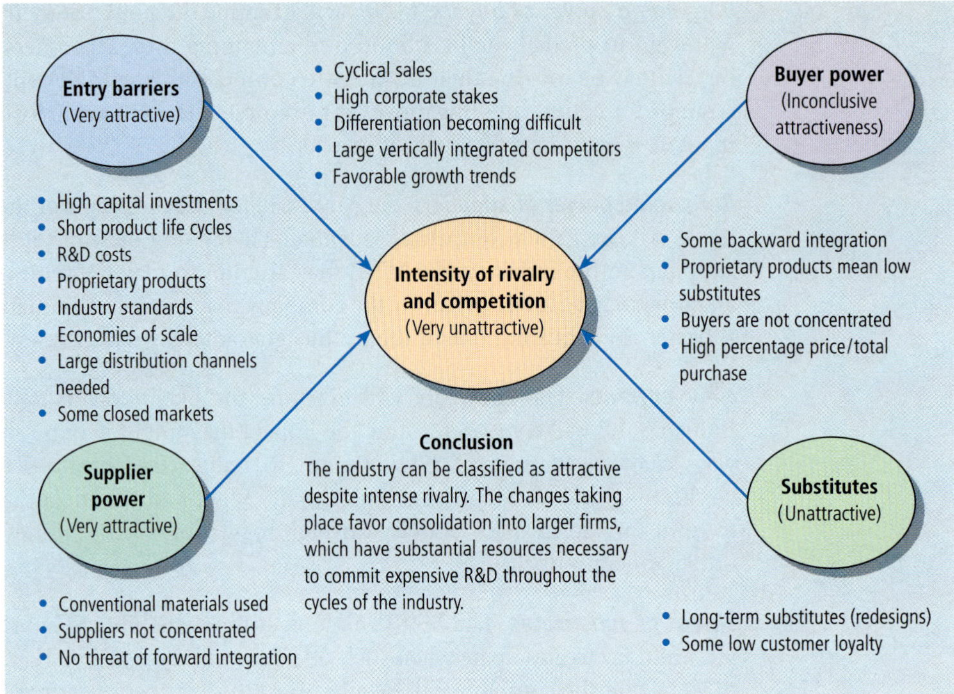

Figure 8.2 The five forces model applied to the semiconductor industry

Source: Scott Beardsley and Kinji Sakagami, *Advanced Micro Devices: Poised for Chip Greatness*, unpublished student paper, Sloan School of Management, MIT, 1988. Reported in Arnoldo C. Hax and Nicolas S. Majluf, *The Strategy Concept and Process: A Pragmatic Approach* (Englewood Cliffs NJ: Prentice-Hall, 1991), p. 46.

example, they could work to develop state-of-the-art semiconductors that might be substituted for the competition's products, and they would attempt to maintain a technological advantage so that the substitute force would not become a problem for them. In the process they would likely be better able to increase their power over the buyers since their products would be so high tech that the customers could not do better by purchasing from a competitor. In summary, environmental assessment, such as that provided by an analysis of competitive forces, is used to determine MNE opportunities and threats and to help identify strategies for improving market position and profitability.

Active learning check 

Review your answer to Active Learning Case question 1 and make any changes you like. Then compare your answer with the one below.

1. Given the competitiveness of the environment, how much opportunity exists for Vodafone in the international mobile phone market?

As seen from the case data, the opportunities in this market are extremely great. One reason is because the market is going to continue growing. The number of mobile phone users in Europe, the US, and Japan will increase sharply during this decade. The key to success in this industry is to have a presence in all of the major markets, primarily the triad countries and others where the cost of mobile phones is within reach of the average person. China, for example, will be an important market because of its large population. However, newly industrialized countries offer even more opportunity because the average GDP is much greater than that of China's. Examples include South Korea, Singapore, and Taiwan. In addition, Australia and New Zealand are going to be important target markets. By focusing on these more affluent markets and offering both state-of-the-art products and competitive prices, Vodafone has a very good chance of outdistancing the competition.

Internal environmental assessment

The internal environmental assessment helps to pinpoint MNE strengths and weaknesses. There are two specific areas that a multinational will examine in this assessment: (1) physical resources and personnel competencies, and (2) the way in which value chain analysis can be used to bring these resources together in the most synergistic and profitable manner.

Physical resources and personnel competencies

The physical resources are the assets that the MNE will use to carry out the strategic plan. Many of these are reported on the balance sheet as reflected by the firm's cash, inventory, machinery, and equipment accounts. However, this does not tell the whole story. The location and disposition of these resources is also important. For example, an MNE with manufacturing plants on three continents may be in a much better position to compete worldwide than a competitor whose plants are all located in one geographic area. Location can also affect cost. In the 1980s it was possible for Japanese steel makers to sell their products in the US at lower prices than their US competitors. During the 1990s US firms improved their steel-producing technology and erected small minimills that were highly efficient, thus offsetting the location advantage of their foreign competitors. Today, however, European steel makers, in particular, have sharply increased their efficiency, and, along with Japanese firms, are now again able to compete in the US market.[17] As a result, American steel makers are again seeking government protection from imports. Location has proven to be but a short-term benefit for US firms.

Strategic business units (SBUs)
Operating units with their own strategic space; they produce and sell goods and services to a market segment and have a well-defined set of competitors

Vertical integration
The ownership of assets involved in producing a good or service and delivering it to the final customer

Another important consideration is the degree of integration that exists within the operating units of the MNE. Large companies, in particular, tend to be divided into **strategic business units (SBUs)**. These are operating units with their own strategic space; they produce and sell goods and services to a market segment and have a well-defined set of competitors.[18] SBUs are sometimes referred to as "businesses within the business". Mitsubishi, the giant Japanese conglomerate, has a host of SBUs that constitute its corporate network. These include steel making, auto production, electronics, and banking. So when a Mitsubishi SBU that manufactures and sells consumer goods is looking for help with financing, it can turn to the banking SBU. If the bank finds that a customer needs a firm to produce a particular electronics product, it can refer the buyer to the electronics SBU.

In fact, some large MNEs use **vertical integration**, which is the ownership of all assets needed to produce the goods and services delivered to the customer. Many large Japanese manufacturing firms, in particular, have moved toward vertical integration by purchasing controlling interests in their suppliers.[19] The objective is to obtain control over the supply and thus ensure that the materials or goods are delivered as needed. Many US and European firms have shied away from this strategy because "captured suppliers" are often less cost effective than independents. For example, a number of years ago *Time* magazine owned the forests for producing the paper it needed. However, the company eventually sold this resource because it found that the cost of making the paper was higher than that charged by large paper manufacturers that specialized in this product. So vertical integration may reduce costs in some instances, but it can be an ineffective strategy in other cases.[20] In particular, one of the major problems with vertical integration is defending oneself from competitors who are less vertically integrated and are able to achieve cost efficiencies as a result. The latter rely heavily on outsourcers and employ **virtual integration**, which is the ownership of the core technologies and manufacturing capabilities needed to produce outputs, while depending on outsourcers to provide all other needed inputs. Virtual integration allows an MNE to operate as if it were vertically integrated, but it does not require the company to own all of the factors of production as is the case with vertically integrated firms.

Virtual integration
A networking strategy based on cooperation within and across company boundaries

Personnel competencies are the abilities and talents of the people. An MNE will want to examine these because they reflect many of the company's strengths and weaknesses. For example, if an MNE has an outstanding R&D department, it may be able to develop high-quality, state-of-the-art products. However, if the company has no sales arm, it will sell the output to a firm that can handle the marketing and distribution. Conversely, if a company lacks a strong R&D department but has an international sales force, it may allow the competition to bring out new products and to rely on its own R&D people to reverse engineer them, that is, to find out how they are built and then develop technologies that can do the same thing, while relying on the sales force to build market share. This strategy has been used by many internationally based personal computer (PC) firms that have taken PC technology and used it to develop similar, but far less expensive, units that are now beginning to dominate the world market.

An understanding of what one does well can help a company to decide whether the best strategy is to lead or to follow close behind and copy the leader. Not every MNE has the personnel competencies to be first in the field, and many are happy to follow because the investment risk is less and the opportunity for profit is often good.

Value chain analysis

Value chain
The way in which primary and support activities are combined in providing goods and services and increasing profit margins

A complementary approach to internal environment assessment is an examination of the firm's value chain.[21] A **value chain** is the way in which primary and support activities are combined in providing goods and services and in increasing profit margins. Figure 8.3 provides the general schema of a value chain. The primary activities in this chain include (1) inbound logistics such as receiving, storing, materials handling, and warehouse activities; (2) operations in which inputs are put into final product form by performing activities such as machining, assembling, testing, and packaging; (3) outbound logistics, which involve distributing the finished product to the customer; (4) marketing and sales, which are used to encourage buyers to purchase the product; and (5) service for maintaining and enhancing the value of the product after the sale through activities such as repair, product adjustment, training, and parts supply. The support activities in the value chain consist of: (1) the firm's infrastructure, which is made up of the company's general management, planning, finance, accounting, legal, government affairs, and quality management areas; (2) human resource management, which is made up of the selection, placement, appraisal, promotion, training, and development of the firm's personnel; (3) technology in the form of knowledge, research and development, and procedures

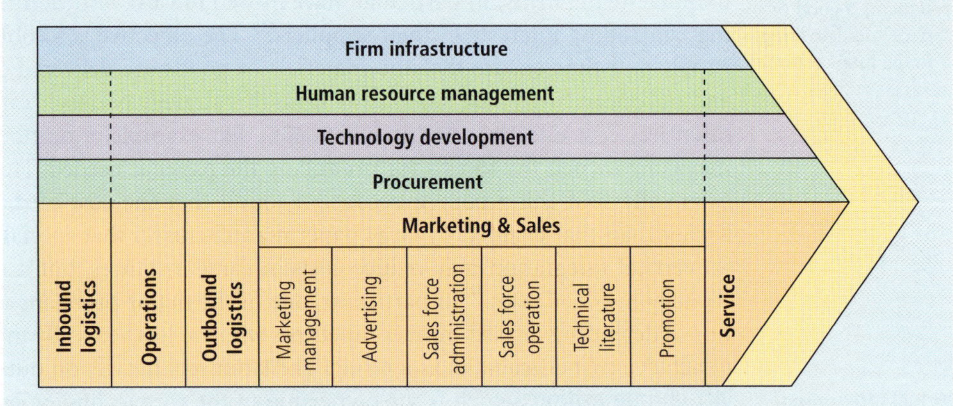

Figure 8.3 A basic value chain

Source: Adapted with the permission of The Free Press, an imprint of Simon & Schuster Adult Publishing Group, from *Competitive Advantage: Creating and Sustaining Superior Performance* by Michael E. Porter. Copyright © 1985, 1998 by Michael E. Porter.

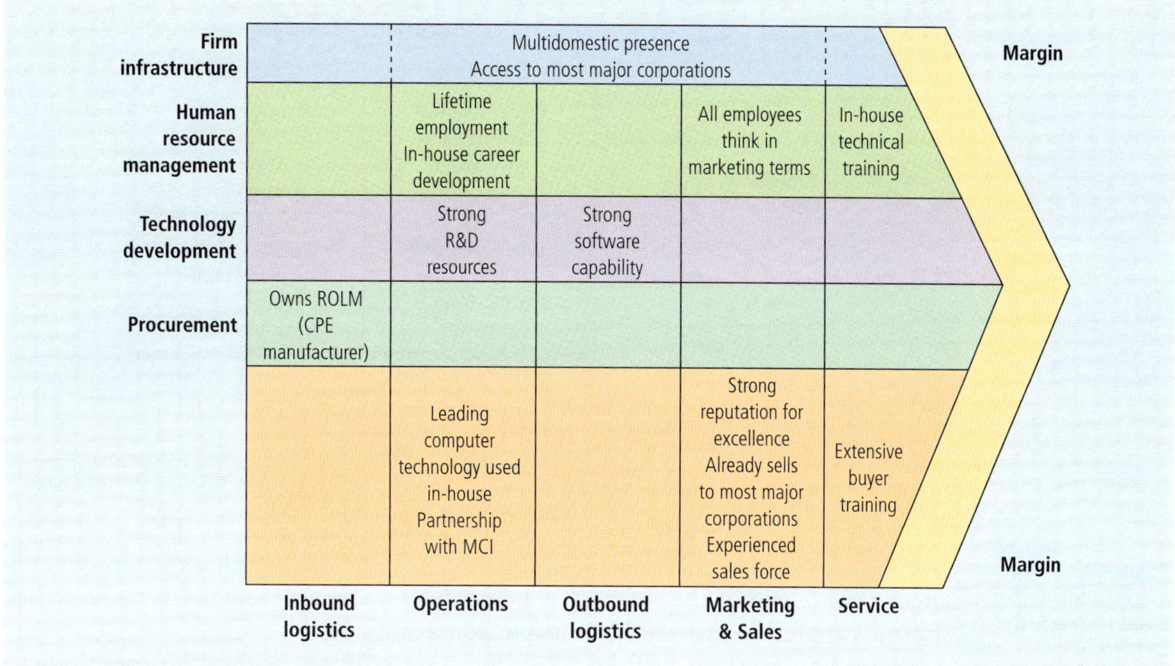

Figure 8.4 The value chain for IBM

Source: Reported in Arnoldo C. Hax and Nicolas S. Majluf, *The Strategy Concept and Process: A Pragmatic Approach* (Englewood Cliffs NJ: Prentice-Hall, 1991), p. 82.

Cost strategy
A strategy that relies on low price and is achieved through approaches such as vigorous pursuit of cost reductions and overhead-control, avoidance of marginal customer accounts, and cost minimalization in areas such as sales and advertising

Differentiation strategy
A strategy directed toward creating something that is perceived as being unique

Focus strategy
A strategy that concentrates on a particular buyer group and segments that niche based on product line or geographic market

that can result in improved goods and services; and (4) procurement, which involves the purchasing of raw materials, supplies, and similar goods.

MNEs can use these primary and support activities to increase the value of the goods and services they provide. As such, they form a value chain. An example is provided in Figure 8.4, which helps to explain why IBM has been so effective in the international market. The company combines the primary and support activities so as to increase the value of its products. IBM's alliance with ROLM and MCI and its strengths in software and hardware technologies have provided the company with a solid foundation for launching successful strategies in the telecommunications industry.

Any firm can apply this idea of a value chain. For example, Makita of Japan has become a leading competitor in power tools because it was the first to use new, less expensive materials for making tool parts and to produce in a single plant standardized models that it then sold worldwide.

Analysis of the value chain can also help a company to determine the type of strategy that will be most effective. In all, there are three generic strategies: cost, differentiation, and focus.[22]

1. **Cost strategy** relies on such approaches as aggressive construction of efficient facilities, vigorous pursuit of cost reductions and overhead control, avoidance of marginal customer accounts, and cost minimization in areas like R&D, service, sales, and advertising.
2. **Differentiation strategy** is directed toward creating something that is perceived as being unique. Approaches to differentiation can take many forms, including the creation of design or brand image, improved technology or features, and increased customer service or dealer networks.
3. **Focus strategy** involves concentrating on a particular buyer group and segmenting that niche based on product line or geographic market. While low-cost and differentiation strategies are aimed at achieving objectives industry-wide, a focus strategy is built around servicing a particular target market, and each functional policy is developed with this in mind.[23]

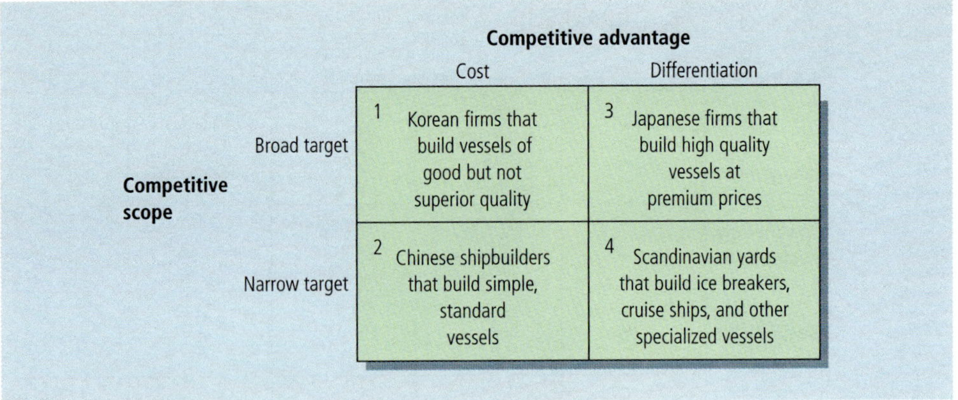

Figure 8.5 Generic strategies in worldwide shipbuilding

Source: Adapted with the permission of The Free Press, an imprint of Simon & Schuster Adult Publishing Group, from *Competitive Advantage: Creating and Sustaining Superior Performance* by Michael E. Porter. Copyright © 1985, 1998 by Michael E. Porter.

Competitive scope
The breadth of a firm's target market within an industry

In addition, the firm will determine its **competitive scope**, which is the breadth of its target market within the industry. Figure 8.5 provides an example of these generic strategies applied to the worldwide shipbuilding industry.

The value chain can help an MNE to create synergies within the organization's activities. For example, by combining the human resource talent of its salespeople with the expertise of its design and styling personnel, firms like PSA Peugeot-Citroen and Volkswagen have been able to increase their auto market share in Western Europe in recent years.[24] In particular, Peugeot and VW have been able to cut costs and offer a wide range of new models. Their overall success is found in their ability to manage the flow of new products, so that the offerings remain reasonably fresh without spending money on excessive investment in updates or redesign. Firms that cannot get this aspect of the product cycle correct have been falling behind in the European market, as seen by Ford, General Motors and, most significantly, Renault.[25] Simply put, by analyzing the ways of combining their primary and support activities, some automotive MNEs have been able to create a strategy that allows them to draw heavily on their strengths while minimizing their weaknesses.[26]

Active learning check 

Review your answer to Active Learning Case question 2 and make any changes you like. Then compare your answer with the one below.

2. What type of generic strategy does Vodafone employ? Defend your answer.

Vodafone uses a focus strategy that is geared toward identifying market niches and meeting the needs of the mobile customers in these target groups. Notice that one of the guidelines it follows in most of its acquisitions is to be the major stakeholder (or at least hold a substantial ownership position) but also have a partner who can help the company deal with the challenges in the local market. As the case notes, in both the Netherlands and France the company has local partners; and in the US it holds 45 per cent of Verizon. So the company targets its market and it also focuses on offering innovative products and a competitive price in order to compete effectively. In Japan, where it is currently unable to match the offerings of DoCoMo, its progress has been slowed, but the company has been successful against KDDI by being able to capture a large percentage of new subscribers. Again, the company's success is a result of a carefully crafted generic strategy that is carefully focused.

Table 8.2 **Typical goals of an MNE**

Profitability	*Marketing*	*Production*	*Finance*	*Human resource management*
Level of products	Total sales volume	Ratio of foreign to domestic production share	Financing of foreign affiliates – retained earnings or local borrowing	Development of managers with global orientation
Return on assets, investment, equity, sales	Market share – worldwide, region, country	Economies of scale via international production integration	Taxation – minimizing the burden globally	Management development of host country nationals
Annual profit growth	Growth in sales volume	Quality and cost control	Optimum capital structure	
Annual earnings per share growth	Integration of country markets for marketing efficiency and effectiveness	Introduction of cost-efficient production methods	Foreign exchange management – minimizing losses from foreign fluctuations	

Source: Adapted from *International Dimensions of Management*, 2nd edition, by A. Phatak © 1989. Reprinted with permission of South-Western College Publishing, a division of Thomson Learning.

Goal setting

The external and internal environmental analyses will provide the MNE with the information needed for setting goals. Some of these goals will be determined during the external analysis, as the company identifies opportunities that it wants to exploit. Others will be finalized after the value chain analysis is complete. In either event one of the outcomes of strategy formulation will be the identification of goals.[27]

There are two basic ways of examining the goals or objectives of international business operations. One is to review them on the basis of operating performance or functional area. Table 8.2 provides an illustration. Some of the major goals will be related to profitability, marketing, production, finance, and human resources. A second way is to examine these goals by geographic area or on an SBU basis. For example, the European group may have a profitability goal of 16 per cent, the North American group's profitability goal may be 17 per cent, and the Pacific Rim group's goal may be 18 per cent. Then there will be accompanying functional goals for marketing, production, and finance. If the MNE has SBUs, each strategic business unit in these geographic locales will have its own list of goals.

This approach uses what is called a "cascading effect" because, like a cascade of water rippling down the side of a hill, it reaches the bottom by moving from one level to the next. The MNE will start out by setting a profitability goal for the overall enterprise. Each geographic area or business unit will then be assigned a profitability goal, which, if attained, will result in the MNE reaching its overall desired profitability. The same approach will be used in other key areas such as marketing, production, and finance. Within each unit, these objectives will then be further subdivided so that every part of the organization understands its objectives and everyone is working toward the same overall goals.

Strategy implementation
The process of attaining goals by using the organizational structure to execute the formulated strategy properly

STRATEGY IMPLEMENTATION

Strategy implementation is the process of attaining goals by using the organizational structure to execute the formulated strategy properly. There are many areas of focus in this process. Three of the most important are location, ownership decisions, and functional area implementation. The box "International Business Strategy in Action: Fuji Xerox saves Xerox" illustrates how these considerations can be used in gaining market entry.[28]

INTERNATIONAL BUSINESS STRATEGY *IN ACTION*

Fuji Xerox saves Xerox

Fuji Xerox was created in 1962 as a joint venture between Xerox and Fuji Photo Film. It is regarded as the most successful partnership between US and Japanese firms. The arrangement developed from a sales operation for Xerox products in Japan into a fully integrated organization with its own R&D and manufacturing and by 1990 its $4 billion revenue constituted 25 per cent of Xerox's worldwide revenues. By then Fuji Xerox had a world product mandate to supply the entire Xerox Group with the low-to-mid-range copiers that were the core of its business. Indeed, as the Xerox monopoly on large copiers began to dwindle in the 1970s, it was its Japanese partner, Fuji Xerox, which rode to the rescue with its new and high quality smaller copiers.

In 1975 Xerox was forced by the US Federal Trade Commission to license its original core copier technology to rivals such as IBM, Kodak, Ricoh, and Canon. If it had not been for Fuji Xerox developing new copier technology, Xerox would have failed. The firm's early monopoly in the world copier business was eroded sharply by intense rivalry from Japanese competitors such as Canon and Ricoh as well as from Kodak and IBM. These rivals produced higher quality, lower priced, more technologically advanced, and more reliable copiers than Xerox.

Fuji Xerox recognized the threat and its managers, acting autonomously, started R&D into new small copiers. The US head office was slow to take on board the technology and products of its Japanese partner. Loss of market share, especially to Canon, however, eventually led to ever closer degrees of cooperation between Xerox and Fuji Xerox. In particular, the high quality standards of Fuji Xerox were spread throughout the Xerox Group, and the total quality management techniques of Fuji Xerox helped Xerox regain market. In this context Xerox was helped by having its partner, Fuji Xerox, based in Japan, the hotbed of TQM and copier innovation in the 1970s and 1980s.

One of the reasons for success in the collaboration between Xerox and Fuji Photo Films was that the latter acted as a silent partner in the 50–50 joint venture and allowed Fuji Xerox to develop its own management cadre, who became skilled in R&D and copier technology, and in the manufacturing and marketing of small copiers. Fuji Xerox also transformed itself from a marketing subsidiary into a full line business, thus ending up being more innovative and responsive to the market than Xerox itself.

Websites: ***www.fujixerox.co.jp***; ***www.xerox.com*** and ***www.fujifilm.com***.

Sources: Adapted from Benjamin Gomes-Casseres and Krista McQuade, *Xerox and Fuji Xerox*, Harvard Business School Case 9-391-156; David T. Kearns and David A. Nadler, *Prophets in the Dark: How Xerox Reinvented Itself and Beat Back the Japanese* (New York: Macmillan, 1992); and Benjamin Gomes-Casseres, "Group Versus Group: How Alliance Networks Compete," *Harvard Business Review*, July/August, 1994, pp. 62–74.

Location

Over the past decade MNEs have greatly expanded their international presence. Some of the areas in which they have begun to set up operations include China, the former Soviet Union, and Eastern Europe.

Location is important for a number of reasons. Local facilities often provide a cost advantage to the producer. This is particularly true when the raw materials, parts, or labor needed to produce the product can be inexpensively obtained close to the facility. Location is also important because residents may prefer locally produced products. For example, many people in the US like to "buy American". Some locations may also be attractive because the local government is encouraging investment through various means such as low tax rates, free land, subsidized energy and transportation rates, and low-interest loans, while imported goods are subjected to tariffs, quotas, or other governmental restrictions, making local manufacture more desirable. Finally, the MNE may already be doing so much business in a country that the local government will insist that it set up local operations and begin producing more of its goods there. This is one of the major reasons that Japanese auto manufacturers began to establish operations in the US.

Although the benefits can be great, there are a number of drawbacks associated with locating operations overseas. One is an unstable political climate that can leave an MNE vulnerable to low profits and bureaucratic red tape. In Russia, for example, the government has encouraged joint ventures, but because of political and economic uncertainty, many businesspeople currently regard such investments as high-risk ventures. A second drawback is the possibility of revolution or armed conflict. MNEs with operations in Kuwait lost just about all of their investment in the Gulf War, and MNEs with locales in Saudi Arabia and other Middle East countries affected by the Gulf War also withstood losses in the region. Most recently, businesses in areas targeted by international terrorists have been making plans to reduce their risks. In some cases firms are finding a way of "hedging their bets", as noted in the following example:

> Some . . . opt for locales where the cost of running a small enterprise is significantly lower than that of running a large one. In this way they spread their risk, setting up many small locations throughout the world rather than one or two large ones. Manufacturing firms are a good example. Some production firms feel that the economies of scale associated with a large-scale plant are more than offset by the potential problems that can result, should economic or political difficulties develop in the country. These firms' strategy is to spread the risk by opting for a series of small plants spread throughout a wide geographic region.[29]

Ownership

Ownership of international operations has become an important issue in recent years. Many Americans, for example, believe that the increase in foreign-owned businesses in the US is weakening the economy. People in other countries have similar feelings about US businesses there. In truth, the real issue of ownership is whether or not the company is contributing to the overall economic good of the country where it is doing business. As one researcher noted, ". . . because the US-owned corporation is coming to have no special relationship with Americans, it makes no sense for the United States to entrust its national competitiveness to it. The interests of American-owned corporations may or may not coincide with those of the American people".[30] Countries that want to remain economically strong must be able to attract international investors who will provide jobs that allow their workers to increase their skills and build products that are demanded on the world market. In accomplishing this objective, two approaches are now in vogue: international joint ventures and strategic alliances.

International joint ventures

International joint venture (IJV)
An agreement between two or more partners to own and control an overseas business

An **international joint venture (IJV)** is an agreement between two or more partners to own and control an overseas business.[31] IJVs take a number of different forms[32] and offer a myriad of opportunities,[33] which helps to explain some of the reasons for the rise in popularity of IJVs in recent years. One of these reasons is government encouragement and legislation that are designed to make it attractive for foreign investors to bring in local partners. A second reason is the growing need for partners who know the local economy, the culture, and the political system and who can cut through red tape in getting things done, something that IJVs often do very well. A third reason is the desire by outside investors to find local partners with whom they can can team up effectively.[34] For example, an MNE might provide a local partner with technology know-how and an infusion of capital that, in turn, will allow the local firm to expand operations, increase market share, and begin exporting. A example is Toyota and PSA Peugeot-Citroen which recently entered into an IJV to jointly develop and build a small fuel-efficient car for the European market. The primary benefit for Toyota is the opportunity to expand its model line-up in Europe. The major advantage for Peugeot is that of gaining a new small car for its European product line while sharing the development costs with Toyota.[35]

Unfortunately, in many cases IJVs have not worked out well. Several studies found a failure rate of 30 per cent for ventures in developed countries and 45–50 per cent in less developed countries.[36] The major reason has been the desire by MNEs to control the operation, which sometimes has resulted in poor decision making and/or conflicts with the local partners. In general, joint ventures are difficult to manage and are frequently unstable.[37] This is why many MNEs have turned to the use of strategic partnerships.

Strategic alliance

Strategic alliance or partnership
An agreement between two or more competitive multinational enterprises for the purpose of serving a global market

A **strategic alliance or partnership** is an agreement between two or more competitive MNEs for the purpose of serving a global market.[38] In contrast to a joint venture where the partners may be from different businesses, strategic partnerships are almost always formed by firms in the same line of business. In recent years these partnerships have become increasingly popular[39] although careful management of these agreements continues to be a critical area of concern.[40] A recent example of a strategic partnership is that of Matsushita Electric Industrial and Hitachi, Japan's two leading electronics manufacturers. These two companies are now jointly developing state-of-the art technology in three areas: smart cards, home network systems, and recyclable and energy-efficient consumer electronics. In the past both firms have developed their own products, but now they are turning to a strategic partnership in order to save money and to shorten development time.[41] Another example of strategic partnerships is that between IBM and NTT. Under the terms of their recent strategic partnership agreement, for the next decade IBM will provide outsourcing services to NTT, Japan's dominant telecommunications carrier. In turn, IBM will be able to use NTT Comware staff in outsourcing and obtaining computer-services contracts with other customers in Japan.[42]

These alliances help to illustrate the growing popularity of international business ownership agreements. Sometimes companies will prefer to invest in another country and maintain 100 per cent ownership. However, this is often a very expensive and risky approach given that the MNE may not have much experience in that particular marketplace and local partners may be very helpful in dealing with all sorts of local barriers. As a result, it is becoming increasingly popular to find MNEs turning to the use of IJVs and strategic partnerships.

Active learning check

Review your answer to Active Learning Case question 3 and make any changes you like. Then compare your answer with the one below.

3. What forms of ownership arrangement is Vodafone using to gain world market share? Explain.

Vodafone uses two basic approaches. The most common is the international joint venture, which is seen by the company's decisions to acquire an ownership position in a local company but have a local partner hold the remainder of the ownership. An example is its 45 per cent stake in Verizon Wireless, which is now the largest US mobile telephone operator in America. In some cases, however, Vodafone opts for total ownership and purchases the entire company. This typically occurs when it feels that it does not need a local partner. An example is Airtouch Communications, where Vodafone acquired the entire firm. In both cases, of course, the ownership arrangement is designed to help Vodafone continue to increase its market share in that geographic region.

Functional strategies

Functional strategies are used to coordinate operations and to ensure that the plan is carried out properly.[43] While the specific functions that are key to the success of the MNE will vary, they typically fall into six major areas: marketing, manufacturing, finance, procurement, technology, and human resources. For purposes of analysis, they can be examined in terms of three major considerations: marketing, manufacturing, and finance.

Marketing

The marketing strategy is designed to identify consumer needs and to formulate a plan of action for selling the desired goods and services to these customers.[44] Most marketing strategies are built around what is commonly known as the "four Ps" of marketing: product, price, promotion, and place. The company will identify the products that are in demand in the market niches it is pursuing. It will apprise the manufacturing department of any modifications that will be necessary to meet local needs, and it will determine the price at which the goods can be sold. Then the company's attention will be devoted to promoting the products and to selling them in the local market.

Manufacturing

The manufacturing strategy is designed to dovetail with the marketing plan and to ensure that the right products are built and delivered in time for sale. Manufacturing will also coordinate its strategy with the procurement and technology people, so as to ensure that the desired materials are available and that the products have the necessary state-of-the-art quality. If the MNE is producing goods in more than one country, it will give attention to coordinating activities where needed. For example, some firms manufacture goods in two or more countries and then assemble and sell them in other geographic regions. Japanese auto firms send car parts to the US for assembly and then sell some of the assembled cars in Canada, Mexico, and South America. Whirlpool builds appliances worldwide with operations in Brazil, Canada, Mexico, the Netherlands, and seven other countries. Such production and assembly operations have to be coordinated carefully.[45]

Finance

Financial strategies used to be formulated and controlled out of the home office. However, in recent years MNEs have learned that this approach can be cumbersome, and, because of fluctuating currency prices, costly as well. Today overseas units have more control over their finances than before, but they are guided by a carefully constructed budget that is in accord with the overall strategic plan. They are also held to account for financial performance in the form of return on investment, profit, capital budgeting, debt financing, and working capital management. The financial strategy often serves both to lead and lag the other functional strategies. In the lead position, finance limits the amounts of money that can be spent on marketing (new product development, advertising, promotion) and manufacturing (machinery, equipment, quality control) to ensure that the desired return on investment is achieved. In the lag position, the financial strategy is used to evaluate performance and to provide insights regarding how future strategy should be changed.

CONTROL AND EVALUATION

The strategy formulation and implementation processes are a prelude to control and evaluation. This process involves an examination of the MNE's performance for the purpose of determining (1) how well the organization has done and (2) what actions should be taken in light of this performance. This process is tied directly to the overall strategy in that the objectives serve as the basis for comparison and evaluation.[46] Figure 8.6 illustrates how this process works.

If the comparison and evaluation show that the strategic business unit or overseas operation is performing according to expectations, then things will continue as before. The objectives may be altered because of changes in the strategic plan, but otherwise nothing major is likely to be done. On the other hand, if there have been problems, the MNE will want to identify the causes and work to eliminate or minimize them.[47] Similarly, if the unit has performed extremely well and achieved more than forecasted, the management may want to reset the objectives to a higher level because there is obviously greater market demand than was believed initially. In making these decisions, the company will use a variety of measures. Some will be highly quantitative and depend on financial and productivity performance; others will be more qualitative and judgmental in nature. The following discussion examines six of the most common methods of measurement used for control and evaluation purposes.

Common methods of measurement

Return on investment (ROI) A percentage determined by dividing net income before taxes by total assets

Specific methods of measurement will vary depending on the nature of the MNE and the goals it has established. However, in most cases **return on investment (ROI)**, which is measured by dividing net income before taxes by total assets, is a major consideration. There are a number of reasons that ROI is so popular as a control and evaluation measure. These include the fact that ROI (1) is a single comprehensive result that is influenced by everything that happens in the business, (2) is a measure of how well the

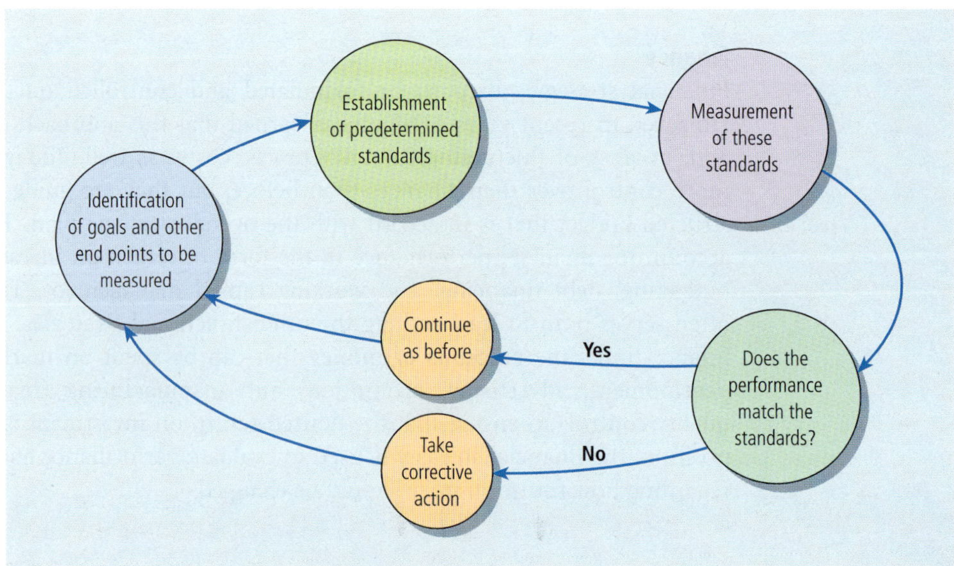

Figure 8.6 **The control and evaluation process**

managers in every part of the world are using the investments at their command, and (3) allows a comparison of results among units in the same country as well as on an inter-country basis. Of course, there are shortcomings in using ROI, such as that (1) if one unit is selling goods to another unit, the ROI of the former is being artificially inflated; (2) the ROI in a growing market will be higher than that in markets which are just getting off the ground or which are maturing, so that a comparison of the ROI performance between units can be misleading; and (3) the ROI is a short-term measure of performance and, if it is relied on too heavily, managers will not develop the necessary long-term time horizons. Despite such shortcomings, however, ROI remains a major measure of performance.

Another measure is sales growth and/or market share. Units will be given sales targets that usually require greater sales this year than last year. If the firm has made an estimate of the total demand, a market share figure will accompany the sales target. The reason for this is two-fold: (1) the MNE wants to increase its sales and (2) the firm wants at least to maintain, if not increase, market share. If the market is judged to be declining, sales targets will be lowered but the MNE will still try to maintain market share.

A third performance area is costs. The MNE will want to achieve increased sales and market share at as low a cost as possible. The firm will also want to maintain close control of production costs. So expenses will be monitored carefully. This is particularly important in declining markets, where the company will want to cut costs as sales decline. For example, if an MNE estimates that it has but three years of product life in the market, it is likely that much of the advertising and promotion expenses will be dropped as the company focuses attention on supplying an ever-decreasing number of customers. This strategy is often successful because the remaining customers are highly loyal and do not need promotional efforts to convince them to buy the product.

New product development is another area of performance measure. This area is extremely important for firms that rely on new offerings. A good example is Nintendo, the Japanese manufacturer of such well-known video games as Mario Brothers: in order to maintain market share and sales growth, the company must continually introduce new product offerings. MNEs in high-tech areas such as electronic goods and computers also fall into this category. In an environment where product improvement or innovation is critical to success, new product development is a key area for control and evaluation.

MNE/host-country relations is another performance area that must be evaluated. Overseas units have to work within the cultural and legal framework of the host country. Many attempt to do this by blending into the community, hiring local managers and employees, adapting their product to the demands of that market, reinvesting part (if not all) of their profits back into the country, and working to improve the economic conditions of the area. As a result, they get on well in the country and there are no problems with the government or other local groups. One thing MNEs know from long experience is that poor host-country relations can seriously endanger profits and may result in a loss of invested capital.

Finally, management performance must be considered. In rating this criterion, the MNE will consider two types of measures: quantitative and qualitative. In the quantitative area, in addition to those discussed above, other common considerations include return on invested capital and cash flow. In the qualitative area, in addition to host country relations, consideration will be given to relations with the home office, the leadership qualities of the unit's managers, how well the unit is building a management team, and how well the managers of the unit have implemented the assigned strategy.

These methods of measurement will be used in arriving at an overall assessment of the unit's performance. Based on the results, the MNE will then set new goals and the international strategic planning process will begin anew.

Active learning check 

Review your answer to Active Learning Case question 4 and make any changes you like. Then compare your answer with the one below.

4. On what basis would a firm like Vodafone evaluate performance? Identify and describe two examples.

There are a number of bases that Vodafone uses in evaluating performance. One is market share. Notice that in evaluating its performance in Japan the company has been keeping track of its success among new subscribers and knows that it has been garnering 60 per cent of this market. Another is overall worldwide market share. In 2001 the company held 15 per cent of the total worldwide mobile phone market. A second way in which Vodafone evaluates performance is in terms of market capitalization. How much is its stock worth? The case data note that after acquiring Airtouch Communications this value stood at $154 billion.

KEY POINTS

1. Strategic planning is the process of determining an organization's basic mission and long-term objectives and then implementing a plan of action for attaining these goals. In carrying out their strategic plan, most MNEs have a specific predisposition. There are four predispositions: ethnocentric, polycentric, regiocentric, and geocentric, and each was described in the chapter.
2. The international strategic planning process involves three major steps: strategy formulation, strategy implementation, and the control and evaluation of the process. Strategy formulation entails the evaluation of the enterprise's environment and the identification of long-range and short-range objectives. The analysis of the external environment typically involves information gathering and information assessment. In this process consideration is given to the five forces that determine industry competitiveness: buyers, suppliers, new entrants to the industry, the availability of substitute goods and services, and rivalry among the competitors. The analysis of the internal environment involves consideration of the firm's physical resources and personnel competencies and the way in which a value chain analysis can be used to bring these resources together in the most synergistic and profitable manner.
3. Strategy implementation is the process of attaining predetermined goals by properly executing the formulated strategy. Three of the most important areas of consideration are location, ownership decisions, and functional area implementation.
4. The control and evaluation process involves an examination of the MNE's performance for the purpose of determining how well the organization has done and for deciding what action now needs to be taken. Some of the most common measures include return on investment, sales growth, market share, costs, new product development, host-country relations, and overall management performance.

KEY TERMS

- strategic planning
- competitive intelligence
- ethnocentric predisposition
- polycentric predisposition
- regiocentric predisposition
- geocentric predisposition
- strategy formulation
- strategic business units (SBUs)
- vertical integration
- virtual integration
- value chain
- cost strategy
- differentiation strategy
- focus strategy
- competitive scope
- strategy implementation
- international joint venture
- strategic alliance or partnership
- return on investment (ROI)

REVIEW AND DISCUSSION QUESTIONS

1. Define the term "strategic planning".
2. In what way can the following basic predispositions affect strategic planning by an MNE: ethnocentric, polycentric, regiocentric, geocentric?
3. How will an MNE carry out an external environmental assessment? Identify and describe the two major steps that are involved in this process.
4. Of what practical value is an understanding of the five forces model presented in Figure 8.1? How would an MNE use this information in the strategic planning process?
5. In conducting an internal environmental assessment, why would an MNE want to identify its physical resources and personnel competencies?
6. What is a value chain? How can this chain be used in an internal environmental assessment?
7. What are the three generic strategies? When would an MNE use each? Use examples to support your answer.
8. What are some typical MNE goals? Identify and briefly describe four major types.
9. One of the most important considerations when implementing a strategy is that of location. What does this statement mean?
10. When are MNEs likely to use an international joint venture? When would they opt for a strategic partnership? Defend your answer.
11. Functional strategies are used to coordinate operations and to ensure that the plan is carried out properly. What are some of the most common types of functional strategies? Identify and describe three.
12. How do MNEs control and evaluate their operations? Describe the basic process. Then discuss some of the common methods of measurement.

REAL CASE

Mountain Equipment Coop

Many people have never heard of the Mountain Equipment Coop (MEC), but it is one of the most successful small businesses in the world. The company currently holds 65 per cent of the Canadian market for outdoor equipment and it far outdistances all other competitive MNEs and retail brands in the country. In fact, MEC is so efficient that its products are lower priced than those of any competitor worldwide.

The Mountain Equipment Coop was founded in 1969 when a group of outdoor enthusiasts decided to get together and purchase expensive outdoor equipment. In 1971 the organization was officially registered as a coop and began operating under a member-elected board of directors that assumed responsibility for setting overall policy and for overseeing management of all operations. Today the MEC has 1.3 million members in Canada, six stores spread across the country, an international mail-order clientele, and a worldwide network of suppliers. And for a one-time $5 dollar fee, members are able to enjoy a wide variety of benefits from an organization that focuses heavily on four primary objectives: keep costs down, offer affordable goods, provide high quality merchandise, and maintain high ethical standards.

Regarding the first of these, the MEC takes a number of steps to control costs and offer affordable products. One is to use the clout of its large membership as a basis for extracting the best possible prices from suppliers, thus being able to offer low cost products. Another is to keep the number of staff to a minimum. Some of the ways it does this is through the use of self-service in all stores and the promotion of its international mail-order business, which can be handled by a small number of personnel. In addition, the coop minimizes overall marketing expenses by relying heavily on customer word-of-mouth and the mail-order network to help promote its products.

The coop also places a great deal of importance on the quality of goods. Its buyers and designers look not only for a low price from suppliers, but also for products that provide both functionality and durability. In addition, the coop offers a lifetime guarantee on most of its products, regardless of whether it manufactured them, had them provided by an outsourcer, or purchased them from a large brand name company.

Coop members are also assured that the company adheres to the highest ethical practices. The organization is an innovator in a number of areas ranging from human rights to the environment. Its stores are designed with the utmost attention to the environment, using as much natural light as possible, high efficiency HVAC (heating, ventilation, and air conditioning), low consumption water fixtures, and recyclable materials. As an example, its Ottawa store uses only half the energy of a conventional building. In addition, the company gives 0.4 per cent of gross sales to environmental and conservation groups. At the same time the coop's retail employees are among the best paid in the country and the firm's buyers and inspectors are charged with ensuring that all factory workers in foreign countries receive a reasonable living wage and work under safe conditions.

Some suppliers, such as Sierra Designs, Salomon, Arc Tyrex, North Face, and Patagonia see the coop as a threat and have refused to sell to it. In many cases, however, this strategy has proven to be counterproductive because it has resulted in MEC designing and manufacturing these products and then successfully competing with the traditional brands that were unwilling to sell to it. In addition, the coop's increased involvement in manufacturing has enabled it to monitor the operations of its suppliers more closely.

Over the past couple of decades, the company's strategy has been more emergent than calculated. Yet it has proven to be a successful business venture that has brought together a large group of dedicated environmentalists and other customers who need products for outdoor activities. In the process, the coop has created a "style" and "brand" presence which appeals to outdoor enthusiasts. In fact, the MEC's outdoor gear has become so popular that even urbanites, highly unlikely to go trekking or camping in the outdoors, are now becoming members. As a result, the company's annual revenues are currently in the range of $150 million and the company is continuing to expand operations across Canada with its seventh store scheduled to be opened in Montreal in the near future.

Websites: **www.mec.ca**; **www.sierra-designs.com**; **www.salomonsports.com**; **www.thenorthface.com** and **www.patagonia.com**.

Sources: **www.mec.ca/**; "Mountain Equipment Co-Op Live With Socially Responsible Retail," *PR Newswire*, May 22, 2001; "One of the Greenest Commercial Buildings in the World," *Sustainable Sport Sourceline*, July 2000.

1. **How does the Mountain Equipment Coop use value chain analysis to increase both its membership and its revenues?**
2. **What is the coop's generic strategy? Describe it.**
3. **How does the company measure its performance? What are two criteria it uses to evaluate how well it is doing?**

REAL CASE

Benetton in the fast lane

Famous for its shocking advertisements Benetton started in 1955 as a small business. Lucianno Benetton and his family started by selling colored sweaters door to door in Treviso, Italy. Over time a regional network of family, friends, and agents set up a closely monitored set of distinctive retail outlets. Over a 15-year period Benetton built up 300 affiliated but independently owned outlets in Italy and a factory with new methods to dye and condition wool. Benetton was not directly involved in the retail outlets, who received high quality products at low costs. Part of the manufacturing savings are realized by outsourcing to neighbouring subcontractors.

Today Benetton has kept this loose network of independent production subcontractors and distribution agents but has now built up to a global network of over 7,000 retail stores. Of these, Benetton owns only about 50 flagship stores and the great majority are operated by independent entrepreneurs. Over 80 per cent of production still takes place in Italy and the company is still 72 per cent owned by the Benetton family.

Benetton is one of those successful global companies that was partly successful because its production and design concept was built on a strong home base. It then expanded the marketing end of its business through closely monitored (but not owned) independent stores. These were able to use the Benetton brand name and distinctive colours and were supported by clever international advertising.

Benetton does not advertise its clothes directly. Rather its advertisements are for a "lifestyle". The "United Colors of Benetton" ads are designed for a homogeneous global consumer interested in fast cars and a fast lifestyle. Benetton goes in for cutting-edge advertising that grabs public attention. This creates an image of new-age awareness, as Benetton advertising has featured Formula 1 cars, AIDS, high art, and "attitude".

How well this plays out globally is uncertain. For example, in 1988 Benetton had 700 retail stores in the US but by 1995 it only had 150. Is this because Benetton has too European an image to succeed in middle America? How can an Italian family firm understand the American lifestyle from its European bases?

Website: **www.benetton.com**.

Sources: Adapted from: *Benetton SpA: Industrial Fashion (A)*, Harvard Business School Case No. 9-685-614; *Benetton (B)*, Harvard Business School Case No. 9-685-020; INSEAD-CEDEP Case No. 01/97-4520, 1996; David Stillit, "Benetton: Italy's Smart Operator," *Corporate Finance*, June 1993; "Benetton's Network," *Ivey Business Quarterly*, 1997.

1. **Is Benetton a multinational enterprise?**
2. **What are the country-specific factors that have helped Benetton be a success?**
3. **What are Benetton's firm-specific advantages?**

ENDNOTES

1 Tim Burt, "GM Outlines Plans to Cut European Capacity," *Financial Times*, September 27, 2001, p. 19.

2 Andrew Park and Peter Burrows, "Dell, the Conqueror," *Business Week*, September 24, 2001, pp. 92–102.

3 Matt Murray, "Merger Machine: Can GE Keep Growing Through Deals?" *Wall Street Journal*, July 31, 2000, pp. C 1, 2.

4 Also see Roland Calori, Leif Melin, Tugrul Atamer and Peter Gustavsson, "Innovative International Strategies," *Journal of World Business*, vol. 35, no. 4 (Winter 2000), pp. 333–354.

5 M. A. Hitt, "The Meaning of Organizational Effectiveness: Multiple Domains and Constituencies," *Management International Review*, vol. 28, no. 2 (Second Quarter 1988), p. 28.

6 David Lei, John W. Slocum, Jr and Robert W. Slater, "Global Strategy and Reward Systems: The Key Roles of Management Development and Corporate Culture," *Organizational Dynamics*, August 1990, p. 29.

7 See David Norburn, Sue Birley, Mark Dunn and Adrian Payne, "A Four Nation Study of the Relationship Between Marketing Effectiveness, Corporate Culture, Corporate Values, and Market Orientation," *Journal of International Business Studies*, vol. 21, no. 3 (Fall 1990), pp. 451–468.

8 For a good example see Keith Bradsher, "Effective Today, Chrysler and Daimler-Benz Are One," *New York Times*,

November 12, 1998, p. C 4 and Tim Burt, "Daimler Chief to Speak on Strategy," *FT.com*, March 4, 2002.

9 For some specific applications of these ideas, see Michael M. Robert, "Managing Your Competitor's Strategy," *Journal of Business Strategy*, March/April 1990, pp. 24–28.

10 M. Carl Drott, "Personal Knowledge, Corporate Information: The Challenges for Competitive Intelligence," *Business Horizons*, March–April 2001, pp. 31–37.

11 Sometimes, of course, competitive intelligence degenerates into corporate spying, as seen in Andrew Edgecliffe-Johnson, "P&G Admits Spying on Unilever," *Financial Times*, August 31, 2001, p. 17.

12 J. E. Preble, P. A. Rau and A. Reichel, "The Environmental Scanning Practices of US Multinationals in the Late 1980s," *Management International Review*, vol. 28, no. 4 (Fourth Quarter 1988), p. 10.

13 For more on this, see R. C. Hoffman, "The General Management of Foreign Subsidiaries in the USA: An Exploratory Study," *Management International Review*, vol. 28, no. 2 (Second Quarter 1988), pp. 41–55.

14 For more on this, see Michael Porter, *The Competitive Advantage of Nations* (New York: Free Press, 1990), Chapter 2.

15 Andrew Pollack, "Nissan Plans to Buy More American Parts," *New York Times*, March 26, 1994, pp. 17, 26.

16 See, for example, Dean Takahashi, "How the Competition Got Ahead of Intel in Making Cheap Chips," *Wall Street Journal*, February 12, 1998, pp. A 1, 11.

17 "A Tricky Business," *Economist*, June 30, 2001, pp. 55–56.

18 Arnoldo C. Hax and Nicolas S. Majluf, *The Strategy Concept and Process: A Pragmatic Approach* (Englewood Cliffs NJ: Prentice-Hall, 1991), p. 416.

19 Also, see Julie Pitta, "Score One for Vertical Integration," *Forbes*, January 18, 1993, pp. 88–90.

20 For an excellent discussion of this topic, see Hax and Majluf (1991) n. 18 above, Chapter 12.

21 C. K. Prahalad and Kenneth Lieberthal, "The End of Corporate Imperialism," *Harvard Business Review*, July/August 1998, pp. 69–79.

22 For the application of these ideas to the European market, see Susan P. Douglas and Dong Kee Rhee, "Examining Generic Competitive Strategy Types in US and European Markets," *Journal of International Business Studies*, vol. 20, no. 3 (Fall 1989), pp. 437–463.

23 Hax and Majluf (1991), n. 18 above, p. 83.

24 Uta Harnischfeger, "Audi Drives Out VW's Gloom, *FT.com*, March 1, 2002.

25 "The Art of Overtaking," *Economist*, September 8, 2001, p. 68.

26 For another good example, see Seth Lubove, "Make a Better Mousetrap," *Forbes*, February 1, 1993, pp. 56–57.

27 Leslie Kaufman, "Avon's New Face," *Newsweek*, November 16, 1998, pp. 59–60.

28 Also, see W. Chan Kim and Peter Hwang, "Global Strategy and Multinationals' Entry Mode Choice," *Journal of International Business Studies*, vol. 23, no. 1 (Summer 1992), pp. 29–53.

29 Richard M. Hodgetts and Fred Luthans, *International Management*, 4th edn (Burr Ridge IL: McGraw/Irwin, 2000), p. 260.

30 Robert B. Reich, "Who Is Us?" *Harvard Business Review*, January/February 1990, p. 59.

31 Audrey Choi, "BMW's Chairman Plans Visit to Honda to Discuss Future of Jointly Held Rover," *Wall Street Journal*, February 18, 1994, p. A 7.

32 Hemant Merchant, "Configurations of International Joint Ventures," *Management International Review*, vol. 40, no. 2 (Second Quarter 2000), pp. 107–140.

33 Hong Liu and Kelvin Pak, "How Important is Marketing in China Today to Sino-foreign Joint Ventures," *European Management Journal*, October 1999, pp. 546–554.

34 Gautam Naik, "AT&T, BT Form World-Wide Alliance," *Wall Street Journal*, July 27, 1998, p. A 3.

35 John Tagliabue, "Toyota and Peugeot in Pact to Produce Car for Europe," *New York Times*, June 30, 2001, p. B 2.

36 Stefan H. Robock and Kenneth Simmonds, *International Business and Multinational Enterprises*, 4th edn (Homewood IL: Irwin, 1989), p. 216.

37 See Sing Keow Hoon-Halbauer, "Managing Relationships Within Sino-Foreign Joint Ventures," *Journal of World Business*, vol. 34, no. 4 (Winter 1999), pp. 344–370.

38 Peter Lorange, Johan Roos and Peggy Simcic Bronn, "Building Successful Strategic Alliances," *Long Range Planning*, December 1992, pp. 10–17.

39 See Masaaki Kotabe, Hildy Teegen, Preet S. Aulakh, Maria Cecilia Coutinho de Arruda, Roberto J. Santillan-Salgado and Walter Greene, "Strategic Alliances in Emerging Latin America: A View from Brazilian, Chilean, and Mexican Companies," *Journal of World Business*, vol. 35, no. 2 (Summer 2000), pp. 114–132.

40 Mitchell Koza and Arie Lewin, "Managing Partnerships and Strategic Alliances: Raising the Odds of Success," *European Management Journal*, August 2000, pp. 146–151.

41 Miki Tanikawa, "Electronics Giants Join Forces in Japan," *Wall Street Journal*, May 24, 2001, p. W 1.

42 Robert A. Guth, "IBM Announces Deal with Japan's NTT," *Wall Street Journal*, November 1, 2000, p. 23.

43 See, for example, Caron H. St. John, Scott T. Young and Janis L. Miller, "Coordinating Manufacturing and Marketing in International Firms," *Journal of World Business*, vol. 34, no. 2 (Summer 1999), pp. 109–127.

44 Matt Marshall, "In Brazil, Coke Sells Foam as Well as Fizz," *Wall Street Journal*, July 28, 1997, p. A 12.

45 Peter Marsh, "Pressing Ahead with Plastic," *FT.com*, March 4, 2002.

46 Jeffrey E. Garten, "Opening the Doors for Business In China," *Harvard Business Review*, May–June 1998, pp. 167–175.

47 Also see John Child and Yanni Yan, "Investment and Control in International Joint Ventures: The Case of China," *Journal of World Business*, vol. 34, no. 1 (Spring 1999), pp. 3–15.

ADDITIONAL BIBLIOGRAPHY

Barkeman, Harry G., Shenkar, Oded, Vermeulen, Freek and Bell, John H. J. "Working Abroad, Working with Others: How Firms Learn to Operate International Joint Ventures," *Academy of Management Journal*, vol. 40, no. 2 (April 1997).

Camuffo, Arnaldo. "Back to the Future: Benetton Transforms its Global Network," *Sloan Management Review*, vol. 43, no. 1 (Fall 2001).

Capon, Noel, Christodoulou, Chris, Farley, John U. and Hulbert, James M. "A Comparison of the Strategy and Structure of United States and Australian Corporations," *Journal of International Business Studies*, vol. 18, no. 1 (Spring 1987).

Cravens, David W., Downey, H. Kirk, and Lauritano, Paul. "Global Competition in the Commercial Aircraft Industry: Positioning for Advantage by the Triad Nations," *Columbia Journal of World Business*, vol. 26, no. 4 (Winter 1992).

Dacin, M. Tina, Hitt, Michael A. and Levitas, Edward. "Selecting Partners for Successful International Alliances: Examination of US and Korean Firms," *Journal of World Business*, vol. 32, no. 1 (Spring 1997).

Davis, Peter S., Desai, Ashay B. and Francis, John D. "Mode of International Entry: An Isomorphism Perspective," *Journal of International Business Studies*, vol. 31, no. 2 (Summer 2000).

Deschamps, Jean-Philippe and Nayak, P. Ranganath. "Competing Through Products: Lessons from the Winners," *Columbia Journal of World Business*, vol. 27, no. 2 (Summer 1992).

Domke-Damonte, Darla. "Interactive Effects of International Strategy and Throughput Technology on Entry Mode for Service Firms," *Management International Review*, vol. 40, no. 1 (First Quarter 2000).

Douglas, Susan P. and Craig, C. Samuel. "Evolution of Global Marketing Strategy: Scale, Scope and Synergy," *Columbia Journal of World Business*, vol. 24, no. 3 (Fall 1989).

Douglas, Susan P. and Rhee, Dong Kee. "Examining Generic Competitive Strategy Types in US and European Markets," *Journal of International Business Studies*, vol. 20, no. 3 (Fall 1989).

Egelhoff, William G. "Great Strategy or Great Strategy Implementation – Two Ways of Competing in Global Markets," *Sloan Management Review*, vol. 34, no. 2 (Winter 1993).

Govindarajan, Vijay and Gupta, Anil K. *The Quest for Global Dominance* (San Francisco CA: Josey-Bass/Wiley, 2001).

Hamel, Gary and Prahalad, C. K. "Do You Really Have a Global Strategy?," *Harvard Business Review*, vol. 65, no. 4 (July/August 1985).

Hitt, Michael A., Hoskisson, Robert E. and Kim, Hicheon. "International Diversification: Effects on Innovation and Firm Performance in Product-Diversified Firms," *Academy of Management Journal*, vol. 40, no. 4 (August 1997).

Hoffmann, Werner H. and Wulf, Schaper-Rinkel. "Acquire or Ally? A Strategy Framework for Deciding Between Acquisition and Cooperation," *Management International Review*, vol. 41, no. 2 (Second Quarter 2001).

Huo, Y. Paul and McKinley, William. "Nation as a Context for Strategy: The Effects of National Characteristics on Business-Level Strategies," *Management International Review*, vol. 32, no. 2 (Second Quarter 1992).

Jones, Robert E., Jacobs, Lester W. and van Spijker, Willem. "Strategic Decision Processes in International Firms," *Management International Review*, vol. 32, no. 3 (Third Quarter 1992).

Kanter, Rosabeth Moss. "Collaborative Advantage: The Art of Alliances," *Harvard Business Review* (July–August 1994).

Kim, W. Chan and Mauborgne, Renne A. "Making Global Strategies Work," *Sloan Management Review*, vol. 34, no. 3 (Spring 1993).

Kim, W. Chan and Mauborgne, Renne A. "Effectively Conceiving and Executing Multinationals' World-wide Strategies," *Journal of International Business Studies*, vol. 24, no. 3 (Third Quarter 1993).

Kotabe, Masaaki and Omura, Glenn S. "Sourcing Strategies of European and Japanese Multinationals: A Comparison," *Journal of International Business Studies*, vol. 20, no. 1 (Spring 1989).

Merchant, Hemant, "Configurations of International Joint Ventures," *Management International Review*, Vol. 40, no. 2 (Second Quarter 2000).

Merchant, Hemant, "Cooperative Strategy: Economic, Business, and Organizational Issues," *Academy of Management Review*, vol. 26, no. 2 (April 2001).

Mintzberg, Henry. "The Fall and Rise of Strategic Planning," *Harvard Business Review*, vol. 72, no. 1 (January/February 1994).

Normann, Richard and Ramirez, Rafael. "From Value Chain to Value Constellation: Designing Interactive Strategy," *Harvard Business Review*, vol. 71, no. 4 (July/August 1993).

Parkhe, Arvind. "Understanding Trust in International Alliances," *Journal of World Business*, vol. 33, no. 3 (Fall 1998).

Porter, Michael E. "The Competitive Advantage of Nations," *Harvard Business Review*, vol. 68, no. 2 (March/April 1990).

Rondinelli, Dennis. "The Struggle for Strategic Alignment in Multinational Corporations: Managing Readjustment During Global Expansion," *European Management Journal*, vol. 19, no. 4 (August 2001).

Roth, Kendall, Schweiger, David M. and Morrison, Allen J. "Global Strategy Implementation at the Business Unit Level: Operational Capabilities and Administrative Mechanisms," *Journal of International Business Studies*, vol. 24, no. 2 (Second Quarter 1993).

Rugman, Alan M. "Multinationals and Global Competitive Strategy," *International Studies of Management and Organization*, vol. 15, no. 2 (Summer 1985).

Sugiura, Hideo. "How Honda Localizes Its Global Strategy," *Sloan Management Review*, vol. 32, no. 1 (Fall 1990).

Tallman, Stephen and Li, Jiatao. "Effects of International Diversity and Product Diversity on the Performance of Multinational Firms," *Academy of Management Journal*, vol. 39, no. 1 (February 1996).

Tallman, Stephe B. and Yip, George S. "Strategy and the Multinational Enterprise," in Alan M. Rugman and Thomas Brewer (eds.), *The Oxford Handbook of International Business* (Oxford: Oxford University Press, 2001).

Thakur, Manab and Das, T. K. "Managing the Growth-Share Matrix: A Four-Nation Study in Two Industries," *Management International Review*, vol. 31, no. 2 (Second Quarter 1991).

Thomas, Howard, Pollock, Timothy and Gorman, Philip. "Global Strategic Analyses: Frameworks and Approaches," *Academy of Management Executive*, vol. 13, no. 1 (February 1999).

Chapter 9

Organizing Strategy

CONTENTS

OBJECTIVES OF THE CHAPTER

The primary purpose of an organizing strategy is to help an enterprise implement its strategic plan. There are a number of basic organization structures from which to choose, although most MNEs tailor-make their design and sometimes use a combination of different structures. Another major area of organizing strategy is the organizational processes of decision making, communicating, and controlling. These processes are fundamental to the efficient operation of the structure, and management will need to decide how they should be carried out. This chapter examines the key elements of organizing strategy.

The specific objectives of this chapter are to:

1. *Examine* organization structures used by enterprises that are just beginning their international expansion.
2. *Describe* the international division and global structures that are used as firms increase their international presence.
3. *Analyze* the key structural variables that influence international organization designs.
4. *Review* the role of the organizational processes in ensuring that the structure is both effective and efficient.

ACTIVE LEARNING CASE

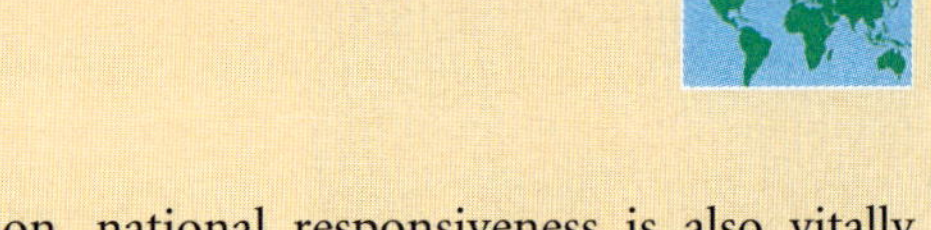

Nortel Networks

Northern Telecom, now called Nortel Networks, transformed itself from a Canadian-based multinational enterprise in the late 1970s to a North American-based MNE by 1987 and by 2000 it had become a transnational corporation. In the process, the company's revenues have increased sharply. Between 1985 and 2000, annual revenue rose from $4.2 billion to $30.3 billion and total worldwide employment increased from 46,500 to 85,000. During this same time period, Nortel began an international expansion. As a result, the company expanded its operations to 150 countries; and, while 90 per cent of its revenues were generated in North America in 1985, by 2000 over 34 per cent of all sales came from outside North America.

Nortel's primary competitive advantage stems from its research and development (R&D) base which allows it to dominate such areas as optical long haul networks, and wireless and metro networks. And in order to maintain its technological advantage, Nortel spends over 13 per cent of annual sales on R&D ($4 billion in 2000). By 2000 the company had 46 worldwide research facilities: 26 in North America, 15 in Europe and the Middle East, four in the Asia-Pacific region, and one in Latin America. In addition, 32 per cent of all employees were involved in R&D work. The company has also relied heavily on joint ventures and on mergers and acquisitions (M&As) to help maintain its strong R&D position.

In the non-triad markets of China, India, and Australia, for example, Nortel's strategy has been to enter joint ventures with domestic partners thus enabling it to use M&As to further its R&D position. For example, in 2000 alone, Nortel acquired 10 companies that allowed it to expand its R&D prowess in high-speed video, data delivery, optical systems, and DSL platforms for Internet access. The company also uses licensing to round out its portfolio and to ensure that it has the best technology in the industry.

While Nortel competes globally in the telecommunications sector, it is careful about the way it operates. In particular, the company caters carefully to both the local culture and to government regulation. Nortel realizes that, despite the fact that there is a growing move in the industry toward global integration, national responsiveness is also vitally important. In fact, far from being one universal market, the telecommunications industry actually consists of a set of regionally separated national markets. And even with the WTO's International Technology Agreement of 1995, there is no single world market for telecommunications. So in order to ensure that its operations are flexible enough to respond to differences in national regulations and consumer tastes, Nortel has adopted a policy of national responsiveness. Strategic decisions in local markets are implemented only after taking into account both technology standards and regulatory factors. As a result of this national responsiveness strategy, Nortel has found that it can be highly responsive to both the customer and to local regulations. In the process, the company has become a transnational corporation. This is clearly seen by three of the steps it has taken.

First, Nortel has decentralized decision making in order to respond effectively to the regional nature of the market. One way it has done this is by giving a large degree of autonomy to both its product-sector and its country managers.

Second, Nortel now employs an internal managerial resource strategy that decentralizes key decision making to some 200 top executives in more than a dozen markets around the world. In 1987, the company was run by 5 to 10 people out of the head office in Mississauga, Ontario. Today, these 200 top managers make the key decisions and have a large degree of autonomy, a characteristic that is typical of a transnational.

Third, the company's decentralized top management structure is held together by heavy use of the Internet for worldwide office communication. Nortel does this through its own specially created internal electronic mail, voice, and data network which is used to a great extent by worldwide managers. As a result, while the firm is highly decentralized, it is able to pull everything together through the use of an effective worldwide communication system.

One of the key managerial challenges for Nortel is that of organizing effective "networks" with its strategic partners across the segmented regional markets that characterize the telecommunications sector. The firm's objective is to be the global resource for digital network solutions and services. By building and integrating both wireline and wireless digital networks on a global basis, and through its recent purchase of Bay Networks, the company has moved toward achieving this objective.

Even the best managed companies can be hit by sectoral downturns. In the year starting in July 2000, Nortel lost over 80 per cent of its stock market value. Its share price fell from over $80 to under $10 a share. The Templeton Global Perfomance Index (TGPI), which ranks firms according to the profitability of their foreign operations, dropped Nortel's ranking from 1st in 1999 to the bottom 10 for the year 2000. The main reason for this was the dot.com bust. Between 1998 and 2000, acquisitions of several US companies for $12.5 billion had increased Nortel's "goodwill" from $423 million to $3,944 million. Several of these acquisitions were financed through exchanges of shares. These shares fell considerably when the dot.com industry bust. In addition, the telecommunications market saw a flood of new entrants in 2000. Nortel's policy was to offer financing to these businesses, allowing them access to Internet infrastructure. The dot.com bust led many upstarts out of business, leaving Nortel unable to reclaim its debts. This has resulted in the company having to lay off over half of its worldwide workforce. However, those who are familiar with the company believe that Nortel will be back thanks to its strong R&D and carefully crafted international organizational arrangement.

Websites: **www.nortelnetworks.com** and **www.nortelnetworks.co.jp**.

Source: Annual Reports of Northern Telecom; Alan Rugman, *The End of Globalization* (London: Random House, 2001); "Twelve Companies Bid for China UNICOM CDMA Deals," *InfoWorld*, April 16, 2001; Michael V. Gestrin, Rory F. Knight and Alan M. Rugman, *The Templeton Global Performance Index 2001* (Templeton: University of Oxford, 2001) at **www.templeton.ox.ac.uk**.

1. **What type of organizational structure would be best for Northern Telecom in pulling together its worldwide operations?**
2. **Why does the company rely so heavily on decentralized decision making?**
3. **In controlling its operations, what are three areas that are paramount for the firm?**

INTRODUCTION

Once an organization decides to go international, it must begin to implement the decision.[1] Some companies do so by simply shipping their goods to a foreign market and having a third party handle sales activities. If the firm's international market continues to grow, however, the enterprise will need to review this strategy and decide whether to play a more active role in the distribution and sale of its products. As this happens, the company's organizing strategy will change.[2]

Major MNEs such as IBM, General Motors,[3] Mercedes, and Mitsubishi have sophisticated global structures that form the basis of their organizing strategies. Sometimes these firms will also have subsidiaries or affiliates that are integrated into the overall structure. For example, Mitsubishi has 28 core groups that are bound together by cross-ownership and other financial ties, interlocking directorates, long-term business relationships, and social and historical ties. Among these are Mitsubishi Bank, Mitsubishi Heavy Industries, Asahi Glass, Tokyo Marine and Fire Insurance, Nikon Corporation, and Kirin Brewery.[4] The Mitsubishi group obviously needs a carefully designed global structure that allows it to integrate and coordinate the activities of these many businesses. Sometimes this undertaking involves more time and effort than the formulation of the strategic plan.

ORGANIZATIONAL STRUCTURES

Multinational enterprises cannot implement their strategies without an effective structure.[5] The strategy sets forth the plan of action, but the structure is critical in ensuring that the desired goals are met efficiently. There are a number of choices available to an MNE when deciding on an organizational arrangement, and a number of factors will influence this choice. For example, firms that are just getting into the international arena are likely to choose a structure that differs from that of firms with seasoned overseas operations. Conversely, companies that use their structures as worldwide sales organizations will have a different arrangement from those that locally manufacture and sell goods in various international markets. International structures will change in compliance with the strategic plan and, if a structure is proving to be unwieldy or inefficient, it will be scrapped in favor of one that addresses these problems.[6] The following discussion examines some of the most common organizational arrangements used by MNEs.

Early organizational structures

When a company first begins international operations, it is typical for these activities to be extensions of domestic operations. The firm's primary focus continues to be the local market, and international involvement is of secondary importance. International transactions are conducted on a case-by-case basis, and there is no attempt to consolidate these operations into a separate department. Under this arrangement international sales are viewed as supplements to the income earned from home country operations.

As international operations increase, however, the MNE will take steps to address this growth structurally. One way is by having the marketing department handle international sales. All overseas operations are coordinated through this department; and if sales warrant it, some of the salespeople will handle international transactions exclusively. In this way the company develops marketing specialists who learn the specific needs and marketing techniques to employ in overseas selling.

An alternative arrangement is to create an export department. This department may report directly to the chief executive officer (CEO) (Figure 9.1, line (*a*)) or be a subdepartment within the marketing area (Figure 9.1, line (*b*)). If the department operates independently of the marketing department (option (*a*)), it is either staffed by in-house marketing people whose primary focus is on the international market or it is operated by an outside export management company that is hired for the purpose of providing

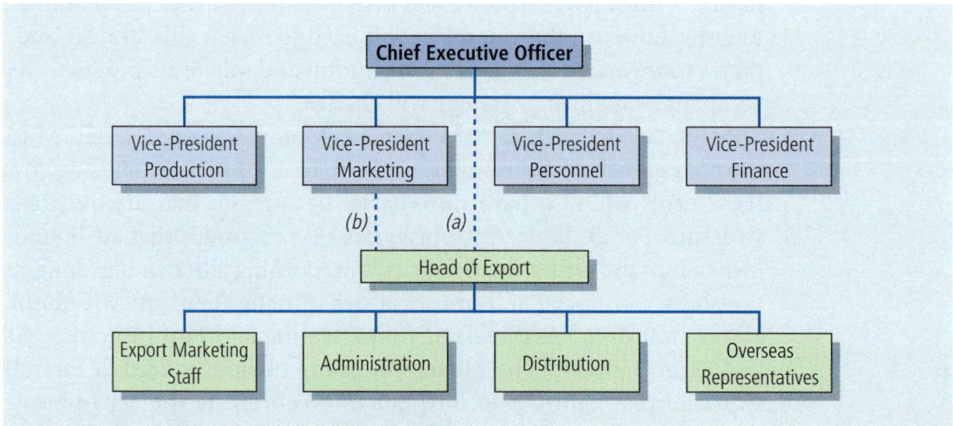

Figure 9.1 **An export department structure**

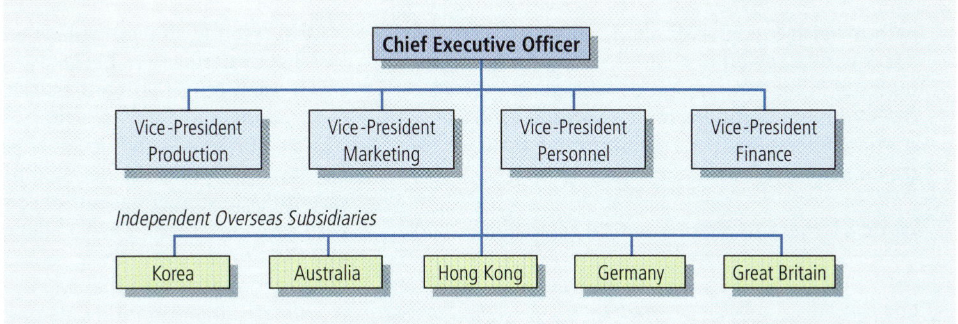

Figure 9.2 **Use of subsidiaries during the early stages of internationalization**

the company with an international arm. Whichever approach is taken, it is important to realize that MNEs planning to increase their international presence must ensure that the export department is a full-fledged marketing department and not just a sales organization.

Another possible arrangement is the use of overseas subsidiaries (see Figure 9.2). This is often a result of individual ventures in various geographic locales in which the head of the venture is given a great deal of autonomy and reports directly to the CEO. As long as the subsidiary shows sufficient profit, it is allowed to operate free from home office interference.

As MNEs become more involved in foreign markets, the export department structure or subsidiary arrangement is generally discarded or supplemented because it cannot meet the changing needs of the organization. As a result, the company will now look into joint ventures[7] and foreign direct investment. As this happens the firm is likely to opt for an international division structure. To examine one company's international organization structure, see the box "International Business Strategy in Action: Rhône-Poulenc organizes for international expansion."

INTERNATIONAL BUSINESS STRATEGY *IN ACTION*

Rhône-Poulenc organizes for international expansion

Rhône-Poulenc is a French-based chemical firm that, through mergers and acquisitions, has managed to become one of the major competitors in its industry. Back in the mid-1980s the company was the twelfth largest chemical firm in the world with 80 per cent of sales being generated in Europe. In this environment, it competed with a large number of firms including US-based giants DuPont and Dow Chemical and leading European chemical companies including Hoechst, BASF, Ciba-Geigy, and ICI.

During this period, the chemical industry was being increasingly structured on a "triad" basis. As a result, Rhône-Poulenc decided to consolidate its successful European base and move into the American market. In the late 1980s the firm made 18 acquisitions in the US including Union Carbide Agrochemical Products and Stauffer Basic Chemicals. These acquisitions made the company into the seventh largest chemical manufacturer in the world, and it was now generating over 20 per cent of its total sales in the American market.

Managing its US operations was not easy. The takeover of Union Carbide worked pretty well because the latter's pesticide products were complementary to those of Rhône-Poulenc's herbicides and fungicides and the corporate cultures of the two companies were similar. However, the Stauffer acquisition proved to be more difficult because there were overlapping product lines and the US managers at Stauffer had little international experience.

In order to improve the efficiency of its diverse US operations, Rhône-Poulenc adapted a highly decentralized organizational structure, consolidating its American business operations into a US country group with headquarters at Princeton, New Jersey. The firm also established English as the official language of the company, even though its parent company was French. And as an intermediate step on the path towards true globalization, the firm's US regional headquarters served to create a strong American presence in the face of vigorous competition from rivals with both efficient production and effective staffing. Rhône-Poulenc's plan for the future was to create a "transnational" structure.

World's largest 10 pharmaceutical companies, 2000

Company	*Country*	*Revenues US $ million*
Merck	Germany	40,363
Pfizer	United States	29,574
Johnson & Johnson	United States	29,139
GlaxoSmithKline	United Kingdom	27,414
Bristol-Myers Squibb	United States	21,331
Novartis	Switzerland	21,207
Aventis	France	20,613
Pharmacia	United States	18,150
AstraZeneca	United Kingdom	18,103
Roche Group	Switzerland	16,982
American Home Products	United States	13,810

Source: Adapted from Fortune, *The Fortune Global 500*, 2001.

Most recently, Rhône-Poulenc has merged with Hoechst of Germany to become Aventis. The merger was a result of increasing pressures within the industry to consolidate in order to achieve further economies of scale in research and development, marketing, and distribution. Today, the new company, Aventis, is the seventh largest pharmaceutical company in the world with revenues totaling $20.6 billion (see the table left) and the firm is now in the process of deciding the organization structure that will best help it coordinate all of its worldwide operations.

Websites: ***www.aventis.com***; ***www.dupont.com***; ***www.dow.com***; ***www.hoechst.com***; ***www.basf.com***; ***www.ciba.com***; ***www.novartis.com*** and ***www.ici.com***.

Sources: Rhône-Poulenc (1996) *Annual Report 1995: Rhône-Poulenc*, Courbevoie Cedex, France; Rhône-Poulenc (1997) *Annual Report 1996*: Rhône-Poulenc (1998) *Annual Report 1997: Rhône-Poulenc*, Courbevoie Cedex, France; H. Banks, "The Road from Serfdom," *Forbes*, October 21, 1996, p. 156; D. Hunter, "Reshaping Rhône-Poulenc," *Chemical Week*, vol. 156, no. 23 (1995), p. 30; D. Owen and D. Green, "Rhône-Poulenc to Focus on Pharmaceuticals Business," *Internet: FT McCarthy*, June 27, 1997, p. 1; Stephen Baker, Inka Resch, Kate Carlisle and Katharine A. Schmidt, "The Great English Divide," *Business Week*, August 13, 2001.

The international division

International division structure
An organizational arrangement in which all international operations are centralized in one division

The **international division structure** centralizes all the international operations (see Figure 9.3). This arrangement provides a number of advantages. One is that it reduces the CEO's burden of direct operation of overseas subsidiaries and domestic operations.[8] A second benefit of this structure is that it raises the status of overseas operations to that of the domestic divisions. All information, authority, and decision making related to foreign efforts is channeled to this division, so there is one central clearing point for international activities. This structure also helps the MNE to develop a cadre of internationally experienced managers.

But the international division structure also has some significant drawbacks. One is that separating operations into two categories, domestic and international, can create rivalries between the two. A second shortcoming is that this arrangement puts pressure on the home office to think in global terms and to allocate resources on the basis of overall market opportunity. This can be extremely difficult for a management that has been domestically focused and makes the majority of its sales in the home market. Despite these drawbacks, the international division structure remains dominant among US MNEs.

Global organizational structures

As MNEs generate more and more revenues from their overseas operations, their strategies become more global in focus and the structures used to implement these strategies follow suit. European firms are a good example. Because their domestic markets are fairly small, these companies have traditionally had global structures. In all, there are six basic types: (1) global product, (2) global area, (3) global function, (4) mixed, (5) matrix, and (6) transnational network.

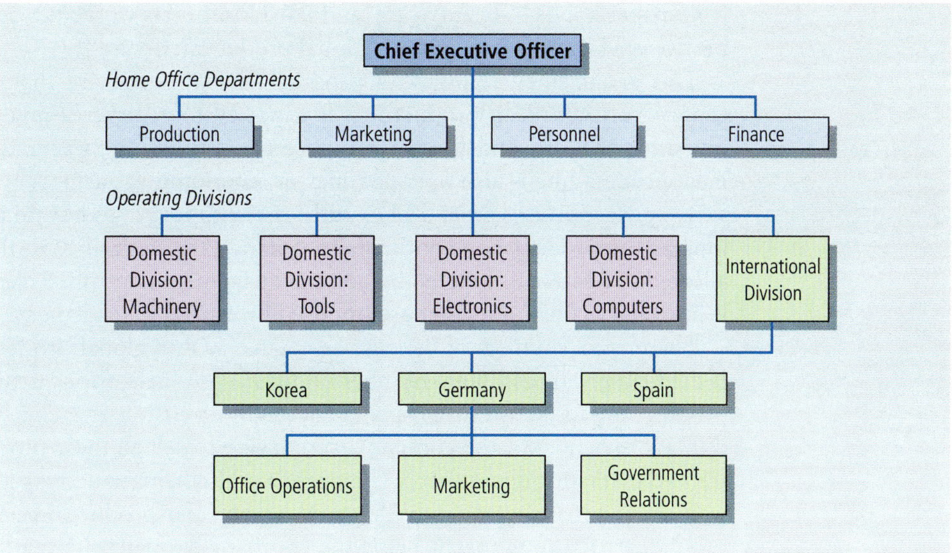

Figure 9.3 **An international division structure**

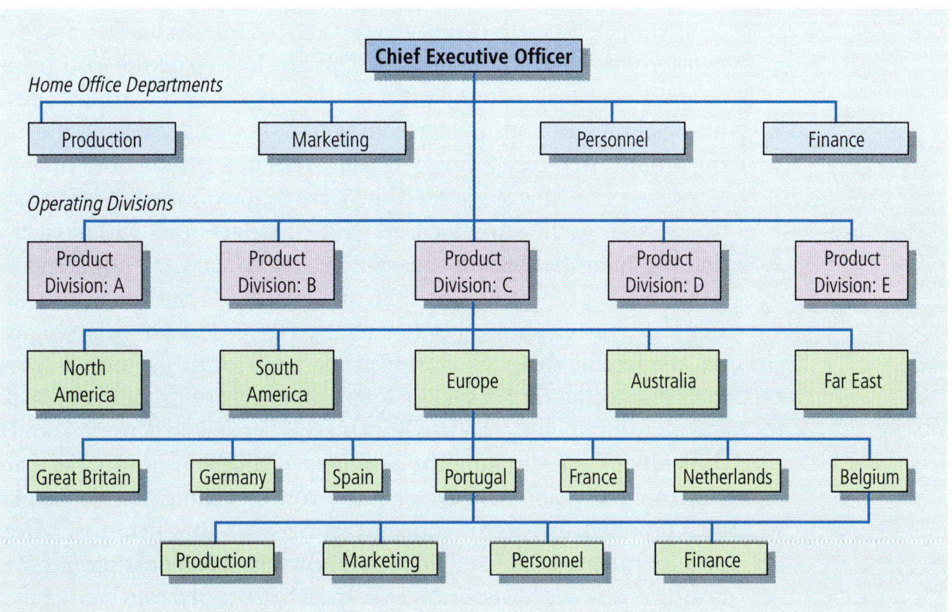

Figure 9.4 **A global product structure**

Global product structure

Global product structure
An organizational arrangement in which domestic divisions are given worldwide responsibility for product groups

A **global product structure** is a structural arrangement in which domestic divisions are given worldwide responsibility for product groups. Figure 9.4 provides an example. In this arrangement each product division sells its output throughout the world. As seen in the case of Product Division C, the European group operates in a host of countries. The same would be true for the other four geographic areas noted in the figure. In each case the manager of the product division would have internal functional support for the entire product line. All production, marketing, personnel, and finance activities associated with Product C would be under the control of this individual. In recent years Procter & Gamble has used this arrangement to market its wide assortment of products from paper goods to beauty care, and Ford Motor has worked to establish a single automotive operation that relies on a global product structure.[9]

This arrangement employs a product division structure that relies on the "profit center" concept. Each product line is expected to generate a predetermined return on investment (ROI), and the performance of each line is measured on this profit basis. Each product line is also operated like an autonomous business, with the product division manager given a great deal of authority with regard to how to run the operation. As long as the product line continues to generate the desired ROI, the division is usually allowed to operate unfettered by home management controls. The only major exception is budgetary constraints that are imposed by central management.

There are a number of benefits associated with a global product division structure. If the firm produces a large number of diverse products, the structure allows each major product line to focus on the specific needs of its customers. This would be particularly difficult to achieve if the company were trying to sell all these products out of one centralized marketing department. This approach also helps to develop a cadre of experienced, well-trained managers who understand a particular product line. A third benefit of the product structure is that it helps the company to match its marketing strategy to the specific needs of the customer. For example, in some areas of the world a product may be in the introduction stage, while in other areas it may be in the growth, maturity, or decline stage. These differing life cycles require close technological and marketing coordination between the home market and the foreign market, and this can be best achieved by a product division approach. The product structure also helps the organization to establish and maintain the necessary link between the product development people and the customer. By continually feeding back information from the field to the home office, the product division personnel ensure that new product offerings meet consumer needs.

At the same time there are drawbacks to the product division arrangement. One is the necessity of duplicating facilities and staff personnel within each division. A second is that products that sell well are often given primary attention and those that need special handling or promotion are often sidetracked, even though this may result in the long-run loss of profit. A third is that an effective product division requires managers who are knowledgeable about the worldwide demand for their products. Most managers know the local market but do not know a lot about international markets. So it takes time to develop the necessary managerial staff to run this type of structure. A fourth shortcoming is the difficulty of coordinating the activities of different product divisions. For example, the electronics division may decide to subcontract components to a plant in Germany, while the computer division is subcontracting work to a firm in France. If the two divisions had coordinated their activities, it might have been possible to have all the work done by one company at a lower price. Finally, lack of cooperation among the various product lines can result in lost sales, given that each division may have information that can be of value to the other. However, because of the profit center concept, each product line operates independently and communication and cooperation are downplayed, if not discouraged.

Global area structure

Global area structure
An organizational arrangement in which primary operational responsibility is delegated to area managers, each of whom is responsible for a specific geographic region

A **global area structure** is one in which primary operational responsibility is delegated to area managers, each of whom is responsible for a specific geographic region. This is a polycentric (host-country-oriented) structure. Figure 9.5 provides an example. Under this arrangement each regional division is responsible for all functions within its area, that is, production, marketing, personnel, and finance. There appears to be some structural similarity between a global area and a global product arrangement; however, they operate in very different ways. With a global product arrangement, each product division is responsible for its output throughout the world. With a global area structure, on the other hand, the individual product lines are subsumed within each of the

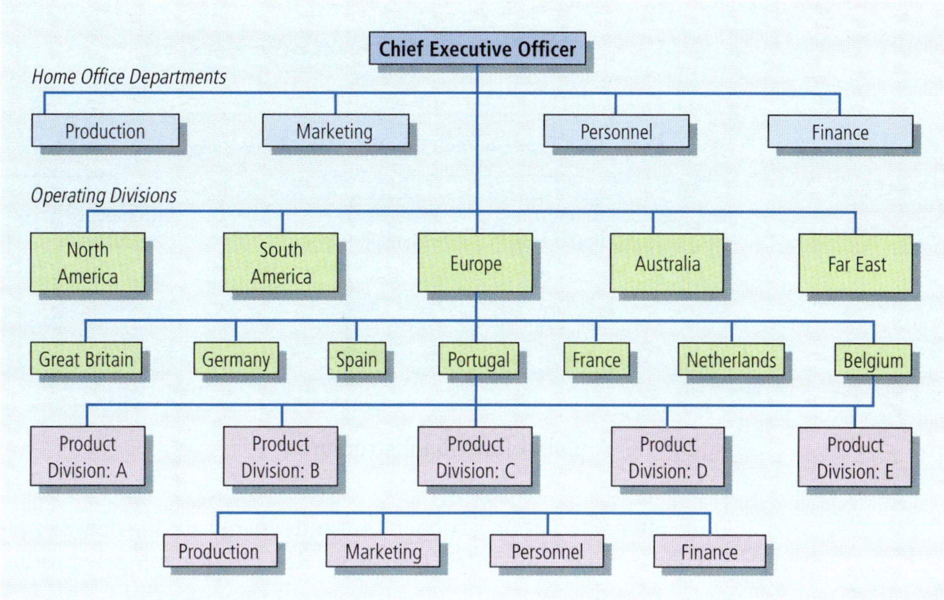

Figure 9.5 **A global area structure**

geographic areas. So the manager in charge of Belgian operations, for example, will be responsible for each of the product lines sold in that region.

A global area structure is commonly used by MNEs that are in mature businesses and have narrow product lines that are not differentiated by geographic area. Food products are a good example:

> In the United States, soft drinks have less sugar than in South America, so the manufacturing process must be slightly different in these two locales. Similarly, in England people prefer bland soups, but in France the preference is for mildly spicy. In Turkey, Italy, Spain, and Portugal people like dark, bitter coffee; Americans prefer a milder, sweeter blend. In northern Europe, Canada, and the United States people prefer less spicy food; in the Middle East and Asia they like more heavily spiced food.[10]

The global area structure provides division managers with the autonomy to make rapid decisions that depend on local tastes and regulations; because of this, the firm can become more "nationally responsive". Also, the company gains a wealth of experience regarding how to satisfy these local tastes and, in the process, often builds a strong competitive advantage. The global area structure works well where economies of scale in production require a region-sized unit for basic production. For example, by setting up operations in the EU, a US company is able to achieve production cost advantages that would not otherwise be possible. Finally, under this structure the company can eliminate costly transportation associated with importing goods produced overseas.

If a product sells well in the US, the company is likely to try to market it worldwide without making any modifications for local taste. Under the area structure the opposite viewpoint holds; the product must be adapted to the local tastes. But this means that the usual product emphasis in a company must be subsumed to the company's geographic orientation and the authority of the area managers. Another shortcoming with this organization structure is the expense associated with duplicating facilities. Each division has its own functional areas and is responsible for both production and marketing. Since production efficiency is often based on the amount of output, small plants are usually less efficient than large ones. Companies using a global area division structure also find it difficult to coordinate geographically dispersed divisions into the overall strategic plan.

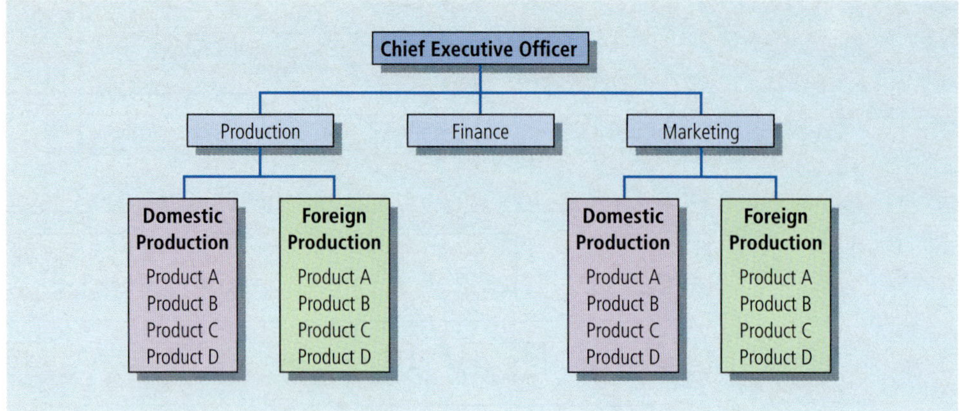

Figure 9.6 **A global functional structure**

Quite often international cooperation and synergy among divisions end up being sacrificed. Finally, companies that rely heavily on R&D to develop new products often find that the global area divisions do not readily accept these offerings. This is because each group is trying to cater to the specific needs of its current market, and new products often require modification to meet the needs of these local customers. Research shows that division managers prefer to sell products that have already been accepted by the market and are reluctant to take on new, untried products. Unfortunately, since most products have fairly short life cycles, this attitude is potentially dangerous to the long-term success of the MNE and the home office must continually fight this "anti-new product" drift.

Global functional structure

Global functional structure
An organizational arrangement in which all areas of activity are built around the basic tasks of the enterprise

A **global functional structure** is one that is built around the basic tasks of the organization. For example, in manufacturing firms production, marketing, and finance are the three primary functions that must be carried out for the enterprise to survive. Figure 9.6 shows such an arrangement.

Under this arrangement the head of the production department is responsible for all domestic and international manufacturing. Similarly, the head of marketing is responsible for the sales of all products here and abroad. This structure is most commonly used by MNEs that have a narrow product line that has reached a stable plateau of global coverage and a level of demand that does not face major changes in a competitive attack.

A primary advantage of the global functional structure is that it allows a small group of managers to maintain control over a wide-reaching organization. A second advantage is that there is little duplication of facilities. Finally, the structure allows tight, centralized control.

A disadvantage of this structural arrangement is that it can be difficult to coordinate the production and marketing areas since each operates independently of the other. This can be particularly troublesome if the MNE has multiple product lines. A second disadvantage is that responsibility for profits rests primarily with the CEO because there is little diffusion of operating authority far down the line.

Researchers have found that the global functional arrangement is most common among raw materials extractors with heavy capital investment. Energy firms also use it. However, this is not a structure that suits many other kinds of businesses.

Mixed structure

Mixed structure
A hybrid organization design that combines structural arrangements in a way that best meets the needs of the enterprise

A **mixed structure** is a hybrid organization design that combines structural arrangements in a way that best meets the needs of the enterprise. Figure 9.7 provides an illustration. Different businesses with different patterns of global demand, supply, and competition

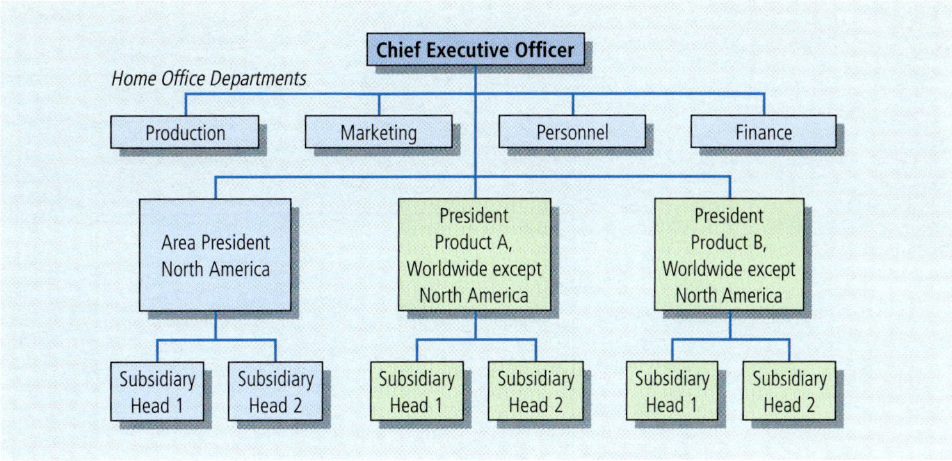

Figure 9.7 **A mixed structure**

demand different management structures. However, sometimes the mixed structure is a temporary one, and the organization opts for a more common form (global product, area, or functional) after a year or two. In other cases the structure remains in place indefinitely or a new mixed structure replaces the old one. The primary advantage of this organizational arrangement is that it allows the enterprise to create the specific types of design that best meets its needs. On the other hand, the arrangement sometimes is so flexible and different from anything the enterprise has used previously that personnel have trouble operating efficiently. Problems emerge with communication flows, chains of command, and groups going their own way. In deciding whether or not to use the mixed structure, MNEs must carefully weigh the benefits and drawbacks.

Matrix structure
An organizational arrangement that blends two organizational responsibilities such as functional and product structures or regional and product structures

Regional managers
In a geocentric matrix, managers charged with selling products in their geographic locale

Product managers
Managers responsible for coordinating the efforts of their people in such a way as to ensure the profitability of a particular business or product line

Matrix structure

A **matrix structure** is an organizational arrangement that blends two organizational responsibilities such as functional and product structures or regional and product structures. The functional emphasis provides attention to the activities to be performed, whereas the product emphasis provides attention to the good that is being produced. This structure is characterized by a dual command system that emphasizes both inputs (functions) and outputs (products). This facilitates development of a globally oriented management attitude. Figure 9.8 illustrates a product-region matrix.

There are three types of managers in this geocentric matrix structure: regional managers, product managers, and matrix managers. **Regional managers** are charged with business in their markets. Budgets for these operations include selling any of the products made by the MNE, subject to the decision of each regional manager. These regional managers have a polycentric focus. **Product managers** are responsible for coordinating the efforts of their people in such a way as to ensure the profitability of a particular

Regions / Products	Country A	Country B	Country C
Product 1			
Product 2			
Product 3			

Figure 9.8 **Geographic matrix structure**

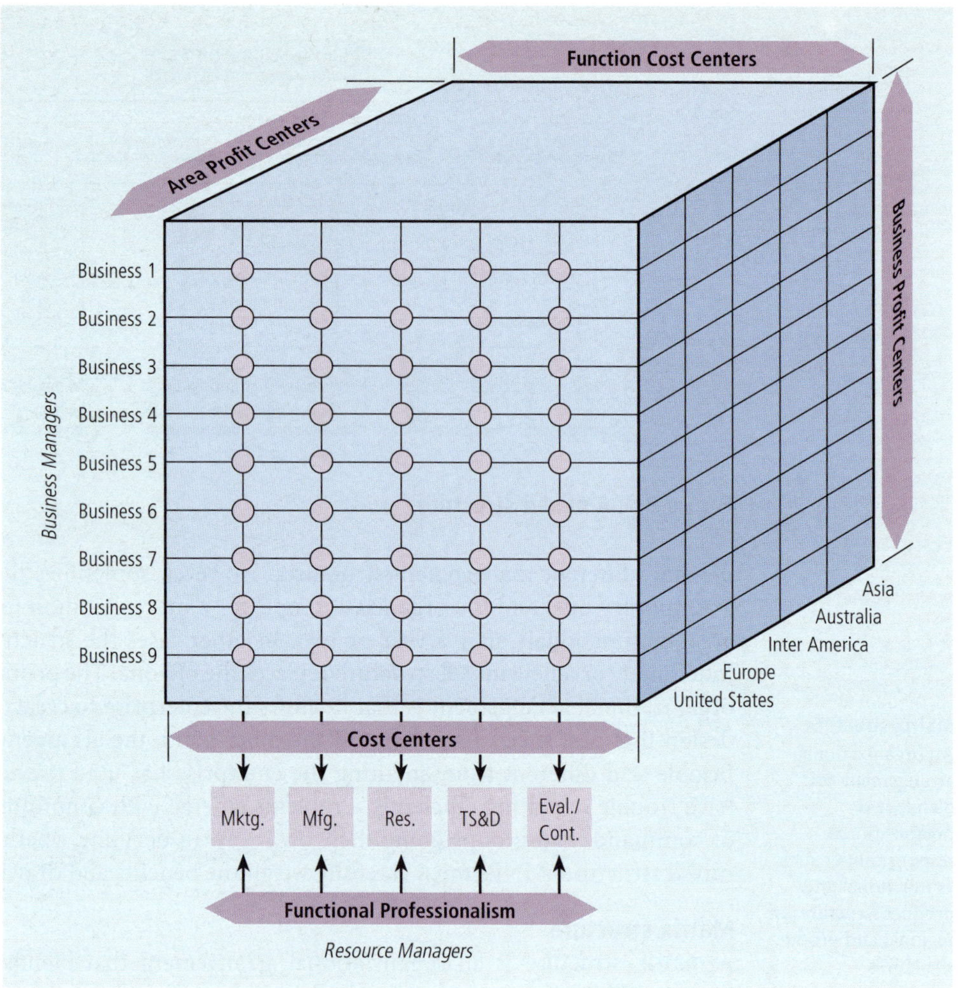

Figure 9.9 A multinational matrix structure

Source: Allan R. Janger, *Matrix Organizations of Complex Businesses* (New York: The Conference Board, 1979), p. 31.

business or product line. These managers have an ethnocentric attitude. The matrix managers are responsible to *both* regional and product managers – they have two bosses.

The matrix design in Figure 9.9 is more complex than that in Figure 9.8, as it has three dimensions. It illustrates how the matrix organizational arrangement can be used to coordinate and manage wide-reaching international operations. **Resource managers** are charged with providing the people for operations, whereas **business managers** are responsible for coordinating the efforts of these people to make profits for the product line. The resource managers are concerned with inputs; the business managers are concerned with outputs. At the bottom of Figure 9.9 there are functional specialists from such areas as marketing, manufacturing, and research. Individuals from each of these areas are assigned to each of the company's nine businesses. In turn these nine profit centers operate in five different areas of the world, including the US, Europe, and Asia. Each business is run by a business board which (although not shown in the figure) reports to senior-level management.

Resource managers
In a matrix structure, managers charged with providing people for operations

Business managers
Managers responsible for coordinating the efforts of people in a corporate organization; for example, in a matrix structure

The matrix design in Figure 9.9 is sometimes referred to as a three-dimensional model because, when it is drawn, it has width, height, and depth. Additionally, it is interesting to note that this multidimensional matrix addresses three major areas: function, product, and geography. So the structure is really a combination of some of the designs discussed earlier.

One of the major advantages of the multinational matrix is that it allows management to address more than one primary area of consideration. In Figure 9.9 the company is able to focus on functional, product, and geographic considerations. MNEs that need to balance a product and a global location strategy can benefit from this type of structure.[11]

On the other hand, there are a number of drawbacks to the use of the matrix structure in international operations. One is the complexity of the design and the use of dual command. This can result in confusion regarding what everyone is responsible for doing and to whom one reports on various matters. A second drawback is the large number of meetings and discussions that often result from efforts to coordinate a variety of different groups, each with its own agenda. A third is that it often takes time for managers to learn to operate in a matrix structure and, if the enterprise has rapid turnover, there is always a significant portion of the personnel who do not fully understand how to function effectively in this environment. The box "International Business Strategy in Action: Making matrix work" describes how some of these problems can be handled.

INTERNATIONAL BUSINESS STRATEGY *IN ACTION*

Making matrix work

Many multinationals use matrix structures in their international operations. Some of these structures work out very well; some do not. The reason for success can often be tied to three important criteria: clarity, continuity, and consistency. If all three are achieved, the matrix tends to work well; if one or more are missing, the structural design is often ineffective.

Clarity refers to how well people understand what they are doing and why they are doing it. If the company's basic objectives are clear, if relationships in the structure are spelled out in direct, simple terms, and the relevance of jobs is enunciated, there is a good chance that clarity will be achieved. A good example is NEC, the giant Japanese MNE that decided to integrate computers and communication and to make this the focus of its business efforts. This message was clearly communicated to the personnel so that everyone in the organization understood what the company wanted to do. On the other hand, competitors like AT&T tried the same strategy but failed to clarify what they were doing. As a result, NEC has been more successful in its pursuit of the computer/communication market.

Continuity means that the company remains committed to the same core objectives and values. This provides a unifying theme and helps to ensure that the personnel are committed. General Electric's Brazilian subsidiary is a good example of how a lack of continuity can hurt. In the 1960s the subsidiary built televisions. During the 1970s it was told to switch to large appliances. Then it was told to focus on housewares. By this time the company's dominant franchise in Brazil's electrical products market had all but dissipated. In contrast, Unilever set up operations in Brazil and, despite volatile changes in the economy, continued to focus its efforts on the electrical products market. Today Unilever has a thriving market in that country.

Consistency relates to how well all parts of the organization are moving in accord with each other. This is often a reflection of how well managers of the various operating divisions are pursuing the same objectives. For example, Philips NV launched an international strategy for its videocassette recording system, the V2000. However, its US subsidiary did not support these efforts because it felt that Matsushita's VHS format and Sony's Beta system were too well established. Because of this, Philips was unable to build the efficiency and credibility it needed to challenge the Japanese dominance of the VCR business.

Matrix structures can be complex organizational arrangements. However, if the MNE is able to achieve clarity, continuity, and consistency, the matrix approach can be very effective.

Websites: **www.nec.com; www.att.com; www.ge.com; www.unilever.com; www.sony.com** and **www.philips.com**.

Sources: Christopher A. Bartlett and Sumantra Ghoshal, "Matrix Management: Not a Structure, a Frame of Mind," *Harvard Business Review*, July–August 1990, pp. 138–145; Courtland L. Bovee et al., *Management* (New York: McGraw-Hill Inc., 1993), pp. 321–323; and Richard M. Hodgetts and Fred Luthans, *International Management*, 4th edn (Burr Ridge IL: Irwin/McGraw, 2000), Chapter 7.

The matrix structure is seldom the first choice of MNEs. The design typically evolves gradually, as the organization realizes that other structural designs are not adequate. However, some companies have abandoned the matrix structure. Skandia, the Swedish insurance firm, for example, has scrapped its matrix design and moved back to a more classical organizational arrangement. As with mixed structures, the matrix is sometimes a temporary arrangement as the enterprise searches for some hybrid design that will help it to operate more efficiently in the international arena.

Transnational network structure

Transnational network structure An organization design which helps MNEs take advantage of global economics of scale while also being responsive to local customer demands

One of the newest forms of international organizational arrangements to emerge is the **transnational network structure** which is designed to help MNEs take advantage of global economies of scale while also being responsive to local customer demands. This structural design combines elements of functional, product, and geographic designs, while relying on a network arrangement to link the various worldwide subsidiaries. At the center of the transnational network structure are nodes, which are units charged with coordinating product, functional, and geographic information. Different product group units and geographical area units have different structures depending on what is best for their particular operations. A good example of how the transnational network structure works is provided by NV Philips, which has operations in more than 60 countries and produces a diverse product line ranging from light bulbs to defense systems. In all, the company has six product divisions with a varying number of subsidiaries in each – and the focus of the latter varies considerably. Some specialize in manufacturing, others in sales; some are closely controlled by headquarters, others are highly autonomous.

The basic structural framework of the transnational network consists of three components: dispersed subunits, specialized operations, and interdependent relationships. *Dispersed subunits* are subsidiaries that are located anywhere in the world where they can benefit the organization. Some are designed to take advantage of low factor costs, while others are responsible for providing information on new technologies or consumer trends. *Specialized operations* are activities carried out by subunits that focus on particular product lines, research areas, and marketing areas, and are designed to tap specialized expertise or other resources in the company's worldwide subsidiaries. Interdependent relationships are used to share information and resources throughout the dispersed and specialized subunits.

The transnational network structure is difficult to draw in the form of an organization chart because it is complex and continually changing. Figure 9.10, which provides a view of NV Philips' network structure, shows how complex the design can be.

Active learning check 

Review your answer to Active Learning Case question 1 and make any changes you like. Then compare your answer with the one below.

1. What type of organizational structure would be best for Northern Telecom in pulling together its worldwide operations?

Nortel is a transnational corporation, so it will need to use some form of transnational network structure. As noted in the case, the company's local operations are designed to address both the culture and national regulations in its various worldwide markets. At the same time, these operations must all be coordinated for worldwide effectiveness. As a result, some of the characteristics of Nortel's structure will include dispersed subunits that are located anywhere in the world where they can be of benefit to the organization; specialized operations that are carried out by these units in order to focus on research, local needs, and product lines; and interdependent relationships that are used for sharing information and resources through the dispersed and specialized subunits.

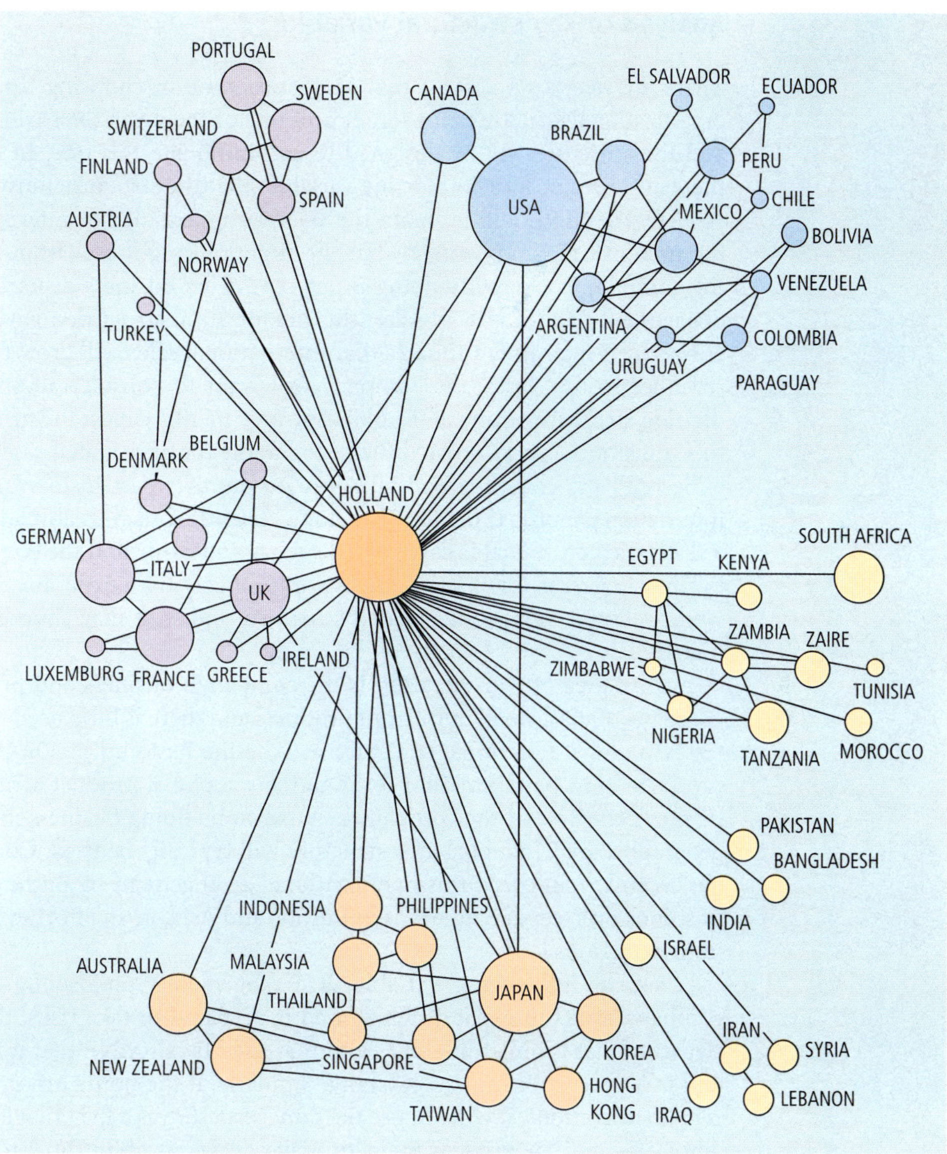

Figure 9.10 The network structure of NV Philips

Source: Academy of Management Review, 'The Multinational Corporation as an Interorganizational Network' by S. Ghoshal and C. A. Bartlett. Copyright 1990 by Academy of Management. Reproduced with permission of Academy of Management in the format textbook via Copyright Clearance Center.

STRATEGIC MANAGEMENT AND ORGANIZING STRATEGY

Research has shown that effective organizations follow the adage "from strategy to structure".[12] They begin by formulating a strategy and only then design a structure that will efficiently implement this plan. In determining the best structure, three questions must be answered:

1. Can the company operate efficiently with domestic divisions or are international divisions also necessary?
2. On what basis should the organization be structured: product, area, function, mixed, or matrix?
3. How can the necessary coordination and cooperation be most effectively achieved?

These answers are usually determined through a careful analysis of five key variables.

Analysis of key structural variables

There are five key variables that MNEs examine in choosing from among alternative organizational structures. In some cases one of these variables will outweigh the others, and the structure will be designed to accommodate this one. In most cases, however, there are three or four interacting variables that the structure must address.

First, the MNE will evaluate the relative importance of international operations at the present time and project what the situation might be within three to five years. If the company is currently doing 5 per cent of its business overseas and has an export department handling these sales, this organization structure may be adequate for now. However, if the MNE estimates that international sales will grow to 25 per cent of total revenues in five years, the company will want to consider adopting an international division structure or one of the global arrangements. Unless the firm is prepared to make this transition, it may prove difficult to handle the anticipated rapid growth.

Second, the company will take into account its past history and experience in the international arena. If the firm has done very little business abroad, it is likely to choose a simple structure that is easy to understand and control. If the company has been doing business overseas for many years, it will probably have experienced managers who can work well in a more sophisticated structure, and so it may choose a mixed design or a matrix.

A third area of consideration is the company's business and product strategy. If the company offers a small number of products and there is little need to adapt them to local tastes, a global functional structure may be the best choice. On the other hand, if the products must be tailored for local markets, a global product arrangement will usually be more effective. If the company is going to be doing business in a number of diverse geographic areas, a global area structure will typically be used. Coca-Cola, for example, has recently reinforced this organizational arrangement by putting new managers into positions overseeing operations in Europe and Asia, in an effort to improve sales growth in these regions.[13]

A fourth influencing variable is management's philosophy of operating. If the company wants to expand rapidly and is prepared to take risks, the firm will choose a structure that is quite different from that used by an MNE that wants to expand slowly and is conservative in its risk taking. Similarly, if the home office wants to keep a tight rein on operations, it will not use the same structure as a firm that gives local subsidiaries autonomy and encourages them to make decisions about how to keep the unit competitive at the local level. French and German subsidiaries, for example, tend to be more centralized than US units. There are also differences in the way operations are controlled. For example, Japanese MNEs like to use face-to-face informal controls while US multinationals prefer budgets, financial data, and other formalized tools.

A final key variable is the enterprise's ability to adjust to organizational changes. As MNE world sales increase, there will be continual modifications in the structure. For example, when the company is small, the domestic divisions will dominate. As the international side of operations grows, the managers of the domestic divisions will have to cede some of their authority and influence. If they are unable or unwilling to do this, the structure will be affected. Similarly, if international executives begin gaining greater authority and there is a need to revamp overseas operations, their willingness to adjust to organizational changes will affect the structure. In some cases MNEs have found that overseas managers, just like their domestic counterparts, build small empires and often are unwilling to give up this power.

The ultimate choice of organization structure rests with top management. However, this group seldom tries to force such a decision on those who will be directly affected.

Instead, there is a give-and-take in which the needs of the enterprise and the personnel are considered.

In recent years the increase in mergers and acquisitions has had an important impact on MNE decision making. Deutsche Telekom's T-Mobile International provides a good example. This company has an ownership position in a large number of mobile phone companies in a host of different countries including Voice Stream (US), One2One (UK), BEN (Netherlands), max.mobil (Austria), and Radio Mobil (Czech Republic). Coordinating the operations of these holdings requires a carefully designed structure coupled with the appropriate amount of decentralized authority.[14] The result is a structure that is both efficient and humanistic. In carrying this out, companies will address the organizational processes that take place within the structure.

Organizational processes

The formal structure provides the skeletal framework within which the personnel operate. The structure is designed to answer the question: What is to be done? The organizational processes – decision making, communicating, and controlling – help to make the structure work efficiently. These processes help to answer the question: Who is to do what, and how will they do it? These processes help to put the organization structure into action.

Decision making

Decision making
The process of choosing from among alternatives

Decision making is the process of choosing from among alternatives. In international operations one of the primary areas of consideration is where the ultimate decision-making authority will rest on important matters. If the home office holds this control, decision making is centralized; if the subsidiary can make many of these important decisions without having to consult the home office, decision making is decentralized. Table 9.1 provides some examples of factors that encourage both these types of decision making.[15]

Table 9.1 Factors that encourage centralization or decentralization of decision making in multinational operations

Encourage centralization of decision making	*Encourage decentralization of decision making*
Large enterprise	Small enterprise
Large capital investment	Small capital investment
Relative importance of the unit to the MNE	Relative unimportance of the unit to the MNE
Highly competitive environment	Stable environment
Strong volume-to-unit-cost relationship	Weak volume-to-unit-cost relationship
High degree of technology	Moderate to low degree of technology
Low level of product diversification	High level of product diversification
Homogeneous product lines	Heterogeneous product lines
High interdependence between the units	Low interdependence between the units
Few highly competent managers in the host country	Many highly competent managers in the host country
High experience in international business	Low experience in international business
Small geographic distance between home office and subsidiary	Large geographic distance between home office and subsidiary

Research shows that decision making in MNE subsidiaries tends to vary from country to country or culture to culture. For example, among British organizations there is a great deal of decentralized decision making. Many upper-level managers do not understand the technical nature of business operations such as financial budgeting or cost control. So they delegate the authority for these matters to middle-level managers while they focus on strategic matters.

French and German subsidiaries tend to be fairly centralized in their decision-making approaches. French senior executives like to maintain control of operations and tend to delegate less authority than do their English counterparts. German managers are hierarchical in their approach and most important decisions are made at the top.

In Scandinavian countries like Norway, Sweden, and Denmark, operations are highly decentralized both in Scandinavian-based firms and abroad. The Scandinavians place a great deal of emphasis on the quality of work life, and they are more interested in the well-being of the worker than in maximizing profit.

Ringsei
Decision making by consensus; this process is widely used in Japan

The Japanese use a combination of decentralization and centralization. They make heavy use of a decision-making process called ***ringsei***, or decision making by consensus:

> Under this system any changes in procedures and routines, tactics, and even strategies of a firm are originated by those directly concerned with these changes. The final decision is made at the top level after an elaborate examination of the proposal through successively higher levels in the management hierarchy and results in acceptance or rejection of a decision only through consensus at every echelon of the management structure.[16]

At the same time top management maintains a great deal of authority over what will be discussed at lower levels. Thus there is both decentralization and centralization exercised by senior-level management.

US MNEs, surprisingly perhaps, tend to use fairly centralized decision making in managing their overseas operations. This is particularly true in areas such as marketing policies, financial matters, and decisions on production capacity. Ford Motor, for example, recently reduced the number of managers reporting to the chief executive officer in order to better control operations.[17] On the other hand, Wal-Mart has been very successful in Canada by using a decentralized approach in order to accommodate the local market.[18] Moreover, this is the current trend worldwide as MNEs work to increase economies of scale and to attain higher operational efficiency. One way in which many MNEs are doing this is through outsourcing, thus simplifying their structures and delegating the authority for some operations to their suppliers.[19]

Active learning check

Review your answer to Active Learning Case question 2 and make any changes you like. Then compare your answer with the one below.

2. Why does the company rely so heavily on decentralized decision making?

The primary reason that the firm relies so heavily on decentralized decision making is that the demands of the local areas are so great that it cannot make all important decisions from headquarters. In particular, over the last decade there have been a number of critical changes in the industry including the need to address local customer needs and the importance of responding effectively to local government regulations.

Communication

Communication The process of transferring meanings from sender to receiver

Communication is the process of transferring meanings from sender to receiver. However, the way in which this is done often varies from one MNE to another. For example, US MNEs use direct communications with their subsidiaries and overseas units.[20] Directives are spelled out clearly and precisely. However, Japanese MNEs prefer more indirect communications in which things are implied and it is up to the listener to determine what to do. The direct approach works well for Americans, whose culture encourages openness and specific communications. The indirect approach works well for the Japanese, whose culture encourages indirect and implied communications.[21] Ouchi, after conducting a series of interviews with Americans working for a Japanese bank in the US, found that this problem can be particularly disconcerting because each side is unable to understand the other's approach, as illustrated by the following:

> *American managers*
> We have a non-stop running battle with the president. We simply cannot get him to specify a performance target for us. We have all the necessary reports and numbers, but we can't get specific targets from him. He won't tell us how large a dollar increase in loan volume or what per cent decrease in operating costs he expects us to achieve over the next month, quarter, or even year. How can we know whether we're performing well without specific targets to shoot for?
>
> *Japanese bank president*
> If only I could get these Americans to understand our philosophy of banking. To understand what the business means to us – how we feel we should deal with our customers and our employees. What our relationship should be to the local communities we serve. How we should deal with our competitors, and what our role should be in the world at large. If they could get that under their skin, then they could figure out for themselves what an appropriate objective would be for any situation, no matter how unusual or new, and I would never have to tell them, never have to give them a target.[22]

These types of culturally based differences can greatly affect the MNE's ability to get things done.

Kinesics A form of non-verbal communication which deals with conveying information through the use of body movement and facial expression

Another communication-based problem is non-verbal messages. In international business these take two major forms: kinesics and proxemics. **Kinesics** deals with the conveying of information through the use of body movement and facial expression. For example, when verbally communicating with someone in the US, it is good manners to look the other party in the eye. However, in many other cultures, such as Arab and Middle East, this is not done, especially if one is talking to a member of the opposite sex. Such behavior would be considered rude and disrespectful.[23]

Proxemics A form of non-verbal communication which deals with how people use physical space to convey messages

Proxemics deals with how people use physical space to convey messages. For example, in the US, businesspeople typically stand two to three feet away from those with whom they are communicating. However, in the Middle East and in many South American countries, it is common to stand right next to the person. This often makes Americans feel very uncomfortable because this space is generally reserved only for family members and close friends. Business is not conducted at this distance. One group of authors summarized the problem this way:

> Americans often tend to be moving away in interpersonal communication with their Middle Eastern or Latin counterparts, while the latter are trying to physically close the gap. The American cannot understand why the other is standing so close; the latter cannot understand why the American is being so reserved and standing so far away; the result is a breakdown in communication.[24]

Another example of proxemics is office layout and protocol. In the US, a large office connotes importance, as does a secretary who screens visitors and keeps away those

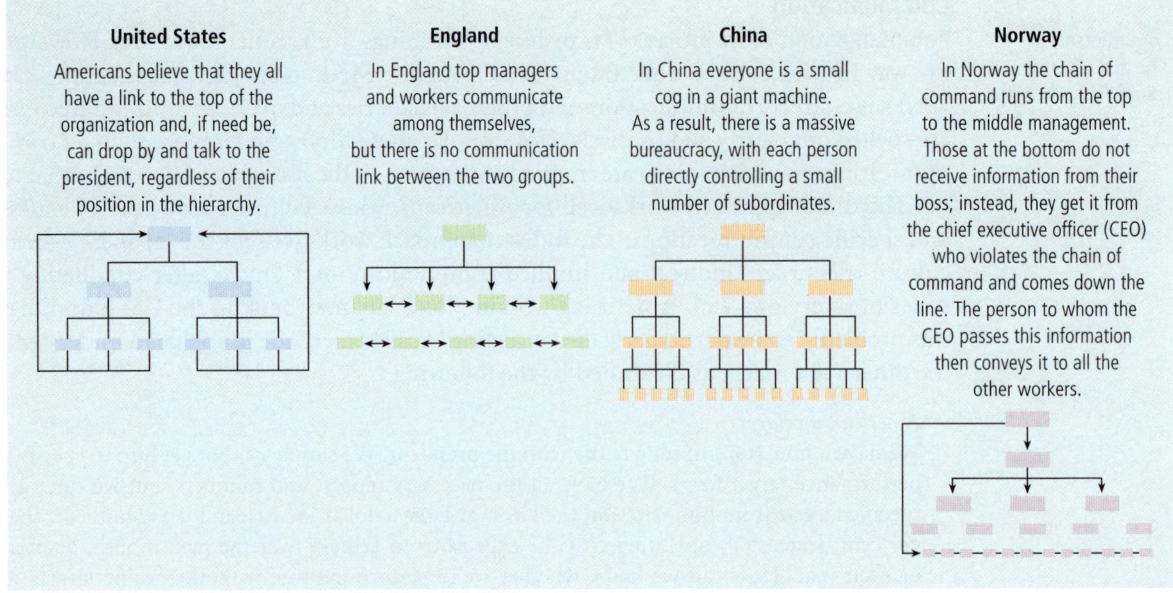

Figure 9.11 Organizational epigrams

An epigram is a terse, witty statement. The organizational epigrams are designed to poke fun at the way communication flows in international organizations. Each was created by an individual with experience in the respective country. The explanation accompanying the respective epigram explains the logic behind the drawing. These epigrams illustrate that communication flows throughout the world are less efficient than the enterprise would like. They also illustrate that each country has its own unique approach to conveying information.

Source: Adapted from Simcha Ronen, *Comparative and Multinational Management*. Copyright © 1986 John Wiley & Sons, Inc. This material is used by permission of John Wiley & Sons, Inc.

whom the manager does not wish to see. In Japan, most managers do not have large offices and, if they do, they spend little time in them since they are generally out talking to the employees and walking around the workplace. If the manager were to stay in the office all day, it would be viewed as a sign of distrust or anger at the work group. In Europe, many managers do not have walled-in offices. The bosses are out in the same large room as their people; there is no one to screen the brokers from the boss.

Every country has some unique communication patterns or behaviors.[25] These behaviors can be particularly troublesome to outsiders who are working locally and are unfamiliar with local approaches to communication. Figure 9.11 provides an interesting example in the form of epigrams that have been drawn from organization structures throughout the world.

Controlling

Controlling
The process of determining that everything goes according to plan

Controlling is the process of determining that everything goes according to plan. This process is to reward performance and it consists of three steps: (1) establishing standards, (2) comparing performance against standards, and (3) correcting deviations. Controlling is closely linked to communication since it is virtually impossible to evaluate performance and make changes without communicating information; many of the same organizational problems discussed above also apply here.

One of the major differences between US and Japanese firms is the use of explicit versus implicit control. One of the major differences between US and European firms is that US MNEs tend to rely more heavily on reports and other performance-related data, whereas Europeans make heavy use of behavioral control. US multinationals compare results of a foreign unit with those of other foreign units, as well as with domestic units, in evaluating performance. European MNEs tend to be more flexible and to judge performance on an individual basis rather than simply making a comparative judgment. Other differences include:

1. Control in US MNEs relies on precise planning and budgeting that are suitable for comparison purposes. Control in European MNEs takes into consideration a high level of company-wide understanding and agreement regarding what constitutes appropriate behavior and how such behavior supports the goals of the subsidiary and the parent company.
2. US multinationals do not encourage their managers to remain in overseas positions for a long period of time. As a result, these companies use large central staffs and centralized information gathering to carry out evaluations. European multinationals, on the other hand, encourage their managers to remain in overseas positions, and these companies rely heavily on these managers to provide input regarding how well the unit is doing.
3. Managers of US MNEs often report to a counterpart back in headquarters who, in turn, conveys information up the line. European multinationals have a more direct reporting channel so that the head of a foreign subsidiary reports to someone who is closer to the top of the structure.[26]

Another major difference is the way in which personnel are evaluated. In the US and in Europe, it is common to single out high performers and to reward them. In Japan, however, credit is given to the entire group and not just to one or two individuals. Singling people out for special attention is not regarded as complimentary. Rather, such attention would make an individual feel that he or she was not regarded as a team player, and this would be insulting. Another important difference is the time period for personnel evaluations. Most US and European firms evaluate their people on an annual basis. However, in Japan, the first major evaluation often does not occur until the employee has been with the firm for almost a decade.[27] These controlling differences greatly affect the way the structure is managed. As a result, running an overseas operation the same way as at home is often difficult.

Active learning check

Review your answer to Active Learning Case question 3 and make any changes you like. Then compare your answer with the one below.

3. In controlling its operations, what are three areas that are paramount for the firm?

There are a number of areas that Nortel needs to control. One of these is profit. As seen in the case, because of the turbulence in the telecommunications industry and the collapse of many dot.com companies, Nortel's stock price has been hard hit. So the company needs to continue focusing on increasing its profit and getting its stock back up. A second, and related, area is cost control. The company recently had to lay off half of its worldwide workforce. Clearly, the firm is now in the process of retrenching and riding out the major changes that are rocking the industry. A third area that the firm will have to monitor continually is its R&D prowess in order to ensure that it remains on the cutting edge so that when industry conditions turn around it will be in a position to capitalize on this development.

KEY POINTS

1. When a company first enters the international arena, it is common to find that these efforts are mere extensions of domestic operations. The MNE will typically handle foreign sales directly through its own marketing department, an export department, or an overseas subsidiary that is the result of a joint venture. As international operations become more important, however, the firm is likely to centralize these operations by adopting an international division structure. This organizational arrangement remains quite popular with many MNEs.
2. As multinationals generate increased revenues from their overseas operations, they are likely to adopt a global organizational structure. There are six basic types: global product, global area, global functional, mixed, matrix, and transnational network. Each type has specific advantages and disadvantages.
3. There are five key variables that MNEs examine in choosing from among alternative organizational structures. These include (a) the relative importance of international operations, (b) past history and experience in the international arena, (c) the company's business and product strategy, (d) management philosophy, and (e) the organization's ability to adjust to organization changes.
4. The formal structure provides the skeletal framework within which the personnel operate. The organization process of decision making, communicating, and controlling make the structure work efficiently. In the decision-making process, one of the key areas of consideration is the amount of centralization or decentralization that will be used by the home office. In communicating, culturally based differences will be of major importance, including non-verbal messages. In controlling, areas of concern include explicit and implicit control and the ways in which personnel will be evaluated.

KEY TERMS

- international division structure
- global product structure
- global area structure
- global functional structure
- mixed structure
- matrix structure
- regional managers
- product managers
- resource managers
- transnational network structure
- business managers
- decision making
- *ringsei*
- communication
- kinesics
- proxemics
- controlling

REVIEW AND DISCUSSION QUESTIONS

1. **How does an export department structure function? Who handles the overseas sales?**
2. **If a company's initial international expansion is conducted through the use of subsidiaries, how closely does it control these subsidiaries? Why?**
3. **Why do MNEs use an international division structure? Are there any drawbacks to this organizational arrangement?**
4. **How does a global product structure work? Why would an MNE opt for this arrangement? What are two drawbacks to using this structure?**
5. **When would an MNE use a global area structure? When would the firm reject this structural arrangement in favor of a different structure?**
6. **How does a global functional structure work? When would it be a popular approach? When would it be of very little value in organizing international operations?**
7. **When would a company opt for a mixed structure? Why? Defend your answer.**
8. **How does a matrix structure work? When would an MNE opt for this organizational arrangement?**
9. **There are five key variables that MNEs examine in choosing from among alternative organizational structures. What are these five? Identify and briefly describe each.**
10. **Why are some overseas operations highly decentralized while others are very centralized? What factors influence this arrangement?**
11. **Why are US international operations more centralized than those in Sweden? Why is the US model becoming more popular among MNEs?**
12. **In what way is implicit versus explicit communication important in understanding how home office managements coordinate international activities?**
13. **What type of control techniques do US MNEs prefer? How does this preference differ from that of the Japanese? Compare and contrast the two.**

REAL CASE

LVMH: organizing luxury products in the international arena

LVMH is a French-based luxury goods group that was founded in 1987 with the merger of Louis Vuitton and Moët Hennessy. In 2000 the group had sales of 11.6 billion euros, up from 8.5 billion euros in 1999. LVMH currently employs around 53,000 people, most of whom work outside France; and the company generates the bulk of its sales in the worldwide market. While 16 per cent of all revenues are earned in France, 26 per cent comes from the US, 18 per cent from the rest of Europe, and 15 per cent from Japan, with the remaining 25 per cent being generated primarily in Asia and Latin America.

Customers everywhere recognize LVMH's famous brand names such as Christian Dior, Dom Perignon, Givenchy, and Moët & Chandon. And LVMH sells its wide array of internationally known products through 1,350 stores worldwide and is so successful that it currently holds 15 per cent of the world market for luxury goods. This market grows by about 10 per cent annually and so it attracts very strong competition. Included in this group are such internationally known firms as Gucci and Bulgari. To be successful in this industry, it is very important to have an effective organizing strategy.

LVMH's organizational arrangement is much more than that of a typical conglomerate. The company has organized itself around its five main lines of business. These groups, which are really strategic business units (SBUs), are set up so that they can sell nationally known, high quality products in a way that both addresses local cultural tastes and takes local rules and regulations into consideration. These five SBUs include:

1. *The LVMH Fashion and Leather Goods* SBU which owns such world famous brand names as Louis Vuitton, Loewe, Celine, Berluti, Kenzo, Givenchy, Christian Lacroix, Marc Jacobs, Fendi, StefanoBi, Emilio Pucci, and Thomas Pink.
2. *The Wines and Spirits* SBU which markets such offerings as Moët & Chandon, Dom Pérignon, Veuve Clicquot, Krug, Pommery, Mercier, Ruinart, Canard duchêne, Château d'Yquem, Chandon Estates, Cloudy Bay, Cape Mentelle, Hennessy, Hine, Newton and MountAdam.
3. *The Perfumes and Cosmetics* SBU which sells Parfums Christian Dior, Guerlain, Parfums Givenchy, Parfums Kenzo, Bliss, Hard Candy, BeneFit Cosmetics, Urban Decay, Fresh, and Make Up For Ever.
4. *The Watches and Jewelry* SBU which markets such brands as TAG Heuer, Ebel, Zenith, Benedom, Fred, Chaumet, and Omas.
5. *The Selective Retailing* SBU which includes a wide variety of operations including Duty Free Shops, Miami Cruiseline, Sephora Europe, Sephora AAP, Le Bon Marché, La Samaritaine, and Solstice.

The profit margin on luxury goods is very high, so control over production, distribution, and advertising is central to profitability. In the manufacture of its high quality merchandise, for example, LVMH ensures that production standards are the highest and the use of its "Made in France" label is used appropriately so as to appeal to its market niches. The company also markets its brand names internationally so that buyers everywhere are familiar with them. One way it does this is by setting aside 11 per cent of all sales to be used exclusively for advertising. On a centralized basis, LVMH also uses a common laboratory for cosmetics research, employs bulk media buys so that it gets the most value for its promotion dollar, and integrates the operations for all of the branch offices in each group to ensure maximum efficiency.

By carefully overseeing major operations from the top while allowing the individual SBUs to make those decisions that directly affect their own local markets, LVMH employs a combination of "tight and loose" control that it uses to maximize its international presence and overall profitability. In the process, the company has found that this type of transnational network structure is particularly effective in ensuring worldwide market growth and increased profitability.

Websites: **www.lvmh.com; www.vuitton.com; www.moet.com; www.dior.com; www.givenchy.com; www.gucci.com; www.bulgari.com** and **www.bulgari.it**.

Sources: Adapted from **www.lvmh.com**; "The Sweet Smell of Success," *Business Week*, July 16, 2001; Carol Matlack, "Identity Crisis at LVMH?" *Business Week*, December 11, 2000.

1. **What type of organizational structure does LVMH have? How do the Duty Free Shops (DFS) fit into its structure?**
2. **What is the role of the SBUs in the organizational structure of LVMH? What problems may arise if each SBU is run independently?**
3. **Compare the organizational structure of LVMH with that of Nortel Networks (see page 242 above). Are there any similarities? How are these organizations different?**

REAL CASE

Command Alkon: a small software business

A successful US small business is Command Alkon based in Birmingham, Alabama. It is the world leader in the design and supply of computer software for the construction business. Command Alkon is only a small MNE, but it has tremendous capabilities in technology standardization and is number 1 in its software in terms of market share, revenues, and distribution. It employs several hundred people and has over 6,000 installations in 75 countries.

It is the result of a merger in December 2000 of Command Data and Alkon, two construction materials software and services firms. The merger was designed to pool these R&D resources in this fast changing computer software business. Their products were already compatible and the merger cut out duplication of effort. Command Data started in 1976 as a command software company offering solutions to the US construction materials industry. As it grew, it acquired ACS in 1985, PSI in 1987, and Vehicom Data in 1997. It now operates offices in Latin America, Australia, and South Africa.

Rival firms are Systech in the US and Dornier in Germany. These are also much larger and more globally integrated than Command Alkon, which has a purely ethnocentric strategy and organizational structure. All decisions are centralized and hierarchical micromanagement is the name of the game. The dominant culture is that of the US home office. There is no customization, and no marketing department, no investment in local offices. Command Alkon, like most small businesses, is driven by its basic product or service, and it replicates its firm-specific advantage overseas. It has either an international division structure or a centralized product structure

Another of the problems for small businesses is that the top management team is, itself, small. Often it is just the founder of the firm, his/her immediate family, and a few friends. Consequently there is little managerial experience and a limited opportunity to develop international business skills. This leads to ethnocentric behavior. Indeed, most small business leaders will not have the internal resources to build an overseer business by foreign direct investment; instead they are drawn to the export mode of foreign entry. This then needs an international division structure.

There are literally thousands, if not hundreds of thousands, of small businesses like Command Alkon. Their business strategy is not as complicated as MNEs; usually SMEs are in one line of business, not many. The international experience of SMEs is usually through licensing and/or exporting. Rarely will they engage in foreign direct investment or develop global organizational structure as the costs of doing business in foreign markets is often too high.

Websites: **www.commanddata.com** and **www.systechsystems.com**.

Sources: **www.commanddata.com**; Gilbert Nicholson, "Command Alkon Found Its Niche and Dug In," *Birmingham Business Journal*, November 2, 2001.

1. **Why does a small business like Command Alkon usually have little or no foreign direct investment? How does it go international?**
2. **What is the typical type of organizational structure for a small business like Command Alkon?**
3. **Why are software businesses usually ethnocentric in their organizational structure?**

ENDNOTES

1 Joanne Lee-Young, "Starbucks' Expansion in China Is Slated," *Wall Street Journal*, October 5, 1998, p. A 27C.

2 See, for example, Yigang Pan and Xiaolian Li, "Joint Venture Formation of Very Large Multinational Firms," *Journal of International Business Studies*, vol. 32, no. 1 (First Quarter 2000), pp. 179–189; and Tim G. Andrews and Nartnalin Chompusri, "Lessons in 'Cross-Vergence': Restructuring the Thai Subsidiary Corporation," *Journal of International Business Studies*, vol. 30, no. 3 (First Quarter 2000), pp. 77–93.

3 Brad Mitchener, "GM Takes a Gamble on Eastern Europe," *Wall Street Journal*, June 23, 1997, p. A 10.

4 William J. Holstein et al., "Mighty Mitsubishi Is on the Move," *Business Week*, September 24, 1990, p. 99.

5 Robert L. Simison, "New Dana Illustrates Reshaping of Auto Parts Business," *Wall Street Journal*, September 2, 1997, p. B 4.

6 A good example is offered by Peter Siddall, Keith Willey and Jorge Tavares, "Building a Transnational Organization for BP Oil," *Long Range Planning*, February 1992, pp. 37–45.

7 For some excellent examples, see Charles H. Ferguson, "Computers and the Coming of the US Keiretsu," *Harvard Business Review*, July–August 1990, pp. 55–70; and Benjamin Gomes-Casseres, "Joint Ventures in the Face of Global Competition," *Sloan Management Review*, vol. 30, no. 3 (Spring 1989), pp. 17–26.

8 Richard M. Hodgetts and Fred Luthans, *International Management*, 4th edn (Burr Ridge IL: McGraw/Irwin, 2000), p. 303.

9 Joann S. Lublin, "Place vs. Product: It's Tough to Choose a Management Model," *Wall Street Journal*, June 27, 2001, pp. A 1, 4.

10 Hodgelts and Luthans (2000) n. 8 above, p. 306.

11 Yves L. Doz, Christopher A. Bartlett and C. K. Prahalad, "Global Competitive Pressures and Host Country Demands," *California Management Review*, Spring 1981, p. 66.

12 Alfred D. Chandler, Jr, *Strategy and Structure* (Garden City, New York: Anchor Books, Doubleday, 1966).

13 Betsy McKay, "Coke Reorganization Puts Three as Contenders for No. 2 Position," *Wall Street Journal*, July 31, 2001, p. B 2.

14 William Boston, "Can Telekom Turn a David into a Goliath," *Wall Street Journal*, June 1, 2001, pp. A 11, 13.

15 Also see Rebecca Blumenstein, "GM Is Building Plants In Developing Nations To Woo New Markets," *Wall Street Journal*, August 4, 1997, pp. A 1, 5.

16 Raghu Nath, *Comparative Management: A Regional View* (Cambridge MA: Ballinger Publishing, 1988), p. 125.

17 Tim Burt and Nikki Tait, "Ford Refines Chain of Command in US," *Financial Times*, Augusts 16, 2001, p. 13.

18 Bernard Simon, "Canada Warms to Wal-Mart," *New York Times*, September 1, 2001, pp. B 1, 3.

19 See, for example, "Japan Inc. on the Treadmill," *Economist*, June 9, 2001, pp. 63–64.

20 Bruce T. Lamont, V. Sambamurthy, Kimberly M. Ellis and Paul G. Simmonds, "The Influence of Organizational Structure on the Information Received by Corporate Strategists of Multinational Enterprises," *Management International Review*, vol. 40, no. 3 (Third Quarter 2000), pp. 231–232.

21 For some excellent insights into how Japanese companies function, see Noboru Yoshimura and Philip Anderson, *Inside the Kaisha* (Boston MA: Harvard Business School Press, 1997).

22 For an excellent contrast of American and Japanese communication problems, see William G. Ouchi, *Theory Z* (Reading MA: Addison-Wesley Publishing, 1981), pp. 33–35.

23 Jane Whitney Gibson, Richard M. Hodgetts and Charles W. Blackwell, "Cultural Variations in Nonverbal Communication," in *Proceedings of the 55th Annual Convention of the Association for Business Communication*, 1990, p. 213.

24 Hodgetts and Luthans (2000) n. 8 above, p. 212.

25 David E. Sanger, "Tokyo's Tips For New York," *New York Times Magazine*, February 6, 1994, pp. 28–29.

26 William G. Egelhoff, "Patterns of Control in US, UK, and European Multinational Corporations," *Journal of International Business Studies*, vol. 15, no. 2 (Fall 1984), pp. 81–82.

27 Ouchi (1981) n. 22 above, p. 22.

ADDITIONAL BIBLIOGRAPHY

Andersson, Ulf and Forsgren, Mats. "In Search of Centre of Excellence: Network Embeddedness and Subsidiary Roles in Multinational Corporations," *Management International Review*, vol. 40, no. 4 (Fourth Quarter 2000).

Barker, Vincent L III. "When Things Go Wrong: Organizational Failures and Breakdown," *Academy of Management Review*, vol. 25, no. 2 (April 2000).

Bartlett, Christopher A. and Ghoshal, Sumantra. "Managing Across Borders: New Organizational Responses," *Sloan Management Review*, vol. 29, no. 1 (Fall 1987).

Bartlett, Christopher A. and Ghoshal, Sumantra. "Matrix Management: Not a Structure, a Frame of Mind," *Harvard Business Review*, vol. 68, no. 4 (July/August 1990).

Bartlett, Christopher A. and Ghoshal, Sumantra, "What Is a Global Manager?" *Harvard Business Review*, vol. 70, no. 5 (September/October 1992).

Beamish, Paul W., Karavis, Lambros, Goerzen, Anthony and Lane, Christopher. "The Relationship Between Organizational Structure and Export Performance," *Management International Review*, vol. 39, no. 1 (First Quarter 1999).

Beldona, Sam, Inkpen, Andrew C. and Phatak, Arvind. "Are Japanese Managers More Long-Term Oriented than United States Managers," *Management International Review*, vol. 38, no. 3 (Third Quarter 1998).

Birkinshaw, Julian. *Entrepreneurship in the Global Firm* (London: Sage, 2000).

Doktor, Robert and Lie, John. "A Systems Theoretic Perspective upon International Organizational Behaviour: Some Preliminary Observations and Hypotheses," *Management International Review*, vol. 31, Special Issue (1991).

Geringer, J. Michael. "Strategic Determinants of Partner Selection Criteria in International Joint Ventures," *Journal of International Business Studies*, vol. 22, no. 1 (First Quarter 1991).

Ghoshal, Sumantra and Bartlett, Christopher A. "The Multinational Corporation as an Interorganizational Network," *Academy of Management Review*, vol. 15, no. 4 (October 1990).

Gregersen, Hal B., Morrison, Allen J. and Black, J. Stewart. "Developing Leaders for the Global Frontier," *Sloan Management Review*, vol. 40, no. 1 (Fall 1998).

Hargadon, Andrew, "Building an Innovation Factory," *Harvard Business Review*, vol. 78, no. 3 (May/June 2000).

Itaki, Masahiko. "Information-Processing Theory and the Multinational Enterprise," *Journal of International Business Studies*, vol. 22, no. 3 (Third Quarter 1991).

Jones, Gary K. and Davis, Herbert J. "National Culture and Innovation: Implications for Locating Global R&D Operations," *Management International Review*, vol. 40, no. 1 (First Quarter 2000).

Kogut, Bruce and Zander, Udo. "Knowledge of the Firm and the Evolutionary Theory of the Multinational Corporation," *Journal of International Business Studies*, vol. 24, no. 4 (Fourth Quarter 1993).

Kotova, Tatiana and Zaheer, Srilata. "Organizational Legitimacy Under Conditions of Complexity: The Case of the Multinational Enterprise," *Academy of Management Review*, vol. 24, no. 1 (October 1999).

Liker, Jeffrey K., "Japanese Automakers, U.S. Suppliers and Supply-Chain Superiority," *Sloan Management Review*, vol. 42, no. 1 (Fall 2000).

Lynn, Leonard H. "Remade in America: Transplanting & Transforming Japanese Management Systems," *Academy of Management Review*, vol. 25, no. 3 (July 2000).

Maljers, Floris A. "Inside Unilever: The Evolving Transnational Company," *Harvard Business Review*, vol. 70, no. 5 (September/October 1992).

Martinez, Jon I. and Jarillo, J. Carlos. "The Evolution of Research on Coordinating Mechanisms in Multinational Corporations," *Journal of International Business Studies*, vol. 20, no. 3 (Fall 1989).

Mills, D. Quinn. "The Decline and Rise of IBM," *Sloan Management Review*, vol. 37, no. 4 (Summer 1996).

Mintzberg, Henry, "Organigraphs: Drawing How Companies Really Work," *Harvard Business Review*, vol. 77, no. 5 (September/October 1999).

Parkhe, Arvind. "Interfirm Diversity, Organizational Learning, and Longevity in Global Strategic Alliances," *Journal of International Business Studies*, vol. 22, no. 4 (Fourth Quarter 1991).

Prahalad, C. K. and Oosterveld, Jan P. "Transforming Internal Governance," *Sloan Management Review*, vol. 40, no. 3 (Spring 1999).

Roehl, Tom. "The Evolution of a Manufacturing System at Toyota," *Academy of Management Review*, vol. 25, no. 2 (April 2000).

Rosenzweig, Philip M. and Singh, Jitendra V. "Organizational Environments and the Multinational Enterprise," *Academy of Management Review*, vol. 16, no. 2 (April 1991).

Roth, Kendall. "International Configuration and Coordination Archetypes for Medium-Sized Firms in Global Industries," *Journal of International Business Studies*, vol. 23, no. 3 (Third Quarter 1992).

Rugman, Alan M. and Verbeke, Alain. "A Note on the Transnational Solution and the Transaction Cost Theory of Multinational Strategic Management," *Journal of International Business Studies*, vol. 23, no. 4 (Fall 1992).

Sanyal, Rajib N. "An Empirical Analysis of the Unionization of Foreign Manufacturing Firms in the US," *Journal of International Business Studies*, vol. 21, no. 1 (First Quarter 1990).

Sullivan, Daniel. "Organization in American MNCs: The Perspective of the European Regional Headquarters," *Management International Review*, vol. 32, no. 3 (Third Quarter 1992).

Westney, Eleanor D. and Zaheer, Srilata. "The Multinational Enterprise," in Alan M. Rugman and Thomas Brewer (eds.), *The Oxford Handbook of International Business* (Oxford: Oxford University Press, 2000), pp. 349–379.

Zahra, Shaker A. "The Dynamic Firm: The Role of Technology, Strategy, Organization, and Regions," *Academy of Management Review*, vol. 24, no. 4 (October 1999).

CONTENTS

Chapter 10

Production Strategy

OBJECTIVES OF THE CHAPTER

Production strategy is critical to effective international operations. Since most goods and services have very limited lives, MNEs must continually provide new offerings, and this can be accomplished only through a well-formulated production strategy. The purpose of this chapter is to examine how MNEs carry out this process. In doing so, we will focus on the entire range of production strategies from research and development to manufacturing, to shipment, and to the final international destination. We will look at the most current approaches, including speed to market, concurrent engineering, and continuous cost reduction.

The specific objectives of this chapter are to:

1. *Examine* the role of research, development, and innovation in production strategy.
2. *Relate* some of the most critical steps in generating goods and services, including global sourcing, costing techniques, quality maintenance, effective materials handling, inventory control, and the proper emphasis on service.
3. *Describe* the nature and importance of international logistics in production strategy.
4. *Review* some of the major production strategies being used by MNEs, including strategic alliances and acquisitions.

ACTIVE LEARNING CASE

The GE production process and Six Sigma

General Electric is a multibillion-dollar, multinational corporation whose products range from 65 cent light bulbs to billion-dollar power plants. In fact, based on revenues, assets, profits, and market value, the firm was recently listed by *Fortune* magazine as number one in the world in 2000. One reason for the company's annual revenue of more than $130 billion is its ability to manage a diverse multiproduct-line operation. Much of its success can be attributed to the production-related concepts that it has employed over the last two decades.

During the 1980s, *work-out*, process mapping, and best practices were the applied concepts. Work-out is a training program designed to empower employees and to implement their problem-solving ideas. In this process a group of 40 to 100 people, picked by management from all ranks and functional areas, attend a three-day meeting. The first day consists of a manager leading the group in roughing out an agenda related to areas where productivity can be increased. Then the manager leaves and for the next $1^1/_2$ days the group breaks into teams to tackle the agenda. On the last afternoon the manager returns and one by one the team members make their proposals for improved productivity. The manager can make only three responses: agree, disagree, or ask for more information – in which case the individual must empower a team to get it by an agreed-upon date. These work-out sessions have proved extremely successful. In one case a group of workers convinced management to allow their factory to bid against an outside vendor for the right to build new protective shields for grinding machines. As a result, the GE group completed the job for $16,000 versus $96,000 for the vendor.

The second method, *process mapping*, involves the creation of a flowchart developed to show all steps, no matter how small, that are used in making or doing something. The map is analyzed for ways of eliminating steps and of saving time and money. In one case a work group was able to reorganize production, cut manufacturing time in half, and reduce inventory by $4 million.

The third method, *best practices*, consists of finding companies that do things better than GE does and then emulating them. In this process GE personnel try to answer the question: What is the secret of this other company's success? Quite often it includes such things as getting products to market faster than anyone else, or treating their suppliers like partners, or having superior inventory management. As a result of best practices, GE is now leaving executives in their jobs for longer periods of time rather than rotating them quickly through new jobs; the best practices process revealed that frequent changes create problems in new product introductions. The company is also learning how to use continuous improvement processes more effectively so that it can bring a new product into the market ahead of the competition and then work on introducing new technologies. In the past the firm would try to perfect all technologies first and then introduce the final version of the product.

These three concepts – work-out, process mapping, and best practices – were the main concepts of GE's production strategy in the 1980s. In the 1990s the dominant production concept is Six Sigma. The name originates from a statistical method for deriving near-perfect quality, equal to 3.4 defects per million operations. The Six Sigma process allows GE to measure how many "defects" there are in a given process and then systematically work to eliminate *them* to approximate "zero defects."

Six Sigma recognizes three elements: the customer, the process, and the employee. The first element, the customer, is the key to defining quality. GE uses the term "Delighting Customers" to generate a mentality whereby customer's expectation on performance, reliability, competitive prices, on-time delivery, service, clear and correct transaction processing, and other customer needs become a key factor in all processes. The second element, the process, promotes "Outside-In Thinking Quality". GE must understand the transaction life cycle from the customer's point of view and identify significant value and improvement from their perspective. Under the banner "Leadership Commitment People", the third element of Six Sigma, the employee, requires that all employees use their talents and energies to satisfy customers. All employees are trained in Six Sigma, including statistical tools, strategy, and techniques of Six Sigma quality. At the core of Six Sigma is a workforce mentality on customer quality expectations, defect reduction, process capability, variation (the customer reacts to the variance not the average results), stability of operations and designing processes to meet customer's expectations.

GE's advantage over failing conglomerates is its ability to transfer knowledge over the whole company. This can be attributed to former CEO Jack Welsh who oversaw GE's transformation from a mainly manufacturing company to a service-oriented knowledge-based company. He defined the company's culture by creating a workforce that can identify opportunities and implement changes.

Website: **www.ge.com**.

Sources: Thomas A. Stewart, "GE Keeps Those Ideas Coming," *Fortune*, August 12, 1991, pp. 40–49; Tim Smart, "What's Wrong with this Profit Picture?" *Business Week*, February 8, 1993, pp. 26–27; Zachary Schiller, "GE's Appliance Park: Rewire, or Pull the Plug," *Business Week*, February 8, 1993, p. 30; "The World Super Fifty," *Forbes*, July 27, 1998, p. 118; **www.ge.com**.

1. **How did General Electric use work-out to increase speed to market?**
2. **How has GE used Six Sigma to reduce cost and to improve quality in a consumer good? In each case, give an example.**
3. **In what way could best practices help GE to develop more effective international strategies? Explain.**

INTRODUCTION

Production management has been responsible for many new goods and services. Examples range from electronic organizers from Sharp to lightweight computers from Dell, to sleekly designed subcompacts from General Motors,[1] to DVD players from Samsung,[2] to five-star hotel operations at the Ritz-Carlton. The nature of production management in the MNE is similar in many respects to that in domestic firms. Both are concerned with the efficient use of labor and capital. Both are also interested in investing in research and development (R&D) and in organizing operations to generate successful new product lines and to increase production and service efficiency.

Backward integration The ownership of equity assets used earlier in the production cycle, such as an auto firm that acquires a steel company

Forward integration The purchase of assets or facilities that move the company closer to the customer, such as a computer manufacturer that acquires a retail chain which specializes in computer products

Horizontal integration The purchase of firms in the same line of business, such as a computer chip firm which acquires a competitor

Like domestic firms, MNEs need to organize their production management so that they can minimize operating costs through the use of logistics and inventory control. A good example is provided by Honda, which has been able to offset the rising value of the yen with cost savings in its factories, thus allowing the firm to hold the price line on many of its new cars.[3] However, pressures from host-country governments or interest groups can affect the multinational's decision making in these areas. For example, host governments often criticize resource-based MNEs for their backward, forward, and horizontal integration. **Backward integration**, which is the ownership of equity assets used earlier in the production cycle, such as an auto firm acquiring a steel company, is criticized for doing little for employment or development in the host nation. **Forward integration**, which is the purchase of assets or facilities that move the company closer to the customer, such as a computer manufacturer that acquires a retail chain that specializes in computer sales, is criticized on the basis that MNEs use this strategy to homogenize consumer tastes to the detriment of national identities. **Horizontal integration**, which is the acquisition of firms in the same line of business, such as a computer chip manufacturer that buys a competitor, is attacked for introducing similar product lines on a worldwide basis and for undercutting the existence of local firms, most of which lack the economies of scale that can be achieved by MNEs.[4]

There are similar challenges in the industrial relations area, where MNEs must take into account different labor practices and wage rates. For example, multinationals are often under pressure from host governments to use local sourcing for their supplies, to hire local workers, to train home country managers and supervisors, and to help improve the production environment in the host nation. These decisions can sometimes result in higher production costs, although most international auto firms, for example, use local suppliers and workers to offset this problem.

The financing of operations is another production-related challenge. The choice between local and international borrowing and the use of internally generated funds to minimize the cost of capital is complicated by foreign exchange risk, international tax laws, and government controls on capital. Additionally, MNEs need to know where they are on their production cost curves in each country, as well as globally, so as to exploit any cost advantages with an appropriate organizational structure. For example, as Toyota's worldwide market share began to stabilize, the firm found that it needed to become increasingly more efficient.[5]

The above examples illustrate some of the common production-related problems facing international firms. However, experienced MNEs have learned how to deal with these challenges. In doing so, they employ a wide gamut of production strategies that address research, development, innovation, global sourcing, costing techniques, and inventory control.[6] The following sections examine each of these production strategies.

RESEARCH, DEVELOPMENT, AND INNOVATION

Production strategies do *not* begin with manufacturing. In the past many MNEs focused most heavily on this aspect of operations, failing to realize that an effective production strategy begins with new product development. This conclusion gains in importance when one considers that many of today's best-selling products and services were unavailable a short time ago. Examples include notebook computers, portable cellular phones, satellite navigation devices, DVD players, broadband DSL lines, and specialized discount stores that cater to selective product lines such as home-related goods or office supplies. Many other products and services have been greatly improved over the last 10 years. Examples include antidepressant medication, automobiles, facsimile machines, hazardous waste treatment services, home delivery food services, medical diagnostic equipment, pacemakers, personal computers, photocopiers, telephones, and televisions. MNEs have come to realize that, if they are not developing new goods and services, they must be improving their current offerings. In either case the focus is on research and development (R&D) and innovation.

New product/service development

There are many new products and services, or improvements of old ones that are introduced every year.[7] Table 10.1 provides a brief list of some of them in which US MNEs excel.

There are also many foreign MNEs that depend heavily on new product and services development. Examples include Toyota, Sony, and Matsushita of Japan; Samsung, Hyundai, and LG International of South Korea; British Petroleum, Imperial Chemical Industries, and AstraZeneca of Great Britain; Volkswagen, Siemens, and Bayer of Germany; TotalFinaElf, Renault, and Peugeot of France; Volvo, Electrolux, and L. M. Ericsson of Sweden; and Nestlé, and Novartis and Roche of Switzerland. Most of these MNEs develop their own goods and services, but some of them rely on others to provide the innovative offerings. A good example is the fairly unknown Kyocera Corporation of Japan. Kyocera manufactures few products under its own name; most products are produced for other firms. For example, Kyocera manufactured some of the first laptop

Table 10.1 America's best offerings: some selected examples

Product/service	*Manufacturers*
Amusement parks	Walt Disney, Six Flags
Artificial heart valves	St Jude Medical
Bulldozers	Caterpillar
Car rental	Avis, Hertz
Communication satellites	General Electric, Hughes Aircraft
Fiber optics	Corning
CT scanners	General Electric
Fast food	Burger King, McDonald's, Pizza Hut
Industrial controls	Honeywell
Large aircraft	Boeing
Media network	CNN
Management consulting	Arthur Andersen, Accenture and McKinsey
Massive parallel supercomputers	Intel, Thinking Machines
Pianos	Steinway & Sons
Razors	Gillette
Soft drinks	Coca-Cola, PepsiCo
Ultralight utility helicopters	Robinson Helicopter

Source: Adapted from *Fortune*, Special edition, Spring/Summer, 1991, pp. 86–87. Updated, December 2001.

computers in the world; they were sold at Radio Shack under the Tandy label. The company is also the major manufacturer of VCRs for Hitachi.[8] MSX international provided much of the development for Ford's Ka, a minicar for the European market.[9] Similarly, many of Nintendo's video games are developed by outside firms that are paid a royalty on sales. In fact, many small, innovative R&D-oriented firms are springing up across Japan, Europe, and the US, and these companies are continually providing large corporations with new products.[10]

In other cases companies are forming alliances to produce and market new products jointly, while continuing to produce still others on their own. For example, Alcatel and Fujitsu are jointly developing 3G mobile systems,[11] Coca-Cola and Procter & Gamble have teamed up to develop a new worldwide juice and snack company,[12] and NEC and Thomson Multimedia are combining their R&D resources to develop plasma display panels, modules, and monitors.[13] The box "International Business Strategy in Action: When the rubber hits the road" provides an example of how the Ford and Firestone partnership broke down.

INTERNATIONAL BUSINESS STRATEGY *IN ACTION*

When the rubber hits the road: Michelin, Ford, and Firestone

Michelin Group, the original radial tire maker, came to North America in the late1960s. Now the French-owned company is the largest tire producer there with 40 per cent of the US market and 96 per cent brand awareness. In Europe, it has 67 per cent of the market. Worldwide it is one of two market leaders with 19.4 per cent market share. Bridgestone, its largest competitor, holds the same market share. Michelin had revenues of 15.4 billion euros in 2000.

The experience of Michelin Tire in expanding to North America illustrates the problem of internationalizing from one part of the triad to another. In 1969, Michelin decided to locate a new plant in Nova Scotia, Canada. The decision was based on the low degree of financial risk resulting from Canadian government tax concessions and direct grants for the project. But, most important, Nova Scotia was a long way from the head offices of the giant US tire producers, in Akron, Ohio. Michelin was reluctant to confront the US tire industry head on, even with its superior technology (at the time radials lasted twice as long as the steel belted tires made by US producers). However, Michelin overlooked the political power of stakeholders like the US government and the US tire industry – and their influence on Canada.

The location in Nova Scotia was based on several country-specific advantages – Canadian financial support ($85 million in loans and grants), importing and exporting benefits (drawbacks and duty-free trade), and a lack of political risk. In addition, Michelin possessed firm-specific advantages (R&D, technology, quality control, production, marketing, management and financing), which made production in Nova Scotia advantageous. Rather than evaluating alternative locations (Quebec, the US), Michelin forged ahead into the Nova Scotian market without sufficient strategic planning.

The choice of Nova Scotia as the location followed from a chance airplane contact in 1967 between the president of Michelin and a representative of Industrial Estates (IEL, the development agency for the Province of Nova Scotia), who stressed the advantages of such a location in serving both US and Canadian markets. Michelin expected to export tires from Canada to the US. There was a very low tariff on such trade, and the US tariffs on imports of tires from Europe were very high.

Michelin's rapid movement into Nova Scotia resulted in retaliation from the US government and a new prohibitive tariff to protect US industry. Michelin's error came in failing to evaluate its alternatives and in not anticipating any retaliation. In February 1973, the US government imposed countervailing duties to the IEL loan of $50 million at a rate of 6 per cent, seeing the loan as an export subsidy. An appeal was heard in 1982, after which the US import tax was reduced but the damage was done. Michelin may as well have entered the US market head on, as the US competitors attacked its presence in Nova Scotia anyway. But today there are several big Michelin plants in the US, and their radials are now being used on many US cars. The Michelin experience illustrates the danger of foreign entry without a long-term triad insight.

Michelin eventually bought Uniroyal and B. F. Goodrich in 1991, some 20 years after its initial entry to North America. At a stroke it achieved massive economies of scale by doubling its sales in North America. It also has an alliance with Goodyear to share R&D costs. Michelin is now a key supplier to original equipment manufacturers (OEMs) such as Peugeot, Citroen, Toyota, Honda, General Motors, and Ford. It also sells business to consumer (B2C) through distributors such as Sears, Wal-Mart, and FeuVert. Its global competitors include Firestone and Pirelli.

In Asia, Michelin is still a minor player compared with Japanese rival Sumitomo/Firestone. It only has 6 per cent of the market in Japan, and little elsewhere in Asia. Michelin has, however, entered into a $200 million joint venture with the Shanghai Tyre and Rubber Company (STRC), the largest tire company in China, to sell its products in China.

Arrayed against Michelin in North America are North American giant Goodyear and Japanese-owned Bridgestone-Firestone. Goodyear has a long-standing relationship with General Motors. Firestone was a supplier to Ford for 97 years until they split in May 2001. This was due to the pressure of litigation involving some 200 deaths and over 750 accidents allegedly due to the separating of tread on Firestone tires on Ford Explorer SUVs. It was found subsequently in a federal study that American cars typically have under-inflated tires. On the Ford Explorer a burst tire can have fatal effects. Ford blamed Firestone and paid to replace 14 million tires on its SUVs. A lot of rubber was burned.

In Venezuela, a similar situation arose with approximately 400 accidents and 100 deaths resulting from locally made tires. Both Ford and Firestone are to be fined for failing to adhere a nylon layer that is required to deal with the high temperatures and bad roads in the country. Ford accused Firestone of failing to meet its own quality standards and to adapt to the Venezuelan market. It later became known in North America that Ford had been aware of other defects in tires in hot countries and had recalled tires in Saudi Arabia and reported troubles in Thailand.

Websites: **www.michelin.com**; **www.michelin.fr**; **www.goodyear.com**; **www.gm.com**; **www.sears.com**; **www.walmart.com**; **www.feuvert.fr**; **www.peugeot.com**; **www.toyota.com**; **www.citroen.com**; **www.honda.com**; **www.ford** and **www.bridgestone-firestone.com**.

Sources: "Tyre Straits," *Economist*, August 2, 2001; Dan Ackman, "Bridgestone Says Don't Tread on Me," *Forbes.com*, May 5, 2001; Michelin, *Annual Report*, 2000; Alan M. Rugman, Donald Lecraw and Laurence Booth, *International Business: Firm and Environment* (New York: McGraw Hill, 1985).

Table 10.2 **The cost of arriving late to market (and still be on budget)**

If the company is late to market by:					
6 months	5 months	4 months	3 months	2 months	1 month
Gross potential profit is reduced by:					
–33%	–25%	–18%	12%	–7%	–3%
If time to market is improved profit will go up by:					
11.9%	9.3%	7.3%	5.7%	4.3%	3.1%
For revenues of $25 million, annual gross profit will increase by:					
$400,000	$350,000	$300,000	$250,000	$200,000	$150,000
For revenues of $100 million, annual gross profit will increase by:					
$1,600,000	$1,400,000	$1,200,000	$1,000,000	$800,000	$600,000

Source: *Academy of Management Executive*, 'The New Competitors: They Think in Terms of "Speed-to-Market"' by Joseph T. Vesey. Copyright 1991 by Academy of Management. Reproduced with permission of Academy of Management in the format textbook via Copyright Clearance Center.

Speed to market

One of the major manufacturing challenges facing MNEs is the speed with which they develop and get new products to market.[14] In recent years many firms have found that a "speed to market" strategy can be extremely profitable. Table 10.2 provides some data to support this statement. Notice from the table that a company that enters the market one month ahead of the competition can increase annual gross profit by $150,000 on a product that generates $25 million and $600,000 on a product that generates $100 million. Simply put, by carefully designing the product and getting it out the door, the company can dramatically increase profitability.

There are a number of steps that MNEs have taken to ensure early delivery of their products. For example, Cisco Systems has outsourced the production of routers and switches to Flextronics, a contract electronics manufacturer. Flextronics receives an electronic order from Cisco Systems, manufactures the product under the Cisco brand, and then delivers it directly to the customers.[15] Sun Microsystems has eliminated its New Products Group, which had centralized control for production development, and made the group part of the manufacturing department. Now both groups work together in designing and manufacturing new products. Next Inc., founded by Steve Jobs of Apple fame, has streamlined the relationship between design and production so that the plant can manufacture a totally new circuit board design in 20 minutes. BMW has combined engineering, development, and production planning in bringing new cars to market in record time.[16]

Time-to-market accelerators
Factors that help reduce bottlenecks and errors and ensure product quality and performance

Modular integrated robotized system (MIRB)
A software-based production process that relies entirely on robots

Concurrent engineering
The process of having design, engineering, and manufacturing people working together to create a product, in contrast to working in a sequential manner

The strategic emphasis is on increasing speed by developing **time-to-market accelerators**, which are factors that help to reduce bottlenecks and errors and to ensure product quality and performance. These accelerators will vary from firm to firm, but they all produce the same results. For example, in 2000, Pirelli, the French tire maker, unveiled its **modular integrated robotized system (MIRB)**. MIRB allows the entire production system to be robotized. Small and flexible, MIRB allows smaller batches to be produced in different locations, potentially locating them next to Pirelli's industrial customers.[17]

In the past many MNEs placed the bulk of their production attention on the manufacturing side of the operation. However, recent research shows that the best way to reduce defective products and to speed delivery is by placing the greatest attention on product design and planning of operations. This is accomplished through what is known as **concurrent engineering**, which involves design, engineering, and manufacturing people working together to create and build the product. Concurrent engineering is

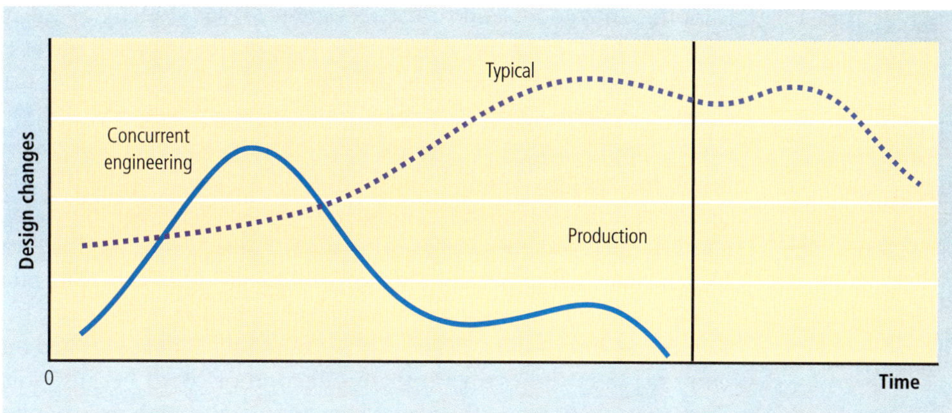

Figure 10.1 Design changes using concurrent engineering versus using a typical approach

Source: *Academy of Management Executive*, 'The New Competitors: They Think in Terms of "Speed-to-Market"' by Joseph T. Vesey. Copyright 1991 by Academy of Management. Reproduced with permission of Academy of Management in the format textbook via Copyright Clearance Center.

useful for two reasons. First, if the product is carefully designed, there are fewer changes needed later on and the good can be swiftly brought to market. (Figure 10.1 provides an illustrative example.) Second, the costs associated with changes increase as the product gets closer to completion; that is, it is almost twice as expensive to correct a problem during production than during product design.

Once a product or service has been planned out, the MNE's attention will turn to production. This strategy is focused very heavily on minimizing costs and increasing quality and productivity.

Active learning check 

Review your answer to Active Learning Case question 1 and make any changes you like. Then compare your answer with the one below.

1. How did General Electric use work-out to increase speed to market?

The primary way that GE used work-out to increase speed to market was by looking for ways to eliminate production bottlenecks and to streamline operations. The strategy of work-out asked the participants: How can we change the operation so that we can get more done in less time? The workers who were familiar with the operations often had a wealth of information to share, and this was sometimes the first time that anyone has asked them their opinions. They were delighted to offer suggestions and recommendations. As a result, the company produced more products in less time than ever before.

GENERATION OF GOODS AND SERVICES

Most people think of the production process as one in which physical goods are produced. However, the process can also be used in generating services, and quite often the two are interlinked.[18] For example, General Motors manufactures cars but the company also offers auto maintenance and repair services[19] and Boeing builds aircraft and services them as well. In other cases services are primary. For example, the Hilton Corporation offers hotel accommodations, Hertz and Avis lease cars, and CNN provides international news coverage.

Sometimes goods and/or services are provided directly by the MNE; other times the firm will have an arrangement with outside firms or suppliers (some of them being direct competitors) to assist in this process. For example, other firms make some of the Hewlett-Packard printers, but HP has its name put on the units and assumes responsibility for marketing the machines.[20] Service organizations follow a similar strategy. Some airlines purchase their in-flight food from companies like Marriott, and some rely on aircraft maintenance firms such as Ryder to service their craft. Many motels subcontract their food service to companies that specialize in this area, including fast-food franchisors such as McDonald's and Burger King. So there is often a mix of product/service strategies at work when generating goods and services. The following discussion examines some of the most important functions that are carried out in this process. The emphasis is most heavily on the production of goods because some of the areas under discussion do not lend themselves to services, although one that does is global sourcing, a primary area of consideration in production strategy.

Global sourcing

Global sourcing
The use of suppliers anywhere in the world, chosen on the basis of their efficiency

In some cases MNEs will produce all the goods and services that they need. However, oftentimes they will use **global sourcing**, by calling upon those suppliers who can provide the needed output more efficiently regardless of where they are geographically located.[21]

There are a number of reasons why global sourcing has become important. The most obvious one is cost. If General Motors (GM) wants to be price competitive in the EU (European Union), one strategy is to build and ship cars from Detroit to Europe at a price equal to, or less than, that charged by EU competitors. Since this is not possible, GM uses overseas suppliers and assembly plants to build much of what it sells in Europe. In deciding who will provide these parts and supplies, the company uses global sourcing, as do other MNEs.

It is important to remember that not all global sourcing is provided by outside suppliers. Some MNEs own their own source of supply or hold an equity position in a supplier. This relationship does not guarantee that the supplier will get the MNE's business on every bid. However, if the supplier is unable to match the cost or quality performance of competitive suppliers, the MNE will eventually terminate the relationship. So there is a great deal of pressure on the supplier to develop and maintain state-of-the-art production facilities. Additionally, since the supplier works closely with the MNE, the company knows how its multinational client likes things done and is able to operate smoothly with the MNE's design and production people.

In recent years some giant MNEs have taken equity positions in a number of different suppliers. Japanese multinationals are an excellent example. These firms often have a network of parts suppliers, subcontractors, and capital equipment suppliers who can be called on. Figure 10.2 provides an illustration for NEC, the giant electronics MNE. A close look at the figure shows that NEC's network of suppliers handle much of the supply needs.

At the same time these suppliers often provide goods and services to other firms. This helps them to maintain their competitive edge by forcing them to innovate, adapt, and remain cost effective. If these suppliers are in similar or complementary industries, as in the case of NEC's suppliers, then technological innovations or revolutionary changes in manufacturing processes will be quickly accepted or copied by others. So the close proximity of the suppliers coupled with their business relationships helps to ensure that they attain and hold positions as world-class suppliers, and this advantage carries over to the customers, who gain both innovative ideas and high-quality, low-

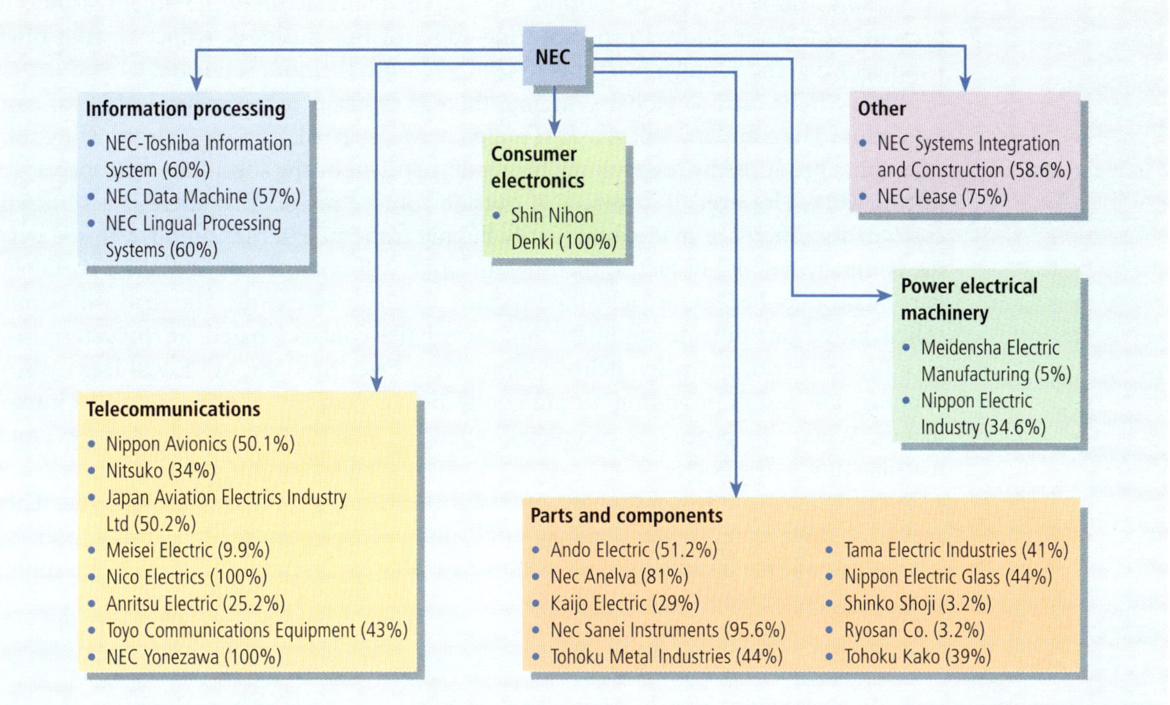

Figure 10.2 **NEC's supply group**

Note: With percentage of supplier owned by NEC in parentheses.

Source: Reprinted by permission of *Harvard Business Review*. Exhibit reported in 'Computer and the Coming of the US Keiretsu' by Charles H. Ferguson, July–August, 1990.

cost supplies. Commenting on the benefit of these domestically based suppliers, Porter notes:

> Perhaps the most important benefit of home-based suppliers . . . is the *process of innovation and upgrading*. Competitive advantage emerges from close working relationships between world-class suppliers and the industry. Suppliers help firms perceive new methods and opportunities to apply new technology. Firms gain quick access to information, to new ideas and insights, and to supplier innovations. They have the opportunity to influence suppliers' technical efforts, as well as to serve as test sites for development work. The exchange of R&D and joint problem solving lead to faster and more efficient solutions. Suppliers also tend to be a conduit for transmitting information and innovations from firm to firm. Through this process, the pace of innovation within the entire national industry is accelerated. All these benefits are enhanced if suppliers are located in proximity to firms, shortening the communication lines.[22]

A good example is the leather footwear industry in Italy. Manufacturers regularly interact with leather suppliers, designers, and producers of other leather goods. As a result, leather footwear manufacturers are extremely knowledgeable regarding industry technology, production techniques, fashion trends, and supply sources.

These advantages also help to explain why many US suppliers are going international. By setting up operations near world-class competitors, these suppliers find it easier to monitor developments, to remain alert to changes in technology and production processes, and to maintain state-of-the-art facilities.[23] In fact, when manufacturers expand operations to another country, it is common to find their major suppliers setting up operations nearby in order to continue serving the manufacturer. The other reason is to prevent local competitors from capturing some of this business, which is what often happens when the supplier attempts to compete from the home country.

When MNEs turn to global sourcing, there is typically a hierarchical order of consideration. The company will give first preference to internal sources, such as having subassemblies produced by the manufacturing department or the subsidiary that specializes in this work. However, if a review of outside sources reveals that there is a sufficient cost/quality difference that would justify buying from an external supplier, this is what the company will do. In fact, sometimes an MNE will not attempt to make a particular part or product because it lacks the expertise to do so efficiently. The firm will simply solicit bids from outside suppliers and award the contract based on predetermined specifications (price, quality, delivery time, etc.). Over time the MNE will learn which suppliers are best at providing certain goods and services and will turn to them immediately. When this process is completed, attention will then be focused on the actual manufacture of the goods.

Recently, environmentalists have reviewed the global supply chains of MNEs. They argue that all suppliers to an MNE should follow environmentally sensitive policies, i.e. be "green". The box "International Business Strategy in Action: Greening the supply chain" examines this issue.

INTERNATIONAL BUSINESS STRATEGY *IN ACTION*

Greening the supply chain

The supply chain is well known in the automobile sector, where most tier one auto parts suppliers have adopted ISO 9000 quality standards over the last decade in order to remain as key suppliers to the OEMs. Less well known is that the supply chain has also been used to introduce environmentally friendly "green" standards. This occurs through the implementation of ISO 14001 standards.

A successful example of this is in Mexico. Despite many NGOs arguing that Mexico is a pollution haven, objective scientific research by Rugman, Kirton, and Soloway (1999) shows that the use of ISO 14000 green processes has unambiguously raised environmental standards in Mexico. When auto suppliers, as well as auto assemblers, have to change their engineering processes to meet ISO 14001 standards in the US and Canada, these new manufacturing processes raise overall environmental performance in Mexico, even if the Mexican government is lagging in enforcing ISO 14000 standards. The "foreign-owned" firms bring in new technologies to poorer countries, including green technologies.

This also occurs in the retail/food sector. A study of the UK retail sector in 2001 found that all along the supply chain firms engage in green purchasing. This occurred across at least three sectors: grocery retailing; furniture; and building materials. The green purchasing was helped by EU environmental regulations. These have led to basic changes in environmental management systems (EMS) of retail companies. The EMS is closely linked to the Denning model of continuous process improvements of quality standards.

The supply chain, or value chain of Porter (1985), typically consists of: supplier management; purchasing; materials management; production scheduling; facilities planning; logistics; and consumer services.

Best practices in UK retail were B&Q (part of the Kingfisher Group) and The Body Shop. Both of these retailers require that their suppliers meet EU environmental standards.

In general, UK grocery retailers (like Sainsbury's, Safeway, Asda) were more engaged in green purchasing than UK furniture and building materials retailers, although both B&Q and The Body Shop had also developed some green capabilities.

Websites: ***www.kingfisher.co.uk***; ***www.the-body-shop.com***; ***www.sainsbury.co.uk***; ***www.safeway.com*** and ***www.asda.co.uk***.

Sources: Linnett M. Mabuku, "Green Purchasing and Corporate Strategy: A Case Study of UK Retail Firms and their International Supply Chains", M.Sc. Dissertation, Environmental Change Institute, University of Oxford, September 2001; Alan M. Rugman, John Kirton and Julie Soloway, *Environmental Regulations and Corporate Strategy* (Oxford: Oxford University Press, 1999); Michael Porter, *Competitive Advantage* (New York: Free Press, 1985).

Manufacturing of goods

MNEs face a variety of concerns in manufacturing goods and services. Primary among these are cost,[24] quality, and efficient production systems.[25]

Cost

Multinationals seek to control their costs by increasing the efficiency of their production processes. Often this means utilizing new, improved technology such as new machinery and equipment. Although these purchases can be expensive, they may be the best way to increase productivity and to lower costs and thus maintain competitive advantage. A good example is provided by the automobile industry in Brazil, which is the heart of the South American automobile market. The country is host to 13 auto makers, including DaimlerChrysler, Volkswagen, and Ford, that are investing over $20 billion to update Brazilian plants to modular manufacturing. **Modular manufacturing** allows suppliers of parts to take on part of the assembly. Dana Corporation, which has set up shop near a Chrysler factory in the city of Curitiba, is now responsible for the assembly of the Dakota's basic skeleton, which represents approximately 30 per cent of the total cost of production. Once this skeleton reaches Chrysler, it is mounted with an engine and a body. Entire assembly lines had to be rebuilt to accommodate this process. Volkswagen, Ford, and General Motors are also developing similar assembly plants to test their efficiency for future implementation to their other factories.[26]

Modular manufacturing
A manufacturing process that consists of modules that can be easily adapted to fit changing demand

A second approach is to tap low-cost labor sources. A good example is the *maquiladora* industry (as discussed in Chapter 6) that has sprung up in Mexico just across the US border. Hundreds of US plants have been established in this area. Examples include TRW Inc., which has a factory where workers assemble seat belts, and Mattel, which has a plant where workers turn out Barbie-doll houses and Disney teething rings.[27] Labor costs in these facilities are less than 20 per cent of those of similar workers in the US. Also, because this is a free trade zone, US duties are levied on the imports only to the extent of the value added in Mexico, so low wage rates in Mexico help to keep down the import duty.

A third approach is the development of new methods used to cut costs.[28] For example, in the US, it is typical for a firm to calculate selling price after a new product is developed. If the price is judged to be too high, the product is sent back to the drawing board to be reworked or the company accepts smaller profit on the product. In Japan, a different system has been introduced (see Figure 10.3). The Japanese begin by determining the target cost of the product *before* going into design, engineering, and supplier pricing. The latter groups then work to bring the product in at the desired price. This unique cost-management system is helping Japanese firms to cut costs and to undersell competitors.[29]

A fourth method that is gaining popularity with MNEs is that of costing products not on an individual basis but as part of a portfolio of related goods. Instead of evaluating the expenses of developing one new soft drink, for example, a company will look at the costs and revenues associated with the entire line of beverages. Coca-Cola of Japan provides an example. Every year there are more than 1,000 new soft drinks, fruit drinks, and cold coffees introduced into the Japanese market. Ninety per cent of them fail, but this does not stop Coke from introducing approximately one new product a month. From a cost accounting standpoint, this is not a profitable strategy. However, as one Coke executive in Japan puts it, "We know that some of these . . . products will survive only a month or two, but our competitors have them, so we have to have them."[30] As a result, Japan is Coca-Cola's most profitable market and the company sells a variety of non-carbonated drinks to complement its main brand.[31]

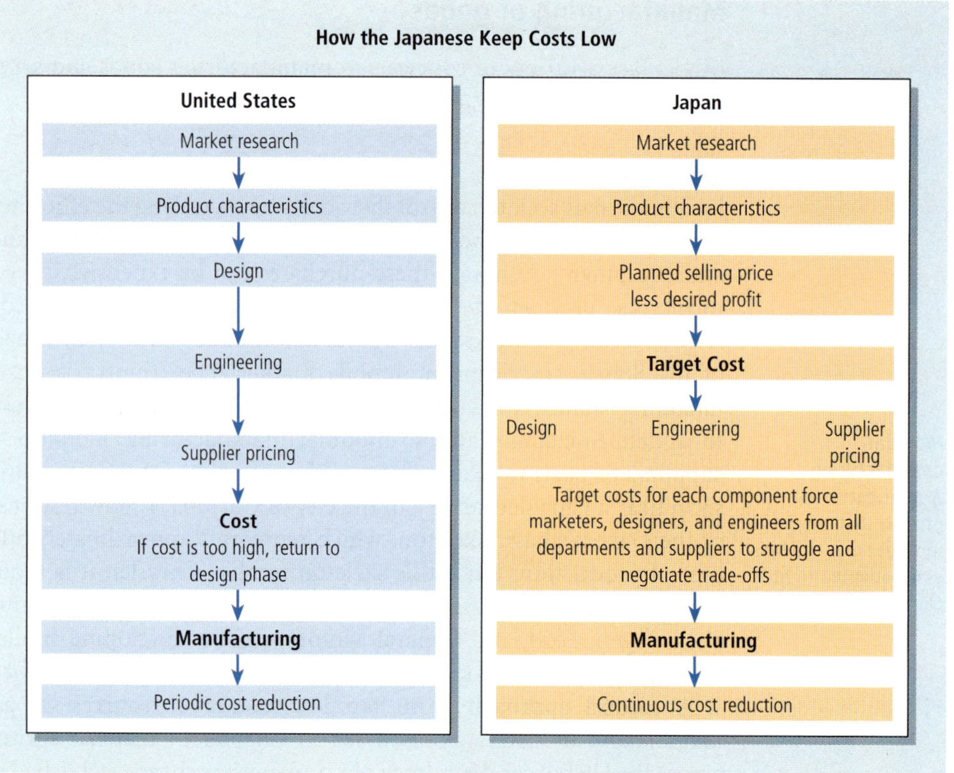

Figure 10.3 Cost reduction approaches: the US versus Japan

Source: Ford S. Worthy, "Japan's Smart Secret Weapon," *Fortune*, August 12, 1991, p. 73.

Quality

For well over a decade quality has been one of the major criteria for business success.[32] As the president of an international consulting firm recently put it, "Products are expected to be nearly perfect."[33] Nowhere is this more clearly reflected than in the auto industry, where the Japanese have garnered a large share of the international market by using what is called ***kaizen***, or continuous improvement.[34] A good example is Toyota Motors, which has continually worked to reduce costs and to improve performance.[35] One way in which the company has achieved this goal is partly through large R&D expenditures. Another important factor has been meticulous design, engineering, and production processes that ensure a proper fit of all parts and overall durability of the unit.[36] In recent years US auto manufacturers (particularly Ford) have also been successful in improving their quality and, as a result, have gained market share. European car makers today are also heavily focused on quality, aware that the Japanese are a major threat to their markets.[37]

Kaizen
A Japanese term which means continuous improvement

Another good example is provided by auto suppliers such as Monroe Auto Equipment, which has continually increased its product quality. Monroe is a major supplier of parts in North America. The company also does a thriving international business, including Ford, Chrysler, and Nissan in Europe and Toyota in Japan.

Other excellent examples of MNEs that have succeeded because of a strong focus on quality include such lesser-known firms as Stanley Works, the WD-40 Co., and A. T. Cross. Stanley Works manufactures tape measures in Asia and then has the accuracy of samples checked by sophisticated laser computers back in New Britain, Connecticut, before selling them worldwide. Stanley Works has also developed a host of other high quality products from double-toothed saws that cut on both the upstroke and the downstroke, for the Asian market, to hammers without claws for carpenters in Central Europe who prefer to use pliers to pull out bent nails, to levels shaped like elongated trapezoids, which the French market prefers.

The WD-40 Co. of San Diego manufactures WD-40, a water-displacing lubricant that fights rust, cleans heel marks from linoleum and walls, and provides a variety of other services around the house. Car mechanics use it to loosen sticky valves and to remove moisture from balky carburetors; handymen apply it to frozen locks and screws. Today the blue-and-yellow spray can be found in stores throughout the world, where it enjoys fanatic customer loyalty. WD-40 is a best-seller in Great Britain and is rapidly gaining market share throughout Europe and Asia.[38]

A. T. Cross of Providence, Rhode Island, has been manufacturing mechanical pens and pencils for almost 150 years. The units are assembled by hand and "every one of the company's hourly employees is a quality control expert who is responsible for checking the tolerances of the engraved grooves to within one ten-thousandth of an inch and for detecting nearly microscopic scratches or the slightest clotting of ink on a pen ball".[39] A. T. Cross's product quality is so high that, despite a lifetime guarantee, less than 2 per cent are ever returned for repair. Today the company's pens and pencils are one of the most popular US-made gifts in Japan.[40]

Production systems

Production system
A group of related activities designed to create value

A **production system** is a group of related activities designed to create value. In the generation of goods and services this system includes location, layout, and materials handling.

Location Location is important because of its impact on production and distribution costs. Many MNEs have found that governments (national and local) are willing to provide tax breaks or other financial incentives to encourage them to set up operations. Accompanying considerations include the availability and cost of labor, raw materials, water, and energy and the development of the country's transportation and communication systems. As noted earlier, many suppliers set up operations near their major customers. So Ford Motor has built up an integrated production network in Western Europe (see Map on Ford Fiesta production network). Ford suppliers are part of this production network in order to maintain their business relationship. Location is also important to service enterprises because they usually require face-to-face contact with their customers. Hotels and airlines are typical examples. Personal service firms such as those of accountants, lawyers, and management consultants also fall into this category.[41]

Layout Plant layout is important because of its impact on efficiency. For example, most auto producers use an assembly line layout in which the workers remain at their station and, as the cars move past them, they perform the necessary functions such as installing radios, air conditioners, interior trim, and so on. In the case of Volvo, the employees work in small teams to build an entire car and the plant is laid out to accommodate this work flow.[42] In other manufacturing settings, however, worldwide competitive firms tend to use U-shaped-cell flow lines because these are more efficient. Schonberger, an internationally known manufacturing expert, has noted that U-shaped production designs enable one person to tend several workstations and to increase the speed with which materials can be delivered and defective parts can be reworked.[43]

In service organizations the layout will vary widely, although it appears to be universal in use. Most hotels, regardless of the country, have the check-in and check-out areas in the same place as such support groups as the bellhops, concierge, and cashier. In fast-food

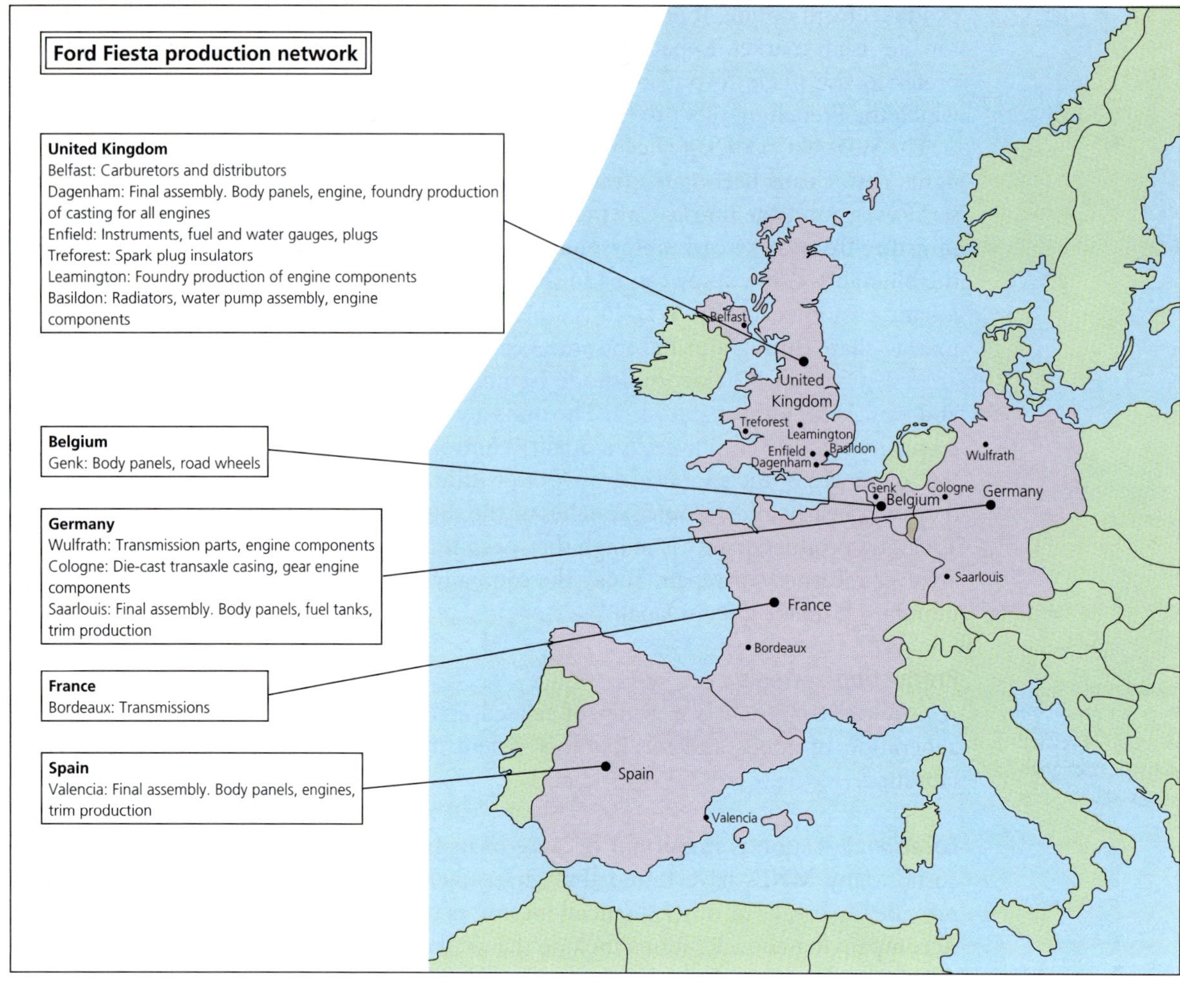

units the food preparation area is situated so that the personnel can quickly serve both in-unit and drive-through customers. In movie houses the concession area is located in the lobby and the projection room at the back of the theater.

Materials handling
The careful planning of when, where, and how much inventory will be available to ensure maximum production efficiency

Process mapping
A flow charting of every step that goes into producing a product

Materials handling **Materials handling** involves the careful planning of when, where, and how much inventory will be available to ensure maximum production efficiency. Part of this is resolved through careful inventory control processes. Part of it is handled when the production layout is determined. For example, General Electric uses **process mapping**, a flowchart that shows every small step that goes into producing a product. As a result, the company is able to study every step in an operation and determine those that are redundant or that can be streamlined. Consequently, the company has been able to reduce work time on some jobs by as much as 50 per cent.[44]

Inventory control

Just-in-time (JIT) inventory
The delivery of parts and supplies just as they are needed

Inventory control has received a great deal of attention in recent years because a well-designed inventory strategy can have dramatic effects on the bottom line.[45] One of the most popular concepts has been **just-in-time inventory** (**JIT** for short), which is based on delivering parts and supplies just as they are needed. If this concept were carried to the extreme, it would mean that manufacturers would not need to store materials because suppliers would be delivering them just in time for shipment to the factory floor.

JIT is an important concept that has been adopted by MNEs throughout the world. However, the degree of use will vary based on the product and the company's production strategy. For example, the Big Three US auto makers use JIT to keep inventory to a minimum. In Japan, firms like Toyota have taken the concept even further and apply it to the way airlines handle reservations: supply is matched directly to demand. Dealers order directly from the factory, which means that customers can get their built-to-order car in 7 to 10 days.

One of the major problems with JIT is that its success rests heavily on the quality and reliability of the suppliers. In Japan, where MNEs often have an equity position in these companies, suppliers will go out of their way to meet the demands of their partners. However, in the US and Europe, most suppliers are independent businesses that work under a contract relationship, so that the bonds are often not as strong between the two parties. This helps to explain why Toyota, which buys US-made parts for cars made in the US, also keeps Japanese-made parts on hand as insurance against defective US materials.[46]

A second problem with JIT is that, while many firms find it works well in managing delivery of parts to the assembly line, few have been able to apply the concept to the entire production process. Most firms still manufacture and ship their output to dealers to sell, in contrast to Toyota's approach of matching supply and demand before producing.

One of the most important things to remember about JIT is that it involves strong support from the workers and the suppliers. Everyone must be operating in unison. If the workers are slow, there will be excess inventory on hand; if the supplier is late, the workers will be sitting by idly.

Demand-Flow™ Technology (DFT)
A production process that is flexible to demand changes

Demand-Flow™ Technology (DFT) is a production process that allows for flexible changes in the middle stages of production. Typically used to produce standardized assembly products, such as computers, DFT permits quick reactions to changes in demand and technology. A surge of demand for Pentium IV computers, for instance, would immediately shift inputs from other computers to be combined with Pentium IV chips to respond to demand. This virtually eliminates inventories.[47] Intermec, a bar code printer and hand held scanner company, reduced inventory by 50 per cent after implementing DFT. The company was also able to consolidate five different printer lines into one flexible mixed-model line, decreasing the amount of manufacturing floor space required by 20 per cent.[48]

Developing a strong service orientation

As noted earlier, many products have a service element associated with them. Sometimes this element is more important than the product itself. For example, many people will not purchase a car or home appliance unless it can be easily serviced. Service is also important when choosing a bank, insurance agent, lawyer, or doctor. Many of the ideas that we have discussed in this section, including sourcing, cost, and quality are also key factors when shopping for services. In addressing this area, MNEs will do two things: (1) consider whether their strategy needs to be oriented toward a product, a service, or a combination of the two, and (2) determine the ideal degree of service to provide.

Determining the product/service balance

Some outputs lend themselves to a strong production orientation; others require much more attention to service. Figure 10.4 offers an illustration. While the figure is designed

Product-dominated businesses	Equally balanced	Service-dominated businesses
Farm produce (corn, wheat, etc.)	Aircraft manufacturing	Advertising agency
Home construction	Fast food unit	Theater production
Auto production	TV network	Teaching

Figure 10.4 **Product- and service-dominated businesses**

more as a point of reference than as a factual source that addresses every firm in the respective industry, it is evident that some MNEs need to have a strong product-dominated focus while others benefit most from a service orientation. A good example is offered by aircraft manufacturers that must be concerned with both ends of the continuum. Olympus and Pentax, both manufacturers of flexible endoscopic equipment, provide another example. To develop their brand names in Latin America, these companies offer medical professionals the surgical training necessary to use their equipment. Since after-sale service is also an important consideration for prospective buyers, which include hospitals, all major endoscope manufacturers have service stations in the region.

On the other hand, there are manufactured products that require far less service than they used to need. A good example is photocopiers. Manufacturers of these machines have improved the quality of their product so substantially that many units are now sold on the basis of price. Service is no longer a major factor because everyone's product is of such high quality.

Knowing whether to sell on the basis of product or service (or a combination of the two) is critical to the success of many MNEs. A mistake at this point can result in emphasis on the wrong sales factors.

Providing the right amount of service

Once the MNE has determined the proper balance of product and service domination, it will evaluate the specific type of service that is warranted. This is particularly important because many MNEs find that the strategy used in their own country does not work overseas. A good example is the Japanese approach to retail services.[49] The amount of personal service that is provided in Japan would surprise many Westerners. For example, auto dealers typically provide pick-up and delivery for repair service customers. They also make new car sales calls to customers' homes. In department stores, it is common to find executives and sales clerks alike line up to bow to the first customers in the store. Japanese banks often help their customers to sell or buy homes, to find distributors for merchandise, and to provide them with tax advice.

While these services help Japanese companies to maintain customer satisfaction, research has found that they are of little value to doing business in other countries. For example, Japanese banks in the US have discovered that US customers want only a limited amount of quality service; they prefer quantity and efficiency in the form of a variety of different services offered at low prices. As a result, Japanese banks here offer the same types of services as do other US banks. Would they be more successful if they changed this strategy and tried to emulate the approach used back home? Given the nature of the US market, they believe that this would be a mistake. The lesson is clear: When competing in terms of service, one must match the competition but not exceed it unless the customer is willing to pay for this service. In the US, the banking customer is not willing.[50]

Active learning check

Review your answer to Active Learning Case question 2 and make any changes you like. Then compare your answer with the one below.

2. How has GE used Six Sigma to reduce cost and to improve quality in a consumer good? In each case, give an example.

Six Sigma allows GE to use process mapping to reduce cost by identifying those activities that can be eliminated or combined in the production process. For example, can an individual who is performing one assembly line task take on other tasks and thus reduce the number of people needed for producing the product? Can inventory be ordered and delivered in smaller amounts, thus making greater use of just-in-time? Consideration of these types of questions can help to reduce cost. In improving product quality, the work group can examine how well all parts of the product fit together, examine the durability of the unit, and look for additional ways of testing the product to ensure that it measures up to quality standards.

INTERNATIONAL LOGISTICS

International logistics The designing and managing of a system to control the flow of materials and products throughout the organization

International logistics is the designing and managing of a system to control the flow of materials and products throughout the firm. This includes the inflow of materials, movement through the production process, and flow out to the wholesale/retail firm or final consumer. International logistics is an important area of strategic consideration because these expenses "currently comprise between 10% and 25% of the total landed cost of an international order".[51] The materials management aspect of international logistics has already been discussed. The following discussion examines three other key topics: transportation, packaging, and storage.

Container ships Vessels used to carry standardized containers that can be simply loaded onto a carrier and then unloaded at their destination without any repackaging of the contents of the containers

Unconventional cargo vessels Vessels used for shipping oversized and unusual cargoes

Roll-on-roll-off (RORO) vessels Ocean-going ferries that can carry trucks that drive onto built-in ramps and roll off at the point of debarkation

Lighter aboard ship (LASH) vessel Barges stored on a ship and lowered at the point of destination

Transportation

In examining international logistics, we will focus on the primary modes of transportation: ocean and air. The others – rail, pipeline, and motor carrier – are of importance in some regions (such as the EU), but they are not as commonly used in moving goods from an MNE's plant to their final destination. Moreover, their use is highly dependent on the infrastructure of the country, that is, the extensiveness and quality of the nation's road system and railroad network. In many non-triad countries the infrastructure is poor and the MNE's use of them is greatly limited.

Ocean shipping

International firms can choose from a fairly wide variety of ocean carriers. The three most common carriers are conventional container ships, cargo vessels, and roll-on-roll-off (RORO) vessels. **Container ships** are used to carry standardized containers that can be simply loaded onto the carrier and then unloaded at their destination, without any repackaging of the contents of the containers. **Unconventional cargo vessels** are used for shipping oversized and unusual cargoes. **Roll-on-roll-off (RORO) vessels** are ocean-going ferries that can carry trucks that drive onto built-in ramps and roll off at the point of debarkation. A carrier similar to the RORO is the **lighter aboard ship (LASH) vessel**, which consists of barges that are stored on the ship and lowered at the point of destination. These individual barges can then operate on inland waterways.

One of the major problems in planning an ocean shipping strategy is the limitations caused by the lack of ports and port services. In developing countries, for example, seaports sometimes lack the equipment necessary to load or unload container cargo, thus limiting the country's ability to export and import. In recent years a number of third world countries have been working to improve their ports so that they can become more active in the international trade arena.

Air shipping

Most countries of the world have airports that can accommodate air freight. The problem with this mode of transportation is its high cost. So, although international air freight has grown dramatically over the last 30 years, it still accounts for less than 1 per cent of the total volume of international shipments. This transportation mode is used in trade more commonly among industrialized nations than any others, and it is usually restricted to high-value items which must reach their destination quickly.

A number of developments have occurred over the past couple of decades that have helped to increase the amount of air shipments. These include more efficient ground facilities, larger aircraft, and better marketing of these services to shippers. In particular, the development by aircraft manufacturers of jumbo cargo jet planes and combination passenger and cargo aircraft has helped immensely.

Choice criteria

In deciding the best transportation mode to use, MNEs tend to focus on four important criteria: time, predictability, cost, and non-economic factors.

Time

The period between departure and arrival of a carrier can vary significantly between an ocean freighter and an aircraft. So one of the questions the firm will have to answer is: How quickly is delivery needed? A number of factors will influence the answer. One is the perishability of the product. Exotic flowers from South America are flown to the US because they would not survive a sea voyage. A second factor is how soon the goods are needed to replenish current stocks. Autos from Japan are brought into the US by ship because the length of the trip will not negatively affect the supply of cars on hand at local dealerships.

In businesses where speed is of the most importance, companies are now coordinating their worldwide supply chains in order to reduce the amount of time needed to get the goods through the production cycle and to the customer. Victor Fung, CEO of Li & Fung, Hong Kong's largest export trading company and an innovator in the development of supply chain management, has provided an example of how this is being done.

> Say we get an order from a European retailer to produce 10,000 garments. It's not a simple matter of our Korean office sourcing Korean products or our Indonesian office sourcing Indonesian products. For this customer we might decide to buy yarn from a Korean producer but have it woven and dyed in Taiwan. So we pick the yarn and ship it to Taiwan. The Japanese have the best zippers and buttons, but they manufacture them mostly in China. Okay, so we go to YKK, a big Japanese zipper manufacturer, and we order the right zippers from their Chinese plants. Then we determine that, because of quotas and labor conditions, the best place to make the garments is Thailand. So we ship everything there. And because the customer needs quick delivery, we may divide the order across five factories in Thailand. Effectively, we are customizing the value chain to best meet the customer's needs.
>
> Five weeks after we have received the order, 10,000 garments arrive on the shelves in Europe, all looking like they came from one factory, with colors, for example, perfectly matched.[52]

Predictability

Although both air and water transportation are basically reliable, they are subject to the vagaries of nature. Bad weather can close an airport; inadequate seaport facilities can slow the loading and unloading of cargo. Because of the great difference in delivery time between the two modes, the choice of mode is often obvious. If a company needs to have a package delivered tomorrow, it will come by air; if the firm wants to clear merchandise out of the warehouse today but the international customer does not need it for 90 days, it will be sent by water. However, certain carriers are more reliable than others, and the MNE will use its experience in determining which companies to choose for delivery. Reliability is particularly important for air shipments, where the difference of one day could significantly influence the saleability of the product.

Cost

The expense associated with shipping is a major consideration when choosing an international transportation mode. Since air freight is significantly more costly than shipment by water, the cost must be economically justifiable. Typically, an MNE will use air shipments only when time is critical and/or the product has high value. For example, if the company has purchased expensive watches in Zurich for its specialty outlets in New York and San Francisco, the watches will be flown to the retailers. Similarly, if a London-based MNE has bought a US-made supercomputer for the home office and wants it installed immediately, the unit will be flown over from the US. On the other hand, if the merchandise is bulky or the cost of air freight is a significant portion of the value of the product, it will be sent by water. For example, autos are exported by ship as are bulk commodities and resources such as oil and coal.

Non-economic factors

Sometimes non-economic factors influence the choice of transportation mode. For example, in the US, all government cargo must use national flag carriers when available. So there is seldom a question of how to send these goods. Similarly, other governments own or subsidize their carriers, and there is pressure on MNEs to use these transportation modes when doing business with these countries. Such political considerations must be taken into account when formulating the transportation strategy.

Packaging

Packaging is important in ensuring that the product is shipped in a safe container and that it arrives undamaged. When goods are transported a long distance or to areas with climates that are different from the one where they are manufactured, the container can prevent spoilage or leakage. Chemicals, for example, must be carefully sealed in containers that can withstand impact and will not crack open if tipped over or dropped. Machines, such as personal computers, must have interior packing that prevents damage during transit.

Packaging is also important because of its direct effect on cost. If units must be shipped in odd-shaped containers, fewer of them can be loaded into the hold of the transport than if they are shipped in square or rectangular containers and can be loaded atop and alongside each other. The weight of the packing material is also important, especially when goods are being shipped by air and costs are based on both distance and weight.

Intermodal containers
Large metal boxes that fit on trucks, railroads, and airplanes and help to reduce handling cost and theft losses by placing the merchandise in an easy-to-move unit that is tightly sealed

Additionally, packaging is important in reducing loading and unloading costs and in minimizing theft and pilferage. In recent years many shippers have begun using **intermodal containers**, which are large metal boxes that fit on trucks, railroad trains, and airplanes and help to reduce handling cost and theft losses by placing the merchandise in an easy-to-move unit that is tightly sealed.

As more goods are shipped internationally, packaging will continue to be a focal point of attention. Such considerations can help an MNE to maximize shipping space and to minimize transportation costs.

Storage

In some cases goods that are shipped internationally have to be stored before being moved to their final destinations. In the US, public storage is widely available. In other countries, including Japan, warehousing facilities are in short supply. Additionally, the configuration of many warehouses is different from that in the US. Ceilings are often lower and there is little automation for handling such common chores as loading and unloading packages or stacking containers on top of each other. In these cases the MNE must decide whether to invest in warehouse facilities or to ship goods only when needed, thus eliminating the warehouse function.

Foreign trade zones
Areas where foreign goods may be held and processed and then re-exported without incurring customs duties (same as a free trade zone)

As discussed in Chapter 6, in some countries there are **foreign trade zones**, which are areas where foreign goods may be held and processed and then re-exported without incurring customs duties (same as a free trade zone). These zones are usually found at major ports of entry (including international air terminals). The effective use of these trade zones can help an MNE: (1) to temporarily store its goods while breaking a large shipment into smaller ones to be shipped to other locales; (2) to combine small shipments into larger ones and then reship them; (3) to process the goods and perform a host of value-added activities before repackaging them for the market; and (4) to give those goods that will remain in the local market a "made in" status so that they can be sold as locally produced products.

An effective storage strategy can be particularly helpful in carrying out the final stages of an MNE's production plan. The strategy can also help to minimize overall product cost, to reduce delivery time, and to increase customer satisfaction.[53]

STRATEGIC MANAGEMENT AND PRODUCTION STRATEGY

MNEs are currently focusing on a number of areas in improving their production strategies. Three that are getting particular attention include: (a) technology and design; (b) continuous improvement of operations; and (c) the use of strategic alliances and acquisitions.

Technology and production design

MNEs are now spending more money on R&D than they have in the past. For example, Ford Motor, General Motors, DaimlerChrysler, and Toyota put 4 per cent of their annual net sales into R&D, and Volkswagen and Honda put 5 per cent.[54] These investments help to explain why auto engineering and quality have improved so much over the last decade. During the 1980s the problem for many US firms was that much of the emphasis was on new R&D, whereas that of their international competitors was on improved R&D. During the 1990s US MNEs began changing their R&D focus and started developing more improved products.

A second current trend is the use of concurrent engineering, which was discussed earlier in the chapter. Many MNEs are now realizing that a team approach to product development, which combines the talents of research, design, and manufacturing people, as well as customers and clients, results in a more successful good. Ford Motor is an excellent example. Ford put together a group called Team Taurus to develop its Taurus and Sable automobile lines. Team members were drawn from designing, engineering, and production and were brought together with customers. Collectively the group discussed how to build the new cars and replaced the sequential approach to manufacturing autos (first design the cars, then produce them, then market them) with a concurrent approach which involved addressing the design, production, and marketing issues all at the same time. The result of this strategy was a Taurus that captured a significant market niche and helped Ford close the gap between itself and the competition.[55]

Empowerment
The process of giving employees increased control over their work

Coupled with these strategies are innovative human resource development programs that are designed around the concept of **empowerment**, which involves giving employees increased control over their work. This strategy is particularly effective because it creates a feeling of pride and ownership in the job and makes employees feel that they are important assets. The use of empowerment is not limited to the research and design areas; it is important in all phases of production, beginning with the creation of the good. Additionally, if things go smoothly at this early stage of the production cycle, there are likely to be fewer problems later on.

Continuous improvement

Due to the success of Japanese MNEs, *kaizen* (continuous improvement) is being emulated by MNEs worldwide. No matter what the good or service is, every day the company tries to do the job better. Some consultants have referred to this strategy as "rapid inch-up",[56] and this certainly captures the essence of the concept. US firms, in particular, have benefited from this idea as reflected by the dramatic increases that have been achieved in productivity. For example, during the 1980s US factories accounted for 23 per cent of the gross national product, thanks to productivity increases of 3.9 per cent annually throughout the decade. This was the best performance of US manufacturers since World War II, and the millennium promises even greater increases.[57]

A large number of firms helped to account for these results. One is Xerox, internationally known for its photocopiers. At the beginning of the 1980s the company was losing market share to overseas competitors. However, the firm then began implementing a production strategy for dramatically improving quality and reducing cost. Today Xerox is again the world's leader in copiers.

Another example is AMP of Harrisburg, Pennsylvania. The company produces high-tech, high-volume commodity electrical and electronic components used in products ranging from aircraft to washing machines. Thanks to new molding and drilling techniques, the company has sharply reduced its reliance on foreign suppliers and currently exports 10 times more than it imports.[58]

As discussed in an earlier section, just-in-time (JIT) is a related concept the MNEs are using to achieve continuous improvement. In the past JIT was used almost exclusively for managing inventory, but now the concept is being employed in other ways. For example, Toyota's use of JIT helps it to assemble a car in 13 man-hours, as compared with 19 to 22 man-hours for Honda, Nissan, and Ford.

Alliances and acquisitions

Another current strategic production trend is the development of alliances and acquisitions.[59] Many MNEs are finding that they cannot compete effectively without entering into joint ventures or other alliances with MNEs that can complement their production strategy.[60] For example, Compaq is well known for its personal computers, but many of the components in these machines are purchased from outside suppliers or are developed by these firms under an alliance agreement. When Compaq needed a hard disk drive for its first laptops, it financed Conner Peripherals, a Silicon Valley start-up with a disk drive already under way, rather than develop the machine in-house. More recently Compaq has ventured into the market for powerful desktop workstations that are used primarily by scientists and engineers. Instead of going head-to-head with market leaders such as Sun Microsystems and Hewlett-Packard, the company assembled a dozen hardware and software firms, including these two computer giants, and put together an alliance aimed at defining a new technical standard for high-speed desktop computing. The objective of the alliance is to develop a standard that will work with any workstation, and thus allow customers the freedom to buy the latest, fastest machine without fear of being tied to any single manufacturer.

Compaq's approach is not unique. The Japanese *keiretsu* system has been using it for years.[61] In fact, some researchers claim that industry alliances account for more of the success of Japanese firms than does just-in-time or any other manufacturing technique. Working in unison with each other, *keiretsu* companies have been able to wield a great deal of power. Many of these firms have monthly meetings in which they exchange information and ideas. Table 10.3 provides a brief overview of six of the country's major *keiretsu* members. Looking closely at the table, we see that it illustrates how valuable cooperation between the members can be. The idea has not been lost on US firms, among others, which are now beginning to put together their own "mini-*keiretsus*". For example, Eastman Kodak has acquired a number of distributors in Japan and has taken small stakes in some 50 suppliers and customers, and IBM is investing venture capital in a host of small European computer-related firms. Motorola has not taken equity positions, but it uses a *keiretsu* approach by developing extremely close ties with suppliers.

Table 10.3 Japan's biggest business groups that regularly attend monthly council meetings

	Mitsubishi	*Mitsui*	*Sumitomo*	*Fuyo*	*DKB*	*Sanwa*
Financial services	Mitsubishi Bank Mitsubishi Trust & Banking Meiji Mutual Life Tokio Marine & Fire	Mitsui Taiyo Kobe Bank Mitsui Trust & Banking Mitsui Mutual Life Taisho Marine & Fire	Sumitomo Bank Sumitomo Trust & Banking Sumitomo Life Sumitomo Marine & Fire	Fuji Bank Yasuda Trust & Banking Yasuda Mutual Life Yasuda Fire & Marine	Dai-Ichi Kangyo Bank Asahi Mutual Life Taisei Fire & Marine Fukoku Mutual Life Nissan Fire & Marine Kankaku Securities Orient	Sanwa Bank Toyo Trust & Banking Nippon Life Orix
Computers, electronics and electrical equipment	Mitsubishi Electric	Toshiba	NEC	Oki Electric Industry Yokogawa Electric Hitachi*	Fujitsu Fuji Electric Yaskawa Electric Mfg. Nippon Columbia Hitachi*	Iwatsu Electric Sharp Nitto Denko Kyocera Hitachi*
Cars	Mitsubishi Motors	Toyota Motor*		Nissan Motor	Isuzu Motors	Daihatsu Motor
Trading and retailing	Mitsubishi	Mitsui Mitsukoshi	Sumitomo	Marubeni	C. Itoh Nissho Iwai* Kanematsu Kawasho Seibu Dept. Store	Nissho Iwai* Nichimen Iwatani International Takashimaya
Food and beverages	Kirin Brewery	Nippon Flour Mills		Nisshin Flour Milling Sapporo Breweries Nichirei		Itoham Foods Suntory
Construction	Mitsubishi Construction	Mitsui Construction Sanki Engineering	Sumitomo Construction	Taisei	Shimizu	Toyo Construction Obayashi Sekisui House Zenitaka

Table 10.3 **(cont'd)**

	Mitsubishi	*Mitsui*	*Sumitomo*	*Fuyo*	*DKB*	*Sanwa*
Metals	Mitsubishi Steel Mfg. Mitsubishi Materials Mitsubishi Aluminum Mitsubishi Cable Industries	Japan Steel Works Mitsui Mining & Smelting	Sumitomo Metal Industries Sumitomo Metal Mining Sumitomo Electric Industries Sumitomo Light Metal Industries	NKK	Kawasaki Steel Kobe Steel* Japan Metals & Chemicals Nippon Light Metal Furukawa Furukawa Electric	Kobe Steel* Nakayama Steel Works Hitachi Metals Nisshin Steel Hitachi Cable
Real estate	Mitsubishi Estate	Mitsui Real Estate Development	Sumitomo Realty & Development	Tokyo Taternono	Tokyo Dome	
Oil and coal	Mitsubishi Oil			Tonen	Showa Shell Sekiyu	Cosmo Oil
Rubber and glass	Asahi Glass		Nippon Sheet Glass		Yokohama Rubber	Toyo Tire & Rubber
Chemicals	Mitsubishi Kasei Mitsubishi PetroChemic Mitsubishi Gas Chemical Mitsubishi Plastics Mitsubishi Kasei Poly	Mitsui Toatsu Chemicals Mitsui Petrochemical Industries	Sumitomo Chemical Sumitomo Bakelite	Showa Denko Nippon Oil & Fats Kureha Chemical Industries	Kyowa Hakko Kogyo Denki Kagaku Kogyo Nippon Zeon Asahi Denka Kogyo Sankyo Shiseido Lion	Ube Industries Tokuyoma Soda Hitachi Chemical Sekisui Chemical Kansai Paint Tanabe Seiyaku Fujisawa Pharmaceuticals
Fibers and textiles	Mitsubishi Rayon	Toray Industries		Nisshinbo Industries Toho Rayon	Asahi Chemical Industry	Unitika Teijin
Pulp and paper	Mitsubishi Paper Mills	Oji paper		Sanyo-Kokusaku Pulp	Honshu Paper	
Mining and forestry		Mitsui Mining Hokkaido Colliery & Steamship	Sumitomo Forestry Sumitomo Coal Mining			
Industrial equipment	Mitsubishi Heavy Industries Mitsubishi Kakoki	Mitsui Engineering & Shipbuilding	Sumitomo Heavy Industries	Kubota Nippon Seiko	Niigata Engineering Iseki Ebara Kawasaki Heavy Industries Ishikawajima-Harima Heavy Industries	NTN Hitachi Zosen Shin Meiwa Industry
Cameras and optics	Nikon			Canon	Asahi Optical	Hoya
Cement		Onoda Cement	Sumitomo Cement	Nihon Cement	Chichibu Cement	Osaka Cement
Shipping and transportation	Nippon Yusen Mitsubishi Warehouse & Transportation	Mitsui OSK lines Mitsui Warehouse	Sumitomo Warehouse	Shawa line Keihin Electric Express Railway Tobu Railway	Kawasaki Kisen Shibusawa Warehouse Nippon Express*	Navix Line Hankyu Nippon Express*

* Companies affiliated with more than one group.

Source: Adapted from *Fortune*, July 15, 1991, p. 81.

Fujitsu offers another interesting production strategy: acquisition coupled with autonomy. In the early 1990s the company purchased Amdahl, the giant Silicon Valley manufacturer of IBM-compatible mainframe computers, and International Computers Ltd, Britain's biggest computer company. Fujitsu realizes that it cannot continue to grow without increasing international sales. At the same time the company knows that growing nationalism is leading many governments to question acquisitions by foreign firms. Additionally, the firm is convinced that Japanese management approaches cannot be universally exported. Companies in other nations have their own way of doing things. So it pays to give overseas acquisitions the autonomy to make most decisions as they see fit. A Fujitsu executive recently put it this way: "Our overseas managers learned to eat T-bone steaks and speak English. But in substantial matters, trying to be worldly isn't enough. A 100% Japanese company simply can't be successful overseas, just as a 100% American or European company can't be in Japan."[62]

Active learning check 

Review your answer to Active Learning Case question 3 and make any changes you like. Then compare your answer with the one below.

3. In what way could best practices help GE to develop more effective international strategies? Explain.

Best practices could help GE to develop more effective international strategies by encouraging the firm to identify those MNEs that are most successful and then to discover how they accomplish that feat. Do these firms manage to develop more new products than do their competitors? Or are they best at quickly getting their new goods into the marketplace? Do they produce the highest quality goods? Or are they lowest-cost producers? What accounts for their ability to achieve such an excellent performance? By asking and answering these questions, GE can gain insights into how it needs to change its own production processes in order to emulate those MNEs successfully.

KEY POINTS

1. Many of today's goods and services will be replaced during the millennium with faster, more efficient, and cheaper substitutes. For this reason, MNEs need to continually research, develop, and bring new offerings to the marketplace. One way in which this is being done is through the use of time to market accelerators. A good example is concurrent engineering.
2. The generation of goods and services entails a number of specific functions. One function is obtaining materials or supplies. Many MNEs have found that global sourcing is the best strategy because it helps to keep down costs while providing a number of other benefits, including ensuring an ongoing source of supply and helping the company to penetrate overseas markets.
3. In the production of goods and services, MNEs focus on a number of key factors, including cost, quality, and well-designed production systems. While these three factors are often interrelated, each merits specific attention. Multinationals have also developed very effective inventory control systems that help to minimize carrying costs and to increase productivity. Attention is also focused on gaining the proper balance between production and service domination. Figure 10.4 illustrates this point.
4. International logistics is the designing and managing of a system to control the flow of materials and products throughout the firm. In addition to inventory control, this involves transportation, packaging, and storing.

5. MNEs are currently focusing on a number of areas in improving their production strategies. Three approaches that have been receiving particular attention include (1) technology and design, (2) continuous improvement of operations, and (3) the use of strategic alliances and acquisitions. These approaches are helping multinationals to meet new product and service challenges while keeping costs down and quality up.

KEY TERMS

- backward integration
- forward integration
- horizontal integration
- time-to-market accelerators
- concurrent engineering
- global sourcing
- *kaizen*
- production system
- materials handling
- process mapping
- Demand-Flow™ Technology (DFT)
- just-in-time (JIT) inventory
- international logistics
- container ships
- unconventional cargo vessels
- roll-on-roll-off (RORO) vessels
- lighter aboard ship (LASH) vessels
- intermodal containers
- foreign trade zones
- empowerment
- modular integrated robotized system (MIRB)
- modular manufacturing

REVIEW AND DISCUSSION QUESTIONS

1. Why are MNEs so interested in new product development? Why do they not simply focus on improving their current offerings?
2. Why is "speed to market" such an important production strategy? Explain.
3. What are "time-to-market accelerators"? In what way is concurrent engineering one of these accelerators?
4. Why do many MNEs use global sourcing? Why do they not produce all the parts and materials in-house? Be complete in your answer.
5. Why are world-class suppliers often located next to world-class manufacturers? What forms of synergy often exist between the two groups?
6. How do MNEs try to reduce production costs? Identify and describe three steps.
7. In what way is the continuous reduction cost method used by Japanese manufacturers (see Figure 10.3) different from the periodic cost reduction method employed by many US firms? Compare and contrast the two.
8. Some MNEs use a production strategy that involves costing a portfolio of related goods rather than just costing each individually. What is the logic behind this strategy?
9. How does *kaizen* help to bring about increased quality? Is this approach limited to Japanese firms or are other MNEs using it as well?
10. What types of issues does an MNE confront when it seeks to improve its production system? Identify and describe three.
11. How does JIT help an MNE to control its inventory? Give two examples.
12. How is employee training an important factor to implementing JIT and DFT production processes?
13. Why would an MNE want to determine the degree to which its primary business was product-dominated and service-dominated? Explain.
14. Why are MNEs concerned with international logistics? How does this help the companies to increase their competitiveness?
15. In recent years MNEs have been focusing on a number of areas in improving their production strategies. What are two of these? Identify and describe each.

REAL CASE

National Cash Register

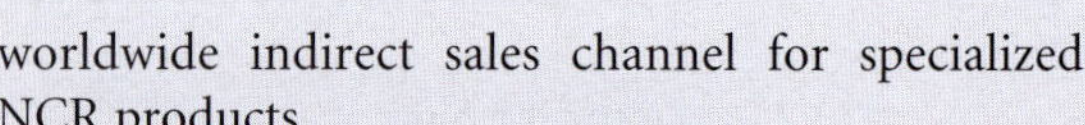

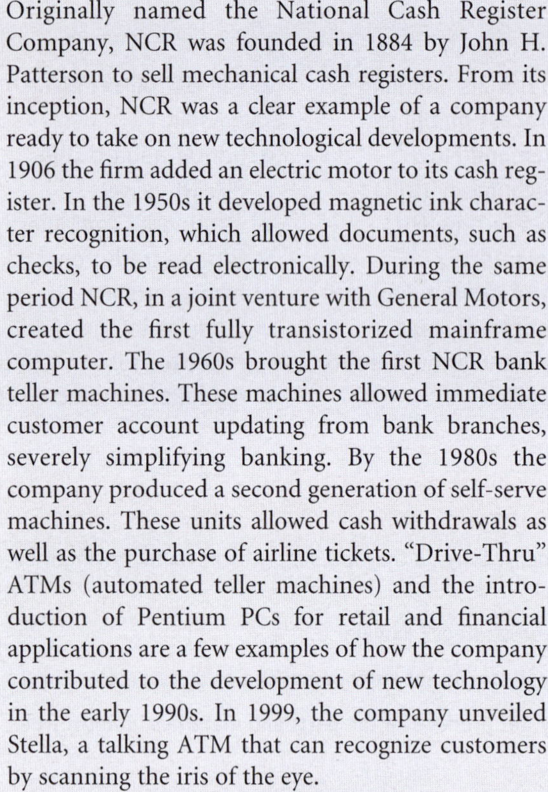

Originally named the National Cash Register Company, NCR was founded in 1884 by John H. Patterson to sell mechanical cash registers. From its inception, NCR was a clear example of a company ready to take on new technological developments. In 1906 the firm added an electric motor to its cash register. In the 1950s it developed magnetic ink character recognition, which allowed documents, such as checks, to be read electronically. During the same period NCR, in a joint venture with General Motors, created the first fully transistorized mainframe computer. The 1960s brought the first NCR bank teller machines. These machines allowed immediate customer account updating from bank branches, severely simplifying banking. By the 1980s the company produced a second generation of self-serve machines. These units allowed cash withdrawals as well as the purchase of airline tickets. "Drive-Thru" ATMs (automated teller machines) and the introduction of Pentium PCs for retail and financial applications are a few examples of how the company contributed to the development of new technology in the early 1990s. In 1999, the company unveiled Stella, a talking ATM that can recognize customers by scanning the iris of the eye.

Nor did NCR lose any time in becoming a multinational. By 1886 the firm began selling abroad and soon had operations in 121 countries. In 2000, 59.3 per cent of NCR's revenue was generated in international markets including such principal locations as Germany, France, Australia, Spain, Italy, Canada, and Switzerland. In Great Britain over 80 per cent of all ATM terminals are NCR's. Furthermore, the company has distribution networks that span the world.

NCR has followed a variety of strategies including the effective use of partnerships. In fact, a recent partnership with APACS from the UK is helping NCR strengthen its already dominant position in the ATM market. This deal will provide customers a myriad of services through a single card built with a microchip (smartcard) replacing the magnetic strip of today's bankcards.

Another approach is the use of distribution partnerships that allow regionally oriented firms to market NCR products. For instance, I. E. Mittwoch & Sons is the sole NCR distributor in Israel, while Hardwood International Corporation functions as a worldwide indirect sales channel for specialized NCR products.

Meanwhile customers serve a dual purpose for the firm. Many of them are multinationals themselves and the application of NCR's products to worldwide operations of companies such as Hallmark, Wal-Mart, and K-Mart contribute to the company's internationalization.

In order to tie the different parts of its global operations, NCR also has developed worldwide customer support networks that are co-administered with its business partners. In 1997 the company announced it would realign global operations within the business units to implement global process efficiency. This new organizational set-up is expected to give more operational freedom to the different business units, decreasing infrastructure and allowing for better communication between the parts.

Competition from new entrants in the 1990s, forced NCR to restructure its business lines. In 1999, the company consolidated 30 business lines into three: ATMs, cash registers, and Teradata. Nearly 70 per cent of the company's revenues came from ATMs, but Teradata, the market leader in warehouse data, is where the company is betting its future. Travelocity, Office Depot, and Lowe's all use Teradata software for marketing and billing purposes. Its biggest competitors in data warehousing are IBM and Oracle.

Website: **www.ncr.com**; **www.gm.com**; **www.hallmark.com**; **www.walmart.com**; **www.teradata.com**; **www.ibm.com** and **www.oracle.com**.

Sources: Adapted from **www3.ncr.com**; Connie Guglielmo, "Here Come The Super-ATMs," *Fortune*, October 14, 1996; NCR, "APACS and NCR Lighten Wallets to Make Britain a Smartcard Leader," Press Release, July 9, 1998; **www.ncr.com**; **www.hardwood-intl.com/**; "First Worlds for Talking Cash Point," *BBC.co.uk*, July 6, 1999; "The Resurrection of NCR," *Forbes*, September 7, 2001.

1. **Why are NCR's operations in developing countries important? How are they different from their principal markets in developed countries?**
2. **Why would NCR choose to maintain distribution partnerships rather than internalize and distribute directly?**
3. **How can customers who are multinationals help market NCR products in other countries?**

REAL CASE

Nike

One of the rules of international production strategy is: manufacture the highest quality product and the world is likely to beat a path to your door. A number of firms help to illustrate this rule. One is Nike, the sports shoe producer. The company makes a wide variety of high quality shoes. The company catalogue lists more than 800 models for use in approximately 25 sports. In 1999 Nike had 35 per cent of the world's market for training shoes (and 45 per cent in the US). In 2000, its sales were over $9 billion. In an effort to keep ahead of the competition, Nike updates each shoe at least every six months. Most of these ideas are generated by Nike's R&D centre in Beaverton, near Portland, Oregon, where physiologists and mechanical engineers study the stresses on an athlete's feet and collaborate with stylists on new shoe ideas.

Although Nike sells its products in over 140 countries and produces in more than 50, it is really a "triad" MNE. Over 92 per cent of its sales are in the triad markets of the US, EU, and "Asia". In 2000 there was a 15 per cent growth of sales in the EU, due mainly to a new distribution facility in Belgium and a new design house in Holland. Nike is still strong in its home market, with 40 per cent of all sales in the US athletic footwear market and over 65 per cent of the basketball footwear market. About 60 per cent of its sales are still in its US home base.

Nike's high quality production is matched by superb marketing skills. The world might be making a path to Nike's door, but the company makes sure the world knows where they are. Nike spends 11 per cent of its revenue on marketing and its "swoosh" brand is recognized the world over. The company continues to use sports stars to endorse its products. Besides US stars like Tiger Woods and Andre Agassi, it has used European soccer players like Eric Catona, cricket players in India, and is now in China preparing for the 2008 Olympic games in Beijing. The idea is: if you can make the "cool" guys wear your products, then the rest will follow.

Perhaps the only thing Nike doesn't like to be remembered for is the bad publicity around its labor practices in Asia. Nike has outsourced all of its production to low wage areas. In 2000, China produced 43 per cent of its footwear; Indonesia 29 per cent; Vietnam 13 per cent; and Thailand 12 per cent. NGOs have criticized the poor working conditions in some of its Asian factories. In 1996, such criticism led to *Life Magazine* publishing a story on Pakistani children stitching Nike's soccer balls. Another famous case occurred in 1997 when a Vietnam factory, owned by a Korean subcontractor, was found to have unsafe working conditions. NGOs in the Western world started campaigns to boycott Nike and demonstrators protested in front of Nike's stores. Allegations of long working hours, bad ventilation, and physical abuse on a mostly young female work force has tarnished Nike's reputation.

Nike's industry dominance was a main reason for its being severely targeted. Many of its competitors were found to have the same labor practices, but were not subjected to the same level of criticism. Nike has a corporate responsibility initiative to improve working conditions in its own factories and to help influence its suppliers. Despite this, the University of Michigan ended use of Nike products in 2001.

Website: **www.nike.com**.

Sources: Adapted from Dylan Jones, "No More Mr. Nike Guy," *Sunday Times Magazine*, August 23, 1998; David Shook, "Why Nike is Dragging its Feet," *Business Week*, March 19, 2001; Sydney H. Schanberg, "On the Playgrounds of America, Every Kid's Goal is to Score: In Pakistan, Where Children Stitch Soccer balls for Six Cents an Hour, the Goal Is to Survive," *Life Magazine*, June 1996; Harry Dunphy, "Nike to Improve Conditions," *Associated Press*, May 12, 1998; Nike, *Annual Report*, 2000.

1. **What is the key to Nike's production strategy? Explain.**
2. **What are the advantages of frequent design changes in Nike's sneakers?**
3. **Why is it important for Nike to clean up its labor practices in Asia? How would you recommend the company approach the issue?**

ENDNOTES

1 Alex Taylor III, "Why GM Leads the Pack in Europe," *Fortune*, May 13, 1993, pp. 83–87.
2 Laxmi Nakarmi and Patrick Oster, "The Korean Tiger Is Out for Blood," *Business Week*, May 31, 1993, p. 54.
3 Doron P. Levin, "Honda to Hold Base Price on Accord Model," *New York Times*, September 2, 1993, p. C 3.
4 Also see Emily Thornton, "Mazda Learns To Like Those Intruders," *Business Week*, September 14, 1998, p. 172.
5 Alex Taylor III, "How Toyota Copes with Hard Times," *Fortune*, January 25, 1993, pp. 78–81 and Joah Muller and Katie Kerwin, "Detroit is Cruising for Quality," *Business Week*, September 3, 2001.
6 For a good example of these challenges, see Ferdinand Protzman, "Daimler's Quest Collides with Slump," *New York Times*, August 3, 1993, pp. C 1, C 5.
7 For some interesting insights into this process, see Christopher Power et al., "Flops," *Business Week*, August 16, 1993, pp. 76–82.
8 Gene Bylinsky, "The Hottest High Tech Company in Japan," *Fortune*, January 1, 1990, pp. 82–88 and Eric Nee, "Kyocera's Dilema," *Fortune*, December 10, 2001.
9 Stuart F. Brown, "New Products from Rented Brains," *Fortune*, September 4, 2000.
10 See Joel Kotkin, "Creators of the New Japan," *Inc.*, October 1990, pp. 96–107 and Daffyd Roderick, "Sega's Dream Past?" *Time Asia*, January 15, 2001.
11 "Alcatel, Fujitsu Unveil Mobile Net Venture," *Industry Standard*, May 3, 2000.
12 "Coca-Cola and P&G in New Venture," *BBC.co.uk*, February 21, 2001.
13 "NEC and Thomson Multimedia Announce Intention to Combine their Worldwide Plasma Displays Businesses in a 50/50 Joint-venture," NEC Press Release, March 14, 2001.
14 See Don Clark, "Intel to Ship Its Next-Generation Chip in 1995, Boosts Outlay for Production," *Wall Street Journal*, January 28, 1994, p. B 5.
15 Gene Bylinsky, "Heroes of US Manufacturing," *Fortune*, March 20, 2000.
16 Also see C. K. Prahalad and Kenneth Lieberthal, "The End of Corporate Imperialism," *Harvard Business Review*, July–August 1998, pp. 69–79.
17 Joseph T. Vesey, "The New Competitors: They Think in Terms of 'Speed-to-Market'," *Academy of Management Executive*, May 1991, pp. 23–33 and "Re-inventing the Wheel," *Economist*, April 20, 2000.
18 Saul Hansell, "Is This the Factory of the Future?" *New York Times*, July 26, 1998, Section 3, pp. 1, 12.
19 Rebecca Blumenstein, "GM Is Building Plants in Developing Nations to Woo New Markets," *Wall Street Journal*, August 4, 1997, pp. A 1, 5.
20 Gene Bylinsky, "Heroes of US Manufacturing," *Fortune*, March 20, 2000.
21 Larry Holyoke, William Spindle and Neil Gross, "Doing the Unthinkable," *Business Week*, January 10, 1994, pp. 52–53; and Andrew Pollack, "Nissan Plans to Buy More American Parts," *New York Times*, March 26, 1994, pp. 17, 26.
22 Michael E. Porter, *The Competitive Advantage of Nations* (New York: Free Press, 1990), p. 103.
23 For more on this, see Earl Landesman, "Ultimatum for US Auto Suppliers: Go Global or Go Under," *Journal of European Business*, May/June 1991, pp. 39–45.
24 Laurie Hays, "IBM's Finance Chief, Ax in Hand, Scours Empires for Costs to Cut," *Wall Street Journal*, January 26, 1994, pp. A 1, A 6.
25 For an interesting development in this area, see Kathy Chen, "Would America Buy A Refrigerator Labeled 'Made in Qingdao'?" *Wall Street Journal*, September 17, 1997, pp. A 1, 14.
26 "The Modular T," *Economist*, September 3, 1998 and David Welch, "Why Detroit is Going to Pieces," *Business Week*, September 3, 2001.
27 Larry Reibstein et al., "A Mexican Miracle?" *Newsweek*, May 20, 1991, p. 42.
28 Ernest Beck, "Why Foreign Distillers Find It So Hard to Sell Vodka to the Russians," *Wall Street Journal*, January 15, 1998, pp. A 1, 8.
29 Ford S. Worthy, "Japan's Smart Secret Weapon," *Fortune*, August 12, 1991, pp. 72–75.
30 Ibid., p. 75.
31 Suh-kyung Yoon, "Working Up a Thirst to Quench Asia," *Far Eastern Economic Review*, February 1, 2001.
32 See Louis Kraar, "Korea Goes for Quality," *Fortune*, April 13, 1994, pp. 153–159; and Gale Eisenstodt, "Sullivan's Travels," *Forbes*, March 28, 1994, pp. 75–76.
33 Erick Calonius, "Smart Moves by Quality Champs," *Fortune*, Spring/Summer 1991, p. 24.
34 See, for example, Christopher Palmeri, "A Process That Never Ends," *Forbes*, December 21, 1992, pp. 52–54.
35 Alex Taylor III, "How Toyota Defies Gravity," *Fortune*, December 8, 1997, pp. 100–108.
36 For more on this, see Thomas A. Stewart, "Brace for Japan's Hot New Strategy," *Fortune*, September 21, 1992, pp. 62–74.
37 Richard A. Melcher and Stewart Toy, "On Guard, Europe," *Business Week*, December 14, 1992, pp. 54–55.
38 Louis S. Richman, "What America Makes Best," *Fortune*, Spring/Summer 1991, p. 80.
39 Ibid., p. 81.
40 Michael Shari and Pete Engardio, "The Sweet Sound of Success," *Business Week*, September 8, 1997, p. 56.
41 See Michael E. McGrath and J. Gordon Stewart, "Professional Service Firms in Europe Move Toward Integrated European Practices," *Journal of European Business*, May/June 1991, pp. 26–30.
42 Steven Prokesch, "Edges Fray on Volvo's Brave New Humanistic World," *New York Times*, July 7, 1991, p. F 5.
43 Richard J. Schonberger, *Building a Chain of Customers* (New York: Free Press, 1990), pp. 50–51.
44 Thomas A. Stewart, "GE Keeps Those Ideas Coming," *Fortune*, August 12, 1991, p. 48.

45 Lucinda Harper, "Trucks Keep Inventories Rolling Past Warehouses to Production Line," *Wall Street Journal*, February 7, 1994, p. B 3.
46 Alex Taylor III, "Why Toyota Keeps Getting Better and Better and Better," *Fortune*, November 19, 1990, p. 79.
47 Gene Bylinsky, "Heroes of U.S. Manufacturing," *Fortune*, March 20, 2000.
48 "Intermec Recognized for its use of Demand Flow[TM] Technology," *Intermec News Release*, May 21, 1997.
49 David A. Aaker, "How Will the Japanese Compete in Retail Services?" *California Management Review*, Fall 1990, pp. 54–67.
50 For still other examples of service-related problems in Japan, see Jon Woronoff, *The Japanese Management Mystique: The Reality Behind the Myth* (Chicago: Probus Publishing, 1992), pp. 120–124.
51 Michael R. Czinkota, Pietra Rivoli and Ilkka A. Ronkainen, *International Business* (Hinsdale IL: Dryden Press, 1989), p. 427.
52 Joan Magretta, "Fast, Global, and Entrepreneurial: Supply Chain Management, Hong Kong Style: An Interview with Victor Fung," *Harvard Business Review*, September–October 1998, pp. 105–106.
53 See, for example, Hellene S. Runtagh, "GE Tracks Transportation and Distribution Opportunities in the EC," *Journal of European Business*, September/October 1990, pp. 22–25.
54 Taylor (1990) n. 46 above, p. 79 and "The Corporate Research and Development Scorecard," *Technology Review*, November/December 2000.
55 Vesey, (1991) n. 17 above.
56 Ibid.
57 See Lucinda Harper, "Productivity in US Jumped by 2.7% in 1992," *Wall Street Journal*, February 5, 1992, p. A 2.
58 Stewart, n. 44 above.
59 Paul Lawrence and Charalambos Vlachoutsicos, "Joint Ventures in Russia: Put the Locals in Charge," *Harvard Business Review*, January/February 1993, pp. 44–54.
60 Stratford Sherman, "Are Strategic Alliances Working?" *Fortune*, September 21, 1992, pp. 77–78; and Thornton (1998) n. 4 above.
61 Robert L. Cutts, "Capitalism in Japan: Cartels and Keiretsu," *Harvard Business Review*, July–August 1992, pp. 48–55.
62 Brenton R. Schlender, "How Fujitsu Will Tackle the Giants," *Fortune*, July 1, 1991, p. 79.

ADDITIONAL BIBLIOGRAPHY

Adler, Paul S. and Cole, Robert E. "Designed for Learning: A Tale of Two Auto Plants," *Sloan Management Review*, vol. 34, no. 3 (Spring 1993).

Beatty, Carol A. "Implementing Advanced Manufacturing Technologies: Rules of the Road," *Sloan Management Review*, vol. 33, no. 4 (Summer 1992).

Bhappu, Anita D. "The Japanese Family: An Institutional Logic for Japanese Corporate Networks and Japanese Management," *Academy of Management Review*, vol. 25, no. 2 (April 2000).

Brouthers, Lance Eliot, Werner, Steve and Matulich, Erika. "The Influence of Triad Nations Environments on Price-Quality Product Strategies and MNC Performance," *Journal of International Business Studies*, vol. 31, no. 1 (Spring 2000).

Cantwell, John. "Innovation and Information Technology in the MNE," in Alan M. Rugman and Thomas Brewer (eds.), *The Oxford Handbook of International Business* (Oxford: Oxford University Press 2001).

Cheng, Joseph L. C. and Bolon, Douglas S. "The Management of Multinational R&D: A Neglected Topic in International Business Research," *Journal of International Business Studies*, vol. 24, no. 1 (First Quarter 1993).

Collins, R. and Schmenner, R. "Taking Manufacturing Advantage of Europe's Single Market," *European Management Journal*, vol. 13, no. 3 (May/June 1995).

Cusumano, Michael A. "Manufacturing Innovation: Lessons from the Japanese Auto Industry," *Sloan Management Review*, vol. 30, no. 1 (Fall 1988).

Deschamps, Jean-Philippe and Nayak, P. Ranganath. "Competing Through Products: Lessons from the Winners," *Columbia Journal of World Business*, vol. 27, no. 2 (Summer 1992).

Douglas, Susan P. and Wind, Yoram. "The Myth of Globalization," *Columbia Journal of World Business*, vol. 22, no. 4 (Winter 1987).

DuBois, Frank L., Toyne, Brian and Oliff, Michael D. "International Manufacturing Strategies of US Multinationals: A Conceptual Framework Based on a Four-Industry Study," *Journal of International Business Studies*, vol. 24, no. 2 (Second Quarter 1993).

Flaherty, M. Therese. "Global Sourcing Strategy: R&D, Manufacturing, and Marketing Interfaces," *Journal of International Business Studies*, vol. 24, no. 1 (First Quarter 1993).

Garvin, David A. "Manufacturing Strategic Planning," *California Management Review*, vol. 35, no. 4 (Summer 1993).

Ghoshal, Sumantra and Bartlett, Christopher A. "Creation, Adoption, and Diffusion of Innovations by Subsidiaries of Multinational Corporations," *Journal of International Business Studies*, vol. 19, no. 3 (Fall 1988).

Hodgetts, Richard, *Measures of Quality and High Performance: Simple Tools and Lessons from America's Most Successful Firms* (New York: Amacom, 1998).

Julian, Scott D. and Keller, Robert T. "Multinational R&D Siting: Corporate Strategies for Success," *Columbia Journal of World Business*, vol. 26, no. 3 (Fall 1991).

Khurana, Anil. "Managing Complex Production Processes," *Sloan Management Review*, vol. 40, no. 2 (Winter 1999).

Kotabe, Masaaki. "The Relationship Between Offshore Sourcing and Innovativeness of US Multinational Firms:

An Empirical Investigation," *Journal of International Business Studies*, vol. 21, no. 4 (Fourth Quarter 1990).

Kotabe, Masaaki and Murray, Janet Y. "Linking Product and Process Innovations and Modes of International Sourcing in Global Competition: A Case of Foreign Multinational Firms," *Journal of International Business Studies*, vol. 21, no. 3 (Third Quarter 1990).

Lei, David and Slocum, John W., Jr. "Global Strategy, Competence-Building and Strategic Alliances," *California Management Review*, vol. 35, no. 1 (Fall 1992).

Levy, David L. "Lean Production in an International Supply Chain," *Sloan Management Review*, vol. 38, no. 2 (Winter 1997).

Patel, Pari and Pavitt, Keith. "Large Firms in the Production of the World's Technology: An Important Case of 'Non-Globalization'," *Journal of International Business Studies*, vol. 22, no. 1 (First Quarter 1991).

Pyke, David. "Manufacturing and Supply Chain Management in China: A Survey of State-, Collective-, and Privately-owned Enterprises," *European Management Journal*, vol. 18, no. 6 (December 2000).

Quinn, James Brian and Hilmer, Frederick G. "Strategic Outsourcing," *Sloan Management Review*, vol. 35, no. 4 (Summer 1994).

Reddy, Prasada. "New Trends in Globalization of Corporate R&D and Implications for Innovation Capability in Host Countries: A Survey from India," *World Development*, vol. 25, no. 11 (November 1997).

Rehder, Robert R. "Building Cars as if People Mattered: The Japanese Lean System vs. Volvo's Uddevalla System," *Columbia Journal of World Business*, vol. 27, no. 2 (Summer 1992).

Rondinelli, Dennis and Berry, Michael, "Multimodal Transportation, Logistics, and the Environment: Managing Interactions in a Global Economy," *European Management Journal*, vol. 18, no. 4 (August 2000).

Rondinelli, Dennis and Vastag, Gyula. "Panacea, Common Sense, or Just a Label?" *European Management Journal*, vol. 18, no. 5 (October 2000).

Rugman, Alan M. and Bennett, Jocelyn. "Technology Transfer and World Product Mandating," *Columbia Journal of World Business*, vol. 17, no. 4 (Winter 1982).

Rugman, Alan M. and Verbeke, Alain. "Subsidiary-specific Advantages in Multinational Enterprises," *Strategic Management Journal*, vol. 22, no. 3 (March 2001).

Serapio, Manuel G., Jr. "Macro-Micro Analyses of Japanese Direct R&D Investments in the US Automotive and Electronics Industries," *Management International Review*, vol. 33, no. 3 (Third Quarter 1993).

Sobek, Durward K. II, Ward, Allen C. and Liker, Jeffrey K. "Toyota's Principles of Set-Based Concurrent Engineering," *Sloan Management Review*, vol. 40, no. 2 (Winter 1999).

Swamidass, Paul M. "A Comparison of the Plant Location Strategies of Foreign and Domestic Manufacturers in the US," *Journal of International Business Studies*, vol. 21, no. 2 (Second Quarter 1990).

Swamidass, Paul M. and Kotabe, Masaaki. "Component Sourcing Strategies of Multinationals: An Empirical Study of European and Japanese Multinationals," *Journal of International Business Studies*, vol. 24, no. 1 (First Quarter 1993).

Vandermerwe, Sandra. "Increasing Returns: Competing for Customers in the Global Market," *Journal of World Business*, vol. 32, no. 4 (Winter 1997).

Yip, George S. "Global Strategy . . . In a World of Nations?" *Sloan Management Review*, vol. 31, no. 1 (Fall 1989).

Young, S. Mark. "A Framework for Successful Adoption and Performance of Japanese Manufacturing Practices in the United States," *Academy of Management Review*, vol. 17, no. 4 (October 1992).

Chapter 11

Marketing Strategy

CONTENTS

OBJECTIVES OF THE CHAPTER

Every multinational has a marketing strategy that is designed to help identify opportunities and to take advantage of them. This plan of action typically involves consideration of four primary areas: the product or service to be sold, the way in which the output will be promoted, the pricing of the good or service, and the distribution strategy to be used in getting the output to the customer. The primary purpose of this chapter is to examine the fundamentals of international marketing strategy. We will look at five major topics: market assessment, product strategy, promotion strategy, price strategy, and place strategy. We will consider such critical marketing areas as product screening, modification of goods and services in order to adapt to local needs, modified product life cycles, advertising, personal selling, and ways in which MNEs tailor-make their distribution systems.

The specific objectives of this chapter are to:

1. *Examine* the process used in conducting international market assessment of goods and services.
2. *Study* the criteria that affect an MNE's decision to alter a good or service in order to adapt the offering to local market tastes.
3. *Describe* some of the ways in which MNEs use advertising and personal selling techniques to promote their product in worldwide markets.
4. *Review* some of the major factors that influence international pricing and distribution strategies.

ACTIVE LEARNING CASE

Worldwide marketing by Volkswagen

During the 1960s German-based Volkswagen AG (VW for short) held more market share in the US than all other auto imports combined, and in the 1970s, despite growing foreign competition, VW sales reached 300,000 units annually. However, the 1980s and early 1990s were not good for the company; annual sales in the US market were down to 150,000 units. In less than 10 years market share had dropped from 3 per cent to 0.5 per cent, and VW had become a minor competitor in the North American part of the triad.

In more recent years, however, Volkswagen has made a stunning comeback in America. Perhaps its biggest success story is the New Beetle, which was introduced in March 1998. By the end of the year the company had sold 55,842 units including 7,516 in December. In all, in 2000 Volkswagen sold 437,000 cars in the US market, an increase of 300 per cent from 1997. In 2000, the New Beetle was the third largest VW seller after the Jetta and the Passat. As a result, the firm's 2000 share of the American car market stood at 2.5 per cent.

Part of this success by VW is accounted for by the fact that cars account for only around 53 per cent of new vehicle sales. The other major group is light trucks where Ford, General Motors, and Chrysler hold 80 per cent of the market. Moreover, in the case of Ford and Chrysler, sales of light trucks are significantly greater than those of automobiles. Yet this growth market has not gone unnoticed by Volkswagen, which recently introduced its EuroVan into the US. The van is built in Hanover, Germany, and comes with a V6 engine and a host of standard equipment and safety features. In 2001, VW sought to take advantage of the 1960s nostalgia that made the New Beetle so successful and began development of the VW Microbus. Still in the concept stage, the Microbus is being designed in Simi Valley, California, to be something of a SUV and a Minivan. If this new entry does well, it will combine with the New Beetle to sharply increase the firm's US market share.

It is the Beetle that holds the greatest promise. In addition to brisk sales the first year, the auto was selected as the 1999 North American Car of the Year by an independent jury of 48 journalists who cover the auto industry for daily newspapers, magazines, television, radio, and the Internet. The award is a comprehensive evaluation of the year's most outstanding new car based on consumer appeal, quality, and driving characteristics. Each jury member is allowed to allot 25 votes to a small selection of finalist cars. The New Beetle garnered 292 votes, more than double the second place finisher, the Honda Odyssey, with 142 votes, and well ahead of the third place car, the Chrysler 300M, with 124 votes. Indeed, Volkswagen is back!

Websites: **www.vw.com**; **www.gm.com**; **www.ford.com** and **www.daimlerchrysler.com**.

Sources: Bernard Avishai, "A European Platform for Global Competition," *Harvard Business Review*, July–August 1991, pp. 103–113; John Templeman and Gail E. Schares, "A Hard U-Turn at VW," *Business Week*, March 15, 1993, p. 47; Audrey Choi, "VW's Lopez Says German Auto Maker is Moving Quickly to Revitalize Itself," *Wall Street Journal*, March 25, 1994, p. A 6; *www.vw.com*; Christine Tierney and Joann Muller, "Another Trip Down Memory Lane," *Business Week*, July 23, 2001; Christine Tierney, Andrea Zammert, Joann Muller and Katie Kerwin, "Volkswagen," *Business Week*, July 23, 2001.

1. **How would VW use market assessment to evaluate sales potential for its cars in the US?**
2. **Does VW need to modify its cars for the US market? Why or why not?**
3. **Would the nature of VW's products allow the company to use an identical promotional message worldwide or would the company have to develop a country-by-country promotion strategy?**
4. **How would currency fluctuations affect VW's profit in the US market?**
5. **What type of distribution system would be most effective for VW in the US?**

INTRODUCTION

International marketing
The process of identifying the goods and services that customers outside the home country want and then providing them at the right price and place

International marketing is the process of identifying the goods and services that customers outside the home country want and then providing them at the right price and place.[1] In the international marketplace this process is similar to that carried out at home, but there are some important modifications that are used to adapt marketing efforts to the needs of the specific country or geographic locale.[2] For example, some MNEs are able to use the same strategy abroad as they have at home. This is particularly true in promotions where messages can carry a universal theme. Some writing implement firms advertise their pens and pencils as "the finest writing instruments in the world", a message that transcends national boundaries and can be used anywhere. Many fast-food franchises apply the same ideas because they have found that people everywhere have the same basic reasons for coming to their unit to eat. In most cases, however, it is necessary to tailor-make the strategy so that it appeals directly to the local customer.

These changes fall into five major areas: market assessment, product decisions, promotion strategies, pricing decisions, and place or distribution strategies. The latter four areas – product, promotion, price, and place – are often referred to as the four Ps of marketing,[3] and they constitute the heart of international marketing efforts.

INTERNATIONAL MARKET ASSESSMENT

International market assessment
An evaluation of the goods and services that the multinational can sell in the global marketplace

International marketing strategy starts with **international market assessment**, an evaluation of the goods and services that the MNE can sell in the global marketplace.[4] This assessment typically involves a series of analyses aimed at pinpointing specific offerings and geographic targets. The first step in this process is called the initial screening.

Initial screening: basic need and potential

Initial screening
The process of determining the basic need potential of the multinational's goods and services in foreign markets

Initial screening is the process of determining the basic need potential of the MNE's goods and services in foreign markets. This screening answers the question: Who might be interested in buying our output?[5] International auto manufacturers will list the EU countries, North America, and Japan as potential buyers. Boeing will target the countries that will be rebuilding their air fleets during the millennium.[6] Kellogg's, General Mills, and Nestlé will be interested in the US and the EU as well as in developing nations that offer potentially new markets.

One way in which initial screening is carried out is by examining the current import policies of other countries and identifying those goods and services that are now being purchased from abroad. A second way is by determining local production. A third way is by examining the demographic changes that are taking place in the country which will create new, emerging markets. These cursory efforts help the MNE to target potential markets. Following the initial screening, the company will begin to narrow its selection.

Second screening: financial and economic conditions

Secondary screening is used to reduce the list of market prospects by eliminating those that fail to meet financial and economic considerations. Financial considerations include inflation rates, interest rates, expected returns on investment, the buying habits of customers, and the availability of credit. These factors are important in determining whether markets that passed the initial, general screening are also financially feasible.

Market indicators Indicators used for measuring the relative market strengths of various geographic areas

Market size An economic screening consideration used in international marketing; it is the relative size of each market as a percentage of the total world market

Market intensity The richness of a market or the degree of purchasing power in one country as compared with others

Market growth The annual increase in sales in a particular market

Trend analysis The estimation of future demand by either extrapolating the growth over the last 3 to 5 years and assuming that this trend will continue or by using some form of average growth rate over the recent past

Estimation by analogy A method of forecasting market demand or market growth based on information generated in other countries, such as determining the number of refrigerators sold in the US as a percentage of new housing starts and using this statistic in planning for the manufacture of these products in other world markets

Regression analysis A mathematical approach to forecasting which attempts to test the explanatory power of a set of independent variables

Cluster analysis A marketing approach to forecasting customer demand; it involves the grouping of data based on market area, customer, or similar variables

Economic considerations relate to a variety of market demand influences, including market indicators. **Market indicators** are used for measuring the relative market strengths of various geographic areas. These indicators focus on three important areas: market size, market intensity, and market growth. **Market size** is the relative size of each market as a percentage of the total world market. For example, industrialized countries account for a sizeable part of the market for cellular telephones, and a few nations such as the US and Japan account for the largest percentage of this total. Nonetheless, non-industrialized with large populations also have a significant market size. In fact, China, the world's largest country in terms of population, is the world's largest mobile phone market in terms of subscribers.[7] **Market intensity** is the "richness" of the market or the degree of the purchasing power in one country, compared with others. For example, the US and Canada are extremely rich markets for automobiles, telephones, and computers, so MNEs selling these products will highlight these two countries. **Market growth** is the annual increase in sales. For example, the market for portable telephones and notebook computers in the US will continue to grow during the millennium, whereas the market for autos will increase much more slowly. However, given the large purchasing power in the US economy, MNEs selling these products will continue to target the US. In recent years other economies, such as Japan, have become increasingly rich in terms of purchasing power, so they too are now target markets for high-tech products. Infrastructure and economic development can also influence market growth. For example, consumers in developing countries, who have not yet been able to acquire a fixed line, might choose instead to purchase a portable phone. It is estimated that, by 2005, one in four Latin Americans will have a portable phone.[8]

Quite often these data are analyzed through the use of quantitative techniques. Sometimes these approaches are fairly simple. **Trend analysis**, for example, is the estimation of future demand either by extrapolating the growth over the last three to five years and assuming that this trend will continue or by using some form of average growth rate over the recent past. A similar approach is **estimation by analogy** through which forecasters predict market demand or growth based on information generated in other countries. For example, if the number of refrigerators sold in the US is 2.5 times the number of new housing starts, a US MNE that is planning to manufacture these products in the EU will estimate demand based on the same formula. A more sophisticated approach is the use of **regression analysis**, a mathematical approach to forecasting which attempts to test the explanatory power of a set of independent variables. In the case of selling refrigerators in the EU, for example, these would include economic growth, per capita income, and the number of births, in addition to other variables including new housing starts. Another sophisticated approach is **cluster analysis**, which is a marketing approach involving the grouping of data on the basis of market area, customer, and so on, based on similar variables. Then a marketing strategy would be formulated for each group. For example, US MNEs providing services in such areas as insurance, legal, financial, and management consulting know that their approaches must often vary from country to country.

Third screening: political and legal forces

The third level of screening involves looking at political and legal forces. One of the primary considerations is entry barriers in the form of import restrictions or limits on local ownership of business operations. Analysis of these barriers often results in identifying loopholes around the various restrictions or data that indicate barriers are far less extensive than initially believed.[9] For example, some MNEs have been able to sidestep legal restrictions by forming joint ventures with local firms. Production restrictions or limitations on profit remittance that restrict operating flexibility must also be considered.

The stability of the government is an important factor in starting a successful operation; however, it is often difficult to predict. Despite the eagerness of investors to flock the Russian market in the early 1990s, auto makers were hesitant to invest in Russia because of the uncertain political and economic environment. It was only in 1998 that Fiat made a commitment to the Russian market.[10] Another consideration is the protection offered for patents, trademarks, and copyrights. In some countries such as China and Taiwan, pirating has been fairly common, resulting in a flooding of markets with counterfeit or look-alike products.

Fourth screening: sociocultural forces

The fourth level of screening typically involves consideration of sociocultural forces such as language, work habits, customs, religion, and values. As noted earlier, culture greatly affects the way people live and MNEs want to examine how well their operations will fit into each particular culture. For example, although Japanese auto manufacturers have set up assembly plants in the US, operations are not identical to those in Japan because of the work habits and customs of Americans. In the US, the work pace is less frantic and most people are unwilling to work the typical $5^1/_2$-day week, which is so common in Japan. Moreover, US managers are accustomed to going home to their families after work, whereas Japanese managers often go out for dinner and drinks and discuss business until late in the evening. MNEs will examine these sociocultural differences in determining where to locate operations.

Fifth screening: competitive environment

The fifth level of screening is typically focused on competitive forces. If there are three or four locations that are equally attractive, the MNE will often make a final choice based on the degree of competition that exists in each locale. In some cases companies do not want to enter markets where there is strong competition. However, in many cases MNEs will decide to enter a competitive market because they believe that potential benefits far outweigh the drawbacks. By going head-to-head with the competition, the company can force itself to become more efficient and effective and thus improve its own competitiveness. The company can do this by taking market share away from a strong competitor and by putting the opposition on the defense. And the MNE can force the opposition to commit more resources to defending the market under attack and to reduce its ability to retaliate effectively. Of course, these conditions do not always hold true, but they help to illustrate why MNEs will consider entering markets that are dominated by competitors.

Final selection

Before making a final selection, MNEs will usually enhance their information by visiting on-site and talking to trade representatives or local officials. Such field trips are very common and can do a great deal to supplement currently available information. Sometimes these trips take the form of a **trade mission**. This is a visit sponsored by commercial officers in a country's local embassy and is designed to bring together executives from MNEs that are interested in examining the benefits of doing business in the particular country.

Based on the outcome of the screenings and the supplemental data, an MNE will make a choice regarding the goods and services to offer overseas.[11] The marketing strategy that is employed in this process revolves around what are commonly called the four Ps of marketing: product, promotion, price, and place.

Active learning check

Review your answer to Active Learning Case question 1 and make any changes you like. Then compare your answer with the one below.

1. How would VW use market assessment to evaluate sales potential for its cars in the US?

There are a number of steps that VW would take. One would be to look at the number of cars being imported into the country, as well as the number being built locally, since this would provide important information regarding current product supply. Another would be to find out the number of auto registrations and how fast this number is growing annually because this would be useful in predicting new sales potential. A third would be to examine the trend of new car sales over the last couple of years and to forecast overall industry sales for the next two to three years. A fourth would be to compare the strengths offered by VW cars with those offered by the competition and to make an evaluation of how the company can position its offering for maximum market penetration.

PRODUCT STRATEGIES

Product strategies will vary depending on the specific good and the customers.[12] Some products can be manufactured and sold successfully both in the US and abroad by using the same strategies. Other products must be modified or adapted and sold according to a specially designed strategy.[13] Figure 11.1 shows a range of possibilities. Products and services located on the left side of the continuum require little modification; those on the right must be modified to fit the market.

Little or no modification

Industrial goods and technical services are good examples of products that need little or no modification. A bulldozer, a notebook computer, and a photocopying machine serve the same purposes and are used the same way in the US as they are in France or in China.[14] Alterations would be minor and include such things as adapting the machine to the appropriate electric voltage or changing the language used for instructions and labels on the machine. The same is true for many types of services. For example, international engineering and construction firms find that their product strategies are

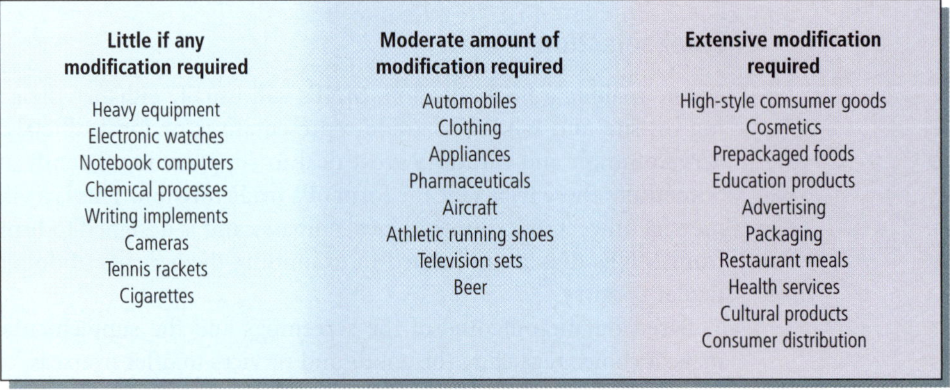

Figure 11.1 **Selected examples of product modification in the international arena**

similar worldwide. People interested in having a dam or a power plant constructed use the same basic concepts and have similar needs throughout the world. In fact, experience is the greatest selling point in convincing clients to hire an MNE in engineering or construction. For example, US firms that had experience in putting out oil well fires in the US and cleaning up the *Exxon Valdez* oil spill in Alaska found a demand for their services in the aftermath of the Gulf War of 1991. Companies with a strong international brand image have also been able to succeed without a differentiation strategy. For example, Chivas Regal, the world-famous Scotch, is sold in many countries, and the product is identical in each case. Similarly, Schweppes (tonic water) and Perrier are internationally known and these respective products are identical worldwide.

Moderate to high modification

A number of factors will result in an MNE using moderate to high product modification. These include economics, culture, local laws, level of technology, and the product's life cycle.

Economics

There are many examples of how economic considerations affect the decision to modify a product. For example, in the US chewing gum packages often contain 10 to 20 sticks. But in many other countries weak purchasing power of the customers necessitates packaging the gum with only five sticks. In many countries consumers must carry their goods home from the store, and so smaller packages and containers are preferable to larger, heavier ones.

Economics is also important when the cost of a product is either too high or too low to make it attractive in another country. For example, in economically advanced countries cash registers are electronic; virtually no one uses hand-cranked machines. However, in many countries of the world electronic cash registers are too expensive and sophisticated for most retail stores and small establishments. So MNEs like National Cash Register continue to manufacture the hand-cranked versions. On the other hand, inexpensive calculating machines are widely employed throughout the world and many stores use hand-held calculators to total customer purchases (although in some places calculations may be cross-checked for accuracy with an abacus).

Similarly, in economically advanced countries products are likely to have frills or extras, whereas in less economically advanced countries only the basic model is offered. For example, in the US, bicycles are used for exercise and recreation and will have a number of special features that make bicycle riding particularly enjoyable. However, in many countries bicycles are a primary source of transportation. So while US bikes are built for comfort and ease of handling, in third world countries they are built for economy and ease of maintenance. As a result, manufacturers will modify the product to fit customer needs.

Culture

In some cases a product must be adapted to different ways people are accustomed to doing things. For example, the French prefer washing machines that load from the top, whereas the British like front-loading units. The Germans prefer high-speed machines that take out most of the moisture in the spin-dry process, whereas the Italians like slower spin speeds because they prefer to hang-dry laundry in the sun. So manufacturers who sell washing machines in the EU must produce a variety of different units.

Food is often an item that must be modified or sold differently. In fast-food franchises like McDonald's, portions of the menu are similar throughout the world and some items are designed to cater specifically to local tastes. For example, coffee in South American units tends to be a much stronger blend than that sold in North America. In certain parts of Europe and Asia, the food is more highly seasoned in keeping with local tastes. For products that are not modified, the marketing focus will be different because of the way the item is used. Schweppes tonic water, for example, typically serves as a mixer in the US and Britain where drinks like gin and tonic are popular. In some countries, France, for example, Schweppes is drunk without alcohol. Clearly, the marketing approaches would be different in these two situations. The marketing message is also important when selling hard liquors. The products remain the same but many places have social customs that frown upon excessive consumption. In these cases MNEs such as Seagram of Canada have tailored their advertising messages along the lines of moderate drinking and the use of mixers to reduce the alcoholic content per serving.

Culture also influences purchasing decisions made on the basis of style or aesthetics. Cosmetics and other beauty aids are good examples. Perfumes that sell well in Europe often have difficulty gaining market share in the US because they do not appeal to American women. Similarly, many products that sell well in the US, such as shampoos and deodorants, have limited market appeal elsewhere. People may not use these products or may have difficulty differentiating the product from local offerings. For example, Gillette has found that it is difficult to develop a distinctive edge in selling toiletries because many people feel that these products are all basically the same.

Convenience and comfort are other culturally driven factors that help to explain the need for product modification. Early Japanese autos in the US were designed to attack other foreign imports, specifically the VW Beetle. Researchers found that the two biggest complaints with the Beetle were the small amount of room in the back seat and the heater, which took too long to warm up the car. Aware that Americans wanted an economical car with these additional features, Japanese imports offered greater leg room for back seat passengers and a heater that was superior to the VW offering. Within a few years these imports began to erode VW's market share. Foreign manufacturers also identified a group that wanted a large number of convenience and comfort features. The result has been the emergence of luxury Japanese and German cars that now compete extremely well with US models in the upper end of the market.

Other culturally based reasons for product modifications include color and language. In the US, the color black is worn for mourning, whereas in other countries white is for mourning and so it is not used for consumer goods. Similarly, most shampoos in the US are light-colored, whereas in some oriental countries consumers prefer dark-colored shampoo. Language can be an important point of modification because a product may need to carry instructions regarding contents or use procedures. In locations where two or more languages are spoken, such as Canada and Switzerland, this information is provided in all appropriate languages. Language is also important in conveying the right image for the product. Quite often it is difficult to replicate the message because the saying or slogan has no meaning in another language.

Local laws

Local laws can require modification of products in order to meet environmental and safety requirements. For example, US emission-control laws have required Japanese and European car importers to make significant model changes before their autos can be sold in the US. Food and pharmaceutical regulations require packaging and labeling that are often quite different from those in the home country. For example, in Saudi Arabia the label of any product containing animal fat or meat must clearly state the kind of animal used and the fact that no swine products were used. Brand-name protection can also require product modification. For example, Ford Motor found that in Mexico it had to rename the Ford Falcon because this brand name was registered to another firm. The same happened to Ford in the case of the Mustang in Germany.

Product life cycle

Another reason for modifying a product is to cope with the limited product life cycle (PLC) of the good. Ford Motor, for example, was extremely profitable in Europe during the 1980s, but those earnings disappeared by the early 1990s because Ford did not develop new, competitive products.[15] This is in contrast to Coca-Cola of Japan, which introduces an average of one new soft drink per month and has the competition scurrying to keep up. Another good example is provided by Gillette, which has been particularly effective in combining technology and marketing to bring new products to market before the market share of old offerings begins to decline significantly. The box "International Business Strategy in Action: Gillette storms the market" describes the company's latest approach.

INTERNATIONAL BUSINESS STRATEGY *IN ACTION*

Gillette storms the market

The razor blade market is extremely competitive, and, while successful products can provide short-run market domination, new products must be introduced every three to five years. In the case of Gillette, for example, the Trac II blade was brought to market in the US in October 1971 and managed to garner almost 30 per cent of the market by 1975. After this time market share began to fall off, but in 1978 the company introduced the Atra blade, and for the next eight years Atra's market share climbed to over 20 per cent before starting to fall. Gillette is a brand-name company that includes its razor and blade business, the Braun small appliances brand, Oral-B, and the Duracell batteries brand. In 2000, Gillette held 80 per cent of the blade and razor market in the US.

During the 1990s Gillette spent $750 million and seven years of research to develop its Mach 3 blade, and this offering has done well as it is completely re-engineered, with a strip to signal the need to change the cartridge. While most new products cannibalize older systems by getting customers to switch from one product to another, the Mach 3 has helped Gillette to capture over 20 per cent of the worldwide market share. A few months after the introduction of the Mach 3, a British supermarket, Asda, introduced its own version which was developed at a fraction of the cost. In 2001, Gillette again was true to its logo "Innovation is Gillette" and announced the launch of the Mach3Turbo, a premium razor to be retailed at $9. The company is expected to invest $300 million in worldwide marketing of this product. About 700 million people around the world use Gillette blades. Today the company has 38 plants in 19 countries and it distributes products in over 200 countries.

The company's strategy of new product introductions also extends to its acquisitions such as Braun AG, world famous for its electric shavers and small appliances. Today Braun's coffee-makers, coffee-grinders, hairdryers, curlers, and dental hygiene products are known for their high quality and sophisticated technology. Braun has also introduced a low-priced shaver that has been a spectacular success. Gillette is also marketing the new Braun Oral-B 3D Excel power plaque remover to attract further market share. In 2000, Braun held 52 per cent of the toothbrush market.

Gillette has not been successful in toiletries such as shampoos or deodorants – products that are extremely difficult to differentiate. However, the company is now offering a new line of brand toiletries for men. This is in keeping with Gillette's overall strategy of continuing to offer new products for the international market, both to replace products that are reaching the end of their product life cycle and to generate demand in new consumer markets that are beginning to emerge. In recent years the firm has been ranked as one of the most admired in America, and it has generated an annual average return on investment of 30 per cent. If Gillette continues "business as usual", it should have no trouble meeting future challenges.

Websites: ***www.gillette.com***; ***www.braun.com***; ***www.oralb.com*** and ***www.duracell.com***.

Sources: Subrata N. Chakravarty, "We Had to Change the Playing Field," *Forbes*, February 4, 1991, pp. 82–86; "Corporate Regulations," *Fortune*, February 8, 1993, p. 60; Susan E. Kuhn, "How to Get High Returns from Top-Quality Stocks," *Fortune*, March 8, 1993, pp. 27–30; ***www.Gillette.com***; ***www.braun.com***; "Gillette, Defying Economy, Introduces a $9 Razor Set," *New York Times*, October 31, 2001.

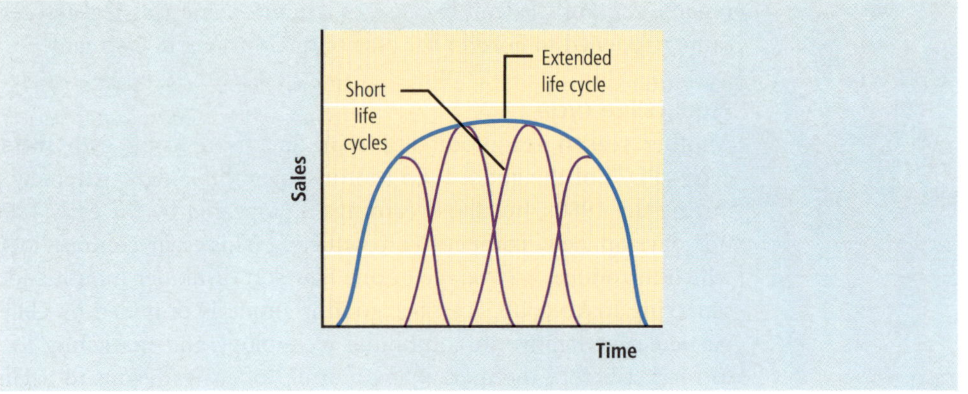

Figure 11.2 **Product life cycles: two different approaches**

One of the most effective strategies has been to shorten the PLC by offering new goods and services before the demand for the old ones has dropped significantly. Figure 11.2 provides a graphic illustration. Note in the figure that there are two types of PLCs. One is the standard PLC, which covers an extended time continuum, often four to five years. The other is a short life cycle that lasts much less. Many companies are discovering that, by shortening the PLC and offering new product adaptations, they are able to capture and retain large market share. This is typically done by offering a new product and then modifying it and bringing out a new version before the competition can effectively combat the first offering. For example, a company will offer a notebook computer with a 64-megabyte internal memory. Then within six months the company will come out with a 128-megabyte internal memory and a built-in modem. Six months later the firm will offer still another version of the product that contains a CD writer and DVD. The video game platform market provides another example of strategic continuous innovation. Nintendo and Sony constantly introduce new products and games to capture the market.[16] In each case the competition is left scurrying to keep up. As long as the firm can continue this adaptation strategy, it can outmode the old product (and those of competitors as well) and maintain market position. At some point the competition may gain the advantage by offering a product that revolutionizes the field, but as long as a product improvement strategy remains viable, the firm will continue to be the product leader, and this strategy is being implemented by MNEs throughout the world.[17]

Active learning check

Review your answer to Active Learning Case question 2 and make any changes you like. Then compare your answer with the one below.

2. Does VW need to modify its cars for the US market? Why or why not?

Based on the case data, it appears that VW needs to make some changes in styling and engineering. The company is convinced that Americans will buy cars that offer German engineering and quality, and in the past VW has made the mistake of producing cars that look "too American". Because of this, many people bought cars from Ford, General Motors, and Chrysler because there were no distinctive qualities that VW could use in attracting these buyers. By modifying its cars and giving them European styling and German engineering, VW can lead from strength and exploit its market advantage.

PROMOTION

Promotion
The process of stimulating demand for a company's goods and services

Promotion is the process of stimulating demand for a company's goods and services.[18] MNEs promote their goods and services through advertising and personal selling. The specific approach that is used, however, will be determined by the nature of the product.

Nature of the product

In promoting a product, a company can use a variety of approaches. The choice will be heavily influenced by whether the firm believes that the same message can be used worldwide or that it needs to be adapted, and whether the product will remain the same or be modified. Here are four variations on this theme:

- *Identical product and identical message.* This approach is used when the MNE intends to sell the same product worldwide and believes that an identical promotional appeal can be used in all markets. A. T. Cross, for example, uses this strategy because writing instruments do not need to be adapted to local markets, so a universal message can be used.
- *Identical product but different message.* This strategy is used when the product satisfies a different need in various markets. For example, in the US, many car companies tout the luxury and convenience of their product, but in other countries the same cars are promoted on the basis of their fuel efficiency or ability to meet basic transportation needs.
- *Modified product but same message.* This strategy is used when the market requires a different version of the product but the needs of the consumer are the same. For example, whether washing machines load from the top or the side, they provide the same function and meet the same customer needs. Similarly, in many countries the seasoning of foods differs from that of foods sold in the US. So while the product is changed, the promotion message remains the same because the needs of the buyer are the same.
- *Modified product and modified message.* When the product use and the buying habits of customers are different from those in the MNE's home market, both the product and promotion message will be modified. For example, breakfast cereal companies such as Kellogg's and General Mills are developing new versions of their popular US cereals for sale in the European market. Since many Europeans do not eat cereal for breakfast, however, the promotion campaign is geared toward changing eating habits rather than (as in the US) getting consumers to switch product loyalty.

Advertising

Advertising
A non-personal form of promotion in which a firm attempts to persuade consumers of a particular point of view

Advertising is a non-personal form of promotion in which a firm attempts to persuade consumers to a particular point of view. In many cases MNEs use the same advertising message worldwide, and since many products fill similar worldwide needs, the company can use a universal message and reduce advertising costs at the same time. However, there are times when the advertising must be adapted to the local market. Two of the most common reasons are that (1) the way in which the product is used is different from that in the home country and (2) the advertising message does not make sense if translated directly. An example of the latter is the Nike commercials that encourage the viewer to "just do it", or Budweiser commercials that ask, "Why ask why?" These make sense to US viewers, but they are too culturally grounded to be used in many other countries. These commercials would leave the viewer confused as to what the advertiser was saying.

As a result, advertisers are very careful to tie the message to buyer needs and wants. On the other hand, there are many advertisements that have been only moderately modified or carried in their entirety because they *do* make sense in other cultures. For example, Marlboro's "cowboy image" has universal appeal, and Nike's ads featuring such internationally known stars as Michael Jordan and Tiger Woods transcend national boundaries, especially after the media exposure they have received. The box "International Business Strategy in Action: IKEA in international markets" provides some examples of how this is being done.

As in the US, MNEs use a number of media to carry their advertising messages. The three most popular media are television, radio, and newspapers. Some of the major differences between the approach used in the US and that employed in other countries include government regulation of media advertising and the fact that many stations do not carry advertising, although in recent years this has been changing. In particular, the use of television advertising has been increasing in Europe, whereas in other areas of the world such as South America and the Middle East newspapers remain the major medium for promotion efforts. However, there are restrictions regarding what can be presented.

INTERNATIONAL BUSINESS STRATEGY *IN ACTION*

IKEA in international markets

In less than 50 years IKEA has grown from a small, private, Swedish furniture retailer to a multinational business with 157 stores in 33 countries and annual sales of $8.5 billion. This internationalization process is all the more remarkable in that IKEA has remained true to the basic philosophy of founder, Ingvar Kamprad, throughout its global expansion. Today IKEA is still a private company.

Initial success can be traced directly to Kamprad, a creative maverick in the furniture business. He redesigned the industry by introducing knock-down kits that customers could take away from the store and assemble themselves. This saved on delivery and changed furniture from its traditional frosty "showroom" mentality to a more "fun" place with children's playpens, nurseries, and cafes in the stores. IKEA also built on the fast growing informal suburban culture by providing abundant parking and by making a trip to the store an entertainment for the family.

This Scandinavian image of relaxed, informal yet efficient service, was extended to Switzerland in 1973, Munich in 1974, to 10 more stores across Germany by 1980 and then throughout the rest of Europe, culminating with entry into Britain in 1987. Internationally, IKEA opened in Australia in 1975 and Canada in 1976. Expansion to the US began in 1985, through the Canadian IKEA operation, into Eastern Europe in the early 1990s, and into Shanghai, China in 1998.

IKEA also brought innovation to the logistics of furniture production by setting up groups of key suppliers to produce components at low cost. These subcontractors, in turn, made money by getting large-volume orders for standardized components from IKEA.

Additionally, the company has kept tight control over product design and quality to maintain its brand name and the distinctive identity of its furniture. And the firm was able to expand rapidly because it did not have to establish expensive manufacturing facilities around Europe, but rather retained centralized control over the subcontractors.

The firm's marketing strategy has been to build on the Swedish home-base stereotype of clean and efficient service. All furniture is well designed, modern, functional, durable, high quality and price competitive. Its image and brand name are well established and have survived numerous imitators. As a result, IKEA has been able to move from its Scandinavian base to being a strong regional player in Europe, and is now competing successfully in the global arena.

In particular, IKEA is a successful multinational business because it has introduced a highly differentiated product into a traditional industry and has now built a globally recognized brand name for high quality, inexpensive, and attractive furniture. It has also combined the generic strategies of differentiation, low cost, and niching and has outsourced both production and delivery components of the value chain.

Website: ***www.ikea.com***.

Sources: Christopher A. Bartlett and Ashish Nanda, *Ingvar Kamprad and IKEA*, Harvard Business School Case 9-390-132; Joseph R. D'Cruz and Alan M. Rugman, "Developing International Competitiveness: The Five Partners Model," *Business Quarterly*, vol. 58, no. 2 (Winter 1993), pp. 60–72; ***www:ikea.com***.

Comparative advertising
The comparing of similar products for the purpose of persuading customers to buy a particular one

Examples include: (1) some countries prohibit **comparative advertising**, in which companies compare their products with those of the competition; (2) some countries do not allow certain products to be advertised because they want to discourage their use (alcoholic beverages and cigarettes, for example) or because they want to protect national industries from MNE competition; and (3) some (such as Islamic) countries censor the use of any messages that are regarded as erotic.

Personal selling

Personal selling
A direct form of promotion used to persuade customers of a particular point of view

Personal selling is a direct form of promotion used to persuade customers to a particular point of view. Some goods, such as industrial products or goods that require explanation or description, rely heavily on personal selling. Avon, the cosmetics company, relies primarily on personal selling and has been very successful with this approach even in countries where people are unaccustomed to buying cosmetics from a door-to-door salesperson. In Mexico, for example, Avon managed to gain acceptance by first introducing the idea of personal selling through a massive advertising campaign so that housewives became aware that the Avon salesperson was not a common door-to-door vendor but, rather, a professional trained to help clients look beautiful. Personal selling is also widely used in marketing products such as pharmaceuticals and sophisticated electronic equipment. For example, Pfizer and Upjohn use salespeople to call on doctors and other individuals who are in a position to recommend their products, and General Electric and Westinghouse salespeople use the same approach in selling overseas that they use in the US.

Because many international markets are so large, some MNEs have also turned to telemarketing. This approach has been very successful in the US, and the overseas subsidiaries of US firms such as IBM, Ford Motor, and Digital Equipment have been using telemarketing to generate new sales. European firms such as Peugeot have also been adopting this approach.

MNEs have also focused attention on recruiting salespeople on an international basis. In some countries this work is not highly regarded, so MNEs have given these people managerial titles that command importance, such as territory or zone manager. Recruiting local talent is extremely important since these people are often better able to sell to local customers. If the product requires special training to sell, MNEs often bring new salespeople to the home office for training, introduce these individuals to those who are manufacturing the products, and create a feeling of teamwork among the field staff and personnel so that the salespeople are energized to go back into the field and sell.

Active learning check

Review your answer to Active Learning Case question 3 and make any changes you like. Then compare your answer with the one below.

3. Would the nature of VW's products allow the company to use an identical promotional message worldwide or would the company have to develop a country-by-country promotion strategy?

This answer will depend on where VW is selling its product. In less developed countries the message would be geared toward economy and efficiency. In more developed countries the message would focus on styling, handling, engineering, and non-economic factors as well. So VW would need to develop a series of different messages because there are a wide number of market niches and no one message will appeal to everyone in the same way.

PRICING

The pricing of goods and services in the international marketplace is often influenced by factors present in home market pricing. These factors include government controls, market diversity, currency fluctuations, and price escalation forces.

Government controls

Every nation has government regulations that influence pricing practices. In some countries there are minimum and maximum prices that can be charged to customers. Minimum prices can help to protect local companies from more efficient international competitors because of a floor on prices that can help to ensure profit for national firms. For example, if the minimum price for a particular type of personal computer is $1,000 and local companies can produce and sell the product for $700, they will make $300 a unit. Foreign competitors may be able to produce and sell the product for $500 and make a $500 profit per unit, but the minimum price laws prevent them from driving out local competition. Without this law, overseas competitors might price the unit at $600 and then raise the price dramatically after local competitors went out of business.

Dumping
The selling of imported goods at a price below cost or below that in the home country

Governments also prohibit **dumping**, or the selling of imported goods at a price below cost or below the cost in the home country. The General Agreement on Tariffs and Trade (GATT) specifically prohibits this practice, which is designed to help MNEs drive out the local competition and then establish a monopoly and subsequently increase prices at will. A number of US firms have been influential in getting the US government to bring dumping charges against Japanese competitors.

Market diversity

Consumer tastes and demands vary widely in the international marketplace, and this results in MNEs having to price some of their products differently. For example, companies have found that they can charge more for goods sold overseas because of the demand. For example, in the US, there is a greater demand for light turkey meat than for dark turkey meat. The latter is typically sold at a lower price and is often purchased by animal food producers. However, the plump dark meat of turkey thighs has a strong market in Europe. As a result, firms like the Shenandoah Valley Poultry Company export thousands of metric tons of dark turkey meat to Europe each year.

A second factor influencing market diversity is the perceived quality of the product. For example, in the US, German auto makers such as Mercedes found that some Americans are willing to pay a premium for German cars. In contrast, the Japanese are not willing to pay a premium for German autos, so Mercedes' pricing structure in Japan is different. More recently Japanese luxury autos have themselves proved to be strong competitors for Mercedes in the US market.

Another factor is the tax laws and attitudes about carrying debt. In the US, some interest payments are tax deductible, and most people have no aversion to assuming at least some debt. In many other countries interest payments are not tax deductible and people are unaccustomed to carrying debt. In Japan, for example, little use is made of consumer credit. In pricing products, MNEs will adjust the local strategy to accommodate the impact of the tax laws and the consumer's willingness to assume debt.

Currency fluctuations

As noted in Chapter 7, when selling products overseas, MNEs often end up assuming the risks associated with currency fluctuations. This risk is particularly important when multinationals have a return on investment target because this objective can become unattainable if the local currency is devalued. For example, if it costs Mercedes $30,000 to manufacture and ship a particular model to the US and the company sells the car to its dealer for $40,000, Mercedes is making a 33 per cent profit on the sale ($10,000/$30,000). However, if the dollar decreases in value by 10 per cent against the German mark, then the company's profit percentage will decline and the firm will have to choose between the following options: (1) to increase the price of the car to the dealer to make up the loss of dollar value, (2) to absorb the loss and leave the price the same, or (3) to absorb part of the loss and increase the price to the dealer to make up the difference. In the mid 1980s, Mercedes absorbed the loss because price increases resulted in sharply lowered demand for the car and even less overall profit for the company. Of course, when the value of the dollar increased against the mark during the 1990s, Mercedes profited accordingly and lowered that price in order to generate additional sales. Beginning in the late 1980s US firms found that their products were becoming much more attractive to European buyers, thanks to the devaluation of the dollar and the accompanying increase in purchasing power of buyers on the Continent. But, the strength of the dollar in the 1990s decreased the demand for US exports. Asian imports, on the other hand, became increasingly price competitive in the US market due to the devaluation of most Asian currencies in the late 1990s.[19]

Price escalation forces

A problem similar to that discussed above is price escalation forces that drive up the cost of imported goods. In the case of Mercedes, for example, if the cost of the car rose from $30,000 to $33,000, the company would want to pass this along to the dealer. In the case of MNEs that sell through a marketing channel where there is a series of middlemen, the effect of a price escalation can be even greater because everyone in the channel will add a percentage increase. For example, if an MNE exports and sells a consumer good for $10 to a large wholesaler and there are five additional middlemen in the channel, each of whom marks up the good by 20 per cent, as seen in Table 11.1, the final price to the consumer is $24.88. If the MNE's cost rises from $10 to $13, the final price to the consumer will now be $32.35, a 30 per cent increase. So price increases by the MNE can dramatically affect what the customer pays, and as long as the multinational continues to export as opposed to manufacture locally, price will be a key marketing consideration because of its effect on consumer demand. In this example it is likely that customer demand would drop substantially unless there are no effective substitutes for this product.

Table 11.1 The effect of MNE pricing on final consumer costs

	Price charged by each middleman				
MNE price	*1*	*2*	*3*	*4*	*5*
$10	$12.00	$14.40	$17.28	$20.74	$24.88
$13	$15.60	$18.72	$22.46	$26.96	$32.35

Ultimate effect of a $3 increase in MNE price: $32.35 – $24.88 = $7.47 or 30 per cent.

Active learning check 

Review your answer to Active Learning Case question 4 and make any changes you like. Then compare your answer with the one below.

4. How would currency fluctuations affect VW's profit in the US market?

Currency fluctuations would affect VW's profit in the US market according to the value of the German mark in relation to the dollar. If the value of the mark were to decline, VW's profit per car sold in the US would rise because these dollars would buy more marks. Conversely, if the value of the mark increased, profit per car would decline because these dollars would buy fewer marks.

PLACE

Distribution
The course that goods take between production and the final consumer

The importance of international logistics was discussed in Chapter 10. The focus of attention here will be on the distribution differences among countries and conditions with which MNEs must be familiar. **Distribution** is the course that goods take between production and the final consumer. This course often differs on a country-by-country basis, and MNEs will spend a considerable amount of time in examining the different systems that are in place, the criteria to use in choosing distributors and channels, and how distribution segmentation will be employed.[20]

Different distribution systems

It is often difficult to standardize the distribution system and to use the same approach in every country because there are many individual differences to be considered. For example, in some countries such as Finland there is a predominance of general line retailers who carry a wide assortment of merchandise. In contrast, the wholesale and retail structure in Italy is characterized by a wide array of stores, many of which specialize or carry limited lines of merchandise. So in distributing goods in these two countries, MNEs need to employ different strategies.

Consumer spending habits can also negate attempts to standardize distribution. In the US, many middlemen are geared to handling credit sales, whereas in Japan, most consumer purchases are on a cash basis. In both Germany and the US, mail-order buying has increased dramatically in recent years, whereas in Portugal and Spain the market is quite small. So the route that the goods take to the consumer will vary.

The location where consumers are used to buying will also influence distribution. In economically developed countries where supermarkets have become commonplace, customers purchase a wide variety of food and other products under one roof. In most countries, however, purchases are made in smaller stores and distribution requires the MNE or the local sales manager to deal with a large number of retailers, each of whom is selling a small amount of merchandise. In recent years some wholesalers and retailers have been expanding their operations to other countries. For example, Wal-Mart, the giant US retailer, has expanded into Mexico and Europe: in 1999 it bought the British supermarket chain, Asda. However, most middlemen operate exclusively within one country, another factor helping to explain why it is still difficult to standardize distribution on an international basis.

Choosing the best distribution system

MNEs use a number of criteria in creating the most efficient distribution system. One is to get the best possible distributors to carry their products. A key factor in evaluating potential distributors is the financial strength of the wholesaler or retailer because the multinational wants to know that the distributor will be able to survive the long run. MNEs that sell goods that require periodic maintenance and servicing will be interested in businesses that can keep sufficient inventory on hand. This is particularly important when selling products such as autos, computers, and electronic equipment. A second factor is how well connected the distributor is in terms of knowing the right people and of providing assistance in handling governmental red tape. This is an important consideration for Coca-Cola when choosing overseas distributors. A third factor is the number and types of product lines the distributor carries currently so that the multinational can identify middlemen who are most likely to give its goods a strong marketing push.

In many cases distributors will have competitive products or feel that they do not need to add any new product lines. If the multinational wants to tap into this distribution system, the company will have to formulate an incentive program that is designed to convince the distributor to carry its products. Some of the ways in which this is done include (1) helping to pay for local promotion campaigns of the product, (2) providing generous sales incentives, (3) conducting marketing research to identify customer niches and sales forecasts to help the distributor to decide how much inventory to carry,[21] and (4) ensuring that unsold or outmoded merchandise can be returned for a full refund.

Depending on the nature of the market and the competition, the multinational may give exclusive geographic distribution to one local seller or may arrange to have a number of sellers jointly selling the product. For example, auto manufacturers will often have more than one dealer in a major metropolis but be willing to give exclusive geographic distribution rights to dealers located in rural areas. This is in contrast to food products that can be sold in a wide variety of outlets and where exclusivity is unnecessary. In these cases the multinational will try to get a variety of distributors to carry the product.

Active learning check 

Review your answer to Active Learning Case question 5 and make any changes you like. Then compare your answer with the one below.

5. What type of distribution system would be most effective for VW in the US?

VW would use the same type of distribution system as that employed by other car manufacturers (i.e. auto dealerships). The big challenge for VW will be to open new dealerships and thus increase market coverage. The market in the US is fairly well blanketed with auto dealerships, but the company could look for successful dealers who would be willing to carry the VW line as well as their current offerings. Another approach is to build VWs in the US and thus reduce the distance the product has to be transported along the distribution system. This not only reduces cost but also helps to ensure faster delivery.

STRATEGIC MANAGEMENT AND MARKETING STRATEGY

Marketing strategies play a key role in helping MNEs to formulate an overall plan of action. Many approaches are directly related to the major areas that have been examined in this chapter, including ongoing market assessment, new product development, and the use of effective pricing. Table 11.2 illustrates the worldwide market penetration of several MNEs that we shall discuss in this section.

Table 11.2 International market penetration: location of subsidiaries, holdings, and joint ventures

General Motors (US)	*Clarins (French)*	*Daewoo (Korean)*	*Mitsubishi Electric (Japanese)*	*Royal Dutch/Shell Group (Dutch/British)*	
		North America			
Canada	Canada	Canada	Canada	Canada	
Mexico	Mexico	Mexico	Mexico	Mexico	
United States	United States	United States	United States	United States	
		Western Europe			
Austria	Austria	Austria	Ireland	Andorra	Spain
Belgium	Belgium	Belgium	Spain	Austria	Sweden
Denmark	Germany	France	Belgium	Belgium	Turkey
Finland	Italy	Germany	France	Denmark	United Kingdom
France	Netherlands	Greece	Germany	Faroe Islands	
Germany	Northern Ireland	Italy	Italy	Finland	
Greece	Rep. of Ireland	Netherlands	Sweden	France	
Ireland	Spain	Norway	Netherlands	Germany	
Italy	Switzerland	Spain	United Kingdom	Gibraltar	
Netherlands	United Kingdom	Sweden		Greece	
Norway		Switzerland		Iceland	
Portugal		Turkey		Ireland	
Spain		United Kingdom		Italy	
Sweden		Vietnam		Luxembourg	
Switzerland				Netherlands	
Turkey				Norway	
United Kingdom				Portugal	
		Central and Eastern Europe			
Croatia		Belarus	Czech Rep.	Albania	Romania
Czech & Slovak Reps.		Bulgaria		Belarus	Russia
Hungary		Croatia		Bulgaria	Slovakia
Russian Fed.		Czech Rep.		Croatia	Slovenia
Slovenia		Hungary		Czech Rep.	Switzerland
Poland		Poland		Estonia	Ukraine
		Romania		Hungary	Yugoslavia
		Russia		Latvia	
		Slovakia		Lithuania	
		Ukraine		Poland	
		Asia and Oceania			
Australia	Australia	Australia	Australia	Australia	Philippines
Hong Kong	Hong Kong	Azerbaijan	Japan	Azerbaijan	Singapore
Indonesia	Japan	Bangladesh	Singapore	Bangladesh	Solomon Islands
Korea	Malaysia	Brunei	China	Brunei	Sri Lanka
New Zealand	Singapore	Burma	Hong Kong	Cambodia	Taiwan
Singapore	South Korea	Cambodia	India	China	Thailand
Thailand	Taiwan	China	Indonesia	Cook Islands	Tonga
China		Hong Kong	Korea	Fiji	Turkmenistan
India		India	Malaysia	French Polynesia	Uzbekistan
Japan		Indonesia	New Zealand	Guam	Vietnam
Malaysia		Japan	Philippines	Hong Kong	Western Samoa
Taiwan		Kazakhstan	Taiwan	India	
		Kyrgyzstan	Thailand	Indonesia	
		Laos	Vietnam	Japan	
		Malaysia		Kazakhstan	
		New Zealand		Korea	
		Pakistan		Laos	
		Philippines		Malaysia	
		Singapore		New Caledonia	
		South Korea		New Zealand	

Table 11.2 ***(cont'd)***

General Motors (US)	*Clarins (French)*	*Daewoo (Korean)*	*Mitsubishi Electric (Japanese)*	*Royal Dutch/Shell Group (Dutch/British)*	
		Sri Lanka Taiwan Thailand Uzbekistan		Niue Island Pakistan Papua New Guinea	
		South America, Central America, and the Caribbean			
Argentina Chile Ecuador Paraguay Venezuela Brazil Colombia Mexico Uruguay		Argentina Brazil Chile Colombia Ecuador El Salvador Panama Peru Puerto Rico Uruguay Venezuela	Argentina Brazil Colombia	Antigua Argentina Bahamas Barbados Belize Bermuda Bolivia Brazil Chile Colombia Costa Rica Cuba Dominican Rep. Ecuador El Salvador Falklands Guatemala Grenada Guadeloupe	Guyana Haiti Honduras Jamaica Neth. Antilles Nicaragua Panama Paraguay Peru Puerto Rico St Kitts St Lucia St Vincent Surinam Trinidad Uruguay Venezuela Virgin Islands UK
		Middle East			
		Iran Jordan Kuwait Saudi Arabia United Arab Emirates	Iran Kuwait Saudi Arabia United Arab Emirates	Iran Jordan Oman Saudi-Arabia Syria	United Arab Emirates
		Africa			
Egypt Nigeria South Africa Kenya Tunisia		Algeria Angola Cameroon Egypt Fritrea Ethiopia Côte d'Ivoire Kenya Libya Mauritius Morocco Nigeria South Africa Sudan Tunisia Yemen Zimbabwe	Egypt South Africa	Angola Benin Botswana Burkina Faso Cameroon Cape Verde Chad Congo Congo (DR) Côte d'Ivoire Djibouti Egypt Eritrea Ethiopia Gabon Gambia Ghana Guinea Guinea-Bissau Kenya	Lesotho Mali Mauritius Morocco Mozambique Namibia Niger Nigeria Reunion Rwanda Senegal South Africa Sudan Swaziland Togo Tunisia Uganda Yemen Zimbabwe

Sources: Adapted from ***www.gm.com***; ***www.shell.com/***; ***www.mitsubishi.com/***; ***www.clarins-financials.com/***; ***www.daewoo.com/***. All data from websites are as available from May 1999.

Ongoing market assessment

One of the major areas that is continuing to receive attention by MNEs is data collection and analysis for the purpose of developing and updating market assessments. In some cases this causes multinationals to change their market approach, while in other cases it supports maintaining a current strategy.

Clarins

The French cosmetics firm Clarins SA is a good example of a firm that is continuing to refine its market strategy based on market assessment data.[22] For over two decades the company has been gathering feedback from customers regarding what they like and do not like about the firm's cosmetics. From these surveys the company has learned that women want makeup that is long-lasting, easy to choose, and easy to apply. This information has been invaluable in helping Clarins to increase market share in an industry where competition is fierce. In fact, the company's growth rate in France has been more than twice the industry average, and Clarins is now achieving similar results in the US market. It is particularly interesting that this growth has been achieved despite the cost of Clarins' products. For example, one of its spray deodorants sells for $10, 50 per cent more than the typical price of similar products available. Another climate-controlled skin treatment which sells for over $30 is a cream that responds to changes in humidity and releases different ingredients under different conditions. Aware of what up-scale customers are willing to buy, Clarins has been very successful in using market assessment information to develop and market high-quality skincare products. One marketing consultant has referred to Clarins as a "Body Shop for rich people", and certainly this target market has paid off well for the company.

Shell Oil

Shell Oil is an MNE whose market assessment has showed the importance of not making significant changes in product or delivery systems.[23] In recent years Shell has limited its product diversification to "tightly linked and synergistic energy and chemical businesses".[24] The company has learned that it is most profitable when staying close to what it knows best. Today Shell works to balance its upstream (exploration and production) and downstream (refining and marketing) and related chemical (industrial, agricultural, and petrochemical) businesses. The company is also developing a strong network of service stations around the world and has learned that its ability to assess situations and to react quickly is an important element in its marketing strategy.

Another approach that Shell uses in improving its assessment skills is to have local operating companies simulate supply disruptions such as dealing with a cut-off of oil from Kuwait. By evaluating these situations, the company was able to bring in alternative, preapproved crudes from other sources after Iraq invaded Kuwait in 1990 and oil from both countries was cut off.

New product development

Another marketing area that is a critical part of many MNEs' strategic management plan is that of new product development. The introduction of new products is helping these firms to maintain market share and to position them for future growth.

General Motors

For much of the 1980s Ford Motor was the leading US auto maker in Europe. However, by the early 1990s General Motors (GM) had taken over this position, thanks to new product development and expansion.[25] In the early 2000s, however, overcapacity in the Western European market shifted GM's energy to cost reduction. European car makers such as VW gained market share against GM through continued product development.[26] At present GM is building Opel engines in Hungary with a local partner and exporting these products to plants in Western Europe where they are swapped for Opels to be sold in Hungary.[27] Meanwhile, in the eastern part of Germany the company opened a 178,000 unit capacity assembly plant.[28] GM is also moving to increase its marketing outlets in Germany by signing up new dealers.[29]

Subaru

Subaru is another example of an auto firm that is turning to new product development for market growth.[30] During the early 1980s the company did extremely well by living up to its advertising slogan: "Inexpensive. And built to stay that way." However, by the latter part of the decade the value of the yen had soared against the dollar, the cost of a Subaru rose sharply, and market share in the US dropped. Now in the millennium Subaru is attempting a comeback through new product development. The company has introduced a new sports coupé with a powerful six-cylinder engine and is offering more options on its four-wheel-drive vehicles. Subaru is also introducing a new device that informs the driver of any sideways variation in driving that might cause an accident.[31] Market share is now beginning to turn around. By 2001, the Subaru Legacy was the market leader in four wheel drive in the US.[32] The company believes that, if it can keep bringing new models into the marketplace, this trend should continue.[33]

IBM

Another example of new product development strategies is offered by IBM, which holds over three-quarters of the world market for top-of-the-line disk drives that are used in mainframe computers. The company recently designated this market as one of its top priorities for the millennium. One reason for this decision is the high profit margins commanded by these disk drives. These margins can run as high as 60 per cent of the selling price. In an effort to stay ahead of the competition, IBM is now introducing higher capacity versions of mainframe disk drives and intends to accelerate the product cycle.[34] This will make it more difficult for competitors to offer lower-priced models because by the time these models are ready for market IBM will be introducing another disk drive. Some industry analysts are predicting the advent of inexpensive disk arrays that will greatly reduce the profitability of the lucrative high end of the disk drive business. However, IBM believes that the complexity of these new drives, which integrate microelectronic controllers and software, will be sufficient to protect margins. The company is also doing well with its new personal computer offerings[35] as well as other telecommunications products.[36]

Effective pricing

Some MNEs use a high-price strategy and skim the cream off the top of the market. Other MNEs employ a low-price strategy designed to penetrate and capture a larger share of the middle and lower parts of the market.[37] Depending on the nature of the market, both strategies can be successful.

Bang & Olufsen

Bang & Olufsen is a Danish electronics company that manufactures stereo components, televisions, and video equipment.[38] The firm aims at the upper end of the market and sells to style-conscious consumers who are unlikely to flinch at paying $4,000 for an audio system, $4,100 for a 28-inch color television with matching video recorder, or $5,600 for a 28-inch video system. One of the primary reasons customers buy from Bang & Olufsen is that the products are well engineered and designed. Televisions, for example, are sleek, thin, and modern-looking. Stereo consoles are trim, polished, and futuristic in design. While many customers prefer to buy less stylish-looking products at one-third the price, Bang & Olufsen continues to have a steady stream of consumers who are willing to pay top dollar. Because of this, the company's worldwide sales now top the *$406 million mark.*[39]

Wal-Mart and Cifra Inc.

In 1997, Wal-Mart acquired a controlling interest in Cifra Inc. of Mexico, the country's biggest retailer.[40] Established in 1957, by the 1990s Cifra sold a wide variety of products, from powdered milk and canned chili to Korean television sets and videocassette recorders. Wal-Mart's acquisition fueled expansion throughout Mexico. Today, Wal-Mart has 545 stores, including department stores, warehouse retailers, clothing stores, and restaurants. One of Wal-Mart Cifra's biggest selling points is low prices. Today the company pushes what is called a "bodega concept": fast-moving, non-perishable goods that are sold in bulk in poor neighborhoods. By keeping gross margins in the range of 10–12 per cent and net profits at 3–5 per cent, the bodegas are able to average over $1 million per store each month. These sales are more than twice those of similar K-Mart and Wal-Mart stores in the US.

KEY POINTS

1. Marketing strategy begins with international market assessment, an evaluation of the goods and services the MNE can sell in the global marketplace. There are a number of steps in this process, including an initial screening that is designed to determine the basic need potential of the company's goods and services, followed by additional screenings that culminate in a final selection of those outputs that the company will market internationally.
2. Product strategies will vary depending on the specific good and the customer. Some products need little or no modification, while others require extensive changes. Some of the factors that influence the amount of modification include economics, culture, local laws, and the product life cycle.
3. There are a number of ways in which MNEs promote their products, although the final decision is often influenced by the nature of the product. The two major approaches used in promotion are advertising and personal selling. Many multinationals try to use the same message worldwide because it is easier and more economical. However, this is not always possible because some messages either have no meaning in other languages or the message lacks the impact of that in other markets. Similarly, while personal selling is used in some markets, in other markets the customer is unaccustomed to this promotion approach and non-personal approaches must be used or the customer must be educated to accept this new form.
4. Pricing in international markets is influenced by a number of factors. Some of these include government controls, market diversity, currency fluctuations, and price escalation forces.

5. Place strategy involves consideration of distribution, or the course that goods will take between production and the final consumer. This course often differs on a country-by-country basis, and MNEs will spend a considerable amount of time in examining the different systems that are in place, the criteria to use in choosing distributors and channels, and how distribution segmentation can be accomplished.
6. There is a variety of marketing strategies that are being used by MNEs when formulating their strategic plans. Three of the most important strategies are ongoing market assessment, new product development, and effective pricing.

KEY TERMS

- international marketing
- international market assessment
- initial screening
- market indicators
- market size
- market intensity
- market growth
- trend analysis
- estimation by analogy
- regression analysis
- cluster analysis
- trade mission
- promotion
- advertising
- comparative advertising
- personal selling
- dumping
- distribution

REVIEW AND DISCUSSION QUESTIONS

1. How does initial screening help an MNE to evaluate those goods and services that might be sold in the international market? What are some ways in which this screening is carried out?
2. After an MNE has completed an initial screening of its goods and services, what other steps will it take in further refining the choice of those products to sell internationally? Briefly describe the remainder of the process.
3. Why can some goods and services be sold internationally without having to undergo much, if any, modification? Explain.
4. What factors influence the need for moderate to high modification of goods and services that have sold well in the home country and will now be marketed overseas? Identify and describe three of the most influential factors.
5. When will an MNE use the same promotion strategy overseas that it uses at home? When will the company modify the approach?
6. Many MNEs find that their advertising messages can be used in overseas markets without much, if any, modification. Why is this so?
7. Why do MNEs sometimes have to modify their personal selling strategies when marketing their goods in international markets?
8. What kinds of factors influence the pricing of goods and services in the international marketplace? Identify and describe three.
9. Why do many MNEs find that they cannot use the same distribution strategy overseas that they employed at home?
10. In choosing the best distribution system, what types of criteria do MNEs use? Identify and discuss three.
11. In what ways are multinationals using the following concepts to help them gain greater international market share: ongoing market assessment, new product development, and effective pricing? In each case, offer an example.

REAL CASE

Citigroup in China

The banking industry faces many barriers to globalization. Overcoming cultural barriers, different regulations and financial systems make establishing a truly global bank very difficult. No one has done it as well as Citigroup's Citibank, which is to banking what Coca-Cola is to the beverage industry. Formed in 1998 by the merger of Citicorp and Travellers Group, in 2000 Citigroup had a presence in over 100 countries around the world. About 67 per cent of its revenue is generated outside North America.

Citibank enters a developing country with its own marketing strategy. In the first stage of development, the bank caters to the global customer (usually a large corporation) by providing short-term loans, cash management, and foreign exchange services. During a country's second stage of development, as demand grows in the face of a burgeoning middle class, Citibank begins to offer personal financial products.

In China, the political climate has restricted Citibank's expansion plans in the Asia region. Citibank opened its first office in China in 1902 but was thrown out by the new Chinese communist government of Chairman Mao in 1949. Even after Citibank was allowed back into the country, its business was mainly restricted to foreign currency. China's market potential, however, always attracted the bank, and, when the country began to show interest in opening its borders and joining the World Trade Organization, Citibank stepped in as a key broker in negotiations with the US government. The bank's efforts are paying off. In the 1990s, the Chinese began to open their economy and make commitments for further reforms. By 2001, import tariffs had been decreased to an average of 15 per cent from 44 per cent in 1992. Import tariffs are expected to continue to decrease and average 9 per cent by 2006. In addition, China is expected to lift most restrictions to foreign investment by 2003, which will allow Citibank to open fully owned branches.

Deregulation is allowing Citibank to fully implement its emerging market marketing strategy in China. In the initial phase, the bank will market to large corporate clients. Today, the bank's revenue from corporate business in China is still one-fifth of that of South Korea. Deregulation will not only allow Citibank to open fully functional branches, it will also attract foreign and local clients. For instance, UPS and FedEx both seek to open 100 per cent-owned delivery systems in China. Home to the largest number of mobile phone subscribers in the world and nowhere near saturation, China is also expected to attract telecom service providers and product manufacturers. With 10 million PCs sold in 2001, the computer industry is also waiting to enter the market. In short, opportunities for foreign investment in China will create a large number of MNE subsidiaries from which Citibank can draw its client pool. In addition, Citibank can benefit from large local companies who seek to do international business. Among these is Legend, a Chinese PC manufacturer that today controls over 25 per cent of the domestic market and is as yet unknown outside the mainland. Other examples include Konka (electronics), Haier (consumer appliances), and China Telecom.

Citibank's second marketing stage for emerging markets is expanding into personal banking. Though personal banking had not yet been deregulated by 2001, Citibank is already applying for a license in China. A significant portion of Citibank's income comes from credit cards. Citibank is hoping that increases in disposable income among middle-class Chinese will prove profitable. Once the credit card market becomes saturated, the bank is likely to move consumers into mortgages, personal loans, pension funds, and other financial products.

Though Citibank has a definite first-mover advantage in the Chinese market, it still faces competition from domestic banks, such as the Industrial and Commercial Bank of China and other large foreign competitors such as the HSBC, which also has extensive experience in the region. As of 2000, there were 71 foreign financial institutions operating in some form in Shanghai.

Websites: **www.citigroup.com**; **www.fedex.com**; **www.ups.com**; **www.legend.com.cn**; **www.konka.com**; **www.haier.com**; **www.chinatelecom.com.cn**; **www.icbc.com.cn** and **www.hsbc.com**.

Sources: Anthony Spaeth, "China's Legend in the Making," *Time.com*, May 8, 2000; "Citigroup Allowed to Build Mansion in Shanghai," *People's Daily*, December 4, 2000; Michael Shari, Brian Bremner, Heather Timmons and Becky Gaylord, "Citibank Conquers Asia," *Business Week* (international edition), February 26, 2001.

1. **How can a foreign organization, such as Citibank, make an initial assessment of a host-country market (such as China) in deciding how to do business there? What is involved in this process?**
2. **What steps can Citibank take in conducting additional screening of the Chinese market before entry? Briefly describe each step and discuss how relevant it is/is not to Citibank.**
3. **Based on the case facts, which of the four Ps of marketing would be relevant for Citibank's entry into China?**

REAL CASE

Brazilian soap operas: a world market

When *Roque Santeiro* aired in Brazil after 10 years of censorship, São Paulo, a city comparable to New York, suddenly came to a halt. The 8 p.m. soap opera has become a ritual in many households, who leave anything they are doing to glue themselves to the TV. Not surprisingly, leading television stations compete heavily for this market. In fact, soap operas are the main source of income for Brazilian TV stations, including TV Globo, Sistema Brasileiro de Televisão (SBT), and Manchete.

Fierce competition has helped Brazilian soap operas become among the very best in the world. *Roque Santeiro* revolutionized editing and launched its scriptwriter as an icon in Brazil. Period-set costumes were used for *Escrava Isaura*. And, in "Torre of Babel", the shopping mall in which most of the action takes place was built for $1.1 million dollars, only to be blown to pieces as the plot developed.

Brazilian soap operas differ from their US counterparts by their running time, and the structure of their plot. While US soap operas can run for up to 10 years, Brazilian soap operas run an average of eight months and tend to have a very specific storyline and plot structure.

With a population of 172 million, Portugese-speaking Brazil is one of the biggest markets for soap operas in the world. It is also one of the biggest producing countries, at nearly 20 soaps per year. And Brazil is a leading exporter of soap operas. Soap operas from Brazil are dubbed into foreign languages and are exported to 128 countries around the world including the US, China, Italy, and Spanish speaking Latin America. In Cuba, the communist government even rescheduled its electric energy rationing to allow citizens to tune into *Escrava Isaura*. Since its Brazilian premiere in 1977, *Escrava Isaura*, the story of a white slave in a Brazilian plantation, has been aired in nearly 80 countries.

Why are Brazilian soaps so successful? One reason is that audiences in other non-triad nations can identify with what is portrayed as Brazilian reality. Since their beginning in the 1960s, Brazilian soap operas have often dealt with such controversial issues as religion, the role of the state, class differences, abortion, sexuality, and racism. These issues were portrayed with due consideration to the predominantly conservative and religious audience of Brazil. TV stations have also tended to borrow from the proven success of stories in other media. The literary works of Mario Benedetti, Mario Vargas Llosa, Jorge Amado, João Guimaraes Rosa, the classics of Greek and Roman literature as well as folk stories, have all inspired soap operas. These universal themes help Brazil to export its soap operas around the world.

TV Globo

In terms of audience, the fourth largest private TV network in the world is Brazil's TV Globo. In 2000, TV Globo held 50 per cent of the Brazilian viewership and over 78 per cent of the television advertising market. TV Globo is part of the Globo Group, which also controls the country's number one radio station, the second largest magazine group, and the cable television company Globo Cabo.

TV Globo had its beginning in 1965, with the inauguration of Channel 4 in Rio de Janeiro. Soon after, the company purchased TV Paulista to broadcast in São Paolo, the biggest city in Brazil. To enter the Belo Horizonte market, the company acquired J. B. Amaral Group in 1968 and in 1971 it expanded to Recife by purchasing the Vitor Costa Group. By 2001, a combination of acquisitions and broadcasting licenses have made TV Globo the largest network in Brazil, with 113 TV stations that reach 99.84 per cent of Brazil's population.

It was in 1966 that TV Globo produced its first two soap operas. These were relatively low budget, but by 2000 production costs reached over $100,000 per one-hour episode, a sizable cost for a Brazilian production. Since a 30-second ad during the 8 p.m. soap opera costs approximately $102,000, soap operas constitute the largest source of income for TV Globo. By 2000, TV Globo had four recording studios, a staff of 1,500 scriptwriters and its soaps were the most successful in the market, capturing upwards of 60 per cent of the audience.

At less than 10 per cent of total sales, foreign sales are a very small, but growing portion of revenues for producers. A one-hour episode of a soap opera can be priced anywhere between $300 in Cuba and $40,000 in Italy. The number of TV sets per capita, the purchasing power of the country, and the amount the stations can earn on advertising determine prices to foreign TV stations.

TV Globo faces competition in various fronts. In the domestic market, SBT and Manchete produce their own soaps to compete with those of TV Globo. Although TV Globo remains by far the most successful, other domestic networks have been able to erode the 80 per cent audience the network enjoyed in the late 1970s. TV Globo's response was to support its own star system, invest in a scriptwriting school in São Paolo, and create stories that are more responsive to TV audiences. The station is very protective of its directors, scriptwriters, and actors and often has them sitting idle under salary, rather than allowing them to go to the competition. Audience panels and rating information are used to change plots of soaps that do not reach desired ratings.

TV Globo also faces competition from established soap opera industries in other Latin American countries, including Mexico, Argentina, Venezuela, and Colombia. Though, these productions have a limited share of the Brazilian market, TV Globo competes with them in their own markets and in non-Latin American markets. These competitors have traditionally made lower quality soaps. Over the last few years, however, improvements in casting, scriptwriting, and directing have begun to increase their notoriety in international markets.

During Ramadan, mosques in Côte d'Ivoire changed the schedule of prayer time to allow the faithful to see the last episode of the Mexican soap *Marimar*. Marimar was also an international hit in Indonesia and the Philippines, where the female lead actress was received with all the honors of royalty.

Another source of competition comes from importing nations, such as Spain, Italy, Greece, and China. Local storylines are being created that are likely to erode TV Globo's market share. Increasing competition from foreign companies is forcing Globo TV to find innovative ways of capitalizing a market. For example, TV Globo recently partnered with a Chinese company to develop a soap opera about a Chinese man who falls in love with a Brazilian woman and goes to Brazil to court her. This guarantees access to the Chinese market.

Thirty-five years of experience in the soap opera market have given Brazil and TV Globo a competitive advantage against new entrants. As production develops in these countries, however, Brazil must adapt to increasing competition to continue its lead. There are a number of ways in which the company can do this, including specializing in some types of soaps, partnering with foreign producers, and moving into other areas of entertainment. In fact, the soap opera business has left Brazil with excellent producers, scriptwriters, directors, camera operators, editors, and actors that can be used to create anything from commercials, drama series, sitcoms, theater, and films. This last has already begun to occur. In 1999 a long acclaimed Brazilian soap opera actress, Fernanda Montegro, was nominated for best actress Oscar for her part in *Central Station*, a movie that was also nominated for best foreign film.

Websites: **http://redeglobo1.globo.com/home** and **www.sbt.com.br**.

Sources: Daniel Mato, "Telenovelas: Transnacionalización de la industria y transformación del género," in N. Garcia Canclini (ed.), *Industrias culturales e integración latinoamericana* (Mexico: Grijalbo, 1999); Nora Mazziotti, *La industria de la telenovela* (Buenos Aires: Paidós, 1996); "Home-grown Films First for Brazil," *BBC.co.uk*, May 8, 2001; "Brazil Media Giant Winks at Wall Street," *Sunday Times*, November 12, 2000.

1. **How is language an issue when marketing Brazilian entertainment to other countries?**
2. **What competitive advantages will Brazil have in the development of a film industry? What types of barriers would this industry face in international markets?**
3. **In what way can foreign capital prove to be a key strategy for TV Globo and the Globo Group?**

ENDNOTES

1 See, for example, Carla Rapoport, "The New US Push Into Europe," *Fortune*, January 10, 1994, pp. 73–74.

2 Susan P. Douglas and C. Samuel Craig, "Evolution of Global Marketing Strategy: Scale, Scope, and Synergy," *Columbia Journal of World Business*, Fall 1989, pp. 47–59.

3 Fred Luthans and Richard M. Hodgetts, *Business*, 2nd edn (Hinsdale IL: Dryden Press, 1993), pp. 378–382.

4 See James Sterngold, "The Awakening Chinese Consumer," *New York Times*, October 11, 1992, Section 3, pp. 1, 6.

5 A good example is provided in Andrew Pollack, "A Translating Phone for Overseas Calls," *New York Times*, January 28, 1993, p. C 3.

6 For more on this development, see Agis Salpukas, "Germans Join Boeing in Jet Study," *New York Times*, January 6, 1993, p. C 5; and Richard W. Stevenson, "A First Step Toward an 800-Seat Jet," *New York Times*, January 28, 1993, p. C 3.

7 "China Goes Mobile Crazy," *BBC.co.uk*, August 15, 2001.

8 Julia Scheeres, "Latin America: The Mobile World," *Wired News*, January 25, 2001.

9 See, for example, Joseph A. McKinney, "Degree of Access to the Japanese Market: 1979 to 1986," *Columbia Journal of World Business*, Summer 1989, pp. 53–59.

10 "Turin Meets Detroit – in the Volga," *Economist*, May 5, 1998.

11 See, for example, James B. Treece et al., "New Worlds to Conquer," *Business Week*, February 28, 1994, pp. 50–52.

12 See Cacilie Rohwedder, "Diet Foods Enjoy a UK Sales Binge, and the Continent May Join Up Soon," *Wall Street Journal*, January 28, 1994, p. A 5.

13 John Templeman and James B. Treece, "BMW's Comeback," *Business Week*, February 14, 1994, pp. 42–44.

14 Also see Daniel McGinn and Adam Rogers, "Operation Supercar," *Newsweek*, November 23, 1998, pp. 48–53.

15 Richard A. Melcher and John Templeman, "Ford of Europe is Going in for Emergency Repairs," *Business Week*, June 17, 1991, p. 48 and Daniel Howes, "Ford's Blue Oval Takes on Added Luster in Europe with Thursfield," *Detnews.com*, December 4, 2001.

16 Mark Borden, "Let the Games Begin," *Fortune*, November 26, 2001.

17 For another look at growth and market share considerations, see Manab Thakur and T. K. Das, "Managing the Growth-Share Matrix: A Four-National Study in Two Industries," *Management International Review*, vol. 31, no. 2 (Second Quarter 1991), pp. 139–159.

18 Luthans and Hodgetts (1993) n. 3 above, p. 381.

19 Also see "The Fate of the Dollar," *BBC.co.uk*, January 19, 2001.

20 Joan Magretta, "Fast, Global, and Entrepreneurial Supply Chain Management, Hong Kong Style," *Harvard Business Review*, September/October 1998, pp. 103–114.

21 See, for example, Robert T. Green and Ajay K. Kohli, "Export Market Identification: The Role of Economic Size and Socioeconomic Development," *Management International Review*, vol. 31, no. 1 (First Quarter 1991), pp. 37–50.

22 John Marcom, Jr., "Forget the Sizzle, Sell the Steak," *Forbes*, August 5, 1991, pp. 86–87.

23 Christopher Knowlton, "Shell Gets Rich by Beating Risk," *Fortune*, August 26, 1991, pp. 79–82.

24 Ibid., p. 82.

25 Also see Keith Naughton et al., "The Global Six," *Business Week*, January 25, 1999, pp. 68–70, 72.

26 "The Art of Overtaking," *Economist*, September 6, 2001.

27 Peter Fuhrman, "A Tale of Two Strategies," *Forbes*, August 6, 1990, p. 42 and "New Opel Transmission Plant to be Built in Hungary," General Motors, Press Release, April 17, 1998.

28 "U.S. President Bill Clinton Visits Open Eisenach Plant," General Motors, Press Release, May 14, 1998.

29 For more on some of General Motors' international expansion, see Jonathan Friedland and Joseph B. White, "GM is Leading an Investment Boom in Mexico," *Wall Street Journal*, December 24, 1998, pp. A 5–6; Lisa Schuchman and Joseph B. White, "Global Consolidations in Autos Heat Up," *Wall Street Journal*, December 21, 1998, p. A 2; and Seth Faison, "GM Opens Buick Plant in Shanghai," *New York Times*, December 18, 1998, pp. C 1, 19.

30 James B. Treece and Karen Lowry Miller, "Subaru Pulls into the Image Shop," *Business Week*, August 19, 1991, pp. 86–87.

31 "Beyond Cruise Control," *Economist*, June 21, 2001.

32 "Subaru Posts Best November in History; Forester and Impreza Set New Monthly Records," *PR Newswire*, December 3, 2001

33 Also see Larry Armstrong, "Revving Up Japan's Also Rans," *Business Week*, December 14, 1998, pp. 135–136.

34 "IBM is First to Ship Products with 'magical' New Material," IBM News Release, May 21, 2001.

35 Catherine Arnst, "The Tiny Shall Inherit the Market," *Business Week*, June 28, 1993, pp. 50–51.

36 Bart Ziegler, "A Giant Stirs: IBM Is Ready to Do Battle. Should Anyone Worry?" *Wall Street Journal*, March 20, 1995, p. R20.

37 See, for example, Jennifer Cody, "Supermarket Giant Ito-Yokado Plans Venture to Import Goods of Wal-Mart," *Wall Street Journal*, January 27, 1994, p. C 3.

38 Peter Fuhrman, "A Beautiful Face Is Not Enough," *Forbes*, May 13, 1991, pp. 105–106.

39 For more on Bang & Olufsen, see Peter Marsh, "Marketing to Be Given a Makeover," *Ft.com*, December 1999.

40 Joel Millman, "The Merchant of Mexico," *Forbes*, August 5, 1991, pp. 80–81 and Matthew Schifrin, "Partner or Perish," *Forbes.com*, May 21, 2001.

ADDITIONAL BIBLIOGRAPHY

Andersson, Ulf, Johanson, Jan and Vahine, Jan-Erik. "Organic Acquisitions in the Internationalization Process," *Management International Review*, vol. 37, Special Issue (1997).

Bonaccorsi, Andrea. "On the Relationship Between Firm Size and Export Intensity," *Journal of International Business Studies*, vol. 23, no. 4 (Fourth Quarter 1992).

Capon, Noel, Berthon, Pierre, Hulbert, James M. and Pitt, Leyland F. "Brand Custodianship: A New Primer for Senior Managers," *European Management Journal*, vol. 19, no. 3 (May 2001).

Cavusgil, S. Tamer, Zou, Shaoming and Naidu, G. M. "Product and Promotion Adaptation in Export Ventures: An Empirical Investigation," *Journal of International Business Studies*, vol. 24, no. 3 (Third Quarter 1993).

Cordell, Victor V. "Effects of Consumer Preferences for Foreign Sourced Products," *Journal of International Business Studies*, vol. 23, no. 2 (Second Quarter 1992).

Craig, C. Samuel and Douglas, Susan P. "Developing Strategies for Global Markets: An Evolutionary Perspective," *Columbia Journal of World Business*, vol. 31, no. 1 (Spring 1996).

Craig, C. Samuel and Douglas, Susan P. "Responding to the Challenges of Global Markets: Change, Complexity, Competition and Conscience," *Columbia Journal of World Business*, vol. 31, no. 4 (Winter 1996).

Cravens, David W., Downey, H. Kirk and Lauritano, Paul. "Global Competition in the Commercial Aircraft Industry: Positioning for Advantage by the Triad Nations," *Columbia Journal of World Business*, vol. 26, no. 4 (Winter 1992).

Dominguez, Luis V. and Sequeira, Carlos G. "Determinants of LDC Exporters' Performance: A Cross-National Study," *Journal of International Business Studies*, vol. 24, no. 1 (First Quarter 1993).

Douglas, Susan P. and Craig, C. Samuel. "Evolution of Global Marketing Strategy: Scale, Scope and Synergy," *Columbia Journal of World Business*, vol. 24, no. 3 (Fall 1989).

Erramilli, M. Krishna and Rao, C. P. "Choice of Foreign Market Entry Modes by Service Firms: Role of Market Knowledge," *Management International Review*, vol. 30, no. 2 (Second Quarter 1990).

Fahy, John, Hooley, Graham, Cox, Tony, Beracs, Jozsef, Fonfara Krysztof and Snoj, Boris. "The Development and Impact of Marketing Capabilities in Central Europe," *Journal of International Business Studies*, vol. 31, no. 1 (Spring 2000).

Hoang, Peter B. "A Causal Study of Relationships Between Firms Characteristics, International Marketing Strategies, and Export Performance," *Management International Review*, vol. 38, Special Issue (1998).

Kale, Sudhir H. and Barnes, John W. "Understanding the Domain of Cross-National Buyer-Seller Interactions," *Journal of International Business Studies*, vol. 23, no. 1 (First Quarter 1992).

Kaynak, Erdener. "A Cross Regional Comparison of Export Performance of Firms in Two Canadian Regions," *Management International Review*, vol. 32, no. 2 (Second Quarter 1992).

Kotabe, Masaaki and Czinkota, Michael R. "State Government Promotion of Manufacturing Exports: A Gap Analysis," *Journal of International Business Studies*, vol. 23, no. 4 (Fourth Quarter 1992).

Kotabe, Masaaki and Okoroafo, Sam C. "A Comparative Study of European and Japanese Multinational Firms' Marketing Strategies and Performance in the United States," *Management International Review*, vol. 30, no. 4 (Fourth Quarter 1990).

Kotabe, Masaaki, "Contemporary Research Trends in International Marketing: The 1990s," in Alan M. Rugman and Thomas Brewer (eds.), *The Oxford Handbook of International Business* (Oxford: Oxford University Press, 2001).

Kramer, Hugh E. "International Marketing: Methodological Excellence in Practice and Theory," *Management International Review*, vol. 29, no. 2 (Second Quarter 1989).

Landry, John T. "Differentiate or Die: Survival in Our Age of Killer Competition," *Harvard Business Review*, vol. 78, no. 3 (May/June 2000).

Lim, Jeen-Su, Sharkey, Thomas W. and Kim, Ken I. "Determinants of International Marketing Strategy," *Management International Review*, vol. 33, no. 2 (Second Quarter 1993).

Liouville, Jacques. "Under What Conditions Can Exports Exert a Positive Influence on Profitability?" *Management International Review*, vol. 32, no. 1 (First Quarter 1992).

Melin, Leif. "Internationalization as a Strategy Process," *Strategic Management Journal*, vol. 24, no. 3 (Third Quarter 1993).

Mitchell, Will, Shaver, J. Myles and Yeung, Bernard. "Performance Following Changes of International Presence in Domestic and Transition Industries," *Journal of International Business Studies*, vol. 24, no. 4 (Fourth Quarter 1993).

Nachum, Lilach. "The Impact of Home Countries on the Competitiveness of Advertising TNCS," *Management International Review*, vol. 41, no. 1 (Spring 2001).

Norburn, David, Birley, Sue, Dunn, Mark and Payne, Adrian. "A Four Nation Study of the Relationship Between Marketing Effectiveness, Corporate Culture, Corporate Values, and Market Orientation," *Journal of International Business Studies*, vol. 21, no. 3 (Third Quarter 1990).

Rugman, Alan M. "The Myth of Global Strategy," *International Marketing Review*, vol. 18, no. 6 (2001), pp. 583–588.

Rugman, Alan M. and Verbeke, Alain. "Trade Policy and Global Corporate Strategy," *Journal of Global Marketing*, vol. 2, no. 3 (Spring 1989).

Ryans, Adrian B. "Strategic Market Entry Factors and Market Share Achievement in Japan," *Journal of International Business Studies*, vol. 19, no. 3 (Fall 1988).

Seringhaus, F. H. Rolf. "Comparative Marketing Behaviour of Canadian and Austrian High-Tech Exporters," *Management International Review*, vol. 33, no. 3 (Third Quarter 1993).

Walters, Peter G. P. "Patterns of Formal Planning and Performance in US Exporting Firms," *Management International Review*, vol. 33, no. 1 (First Quarter 1993).

Walters, Peter G. P. and Zhu, Mingxia. "International Marketing in Chinese Enterprises: Some Evidence from the PRC," *Management International Review*, vol. 35, no. 3 (Third Quarter 1995).

Yan, Rick. "To Reach China's Consumers, Adapt to Guo Qing," *Harvard Business Review* (September–October 1994).

Yavas, Ugur, Verhage, Bronislaw J. and Green, Robert T. "Global Consumer Segmentation Versus Local Market Orientation: Empirical Findings," *Management International Review*, vol. 32, no. 3 (Third Quarter 1992).

CONTENTS

Chapter 12

Human Resource Management Strategy

OBJECTIVES OF THE CHAPTER

Human resource management strategy provides an MNE with the opportunity to truly outdistance the competition. For example, if IBM develops a laser printer that is smaller, lighter, and less expensive than competitive models, other firms in the industry will attempt to reverse engineer this product to see how they can develop their own version of the printer. However, when a multinational has personnel who are carefully selected, well trained, and properly compensated, the organization has a pool of talent that the competition may be unable to beat. For this reason, human resource management is a critical element of international management strategy. This chapter considers the ways in which multinationals prepare their people to take on the challenge of international business. We focus specifically on such critical areas as selection, training, managerial development, compensation, and labor relations.

The specific objectives of this chapter are to:

1. *Define* the term *international human resource management* and discuss human resource strategies in overseas operations.
2. *Describe* the screening and selecting criteria often used in choosing people for overseas assignments.
3. *Relate* some of the most common types of training and development that are offered to personnel who are going overseas.
4. *Discuss* the common elements of an international compensation package.
5. *Explain* some of the typical labor relations practices used in the international arena.
6. *Describe* some of the human resource management strategies that are currently receiving a great deal of attention from MNEs.

ACTIVE LEARNING CASE

The Coca-Cola Company thinks local

The Coca-Cola Company has been operating internationally for most of its 100-year history. Today the company has operations in 200 countries and employs over 400,000 people. The firm's human resource management (HRM) strategy helps to explain a great deal of its success. It now follows a strategy of "national responsiveness" by adapting to local market conditions. In one recent year The Coca-Cola Company transferred more than 300 professional and managerial staff from one country to another under its leadership development program, and the number of international transferees is increasing annually. One senior-level HRM manager explained the company's strategy by noting:

> We recently concluded that our talent base needs to be multilingual and multicultural. . . . To use a sports analogy, you want to be sure that you have a lot of capable and competent *bench strength*, ready to assume broader responsibilities as they present themselves.

In preparing for the future, The Coca-Cola Company includes a human resource recruitment forecast in its annual and long-term business strategies. The firm also has selection standards on which management can focus when recruiting and hiring. For example, the company likes applicants who are fluent in more than one language because they can be transferred to other geographic areas where their fluency will help them to be part of The Coca-Cola Company's operation. This multilingual, multicultural emphasis starts at the top; of the 21 members of the board, only four are Americans.

The firm also has a recruitment program that helps it to identify candidates at the college level. Rather than just seeking students abroad, The Coca-Cola Company looks for foreign students who are studying in the US at domestic universities. The students are recruited in the US and then provided with a year's training before they go back to their home country. The Coca-Cola Company also has an internship program for foreign students who are interested in working for the company during school breaks, either in the US or back home. These interns are put into groups and assigned a project that requires them to make a presentation to the operations personnel on their project. This presentation must include a discussion of what worked and what did not work. Each individual intern is then evaluated and management decides the person's future potential with the company.

The Coca-Cola Company believes that these approaches are extremely useful in helping the firm to find talent on a global basis. Not only is the company able to develop internal sources, but its intern program provides a large number of additional individuals who would otherwise end up with other companies. The Coca-Cola Company earns a greater portion of its income and profit overseas than it does in the US. The company's human resource management strategy helps to explain how, despite the success of its HRM policies, The Coca-Cola Company found itself facing a series of problems as it entered the millennium. During the 1980s the firm expanded its global reach and so the company began to centralize control and to encourage consolidation among all bottling partners. In the 1990s, however, the world began to change. Many national and local leaders began seeking sovereignty over their political, economic, and cultural futures. As a result, the very forces that were making the world more connected and homogeneous were also triggering a powerful desire for local autonomy and the preservation of unique cultural identity. Simply put, the world was demanding more nimbleness, responsiveness, and sensitivity from MNEs, while The Coca-Cola Company was centralizing decision making, standardizing operating practices, and insulating itself from this changing environment. The Coca-Cola Company was going global, when it should have been going local according to CEO Douglas Daft.

Today, The Coca-Cola Company is beginning to turn things around. In particular, the firm has begun implementing three principles that are designed to make it more locally responsive. First, The Coca-Cola Company is instituting a strategy of "think local, act local" by putting increased decision making in the hands of local managers. Second, the company is focusing itself as a pure marketing company that pushes its brands on a regional and local basis. Third, the firm is working to become a model citizen by reaching out to the local communities and getting involved in civic and charitable activities. In the past The Coca-Cola Company succeeded because it understood and appealed to global commonalities. In the future it hopes to succeed by better understanding and appealing to local differences. The Coca-Cola Company is able to achieve this feat.

Websites: ***www.cocacola.com*** *and* ***www.cokecce.com***.

Sources: Richard M. Hodgetts and Fred Luthans, "US Multinationals' Expatriate Compensation Strategies," *Compensation & Benefits Review*, January/February 1993, p. 60; Nikhil Deogun, "A Coke and a Perm? Soda Giant is Pushing into Unusual Locales," *Wall Street Journal*, May 8, 1997, pp. A 1, 8; ***www.cocacola.com***; "The Coca-Cola Company Elects Charlene Crusoe-Ingram Vice President," *PRNewswire*, October 17, 2001; Douglas Daft, "Back to Classic Coke", *Financial Times*, March 27, 2000, p. 20.

1. **Does The Coca-Cola Company have a local perspective regarding the role of human resource management?**
2. **On what basis does The Coca-Cola Company choose people for international assignments? Identify and describe two.**
3. **What type of training does the firm provide to its interns? Of what value is this training?**
4. **How useful is it for The Coca-Cola Company managers to be fluent in more than one language? Why?**

INTRODUCTION

International human resource management (IHRM) The process of selecting, training, developing, and compensating personnel in overseas positions

Home country nationals Citizens of the country where the multinational resides

Expatriates Individuals who reside abroad but are citizens of the parent country of the multinational; they are citizens of the home, not of the host country

Host country nationals Local people hired by a multinational

Third country nationals Citizens of countries other than the one in which the multinational is headquartered or the one in which they are assigned to work by the multinational

International human resource management (IHRM) is the process of selecting, training, developing, and compensating personnel in overseas positions. This chapter will examine each of these activities. Before doing so, however, it is important to understand the general nature of this overall process, which begins with selecting and hiring.

There are three basic sources of personnel talent that MNEs can tap for positions.[1] One is **home country nationals**, who reside abroad but are citizens of the parent country of the multinational. These individuals are typically called **expatriates**. An example is a US manager assigned to head an R&D department in Tokyo for IBM Japan. A second is **host country nationals**, who are local people hired by the MNE. An example is a British manager working for Ford Motor in London. The last is **third country nationals**, who are citizens of countries other than the one in which the MNE is headquartered or the one in which they are assigned to work by the multinational. An example is a French manager working for Sony in the US.

Staffing patterns may vary depending on the length of time that the MNE has been operating. Many MNEs will initially rely on home country managers to staff their overseas units, gradually putting more host country nationals into management positions as the firm gains experience. Another approach is to use home country nationals in less developed countries and employ host country nationals in more developed regions. This pattern has been found fairly prevalent among US and European MNEs.[2] A third pattern is to put a home country manager in charge of a new operation, but, once the unit is up and running, turn it over to a host country manager. Figure 12.1 provides an illustration of the types of managers, by nationality mix, required over the stages of internationalization. When MNEs are exporting into a foreign market, host country nationals will handle everything. As the firm begins initial manufacture in that country, the use of expatriate managers and third country nationals begins to increase. As the company moves through the ensuing stages of internationalization, the nationality mix of the managers in the overseas unit continues to change to meet the changing demands of the environment.

In some cases staffing decisions are handled uniformly. For example, most Japanese MNEs rely on home country managers to staff senior-level positions. Similarly, some European MNEs assign home country managers to overseas units for their entire career. US MNEs typically view overseas assignments as temporary, and so it is more common to find many of these expatriates working under the supervision of host country managers.

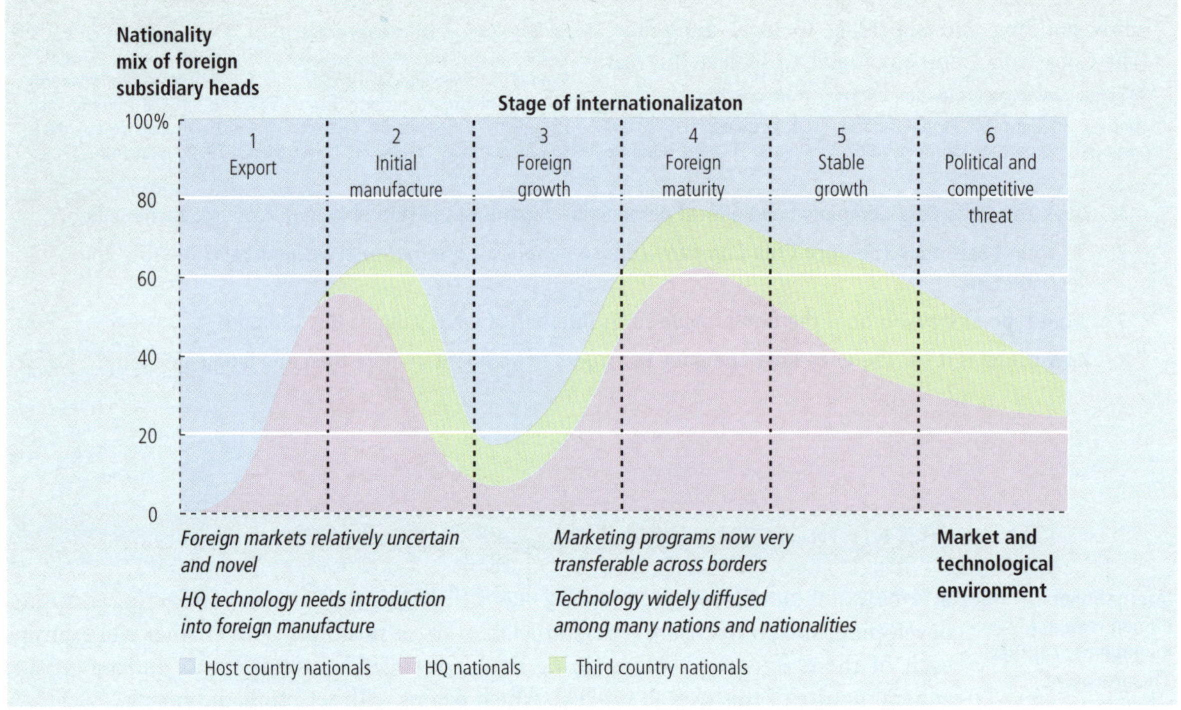

Figure 12.1 The management of multinational enterprises

Source: Reprinted from *Columbia Journal of World Business*, Summer 1973, Lawrence G. Franko, "Who Manages Multinational Enterprises?", page 33, Copyright 1973, with permission from Elsevier Science.

The size of the compensation package also plays an important role in personnel selection and placement. As the cost of sending people overseas has increased, there has been a trend toward using host country or third country nationals who know the local language and customs. For example, in recent years many US multinationals have hired English or Scottish managers for the top positions at subsidiaries in former British colonies such as Jamaica, India, the West Indies, and Kenya.[3]

The above factors influence IHRM strategies and help MNEs to integrate an international perspective into their human resource policies and practices.[4]

Active learning check

Review your answer to Active Learning Case question 1 and make any changes you like. Then compare your answer with the one below.

1. Does The Coca-Cola Company have a local perspective regarding the role of human resource management?

The company certainly does have a local perspective regarding the human resource management role. The Coca-Cola Company is interested in recruiting people from anywhere in the world, training and developing them, and then sending them to assignments throughout the globe. The company does not confine itself to recruiting, training, developing, or promoting people from any one particular region or country. Both Americans and non-Americans have equal opportunities in the firm, further reinforcing this international perspective.

SELECTION AND REPATRIATION

Two of the major human resource management challenges facing MNEs are those of selecting qualified people for overseas assignments and, in the case of home country nationals, then effectively repatriating them into the workforce upon their return. Each presents a significant challenge.

International screening criteria and selection procedures

International screening criteria
Factors used to identify individuals regarded as most suitable for overseas assignments

International screening criteria are those factors that are used to identify individuals regarded as most suitable for overseas assignment. Some MNEs use an extensive list; others rely on only a handful of factors. There are a number of screening criteria that are commonly used in determining whom to send overseas. These criteria focus on both individual and family considerations.

Adaptability

One screening criterion is an individual's ability to adapt to cultural change.[5] Research shows that many managers are initially pleased to learn that they are being sent overseas. However, within a few months many of these expatriates begin to suffer from culture shock brought on by the large number of changes to which they are subjected.[6] This often results in a decline in job satisfaction. However, as the managers continue their overseas assignment, satisfaction goes back up. Torbiorn, for example, reports that by the end of the first year most managers are through the cultural change phase and are beginning to adjust to their new conditions. For those who stay overseas two or more years, Torbiorn has found that satisfaction reaches new heights and continues rising.[7] Researchers have also found that men tend to adjust slightly faster than women, and people over the age of 35 have somewhat higher levels of satisfaction after the first year.

In determining how well an individual will adapt to cultural change, MNEs examine a number of characteristics, including (1) work experiences with cultures other than one's own, (2) previous overseas travel, (3) knowledge of foreign languages (fluency is not generally necessary), (4) the ability to solve problems within different frameworks and from different perspectives, and (5) overall sensitivity to the environment.[8]

Self-reliance

Managers who are posted to overseas assignments must be self-reliant and independent because they often have to make on-the-spot decisions without consulting the home office. In determining self-reliance, MNEs will evaluate the amount of field experience an individual has had, as well as special project and task force experience, since such assignments often require and nurture self-reliance. Consideration is also given to hobbies or avocations that require a high degree of personal independence.

Age, experience, and education

MNEs often find that young managers are eager for international assignments and want to learn more about other cultures. On the other hand, older managers have more experience and maturity to bring to the assignment. In order to balance the strengths of the two groups, many firms send both young and seasoned personnel to the same overseas post so that each can learn from the other.

Some MNEs believe that a college degree, preferably a graduate degree, is important for international managers. However, there is no universal agreement on this point. Multinationals that sell highly technical products tend to prefer people with science degrees. Other MNEs feel that a good education helps to develop logical thinking, creative ideas, and a broad perspective of the world, so these firms prefer individuals with a liberal arts education. However, the best overall combination seems to be an undergraduate degree coupled with an MBA from a recognized business school.[9]

Health and family status

Expatriates must have good physical and emotional health. Those with physical problems that will limit their activities are screened from consideration. So are those who are judged less likely to withstand the culture shock.

Multinationals also take into account the person's family situation. An unhappy family life will negatively affect employee productivity. One survey of US multinationals found that the primary reason for expatriate failure was the inability of the manager's spouse to adjust to a different physical or cultural environment. For this reason, some firms interview both the spouse *and* the manager before deciding whether to approve the assignment.[10]

The increasing number of dual-career families in Western countries creates a further challenge for MNEs. Equally career minded spouses might experience a career interruption during their spouse's overseas assignment. In fact, a study of 332 repatriates and spouses found most dissatisfaction with MNEs resulted from lack of employment support for the trailing spouse.[11]

Motivation and leadership

Another selection criterion is the individual's desire to work abroad and the person's potential commitment to the new job. Many people who are unhappy with their position at home will consider an overseas assignment, but this is not sufficient motivation. Motivational factors include a desire for adventure, a pioneering spirit, a desire to increase one's chances for promotion, and the opportunity to improve one's economic status.[12]

Additionally, one group of researchers recently examined the factors associated with employee willingness to work overseas and concluded that:

1. Unmarried employees are more willing than any other group to accept expat assignments.
2. Married couples without children at home or those with non-teenage children are probably the most willing to move.
3. Prior international experience appears associated with willingness to work as an expatriate.
4. Individuals most committed to their professional careers and to their employing organizations are prone to be more willing to work as expatriates.
5. Careers and attitudes of spouses will likely have a significant impact on employee willingness to move overseas.

Employee and spouse perceptions of organizational support for expatriates are also critical to employee willingness to work overseas.[13]

Applicants are also evaluated on the basis of their leadership potential since most expatriates will end up supervising others. While this is a difficult factor to assess, there are a number of characteristics that are commonly sought when making this evaluation, including maturity, emotional stability, the ability to communicate well, independence, initiative, and creativity. These characteristics are good indications of leadership potential.[14]

Selection procedures

The most common selection procedure is the interview. However, some companies also use tests to help in making the final choice for overseas assignments.

One international management expert has reported that extensive interviews of candidates and their spouses by senior executives still ultimately provide the best method of selection.[15] Other researchers agree. For example, 52 per cent of the US MNEs that Tung surveyed conducted interviews with both the manager and the spouse, while 47 per cent conducted interviews with the candidate alone. In the case of technically oriented positions, these percentages were 40 and 59 per cent. Other MNEs follow a similar pattern. Based on her research, Tung has concluded that multinationals are becoming increasingly cognizant of the importance of interviewing in effective performance abroad.[16]

Some MNEs also use tests to help predict those most likely to do well in international assignments. However, this approach has not gained a great deal of support because it is expensive and many MNEs feel that tests do not improve the selection process. As a result, the candidate's domestic record and evaluations from superiors and peers, along with the interview, tend to be relied on most heavily.

Repatriation of expatriates

Repatriation
The process of returning home at the end of an overseas assignment

For US expatriates an overseas assignment is usually two to three years, although some companies are now encouraging their people to consider making the international arena a lifetime career choice. **Repatriation** is the process of returning home at the end of an overseas assignment. One reason is the change in the standard of living. While overseas many expatriates have generous living allowances and benefits that they cannot match back home. An accompanying problem is the change in cultural lifestyle. For example, a person who is transferred from a cosmopolitan city such as Vienna to a small town in Middle America will find it necessary to make major adjustments, ranging from social activities to the pace of life in general. Additionally, it is common to find that those who sold their house before leaving and have been overseas from three to five years are stunned by the high price of a replacement home. Not only have they lost a great deal of equity by selling, but also they must come up with a substantial down payment and much larger monthly mortgage payments.

Reasons for repatriation

Managers are repatriated for a number of reasons. The most common one is that the predetermined time assignment is completed. Another is the desire to have their children educated in the home country. The expatriate may be unhappy overseas, and the company may feel there is more to be gained by bringing the person back than in trying to persuade the individual to stay on. Finally, as in any position, if the manager has performed poorly, the MNE may decide to put someone else in the position.

Readjusting

Although many expatriates look forward to returning, some find it difficult to adjust. A number of reasons can be cited. One is that the home office job lacks the high degree of authority and responsibility that expatriates had in their overseas job. Another is that they feel the company does not value international experience and the time spent overseas seems to have been wasted in terms of career progress.[17] Some companies do not have plans for handling returning managers. If these individuals are assigned jobs at random, they can find their career progress jeopardized.

Recent research shows that the longer people remain overseas, the more problems they are likely to have being reabsorbed into the operations back home. In addition to the factors considered above, several factors make repatriation after longer periods difficult. These include (1) they may no longer be well known among people at headquarters, (2) their old job may have been eliminated or drastically changed, or (3) technological advances at headquarters may have rendered their existing skills and knowledge obsolete.[18]

In many cases it takes from 6 to 12 months before a returning manager is operating at full effectiveness. Adler reports that many expatriates have moderate to low effectiveness for the first 60 to 90 days, but the increase in effectiveness continues month after month as the person readjusts to life back home.

Adjustment strategies

Transition strategies
Strategies designed to help smooth the move from foreign to domestic assignments

Repatriation agreement
An agreement which spells out how long a person will be posted overseas and sets forth the type of job that will be given to the person upon returning

In recent years MNEs have begun to address adjustment problems faced by returning expatriates. Some organizations have now developed **transition strategies** that are designed to help smooth the move from foreign to domestic assignments.

One of these strategies is the **repatriation agreement**, which spells out how long the person will be posted overseas and sets forth the type of job that will be given to the person upon returning. The agreement typically does not spell out a particular position or salary, but it does promise a job that is at least equal in authority and compensation to the one the person held overseas. This agreement relieves a great deal of the anxiety that expatriates encounter because it assures them that the MNE is not going to forget them while they are gone and that there will be a place for them when they return.

A second strategy is to rent or maintain the expatriate's home during the overseas tour. Both Union Carbide and the Aluminum Company of America have such arrangements. These plans help to reduce the financial burden that managers face when they learn that their monthly mortgage will now be hundreds of dollars higher than when they left for a three-year tour.

A third strategy is to assign a senior executive as a sponsor for each manager who is posted abroad. In this way there is someone looking after each expatriate and ensuring that his or her performance, compensation, and career path are on track. When the person is scheduled to return home, the sponsor will begin working internally to ensure that there is a suitable position for the expatriate. Companies such as IBM and Union Carbide use this form of the mentoring process, and it is proving to be very effective.

A fourth strategy is to maintain ongoing communications with expatriate managers, thereby ensuring that they are aware of what is happening in the home office. In addition, if the individuals are scheduled to be home on leave for any extended period of time, the company will work them into projects at headquarters. In this way the expatriates are able to maintain their visibility at headquarters and to increase the likelihood that they are viewed as regular members of the management staff rather than as outsiders.

These expatriate strategies help MNEs to maintain a proactive approach in dealing with expatriate concerns, and they are becoming more widespread. For example, Tung reports that the best-managed US, European, Japanese, and Australian firms she studied had (1) mentor programs consisting of one-on-one pairing of an expatriate with a member of the home office senior management staff, (2) a separate organization unit with primary responsibility for the specific needs of expatriates, and/or (3) maintenance of constant contacts between the home office and the expatriate.[19]

Active learning check

Review your answer to Active Learning Case question 2 and make any changes you like. Then compare your answer with the one below.

2. On what basis does The Coca-Cola Company choose people for international assignments? Identify and describe two.

One of the bases on which the company chooses people is the ability to speak at least two languages fluently. A second is familiarity with at least two cultures. Both are viewed as critical for success in international assignments.

TRAINING AND DEVELOPMENT

Training The process of altering employee behavior and attitudes in a way that increases the probability of goal attainment

Managerial development The process by which managers obtain the necessary skills, experiences, and attitudes that they need to become or remain successful leaders

Standardized training programs Generic programs that can be used with managers anywhere in the world

Tailor-made training programs Programs designed to meet the specific needs of the participants, typically including a large amount of culturally based input

Training is the process of altering employee behavior and attitudes in a way that increases the probability of goal attainment. **Managerial development** is the process by which managers obtain the necessary skills, experiences, and attitudes that they need to become or remain successful leaders. Training programs are designed to provide individuals who are going overseas with information and experience related to local customs, cultures, and work habits and thus help these managers to interact and work more effectively with the local workforce.[20] Development is typically used to help managers improve their leadership skills, keep up to date on the latest management developments, increase their overall effectiveness, and maintain high job satisfaction.[21]

Types of training

MNEs use a number of types of training and development programs.[22] These can be grouped into two general categories: standardized and tailor-made.

Standardized training programs are generic and can be used with managers anywhere in the world. Examples include programs for improving quantitative analysis or technical skills that can be used universally. Research reveals that many behaviorally oriented concepts can also be handled with a standardized program (although follow-on programs must be tailor-made to meet the specific needs of the country). Examples include programs designed to acquaint the participants with the fundamentals of how to communicate, motivate, or lead people. Another form of standardized training presently offered by large MNEs addresses cultural differences on a global scale. For instance, with operations in 200 countries, managers of Colgate-Palmolive are often exposed to more than one foreign culture. To address this, the company offered cultural diversity training to its managers.[23]

Tailor-made training programs are designed to meet the specific needs of the participants and typically include a large amount of culturally based input. These programs are more commonly developed by large MNEs and by multinationals that need a working knowledge of the local country's beliefs, norms, attitudes, and work values. Quite often the input for these programs is provided by managers who are currently working in the country (or have recently worked there) and by local managers and personnel who are citizens of that country. In most cases this training is provided to expatriates before they leave for their assignment, but in some cases it is provided on-site.

Research shows that the following six types of programs are most popular:

1. Environmental briefings used to provide information about such things as geography, climate, housing, and schools.
2. Cultural orientation designed to familiarize the individual with cultural institutions and value systems of the host country.
3. Cultural assimilators using programmed learning approaches designed to provide the participants with intercultural encounters.
4. Language training.
5. Sensitivity training designed to develop attitudinal flexibility.
6. Field experience, which sends the participant to the country of assignment to undergo some of the emotional stress of living and working with people from a different culture.[24]

Typically, MNEs will use a combination of the above programs, tailoring the package to fit their specific needs. A good example is provided by Underwriters Laboratories Inc., which uses a two-day, in-house program to provide training to those personnel who will be dealing extensively with Japanese clients in the US. The program is designed around a series of mini-lectures that cover a wide range of topics from how to handle introductions to the proper way to exchange gifts. The program employs a variety of training techniques, including lectures, case studies, role-playing, language practice, and a short test on cultural terminology. The two-day training wraps up with a 90-minute question-and-answer period during which participants are given the opportunity to gain additional insights into how to develop effective client relationships.

Some firms extend their training focus to include families. In addition to providing language training, firms such as General Electric Medical Systems Group (GEMS), a Milwaukee-based firm that has expatriates in France, Japan, and Singapore, will match up the family that is going overseas with another family that has been assigned to this country or geographic region. The latter will then share many of the problems that it faced during the overseas assignment and relate some of the ways that these situations were resolved. It is also common to find MNEs offering cultural training to all members of the family, not just to the executive. This helps to create a support group that will work together to deal with problems that arise during the overseas assignment. The box "International Business Strategy in Action: P&O cruise ships" details how an MNE's IHRM training is tightly related to its global expansion.

INTERNATIONAL BUSINESS STRATEGY *IN ACTION*

P&O cruise ships

Few people know that the "Princess" cruise ships, which were the "love boats" of TV fame, are owned by a British company, P&O Princess Cruises plc. While the company operates under the P&O Cruises brand in all its markets, the following brands are also used in Europe: Swan Hellenic, Aida Cruises, A'ROSA, and Seetours International. P&O Princess Cruises is the third largest cruise line in the world. This is a $2 billion service business that is one of Britain's most international companies.

The Peninsular and Orient Steam Navigation Company, known as P&O, was the sea transportation backbone of the old British Empire. In the 19th century it won British government contracts to deliver mail (post) to the Spanish peninsula and (via Africa and the Indian subcontinent) to Australia and the Far East. In the past P&O's ships have been commandeered by the British government in wartime to serve as transport vessels. As recently as the Falklands War of 1982 its large flagship, *Canberra*, played a central role in the British war effort.

In 2000, P&O Princess Cruises spun off from P&O and began to be traded in the New York Stock Exchange. The company is using the familiar P&O brand name as a base for its British Commonwealth cruise ships. Acquired in 1974, the Princess cruise ships are operated separately in North America. These cruise ships include *Sun Princess*, *Dawn Princess*, *Grand Princess*, and the new giant, *Golden Princess*. With an older population of North America "baby boomers", the growth of cruises has been striking. Occupancy on P&O is usually at 100 per cent of capacity. P&O is the leading cruise tour operator along the North American West Coast to Alaska. Cruises are sold through 28,000 travel agents. The *Canberra* served the British cruise market until its withdrawal in 1997 after 36 years' service. In 2001, there are five newer ships serving Britain, including: *Arcadia*, *Minerva*, and *Aurora*. To enter the continental Europe market, P&O purchased a majority stake in Germany's AIDA in 1999 and the remaining stake in 2000. P&O Cruises also purchased Germany's Seetours, a competing cruise line with 40 years of experience, and merged it with AIDA. Since then, AIDA has become the best-known cruise line in Germany.

P&O has an interesting strategic challenge of integrating diverse business, from trucks to boat shows. In particular it needs to link its very capital-intensive cargo ships, which require good information technology and operational efficiency, with its cruise ships, which are in the leisure and entertainment business. The molding of an engineering and technical culture with the marketing, sales, and service activities of the cruise ships is an interesting managerial challenge. P&O has tackled this by extensive programs of management training. For example, it has developed a series of senior management programs at Templeton College, Oxford University, over the last 10 years. These have both improved business efficiency and also moved managers into new areas of customer service, such as environmental and regulatory issues. As a result, P&O is a successful and growing business with a global mindset in its managers.

In November 2001, P&O and Royal Caribbean agreed to a merger that would create a $6.8 billion company. With 41 ships, the new company will dethrone Carnival Cruise Line to become the largest cruise line in the world. Although operations will be merged, P&O and Royal Caribbean will remain as holding companies holding 50.7 and 49.3 per cent respectively of P&O/Royal Caribbean.

Websites: **www.poprincesscruises.com**.

Sources: Annual Reports of P&O; **www.poprincesscruises.com**; Scheherazade Daneshkhu, "Caribbean and P&O Chart Merger Course," *Financial Times*, November 21, 2001.

Active learning check

Review your answer to Active Learning Case question 3 and make any changes you like. Then compare your answer with the one below.

3. What type of training does the firm provide to its interns? Of what value is this training?

The company puts interns into groups and assigns projects that require them to investigate or study certain areas of operations. The interns are then evaluated on the outcome. This training is useful in helping the firm to identify those individuals who offer the most promise for the company.

COMPENSATION

In recent years compensation has become a primary area of IHRM attention.[25] On the one hand, multinationals want to hire the most competent people. On the other hand, they want to control costs and to increase profits. Sometimes these two objectives are not compatible; it can be expensive to relocate an executive overseas. A close look at the breakdown of international compensation packages helps to make this clear.

Common elements in an international compensation package

A typical international compensation package includes base salary, benefits, and allowances. Additionally, most packages address the issue of tax protection and/or tax equalization. The following examines these four elements.

Base salary

Base salary is the amount of cash compensation that an individual receives in the home country. This salary is typically the benchmark against which bonuses and benefits are calculated. Survey research reveals that the salaries of expatriates are tied to their home country, so a German manager working for a US MNE and assigned to Spain will have a base salary tied to the salary structure in Germany.[26] This salary is usually paid in either home currency, local currency, or a combination of the two.

In recent years base salary has become an issue when foreign firms have merged or acquired companies in other countries where salaries are significantly higher. For example, when Chrysler and Daimler-Benz merged, the Chairman and CEO of Chrysler had a salary of $1.6 million in contrast to his Daimler-Benz counterpart who was earning $1.1 million.[27] Moreover, a recent comparison of the base salaries of chief executive officers of industrial companies with annual revenues of $250 to $500 million found the following:

United States	$490,000
Brazil	$480,000
United Kingdom	$430,000
Hong Kong	$390,000
France	$360,000
Mexico	$340,000
Japan	$320,000
Germany	$300,000
South Korea	$120,000.[28]

So, indeed, base salary can present problems in the international arena.

Benefits

Benefits often make up a large portion of the compensation package. Additionally, there are a number of difficult issues which typically must be resolved. These include how to handle medical coverage, what to do about social security, and how to handle the retirement package. Some of the specific issues that receive a great deal of attention include:

1. Whether or not to maintain expatriates in home country programs, particularly if the company does not receive a tax deduction for it.
2. Whether companies have the option of enrolling expatriates in host country benefit programs and/or making up any difference in coverage.
3. Whether host country legislation regarding termination affects benefit entitlements.
4. Whether expatriates should receive home country or host country social security benefits.
5. Whether benefits should be maintained on a home country or host country basis, who is responsible for the cost, whether other benefits should be used to offset any shortfall in coverage, and whether home country benefit programs should be exported to local nationals in foreign countries.[29]

Most US MNEs include their expatriate managers in the company's benefit program and the cost is no more than it would be back home. In those cases where a foreign government also requires contribution to a social security program, the company picks up this expense for the employee. Fortunately, in recent years a number of international agreements have been signed that eliminate requirements for dual coverage.

MNEs also provide vacation and special leave to expatriates. This often includes company-paid air fare back home for the manager and family on an annual basis, as well as emergency leave and expense payments in case of death or illness in the family.

Allowances

Cost-of-living allowance
A payment to compensate for differences in expenditures between the home country and the foreign location

Allowances are another major portion of some expatriate compensation packages. One of the most common is the **cost-of-living allowance**, which is a payment to compensate for differences in expenditures between the home country and the foreign location. This allowance is designed to provide the employee with the same standard of living that he or she enjoyed in the home country. This allowance can cover a wide variety of areas, including relocation, housing, education, and hardship.

Relocation expenses usually include moving, shipping, and storage charges associated with personal goods that the expatriate is taking overseas. Related expenses can include perquisites such as cars and club memberships, which are commonly provided to senior-level managers.

Housing allowances cover a wide gamut. Some firms will provide the manager with a residence while overseas and pay all expenses associated with running the house. Other firms will give the individual a predetermined amount of money each month and the manager can make the housing choice personally. Some MNEs will also help the individual to sell his or her house back home or to rent it until the manager returns. The company usually pays expenses associated with these activities. Other MNEs such as General Motors encourage their people to retain ownership of their home by paying all rental management fees and reimbursing the employee for up to six months' rent if the house remains unoccupied.

Education allowances for the expatriate's children are an integral part of most compensation packages. These expenses cover such things as tuition, enrollment fees, books, supplies, transportation, room, board, and school uniforms. In some cases attendance at post-secondary schools is also provided.

Hardship allowance
A special payment made to individuals posted to geographic areas regarded as less desirable

A **hardship allowance** is a special payment made to individuals who are posted to areas that are regarded as less desirable. For example, individuals posted to Eastern Europe, China, and some Middle East countries typically receive a hardship premium as an inducement to accept the assignment. These payments can be in the form of a lump sum ($10,000 to $25,000) or a percentage (15 to 50) of the individual's base compensation.

Taxation

MNEs also provide tax protection and/or tax equalization for expatriates. For example, a US manager who is sent abroad can end up with two tax bills: one for income earned overseas and the other for US taxes on these monies. Section 911 of the US Internal Revenue System code permits a deduction of up to $70,000 on foreign earned income. For some executives, however, there still might be some US taxes due. In handling these situations, most MNEs have a tax equalization program under which they withhold an amount equal to the home country tax obligation of the manager and then pay all taxes in the host country. Another approach is that of tax protection; the employee pays up to the amount of taxes equal to those he or she would pay based on compensation in the home country. In this case the individual is entitled to any difference if total taxes are less in the foreign country than in the home country. Other MNE tax considerations involve state and local tax payments and tax return preparation.[30]

The most common approach is for the MNE to determine the base salary and other extras (bonuses, etc.) that the manager would make if he or she were living in the home country. The taxes on this income are then computed and compared with the total due on the expatriate's income. Any taxes over and above that that would have been due in the home country are then paid by the multinational.

Current compensation trends

In terms of compensation, the MNE's objective is to ensure that the expatriate does not have to pay any additional expenses as a result of living abroad. Figure 12.2 illustrates this idea. The income taxes, housing, goods and services, and reserve that the person has in the home country are protected so that the individual's out-of-pocket expenses remain the same. As we see from the figure, the overall package can be substantial. This is why currently there is a trend toward not sending expatriates to overseas positions unless there is a need for their specific services. In fact, the costs have become so prohibitive that firms like Dow Jones & Company, owner of the *Wall Street Journal*, have now radically revised their formula for paying allowances for housing, goods, and services.[31] In addition, MNEs are increasingly replacing permanent relocation and long-term assignment with as-needed short trips that typically last less than a year.[32]

Another trend is the creation of special incentive systems designed to keep expatriates motivated. In the process, a growing number of MNEs are now dropping bonuses or premiums for overseas assignments and replacing them with lump-sum premiums. This approach has a number of benefits. One is that expatriates realize that they will be given this payment just once – when they move to the international locale. So the payment tends to retain its value as an incentive. A second is that the costs to the company are less because there is only one payment and no future financial commitment.

The specific incentive program that is used will vary. Researchers have found that some of the factors that influence the type and amount of incentive include whether the person is moving within or between continents and where the person is being stationed. Table 12.1 provides some of the latest survey information related to these incentive practices.

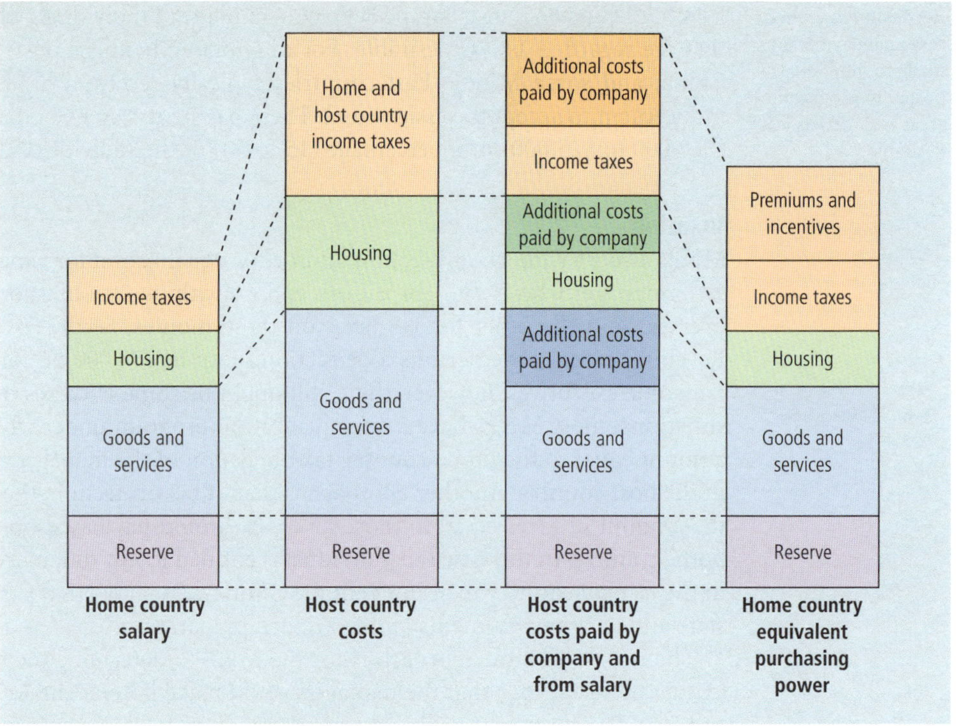

Figure 12.2 Cost of expatriate managers

Source: C. Reynolds, "Compensation of Overseas Personnel," in J. J. Famularo (ed.), *Handbook of Human Resource Administration*, 2nd edn (New York: McGraw-Hill, 1986), p. 51. Reproduced with permission of The McGraw-Hill Companies.

Table 12.1 Employer incentive practices around the world

Type of premium	*Asia* %	*Europe* %	*North America* %	*Total* %
Respondents paying for moves within continents				
Ongoing	62	46	29	42
Lump sum	21	20	25	23
None	16	27	42	32
Respondents paying for moves between continents				
Ongoing	63	54	39	49
Lump sum	24	18	30	26
None	13	21	27	22

Source: Geoffrey W. Latta, "Expatriate Incentives: Beyond Tradition," *HR Focus*, March 1998, p. S 4. Reprinted by permission © *HRfocus*, March 1998. 212/244–0360. http://www.ioma.com

Finally, it is important to realize that many companies are beginning to phase out incentive premiums. Instead, they are focusing on creating a cadre of expats who are motivated by non-financial incentives.

> More companies are starting to take an entirely different approach, paying *no* premiums to expatriates regardless of where they send them. According to this philosophy, an assignment itself is its own reward. It's an opportunity for an employee to achieve personal and career growth. In some organizations, succession planning for senior-level positions requires international experience. Others view expatriate assignments as a step toward achieving globalization. Companies that subscribe to the philosophy of paying no premiums only consider cost-of-living issues, not motivational rewards, when designing pay packages.[33]

LABOR RELATIONS

One of the major challenges facing MNEs is that of orienting their strategy to meet the varying demands of organized labor around the world (see Figure 12.3). National differences in economic, political, and legal systems create a variety of labor relations systems, and the strategy that is effective in one country or region can be of little value in another country.[34]

In managing labor relations, most MNEs use a combination of centralization and decentralization with some decisions being made at headquarters and others being handled by managers on-site.[35] Researchers have found that US MNEs tend to exercise more centralized control in contrast to European MNEs such as the British. A number of factors have been cited to explain this development, including: (1) US companies tend to rely heavily on formal management controls and a close reporting system is needed to support this process; (2) European companies tend to deal with labor unions at an industry level compared with US MNEs that deal at the company level; and (3) for many US firms the domestic market represents the bulk of their sales (a situation that is not true for many European MNEs) and the overseas market is managed as an extension of domestic operations.[36]

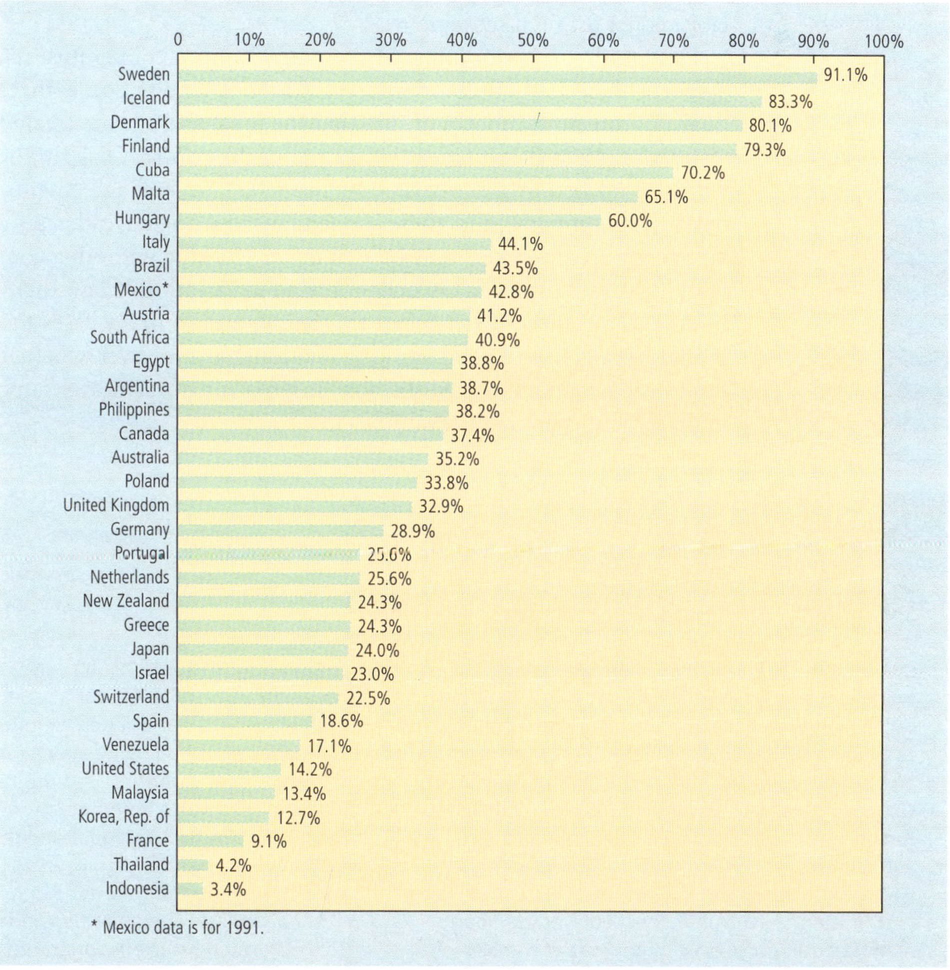

Figure 12.3 Labour unions worldwide, 1995 (% of labour force that is unionized)

Source: International Labor Organization, *World Labour Report*, November 1997.

Labor relations practices

Labor relations practices vary widely. In some countries the economy is strong and unions are able to make major demands; in other countries the economy is weak and the union's ability to bargain is diminished. Similarly, some countries have strong pro-management governments while others are heavily union-oriented. A third factor is the willingness of unions to strike or walk out as opposed to continuing to talk with management in the hopes of resolving differences. Germany and Japan provide some interesting contrasts.

Germany

Labor unions have been traditionally strong in Germany. Although a minority of the labor force is organized, unions set the pay scale for about 90 per cent of the country's workers with wages determined by job classifications.[37] Union membership is voluntary, but there is only one union in each major industry. This union will negotiate a contract with the employers' federation for the industry, and the contract will cover all major issues, including wages and terms of employment. If there is a disagreement over the interpretation or enforcement of the contract, the impasse is typically resolved between the company and the worker with the participation of a union representative or work council. If this procedure is unsuccessful, the matter can then be referred to a German labor court for final settlement.

Despite their power, unions have a much more cooperative relationship with management than do their counterparts in the US. One reason is that workers serve on the board of directors and can ensure that the rank-and-file are treated fairly.

If there is a strike, it tends to occur after the contract has run out and a new one has yet to be ratified by the workers. As in the US, several agreements may be in force in a particular company, and these agreements do not have the same termination dates. So one group of workers may be striking or working without a contract while another is working under contract. On occasion, and in violation of law, there may be strikes in the middle of a contract period, but this is rare and in many cases the union and management typically have a good working relationship. However, whether this will continue in the future is difficult to say; the box "International Business Strategy in Action: German management gets tough" examines this.

INTERNATIONAL BUSINESS STRATEGY *IN ACTION*

German management gets tough

During the 1970s and 1980s German manufacturing workers made substantial gains at the bargaining table. However, these successes are now coming back to haunt both them and their unions. In 1990, the average hourly manufacturing cost in the US was $15 while Germany's was $22. Between 1985 and 1990, manufacturing cost in US dollars in Germany increased by 130 per cent. This was a result of the strength of Germany currency and a 28 per cent increase in labor costs in German currency. By 2000 average hourly manufacturing cost in Germany was at the $23 level, but still above the $15 level in Italy, $16 in the UK, and $20 in the US. In 1999, Volkswagen was prevented from laying off some 30,000 excess German workers by tough unions and labour laws. Job security and high wages are not the only labor disadvantages for German firms who receive shorter labor-hour weeks, six weeks paid vacations, and a very generous sick leave plan that promotes absenteeism. As a result, German products were having trouble finding international markets. In response, employers began looking for ways of turning things around.

In particular, companies began demanding wage concessions and started working to eliminate jobs. IBM's German subsidiary, which had almost 25,000 employees, divided itself into five companies, leaving only the 6,000 workers in the production unit working under a union contract. The remainder of the employees were not covered by the collective agreement, allowing the company to increase their work week to 40 hours. Other companies began implementing similar strategies, convinced that labor leaders would make concessions in order to ensure the long-run survival of the business. In particular, managers pointed to the fact that international competition was threatening German jobs, and, unless productivity could be increased, there was a good chance that more and more local firms would go out of business. This strategy, and a decrease in the exchange rate, have led to real wage decreases and a restructuring of the labor market over the last few years.

There are a growing number of companies that are now winning concessions from their unions. One is CED Informationstechnik GmbH, a small firm that assembles personal computers. The company's union contract allows it to cut back the workforce when orders are weak. And since CED focuses on delivery of computers within 24 hours of receiving an order, it has no need to build inventory. So the workforce size is tied directly to the amount of orders on hand, thus allowing CED to operate with a basic crew of only 200 people. In turn, another group of approximately 40 workers has contracts guaranteeing them at least 1,000 hours of work annually, so these people can count on approximately 20 hours a week on average – although this is all tied to work orders. The remaining 300 employees at CED work as needed and can find after a month or two of large orders that things dry up and they have no work for the next couple of months. It is a chance they have to take.

A 9.5 per cent unemployment rate and the relocation of operations outside Germany by both domestic and foreign companies have increased pressure on unions to accept less favorable contracts. While all of this is a big change from the days when the unions used to dictate terms, it is one that is accepted by both the workers and the CED's worker council. This attitude is reflective of a growing number of unions. In 1999, when Wacker-Chemie workers were in danger of losing their jobs because the company was losing millions of dollars, the union proactively allowed the adjustment of wages and an adjustment in workers hours. As a result jobs were saved and Wacker-Chemie was allowed to get back on its feet. Thanks to compromise on the part of its union, management in the chemical sector can, upon consultation with workers, decrease wages by up to 10 per cent per year, eliminate Christmas bonuses, and adjust the hours of work. In 2000, workers at Philipp Holzmann, a construction firm undergoing problems, bargained a wage decrease with the condition that workers will share the company's future gains. This new-founded flexibility offers the promise of making German industry more competitive than it has been in a long time!

Websites: ***www.vw.com***; ***www.volkswagen.de***; ***www.ibm.com*** and ***www.wacker.de***.

Sources: John Templeman, "Crunch Time for Germany's Unions," *Business Week*, June 7, 1993, p. 47; Greg Steinmetz, "Under Pressure, Germany's Unions Bend," *Wall Street Journal*, July 29, 1997, p. A 10; Dagmar Aalund, "Germany's Jobless Rate Worsens, Inspiring Worry Over a Showdown," *Wall Street Journal*, December 9, 1998, p. A 17; Howard Banks, "German Industry Is Fleeing Germany. Why?" *Forbes*, May 5, 1997; Michael Calabrese, "Should Europe Adopt the American Economic Model?" *IntellectualCapital.com*, August 6, 1998; David Fairlamb et al., "Europe's Big Chance," *Business Week*, September 27, 1999, pp. 62–64; Jack Ewing, "This Union Leader Cuts Germany's Bosses Some Slack," *Business Week*, September 10, 2001; "Unions' Unions," *Economist*, April 27, 2000.

Japan

In Japan, union–management relationships are extremely cooperative. Social custom dictates non-confrontational behavior. So although labor agreements are often general and vague, disputes regarding interpretations tend to be settled in an amicable manner. Sometimes it is necessary to bring in third-party mediators or arbitrators, but there are no prolonged, acrimonious disputes that end up in a plant being closed down because the two sides cannot work together. Typically, a strike is used merely to embarrass the management and seldom lasts longer than one week. While it is possible to resort to legal action in resolving strikes, this is typically frowned upon by both labor and management and both sides try to stay away from using this means of bringing about solutions to their problems.[38]

Japanese unions are most active during the spring and at the end of the year, the two periods during which bonuses are negotiated. However, these activities do not usually end up in a union–management conflict. If there is a strike, it is more likely at a time when a Japanese union is negotiating with management during industry-wide negotiations. Even here, the objective is to show that the workers are supportive of the union and not to indicate a grievance or complaint with management. In overall terms, Japanese workers tend to subordinate their interests and identities to those of the group. This cultural value helps to account for a great deal of the harmony that exists between unions and management.[39]

Industrial democracy

Industrial democracy The legally mandated right of employees to participate in significant management decisions

Unlike the US, many countries have **industrial democracy**, which is the legally mandated right of employees to participate in significant management decisions. This authority extends into areas such as wages, bonuses, profit sharing, work rules, dismissals, and plant expansions and closings. Industrial democracy can take a number of different forms.

Forms of industrial democracy

At present there are a number of forms of industrial democracy. In some countries one form may be more prevalent than others, and it is common to find some of these forms existing simultaneously. The following describes three of the most popular forms.

Codetermination A legal system that requires workers and their managers to discuss major strategic decisions before companies implement the decisions

Codetermination **Codetermination** is a legal system that requires workers and their managers to discuss major strategic decisions before companies implement them. Codetermination has brought about worker participation on boards of directors and is quite popular in Europe where in Austria, Denmark, Holland, and Sweden there is legally mandated codetermination. In many cases the workers hold one-third of the seats on the board, although it is 50 per cent in private German companies with 2,000 or more employees. On the negative side, some researchers report that many workers are unimpressed with codetermination and feel that it does not provide sufficient worker input to major decisions.

Work councils Groups that consist of both worker and manager representatives and are charged with dealing with matters such as improving company performance, working conditions, and job security

Work councils **Work councils** are groups that consist of both worker and manager representatives and are charged with dealing with matters such as improving company performance, working conditions, and job security. In some firms these councils are worker- or union-run, whereas in other companies a management representative chairs the group. These councils are a result of either national legislation or collective bargaining at the company–union level, and they exist throughout Europe. However, the power of these councils varies. In Germany, the Netherlands, and Italy, work councils are more powerful than they are in England, France, and Scandinavia.

Shop floor participation

Shop floor participation takes many forms, including job enrichment programs, quality circles, and various other versions of participative management. These approaches provide the workers with an opportunity to make their voices heard and to play a role in identifying problems and resolving them. Shop floor participation is widely used in Scandinavian countries and has spread to other European nations and to the US over the last two decades.

Industrial democracy in action

Industrial democracy can be found in different forms throughout the US, Europe, and Asia. The following discussion examines three examples.[40]

Germany

Industrial democracy and codetermination are both very strong in Germany, especially in the steel and auto industries. Private firms with 2,000 or more employees (in the steel industry it is 1,000 employees) must have supervisory boards (similar to a board of directors in the US) composed of workers as well as managers. There must also be a management board which is responsible for daily operations, and company employees elect members to this board.

Researchers have found that codeterminism works well in Germany. Some critics have argued that there are too many people involved in the decision-making process, and this slows things down, thus resulting in inefficiencies. However, Scholl reports that a study he conducted of both managers and work councils found no such problems.[41] In fact, the millennium is likely to see even greater efforts toward codeterminism in the unified Germany.

Denmark

Industrial democracy in Denmark gives workers the right to participate in management on both a direct and an indirect basis. The direct form maintains that employees are members of semiautonomous work groups that provide ideas on how to enhance productivity and quality and schedule work. In indirect form there are shop stewards on the floor who represent the workers, fellow workers on the board of directors, and cooperation committees that consist of both management and worker representatives. Industrial democracy works exceptionally well in Denmark, where researchers have found that cooperation committees contribute substantially to openness, coordination of effort, and a feeling of importance on the part of workers.[42]

Japan

Japan's use of industrial democracy concepts is not tied to political philosophy as is the case in Europe; rather, it is oriented more to Japanese culture and the belief in group harmony. Moreover, Japanese industrial democracy is not as extensive as that in the West. Japanese workers are encouraged to identify and help to solve job-related problems associated with quality and the flow of work. Management in turn is particularly receptive to worker ideas that will produce bottom-line results. This process is carried out in a paternalistic setting in which the company looks after the employees and the latter respond appropriately.

Unions play virtually no role in promoting industrial democracy or participative management because they are weak and, in many cases, only ceremonial. One group of researchers put it this way:

> In truth, most workers think of themselves as company employees who are simply associated with the union. Moreover, it is not uncommon to find a union strike in a company with two or three work shifts and no loss of work output. This is because, when the strikers are done picketing or marching, they then go to work and the group coming out of the factory takes up the strike activity. In a factory with three shifts, a line employee will work a full shift, picket for a while, go home to eat and sleep, and then return to the factory for her or his shift.[43]

As a result, Japanese MNEs face the greatest challenge from industrial democracy because they are least accustomed to using the idea. On the other hand, as Japanese firms continue to expand into Europe and the US, it is likely that there will be a growing use of authority-sharing concepts such as codetermination, work councils, and other approaches that are becoming so common in Western firms.

STRATEGIC MANAGEMENT AND IHRM STRATEGIES

There are a number of human resource management (HRM) strategies currently receiving attention from MNEs.[44] While there are too many to address here, three that warrant consideration are language training, cultural adaptation, and competitive compensation.

Language training

English is the primary language of international business. However, training in the host country language can be particularly useful because it allows managers to interact more effectively with their local colleagues and workers and to communicate more directly with suppliers and customers. Another advantage of language training is that it allows the manager to monitor the competition more effectively. For example, in recent years a growing number of US MNEs have set up operations in Japan. Included in this group are DuPont, Eastman Kodak, Hewlett-Packard, IBM, Procter & Gamble, and Rockwell International. Many of these MNE expatriate managers and R&D personnel have been given language training, and it has paid off handsomely. For example, when Rockwell International entered into negotiations with a Japanese firm regarding royalties on a patent it holds on advanced semiconductor processing technology, the Japanese company said that it had no intention of using Rockwell's patent. However, the company negotiators were able to show the Japanese an article from a Japanese newspaper in which their company had boasted about using the new technology. As a result, Rockwell now receives royalties on the use of this technology by the Japanese company.[45] In fact, thanks to language training, Rockwell was able to discover a host of patent infringements on the same technology by other Japanese firms.

Language training is also useful in recruiting local talent and developing good relations with local organizations. IBM Japan, for example, hires 30 per cent of its research scientists from Japanese universities or companies. Other US firms follow a similar pattern, offering large salaries ($150,000 and up) to attract senior Japanese scientists who can help to create new high-tech products. Language training also comes in handy in developing and sustaining relationships with universities and governmental agencies. In fact, Dow Chemical has created a team for just this purpose.

Another benefit of language training is for monitoring competition. MNEs often locate near their major competitors because new developments by these firms are most likely to be reported in local newspapers and in other sources. It is frequently possible to learn more about what a competitor is doing through local news media than one could ever find out if the investigation were conducted from MNE headquarters. Many foreign MNEs have personnel who are fluent in English, peruse the *Wall Street Journal*, *New York Times*, and US industry publications on a daily basis, and then compile a thick folder on the strategies of their US competitors.

Language training is also useful in helping to learn about the culture of the country and in interacting socially with the people. Recent research reports that most US expatriate managers give low importance to the value of a second language. In contrast, executives from South America, Europe, and Japan place a high priority on speaking more than one language. One research study concluded by noting "these results provide a poignant indication of national differences that promise to influence profoundly the success of US corporations".[46] Fortunately, universities in the US are now stepping in to help out. For example, the Massachusetts Institute of Technology, as well as other institutions of higher learning, now offers courses in how to read technical Japanese and understand the Japanese research culture; this educational focus is likely to expand to other countries during the millennium. For the moment, however, language training continues to be a weak link in the development of an effective IHRM strategy for many MNEs.

Active learning check 

Review your answer to Active Learning Case question 4 and make any changes you like. Then compare your answer with the one below.

4. How useful is it for The Coca-Cola Company managers to be fluent in more than one language? Why?

The Coca-Cola Company's managers must be fluent in other languages because the company feels that this allows the individuals to operate effectively in at least two different cultures. This permits the company to transfer managers from one geographic region to another and to know that the manager will be able to become acculturated within a minimum time period. Moreover, since there are common languages in many regions of the world, a manager who is fluent, for example, in English and Spanish could be transferred to countries throughout North America, South America, Europe, Africa, and Australia. Thus bilingualism provides the company with a cadre of managers who can literally span the globe.

Cultural adaptation

Closely tied to language training is the need for managers to understand the culture of the country to which they are assigned. The importance of culture was discussed in Chapter 5, where it was noted that there are major differences between cultural clusters. In preparing managers for overseas positions, MNEs are now using three basic approaches. The simplest and least expensive approach is to design a program that provides cultural orientation by familiarizing the individual with the cultural institutions and value systems of the country. This is often done through a formal training program and/or meetings with company personnel who have just returned from a posting in that country. The second is to provide the individual with language training and, if time and money permit, allow the person to visit the country. Some MNEs tie this approach to the manager's assignment by setting aside the first couple of weeks on-site for orientation and acculturation. A third approach that is fairly expensive but has received high marks for its value is the use of cultural assimilators.

Cultural assimilators

Cultural assimilator
A programmed learning technique designed to expose members of one culture to some of the basic concepts, attitudes, role perceptions, customs, and values of another culture

A **cultural assimilator** is a programmed learning technique that is designed to expose members of one culture to some of the basic concepts, attitudes, role perceptions, customs, and values of another culture. Cultural assimilators are developed for pairs of cultures such as familiarizing managers from the US with the culture in Germany. Of course, an assimilator can be developed for expatriates who are assigned to any culture in the world, and the approach almost always takes the same format: The person being trained is asked to read a short episode of a cultural encounter and then to choose an interpretation of what has happened and why. If the person's response is correct, the individual goes on to the next episode. If not, the person is asked to reread the episode and then to make another choice. Table 12.2 provides an illustration.

Cultural assimilators use critical incidents as the basis for the training. These incidents are typically ones in which (1) the expatriate will be interacting with a host nation, (2) the situation may be misinterpreted or mishandled if the individual is not properly

Table 12.2 A cultural assimilator situation

Sharon Hatfield, a school teacher in Athens, was amazed at the questions that were asked of her by Greeks whom she considered to be only casual acquaintances. When she entered or left her apartment, people would ask her where she was going or where she had been. If she stopped to talk, she was asked questions like, "How much do you make a month?" She thought the Greeks were very rude.

Page X-2

Why did the Greeks ask Sharon such "personal" questions?

1. The casual acquaintances were acting like friends do in Greece, although Sharon did not realize it.

   Go to page X-3

2. The Greeks asked Sharon the questions in order to determine whether she belonged to the Greek Orthodox Church.

   Go to page X-4

3. The Greeks were unhappy about the way in which she lived and they were trying to get Sharon to change her habits.

   Go to page X-5

4. In Greece such questions are perfectly proper when asked of women, but improper when asked of men.

   Go to page X-6

You selected 1: The casual acquaintances were acting like friends do in Greece, although Sharon did not realize it.

Correct. It is not improper for in-group members to ask these questions of one another. Furthermore, these questions reflect the fact that friendships (even "casual" ones) tend to be more intimate in Greece than in America. As a result, friends are generally free to ask questions which would seem too personal in America.

Go to page X-1

Page X-4

You selected 2: The Greeks asked Sharon the questions in order to determine whether she belonged to the Greek Orthodox Church.

No. This is not why the Greeks asked Sharon such questions. Remember, whether or not some information is "personal" depends on the culture. In this case the Greeks did not consider these questions too "personal." Why? Try again.

Go to page X-1

You selected 3: The Greeks were unhappy about the way in which she lived and they were trying to get Sharon to change her habits.

No. There was no information given to lead you to believe that the Greeks were unhappy with Sharon's way of living. The episode states that the Greeks were acquaintances of Sharon.

Go to page X-1

You selected 4: In Greece such questions are perfectly proper when asked of women, but improper when asked of men.

No. Such questions are indeed proper under certain situations. However, sex has nothing to do with it. When are these questions proper? Try to apply what you have learned about proper behavior between friends in Greece. Was Sharon regarded as a friend by these Greeks?

Go to page X-1

Source: Adapted from Fred E. Fiedler, Terence Mitchell and Harry C. Triandis (1971) "The Culture Assimilator: An Approach to Cross-Cultural Training," *Journal of Applied Psychology*, April 1971, **55**, 97–98. Copyright © 1971 by the American Psychological Association. Adapted with permission.

trained, and (3) the event is relevant to the expatriate's task or mission requirements.[47] The incidents are provided by expatriates who have served in this particular country, as well as by members of the host nation. Once the incidents are written, they are tested on people who have had experience in this country in order to ensure that the responses are realistic and that one choice is indeed preferable to the others. Typically, 150 to 200 incidents will be developed and then the list will be pruned to 75 to 100 incidents, which are eventually included in the assimilator booklet.

Assimilators can be expensive to create. The typical cost for developing one is approximately $50,000. However, for MNEs that are continually sending people to a particular overseas location, the cost can be spread over many trainees and the assimilator can remain intact for a number of years. A $50,000 assimilator that is used with 500 people over a five-year period will cost the company only $100 per person, and the cost of revising the program is often quite small, so over the long run cultural assimilators can be very cost effective.

Competitive compensation

MNEs are also beginning to evaluate more carefully the cost of sending people overseas as well as to review the expense of maintaining executive talent in the international arena. The first of these concerns focuses on all expatriates. The second addresses top-level managers only.

Compensation costs vary widely because goods and services in some countries of the world are sharply higher (or lower) than in others. For example, food, clothes, and entertainment in the US *are* fairly inexpensive when compared with Japan, Hong Kong, Taiwan, or Great Britain (see Table 12.3). In particular, the cost-of-living allowance for managers in Europe and Japan adds significantly to the MNE's overhead. For this reason, major MNEs from General Motors to IBM to TRW are looking for ways of recruiting and developing local talent to staff operations and thus reducing their reliance on expatriates.

The other major area of compensation that is receiving increased attention is that of hiring and retaining top management talent. Research shows that the cost of hiring senior-level managers is extremely high, and in most cases these individuals received a substantial salary raise when they moved into their new position. Moreover, as the demand for talented executives increases, the salaries of international managers will continue to rise. This is one reason that many MNEs are now hiring people for specific

Table 12.3 Cost of living in select cities (New York = 100)

Location	*Cost*	*Location*	*Cost*	*Location*	*Cost*
Tokyo	140	Moscow	85	Kuala Lumpur	60
Taipei	120	Boston	84	Prague	57
Hong Kong	116	Brussels	79	Istanbul	56
London	102	Cleveland	79	Bogota	56
New York	100	Caracas	77	Bangkok	55
Singapore	97	Athens	69	Jakarta	53
Tel Aviv	97	Lisbon	68	Budapest	49
Beijing	96	Warsaw	65	Johannesburg	47
Buenos Aires	90	São Paolo	61	Manila	44
Seoul	90	Santiago	63	New Delhi	40
Mexico City	86				

Source: Adapted from *The Economist*, 7.7.01.

locations and leaving these individuals in place for extended periods of time. This strategy is less costly than continually moving managers from one geographic location to another.

During the millennium human resource management strategy will become an increasingly important part of the overall MNE strategic plan. Rising compensation costs are one of the major reasons for this trend.

Specially designed HRM programs

Another emerging trend is specially designed human resource management (HRM) programs. In recent years a growing number of MNEs have begun to realize that HRM practices have to be tailor-made. This has been clearly illustrated by Sparrow and Budhwar, who compared data from 13 different countries on the basis of HRM factors. Five of these factors included the following:

1. Structural empowerment which is characterized by flat organization designs, wide spans of control, the use of flexible cross-functional teams, and the rewarding of individuals for productivity gains.
2. Accelerated resource development which is characterized by the early identification of high potential employees, the establishment of both multiple and parallel career paths, the rewarding of personnel for enhancing their skills and knowledge, and the offering of continuous training and development education.
3. Employee welfare emphasis which is characterized by firms offering personal family assistance, encouraging and regarding external volunteer activities, and promoting a culture that emphasizes equality in the workplace.
4. An efficiency emphasis in which employees are encouraged to monitor their own work and to continually improve their performance.
5. Long-termism which stresses long-term results such as innovation and creativity rather than just weekly and monthly short-term productivity.[48]

When Sparrow and Budhwar used these HRM approaches on a comparative country-by-country basis, they found that there were worldwide differences in HRM practices. Table 12.4 shows the comparative results, after each of the 13 countries was categorized as being either high or low on the respective factors.

These findings reveal that countries are unique in their approach to HRM. What works well in the US may have limited value in France. In fact, a close analysis of Table 12.4 shows that none of the 13 countries had the same profile; each was different. This was even true in the case of Anglo nations such as the US, Canada, Australia, and the UK where differences in employee welfare emphasis, accelerated resource development, long efficiency orientation, and long-termism resulted in unique HRM profiles for each. Similarly, Japan and Korea differed on two of the factors, as did Germany and France; and India, which many people might feel would be more similar to an Anglo culture than to an Asian one, differed on two of the factors with both the US and the UK, with three of the factors with Canada, and on all four factors with Australia.

These findings point to the fact that MNEs in the millennium will have to focus increasingly on HRM programs designed to meet the needs of local personnel. A good example is provided in Eastern Europe where international managers are discovering that in order to effectively recruit college graduates their firms must provide training programs that give these new employees opportunities to work with a variety of tasks and to help them specialize in their particular fields of interest. At the same time the MNEs are discovering that these recruits are looking for companies that offer a good social working environment. A recent survey of over 1,000 business and engineering students from Poland, the

Table 12.4 **Human resource management practices in select countries**

	Structural empowerment		*Accelerated resource development*		*Employee welfare emphasis*		*Efficiency emphasis*		*Long-termism*	
	High	*Low*	*High*	*Low*	*High*	*Low*	*High*	*Low*	*High*	*Low*
United States	X			X	X		X			X
Canada	X			X	X			X		X
United Kingdom	X			X		X		X		X
Italy		X		X		X		X		X
Japan		X		X	X		X		X	
India		X		X	X			X	X	
Australia	X		X			X	X		X	
Brazil	X		X		X			X	X	
Mexico	X		X		X			X		X
Argentina		X	X		X			X		X
Germany		X	X			X		X	X	
Korea		X	X			X	X		X	
France		X	X			X	X			X

Source: Adapted from *Journal of World Business*, Vol. 32, No. 3, 1997, Paul R. Sparrow and Pawan S. Budhwar, "Competition and Change: Mapping the Indiana HRM Recipe Against World-Wide Patterns", p. 233, Copyright 1997, with permission from Elsevier Science.

Czech Republic, and Hungary found that almost two-thirds of the respondents said that they wanted their boss to be receptive to their ideas; 37 per cent were looking for managers who had strong industry experience; and 34 per cent wanted a boss who was a good rational decision maker. These findings indicate that multinational human resource management is now becoming much more of a two-way street: both employees and managers need to adjust continually to emerging demands.[49]

KEY POINTS

1. International human resource management (IHRM) is the process of selecting, training, developing, and compensating personnel in overseas positions. IHRM strategies involve consideration of staffing, selecting, training, compensating, and labor relations in the international environment.
2. There are a number of screening criteria that are used in choosing people for international assignments. These include adaptability, self-reliance, age, experience, education, health, family status, motivation, and leadership. The most common selection procedure is the interview, although some firms also use testing. In recent years MNEs have also begun formulating repatriation strategies for integrating returning managers back into the work place at home.
3. Training and development programs are another key part of IHRM strategies. There are a wide variety of these programs, ranging from environmental briefings to language training.
4. There are a number of common parts in a typical international compensation package, including base salary, benefits, allowances, and tax protection and/or equalization. In essence, the package's objective is to ensure that the expatriate does not have to pay any additional expenses as a result of living abroad.

5. Labor relations practices vary widely in the international arena. For example, union–management relations and industrial democracy approaches are different throughout Europe, and these differ dramatically from those in Japan.
6. There are a number of human resource management strategies that currently are receiving a great deal of attention from MNEs. Three of these are language training, cultural adaptation, and competitive compensation.

KEY TERMS

- international human resource management (IHRM)
- home country nationals
- expatriates
- host country nationals
- third country nationals
- international screening criteria
- repatriation
- transition strategies
- repatriation agreement
- training
- managerial development
- standardized training programs
- tailor-made training programs
- cost-of-living allowance
- hardship allowance
- industrial democracy
- codetermination
- work councils
- cultural assimilator

REVIEW AND DISCUSSION QUESTIONS

1. Many US MNEs are accused of not focusing their efforts sufficiently on internationalization. How can these MNEs develop an international perspective among their managers? Offer three suggestions.
2. What are some of the most common screening criteria for individuals being chosen for international assignments? Identify and discuss four of them.
3. Why do MNEs tend to prefer interviews to testing when selecting people for international assignments?
4. In what way is repatriation proving to be a major problem for MNEs? How can they deal with this issue? Offer two substantive recommendations.
5. What are some of the most common forms of training and development offered to people going international or already operating there? Identify and describe three of them.
6. What are the most important parts of an international compensation package? Identify and describe three of them.
7. Why do some compensation packages have a hardship allowance?
8. In terms of compensation, why do many MNEs prefer to use a local manager rather than to bring in an expatriate?
9. What are some of the primary differences in labor relation practices between Germany and Japan? Identify and discuss two of them.
10. How does industrial democracy work? Compare and contrast its use in Denmark, Germany, and Japan.
11. How are MNEs attempting to improve the language training that is given to their personnel being posted overseas?
12. How would an MNE use a cultural assimilator to prepare people for overseas assignments?
13. What are some of the latest trends in competitive compensation in the international arena? Identify and describe two of them.

REAL CASE

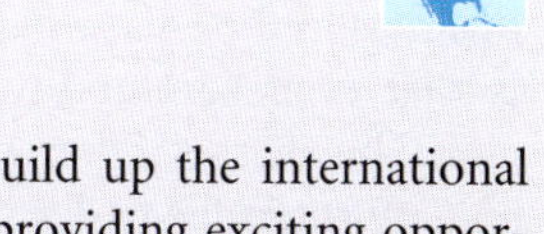

Enron – recruiting the best

Working for Houston-based Enron, a US utility company producing and trading natural gas, was not seen as an exciting career move for top-quality MBAs. Indeed, in 1990 new CEO Kenneth Lang found that Enron did not even recruit from the top US business schools such as Harvard, Stanford, and Chicago. Instead, Enron went to second- and third-tier schools, as its experience was that these MBAs were more stable and it found that these graduates were very committed to careers in the gas utility business. However, Lang fired the human resource (HR) director who was failing to recruit top-class people. During the 1990s Lang spent a large amount of his time in recruitment, and he believed that to be a world-class company it was necessary to recruit world-class people. Enron began to compete with consulting firm McKinsey for MBAs from Harvard and other top business schools in the world. This change in hiring criteria came at the same time as Lang began injecting enthusiasm and vision into the company. In 1990, 80 per cent of the company's revenue came from pipelines and the remaining 20 per cent from oil and gas exploration. But, with deregulation of the US energy business came the opportunity to market natural gas and electricity from various suppliers. By 2000, only 20 per cent of Enron's revenue came from pipelines and exploration. The remaining 80 per cent were new businesses, including wholesale of energy, retail of energy, and telecommunications. Naturally, as the company's core strategy changed, its human resources needs also changed. During that time, the company was injected with MBAs who could help turn the company into a flexible and innovative marketer.

When Enron was formed in 1985 in a merger of two US gas companies, it became the largest natural gas utility in the US with the largest gas pipeline system and more gas-fired independent power plants than any other company in the world. In 2000, Enron's revenues were over $100 billion. At this time it had 20,000 employees and operations in over 40 countries. Among its international operations, the company became the leading distributor and marketer of natural gas in South Korea. In 2001 Enron was building a 3,000 kilometer natural gas pipeline from Bolivia to Brasil. One of Kenneth Lang's strategies was to build up the international side of Enron's business, providing exciting opportunities and responsibilities for fast-track MBA recruits.

Launched in November 1999, EnronOnline was a clear example of the company's achievement in creating a flexible and innovative workforce. In early 1999, 380 employees started developing the concept of an online natural gas and electricity trading system. The research and development of the site was funded by allocated funds, which meant there was no need to consult with top management to start off the project. Enron's CEO and then president Jeffrey K. Skilling were only consulted once the projected was close to launch. In less than a year, EnronOnline had traded over $90 billion in energy and financial products. By mid 2000, 60 per cent of Enron's transactions were being traded through EnronOnline. Skilling saw the project through and established Enron Net Works to look at other online opportunities. The company expanded outside its traditional industry and sought to trade products ranging from chemicals to airport landing rights.

Skilling was also behind Enron's entry into the telecommunications business. In 1998, he wanted to buy a high speed connection that would allow a few hours of daily teleconferencing from the headquarters in Houston to the company's New York office. The cost was estimated at $20,000 per month, regardless of use. Skilling immediately saw parallels to the pre-deregulation natural gas market and Enron Broadband Services (EBS) was launched. EBS developed a fibre-optic network to connect various companies and allow for the trading of bandwidth. Just as in the case of gas, a customer would be able to purchase bandwidth from Enron who would then use any of its suppliers to deliver the information. Enron guaranteed the quality of its suppliers and could achieve best allocations by combining resources from multiple suppliers.

Enron also developed a new core competence (firm-specific advantage) in organizational learning and managing political risk. It was one of the first firms in a stable and traditional energy-related sector to develop a knowledge-based business with skilled and well-trained people. These individuals were managers rather than engineers. This gave Enron a competitive advantage compared with the average business in the energy field. The lesson to be learned is that even commodity-type utilities can become global businesses if they are willing to spend the time and effort needed to develop dynamic organizational capabilities.

In November 2001 Enron's stock market capitalization tumbled after public disclosure of dubious financial practices by its senior financial officers. Its CFO resigned and its annual reports were restated to show a loss of over half a billion dillars in the previous five years. Its share price fell from $90 to $1 a share in six weeks. It declared bankruptcy on November 30, 2001. Perhaps Enron's management was not so good after all.

Website: **www.enron.com**.

Source: Enron Annual Reports; Andrew Inkpen, "Enron Development Corporation," in Paul W. Beamish, Allen Morrison and Philip M. Rosenzweg (eds), *International Management: Text and Cases* (Chicago IL: Irwin, 1997); Sumantra Ghoshal and Christopher A. Bartlett, "Play the Right Cards to Fit the Aces in the Pack," *Financial Times*, July 28, 1998; Sumantra Ghoshal and Christopher A. Bartlett, *The Individualized Corporation* (New York: Harper Business, 1997); **www.enron.com**; Wendy Zellner, "Enron Electrified," *Business Week*, July 24, 2000; *Financial Times*, December 30, 2001.

1. **What type of services should Enron have made available to expatriates and their spouses?**
2. **How should expatriate services be tailored to the host country?**
3. **What steps could Enron have taken to minimize overseas assignment expenses?**

REAL CASE

Executive search firms

Commonly known as headhunters, Executive Search Firms (ESFs) are a specialized branch of management consulting. They work directly with clients, usually MNEs, to identify, evaluate and recruit senior executives. In 2000, an estimated 73 per cent of Fortune 1,000 companies used an executive search firm to fill positions ranging from entry-level to CEO and board member. Worldwide ESFs are a $10 billion industry. ESFs fees are a percentage of the salary (including equity) the chosen candidate will receive in the first year of employment. This creates the right incentives for bargaining for high salaries by their executives. The largest firms are shown in the table below. These firms are highly competitive, particularly in North America and Europe. There are also many small local boutique firms, but these often work with the major international chains for MNE recruiting.

World's largest Executive Search Firms, 2000

Executive search firm	*Revenue $*	*Number of offices*
Korn/Ferry International	576	74
Heidrick & Struggles	574	78
Spencer Stuart	345	52
Egon Zehnder International	319	55
Russell Reynolds Assoc.	305	35
TMP Worldwide	180	33
Ray & Berndtson	176	47
Hever Amrop Alliance	129	75

Note: These numbers do not include revenues from online businesses.
Source: *FT.com*.

Korn/Ferry is the largest ESF in the world with revenues totaling $576 million in 2000. The company is a franchise business, with offices in North America, Europe, Asia Pacific, and Latin America. In each region, the company evaluates staffing needs and then specializes in a few core areas. In Europe and North America, Korn/Ferry serves the e-business industry, but not in Latin America, where e-business is not as common.

The second largest ESF is Heidrick & Struggles (H&S). Unlike Korn/Ferry, H&S is completely integrated. Over the last eight years the company has grown an average of 25 per cent per year to become the second largest ESF in the world.

After several years of dot.com driven prosperity, the slowdown of the world economy has hit the ESFs hard. Between 1998 and 2000, the industry enjoyed a boom with annual growth of over 20 per cent. In the US, growth was even higher at 31 per cent in 2000. In 2001 ESFs were reporting losses and many headhunters were looking for work themselves. Korn/Ferry restructured and reduced its workforce by 20 per cent. Its largest competitor H&S is also cutting its employees by 13 per cent. Ironically, this is occurring at the same time as the number of people seeking their employment services has skyrocketed. ESFs revenues, however, are not dependent on the supply of executives, but on the demand, and this has fallen considerably.

To offset the strong dependence on the business cycle, ESFs are increasingly diversifying. In 2001, a third of Egon Zehnder International's revenues came from non-search work. The company has become a consultant for private investors who want to evaluate a firm's quality of management. It has also entered the human resource development business by providing mid-size MNEs with an assessment team. Whitehead Mann has also acquired non-search related HR businesses that it is developing. Diversification has allowed these companies to avoid much of the recession. Branching into consulting is unlikely to provide much respite for ESF since consulting firms are also facing similar challenges.

According to H&S, the economic slowdown has led to a contraction of the executive search business, but has increased the number of high-level positions that are available. The company reported a decline of 38 per cent in the number of executive searches in the third quarter of 2001. Dissatisfaction with CEOs and other top ranking managers has increased the average fee per search by 12 per cent.

Korn/Ferry is also diversifying its portfolio of industry sectors in executive searching. Its International Homeland Defense Security Practice division staffs the need of organizations requiring "high-level security executives". Demand has boomed since the attack on the World Trade Center on September 11, 2001.

Websites: **www.kornferry.com**; **www.heidrick.com**; **www.spencerstuart.com**; **www.russreyn.com**; **www.zehnder.com**; **www.tmp.com**; **www.rayberndtson.com** and **www.amrophever.com**.

Sources: **www.kornferry.com**; "The Fading Appeal of the Boardroom," *Economist*, February 8, 2001; Michael Skapinker, "Search Firms Look High and Low for Business,"*FT.com*, November 14, 2001; Richard Donkin, "Korn/Ferry is back on top," *FT.com*, May 14, 2001.

1. **When staffing the needs of the foreign subsidiary of a German company, what pool of candidates can the ESF choose from? Why would an international ESF be more capable of performing this task than the MNE's internal human resources department?**
2. **How would compensation negotiations be different for home, host, and third country candidates?**
3. **What types of factors would the ESF use to identify a potential candidate for an overseas assignment?**

ENDNOTES

1 Brian O'Reilly, "Your New Global Work Force," *Fortune*, December 14, 1992, pp. 52–66.

2 Rosalie L. Tung, "Selection and Training Procedures of US, European, and Japanese Multinationals," *California Management Review*, vol. 25, no. 1 (Fall 1982), p. 59.

3 Richard M. Hodgetts and Fred Luthans, *International Management*, 4th edn (Homewood IL: Irwin/McGraw, 2000), p. 430.

4 Ellen Brandt, "Global HR," *Personnel Journal*, March 1991, pp. 38–44; and Stephanie Overman, "Shaping the Global Workplace," *Personnel Administrator*, October 1989, pp. 41–44.

5 Rosalie L. Tung and Edwin L. Miller, "Managing in the Twenty-first Century: The Need for Global Orientation," *Management International Review*, vol. 30, no. 1 (First Quarter 1990), pp. 5–18.

6 Indrei Ratiu, "Thinking Internationally: A Comparison of How International Executives Learn," *International Studies of Management & Organization*, Spring/Summer 1983, pp. 139–150.

7 Ingemar Torbiorn, *Living Abroad* (New York: Wiley, 1982), p. 98.

8 Hodgetts and Luthans, (2000) n. 3 above, p. 434.

9 Jean E. Heller, "Criteria for Selecting an International Manager," *Personnel*, May/June 1980, p. 48.

10 Jeffrey L. Blue and Ulric Haynes, Jr, "Preparing for the Overseas Assignment," *Business Horizons*, June 1977, p. 62.

11 Michael Harvey, "Dual Career Expatriates: Expectations, Adjustments and Satisfaction With International Relocation," *Journal of International Business Studies*, vol. 28, no. 3 (Winter 1997).

12 Torbiorn (1982) n. 7 above, pp. 156–161.

13 Patricia C. Borstorff, Stanley G. Harris, Hubert S. Field and William F. Giles, "Who'll Go? A Review of Factors Associated with Employee Willingness to Work Overseas," *Human Resource Planning*, vol. 20, no. 3 (1997), p. 38.

14 See also Agis Salpukas, "From Brooklyn, Around the World, to Mobil's Top Job," *New York Times*, February 6, 1994, p. F 8.

15 Heller (1980) n. 9 above, p. 53.

16 Tung (1982) n. 2 above, p. 64.

17 Gary R. Oddou and Mark E. Mendenhall, "Succession Planning for the 21st Century: How Well Are We Grooming Our Future Business Leaders?" *Business Horizons*, January/February 1991, pp. 26–34.

18 Rosalie L. Tung, "Career Issues in International Assignments," *Academy of Management Executive*, August 1988, p. 242.
19 Ibid., p. 243.
20 See, for example, J. Bernard Keys and Robert M. Fulmer, *Executive Development and Organizational Learnings for Global Business* (New York: International Business Press, 1998), pp. 1–9.
21 Stephen H. Rhinesmith, John N. Williamson, David M. Ehlen and Denise S. Maxwell, "Developing Leaders for the Global Enterprise," *Training and Development Journal*, April 1989, pp. 25–34; Patricia A. Galagan, "Executive Development in a Changing World," *Training and Development Journal*, June 1990, pp. 23–35; and Madelyn R. Callahan, "Preparing the New Global Manager," *Training and Development Journal*, March 1989, pp. 29–32.
22 See Steven H. Rhinesmith, "An Agenda for Globalization," *Training and Development Journal*, February 1991, pp. 22–29; Benton Randolph, "When Going Global Isn't Enough," *Training*, August 1990, pp. 47–51; and Ronald Henkoff, "Companies That Train Best," *Fortune*, March 22, 1993, pp. 62–75.
23 "Company Culture in the Global Village," *Philips' What's Up Archive*, July 12, 1999.
24 Tung (1982) n. 2 above, p. 65.
25 See Lin P. Crandall and Mark I. Phelps, "Pay for a Global Work Force," *Personnel Journal*, February 1991, pp. 28–33.
26 Peter J. Dowling and Randall S. Schuler, *International Dimensions of Human Resource Management* (Boston MA: PWS-Kent Publishing, 1990), p. 121.
27 Greg Steinmetz and Gregory L. White, "Chrysler Pay Draws Fire Overseas," *Wall Street Journal*, May 26, 1998, p. B 1.
28 Adam Bryant, "American Pay Rattles Foreign Partners," *New York Times*, January 17, 1999, Section 4, p. 1.
29 Dowling and Schuler (1990) n. 26 above, p. 125.
30 Ibid., p. 123.
31 Alex S. Jones, "Dow Jones Plans to Tighten Foreign Policy for Workers," *New York Times*, September 9, 1991, p. C 6.
32 "Nasty, Brutish and Short," *Economist*, December 14, 2000.
33 Geofferey W. Latta, "Expatriate Incentives: Beyond Tradition," *HR Focus*, March 1998, p. S 4.
34 A good example is workplace discrimination, which is a major issue in the US but not in many other countries. See Susan Antilla, "Workplace Discrimination? Don't Try It Around Here," *New York Times*, February 13, 1994, p. F 7.
35 See, for example, Laurie Hays, "IBM's Finance Chief, Ax in Hand, Scours Empires for Costs to Cut," *Wall Street Journal*, January 26, 1994, pp. A 1, A 6.
36 C. K. Prahalad and Y. L. Doz, *The Multinational Mission: Balancing Logical Demands and Global Vision* (New York: Free Press, 1987).
37 Ferdinand Protzman, "Rewriting the Contract for Germany's Vaunted Workers," *New York Times*, February 13, 1994, p. F 5.
38 Keith Atkinson, "State of the Unions," *Personnel Administrator*, September 1986, p. 58.
39 For additional insights into Japanese labor management practices, see Karen Lowry Miller and Larry Armstrong, "How Honda Hammered Out Its New Accord," *Business Week*, December 21, 1992, p. 86; and David E. Sanger, "Layoffs and Factory Closings: Shaking the Japanese Psyche," *New York Times*, March 3, 1993, pp. A 1, C 16.
40 For a European country comparison of labor involvement in industrial decision making, see Mark Fenton-O'Creevy, "Survey – Mastering People Management," *Ft.com*, November 26, 2001.
41 Wolfgang Scholl, "Codetermination and the Ability of Firms to Act in the Federal Republic of Germany," *International Studies of Management & Organization*, Summer 1987, pp. 27–37.
42 Reinhard Lund, "Industrial Democracy in Denmark," *International Studies of Management & Organization*, Summer 1987, pp. 27–37.
43 Hodgetts and Luthans (2000) n. 3 above, p. 504.
44 For specific examples of HRM practices throughout the world, see Michael J. Marquardt and Dean W. Engel, *Global Human Resource Development* (Englewood Cliffs NJ: Prentice-Hall, 1993).
45 Susan Moffat, "Picking Japan's Research Brains," *Fortune*, March 25, 1991, p. 94.
46 Reported in "Report: Shortage of Executives Will Hurt US," *Omaha World Herald*, June 25, 1989, p. 1-G.
47 Fred E. Fiedler, Terence Mitchell and Harry C. Triandis, "The Culture Assimilator: An Approach to Cross-Cultural Training," *Journal of Applied Psychology*, April 1971, p. 95.
48 Paul R. Sparrow and Pawan S. Budhwar, "Competition and Change: Mapping the Indian HRM Recipe Against World-Wide Patterns," *Journal of World Business*, vol. 32, no. 3 (Fall 1997), p. 231.
49 Bodil Jones, "What Future European Recruits Want," *Management Review*, January 1998, p. 6.

ADDITIONAL BIBLIOGRAPHY

Abramson, Neil R., Lane, Henry W., Nagai, Hirohisa and Takagi, Haruo. "A Comparison of Canadian and Japanese Cognitive Styles: Implications for Management Interaction," *Journal of International Business Studies*, vol. 24, no. 3 (Third Quarter 1993).

Adler, Nancy J. and Bartholomew, Susan. "Academic and Professional Communities of Discourse: Generating Knowledge on Transnational Human Resource Management," *Journal of International Business Studies*, vol. 23, no. 3 (Third Quarter 1992).

Banai, Moshe and Reisel, William D. "Expatriate Managers' Loyalty to the MNC: Myth or Reality? An Exploratory Study," *Journal of International Business Studies*, vol. 24, no. 2 (Second Quarter 1993).

Beaumont, Philip, "New Challenges for European Human Resource Management," *European Management Journal*, vol. 19, no. 4 (August 2001).

Black, J. Stewart and Gregersen, Hal B. "The Other Half of the Picture: Antecedents of Spouse Cross-Cultural Adjustment," *Journal of International Business Studies*, vol. 22, no. 3 (Third Quarter 1991).

Black, J. Stewart and Mendenhall, Mark. "Cross-Cultural Training Effectiveness: A Review and a Theoretical Framework for Future Research," *Academy of Management Review*, vol. 15, no. 1 (January 1990).

Boyacigiller, Nakiye. "The Role of Expatriates in the Management of Interdependence, Complexity and Risk in Multinational Corporations," *Journal of International Business Studies*, vol. 21, no. 3 (Third Quarter 1990).

Camuffo, Arnaldo and Costa, Giovanni. "Strategic Human Resource Management – Italian Style," *Sloan Management Review*, vol. 34, no. 2 (Winter 1993).

De Cieri, Helen and Dowling, Peter J. "Strategic International Human Resource Management: An Asia-Pacific Perspective," *Management International Review*, vol. 37, Special Issue (1997).

Ebrahimpour, Maling and Cullen, John B. "Quality Management in Japanese and American Firms Operating in the United States: A Comparative Study of Styles and Motivational Beliefs," *Management International Review*, vol. 33, no. 1 (First Quarter 1993).

Feldman, Daniel C. and Thomas, David C. "Career Management Issues Facing Expatriates," *Journal of International Business Studies*, vol. 23, no. 2 (Second Quarter 1992).

Geringer, J. Michael and Frayne, Colette A. "Human Resource Management and International Joint Venture Control: A Parent Company Perspective," *Management International Review*, vol. 30, Special Issue (1990).

Haigh, Robert W. "Building a Strategic Alliance – The Hermosillo Experience as a Ford-Mazda Proving Ground," *Columbia Journal of World Business*, vol. 27, no. 1 (Spring 1992).

Harvey, Michael. "The Selection of Managers for Foreign Assignments: A Planning Perspective," *Columbia Journal of World Business*, vol. 31, no. 4 (Winter 1996).

Harvey, Michael, "Dual Career Expatriates: Expectations, Adjustments and Satisfaction With International Relocation," *Journal of International Business Studies*, vol. 28, no. 3 (Fall 1997).

Jun, Sunkyu, Gentry, James W. and Hyun, Yong J. "Cultural Adaptation of Business Expatriates in the Host Marketplace," *Journal of International Business Studies*, vol. 32, no. 2 (Summer 2001).

Kayworth, Timothy, "The Global Virtual Manager: A Prescription for Success," *European Management Journal*, vol. 18, no. 2 (April 2000).

Lado, Augustine A. "Strategic Human Resource Management," *Academy of Management Review*, vol. 25, no. 3 (July 2000).

Milliman, John, Von Glinow, Mary Ann and Nathan, Maria. "Organizational Life Cycles and Strategic International Human Resource Management in Multinational Companies: Implications for Congruence Theory," *Academy of Management Review*, vol. 16, no. 2 (April 1991).

Roth, Kendall and O'Donnell, Sharon. "Foreign Subsidiary Compensation Strategy: An Agency Theory Perspective," *Academy of Management Journal*, vol. 39, no. 3 (June 1996).

Sanyal, Rajib N. "An Empirical Analysis of the Unionization of Foreign Manufacturing Firms in the US," *Journal of International Business Studies*, vol. 21, no. 1 (First Quarter 1990).

Schuler, Randall S. and Rogovsky, Nikolai. "Understanding Compensation Practice Variations Across Firms: The Impact of National Culture," *Journal of International Business Studies*, vol. 29, no. 1 (First Quarter 1998).

Sergeant, Andrew and Frenkel, Stephen. "Managing People in China: Perceptions of Expatriate Managers," *Journal of World Business*, vol. 33, no. 1 (Spring 1998).

Shaffer, Margaret A. "Dimensions, Determinants, and Differences in the Expatriate Adjustment Process", *Journal of International Business Studies*, vol. 30, no. 3 (Fall 1999).

Shenkar, Oded and Zeira, Yoram. "Human Resources Management in International Joint Ventures: Directions for Research," *Academy of Management Review*, vol. 12, no. 3 (July 1987).

Stark, Andrew. "What's the Matter with Business Ethics?" *Harvard Business Review*, vol. 71, no. 3 (May/June 1993).

Sullivan, Jeremiah J. and Peterson, Richard B. "A Test of Theories Underlying the Japanese Lifetime Employment System," *Journal of International Business Studies*, vol. 22, no. 1 (First Quarter 1991).

Taylor, Sully, Beechler, Schon and Napier, Nancy. "Toward an Integrative Model of Strategic International Human Resource Management," *Academy of Management Review*, vol. 21, no. 4 (October 1996).

Tung, Rosalie L. and Miller, Edwin L. "Managing in the Twenty-First Century: The Need for Global Orientation," *Management International Review*, vol. 30, no. 1 (First Quarter 1990).

Tung, Rosalie L. "American Expatriates Abroad: From Neophytes to Cosmopolitans," *Journal of World Business*, vol. 33, no. 2 (Summer 1998).

Vanderbroeck, Paul. "Long-Term Human Resource Development in Multinational Organizations," *Sloan Management Review*, vol. 34, no. 1 (Fall 1992).

CONTENTS

Chapter 13

Political Risk and Negotiation Strategies

OBJECTIVES OF THE CHAPTER

Political change often has a tremendous impact on the business climate. Yet it is frequently difficult to predict. For example, who could have guessed that during the late 1980s the former Soviet Union would begin to move toward a market economy[1] or that in the early 1990s the Soviet Union would break up completely? These developments were greeted enthusiastically by Western businesspeople, who now see the newly independent republics as countries with great economic potential. At the same time many Western business executives are reluctant to invest heavily in these countries because of the uncertainty of how far the market-based economic reforms will go. Even when political changes appear to move in a direction that is favorable to market forces, there are political risks. This chapter examines political risk, how multinational enterprises (MNEs) forecast this risk, and how they use negotiating tactics to minimize their political risk.

The objectives of this chapter are to:

1. *Examine* the nature of political risk.
2. *Discuss* some of the most common ways that multinationals go about managing their political risk.
3. *Review* typical negotiation strategies and tactics used in "hammering out" agreements.
4. *Present* some of the strategies used by MNEs to protect their overseas investments.

ACTIVE LEARNING CASE

Singapore Airlines

Singapore Airlines (Singapore for short) is one of the most successful airlines in the industry. While companies like Eastern Airlines, Pan American, and TWA have been closing their doors or taking big financial losses, Singapore has been profitable. In 2001, for example, the company netted over S $1.55 billion (US $855 million) in profits.

One of the main reasons for this success is its high quality service. Singapore pioneered many of the in-flight services that are now the industry standard, such as providing free drinks and headsets. More recently, Singapore has added telephones and extra legroom so that customers will be comfortable during their international flights. And the airline has installed seats in business class that have four additional inches of pitch, thus providing travelers a more restful position during a long flight. In 2001, Singapore was the first airline to provide in-flight e-mail and web browsing to its passengers. The company also has one of the best entertainment systems in the air, allowing a customer to choose the movie or a CD it wants and project it to a seat side screen. It also allows customers to play Nintendo games interactively with other passengers.

Company policy requires that flight attendants learn everyone's name, even of those passengers who are flying in the coach section. Additionally, Singapore is working to develop an information system that will tell flight attendants what drink a certain frequent traveler prefers. Also, Singapore requires that most employees take annual training, thus making sure that the highest levels of service are maintained both in the air and on the ground.

Singapore is now expanding its routes to cover the Atlantic, as well as more of Asia. For example, it has instituted coverage from New York to Singapore. The airline had been operating out of Los Angeles, San Francisco, and Honolulu, but this was its first venture to the east coast of the US. The Singapore flight stops in Frankfurt, which is already one of its European hubs; however, the passengers do not have to change planes. This was the first direct air service from New York to East Asia via the Atlantic and the initial prices were quite high. However, Singapore filed with the requisite governmental agencies to lower these fares. For this to happen, the other carriers that fly this transatlantic leg would have to accept the new rates, something that they would be reluctant to do because it would dilute their own revenue. Additionally, governments that usually act to support the best interests of their own carriers set international fares.

In 1999, Singapore was also lobbying the British government to liberalize transatlantic flight. The airline wants to fly to America from London, but the British government has been sluggish at deregulation. The company also wants to move into the Australian and New Zealand market, but has again stumbled against government protectionism. Yet Singapore does not seem concerned. The airline has over $500 million in cash, more than enough resources to continue operating while it works to gain government approvals that will help to expand its international market. The company has also sought equity as a way to enter these markets. In 2000, it purchased a 49 per cent share of British Virgin Atlantic Airways and secured a 25 per cent stake in Air New Zealand. In 2001, Singapore was negotiating a possible entry into the Australian market after the collapse of Australia's Ansett, which is partly owned by Air New Zealand. Singapore expects to become a minority shareholder in a new Ansett. In addition, Singapore has now created strategic alliances with a host of different airlines.

In 2000, Singapore joined the Star Alliance, a network of international airlines that controls over 20 per cent of world travel and includes Air Canada, Air New Zealand, All Nippon Airways, Ansett Australia, Austrian Airlines, British Midland, Lauda Air, Lufthansa, Mexicana, SAS Scandinavian, Singapore Airlines, Thai Airways, Tyrolean Airways, United Airlines, and Varig Brazilian Airways. By working with these partners Singapore can offer customers access to 93 destinations in 42 countries.

Websites: ***www.singaporeair.com***; ***www.aa.com***; ***www.virgin-atlantic.com***; ***www.ansett.com.au***; ***www.airnz.com*** and ***www.star-alliance.com***.

Sources: Adapted from Agis Salpukas, "For Singapore Air, a New Direction," *New York Times*, July 11, 1991, pp. C 1, C 6; Patricia Sellers, "Companies that Serve You Best," *Fortune*, May 31, 1993, p. 75; Kenneth Labich, "Air Wars Over Asia," *Fortune*, March 4, 1994, pp. 93–98; ***www.singaporeair.com***; "One Down, More to Go?" *Economist*, September 17, 1998; "The Air War," *Economist*, September 9; Alan Hall, "You've Got Mail – at 30,000 Feet, *Business Week*, May 17, 2001

1. **Briefly describe one macro political risk and one micro political risk that Singapore Airlines faces.**
2. **In what way would doing business in the US pose a political risk for Singapore Airlines? How would doing business in a country like China pose such a risk?**
3. **What strengths would Singapore Airlines have if it were negotiating for the rights to operate out of Heathrow airport in London? What needs would such an arrangement fill for the UK? What needs would it fill for Singapore?**
4. **Why would the management of Singapore Airlines need to understand cultural differences in negotiating behavior? Would this need be greater than that of a brewer in Amsterdam who wants to negotiate the acquisition of a winery in Madrid? Why?**

INTRODUCTION

Political risk
The probability that political forces will negatively affect a multinational's profit or impede the attainment of other critical business objectives

Political risk is the probability that political forces will negatively affect an MNE's profit or impede the attainment of other critical business objectives. The study of political risk addresses changes in the environment that are difficult to anticipate. Common examples include the election of a government that is committed to nationalization of major industries or one that insists on reducing foreign participation in business ventures.

Most people believe that political risk is confined to third world countries or to those with unstable governments. However, the policies of some past EU governments, such as France, toward limiting Japanese investment illustrate that political risk is also an issue for firms doing business in highly industrialized nations. Another example is the previous restrictions of foreign investment in the energy and communications industries in Canada. US regulations that restrict foreign investment in the banking and commercial airline industries reflect political risk as well.[2]

In addition, there are cultural barriers that can increase political risk. For example, many MNEs feel that it is difficult to crack the Japanese market because the value system of the country discourages purchasing from foreign producers, and the government supports this system. There are also political agreements that can create risks for foreign firms such as the European Airbus consortium that is now cutting into the world dominance of US aircraft manufacturers.[3]

These examples indicate the pervasiveness of political risk. Given the large number of international markets in which US firms operate (see Table 13.1), political risk is going

Table 13.1 The Top 10 US export markets

Market	*2000 annual sales (in millions of US $)*
Canada	178.9
Mexico	111.4
Japan	64.9
United Kingdom	41.6
Germany	29.4
South Korea	27.8
Taiwan	24.4
Netherlands	21.8
France	20.3
Singapore	17.8

Source: US Census Bureau, 2000.

to remain an area of concern for US MNEs.[4] In dealing with this issue, effective negotiating can help to reduce and contain problem areas. This linkage will be explained later in the chapter.

THE NATURE OF POLITICAL RISK

Political risk includes both macro- and microfactors. MNEs often begin by examining the macrofactors and then determining how the microfactors further influence the risk.

Macro political risk

Macro political risk
A risk that affects all foreign enterprises in the same way

Expropriation
The governmental seizure of private businesses coupled with little, if any, compensation to their owners

Indigenization laws
Laws which require that nationals hold a majority interest in all enterprises

A **macro political risk** is one that affects all foreign enterprises in the same general way. **Expropriation**, the governmental seizure of private businesses coupled with little, if any, compensation to the owners, is an example of a macro political risk. Communist governments in Eastern Europe and China expropriated private firms following World War II. Fidel Castro did the same in Cuba from 1958 to 1959. In more recent years governments in Angola, Chile, Ethiopia, Peru, and Zambia have expropriated private enterprises. In all these cases both large and small businesses felt the impact of the political decision.

Macro political risk can also be the result of political boycotts.[5] Since 1955 a number of Arab countries have boycotted firms with branches in Israel or companies that have allowed the use of their trade name there. Macro political risk can also come about because of **indigenization laws**, which require that nationals hold a majority interest in all enterprises.

In recent years the macro political risk in many nations has changed.[6] For example, Eastern European countries, such as Poland, Hungary, and the Czech Republic, now welcome and encourage private investments,[7] as does Russia.[8] In Asia, China's entry into the World Trade Organization in December 2001 was the result of two decades of market reform.[9] Meanwhile, Vietnam recently negotiated a trade agreement with the US.[10] These developments have reduced macro political risk and may well encourage foreign investments.[11] However, there is still micro political risk to be considered.

Micro political risk

Micro political risk
A risk that affects selected sectors of the economy or specific foreign businesses

A **micro political risk** is one that affects selected sectors of the economy or specific foreign businesses. These risks are typically a result of government action in the form of industry regulation, taxes on specific types of business activity, and local content laws.[12] Canada's 1981 decision (now rescinded) to reduce foreign ownership in its petroleum industry from 75 to under 50 per cent is an example. Peru's decision to nationalize its copper mines is another good example. The US decision to tax textile imports is a third.

A number of factors help to determine the degree of micro political risk. One is the dominance of foreign firms. For example, in recent years the US government has insisted that Japanese auto makers establish manufacturing facilities in the US. When the Japanese auto firms were small, they did not attract much attention. Now that they are a large part of the US market, there is more interest in regulating them. Similarly, in the early 1990s, Nintendo, which held a dominant share of the video game market in the US, became the target of antitrust lawsuits.[13]

A second factor is the ease with which the MNE's operations can be managed. If a government can run a factory just as efficiently as the foreign owner, the operation may be nationalized. However, if special skills or training are required, the risk of takeover is smaller. Likewise, if the operation needs a continual inflow of new technology from the home office in order to maintain competitive efficiency, the risk is lower because the MNE will halt technology inflow if the operation is seized. On the other hand, if the necessary technology can easily be acquired elsewhere, the risk is much higher.

Retaliation is another source of micro political risk. If the MNE is not in a position to strike back, the micro political risk increases. For example, when Iran under the Ayatollah Khomeini took over US firms in that country, Iranian assets in the US were frozen as part of a retaliatory legal action. If the multinational is large or highly influential, the backlash can be severe. Some third world countries have seized banks and found to their dismay that the international financial community has refused to do any more business with them.

A fourth factor is the changing priorities of the country. As the countries of the former Soviet Union work to reform their economies, the political risk in industries such as high-tech, petroleum, and manufacturing are likely to lessen because the governments are trying to encourage investment in these areas.

Finally, competing political philosophies affect micro political risk. The Russian Commonwealth consists of a host of groups with different political beliefs. Most of them have renounced communism, some want to modify the principles of that ideology, and some still want to adhere to the basic beliefs with which they have grown up. As a result, many MNEs believe that there will be different rules applied to different industries in different geographic locales, depending on which political group has the most influence over their operations.

Active learning check 

Review your answer to Active Learning Case question 1 and make any changes you like. Then compare your answer with the one below.

1. Briefly describe one macro political risk and one micro political risk that Singapore Airlines faces.

One macro political risk is that some of the countries in which Singapore Airlines does business will require all foreign operations to have local partners. One micro political risk is that the airline industry in some countries will prevail on their government to protect them from competition by not letting Singapore lower its rates to match their own.

Sources of political risk

There are a number of sources of political risk. Table 13.2 presents some important sources and their effects.

The major risk is a change in the political philosophy of those who are running the country. This can be a result of one government being ousted by another, as when Castro replaced Batista in Cuba, or a change in government actions such as when the Chinese government suddenly squelched the student movement in Tiananmen Square and imprisoned its leaders. These actions send a clear message to businesses that are operating or considering doing business there. Conversely, a change in government philosophy toward encouraging foreign investments can have an impact. For example, when Michael Manley was prime minister of Jamaica in the 1970s, the country moved toward socialism and US investment dried up. Manley's subsequent defeat at the polls was a result of strong local interests and a populace that became convinced that, without outside

Table 13.2 **Political risk: sources, agents, and effects**

Sources of political risk	*Groups that can generate political risk*	*Effects of political risk*
• Political philosophies that are changing or are in competition with each other • Changing economic conditions • Social unrest • Armed conflict or terrorism • Rising nationalism • Impending or recent political independence • Vested interests of local business groups • Competing religious groups • Newly created international alliances	• Current government and its various departments and agencies • Opposition groups in the government that are not in power but have political clout • Organized interest groups such as teachers, students, workers, retired persons, etc. • Terrorist or anarchist groups operating in the country • International organizations such as the World Bank or the United Nations • Foreign governments that have entered into international alliances with the country or that are supporting opposition to the government	• Expropriation of assets (with or without compensation) • Indigenization laws • Restriction of operating freedom concerning, e.g., hiring policies and product manufacturing • Cancellation or revision of contracts • Damage to property and/or personnel from terrorism, riots, etc. • Loss of financial freedom such as the ability to repatriate profits • Increased taxes and other financial penalties

investors and US tourism, the economy would never turn around. In the late 1980s Manley was returned to power and moved much closer to the center of the political continuum than before.

Sometimes, however, pressure is applied for a "get tough" approach. After the Muammar Qaddafi regime assumed control in Libya in the late 1960s, that country began taking steps to revise its agreements with the international oil companies. One reason was to show the populace that the government was strong. Another was to undermine the position of the oil firms by blaming them for corrupting the previous government with bribes.

So a variety of motivations help to explain political risk. The MNE's challenge is to identify these motivations and then to decide how to manage them.

FORECASTING AND MANAGING POLITICAL RISK

MNEs use a number of strategies in managing political risk. A typical approach is to first forecast the specific risks and then determine how to reduce or eliminate those risks that are considered unacceptable.

Forecasting political risk

Some MNEs use an informal approach to assessing risk, whereas others employ formal systematic procedures. Some MNEs will create an ad hoc group to deal with these issues, whereas others will have a standing committee that is charged with this responsibility. In each case, however, those making the assessment will focus on two areas: (1) the political system in which the company will be doing business and (2) the goods to be produced and the operations to be carried out. Based on this evaluation, the MNE will determine its risk vulnerability.

Examining the political system

An MNE needs to understand the host country's political system because politics greatly influences the economy and political risk.[14] This linkage helps to explain why many MNEs are interested in doing business in the countries of the former Soviet Union but remain cautious about making any major investments there. The MNEs are concerned that another change in the political climate would result in massive financial losses. Similar reasoning can be used in explaining MNE hesitation about investing in China and other countries where the government still exercises totalitarian control.

MNEs will also cast a critical eye on governments that seem to give home country companies a decided advantage over foreign firms. MNEs have become more involved in lobbying both home and host governments, and over the last decade trade negotiations between many countries have started to deal with investment and trade issues of direct relevance to MNEs.[15] The US free trade agreements with Canada and Mexico are examples,[16] as is the Pacific Islands Countries Trade Agreement (PICTA) initiative that will likely include Australia, New Zealand, and 14 Pacific Islands.[17]

Other forms of governmental action have also proved useful. For example, the US role in the Gulf War of 1991 increased its influence in that region and helped to ensure the sale of US goods and services in Kuwait and Saudi Arabia.[18] Another example is the pressures that industrialized nations have put on countries like the Russian Commonwealth and China, in which economic assistance is tied to political and economic reform.[19]

MNEs will evaluate the impact of these changes. They will also examine the political clout that host country firms have with their own government. In the US, for example, lobbyists and special interest groups in areas such as steel, textiles, softwood lumber, and semiconductors have been particularly effective in securing protection from imports.[20]

Active learning check 

Review your answer to Active Learning Case question 2 and make any changes you like. Then compare your answer with the one below.

2. In what way would doing business in the US pose a political risk for Singapore Airlines? How would doing business in a country like China pose such a risk?

The primary political risk that Singapore Airlines faces in the US is that the government would not want the airline to take too much business away from US international carriers, especially because many US carriers are in poor financial straits. However, there are minimum risks for the airline in the US. Doing business in China, however, is a different story. Here the airline might find that the government makes much greater demands such as allowing local residents to pay for their tickets in Chinese currency, insisting that the airline fly certain internal routes even if there is limited traffic on those routes, and staffing most of its China-based facilities with local personnel. Additionally, there is the risk associated with the stability of the Chinese political system. So political risk would be of much greater concern to Singapore Airlines if it wanted to open up routes in China than if it wanted to secure landing sites in the US.

Evaluating products and operations

Products and operations also face political risk. One example is government restrictions on local ownership. If the government requires joint ventures or local participation in operations, the MNE must determine the degree of risk associated with doing business under these conditions. Some firms have never agreed to joint ventures, whereas others have tried to minimize this risk by limiting local control of operations.

A related risk is that the joint partner will steal product knowledge or technology. A good example is publishing ventures in China. US firms no longer enter into such ventures because they have learned that copyrights are not legally enforceable in China; there is no way of preventing Chinese partners from publishing translated works as their own. Technology theft is another example. If local laws do not protect patent infringement, a joint venture participant may simply steal the other's technology without any fear of retaliation.[21]

A third example is government policy regarding the purchase of foreign-made goods. If the government buys only locally produced goods and encourages a "buy local" policy, the political risk increases accordingly.

Product and operation risk can also grow out of a government's approach to pricing practices, monopolies, and collusion among competitors. In the US, there are antitrust laws that encourage competition. In many other countries, however, collusion and the formation of cartels are legal. In recent years the US government has brought pressure on countries like Japan to prohibit price fixing and other practices that reduce the ability of US MNEs to crack this market. One result has been the recent publication of new trade laws that promise to make the market more accessible to outsiders. Some specific changes that have been introduced are: (1) companies are forbidden from enforcing "suggested retail prices", thus opening the way for discount stores; (2) firms cannot join together to boycott firms trying to enter a market; (3) dominant companies are not allowed to use their influence to force clients to shun competitive goods; and (4) the Japanese Fair Trade Commission can order a company to sell its stock holdings in another firm, if such action is deemed necessary to eliminate violation of the Antimonopoly Act.[22]

Quantifying risk vulnerability

After an MNE examines the political system and the risks inherent in going international, the company will try to express this risk in explicit terms. Table 13.3 provides an illustration of select criteria that can be used in this procedure. This process allows the firm to compare the political risk of doing business in one country with that of doing business in another nation. For example, it is possible to compare the political risks associated with starting a joint venture in the former Soviet Union versus Poland, Chile versus Venezuela, or France versus Germany. Or the company can develop a list of countries with political risk scores, ranging from the highest to the lowest and can decide which scores fit within its "range of acceptance".

The factors that are quantified in Table 13.3 are not all-inclusive, but they do illustrate the types of criteria that are considered when assessing political risk. As seen in the table, some criteria have wider minimum and maximum ranges than others because the risk varies more widely. However, the important result is the overall score for a particular country. If this score is too high, the MNE will drop it from further consideration unless there are ways of reducing the risks associated with some of the criteria. For example, it may be impossible to influence the first criterion in Table 13.3 (stability of the political system), but it may be possible to strike a deal with the local union (number 8 in the table) and thus improve the chances of good labor relations. It may also be possible to negotiate an improvement in restrictions on imports, exports, and monetary transfers

Table 13.3 An illustration of select criteria for evaluating political risk

Major area	Criteria	Scores: Minimum	Scores: Maximum
Political economic environment	1 Stability of the political system	3	14
	2 Imminent internal conflicts	0	14
	3 External threats to stability	0	12
	4 Degree of control of the economic system	5	9
	5 Reliability of the country as a trading partner	4	12
	6 Constitutional guarantees	2	12
	7 Effectiveness of public administration	3	12
	8 Labor relations and social peace	3	15
Domestic economic conditions	9 Size of the population	4	8
	10 Per capita income	2	10
	11 Economic growth over the last 5 years	2	7
	12 Potential growth over the next 3 years	3	10
	13 Inflation over the past 2 years	2	10
	14 Accessibility of the domestic capital market to outsiders	3	7
	15 Availability of high-quality local labor force	2	8
	16 Possibility of employing foreign nationals	2	8
	17 Availability of energy resources	2	14
	18 Legal requirements regarding environmental pollution	4	8
	19 Infrastructure, including transportation and communication systems	2	14
External economic relations	20 Import restrictions	2	10
	21 Export restrictions	2	10
	22 Restrictions on foreign investments	3	9
	23 Freedom to set up or engage in partnerships	3	9
	24 Legal protection for brands and products	3	9
	25 Restrictions on monetary transfers	2	8
	26 Revaluation of the currency during the last 5 years	2	7
	27 Balance of payments situation	2	9
	28 Drain on foreign funds through oil and energy imports	3	14
	29 International financial standing	3	8
	30 Restriction on the exchange of local money into foreign currencies	2	8

Source: Adapted from E. Dichtl and H. G. Koeglmayr, "Country Risk Ratings," *Management International Review*, vol. 26, no. 4 (Fourth Quarter 1986), p. 6.

(numbers 20, 21, and 25 in the table). As a result, the political risk score might be reduced to an acceptable level.

If a country is highly interested in having an MNE set up operations there, the government may offer special concessions that will reduce the political risks for this company but not for others. This is particularly valuable because it provides the firm with a competitive advantage. On the other hand, if negotiations with the country end up reducing political risk for all global firms doing business there, the MNE will want to consider the impact of this action on its competitive stance and profitability. This is where effective negotiating strategies enter the picture. MNEs might also choose not to do business with a country when it deems the terms of trade to be detrimental to overall profitability. One such a case is Pfizer's threat to boycott France unless the country agrees to increase drug prices.[23]

NEGOTIATION STRATEGIES

There are two key steps in developing effective negotiating strategies. First, the MNE will evaluate its own position and that of the other group(s) in order to determine how the interests of both can fit together. For example, Apple examined Sony's manufacturing ability and competitive challenge before deciding to have Sony build the low-end models of the Apple Powerbook computer. Second, the company will examine the behavioral characteristics of the other parties in order to understand their style of negotiating. For example, when negotiating with the Japanese media for the rights to provide Olympic game coverage in Japan, Olympic committee negotiators have continually found that these media executives always begin the process with very low bids. So the Olympic negotiators always start with very high offers.

Evaluation of positions

Sometimes an MNE will enter negotiations with a host country in order to secure a variety of guarantees such as low taxes, the right to repatriate profits, and a promise regarding freedom of operations. At other times these negotiations will be directed toward a potential partner, such as working out the terms of a joint venture. Still other times the MNE will negotiate with a host of parties: country officials, potential partners, and the like. In all these cases the first step is to evaluate the strengths and needs of all parties.

Strengths

The strengths of the parties are those assets or benefits that each brings to the bargaining table. In the case of an MNE, examples include technology, products, services, managerial expertise, and capital. For example, when General Motors sets up a new operation in Mexico, the company invests capital, uses modern technology to build the autos, and employs managerial expertise in getting the operation off and running. When the Hilton Corporation builds a new hotel in Germany, it invests capital, employs managerial expertise, and offers a variety of world-class hospitality services to the guests. MNEs also hire local personnel, stimulate the economy, and in industries such as manufacturing, textiles, and mining help to generate exports for the country.

The bargaining strengths of the country will include such factors as large consumer markets, economic and political stability, sources of capital, tax breaks, and an appropriate labor force. The US, for example, offers all these strengths to MNEs. As a result, the bargaining position of foreign MNEs vis-à-vis the US government is diminished. This is in comparison with the situation faced by companies looking to set up operations in third world countries where the latter have a weak bargaining position because of their small consumer market, political instability, and/or financial strength.

The bargaining strengths of parties will depend on their specific contributions. For example, in many cases a local partner knows the market and has conducted business there for years. This makes the partner valuable to the MNE. Other contributions of local partners can include capital, a well-trained workforce, factories or retail outlets for moving the goods to the customer, and government contractors who can help to eliminate red tape.

Other parties to the transaction can include stockholders or other interest groups that monitor the company's operations. During the 1980s many MNEs stopped doing business in South Africa because of pressure from these investor groups (see the box "International Business Strategy in Action: De Beers"). Companies involved in manufacturing war material, producing chemicals, and building nuclear energy plants have also come under investor and social pressure. MNEs may also encounter complaints from partners in other joint ventures who feel that this latest investment will negatively affect their current venture.

INTERNATIONAL BUSINESS STRATEGY *IN ACTION*

De Beers

Across the world, the De Beers name is synonymous with diamonds. Established in 1888 in Johannesburg, South Africa, De Beers is the largest mining company in the world, accounting for 45 per cent of world production. Through the De Beers Groups Diamond Trading Company (DTC) – formerly the Central Selling Organization (CSO) – De Beers controls an even higher percentage of world trading. Its own production and a network of smaller producers allow the company to trade approximately 66 per cent of world diamonds.

Yet De Beers faces political risk as its entry to the triad markets of North America and Europe is threatened by government competition policy. The establishment of the DTC came as a response to increased competition and government regulation. In 1991, De Beers controlled nearly 85 per cent of the world's diamond market. Yet De Beers is banned from directly entering the US market because of an antitrust legal ruling that sees it as a monopoly. Under the CSO, the group's market dominance had allowed it to manipulate market prices by accumulating inventory. While De Beers is still allowed to operate in the EU, it worries that antitrust proceedings could commence at any time.

In the past, De Beers has come under attack from antiglobal activists for purchasing diamonds from war-torn nations, such as Sierra Leone, Angola, and the Democratic Republic of Congo. It is accused of financing both sides of a conflict. In 2000, De Beers resolved to stop purchasing what has been termed "blood diamonds". While this improves the brand name image of De Beers, these diamonds are likely to find their way to the market by other means, further decreasing the company's share of the diamond distribution market.

The establishment of the DTC, and its new sourcing policy, are meant to ease entry restrictions to triad markets and develop the De Beers brand name. Threats to erode De Beers' dominance include: increasing competition from man-made diamonds; new technology that allows diamonds to be extracted from remote areas – such as the bottom of the sea; and the discovery of new natural sources of diamonds.

De Beers understands that its future will heavily depend on the development of its brand name, particularly as a luxury brand. LVMH (Louis Vuitton and Moët Hennessy) and the De Beers Group entered into a strategic partnership in 2001. The two companies will create a new independent joint venture that will market premium luxury diamonds under the De Beers name. This new company will not exclusively purchase from De Beers, but will source from worldwide distributors. De Beers provides its brand name rights and expertise on diamond appraisal to maintain the high standards required for the luxury market. LVMH will market the product.

De Beers company is moving away from monopolistic supply-side market manipulation and towards marketing to influence demand. The "A Diamond is Forever" TV campaign aims to increase demand for diamonds. Interestingly, competitors also benefit from this type of marketing. This is not presently very important for a dominant player of the size of De Beers.

Websites: ***www.debeersgroup.com***; ***www.lvmh.com*** and ***www.adiamondisforever.com***.

Sources: "De Beer's Worst Friend," *Economist*, August 20, 1998; Rodney Smith, "Diamond's Are Not Forever," *BBC.com*, July 26, 2001; ***www.debeersgroup.com***.

Needs

The needs of the parties in the negotiation will also influence the agreement. An MNE may want to set up operations in Belgium in order to secure entry into the EU, to sidestep import tariffs, and to be able to compete in one of the world's largest and fastest growing consumer markets. The company may also have an annual 15 per cent sales growth target and be unable to achieve this goal without entering the EU. So the firm's need to expand is quite strong.

The host country may have a need for the type of technology or product that the company is planning to produce. If the MNE sets up operations here, the country may also find that the firm is prepared to invest capital and to hire and train local personnel. Additionally, as a result of these operations, exports may increase and the general economy will benefit. On the other hand, if the MNE has nothing special to offer, the host country may be willing to give few, if any, incentives.

The needs of other groups will also influence the negotiation. For example, if the stakeholders want to see vigorous expansion into the European market, they may be willing to have the company make large initial concessions because of the strong future growth potential offered in the market. If the MNE is going to be working in the host country with local partners or purchasing from local suppliers, there is pressure on that country to let the company in.

Active learning check

Review your answer to Active Learning Case question 3 and make any changes you like. Then compare your answer with the one below.

3. What strengths would Singapore Airlines have if it were negotiating for the rights to operate out of Heathrow airport in London? What needs would such an arrangement fill for the UK? What needs would it fill for Singapore?

Some of the strengths that Singapore Airlines would bring to the negotiating table include employment opportunities for local personnel, potential capital investment in local facilities, and the providing of first-class air service to the Orient. Some of the needs it would fill for the UK include an increase in tourists and other visitors to the country, the opening up of more direct routes to the Orient for business travelers, and the generation of income. Some of the needs the arrangement would fill for Singapore include increased revenues, a greater international presence, and the opportunity to develop new routes.

Behavioral characteristics of the participants

Next, the MNE will examine the negotiating behaviors of the parties. What can be expected in terms of offers, counteroffers, ploys, and other stratagems? These answers will help the MNE to minimize surprises.

Cultural differences

Although the objective of the negotiation process may be universal (strike as good a deal as possible), the way in which the process is carried out will be greatly influenced by the cultural values and norms of the participants. Commenting on the difference between Arab and US negotiators, one group of researchers noted:

> . . . [Arabs] treat deadlines as only general guidelines for wrapping up negotiations. They tend to open negotiations with an extreme initial position. However, the Arabs believe strongly in making concessions, they do so throughout the bargaining process, and they almost always reciprocate an opponent's concessions. They also seek to build a long-term relationship with their bargaining partners. For these reasons, Americans typically find it easier to negotiate with Arabs than with representatives from many other regions of the world.[24]

One of the major differences is the amount of authority that the negotiator has to approve an agreement. In some societies, such as the US and Great Britain, negotiators are given authority to make deals or at least to express agreement on the basic arrangement that is being negotiated. This approach works well when doing business with many Western firms, as well as with Chinese negotiators (see the box "International Business Strategy in Action: Doing business in China"). However, it is often of limited value when dealing with people from other cultures. In fact, the other parties may not have the authority to give the go-ahead on anything. For example, Japanese and Russian negotiators are often lower-level personnel who are not authorized to approve agreements. This can be frustrating to Americans who feel that they are wasting their time. The lack of face-to-face interaction with those who will be making the final decision can be unsettling. On the other hand, many foreign negotiators use this ploy because they have learned that it often leads to greater concessions from US businesspeople, who become anxious to sign a deal and thus are more flexible on terms.

INTERNATIONAL BUSINESS STRATEGY *IN ACTION*

Doing business in China

China promises to be a major market for MNEs during the millennium. However, doing business in this country can present major problems since many international managers have had, at best, limited experience in dealing with Chinese managers. What are some steps that can help to ensure success? One China expert recently noted the following:

1. Doing business in China requires a long-term commitment. Firms that are hoping for fast profit will be disappointed. It may take 5 to 10 years, in some cases, before a company will begin to earn a return on its investment.
2. Personal connections are important. Companies that want to be successful have to meet the right people and persuade them to help the business. If this happens, the MNE will find that a great deal of red tape can be eliminated.
3. While many firms like to set up joint ventures, companies that establish direct operations that tap China's pool of inexpensive labor often do much better because they have control over their own operations and are helping the government to keep the workforce employed.
4. The Chinese like to deal with negotiators who have authority to make decisions. They respect people with authority and are disappointed if the negotiators have to contact the home office continually regarding how to proceed.
5. On the other hand, negotiators have to understand that the Chinese are not rapid decision makers. Determination and patience are important because the Chinese are thorough and methodical in their evaluation of a project or proposal.
6. Written contracts tend to be shorter than those in the West because the Chinese do not believe that everything must be written down. Friendship and trust between the parties is used to resolve any disputes. As a result, written agreements are similar to what in the West are known as "memos of general understanding." However, these agreements do contain the obligations and duties of each party and stipulations regarding how any differences will be resolved, so they are not as open-ended as one might think.

Sources: Adapted from L. S. Tai, "Doing Business in the People's Republic of China: Some Keys to Success," *Management International Review*, vol. 28, no. 1 (First Quarter 1988), pp. 5–9; Amy Borrus, "The Best Way to Change China Is from the Inside," *Business Week*, May 17, 1993, p. 69; Philip R. Harris and Robert T. Moran, *Managing Cultural Differences*, 4th edn (Houston TX: Gulf Publishing, 1996), pp. 252–257; Fons Trompenaars and Charles Hampden Turner, *Riding the Waves of Culture: Understanding Diversity in Global Business*, 2nd edn (New York: McGraw-Hill, 1998); Jeanne M. Brett, Debra L. Shapiro and Anne L. Lytle, "Breaking the Bonds of Reciprocity in Negotiations," *Academy of Management Journal*, August 1998, pp. 410–424; Elisabeth Rosenthal, "US Trade Official Says China Market Is Closed Tighter," *New York Times*, September 23, 1998, p. C 2.

Another cultural difference in negotiating style is the objective of the negotiators. US businesspeople tend to be very practical and to focus on short-term results. Negotiators from the Far East tend to move more slowly, like to get to know the other party, and have a more long-run focus.

Social custom plays an important part in negotiations between people of different cultural backgrounds. Many Americans and other Western businesspeople are not accustomed to giving gifts to those with whom they are doing business. However, in some parts of the world it is common to exchange presents to create an initial bond of friendship, and a failure to do so is considered to be bad manners.

A fourth factor is language. When negotiators do not speak the same language and must use interpreters, there are more chances for a misinterpretation or misunderstanding to occur. This problem also exists in written communications. Schermerhorn, for example, has found that, when documents are translated from one language to another and then translated back to check for accuracy, there are interpretation problems.[25] The original translation appears to convey the desired information, but, when another person is called in to translate the document back into the original language, some parts of it are different from that intended initially.

A related cultural problem is the use of written documents. In some countries a written document is used as a basis for establishing what is to be done. As a result, the document is detailed and factual. In other countries a written document is viewed as the basis for a general agreement and the parties then negotiate the implementation as they go along. US MNEs prefer a more detailed document because they feel that everything should be spelled out in writing. Chinese and other Far East negotiators often view this as a sign of distrust and believe a more open-ended agreement should be used.

Active learning check

Review your answer to Active Learning Case question 4 and make any changes you like. Then compare your answer with the one below.

4. Why would the management of Singapore Airlines need to understand cultural differences in negotiating behavior? Would this need be greater than that of a brewer in Amsterdam who wants to negotiate the acquisition of a winery in Madrid? Why?

The management of Singapore Airlines would need to understand cultural differences in negotiating behavior because they do business with people in a wide variety of cultures. The airline has routes in the Far East, the US, and Europe and so is continually negotiating with individuals who use a wide variety of different negotiating tactics and styles. The airline's need to understand these differences is greater than that of the brewer in Amsterdam because the negotiation for the acquisition of the winery will not be continually repeated. It is basically a "one-shot deal". Moreover, while managing the winery will require that the brewer continually negotiates with people from a different culture, this is only one culture. Singapore Airlines continually negotiates with people from a variety of diverse cultures.

Negotiating an agreement

When negotiating an agreement, three areas are of major importance: acceptance zones, renegotiation, and general negotiating behaviors. To the extent that MNE negotiators are knowledgeable regarding these areas, their efforts will be successful.

Acceptance zones

Acceptance zone
An area within which a party is willing to negotiate

Each party to a negotiation will have an **acceptance zone** or an area within which it is willing to negotiate. For example, if Anheuser-Busch, the giant US brewer, wants to buy a brewery in Düsseldorf, Germany, the US MNE will determine three prices: the highest price it is willing to pay, the price it would like to pay, and the offer at which it will begin the bargaining. For purposes of illustration, assume that Anheuser-Busch (AB) is willing to pay up to $25 million for the company but hopes to make the acquisition for $23 million and intends to start the negotiation at $20 million.

Will AB be successful? This depends on the acceptance zone of the Düsseldorf brewer. If the company will not sell for less than $27.5 million, there will be no deal because the buyer's maximum offer is less than the seller's minimum acceptance. However, assume that the German firm will not sell for less than $21 million, would like to get $24 million, and intends to start the negotiation at $28 million. In this case the two sides should be able to strike a deal since they have overlapping zones of acceptance, as illustrated in Figure 13.1.

Notice from Figure 13.1 that, when the acceptance zones of the two parties overlap, there is common ground for negotiating. Additionally, keep in mind that, if the zones do not overlap, negotiations will not always end in a stalemate. After listening to each other the parties may agree to change their respective bids and offers, adjust the acceptance zones, and end up with common negotiating ground.

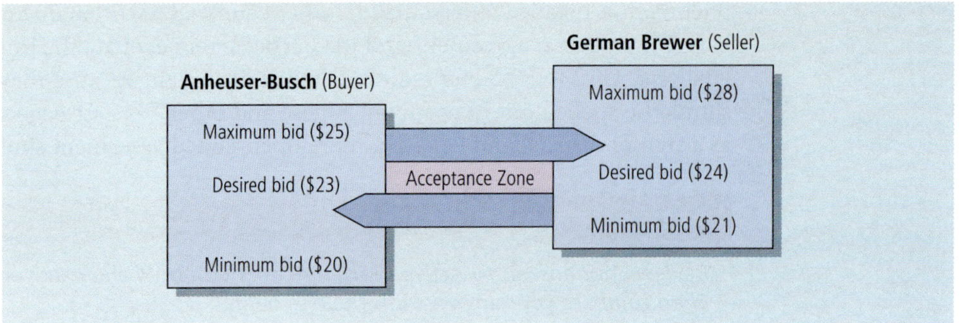

Figure 13.1 Zones of acceptance in the negotiating process (in millions of US $)

In the case of Figure 13.1 the two parties would eventually negotiate within a range of $21 million (the least amount the seller will take) and $25 million (the most the buyer will pay). It is not possible to say what the final price will be because this will depend on how willing each side is to concede ground to the other. However, whatever the final price, the seller is going to get at least the desired minimum and the buyer will not pay more than the established maximum.

Renegotiation

In the above example the negotiation process focused on one issue: acquisition of a brewery. When the purchase price is agreed upon, the process comes to an end. However, many MNE's negotiations with an individual or group will be repeated in the future. For example, Ford Motor may negotiate with a parts supplier in Brussels and sign a two-year contract. During the ensuing 24 months, the two parties may negotiate changes in the agreement, and at the end of this time the parties may renegotiate the overall agreement and settle on a new two-year contract. So in negotiating the MNE must remember that, if the other side feels that it gave up more than it should have, then it will expect reciprocity in the future.

It is also important to remember that initial negotiations often lead to one party gaining the upper hand. For example, if Brazil wants Cummins Engine to set up a plant in Brasilia, the country may make a very enticing offer. However, at some point in time the country may begin to bring pressure on Cummins to allow local ownership in the operation or to invest more money in plant and equipment and to expand the facilities. If Cummins wants to remain in Brazil, the two parties will then begin renegotiating their agreement. In this case Cummins may accede to the government's request in turn for allowing the company to repatriate more of its profits back to the US or to set up operations in other locales around the country.

Negotiating behaviors and tactics

During the negotiations it is common to find a wide variety of behaviors and tactics employed. For example, in some countries a great deal of time is spent building interpersonal relationships and getting to know the other parties to the negotiations. This approach is not widely used by US negotiators. But, as Adler points out, this can be an important activity.

> Effective negotiators must view luncheon, dinner, reception, ceremony, and tour invitations as times for interpersonal relationship building, and therefore as key to the negotiating process. When US negotiators, often frustrated by the seemingly endless formalities, ceremonies, and "small talk," ask how long they must wait before beginning to "do business," the answer is

simple: wait until your opponents bring up business (and they will). Realize that the work of conducting a successful negotiation has already begun, even if business has yet to be mentioned.[26]

Another common behavior or tactic is to learn the time limits of the other party. For example, if the German brewer learns that AB would like to buy a brewery within the next 90 days, the seller can use this information to gain an advantage. By delaying the negotiation until the end of this time period, the German company can then dig in its heels and ask for a price that is on the high side of AB's acceptance zone.

Another tactic is the use of reciprocity. Arab and US negotiators tend to reciprocate by trading favors. If one side gives way on an issue, the other side will respond by giving way on something else. However, researchers have found that this is not always the case. Brazilians, for example, are likely to make initial concessions but then dig in and hold their ground. If the negotiator knows the likelihood of reciprocity, he or she is in a better bargaining position.

Still another tactic is the use of extreme offers or requests such as asking $60 million for a company that is worth half that amount or, conversely, offering $10 million for the firm. Researchers have found that Chinese, Arab, and Russian negotiators often use extreme behaviors, in contrast to US and Swedish negotiators whose initial position is fairly close to the one they are seeking.[27] However, US negotiators have been known to use extreme positions. When Peter Ueberroth managed the Olympic games in the US in 1984, he turned a profit of over $100 million by using extreme position bargaining, among other ways. For example, when the Japanese offered $6 million for the right to televise the games in Japan, Ueberroth countered by asking for $90 million. The two sides eventually agreed on $18.5 million, which was far higher than the $10 million the Olympic Committee hoped to get.[28]

Other common bargaining tactics include promises, threats, rewards, commitments, and the use of self-disclosure. Table 13.4 provides illustrations of some of these negotiating behaviors by Japanese, US, and Brazilian negotiators. The table shows that each

Table 13.4 Twelve examples of the differences in verbal behaviors among Japanese, US, and Brazilian negotiators

	Number of times behavior was used in a 30-minute negotiating session by members of each group		
Behavior (description)	*Japanese*	*US*	*Brazilian*
1 Making promises	7	8	3
2 Making threats	4	4	2
3 Making recommendations	7	4	5
4 Giving warnings	2	1	1
5 Offering rewards	1	2	2
6 Making commitments	15	13	8
7 Asking questions	20	20	22
8 Giving commands	8	6	14
9 Revealing personal information about oneself	34	36	39
10 Making a first offer	61.5	57.3	75.2
11 Granting initial concessions	6.5	7.1	9.4
12 Using the word "no"	5.7	9.0	83.4

Source: Adapted from John L. Graham (1985) "The Influence of Culture on the Process of Business Negotiations: An Exploratory Study," *Journal of International Business Studies*, Spring, p. 88. Adapted and reprinted with permission.

group has a series of behaviors that make it different from the other two. For example, the Japanese like to make recommendations, the Americans make wide use of promises, and the Brazilians rely heavily on self-disclosure.[29]

Another important negotiating area is non-verbal behavior. This is characterized by such actions as silent periods, during which the negotiator says nothing, and facial gazing, during which the person stares at the other individual. Researchers have found that the Japanese and the Americans are more likely to use silence, whereas the Brazilians are more likely to use facial gazing.

These behaviors and tactics are often used in international negotiations. Effective negotiators learn how to use them and how to counteract their use by the opposition. Some examples are provided in the next section.

STRATEGIC MANAGEMENT AND POLITICAL RISK

MNEs take many steps to ensure that their strategies do not go awry because of unexpected developments. Two of the most beneficial steps are the use of integrative and protective/defensive techniques and the strategic use of joint ventures and partnerships.[30] The following section examines both.

Use of integrative and protective/defensive techniques

Integrative techniques
Strategies designed to help a multinational become a part of the host country's infrastructure

There are a variety of stratagems that MNEs employ in reducing risk. Some are collectively known as **integrative techniques**, which are designed to help the MNE become a part of the host country's infrastructure.[31] The objective of an integrative technique is to help the company blend into the environment and to become less noticeable as a "foreign" firm. One of the simplest ways is to use a name that is not identified with an overseas company and, if an acquisition is made, keep the old name in place. For example, Bridgestone is a Japanese tire company, but no one would know this based on the name of the company. Additionally, Bridgestone owns Firestone Tire & Rubber, but few Americans are aware of this fact. Similarly, Hoechst of Germany owns the Celanese Company, and most people do not know this. Nor do many people realize that almost 25 per cent of the banks in California are Japanese owned; their names provide no clues to their real owners. This tactic deflects public attention and concern that US assets are being swallowed up by overseas investors.

Another common integrative technique is to develop good relations with the host government and other political groups and to produce as much of the product as possible locally. In turn the MNE will hire and promote local personnel and use them to run a large portion of the operations. This strategy endears the company to the government and, if any action is taken against foreign firms, these firms are likely to be spared.

A good example of an MNE that uses integrative techniques is IBM, which has consistently attempted to immerse itself into the host country's environment and to serve as a major export arm. As a result, the giant computer firm has been very successful in dealing with foreign governments and extracting major concessions from them. For example, IBM does not take on local partners, and host countries have always agreed to this demand.

Protective and defensive techniques
Strategies designed to discourage a host country from interfering in multinational operations

Protective/defensive techniques

Protective and defensive techniques are strategies that are designed to discourage a host country from interfering in multinational operations. In contrast to integrative techniques, protective and defensive measures are aimed at fostering *non-integration* of the MNE into the local environment. A good example is conducting research and development (R&D) at other geographic locales and importing this knowledge as needed. Should the government suddenly decide to seize the firm's facilities, the company's R&D base would not be threatened.

Another protective and defensive technique is to limit the role of the local personnel to those operations that are not vital to the running of the facility. So if the government decides to take over the operation, the host country personnel will not be able to handle things efficiently. Those with the requisite knowledge and training are overseas personnel who are sent on-site by the multinational.

A third technique is to raise as much capital as possible from the host country and local banks. When this happens, the government is reluctant to interfere in operations because this may threaten its own investment and that of the home country banks. In a manner of speaking, this strategy co-opts the government and brings it onto the MNE's team. Any strike against the multinational is a blow against the host country.

A fourth technique is to diversify production among a number of countries. In this way, if the government seizes the MNE's facilities, only one area of production is disrupted. The company can then reallocate production and get back on stream in short order.

Combination strategies MNEs often use a combination of integration and protective/defensive techniques to reduce and manage their political risk. Figure 13.2 provides an example of how companies can do this. In the case of the low-technology manufacturing firm (#1 in Figure 13.2), the only way to employ a protective/defensive strategy is to raise capital locally. As a result, this firm will work to integrate itself into the country and to act very much like a local firm.

An international air carrier (#2 in Figure 13.2) will use an integrative strategy by setting up local operations and by hiring people to staff the facilities, to maintain the planes, and to handle arrivals and departures. The airline will also help to generate money for the country by bringing in tourists and businesspeople. At the same time the company will seldom have more than a small percentage of its planes in this locale on any one

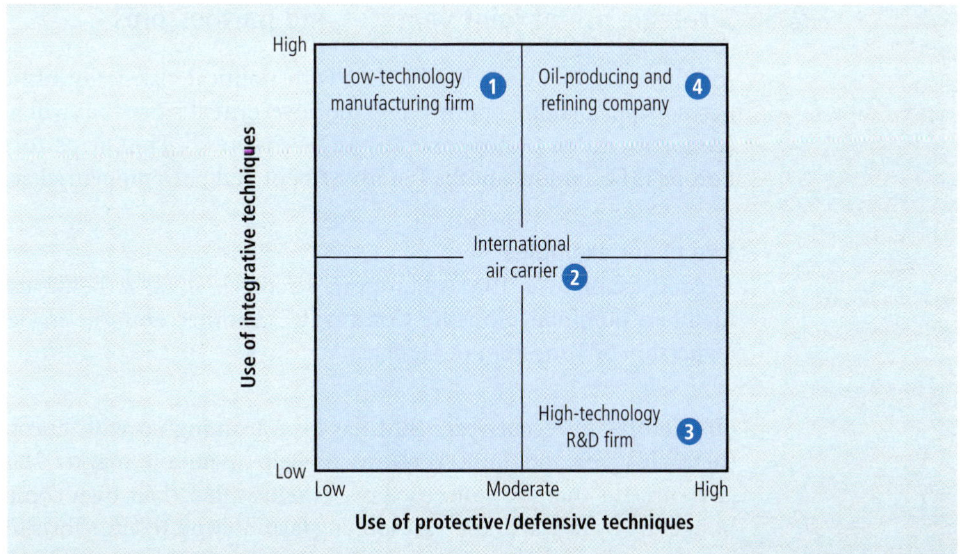

Figure 13.2 Select examples of the use of integrative and protective/defensive techniques

day. Additionally, the pilots will often come from other countries and be highly skilled individuals, and the top management team will be operating out of headquarters in the home country. So while the air carrier will take some steps to accommodate the country, it will also be well positioned should the country decide to seize its aircraft or to increase taxes or airport fees. Moreover, aside from facilities at the airport, the company will usually have no other fixed assets except for the planes. Therefore any crackdown on the airline might result in retaliatory action by other airlines, which would refuse to fly into the country. Such action could seriously hamper the country's economic growth. Consequently, a strategy that provides for the intermediate use of both integrative and protective/defensive techniques often works extremely well.

A high-technology R&D firm (#3 in Figure 13.2) will not put much emphasis on integrative techniques because it does not want to become integrated into the local economy. The firm may be situated where it is because the company finds that it is easier to recruit top talent to live in that region. Or other competitors may be headquartered there, and the company finds that it's easier to keep tabs on these firms by situating nearby. So while the company may hire local people to staff basic operations, personnel from other countries who live locally will handle all the R&D and other sophisticated functions. If the firm should hire local people for some of these R&D positions, the company will work to keep them loyal to the firm and not to the country. Thus if there is an attempt to seize the firm's R&D facilities, the loss will be minimized.

In the case of an oil-producing and refining company (#4 in Figure 13.2), the firm is likely to make strong use of both integrative and protective/defensive techniques. The company will need to get on well with the government since it is tapping the country's natural resources. There is likely to be a great deal of hiring of local personnel for routine jobs. The firm will also work hard to generate as much revenue as possible since the government is unlikely to interfere with the operations of a revenue-producing firm. At the same time the MNE will maintain control of the more sophisticated jobs so that these cannot be carried out by anyone else. If the company were to be taken over, local workers would be unlikely to know how to operate the machinery and equipment efficiently.

Strategic use of joint ventures and partnerships

Another way in which MNEs deal with political risk is by using joint ventures and partnerships that are approved by the government since that will help to build the local economy and/or to support current businesses.[32] This helps to explain why Eastern Europe is becoming a hotbed of investment and entrepreneurial activity.[33]

Two major examples

A good example is IBM's European strategy, which is being used to help the firm maintain dominance on the Continent.[34] Another example is General Electric's joint ownership of Tungsram of Hungary.[35]

IBM Europe In recent years IBM has been teaming up with European firms and using these alliances and joint ventures to help maintain market share. Many European governments that are concerned over the fact that their own computer firms are being bought up by the Japanese[36] are looking favorably on IBM's efforts to cement ties with the remaining firms. IBM teamed up with Siemens of Germany to develop high-capacity 64-megabit memory chips, and the two are now working on other projects.[37] IBM is also stepping up production so that it can sell microchips, finished subsystems, disk drives, and telecommunications equipment to companies like Siemens and Groupe Bull, and the firm is not stopping here:

> In an effort to forge new links, IBM has become a major source of venture capital for independent suppliers of software and services. . . . Recently IBM Europe has plowed more than $100 million into nearly 200 joint ventures and partnerships, from a German software maker to a Danish supplier of network services.[38]

General Electric General Electric (GE) and Tungsram, the giant Hungarian light bulb manufacturer, have joined forces in an agreement in which GE paid $150 million for 50.1 per cent of the company and then eventually bought full ownership. Prior to the agreement GE held only 2 per cent of the Western European light bulb market. After the purchase this jumped to 9 per cent.

GE is introducing more modern technology into the plant while studying some of the technological breakthroughs that the R&D people at Tungsram have already achieved, including their work on tungsten filaments. These breakthroughs help to explain why GE wanted Tungsram; despite having to operate under a communist regime that took away most of its profits, the firm had managed to produce some excellent products and to make some important technological discoveries.[39]

GE believes that, with Tungsram in its corner, it can increase its European market share during the millennium and perhaps replace Philips as the major firm on the continent. Given the manner in which it has approached the project, the Hungarian government is solidly behind GE's efforts and political risk has been minimized.

Minimizing failure of cooperative efforts

While joint ventures and joint ownership are important ways of dealing with political risk, MNEs are also aware of the problems that can result if there is a falling out between the partners.[40] This can be particularly troublesome if the local government were to support the home company's actions. For this reason, MNEs often make use of two strategic factors when deciding on a joint venture or joint ownership arrangement: (1) compatibility of firm-specific advantages and (2) safeguards against unethical behavior.[41]

Firm-specific advantages

Firm-specific advantages (FSAs) Strengths or benefits specific to a firm and a result of contributions that can be made by its personnel, technology, and/or equipment

Firm-specific advantages (FSAs for short) are the strengths or benefits specific to the firm that each partner brings to a joint venture or ownership arrangement. For example, IBM can offer venture capital to small firms in Europe while they can provide IBM with product technology. GE can offer capital, technology, and management expertise to Tungsram and the latter can provide a reputation for quality-produced goods, a factory, and a labor force. If the FSAs of the parties complement each other, the arrangement can be profitable for both. However, there is one other key consideration. What will happen if one party to the agreement takes advantage of the other, for example by stealing technology, breaking the deal, and going its own way? If the local partner does this, the MNE must hope that the local government will provide the necessary protection and return of its assets, patents, and so on.

Many MNEs believe that, if there is a breakdown between the two partners to a joint venture agreement, the local company will come out ahead, so they take steps to prevent such an occurrence by protecting themselves from the start. For example, if the local partner steals the technology and begins producing the product under a different name or trademark, the MNE will have plans to retaliate by finding another local partner with whom to do business and possibly to drive the initial partner from the market. If the

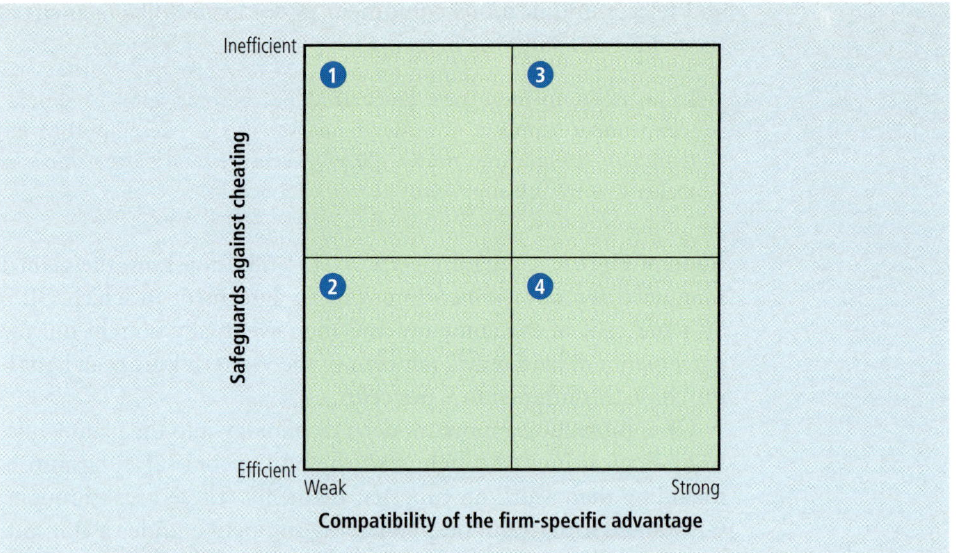

Figure 13.3 **Ensuring the success of a joint venture or an ownership agreement**

local partner takes venture capital funds and spends them on R&D activities that have no relationship to the venture, the MNE will refuse to commit more money to the project. In each of these cases the MNE is able to retaliate effectively. Aware of this, the partner is unlikely to undertake unethical behavior.

Figure 13.3 provides an illustration of how the compatibility of FSAs and the safeguards against cheating can result in a successful or an unsuccessful venture or ownership agreement. Only in quadrant 4 do things work out to the MNE's advantage. For this reason, it will work to develop agreements that meet the two conditions in this quadrant.[42] We make further use of this FSA framework in Chapter 20.

KEY POINTS

1. **Political risk is the probability that political forces will negatively affect an MNE's profit or impede the attainment of other critical business objectives. This risk can be examined in terms of macro- and microfactors. A macro political risk is one that affects foreign enterprises in the same general way. Expropriation of foreign firms is an example. A micro political risk is one that affects selected sectors of the economy or specific foreign businesses. A government decision to reduce foreign ownership in the airline business is an example.**

2. **There are a number of sources of political risk. Among others, these include the political philosophy of the government in power, changing economic conditions, rising nationalism, social unrest, terrorism, the vested interests of local business groups, and newly created international alliances.**

3. **MNEs use a number of approaches in managing political risk. One is to forecast this risk by examining the political system and by evaluating the overall risk. Another approach is to examine the impact of this risk on company products and operations. Based on the results, the company will then determine the risk vulnerability. In some cases, as seen in Table 13.3, this vulnerability is quantified.**

4. There are three key steps in developing effective negotiating strategies. First, the MNE will evaluate its own position and that of the other parties to the negotiation. Second, the firm will examine the behavioral characteristics of the other parties in order to better understand their style of negotiation. Third, the MNE will use this information to hammer out an agreement that is acceptable to both sides. In carrying out the latter step, the MNE will give particular attention to identifying the acceptance zone of the other party and to using behaviors and negotiating tactics that will result in both sides feeling that they are getting what they want.
5. MNEs tend to use a combination of integrative and protective/defensive techniques in minimizing political risk. They also rely on the strategic use of joint ventures and partnerships and carefully analyze each situation before entering into the agreement.

KEY TERMS

- political risk
- macro political risk
- expropriation
- indigenization laws
- micro political risk
- acceptance zone
- integrative techniques
- protective and defensive techniques
- firm-specific advantages

REVIEW AND DISCUSSION QUESTIONS

1. What is meant by the term "political risk"? Is there political risk in every country of the world? Explain.
2. How does macro political risk differ from micro political risk? Compare and contrast the two.
3. What are some factors that help to determine the degree of micro political risk? Identify and describe three of them.
4. Drawing on the information in Table 13.2, what are three major sources of political risk? What is the likely effect of each source?
5. When predicting political risk, why will an MNE be interested in examining the political system of the country?
6. When an MNE evaluates the political risk associated with its products and operations, what areas will it investigate? Identify and discuss three of them.
7. How can an MNE quantify its political risk vulnerability? Use Table 13.3 as a point of reference.
8. If Citicorp were thinking about opening startup operations in a country in Eastern Europe, how would the firm evaluate its own strengths and needs when preparing for the negotiations?
9. Why will an MNE be interested in the behavioral characteristics of the participants to a negotiation? How can such information help to improve its negotiating position?
10. In a negotiation, why would an MNE be interested in the acceptance zone of the other party?
11. What are some bargaining tactics that are used in international negotiating? Identify and describe three of them.
12. How do MNEs use integrative techniques in order to reduce their political risk? Describe an example.
13. How do MNEs use protective/defensive techniques in order to reduce their political risk? Describe an example.
14. How could an MNE ensure the success of a joint venture or ownership agreement through consideration of firm-specific advantages and safeguards against cheating? Give an example.

REAL CASE

Investing in Russia

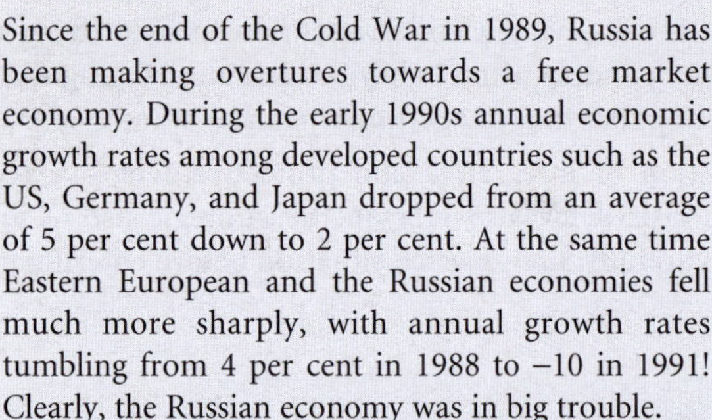

Since the end of the Cold War in 1989, Russia has been making overtures towards a free market economy. During the early 1990s annual economic growth rates among developed countries such as the US, Germany, and Japan dropped from an average of 5 per cent down to 2 per cent. At the same time Eastern European and the Russian economies fell much more sharply, with annual growth rates tumbling from 4 per cent in 1988 to −10 in 1991! Clearly, the Russian economy was in big trouble.

Investment from the West was seen as a way to improve the economy. However, significant changes needed to take place to reduce political risk in Russia. Initially, five steps were recommended by outside experts: (1) change the relationship between the national government and the republics in order to set up a federal political system in which central powers are limited; (2) eliminate or slash most state subsidies, including defense spending, and create a uniform sales tax and personal and corporate income tax system; (3) establish a commercial banking system, boost interest rates, and create an independent bank that will halt current inflationary practices; (4) break up state monopolies and industrial cartels; and (5) free the price of most goods immediately and gradually add to this list those changes that must be phased in more slowly: energy, public transportation, housing, and basic consumer goods such as milk, bread, and meat.

By the mid-1990s things looked good; the republics had become more autonomous from the central government and new private banks had begun to emerge. Most importantly, by 1997, the private sector accounted for more than half of Russia's output. Some 18,000 industrial firms had been privatized and over 1 million new businesses were created. The old Russia, its ideology and institutions, had ceased to exist.

Yet the late 1990s proved to be a wake-up call to foreign investors in Russia. The Asian crisis left many feeling Russia could be next and it would have been had the IMF and the World Bank not been ready to bail the country out. The Russian government had pegged the ruble to the US dollar and used interest rates to defend the exchange rate. This led to skyrocketing interest rates that reached over 50 per cent in peak periods. When the government allowed the ruble to float, investors lost on the devaluation what they had earned on interest rates.

What brought this about? While Russia's steps towards liberalization have been significant, the country is only mid-way to becoming a truly democratic free market. The new private banks are not real banks. They offer no real credit system. They lack credibility, which makes Russians more likely to hold currency or send their savings to foreign banks than to deposit them in these new banks. A large bureaucratic web still exists and a small corrupt mafia is proving difficult to police.

Despite all setbacks, Russia is bound to turn itself around. In 2001, for the first time since the end of communism Russia had a balanced budget, a trade surplus, reserves, and a growing economy. In 2000, the economy grew by 8 per cent. This growth, however, has done little to lure foreign investors who would rather flock to the Chinese market than face the volatility and corruption of the Russian economy.

Sources: Adapted from Leonard Silk, Rose Brady et al., "Can Gorbachev Pound Missiles into Plowshares?" *Business Week*, July 29, 1991, pp. 42–43; Steven Erlanger, "To Russia, with Good Ol' American Know-How," *New York Times*, June 13, 1993, p. F 5; Rob Norton and Kerry L. Hubert, "The Good News About Russia," *Fortune*, April 14, 1997, p. 32; Steve H. Hanke, "Is the Ruble Next?" *Forbes*, March 9, 1998, p. 64; Danie Yergin and Thane Gustafson, "Don't Write Off Russia – Yet," *Fortune*, September 28, 1998, pp. 99–102; Domingo F. Cavallo, "The Immensity of Russia's Problems," *Forbes*, August 24, 1998, p. 263; Steve H. Hanke, "Capitalism Without Banks," *Forbes*, September 7, 1998, pp. 150–151; "Russia's Economic Quagmire," *Economist*, April 24, 1999, pp. 69–70; "Good in Part," *Economist*, July 19, 2001.

1. **What political risks do MNEs face in Russia? Identify and describe three of them.**
2. **What strengths would a consumer goods manufacturing firm bring to the country? What Russian needs would it help to meet?**
3. **How could this manufacturer employ integrative or protective/defensive techniques in the country? Identify and describe one approach that could be used for each.**

REAL CASE

Enron in India

In 1992 Enron Development Corporation (EDC) signed a contract for $2.8 billion to develop the Dabhol Project for a gas-fired power plant in the Indian state of Maharashtra. The plant was to supply natural gas and naphtha to the region's industry. In 1995 the new BJP government of Maharashtra canceled the project. The project was one-third complete at the time of cancellation and employed 2,600 people. The head of EDC, Rebecca Mark, renegotiated the project and Enron was eventually allowed to complete the project. However, this was only one of a series of confrontations involving Enron, national and local governments, and activists during the lifetime of the project.

Enron originally entered the Indian energy market to become a first mover in a growing market. India requires up to 10,000 Mw of new electricity capacity per year to keep up with economic growth at its present level of 6–8 per cent. In 2001, the country had 90,000 MW in capacity, which only allows it to supply electricity to 65 per cent of the population. Even those lucky enough to have power must endure rationed blackouts throughout the day. Establishing the plant allowed Enron a power source while awaiting deregulation of the energy market. After this, Enron would concentrate in marketing energy from different sources to users across the country.

The project was off to a bad start when activists claimed that government officials had been bribed to approve the project and that Enron allowed police brutality against activists who opposed the project. The courts cleared Enron but the local public remained unconvinced. In the process, the local government that approved the project was voted out of power and Enron saw its reputation shattered in the region.

Enron's investment had government assurances and a mutually agreed upon formula for calculating energy prices. The sole client of Enron's Dabhol Power Company is the state government. The Maharashtra State Electricity Board (MSEB) is forced to pay the plant a fixed monthly rate of 940 million Rupees whether or not the MSEB purchases any electricity or not. This rate is calculated to cover the plant's debt, fixed running costs, and the profits of Enron and other shareholders. The contract between Enron and the state of Maharashtra was meant to diminish the risk to Enron, but it also decreased its sensitivity to the local environment. A sudden devaluation of the Rupee and a rise in oil prices made Enron's energy prices increase to four times that of local producers and the MSEB was unable to cover the costs. Suddenly, the MSEB could not meet its obligations under the contract, but was still required to pay the fixed costs.

In 2001, Enron was close to closing the plant. The MSEB stopped paying its bills in May 2001. By September 2001, it owed $185 million to Enron. The MNE states that its contract with MSEB is legal and has been approved on 25 occasions in Indian courts. Enron and its partners Bechtel and GE are seeking $1 billion in compensation for costs already incurred in the plant and up to $5 billion if its contract is cancelled.

Enron's experience in India made it reconsider its expansion plans in third world countries. Yet much of the blame rests on Enron itself. The company underestimated the political risk despite the widespread discontent with the contract's approval. It was also unable to adapt to a changing economic environment. Despite the general perception that Enron's plant was too much for Maharashtra's economy, supplying quality energy at a cost that could send the state into bankruptcy, India cannot afford to let Enron's project fail as it risks compromising future FDI. By late 2001, a disillusioned Enron was bargaining with private and public investors to sell the plant. In October, it sold its upstream assets to BG, the UK oil group. In November 2001, Enron went bankrupt, due to unrelated financial problems in its home base.

Websites: **www.enron.com**; **www.bechtel.com** and **www.ge.com**.

Source: Jonathan Karp and Kathryn Kranhold, "Enron's Plant in India Was Dead; This Month, It Will Go On Stream," *Wall Street Journal*, February 5, 1999, pp. A 1, 6; "India to Hold Inquiry into Enron Affair", *Financial Times*, September 20, 2001, p. 9; "Enron, and on, and on," *Economist*, April 19, 2001; "Generation Gaps," *Economist*, January 11, 2001. Mathew Jones "BG Buys Enron's Indian Upstream Assets for $388m," *FT.com*, October 3, 2001; Julie Earle, "Enron Wants out of Indian Power Project," *FT.com*, July 26, 2001.

1. **Did Enron do an appropriate risk assessment when entering into the Maharashta project?**
2. **Enron's agreement with the government of Maharashta was declared legal on 25 occasions in Indian courts. Most firms, however, chose not to draft agreements that would guarantee profits to investors regardless of the situation. Why is this not a generally practiced strategy?**
3. **After rumors began to emerge about bribery and corruption in the Enron affair, was Enron's decision to continue with the operation justified?**

ENDNOTES

1 Serge Schmemann, "Gorbachev Offers Party a Charter that Drops Icons," *New York Times*, July 26, 1991, pp. A 1, A 5.

2 Also, see Douglas Harbrecht et al., "Tough Talk," *Business Week*, February 28, 1994, pp. 26–28.

3 Also, see Richard W. Stevenson, "Europeans Join to Build a Fast Plane," *New York Times*, April 8, 1994, pp. C 1–C 2 and Charles Goldsmith, "After Trailing Boeing for Years, Airbus Aims for 50% of the Market," *Wall Street Journal*, March 16, 1998, pp. A 1, 8.

4 For a discussion of US exports, see James Beeler, "Exports: Ship 'Em Out," *Fortune*, Special edn, Spring/Summer 1991, p. 58.

5 Barnaby J. Feder, "Honeywell's Route Back to South Africa Market," *New York Times*, January 31, 1994, pp. C 1, C 4.

6 Keith Bradsher, "Push by US to Cut Tariffs Is Reported," *New York Times*, January 8, 1993, pp. C 1, C 10.

7 However, these countries are also concerned with quid pro quo, as seen in Richard W. Stevenson, "East Europe Says Barriers to Trade Hurt Its Economies," *New York Times*, January 25, 1993, pp. A 1, C 8.

8 See Zbigniew Brzezinski, "Help the New Russian Revolution," *New York Times*, July 14, 1991, p. F 13. For more on Russia's reform difficulties, see Robert Cottrell, "The Promise of Capitalism has Yet to Be Realised," *Ft.com*, November 30, 2001.

9 James Kynge, "China Enters WTO Dawn with Mixed Expectations, *Ft.com*, December 10, 2001; and "Surveys: China," *FT.com*, November 13, 2000.

10 Amy Kazmin, "Vietnam Ratifies Trade Agreement with the US," *FT.com*, November 28, 2001.

11 Also, see Thomas L. Freedman, "Bentsen Seeks Freer Asian Markets," *New York Times*, January 19, 1994, pp. C 1–C 2 and "New Challenges for G7 Chiefs," *BBC.co.uk*, April 14, 2000.

12 Richard M. Hodgetts and Fred Luthans, *International Management*, 4th edn (Burr Ridge IL: McGraw/Hill, 2000), pp. 277–278, and Jonathon Sapsford, "Japanese Firms Brace for First Laws on Consumer Rights and Insurers Gain," *Wall Street Journal*, March 8, 1994, p. A 13.

13 *Atari and Tengen v Nintendo*, United States Court Of Appeals for the Federal Circuit, September 10, 1992.

14 Douglas Jehl, "Clinton Drops 19-Year Ban on US Trade with Vietnam: Cites Hanoi's Help on MIAs," *New York Times*, February 4, 1994, pp. A 1, A 6.

15 As an example, see Keith Bradsher, "New US–Japan Chip Pact Approved," *New York Times*, June 5, 1991, p. C 11.

16 Clyde H. Farnsworth, "Trade Focus Has Changed," *New York Times*, May 28, 1991, pp. C 1, C 9.

17 "Pacific Islands to Sign Trade Pact," *BBC.co.uk*, August 14, 2001.

18 Also, see Louis Uchitelle, "Gulf Victory May Raise US Influence in OPEC," *New York Times*, March 5, 1991, pp. C 1, C 8.

19 R. W. Apple, Jr., "Leaders Express Support for Gorbachev," *New York Times*, July 17, 1991, pp. A 1, A 6; Andrew Rosenthal, "Bush Renewing Trade Privileges for China, but Adds Missile Curbs," *New York Times*, March 28, 1991, pp. A 1, A 4; and "Tricky Moves for the Bank and the Fund," *Economist*, February 15, 2001.

20 See, for example, David B. Yoffie, "How an Industry Builds Political Advantage," *Harvard Business Review*, vol. 66, no. 3 (May/June 1988), pp. 82–89. Also, see Alan M. Rugman and Alain Verbeke, *Global Corporate Strategy and Trade Policy* (London and New York: Routledge, 1990), Pat Choate, *Agents of Influence* (New York: Knopf, 1990); and "Pettigrew Plans to Lobby Washington on Lumber," *Toronto Star*, September 7, 2001.

21 For more on this, see Lee T. Brown, Alan M. Rugman and Alain Verbeke, "Japanese Joint Ventures with Western Multinationals: Synthesising the Economic and Cultural Explanations of Failure," *Asia Pacific Journal of Management*, vol. 6, no. 2 (1990), pp. 225–242; and Richard McGregor, "Microsoft Strikes Accord in China against Piracy," *Ft.com*, December 6, 2001.

22 David E. Sanger, "Japan Sets Tough Rules on Business," *New York Times*, July 15, 1991, pp. C 1–C 2.

23 Geoff Dyer, Adrian Michaels and Raphael Minder, "Pfizer Threatens Boycott of New Drugs in France," *Ft.com*, December 10, 2001.

24 Hodgetts and Luthans (2000) n. 12 above, p. 287.

25 John R. Schermerhorn, Jr, "Language Effects in Cross-Cultural Management Research: An Empirical Study and a World of Caution," *National Academy of Management Proceedings*, 1987, pp. 102–105.

26 Nancy J. Adler, *International Dimensions of Organizational Behavior*, 2nd edn (Boston MA: PWS-Kent Publishing, 1991), p. 197.

27 Hodgetts and Luthans (2000) n. 12 above, pp. 287–288.

28 Ibid., pp. 290–291.

29 For additional insights into negotiating, see Brian Mark Hawrysh and Judith Lynne Zaichkowsky, "Cultural Approaches to Negotiations: Understanding the Japanese," *International Marketing Review*, vol. 7, no. 2 (1990), pp. 28–42.

30 For a detailed discussion of protective/defensive techniques, see Ann Gregory, "Political Risk Management," in Alan M. Rugman (ed.) *International Business in Canada* (Toronto: Prentice-Hall, 1989) pp. 310–329.

31 For a good example of how Japan does this, see Andrew Pollack, "Japan Takes a Pre-emptive Step on Auto Exports," *New York Times*, January 9, 1993, pp. 17, 26; and Richard W. Stevenson, "Japanese Cars Get British Accents," *New York Times*, February 25, 1992, pp. C 1, C 14.

32 Stephen O. Spinks and Robert C. Stanley, "Joint Ventures Under EC Antitrust and Merger Control Rules: Concentrative or Cooperative," *Journal of European Business*, March/April 1991, pp. 29–34; and Edmund

L. Andrews, "Sprint Forms Joint Venture with Alcatel," *New York Times*, February 4, 1993, p. C 3.

33 Paul Hofheinz, "New Light in Eastern Europe?" *Fortune*, July 29, 1991, pp. 145–152 and "President Invites Foreign Investors to Ukraine," *BBC Monitoring Service*, December 7, 2001.

34 Carol J. Loomis, "Can John Akers Save IBM?" *Fortune*, July 15, 1991, pp. 40–56; Douglas Harbrecht, Neil Gross and Peter Burrows, "Suppose They Have a Trade War and Nobody Came," *Business Week*, March 29, 1993, p. 30; and Gary McWilliams and Neil Gross, "DEC: New Chip, New Partner, New Ball Game?" *Business Week*, March 29, 1993, p. 31.

35 Gail E. Schares, Zachary Schiller and Patrick Oster, "GE Gropes for the On-Switch in Hungary," *Business Week*, April 26, 1993, pp. 102–103.

36 Jonathan B. Levine and Gail E. Schares, "IBM Europe Starts Swinging Back," *Business Week*, May 6, 1991, p. 52.

37 "Siemens Signs Alliance Partnership Agreement with Tivoli Systems," IBM News Release, Ocrober 21, 1999; and "Siemens Announces Partnership to Develop and Distribute Meta Directory for IBM System 390," Siemens News Release, September 24, 2001.

38 Jonathan B. Levine and Gail E. Schares, "IBM Europe Starts Swinging Back," *Business Week*, May 6, 1991, p. 52.

39 See Steven Greenhouse, "Running on Fast-Forward in Budapest," *New York Times*, December 16, 1990, Section 3, pp. 1, 8.

40 Jordan D. Lewis, "How to Build Successful Strategic Alliances," *Journal of European Business*, November/December 1990, pp. 18–29; and Tom Lewis and Mark Turley, "Strategic Partnering in Eastern Europe," *International Executive*, January/February 1991, pp. 5–9.

41 See Brown, Rugman and Verbeke (1990) n. 21 above.

42 For additional insights, see Peter J. Pettibone, "Negotiating a Business Venture in the Soviet Union," *Journal of Business Strategy*, January/February 1991, pp. 18–23; Keith A. Rosten, "Soviet–US Joint Ventures: Pioneers on a New Frontier," *California Management Review*, Winter 1991, pp. 88–108.

ADDITIONAL BIBLIOGRAPHY

Brett, Jeanne M. and Okumura, Tetsushi. "Inter- and Intracultural Negotiations: US and Japanese Negotiators," *Academy of Management Journal*, vol. 41, no. 5 (December 1998).

Brewer, Thomas L. "Government Policies, Market Imperfections, and Foreign Direct Investment," *Journal of International Business Studies*, vol. 24, no. 1 (First Quarter 1993).

Brewer, Thomas L. "An Issue-Area Approach to the Analysis of MNE–Government Relations," *Journal of International Business Studies*, vol. 23, no. 2 (Second Quarter 1992).

Chi, Tailan. "Business Strategies in Transition Economies," *Academy of Management Review*, vol. 26, no. 2 (April 2001).

Cosset, Jean-Claude and Roy, Jean. "The Determinants of Country Risk Ratings," *Journal of International Business Studies*, vol. 22, no. 1 (First Quarter 1991).

Gavin, Joseph G. III. "Environmental Protection and the GATT: A Business View," *Columbia Journal of World Business*, vol. 27, nos. 3, 4 (Fall/Winter 1992).

Geringer, J. Michael. "Strategic Determinants of Partner Selection Criteria in International Joint Ventures," *Journal of International Business Studies*, vol. 22, no. 1 (First Quarter 1991).

Geringer, J. Michael and Hebert, Louis. "Measuring Performance of International Joint Ventures," *Journal of International Business Studies*, vol. 22, no. 2 (Second Quarter 1991).

Gomes-Casseres, Benjamin. "Joint Ventures in the Face of Global Competition," *Sloan Management Review*, vol. 30, no. 3 (Spring 1989).

Grosse, Robert. "Restrictive Business Practices in International Service Industries: Examples from Latin America," *Transnational Corporations*, vol. 6, no. 2 (August 1997).

Hillman, Amy and Keim, Gerald. "International Variation in the Business–Government Interface: Institutional and Organizational Considerations," *Academy of Management Review*, vol. 20, no. 1 (January 1995).

Horrigan, Brenda D. "Debt Recovery by Foreign Investors in Post-crisis Russia," *European Business Journal*, vol. 11, no. 2 (1999).

Inkpen, Andrew C. and Beamish, Paul W. "Knowledge, Bargaining Power, and the Instability of International Joint Ventures," *Academy of Management Review*, vol. 22, no. 1 (January 1997).

Kogut, Bruce. "A Study of the Life Cycle of Joint Ventures," *Management International Review*, vol. 28, Special Issue (1988).

Lee, Suk Hun. "Relative Importance of Political Instability and Economic Variables on Perceived Country Creditworthiness," *Journal of International Business Studies*, vol. 24, no. 4 (Fourth Quarter 1993).

Li, Jiatao and Guisinger, Stephen. "Comparative Business Failures of Foreign-Controlled Firms in the United States," *Journal of International Business Studies*, vol. 22, no. 2 (Second Quarter 1991).

Lin, Xiaohua and Germain, Richard. "Sustaining Satisfactory Joint Venture Relationships: The Role of Conflict Resolution Strategy," *Journal of International Business Studies*, vol. 29, no. 1 (First Quarter 1998).

Luo, Yadong. "Joint Venture Success in China: How Should We Select a Good Partner," *Journal of World Business*, vol. 33, no. 2 (Summer 1998).

Makhija, Mona Verma. "Government Intervention in the Venezuelan Petroleum Industry: An Empirical Investigation of Political Risk," *Journal of International Business Studies*, vol. 24, no. 3 (Third Quarter 1993).

Miller, Kent D. "Industry and Country Effects on Managers' Perceptions of Environmental Uncertainties," *Journal of International Business Studies*, vol. 24, no. 4 (Fourth Quarter 1993).

Nigh, Douglas and Smith, Karen D. "The New US Joint Venture in the USSR: Assessment and Management of Political Risk," *Columbia Journal of World Business*, vol. 24, no. 2 (Summer 1989).

Ofori-Dankwa, Joseph. "Murray and Reshef Revisited: Toward a Typology/Theory of Paradigms of National Trade Union Movements," *Academy of Management Review*, vol. 18, no. 2 (April 1993).

Peng, Mike W. "Controlling the Foreign Agent: Case Studies of Government–MNE Interaction in a Transition Economy," *Management International Review*, vol. 40, no. 2 (Summer 2000).

Rajan, Mahesh N. and Graham, John L. "Nobody's Grandfather Was a Merchant: Understanding the Soviet Commercial Negotiation Process and Style," *California Management Review*, vol. 33, no. 3 (Spring 1991).

Rice, Gillian and Mahmoud, Essam. "A Managerial Procedure for Political Risk Forecasting," *Management International Review*, vol. 26, no. 4 (Fourth Quarter 1986).

Rolfe, Robert J., Ricks, David A., Pointer, Martha M. and McCarthy, Mark. "Determinants of FDI Incentive Preferences of MNEs," *Journal of International Business Studies*, vol. 24, no. 2 (Second Quarter 1993).

Rugman, Alan M. and Verbeke, Alain. "Mintzberg's Intended and Emergent Corporate Strategies and Trade Policy," *Canadian Journal of Administrative Sciences*, vol. 8, no. 3 (September 1991).

Sebenius, James K. "Negotiating Cross-Border Acquisitions," *Sloan Management Review*, vol. 39, no. 2 (Winter 1998).

Shan, Weijian. "Environmental Risks and Joint Venture Sharing Arrangements," *Journal of International Business Studies*, vol. 22, no. 4 (Fourth Quarter 1991).

Shi, Xinping. "Antecedents of International Business Negotiations in the China Context," *Management International Review*, vol. 41, no. 2 (Summer 2001).

Singer, S. Fred. "Sustainable Development vs. Global Environment: Resolving the Conflict," *Columbia Journal of World Business*, vol. 27, no. 3 (Fall/Winter 1992).

Stewart, Sally and Keown, Charles F. "Talking with the Dragon: Negotiating in the People's Republic of China," *Columbia Journal of World Business*, vol. 24, no. 3 (Fall 1989).

Tallman, Stephen B. "Home Country Political Risk and Foreign Direct Investment in the United States," *Journal of International Business Studies*, vol. 19, no. 2 (Summer 1988).

Chapter 14

International Financial Management

CONTENTS

OBJECTIVES OF THE CHAPTER

International business operations can be extremely complex. One reason is that the impact of financial decisions or developments in one locale can affect the operations or performance of subsidiaries in other locales, as well as in the MNE at large. For example, a Japanese subsidiary in the US may have a sales goal of 300 million yen based on an exchange rate of 110 yen to the dollar. However, if the yen's value declines to 125 per dollar, the subsidiary is faced with a number of financial decisions, including whether to raise or lower prices, whether to increase or decrease the amount of inventory being imported from Japan, and whether to speed up or slow down the collection of receivables from US vendors. In this chapter we will focus on some of the major financial strategies and techniques that are used to manage international operations and to protect the MNE against wide fluctuations in local currencies.

The objectives of this chapter are to:

1. *Compare* and *contrast* how polycentric, ethnocentric, and geocentric solutions are used in determining the financial planning and controlling authority that is given to subsidiaries.
2. *Study* some of the most common techniques that are used in managing global cash flows, including funds positioning and multilateral netting.
3. *Examine* foreign exchange risk strategies that are used to protect the multinational against financial losses.
4. *Explain* how capital expenditure analysis and capital budgeting are carried out.
5. *Provide* examples of international financial strategies currently being used by multinationals.

ACTIVE LEARNING CASE

British Airways' expansion plans

By the end of the 1990s there were only three dominant airlines in the US: American, Delta, and United. The others were either smaller carriers or were facing big financial problems. Throughout the 1990s, British Airways (BA) has been seeking to merge with a US airline to create a giant transatlantic alliance. In mid-1992, BA announced it was entering an arrangement with USAir (the former name of US Airways) that would have allowed passengers to travel throughout Europe and the US by relying on just one carrier: BA/USAir. The alliance would have coordinated ticket pricing, catering, advertising, and the network of flights and connections. The Big Three asked the US government to block this arrangement because it gave too much of the US market to a foreign company. After failed negotiations with the US and British governments, BA decided instead to hold a 24.6 per cent minority of the voting shares in USAir. The US restricts foreign ownership of voting shares in an airline to 25 per cent.

In 1997, BA announced it would sell its share of USAir and instead seek an alliance with American Airlines (AA). The proposed alliance would have allowed BA and AA to code share, coordinate routes and schedules and integrate frequent flyer programs. Rival US airlines denounced the move, claiming it would reduce competition and allow the alliance a large share of the transatlantic traffic. To allow the merger to continue, EU antitrust authorities demanded the alliance give up 267 weekly slots in London's Heathrow, or 10 per cent of their total. BA/AA refused to do this, claiming it would hamper their competitiveness. The two airlines' cooperative efforts were thus reduced to their mutual participation in the Oneworld international alliance.

Four years after their initial proposal, BA/AA once again tried to win antitrust immunity. In 2001 the two airlines approached regulators, claiming that a new set of factors had emerged to support their case. These factors included: the continued expansion of Open Skies agreements between the US and many European nations that had increased competition; the emergence of international alliances that provide global networks; the relative decrease in Heathrow's European dominance as airports in Frankfurt, Amsterdam, and Paris increased traffic; and the development of similar alliances among competitors.

US competitors, Delta, Continental, and Northwest, once again asked the US Department of Transportation to hold a judicial hearing, arguing that most of the concerns were the same as in 1996 and that the case must be evaluated by an independent arbiter. Ironically, two of the three companies opposing the deal have similar deals of their own with other European carriers. The Delta–Air France and KLM–Northwest alliances are very similar to what BA/AA are proposing. Why then all the fuss over another alliance? BA is the largest European airline with $13.7 billion in revenue in 2000 and serves 230 destinations in 94 countries. AA is the second largest airline in the US with $19.7 billion in revenues in 2000 and serves 242 destinations in 52 countries. The alliance would create a dominant company with control over transatlantic flights. BA and AA each have 263 and 273 US–Europe flights respectively and, between them, they control 38 per cent of Heathrow's slots.

In Europe, the UK's Office of Fair Trading and the European Commission's competition directorate are examining the proposal. The loudest opposition by a competitor comes from Britain's Virgin Atlantic. News of the new proposal resurrected Virgin's No Way BA/AA campaign. Virgin contends that BA/AA would hold 60 per cent of all Heathrow–US service and fly 50 per cent of all passengers traveling between the US and the UK. Together, BA/AA fly 9 million passengers between the UK and the US; the next biggest carrier flies 3.5 million. Virgin claims that this dominance would effectively eliminate smaller airlines from the transatlantic market.

At the center of the proposal is BA's access to US market and US carriers' access to London's Heathrow. Presently, BA flies to 25 American airports but it cannot pick up passengers in one US city to fly them to another US city. If the deal with AA goes through, BA/AA would have total access to US and EU markets. US carriers have the opposite problem. Only two US airlines, American and United, have access to Heathrow airport. For years the US and British governments have been negotiating an "Open Skies" agreement without much progress. The proposed alliance has added momentum to Open Skies. The British government has indicated that it would be willing to negotiate an Open Skies agreement if the BA/AA is granted antitrust immunity.

Though some competitors welcome deregulation of the US and UK market, they criticize the use of Open Skies as a bargaining chip for the proposed BA/AA deal. They contend that Open Skies would be irrelevant if the BA/AA agreement gives one company a virtual monopoly in the US–UK market and that competition would be better served by preventing the merger.

In 2002, the US government approved the merger of British Airways and American Airlines on condition that the merged company surrender over 200 slots in Heathrow Airport. Both airlines announced that they would not merge due to the excessive strategic cost imposed by regulators.

Websites: ***www.aa.com***; ***www.british-airways.com***; ***www.usairways.com***; ***www.oneworldalliance.com***; ***www.delta.com***; ***www.nwa.com***; ***www.airfrance.com***; ***www.continental.com*** and ***www.klm.com***.

Sources: Adapted from Paula Dwyer et al., "Air Raid: British Air's Bold Global Push," *Business Week*, August 24, 1992; Agis Salpukas, "The Big Foreign Push to Buy into US Airlines," *New York Times*, October 11, 1992; Adam Bryant, "British Air Halts Move into USAir," *New York Times*, March 8, 1994; "Predators in the Air," *Economist*, June 8, 2000; Peter Spiegel, "US Rivals Call for Hearing on Deal by BA and American," *Financial Times*, November 20, 2001; "Branson Slams BA/AA Alliance," Virgin Atlantic News Release, November 12, 2001; "Let Fly," *Economist*, March 8, 2001.

1. **Is the BA/AA alliance going to use a polycentric, ethnocentric, or geocentric solution to handling operations?**
2. **If the two carriers complete their merger and the US dollar then weakens against the British pound, how will this affect the financial statements of the company?**
3. **If BA believed that the British pound was going to appreciate in relation to the German mark, how could the company use a lead and lag strategy to its advantage?**
4. **How great is the political risk that BA faces in the US? Explain.**

INTRODUCTION

International financial management encompasses a number of key areas. These include the management of global cash flows, foreign exchange risk management, and capital expenditure analysis and capital budgeting. Decisions in each of these areas can significantly impact the others. For example, if the exchange rate of the Mexican peso sharply declines against the dollar, the multinational may decide to transfer more dollars to its Mexican subsidiary so that the unit can continue paying for imports from the US. At the same time the MNE may decide not to allow the subsidiary to renovate the administrative offices because the unit's profitability (in dollars) is going to be below expectations. The manager of the Mexican unit cannot be blamed for the declining peso, but this development has resulted in the parent company making decisions that affect local operations.

The objective of international financial management strategies is to provide assistance to all geographic operations and to limit financial losses through the use of carefully formulated cash flow guidelines, the timely execution of foreign exchange risk management strategies, prudent capital expenditures, and careful capital budgeting. The responsibility for these activities is spread throughout the organization, and some of these decisions are made on a day-to-day basis, whereas others are determined only periodically. Additionally, some of these decisions are made by the parent company, whereas others fall within the purview of the subsidiary. In an effort to ensure that each group understands its limits of financial authority, it is common to find financial management planning beginning with a determination of parent–subsidiary relationships.

DETERMINING PARENT–SUBSIDIARY RELATIONSHIPS

Because finance is such an important area of operations, it is critically important that parent companies firmly establish the relationships that will exist regarding financial planning and control authority. On the one hand, each branch or subsidiary should be responsible for its own planning and control system. On the other hand, there must be some central control in order to coordinate overall operations and to ensure both efficiency and profitability. In addressing this challenge, MNEs tend to opt for one of three solutions: polycentric, ethnocentric, or geocentric.

Polycentric solution

Polycentric solution
An approach to determining parent–subsidiary relations; it involves treating the MNE as a holding company and decentralizing decision making to the subsidiary levels

A **polycentric solution** is to treat the MNE as a holding company and to decentralize decision making to the subsidiary levels. In this arrangement financial statements are prepared according to generally accepted accounting principles in both the overseas subsidiary's and the parent's home country, and the subsidiary's performance is evaluated against that of similar domestic and foreign concerns.

The advantages of the polycentric approach are those commonly obtained with decentralization. Decisions are made on the spot by those most informed about market conditions, and international subsidiaries tend to be more flexible, motivated, efficient, and competitive. On the other hand, this solution reduces the authority of the home office, and senior corporate management often dislike this dilution of their authority. Additionally, an MNE may find that a polycentric approach results in competition between different international subsidiaries and lowers overall profits for the company.

Ethnocentric solution

Ethnocentric solution
An approach to determining parent–subsidiary relations; it involves treating all foreign operations as if they were extensions of domestic operations

The **ethnocentric solution** is to treat all foreign operations as if they were extensions of domestic operations. In this case each unit is integrated into the planning and control system of the parent company.

The advantage of this system is that management is able to coordinate overall operations carefully. This usually results in centralization of the finance function so that cash not needed for day-to-day operations can be invested in marketable securities or transferred to other subsidiaries or branches that need working capital. The primary drawback of this solution is that it can cause problems for the individual subsidiary, which may feel that it needs more cash than is left on hand or that it is hindered in its efforts to expand because the parent company is siphoning off necessary resources.

Geocentric solution

Geocentric solution
An approach to determining parent–subsidiary relations; it involves handling financial planning and controlling decisions on a global basis

The **geocentric solution** is to handle financial planning and controlling decisions on a global basis. These decisions are typically influenced by two factors. One is the nature and location of the subsidiary. For example, British investment in North America has predominantly been via holding companies, the polycentric approach, since the quality of local management largely rewards decentralization. Conversely, investment in developing countries has typically been centralized, with the parent company maintaining close control of financial expenditures. A second influencing factor is the gains that can be achieved by coordinating all units in a carefully synchronized way. When an MNE's overseas units face a myriad of tax rates, financial systems, and competitive environments, it is often more efficient to centralize most of the financial control decisions because this is the best way to ensure that profit and efficiency are maximized. For example, if there are two subsidiaries which are equally able to sell a particular product to a major customer, with centralized financial planning the parent company could ensure that the sale would be made by the unit located in the country with the lowest corporate income tax rate. Additional examples of the ways in which financial operations could be directed by using a geocentric solution are seen in the management of global cash flows.

Active learning check

Review your answer to Active Learning Case question 1 and make any changes you like. Then compare your answer with the one below.

1. Is the BA/AA alliance going to use a polycentric, ethnocentric, or geocentric solution to handling operations?

The alliance is going to use a geocentric solution to handling operations. This is clear from the way in which the two air carriers are beginning to merge their operations so that they are both working in harmony. An alliance of equals, BA/AA can capitalize on their individual regional/triad strengths.

MANAGING GLOBAL CASH FLOWS

One of the key areas of international financial management is the careful handling of global cash flows. There are a number of ways in which this is done. Three of the most important ones include the prudent use of internal funds flows, the use of funds positioning, and the use of multilateral netting. The following sections examine each of these three.

Internal funds flows

Working capital The difference between current assets and current liabilities

When an MNE wants to expand operations or fund activities, one of the simplest ways of obtaining the needed monies is by getting them from internal sources such as **working capital**, which is the difference between current assets and current liabilities. For example, if General Motors' German subsidiary wants to hire more employees, it may be able to pay for this payroll increase out of the funds it generates from ongoing operations. Another way of raising money internally is by borrowing from a local bank or from the parent company. For example, an MNE's Chilean subsidiary will get a loan from the parent company or the German subsidiary and then repay the money with interest out of operations. A third way is by having the parent company increase its equity capital investment in the subsidiary. In turn the subsidiary could pay the parent dividends on the investment. These examples are illustrated in Figure 14.1 and help to show that there are many ways for multinational firms to generate internal cash for operations.

Which method is most likely to be used? The answer will depend on a number of factors, including government regulations regarding intercompany lending. For example, when tax rates are high for a profitable subsidiary, it is common to find those units willing to lend money at low rates of interest to other subsidiaries in the MNE that need

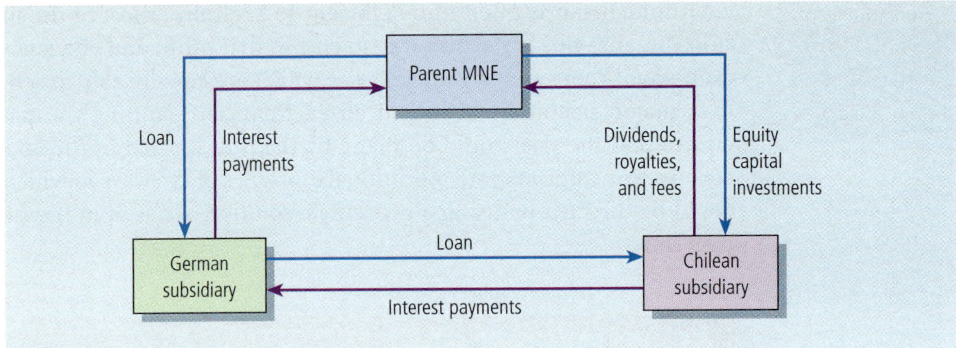

Figure 14.1 **Common example of internal sources and flows of funds**

funds to expand into growth markets. The logic behind this strategy is quite simple: the highly profitable unit does not need to charge a high interest rate because much of this interest will be taxed away by the government. Conversely, the subsidiary that is borrowing the money needs low interest rates so as to conserve its cash for expansion purposes. By shifting the money around in this fashion, the MNE is able to support expansion efforts, to minimize taxes, and to increase the sales potential of the subsidiaries. In an effort to prevent multinationals from taking advantage of such tax loopholes, in recent years some governments have changed their tax laws and established a minimum rate that can be charged on these intercompany loans.

Another area of concern is government limits on a parent company's ability to charge subsidiaries a licensing or royalty fee for the use of technology or to assess a management fee that covers the subsidiary's fair share of corporate overhead. When there are no government restrictions in these areas, the MNE has greater freedom in drawing funds from subsidiary operations, thus providing the parent with a pool of money that can be used for other worldwide operations. The ways in which this is done are commonly referred to as funds positioning techniques.

Funds positioning techniques

Funds positioning techniques
Strategies used to move monies from one multinational operation to another

Funds positioning techniques are strategies that are used to move monies from one multinational operation to another. While there are a variety of approaches, three of the most common are transfer pricing, tax havens, and fronting loans.

Transfer pricing

Transfer price
An internal price set by a company in intrafirm trade, such as the price at which one subsidiary will sell a product to another subsidiary

A **transfer price** is an internal price that is set by a company in intra-firm trade such as the price at which the Chilean subsidiary will purchase electric motors from the German subsidiary. An initial conclusion would be that the German firm will sell the motors at the same price as it would to any outside purchaser. A second conclusion is that the Chilean subsidiary will receive a discount because it is an intra-firm transaction and the parent will not allow its subsidiaries to profit at the expense of each other. However, both of these conclusions are incorrect when a transfer pricing strategy is employed. The final price will be determined by local regulations and will be set at a level that allows the MNE to achieve certain desired goals such as to increase profit, to reduce costs, and/or to move money among the subsidiaries.

Table 14.1 **Shifting profits by transfer pricing**

	Arm's length price		*Transfer price*	
	Country A	*Country B*	*Country A*	*Country B*
Sales	$10,000 exports	$12,000	$12,000 exports	$12,000
Costs of sales	8,000	10,000	8,000	12,000
Profit	2,000	2,000	4,000	Nil
Tax rate (A: 40%, B: 50%)	800	1,000	1,600	Nil
Net profit	1,200	1,000	2,400	Nil

Arm's length price
The price a buyer will pay for merchandise in a market under conditions of perfect competition

A good example is provided by a multinational that has a subsidiary located in Country A, which has a low corporate income tax and is selling goods to a subsidiary located in Country B, which has a high corporate income tax. If the transfer price is set carefully, it is possible to reallocate taxable income away from the highly taxed subsidiary to the subsidiary with the low tax rate. Table 14.1 provides an example by contrasting arm's length pricing with transfer pricing. An **arm's length price** is the price a buyer will pay for merchandise in a market under conditions of perfect competition. As seen in the table, it cost the subsidiary in Country A $8,000 for the goods it is selling to the subsidiary in Country B. Under an arm's length price the seller is adding $2,000 for profit and selling the goods for $10,000. In turn the second subsidiary is selling these goods for $12,000. Thus both subsidiaries are making a profit of $2,000. As also seen in the table, the tax rate in Country A is 40 per cent, whereas in Country B it is 50 per cent. So the first subsidiary will have a net profit of $1,200, whereas the second subsidiary will net $1,000.

Under a transfer price arrangement, however, the objective is to maximize profits in the low tax rate country and to minimize them in the high tax rate country. In this case, as seen in Table 14.1, the first subsidiary sells the goods for $12,000, and after paying 40 per cent tax on the $4,000 profit, it ends up with a net profit of $2,400. The second subsidiary sells the goods for $12,000 and makes no profit. However, thanks to the transfer pricing strategy, the multinational's overall profit is greater than it was with arm's length pricing ($2,400 versus $2,200).

One of the obvious benefits of transfer pricing is that it allows the multinational to reduce taxes. A second benefit is that the strategy lets the firm concentrate cash in specific locales such as with the first subsidiary. One of the problems with transfer pricing is that the financial statements do not accurately reflect subsidiary performance because the profit margins are manipulated. A second problem is that the strategy does not encourage efficient performance by the seller, whose primary objective is to unload merchandise on the other subsidiary at a profit as high as can be justified.

In recent years countries have been rewriting their tax codes to prevent arbitrary transfer pricing. In the US, for example, the Internal Revenue Service (IRS) now asks multinationals to apply for an advanced determination ruling (ADR) before establishing a transfer pricing policy. After the firm submits the ADR request, the IRS will determine whether or not the policy is appropriate. The objective of the tax agency is to ensure that MNEs charge their overseas subsidiaries the same price for components and products as they charge independent third parties, thus effectively eliminating price manipulation for tax purposes.[1]

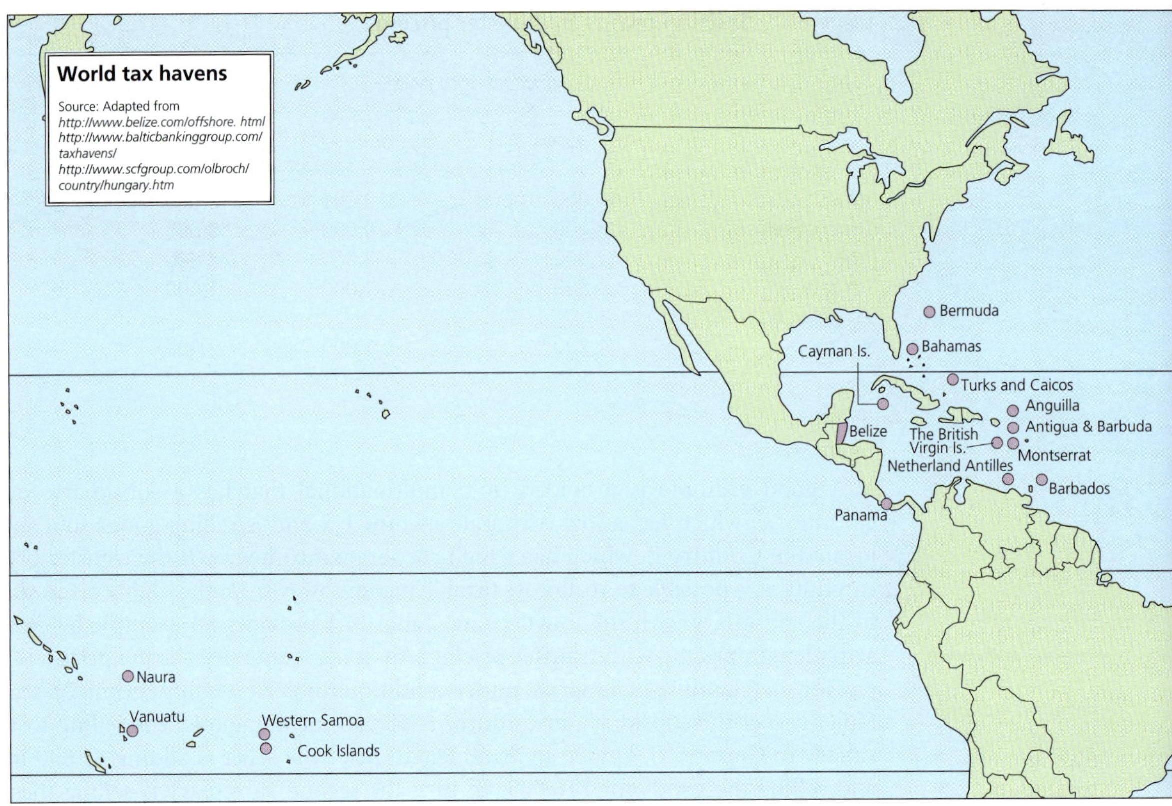

Tax havens

Tax havens
Low-tax countries that are hospitable to business

A second funds positioning technique is the use of **tax havens**, which are low-tax countries that are hospitable to business (see accompanying map). This strategy is typically used in conjunction with transfer pricing and involves a subsidiary selling its output at a very low cost to a subsidiary in a tax haven which in turn sells the merchandise at a very high price to a third subsidiary.[2] Table 14.2 provides an example, which is similar to that in Table 14.1, except that the sales are now routed through a subsidiary located in a tax haven, Country B, where no tax is paid at all. The result of the example in the table is a net profit of $4,000. This is greater than that illustrated in Table 14.1, where a simple case of transfer pricing was employed. For more on the matter of tax havens, see the box "International Business Strategy in Action: Tax havens."

Table 14.2 Transfer pricing through tax havens

	Country A subsidiary	*Country B subsidiary (tax haven)*	*Country C subsidiary*
Sales	$8,000 exports →	$12,000 exports →	$12,000
Costs of sales	8,000	→ 8,000	→ 12,000
Profit	—	—	—
Tax rate (A: 40%, B: 0%, C: 50%)	—	—	—
Net profit	0	4,000	0

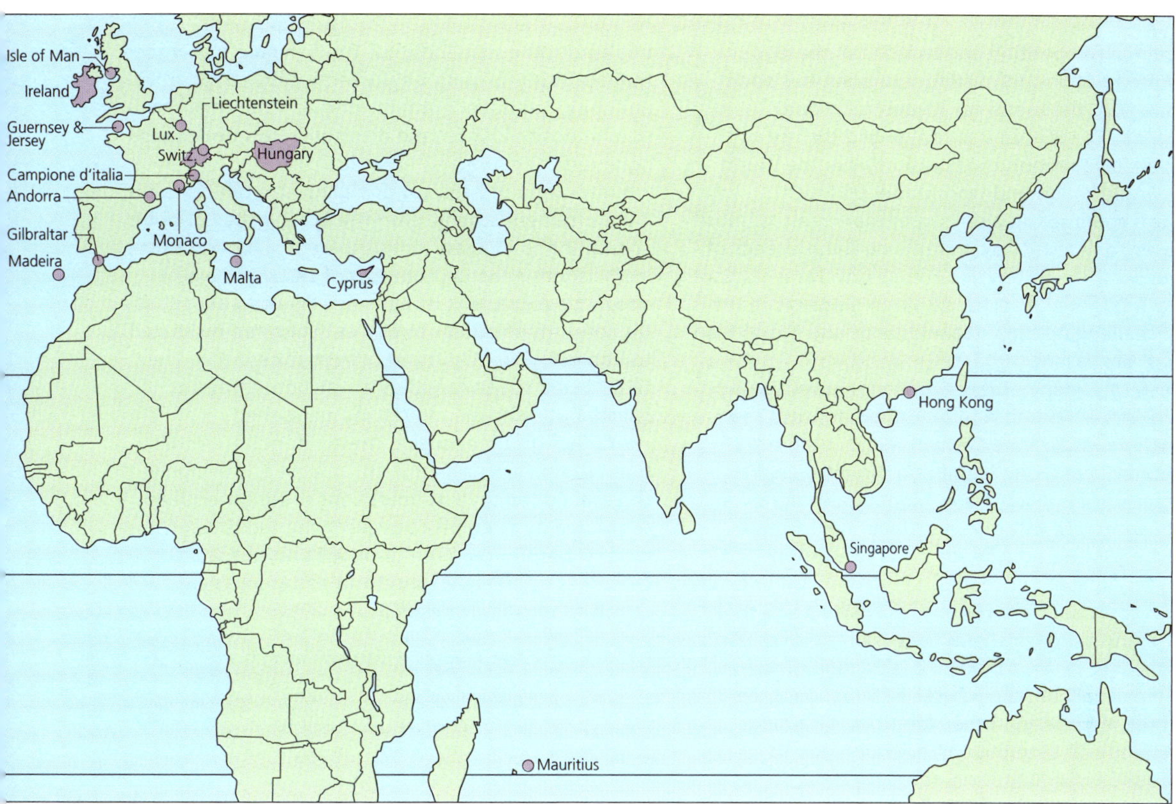

INTERNATIONAL BUSINESS STRATEGY *IN ACTION*

Tax havens

What do Switzerland, the Bahamas, Monaco and Andorra have in common? By some definition, they are all considered to be tax havens. In general, a tax haven is a country or a jurisdiction that allows individuals or corporations to set up a subsidiary and to avoid paying taxes in their country of residence, thus depriving their home governments of some tax revenues that are used to provide government services.

One of the underlying problems that led to the creation of tax havens in the first place is that there is no single international tax standard. Individual governments have different tax policies, so MNEs have an incentive to deploy their overall financial assets around their worldwide network of subsidiaries in order to minimize taxation. It would not be possible for MNEs to do this if there were a common unitary world tax system. The MNEs are reacting to the lack of a global standard in government tax policy, yet governments are blaming them for using perfectly legal tax havens.

Each tax haven jurisdiction has its own sets of laws on taxation and transparency. Tax havens are also sometimes accused by NGOs like Oxfam as being a means for money laundering and of hiding the proceeds of criminal activity, including political corruption, illicit arms dealing, and drug trafficking. In fact, there is little evidence of the latter activity, other than in movies and pop literature.

The OECD lists a number of factors used to identify a tax haven. Among these, a tax haven is a country or jurisdiction that (i) imposes no or nominal taxes and is used by foreigners to escape taxes in their own countries (this includes "ring fencing" jurisdictions that reserve preferential treatment to foreigners, thus shielding itself from tax avoidance by its own residents); (ii) has laws or administrative practices which prevent the exchange of information with other governments on taxpayers benefiting from low taxation; (iii) lacks transparency; (iv) does not require substantial productive operations in the country, suggesting policies geared to attracting income only on a preferential tax basis. Of all these factors, only the first one is necessary for the identification of a tax haven.

In recent years, the OECD has been pressuring countries and jurisdictions to reverse what it calls harmful tax competition and lack of transparency. The United Nations, for different reasons, has been trying to curb the use of tax havens for money laundering. The EU has also challenged the use of unfair tax competition by US exporters in the World Trade Organization and won. Under US law, US exporters could set up a sales operation in an offshore tax haven, and avoid paying taxes on the proceeds of this business. The British and French governments have also each targeted its own tax haven jurisdiction, the British challenging the Channel Islands and Isle of Man offshore tax havens.

Reluctantly, many of these countries have reacted to OECD pressures and reformed their policies. The Channel Islands and the Cayman Islands both have anti-money laundering legislation. Under pressure from the French government, Monaco also signed an agreement to prevent money laundering, increase transparency, and remove some tax concessions.

Yet, the total eradication of tax havens will not come without confrontation. For one, tax havens and their financial institutions depend heavily on these deposits. The Bahamas, which considers itself a major international financial hub, can foresee a tremendous loss of income, especially if other countries, including Switzerland and Luxembourg, are not ready to implement the same policies. The Bahamas has argued that the OECD is using a two-tier system, cooperatively designing legislation with its member countries and then imposing this regime on smaller, less developed, non-member countries.

Switzerland, for its part, is willing to work out a tax reimbursement scheme with the EU and the US, but is not willing to increase its transparency. Though this might address the tax concerns of OECD nations, it does little to prevent criminal activity or to address the tax concerns of poorer countries, which are estimated to lose over $50 billion a year from tax evasion. The OECD listed the Bahamas as an uncooperative tax haven, but Switzerland was not mentioned.

Another group opposing these reforms are MNEs that use tax havens. In Britain, at least one company threatened to move its operations if the government continued its attempts to prevent the use of tax havens. Despite this type of opposition, the OECD continues to pressure for reform and expects all countries to comply by 2005.

Websites: **www.oecd.org** and **www.oxfam.org**.

Sources: OECD, *Harmful Tax Competition*, 1998; "Offshore Financial Centers Hit at OECD Tax Competition," *Financial Times*, November 21, 2001; Oxfam, *Oxfam Policy Papers – Tax Havens*, June, 2000.

Fronting loans

Fronting loan
A funds positioning strategy that involves having a third party manage the loan

A **fronting loan** is a funds positioning strategy that involves having a third party manage the loan. For example, if a US multinational decided to set up operations in China, the MNE might be concerned with the political risk that accompanies such a decision. Is it possible that the government might expropriate the subsidiary's assets, including all the cash on hand? In an effort to protect their investments, the parent company could deposit funds with a major international bank that has strong ties to China and is on good terms with the government. In turn the subsidiary would apply for a loan with this bank and the multinational company's deposit would be given to the subsidiary in the form of a loan. It is highly unlikely that the Chinese government would expropriate the subsidiary and endanger the loan or its relationship with the international bank. Thus the MNE has successfully positioned its funds.

Funds positioning strategies are important in moving money around a multinational, as well as in helping the MNE to cope with political and legal roadblocks that stand in the way of such action. However, an internally operated netting process that controls the flow of funds and ensures that bills are paid promptly always complements these strategies. This process is often collectively referred to as multilateral netting.

Multilateral netting

When subsidiaries do business with each other, each may owe money to the others and in turn be owed money by them. Figure 14.2 provides an example of four subsidiaries that have both amounts due and amounts payable from each of the others. Over time, of course, these obligations will be resolved by the individual subsidiaries. In an effort to make the process more efficient, however, many multinationals have now set up clearing

Table 14.3 **Net cash positions of subsidiaries**

Subsidiary	*Total receivables*	*Total payables*	*Net positions*
German	$300,000	$225,000	$75,000
Chilean	125,000	150,000	–25,000
Japanese	200,000	275,000	–75,000
Mexican	225,000	200,000	25,000

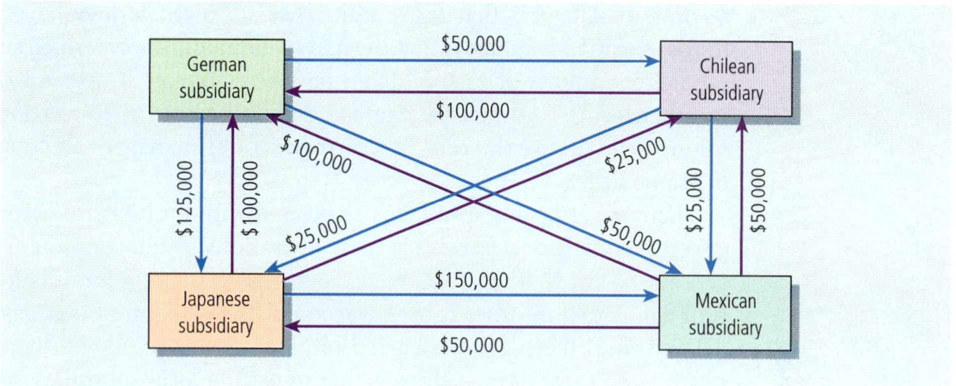

Figure 14.2 **Multilateral dollar flows between subsidiaries**

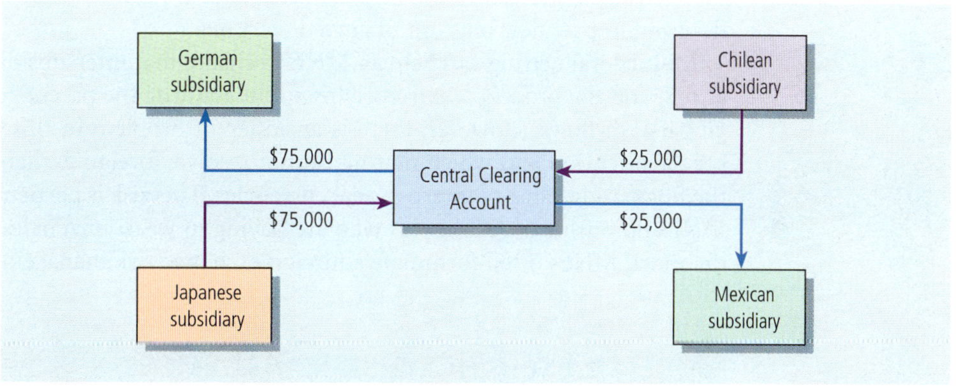

Figure 14.3 **Centralized netting process in action**

Multilateral netting
The process of determining the net amount of money owed to subsidiaries through multilateral transactions

accounts in a certain location and assigned the manager at this location the authority to make the transfers that are necessary to pay intra-company subsidiary obligations. This process of **multilateral netting**, which involves a determination of the net amount of money owed to subsidiaries through multilateral transactions, begins with a computation of the amounts owed to each. Table 14.3, which has been constructed based on the information in Figure 14.2, shows these net positions. Based on this information, those that owe money are required to transfer it to a centralized clearing account (see Figure 14.3), whereas those that are owed money are paid from this central account.

The clearing account manager is responsible for seeing that this process occurs quickly and correctly. Typically, this individual will receive monthly transaction information from all the subsidiaries and will use these data to determine the net position of each unit. The manager will then see that the necessary transfers are made. These transfers usually take place in the currency of the payer, so the German subsidiary will pay its obligation in DMs, whereas the Mexican subsidiary will pay in pesos. The clearing account manager's staff will handle the process.

There are a number of reasons that multilateral netting has become popular. One advantage is that it helps the parent company to ensure that financial interactions between the units are quickly brought to completion. If bills are allowed to be outstanding for months at a time, it can result in the other units not wanting to do business with slow-paying subsidiaries. Netting helps to reduce the likelihood of such problems. A second advantage is that those units that are owed money have faster access to their funds. A third advantage is that the parent company knows which subsidiaries are amassing large amounts of cash and can tap these sources if necessary to support activities in other locales. A fourth advantage is that the cost of converting foreign exchange is minimized because the central clearing account manager can convert large amounts at the same time.

There are also some problems associated with multilateral netting. One is that many governments place controls on these operations by allowing them only for trade transactions. So the MNE's ability to use netting for moving funds can be limited. A second problem is that in other cases governments have required that payment for imports be delayed until these goods clear customs, thus slowing down the netting process by as much as 60 to 90 days. A third is that of getting local subsidiary managers to cooperate and keep the central clearing account manager fully apprised of all transactions affecting this process. Sometimes there is a reluctance to cooperate on the part of those managers whose cash outflows are substantially larger than their inflows. Under a netting process they can no longer delay payments for three or four months while working to reverse the flow and to pay their bills out of current earnings.

Multilateral netting can help an MNE to ensure that intersubsidiary accounts are balanced, and the process is extremely useful in assisting the parent company in managing global cash flows. However, there is an inherent problem in this process that requires special attention and which netting cannot resolve: foreign exchange risk as typified by the fluctuating value of international currencies. This risk is particularly important when MNEs do business with buyers who are paying in weak currencies. In dealing with this dilemma, MNEs often formulate a foreign exchange risk management strategy.

FOREIGN EXCHANGE RISK MANAGEMENT

There are a number of ways that multinationals try to manage their foreign exchange risk. For example, if the company believes that Mexico is going to devalue the peso, it will reduce the amount of those pesos being held by the central clearing account by using them to pay bills. Conversely, if the peso is forecast to gain in strength against the dollar, the MNE will hold on to those pesos but will reduce its holdings of dollars. This is only one simple example, but it illustrates that foreign exchange risk strategies are important to effective multinational financial management.

A number of areas merit attention when examining foreign exchange risk management. One is inflation and its impact on the value of foreign exchange. A second is the types of exposure that exchange rates create. A third is hedging strategies that can be used to minimize risk. A fourth is the types of forecasting and reporting systems that must be developed in order to plan and control company response. The following sections examine each of these four areas.

Inflation

Every nation faces varying degrees of annual inflation. On the positive side, inflation can make financial liabilities attractive. For example, if General Electric (GE) were to buy an office building in Monterrey, Mexico, for 3 million pesos and the bill is due in three annual installments, inflation can influence the overall value of the deal. Among other things, if inflation were to run at 10 per cent annually, the building would be worth a great deal more than 3 million pesos at the end of this three-year period. So inflation encourages buyers to purchase now while prices are lower. On the other hand, inflation affects interest rates (see the international Fisher effect discussed in Chapter 7) by driving up the cost of loans. Inflation also affects the value of local currency in the international marketplace. So there is a downside to inflation. See the box "International Business Strategy in Action: Buying a Big Mac".

INTERNATIONAL BUSINESS STRATEGY *IN ACTION*

Buying a Big Mac

One of the most interesting ways of determining whether a subsidiary's value is affected by inflation is to compare the value of the local currency and that in the home country. For example, as the Swiss franc strengthens against the dollar, US multinationals with operations in Switzerland will benefit from the profits generated from a greatly enhanced dollar value of that unit.

Another interesting way of gauging these values is to examine the purchasing power parity (PPP) of the overseas currency and the US dollar by comparing the cost of food in the two countries. Some international analysts also point out that this is a good way of determining whether a currency is undervalued or overvalued. For example, if a Big Mac costs $2.54 in the US and 294 yen in Japan, the official exchange rate should be 116 yen to the dollar (294/2.54), assuming that the Big Mac is an accurate form of PPP comparison. If the official exchange is less than 116 to the dollar, then the dollar is undervalued. Conversely, if the exchange rate is more than 116 to the dollar, the US currency is overvalued. This same logic can be applied throughout the world, thus obtaining some insights into how closely the purchasing power of the dollar comes to the actual exchange rate. The table below provides some recent information on this subject.

The Hamburger Standard

	Big Mac prices				
Country	*In local currency*	*in dollars*	*Implied PPP* of the dollar*	*Actual $ exchange rate 17/04/01*	*Under (–)/over (+) valuation against the dollar, %*
United States†	$2.54	2.54	—	—	—
Argentina	Peso 2.50	2.50	0.98	1.00	–2
Australia	A $ 3.00	1.52	1.18	1.98	–40
Brazil	Real 3.60	1.64	1.42	2.19	–35
Britain	Pound 1.99	2.85	1.28‡	1.43‡	+12
Canada	C $ 3.33	2.14	1.31	1.56	–16
Chile	Peso 1260	2.10	496	601	–17
China	Yuan 9.90	1.20	3.90	8.28	–53
Czech Rep	Koruna 56.00	1.43	22.0	39.0	–44
Denmark	DKr 24.75	2.93	9.74	8.46	+15
Euro area	Euro 2.57	2.27	0.99§	0.88§	–11
France	FFr 18.50	2.49	7.28	7.44	–2
Germany	DM 5.10	2.30	2.01	2.22	–9

(cont'd)

Country	Big Mac prices in local currency	Big Mac prices in dollars	Implied PPP* of the dollar	Actual $ exchange rate 17/04/01	Under (–)/over (+) valuation against the dollar, %
Italy	Lire 4,300	1.96	1,693	2,195	–23
Spain	Pta 395	2.09	156	189	–18
Hong Kong	HK $ 10.70	1.37	4.21	7.80	–46
Hungary	Forint 399	1.32	157	303	–48
Indonesia	Rupiah 14,700	1.35	5,787	10,855	–47
Japan	Yen 294	2.38	116	124	–6
Malaysia	M $ 4.52	1.19	1.78	3.80	–53
Mexico	Peso 21.9	2.36	8.62	9.29	–7
New Zealand	NZ $ 3.60	1.46	1.42	2.47	–43
Poland	Zloty 5.90	1.46	2.32	4.03	–42
Russia	Ruble 35	1.21	13.8	28.9	–52
Singapore	S $ 3.30	1.82	1.30	1.81	–28
South Africa	Rand 9.70	1.19	3.82	8.13	–53
South Korea	Won 3,000	2.27	1,181	1,325	–11
Sweden	SKr 24.0	2.33	9.45	10.28	–8
Switzerland	SFr 6.30	3.65	2.48	1.73	+44
Taiwan	NT $ 70.0	2.13	27.6	32.9	–16
Thailand	Baht 55.0	1.21	21.7	45.5	–52

Source: Adapted from *The Economist*, 3.4.99.
* Purchasing power parity: local price divided by price in US.
† Average of New York, Chicago, San Francisco, and Atlanta.
‡ Dollars per pound.
§ Dollars per euro.

As seen from the table, the dollar is undervalued in Britain, Denmark, and Switzerland. From the viewpoint of global macroeconomic stability the US would want these countries to revalue their currency, although this would negatively affect the ability of US firms to sell abroad. On the other hand, most other currencies are undervalued against the dollar mainly as a result of the US boom of 1998–2000. The most undervalued currencies are found in China, Malaysia, the Philippines, and South Africa. This makes products from these countries cheaper in the international markets. Additionally, there are a number of reasons that PPP prices are higher or lower than expected, including local taxes, transportation costs, property costs, and, as in the case of Germany and Japan, typically high retail markups. However, the Big Mac example does provide some interesting insights regarding the purchasing power of the local currency.

Source: Adapted from "Big MacCurrencies," *Economist*, April 18, 1992, p. 81; "Big MacCurrencies," *Economist*, April 17, 1993, p. 79; "Big MacCurrencies," *Economist*, April 11, 1998; Kevin Kelly, Neil Gross and James B. Treece, "Besting Japan," *Business Week*, June 7, 1993, pp. 26–28; "Currency Markets," *New York Times*, December 28, 1993; "Big MacCurrencies," *Economist*, April 3, 1999, p. 90; "Ten Years of the Big Mac Index," *Economist*, April 19, 2001.

When MNEs do business in a country that is facing rapid inflation, there are a number of financial strategies that they often use. These include (1) rapid depreciation of fixed equipment so as to recover the value of these assets as quickly as possible; (2) slower payment of outstanding accounts to sellers who are taking payment in local currency – since the value of this currency is declining and the longer payment is postponed, the better it is for the subsidiary; (3) greater emphasis on collecting current receivables since this currency is losing value each month; (4) holding minimum amounts of local currency while transferring the rest of these funds into more stable or appreciating currencies; and (5) looking for other sources of capital since local borrowers are going to be increasing the interest rate in order to protect their real return on investment. Multinationals will also consider raising their prices so as to protect their profitability in the face of inflation.

Addressing exchange rate fluctuations

Multinationals will also want to reduce their exposure to exchange rate fluctuations. The most common forms of exposure are translation, transaction, and economic.

Translation exposure

Translation
The process of restating foreign financial statements in the currency of the parent company

Consolidation
The combining of the major financial statements of subsidiaries into composite statements for the parent firm

Translation exposure
The foreign exchange risk that a firm faces when translating foreign currency financial statements into the reporting currency of the parent company

Translation is the process of restating foreign financial statements in the currency of the parent company. For example, PepsiCo will translate the balance sheets and income statements of its subsidiaries into dollars. In this way management and the stockholders can see how each unit is doing. The company will also combine the major financial statements of subsidiaries into composite statements for the parent firm through a process known as **consolidation**. The procedures that US firms follow in this process are found in Financial Accounting Standards Board (FASB) Statement No. 52, which deals with foreign currency translation. Statement 52 requires that sales be recorded at the spot exchange rate that is in effect on the date of the transaction. Receivables and payables are recorded at subsequent balance sheet dates at the spot exchange rate on those dates. Any foreign exchange gains and losses that arise from these transactions are then reflected directly on the income statement.

Translation exposure is the foreign exchange risk that a firm faces when translating foreign currency financial statements into the reporting currency of the parent company. A good example of this exposure for a US MNE is when the currency of a local country weakens in relation to the dollar. For example, if the Chilean peso declined by 10 per cent against the dollar, the value of the Chilean subsidiary's peso account at the local bank would also decline when translated into dollars in the consolidation process. If the company had the equivalent of $100,000 (US) on deposit, this account would now be worth $90,000 in translation and consolidation. Of course, this decline would not affect the number of pesos on deposit, and the local purchasing power of these pesos, at least in the short run, would remain the same. However, the decline would negatively affect the subsidiary's ability to purchase imports from countries with strong currencies since it would now take more pesos than before to buy these goods.

Transaction exposure

Transaction exposure
The risk that a firm faces when paying bills or collecting receivables in the face of changing exchange rates

Transaction exposure is the risk that a firm faces when paying bills or collecting receivables in the face of changing exchange rates. For example, if a US retailer were to purchase 10,000 shirts from a Mexican manufacturer for $90,000 and agree to pay the bill in 90 days in pesos (assuming a current exchange rate of 10 pesos to the dollar), the transaction exposure would be the risk that the peso would strengthen against the dollar. If the US firm were to pay the bill immediately, it would remit 900,000 pesos to the manufacturer. If it waits until the end of 90 days and the exchange rate is now 8.9 pesos to the dollar, the company would still pay 900,000 pesos but the cost in dollars is $101,235.90 (900,000/8.9), higher than it was initially. On the other hand, if a US manufacturer had sold goods to a Mexican firm and payment was due in pesos, the increasing value of the peso would result in a gain to the US company. For example, if the multinational had sold household appliances valued at 7 million pesos, the original sale would have generated $700,000 (7,000,000/10), but by the time the Mexican firm remitted the pesos, the company would have received $786,516.85 (7,000,000/8.9) for an additional gain of $86,516.85. So in international sales and purchases there is transaction exposure on the part of both the buyer and the seller.

Economic exposure

Economic exposure
The foreign exchange risk involved in pricing products, sourcing parts, or locating investments to develop a competitive position

Economic exposure is the foreign exchange risk involved in pricing products, sourcing parts, or locating investments in order to develop a competitive position. Economic exposure covers a wide gamut of risk. In the case of pricing products, when the currency of a foreign buyer changes in relation to that of the seller, the latter will have to decide how to deal with the accompanying risk. For example, if the Japanese yen strengthens against the dollar, should a US firm that is selling to a Japanese supplier lower its price? If all sales are in yen, the US firm will gain more dollars by leaving the price alone. On the other hand, if the US company lowers the price, may that stimulate more demand from the buyer? Conversely, if the yen weakens against the dollar, should the US seller hold the price line or raise it to ensure dollar sales and profit margins? The fluctuating yen/dollar relationship creates a risk for the US firm.

A related decision deals with subsidiary assets. If the value of the local currency strengthens, the sale of inventory will generate larger dollar profits. However, would it be wiser to lower price, to take less profit per item, but to generate more demand? Similarly, would it be wise now to sell fixed assets such as buildings or factories and then to lease them back from the purchaser? Some US firms in Tokyo found that by the early 1990s the land and buildings that they had bought years before were now worth hundreds of times their original purchase price. Believing that the local real estate market was as high as it was going to go and feeling that it would be more advisable to sell the properties and rent them back, these firms sold their office buildings and made tremendous profits. The ensuing decline of Tokyo real estate prices showed that these firms had made very wise decisions.[3]

Another example of economic exposure is the risk that companies take when selling to a country with a weakening currency. In this case many MNEs have sought to increase their own production efficiency, lower their costs, and continue to generate acceptable profit.[4] Firms such as Honda, Nissan, and BMW have complemented this strategy by setting up operations in the US, their largest international market.[5] In the process the firms have reduced their economic exposure.

As seen here, there are a variety of ways that MNEs deal with exchange rate changes. Another way, used particularly by multinationals that conduct a large amount of business in the international arena, is hedging strategies.

Active learning check

Review your answer to Active Learning Case question 2 and make any changes you like. Then compare your answer with the one below.

2. If the two carriers complete their merger and the US dollar then weakens against the British pound, how will this affect the financial statements of the company?

This will depend on whether the two carriers continue to issue separate financial statements. If they do, AA's financials will be affected only by the amount of sterling that it has on hand. Otherwise there will be no effect, since changes in the pound do not affect the cost to AA of doing business in the US. In the case of BA the accounts payable that are due in dollars will negatively affect the airline's financials. If the two carriers combine their statements into one, the overall effect will be a result of how these transactions net out. This would be determined based on the rules in FASB Statement No. 52.

Hedging strategies

Hedge
A form of protection used against an adverse movement of an exchange rate

A **hedge** is a form of protection against an adverse movement of an exchange rate. If a multinational would suffer a large financial loss if the dollar were to weaken against the yen, the company would likely hedge its position to ensure that, if the dollar did weaken, the firm would not suffer a major loss. A hedge, therefore, is a form of insurance that helps to minimize the risk of loss. The following sections examine some of the most common forms of hedging.

Operating financial strategies

Operating financial strategies are designed to minimize the effect of changing exchange rates on the local unit's profitability. In an economy suffering from severe inflation and whose currency is expected to depreciate, for example, local subsidiaries will limit credit sales and will try to collect their receivables as quickly as possible because prices are constantly rising and eroding the purchasing power of these funds. Conversely, these companies will delay paying obligations that are denominated in local currency because it is cheaper to do so, but they will promptly pay all bills that are denominated in strong currencies. At the same time subsidiaries will consider buying fixed assets that are likely to benefit from inflation.

Lead strategy
A hedging strategy that calls for collecting foreign currency receivables before they are due if the currency is expected to weaken, and paying foreign currency payables before they are due if the currency is expected to strengthen

Lag strategy
A hedging strategy that calls for delaying the receipt of foreign currency payment if this foreign currency is expected to strengthen and delaying foreign currency payables when the local currency is expected to weaken

Closely linked to the above discussion is the use of lead and lag strategies, which are used to protect cash flows. A **lead strategy** calls for collecting foreign currency receivables before they are due if the currency is expected to strengthen and paying foreign currency payables before they are due if the currency is expected to strengthen. The logic behind a lead strategy is obvious: the company wants to obtain a currency before its value increases and to pay promptly bills due in a currency that is going to strengthen. A **lag strategy** calls for a company to delay receiving foreign currency payments if the currency is expected to strengthen and to delay paying foreign currency payables when this currency is expected to weaken. The logic is the reverse of that used with a lead strategy.

Inventory decisions will be based on the subsidiary manager's reading of the situation. If inflation is rapidly driving up prices, the subsidiary will minimize the amount being carried while profiting from the price increases. If inventory is being imported, the manager will try to stock up on these goods before the local currency weakens. If local currency is strengthening, however, the manager will spread out the purchases so that the goods being bought can be purchased with a stronger currency. Some multinationals supplement these inventory and selling strategies by following this rule: make purchases in a weak currency and sales in a strong currency.

Debt strategies will also be handled on a contingency basis. Although some firms prefer to borrow as much as possible from local sources and to minimize their reliance on other sources, this strategy has shortcomings. For example, during inflationary periods the cost of local borrowing will be very high. Similarly, the use of weak local currency limits the firm's ability to purchase from countries with strong currencies. Because a number of factors need to be carefully weighed, most MNEs make these decisions on a case-by-case basis.

Forward exchange contract A legally binding agreement between a firm and a bank that calls for the delivery of foreign currency at a specific exchange rate on a predetermined future date

Forward exchange contracts

A **forward exchange contract** is a legally binding agreement between a firm and a bank that calls for the delivery of foreign currency at a specific exchange rate on a predetermined future date. The purpose of such a contract is to minimize the risk associated with foreign exchange fluctuations. A case example would be a US supplier that sells equipment to a Japanese firm for 50 million yen with payment due in 90 days. If the spot exchange rate is 104 yen to the dollar, the value of the contract is $480,769.23 (50,000,000/104).

However, what will the exchange rate be in 90 days? If the US firm does not want to take a chance that the yen will strengthen, it will purchase a forward contract from the bank for, say, 106 yen to the dollar. So the supplier is willing to take a guaranteed $471,698.11 (50,000,000/106) in 90 days in exchange for the 50 million yen that the Japanese are paying. In the interim, if the value of the yen were to weaken and go above 106 yen per dollar, the company will have saved money. If the price remains at 104 yen per dollar, the company gives up $9,701.12 ($480,769.23 minus $471,698.11) for the guarantee. Of course, if the yen were to strengthen to 100 per dollar by the end of the 90 days, the forward exchange contract would have cost the firm a total of $28,301.89 ($500,000 minus $471,698.11) and the company would have been better off accepting the risk. On the positive side, forward exchange contracts provide safety against the decline of the buyer's currency. On the negative side, these contracts can sometimes prove costly.

Currency options

Currency option
An instrument that gives the purchaser the right to buy or sell a specific amount of foreign currency at a predetermined rate within a specified time period

A **currency option** is an instrument that gives the purchaser the right to buy or sell a specific amount of foreign currency at a predetermined rate within a specified time period. Currency options are more flexible than forward exchange contracts because the buyer does not have to exercise the option. Using the above example, the seller wants to protect the value of the 50 million Japanese yen. This could be done by purchasing an option to deliver 50 million yen for dollars at a predetermined exchange rate of, say, 104 yen per dollar in 90 days. The company would have to pay an option cost (assume it is $25,000) for this right, but then the currency's value would be protected. No matter what happens to the exchange rate between the dollar and the yen, the company can turn the 50 million yen over to the person who sold the option and the individual must give the firm $480,769.23 (50,000,000/104). Of course, the company will exercise this option *only* if the value of the yen in 90 days is less than this amount. If the yen were to increase in value to 102 per dollar, the currency would be worth $490,196.07 (50,000,000/102) and the firm would not exercise its option. On the other hand, if the yen declined in value to 106 per dollar, the 50 million yen would be worth only $471,698.11 (50,000,000/106) and the firm *would* exercise its option. Regardless of what happens to the yen per dollar exchange rate, however, the company must deduct $25,000 from its revenues because this is the price for the option. Many firms feel that this is a reasonable price to pay in order to ensure that they will not suffer the ill-effects of a rapidly declining yen.

Developing forecasting and reporting systems

The management of foreign exchange risk can be both complex and cumbersome. A multinational with 20 subsidiaries can present a formidable challenge to the parent company because so many foreign exchange risk decisions need to be made and monitored. However, there are a number of steps that MNEs typically take in creating the necessary system for managing these decisions. They may:

1. Decide the types and degrees of economic exposure that the company is willing to accept.
2. Develop the necessary expertise (in-house personnel and/or outside economists or consultants) for monitoring exchange rates and for forecasting those rates that are applicable to the identified exposures.
3. Construct a reporting system that allows the firm to identify exposed accounts, to measure this exposure, and to feed back information on what the firm is doing and the status of these decisions.
4. Include all MNE units in this reporting system so that each better understands the risks it is assuming and is aware of the actions that must be taken to deal with these risks.

5. Keep senior-level management fully apprised of what is going on in each area of responsibility so that every regional or divisional manager is able periodically to revise the exposure risk and to make those strategy changes that will help more effectively to manage the process.

As firms begin to implement these five steps, they are better able to deal with the management of foreign exchange risk. Another financial area that receives considerable attention is capital expenditure analysis and capital budgeting.

Active learning check 

Review your answer to Active Learning Case question 3 and make any changes you like. Then compare your answer with the one below.

3. If BA believed that the British pound was going to appreciate in relation to the German mark, how could the company use a lead and lag strategy to its advantage?

If BA believed that the pound was going to get stronger against the mark, and if it were owed marks, the firm would try to collect them immediately before their value declined. At the same time BA would delay payment of those obligations that were fixed in marks, for it would be getting more marks per pound after the appreciation, thus making it easier to pay those bills. The firm would lead collections and lag payables.

CAPITAL EXPENDITURE ANALYSIS AND CAPITAL BUDGETING

Capital expenditures Major projects in which the costs are to be allocated over a number of years

Capital expenditures are major projects in which the costs are to be allocated over a number of years. Examples include major acquisitions, the building of new plants, and the refurbishing of existing equipment. Because the firm has to live with the results of these decisions for a long period of time, mathematical techniques of analysis are often used, including discounted cash flow techniques such as net present value (NPV) and internal rate of return. Traditional methods such as payback period and accounting rate of return are also employed, either as a first-cut approximation technique or to provide additional information. In fact, the basic techniques that are appropriate to domestic analysis are often applied to capital expenditure analysis in multinationals as well as to foreign projects in general.

In contrast to domestic projects, however, one basic question must be answered: Who should conduct the analysis, the parent or the foreign subsidiary? Typically, the initial analysis is done at the subsidiary or branch level and then passed up to the head office for modification and/or approval. For example, two subsidiaries may both want to build a new tire plant and sell to the same market. Without coordination, they would compete against each other and the expected profits would not materialize. So the parent corporation will make a decision that benefits the entire organization. In this latter role the parent may have to turn down a positive NPV project from one subsidiary in favor of a higher NPV project from another subsidiary. The same process applies in reverse to plant closures; the shutdown will be at the plant with the largest negative NPV. Similarly, factories or holdings that do not generate sufficient profit may be sold.[6]

Use of net present value

The parent company will review expenditure proposals because it has the necessary overall information to make these decisions. Moreover, such expenditure decisions will often be different from those of the subsidiary because the latter may use faulty valuation techniques or fail to address adequately the impact of political risk. In explaining why these differences occur, we must first review the basic NPV criterion. This criterion separates the financing and operating parts of the problem by discounting operating cash flows by a weighted average cost of capital that embodies the financing decision. The NPV equation is

$$\text{NPV} = \sum_{t=0}^{T} \frac{I_t + C_t}{(1 + K_A)^t} \qquad \text{(Eq. 14.1)}$$

where

$$K_A = k_e \frac{S}{V} + k_d(1 - t_x)\frac{D}{V} \qquad \text{(Eq. 14.2)}$$

The definitions of the terms are:

I_t = investment cash outlays in year t
C_t = cash inflows in year t
T = terminal date or end of project
K_A = weighted average cost of capital
k_e = cost of equity capital
k_d = cost of debt financing
t_x = tax rate
D/V, S/V = debt and equity ratios, respectively
NPV = incremental net present value for the project.

In examining what determines the NPV, we must realize that disagreement between parent and subsidiary can arise because of the discount rate K_A, investment cost, and annual cash flows. Political risk can also affect all values. For example, the risk of foreign currency controls can cause some of the future cash flows to be largely ignored by the parent. From the parent's perspective, if funds can no longer be remitted, their value is substantially reduced since they are not available for dividend payments or for reinvestment elsewhere. Conversely, once foreign exchange controls are in place, the parent will often treat blocked funds as being less valuable. From the parent's perspective, the cost of future investments in the country, financed by these blocked funds, is reduced. In both cases the subsidiary is not directly concerned with the problem of foreign exchange controls, and it will discount all cash flows that are incremental from its own perspective.

Similarly, political risk may cause the parent to increase the discount rate or required return to reflect that risk. However, if the subsidiary does not agree with that perception, it will not increase the discount rate, so its calculation of the present value of the cash inflows and NPV will be higher. Moreover, if foreign exchange controls are enforced, the local capital markets can be isolated from the international capital market. From the subsidiary's perspective, the result may be lower local real interest rates, which make local investment opportunities seem attractive. However, the parent, looking at global opportunities, may decide that it will make more sense to draw capital out of the country for reinvestment elsewhere.

Another reason that parent and local NPVs may differ is faulty application of the NPV framework. The most common errors are in incorrectly choosing t_x and K_A. The tax rate t_x is relevant in two places, the incremental tax that results from the incremental profits and the incremental tax shield that results from debt financing. Here, the errors usually come from a failure to determine the incremental tax rate. From the subsidiary's perspective the tax rate is the extra tax that it pays locally. However, the parent must also consider any incremental tax that it will pay once dividends are remitted.

In determining the discount rate K_A, several problems emerge. First, it is common that discount rates differ by several percentage points. The reason is obvious: inflation differs across different countries, and thus the inflationary premium built into the discount rate will differ. What the firm can never do is to use a discount rate from one country to evaluate cash flows denominated in another currency. The correct procedure is to calculate the real discount rate and then to "gross it up" for the inflationary expectations of the relevant country.

Additionally, debt ratios differ across subsidiaries, and the weights in Equation 14.2 may alter the cost of capital. This will inevitably occur if the multinational maximizes the use of debt financing in a country with subsidized borrowing rates. However, the debt ratio of that country is then not appropriate for determining the cost of capital since the excess debt can be carried only because that subsidiary is part of a multinational. Similarly, it is a mistake to use the local real cost of debt to determine the cost of capital. In both these examples, if the MNE uses local debt norms and local debt costs, it is negating the advantage of being a multinational. That advantage is the ability to raise debt internally where it is the cheapest. As a result, in a country with a high debt cost the firm may have very little debt, whereas in a country with subsidized interest costs it may have a large amount of debt. In both cases there is no effect on the overall cost of funds to the multinational. Hence local debt norms and interest costs will be ignored unless local regulations restrict the use of debt funds to projects within that country. In this instance, if the firm accepts a local project, it can also raise more subsidized foreign debt. If the money cannot be removed from the country by transfer pricing or whatever, then its cost is relevant in Equation 14.2.

In general, the financing options open to a multinational are greater than those of a domestic firm. The Eurobond market and foreign bond markets give the multinational the ability to raise funds where the cost is the cheapest. Moreover, the extensive national network of the MNEs enables them to take advantage of local incentive programs. These include regional investment incentives, tax holidays for new investments, export insurance, and loan guarantees. The result is a lower overall cost. However, in the analysis of any particular project the discount rate should reflect only the subsidized rates that would not be available unless the project was undertaken. The latter application errors are frequently made and can serve to drive a wedge between the parent and the subsidiary, often resulting in considerable acrimony between the respective staffs.[7]

Institutional features

Thus far the focus has been on the technical question of how to evaluate capital expenditures. However, there are two institutional factors that warrant attention: government subsidies and controls, and political risk insurance.

Government subsidies and controls

Government intervention can affect the profitability of a project or its financing. For example, in considering foreign investments, countries such as Australia and Canada have **foreign investment review agencies**, which review these investments to ensure that they benefit the local economy. As a result, foreign investment is often contingent on factors such as local employment quotas, local sourcing of components, the transfer of technology, and a degree of local ownership. This intervention can obviously complicate capital expenditure analysis. Frequently the result is to forecast specific, quantitative outcomes. For example, if technology is locally licensed, what is the possible impact of its being leaked to different countries? If the MNE has to train local middle management and to sell shares locally, how does this affect the probability of forcible divestiture at some future date? In many cases the result of local content regulations is to expropriate all the advantages possessed by the multinational. One of the particular problems here is

Foreign investment review agencies
Agencies which review foreign investments to ensure that they benefit the local economy

local ownership requirements. The parent's viewpoint is dominant on the assumption that the objective of the firm is to maximize its market value, which is owned by shareholders in the home country. However, once joint ventures and significant minority shareholdings are traded locally, this solution breaks down. The problem now becomes whose market value should be maximized. The result is that while minority ownership reduces the political risk of expropriation, it restricts the multinational's freedom of action. It is, therefore, not surprising that, where political risk is lowered, minority shareholders get bought out. For example, Ford acquired its British minority shareholdings in 1961, and Shell bought out its minority US shareholdings in 1984.

However, government regulation is not all bad. Outside North America the interventionist approach of most governments creates unique opportunities for the MNE. For example, most countries provide concessionary financing that is contingent on the use of certain local resources. The **British Export Credits Guarantee Department (ECGD)** has some of the lowest cost money for export financing as long as the borrower uses British equipment. By structuring an investment to use British equipment, a multinational might be able to borrow $10 million at 3 per cent interest instead of at a market rate of, say, 9 per cent. In effect, this subsidized loan represents a gift by the British taxpayers. This value has to be factored into the analysis. The inclusion of subsidies also occurs in domestic capital expenditure analysis, for example with the proliferation of small business financing programs. However, in an international project, rather than being unusual, it is rare *not* to determine the value or cost of a particular government program. Recently government regulation of MNEs has been falling, leading to more cross-listings on the world stock exchange.

British Export Credits Guarantee Department (ECGD)
A governmental agency that lends money for export financing of British equipment

Political risk insurance

Political risk insurance is available in most countries for exports and foreign direct investment. In the US, the **Overseas Private Investment Corporation (OPIC)** was established in January 1971 to provide insurance for US foreign investment against blocked funds, expropriation and war, and revolution and insurrection.[8] The terms of political risk insurance are similar across different countries. Usually there is approval by the host government of the investment, some type of bilateral agreement on foreign investment, and coverage limited to some multiple of the initial investment for up to 20 years. For specific types of risk this coverage can be insured separately. In the US, it is estimated that about 70 per cent of foreign investment in less developed countries is insured through OPIC.

Overseas Private Investment Corporation (OPIC)
An organization that provides insurance of US foreign investment against blocked funds, expropriation and war, and revolution and insurrection

Political risk insurance creates another option that is available for analysis. In effect, the company has to decide the incremental value of this insurance. This is typically done by considering how the MNE can restructure the foreign investment, such as by fronting loans or long-term contracts at high transfer prices as alternatives to political risk insurance. The ultimate decision will reflect the optimum structuring of the proposal under analysis.

Active learning check 

Review your answer to Active Learning Case question 4 and make any changes you like. Then compare your answer with the one below.

4. How great is the political risk that BA faces in the US? Explain.

The company certainly faces some risk in that there is growing pressure not to allow the merger. On the other hand, if this opposition is based on gaining a quid pro quo arrangement in which US carriers are given broader access to the European market, then the risk is quite small. The concern that is being evinced is merely a smokescreen by the US airlines for gaining a better bargaining position.

STRATEGIC INTERNATIONAL FINANCE

There are a number of ways that MNEs apply the international financial concepts that have been discussed in this chapter. One way is by employing a geocentric approach that helps to coordinate subsidiary operations and ensures that there is a uniform, harmonious strategy.[9] This approach is particularly evident in the way that some multinationals are now closing local operations in favor of overseas production and are using joint ventures and other partnership arrangements to reduce their financial risk.[10] Another approach is the manner in which financial management analysis is used in choosing sites for overseas operations. This is particularly true for foreign firms with strong currencies.

Establishing overseas operations

Because the US is a major market for many international firms, foreign MNEs have been particularly concerned about the value of the US dollar. For example, when Ford Motor acquired Volvo's automotive business, the Swedish firm insisted on receiving the purchase price in krona.[11] This concern has also resulted in foreign firms setting up operations in the US in order to offset the competitive impact associated with having a currency that is very strong vis-à-vis the American dollar. For example, BMW built an auto production facility in South Carolina because it found it was 20 per cent less costly to produce cars in South Carolina than to bring them in from Germany.[12] Other companies have made acquisitions in the US market in order to protect their overall profitability. For example, BASF has acquired a Mobil plastic unit for $330 million; Benckiser purchased Coty, the fragrance maker, from Pfizer for $440 million; Siemens spent $1.2 billion to purchase ROLM, a manufacturer of telecommunications equipment, from IBM, and Daimler-Benz bought Chrysler for almost $40 billion.[13]

At the same time US firms are continuing to move abroad, especially since many Asian currencies are at a low ebb and purchase prices have fallen. General Motors, for example, is now producing light trucks in China, has 16 ventures there related to producing auto components, and has opened a Buick plant in Shanghai. As of the end of 1998 the company was assembling close to 500,000 cars annually, most of which were small sedans or subcompacts.[14] At the same time Atlantic Richfield and Phillips China have invested in ventures for drilling for methane gas, IBM is expanding its investment there in the computer business, Telluride International Energy is building a power plant, and Lucent Technologies has earmarked millions of dollars to expand its Internet backbone in the country.[15]

European and US firms are not alone in their efforts to establish overseas operations. Pacific-based MNEs are also realizing the benefits of going local, and this group is not limited to auto makers. South Korean firms such as LG Group and Samsung are now using direct investment and joint ventures to help open markets in Europe and the US. High labor costs, runaway interest rates, and low-cost competition are battering these firms at home, and local content laws have been holding down market acceptance abroad. In an effort to circumvent these problems, LG is using alliances to widen its market share, as seen by its collaboration with Gepi of Germany and Iberna of Italy to produce refrigerators for the European market. LG designs the units in its Ireland facility, Gepi supplies the components, and Iberna assembles the finished products. Samsung has purchased Werk für Fernsehelektronik, a former East German picture tube maker, and is spending $120 million to upgrade the plant, which will be capable of turning out 1.2 million television sets annually. The company is also negotiating to buy an even larger German television maker, RFT, and has moved its Portuguese and Spanish color television plants to England and its videocassette recorder plant from England to Spain in order to lower operational costs, to improve quality, and to increase employment.[16]

Reducing financial risk

Although some of the above strategies are useful in reducing risk, there are other tactics that are also particularly useful, including mergers, acquisitions,[17] joint ventures for new, high-risk projects, partnering with established MNEs in order to gain international market share, and cutting operating costs through new plant design.[18]

Alliances

In recent years an increasing number of MNEs have been joining together to share the costs of high-tech projects. This sharing involves not only research and development expenses, but also the costs of manufacturing and selling the finished products.

One example is provided by Microsoft, which has entered into an alliance with Sony to link personal computers and consumer electronics devices, thus moving closer together on technology standards for digital television and other consumer products. The two firms have endorsed a technology that can connect videocassette recorders, camcorders, personal computers, and other devices.[19] Another example is GM and Isuzu, which are now extending their alliance in advanced vehicle technologies such as electric vehicles and fuel cells.[20] A third example is Kita Kyushu Coca-Cola Bottling and Sanyo Coca-Cola Bottling, two major bottlers in southwest Japan which have agreed to merge their operations and thus combine a somewhat fragmented distribution system into a smoother, seamless approach that should boost profitability.[21] A fourth example is Citigroup, which acquired 15 per cent equity in Taiwan's Fubon Group. This alliance will serve as a springboard for future expansion in the Asian region.[22]

Cost-cutting

Another key financial strategy is cutting costs[23] and investing in new plant and equipment,[24] resulting in higher productivity and lower expenses. Still another strategy is the renegotiation of labor contract agreements in high-cost areas of the world.

Investment in new plant and equipment will be critical to the success of MNEs during the millennium. This is particularly true in Japan, where many auto manufacturers are finding it increasingly difficult to hire new people. Worse yet, the turnover rate in some factories runs as high as 50 per cent annually. In explaining the reason for this turnover, many workers refer to the three Ks: *kiken* (dangerous), *kitsui* (difficult), and *kitanai* (dirty). Young people, in particular, prefer the slower-paced world of office work where people wear suits and ties, take leisurely lunch hours, and are not exhausted at the end of a long day.

In an effort to deal with this problem, Nissan Motor has built a new factory that promises to be far less stressful on the workers than anything yet. Company officials refer to it as a "dream factory" and claim that it is designed to reduce many of the pitfalls of past manufacturing plants. The latter, for example, are characterized by the traditional conveyor belt from which cars are suspended. When the car reaches the workers, the employees scramble to install parts and to complete their tasks as quickly as possible. This typically involves squatting on the floor, stretching across the seat or the hood, ducking under the car, or reaching across the top of the vehicle to install or tighten something. If the workers are unable to keep up with the line, the conveyer belt must be stopped until they finish because all cars advance in lockstep. In contrast, Nissan's new plant has done away with the conveyer belt. All cars are now placed on motor-driven dollies. These dollies can be raised or lowered so that the workers do not have to stretch or squat. Additionally, even if it takes longer than usual to complete a particular task, this creates no problem for the factory. The workers can simply scoot the dolly up to the next station as soon as they are finished.

Another difference between the Nissan plant and more conventional ones is that the work area is brightly lit with natural sunlight filtering in through skylights, compared with the poorly lit work environments in other plants. Additionally, the factory is air conditioned and the temperature is kept at 77°F (degrees Fahrenheit), in contrast to other auto plants where there is no air conditioning. Another welcome feature is the use of robots to perform the dirtiest and most difficult jobs, painting and welding. And to reduce worker exhaustion, robots carry out a large percentage of the actual assembly. A huge robot arm, for example, grabs seats from an overhead rack and swings them into the car with a flick of its mechanical wrist. Then a small robot arm bolts the seat to the floor. Nissan contends that this new plant will not only cut down on worker absenteeism and turnover, but that the factory will be 30 per cent more efficient than those of the competition.[25]

Other Japanese manufacturers are also heavily focused on cost-cutting. For example, Honda and Toyota operations in the US have been simultaneously reducing costs while increasing quality. The result is that car prices for many of their models have remained the same or dropped slightly in recent years, while the number of features have increased. This "more value for your money" concept has been influential in helping both auto makers to increase their US market share and profitability.[26] Ford has been following a similar approach through a vigorous outsourcing program and by seeking to cut $1 billion from its costs, thus boosting its return on investment from the North American market and, hopefully, helping drive up stock price as well.[27] Simply put, cost-cutting is now a critical part of many financial investment strategies.

KEY POINTS

1. **International financial management encompasses a number of critical areas, including the management of global cash flows, foreign exchange risk management, capital expenditure analysis, and capital budgeting. In carrying out these financial activities, MNEs can use three approaches or solutions: polycentric, ethnocentric, or geocentric.**
2. **There are three main areas of consideration in managing global cash flows. One is the movement of cash so that each subsidiary has the working capital needed to conduct operations. A second area is the use of funds positioning techniques that can help to reduce taxes and to deal with political and legal roadblocks that impede cash flows. A third is multilateral netting, which ensures that transactions between the subsidiaries are paid in a timely manner.**
3. **Foreign exchange risk management encompasses a variety of financial strategies that are designed to limit the multinational's exposure to exchange rate fluctuations. In particular, the MNE will want to reduce translation, transaction, and economic exposure. One of the most common ways of doing this is through hedging. Examples include lead and lag strategies, the purchase of forward exchange contracts, and the use of currency options.**
4. **A third major strategic financial issue is capital expenditure analysis. This entails computation and deliberation of such matters as the weighted cost of capital and the degree of political risk that is being assumed. Some of the methods of dealing with these issues were discussed with attention given to the fact that the final decision on capital expenditures is often affected by subjective considerations as well as by objective evaluations.**
5. **At present MNEs are taking a number of important international financial steps. Some of the primary ones include establishing overseas operations, creating joint ventures, and cutting operating costs.**

KEY TERMS

- polycentric solution
- ethnocentric solution
- geocentric solution
- working capital
- funds positioning techniques
- transfer price
- arm's length price
- tax havens
- fronting loan
- multilateral netting
- translation
- consolidation
- translation exposure
- transaction exposure
- economic exposure
- hedge
- lead strategy
- lag strategy
- forward exchange contract
- currency option
- capital expenditures
- foreign investment review agencies
- British Export Credits Guarantee Department (ECGD)
- Overseas Private Investment Corporation (OPIC)

REVIEW AND DISCUSSION QUESTIONS

1. In determining parent–subsidiary relationships, how does a polycentric solution differ from an ethnocentric or geocentric solution? Compare and contrast all three.
2. What is meant by the term "working capital," and what are two of the most common ways that parent companies can provide this capital to their subsidiaries? What are two ways in which the parent can obtain funds from the subsidiaries?
3. How can an MNE shift profits through the use of transfer pricing? Provide an example.
4. Of what value is multilateral netting in helping MNEs to manage cash flows? Give an example.
5. If a foreign country is facing high inflation, what are three financial strategies that the local multinational unit might employ? Identify and describe each.
6. Why are MNEs interested in translation and consolidation of financial statements? Of what practical value is this activity to the company?
7. Under what conditions will an MNE face translation exposure? What financial strategy might the organization use to minimize this exposure?
8. When might an MNE face transaction exposure? What is a financial strategy that the firm could use to minimize this risk?
9. What is meant by the term "economic exposure"? What is a financial strategy that an MNE could use to minimize this risk?
10. When would a multinational use a lead strategy to hedge a risk? When would a multinational use a lag strategy for this purpose? In each case, give an example.
11. When might an MNE use a forward exchange contract? Why might the firm decide to forgo this strategy in lieu of purchasing a currency option?
12. What role does net present value (NPV) play in the review of capital expenditure proposals? Give an example.
13. How can political risk affect the computation of NPV? Will the risk result in the MNE wanting a higher or a lower NPV? Explain.
14. Why do parent and local subsidiaries sometimes differ in their calculation of NPV for a particular project or expenditure? How can this difference be resolved?
15. How does the availability of political risk insurance change the structure of the capital expenditure analysis process? Give an example.

REAL CASE

Brazil: State-owned enterprises are privatized

Between 1997 and 2001, the Brazilian government raised over $150 billion through privatization of state-owned companies like Telebras, Petrobras, and Paraiban. Large companies in mining, banking, and utilities were sold as part of the Brazilian government's National Privatization Programme beginning in the early 1990s, privatization aimed to reduce the strategic position of the Brazilian government in the economy, to raise funds to reduce public debt, and to provide a more efficient infrastructure needed to develop the country's industrial sector.

Brazil enjoys a relatively high level of per capita GDP, infrastructure, and entrepreneurship. At $800 billion, Brazil is the largest economy in South America and the eighth largest in the world. It is also one of the largest countries in terms of population. The city of São Paolo alone has a population equal to that of Australia. Though the economy is still relatively underdeveloped, foreign investors see it as the largest potential market in Latin America. This is nothing new. During the mid 20th century, Brazil was able to negotiate favorable deals with foreign investors who were eager to enter the market. This was particularly true of the automotive market, where Brazil was able to enforce domestic content rules that generated backward linkages and led to the development of a related industrial sector. Not surprisingly, when privatization began, investors flocked to purchase public companies in the key sectors of telecommunications, oil and gas, power, mining, and banking.

Banking

During the 1980s and early 1990s, governments had used Brazilian state-owned banks to finance their projects. This policy was partly responsible for inflation reaching over 2,000 per cent in 1993. The banks lacked financial discipline and were on the verge of collapse when Brazil's federal government began restructuring them in the mid 1990s. The government invested approximately $30 billion in stabilizing banks to then have them auctioned to private investors.

Trade unionists and students protested the privatizations of banks. This did not deter foreign and domestic investors from buying the disreputable banks. Only 25 per cent of all Brazilians hold a bank account, and foreign investors are betting on the growth potential. Among the largest foreign investors are Bilbao Vizcaya (Spain), Santander Banks (Spain), HSBC (UK), and ABN Amro (Dutch).

ABN Amro purchased Banco Real (1998), Bandepe (1998), Paraiban (2001), and is expected to bid for Besg in December 2001. The total purchase price for Paraiban was $29.4 million. Paraiban and Bandepe have operations in Brazil's North East, where banking is still underdeveloped. The Dutch bank is hoping to build a banking network in the region. HSBC entered the market with the acquisition of Banco Bamerindus (1997). By 2001, HSBC was the second largest private banking group in Brazil with 1,000 branches in 600 cities. Spanish banks are also buying state-owned banks. In November 2000, Santander Central Hispano bid $3.6 billion for a controlling stake in Banco do Estado de São Paolo. Banco Bilbao Vizcaya put up $463 million for Banco Excel Economico (1998).

Telecommunications

Amid numerous protests and lawsuits, Telebras was sold to private investors in 1998 for a total of $19 billion (a $5 billion premium on the government's opening price). The company had been divided into 12 subsidiaries that were each auctioned separately. These included eight mobile operators, three regional carriers, and one long distance operator. Telefónica of Spain purchased Telesp, São Paolo's regional carrier, for $5 billion. MCI of the US purchased the long distance operator for $2.3 billion.

For Telefónica, all is not well. As part of its bid it had promised to increase the number of phone lines by 400,000 in the first three months after taking control. To do this, it hired inept engineers and poorly trained subcontractors that disconnected lines and unplugged entire neighborhoods. Telefónica's offices were flooded with angry customers and the media attacked the company and the government's privatization plan. The Justice Ministry and Anatel, the country's telecommunications regulator, fined Telefónica R$8 million. Despite all setbacks, by 2001 the privatization of Telebras had substantially increased the number of lines and the quality of telecommunications in Brazil.

Power

The electric power sector has experienced very little reform because different levels of government own different segments of the business. In 2001, Copel, a power company, had its auction postponed twice. No new date has been set for the auction. The company is profitable, and already has a sizable portion of the domestic power market. It generates 7 per cent of the country's electricity. Initial bidders withdrew their offers, claiming the asking price of $1.94 billion was too high and that the regulations in the sector would prove an obstacle to profitability.

Copel's auction failure has raised concerns about investor's confidence. A recession in the Mercosur region and the devaluation of the real are partly to blame. On January 1999, Brazil's Central Bank allowed the real to float. Despite initial fears of inflation, investors reacted relatively favorably. By January 2001, the real had fallen by 40 per cent, giving a blow to FDI. These companies must pay for equipment in US dollars but bill in local currencies.

After massive restructuring, the state-owned oil company, Petrobras, was also open to private capital. The government, however, continues to retain 55 per cent of all voting shares.

Websites: **www.petrobras.com.br**; **www.telebras.com.br**; **www.paraiban.com.br**; **www.bbv.es**; **www.santander.com.br**; **www.gruposantander.com**; **www.hsbc.com**; **www.abnamro.com**; **www.telefonica.es**; **www.mci.com** and **www.copel.com**.

Sources: "Telecoms: Beginning to Be Untangled", *Financial Times Survey – Brazil*, 1999; "ABN Amro Buys Paraiban", *FT.com*, November 9, 2001; "Copel Privatization Doubt as Auction is Again Put Off," *FT.com*, November 7, 2001; "Privatization in Brazil: The Case of Public Utilities," *OECD Observer*, August 1, 1999; Thierry Ogier, "Gros Named Next Petrobras Head," *FT.com*, December 2, 2001.

1. **What benefits can Brazil expect from the privatization of public banks?**
2. **How are banks operating in Brazil affected by the devaluation of the real?**
3. **How is the competitiveness of a foreign telecommunications company affected by a depreciation of the real?**

REAL CASE

Global accounting standards

Most people traveling across Europe have suffered the inconvenience of electrical plugs that do not fit sockets. The lack of an international standard is not only a traveling inconvenience but it also creates barriers to trade, since companies must change their production to fit the country's standard. The EU has sought to standardize plugs and sockets but many countries argue that their sockets are safer or of better quality and theirs should be the EU's standard. It is understandable since countries that must change their standard will be burdened with the expense of adapting plugs, sockets, and manufacturing facilities.

Accounting practices have also become an issue of international contention. The purpose of financial information is to allow investors to make sound decisions. Like the plug that cannot fit into the socket, international investors cannot translate international financial information because of different practices. Take for instance the case of mergers. The US uses the pooling method, which allows merging companies to add their accounts together without consideration for the cost of the acquisition. Europeans commonly use the purchase method, in which one company must be the buyer, and the difference between the price paid and the book value is called "goodwill". The goodwill must be amortized over a few years, reducing profits. A similar transaction using the US method would yield a different financial statement for years to come from if the European method is used. In 2001, the US was studying whether or not it would adopt the purchase method over the pooling method, but critics of the reform argued that it would deflate a company's profits during the years of amortization.

Further from the triad, the differences are even more dramatic. When Daewoo filed for bankruptcy in 1999, investors were taken by surprise. The company had inflated assets and $34 billion in hidden debt. Granted most of this was attributed to outright fraud, the country's accounting standards did not help either. In South Korea, companies can record as assets payments that are not due for more than a year. So a balance sheet under US standards would show much lower assets than under South Korean standards. In China, foreign investment is hindered by the belief that the communist legacy of "creative accounting" to meet centrally planned quotas continues to prevail. Russia also has its own accounting standards and while some companies, like Sibneft and Yukos, have officially adopted International Accounting Standards to improve their image, their reporting has continued to be poor and unreliable.

As in the case of plugs and sockets, there is a drive to find a common accounting standard. The EU and the US are debating which standard to adopt, the US GAAP (Generally Accepted Accounting Principles) or the International Accounting Standards (IAS).

In February 2001, the European Commission presented the European Parliament and the Council of Ministers with a proposal to consolidate accounts of all companies listed on regulated markets in accordance with IAS. If this goes through, the new law would be effective by 2005 at the latest. The EU also maintains open consultation with IAS with regards to the adoption of standards. This will ensure the relevance of the standards to Europe's business environment.

The inclusion of the US is crucial to the development of international standards – in particular because non-triad companies hoping to enter the US capital markets would be more willing to conform to international standards. The US is hesitant to adopt IAS. Critics of adopting IAS argue that the US GAAP is an efficient and transparent form of accounting and any change would be detrimental since foreign standards are not sufficiently tough. More moderate critics believe that the IAS and the US GAAP are comparable in efficiency but that they both lack in areas such as reporting derivatives.

As long as regional and national standards prevail, the world's capital markets will remain fractured. The global standard to be adopted must be transparent, comparable, and be fitted to function in an international business environment. While both US GAAP and IAS are considered transparent and comparable, the IAS has an advantage in that it was specifically tailored for international business.

Finally, the differences in international accounting standards mean that the profits of MNEs need to be recalculated carefully, using subsidiary level data. The only source on this is the Oxford University *Templeton Global Performance Index* of the foreign assets and foreign profits of the largest 500 MNEs for whom accounting data are available – about 200 to 250. These data were published in 1998, 2000, and 2001.

Websites: **www.iasc.org.uk**.

Sources: **www.iasc.org.uk**; "Korean Murk," *Economist*, May 29, 2001; "A Hill of Beans," *Economist*, January 15, 1998; "Draining the Pool," *Economist*, September 9, 1999; "America vs. the World," *Economist*, January 15, 1998; "Russia's Cooked Books," *Economist*, September 7, 2000; *The Templeton Global Performance Index*, Templeton College, University of Oxford; **www.templeton.ox.ac.uk**.

1. **Are there geocentric accounting standards? Or are they ethnocentric?**
2. **Why are there different accounting standards across the triad?**
3. **If there are different accounting standards, how can the worldwide profits of MNEs be properly assessed?**

ENDNOTES

1 Edward Neumann, "MNCs Start Taking IRS Surveillance of Transfer Pricing More Seriously," *Business International Money Report* (New York: Business International Corporation, May 7, 1990), p. 167.

2 For more on tax havens, see "Gimme Shelter," *Economist*, January 7, 2000.

3 Also, see Neil Weinberg, "Rent Shokku," *Forbes*, June 7, 1993, p. 108.

4 Doron P. Levin, "Honda to Hold Base Price on Accord Model," *New York Times*, September 2, 1993, p. C 3.

5 For more on Honda, see Alex Taylor III, "How Toyota Copes with Hard Times," *Fortune*, January 25, 1993, pp. 78–81.

6 See John Rossant, "Privatize the Beast," *Business Week*, May 24, 1993, p. 54.

7 For more detailed discussion of the strategic aspects of the capital budgeting decision and the manner in which decisions can be centralized or decentralized, see Alan M. Rugman and Alain Verbeke, "Strategic Capital Budgeting Decisions and the Theory of Internalization," *Managerial Finance*, vol. 16, no. 2 (1990), pp. 17–24.

8 For more on the Overseas Private Investment Corporation (OPIC), see **www.opic.gov**.

9 See William C. Symonds et al., "High-Tech Star," *Business Week*, July 27, 1992, pp. 54–58.

10 See Brian Coleman and Thomas R. King, "Euro Disney Rescue Package Wins Approval," *Wall Street Journal*, March 15, 1994, p. A 3.

11 "Ford to Pay $6.47 Billion in Volvo Deal," *Wall Street Journal*, January 29, 1999, Section A, pp. 3, 6.

12 Also, see John Templeman and James B. Treece, "BMW's Comeback," *Business Week*, February 14, 1994, pp. 42–44.

13 Keith Bradsher, "Industry's Giants Are Carving Up the World Market," *New York Times*, May 8, 1998, pp. C 1, 4; and Robyn Meredith, "A Joining of Opposites Could Help Customers," *New York Times*, May 8, 1998, p. C 4.

14 Seth Faison, "GM Opens Buick Plant in Shanghai," *New York Times*, December 18, 1998, pp. C 1, 19.

15 "Opening the Door a Crack," *New York Times*, June 30, 1998, p. A 10.

16 Laxmi Nakarmi and Igor Reichlin, "Daewoo, Samsung, and Goldstar: Made in Europe?" *Business Week*, August 24, 1992, p. 43.

17 Rita Koselka, "A Tight Ship," *Forbes*, July 20, 1992, pp. 141–142, 144.

18 Craig Torres, "TRW Plans Mexican Venture to Start a Credit Operation in Guadalajara," *Wall Street Journal*, January 7, 1994, p. A 5.

19 Don Clark and David Bank, "Microsoft, Sony to Cooperate On PCs, Devices," *Wall Street Journal*, April 8, 1998, p. B 6.

20 Lisa Shuchman and Joseph B. White, "Global Consolidations in Autos Heat Up," *Wall Street Journal*, December 21, 1998, p. A 2.

21 Nikhil Deogun, "Coca-Cola to Put Together the Merger of Two Bottlers in Japan to Lift Sales," *Wall Street Journal*, January 14, 1999, p. A 4.

22 "Citigroup and Taiwan's Fubon Group Announce a Powerful Strategic Partnership," Citigroup Press Release, May 6, 2000.

23 See, for example, John Templeman, Stewart Toy and Paula Dwyer, "How Many Parts Makers Can Stomach the Lopez Diet?" *Business Week*, June 28, 1993, pp. 45–46.

24 See Richard W. Stevenson, "Lopez Plan for Factory Is Studied," *New York Times*, June 15, 1993, pp. C 1, C 19.

25 Andrew Pollack, "Assembly-Line Amenities for Japan's Auto Workers," *New York Times*, July 20, 1992, pp. A 1, C 5. For more on Nissan cost-cutting strategies see, "Renault's Alliance with Nissan," *Economist*, August 16, 2001.

26 Valerie Reitman, "Honda Sees Performance and Profits from New Accord," *Wall Street Journal*, August 27, 1997, p. B 4.

27 Fara Warner and Joseph B. White, "Ford Plans to Reduce Costs by Another $1 Billion," *Wall Street Journal*, January 8, 1999, p. A 3.

ADDITIONAL BIBLIOGRAPHY

Adler, Michael and Dumas, Bernard. "Exposure to Currency Risk: Definition and Management," *Financial Management* (Summer 1984).

Ahadiat, Nasrollah. "Geographic Segment Disclosure and the Predictive Ability of the Earnings Data," *Journal of International Business Studies*, vol. 24, no. 2 (Second Quarter 1993).

Albach, Horst. "Financial Planning in the Firm," *Management International Review*, vol. 32, no. 1 (First Quarter 1992).

Batten, Jonathan, Mellor, Robert and Wan, Victor. "Foreign Exchange Risk Management Practices and Products Used by Australian Firms," *Journal of International Business Studies*, vol. 24, no. 3 (Third Quarter 1993).

Booth, Laurence D. "Hedging and Foreign Exchange Exposure," *Management International Review*, vol. 22, no. 1 (1982).

Bowe, Michael and Dean, James W. "International Financial Management and Multinational Enterprises," in Alan M. Rugman and Thomas L. Brewer (eds.), *The Oxford Handbook of International Business* (Oxford: Oxford University Press, 2001).

Choi, Frederick D. S. "Accounting and Control for Multinational Activities: Perspective on the 1990s," *Management International Review*, vol. 31, Special Issue (1991).

Clark, Terry, Kotabe, Masaaki and Rajaratnam, Dan. "Exchange Rate Pass-Through and International Pricing Strategy: A Conceptual Framework and Research Propositions," *Journal of International Business Studies*, vol. 30, no.2 (Summer 1999).

Damanpour, Faramarz. "Global Banking: Developments in the Market Structure and Activities of Foreign Banks in the United States," *Columbia Journal of World Business*, vol. 26, no. 3 (Fall 1991).

Doupnik, Timothy S. and Salter, Stephen B. "An Empirical Test of a Judgemental International Classification of Financial Reporting Practices," *Journal of International Business Studies*, vol. 24, no. 1 (First Quarter 1993).

Dufey, Gunter and Giddy, Ian H. "Innovation in the International Financial Markets," *Journal of International Business Studies* (Fall 1981).

Eden, Lorraine. "Taxes, Transfer Pricing, and the Multinational Enterprise," in Alan M. Rugman and Thomas L. Brewer (eds.), *The Oxford Handbook of International Business* (Oxford: Oxford University Press, 2001).

Egelhoff, William G., Gorman, Liam and McCormick, Stephen. "How FDI Characteristics Influence Subsidiary Trade Patterns: The Case of Ireland," *Management International Review*, vol. 40, no. 3 (Fall 2000).

Eiteman, David K. and Stonehill, Arthur I. *Multinational Business Finance*, 5th edn (Reading MA: Addison-Wesley, 1989).

Forester, Stephen R. and Karolyi, G. Andrew. "International Listings of Stocks: The Case of Canada and the US," *Journal of International Business Studies*, vol. 24, no. 4 (Fourth Quarter 1993).

George, Abraham M. and Schroth, C. William. "Managing Foreign Exchange for Competitive Advantage," *Sloan Management Review*, vol. 32, no. 2 (Winter 1991).

Hekman, Christine. "A Financial Model of Foreign Exchange Exposure," *Journal of International Business Studies* (Summer 1985).

Holland, John. "Capital Budgeting for International Business: A Framework for Analysis," in Robert Kolb (ed.), *The International Finance Reader* (Miami FL: Kolb Publishing, 1990).

Jacque, Laurent L. "Management of Foreign Exchange Risk: A Review Article," *Journal of International Business Studies* (Spring/Summer 1981).

Jesswein, Kurt R., Kwok, Chuck C. Y. and Folks, William R., Jr. "Corporate Use of Innovative Foreign Exchange Risk Management Products," *Columbia Journal of World Business*, vol. 30, no. 3 (Fall 1995).

Khoury, Sarkis J. *Recent Developments in International Banking and Finance* (New York: North-Holland, 1990).

Kwok, Chuck C. Y. and Brooks, LeRoy D. "Examining Event Study Methodologies in Foreign Exchange Markets," *Journal of International Business Studies*, vol. 21, no. 2 (Second Quarter 1990).

Lessard, Donald R. *International Financial Management*, 2nd edn (New York: Wiley, 1985).

Lubecke, Thomas H., Markland, Robert E., Kwok, Chuck C. Y. and Donohue, Joan M. "Forecasting Foreign Exchange Rates Using Objective Composite Models," *Management International Review*, vol. 35, no. 2 (1995).

Luehrman, Timothy A. "The Exchange Rate Exposure of a Global Competitor," *Journal of International Business Studies*, vol. 21, no. 2 (Second Quarter 1990).

Mokkelbost, Per B. "Financing the New Europe with Participating Debt," *Management International Review*, vol. 31, no. 1 (First Quarter 1991).

Parkhe, Arvind. "International Portfolio Analysis: A New Model," *Management International Review*, vol. 31, no. 4 (Fourth Quarter 1991).

Randøy, Trond, Oxelheim, Lars and Stonehill, Arthur. "Corporate Financial Strategies for Global Competitiveness," *European Management Journal*, vol. 19, no. 6 (December 2001).

Rugman, Alan M. *International Diversification and the Multinational Enterprise* (Lexington MA: D. C. Heath, 1979).

Rugman, Alan M. "Implications of the Theory of Internalization for Corporate International Finance," *California Management Review*, vol. 23, no. 2 (Winter 1980).

Rugman, Alan M. "International Diversification and Multinational Banking," in Sarkin J. Khoury and Alo Gosh (eds.), *Recent Developments in International Banking and Finance* (Lexington, MA: D. C. Heath, 1987).

Rugman, Alan M. and Anderson, Andrew. "Globalization of Banking Services: Canada's Strategies in the Triad," in Yair Aharoni (ed.), *Coalitions and Competition: The Globalization of Professional Business Services* (London: Routledge, 1993).

Rugman, Alan M. and Eden, Lorraine. *Multinationals and Transfer Pricing* (London: Croom Helm and New York: St Martin's Press, 1985).

Shapiro, Alan C. *Multinational Financial Management*, 3rd edn (Boston MA: Allyn & Bacon, 1989).

Stanley, Marjorie T. "Capital Structure and Cost of Capital for the Multinational Firm," *Journal of International Business Studies*, vol. 21, no. 2 (Spring/Summer 1981).

Tsetsekos, George P. and Gombola, Michael J. "Foreign and Domestic Divestments: Evidence on Valuation Effects of Plant Closings," *Journal of International Business Studies*, vol. 23, no. 2 (Second Quarter 1992).

Wallace, Wandaa. "The Value Relevance of Accounting: The Rest of the Story," *European Management Journal*, vol. 18, no. 6 (December 2000).

PART FOUR

International Business Strategies in Action

Chapter 15

Corporate Strategy and National Competitiveness

CONTENTS

OBJECTIVES OF THE CHAPTER

The primary objective of this chapter is to provide an overall framework for understanding how both nations and MNEs must fashion their strategies to achieve international competitiveness. In doing so, we give particular consideration to Canada and Mexico.

The objectives of this chapter are to:

1. *Examine* the determinants and external variables in Porter's "diamond" model of national competitiveness and critique and evaluate this model.
2. *Present* a "double diamond" model that illustrates how firms in non-triad countries such as Canada are using their diamond to design corporate strategies for the North American market.
3. *Discuss* the benefits and effects of a free trade agreement and a North American Free Trade Agreement on both Mexico and Canada.
4. *Describe* how Mexico is using a double diamond model to tap into the North American market.
5. *Define* the terms *economic integration* and *national responsiveness* and relate the importance of these two concepts to MNE strategies throughout the world.

ACTIVE LEARNING CASE

Worldwide operations and local strategies of ABB

Asea Brown Boveri (ABB) is headquartered in Zurich, Switzerland, and is one of Europe's major industrial firms. Since the merger in 1987 that created the company, ABB has been acquiring or taking minority positions in a wide number of firms throughout the world. In recent years it has purchased Westinghouse's transmission and distribution operations and Combustion Engineering, the manufacturer of power-generation and process-automation equipment. In Mexico, ABB acquired FIP SA in 2001, an oil and gas production equipment company. The conglomerate, which currently employs 160,000 people worldwide, has annual revenues in excess of $23 billion. Fifty-five per cent of its revenues come from Europe, 25 per cent the Americas, and 12 per cent from Asia. The remainder comes from Africa and the Middle East.

The company operates on both local and global terms. On the one hand, the firm attempts to maintain deep local roots wherever it operates so that it can modify both products and operations to that market. For example, managers are trained to adapt to cultural differences and to learn how to communicate effectively with local customers. At the same time ABB works to be global and to make products that can be sold anywhere in the world because their technology and quality give them a worldwide appeal.

A good example of a business that demonstrates ABB advantages is transportation. The company generates $2 billion a year in revenues from such products as subway cars, locomotives, suburban trains, trolleys, and the electrical and signaling systems that support these products. This is possible for four reasons: (1) the company's research and development makes it a technology leader in locomotives and power electronics, enabling the firm to develop and build high-speed trains and rail networks throughout the world; (2) the company's operations are structured to take advantage of economies of scale and thus keep prices competitive; (3) the company adapts to local environments and works closely with customers so that it is viewed as a national, not a foreign, company; and (4) the company works closely with companies in other countries that are favored by their own government but need assistance in financing and producing locomotive equipment for that market. As a result, ABB is able to capitalize on its technological and manufacturing expertise and to develop competitive advantages in both triad and non-triad markets.

In some cases ABB has gone as far as taking an ownership position in companies that are located in emerging economic markets. For example, the firm purchased 76 per cent of Zamech, Poland's leading manufacturer of steam turbines, transmission gears, marine equipment, and metal castings. ABB has bought into two other Polish firms that make a wide range of generating equipment and electric drives. ABB is now in the process of reorganizing these firms into profit centers, transferring its own expertise to local operations, and developing worldwide quality standards and controls for production. If all goes according to plan, ABB will soon have a thriving Polish operation that will be helping to rebuild Eastern Europe.

The company works hard to be a good "citizen" of each country in which it operates, while also maintaining its supranational status. As a result, ABB is proving that it is possible to have worldwide operations and local strategies that work harmoniously.

Website: ***www.abb.com***.

Sources: Adapted from William Taylor, "The Logic of Global Business: An Interview with ABB's Percy Barnevik," *Harvard Business Review*, March/April 1991, pp. 91–105; Carla Rapoport, "A Tough Swede Invades the US," *Fortune*, June 29, 1992, pp. 76–79; Carol Kennedy, "ABB: Model Merger for the New Europe," *Long Range Planning*, vol. 25, no. 5 (1992), pp. 10–17; Edward L. Andrews, "ABB Will Cut 10,000 Jobs and Switch Focus to Asia," *New York Times*, October 22, 1997, p. C 2; ***www.abb.com***.

1. **In what way does ABB's strategy incorporate Porter's four country-specific determinants and two external variables?**
2. **Why did ABB buy Zamech? How can the company link Zamech to its overall strategic plan?**
3. **How does ABB address the issues of globalization and national responsiveness? In each case, cite an example.**

INTRODUCTION

Some multinational firms rely on their home market to generate the research, development, design, or manufacturing that is needed to sell their goods in international markets. More and more, however, MNEs are finding that they must focus on the markets where they are doing business and on strategies for tapping the resources of these markets and gaining sales entry. In short, multinationals can no longer rely exclusively on the competitive advantage that they hold at home to provide them with a sustainable advantage overseas.

In addition, many small countries realize that they must rely on export strategies to ensure the growth of their economies. Those that have been most successful with this strategy have managed to tap into markets within triad countries. Good examples are Canada and Mexico; both have found the US to be a lucrative market for exports and imports. As a result, many successful business firms in these two countries have integrated themselves into the US economy, and in the process have created what some international economists call a North American market. In the future many more MNEs are going to be following this pattern of linking into the economies of triad members.

The basic strategy that these MNEs are following can be tied directly to the Porter model that was presented in Chapter 1, although some significant modifications of this model are in order. We will first examine Porter's ideas in more detail and then show how these ideas are serving as the basis for developing firm strategies and international competitiveness in Canada and Mexico.

PORTER'S DIAMOND

In Chapter 1 we identified four determinants of national competitive advantage, as set forth by Porter (see Figure 1.1). We noted that these factors can be critical in helping a country to build and maintain competitive advantage. We will now return to Porter's "diamond" framework in more depth, see how his findings apply specifically to triad countries, and then determine how these ideas can be modified and applied to nations that are not triad members.

Determinants and external variables

Porter's "diamond" model is based on four country-specific determinants and two external variables. The determinants include:

1. *Factor conditions.* These include (1) the quantity, skills, and cost of the personnel; (2) the abundance, quality, accessibility, and cost of the nation's physical resources such as land, water, mineral deposits, timber, hydroelectric power sources, and fishing grounds; (3) the nation's stock of knowledge resources, including scientific, technical, and market knowledge that affect the quantity and quality of goods and services; (4) the amount and cost of capital resources that are available to finance industry; and (5) the type, quality, and user cost of the infrastructure, including the nation's transportation system, communications system, health-care system, and other factors that directly affect the quality of life in the country.
2. *Demand conditions.* These include (1) the composition of demand in the home market as reflected by the various market niches that exist, and buyer sophistication and how well the needs of buyers in the home market precede those of buyers in other markets; (2) the size and growth rate of the home demand; and (3) the ways through

which domestic demand is internationalized and pulls a nation's products and services abroad.

3. *Related and supporting industries.* These include (1) the presence of internationally competitive supplier industries that create advantages in downstream industries through efficient, early, or rapid access to cost-effective inputs and (2) internationally competitive related industries that can coordinate and share activities in the value chain when competing or those that involve complementary products.
4. *Firm strategy, structure, and rivalry.* These include (1) the ways in which firms are managed and choose to compete, (2) the goals that companies seek to attain as well as the motivations of their employees and managers, and (3) the amount of domestic rivalry and the creation and persistence of competitive advantage in the respective industry.

The four determinants of national advantage shape the competitive environment of industries. However, two other variables, chance and government, also play important roles:

1. *The role of chance.* Chance events can nullify the advantages of some competitors and bring about a shift in overall competitive position because of developments such as (1) new inventions, (2) political decisions by foreign governments, (3) wars, (4) significant shifts in world financial markets or exchange rates, (5) discontinuities in input costs such as oil shocks, (6) surges in world or regional demand, and (7) major technological breakthroughs.
2. *The role of government.* Government can influence all four of the major determinants through actions such as (1) subsidies, (2) education policies, (3) the regulation or deregulation of capital markets, (4) the establishment of local product standards and regulations, (5) the purchase of goods and services, (6) tax laws, and (7) antitrust regulation.[1]

Figure 15.1 provides an illustration of the complete system of these determinants and external variables. Each of the four determinants affects the others and all in turn are affected by the role of chance and government.

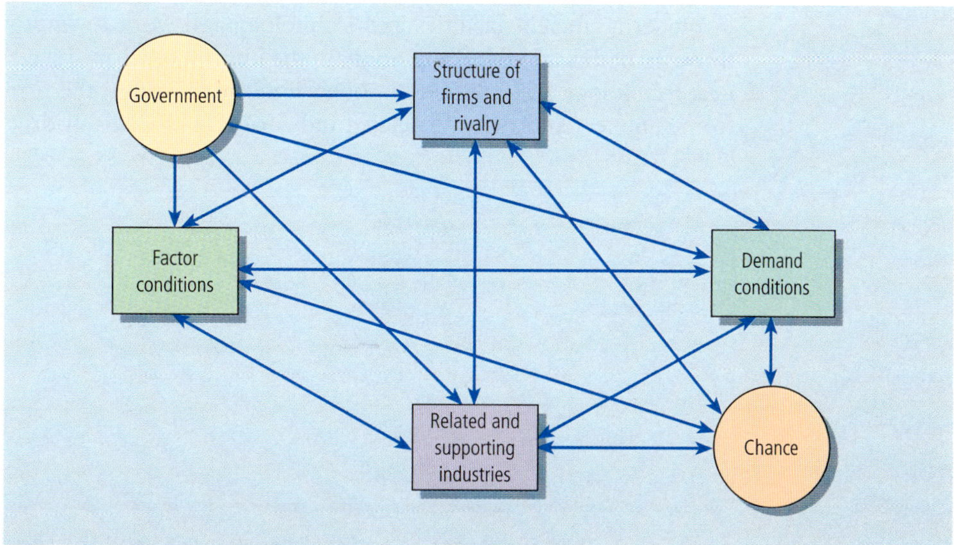

Figure 15.1 Porter's single diamond framework

Source: Adapted with the permission of The Free Press, an imprint of Simon & Schuster Adult Publishing Group, from *The Competitive Advantage of Nations* by Michael E. Porter. Copyright © 1990, 1998 by Michael E. Porter.

Critique and evaluation of the model

In applying this model to international business strategy, we must first critique and evaluate Porter's paradigm and supporting arguments. First, the Porter model was constructed based on statistical analysis of aggregate data on export shares for 10 countries: Denmark, Italy, Japan, Singapore, South Korea, Sweden, Switzerland, the UK, the US, and West Germany. In addition, historical case studies were provided for four industries: the German printing press industry, the US patient-monitoring-equipment industry, the Italian ceramic tile industry, and the Japanese robotics industry. In each case the country is either a member of the triad or an industrialized nation. Since most countries of the world do not have the same economic strength or affluence as those studied by Porter, it is highly unlikely that his model can be applied to them without modification.

Second, the government is of critical importance in influencing a home nation's competitive advantage. For example, it can use tariffs as a direct entry barrier to penalize foreign firms, and it can employ subsidies as an indirect vehicle for penalizing foreign-based firms. Government actions such as these, however well intentioned, can backfire and end up creating a "sheltered" domestic industry that is unable to compete in the worldwide market.[2]

Third, although chance is a critical influencing factor in international business strategy, it is extremely difficult to predict and guard against. For example, until the day Saddam Hussein invaded Kuwait in 1991, the US government was predicting that there would be no invasion. In a similar vein, technological breakthroughs in computers and consumer electronics have resulted in rapid changes that, in many cases, were not predicted by market leaders.

Fourth, in the study of international business Porter's model must be applied in terms of company-specific considerations and not in terms of national advantages. As Porter so well notes in his book, "Firms, not nations, compete in international markets."[3]

Fifth, in support of his model, Porter delineates four distinct stages of national competitive development: factor-driven, investment-driven, innovation-driven, and wealth-driven (see Figure 15.2). In the factor-driven stage, successful industries draw their advantage almost solely from the basic factors of production such as natural resources and the nation's large, inexpensive labor pool. Although successful internationally, the industries compete primarily on price. In the investment-driven stage, companies invest in modern, efficient facilities and technology and work to improve these investments through modification and alteration. In the innovation-driven stage, firms work to create new technology and methods through innovation within the firm and with assistance from suppliers and firms in related industries. In the wealth-driven stage, firms begin

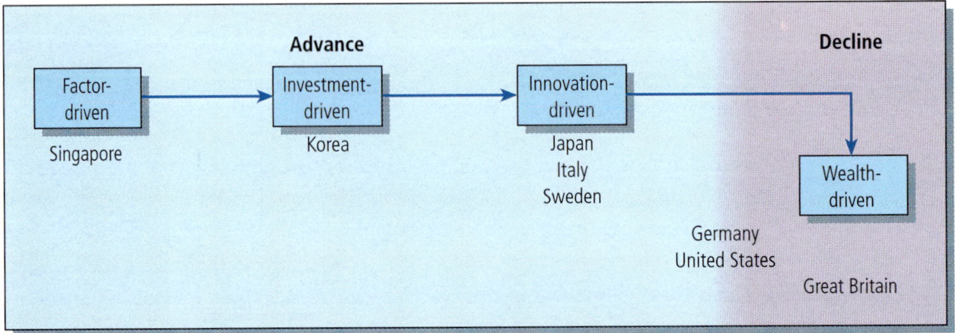

Figure 15.2 The four stages of national development and the current position of select nations

Source: Adapted with the permission of The Free Press, an imprint of Simon & Schuster Adult Publishing Group, from *The Competitive Advantage of Nations* by Michael E. Porter. Copyright © 1990, 1998 by Michael E. Porter.

to lose their competitive advantage, rivalry ebbs, and there is a decline in motivation to invest. As seen in Figure 15.2, Porter believes that Singapore is in the factor-driven stage, Korea is investment-driven, Japan is innovation-driven, Germany and the US are between innovation and wealth-driven, and Great Britain is wealth-driven. Since the stage of development greatly influences the country's competitive response, the placement of countries in Figure 15.2 is critical. So too is the logic that countries move from one stage to another, rather than spanning two or more of these stages because there are likely to be industries or companies in all major economies that are operating at each of these stages.

Sixth, Porter contends that only outward FDI is valuable in creating competitive advantage, and inbound foreign investment is never the solution to a nation's competitive problems. Moreover, foreign subsidiaries are not sources of competitive advantage and "widespread foreign investment usually indicates that the process of competitive upgrading in an economy is *not entirely healthy* because domestic firms in many industries lack the capabilities to defend their market positions against foreign firms."[4] These statements are questionable and have already been rejected in this text. For example, Canadian-based scholars such as Safarian,[5] Rugman,[6] and Crookell[7] have all demonstrated that research and development undertaken by foreign-owned firms is not significantly different from that of Canadian-owned companies. Additionally, Rugman has found that the 20 largest US subsidiaries in Canada export virtually as much as they import (the rate of exports to sales is 25 per cent, whereas that of imports to sales is 26 per cent).[8]

Seventh, as seen in Figure 15.2, reliance on natural resources (the factor-driven stage) is viewed by Porter as insufficient to create worldwide competitive stature.[9] However, Canada, for one, has developed a number of successful megafirms that have turned the country's comparative advantage in natural resources into proprietary firm-specific advantages in resource processing and further refining, and these are sources of sustainable advantage.[10] Moreover, case studies of the country's successful multinationals such as Alcan, Noranda, and Nova help to illustrate the methods by which value added has been introduced by the managers of these resource-based companies.[11]

Eighth, the Porter model does not adequately address the role of MNEs. Researchers such as Dunning[12] have suggested including multinational activity as a third outside variable (in addition to chance and government). Certainly there is good reason to question whether MNE activity is covered in the "firm strategy, structure, and rivalry" determinant, and some researchers have raised the question regarding how the same rivalry determinant can both include multinationality for global industries and yet exclude it for multidomestic industries. As Dunning notes, "there is ample evidence to suggest that MNEs are influenced in their competitiveness by the configuration of the diamond in other than their home countries, and that this in turn may impinge upon the competitiveness of home countries."[13] For example, Nestlé earns 98 per cent of its sales outside Switzerland.[14] Thus the Swiss diamond of competitive advantage is less relevant than that of the countries in which Nestlé operates. This is true not only for MNEs in Switzerland but for 95 per cent of the world's MNEs as well. For example, virtually all of Canada's large multinationals rely on sales in the US and other triad markets. Indeed, it could be argued that the US diamond is more relevant for Canada's industrial multinationals than Canada's own diamond; over 70 per cent of Canadian MNE sales take place in the US. Other nations with MNEs based on small home diamonds include Australia, New Zealand, Finland, and most, if not all, Asian and Latin American countries as well as a large number of other small countries. Even small nations in the EU, such as Denmark, have been able to overcome the problem of a small domestic market by gaining access to one of the triad markets. So in applying Porter's framework to international business at large, one conclusion is irrefutable: *different diamonds need to be constructed and analyzed for different countries.*

Active learning check 

Review your answer to Active Learning Case question 1 and make any changes you like. Then compare your answer with the one below.

1. In what way does ABB's strategy incorporate Porter's four country-specific determinants and two external variables?

The strategy incorporates Porter's country-specific determinants as part of a well-formulated global strategy that is designed to tap the strengths of various markets. For example, the company draws on the factor conditions and demand conditions in Europe to support its transportation business. The company also draws on supporting industries to help sustain its worldwide competitive advantage in that industry. At the same time the company's strategy, structure, and rivalry are designed to help it compete at the local level. The strategy incorporates the external variable of government by considering relations between countries as a lubricant for worldwide economic integration. The strategy addresses the variable of chance by operating globally and thus reducing the likelihood that a war or a regional recession will have a major negative effect on operations. The firm's heavy focus on core technologies and research and development also helps to minimize this chance variable.

OTHER "DIAMOND" MODELS: TWO CASE EXAMPLES

Researchers have recently begun using the Porter diamond as a basis for analyzing the international competitiveness of smaller countries. This approach builds on Porter's theme of corporate strategy and process as a source of competitive advantage for a nation.

Canada and the double diamond

Figure 15.3 illustrates how Porter's single diamond would look if it were applied to Canada's case.[15]

Two themes have recurred consistently in Canadian industrial policy: export promotion for natural resource industries and import substitution in the domestic arena. The Canadian market has always been seen as too small to support the development of economies of scale that are required in modern industry. Hence it has been the practice in Canada to provide the base for developing large-scale resource businesses that are designed to exploit the natural resources found in the country. Export strategies have placed emphasis on commodity products that have been developed in isolation from major customers. In the past these strategies had been encouraged by US government policies that removed or eliminated tariffs on imports of commodities that are not produced extensively in the US. The Canadian government's role had been to help leading Canadian-based businesses by establishing relatively low taxes on resource extraction and by subsidizing the costs of capital through grants, low-interest loans, and loan guarantees.

With respect to import substitution, the Canadian goal had been to use tariff and non-tariff measures to provide a protected environment for development of secondary industry. Under this arrangement the country's approach to business was largely focused inwardly; it relied solely on the extent and quality of national resources as the base for the creation of wealth.

By the mid-1960s, however, it became clear that a more international focus was needed. The 1967 Canada–United States Auto Pact demonstrated that significant economic benefits would result from the elimination of tariffs on trade between the two countries in autos and parts. This agreement eventually became the model for the United States–

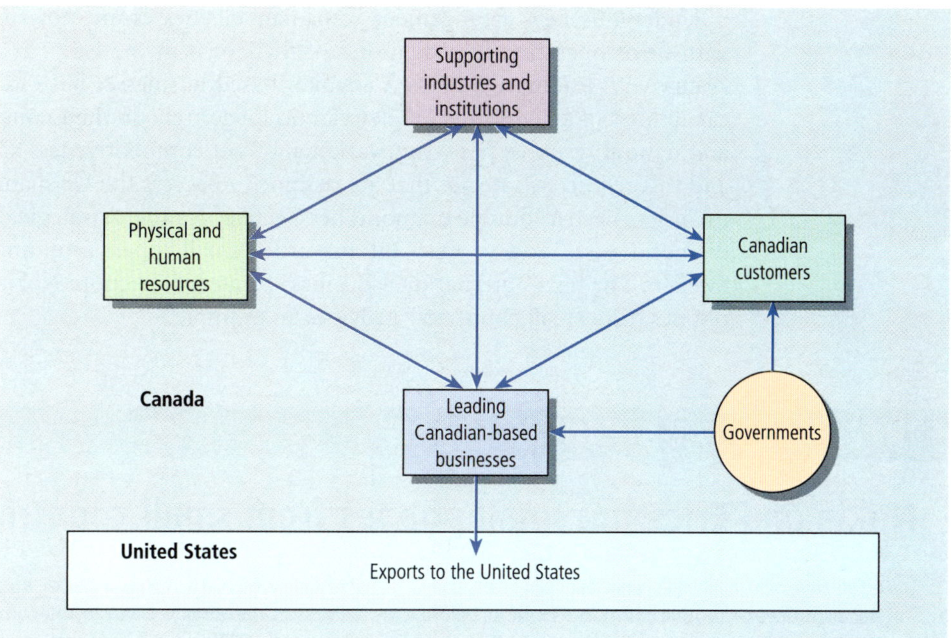

Figure 15.3 The single diamond view

Source: Adapted from Alan M. Rugman and Joseph R. D'Cruz, *Fast Forward: Improving Canada's International Competitiveness* (Toronto: Kodak Canada, 1991), p. 35.

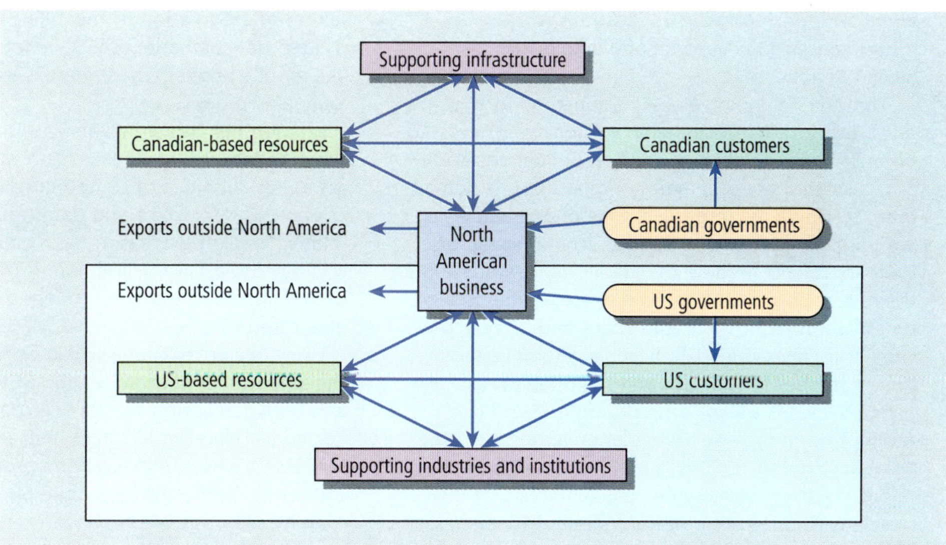

Figure 15.4 Canadian–US double diamond

Source: Adapted from Alan M. Rugman and Joseph R. D'Cruz, "The 'Double Diamond' Model of International Competitiveness: the Canadian Experience," *Management International Review*, vol. 33, Special Issue 2 (1993), p. 32.

Canada Free Trade Agreement.[16] In the process Canadian plants gained economies of scale by producing for the North American market as a whole rather than for the Canadian market alone. For corporate strategy, the result of North American economic integration has been the development of a Canadian US "double diamond". This double diamond shows that the two countries are integrated for strategy purposes into a single market (see Figure 15.4).

Under this new arrangement Canadian businesses are now in direct competition with firms operating in a diamond of their own in the US.[17] In order to survive this rivalry with leading US firms, Canadian-based businesses have to develop competitive capabilities of a high order.[18] They can no longer rely on their country's home diamond and natural resource base. Innovation and cost competitiveness are equally important, and this requires strategies that are designed to access the US diamond. Now Canadian managers need a "double diamond perspective" for their strategic decisions. The double diamond is, of course, relevant for other small, open economies like Finland and Sweden. The box "International Business Strategy in Action: Nokia and Ericsson: small phones from small countries" provides an example.

INTERNATIONAL BUSINESS STRATEGY *IN ACTION*

Nokia and Ericsson: small phones from small countries

Based in one of the world's smallest countries, the largest producer of mobile phones is Finland's Nokia. Founded in 1865, Nokia was a major manufacturer of paper products before it transformed itself into a high-tech producer of electronic products, especially cellular phones, starting in the 1970s. By 2000, Nokia was the largest company in Finland with sales of nearly US $28 billion. Production facilities span 10 countries and R&D is performed in 15 locations worldwide. It had sales in 130 countries and employed 60,000 people.

From the beginning Nokia has pursued foreign sales. This internationalization strategy was necessary because Finland only has 3 million people and today only a small share of its sales originates in its home base. So Nokia became the mobile phone leader in Scandinavia, despite competition from Ericsson of Sweden. Next it became the leader in Britain and then the rest of Europe and formed strategic alliances with US distributors such as Radio Shack and US telecom companies like AT&T. The firm has also developed special phones for Chinese and Japanese users.

Nokia spends a large amount on R&D and it is attempting to provide mobile phones which enable "global roaming" by being usable across different telecom systems worldwide. This requires that it work closely with different political regimes in order to try and develop an industry standard. In this venture it works with its great rival, Ericsson. They are attempting to establish GSM as the standard for mobile phones across Europe, and as one of the global standards. The next generation of mobile phones may build on a system like GSM.

L. M. Ericsson has over 105,000 employees and sales of US $30 billion in the 140 countries in which it operates. In 1997, Ericsson was the world's largest producer of digital mobile phones. Over 50 per cent of its sales are in Europe, 21 per cent in Asia, 13 per cent in North America, and 16 per cent in South America. Unlike Nokia, which started as a paper and rubber producer, Ericsson has always been in telecommunications, starting in 1876 as a telephone manufacturer. It has always been innovative and, today, one in four employees works in R&D. In other areas of business it developed telephone switches in which it competes with firms such as Canada's Nortel and France's Alcatel. Ericsson was well positioned to benefit from the telecom deregulation of the 1980s and 1990s. This has created new demand, especially for new equipment like mobile phones where there were few local monopoly producers.

Ericsson has formed alliances with Compaq, Intel, Hewlett Packard, and Texas Instruments. These firms act as key suppliers of components and products that Ericsson uses for voice and data transmission. The relative weakness Ericsson has, compared with Nokia and Motorola, is its brand name. The firm has strong production technology but needs to improve on its marketing side.

Firms like Ericsson and Nokia will benefit from the alliance between AT&T and British Telecom, and between Sprint, France Telecom, and Deutsche Telekom. These big alliances help set standardized services to which mobile phone producers can respond efficiently. In the future mobile phones will become even smaller, but the two producers from small countries, Nokia of Finland and Ericsson of Sweden, will become even bigger.

Websites: ***www.nokia.com***; ***www.ericsson.com***; ***www.motorola.com***; ***www.nortelnetworks.com***; ***www.alcatel.fr***; ***www.att.com***; ***www.compaq.com***; ***www.hp.com***; ***www.intel.com*** and ***www.ti.com***.

Sources: Annual Reports; Richard Hylton, Nick Moore and Roger Honour, "Making Money in the Tech Market," *Fortune*, May 13, 1996; Erick Schonfeld, "Hold the Phone: Motorola Is Going Nowhere Fast," *Fortune*, March 30, 1998; Caroline Daniel, "World's Most Respected Companies," *FT.com*, December 17, 2001; ***www.nokia.com***; ***www.ericsson.com***.

The Free Trade Agreement has also created a series of unique pressures on the Canadian subsidiaries of US multinationals. Many of these subsidiaries were created for the purpose of overcoming Canadian tariff barriers that were designed to encourage development of local operations. These businesses are now unnecessary, and many of them are currently in direct competition with their US-based parent. If they cannot compete successfully, future business will go south of the border.[19]

Meanwhile, major Canadian firms are working to develop competitive positions in the US as well as worldwide.[20] A good example is Nortel Networks, the country's leading manufacturer of telephone equipment. The firm has now established a significant manufacturing and product development presence in the US from which it sources a large part of its product line. The company has two major operating centers: one in Canada outside Toronto and the other near Washington DC. Vigorous rivalry between operations in both countries has helped Nortel Networks to develop global competitiveness, as recently demonstrated by its success in winning a large contract with Japan's Nippon Telephone and Telegraph.[21]

Bombardier Inc. provides another example. Beginning as a Canadian manufacturer of snow-going equipment, the company has now grown into a multinational firm with interests in aviation, transportation, and financial services. In the aviation/aerospace business, Bombardier has major operations in Canada and the US, among other locations, and manufactures corporate jets, small airliners, amphibious planes, weapons systems, and space systems. The company's transportation operations have locations throughout North America and Europe and make passenger trains, mass transit railcars, and engines. Its recreational products division, located primarily in North America, manufactures snowmobiles, boats, all-terrain vehicles, and small electric cars. The firm's business/financial service operations, which are also heavily based in Canada and the US, provide business and consumer financial assistance.[22]

Other major Canadian firms are following suit, operating from a North American perspective in order to lay the groundwork for becoming globally competitive.[23] This involves viewing the US and Canada as home-based markets and integrating the use of both "diamonds" for development and implementation of strategy. In particular, this requires:

1. developing innovative new products and services that simultaneously meet the needs of the US and Canadian customer, recognizing that close relationships with demanding US customers should set the pace and style of product development;
2. drawing on the support industries and infrastructure of both the US and Canadian diamonds, realizing that the US diamond is more likely to possess deeper and more efficient markets for such industries; and
3. making free and full use of the physical and human resources in both countries.[24]

Strategic clusters in the double diamond

The primary advantage of using the double diamond is that it forces business and government leaders to think about management strategy and public policy in a more productive way. Rather than viewing the domestic diamond as the unit of analysis, it encourages managers from smaller countries always to be outward looking. Doing well in a double diamond is the first step toward global success.

Strategic cluster
A network of businesses and supporting activities located in a specific region, where flagship firms compete globally and supporting activities are home-based

Once a country has recognized the benefit of the double-diamond perspective, it should first identify successful and potentially viable clusters of industries within its borders and then examine their linkages and performance across the double diamond. A **strategic cluster** is a network of businesses and supporting activities located in a specific region, where the flagship firms compete globally and the supporting activities are home-based, although some of them can be foreign-owned. In addition, some of the critical business inputs and skills may come from outside the country with their relevance and usefulness being determined by the membership of the strategic cluster. A successful strategic cluster will have one or more large MNEs at its center. Whether these are home- or foreign-owned is irrelevant so long as they are globally competitive. These MNEs are flagship firms on which the strategic cluster depends. Ideally, they operate on a global basis and plan their competitive strategies within the framework of global competition. A vital component of the cluster is companies with related and supporting activities, including both private and public sector organizations. In addition, there are think tanks, research groups, and educational institutions. Some parts of this network can even be based outside the country, but the linkages across the border and the leadership role of the nation's flagships result in world-class competitive multinationals.[25]

Currently there are several strategic clusters in Canada. One is the auto assembly and auto parts industry in southwestern Ontario, led by the big three US auto multinationals with their related and affiliated suppliers and distributors. There are linkages to various high-tech firms and research groups; these linkages span the border, as does the auto assembly industry itself. Other strategic clusters are based in banking and financial services in Toronto, the advanced manufacturing and telecommunications strategic cluster in Toronto, the forest products industries in western and eastern Canada, the energy clusters in Alberta, and the fisheries in Atlantic Canada. Some of these clusters are led by flagship Canadian-owned multinationals such as Nortel, Nova, or Bombardier; others are led by, or include, foreign-owned firms such as IBM Canada and DuPont Canada.[26]

Many Canadian-based clusters are resource-based. The challenge for managers in these clusters is to continue to add value and to eliminate the commodity nature of Canada's resource industries. One way to do this is by developing a global marketing strategy that builds on the Canadian–US double diamond instead of remaining as the extractor or harvester of resources. To implement such a global strategy requires a large investment in people who will bring strong marketing skills and develop a global intelligence network to identify the different tastes and preferences of customers. This network provides a role for smaller knowledge-intensive marketing research and consulting firms to participate in the resource-based cluster. There is also the potential for collaborative ventures.

A 1998 World Economic Forum Report ranks Canada as the fifth most competitive in the world with Singapore, Hong Kong, the US, and the UK ahead of it.[27] The big problem Canada now faces is that of raising its productivity levels. According to the Organization for Economic Cooperation and Development, since 1990 this level has increased less than half as fast as that of the US.[28]

Further research is required to investigate Canadian-based strategic clusters and their competitive advantages, compared with rival clusters within North America and also around the world. This will require two types of work. First, the intra-firm competition of clusters within North America needs new data that do not ignore the nature of foreign ownership and whether US and Canadian foreign direct investment (FDI) by sector is inbound or outbound. Instead, direct investment in North America must be regarded as "domestic" and be contrasted with "external" direct investment from Japan[29] and the EU.[30] Similarly, trade flows between Canada and the US must be thought of as intra-firm when they occur between components of a cluster or even between and among clusters.

This approach is so radical that many existing concepts must be rethought. For example, the level and extent of subsidies available to clusters located in the US (for example, in the Great Lakes states) must be related to those paid by provinces in Canada (such as Ontario). Yet there is little or no published work on state or provincial subsidies; even the work on federal subsidies in either country is extremely thin.

Finally, the real sources of Canadian competitive advantage are to be discovered not only by statistical analysis, but also by interviews of managers and officials, that is by fieldwork in the strategic clusters. Such "hands-on" research is exceptionally time-consuming and expensive. However, to make the task feasible, a number of important strategic clusters can be selected for analysis, self-audits should be made, conferences should be held, and so on. The future success of these efforts will depend heavily on leadership by Canadian business leaders and government officials.

Mexico and the double diamond

We can also adapt the Porter diamond to analyze firm strategies and international competitiveness in Mexico. The basic concepts in this framework are the same as those discussed in the Canadian diamond.

Linking to the US diamond

Mexico's linkage to the US diamond is somewhat different from Canada's. One reason is the fact that there are few home-based MNEs that have the capital to invest in the US or Canada.[31] (Review Chapter 3 for information on how and why FDI is used by MNEs.) In fact, as seen in Table 15.1, during the 1990s Mexico's FDI in the US increased by only $1.5 billion and it remained negligible in Canada. In contrast, by 2000 Canada had just under $2 billion invested in Mexico and the US had over $34 billion there.[32] More importantly, US FDI in Canada reached over $110 billion and Canada's FDI in the US was $90 billion. Thus Mexico's strategy with its North American neighbors relies more heavily on trade than on FDI for outward market access, while using inward FDI to help promote internal development.

As seen in Figure 15.5, Mexico and the US conduct over $267 billion of trade every year and Canada and Mexico do over $5 billion of business. Additionally, Mexico is

Table 15.1 **Stocks of FDI by Canada, the US, and Mexico, 1988–1999 (in millions of US $)**

	Canada's FDI in:		*US FDI in:*		*Mexico's FDI in:*	
Year	*United States*	*Mexico*	*Canada*	*Mexico*	*Canada*	*United States*
1988	39,602	165	62,656	5,712	25.2	218
1989	44,495	202	63,948	8,264	10.1	350
1990	51,544	212	69,508	10,313	—	575
1991	55,353	176	70,711	12,501	—	747
1992	53,418	375	68,690	13,730	49.7	1,289
1993	52,565	413	69,922	15,221	120.4	1,244
1994	56,236	783	78,018	16,169	130.4	2,069
1995	62,975	823	85,441	15,980	144.0	1,850
1996	68,971	1,416	91,301	19,900	—	1,436
1997	72,140	1,555	99,859	25,395	—	1,723
1998	83,859	1,826	101,871	28,396	—	2,055
1999	90,394	1,901	111,707	34,265	—	1,730

Source: Adapted from OECD (2000) *International Direct Investment Statistics Yearbook, 2000*. Copyright OECD, 2000. Numbers for Mexico, 1998 to 1999 are from United States, Bureau of Economic Analysis, 1998–2000.

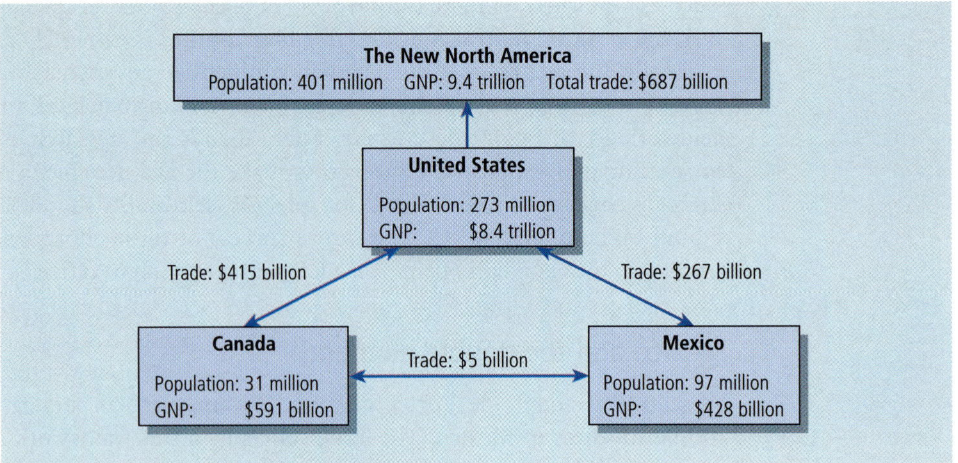

Figure 15.5 The shape of North America

Source: Adapted from World Bank, *World Development Report 2000, 2001* and IMF, *Direction of Trade Statistics Yearbook, 2001*.

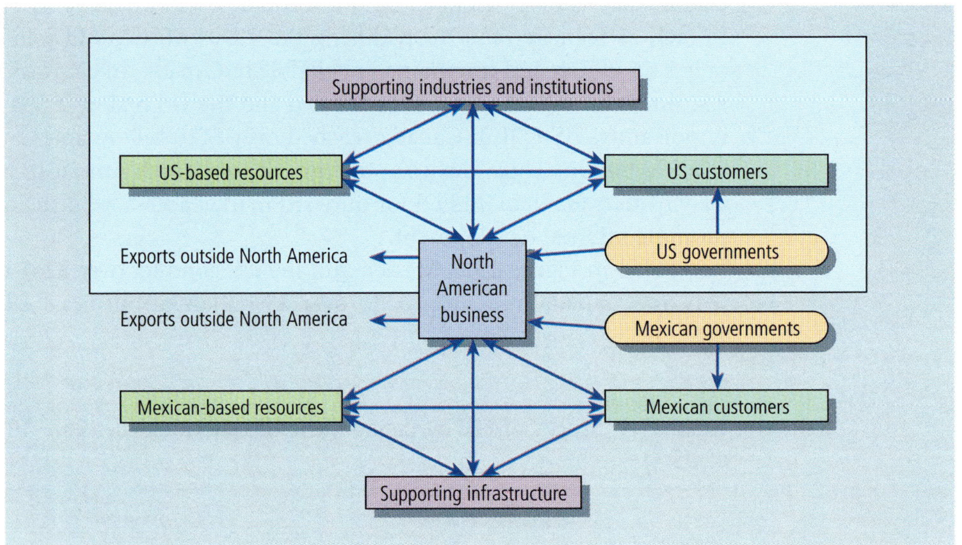

Figure 15.6 US–Mexican double diamond

Source: Richard M. Hodgetts, "Porter's Diamond Framework in a Mexican Context," *Management International Review*, vol. 33, Special Issue no. 2 (1993), p. 48.

the third largest trading partner of the US, and, while the country has a negative trade balance with the world, it runs a positive balance with the US. In fact, in recent years the latter has accounted for over 70 per cent of Mexico's exports *and* imports. The next most important trading partner is Japan, with a mere 0.6 per cent of Mexico's exports and 3.7 per cent of its imports. So Mexico is closely linked with the US economy, and its economic growth will depend heavily on participation in this North American market.[33] Figure 15.6 illustrates this idea with the US–Mexican double diamond.

Mexico is linking itself to the US diamond in a number of ways.[34] One is by serving as a customer for outside goods. For example, Caterpillar is the main supplier of heavy equipment for road building in Mexico; General Electric exports to Mexico over

$100 million of goods annually, including locomotives, power-generation equipment, and diagnostic imaging equipment; and Kodak exports over $125 million annually of cameras, film, and other products.[35]

At the same time Mexican businesses are working to expand their links in the US market. Between 1994 and 2000 exports to the US market increased from $50 billion to almost $150 billion. Much of this output is in the form of manufactured goods, in particular automobiles. In fact, auto production in Mexico accounts for employment of over 450,000 workers and generates close to 1.9 million vehicles, most of which are targeted for the US market.[36] General Motors, for example, has invested over $1 billion since 1993 in setting up local operations and is becoming one of the major producers of cars in Mexico.[37] At the same time US firms are also investing in a wide array of non-automotive projects.[38] IBM, for example, now produces magnetic readers for computer hard-disk drives in Guadalajara and air ships them to California on a daily basis. Asian firms are no longer able to compete effectively in this market. The same is true in textiles, where Mexican firms are now proving dominant.

> In 1996 Mexico overtook China as the largest supplier of textiles and garments to the US. Now, US mills are rushing to invest. In Altamira on the Gulf of Mexico, for example, Guilford Mills Inc., based in Greensboro, NC, is building a $100 million knitting, dyeing, and finishing plant. In Puebla, several Mexican families set up a venture, Skytex, which is turning out two million yards of polyester fabric per month. Half of it goes the to US. "This plant was conceived for NAFTA," says Deputy Sales Director Alberto Serur: "I can ship to the border in 18 hours, while the Asians take 21 days."[39]

Maquiladoras

In 1965 the Mexican government established the *maquiladora* industry to attract foreign manufacturing operations. Imported products for the *maquiladoras*' production are exempt from Mexican duties as long as they are used for exports. In recent years certain items such as transportation equipment and computers, not directly involved in production, have also been made exempt from duties. Additionally, *maquiladoras* are no longer restricted to the border zone, and some have been permitted to settle inland and to sell finished products on the domestic market.

Today the *maquiladora* industry is one of the country's largest sources of hard currency earnings from exports, after oil. In 1965 there were 12 *maquiladora* plants and by 1990 this number had increased to 3,562.[40] These businesses, which are principally US-owned, are widely considered to have established a basis for more intensified economic cooperation anticipated under an FTA (Free Trade Agreement).[41] At the same time the growth of these companies is creating friction because many Americans feel that the low wage rates in Mexico are causing firms to transfer work there and to lay off employees back home.

What will the future hold regarding Mexico and North America? The most likely developments will be continued investment by US and Canadian firms and the establishment of worldwide competition there. By the year 2005 Mexico is likely to be manufacturing and shipping many more products back north as well as exporting to more countries than they are doing today. In contrast to Canada, which is trying to create and nurture Canadian-owned MNEs that will compete worldwide, Mexico will build these businesses internally with financial and technological investments, primarily from its North American neighbors.[42]

The double diamond examples of Canada and Mexico help to explain how MNEs can use Porter's ideas to formulate strategies. However, these firms also need to address the issue of national responsiveness, the focus of the discussion in the next section.

Active learning check

Review your answer to Active Learning Case question 2 and make any changes you like. Then compare your answer with the one below.

2. Why did ABB buy Zamech? How can the company link Zamech to its overall strategic plan?

ABB bought Zamech for a number of reasons. The company provides a springboard to the Eastern European market, which is likely to grow dramatically during the coming decade. ABB links Zamech to its overall strategic plan by using the same approach that US firms are employing with Mexico. The company has purchased an equity position and is helping to set up a manufacturing operation that can provide goods for the local market as well as for other markets in both Eastern and Western Europe.

GLOBALIZATION AND CORPORATE STRATEGY

Globalization
The production and distribution of products and services of a homogeneous type and quality on a worldwide basis

National responsiveness
The ability of MNEs to understand different consumer tastes in segmented regional markets and to respond to different national standards and regulations imposed by autonomous governments and agencies

A major trend that has affected the thinking of corporate MNE strategists over the last 10 years is that of balancing a concern for "globalization" (or economic integration) with national responsiveness. **Globalization** can be defined as the production and distribution of products and services of a homogeneous type and quality on a worldwide basis.[43] To a large extent MNEs have homogenized tastes and help to spread international consumerism. For example, throughout North America, the wealthier nations of Europe, and Japan, there has been a growing acceptance of standardized consumer electronic goods, automobiles, computers, calculators, and similar products. However, the goal of efficient economic performance through a universal globalization strategy has left MNEs open to the charge that they are overlooking the need to address national concerns. **National responsiveness** is the ability of MNEs to understand different consumer tastes in segmented regional markets and to respond to different national standards and regulations that are imposed by autonomous governments and agencies. Throughout this decade multinationals will continually have to deal with the twin goals of economic integration and national responsiveness.[44] See the box "International Business Strategy in Action: Tate & Lyle as a transnational."

INTERNATIONAL BUSINESS STRATEGY *IN ACTION*

Tate & Lyle as a transnational

The dominant firm in the sugar industry is Tate & Lyle plc, a British MNE founded in 1921. Its early success was based upon processing sugar from plantations in the Caribbean. It is the major sugar provider to Europe, is also present in North America, and now finds its fastest growing market in Asia, especially China, and in developing third world economies.

Tate and Lyle's firm-specific advantages are based on its brand name and reputation for quality and also on economies of scale in its very large sugar refinery plants. Since sugar producers (such as beet farmers in the US) are highly protected, Tate & Lyle needs to be nationally responsive to local regulations as well as highly globalized, i.e. it has to operate as a "transnational" firm. It has therefore developed a decentralized "regional" organizational structure to help develop responsiveness to local market demands and regulations.

The demand for sugar in wealthy Western economies is slowing down due to health concerns and the arrival of sugar substitutes in the form of artificial sweeteners and starches. In the 1980s Tate & Lyle made numerous acquisitions in the US, such as Staley (now Western Sugar). However, the company divested its US operations in 2001 after a decade long drop in the price of sugar. This has encouraged Tate & Lyle to broaden its market to Asia and the emerging economies of Eastern Europe, as well as to diversify into associated product areas, such as sweeteners, where it markets sucralose.

Websites: ***www.tate-lyle.co.uk***.

Sources: Tate & Lyle Annual Reports 1995, 1996, 1997; ***www.hoovers.com/capsules/42402.html***, "Hoover's Company Capsule – Tate & Lyle PLC"; Rene Pastor, "Domino Buyers See Promise in US Sugar Market", *Standard*, July 26, 2001.

Integration versus national responsiveness

Conceptually, the twin issues of integration and national responsiveness can be analyzed through the use of Figure 15.7, which has been adapted from Bartlett[45] and Bartlett and Ghoshal. Transnational MNEs need to reconcile these twin issues.

The vertical axis measures the need for globalization, frequently called "economic integration". Movement up the axis results in a greater degree of economic integration; this generates economies of scale as a firm moves into worldwide markets, selling a single product or service. These economies are captured as a result of centralizing specific activities in the value-added chain. They also occur by reaping the benefits of increased coordination and control of geographically dispersed activities.

The horizontal axis measures the need for corporations to be nationally responsive. Companies must address local tastes and government regulations. This may result in a geographical dispersion of activities or a decentralization of coordination and control for individual firms.

On the basis of the two axes in Figure 15.7, four situations can be distinguished. Quadrants 1 and 4 are the simplest cases. In quadrant 1 the need for integration is high and the need for awareness of sovereignty is low. This focus on economies of scale leads to competitive strategies that are based on price competition. In this environment mergers and acquisitions often occur.

The opposite situation is represented by quadrant 4, where the need for national responsiveness is high but the integration concern is low. In this case niche companies adapt products to satisfy the high demands of sovereignty and to ignore economies of scale since integration is not very important.

Quadrants 2 and 3 reflect opposite situations. Quadrant 2 incorporates those cases where the need for both integration and national responsiveness is low. Both the potential to obtain economies of scale and the benefits of being sensitive to sovereignty are of little value. Typical strategies in quadrant 2 are characterized by increased international

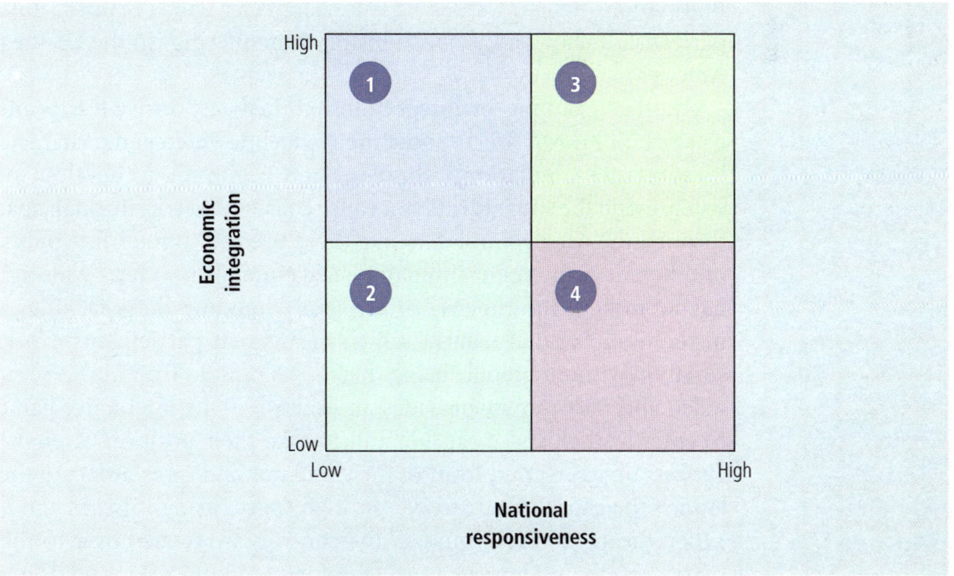

Figure 15.7 Integration and national responsiveness

Source: Reprinted by permission of Harvard Business School Press. Adapted from C. A. Bartlett, "Building and Managing the Transnational: the New Organizational Challenge", in *Competition in Global Industries* edited by M. E. Porter, Boston, MA 1986. Copyright © 1986 by the Harvard Business School Publishing Corporation; all rights reserved; and *Managing Across Borders: The Transnational Solution*, 2nd edn. by C. A. Bartlett and S. Ghoshal, Boston, MA 1998. Copyright © 1998 by Harvard Business School Publishing Corporation; all rights reserved.

standardization of products and services. This can lead to lower needs for centralized quality control and centralized strategic decision making, while simultaneously eliminating requirements to adapt activities to individual countries.

In quadrant 3 the needs for integration and national responsiveness are both high. There is a strong need for integration in production, along with higher requirements for regional adaptations in marketing. Quadrant 3 is the most challenging quadrant and one in which many successful "transnational" MNEs operate. Using this framework, we can analyze the impact of various exogenous policy shocks and trends on different industries, firms, banks, and other private sector institutions.

Balancing the trade-offs

MNEs in every industry apply the ideas in Figure 15.7, but they do so in a variety of ways. The following are select examples from three different industries: entertainment, personal computers, and automobiles.

Entertainment

One of the most successful entertainment firms in the world is the Walt Disney Company. Its Disneyland Paris operation in France is a good example of how integration and national responsiveness are balanced. The park offers many of the same features (integration) found in Disney's Orlando (Florida), Anaheim (California), and Tokyo operations, including amusement rides and cartoon characters such as Mickey Mouse, Goofy, and Donald Duck. The company has recently expanded the European facilities along the lines of its MGM studios near Orlando.[46] This integration focus which stresses uniformity among the geographically scattered parks is supplemented by national responsiveness that is designed to appeal to European visitors. English and French are the official languages of the park, and there are multilingual guides who are conversant in Dutch, German, Spanish, and Italian. A second example of national responsiveness is found in the international emphasis that the company has given to its Disney characters: Pinocchio is Italian, Cinderella is French, Peter Pan is British. At its movie theater in the park Disney shows a European history film offering (in the US the film is a travelogue of America).

Another example of integration/national responsiveness is offered by Sega Enterprises, best known for its Sonic the Hedgehog video game character. Sega is now taking its computer simulation technology and beginning to develop small theme parks that will provide the same thrills as a roller coaster or a trip through space. This is being done through the use of simulators like those used to train airline pilots. By building a series of different amusement simulators, Sega intends to offer a wide array of "rides" without having to bear the expense of physically building these facilities. The idea is captured in the term "virtual reality," which means that participants experience the effects of a situation without literally being there.[47] "Scramble Training", a Sega simulator that is part video and part movie, provides an example. This interactive game allows eight players to enter a small space capsule and to take their position as pilot trainees. The captain appears on a screen in front of the simulator and gives orders to the players, who in turn launch the capsule and swerve through space, firing missiles and competing for points. When the captain is wounded, the controls are turned over to the player with the best score, who then steers the capsule in for a landing. Sega intends to develop a host of different interactive simulators that will allow it to compete with amusement parks such as Disney. (In fact, Sega's concept is often referred to as "Disney in a Box".) The simulators are uniform in design and construction, thus allowing the company to employ an integration emphasis. However, the types of games will vary from country to country (national responsiveness) depending on the entertainment interests of the local populace. For example, Sega has found that Americans are very sports-oriented, so there is likely to be an opportunity for players to participate in a world series simulation. In Europe, this game would have little attraction, but many players there would like to participate in the World Cup soccer finals. Thus the company can modify its product characteristics to meet the needs of the customer.[48]

Personal computers

Most personal computer (PC) makers compete on the bases of technology and price. They offer state-of-the-art machines and try to hold down their costs by outsourcing components and by improving assembly efficiency. This strategy is particularly important in markets such as Japan, where, in the early 1990s, less than 25 per cent of the population owned PCs and local demands, such as a need to write in *kanji*, had discouraged foreign competition.

In recent years, however, US firms have been making major headway in this market, thanks to their ability to exploit both integration and national responsiveness.[49] For example, Compaq and Dell have entered this market with low-priced units that were the same as those sold elsewhere (integration) but offered sharply lower prices (national responsiveness). As a result, both firms have been able to garner market share. IBM has employed a similar strategy in addition to addressing the desire of local customers to write in *kanji*. The company has now perfected a bilingual version of Microsoft's DOS, the standard operating system that controls approximately 80 per cent of PCs in the world. IBM's version allows these machines to prepare or search documents with Japanese characters, the Western alphabet, or both. Apple is also having very good success in Japan, thanks to its willingness to adapt to local needs. For example, the company has a Japanese management team that has helped to surmount local barriers to "buying foreign". The company has also cultivated a strong network of dealers and worked to develop an image as an innovator, both of which are of critical importance in the Japanese market. As a result of this careful balance of integration and national responsiveness, Apple and IBM alone account for almost 16 per cent of the Japanese PC market.[50]

Other US firms are also using a carefully formulated integration/national responsiveness strategy to gain market share. For example, Microsoft, designer of Windows, one of the most popular PC software programs of all time, has written a special version for the Japanese market. Until 1993 only 440,000 copies of the program had been sold, but when the company unveiled its new version of Windows, over 65,000 copies were sold in two days. Summing up the current situation, one observer has noted, "For now, American PC vendors feel the wind at their backs. Not only is the software finally available to help them attack the Japanese market with a coherent strategy, but, in addition, the strengthening yen lets them further undercut the prices of their Japanese counterparts."[51]

Automobiles

Every car manufacturer uses economic integration by producing autos that can be made and marketed around the world. In a few cases, the Volkswagen Beetle being the best example, a car will not need to be modified for the local market.[52] In most cases, however, an integration strategy is complemented by national responsiveness in the form of design, engineering, and manufacturing changes. Ford Motors' Mondeo provides a good example. This car has been developed for the world market and has uniform worldwide engineering standards with almost every specification expressed in the metric system. The company also has created uniform standards for raw materials, design, procurement, and manufacture of individual parts. Identical production tools are used at both European and US locations so that economies of scale can be maximized. At the same time, Ford has taken national responsiveness into consideration. European buyers prefer manual transmissions, while US buyers like automatic drive. Europeans demand cars that handle well, while this is not a priority issue with US customers. On the other hand, Americans want air-conditioned cars, while many European buyers do not. The overall cost of developing the Mondeo was $6 billion. However, initial sales in Europe were brisk and the company believed that it could maintain this momentum in the US market. Ford also believed that it could create additional car models from the Mondeo program and thus develop a series of new offerings. If this is true, the integration and national responsiveness strategies used for the Mondeo will help to smooth the way for future auto sales and help the company to recoup this enormous investment.[53]

Honda offers another example of integration and national responsiveness strategies. The firm now builds a variety of different car sizes from one production platform by bending and stretching the autos to fit the demands of the market. As a result, Honda is able to build cars in the US that are longer and roomier, while offering smaller, more compact models of the same car in Japan. The company is now using this same approach to build sports utility vehicles for the world market.[54]

General Motors (GM) offers yet another example of integration and national responsiveness strategies. Like Ford, GM often develops cars for the European market and then introduces them into the US. As a result, the cars are frequently identical in styling and design but have different features to accommodate local tastes. The Celta, a new subcompact offering in Brazil, has fewer features and 50 per cent fewer parts than competitive models. In collaboration with its suppliers, GM created a modular assembly plant with just-in-time supplier delivery. Efficiency costs of such an integration strategy allowed for an inexpensive subcompact for developing markets where price and reliability are most important.[55] When the auto is made in another developing market, it will be possible to build and assemble each unit quickly because the process will have been perfected in Brazil. This integration focus is complemented by national responsiveness. In Brazil, marketing of the Celta stresses security locks and anti-theft devices, while in safer developing countries, the car's suspension system and handling in tough roads will be more stressed.

Competitiveness in the triad

From the viewpoint of MNEs, one of the most important business decisions regards the trade-off between integration and national responsiveness. Successful MNEs know that they can no longer afford to ignore the latter and to concentrate solely on globalization through economic integration.

In the US

The US experiences considerable decentralization in economic decision making. It is a country in which subnational units (states and provinces) continue to increase in importance. This issue should not be confused with pluralism. A variety of political opinions and parties is a strength of democracy. The problem arises when the institutional structure of the nation and its businesses cannot operate in an efficient manner, relative to global competitors.

The US Constitution was designed to allow Congress to be a broker for regional and special interests. On occasions the Congress works with the Executive branch, and a coordinated economic and even social policy can be both formulated and implemented. Examples of social reform and government economic activity in the Kennedy–Johnson years can be contrasted with a return to more market-based principles and a somewhat reduced role for government in the Reagan years.

However, in many areas affecting the private sector today the overwhelming characteristic of doing business in the US is the responsiveness of governments to special interest groups and lobbies. The more decentralized the level of government is the more responsive will be the regulatory activity to the lobbyist. On occasions, businesses themselves can be lobbyists, but there are many other groups, such as environmentalists and social activists, who seem to be growing in power. Examples of conflicts in business lobbying occur in the areas of administration of US trade remedy laws and in the current US debate about the possible regulation of inward foreign direct investment (FDI).

It has been demonstrated by Rugman and Anderson,[56] as well as by others, that the current administration of US countervailing duty (CVD) and antidumping (AD) laws is highly responsive to domestic producer interests and biased against foreign firms. It has been found that US corporations use CVD and AD as a competitive strategy to erect entry barriers against rival firms.[57] Since 1980, the US has initiated 1,022 CVD and AD cases (see Table 15.2). Thus, even when the US government was pursuing negotiations for free trade with Canada, individual US corporations were still using the CVD and AD laws to help restrict Canadian imports. This is a clear example of the US national interest being offset by selective producer interests. Examples have occurred in the softwood lumber, pork, fish, steel, and related industries – there were over 22 CVD and AD cases against Canada in the 1990s.[58] More of the same is in store in the future, although Canadian concerns about the administration of CVD and AD laws have been somewhat answered by the establishment of binational panels under the terms of the FTA and then NAFTA.

Another area of concern is inward FDI, which some congressional leaders now wish to restrict, and some Americans seem concerned with the growing amount of Japanese FDI. Some members of Congress have urged more screening of such FDI, and there is a strong "Japan-bashing" stance in US trade policy. Yet at the same time state officials have been actively seeking Japanese FDI because they want the jobs and the tax base. This potential clash between Washington "beltway" thinking (anti-Japanese) and state-level activity (pro-Japanese) parallels Canada's experience with the regulation of FDI.

The US seems destined in the next 10 years to repeat many of the mistakes made in Canada over the last 30 years. In 1974 the Trudeau government introduced the Foreign Investment Review Agency (FIRA), which was designed to screen FDI on economic criteria to assess if there was a net benefit to Canada. Over the 1974 to 1985 period FIRA responded to Ottawa's political winds, at times rejecting as much as 30 per cent of applications but at other times (especially 1982 to 1985) approving virtually everything.[59] The administrators at FIRA and the responsible ministers made political decisions just as the US International Trade Commission and the US Commerce Department do today in US trade law cases.

In 1985 FIRA was abolished and a new agency, Investment Canada, was created with the mandate to attract FDI rather than scare it away.[60] This change in thinking about FDI came with a change in government. In 1984 the Progressive Conservative government was elected with a mandate of job creation. Throughout the lifetime of FIRA most provinces, especially those in Atlantic Canada, wanted FDI for jobs and taxes. The clash between the provinces that favored FDI and the central Canadian economic nationalists

Table 15.2 United States countervailing and antidumping cases initiated, 1980–2000*

Country	GATT (1980–1994)	WTO (1995–2000)	Total (1980–2000)	% of total	Country	GATT (1980–1994)	WTO (1995–2000)	Total (1980–2000)	% of total
Japan	73	19	92	9.0	Costa Rica	7	0	7	0.7
South Korea	51	18	69	6.8	Australia	6	0	6	0.6
China	52	16	68	6.7	Germany East	6	NA	NA	0.6
Brazil	57	5	62	6.1	Hungary	6	0	6	0.6
Taiwan	47	11	58	5.7	Chile	3	2	5	0.5
Canada	46	8	54	5.3	Norway	5	0	5	0.5
Mexico	45	6	51	5.0	Peru	5	0	5	0.5
Italy	38	10	48	4.7	Finland	4	0	4	0.4
France	29	4	33	3.2	Hong Kong	4	0	4	0.4
Spain	28	3	31	3.0	Iran	4	0	4	0.4
United Kingdom	27	2	29	2.8	Trinidad and Tobago	2	2	4	0.4
Venezuela	25	4	29	2.8	Ukraine	3	1	4	0.4
India	17	6	23	2.3	Ecuador	3	0	3	0.3
Thailand	21	2	23	2.3	Philippines	3	0	3	0.3
Germany West	22	NA	NA	2.2	Switzerland	3	0	3	0.3
Belgium/Luxembourg	17	2	19	1.9	Bangladesh	2	0	2	0.2
Argentina	17	1	18	1.8	Czechoslovakia	2	NA	NA	0.2
Germany (after 1990)	12	6	18	1.8	Czech Republic	NA	2	NA	0.2
Israel	15	0	15	1.5	Denmark	0	2	2	0.2
Singapore	14	0	14	1.4	El Salvador	2	0	2	0.2
South Africa	8	6	14	1.4	Greece	2	0	2	0.2
Turkey	10	3	13	1.3	Kazakhstan	1	1	2	0.2
Netherlands	12	0	12	1.2	Kenya	2	0	2	0.2
Austria	10	1	11	1.1	Macedonia	0	2	2	0.2
Indonesia	1	10	11	1.1	Saudi Arabia	2	0	2	0.2
Malaysia	11	0	11	1.1	Egypt	1	0	1	0.1
Russia	7	4	11	1.1	Ireland	1	0	1	0.1
New Zealand	10	0	10	1.0	Pakistan	1	0	1	0.1
Poland	10	0	10	1.0	Panama	1	0	1	0.1
Romania	9	1	10	1.0	Slovakia	0	1	1	0.1
Sweden	9	1	10	1.0	Sri Lanka	1	0	1	0.1
Colombia	9	0	9	0.9	UAE	1	0	1	0.1
Portugal	9	0	9	0.9	Uruguay	1	0	1	0.1
Yugoslavia	8	0	8	0.8	Total	787	143	930	91.0

* Does not include cases initiated in 2000.

Source: US Department of Commerce, International Trade Administration *United States Countervailing and Antidumping Cases Initiated, 1980–2000*.

led to the federal government giving up many of its powers to regulate FDI by buying into the agenda of the provinces, especially their overwhelming priority about jobs. Perhaps this is some evidence of the triumph of decentralized economic power. But a paradox emerges. In Canada, the economic nationalists, who have used central government power, are in retreat, while it appears that in the US economic nationalism is just beginning to take off. If Japan-bashing continues, then the US proponents of restrictions on FDI will have the same unhappy experience with the FIRA as did Canada. Private sector US corporate strategists will, therefore, need to respond to a large dose of economic nationalism and its associated protectionist inefficiencies.

In Eastern Europe

Another example of the use of sovereignty and the destruction of centralized economic power and values was the 1989 revolution in central Europe and the collapse of the Soviet Union in 1991. The rejection of totalitarian communist regimes by the people of countries such as Romania, Belarus, and Russia will have many implications for business. The key point is that these countries are currently very poor, with inefficient economic and financial systems. The economic development of these nations will probably be through FDI rather than through joint ventures. Popular wisdom to the contrary, joint ventures between poor nations and wealthy corporations rarely work. The preferable mode of international business is FDI since Western firms can then control their proprietary advantages and not risk dissipation through joint ventures.[61] In the literature on joint ventures in developing countries it has been found that there exists a great deal of instability and joint venture failure.[62] Multinationals prefer FDI and countries such as India and Mexico, which once greatly restricted FDI, experienced inefficient economic development and eventually had to lift such regulations. This experience is relevant for Eastern Europe.

Doing business in Eastern Europe for the next 5 to 10 years will be dominated by the need for economic efficiency. The globalization concept will overwhelm concerns about adapting products for sovereignty. It is in the EU nations that national responsiveness will be important for corporations. In the wealthy triad powers, adapting to sovereignty matters; in the third world and in Eastern Europe, economic efficiency is what matters.

In Japan

A key explanation for the success of Japanese MNEs is that they benefit from a highly centralized home market economy. This has permitted Japan to use levers of industrial policy and strategic trade policy that could not be implemented successfully in the other areas of the triad.

Centralized government policy is critical to implementing effective corporate strategy.[63] The Japanese cultural, religious, social, and political system is much more centralized in nature than other triad blocs. This has enabled Japanese MNEs to follow globalization strategies. So, for example, after the two OPEC oil crises of the 1970s Japanese industry was rapidly transformed out of shipbuilding, heavy engineering, and other energy-intensive manufacturing and into computer-based manufacturing, consumer electronics, and high value-added services, including banking and financial services. The government and the MNEs worked together to implement a new industrial strategy in an effective and efficient manner.

Such radical restructuring through industrial policy is unlikely to work in North America and Europe because of the decentralized nature of economic power. Attempts by the US or Canada to implement a new industrial policy are unlikely to be successful. Whatever government incentives and subsidies are made available will be appropriated by industries seeking shelter from competitors in the triad. To erect entry barriers against foreign competitors, companies will use the decentralized nature of the economic system. This has already occurred in the US with companies seeking protection from competitors through the use of CVD and AD laws. US steel, forest products, fish, and semiconductor industries, among others, have been using short-term legal remedies instead of investing in the development of sustainable, proprietary, firm-specific advantages.

What are the implications for corporate strategy of these asymmetrical developments in the triad? Japanese MNEs will continue to pursue an integration/globalization strategy, but these MNEs may face difficulties when they need to operate in the decentralized environments of North America and Europe since marketing-type skills will become more important than production skills. Over the last decade MNEs from Europe and North America have often abused the nature of their home country decentralized systems, and sovereignty has hindered efficient corporate development. However, MNEs from North America and Europe have a potential competitive advantage over Japanese MNEs if they can learn from their past mistakes. Awareness of sovereignty can make the former companies better equipped in the future to be more nationally responsive than their Japanese counterparts. Indeed, Japanese MNEs may become locked into a "globalization only" strategy, just as the world begins to demand much more corporate responsiveness to sovereignty.

Active learning check 

Review your answer to Active Learning Case question 3 and make any changes you like. Then compare your answer with the one below.

3. How does ABB address the issues of globalization and national responsiveness? In each case, cite an example.

ABB addresses the issue of globalization by producing state-of-the-art products for worldwide markets. For example, the same high-speed trains that can carry passengers and goods through the Alps can be used for transporting people and goods across the plains of the US or the steppes of Russia. It may be necessary to make modifications to address local geographic and climatic conditions, of course, but the basic technology and manufacturing techniques are similar. At the same time ABB addresses national responsiveness by trying to be a local firm that is interested in the needs of that market. As a result, the company balances globalization and sovereignty – a feat that is not accomplished very well by most MNEs.

KEY POINTS

1. Porter's diamond model is based on four country-specific determinants and two external variables (chance and government). This model is extremely useful in examining strategies among triad and other economically developed countries. However, when applying the model to smaller, open, trading economies, a modification of the model is in order.
2. Canada's economic success will depend on its ability to view itself as part of the North American market and to integrate itself into this overall market. This requires the use of a "double diamond" model for corporate strategy. This is resulting in Canadian firms developing competitive capabilities that allow them to compete successfully with US firms in the US. This is being done by (a) developing innovative products and services that simultaneously meet the needs of the US and Canadian customer, (b) drawing on the support industries and infrastructure of both the US and Canadian diamonds, and (c) making free and full use of the physical and human resources in both countries.
3. Mexico's economic success also depends on its ability to integrate itself into the North American market. However, this strategy is different from that of the Canadians because Mexico does not have the FDI to invest in the US market. Much of its linkage is a result of low labor costs that allow the country to produce inexpensive goods and to export them into the US. The North American Free Trade Agreement worked out with the US and Canada in 1993 will determine part of the country's future economic success.

4. A major trend that has affected the thinking of corporate MNE strategists over the last 10 years is that of balancing a concern for economic integration and globalization with that of national responsiveness. Many MNEs have focused on integration without giving sufficient attention to the sovereignty issue. However, there will have to be a reversal of this trend and MNEs will become much more interested in national responsiveness if they hope to succeed in overseas markets.

KEY TERMS

- strategic cluster
- globalization
- national responsiveness

REVIEW AND DISCUSSION QUESTIONS

1. The Porter diamond is based on four country-specific determinants and two external variables. What does this statement mean? Put it in your own words.
2. Porter notes that "Firms, not individual nations, compete in international markets." How does this statement help to explain some of the major challenges facing MNEs?
3. Using Figure 15.2 as your point of reference, how does the current national development of the US differ from that of Korea? How does Great Britain's differ from that of Singapore?
4. Why does the Porter diamond need to be modified in explaining the international competitiveness of countries such as Canada and Mexico?
5. How does the double diamond, as illustrated in Figure 15.4, help to explain international competitiveness in Canada?
6. How can Canadian firms view the US and Canada as home-based markets and integrate the use of both diamonds for development and implementation of strategy? Be complete in your answer.
7. Of what value are strategic clusters in the double diamond? Explain.
8. How does the double diamond in Figure 15.6 help to explain Mexico's international business strategy? Explain.
9. How important are the *maquiladoras* to the growth of the Mexican economy? In what way do these businesses link Mexico with the Canadian–US double diamond?
10. In what way are economic integration/globalization and national responsiveness important to MNE strategies?
11. In the entertainment industry, which is more important, integration or national responsiveness?
12. Based on current developments in the PC market in Japan, which is more important for US MNEs, integration or national responsiveness? Why?
13. Which is more important for US auto makers doing business in Europe, integration or national responsiveness? Why?

REAL CASE

There is no global beer; it is local

Beer is a good example of an industry that is not globalized. The world's largest brewery, Anheuser-Busch, still sells 90 per cent of Budweiser in the US. Heineken still generates 61 per cent of its profits within the EU. Perhaps the Belgian brewery, Interbrew, has done best in expanding from its EU base into North America by the purchase of Canada's largest brewer, Labatt, in 1993.

Beer is stubbornly local. While Budweiser is the world's single largest beer brand, it accounts for only 3.6 per cent of the world's sales of beer each year. Beer is local as it is bulky and too expensive to export; as a result beer is brewed domestically and foreign producers will license their brand name products to local producers to gain a local market presence. In addition, imports of alcoholic beverages are traditionally heavily taxed. Rival domestic producers usually tie up local distribution channels. Governments also protect domestic breweries, for example in Germany, where the Reinheitsgebot purity rules have protected indigenous beer for over 400 years.

Also in Canada, domestic brewers were exempted from the national treatment provision of the United States–Canada Free Trade Agreement of 1989 (and later from NAFTA in 1993). The reason is that, initially, each Canadian company needed to have a brewery in each province, resulting in rather small and inefficient breweries in the small population Atlantic Provinces. Of course, such breweries in Canada were protected from imports and were inefficient, so Labatt was taken over by the Belgian brewery, Interbrew. Molson was also doing badly by 2001.

The local and fragmented nature of the brewing industry can be offset by acquisitions. The half dozen leading world brewers are constantly attempting to increase their market share in both developed and developing countries. The world leader, Anheuser-Busch, makes Budweiser, but, as already noted, most of its sales are in the US. A brewer from the small economy of Belgium, Interbrew, has made huge gains in the last few years, buying up many companies including Bass Brewers of the UK, Becks of Germany, and Labatt in Canada. Its major product line is Stella Artois. South African Breweries (SAC) was reported in late 2001 to be looking into a merger with Interbrew or Miller. The table below lists the world's largest brewers.

There are a few premium "designer" beers (i.e. high-end beers that have been developed into global brands), but these are usually produced under license. This has led to cross-licensing and distribution arrangements as well as to mergers and to acquisitions. Today there is some consolidation in this segment to a few large brewers such as Heineken, Interbrew, Guinness/UDV, and Anheuser-Busch. But the premium lager segment is a minority of the total world beer market, which still has mainly local beer.

Largest worldwide brewers

Name	*Volume MHL*
Anheuser-Busch	150.0
Interbrew	76.2
Heineken	72.0
SAB (South African Business)	56.0
Ambev	56.0
Miller	53.0
Carlsberg	46.0
S&N (Scottish & Newcastle)	35.8
Asahi	35.0
Kirin	32.0

Source: *Financial Times*, November 29, 2001, p. 19.

Websites: ***www.molson.com***; ***www.labatt.com***; ***www.anheuser-busch.com***; ***www.ambev.com***; ***www.heineken.com***; ***www.interbrew.com***; ***www.sabplc.com***; ***www.millerbrewing.com***; ***www.carlsberg.com***; ***www.asahi.com*** and ***www.kirin.com***.

Sources: Adam Jones et al. "A Game of Musical Chairs is Brewing," *Financial Times*, November 29, 2001; "Battling Brewers", *Economist*, March 16, 2000; "The Big Pitcher", *Economist*, January 18, 2001.

1. **Is the production and distribution of beer nationally responsive?**
2. **If beer is mainly local why are there mergers and acquisitions of beer companies?**
3. **In the integration/responsiveness matrix of Chapter 15, where would you position the world's largest brand name beer companies and why?**

REAL CASE

S. C. Fang Brothers

Many large US retail stores buy goods that are produced abroad. Good examples include Sears and Wal-Mart. However, very few people know the names of the manufacturers, despite the fact that some of these firms are extremely large. For example, not many people have ever heard of S. C. Fang Brothers, but a large number of them have worn products produced by this company. The Fangs are one of the families that dominate the textile industry in Asia, and for the last decade they have supplied T-shirts to Gap and blouses to Calvin Klein, to name but two of their customers. The family began the business after it fled from mainland China in 1949. The Fangs had ordered hundreds of the newest, most technologically advanced cotton spindles to be shipped to Hong Kong. They then escaped from China to Hong Kong and started their business.

At first the company moved into cotton spinning and did very well. However, by the mid-1960s competitors turned to yarn and textiles, and the company changed strategy. It moved into apparel, producing sweaters on a private-label basis for stores in the UK. Soon the Fangs were major players in the apparel trade, including a large market in the US, but this did not last long. Labor costs in Hong Kong began to escalate and the US government started imposing restrictions on the quantities of cheap sweaters that could be brought in from Hong Kong. It was time for another change in strategy.

The Fangs spread manufacturing operations across nine countries. By the mid-1990s they made T-shirts in the Philippines and Panama, trousers in Thailand, sweaters in Malaysia, and knit garments in South Carolina. They have also opened retail stores, the best known being the Episode Stores chain. A large percentage of the clothing sold in these stores is made by the Fangs in their worldwide factories. One of their most popular offerings has been what is called "bridge clothing," which is less expensive than designer outfits but which is still of high quality. This move upmarket has made Fang Brothers more responsive to foreign customers, compared with their early days of exporting alone from Hong Kong.

When the island of Hong Kong reverted from British to Chinese control in 1997, many business people there left as they were worried about the possible adverse economic consequences of integrating a capitalist society into a communist one. The Fang family decided to keep Hong Kong as its home and headquarters. However, if conditions under the Chinese had required them to move, it would not have been too difficult because the company is now situated worldwide. As their factories and revenues are now diversified globally the business is no longer dependent on Hong Kong as its home base.

Websites: **www.gap.com**.

Sources: Adapted from Phyllis Berman and Jean Sherman Chatzky, "Closer to the Consumer," *Forbes*, January 20, 1992, pp. 56–57; Bill Saporito, "David Glass Won't Crack Under Fire," *Fortune*, February 8, 1993, pp. 75–80; and Kevin Kelly, "The Big Store May Be on a Big Roll," *Business Week*, August 30, 1993, pp. 82–85.

1. **What factor conditions are most important to this company? How has the firm managed to maintain access to these factors?**
2. **How have the Fang brothers managed to link their operations into triad markets? Describe two examples.**
3. **How does the company deal with the issue of national responsiveness? Give two examples.**

ENDNOTES

1 For a detailed discussion of these variables and determinants, see Michael E. Porter, *The Competitive Advantage of Nations* (New York: Free Press, 1990), pp. 69–130.
2 Alan M. Rugman and Alain Verbeke, *Global Corporate Strategy and Trade Policy* (London and New York: Routledge, 1990).
3 Michael E. Porter, *The Competitive Advantage of Nations* (New York: Free Press, 1990), p. 33.
4 Ibid., p. 671.
5 A. E. Safarian, *Foreign Ownership of Canadian Industry* (Toronto: McGraw-Hill Inc., 1968).
6 Alan M. Rugman, *Multinationals in Canada: Theory, Performance and Economic Impact* (Boston MA: Martinus Nijhoff, 1980).
7 Harold Crookell, *Canadian–American Trade and Investment Under the Free Trade Agreement* (Westport, CT: Quorum Books, 1990).
8 Alan M. Rugman, *Multinationals and Canada–United States Free Trade* (Columbia SC: University of South Carolina Press, 1990).
9 See Alan M. Rugman, "Strategies for National Competitiveness," *Long Range Planning*, vol. 20, no. 3 (1987), pp. 92–97.
10 Alan M. Rugman and John McIlveen, *Megafirms: Strategies for Canada's Multinationals* (Toronto: Methuen/Nelson, 1985).
11 Ibid.
12 John H. Dunning, "Dunning on Porter." Paper presented at the Annual Meeting of the Academy of International Business, Toronto, October 1990, and published in John H. Dunning, *The Globalization of Business* (London and New York: Routledge, 1993); and John H. Dunning, "Internationalizing Porter's Diamond," *Management International Review*, vol. 33, Special Issue no. 2 (1993), pp. 7–16.
13 Ibid., 1990, p. 11.
14 United Nations, *World Investment Report* (New York: United Nations, 2000).
15 Alan M. Rugman and Joseph R. D'Cruz, *Fast Forward: Improving Canada's International Competitiveness* (Toronto: Kodak Canada, 1991); and Alan M. Rugman and Joseph R. D'Cruz, "The 'Double Diamond' Model of International Competitiveness: The Canadian Experience," *Management International Review*, vol. 33, Special Issue 2 (1993), pp. 17–40.
16 For another view of the FTA, see John N. Turner, "There Is More to Trade Than Trade: An Analysis of the US/Canada Trade Agreement 1988," *California Management Review*, Winter 1991, pp. 109–119.
17 Alan M. Rugman, "The Free Trade Agreement and the Global Economy," *Business Quarterly*, Summer 1988, pp. 13–20.
18 Alan M. Rugman and Alain Verbeke, "Strategic Responses to Free Trade," *Hitotsubashi Journal of Commerce and Management*, December 1988, pp. 69–79; and Alan M. Rugman and Alain Verbeke, "Foreign Subsidiaries and Multinational Strategic Management: An Extension and Correction of Porter's Single Diamond Framework," *Management International Review*, vol. 33, Special Issue 2 (1993), pp. 71–84.
19 See, for example, Joseph R. D'Cruz and James Fleck, *Yankee Canadians in the Global Economy* (London, Ontario: National Centre for Management Research and Development, 1987); and Alan M. Rugman and Joseph D'Cruz, *New Visions for Canadian Business: Strategies for Competing in the Global Economy* (Toronto: Kodak Canada, 1990).
20 See Andrew Solocha, Mark D. Soskin and Mark J. Kasoff, "Determinants of Foreign Direct Investment: A Case of Canadian Direct Investment in the United States," *Management International Review*, vol. 30, no. 4 (Fourth Quarter 1990), pp. 371–386.
21 Also, see "The Spreading Maple Leaf," *Economist*, January 15, 1994, p. 68.
22 Anthony De Palma, "The Transportation Giant Up North," *New York Times*, December 26, 1998, pp. C 1, 3.
23 See, for example, Tamsin Carlisle, "Calgary Becomes Outpost on High-Tech Frontier," *Wall Street Journal*, March 24, 1998, p. A 19.
24 Also, see Alan M. Rugman and Alain Verbeke, "Multinational Corporate Strategy and the Canada–US Free Trade Agreement," *Management International Review*, vol. 30, no. 3 (Third Quarter 1990), pp. 253–266; and Alan M. Rugman and Alain Verbeke, "How to Operationalize Porter's Diamond of International Competitiveness," *International Executive*, vol. 35, no. 4, July/August (1993), pp. 283–299.
25 For more details of this business network approach, see Joseph R. D'Cruz and Alan M. Rugman, *New Compacts of Canadian Competitiveness* (Toronto: Kodak Canada, 1992); Joseph R. D'Cruz and Alan M. Rugman, "Business Networks for International Competitiveness," *Business Quarterly*, vol. 56, no. 4 (Spring 1992), pp. 101–107; and Joseph R. D'Cruz and Alan M. Rugman, "Developing International Competitiveness: The Five Partners Model," *Business Quarterly*, vol. 58, no. 2 (Winter 1993), pp. 60–72.
26 D'Cruz and Rugman, *New Compacts of Canadian Competitiveness* (1992) n. 25 above, pp. 29–36.
27 World Economic Forum, 1998.
28 Christopher J. Chipello and Roger Ricklefs, "How Productivity Clouds Canada's Competitiveness, Living Standards," *Wall Street Journal*, February 9, 1999, p. A 19.
29 Alan M. Rugman, *Japanese Direct Investment in Canada* (Ottawa: Canada–Japan Trade Council, 1990).
30 See Alan M. Rugman and F. Bill Mohri, "Trade and Investment Among Canada and the Triad," Working paper, University of Toronto, July 1991; and Alan M. Rugman (ed.), *Foreign Investment and NAFTA* (Columbia SC: University of South Carolina Press, 1994).

31 Alan M. Rugman and Alain Verbeke, "Foreign Direct Investment in North America: Current Patterns and Future Relationships in Canada, the United States, and Mexico," Ontario Centre for International Business, Research program working paper, no. 57, November 1991, p. 4, published in Khosrow Fatemi and Dominick Salvatore (eds.), *North American Free Trade Agreement* (London: Pergamon Press, 1994).

32 In contrast, Japanese FDI between 1986 and 1991 dropped from $225 million to $150 million. See Stephen Baker and Karen Lowry Miller, "Why Japan Inc. Is Steering Clear of Mexico," *Business Week*, December 2, 1991, pp. 50–52.

33 Also, see Anthony DePalma, "Mexico Slips into Recession," *New York Times*, March 16, 1994, pp. C 1, C 5.

34 Bob Ortega, "Some Mexicans Charge North in NAFTA's Wake," *Wall Street Journal*, February 22, 1994, pp. B 1, B 5; and Craig Torres, "TRW Plans Mexican Venture to Start a Credit Operation in Guadalajara," *Wall Street Journal*, January 7, 1994, p. A 5.

35 Sandra Masur, "The North American Free Trade Agreement: Why It's in the Interest of US Business," *Columbia Journal of World Business*, Summer 1991, pp. 99–103.

36 "Why Mexico Scares the UAW," *Business Week*, August 3, 1998, p. 37 and "U.S. Slowdown Adds to Mexican Auto Industry's Woes," *Forbes.com*, April 19, 2001.

37 Jonathan Friedland and Joseph B. White, "GM Is Heading An Investment Boom in Mexico," *Wall Street Journal*, December 24, 1998, pp. A 5, 6.

38 Joel Millman, "High-Tech Jobs Transfer to Mexico with Surprising Speed," *Wall Street Journal*, April 9, 1999, p. A 18.

39 Geri Smith and Elisabeth Malkin, "Mexican Makeover," *Business Week*, December 21, 1998, p. 52.

40 Alan Rugman and Alain Verbeke, "Foreign Direct Investment in North America," n. 31 above, p. 12 and Federal Reserve Bank of Dallas, "Maquiladoras 2000: Still Growing," *Business Frontiers* (El Paso: Federal Reserve Bank of Dallas, 2000).

41 United States International Trade Commission, *The Likely Impact on the United States of a Free Trade Agreement with Mexico*, USITC Publication 2353, February 1991, pp. 1–5.

42 Also, see *Lloyd Economic Report* (Guadalajara, Mexico), March 1994.

43 For a discussion of various definitions of globalization, see Chapter 1 of Alan M. Rugman, *The End of Globalization* (London: Random House, 2000 and New York: McGraw Hill/Amacom, 2001).

44 See Alan M. Rugman and Karl Moore, "How Global is Globalisation," *FT Mastering Management Online*, November 2001.

45 Christopher A. Bartlett, "Building and Managing the Transnational: The New Organizational Challenge," in M. E. Porter (ed.), *Competition in Global Industries* (Boston MA: Harvard Business School Press, 1986), pp. 367–401 and Christopher A. Bartlett and Sumantra Ghoshal, *Managing Across Borders: The Transnational Solution* (Boston MA: Harvard Business School Press, 1989).

46 "Disney's Euro Problem," *Miami Herald*, July 9, 1993, p. C 3.

47 Andrew Pollack, "Sega Takes Aim at Disney's World," *New York Times*, Section 3, July 4, 1993, pp. 1, 6.

48 For more on Sega, see Irene M. Kunii, "Sega: 'We're Going to Blow Them Out of the Water'," *Business Week*, December 7, 1998, p. 108.

49 Brenton R. Schlender, "US PCs Invade Japan," *Fortune*, July 12, 1993, pp. 68–73.

50 See also "PC Market Has Ups and Downs," *Asia Times*, December 5, 2001; and Apple, *Guide to Japan for Macintosh Developers*, 2000 Edition.

51 Schlender (1993) n. 49 above, p. 73.

52 Gabriella Stern, "VW's US Comeback Rides on Restyled Beetle," *Wall Street Journal*, May 6, 1997, pp. B 1–2.

53 Alex Taylor III, "Ford's $6 Billion Baby," *Fortune*, June 28, 1993, pp. 76–81.

54 Keith Naughton et al., "Can Honda Build a World Car?" *Business Week*, September 8, 1997, pp. 100–108.

55 "GM do Brasil Launches de Chevrolet Celta," *Automotive Intelligence News*, September 5, 2000.

56 Alan M. Rugman and Andrew Anderson, *Administered Protection in America* (London and New York: Routledge, 1987).

57 Rugman and Verbeke (1990) n. 2 above.

58 International Trade Administration, *Antidumping and Countervailing Duty Cases Initiated Since January 01, 1980 Current Through January 01, 2000*, January 2000.

59 Alan M. Rugman, *Multinationals in Canada: Theory, Performance and Economic Impact* (Boston MA: Martinus Nijhoff, 1980).

60 Alan M. Rugman and Leonard Waverman, "Foreign Ownership and Corporate Strategy," in Leonard Waverman (ed.), *Corporate Globalization Through Mergers and Acquisitions* (Calgary: University of Calgary Press, 1991), pp. 59–87.

61 Alan M. Rugman, *Inside the Multinationals: The Economics of Internal Markets* (London: Croom Helm and New York: Columbia University Press, 1981).

62 Paul W. Beamish, *Multinational Joint Ventures in Developing Countries* (London and New York: Routledge, 1989).

63 Alan M. Rugman and Alain Verbeke (1990) n. 2 above.

ADDITIONAL BIBLIOGRAPHY

Akers, John F. "Ethics and Competitiveness – Putting First Things First," *Sloan Management Review*, vol. 30, no. 2 (Winter 1989).

Bartlett, Christopher and Ghoshal, Sumantra. *Managing Across Borders: The Transnational Solution* (Boston MA: Harvard Business School Press, 1989, 1998).

Bartlett, Christopher and Ghoshal, Sumantra. *Transnational Management* (Boston MA: Irwin, 1992).

Birkinshaw, Julian. "Strategy and Management in MNE Subsidiaries," in Alan M. Rugman and Thomas L. Brewer (eds.), *The Oxford Handbook of International Business* (Oxford: Oxford University Press, 2001).

Birkinshaw, Julian and Hood, Neil. "Characteristics of Foreign Subsidiares in Industry Clusters," *Journal of International Business Studies*, vol. 31, no. 1 (First Quarter 2000).

Boyd, Gavin (ed.). *The Struggle for World Markets: Competition and Cooperation Between NAFTA and the EU* (Cheltenham: Elgar, 1998).

Cho, Dong-Sung and Moon, Hwy-Chang. *From Adam Smith to Michael Porter: Evolution of Competitiveness Theory* (Singapore: River Edge NJ, 2000).

Choate, Pat. "Political Advantage: Japan's Campaign for America," *Harvard Business Review*, vol. 68, no. 5 (September/October 1990).

Dickson, Peter R. and Czinkota, Michael R. "How the United States Can Be Number One Again: Resurrecting the Industrial Policy Debate," *Columbia Journal of World Business*, vol. 31, no. 3 (Fall 1996).

Dunning, John H. "Internationalizing Porter's Diamond," *Management International Review*, vol. 33, no. 2 (Second Quarter 1993).

Dunning, John H. "The Geographical Sources of Competitiveness of Firms: Some Results of a New Survey," *Transnational Corporations*, vol. 5, no. 3 (December 1996).

Kline, John M. "Trade Competitiveness and Corporate Nationality," *Columbia Journal of World Business*, vol. 24, no. 3 (Fall 1989).

Kotler, Philip. *The Marketing of Nations* (New York: The Free Press, 1997).

Kuttner, Robert. "How 'National Security' Hurts National Competitiveness," *Harvard Business Review*, vol. 69, no. 1 (January/February 1991).

Leong, Siew Meng and Tan, Chin Tiong. "Managing Across Borders: An Empirical Test of the Bartlett and Ghoshal (1989) Organizational Typology," *Journal of International Business Studies*, vol. 24, no. 3 (Third Quarter 1993).

Lodge, George C., Decker, Hans W., Tonelson, Alan, Brown, John Seely, Pennington, Hilary, Hale, David, Raduchel, William J., Shapiro, Robert J., Gilder, George and Branscomb, Lewis M. "How Real Is America's Decline?" *Harvard Business Review*, vol. 70, no. 5 (September/October 1992).

Martinez, Jon I. and Jarillo, J. Carlos. "Coordination Demands of International Strategies," *Journal of International Business Studies*, vol. 22, no. 3 (Third Quarter 1991).

Merrills, Roy. "How Northern Telecom Competes on Time," *Harvard Business Review*, vol. 67, vol. 4 (July/August 1989).

Narula, Rajneesh. "Technology, International Business and Porter's 'Diamond': Synthesizing a Dynamic Competitive Development Model," *Management International Review*, vol. 33, no. 2 (Second Quarter 1993).

Ostry, Sylvia. "Government and Corporations in a Shrinking World: Trade and Innovation Policies in the United States, Europe & Japan," *Columbia Journal of World Business*, vol. 25, nos. 1, 2 (Spring/Summer 1990).

Porter, Michael E. "The Competitive Advantage of Nations," *Harvard Business Review*, vol. 68, no. 2 (March/April 1990).

Porter, Michael E. *On Competition* (Boston MA: Harvard Business School Press, 1998).

Radosevich, Raymond and Kassicieh, Suleiman. "Strategic Challenges and Proposed Responses to Competitiveness Through Public-Sector Technology," *California Management Review*, vol. 35, no. 4 (Summer 1993).

Roth, Kendall. "International Configuration and Coordination Archetypes for Medium-Sized Firms in Global Industries," *Journal of International Business Studies*, vol. 23, no. 3 (Third Quarter 1992).

Roth, Kendall and Morrison, Allen J. "An Empirical Analysis of the Integration–Responsiveness Framework in Global Industries," *Journal of International Business Studies*, vol. 21, no. 4 (Fourth Quarter 1990).

Ruhli, Edwin and Schuppisser, Stefan. "Switzerland and Its Industry in International Competition," *Columbia Journal of World Business*, vol. 29, no. 4 (Winter 1994).

Rugman, Alan M. "Diamond in the Rough," *Business Quarterly*, vol. 55, no. 3 (Winter 1991).

Rugman, Alan M. "Porter Takes the Wrong Turn," *Business Quarterly*, vol. 56, no. 3 (Winter 1992).

Rugman, Alan M. and D'Cruz, Joseph. "The Double Diamond Model of International Competitiveness: The Canadian Experience," *Management International Review*, vol. 33, no. 2 (Second Quarter 1993).

Rugman, Alan M. and Verbeke, Alain. *Research in Global Strategic Management: Volume 4: Beyond the Three Generics* (Greenwich, CT: JAI Press, 1993).

Rugman, Alan M. and Verbeke, Alain. "Foreign Subsidiaries and Multinational Strategic Management: An Extension and Correction of Porter's Single Diamond Framework," *Management International Review*, vol. 33, no. 2 (Second Quarter 1993).

Rugman, Alan M. and Verbeke, Alain. "How to Operationalize Porter's Diamond of Competitive Advantage," *International Executive*, vol. 35, no. 4 (July/August 1993).

Rugman, Alan M. and Waverman, Leonard. "Foreign Ownership and Corporate Strategy," in Leonard Waverman (ed.). *Corporate Globalization Through Mergers and Acquisitions* (Calgary: University of Calgary Press, 1991).

Scott, Bruce R. "Competitiveness: Self-Help for a Worsening Problem," *Harvard Business Review*, vol. 67, no. 4 (July/August 1989).

Smitka, Michael. "Are US Auto Exports the Growth Industry of the 1990s?" *Sloan Management Review*, vol. 35, no. 1 (Fall 1993).

CONTENTS

Chapter 16

European Union

OBJECTIVES OF THE CHAPTER

The European Union (EU) is one of the world's largest markets. Future expansion to include Central and Eastern Europe emerging economies will not only increase the size of the market, but also its growth potential. As a result, many MNEs are now doing business in the EU or are targeting the area in their expansion plans. This chapter examines the EU environment and reviews some of the major strategy considerations that must be addressed by companies doing business in this economic bloc.

The objectives of this chapter are to:

1. *Describe* the emerging single European market and the competitive status of the EU in relation to other triad members.
2. *Discuss* how firms carry out an overall strategic analysis of the EU market in terms of competitive intelligence and evaluation of location.
3. *Relate* some of the major strategy issues that must be considered when doing business in the EU, including exporting, strategic alliances and acquisitions, manufacturing considerations, marketing approaches, and management considerations.

ACTIVE LEARNING CASE

France Telecom

France Telecom is a good example of an organization that has become very strong in its home part of the triad. France Telecom has built up a major presence in the EU by first strategic alliances and more recently acquisitions of competitors. It can now use its strong EU home base as a staging ground to enter the North American and Asian markets, as was discussed in the earlier case on Vodafone (in Chapter 8).

With $31.1 billion in revenues in 2000, the state-owned France Telecom is Europe's second largest telecommunications company. France Telecom has come a long way since 1995, when 75 per cent of its revenues were from fixed-line operations and foreign sales accounted for only 2 per cent of revenues. Today, the French fixed-line business accounts for only 33 per cent of the company's revenues and by 2003 foreign sales are expected to account for over 50 per cent of total revenues.

The rise of France Telecom in the European market and its expansion into wireless and Internet are the result of a combination of R&D expenditures, alliances, and strategies. France Telecom R&D is the largest research center in Europe with 4,250 employees and holds 3,287 patents worldwide. R&D efforts strive to facilitate human interaction through telecommunications. This includes preparing for the introduction of 3G mobile phones, improving network infrastructure, combining telecommunication products and services into one platform, and improving Internet service.

R&D has helped France Telecom to secure a place in the European market. However, the fractured nature of the European market made strategic alliances a necessary element in France Telecom's international strategy. The EU's 15 members not only lack a common language but also a common regulatory system. Each country awards its own mobile licenses, forcing new entrants to make alliances with license holders. In addition, the previous fixed-line companies continue to own much of the local telecommunications infrastructure, increasing the benefits of partnering up.

In 1995, France Telecom joined Telekom and Sprint to form the Global One alliance. The alliance was expected to serve as a springboard into the US market while protecting France Telecom's home market from competition by Telekom. In 1999, Sprint was purchased by MCI World, effectively voiding the alliance. In the same year, Deutsche Telekom also rescinded its obligations when it sought a merger with Telecom Italia. As a result, France Telecom redesigned its international strategy and began to compete directly with Deutsche Telekom in the German market. This was done through purchase of 17 per cent of E-plus, the country's third largest mobile phone operator. This marked a turning point for France Telecom's international strategy. The company will now favor acquisitions over alliances.

In January 2000, France Telecom purchased the Global One alliance from its partners. This was the beginning of a purchasing spree. Later that year, France Telecom purchased Orange (UK) from Vodafone. The company had a presence in 20 countries around the world, including 13 in Europe. France Telecom combined its own mobile business with that of Orange to create Europe's second largest mobile phone company. This acquisition was also a strategic move into the UK market. Its biggest competitor, Deutsche Telekom, had already purchased One2One in the UK. With 12.2 million active customers, Orange was the largest mobile operator in the UK, catapulting France Telecom into the big leagues.

France Telecom also purchased Equant NV and Freeserve in 2000. Equant NV was combined with Global One under the name Equant. The new company is a corporate service provider in 220 countries and has 3,700 large business customers. Freeserve, the UK's largest Internet service provider, was purchased by Wanadoo, France Telecom's Internet subsidiary.

In 2001, like other telecoms, France Telecom experienced a sharp decrease in share value. In less than one year, its share price dropped by 70 per cent. This was a result of the dot.com bust; the cost of buying 3G mobile licenses in Britain, Germany, France, and Italy among others; and a debt totaling over $54 billion. This debt is the cost of its acquisitions and the lack of a strong market that would allow it to raise fund through the sale of equity. Notwithstanding, France Telecom has succeeded in its plan to become a major European competitor. The company is now strategically prepared to take advantage of future profits from 3G mobiles, the deregulation of telecommunications and increased competition in local markets, economies of scale on ISP, and the increasing integration of the EU market. In addition, its debt is comparable to that of its major competitors, Deutsche Telekom and British Telecom.

Websites: **www.francetelecom.com**; **www.sprint.com**; **www.equant.com**; **www.mci.com**; **www.one2one.co.uk**; **www.orange.co.uk**; **www.freeserve.com**; **www.wanadoo.fr** and **www.bt.com**.

Sources: **www.francetelecom.com**; "France Telecom: Battling Debt," *BBC.co.uk*, April 19, 2001; "French Giant Targets Alliance," *BBC.co.uk*, October 12, 1999; "France Telecom Clinches Orange Deal," *BBC.co.uk*, May 30, 2000; "France Telecom Takes Over Equant," *BBC.co.uk*, November 20, 2000; Richard Tomlinson, "Michel Bon is on the Line," *Fortune*, February 19, 2001; Richard Tomlinson, "5 Moves to Win the Telecom Game," *Fortune*, January 7, 2002.

1. **Describe the stages by which France Telecom has built up a successful strategic base in the EU. What barriers to integration had to be overcome in the EU before France Telecom could buy up rival companies?**
2. **To what extent is the triad strategy of France Telecom the same as that of Vodafone (in Chapter 8)? Are there any differences?**
3. **In what ways will globalization and localization (sovereignty) be important issues for conducting mergers in the EU?**
4. **In what ways will both pricing and positioning be important for companies like France Telecom doing business in the EU?**

THE EU ENVIRONMENT

The EU currently consists of 15 countries that are closely linked both economically and politically, 12 of whom have agreed to use the euro as their basic currency.[1] Doing business in this bloc offers great opportunities, and many MNEs are interested in tapping this giant potential (see Table 16.1). Before examining the current EU environment, we need to realize that in the early years of the millennium this market will expand to incorporate other countries. This expanded EU will create a "greater Europe," comprising a trading area of some 550 million people in 28 countries (see accompanying map).[2] At the same time, many Eastern European countries are seeking associate status with the EU or have trade agreements with the bloc.[3] So the EU is already emerging as a strong rival triad power to that of the US and Japan. In the future an expanded European economic market may well become the largest of the triad powers.

Emergence of a single European market

The origins of the EU go back to the formation of the European Economic Community (EEC) in the late 1950s, at which time there were six founding members: France, West Germany, Italy, Belgium, the Netherlands, and Luxembourg. By the late 1990s, the EU had grown to include Austria, Finland, Great Britain, Ireland, Denmark, Greece, Spain, Sweden, and Portugal. Over the last 40 years rapid economic growth has led to a high degree of political and social integration.

The objectives of the EU are:

1. Elimination of customs duties among member states.
2. Elimination of obstacles to the free flow of import and/or export of goods and services among member states.
3. Establishment of common customs duties and unified industrial/commercial policies regarding countries outside the community.
4. Free movement of persons and capital within the bloc.
5. Acceptance of common agricultural policies, transport policies, technical standards, health and safety regulations, and educational degrees.

Source: Adapted from *The World Factbook, 1993–1994*; *The Europa World Yearbook, 2002*.

Single European Act (SEA) An Act passed by the EU which contains many measures to further integrate the member states, along economic and political dimensions, and which allows the Council of Ministers to pass most proposals by a majority vote, in contrast to the unanimous vote that was needed previously

Council of Ministers The major policy decision-making body of the EU; it consists of one minister from each of the 12 member states and is one of four major institutions of the EU

6. Common measures for consumer protection.
7. Common laws to maintain competition throughout the community and to fight monopolies or illegal cartels.
8. Regional funds to encourage the economic development of certain countries/regions.
9. Greater monetary and fiscal coordination among member states and certain common monetary/fiscal policies.[4]

In December 1985 EU leaders adopted a White Paper that contained 279 proposals aimed at achieving a single unified European market by December 31, 1992. Less than two years later the **Single European Act (SEA)** was enacted.[5] One of the most important parts of the SEA was the EU **Council of Ministers**, one of the four major institutions of the EU. For each field of discussion, the EU Council of Ministers consists of one minister from each of the member states and is responsible for making major policy decisions for union. The Council could now pass most proposals with a majority vote, in contrast to the unanimous vote that was needed previously. This opened the door for much faster progress toward political, as well as economic, integration among member countries. The EU has now adopted a single European currency. It has also committed to a social charter, complete harmonization of social and economic policies, a common defense policy, and related measures that increase the power of the EU bureaucracy in Brussels.

Table 16.1 **Economic profile of the big three (in US dollars)**

	United States	*Japan*	EU15
The economy			
Gross domestic product (2000)	$9.8 trillion	$4.8 trillion	$7.9 trillion
Industrial output trend	–6.3%	–12.2%	–1.1%
Retail sales trend	+9.8%	+1.5%	–2.1%
Consumer prices trend	+2.1%	–0.8%	+2.3%
Producer prices trend	–1.0%	–1.3%	–0.6%
Government consumption trend (1999)	+2.4%	+1.3%	–2.0%
Gross fixed-investment trend (1999)	+9.1%	+1.1%	+4.4%
Workforce			
Labor-force participation (1999)	67.1%	62.4%	56.8% (1)
Civilian employment growth trend	–0.6%	–1.6%	+1.2%
Labor cost per hour	$20.03	$22.22	$17.68
Compensation per employee trend	+3.3%	–0.4%	+2.6%
Unit labor costs trend (1990–1998)	+0.1%	+1.4%	–0.6% (2)
Unemployment rate	5.4%	5.4%	7.7%
Trade			
Current-account balance (% of GDP)	–3.7%	+2.5%	+0.1%
Export of goods/services trend	–16.4%	–18.6%	+1.5%
Import of goods/services trend	–14.6%	–14.6%	–0.5%
Public sector			
Public spending (% of GDP)	32.7%	30.0%	43.8%
Government debt (% of GDP)	61.5%	108.8%	66.3%
Consumers			
New car sales	8.9 million	4.3 million	11.6 million
Household savings ratio	–0.3%	12.4%	12.5% (3)
Stock market			
Stock market capitalization (1999)	$16.6 trillion	$4.5 trillion	$9.4 trillion
2001 share prices performance	–11.1%	–25.7%	+29.8%
Capital market			
Short-term interest rates	1.9%	0.5%	3.5% (3)
Long-term interest rates	5.7%	1.3%	4.7% (3)

Notes: GDP figures are at current prices and exchange rates.

(1) Calculated using the weighted average of labor participation in France, Germany, Italy, Netherlands, Sweden, and the UK.

(2) Calculated using the weighted average of labor participation in Belgium, France, Germany, Italy, Netherlands, Sweden, and the UK.

(3) Refers to Eurozone

Sources: Adapted from OECD, *National Account of OECD Countries*, vol. 1, 2001; OECD, *Main Economic Indicators*, 2001; OECD, *OECD in Figures*, 2001; Economist Intelligence Unit (***www.economist.com***); Bureau of Economic Analysis, *Survey of Current Business*, February 2001 (***www.bea.doc.gov***); OECD, *OECD in Washington*, February 2001; World Bank, *World Development Report*, 2000/2001.

Single European market (SEM)
A market consisting of all members of the EU, bound together by a single currency, a special charter, complete harmonization of social and economic policies, and a common defense policy

Will the EU eventually bring about a **single European market (SEM)** in which the above stated goals are achieved? This will depend on the extent of progress in the area of free movement of goods, changes in financial and banking services, and the practice of government procurement.

Free movement of goods

There have been no customs duties between most EU members since March 1, 1986. However, free movement of goods has been hampered by a host of non-tariff barriers that help local industries by obstructing the import of goods. These barriers have included technical standards, administrative barriers, and fragmented local markets.

In the case of technical standards, for example, goods can be shipped to another EU country but they might not be sold if they fail to conform to technical, safety, or other standards and regulations of the importing country. Today these individual standards are being phased out and replaced with common EU standards.

Administrative barriers include such things as refusal to admit food products that contain additives or substitutes that are judged detrimental to the consumer's health. These barriers are also being phased out.[6]

Fragmented local markets have been created by exploiting language differences between countries and by setting artificially high prices for goods. With the growth of discount stores, mail order houses, cross-border buying deals, and e-commerce, these differentials are also being gradually eliminated.

Changes in financial and banking services

Since July 1990, with the exception of a few EU countries, there has been free capital movement among members. This has resulted in the emergence of more Europe-wide financial service corporations. So, for example, an English building association can now sell mortgage loans in Rome through the mail and a French company can sell life insurance to Belgians through a branch in Frankfurt. There will also be a unified equity market and stockbrokers will be able to operate freely in every city in the EU. The combined capitalization of the entire EU is over $5 trillion, approximately one-third of that of the US.[7] The combined EU equity market will create tremendous opportunities, making it easier for companies to raise money by selling stock and giving investors greater access to security issues throughout the EU. There will also be greater uniformity in retail financial areas such as banking services and credit cards. Commenting on the future of the financial services industry in the EU, one group of researchers has predicted that:

> As financial intermediaries consolidate in type and number at a European level, operationally inefficient and uninnovative banks and securities houses that are financially viable only under protected circumstances will find themselves restructured in some form or another. The cross-shareholdings and strategic alliances under which these players are now taking refuge may end up in outright mergers and acquisitions, as financially healthier intermediaries with new value-propositions to the end-clients become bolder in the pan-European arena. And the buyers of their financial products will certainly gain from being served by more innovative and efficient intermediaries who will now be faced with competitive pressures at a European, rather than national, level . . .[8]

The EU has also created a single currency, the euro,[9] which some believe will challenge the US dollar's dominance of international trade and finance.[10] In January 2002, the euro officially replaced individual countries' coins and bank notes.[11] The common currency, originally used as a benchmark and now as the only currency, has allowed buyers to use comparative shopping in seeking the lowest prices.[12] In the process, this development has helped generate new opportunities for both EU businesses as well as for foreign MNEs doing business in the EU.[13]

Practice of government procurement

EU government procurements account for close to 11 per cent of the union's gross domestic product (GDP). In the past it has been common to find governments awarding contracts to national firms. However, with the emergence of the SEM and the Government Procurement Agreement (GPA), this is diminishing. The result will be greater efficiency, lower cost, and an economically stronger common market. On the other hand, it is important to realize that, in implementing this strategy, many companies are likely to find themselves losing business to competitors in other EU countries who can provide higher quality and service and lower cost. This development will also probably be somewhat slow in coming because of the possible negative impact of the economic growth of individual countries and the desire to favor national firms when awarding government contracts. For instance, despite the GPA, which obligues EU members to publish large tenders, in 1999 the European Commission sent "reasoned opinions" for not publishing tenders – the second stage on infringement procedures – to seven member states.[14]

The EU is also seeking ways of standardizing the procurement process to overcome language barriers. For example, in 2001, the European Commission proposed a common vocabulary to be used in all public procurement notices that would standardize the procurement process and increase competition.[15]

Active learning check

Review your answer to Active Learning Case question 1 and make any changes you like. Then compare your answer with the one below.

1. Describe the stages by which France Telecom has built up a successful strategic base in the EU. What barriers to integration had to be overcome in the EU before France Telecom could buy up rival companies?

As a state-owned monopoly, France Telecom originally had a strong presence in its own market but relied heavily on fixed-line operations and had no significant international presence. Faced with deregulation, France Telecom sought to compete regionally but understood that to do so it had to have competitive products and access to international markets. Investment in R&D allowed the company to expand its product line while strategic alliances were sought to protect its market and expand into other markets. The Global One alliance with Telekom provided a period of competitive shelter from one of its major EU competitors. By the time this alliance was dissolved in 1999, France Telecom had the capacity to compete alone against major EU telecommunication companies and had begun to acquire companies to solidify its product line and to enter new EU markets.

For France Telecom to be able to purchase rival firms, deregulation of telecommunication markets of individual countries in the EU had to occur. In addition, France Telecom acquisitions must overcome antitrust legislation in the EU.

The competitive status of the EU

The eventual emergence of an integrated EU will help greater Europe to compete more effectively with the other triad members.[16] However, several EU countries are currently at a competitive disadvantage in some areas.

Productivity

High wages, salaries, and fringe benefits put some EU firms at a disadvantage in competing with their US and Japanese counterparts. Labor laws in all EU countries make it extremely difficult to fire employees once they have been employed for a year. US companies have much greater freedom and flexibility in hiring and firing their workers on short notice. This means that employees must remain productive to retain their jobs and that companies can adjust more readily to changes in demand for their product or service. Japanese firms tend to treat their workers as a fixed cost and so find the practice of firing to be unnecessary; employees are grateful to their employers and are willing to work hard to upgrade their skills and to increase the economic performance of their companies.

Table 16.2 **Hourly compensation costs in manufacturing, 1991–2000**

	1991	*2000*	*% change (1991–2000)*
European Union	17.73	18.33	3.38
of which			
France	15.65	16.38	4.66
Germany (1)	22.55	23.50	4.21
Italy	18.32	14.66	–19.98
Spain	12.29	10.85	–11.72
United Kingdom	13.74	15.88	15.57
United States	15.58	19.86	27.47
Japan	14.67	22.00	49.97

Notes: GDP figures are at current prices and exchange rates.

(1) For 2000, the hourly compensation is calculated by averaging the average compensation in the former West Germany ($24.01) and East Germany ($23.99).

Source: US Department of Labor, Bureau of Labor Statistics, September 2001.

With some success, European firms are working to increase their productivity and to match that of their major triad competitors. In the early 1990s the EU's hourly compensation for production workers was 14 per cent higher than in the US and 15 per cent higher than in Japan. However, by 2000, this was reversed and the EU had the lowest labor costs in the triad (see Table 16.2). Much of the decrease can be attributed to a decrease in the value of EU currencies against the dollar during the period. Nonetheless, European firms were also able to negotiate better contracts with labor unions and to successfully lobby the government for more flexibility.[17] (Also see the box "International Business Strategy *in Action*: German management gets tough" in Chapter 12.)

Investment spending

Investment spending in EU countries has traditionally lagged behind. Part of this can be explained by rapid increases in wages and benefits during the 1980s which were not offset by increases in productivity. As a result, EU firms found themselves without the capital to invest and had to resort to borrowing. Demands for loans resulted in higher interest rates, which also put a strain on investors. By the late 1980s EU government spending had risen to approximately 50 per cent of GDP (in contrast to about 30 per cent for the US and Japan).[18] Because of this, taxes were raised, thus limiting funds and forcing interest rates to go even higher. More recently EU economies have been doing much better, stabilizing government spending. Despite this, most European countries continue to perform below the US level in terms of both annual increases and overall productivity. (See Figure 16.1.)

Education

Another area where EU countries have failed to maintain a competitive edge is education. While all three triad groups spend approximately 5 per cent of GDP on education, the approaches are different. In Europe, most vocational training is provided at the high school level, whereas in the US and Japan it is done later. In addition, in the US, a higher percentage of the population attends college than in Europe or Japan. The European university curriculum is more theoretical than in either the US or Japan. European educational institutions are also more rigid and less able to adapt to the changing needs of business. There is less interaction between European educational institutions and industry than in the US and Japan. As a result, many European students receive training that is inappropriate for the employment needs of European business and industry. This,

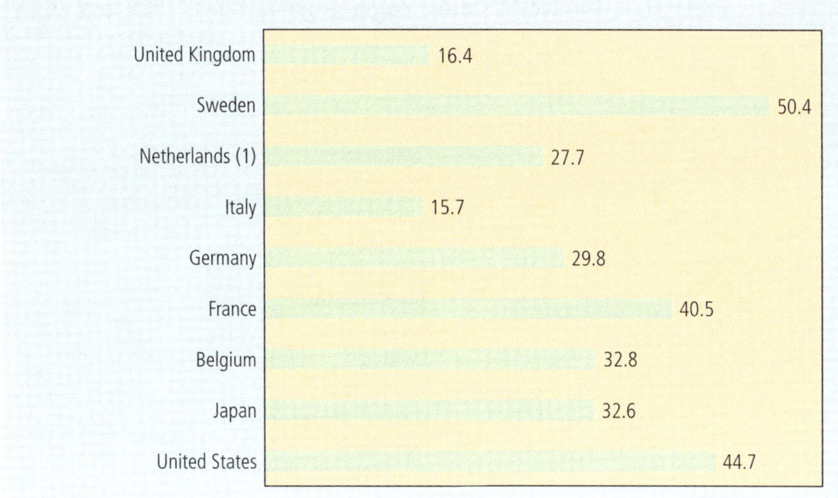

Figure 16.1 **Productivity: percentage increase in output per hour, 1992–2000**

Source: US Department of Labor, Bureau of Labor Statistics, August 2001.

in part, explains the extremely high unemployment rates in the age group under 25 in many regions of Europe.

The major challenge for European countries will be to modify their education systems and to make them more flexible, more practical, and better able to adapt to the changing demands of industry.

Overall evaluation

In overall terms, the EU has traditionally lagged behind its triad competitors. As Table 16.3 shows, in 1989 the 15 EU countries ranked in the top 22 most competitive nations in the world. By 2001 only 10 of the group were on this list. The world is becoming a more competitive place, and some EU countries are finding it hard to keep up.

What changes are likely to occur in the future? One is an increase in acquisition and mergers among EU firms and between them and companies from outside the bloc. A seond change is the emergence of new technologies that will be developed in EU laboratories. A third is additional free trade agreements and other economic arrangements among European countries that are designed to make the EU a stronger, more competitive market.

Active learning check 

Review your answer to Active Learning Case question 2 and make any changes you like. Then compare your answer with the one below.

2. To what extent is the triad strategy of France Telecom the same as that of Vodafone (in Chapter 8)? Are there any differences?

Both Vodafone and France Telecom have a stronger presence in the European market than in any other triad market. Acquisitions have been a major part of both their strategies to gain technology and market share in their own triad region and in other triad markets. One difference is Vodafone's continued reliance for alliances, such as its joint venture with Bell Atlantic, while France Telecom no longer seeks alliances but equity in competitors. Another difference is that the extent of Vodafone's international expansion is much larger than France Telecom's, including not only a strong presence in Japan but also an investment in non-triad countries.

Table 16.3 **The world's most competitive nations, 1989 and 2001**

Rank	*1989*	*2001*
1	Japan	USA
2	Switzerland	Singapore
3	United States	**Finland**
4	Canada	**Luxembourg**
5	**Germany**	**Netherlands**
6	**Finland**	Hong Kong
7	**Netherlands**	**Ireland**
8	**Sweden**	**Sweden**
9	Norway	Canada
10	Australia	Switzerland
11	**United Kingdom**	Australia
12	**Denmark**	**Germany**
13	**France**	Iceland
14	**Belgium/Luxembourg**	**Austria**
15	**Austria**	**Denmark**
16	**Ireland**	Israel
17	New Zealand	**Belgium**
18	**Spain**	Taiwan
19	**Italy**	**United Kingdom**
20	Turkey	Norway
21	**Portugal**	New Zealand
22	**Greece**	Estonia

Sources: Adapted from IMD and World Economic Forum, *The World Competitiveness Report 1989*, and IMD, *The World Competitiveness Report 2001* (***www.imd.ch***).

CONDUCTING A STRATEGIC ANALYSIS

As we have seen, the EU is likely to be a very competitive market in the future.[19] In preparing to do business in the EU, foreign MNEs must first conduct an overall strategic analysis.[20] This analysis should focus on the competitive nature of the industry that is being targeted. Assuming that the enterprise intends to set up operations by FDI or alternative investments rather than merely export to the market, the analysis must also evaluate location. The following section examines both of these activities.

Using competitive intelligence

Competition in the EU has increased over the last five years. Some of the specific strategies that have been employed include careful market segmentation, increased research and development, and the use of mergers, acquisitions, and alliances to help build market share and to improve competitive strength. By the late 1990s, for example, US car makers such as Ford Motor and General Motors were well positioned to compete successfully in the EU;[21] IBM was reorganizing and seeking to capitalize on its strong European holdings; and companies such as Coca-Cola, Colgate, Gillette, and Procter & Gamble were making plans to build market share. Competitor intelligence has been an essential part of these developments. This approach employs two complementary paths: external information gathering and internal infrastructural analysis.

External information gathering

The information that is critical for competitor analysis is typically located in a variety of sources.[22] For example, in Great Britain, Denmark, and Ireland, centralized government-controlled company registration offices provide financial information on registered firms. Other useful sources of competitive information include the Department of Trade and Industry (DTI), trade associations, business information services, and regional and local publications. In France, a great deal of registration information is commonly found in local courthouses. This is also the case in Germany and Italy, where companies must register with the local civil courts in the region where they are headquartered. In these countries chambers of commerce are also excellent sources of information since these organizations work much more closely with business firms than do their counterparts in the US. Central databases created by the EU Commission can be used to keep abreast of changes in national legislation, thus helping companies to remain aware of new laws and regulations. An understanding of the legal, technical, and cultural barriers often used to keep foreign competition at bay can be particularly important in an environmental analysis. The box "International Business Strategy in Action: Toys 'Я' Us in Europe" illustrates this point.

INTERNATIONAL BUSINESS STRATEGY *IN ACTION*

Toys "Я" Us in Europe

Many multinationals like to set up operations in Europe, particularly in the largest economy, Germany. Despite its economic downturn in the 1990s, this country has a very strong economy and it greatly influences what happens in the rest of the EU. However, breaking down technical and cultural barriers in Germany can be a major chore. Toys "Я" Us offers an excellent case example.

When the company decided to enter the German market, it was greeted by a partial boycott and a public relations blitz that condemned the concept of a self-service toy supermarket as being alien and wrong. Even though the managing director of Toys "Я" Us was a German, strong objections were directed against a US retailer wanting large-area sales space in Germany. The company soon learned that legal and cultural barriers could be effectively used to block foreign competition. When Toys "Я" Us applied for a construction permit in Cologne, the city fathers asked the local chamber of commerce and retailers' association how they felt about the application. The latter replied that a toy store belongs in the center of the city, not on the edge of town. Yet this is exactly where Toys "Я" Us needed to be located so that it could build a sprawling store and a parking lot that was the size of a football field. In addition, the German Toy Manufacturers Association questioned why a toy store would sell so many non-toy items.

The managing director for Toys "Я" Us refused to allow these early setbacks to thwart his efforts. He continued making the rounds of trade shows, negotiating for store sites, and presenting the company's plans to local officials; eventually he wore down the resistance. Even the competition began to realize that successful large toy stores could spark a boom in the toy market. This is exactly what happened. By the 1990s the toy industry in Germany was increasing at an annual rate of 10 per cent. In addition, competitors began copying some of the approaches used by Toys "Я" Us, such as piling shelves at the back of the store with baby food and diapers. They now realize that parents who come in to get diapers or baby food seldom leave without buying a toy for the child.

By 1995 Toys "Я" Us had 59 stores in Germany and it held the largest share of the toy market in Germany. It had another 149 outlets in Europe, including 61 in the UK, 44 in France, and 29 in Spain. By 2000, 30 per cent of Toys "Я" Us stores were located outside the US. After an initial failure in the international market that saw the closing of 50 stores in 1998, the toy retailer redefined its strategy and over the next two years opened as many stores in key markets in Europe and Asia. The German experience has taught the management that despite cultural, legal, and technical barriers, a retail company can succeed in Europe if it is patient, maintains a strong consumer-oriented marketing focus, and is nationally responsive.

Websites: ***www.toysrus.co.uk***; ***www.toysrus.fr***; ***inc.toysrus.com*** and ***www.toysrus.de***.

Sources: Adapted from Ferdinand Protzman, "Greetings from Fortress Europe," *New York Times*, August 18, 1991, Section 3, pp. 1, 6; John Templeman et al., "Germany Fights Back," *Business Week*, May 31, 1993, pp. 48–51; ***www.toysrus.com***; Paul Klebnikov, "Trouble in Toyland," *Forbes*, June 1, 1998, pp. 56–60; Michael V. Gestrin, Rory F. Knight and Alan M. Rugman, *The Templeton Global Performance Index* (Templeton College, University of Oxford, 1998).

Internal infrastructural analysis

The second step that MNEs take is an analysis of how to manage their infrastructure. Prescott and Gibbons have described four types of infrastructures that can be used to compete effectively: coordinated, market coordination, resource point sharing, and autonomous.[23] The choice of infrastructure is determined by the similarity of national markets among the MNE's businesses and the extent of resource sharing across businesses.

Coordinated infrastructure
An infrastructure used when there is a high degree of similarity among national markets and business units share resources in an effort to help each other to increase overall sales

Market coordination infrastructure
An infrastructure used by firms that compete in similar national markets but do little resource sharing among their businesses

Resource-sharing infrastructure
An infrastructure used by firms that compete in dissimilar national markets but share resources such as R&D efforts and manufacturing information

Autonomous infrastructure
An infrastructure used by multinationals that compete in dissimilar national markets and do not share resources

The **coordinated infrastructure** is used when there is a high degree of similarity among national markets and business units share resources in an effort to help each other increase overall sales. Computer firms often use this approach. Firms that compete in similar national markets but do little resource sharing among their businesses use a **market coordination infrastructure**. This approach is employed by companies that set up each operation as a separate, independent business. Small firms that are geographically dispersed sometimes use this approach. Firms that compete in dissimilar national markets but share resources such as R&D efforts and manufacturing information use a **resource-sharing infrastructure**. Auto manufacturers use this approach. An **autonomous infrastructure** is used by MNEs that compete in dissimilar national markets and do not share resources. Highly diversified MNEs use this approach.

Evaluating locations

Many companies are finding that they need to expand globally if they are to remain competitive. Auto suppliers are a good example. By the beginning of the 1990s North American auto suppliers had seen their world market share decline from 32 to 28 per cent, whereas Western Europe's world market share rose from 30 to 39 per cent. An international survey reveals that US auto suppliers believed that Europe promised the greatest potential for them because it is the largest single market in the world, has an industry structure that is similar to that in the US, and offers a source of low-cost manufacturing.[24] As a result, firms like General Motors and Ford Motor expanded their European presence through greater foreign direct investment and strategic alliances. Companies in a host of other industries, from computers to consumer goods, are following suit, and many are finding that regions and municipalities are prepared to provide investment incentives to encourage this activity.

Table 16.4 Comparison of investment incentives in selected EU countries based on an actual project evaluation

	Spain		*Italy*		*France*		*United Kingdom*	
	Application area	*Level*	*Application area*	*Level*	*Application area*	*Level*	*Application area*	*Level*
Grants	Available in parts of the country only	Very attractive	Available in parts of the country only	Attractive	Available in parts of the country only	Attractive	Available in whole country	Slightly attractive
Employment subsidies	Available in whole country	Very attractive	Available in whole country	Attractive	Available in whole country	Slightly attractive	Available in parts of the country only	Attractive
Tax breaks	Available in whole country	Attractive	Available in parts of the country only	Very attractive	Available in whole country	Very attractive	Available in parts of the country only	Attractive
Soft loans	Available in parts of the country only	Slightly attractive	Available in parts of the country only	Slightly attractive	Available in parts of the country only	Slightly attractive	Available in parts of the country only	Slightly attractive

Application area: Available in whole country; Available in parts of the country only

Level: Slightly attractive; Attractive; Very attractive

Source: Adapted from Maria Brindlmayer, "Comparing EC Investment Incentives and Getting the Best Deal," *Journal of European Business*, November/December, 1990, p. 38.

Regional incentives

Investment incentives take a number of forms, including grants, low-interest loans, reduced land prices, and training support for personnel. Table 16.4, which was constructed for the purpose of evaluating a specific project, provides a general comparison of investment incentives in several major EU countries. It shows that incentives vary from country to country. Some of these incentives are available only for several years, whereas others remain in effect for a much longer time.

Typically, incentives will be higher when (1) the region is economically depressed, (2) many jobs are being created, (3) the company is making a large investment, and/or (4) the investment is likely to attract other investors. Before agreeing to any contract, however, it is important that the deal be "locked in" and that any repayment of subsidies be made clear up front.

Other evaluation criteria

While subsidies can be important incentives, most MNEs doing business in the EU consider them as just one element in the evaluation process. Some of the other conditions and costs are described in Table 16.5. They include operational costs such as labor,

Table 16.5 Comparison of location factors: one example

	Port city X (France)	*Port city Y (UK)*
Labor		
Availability	More attractive	Less attractive
Wages (incl. fringes)	Less attractive	More attractive
Strike level	More attractive	Less attractive
Utilities		
Telephone penetration	Approximately equal	Approximately equal
Price	Less attractive	More attractive
Transport		
Road access	More attractive	Less attractive
Rail access	More attractive	Less attractive
Air access	Approximately equal	Approximately equal
Water access	Approximately equal	Approximately equal
Location		
Distance from Germany	More attractive	Less attractive
Land		
Costs/square yard	More attractive	Less attractive
Other		
English language education	Less attractive	More attractive

Between the two sites: Less attractive / Approximately equal / More attractive

Source: Adapted from Maria Brindlmayer, "Comparing EC Investment Incentives and Getting the Best Deal," *Journal of European Business*, November/December, 1990, p. 38.

utilities, transportation, and distance from major markets. A recent survey conducted among 1,000 European companies that were not seeking financial assistance revealed that the most important location factors, in order of importance, were (1) access to customers, (2) quality of labor, (3) expansion prospects, (4) level of wage costs, (5) attractive environment, (6) access to suppliers, (7) non-financial regional assistance, (8) absence of restrictions for expansion, (9) infrastructure, (10) level of rents, and (11) public transportation.[25] Another factor that is often mentioned is the ease with which a company that is not doing well can withdraw. This includes laying off workers and selling facilities, and other factors involved in exiting a market. Gathering location data and the negotiating terms can take a considerable amount of time, but the results often justify the investment.

STRATEGY ISSUES

Many issues have been addressed in this book. We now focus on those strategies that need to be considered when doing business in the EU. These issues include (1) an overall strategic analysis, (2) the feasibility of exporting, (3) the value of strategic acquisitions and alliances, (4) marketing considerations, (5) manufacturing approaches, and (6) management considerations. The following section briefly examines each issue.

Overall strategic analysis for the EU

In formulating a strategy for doing business in the EU, we should look at both the process of globalization through economic integration and the need for a firm to be **nationally responsive**.[26] This is done on the matrix in Figure 16.2. The horizontal axis represents political sovereignty, and the need for a firm to be nationally responsive. We call this the "national responsiveness" axis. It is a political axis and takes into account both consumer tastes and government regulations. The vertical axis represents globalization through economic integration. We call this the "integration" axis. This includes the need to develop economies of scale, to use a value-added strategy, and to reap the benefits of increased coordination and control of geographically dispersed activities.

National responsiveness
The ability of MNEs to understand different consumer tastes in segmented regional markets and to respond to different national standards and regulations imposed by autonomous governments and agencies

Quadrants 1 and 4 in Figure 16.2 present relatively simple strategy situations. Quadrant 1 requires a strategy in which the MNE does not need to be concerned with national

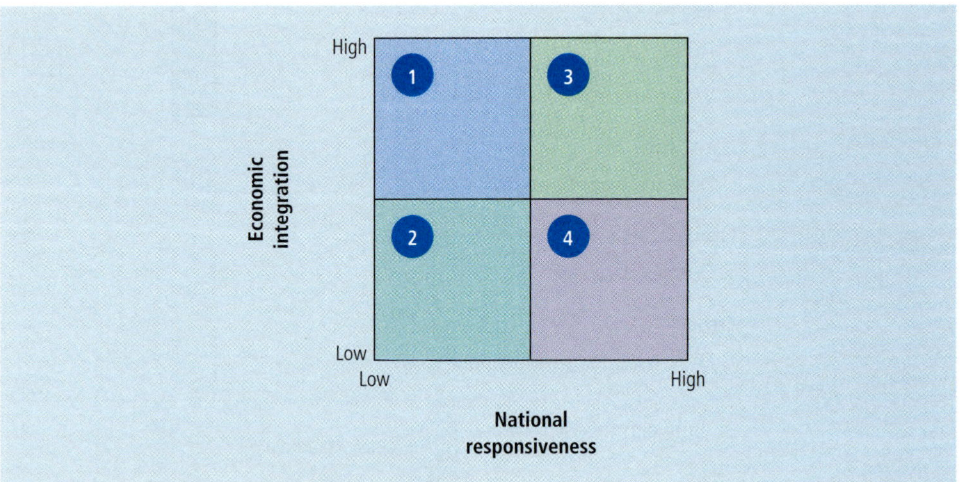

Figure 16.2 Business strategies for the EU

Source: Alan M. Rugman and Alain Verbeke, "Europe 1992 and Competitive Strategies for North American Firms," *Business Horizons*, November/December 1991, p. 77.

responsiveness. The company is in a market driven by high integration and its strategy must be on achieving price competitiveness. Firms operating in this quadrant are often centralized in structure and thus can use mergers and acquisitions to benefit from high economic integration. Companies selling microcomputers frequently operate in quadrant 1.

In quadrant 4 economic integration is less important than national responsiveness, so the MNE must focus on adapting products to satisfy the specific demands of each country. In this case integration is minimized in favor of a decentralized strategy of national responsiveness that is designed to appeal to select niches and target groups. Companies selling food products and designer clothes use this approach.

In quadrant 2 there is low integration and low national responsiveness. The potential of obtaining economies of scale and benefits of national or regional responsiveness are both small. MNEs operating in this quadrant are vulnerable to triad competitors. In this quadrant there is no advantage in centralized quality control or economies of scale and no ability to adapt activities to individual countries. MNEs selling inexpensive toys that are undifferentiated fall into this quadrant.

MNEs in quadrant 3 use a strategy of high integration and high national responsiveness that is characterized by strong price competitiveness and select target positioning. This is the most challenging quadrant to implement as the firm's organization structure is complex, but it is the one in which many successful triad-based adaptive multinationals operate. Auto firms fall into this quadrant.

A close look at events in the EU reveals that Brussels' administrators designed a strategy to help European firms move into quadrant 1. This plan is designed to create a natural barrier to entry for outside firms and to help ensure the success of local competitors. A survey of the top management of Europe's 300 largest corporations has confirmed this tendency toward integration. The survey found that European managers anticipate increased integration due to such developments as strategic partnerships, mergers, and takeovers as well as increasing economies of scale.[27] As a result, the managers expect the development of more efficient modern industries. The survey also found that European managers were confident that economic integration was a viable strategy for them, but that it would be detrimental to non-European MNEs. Only 9 per cent of the managers believed that US firms would gain ground in Europe, while 42 per cent said that US firms would lose competitive strength.

Exporting firms operate in quadrant 4. As outsiders in the EU, US firms will find it increasingly difficult to export to Europe and to compete on economies of scale in the face of integration by rival firms in the EU. Not only will costs be higher for exporters, but locally based competitors will have more access to competitive information. As a result, during the millennium many exporting firms will be switching to FDI from exporting in order to meet the new nature of competition in Europe.

Active learning check

Review your answer to Active Learning Case question 3 and make any changes you like. Then compare your answer with the one below.

3. In what ways will globalization and localization (sovereignty) be important issues for mergers in the EU?

Companies successfully operating in different EU countries will seek mergers to achieve some economies of scale in R&D, design, sourcing, and distribution among others. Nonetheless, the benefits of economies of scale have to be weighted against the need to tailor-make products for customers in different markets. Globalization will therefore occur only in some sectors of the merged company.

Exporting

Those firms that continue to export to the EU will have to address a number of legal/financial matters. The following sections examine some of the most important issues. (See Table 16.6.)

Customs duties and taxes

Goods manufactured outside the EU are subject to customs duties at the point of entry. These duties are determined by an EU-wide tariff system that establishes common rates

Table 16.6 Direction of EU trade, 1991–2000

	Exports to				*Imports from*			
	1991		*2000*		*1991*		*2000*	
Country/region	*(billions of US $)*	*% of total*	*(billions of US $)*	*% of total*	*(billions of US $)*	*% of total*	*(billions of US $)*	*% of total*
European Union*	1,005.4	67.5	1,416.8	62.1	992.9	62.8	1,321.9	57.9
Austria	36.8	2.5	48.0	2.1	28.4	1.8	35.3	1.5
Belgium/Luxembourg	92.0	6.2	126.2	5.5	96.1	6.1	125.1	5.5
Denmark	22.6	1.5	29.1	1.3	24.6	1.6	28.1	1.2
Finland	12.9	0.9	22.2	1.0	17.0	1.1	24.4	1.1
France	161.2	10.8	221.7	9.7	148.9	9.4	180.6	7.9
Germany	222.2	14.9	283.6	12.4	237.9	15.1	296.8	13.0
Greece	13.3	0.9	20.4	0.9	6.5	0.4	5.1	0.2
Ireland	14.9	1.0	32.6	1.4	18.0	1.1	46.0	2.0
Italy	105.9	7.1	135.3	5.9	107.1	6.8	119.2	5.2
Netherlands	93.0	6.2	121.4	5.3	112.0	7.1	161.8	7.1
Portugal	19.1	1.3	32.2	1.4	14.1	0.9	20.2	0.9
Spain	61.4	4.1	109.8	4.8	44.1	2.8	77.3	3.4
Sweden	31.0	2.1	48.4	2.1	35.4	2.2	47.9	2.1
United Kingdom	119.1	8.0	185.7	8.1	102.8	6.5	154.0	6.7
Other Western Europe	75.0	5.0	90.7	4.0	73.8	4.7	100.7	4.4
Iceland	1.0	0.1	1.6	0.1	1.2	0.1	1.6	0.1
Norway	17.4	1.2	23.4	1.0	27.2	1.7	43.1	1.9
Switzerland	56.6	3.8	65.7	2.9	45.4	2.9	56.0	2.5
Central and Eastern Europe	71.3	4.8	175.5	7.7	68.9	4.4	164.8	7.2
of which								
Czech Republic*	5.7	0.4	22.0	1.0	5.9	0.4	19.9	0.9
Hungary	5.8	0.4	21.2	0.9	5.8	0.4	20.8	0.9
Poland	11.0	0.7	31.1	1.4	8.9	0.6	21.7	0.9
Russia	NA	NA	18.2	0.8	NA	NA	6.4	0.3
Turkey	10.8	0.7	28.8	1.3	8.2	0.5	17.1	0.7
Others	38.0	2.5	54.1	2.4	40.1	2.5	78.9	3.5
Total Europe	1,151.7	77.3	1,683.0	73.7	1,135.6	71.9	1,587.4	69.5
Non-European	338.6	22.7	600.0	26.3	444.6	28.1	697.5	30.5
of which								
United States	94.8	6.4	213.4	9.3	120.1	7.6	188.4	8.2
Japan	29.5	2.0	41.3	1.8	72.1	4.6	82.0	3.6
Total	1,490.3	100.0	2,283.0	100.0	1,580.2	100.0	2,284.9	100.0

* Exports and imports from and to the EU refer to intra-EU trade.
For 1991, Czech Republic numbers include trade performed with the Slovak Republic (Czechoslovakia). Numbers might not add up due to rounding.

Source: IMF, *Direction of Trade Statistics Yearbook, 1996, 2001.*

regardless of entry point. Most duties are based on the value of the good ad valorem, and this value depends on the stage of assembly or completion of the end product.

Excise taxes are levied on certain types of goods such as alcohol, tobacco, and gasoline. These rates are determined by each member state, although the EU is now working on establishing uniform excise duties throughout the bloc.[28]

Product standards

Products exported to the EU must meet standards and technical regulations. Many of these are common throughout the bloc, but, when they are not, the product must meet the standards of the country to which it is exported. In many cases products produced in outside countries must be modified in order to gain EU entry.[29]

Conducting export operations

In recent years many US exporters of both goods and services have consolidated their operations with those of European companies, thus helping them to surmount EU barriers. For example, US accounting firms typically operate through local partnerships. Other examples are management consulting firms that have international operations that help them to address the needs of local clients and law firms with overseas offices.

Those MNEs that do choose to export to the EU must carefully select their agents and distributors. Five steps are critical to this process:

1. Examine the legal and business considerations involved in appointing foreign intermediaries and establish criteria that reflect the particular geographic market.
2. Assemble a list of potential candidates by using the various directories and by consulting with other sources of information.
3. Qualify such candidates by applying certain criteria and by conducting a preliminary interview.
4. Visit the proposed intermediary to obtain additional information about its resources and facilities, to get a proper feeling for the intermediary's compatibility with the organization, and to check the objectives of the agent or distributor.
5. After selecting an agent or distributor, (a) negotiate an agreement that is fair and mutually beneficial, (b) comply in good faith with the terms of the agreement, (c) continue communication between the parties, and (d) make occasional adjustments in the relationship in response to changing circumstances.[30]

Many small and intermediate size MNEs will continue to export to the EU because it is too expensive for them to use any other route. Large MNEs, on the other hand, are turning more and more to strategic acquisitions and alliances.

Strategic acquisitions and alliances

Two of the most popular ways of gaining a foothold in the EU are through strategic acquisitions or alliances. (See the box "International Business Strategy in Action: Kingfisher as a European retailer.") A *Harvard Business Research* study analyzed 49 strategic alliances and concluded that the chances of success are improved if the parties keep five guidelines in mind: (1) acquisitions work better than alliances when developing core businesses; (2) alliances are effective when firms want to gain entry into new geographic markets or businesses that are tangential to the core business; (3) alliances between strong and weak companies typically do not work well; (4) alliances that last are characterized by an ability to move beyond the initially established expectations and objectives; and (5) alliances are more likely to be successful when both sides hold an equal amount of financial ownership. In addition, more than three-quarters of the alliances that were studied ended with one of the parties acquiring full control.[31]

INTERNATIONAL BUSINESS STRATEGY *IN ACTION*

Kingfisher as a European retailer

In a recent study of the profitability of foreign assets, a British retailer, Kingfisher, came top of the pack. Its average return on foreign assets was 32 per cent for 1996 and 1997, well above the average of 4.78 per cent for the world's top 500 MNEs. What's more, in that period, Kingfisher only had 9 per cent of its total assets in foreign markets, but by 1999 had increased this to 40 per cent.

Kingfisher is a company that is leveraging its foreign assets to promote growth. Its first successful acquisition was of French electrical retailer Darty, followed in 1998 by a merger with French do-it-yourself retailer Castorama. Kingfisher also has other operations across Europe: in Belgium, the Netherlands, and Germany. It has moved into Asia with the acquisition of an electrical retail chain in Singapore in 1998, and is also in Taiwan.

Kingfisher was only formed in 1989, and consists of the British Woolworths Stores, Comet (electrical products), Superdrug, and B&Q (home improvement stores). In 1998 total sales revenues for Kingfisher were £6.4 billion (about US $10 billion). There were 2,500 stores in 13 countries, principally in Britain and France. These retail brand stores operate in chains across Britain. The CEO, Sir Geoffrey Mulcahy, has led the growth drive. He tried to consolidate Kingfisher's leading position in Britain by merging with the large supermarket chain Asda. In 1999, Asda was the third largest British supermarket chain behind Sainsbury and Tesco. However, Wal-Mart has now bought Asda.

Sir Geoffrey Mulcahy also has provided leadership in the foreign expansion through patience and strategic initiative. The merger with Castorama took five years to negotiate, as did the earlier one with Darty. The French managers and workers keep their jobs as "retail is detail" and local knowledge is vital. While its foreign businesses operate autonomously, there are logistical savings and scale economies in purchasing that arise for the Kingfisher group as a whole. Sir Geoffrey has positioned Kingfisher to ride the wave of growth through profitable international expansion.

Another popular way of doing business in the EU is through the use of strategic alliances. Experts agree that four of the most important steps include:

1. Pick a compatible partner and take the time to get to know and trust this company.
2. Choose a partner with complementary products or markets, rather than one who competes directly.
3. Be patient and do not rush into a deal or expect immediate results.
4. Learn about the partner's technology and management but try not to give away your own core secrets.

In some alliances one partner has taken advantage of the other by stealing technology or forcing the partner into a position where it had to sell out to the other. However, this will not happen if both sides make substantive contributions to the undertaking and each realizes that it needs the other. Moreover, even when alliances have not worked out, companies have found it in their best interest to continue looking for other partners for other deals.

Websites: ***www.kingfisher.co.uk***; ***www.asda.co.uk***; ***www.j-sainsbury.co.uk***; ***www.tesco.com*** and ***www.walmart.com***.

Sources: Michael V. Gestrin, Rory F. Knight and Alan M. Rugman, *The Templeton Global Performance Index* (Templeton College, University of Oxford, 1998); Kingfisher, *Annual Report and Accounts*, 1997, 1998; Corporate Profile: Kingfisher; *The Times*, London, February 1, 1999, p. 44; *Financial Times*, May 18, 1988, December 12, 1989; Bernard M. Wolf, "The Role of Strategic Alliances in the European Automotive Industry," in Alan M. Rugman and Alain Verbeke (eds.), *Research in Global Management*, vol. III (Greenwich, CT: JAI Press, 1992), pp. 143–163.

Making strategic alliances work

It is more common to find MNEs using strategic alliances than using acquisitions, and there are several important steps in making these arrangements work. One is that each partner must complement the other.[32] If one company is strong in research and development (R&D) and the other's strengths are in manufacturing and marketing, the alliance may be ideal. On the other hand, if both are strong in R&D and weak in manufacturing and marketing, there is no synergy and the two may end up trying to steal secrets from each other and competing rather than cooperating. Second, the goals of the two groups must be carefully spelled out. Once the partners have agreed upon the primary criteria such as new product development, increased market share, and return on investment, they can then decide how to commit their resources. These goals provide a basis for overall direction.

The key people from each firm must get to know each other. Building working relationships across the two firms is essential for resolving problems and issues that come up. Communication, networking, and interpersonal relationships are extremely useful in ensuring that the spirit of the alliance is kept alive.

Each group must understand how the other works so that differences can be accommodated. If one partner is responsible for making certain parts and for providing them to the other, there must be a clear understanding regarding such matters as product quality and delivery time. If the partner receiving products prefers to accumulate inventory to prevent stockout problems, the other must develop a manufacturing plan that addresses this need.

The parties must hold frequent meetings and develop a trust. The successful alliance between General Electric and Snecma was a result of mutual respect and dependence. The two companies cooperated fully in developing, manufacturing, and marketing commercial jet engines. As a result, today the joint venture makes one of the best-selling commercial jet engines in the world.

Marketing considerations

As the EU develops towards a true economic union, internal barriers to entry and mobility barriers within the bloc will disappear. This will create both challenges and opportunities. In particular, competition is likely to increase as it becomes easier for competitors to invade each other's territories. As a result, marketing strategies in the millennium will have to reflect concern for both pricing and positioning.

Pricing

The European Commission has estimated that the price of goods and services throughout the EU will decline. Five specific developments will make this work: (1) decreasing costs of doing business, now that internal barriers and restrictions have been removed, (2) the opening up of public procurement contracts to broader competition, (3) foreign investment that will increase production capacity, (4) more rigorous enforcement of competition policy, and (5) general intensified competition brought about by economic reforms.[33]

Price will become an even more important marketing factor to the extent that EU customers develop similar tastes and are willing to accept globally standardized products. As this happens, MNEs will be able to sell the same product throughout the bloc without having to make modifications for local tastes. Unfortunately, while some goods can be marketed with this strategy, many will require careful positioning for select target groups.

Positioning

Some global products such as Coca-Cola, Pepsi, and Marlboro cigarettes have universal appeal, but these are more the exception than the rule. For example, in the UK the Renault is viewed as a good economy car, but in Spain it is perceived as a luxury automobile. Similarly, in Great Britain and Holland, toothpaste is viewed as a hygiene product and sells much better than in Spain and Greece, where it is marketed as a cosmetic.[34]

As a result, the marketing motto, "plan globally, act locally", will continue to be a useful dictum. A good example is provided by the EU cellular communications market, which offers tremendous opportunities but is also extremely competitive because there are so many submarkets throughout the community. As a result, it is likely that the mobile communications market will end up being divided among a host of major competitors, each of which positions itself for a particular local or regional target group.

Active learning check

Review your answer to Active Learning Case question 4 and make any changes you like. Then compare your answer with the one below.

4. In what ways will both pricing and positioning be important for companies like France Telecom doing business in the EU?

Companies like France Telecom must be prepared to take full advantage of the economies from EU integration. Costs must decrease to increase market share in the more competitive EU market. At the same time, companies must have access to markets of the EU and market their products according to both the expectation of customers and the maximization of profits.

Direct marketing

Another strategy that is likely to receive a great deal of attention is direct marketing. Most EU firms tailor their products to narrow markets and direct mail is only now gaining attention. Unlike the US where businesses have been using telemarketing and other non-traditional channels for well over a decade, this is a new approach for European consumers, and there are a number of challenges that MNEs will have to surmount if they hope to direct market their product, such as: (1) consumers speak different languages, so a universal message or strategy will not work throughout the bloc; (2) inclusion of direct-response telephone numbers in television spots is forbidden by the privacy laws of some member states such as Germany; (3) information about potential clients is fragmented and not easily obtainable; and (4) the infrastructure for direct marketing is weak because credit cards, toll-free numbers, and computer bases are still in their infancy in Europe.[35] In addition, a high credit card fraud rate has slowed down the growth potential of e-commerce.[36] Nevertheless, direct marketing is likely to play a major role in MNE efforts to create a pan-European marketing strategy.

Manufacturing considerations

As individual country regulations are eliminated and EU members continue to standardize rules and regulations, it will be possible to produce uniform goods for the entire market. This will not come about immediately because of the time needed to change such things as electric systems so that toasters, television sets, and other home appliances can all be manufactured with the same type of plugs. However, MNEs will eventually be able to produce many products with standard parts that work in all EU countries. At the same time manufacturers will continue producing goods that appeal to local market tastes. For example, appliance makers now manufacture self-cleaning ovens for the French because of their tradition of high-temperature cooking. However, they typically leave out this option for the German market where food is generally cooked at lower temperatures. Some major manufacturing considerations that warrant attention by those doing business in the EU include reducing costs, building factory networks, and entering into R&D alliances.

Reducing costs

One manufacturing benefit of producing for a market with 375 million consumers is the ability to reduce cost per unit through the use of standardized components and large production runs. Under this arrangement the cost of the components is kept to a minimum and the large production runs allow the company to spread fixed costs over more units. This means cost per item can be sharply reduced. Moreover, economies of

Delayed differentiation
A strategy in which all products are manufactured in the same way for all countries or regions until as late in the assembly process as possible, at which time differentiation is used to introduce particular features or special components

scale can be achieved even when production has to be tailored to local conditions. This is accomplished through the use of **delayed differentiation**, in which all products are manufactured in the same way for all countries of regions until as late in the assembly process as possible. In these final stages differentiation is then used to introduce particular features or special components.

MNEs are also using outsourcing and just-in-time inventory systems to reduce the cost of carrying parts and supplies. By tailoring deliveries and shipments to the production schedule, factories are able to minimize their investment in materials and work-in-process. This system is also used by large retailers such as Marks & Spencer of the UK, which employs its electronic network system to keep track of inventory at each store in England, as well as on the Continent, and to replenish its outlets as needed.[37]

Another way in which costs are being controlled is by redesigning production processes, thus scrapping old, inefficient techniques in favor of more streamlined methods. This includes careful study of competitive firms in order to identify and copy their successful approaches to cost control. It also entails the elimination of red tape and the use of well-trained, highly motivated work teams.

Factory networks

MNEs in Europe are now beginning to create sophisticated networks of factories that both produce components and finished goods and provide distribution and after-sales services. For example, the Philips television factory in Bruges, Belgium, uses tubes that are supplied from a factory in Germany, transistors that come from France, plastics that are produced in Italy, and electronic components that come from another factory in Belgium.

These factory networks are also integrated with computer software packages that can operate in multiple European countries without the need for modification. Figure 16.3 provides an illustration. The software packages allow companies to make supply,

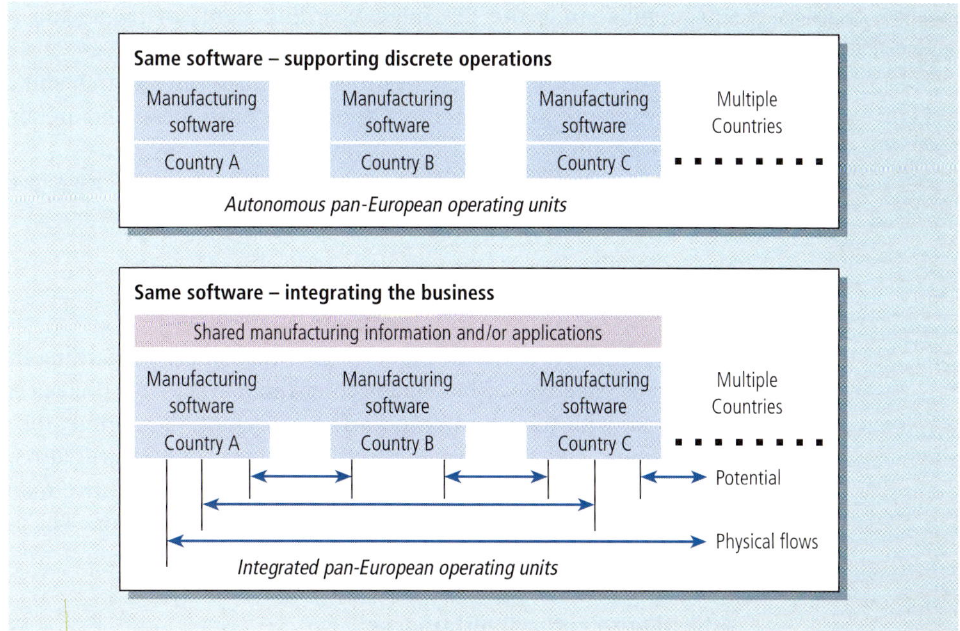

Figure 16.3 Pan-European manufacturing systems

Source: Adapted from Nigel Dunham and Robin Morgan, "The Search for a Truly Pan-European Manufacturing System," *Journal of European Business*, September/October 1991, p. 44.

production, and distribution decisions while at the same time satisfying the requirements of the different legal entities in the countries where they operate. Some specific functions that they help companies to perform include forecasting, logistics planning, inventory planning, production planning, and central updating of bills of materials. The software provides each factory manager with the specific information needed and does so in that individual's own language. As a result, MNEs are able to coordinate multiple activities and thus to develop an effective pan-European manufacturing system.

Research and development alliances

Another emerging manufacturing strategy is participation in cooperative R&D programs. In the EU this is taking two complementary paths. First, many companies are teaming up to share R&D expenses. Siemens and Philips have used this approach to develop computer chips and IBM has a number of agreements with European firms for developing advanced computer technology.

Second, many firms are trying to get some of these costs funded by participating in European cooperative R&D programs. The EU is providing European industry with funding for research in such areas as information technology, biotechnology, and energy. The objective of the program is to stimulate cross-border cooperation and to make Europe more productive and competitive in the world market. One of the best-known programs is the **European Research Cooperation Agency** (Eureka, for short), which was launched in 1985 and which emphasizes projects in the fields of energy, medicine, biotechnology, communications, information technology, transport, new materials, robotics, production automation, lasers, and the environment.[38] This program has helped to develop a European standard for high-definition television and has funded semiconductor research. To date more than 2,000 organizations have participated in Eureka-related projects. Those firms that are interested in participating in these cooperative programs typically do so by carrying out six steps:

European Research Cooperation Agency
A research and development alliance which emphasizes projects in the fields of energy, medicine, biotechnology, communications, information technology, transport, new materials, robotics, production automation, lasers, and the environment

1. Find out if the company is eligible for EU-funded programs.
2. Carefully study the EU rules regarding rights of ownership and dissemination of results.
3. Carefully choose the best location for a European research and development center.
4. Determine those competitors and major customers who are already participating in the program.
5. Gather recommendations from the firm's EU and local management.
6. Put together the company's application for funding.[39]

Management considerations

As more firms enter the EU, there is growing concern regarding their ability to manage Europeans effectively. Many firms enter the market with preconceived ideas about how to interact with their European partners or employees. Some, for example, believe that management styles that were effective in their country will also work well in Europe. However, as the Japanese have discovered in the US, effective management approaches must be tailor-made to meet the needs of the local situation. The primary focus must be on adjusting to cultural differences.

Adjusting to cultural differences

There are a number of differences between US and European workers. For example, Europeans are more accustomed to participating in decision making. They have a long history of worker participation programs and of holding seats on the board of directors.

Another difference is employee motivation. Researchers have found that quality of work life is extremely important in Scandinavian countries, whereas opportunities for individual achievement are of particular importance in the UK. French workers are interested in individual achievement but place strong emphasis on security. German workers place high value on both advancement and earnings.[40] Clearly, no universal list of motivators can be applied throughout the EU. These facts illustrate the importance of MNEs having a global perspective as well as having managers who are focused on the country-specific needs of the area where they are working.

Barriers to EU market access

Throughout the book we have explored the need for access to triad markets. Unfortunately, while the EU has become the world's largest market, some EU-based MNEs have sought to restrict access to this area. Although the overall trend during the postwar period has been toward an increasingly liberalized trade environment, international managers must know how to deal with, or at least anticipate, the use of administrative barriers in foreign markets.

The two most common trade law entry barriers are countervailing duty laws (CVD) and antidumping laws (AD). (These were discussed earlier in Chapters 6 and 15.) While the US uses CVD as an entry barrier (it had 90 per cent of the world's CVD cases in the 1980s), the EU uses AD as an entry barrier. Both **countervailing duties (CVD)** and **antidumping duties (AD)** are import tariffs that are intended to protect domestic producers from harmful dumping and subsidization by foreign governments. However, it has been demonstrated in several studies that these laws have been "captured" and used by weak firms seeking shelter from strong competition by rival MNEs in the triad.[41]

Countervailing duties (CVD)
Import tariffs intended to protect domestic producers from harmful subsidization by foreign governments

Antidumping duties (AD)
Import tariffs intended to protect domestic producers from foreign products sold at less than their cost of production or at lower prices than in their home market

Table 16.7 shows both the high number of AD cases that were launched and the tendency toward sectoral concentration in the use of AD by EU firms during the period from 1996 to 2000. Many AD cases were brought in the chemical, electronics, iron and steel, and other "mature" sectors that have weak firm-specific advantages (FSAs).

The use of these trade law instruments to provide shelter is by no means unique to the EU, as the earlier discussion of AD and CVD in Chapter 15 showed.[42] However, from Table 16.7 it is clear that non-EU firms in the chemical, electronics, and iron and steel sectors should probably anticipate some resistance if they plan to begin exporting to the EU market with a view to competing with domestic producers.

Table 16.7 **EU antidumping cases by sector, 1996–2000**

Description	*1996*	*1997*	*1998*	*1999*	*2000*
Chemicals and allied products	0	8	0	28	17
Textile and allied products	10	8	9	11	0
Wood and paper	0	7	0	0	0
Electronics	0	14	0	12	2
Other mechanical engineering	0	1	0	5	1
Iron and steel	9	4	19	25	7
Other metals	1	1	0	0	2
Other	5	2	1	5	2
All products listed	**25**	**45**	**29**	**86**	**31**
Of which antidumping	24	42	21	66	31
Of which antisubsidy	1	3	8	20	0

Sources: Commission of the European Communities, *Nineteenth Annual Report from the Commission to the European Parliament on the Communities Anti-Dumping and Anti-Subsidy Activities*, 2000.

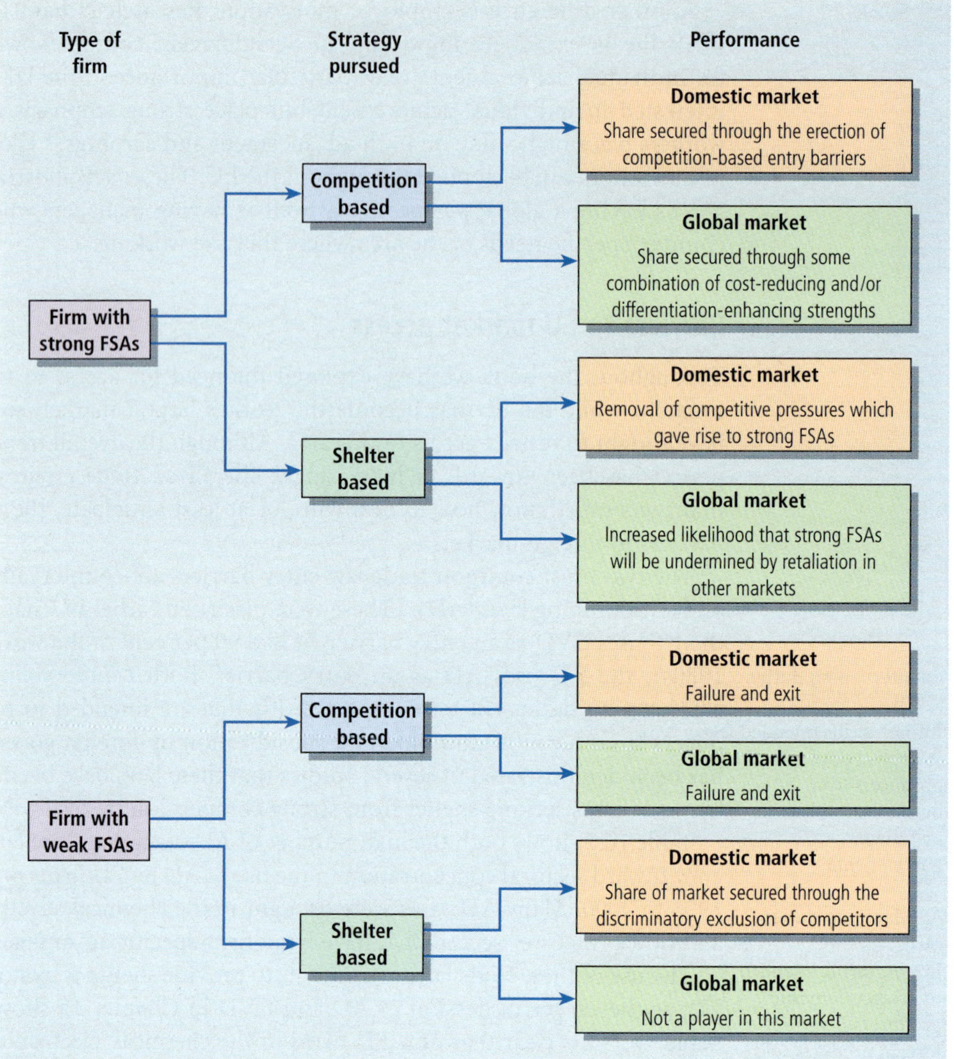

Figure 16.4 **Competition and shelter-based strategies**

Figure 16.4 shows the rationale for the use of AD and CVD laws by particular firms. As with all free-market economies, the EU economy has, at any given point in time, a significant number of firms in difficulty due to the pressure of global competition. These firms are barely able to compete with their more efficient global rivals and find themselves on the verge of exit from the industry. If the main reason for this is international competition, and domestic administrative instruments are in place that would allow such a firm to continue operating by limiting foreign competition, the company is likely to use these instruments. Such a situation is a rare instance when it is logical for a firm to spend time and money on an activity that is not productive from a competitiveness standpoint. By using AD or CVD laws, the uncompetitive firm is able to remain in operation not by improving its firm-specific advantages but, rather, by artificially raising the price at which foreign competitors must sell in the domestic market.

The abusive use of AD and CVD is a particular problem for non-triad members and for MNEs from other parts of the triad. The reason is that the administration of these trade laws is discretionary and subject to political pressures. Moreover, there is now strong evidence that the administration of these trade laws is biased in favor of domestic plaintiffs and against foreign firms.[43] The technical test of "material injury" due to the subsidies or dumped exports is routinely abused by the responsible administrative agencies in both the EU and the US.[44] This is an extremely serious problem for global business and it serves to reinforce the existence of the triad at the expense of a liberalized world trade and investment system.

KEY POINTS

1. The overall objective of the EU is to create a market in which there are no economic barriers to trade between the member countries. When this is achieved, the EU will be the largest economic bloc in the world. However, there are three areas, in particular, where additional progress must be made: free movement of goods, changes in financial and banking services, and the practice of government procurement.
2. The current competitive status of the EU lags that of the US and Japan in a number of areas, including productivity, investment spending, and education. Greater economic strides will be needed if the EU is to compete effectively with its triad counterparts.
3. In preparing to do business in the EU, MNEs should focus on the competitive nature of the industry that is targeted and on evaluation of location. Competitive intelligence gathering involves external information gathering and internal infrastructural analysis. Location evaluation entails consideration of such factors as regional incentives, operating costs, and distance from major markets.
4. There are many aspects of strategy that need to be considered when doing business in the EU. These include (1) an overall analysis of the environment, (2) the feasibility of exporting, (3) the value of strategic alliances and acquisitions, (4) marketing considerations, (5) manufacturing approaches, and (6) management considerations. Managers need to weigh the choices of economic integration and/or national responsiveness very carefully.
5. The EU has a large internal market. Firms located in the EU can use a new type of non-tariff barrier to entry to keep out rival firms, namely trade remedy legislation such as countervailing duty laws (CVD) and antidumping (AD) laws. Recent research has found that the use of both CVD and AD is a "shelter" strategy that is designed to protect uncompetitive domestic firms. However, the more successful EU firms concentrate on the development of sustainable firm-specific advantages rather than on the use of CVD and AD laws.

KEY TERMS

- Single European Act (SEA)
- EU Council of Ministers
- single European market (SEM)
- coordinated infrastructure
- market coordination infrastructure
- resource-sharing infrastructure
- autonomous infrastructure
- delayed differentiation
- European Research Cooperation Agency
- countervailing duties (CVD)
- antidumping duties (AD)
- national responsiveness

REVIEW AND DISCUSSION QUESTIONS

1. What are the ultimate objectives of the EU? Identify and describe them.
2. Will the EU bring about a single European market? What type of changes will have to take place in order for this to happen? Identify and describe three of them.
3. What is the competitive status of the EU in terms of labor productivity and investment spending? Based on your answer, what is your overall evaluation of this status?
4. How can firms doing business in the EU use competitive intelligence? Identify and describe two major steps that can be used in this process.
5. What types of regional incentives do countries offer MNEs willing to set up operations in their locales? Identify and describe two of them.
6. In addition to regional incentives, what other evaluation criteria should MNEs employ when deciding where in the EU to establish operations? Identify and describe three of them.
7. In formulating a strategy for doing business in the EU, there are two primary areas of initial consideration: national responsiveness and economic integration. What does this statement mean? Be sure to include a discussion of Figure 16.2 in your answer.
8. What do companies that want to export to the EU need to know about doing business there? Discuss five facts or strategies that would be of value to them.
9. In gaining a foothold in the EU, when is it most effective to opt for an acquisition over an alliance? When is a strategic alliance a better choice? In each case, provide an example.
10. Why will marketing strategies in the EU have to reflect a concern for pricing? A concern for positioning? Give an example of when each would be the most important consideration.
11. What is the likely future of direct marketing in the EU? Defend your answer.
12. What are three major manufacturing considerations for companies doing business in the EU? Identify and describe each.
13. How important is it for EU managers to have a global perspective? Be complete in your answer.
14. How can trade laws be used by EU firms to keep out global competitors?
15. What evidence is there that EU firms use antidumping laws?

REAL CASE

Accor budget hotels

The largest manager of budget-priced hotels in the world is the French hotel management company, Accor. In 2000, the company had 7 billion euros in revenue and 145,000 employees worldwide. Altogether it manages a portfolio of 3,600 hotels in 90 countries, of which 2,000 are in the budget and economy class. It runs all the US Red Roof Inns as well as the Motel 6 chain. In Europe, it manages budget hotels such as Ibis, Formule 1, and Etape Hotels. It also runs all the Novotel, Sofitel, and Mercure hotels in the upper and medium price range.

Accor has developed international capabilities in being a major services provider to the tourist, business travel, and food business sectors. It is developing an international brand name for the group's activities in these areas. It uses B2B and B2C Internet services. There are 860,000 restaurant managers, supermarket suppliers, and other affiliated workers using its B2B services, along with another 300,000 customers/small business people using B2C.

The company began operations in 1967 and rapidly expanded its Novotel hotels across France. The acquisition of another hotel chain in 1974, Courtepailles, established Accor as a major player in the French market. During the next two years the company moved to develop a market presence in the two- and three-star hotel market segment. This was done through the opening of an Ibis two-star hotel in Bordeaux and the acquisition of the three-star Mercure hotel chain.

The first significant expansion outside France was the 1973 opening of Novotel in Warsaw, Poland. In 1976 Accor opened its first hotel in Brazil and over the next year began to rapidly develop in Latin America. In 1979, Accor entered the US market with hotels in Minneapolis and New York and in 1984 a large Novotel was erected in Broadway. To enter the affordable US hotel market, the Motel 6 chain was purchased in 1990. By acquiring Sofitel in 1980 the company entered the African market and also strengthened its position in the European market. In 1986, Accor began development in Asia, including China and Thailand. In preparation for the 2008 Olympic games, Accor has entered a joint venture with the Beijing Tourism Group to manage 50 hotels by 2008.

Accor is also in the travel industry business. In France it owns Carlson Wagonlit Travel and Frantour. Acquiring international travel companies allowed Accor to complement its international hotel expansion plans. The acquisition of Africatours in 1984 allowed Accor to control the stream of tourism in the region. In 1987, Africatours acquired Asia tours and America tours. In 2000, Accor purchased a 38.5 per cent stake in Go Voyages, an e-travel planner that targets the European traveler.

Growing expertise in the hospitality business has also allowed the company to diversify into other areas, including restaurants and casinos. In 2000 it operated over 100 branches of the Courtepaille restaurants–grills and a dozen Accor casinos, mainly in France.

In December 2001, Accor agreed to purchase Compagnie Européenne de Casinos (CEC) for \$233.7 million. In January, however, the competing Groupe Partouche began acquiring CEC shares at a higher per share price. This boosted the expected price per share and has left Accor struggling to reformulate a deal. CEC has 24 casinos across Europe with the majority in France. The move comes at a time of consolidation in the casino industry. In 1996, major chains owned only 20 per cent of French casinos; by 2002 it had increased to 80 per cent. If Accor succeeds in purchasing CEC, its market share would increase to 21 per cent in France. France has 170 casinos with revenues totaling 1.895 billion euros and accounts for 40 per cent of the European market. Accor, Européenne de Casinos, Partouche, and Tranchant account for 45 per cent of the French market.

Accor makes one-third of its profits in the US. It lost one-third of its market capitalization in the week after the September 11 terrorist attack on the World Trade Center. As a result its profits in 2001 were the same as in 2000, at about \$650 million.

Foreign owners dominate the US hotel business at the high end. Four Seasons, a Canadian-founded chain, is the top of the line executive-class hotel chain. The UK hotel group, Six Continents (formerly the Bass group), operates Holiday Inn and the Inter-Continental hotel chains.

Websites: ***www.accorhotels.com***; ***www.accor.com***; ***www.fourseasons.com*** and ***www.sixcontinents.com***.

Sources: ***www.accorhotels.com***; Raphael Minder, "Accor May Have to Rethink Casino Offer," *FT.com*, January 3, 2002; Raphael Minder, "Accor to Acquire Casino Group for E258m," *FT.com*, December 17, 2001; "Casinos on Threshold of Recomposition," *La Tribune*, January 3, 2002, "Accor Agrees Chinese JV to Manage Around 50 Hotels by 2008," *AFX Europe*, December 12, 2001 and Anaïs Jouvancy, "European E-Travel Takes Off," *Le Monde Interactif*, November 8, 2000.

1. **Why did Accor concentrate on the French and European market before expanding into other regions?**
2. **How are acquisitions an important part of Accor's expansion strategy?**
3. **What are the advantages of increasingly relying on the Internet for B2B and B2C?**

REAL CASES

Pharmaceutical mergers

Pharmaceutical mergers are the result of an industry hungry for innovation and market expansion. Over the last few years, pharmaceutical companies have increasingly faced pressure from third party drug reimbursement programs and regulators. In addition, the industry is battling with the expiration of patents in some of their most profitable drugs. The patent for Prozac, an anti-depressant manufactured by Eli Lilly, expired in August 2001 and within three weeks the company's market share dropped by two-thirds to generics. There is a pressing need to develop new drugs in order to maintain an income source. Mergers allow large pharmaceutical companies to achieve economies of scale in R&D while increasing their overall R&D budget. In addition, mergers allow access to a partners, markets, and the distribution systems of well-established rivals. The large pharmaceutical companies are fighting to choose partners for a strategic game of innovation.

Aventis is the result of the 1999 merger of German Company Hoechst and French firm Rhône-Poulenc, both successful chemical companies that had existed for over 100 years. Aventis, a French company, is now a world leader in pharmaceuticals. It has acquired Institut Merieux, Union Carbide's agriculture division, Celenan Corporation, and Connaught Laboratories, among others. The lead office of Aventis is in Strasbourg. Aventis had sales of US $20.6 billion in 2000 which made it the fourth largest European pharmaceutical company, after Merck, GlaxoSmithKline, and Novartis. But Aventis is larger than AstraZeneca and Roche.

Aventis is just one of a wave of mergers, joint ventures, and strategic alliances in the pharmaceutical industry (see the table below). In 1995, Glaxo and Wellcome and then Pharmacia and Upjohn merged to create two of the world's largest pharmaceutical companies. In 1999, British company Zeneca merged with Swedish Astra to create AstraZeneca, and Monsanto and Pharmacia Upjohn merged under the name Pharmacia. Bayer and Roche merged their US operations and Roche has been busy acquiring Genetech in 1990 and the Corange Group in 1997. Switzerland's Ciba-Geigy and Sandoz merged in 1996 to create Novartis.

Yet pharmaceutical mergers tend to be difficult to secure. Glaxo Wellcome and SmithKline Beecham called off a merger, angering shareholders and creating large stock market loses. Glaxo Wellcome has since attempted a similar merger with US pharmaceutical company Brystol Myers, but managers were unable to reach an agreement. American Home

World's largest 10 pharmaceutical companies, 2000

Company	*Country*	*Revenues*	*Merger activity*
Merck	Germany	40,363	
Pfizer	United States	29,574	Merged with Warner-Lambert
Johnson & Johnson	United States	29,139	
GlaxoSmithKline	United Kingdom	27,414	Merger between Glaxo Wellcome and SmithKline Beecham
Bristol-Myers Squibb	United Kingdom	24,414	Failed merger with Glaxo Wellcome
Novartis	Switzerland	21,207	Merger of Ciba-Geigy and Sandoz
Aventis	France	20,613	Merger of Hoechst and Rhône-Poulenc
Pharmacia	United States	18,150	Merger of Pharmacia and Upjohn and Monsanto
AstraZeneca	United Kingdom	18,103	Merger of Astra and Zeneca
Roche Group	Switzerland	16,982	Acquired Genetech and Corange Group
American Home Products	United States	13,810	Failed merger with Warner-Lambert

Source: Adapted from Fortune, *The Fortune Global 500*, 2001 and other sources.

Products (AHP) is also on the lookout for a partner. In 1998 talks with SmithKline proved unfruitful. By 1999 AHP was holding talks with Warner-Lambert. Pfizer then started a bid for Warner-Lambert, successfully outbidding AHP.

Merck, the German MNE, is one of the five largest pharmaceutical companies in the world. It has 209 subsidiaries in 52 countries and produces at 60 locations in 26 countries. Merck is also in specialty chemicals and in laboratory research and distribution. It produces antidiabetics, cardiovascular drugs, and generic drugs. The company has chosen against mergers and is instead concentrating its efforts in the development of new drugs.

Merck builds on the German "diamond" factor conditions of highly skilled resources and chemical engineers in a knowledge cluster of pharmaceuticals in Germany. This cluster also partly explains the success of another German MNE, Bayer AG. Both Merck and Bayer have grown with the expansion of the EU to 15 member states.

Bayer is a major supplier of diagnostic systems, drugs for infections, respiratory and central nervous system diseases. Bayer is in different market segments from Merck, and, although they come from the same German pharmaceutical cluster, they do not compete head to head.

Both Merck and Bayer have strong brand names for their products. Merck also emphasizes responsible care and environmental sustainable development.

Websites: **www.merck.com**; **www.pfizer.com**; **www.jnj.com**; **www.gsk.com**; **www.bms.com**; **www.novartis.com**; **www.pharmacia.com**; **www.astrazeneca.com**; **www.roche.com**; and **www.ahp.com**.

Sources: "Eli Lilly's Drug-induced Depression," *Economist*, August 10, 2000; Mark Jewell, "Prozac Losing Market Share to Generics," *Associated Press*, September 6, 2001; Kerry Capell, "An About-Face at Aventis," *Business Week Online*, November 27, 2000; Alan Rugman, *The End of Globalization* (Washington DC: Random House, 1999).

1. **What benefits are pharmaceutical companies seeking by merging? Do pharmaceuticals face any disadvantages as a result of these mergers?**
2. **How does the risk associated with the R&D provide an incentive for industry consolidation?**
3. **What are the advantages and disadvantages to consumers of having a consolidated industry?**

ENDNOTES

1 "European Central Bank," *BBC.co.uk*, May 31, 2001.

2 The 13 countries presently seeking accession into the European Union are: Bulgaria, the Czech Republic, Estonia, Cyprus, Latvia, Lithuania, Hungary, Malta, Poland, Romania, Slovenia, Slovakia, and Turkey. In January 2002, 12 were already negotiating their entry into the union. European Commission, *Enlarging the European Union*, 2001.

3 "Emerging opportunities in Central Europe," *FT.com*, January 14, 2002.

4 Spyros G. Makridakis and Michelle Bainbridge, "Evolution of the Single Market," in Spyros G. Makridakis (ed.), *Single Market Europe: Opportunities and Challenges for Business* (San Francisco CA: Jossey-Bass, 1991), p. 9.

5 Also see Trevor Merriden, "How 'Single' is the Single Market?" *Management Review*, March 1998, pp. 27–31.

6 "New Labeling Proposal Puts Spotlight on GM Food and Feed," *European Business News*, August 1, 2001.

7 "The Case for Europe," *Asiaweek.com*, February 9, 2001.

8 Gabriel Hawawini and Eric J. Rajendra, "Integrating and Legislating Rapid Changes in the Financial Services Industry," in Spyros G. Makridakis (ed.), *Single Market Europe: Opportunities and Challenges for Business* (San Francisco CA: Jossey-Bass, 1991), pp. 323–324.

9 Edmund L. Andrews, "11 Countries Tie Europe Together in One Currency," *New York Times*, January 1, 1999, pp. A 1, 8.

10 Thomas Kamm, "Emergence of Euro Embodies Challenge and Hope for Europe," *Wall Street Journal*, January 4, 1999, pp. A 1, 4.

11 Tatiana S. Boncompagni, "Europe's Retailers Prepare to Switch to the Euro, Seeking to Gain Customers," *Wall Street Journal*, November 9, 1998, p. B 13A and "Euro Used for 75% of Payments," *BBC.co.uk*, January 8, 2002.

12 Edmund L. Andrews, "Sticker Shocks in Euro Land," *New York Times*, December 27, 1998, Section 3, pp. 1, 6.

13 Michael Hickins, "US Business Blinks at the Euro," *Management Review*, April 1998, pp. 33–37.

14 European Commission Spokesman's Briefing for August 9, 1999.

15 "New 'Common Vocabulary' Proposed for Public Procurement," *European Business News*, August 13, 2001.

16 Herbert A. Henzler, "The New Era of Euro-capitalism," *Harvard Business Review*, vol. 70, no. 4 (July/August 1992), pp. 57–68.

17 Jack Ewing, "This Union Leader Cuts Germany's Bosses Some Slack," *Business Week*, September 10, 2001.

18 US Census Bureau, *Statistical Abstract of the United States*, 2000, p. 837.

19 Douglas Lavin, "France, Germany Must Cut More Jobs to Improve Efficiency, Report Suggests," *Wall Street Journal*, March 14, 1997, p. B 3A.

20 Jonathan B. Levine, "Grabbing the Controls in Mid-Tailspin," *Business Week*, January 17, 1994, pp. 45–46.

21 Rebecca Blumenstein, "Cadillac Has Designs on Europe's Luxury-Car Buyers," *Wall Street Journal*, September 9, 1997, pp. B 1, 14.

22 Virginia O'Brien, "Competitor Intelligence in the European Community," *Journal of European Business*, September/October 1990, pp. 17–21.

23 John E. Prescott and Patrick T. Gibbons, "Europe '92 Provides New Impetus for Competitive Intelligence," *Journal of Business Strategy*, November/December 1991, pp. 20–26.

24 Earl Landesman, "Ultimatum for US Auto Suppliers: Go Global or Go Under," *Journal of European Business*, May/June 1991, pp. 39–45.

25 Ibid., pp. 40–41.

26 Alan M. Rugman and Alain Verbeke, "Europe 1992 and Competitive Strategies for North American Firms," *Business Horizons*, November/December 1991, pp. 76–81.

27 Ibid., p. 78.

28 "European Taxes: Fear or Fantasy?" *BBC.co.uk*, May 24, 2001.

29 For more specifics on standards, please visit ***www.eurunion.org/legislat/standard/standard.htm***.

30 Thomas F. Clasen, "An Exporter's Guide to Selecting Foreign Sales Agents and Distributors," *Journal of European Management*, November/December 1991, pp. 28–32.

31 Joel Bleeke and David Ernst, "The Way to Win in Cross-Border Alliances," *Harvard Business Review*, vol. 69, no. 6 (November/December 1991), pp. 127–128.

32 See, for example, Bill Vlasic et al., "The First Global Car Colossus," *Business Week*, May 18, 1998, pp. 40–43.

33 Gianluigi Guido, "Implementing a Pan European Marketing Strategy," *Long Range Planning*, October 1991, p. 27.

34 Ibid., p. 30.

35 Ibid., pp. 31–32 and "Credit Card Boom Warning," *BBC.co.uk*, January 9, 2001.

36 "Credit Card Fraud Rises by 50%," *BBC.co.uk*, February 20, 2001.

37 Heather Ogilvie, "Electronic Ties That Bind: Marks & Spencer's Pan-European JIT Inventory System," *Journal of European Business*, September/October 1991, pp. 48–50.

38 Jean-Claude Goldenstein and Sandra Thompson, "Participating in European Cooperative R&D Programs," *Journal of European Business*, September/October 1991, p. 51.

39 Ibid., p. 52.

40 For more on this, see Richard M. Hodgetts and Fred Luthans, *International Management*, 4th edn (Homewood IL: Irwin/McGraw, 2000), Chapter 13.

41 The theory of shelter has been developed in Alan M. Rugman and Alain Verbeke, *Global Competitive Strategy and Trade Policy* (London: Routledge, 1990). A study on the use of EC trade law measures as a shelter strategy is by Alan M. Rugman and Michael Gestrin, "EC Anti-Dumping Laws as a Barrier to Trade," *European Management Journal*, vol. 9, no. 4 (December 1991), pp. 475–482. Related data and analysis of EC trade law cases are reported in Patrick A. Messerlin, "Anti-Dumping Regulations or Procartel Law?: The EC Chemical Case," *World Economy*, vol. 13, no. 4 (December 1990), pp. 465–492.

42 For an application of the concept of shelter by the use of US trade laws, see Alan M. Rugman and Michael Gestrin, "US Trade Laws as Barriers to Globalization," *World Economy*, vol. 14, no. 3 (December 1991), pp. 335–352. For earlier data and studies of US trade law cases used as a barrier to entry against rival Canadian firms, see Alan M. Rugman and Andrew D. M. Anderson, *Administered Protection in America* (London and New York: Routledge, 1987).

43 For an excellent discussion of triad power and the use of trade laws as barriers to entry, see Sylvia Ostry, *Governments and Corporations in a Shrinking World* (New York and London: Council on Foreign Relations Press, 1990).

44 For evidence of the abuse of US trade law procedures, see Richard Boltuck and Robert Litan (eds.), *Down in the Dumps: Administration of the Unfair Trade Laws* (Washington DC: Brookings Institute, 1991). For recent legal and economic research on this issue, see Michael J. Trebilcock and Robert C. York (eds.), *Fair Exchange: Reforming Trade Remedy Laws* (Toronto: C. D. Howe Institute and McGraw-Hill Ryerson, 1990).

ADDITIONAL BIBLIOGRAPHY

Czinkota, Michael. "The EC '92 and Eastern Europe: Effects of Integration vs. Disintegration," *Columbia Journal of World Business*, vol. 26, no. 1 (Spring 1991).

Deschamps, Jean Claude. "The European Community, International Trade, and World Unity," *California Management Review*, vol. 35, no. 2 (Winter 1993).

Douglas, Susan P. and Rhee, Dong Kee. "Examining Generic Competitive Strategy Types in US and European Markets," *Journal of International Business Studies*, vol. 20, no. 3 (Fall 1989).

Dowling, Michael and Leidner, Alfred. "Technical Standards and 1992: Opportunity or Entry Barrier in the New Europe? *Columbia Journal of World Business*, vol. 25, no. 3 (Fall 1990).

Kidd, John B. and Teramoto, Yoshiya. "The Learning Organization: The Case of the Japanese RHQs in Europe," *Management International Review*, vol. 35, Special Issue (1995).

Lawton, Thomas C. "Evaluating European Competitiveness: Measurements and Models for a Successful Business Environment," *European Business Journal*, vol. 11, no. 4 (1999).

Lowson, Robert, "Analysing the Effectiveness of European Retail Sourcing Strategies," *European Management Journal*, vol. 19, no. 5 (October 2001).

Mayrhofer, Ulrike. "Franco–British Strategic Alliances: A Contribution to the Study of Intra-European Partnerships," *European Management Journal*, vol. 20, no. 1 (February 2002).

Miller, Alan N. "British Privatization: Evaluating the Results," *Columbia Journal of World Business*, vol. 30, no. 4 (Winter 1995).

Millington, Andrew I. and Bayliss, Brian T. "The Process of Internationalisation: UK Companies in the EC," *Management International Review*, vol. 30, no. 2 (Second Quarter 1990).

Millington, Andrew I. and Bayliss, Brian T. "Non-Tariff Barriers and UK Investment in the European Community," *Journal of International Business Studies*, vol. 22, no. 4 (Fourth Quarter 1991).

Millington, Andrew and Bayliss, Brian T. "The Strategy of Internationalization and the Success of UK Transnational Manufacturing Operations in the European Union," *Management International Review*, vol. 37, no. 3 (Third Quarter 1997).

Nitsch, Detlev, Beamish, Paul and Makino, Shige. "Entry Mode and Performance of Japanese FDI in Western Europe," *Management International Review*, vol. 36, no. 1 (First Quarter 1996).

Papanastassiou, Marina and Pearce, Robert. "Technology Sourcing and the Strategic Roles of Manufacturing Subsidiaries in the UK: Local Competence and Global Competitiveness," *Management International Review*, vol. 37, no. 1 (First Quarter 1997).

Pelkmans, Jacques, "Making EU Network Markets Competitive," *Oxford Review of Economic Policy*, vol. 17, no. 3 (Autumn 2001).

Quelch, John A. and Buzzell, Robert D. "Marketing Moves Through EC Crossroads," *Sloan Management Review*, vol. 31, no. 1 (Fall 1989).

Rehder, Robert R. and Thompson, Judith Kenner. "Nissan UK: The Japanese Transplant Beachhead in Europe," *Columbia Journal of World Business*, vol. 29, no. 3 (Fall 1994).

Rugman, Alan M., Theil, Rita and Verbeke, Alain. "Entry Barriers and Bank Strategies for the Europe 1992 Financial Directives," *European Management Journal*, vol. 10, no. 3 (September 1992).

Rugman, Alan M., Verbeke, Alain and Campbell, Alexandria. "Strategic Change in the European Flexible Manufacturing Industry," *European Management Journal*, vol. 8, no. 3 (September 1990).

Rugman, Alan M. and Verbeke, Alain. "Environmental Change and Global Competitive Strategy in Europe," in *Research in Global Strategic Management: Volume 2: Global Competition and the European Community* (Greenwich CT: JAI Press, 1991).

Rugman, Alan M. and Verbeke, Alain. *Research in Global Strategic Management: Volume 2: Global Competition and the European Community* (Greenwich CT: JAI Press, 1991).

Rugman, Alan M. and Verbeke, Alain. "Competitive Strategies for Non-European Firms," in B. Burgenmeier and J. L. Mucchielli (eds.), *Multinationals and Europe 1992: Strategies for the Future* (London and New York: Routledge, 1991).

Rugman, Alan M. and Verbeke, Alain. "Europe 1992 and Competitive Strategies for North American Firms," *Business Horizons*, vol. 34, no. 6 (November/December 1991).

Taggart, James H. "An Evaluation of the Integration-Responsiveness Framework: MNC Manufacturing Subsidiaries in the UK," *Management International Review*, vol. 37, no. 4 (Fourth Quarter 1997).

Welfens, Paul J. J. "Foreign Investment in the East European Transition," *Management International Review*, vol. 32, no. 3 (Third Quarter 1992).

Chapter 17

Japan

CONTENTS

OBJECTIVES OF THE CHAPTER

Japan is one of the world's leading economic powers. Each year the EU and the US buy billions of dollars of cars, computers, and electronic goods that are made in Japan. Many other nations also rely heavily on Japanese industry to provide them with a wide array of products. At the same time, Japan is becoming a major market for multinational enterprises (MNEs), which see a growing demand for goods and services accompanying the country's dramatic economic prosperity. These MNEs have also come to realize that, in order to be a world-class competitor, they need to do business in Japan.

The specific objectives of this chapter are to:

1. *Examine* the nature of the Japanese economy and present some of the most important factors that need to be considered when doing business there.
2. *Describe* some of the major characteristics of the Japanese economic system that are critical to doing business in that country.
3. *Relate* six basic steps taken by firms that have successfully entered the Japanese market.
4. *Compare* and *contrast* the benefits and drawbacks associated with start-up strategies, including exporting, licensing agreements, joint ventures, acquisitions, and Japanese subsidiaries.
5. *Discuss* how to manage on-site operations, with particular attention to recruitment, location, organization, and financing.

ACTIVE LEARNING CASE

Figuring out how to do business in Japan

Doing business in Japan presents many challenges to foreign MNEs. One of the biggest is how to carve out a market in a country where *keiretsus* and other cartel-like arrangements are so common. At first, many MNEs entering Japan find it difficult to compete effectively. Major *keiretsus* or cartels are billion-dollar firms with business ties that turn them into huge, vertically integrated companies. Some of these cartels own or have business dealings with a host of other companies that ensure that the *keiretsu* can manufacture and sell its products without ever relying on a firm outside this circle of firms. There are even distribution cartels in Japan that are so encompassing that they can control the flow of products, accessories, services, and prices from the factory floor all the way to the consumer. A good example is Matsushita.

Matsushita manufactures Panasonic, National, Technics, and Quasar products. The firm also controls a chain of approximately 18,000 national retail stores throughout the country. These stores sell a wide variety of products, from batteries to refrigerators. Most importantly, they agree to sell at manufacturers' recommended prices. In turn Matsushita ensures the survival of these stores by giving them a 25 per cent retail margin on sales. This margin is a result of fixed retail prices, manufacturing rebates, advertising subsidies, and protected sales territories from other Matsushita dealers. Other Japanese firms have similar arrangements. Examples include Toshiba, Hitachi, Mitsubishi, Sanyo, and Sony.

Despite such a major obstacle, foreign MNEs are learning that there are a number of useful strategies that can help them to break into the Japanese market. In the case of suppliers, for example, it is important to be patient and to continue to bid for business. At first, many *keiretsus* turn down foreign companies because they want to stay within their cartel-like arrangement. However, these *keiretsus* are also interested in pushing out their major competitors, and a foreign supplier with high quality products will often find that one of the major *keiretsus* will break with tradition and make a deal. Additionally, many small *keiretsus* are trying to get off the ground and to gain market share. These too are interested in developing relations with high quality suppliers. Moreover, because the best local suppliers are usually already tied to *keiretsus*, foreign sources are often very attractive to these fledgling cartels.

A second strategy is to link forces with established Japanese firms in the form of joint ventures. For example, T. Row Price Associates recently entered into a joint venture with Daiwa Securities and the Sumitomo Bank. The venture will focus on mutual-fund management. And the Swiss Bank Corporation has now formed a host of new joint ventures with the Long-Term Credit Bank of Japan. While there are drawbacks to these ventures, two of the major advantages are sharing the risk and achieving rapid market access.

A third strategy is to team up with Japanese firms to help develop or manufacture new products. One recent example is Motorola and Texas Instruments (TI), which have an arrangement with Sony. TI provides signal processors for Sony compact disk players and Motorola manufactures the chips that go into Sony camcorders. Another example is AT&T's Bell Laboratories and AT&T's Microelectronics, which have a working relationship with NEC. Bell is helping NEC to design products and Microelectronics is making and supplying the chips for these units.

A fourth, and more recent, strategy is acquisition and merger. GE Capital, for example, has bought the leasing businesses of the Japan Leasing Corporation, purchased NC Card Sendai, specialists in financing for installment sales and consumer credit, and set up a merger with a Japanese firm to expand a ship container leasing business. Another example is Wal-Mart, which in 2001 entered the Japanese general merchandiser market by purchasing 30 stores from bankrupt Mycal, Japan's fourth largest retailer.

A number of developments are changing the Japanese retailing landscape with profound implications to foreign companies. In the political sphere, bilateral negotiations between the US and Japan have continued to open the way for foreign MNEs. In 1989, the Japanese government reformed the Large Retail Store Law to allow Toys "Я" Us to open a superstore. See "Real Case: Toys "Я" Us in Japan" at the end of this chapter. In just six years the company opened 64 stores. However, the Large Retail Store Law remained to protect small retailers. The law also protected the distribution networks of large *keiretsus*, creating barriers for the development superstores that could carry foreign products. Working within this framework, Gap, Foot Locker, Nike, Pier 1 Imports, Tower Records, and Warner Bros continued to open superstores throughout the 1990s. The Large Retail Store Law was once again reformed in 2000. The new law transferred the responsibility of deciding whether a superstore could be constructed from the Ministry of International Trade and Industry (MITI) to the country's local governments. Japan's 47 prefectures and 12 major metropolitan regions can still deny permits for large store development if they find such business might create a problem in the local environment. Local environmental analysis, however, is now restricted to issues of traffic, parking, and trash and cannot ban a development based on the effects to small local retailers.

Large foreign retailers, B2C retailing, and the rise of Chinese imports are also putting pressure on local *keiretsus* to reform their distribution networks and become more price-competitive. Today, Costco and Wal-Mart from the US and Carrefour of France are aggressively challenging traditional network structures and attempting to eliminate the wholesalers. Large Japanese manufacturers, however, are reluctant to sell directly to these companies and often prefer to maintain their traditional alliances with wholesalers. Out of necessity, foreign retailers continue to purchase large amounts from wholesalers but retain a long-term goal of eliminating them. For this, they reach (or are reached by) manufacturers in financial trouble who are willing to negotiate direct contracts in exchange for financial relief. Foreign outsourcing, particularly from nearby Asian nations such as China, has also been a way of bypassing Japan's powerful wholesalers.

By allowing Japanese customers direct access to retailing over the Internet, B2C retailing is putting pressure on large local MNEs to shed their traditional distribution networks. Mom and pop stores must now be price-competitive with the Internet and many cannot continue to offer the manufacturer's suggested price. Despite a long tradition of small retailer fostering, Matsushita is now moving its Panasonic division into direct B2C. During the 1990s, Matsushita's small retail shop network decreased by 30 per cent, partly as a result of a lack of prospective shopkeepers. Those retailers that continue to work for Matsushita are increasingly uneasy about charging the manufacturer's suggested price.

There are a number of reasons that MNEs want to do business in Japan. One is the growing market. A second is that Japan is a major economic force in the Pacific and this power is likely to grow over the ensuing decades. By maintaining a presence in Japan, worldwide competitors are in the best position to monitor these strategies and to respond with countermeasures. For these multinationals, doing business in Japan is critical to the growth of their enterprises. So it is critical for them to learn how to do business here.

Websites: **www.gap.com**; **www.ti.com**; **www.motorola.com**; **www.walmart.com**; **www.pier1.com**; **www.costco.com**; **www.carrefour.fr**; **www.footlocker.com**; **www.panasonic.co.jp**; **www.nike.com**; **www.towerrecords.co.jp**; **www.warnerbros.co.jp**; **www.toshiba.co.jp**; **www.hitachi.co.jp**; **www.hitachi.com**; **www.mitsubishi.com**; **www.sanyo.com**; **www.sony.com**; **www.sony.co.jp** and **www.daiwa.com**.

Sources: Adapted from Robert L. Cutts, "Capitalism in Japan: Cartels and Keiretsu," *Harvard Business Review*, vol. 30, no. 4 (July/August 1992), pp. 48–55; Emily Thornton, "Will Japan Rule a New Trade Bloc?" *Fortune*, October 5, 1992, pp. 131–132; Bill Spindle, "GE Capital Seeks Out Niches in Japan," *Wall Street Journal*, January 5, 1999, p. A 17; Jonathan Sapsford, "GE Capital to Buy $7 Billion in Japanese Assets," *Wall Street Journal*, January 25, 1999, pp. A 13, 15; and Jonathan Sapsford, "US Financial Firms Delve Deeper Into Japan," *Wall Street Journal*, January 26, 1999, pp. A 13, 15; "Retail Collapse Hits Japan's Biggest Bank," *BBC.co.uk*, September 16, 2001; Ken Belson, "Matsushita Keeps Its Old-School Ways," *Fortune*, January 7, 2002; Susan MacKnight, "Weekly Review," *Japan Economic Institute Review*, September 15, 2000; Irene M. Kunni, "A Bold Mechanic for Matsushita's Creaky Machine," *Business Week*, July 21, 2000; Adam Creed, "Panasonic to Sell Over the Web in Japan," *Washington Post*, July 11, 2000.

1. **Why do MNEs need to understand the role of *keiretsus* in the Japanese economy?**
2. **How can foreign MNEs use *keiretsus* to their own advantage? Give an example.**
3. **Why are joint ventures so popular among foreign MNEs? Cite two reasons.**
4. **Why is Japan likely to remain a target market for international MNEs? Cite two reasons.**

PROFILE OF JAPAN

Japan consists of four main islands (Hokkaido, Honshu, Shikoku, and Kyushu) and a number of smaller islands (see accompanying map). The country is approximately the size of California, and over the last three decades it has become a major industrial power. Today the Japanese yen is one of the strongest currencies in the world as the nation's massive international trade has helped it to maintain vigorous, sustained economic growth.[1]

Political and legal system

The branches of the Japanese government are very similar to those in the US: legislative, executive, and judicial. Legislative power is vested in the **Diet**, which consists of a popularly elected House of Representatives and House of Councillors. There are five major political parties. The strongest of these is the Liberal-Democratic party, which is conservative and generally supported by the two most powerful groups in the country: business and agriculture.[2]

Diet
The branch of the Japanese government in which legislative power is vested; it consists of a popularly elected House of Representatives and House of Councillors

Japan 2000

Population	127.4 million
GDP	US $ 4677 billion
GDP per capita	US $ 36,712
Inflation rate	−0.6%
Trade balance	100.1 billion
Unemployment rate	4.7%

Source: Statistics Bureau and Statistics Center, Ministry of Public Management, Home Affairs, Posts and Telecommunications, *Labour Force Survey*, January 30, 2001; World Bank, *Japan at a Glance*, September 19, 2001.

Executive power rests with the Cabinet, which is organized and headed by the prime minister, who is elected by the Diet.[3] In addition to the office of the prime minister, there are 17 ministerial divisions in the executive branch.[4]

The judicial power is vested in the Supreme Court. In addition, there are eight high courts and a host of district courts throughout the country.

Japan is divided into 47 prefectures, somewhat similar to US states. Each local political subdivision, including cities, towns, and villages, has its own executive power and operates within the scope of the national law.

Population and social patterns

There are approximately 127 million people in Japan – the population is densely concentrated, with 50 per cent of the population living in or around the three largest metropolitan areas of Tokyo, Osaka and Nagoya.

The standard dialect of Japanese is understood throughout the country, even though there are some local differences. English is the most frequently taught foreign language, and in business circles visitors can generally communicate in English, although involved negotiations typically require an interpreter.

Education is mandatory in Japan until the age of 14. Primary school lasts six years and junior high school three years. Though further education is optional almost 40 per cent of Japanese students go to college or university.[5] Admission to first-tier public universities such as Tokyo University and Kyoto University and private universities such as Keio University and Waseda University is extremely competitive. Students hoping to gain entrance to these schools begin preparations very early in their school years, often working many extra hours. Graduation from these first-tier universities is often a stepping-stone to a good job and career.

Living standards are high, although houses and apartments are typically much smaller than those in the US. In addition to salaries, employees receive various social insurance benefits, paid holidays and vacations, and retirement pay.

Some social patterns are distinctly different from those in the West.[6] The Japanese are a group-oriented people. This social behavior carries over to business relationships as well, where school ties and friendships are often major factors. The Japanese also place a strong emphasis on harmony, orderliness, and respect for others.[7] Because of these values, the Japanese often seem ambiguous or non-committal in situations such as contract negotiations. These efforts to avoid direct confrontation are frequently misunderstood by businesspeople sitting across the negotiation table.[8]

Japanese employees place a high value on the work ethic. Unlike the culture in many Western countries, job attendance is viewed as mandatory and everyone shows up every day. Managers are required to stay late and work on weekends; this is part of the job and is well accepted by the rest of society. Commenting on the work schedule of these employees, two experts on Japan have explained that, "To this day, it is considered shameful for a husband to be home before ten o'clock in the evening on a workday. Even weekends are spent in the office or on work-related outings – golf trips, company meetings, and travel with customers."[9]

Gairojin
A Japanese person who leaves his or her company to work for a foreign firm

Gaijin
A Japanese word which means "outsider"; it is used to refer to foreigners doing business in Japan

There is also a strong bond between workers and their companies. Employees identify with their firms and are often unwilling to leave even when they are offered more money to join foreign firms.[10] In fact, there is often a stigma attached to making such a career move. This is reflected in the way that the Japanese describe people who leave to work for foreign firms. A Japanese who leaves his company to work for a foreign company is known as a **gairojin**, stemming from the word **gaijin**, which means literally "outsider". Because of this attitude, local recruiting is a major problem for most foreign companies.[11]

The Asian Crisis of 1997–1998 and the Japanese economic slowdown of 2001–2002 helped to change labor market relations in Japan. The traditional system of lifetime employment slowly dismantled in key sectors and, as unemployment rose, displaced workers and those who no longer felt they had job security increasingly became receptive to changing jobs, even working with foreign companies. In addition, many bankrupt Japanese companies were purchased outright by foreign MNEs. Nonetheless, loyalty continues to be an important part of the employee–company relationship.

Japan is a hierarchical society. Social ranking determines the amount of respect given and the amount of effort that is made in maintaining relationships, in greeting and bowing, and even in framing everyday speech. Social relationships are also greatly influenced by the power of obligation. When someone is a member of a group, the individual is expected to assume certain responsibilities to the other members. For example, many senior managers will spend three or four weekends a year attending the weddings of their employees. In addition, there are business-related responsibilities such as giving gifts to key employees, suppliers, and customers, exchanging critical information with clients, and participating in joint venture arrangements with partners. The burden of such social/business obligations helps to explain why many Japanese shy away from making new social relationships. The accompanying responsibilities are simply too time demanding. It also helps to explain why doing business in Japan often takes much longer than in other countries. Japanese managers already have so many things to do that they are frequently in no hurry to enter into new relationships.

Business and the economy

Japan has a gross domestic product (GDP) of approximately $4.7 trillion and one of the largest per capita incomes in world. However, in recent years Japan has also faced a prolonged economic slowdown. In particular, the nation's banks were awash in red ink[12] with bad debts in excess of $1 trillion in 1998.[13] In 2001, the bank's non-performing or questionable debt was estimated at anywhere between $145 billion and $845 billion and by 2002 the government was scuffling to avert a banking crisis.[14] (See the box "International Business Strategy in Action: The Japanese banking crisis".) At the same time, the jobless rate increased to 4.7 per cent,[15] firms such as Fujitsu and NEC announced layoffs and plant closings,[16] and GDP growth was declining.[17] Table 17.1 provides some additional contrasting data that show how far the Japanese economy had slid over the 1990s. At the same time, the economy has a great deal of underlying strength. A number of factors account for this. One is the role of governmental agencies and ministries in promoting economic growth.

Ministry of International Trade and Industry

Ministry of International Trade and Industry (MITI) A Japanese ministry charged with providing information about foreign markets and with encouraging investment in select industries and, in the process, helping to direct the economy

The **Ministry of International Trade and Industry (MITI)** serves as the coordinating body of the country's powerful commercial machinery. It is MITI's job to identify and rank national commercial pursuits and business opportunities and to guide the distribution of national resources to meet these goals. MITI encourages Japanese companies to pursue targeted opportunities such as developing advanced computer technology, high-tech industrial and agricultural machinery, optical electronics, and world-class auto manufacturing. Firms that are willing to enter these industries are provided with government subsidies and market protection.

When MITI identifies an area where it would like to expand business efforts, it is able to gain support for three reasons: (1) *financial incentives* – as noted earlier, these are

Table 17.1 Japan's changing economic status in recent years

	1990	*2000*	*Change*
Business and the economy			
Unemployment rate	2.1%	4.7%	124%
GDP growth	5.1%	1.9%	–63%
Inflation	3.1%	–0.6%	–119%
Motor vehicle production	13.5 million	10.1 million	–25%
Floor area of new construction put in place (1000s of square meters)	279,116	194,481	–30%
Annual sales of large-scale department stores	11.5 trillion yen	10.0 trillion yen	–13%
Society			
Golf club membership cost (at the upscale Koganei Golf Club)	440 million yen (1989)	61 million yen (1999)	–86%
Residential land prices in Tokyo (average per square meter)	514,200 yen	232,400 yen	–55%
Residential land prices in Osaka (average per square meter)	534,400 yen	206,700 yen	–61%

Sources: Ministry of Finance, *Balance of Payments*, December 13, 2001; Statistics Bureau and Statistics Center, Ministry of Public Management, Home Affairs, Posts and Telecommunications, *Labour Force Survey*, January 30, 2001; World Bank, *Japan at a Glance*, September 19, 2001; International Department, Bank of Japan, "Comparative Economic and Financial Statistics, Japan and Other Major Countries," December 22, 2000; Policy Bureau, Ministry of Land, Infrastructure and Transport, Construction Research and Statistics Division, Information and Research Department, September 2001; Ministry of Land, Infrastructure and Transport, Land and Water Bureau, Land Price Research Division, *Prefectural Land Prices Survey*, September 20, 2001.

made available to companies that are prepared to commit resources; (2) *personal relationship* – most MITI ministers have attended the major universities, and so they have school ties to the captains of industry; and (3) *location* – MITI offices and those of most corporate and financial giants are located in the same area of Tokyo, and so it is common to find the two groups interacting and sharing ideas.

Today MITI coordinates a wide variety of programs spread among regional governments in each prefecture, university, and industry. Primary consideration is now being given to ABCD industries: automation, biotechnology, computers, and data processing. Certain regions of the country have their own market niche, such as Hokkaido for marine technology, Kumamoto for applied machinery, and Okayama for biotechnology. Companies doing business in Japan must be aware of the impact of MITI and its efforts to coordinate and direct business efforts.

Keiretsus

Keiretsu
A Japanese term for a business group consisting of a host of companies and banks linked together through ownership and/or joint ventures

Before World War II the Japanese economy was dominated by 10 large family-led business giants, which included Mitsui, Mitsubishi, Sumitomo, and Yasuda. After the war the Americans broke up these conglomerates. They have since reappeared in the form of ***keiretsus***, which are massive, vertically integrated corporations. There are three main types of *keiretsus*: banks or financial firms, manufacturing companies, and industrial companies, which are usually led by a trading company.

Three of the 25 biggest commercial and savings banks in the world are Japanese-owned (see Table 17.2). Manufacturing *keiretsus* include Toyota, Nippon Steel, and

INTERNATIONAL BUSINESS STRATEGY *IN ACTION*

The Japanese banking crisis

The under-reporting of non-performing loans in the Japanese banking industry is now well known. Together, Japan's 14 biggest banks are believed to have bad loans of 6 trillion yen ($48.9 billion). In 2001, bad loans caused 50 small deposit-taking institutions to go bankrupt. In other words, Japan is virtually broke.

In November 2001, Japan's second-largest bank, Sumitomo Mitsui, increased its expected bad-loan provision from 400 billion yen to 1,000 billion yen ($8 billion). The announcement came a day after Asahi Bank made similar news by revising its bad debt expectations to 400 billion yen from 100 billion yen. As a result of these adjustments, profits for 2001–2002 were also reassessed to a net loss of 150 billion yen for Sumitomo Mitsui and 530 billion yen for Asahi. Investors reacted positively to the news, driving share prices up.

Increasingly, Japanese banks are being pressured to acknowledge non-performing loans. After inspecting 10 large banks, the Financial Services Agency (FSA), Japan's banking regulator, announced that credit risks had not been properly assessed for 15 per cent of all corporate borrowers. The Japanese Bankers Association confirmed that, between April and September of 2001, 135 of its members recorded losses of 983.1 billion yen ($7.7 billion). In the stock market, banks' shares dropped by up to 80 per cent in 2001. The official announcement of losses by two of Japan's largest banks sent clear indications among investors that they were now ready to deal with the burden of their bad loans. Other banks followed suit and amended their accounts.

A continued recession that saw the Japanese stock market drop by 24 per cent in 2001 underlies the banks' afflictions. Weak global and domestic demand decreased manufacturing activity by over 13 per cent in November 2001, the largest drop in 26 years. Car production dropped by 5.1 and vehicle exports dropped by 2.5 per cent compared with the previous year. Retail activity also fell by 2.7 per cent. Not surprisingly, bankruptcies were at their highest in 17 years and companies are struggling to restructure, slash inventories, and cut jobs. At 5.5 per cent, unemployment is at its highest since it began to be recorded.

The FSA, the Japanese government, and the banks are all attempting to avert a banking crisis that would have global and regional repercussions. By continuing to pressure banks to increase transparency and recognize non-performing debt, the FSA hopes to bring back confidence to banking. In December 2001, the Japanese government announced that it would take measures to prevent a banking crisis, including providing public funds to bail out the banking system. One major concern is that the expected removal of blanket protection for bank depositors in April 2002 could lead to a run on the banks. Sumitomo Mitsui is leading the banking restructuring process by promising to close down 177 of its 578 domestic branches and lay off 4,900 employees by 2004.

The restricting of the Japanese banking system has been delayed for too long – let's hope that Japan sorts out its problems before causing a major world financial crisis.

Websites: **www.smbc.co.jp** and **www.asahibank.co.jp**.

Source: Bayan Rahman, "Japan Tries to Calm Fears of Banking Crisis," *FT.com*, December 28, 2001; Bayan Rahman, "Japan May Use Public Cash to Bolster Banks," *FT.com*, December 27, 2001; Bayan Rahman, "Grim Industrial Data Underline Depth of Japan's Woes," *FT.com*, December 27, 2001; David Ibison, "Sumitomo Mitsui Comes Clean on ¥1,000 bn loan losses," *FT.com*, November 21, 2001; David Ibison, "Japan's Asahi Bank Suffers Rise in Loan-Loss Charges," *FT.com*, November 20, 2001; "Fitch Sees Japanese Banks Remaining Weak in 2002, into 2003," *AFX Europe*, January 8, 2002.

Matsushita, well known for a wide variety of products from cars to consumer goods. Trading companies such as Mitsui and Mitsubishi do billions of dollars in imports and exports, and this trading volume accounts for almost 25 per cent of Japan's GDP.

Keiretsus are so powerful that they often provide all of their own financing and operating needs from internal sources. Foreign MNEs competing in Japan need to evaluate the power of these firms, in terms of both competitiveness and the opportunity for strategic alliances and joint ventures.[18] They also need to evaluate the possibilities and benefits of working with small and medium-size suppliers that are now beginning to gain ground in their battle with these *keiretsus*. See box "International Business Strategy in Action: Kirin Beer goes international".

Table 17.2 The world's 25 largest commercial and savings companies, 2000

Rank	*Bank*	*Country*	*Revenues (in millions of US $)*
1	Deutsche Bank	Germany	67,133
2	J. P. Morgan Chase & Co.	United States	60,065
3	Crédit Suisse	Switzerland	59,316
4	Bank of America Corp.	United States	57,747
5	BNP Paribas	France	57,612
6	Mizuho Holdings	Japan	52,069
7	HSBC Holdings	Britain	48,633
8	UBS	Switzerland	47,316
9	Fortis	Belgium/Netherlands	43,831
10	ABN AMRO Holding	Netherlands	43,390
11	Crédit Agricole	France	34,685
12	Hypovereinsbank	Germany	32,136
13	Santander Central Hispano Group	Spain	31,928
14	Royal Bank of Scotland	Britain	29,770
15	Wells Fargo	United States	27,568
16	Bank of Tokyo-Mitsubishi	Japan	26,347
17	Bank One Corp.	United States	25,168
18	Barclays	Britain	25,097
19	Sumitomo Bank	Japan	24,669
20	First Union Corp.	United States	24,246
21	Société Générale	France	24,224
22	Dresdner Bank	Germany	23,777
23	Westdeutsche Landesbank	Germany	23,540
24	Lloyds TSB Group	Britain	23,526
25	Fleetboston Financial	United States	22,608

Source: Adapted from *Fortune*, "The Fortune Global 500 Ranked within Industries," 2001.

Active learning check

Review your answer to Active Learning Case question 1 and make any changes you like. Then compare your answer with the one below.

1. Why do MNEs need to understand the role of *keiretsus* in the Japanese economy?

MNEs need to understand the role of *keiretsus* so that they realize some of the difficulties inherent in breaking into the Japanese market. These cartel-like arrangements involve hundreds of companies that are tied together through business relations (and sometimes social relations) and those that are not associated with one of these groups are often at a distinct disadvantage.

Large Retail Store Law
A Japanese law that limits the size of retail stores and requires that local competitors approve the opening of any facility that is more than 500 square meters

Barriers to business

Although Japan has removed many of its import quotas and duties, major non-tariff barriers still prevent foreign firms from gaining a market foothold. For example, since 1973 the **Large Retail Store Law** has limited the size of retail stores and required that local competitors approve the opening of any facility that is more than 500 square meters. The US tried to negotiate a repeal of this law and was partly successful. In 2001, large-store approval was deferred to local prefectures and major metropolises, who had to evaluate the environmental impact of the store but could not take into account the economic

INTERNATIONAL BUSINESS STRATEGY *IN ACTION*

Kirin Beer goes international

Kirin Beer has been Japan's largest brewer for over 130 years. However, in recent years the company has been having its share of problems. These all started back in the 1970s when Kirin held 70 per cent of the national market. At this time antitrust regulators decided to open the local market to other brewers. As a result, Asahi Beer quickly became the country's second largest brewer, and since then Asahi has continued to erode Kirin's market share with: (1) a combination of fresher tasting brews; (2) a successful marketing strategy with commercials aimed at young, active individuals; and (3) a distribution network that introduced what has turned out to be a growing trend among beer consumers – canned beer sold in large supermarkets.

In retrospect, one of Kirin's biggest mistakes was that it was too slow in reacting to competition in a market that it long took for granted. For example, despite Asahi's tactics, Kirin continued to rely heavily on its traditional sales approach and its long-established network of "mom-and-pop" stores across the country. In truth, the company was confused regarding how to deal with competition and, as a result, made a number of mistakes. For example, when the giant brewer decided to increase its marketing effort and create television ads directed at young people, the strategy was perceived by many viewers as a poor imitation of Asahi's own advertising strategy and the campaign flopped. As a result of such missteps by Kirin, Asahi continued to gain market share and by 2001 the company held 36 per cent of the Japanese beer market compared with Kirin's 38 per cent. Commenting on his company's inability to exploit its advantages, one of the managers in Kirin's marketing research department noted, "We are a good example of bad brand management."

Most recently, in an effort to maintain its position in the Japanese market, Kirin has been working to exploit its traditional image. Kirin Lager, Japan's oldest brew, is now being promoted as the classic Japanese premium beer, the type of beer to enjoy with family and friends. And to promote this image with its other brews as well, Kirin has begun increasing its advertising budget. Unfortunately, this new effort faces a number of challenges. The biggest one may well be that most Japanese beer drinkers admit that all beers taste the same to them – so increased advertising may not generate the desired results.

Kirin has also been expanding its international efforts. Today its products are available in 40 nations including the US, the EU, China, Taiwan, and a host of other Asian countries. In most instances Kirin has teamed up with a local brewer. For example, in 1998 the company entered into a partnership with Anheuser-Busch that allowed Kirin Beer to be brewed in Los Angeles and then shipped to the rest of the country. By 2001 this strategy was paying off. US sales tripled within these three years.

Kirin has also been actively expanding in Asia. China (by consumption, the second largest beer market after the US) is one of Kirin's most important foreign markets. In gaining a foothold here, the company has partnered with a local brewer and since then its sales in China have been increasing each year. And in Taiwan, Kirin Beer is now the top imported beer. So the company is off to a good international start. Competitors, however, are also expanding internationally, creating an ongoing need for product differentiation and good brand marketing. So Kirin still has a long way to go.

One of the things that may help the company is that it is part of Mitsubishi, Japan's largest *keiretsu*. Today the Mitsubishi group has annual sales in excess of $110 billion, and there are approximately 30 core members who are bound together by cross-ownership and other financial ties (see Table 10.4 for a complete list of this *keiretsu*). Although the members of Mitsubishi operate independently, they can call upon one other for help. For example, when Akai Electric had financial problems, Mitsubishi Bank rescued it. When Mitsubishi Heavy Industries' shipbuilding business ran into trouble, it was able to find work at other group companies for those personnel who were laid off. And the cross-holding structure has also come in handy when warding off takeovers. For example, when Texaco bought Getty Oil, it was prepared to sell Getty's 50 per cent share of Mitsubishi Oil to Kuwait Petroleum. However, the members of the Mitsubishi group got together and outbid the Kuwaitis for Getty's shares. The group has also made important acquisitions and struck major deals in a variety of areas. Mitsubishi companies have participated in the $940 million purchase of the Pebble Beach golf course in California, won a $400 million power plant deal in Virginia, and launched a $150 million futures trading joint venture in Chicago. Overall, Mitsubishi has hundreds of interdependent companies and they are building an empire that stretches from Asia to Europe to the US. With their help, Kirin may be able to become a major international brewer.

Websites: ***www.kirin.co.jp***; ***www.mitsubishi.com*** and ***www.asahibeer.co.jp***.

Sources: ***www.rolf.ru/***; ***www.mitsubishi.com/***; ***www.hoovers.com/capsules/41773.html***; William J. Holstein et al., "Mighty Mitsubishi Is on the Move," *Business Week*, September 24, 1990, pp. 98–107; "Japan's Automakers: A Controlled Skid," *Fortune*, May 17, 1993, p. 12; Emily Thornton, "Japan's Struggle to Restructure," *Fortune*, June 28, 1993, pp. 84–88; "Japan's Beer Wars," *Economist*, February 26, 1998; and "A Right Old Brewhaha in Japan," *Economist*, February 22, 2001 and ***mitsubishi.com/ghp_japan/financial/financial.html***.

effect on local retailers. The definition of a large retail store also increased floorsize to 1,000 square meters.[19] Though the new law is still a barrier for foreign businesses and enforcement will likely show regional differences, its impact has been effectively lessened and MNEs such as Costco and Carrefour have successfully entered the Japanese market and Wal-Mart is expected to follow suit.[20] In fact, Carrefour's first superstore in Makuhari, North East of Tokyo, had a total floor area of 30,000 square meters.[21]

A second barrier is the informal job-bidding system that goes on behind closed doors. This system eliminates foreign competition and ensures maximum profits for the local participants, who are the only ones allowed to bid. An accompanying problem is a common Japanese practice of below-cost bidding such as offering to provide computer hardware for a low price on a project where costs are as high as $1 million. Then, after securing the contract, the Japanese business will make up the loss by selling the software at astronomical prices. These practices have excluded many international computer firms from the Japanese market (although IBM Japan is an obvious exception). The Japanese government is now beginning to crack down on these practices, but for the time being, at least, non-tariff barriers remain major problems for foreign MNEs.[22]

Trade imbalances

The key business-related issue that dominates the economic scene is the friction over trade imbalances between Japan and the rest of the world. As seen in Figure 17.1 the US continues to run major trade deficits with Japan. The US is not alone. To a much smaller extent Japan is now running large surpluses with the EU as well. As a result, more and more countries are putting pressure on Japan to open up its markets. If this does not

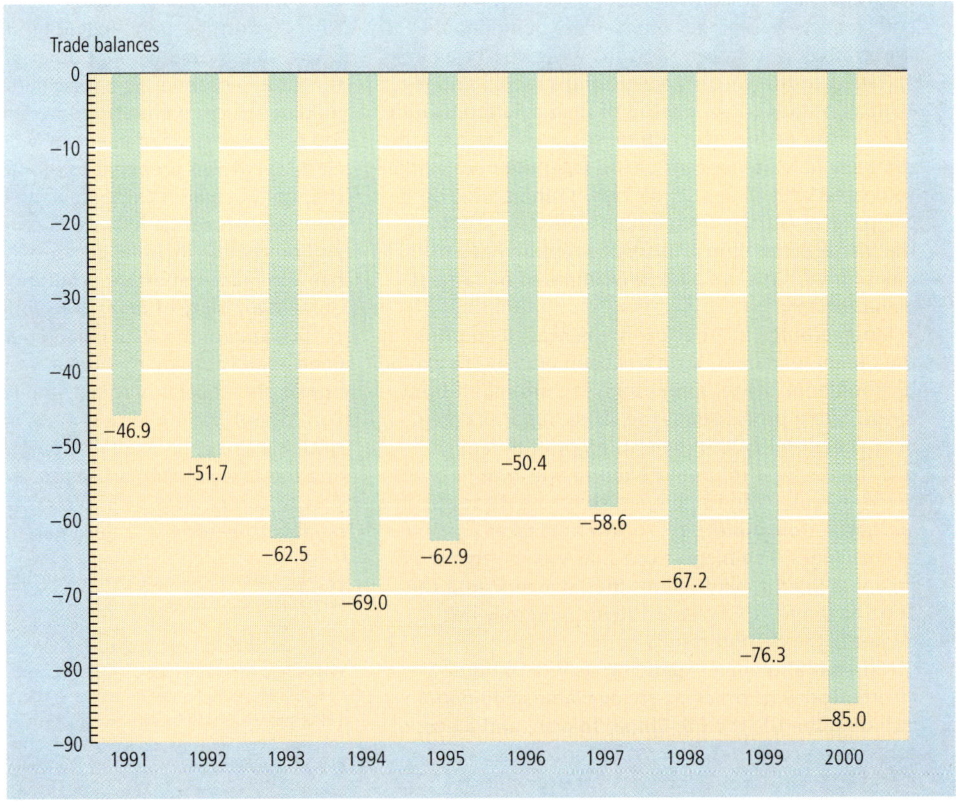

Figure 17.1 The US trade balances with Japan (in billions of US $)

Source: Adapted from IMF, *Direction of Trade Statistics Yearbook, 1996, 2001*.

happen, new trade barriers will probably be instituted in the US, where Japanese auto firms could be badly hurt, and in Europe, where the EU is demanding trade reciprocity as a condition for opening up its bloc market. Because of these reciprocity demands, MNEs who want to do business in Japan see the potential for new business opening up in the next few years.

US impatience with Japanese trading practices is nothing new; for many years people have considered Japanese trade practices to be unfair. Japan was even kept out of GATT until 1955, eight years after the Agreement was signed. At that time the main lobbyist for Japan's membership was the US. Whereas many European nations were fearful of Japan joining GATT, the US, as the dominant player in world trade, saw no threat.

Now that Japan is a trading powerhouse, appeals for protectionism are often heard in the US in some quarters,[23] but many economists do not agree with these sentiments. They believe that the popularity of Japanese products shows the ability of the Japanese to deliver what the US customer demands and that the US industry has not been responsive enough to these consumers. These economists maintain that the key to reducing the trade deficit with Japan lies not in protectionism but, rather, in US companies working harder to meet customer needs.[24] At the same time deregulation of industries such as the financial markets has resulted in an influx of Wall Street firms that are now finding growing opportunities in Japan.[25]

Though the issue of the trade imbalance between the US and Japan continues to drive bilateral negotiations, its relevance has decreased. This can be attributed to two factors, the efforts of the Japanese government to open its market and the declining role of Japan's trade surplus in the US economy. In 2000, Japan accounted for only 17 per cent of the US $486 billion trade deficit with the world. In fact, for the same year, the US trade deficit with the EU was much larger, accounting for 46 per cent of the US trade imbalance. In addition, US and EU trade diplomats are shifting their focus in the region to China, which has a growing trade surplus with the triad.[26]

ACHIEVING SUCCESS IN JAPAN: SEVEN BASIC STEPS

Despite the challenges, many foreign firms have been successful in the Japanese market. Amway, Carrefour, Exxon, HSBC, Hewlett-Packard, IBM, Intel, McDonald's, Merck, Pfizer, and Xerox all do millions of dollars of business in Japan every year.[27] The US alone sells over 50,000 products in Japan and MITI estimates that there are over 1,000 US firms in the country, operating through subsidiaries or joint ventures. Annual sales by US firms are in the neighborhood of $100 billion. How has this been possible? Researchers have found that foreign MNEs that are most successful in Japan tend to follow seven basic steps.[28]

First: Research the Japanese market

The initial step that successful firms undertake is to research the market. As discussed in Chapter 15, this includes a preliminary analysis of potential customers, the nature of the industry, likely competitors, and firms with whom strategic alliances can be created. It also includes initial estimates of the start-up capital and human resources that will be needed. Next comes a detailed plan regarding how to establish a presence in the market and how to differentiate the company's goods and services from those currently offered.

A number of successful firms have supplemented this approach with cultural training. This training typically covers Japanese history, customs, culture, and business practices. Additionally, for those who will be directly involved in on-site operations, rudimentary conversational Japanese is often included. The company Applied Materials Japan does this through an orientation program that includes (1) specially chosen reading on Japan, (2) talks by Japanese executives who are in the US on assignment, and (3) weekly visits by groups of four to five managers and engineers from Japan's semiconductor companies. Through this process each executive is immersed in Japanese culture, customer demands, manufacturing technology, quality principles, geography, and everyday language skills.

When the orientation program is complete, Applied Materials sends its top people to Japan for further acculturation and to learn firsthand how things are done there. This also helps the managers to get a better understanding of the market and to formulate ideas for local operations.

Second: Put the customer first

In the Japanese market customer service is used as a strategic weapon to beat the competition. Every firm tries to outdo its competitors in pleasing the buyer, and this results in outstanding service. For example, when a customer buys a new car in Japan, the auto dealer delivers it to the buyer. If there is a problem with the car and servicing is required, the dealer will have the auto brought in and will provide a replacement while the car is being fixed.

Service is so important that many Japanese customers will not buy from a company that they feel is unable to provide support for what it sells. This extends from consumer goods to industrial parts that are purchased by manufacturing firms.

The emphasis on service also provides companies with a competitive edge when doing business elsewhere in the world. This is why many firms want to do business in Japan; it helps them to improve their customer service focus and so to compete more effectively in the international arena.

Third: Maintain control of operations

Successful MNEs have found that it pays to operate as close to the customer as possible in Japan. This means eliminating third party agents. So while exporting, licensing, and distributorships are often employed to help firms break into the Japanese market, the most successful foreign companies limit their use. Rather, they opt for joint ventures or direct operating subsidiaries with their own Japanese management and local sales, marketing, manufacturing, and development capability. Other reasons for using the most direct channel possible include (1) the firm is better able to develop an image as a Japanese company and thus to increase the opportunity for more local business, (2) profits are increased by eliminating middlemen, and (3) local Japanese firms that are unable or unwilling to spend more money to protect their domestic market share lose out to these foreign competitors.

Foreign firms that have followed this approach include Kodak Japan. The company has constructed a large research and development center in Yokohama, consolidated all Japanese operations at this location, increased its investment and advertising expenditures, and is now a major market force in Japan. Kodak claims that this approach has kept its competitors at bay. Having to compete in a highly dynamic market has helped the firm to increase efficiency and effectiveness.

IBM Japan is another good example. The firm started operations in Japan in 1925 and now has over 22,000 employees, several major factories, a world-class semiconductor fabrication center, sales offices throughout the country, and central research laboratories nationwide. Today IBM Japan is one of the largest foreign MNEs in the country, although most Japanese regard the company as a local firm because it has done such a good job of immersing itself in the economy and the culture.

Fourth: Offer the right products

Successful foreign-owned MNEs realize that many products sold elsewhere in the world must be re-engineered and specially tailored for the Japanese market. For example, Kentucky Fried Chicken (KFC) Japan customized its product from the very start. Units are positioned as upscale, trendy stores rather than fast-food outlets. The Japanese menu includes fried fish and smoked chicken, coleslaw has a reduced sugar content, and french fries are substituted for mashed potatoes. These adaptations for the Japanese market have made KFC Japan extremely successful. In contrast, Pharmacia has always worked closely with Japanese hospitals and pharmacies in order to obtain feedback on product requirements, to gain acceptance for new products through the regulatory process, and to research new chemicals and processes. Today their Japanese subsidiary is highly profitable.[29]

In other cases adjustment has been a response to poor performance. When Swatch, the Swiss maker of inexpensive, colorful watches entered Japan, its sales were dismal. The Japanese had not been accustomed to wearing watches as a fashion accessory. The company had to develop custom Japanese-designed Swatches and to educate the young people about using them.

Fifth: Attack and counterattack

MNEs doing business in Japan have learned that no product is immune from attack for more than six months. For example, soon after McDonald's entered the market, a host of competitive hamburger chains began springing up. As a result, McDonald's Japan had to modify its menu continually, introduce aggressive advertising, and use discounting campaigns. In this way the firm has been able to maintain market leadership.

Procter & Gamble (P&G) faced a similar situation. For the first few years after it introduced disposable diapers the company held most of the market. By the mid-1980s, however, competitors had beaten the company's market share down to 5 per cent by offering new, improved products. Since then P&G has introduced product changes at a much faster rate than in the US and has managed to garner 25 per cent of the Japanese market.

In the case of Fuji Xerox, by the late 1970s the partnership realized that competition was increasing rapidly. So it began intensely investigating the market and investing heavily in R&D. This was followed by renewed manufacturing emphasis on quality control, vigorous reduction of inventory and production costs, and the introduction of a variety of new office products, including high-speed, low-end copiers. By the mid-1980s Fuji Xerox had stopped IBM from making inroads into the copier market and was taking market share away from both Canon and Ricoh. Today the company is regarded as the strongest in that industry in Japan.

Sixth: Stay the course

One of the most important challenges that successful firms have to meet is "staying the course" when market share is small and the competition is strong. This has been particularly true in the case of small firms looking to gain an initial foothold. Allen-Edmonds, a small high-quality footwear manufacturer from Wisconsin, found that it had to persevere in the market and to keep plugging away despite the strong competition. Today Japan is a major market for its products. In other cases a partnership arrangement has proved helpful. For example, Sun Microsystems has partnership agreements with Fujitsu, Toshiba, and Fuji Xerox that provide it with access to technology and markets;

IBM has partnership agreements with Ricoh and Nippon Steel for selling and servicing IBM equipment in Japan. In still other cases firms have found that a piggyback arrangement can be ideal. For example, Blue Diamond Almond Growers of California has an agreement with Coca-Cola Bottling in Japan whereby the latter uses its distribution channels to sell almonds, and General Foods (GF) has teamed up with Ajinomoto, a Japanese food processing company, which adapts GF products for the Japanese market.

Seventh: Use Japan as a jumping off point

Many successful MNEs establish Japanese operations because they believe that this provides them with the experience and competitive edge that can be used worldwide.[30] For example, Texas Instruments (TI) was one of the only surviving US manufacturers of dynamic random access memories (DRAMs), the largest single segment of the semiconductor market. One reason that it had been able to achieve this feat was due to what TI had learned about manufacturing from its Japanese subsidiary and promoted throughout the rest of the company. By bringing in Japanese consultants to teach its workers how to achieve total quality management and by introducing an employee suggestion system, TI was able to improve productivity and empower the workers to control production. The results were astounding. Within five years from the time it started, TI had driven its defect rate from more than 5,000 parts per million (ppm) to less than 20 ppm. In the process the company won the Deming Quality Award, the first non-Japanese firm to win this prize.

Active learning check 

Review your answer to Active Learning Case question 2 and make any changes you like. Then compare your answer with the one below.

2. How can foreign MNEs use *keiretsus* to their own advantage? Give an example.

Foreign MNEs can use *keiretsus* in two ways. One is by teaming up with a *keiretsu* in a form of joint venture arrangement, thus gaining access to the *keiretsu's* manufacturing and marketing prowess. A second is by pitting two or more *keiretsus* against each other in an effort to make a deal with the MNE, thus gaining the best possible business terms.

CHOOSING A START-UP STRATEGY

Many companies that want to do business in Japan cannot afford to keep control of operations. The following sections examine some of the most common alternative start-up strategies.

Exporting

The Japanese government is now taking numerous steps to encourage exporters. Import tariffs have been eliminated on a wide number of products in areas such as agricultural machinery, base metals, chemicals, combustion engines, furniture, glass, home appliances, pharmaceutical products, precious metals, satellites, and sporting goods. The fact that Japan is the third largest US export market after Canada and the EU, and the third largest EU export market after the US and Switzerland, helps to explain why exporting will continue to be a viable strategy for many firms.

MITI has also unveiled a policy of encouraging imports to Japan by offering tax incentives for manufactured imports, making public funds available to finance these goods, increasing the budget for import promotion programs, and focusing on additional steps toward tariff reduction and elimination.

JETRO

Japan External Trade Organization (JETRO)
A non-profit, government-supported organization dedicated to the promotion of mutually beneficial trade between Japan and other nations

The government has also created the **Japan External Trade Organization (JETRO)**, which is a non-profit, government-supported organization dedicated to the promotion of mutually beneficial trade between Japan and other nations. The organization's headquarters are in Tokyo, but it has a worldwide staff of over 1,200 people and a network of 36 offices throughout Japan and 80 other countries.[31] Each of these offices is a comprehensive information center on business and economic relations between the host country and Japan.

JETRO provides a number of services to exporters. These include (1) general information on the Japanese market in the form of economic data such as consumption trends, trading conditions, and distribution channels, (2) information on market trends for various products such as clothing, food, household products, and sporting goods, (3) trade fairs that are held in Japan and designed to help overseas businesses to find trading partners and investigate sales channels, and (4) information databases that are available to potential exporters.

The goal of these efforts is to form distribution agreements between US exporters and Japanese importers. In many cases the importers are large specialty trading companies that buy and sell thousands of products through various divisions in each industrial sector and have their own networks of group companies and subdistributors for a nearly unlimited variety of products.

Before agreeing to any such arrangement, these companies need to understand the advantages and disadvantages of this approach. On the positive side, a distributor arrangement (1) provides instant market access, (2) minimizes the start-up costs and risk of doing business in Japan, (3) ensures that a company which has credibility with the customer is selling the product, and (4) offers a fast, reliable source of cash flow. On the negative side, the distributor (1) may be unfamiliar with the company's specific product or technology, (2) may have a large number of products to sell and devote limited time to this one, (3) may have limited access to the specific customers who are most likely to purchase this product, and (4) will not provide the opportunity for the foreign firm to deal face-to-face with the customer.

Licensing agreements

Licensing agreement
An arrangement whereby one firm gives another firm the right to use certain assets such as trademarks, patents, or copyrights in exchange for a fee

A **licensing agreement** is an arrangement whereby one firm gives another firm the right to use certain assets such as trademarks, patents, or copyrights in exchange for the payment of a fee. This approach has been extremely common in Japan.

Overall, there are two basic advantages to licensing. First, it can help a company to establish a market and to set operating standards for new technologies and products. Second, it is a method of earning short-term fees with the promise of longer-term profits. Sun Microsystems (Sun), for example, has licensed its microprocessor technology to Toshiba and to other leading computer manufacturers in Japan in order to promote its Sparc/Unix technology as a standard for the entire computer industry. By sharing the basic aspects of the technology with these firms, Sun has been able to expand its own opportunities by preventing the adoption of standards that would have deterred sales growth.

INTERNATIONAL BUSINESS STRATEGY *IN ACTION*

Japan and foreign direct investment

As one of the triad economic powers, Japan has both inward and outward foreign direct investment. In this special case, we first discuss some of the impediments to inward FDI in Japan in the first box below, and the common barriers for inward foreign direct investment in Japan. In the second box, we discuss the success of Japanese outward FDI, with special reference to productivity.

Common barriers for inward foreign direct investment in Japan:

- *Inadequate information systems for foreign companies wishing to invest in Japan.* The country does not have a one-stop source of information and provides very little information in English.
- *Few industrial park sites for lease in Japan.* Constructed by local governments, most industrial parks are only available for purchase, not for rent. The sale price for such properties tends to be much higher than in western countries, increasing the initial investment costs and the risk of withdrawal.
- *Complex land-use regulations.* Multiple and multilayered regulations arise from the National Land Use Planning Act, and other laws which apply to land use. When conversion of land to commercial use is permitted, development permission must be gained under each regulation separately.
- *Costly legal and accounting services.* Foreign companies must complete procedures for applying for work permits and setting up corporations. Specialists are available, but it is difficult for a foreign firm to judge which type of paralegal to turn to for each of its needs and few of them can provide English services. Foreign firms then hire lawyers at higher costs, who then outsource the job to relevant specialists. In addition, there are no one-stop joint legal-accounting services.
- *Strict work permit/visa requirements.* Japan requires that there is a place of business employing two or more full-time staff for the applicants of an investor/business manager work permit. Applicants for an engineer work permit must have at least a university degree or have ten years of practical experience. Intra-company transferee work permits require that the individual has worked for the company for at least a year directly prior to the assignment.
- *Certificate of Seal Registration.* To register a new company, Japanese companies must fill a "certificate seal registration". Though, foreign firms may submit a "certification of signature," many regional register offices will only accept a "certificate of seal registration." For this to be granted there must be an established residence. This is difficult to do for companies that have not yet been established.
- *Japan's distinctive guarantee system.* A business practice that requires personal guarantees on securing credit for a corporation. It is often difficult for a foreign firm or individual to find a Japanese guarantor.

Source: JETRO, *The Survey on Actual Conditions Regarding Access to Japan: Inward Foreign Direct Investment*, 2000.

Japanese outward FDI increases world productivity

Japanese manufacturing is famous for its productivity. In 2000, it took Nissan 17.4 hours to make a car in North America, compared to 25.7 hours for Ford, 26.8 hours for GM and 31.3 hours for DaimlerChrysler. In 2001, it was Honda that topped the list with 95 vehicles per employee at its Marysville factory in Ohio. Nissan's Sunderland plant in the United Kingdom tops the European productivity list with 95 vehicles per employee in 2001. Ford's Melfi plant in Italy and Toyota's Burnaston plant in the United Kingdom tail in second place at 87 units per employee, (see accompanying Table). Worldwide, of the top 10 car plants in the world ranked by vehicles per employee, the first nine are Japanese and the tenth is South Korean. This isn't at all surprising. It was, after all, the Japanese that pioneered just-in-time and quality control production techniques that have now been adopted by manufacturing plants across the triad.

In an effort to narrow the productivity gap with Japanese competitors, European and North American carmakers have begun restructuring, closing down inefficient plants and cutting down surplus capacity. Most importantly, they are responding to Japanese FDI by adopting Japanese lean production processes.

In Europe, Ford cut its capacity by 20 per cent in two years, closed a number of inefficient plants and introduced "flex manufacturing" to allow for the production of multiple models on the same line. Ford's plant in Saarlouis, Germany, saw its productivity rise from 58 vehicles per employee in 1998 to 87 units per employee in 2001. Although, three of General Motors' plants ranked in the top ten in Europe, it is still making losses

European automotive productivity index, 2002

Rank	Manufacturer	Plant	Country	Vehicles Produced 2001	Vehicles per employee 2000	Vehicles per employee 2001	% Change
Top 10							
1	Nissan	Sunderland	United Kingdom	296,489	101	95	(5.9)
2	Ford	Saarfouis	Germany	408,405	81	87	7.4
3	Toyota	Burnaston	United Kingdom	156,000	86	87	1.2
4	Fiat	Melfi	Italy	350,756	76	82	7.9
5	General Motors	Eisenach	Germany	137,272	77	77	–
6	Renault	Valladolid	Spain	277,188	77	77	–
7	General Motors	Antwerp	Belgium	313,722	77	76	(1.3)
8	General Motors	Zaragoza	Spain	358,040	76	75	(1.3)
9	Renault	Flins	France	376,396	70	73	4.3
10	Ford	Valencia	Spain	318,423	77	70	(9.1)
Bottom 10							
1	PSA	Madrid	Spain	151,048	40	43	7.5
2	PSa	Mangualde	Portugal	50,162	40	42	5.0
3	Volvo	Torslanda	Sweden	136,600	40	40	–
4	Renault	Sandouville	France	271,141	32	40	25.0
5	Renault	Bursa	Turkey	96,860	51	39	(23.5)
6	PSA	Rennes	France	305,472	33	38	15.2
7	Volvo	Born	Netherlands	122,071	40	36	(10.0)
8	General Motors	Russelsheim	Germany	165,009	34	36	5.9
9	PSA	Sochaux	France	384,644	34	36	5.9
10	Volkswagen	Emden	Germany	258,600	27	32	18.5

Source: Tim Burt, "Japanese car plants top productivity table," *Financial Times*, July 8, 2002.

in the region. The company has decided to reduce its capacity by 400,000 and reduce its workforce by 3,500–4,000 in Europe alone.

North American car manufacturers are applying these measures across their entire operations. In their home market, Ford is planning to close five plants and decrease its North American workforce by 22,000. General Motors is also cutting thousands of jobs, however, the company is also increasing US output to utilize about 1 million units of idle capacity.

Critics of vehicle-per-employee comparisons point out that brand value and vehicle quality are just as important as quantity. Peugeot Citroën of France (PSA), with four plants in the top 10 under-performers with respect to vehicle per employee is the most profitable volume carmaker in Europe. Nissan, Ford, Toyota, GM and Fiat, which own eight of the top 10 auto plants in term of units, are either showing loses in the European market or are breaking even. In fact, by using the right combination of labour and capital, PSA has become the lowest-cost producer in Europe.

Nissan's productivity contrasts with the relatively low quality of its vehicles. In 2002, Nissan had 152 defects per 100 vehicles. The top carmakers, in terms of quality, were Toyota and Honda, with 107 and 113 defects per 100 vehicles respectively. GM, DaimlerChrysler and Ford, ranked above Nissan, but below Toyota and Honda (see Table right). For Ford, the implementation of Six Sigma and a Toyota-style Quality Operating System are responsible for the company's rise to fifth place. Between 2001 and 2002, Ford reduced its defects from 162 per 100 vehicles in 2001, to 143 in 2002. By the same measure, General Motors improved its quality by 30 per cent over the same period.

Automakers' manufacturing quality, 2002

Rank	Manufacturer	defects per 100 units 2002
1	Toyota	107
2	Honda	113
3	General Motors	130
4	DaimlerChrysler	141
5	Ford	143
6	Volkswagen	152
7	Nissan	152

Source: Kathleen Kerwin, "From Ford, a Less-Tinny Lizzie," *Business Week*, May 30, 2002.

Source: Tim Burt, "Japanese car plants top productivity table," *Financial Times*, July 8, 2002; Earle Eldridge, "Japan carmakers still most productive," *USA Today*, June 15, 2001; GM cuts 5,000 more jobs, *BBC.co.uk*, January 7, 2002; Joseph White and Gregory L. White, "Toyota, Honda tops in quality study," *The Wall Street Journal*, May 30, 2002 and Kathleen Kerwin, "From Ford, a Less-Tinny Lizzie," *Business Week*, May 30, 2002.

There are four disadvantages to licensing: (1) competitors are given new technology, processes, or information without having to spend any money on R&D; (2) the licensor typically has no local presence but, rather, relies exclusively on the licensee; (3) there is no chance for complementary opportunities of any kind such as identifying local demand for goods that could be produced by spinning off this technology; and (4) competitive obsolescence is virtually guaranteed as the licensee seeks methods of improving the technology and striking out on its own.

In deciding on a licensing agreement, the participating firms must weigh the advantages and disadvantages carefully. Restrictive Japanese laws that made licensing and technology sharing mandatory have now been relaxed. However, their inability to prevent licensees from copying and improving MNE technology has led many multinationals to be more cautious in the case of licensing agreements.

Joint ventures

Joint ventures are another popular method of tapping into the Japanese market. In recent years many Japanese firms have recognized the need to diversify operations and to offer additional goods and services, thus expanding their base of operations. Often a joint venture has provided this opportunity. Some benefits associated with joint ventures include (1) reduction of risk of failure by sharing the burden with a partner, (2) rapid market access and the opportunity for quick profits, and (3) an increase in company and product acceptance brought about by having a local firm serve as the direct interface with the customer. Some primary drawbacks to joint ventures include (1) domination of the local market by the partner, thus effectively insulating the foreign firm from direct contact with the customer; (2) creation of business outlets by the local partner which are in direct competition with the joint venture; and (3) inability to work well with the foreign partner, resulting in either a sellout to the latter or a cessation of the arrangement.

One of the most important steps in creating a joint venture is to research the partner and to learn about its resources and abilities to contribute to the arrangement. Particular attention needs to be focused on the partner's

1. Distribution channels and large customer associations.
2. Recognized technical leadership in the field.
3. Support and service capabilities.
4. Geographic coverage.
5. Market image and reputation.
6. Complementary/competitive product fit.
7. Industrial ranking – first-, second-, or third-tier.
8. Willingness to accept a non-exclusive arrangement.
9. Industrial or banking group associations.
10. Long-term synergies.[32]

Many foreign firms have found that large, nationally respected Japanese firms offer the most advantages because they best meet the above criteria. However, sometimes the size of the other party also puts it in a position to dominate the relationship and eventually to squeeze out its smaller partner. This is one reason for choosing smaller partners with whom a true 50/50 relationship can be created. The profits and market growth are not likely to be as great, but the long-range relationship can be more stable and lasting.

It is also important to realize the significance of being an active partner. Foreign MNEs that do not make an equal contribution to the business and play an active role in the operation of the enterprise often lose out to their local partner. For example, when the financial or operating contribution by the foreign partner is less than 50 per cent, the other side frequently takes over more and more control of the venture. Eventually the more active partner will either attempt to buy out the other or to terminate the agreement because it no longer needs the partner.

The most successful joint ventures have been those in which each side views the partnership as a long-run commitment and is determined to succeed as a team. There are a number of important steps that must be carried out in accomplishing this objective, including (1) each must be prepared to accept responsibility for the success of the venture, (2) each must be sensitive and hospitable to the other in day-to-day dealings, (3) the two sides must meet informally so that each gets to know the other on a personal level and to create a deep sense of trust between them, (4) personnel at all levels of the organization must interact and work together, and (5) victories and successes should be celebrated together.

Active learning check 

Review your answer to Active Learning Case question 3 and make any changes you like. Then compare your answer with the one below.

3. Why are joint ventures so popular among foreign MNEs? Cite two reasons.

Joint ventures are popular because they give a company an opportunity for immediate market access and the opportunity for rapid profits. There is also a reduction of the risk of failure since both sides jointly share that risk.

Acquisitions

In the US, acquisitions are often used as a means of creating synergy and adding value to a company. In recent years acquisitions have become a very attractive way of entering the Japanese market. This is quite different from the situation in the early 1990s when high stock prices and the increasing value of the yen made it prohibitive for foreign buyers to purchase Japanese firms. As a result, in recent years the Travelers Group has purchased 25 per cent of Nikko Securities, Japan's third largest brokerage firm, and foreign investors now have substantial ownership in Japanese firms.[33] For example, 45 per cent of Sony is now held by foreigners, as is 42 per cent of Rohm, 39 per cent of Canon, and 36 per cent of Fuji.[34]

Firms that do acquire Japanese companies must learn how to manage the workforce. The personnel have been so long accustomed to working for the previous management that new managers have many barriers to overcome. Bridging the cultural gap and differences in management philosophies after acquiring a Japanese company is often too great a challenge.[35] As a result, acquisitions remain one of the least used approaches for getting into the Japanese market.

Creating a local subsidiary

One of the most popular approaches to doing business in Japan is the wholly-owned or majority-owned Japanese subsidiary. In addition to those already mentioned in this chapter, US firms with Japanese subsidiaries include Alcoa, American Express, Amway, Apple Computer, Dow Chemical, Ford Motor, Hewlett-Packard, Philip Morris, Revlon, Tandy, and Warner-Lambert.

Some advantages of a subsidiary include (1) the achieving of closeness to the customer and thus improving market responsiveness and the ability to assess future opportunities, (2) the creation of a unified strategy and objectives on a worldwide basis, and (3) the attainment of world-class performance. Some drawbacks of the approach include (1) heavy fixed expenses and start-up costs, (2) the need to generate sales from the ground up, (3) the difficulty of finding a reliable minority partner, (4) the challenge of hiring local personnel, and (5) the problems associated with managing local operations.

While the pros and cons of this strategy must be carefully weighed, the reasons that the subsidiary approach has proven popular with many foreign firms include the opportunity for future growth and the ability to develop world-class approaches that can be used globally. The following section examines the steps that must be met by those firms opting for this approach.

MANAGING ON-SITE OPERATIONS

Managing on-site operations requires attention to a number of important areas. Primary among these are recruiting, choosing site facilities, organizing the business, and financing operations.

Recruiting

One of the first, and certainly the most difficult, tasks for subsidiaries managing on-site operations in Japan is that of recruiting personnel. Unlike the US where top managers are often recruited from other firms, in Japan it is difficult to get executives to change companies. As we have seen, Japanese workers are closely aligned with their employers and take pride in their identity as company employees. One of the most effective strategies is first to recruit a top manager and other members of the management team. They in turn will work to attract other managerial and key personnel. Commenting on the challenge of recruiting these people, two Japanese experts have noted:

> Hiring a good manager is not easy; it is an intricate and slow-moving process. It often takes six months to a year (or more) after initial agreement with an individual before he or she actually comes on board. Hiring managers from large Japanese companies, especially when they are your customers, is a sensitive situation, far more so than in America. The hiring dance typically begins with one of your company's top executives meeting with the candidate's employer and even his family to request permission to negotiate with the individual and to provide assurance of his future position, security, and opportunities. From there, several meetings must take place over a long period of time.[36]

One of the prime sources of recruiting is college graduates. Every year recruiters from industry work feverishly to attract these individuals. The problem for foreign firms is that most graduates of the first-tier universities such as Tokyo University, Kyoto University, and Waseda University prefer to work for Japanese companies. In order to recruit effectively in Japan, the foreign firm needs to gain acceptance in the academic community. College professors play the role of mentor to many students, and these professors must be won over if a company is to be successful in generating interest among the students.

Many firms are now supplementing their managerial and college recruiting strategies with compensation packages that are designed to attract working women. Included in these packages are day-care centers for young children, one-year leave policies for new parents, higher wages, and shorter working hours. US firms have been doing so well in this area that Japanese companies have now begun to respond. Saison, which runs department stores and supermarkets, offers low-cost day-care services and meals for the children of employees. Toyota Motor has a one-year parental leave program, and Nissan Motor offers its people a five-year program. With the growing labor shortage in Japan and the fact that by the early 1990s Japanese women were making less than were 60 per cent of their male counterparts, such competitive measures were predictable. The future will see even more vigorous recruiting competition between Japanese and locally based foreign subsidiaries.

Choosing location and organization

Two of the major operating decisions that must be made are where the firm will be located and how local operations will be organized. Because of the importance of location, this decision is typically made first.

Making a location decision

The cost of doing business in Japan can be prohibitive, especially if the firm wants a location in Tokyo. Land here is costly, construction rates are high, and rents are steep. Rental costs in Tokyo in recent years have been more than double those of many other locations.[37] As a result, many companies now bypass Tokyo (except, perhaps, for a small office that is used more for public relations than for operations) in favor of sites that are closer to the customers and/or labor supply. Manufacturing firms, for example, can now be found in cities like Nagoya, Osaka, Hiroshima, and Kumamoto, and there are new centers of commerce continually springing up throughout the country. In making a final location choice, it is advantageous to talk to the local government and to determine how the company's needs match those of the area. Some prefectures offer small and rural settings, while others have major centers of commerce. These governments are all interested in attracting business and industry and provide a variety of forms of assistance.

Organizing for operations

There are a number of differences between the way that the Japanese manage their operations and the way that this is done in most other countries. One is the relationship that exists between managers and employees. Managers are extremely paternalistic and concerned about the well-being of their people. In turn the employees are loyal, dedicated, and hard working. Firms like IBM Japan have succeeded, in part, because the philosophy of the parent company contains many of the same values that are present in Japanese firms. MNEs setting up operations in Japan must use a similar, highly protective leadership approach. Otherwise it is extremely difficult to recruit and retain personnel.

A second important guideline is that of delegating operating authority to the subsidiary. There are two reasons for this. First, home office personnel typically do not know how to interact effectively with Japanese clients and customers. Unless the top staff at headquarters have received extensive cultural training and on-site experience, it is often best to defer local decisions to the subsidiary managers. Second, the subsidiary must gain and maintain credibility in the local market, and this will not happen if customers or clients deal directly with headquarters staff. When headquarters remains in the most visible position, the Japanese conclude that top management views the subsidiary as weak and ineffective. Customers, clients, and competitors must all see a united front in which the subsidiary is the representative of the company and all important matters, at least publicly, are referred to the local organization.

In order to ensure that the subsidiary is not relegated to a minor place in the organizational hierarchy, many MNEs have the head of the unit report directly to the chief executive officer of the multinational. It is also common to find the subsidiary manager actively participating in all worldwide corporate strategy meetings, thus ensuring that Japanese operations are strategically integrated into the overall plan. This organizational arrangement is also a sign of commitment and helps to build trust and cooperation between the subsidiary and the headquarters staff.

Another operating objective is to immerse the company in the local market so that it is seen as inherently Japanese. When this is accomplished, the firm is regarded as having high quality production, reliable service, and genuine concern for the personnel. Applied Materials, Avon, IBM, TI, and Xerox, among others, are examples of companies that have achieved this objective. When this happens, many barriers that face foreign subsidiaries from recruiting to winning sales contracts begin to fall.

A supplemental approach is the development of formal communication links between the two groups. These interactions typically range from daily phone calls to teleconferences to on-site visits. Executives from the home office will often spend a large amount of their time each year in Japan and subsidiary managers will come to headquarters to discuss operations and strategy. Some firms supplement these meetings with on-site assignments so that personnel from each group work in the other's locale. This helps each to understand the other and is useful in creating long-run harmony.

Financing operations

There are two major areas of financial consideration when doing business in Japan. The first is establishing a banking relationship to handle day-to-day and short-term financial demands. The other is deciding how to finance long-term operations.

Banking relationships

Banking in Japan is based on personal relationships. Of course, it is possible to walk into a Japanese bank, deposit funds, and start paying bills and handling other financial obligations that are associated with running the subsidiary. However, the most effective approach is to use a facilitator to introduce the company to a bank. Many people can perform this function: businesspeople, other bankers, and government officials. Major MNEs often accomplish this through their dealings with a Japanese bank elsewhere in the world. For example, a company in San Francisco that is doing business with a Japanese-owned bank in the city will call on its banker to help establish a relationship with a bank in Japan. If the San Francisco bank is directly affiliated with a bank there, this is quite easy. Otherwise the banker will contact a counterpart in Japan and provide a history and working relationship of the company. In turn the Japanese bank will help the foreign subsidiary to handle its financial needs and, if additional services are needed that are outside the scope of the bank, will provide the necessary introductions to other parties. This can be particularly important when the subsidiary is setting up operations in areas where the main bank does not have offices or if the subsidiary wants to apply for assistance or funding from organizations such as the Japan Development Bank.

Development Bank of Japan (DBJ)
A publicly funded financial institution with a mandate to advance business projects in accordance with the government's social and economic policies (previously known as the Japan Development Bank)

The **Development Bank of Japan (DBJ)** (previously known as the Japan Development Bank) is a government-owned institution whose primary objective is to promote industrial development nationwide. Funds from the bank can be spent in a variety of ways such as funding for foreign research and development projects, providing assistance to companies setting up new factories, and lending money to firms that are helping to promote exports. The DBJ also functions to promote private investment in areas of public interest. In Japan, there are not as many sources of capital as there are in the US, but once a company is in the mainstream of financing opportunities, the supplies of capital are usually quite plentiful. These extend from commercial banks to local banks to insurance companies to pension funds.[38]

Raising capital

Most MNEs finance their initial foray into the Japanese market with funds from abroad. However, once the operation is established, the company can consider raising long-term capital in the local market. A number of foreign firms that have gone international in recent years have been quite successful in floating local stock issues to cover the costs of their Japanese operations. For example, Avon Products raised over $240 million with its Japanese issue, $92 million for Shaklee, $90 million for Levi Strauss, and $42 million for Baskin Robbins. During the millennium an increasing number of foreign MNEs will use the local equity markets to help them finance the costs of doing business in Japan.

JAPAN AS A TRIAD POWER

It is important to remember that Japan is a triad power. The country has experienced the fastest and longest period of sustained economic growth in world history over the last 40 years. Although the rate of growth began to slow in the 1990s, Japan's momentum will keep it going into the 21st century. Indeed, this century may be the Pacific century, with other Asian nations following the Japanese model of rapid growth and development.

Japan's role as a triad power is confirmed by the data in Table 17.3. This table brings together information presented earlier in this book on Japan's share of the triad's trade, FDI, and proportion of global firms.

Table 17.4 reports changes in the direction of Japan's trade over the last 10 years. Exports have become even more focused on the US, the EU, and the rest of Asia. While the value of Japanese exports to the US increased 56 per cent, from $92,200 million to $144,009 million, during this period the value of Japanese exports to the rest of Asia increased by 111 per cent, and to the EU by 22 per cent during the same period. The share of "all others" decreased by 23 per cent.

In terms of shares of Japanese imports, Table 17.4 also shows that imports from the rest of Asia and from other non-triad countries increased the most, at 94 per cent and 47 per cent respectively over the period. The share of imports originating from the US and EU decreased over the same period. This decline can be explained by the devaluation of the yen during the Asian crisis that made imports from the US and the EU relatively expensive for Japanese consumers. Similarly, the increase in exports to triad nations is the result of a drop in the price of Japanese imports relative to that of other countries.[39]

Table 17.3 Japan's role in the triad

	Exports				*FDI**				*500 largest MNEs*†			
Triad powers	*1990 (in billions of US $)*	*% of world total*	*1999 (in billions of US $)*	*% of world total*	*1990 (in billions of US $)*	*% of world total*	*1999 (in billions of US $)*	*% of world Total*	*1989 no.*	*% of world total*	*2000 no.*	*% of world total*
Japan	243	10.0	419.2	7.4	201.4	11.7	292.8	6.2	111	22.2	104	20.8
United States	264	10.9	690.7	12.2	430.5	25.1	1,131.5	23.8	167	33.4	185	37.0
European Community‡	915	37.8	2,189.6	38.8	789.4	46.0	2,337.0	49.1	127	25.4	141	28.2

* Refers to FDI outward stock.

† 1990 is the year the Global 500 list was introduced in *Fortune*. Also, prior to 1995 the Global 500 included only industrial corporations. In 1995 it combined service and industrial corporations.

‡ The European Community refers to the EU prior to 1995. Data for EU do not include Finland, Austria, and Sweden prior to 1995, the year these countries joined the union.

Source: IMF, *Direction of Trade Statistics Yearbook, 1996*; United Nations, *World Investment Report, 2000*; Fortune, *The Fortune 500*, 1990, 1995, and 1997.

Table 17.4 Direction of Japan's trade, 1991–2000

	Exports to				*Imports from*			
	1991		*2000*		*1991*		*2000*	
Country/region	*(millions of US $)*	*% of total*	*(millions of US $)*	*% of total*	*(millions of US $)*	*% of total*	*(millions of US $)*	*% of total*
United States	92,200	29.3	144,009	30.2	53,634	22.7	72,514	19.2
Canada	7,258	2.3	7,474	1.6	7,691	3.3	8,698	2.3
European Union	64,104	20.4	78,457	16.4	34,422	14.5	46,813	12.4
Other Asia	97,732	31.0	206,323	43.2	89,318	37.7	173,439	46.0
All others	53,551	17.0	41,070	8.6	51,547	21.8	75,689	20.1
Total	314,845	100.0	477,333	100.0	236,612	100.0	377,153	100.0

Source: Adapted from IMF, *Direction of Trade Statistics Yearbook, 1996, 2001*.

Table 17.5 Japan's trade with East Asia

	Exports to				*Imports from*			
	1991		*2000*		*1991*		*2000*	
Country/region	*(millions of US $)*	*% of total*	*(millions of US $)*	*% of total*	*(millions of US $)*	*% of total*	*(millions of US $)*	*% of total*
NIE	66,928	59.0	114,697	55.6	27,352	22.7	46,439	26.8
Singapore	12,228	10.8	20,830	10.1	3,417	2.8	6,426	3.7
Hong Kong	16,337	14.4	27,187	13.2	2,066	1.7	1,668	1
South Korea	20,088	17.7	30,703	14.9	12,381	10.3	20,454	11.8
Taiwan	18,275	16.1	35,977	17.4	9,488	7.9	17,891	10.3
ASEAN (not NIE)	25,833	22.7	47,681	23.1	29,067	24.0	53,119	30.6
Brunei Darussalam	129	0.1	56	0	1,501	1.2	1,653	1
Indonesia	5,618	5	7,604	3.7	12,783	10.6	16,371	9.4
Malaysia	7,649	6.7	13,886	6.7	6,458	5.4	14,490	8.4
Philippines	2,662	2.3	10,257	5	2,347	1.9	7,190	4.1
Thailand	9,446	8.3	13,634	6.6	5,258	4.4	10,595	6.1
Vietnam	218	0.2	1975	1	662	0.5	2,637	1.5
Other ASEAN	111	0.1	269	0.1	58	0	183	0.1
Other Asia	20,727	18.3	43,945	21.3	64,268	53.3	73,881	42.6
of which								
Australia	6,504	5.7	7,748	3.8	12,965	10.7	12,397	7.1
India	1,525	1.3	2,488	1.2	2,186	1.8	2,637	1.5
New Zealand	1,082	1	1,264	0.6	1,820	1.5	2,194	1.3
Pakistan	1,362	1.2	604	0.3	650	0.5	251	0.1
P.R. of China	8,605	7.6	30,356	14.7	14,248	11.8	55,156	31.8
Asia total	113,488	100	206,323	100	120,687	100	173,439	100

Note: Numbers in Asia total might not add up due to rounding.

Source: Adapted from IMF, *Direction of Trade Statistics Yearbook, 1996, 2001*.

Table 17.5 provides a closer look at Japan's trade relationship with its Asian neighbors. All the newly industrialized economies (NIEs) have negative balance-of-payment positions with Japan, the overall value of Japanese exports to these four countries being 146 per cent higher than its imports in 2000. It is only when Japan's trading relationship with the poorer, primary resource-producing economies of ASEAN is considered that the trade balance evens out. In fact, once the NIEs were excluded, Japan's imports from the rest of Asia ($127 billion) were nearly 40 per cent higher than its exports ($92 billion). This highlights how Japan's competitiveness and success in penetrating markets with its exports have been concentrated in manufacturing, and the extent to which an economic powerhouse like Japan can run large trade surpluses with its competitors but still be dependent on and run trade deficits with other countries.

Figure 17.2 reports data on Japan's foreign direct investment (FDI) and the rapid expansion of Japanese FDI stocks abroad. This table shows the distribution of these stocks in different countries and regions of the world (OECD accounting practices differ considerably from those in the US, and, as such, the figures reported in Figure 17.2 are not directly comparable with the US Department of Commerce data used elsewhere in this book). Briefly, the US share of FDI stocks in 1998 is by far the highest, at 41 per cent, followed by the rest of Asia at 29.6 per cent and Europe at 19.2 per cent. The total value of Japanese FDI stocks, as reported by the OECD, is around $238.2 billion. These data help to illustrate why Japan is an economic superpower and why many non-triad nations want to establish linkages with this country.

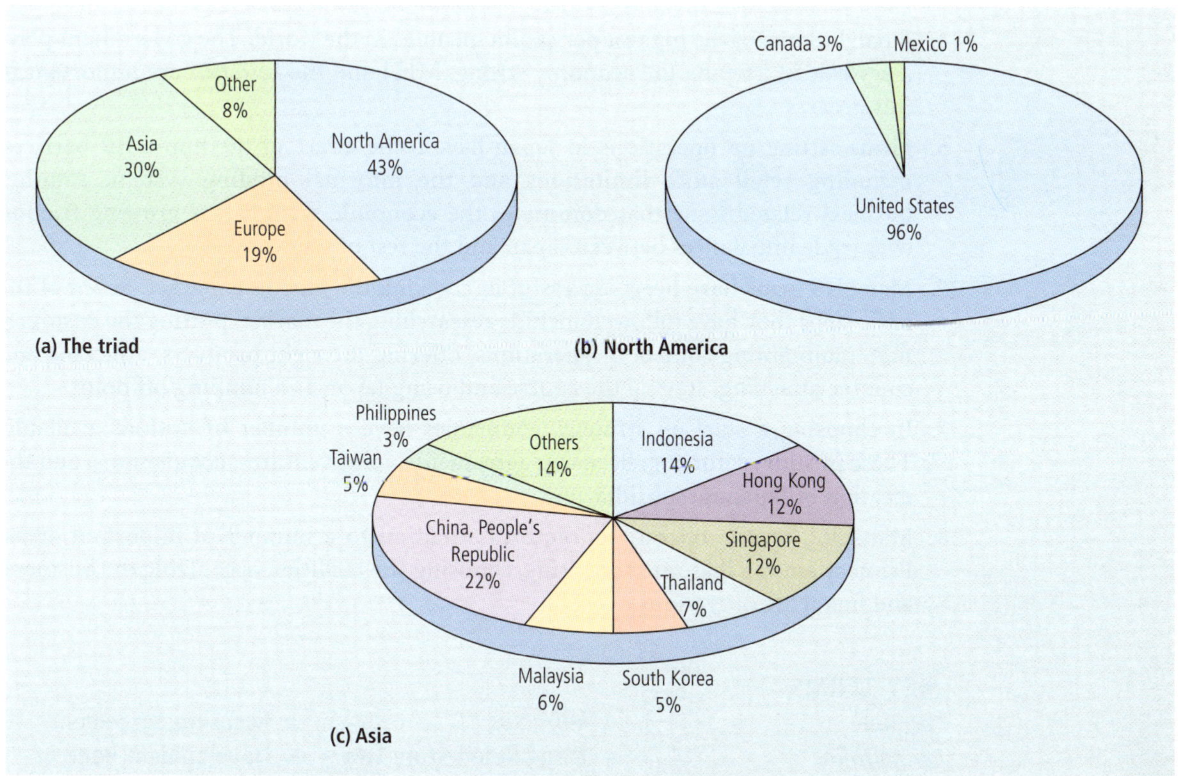

Figure 17.2 **Japan's foreign direct investment: position at year-end, 1998**

Note: Asia includes Australia and New Zealand.

Source: Adapted from OECD (2000) *International Direct Investment Statistics Yearbook, 2000*. Copyright OECD, 2000.

Active learning check 

Review your answer to Active Learning Case question 4 and make any changes you like. Then compare your answer with the one below.

4. Why is Japan likely to remain a target market for international MNEs? Cite two reasons.

Japan is likely to remain a target market for international MNEs because of its large growing economy and affluent consumer base. A second reason is the value of monitoring Japanese world-class competitors by having local operations that compete head-to-head, thus helping the MNE to maintain a strong, competitive posture.

KEY POINTS

1. The branches of the Japanese government are similar to those of the US: legislative, executive, and judicial. Legislative power is vested in the Diet, a bicameral body. Executive power rests with the Cabinet. Judicial power is vested in the Supreme Court.
2. There are approximately 127 million Japanese. There is mandatory education at the lower levels, and general living standards are good.
3. Social patterns are distinctly different from those in the West. Japan is a group-oriented society. Strong emphasis is given to harmony, orderliness, and the respect of others. Social ranking and the power of obligation are both extremely important.
4. Japan has one of the highest per capita incomes in the world. The government plays a key role in keeping the economy strong. MITI and the *keiretsus* are important in this process.
5. Firms setting up operations in Japan have to be aware of the non-tariff barriers, including retail store limitations and the informal bidding system. Another business-related issue that dominates the economic scene is the growing friction over trade imbalances between Japan and the rest of the world.
6. Many US firms have been successful in cracking the Japanese market. Seven of the basic steps they have followed include researching the market, putting the customer first, maintaining control of operations, offering the right products, attacking and counter-attacking, staying the course and using Japan as a jumping off point.
7. In choosing a start-up strategy, companies have a number of options available. These include exporting, licensing agreements, joint ventures, acquisitions, and the creation of Japanese subsidiaries.
8. Managing on-site operations requires attention to a number of important areas. Primary among these are recruiting, choosing site facilities, organizing the business, and financing operations.

KEY TERMS

- Diet
- *gairojin*
- *gaijin*
- Ministry of International Trade and Industry (MITI)
- *keiretsus*
- Large Retail Store Law
- Japan External Trade Organization (JETRO)
- licensing agreement
- Development Bank of Japan (DBJ)

REVIEW AND DISCUSSION QUESTIONS

1. How important to the Japanese is harmony and the respect of others? What implication does this have for MNEs doing business in Japan?
2. How does the power of obligation influence Japanese business practices? Give an example.
3. What role does MITI play in Japan? Explain.
4. What are some non-trade barriers to doing business in Japan? Identify and describe three of them.
5. How can MNEs doing business in Japan do the following: research the market, put the customer first, and maintain control of operations? In each case, give an example.
6. How can MNEs doing business in Japan do the following: offer the right products, attack, counterattack, and use Japan as a jumping off point? In each case, give an example.
7. What are some of the steps that should be taken by companies interested in exporting to Japan? Identify and describe three of them.
8. How does a licensing agreement differ from a joint venture? Compare and contrast the two and discuss three advantages associated with each.
9. Why is an acquisition strategy for entering the Japanese market often a poor one?
10. When choosing a start-up strategy, why do many successful MNEs create a Japanese subsidiary? What are some of the primary advantages of this approach?
11. Why is it difficult to recruit graduating college students in Japan? How can MNEs overcome these problems?
12. What are three useful guidelines that MNEs should follow when organizing operations in Japan? Discuss each.
13. How can the Development Bank of Japan be of value to MNEs operating in Japan?
14. How can MNEs in Japan raise long-term capital locally? Explain.

REAL CASE

Toys "Я" Us in Japan

Toys "Я" Us was founded in 1957 by Charles Lazarus. His family business focused on the rebuilding and selling of bicycles, and later he began selling children's furniture. Over time, he began to realize that selling toys was a superior business opportunity, and he founded the "children's Supermarket" chain. In 1966 Lazarus sold the chain (which at the time owned four stores) to Interstate Store for $7.5 million, but he retained a seat on the company's board. When Interstate folded in 1978, Lazarus rescued his company, with the goal of making it a national chain. By 1988 the company had captured 20 per cent of the US toy market, with sales surpassing $4 billion. Toys "Я" Us opened its first international outlet in Canada in 1984, and then they moved into Europe, Hong Kong, and Singapore, where the "discount formula" was as popular as in the US.

Due to its sourcing from manufacturers, Toys "Я" Us is able to offer prices 10–20 per cent lower than other retailers. It has a "killer category" firm-specific advantage. The company offers a wide variety of 15,000 items in a warehouse of an average size of 54,000 square feet, and it applies the same store design and layout everywhere. Central control is a key feature of the organization because the extensive computer network ensures almost automatic replacement of every toy sold, maintaining predetermined inventory levels.

According to the Bank of Japan, annual retail sales grew 94 per cent during the 1980s, while Japan's GDP grew at an average annual rate of 7 per cent. Children's products accounted for a significant proportion of consumer spending in Japan. In this context, by 1991 the Japanese toy market had become the second largest in the world at $7.1 billion, behind only the US.

These market characteristics suggested that the Japanese toy market offered an attractive opportunity for Toys "Я" Us, but on the other hand there were some major hurdles to overcome. Despite the rapid growth it had experienced, Japan's toy industry remained highly fragmented and locally focused. The Japanese shopper reportedly preferred personal attention from the shop keeper rather than low prices (one of the main characteristics of the Toys "Я" Us business model).

In addition to customers' habits and personal loyalties, Japan's retail structure was also bolstered by a series of laws restricting the spread of larger retail stores. Younger generations were realizing that they were paying inflated prices for many consumer goods, however. Slowly, their demands for fewer commercial restrictions and lower prices began to influence the political process.

A typical Japanese toy store was less than 3,200 square feet in area. Nearly all retail shops were domestically owned and bought their toys from local wholesalers, usually for 75–80 per cent of the manufacturer's "suggested price". Retailers then sold the toys for the suggested price, deviating from it only rarely. Fragmented wholesalers served these shops. These wholesalers sold their products through a complex distribution system that typically involved between three and five layers of intermediaries. On the other hand, the business model of Toys "Я" Us is characterized by the lack of middlemen, larger size of the stores, great variety, and low price.

Toys "Я" Us began its international expansion in 1984, opening its first store in Canada. Once the company proved its success, it started a global expansion, opening stores in Singapore, Hong Kong, and Europe. The international business model was the same as the company used in the US: the stores resembled each other, and each store had a self-service supermarket format that offered a great variety of toys sold at low prices. Overcoming protests in some of the markets it expanded into, the company continued its global expansion, and by 1991 Toys "Я" Us had 97 international stores, accounting for 14 per cent of total revenues.

The company seemed to use a regional approach initially but then it moved into a "global" strategy. Since the business model that the company applied was exactly the same in all countries, Toys "Я" Us was located within the first quadrant of the Chapter 15 matrix where it had high economic benefits with low national responsiveness. In 1991, however, Toys "Я" Us faced a new challenge in entering the Japanese market. This new market represented great possibilities but also involved a high risk of failure, especially if the company did not change its business model.

Should Toys "Я" Us make changes in its international strategy in order to conquer challenges for its success in Japan? Should Toys "Я" Us shift its international strategy to a transnational strategy by making appropriate changes? Can it do so without damaging its firm-specific advantages in its "killer category" variety, novelty of toys and competitive prices?

A local partner was required to overcome the problems of Japanese culture and history being incompatible with the Toys "Я" Us business model. A strategic alliance with Den Fujita, who had successfully run McDonald's Japan, was critical for the success of Toys "Я" Us. He is the only Japanese business leader who has succeeded in bringing foreign retail business into the restrictive Japanese market, except for brand-oriented retailers with value-added prices such as Hermes and Louis Vuitton.

The alliance with Den Fujita may also help the Japanese government to allow Toys "Я" Us' expansion in Japan, because he is a powerful opinion leader who affects government policy making. US and Japanese negotiators have developed SII (Structural Impediments Initiative) to bring about the greater opening of the Japanese market to foreign players. Toys "Я" Us should build a closer relationship with the US government to take full advantage of SII.

Building close relationships with local manufacturers is critical in order for Toys "Я" Us Japan to realize its competitive prices and variety. Again, Den Fujita's influence in Japanese business is useful. Moreover, Toys "Я" Us can leverage its status as an international retailer to build relationships with Japanese manufacturers interested in international expansion. Building stores large enough to maintain the variety of toys is crucial. On the other hand, land prices in Japan are too high to have the same size of stores as in the US. Toys "Я" Us needs to determine an optimal size for Japanese stores that sustains its competitive advantage with reasonable rent expense.

As of 2001, Toys "Я" Us Japan has been a high success; it is the top toy retailer with approximately

10 per cent market share. The phrase "category killer", which represents foreign retailers with large stores and cheaper prices, was relevant to Toys "Я" Us' success in Japan. Toys "Я" Us Japan now has 111 stores and is planning to expand the number of stores to 200 by 2010. It also successfully completed its Initial Public Offering (IPO) in April 2000. Worldwide, Toys "Я" Us has 1,090 stores in the US (710 Toys "Я" Us and 380 other types such as Kids "Я" Us), and 491 stores in 27 countries, including 111 in Japan, 63 in the UK, and 51 in Germany. It has become a much more transnational company than it was in 1991.

Websites: ***www.toysrus.co.jp*** and ***inc.toysrus.com***.

Sources: Adapted from Debora L. Spar, "Toys 'Я' Us in Japan," Harvard Business School case 796–077, 1995; Debora L. Spar, "National Policies and Domestic Politics," in Alan M. Rugman and Thomas Brewer (eds), *The Oxford Handbook of International Business*, Oxford: Oxford University Press, 2001, pp. 206–231; Debora L. Spar, *Ruling the Waves* (New York: Harcourt, 2002).

1. **What are the firm-specific advantages of Toys "Я" Us?**
2. **What is the strategic risk for Toys "Я" Us in entering the Japanese market? What specific cultural and political barriers to entry does it face?**
3. **Why was Toys "Я" Us more successful in Japan than in the earlier case (in Chapter 16) dealing with Toys "Я" Us in Germany?**

REAL CASE

The Asian financial crisis

With the Asian financial crisis of 1997–1998, most of the Asian Tigers took a big blow. These countries had enjoyed phenomenal growth over the last decades and were models for industrial growth. But, in 1997, the Asian stock markets lost about $400 billion dollars in value. Malaysia, Indonesia, and Thailand were hit hardest and saw their currencies devalued by 33 per cent, 53 per cent, and 58 per cent respectively. In Indonesia, 500,000 jobs were lost in the construction business alone and similar unemployment burdened Malaysia and Thailand. Meanwhile, banks and corporations could not borrow money. Asia's banks had close to $200 billion of bad debts, without including Japan and China. The irony was that the financial system that had allowed these countries to grow was also one of the main reasons for the crisis. Some banks had been lending not on the basis of profitability but due to political ties and they expected the government to bail out any poorly performing companies.

Japan is the second largest economy in the world, and it is the economic center of the Asia Pacific region. Most Asian countries depend on it for trade and investment and 44 per cent of Japan's exports go to Asian Pacific countries. As the Asian region is interlocked, the Japanese financial system was also affected by the Asian crisis. The Japanese model of growth involves lending to handpicked companies at low interest rates in cooperation with the government. In 1997, bad debt in Japan was estimated to be in the range of $624 to $800 billion. By 1998 the yen had fallen to 147 to the US dollar compared with 80 to the US dollar in mid-1995.

Japan suffered a financial and real estate bust but has warded off an industrial one. The Japanese banks and insurance companies were riddled with bad debt. Tokyo City Bank, the 40th largest in Japan, and Sanyo Securities, among others, filed for bankruptcy in late 1997. The Japanese government, pressured by the crisis, had to open up its financial sector, and outside financial companies helped to upgrade the financial industry. Fidelity Investments partnered with three Japanese banks to sell mutual funds. Citibank is taking a big share of Japanese retail banking. GE Capital entered into a joint venture with an almost bankrupt Toho Mutual Life. Meanwhile, Merrill Lynch acquired a 2,000-branch network from one of Japan's largest brokerage firms, Yamaichi Securities, which went out of business during the crisis. The government also unveiled a $228 billion financial stabilization in 1998 to inject funds into the ailing banking system.

For their part, Japanese financial institutions are also changing their ways. Nomura Securities of Japan was considering selling off its huge portfolio of bank shares, thereby dismantling a traditional system of cross-share ownership that has defined business in Japan. Meanwhile, the Long-Term Credit Bank of Japan has cut its board of directors by two-thirds and its staff by 20 per cent for savings of

$1.6 billion. The liberalization is expected to make Japan's financial sector as free as that of Britain by the year 2001. After this shake-up things will never be the same in Japan.

Websites: ***www.citigroup.com***; ***www.ml.com*** and ***www.nomura.co.jp***.

Sources: Adapted from "Asia's Fall from Grace," *Economist*, April 12, 1997, pp. 32–36; Joshua Cooper Ramo, "When Currencies Collide," *Time.com*, August 24, 1998, Alan M. Rugman and Rory Knight, "A Regional Fix for Multinationals," *Global Finance*, vol. 12, no. 2 (December 1998), p. 30; Sandra Sugawara, "Japan Approves Bank Rescue Plan," *Washington Post*, February 17, 1998.

1. **How has the Asian financial crisis affected the Japanese banking system?**
2. **What was the role of Japanese banks in the *keiretsu* system?**
3. **Why are Western financial institutions investing in Japan?**

ENDNOTES

1 For more on this subject, see *Doing Business in Japan* (Japan: Price Waterhouse, 1998) and *Financial Times*, Country Surveys: Japan 2001 at ***http://surveys.ft.com/japan2001/***.

2 For more on Japan's political parties, see: Tim Ito, "Major Political Parties in Japan," *Washington Post*, July 1998.

3 Also, see Robert Neff, William J. Holstein and Amy Borrus, "Japan: Who's in Charge?" *Business Week*, April 25, 1994, pp. 48–49.

4 For more on Japan's elected prime minister and the Cabinet, see "New Japan Cabinet Causes Stir," *BBC.co.uk*, April 26, 2001.

5 The Asahi Shimbun, *Japan Almanac*, 2002.

6 David E. Sanger, "Tokyo's Tips for New York," *New York Times Magazine*, February 6, 1994, p. 29.

7 Noboru Yoshimura and Philip Anderson, *Inside the Kaisha* (Boston MA: Harvard Business School Press, 1997).

8 James C. Morgan and J. Jeffrey Morgan, *Cracking the Japanese Market* (New York: Free Press, 1991), p. 20.

9 Ibid., p. 68 and "Japan's Workaholic Culture," *BBC.co.uk*, April 4, 2000.

10 Much of this loyalty is not a result of culture but, rather, a result of guaranteed employment, as explained in Jeremiah J. Sullivan and Richard B. Peterson, "A Test of Theories Underlying the Japanese Lifetime Employment System," *Journal of International Business Studies*, vol. 22, no. 1 (First Quarter 1991), p. 94.

11 For an interesting comparative view, see John E. Rehfeld, "What Working for a Japanese Company Taught Me," *Harvard Business Review*, vol. 28, no. 6 (November/December 1990), pp. 167–176.

12 Jonathon Sapsford, "Japan's Banks Are Awash in Red Ink," *Wall Street Journal*, May 26, 1998, p. A 14.

13 David E. Sanger, "Japan's Bad Debt is Now Estimated Near $1 Trillion," *New York Times*, July 30, 1998, pp. A 1, 8.

14 Brian Bremner, "All Eyes on Japan's Teetering Economy," *Business Week Online*, September 17, 2001.

15 Ministry of Public Management, Home Affairs, Posts and Telecommunications, *Labour Force Survey*, January 30, 2001. For information on the monthly unemployment rates, that hit their highest in history at 5.4 per cent in November 2001, see: "Japan Jobless Rate Hits New High," *BBC.co.uk*, November 29, 2001.

16 "Fujitsu Says to Cut Workforce by 16,400," *CNN.com*, August 20, 2001 and Jonathan Sprague and Suvendrini Kakuchi, "Labor Pains," *AsiaWeek.com*, September 7, 2001.

17 Bill Spindle, "Japan's Weak GDP Suggests Little Hope Soon," *Wall Street Journal*, September 14, 1998, p. A 24.

18 Larry Holyoke, William Spindle and Neil Gross, "Doing the Unthinkable," *Business Week*, January 10, 1994, pp. 52–53.

19 Susan MacKnight, *Weekly Review of the Japan Economic Institute*, September 15, 2000.

20 "Wal-Mart to Buy some Japan Mycal Stores," *Forbes.com*, November 11, 2001.

21 "Retailing Revolution: Foreign Megastores Open Their First Japanese Outlets," *Japan Information Network: Trends in Japan*, February 6, 2001 (see: ***http://jin.jcic.or.jp/***).

22 For an overview of Japanese procurement policies, see Department of Foreign Affairs and International Trade (DFAIT) of Canada, *Japan – Summary Information on Government Procurement*, 2001 at (***www.dfait-maeci.gc.ca/ni-ka/business/procurement-e.asp***).

23 Robert S. Greenberger and Laura Johannes, "US Urges Japan to Further Open Its Film Market," *Wall Street Journal*, August 20, 1998, p. A 4.

24 Also, see Bill Spindle, "Japanese 'Big Bang' Is Leading to Big Boon for US High-Tech," *Wall Street Journal*, September 16, 1997, pp. A 1, 13; Asra Q. Nomani and Douglas A. Blackmon, "How Maneuvering by Airlines Shaped US–Japan Accord," *Wall Street Journal*, February 2, 1998, pp. A 1, 19; Martin Crutsinger, "Japan at Forefront in Deal to Lower Trade Barriers," *Miami Herald*, November 16, 1998, p. 6a.

25 Robert Steiner, "Tokyo Regains Its Place as a Finance Hub," *Wall Street Journal*, May 29, 1997, p. A 12.

26 See IMF, *Direction of Trade Statistics Yearbook, 2001*.

27 *Handy Facts on US–Japan Economic Relations* (Tokyo: Japan External Trade Organization, 1998).

28 Also, see Nagami Kishi, "How Foreign Firms Can Succeed," *Journal of Japanese Trade & Industry*, no. 6 (1990), pp. 12–14.

29 For more on Pharmacia in Japan, see ***www.pharmacia.co.jp/index_e.html***.

30 Also, see Mark Mason, "United States Direct Investment in Japan: Trends and Prospects," *California Management Review*, Fall 1992, pp. 98–115.

31 See ***www.jetro.go.jp/top/cat1/abjtr.html***.

32 Also, see Gale Eisenstadt, "Information Power," *Forbes*, June 21, 1993, pp. 171–172.

33 Sheryl WuDunn, "Japan Braces For Arrival of 'Big Bang'," *New York Times*, June 4, 1998, pp. C 1, 6.

34 Maki Tanikawa, "Shareholder Rights? In Japan?" *Business Week*, November 9, 1998, pp. 70, E 12.

35 Also, see Andrew Pollack, "Mazda Shows Improvement Under Ford's Leadership," *New York Times*, May 24, 1997, p. 22.

36 Morgan and Morgan (1991) n. 8 above, p. 187.

37 *Investment in Japan: Facts and Figures* (Tokyo: JETRO, 1998).

38 For more on Japanese banking and finance, see *Financial Times, Financial Times Surveys: Japanese Banking and Finance*, 2001.

39 "The Big Yen Headache," *BBC.co.uk*, June 11, 1998.

ADDITIONAL BIBLIOGRAPHY

Abegglen, James C. and Stalk, George. *Kaisha, the Japanese Corporation* (New York: Basic Books, 1985).

Balassa, Bela and Noland, Marcus. *Japan in the World Economy* (Washington DC: Institute for International Economics, 1988).

Bhappu, Anita D. "The Japanese Family: An Institutional Logic for Japanese Corporate Networks and Japanese Management," *Academy of Management Review*, vol. 25, no. 2 (April 2000).

Black, J. Stewart. "Work Role Transitions: A Study of American Expatriate Managers in Japan," *Journal of International Business Studies*, vol. 19, no. 2 (Summer 1988).

Brouthers, Lance Eliot and Werner, Steve. "Are the Japanese Good Global Competitors?" *Columbia Journal of World Business*, vol. 25, no. 3 (Fall 1990).

Burton, F. N. and Saelens, F. H. "Japanese Strategies for Serving Overseas Markets: The Case for Electronics," *Management International Review*, vol. 27, no. 4 (Fourth Quarter 1987).

Cutts, Robert L. "Capitalism in Japan: Cartels and Keiretsu," *Harvard Business Review*, vol. 70, no. 4 (July/August 1992).

Czinkota, Michael R. and Woronoff, Jon. *Unlocking Japan's Markets* (Chicago. Probus 1991).

Daniel, Shirley J. and Reitsperger, Wolf D. "Management Control Systems for JIT: An Empirical Comparison of Japan and the US," *Journal of International Business Studies*, vol. 22, no. 4 (Fourth Quarter 1991).

Dyer, Jeffrey H. and Ouchi, William G. "Japanese-Style Partnerships: Giving Companies a Competitive Edge," *Sloan Management Review*, vol. 35, no. 1 (Fall 1993).

Fahy, John and Taguchi, Fuyuki. "Reassessing the Japanese Distribution System," *Sloan Management Review*, vol. 36, no. 2 (Winter 1995).

Friedman, George and Lebard, Meredith. *The Coming War with Japan* (New York: St Martin's Press, 1991).

Gundling, Ernest. "Ethics and Working with the Japanese: The Entrepreneur and the 'Elite Course'," *California Management Review*, vol. 33, no. 3 (Spring 1991).

Hanssens, Dominique M. and Johansson, John K. "Rivalry as Synergy? The Japanese Automobile Companies' Export Expansion," *Journal of International Business Studies*, vol. 22, no. 3 (Third Quarter 1991).

Helper, Susan R. and Sako, Mari. "Supplier Relations in Japan and the United States: Are They Converging?" *Sloan Management Review*, vol. 36, no. 3 (Spring 1995).

Johansson, Johny K. and Nonaka, Ikujiro. "Market Research the Japanese Way," *Harvard Business Review*, vol. 65, no. 3 (May/June 1987).

Johnson, Chalmers. "Comparative Capitalism: The Japanese Difference," *California Management Review*, vol. 35, no. 4 (Summer 1993).

Johnson, Jean L., Sakano, Tomoaki and Onzo, Naoto. "Behavioural Relations in Across-Culture Distribution System: Influence, Control and Conflict in US–Japanese Marketing Channel," *Journal of International Business Studies*, vol. 21, no. 4 (Fourth Quarter 1990).

Kaikati, Jack G. "Don't Crack the Japanese Distribution System – Just Circumvent It," *Columbia Journal of World Business*, vol. 28, no. 2 (Summer 1993).

Kearns, Robert L. *Zaibatsu America* (New York: Free Press, 1992).

Kotabe, Masaaki and Omura, Glenn S. "Sourcing Strategies of European and Japanese Multinationals: A Comparison," *Journal of International Business Studies*, vol. 20, no. 1 (Spring 1989).

Kriger, Mark P. and Solomon, Esther E. "Strategic Mindsets and Decision-Making Autonomy in US and Japanese MNCs," *Management International Review*, vol. 32, no. 4 (Fourth Quarter 1992).

Lee, Jangho, Roehl, Thomas W. and Choe, Soonkyoo. "What Makes Management Style Similar and Distinct Across Borders? Growth, Experience and Culture in Korean and Japanese Firms, *Journal of International Business Studies*, vol. 31, no. 4 (Winter 2000).

Makino, Shige and Neupert, Kent E. "National Culture, Transaction Costs, and the Choice Between Joint Venture and Wholly Owned Subsidiary," *Journal of International Business Studies*, vol. 31, no. 4 (Winter 2000).

Mason, Mark. "United States Direct Investment in Japan: Trends and Prospects," *California Management Review*, vol. 35, no. 1 (Fall 1992).

McMillan, Charles J. *The Japanese Industrial System* (Berlin: Walter de Gruyter, 1984).

Mirza, Hafix, Buckley, Peter J. and Weir, David T. H. "European Direct Investment in Japan," *Management International Review*, vol. 35, no. 1 (First Quarter 1995).

Morita, Akio. "Partnering for Competitiveness: The Role of Japanese Business," *Harvard Business Review*, vol. 70, no. 3 (May/June 1992).

Mowery, David C. and Teece, David J. "Japan's Growing Capabilities in Industrial Technology: Implications for US Managers and Policymakers," *California Management Review*, vol. 35, no. 2 (Winter 1993).

Nishiguchi, Toshihiro and Brookfield, Jonathan. "The Evolution of Japanese Subcontracting," *Sloan Management Review*, vol. 39, no. 3 (Fall 1997).

Rugman, Alan M. and Anderson, Andrew. "Japanese and Canadian Direct Investment in the United States," *Singapore Economic Review*, vol. 26, no. 2 (October 1991).

Rugman, Alan M., Brown, Lee and Verbeke, Alain. "Japanese Joint Ventures with Western Multinationals: Synthesizing the Economic and Cultural Explanations of Failure," *Asia-Pacific Journal of Management*, vol. 6, no. 2 (April 1989).

Rugman, Alan M. and Verbeke, Alain. "Trade Policy for the Asia-Pacific Region: A US–Japan Comparison," *Journal of Business Administration*, vol. 17, nos. 1–2 (1987/88).

Taylor, Sully and Napier, Nancy. "Working in Japan: Lessons from Women Expatriates," *Sloan Management Review*, vol. 37, no. 1 (Spring 1996).

Tezuka, Hiroyuki. "Success as the Source of Failure? Competition and Cooperation in the Japanese Economy," *Sloan Management Review*, vol. 38, no. 2 (Winter 1997).

Tyson, Laura D'Andrea. *Who's Bashing Whom?: Trade Conflict in High Technology Industries* (Washington DC: Institute for Research in International Economics, 1992).

Westney, D. Eleanor. *Imitation and Innovation* (Cambridge MA: Harvard University Press, 1987).

Yoshino, M. Y. and Lifson, Thomas B. *The Invisible Link* (Cambridge MA: MIT Press, 1986).

Chapter 18

North America

CONTENTS

OBJECTIVES OF THE CHAPTER

The US, Canada, and Mexico constitute a thriving economic bloc. Over 32 per cent of all US trade is with Canada and Mexico; both of these countries conduct well over 75 per cent of their international trade with the US (see Tables 18.1, 18.2, and 18.3). Yet Canada and Mexico are very different from the US and both have distinctive business practices. Doing business in these countries requires just as much research and attention to institutional detail as doing business in the EU or Japan.

The specific objectives of this chapter are to:

1. *Examine* the nature of the Canadian and Mexican political and economic systems and their implications for business strategy.
2. *Review* the business environment with primary attention on the industrial, regulatory, banking and finance, and labor relations areas.
3. *Investigate* major economic opportunities that exist in Canada and Mexico and some of the ways of conducting business in these nations.
4. *Consider* specific institutional arrangements, namely, the United States–Canada Free Trade Agreement (FTA) and the North American Free Trade Agreement (NAFTA), which play an important role in shaping opportunities and the business environment in North America.

ACTIVE LEARNING CASE

The Free Trade Area of the Americas builds on NAFTA

The United States–Canada Free Trade Agreement (FTA) of 1989 had a dramatic effect on the strategies of many companies in both countries. One of the most common developments was a consolidation of operations, improving the efficiency of production and distribution in the more integrated market. But many inefficient Canadian plants of uneconomic size closed down.

As a result, some Canadians worry that Canada will be unable to take advantage of the benefits of free trade between the two countries, and that US business will dominate the market. Canadian unions, in particular, are strongly opposed to the FTA; they attribute plant closings and layoffs caused by the recession of 1990 to 1992 solely to the FTA. On the other hand, many individuals argue that these are only short-run setbacks and that in the long run the economies of both countries will benefit from free trade. They also point out that most people are relatively immobile and will continue to buy goods made in their own country. Thus the likelihood of US firms dominating the Canadian economy is remote. Additionally, they point out that the market for Canadian goods in the US is much larger than the market for US goods in Canada. So Canadians have more to gain than to lose from the FTA. In practice, the depreciation of the Canadian dollar by over 25 per cent in the 1990s kept Canadian manufacturing going as an export supplier to the US, particularly in the auto sector.

The signing of the North American Free Trade Agreement (NAFTA) in 1993 has extended the FTA to include Mexico. The NAFTA has helped Mexico to continue to open up its markets to free trade and has helped to increase its rate of economic growth. The country is also doing well in attracting outside investment by such major firms as General Motors and DaimlerChrysler, which have collectively invested well over $500 million there.

Over the past five years triad countries have been setting up operations in Mexico to tap a growing local market. The Mexican middle and upper classes are spending more, especially on big ticket items. US autos, which often cost three times as much as they do in the US, are a popular purchase. Moreover, although Japanese cars sell well in most places, many Mexicans prefer US-made products; Japanese are seen as lower status in Mexico. Many other retail businesses such as clothing and home appliances are seeing equal growth.

Talks are also under way for a Free Trade Area of the Americas (FTAA). This will build in the principles of NAFTA, which eliminated tariffs and introduced the principle of national treatment for foreign direct investment. In 2001, at the Quebec City Summit, the US government sought to renew negotiations with Latin American countries, which had not progressed very far since the Miami Summit in 1991. This was received with mixed feelings by Latin American countries, but it was agreed to launch the FTAA in 2005. Brazil is hesitant to joint the FTAA, but most other countries are keen to access the huge US market. Some misinformed antiglobalization groups have emerged to protest at what they perceive as an imperialist move that will strengthen US multinationals at the expense of local interests. Others share in the dislike of US farm subsidies and of clauses intended to protect labor and environmental laws.

US farm subsidies hinder free trade in one of the industries in which developing countries have a competitive advantage. Not surprisingly the US agricultural sector opposes eliminating these subsidies and counter argues (on a triad basis) that, since Japanese and EU subsidies would not be removed at the same time, they would face a competitive disadvantage. Yet, whether or not the EU and Japan eliminate subsidies, the agricultural sector will be heavily hit by the entry of competitive agricultural products from developing countries.

Latin American countries are also suspicious of US-led clauses on labor and environmental protection (which the US Congress insists on). They argue that these clauses might be used more as non-tariff barriers to trade than as genuine labor and environmental protection. Nonetheless, if countries of the Americas successfully negotiate the FTAA it would create the largest trade block in the world encompassing 738 million people from Canada to Chile. Indeed, given the success of the EU, and the logic of the triad, an FTAA is inevitable.

Sources: Stephen Baker, Elizabeth Weinger and Mike Zellner, "Can Latin America Move from the Third World to the First?" *Business Week*, October 21, 1991, pp. 54–56; Louis R. Richman, "How NAFTA Will Help America," *Fortune*, April 19, 1993, pp. 95–102; John Urquhart, "Canada Pursues Latin American Trade," *Wall Street Journal*, November 7, 1997, p. A 15; Jonathan Friedland and Joseph B. White, "GM Is Leading an Investment Boom in Mexico," *Wall Street Journal*, December 24, 1998, pp. A 5–6; "FTAA Talks Enter Cyclical Stage," *BBC.co.uk*, April 6, 2001; "Brazil Skeptical of Free Trade Deal," *BBC.co.uk*, April 19, 2001; "United States Singled Out as World's Largest Polluter in Hague Conference," *CNN.com*, November 20, 2000.

1. **How did the Free Trade Agreement help the Canadian economy?**
2. **Will NAFTA see an increase in exports between the US and Canada? Why or why not?**
3. **In what way is Mexico's economic progress creating a market for US products?**
4. **Will an FTAA lead to increased trade in the Americas; why or why not?**
5. **Should environmental laws be included in the FTAA, and why or why not?**

Table 18.1 Direction of US trade

	Exports to				*Imports from*			
	1991		*2000*		*1991*		*2000*	
Country/region	*(billions of US $)*	*% of total*	*(billions of US $)*	*% of total*	*(billions of US $)*	*% of total*	*(billions of US $)*	*% of total*
Canada	85.1	20.2	174.6	22.6	93.8	18.4	229.2	18.5
Mexico	33.3	7.9	108.8	14.1	31.9	6.3	135.1	10.9
Japan	48.1	11.4	64.5	8.4	95.0	18.7	149.5	12.1
EU*	108.4	25.7	164.6	21.3	96.6	19.0	223.3	18.0
All others	275.0	65.2	512.5	66.4	317.3	62.3	737.1	59.5
Total	421.7	100.0	772.0	100.0	509.3	100.0	1,238.2	100.0

* EU refers to the European Economic Community for 1991 and the European Union for 2000.

Source: IMF, *Direction of Trade Statistics Yearbook, 1996, 2000.*

Table 18.2 Direction of Canada's trade

	Exports to				*Imports from*			
	1991		*2000*		*1991*		*2000*	
Country/region	*(billions of US $)*	*% of total*	*(billions of US $)*	*% of total*	*(billions of US $)*	*% of total*	*(billions of US $)*	*% of total*
United States	95.6	75.8	240.7	87.0	75.0	62.3	153.7	64.4
EU*	10.3	8.1	12.3	4.4	15.1	12.6	24.8	10.4
Japan	6.2	4.9	5.9	2.1	8.9	7.4	11.2	4.7
Triad	112.0	88.8	258.9	93.6	99.0	82.2	189.7	79.4
Mexico	0.4	0.3	1.4	0.5	2.3	1.9	7.7	3.2
All others	13.7	10.9	16.4	5.9	19.1	15.8	41.4	17.3
Total†	126.2	100.0	276.7	100.0	120.5	100.0	238.9	100.0

* EU for 1987 refers to 12 countries in the EC; EU for 1996 includes Sweden, Finland, and Austria, which joined in 1995.
† Numbers might not add up to totals and percentages might not add up to 100 due to rounding.

Source: IMF, *Direction of Trade Statistics Yearbook, 1996, 2000.*

Table 18.3 Direction of Mexico's trade

Country/region	*Exports to*				*Imports from*			
	1991		*2000*		*1991*		*2000*	
	(billions of US $)	*% of total*	*(billions of US $)*	*% of total*	*(billions of US $)*	*% of total*	*(billions of US $)*	*% of total*
United States	18.7	69.5	147.7	88.7	24.6	64.6	127.5	73.1
Canada	0.6	2.1	3.4	2.0	0.8	2.0	4.1	2.3
North America*	19.3	71.6	151.0	90.7	25.4	66.7	131.6	75.4
Western hemisphere†	2.0	7.4	6.5	3.9	1.9	5.0	5.4	3.1
EU‡	3.4	12.5	5.6	3.4	6.8	17.8	16.3	9.3
Japan	1.2	4.6	0.9	0.6	2.1	5.4	6.5	3.7
Other Asia	0.3	1.0	1.2	0.7	1.2	3.0	13.7	7.8
All others	0.8	2.9	1.2	0.7	0.8	2.1	1.1	0.6
Total	26.9	100.0	166.5	100.0	38.1	100.0	174.5	100.0

* Excluding Mexico.
† Excluding Mexico, Canada, and the US.
‡ EU for 1987 refers to 12 countries in the EC; EU for 1996 includes Sweden, Finland, and Austria, which joined in 1995.

Source: IMF, *Direction of Trade Statistics Yearbook, 1996, 2000.*

INTRODUCTION

In Chapter 15 we saw that governments and the various institutions through which they wield their powers are important external factors in the international business environment. This chapter will focus on institutional factors in the North American market that must be considered when looking at the Canadian and Mexican markets. The North American Free Trade Agreement (NAFTA) has not abolished all trading barriers between the US, Canada, and Mexico. There are still major impediments to trade and investment. Furthermore, each of the partners retains its own trade laws. A legal mechanism to appeal trade decisions exists, but this is a compromise position. In contrast, EU member states cannot use trade laws against their partners. So although NAFTA is a step toward trade liberalization, business decisions should not assume that "free trade" makes Canada and Mexico identical to the US.

CANADA

Canada, with a land area of almost 3.6 million square miles, is second in size only to Russia. The country is divided into 10 provinces and three territories (see accompanying map). Canada is so large that it encompasses four time zones. The French and British fought over the country, with control passing into British hands in 1763. Canada became a separate nation in 1867, although it did not fully repatriate its constitution until 1982. Today it remains a leading member of the British Commonwealth.

Canada's economy

Canada's 32 million people enjoy one of the highest standards of living in the world. Consumer tastes and disposable wealth in Canada are very similar to those in the US.

Approximately two-thirds of all families own their own homes, and large percentages own durable goods such as radios (99 per cent), refrigerators (99 per cent), telephones (97 per cent), washing machines (77 per cent), and videocassette recorders (25 per cent).

Gross domestic product in 2000 was about $775 billion, in US dollars and at purchasing parity. The rate of economic growth during the 1990s was in the 2–3 per cent range for most years, partly as a result of a major recession in the early 1990s. In the later part of the 1990s, GDP growth was in the 3–4 per cent range. Canada has typically had a positive balance of payments, thanks to its food, energy, and motor vehicle exports. Canada's primary trading partner is the US, which provided over 64 per cent of Canada's imports and accounted for 87 per cent of the country's exports in 2000 (see Table 18.2).

Canada's economic growth has been historically based on the export of agricultural staples, especially grains, and on the production and export of natural resource products such as minerals, oil, gas, and forest products. However, major secondary industries have also emerged; Canada now ranks as one of the top 10 manufacturing nations of the world. The service industry is also expanding rapidly, especially financial services in Toronto. However, the country still faces a major productivity challenge. Recent studies show that Canada's productivity growth is threatening to draw down the nation's standard of living for decades to come.[1]

Almost 80 per cent of manufacturing activity is located in Ontario and Quebec, including the entire motor vehicle industry, which is Canada's largest segment, while Calgary has now become a major high-tech center.[2] Almost one-quarter of all Canada's exports (and imports) are in autos and auto-related products. The Canada–United States Automotive Products Trade Agreement (Autopact) has encouraged this two-way trade over the last 35 years. This allowed free trade in autos assembled in Canada or the US, provided there was 50 per cent value added in Canada. (Under the NAFTA the content provision increased to 62.5 per cent.) Financial institutions and other business service industries are also concentrated in central Canada. The eastern and western areas of the country are more dependent on primary industries: fishing, forestry, and mining in the east; agriculture, ore, and mineral fuels in the west. Canada's growth was helped by large inflows of FDI; today 40 per cent of the primary and secondary industries are foreign-owned. Yet Canada is wealthy enough now, and its economy is sufficiently mature, to have substantial outward FDI, particularly in the US.

The US has more FDI in Canada than in any other country, including Great Britain. Since 1988 this investment has doubled, and today it stands at about $126 billion. At the same time Canada has invested $101 billion in the US, more than in any other country.[3] We can see these relationships within individual industries. For example, many US airlines, including American, Delta, and Northwest, fly to Canada, and Air Canada and Canadian Airlines, which recently merged, among others, have US routes. So part of the US international airline strategy involves competing with Canadian carriers that are vying for the US market (see the box "International Business Strategy in Action: Open Skies"). There are many other examples of Canadian investment in the US. Canadian Pacific has purchased the Delaware & Hudson Railway and Bombardier Inc. bought the Learjet Corporation of Wichita, Kansas. Many other acquisitions are even larger.

INTERNATIONAL BUSINESS STRATEGY *IN ACTION*

Open Skies

Over the past few years US and Canadian airline carriers have begun to try to improve their competitive positions through a series of alliances. For example, Air Canada has become part of Star Alliance, a collection of 15 international airlines – including United Airlines from the US – that account for 21 per cent of the global market. Similarly, prior to merging with Air Canada in 2000, Canadian Airlines had joined American Airlines and its code-sharing partners around the world in the Oneworld alliance. This is a result of a trend that is grouping the international airline business into several large alliances to compete against each other.

For the North American Airline market this means an increase in efficiency. In 1993 US carriers were authorized to serve only 44 routes in Canada, and Canadian carriers had a mere 28 routes in the US. A study at the time revealed that, if the skies between the two countries were allowed to open up, air traffic would double within the next few years. The study also estimated that the resulting increase in tourism and trade would generate $10.3 billion in additional economic activity. These statistics indicate why a new Open Skies agreement between the countries was enacted in 1995. The agreement liberalized the regulatory environment for airlines in both countries. Since the establishment of Open Skies in 1995, transborder traffic has increased from 13 million passengers in 1994 to 20 million in 2000. Nonetheless, the 1995 treaty comes short of a full Open Skies agreement because of restrictions on cargo and third country rights.

As the North American Free Trade Agreement (NAFTA) also came into effect on January 1, 1994, there was a further incentive to liberalize trade in services such as airline travel. However, under the restricted transportation provisions of NAFTA, national treatment does not apply. This means that a US airline can only do business across the Canadian borders on a point-to-point basis, from, say, La Guardia in New York to Toronto. It cannot pick up any passengers within Canada. Similarly, Air Canada can fly from Montreal to New York to Miami, but it cannot compete with US airlines on the internal US New York to Miami route.

Despite the lack of national treatment, since the Open Skies agreement, Air Canada has doubled its flights to the US and more than tripled its number of routes. Today, Air Canada handles over 40 per cent of the Canada–US traffic and it attributes close to 3,000 new jobs to the agreement. Air travel was further eased in 1998 by a bilateral agreement to facilitate preclearance of customs and immigration services. This will reduce double inspections by customs and immigration officers in both countries. The large success of these agreements has led both governments to negotiate similar agreements with other countries around the globe.

Websites: ***www.aircanada.com*** *and* ***www.oneworldalliance.com***.

Sources: Adapted from William C. Synods and Seth Payne, "Clear the Air Between the US and Canada," *Business Week*, June 21, 1993, p. 59; Randall Litchfield, "Sacred Cows of Nationhood," *Canadian Business*, January 1993, p. 13; Claude I. Taylor, "Critical Mass, Competitiveness and the New Economic Order," *Canadian Business Review*, Spring 1992, pp. 38–40; Alan M. Rugman, *Foreign Investment and NAFTA* (Columbia SC: University of South Carolina Press, 1994); ***www.aircanada.ca***; Air Canada, "Air Canada President and CEO Urges U.S. AirLine CEOs Towards Further Liberalization of U.S.–Canada Market," Press Release, December 13, 2001; Canada, Ministry of Transportation, *Canada Transportation Act Review*, July 18, 2001.

Active learning check

Review your answer to Active Learning Case question 1 and make any changes you like. Then compare your answer with the one below.

1. How did the Free Trade Agreement help the Canadian economy?

The Free Trade Agreement will eliminate tariffs and make it easier for efficient Canadian firms to operate competitively in the US. At the same time the Agreement will allow efficient US firms to ship their goods into Canada without paying any tariffs and, in the process, will help to drive down prices. So the Free Trade Agreement can help the Canadian economy by encouraging efficiency, lowering prices, and opening up new markets in the US.

Differences in the business environment

Although there are many similarities between the business environments of the US and Canada, there are also some important differences.

Canada's industrial climate

The Canadian economy is characterized by private enterprise. However, some industries, such as broadcasting and public utilities, are government-owned or subject to substantial government regulation.[4] Over the last decade the trend has been toward privatization and deregulation. In fact, there is a federal government minister who oversees privatization; this individual has been responsible for selling companies that the government feels are no longer essential to meet public policy goals. Firms that have been privatized in include Canadair, the deHavilland Aircraft Company, Canadian National Railway's trucking division, Fisheries Products International, and Air Canada.

Small business is a major part of the economy and accounts for almost 80 per cent of all new employment in manufacturing. The service and retail trade industries are characterized by a large number of companies that vary in size. Seventy per cent of Canadians work in service industries.

Canada's regulatory environment

Commerce and industry in Canada is regulated at every level of government: federal, provincial, and municipal. Many of these regulations are similar to those in the US.

Competition Act
A Canadian federal law which regulates anticompetitive practices and prohibits actions that will substantially lessen or prevent competition; it is similar to US antitrust laws

Competition Regulation of competition is under the jurisdiction of the federal Parliament. Legislation in this area was revised in the late 1980s in order to eliminate restrictive trade policies, to stimulate production, and to promote the international competitiveness of Canadian business. Although there are no price controls in Canada, there is regulation to review monopolies, acquisitions, and mergers. The regulation of anticompetitive practices is handled under the **Competition Act**. This Act prohibits individuals and companies from practices that will substantially lessen or prevent competition in the marketplace. The Act outlaws bid-rigging, price discrimination, or conspiring to unduly lessen competition. It also provides for regulation of acquisitions and mergers. If the purchase price is $400 million or more, the parties must refrain from completing the transaction for a time period ranging from 7 to 21 days. During this time the government will review the situation and decide if the purchase will prevent or lessen competition (using international comparisons) and thus be non-competitive in nature. A ruling will then be made.

Active learning check 

Review your answer to Active Learning Case question 2 and make any changes you like. Then compare your answer with the one below.

2. Will NAFTA see an increase in exports between the US and Canada? Why or why not?

In the future, US–Canada trade will increase as a result of NAFTA. Three reasons can be cited. First, the elimination of all tariffs under the FTA is going to encourage exports. Second, under the FTA arrangements both countries are more likely to produce those goods and services for which they have a competitive advantage and to buy the others from their neighbor. Third, as the economies of the two countries grow, so will the amount of trade as each begins to adapt operations to the desires of the other and starts to tap this market further.

Exports and imports Export permits are required for the shipment of goods having strategic value, such as uranium. They are also required to implement the provisions of various international agreements into which Canada has entered. Import documentation is also required, as well as payment of a goods and sales tax (GST).[5] This tax, which went into effect on January 1, 1991, is a value-added tax. On imports, this tax is collected by Canadian Customs. The GST was set at 7 per cent of the value of the goods plus any import duties.[6]

Francization in Quebec The Canadian federal government has a bilingual policy.[7] But in the province of Quebec, French is the official language for business and education. All firms employing 50 or more employees in Quebec must use French at all levels of the organization. Other regulations related to the use of French in Quebec are that (1) all product labels must be in French; translations cannot be given greater prominence than the French portion; (2) company names and signs must be in French, but a version of the firm's name in another language may accompany the French version for use outside Quebec; and (3) all signs on the outside of stores must be in French only.[8] In addition, all education, health services, and all other services under provincial jurisdiction are delivered in French. Some exceptions to the French language and sign law policies accommodate the one-fifth of the Quebec population that speaks English. For example, McGill University and Concordia University can operate in English, and English signs can be displayed inside stores, provided they are smaller than French signs.[9]

Banking and finance

Banks in Canada offer a full range of financial services. There are six large Canadian chartered banks with extensive national branch networks that account for 90 per cent of the nation's banking industry assets. There also many smaller (often foreign-owned) banks.[10] These banks respond to the actions of the central bank, the Bank of Canada. This federal government institution is directly responsible for the nation's monetary policy, including (1) regulating credit and currency, (2) controlling and protecting the external value of the Canadian dollar, and (3) regulating the general level of production, trade, prices, and employment, within the scope of monetary policy.

In carrying out its functions, the Bank of Canada buys and sells foreign exchange and sets the interest rate that is charged to commercial banks. These functions are similar to those carried out by the Federal Reserve in the US, which helps to monitor the US monetary system. The Bank of Canada is also responsible for issuing the country's notes and coins and for managing the federal debt. Canadian interest rates and its exchange rate closely follow those set in the US, especially in relation to non-North American interest and exchange rates.

Banks operate within the confines of the Bank Act. There are two types of banks: Schedule A and Schedule B. Schedule A banks are Canadian-owned and no shareholder has more than 10 per cent of the voting stock. Schedule B banks are closely held Canadian-owned or foreign banks. These are allowed to carry on normal banking activities. However, foreign-owned banks cannot, as a group, own more than 16 per cent of the total domestic assets of the Canadian banking system. Subsidiaries of US banks are not subject to this restriction because of the United States–Canada Free Trade Agreement. In addition, Canadian banks are allowed to operate across the country.

There is also a host of specialized financial institutions that provide limited services throughout the provinces. Examples include savings banks, cooperative credit unions, loan companies, mortgage companies, and insurance companies. Investment bankers provide short-term funds to companies for acquisition or reorganization purposes.

Canada has four major stock exchanges: Toronto, Montreal, Vancouver, and Calgary. Toronto is the major exchange; it accounts for approximately 95 per cent of dollar trading volume. Toronto is also the financial center of the country.[11]

Labor relations

Labor relations are governed by both federal and provincial labor legislation. The **Canada Labor Code** is the federal law that covers such matters as wages, employment practices, work safety, and conciliation in the event of a labor dispute. Province governments have similar laws to cover employer–employee relations at the local level.

Canada Labor Code
A federal law that covers areas such as wages, employment practices, work safety, and conciliation of labor disputes

Unions With the exception of farmers, domestic help, and white-collar workers, the work force is heavily unionized. Approximately 30 per cent of the total labor force is unionized, in contrast to approximately 13.5 per cent in the US.[12] In some instances the workers are free to choose or reject union membership. In other cases they must become members in order to keep their jobs. The labor–management contract determines these conditions.

As in the US, once a union has been certified to represent the workers, management must bargain in good faith. The result of such bargaining is a labor–management agreement that determines wage rates, fringe benefits, working conditions, and management rights. Economic nationalism is a strong component of Canadian unionization, and the unions have been major opponents of the FTA, NAFTA and other economic and political relationships with the US.

Active learning check 

Review your answer to Active Learning Case question 3 and make any changes you like. Then compare your answer with the one below.

3. In what way is Mexico's economic progress creating a market for US products?

Mexico's progress under the NAFTA will create a market for US goods in that, as the middle and upper classes in the country increase their purchasing power, they will turn more and more to the purchase of US-made goods. From cars to television sets to home appliances, Mexican consumers will be buying products sold by US MNEs. Additionally, the sale of these goods will create increased interest in Mexico by US multinationals, and this will mean even greater opportunities for US firms – and Mexican consumers. The elimination of tariffs under the NAFTA ties Mexico into the North American triad.

Working conditions All provinces have legislated minimum wage rates and they are periodically adjusted. However, in most sectors wages and salaries are similar to US levels.

There is a national compulsory contributory pension plan that provides retirement benefits to contributors, generally at the age of 65. This age limit varies, however, and there is growing pressure to relax mandatory retirement rules.[13] In addition, many private pension plans are in effect. Other benefits include group life insurance, medical insurance, and subsidized food and housing. Most provincial legislation limits daily or weekly working hours, with mandatory overtime pay for hours worked in excess of these limits. The government also mandates minimum annual paid vacations in almost all industries. This typically is two weeks following one year of employment and increases up to three or four weeks after longer employment. There are also legislated holidays, which, depending on the city and the province, usually vary between 8 and 12 days.

All provinces prohibit employment discrimination on the basis of race, religion, national origin, color, sex, age, or marital status. There are also equal pay for equal work provisions, which vary across provinces. They are designed to prevent gender bias in pay levels, and in recent years Canada has taken significant strides in reducing the earnings gap between men and women who do the same types of work.[14] For example, Ontario has specific "pay equity" legislation that requires employers to remove gender bias in pay levels; salary adjustments were phased in, starting in 1990. Similar legislation has been enacted in a number of other provinces, including Quebec and Saskatchewan.

Investments

Investment Canada Act (ICA)
An act designed to create a welcome climate for foreign investment by significantly loosening previous restrictions

The **Investment Canada Act (ICA)** came into effect on June 30, 1985 and is designed to create a welcome climate for foreign investment by significantly loosening previous restrictions. At the same time, however, some regulations still remain in effect. As noted earlier, investments in certain industries are restricted. For example, a license to operate a broadcasting station can be granted only to a Canadian citizen or corporation whose stock is 80 per cent owned by Canadian citizens or Canadian-controlled corporations. Generally, non-residents cannot hold more than 25 per cent of the issued and outstanding shares of a chartered bank, a life insurance company, a sales finance company, a loan company, or a trust company. Nor can a single non-resident together with his or her associates hold more than 10 per cent of the issued and outstanding shares of these types of companies. Limits are much less stringent in the securities industry, but the government must be kept apprised of such ownership.

Under the ICA a non-Canadian wishing to acquire a Canadian firm must make an application to the ICA for review and approval, if the assets are valued at more than $5 million or the business relates to Canada's cultural heritage or national identity. In the case of US firms buying Canadian operations, under the provisions of the Free Trade Agreement, the ICA review takes place at the $150 million level. So the investment climate is much more conducive to US investors than to any others. When the ICA does conduct a review, a number of factors are considered in determining whether the investment will benefit Canada. These include employment, technological benefits, and product innovation.

In addition, there are numerous provincial statutes that place restrictions on foreigners seeking to invest in particular industries or activities. For example, in most provinces individuals have to be Canadian residents for at least a year in order to be registered securities dealers. Similarly, foreigners who are registering ownership of land must disclose their citizenship. In Alberta, British Columbia, Manitoba, Ontario, and Saskatchewan, a majority of the board of directors of corporations must be resident Canadians. However, an indirect takeover of a foreign-owned publisher will require that the firm be sold to a Canadian owner, according to the "Baie Comeau policy".

Canada's multinationals

It is useful to identify Canada's major companies against the background of global competition and triad power. Some larger Canadian companies like Nortel Networks and Bombardier are well known in the US.

Table 18.4 ranks the 20 largest Canadian-owned companies in decreasing order of size measured by their sales in 2000. The largest firm, Nortel Networks, with sales of

Table 18.4 The largest Canadian-owned companies by size

Rank	*Firm*	*Industry*	*2000 sales (in millions of Canadian $)*	*F/T**
1	Nortel Networks	High-tech manufacturing	44,958	0.95
2	Onex	Conglomerates	24,531	0.77
3	CIBC	Banks	23,124	0.33
4	Royal Bank of Canada	Banks	22,841	NA
5	George Weston	Conglomerates	22,344	0.07
6	TransCanada Pipelines	Gas/electrical utilities	21,156	0.38
7	Toronto-Dominion Bank	Banks	20,075	NA
8	Bank of Nova Scotia	Banks	18,996	0.37
9	Bank of Montreal	Banks	18,629	NA
10	BCE	Telecommunications	18,094	0.11
11	Power Corp. of Canada	Conglomerates	16,906	0.36
12	Sun Life Financial Services of Canada	Diversified financials	16,206	0.76
13	Canadian Pacific	Conglomerates	16,102	0.53
14	Bombardier	Information technology	16,101	0.90
15	Magna International	Motor vehicles and parts	15,612	0.64
16	Manulife Financial	Diversified financials	14,152	0.66
17	Alcan Aluminium	Mining	13,585	0.93
18	Hydro-Québec	Gas/electrical utilities	11,429	0.22
19	Empire	Food and drugstores	11,164	NA
20	Quebecor	Multimedia	10,915	NA
Average			18,846	
Total			376,919	

* F/T refers to foreign exports and sales divided by total sales.

Source: Adapted from "The Financial Post 500," *National Post*, 2001.

Table 18.5 The largest foreign-owned companies in Canada, by size

Rank	*Firm*	*Industry*	*2000 sales (in millions of Canadian $)*	*F/T**	*Ownership*
1	General Motors of Canada	Motor vehicles and parts	42,015	NA	US (100)
2	Ford Motor Co. of Canada	Motor vehicles and parts	24,638	0.68	US (100)
3	Seagram Co.	Conglomerates	23,105	0.97	France (100)
4	DaimlerChrysler Canada	Motor vehicles and parts	21,902	NA	US (100)
5	Imperial Oil	Oil and gas production	16,635	0.16	US (70)
6	Honda Canada	Motor vehicles and parts	8,900	0.60	Japan (100)
7	Shell Canada	Oil and gas production	8,100	NA	Netherlands (78)
8	Canadian Ultramar	Oil and gas production	6,406	NA	US (100)
9	Sears Canada	General merchandisers	6,356	NA	US (55)
10	IBM Canada	High-tech manufacturing	5,700	NA	US (100)
11	Canadian National Railway	Transportation/courier	5,428	0.33	Foreign (60)
12	Canada Safeway	Food and drugstores	5,122	NA	US (100)
13	Husky Energy	Oil and gas production	5,090	NA	Barbados (68)
14	Inco	Mining	4,328	0.98	US (55)
15	Medis Health and Pharmaceutical Services	Wholesalers/distribuitors	4,072	NA	US (100)
16	Mitsui of Canada	Chemicals and fertilizers	3,716	NA	Japan (100)
17	Cargill	Agriculture	3,527	0.70	US (100)
18	Costco	General merchandisers	3,436	NA	US (100)
19	Great Atlantic and Pacific Co of Canada	Food and drugstores	3,202	NA	US (100)
20	Toyota Canada	Motor vehicles and parts	3,186	NA	Japan (100)
Average			10,243		
Total			204,864		

* F/T refers to foreign exports and sales divided by total sales.

Source: Adapted from "The Financial Post 500," *National Post*, 2001.

nearly $45 billion, is widely recognized as being one of Canada's most successful multinationals, although its stock price plunged in 2001 due to the dot.com bust and the overcapacity of telecom lines. With revenues of $24.5 billion, Onex Corporation is a global conglomerate that operates in multiple industries, including sugar refining, investment, telecommunications, and automotive parts. Other well-known Canadian industrial multinationals at the top of the list are BCE, Bombardier, and Magna International.

Table 18.5 lists the 20 largest foreign-owned firms in Canada. These firms also contribute to the performance of the country, creating jobs and wealth for Canadians. However, all foreign-owned firms must be examined in terms of their relationship to their parent firms. A high degree of autonomy, or development of world-class products in Canada, is necessary for a foreign-owned firm to provide sustained benefits to Canada. The Big Three auto firms have not done this. However, some energy firms, such as Imperial Oil (owned by Exxon), have a history of Canadian development, whereas others such as IBM Canada already operate divisions in Canada on a global basis. Others, such as Asea Brown Boveri (ABB), have a decentralized organizational structure with a large degree of local autonomy. These smaller (ABB is not on the list) but more autonomous Canadian firms have learned to survive within the global networks of their parent organizations, and their managers can help to provide leadership to Canadians.

Table 18.6 **The largest Canadian-based firms, by degree of multinationality**

Rank	*Company*	*Industry*	*2000 (in millions Canadian $)*	*% Sales outside of Canada*
1	Inco	Mining	4,398	0.98
2	Seagram Co.	Conglomerates	23,105	0.97
3	United Dominion Industries	General manufacturing	3,514	0.96
4	Potash Corp. of Saskatchewan Inc.	Chemicals and fertilizers	3,315	0.96
5	Nortel Networks Corp.	High-tech manufacturing	44,958	0.95
6	Thomson Corp.	Multimedia	9,673	0.94
7	Alcan Aluminium Ltd	Mining	13,585	0.93
8	Bombardier Inc.	Information technology	16,101	0.90
9	Moore	Publishing and printing	3,353	0.90
10	Canadian Wheat Board	Agriculture	4,505	0.89
11	Laidlaw	Transportation/courier	4,330	0.89
12	Pratt & Whitney Canada	General manufacturing	2,290	0.85
13	Tembec	Paper and forest products	2,598	0.79
14	Brookfield Properties	Real estate	3,051	0.78
15	Onex Corp.	Conglomerates	24,531	0.77
16	Sun Life Financial Services of Canada	Diversified financials	16,206	0.76
17	Noranda	Mining	6,957	0.76
18	Cargill	Agriculture	3,527	0.70
19	Ford Motor Co. of Canada	Motor vehicles and parts	24,638	0.68
20	Manulife Financial Corp.	Diversified financials	14,152	0.66
Average			11,439	
Total			228,786	

Note: These data were compiled using only the Top 100 Canadian companies based on revenues. The data for foreign sales are limited and companies that might otherwise be in the list might be excluded.

Source: Adapted from "The National Post 500," *National Post*, 2001.

Another indicator of the nature of international expertise among these firms comes from the degree of their exports. Table 18.4 also reports data on the foreign sales of the largest 20 Canadian owned firms. Exports from Canadian sales of subsidiaries in the US and others offshore (excluding the US) are shown. According to the table, these large companies sell approximately 50 per cent of their output abroad. The foreign-owned firms in Canada (Table 18.5) also sell abroad, but information on foreign sales is not readily available. Nonetheless, the seven companies that do report this information export about 60 per cent of their output.

Table 18.6 shows Canadian-based firms ranked according to overseas sales. The largest, Inco, exports virtually everything. Additionally, most of Seagram's sales are outside Canada, as are those for the United Dominion Industries, the Potash Corporation, Nortel Networks, the Thomson Corporation, and Alcan. Notably, the top three most export oriented firms are foreign-owned companies. Seagram, which until recently was Canadian, was first purchased by French Vivendi and then resold to Diageo and Pernod Ricard in 2001.[15] For these large 20 firms the average ratio of foreign to total sales is 85 per cent. This demonstrates the tremendous attraction of foreign markets for larger companies in a relatively small market like Canada's. This provides further evidence that access to a triad market (in this case the US) is critical for success in a global market.

Multilateral Agreement on Investment (MAI)

Canada will benefit from any type of multilateral agreement on investment. An attempt to negotiate an MAI was made in Paris at the Organization for Economic Cooperation and Development (OECD) over the 1995 to 1998 period. The draft MAI was based on the lines of the North American Free Trade Agreement (NAFTA). The millennium round of the WTO may take up the need for an MAI.

An MAI will include the principle of national treatment, i.e. equal access for foreign investors to the host country's market (but according to host country rules). A number of sectors will be exempted from the national treatment principle. Canada, in the same spirit of the FTA and NAFTA, insists on exemptions on health care, education, social services, cultural industries, and transportation. All regulations on investment will be identified as will be all exemptions to the principle of national treatment. Additionally, dispute settlement mechanisms will be put in place, to allow individual investors (and companies) to appeal against government regulations and bureaucratic controls. The MAI will help countries to harmonize their regulations, although, in the areas of competition policy and tax policy, not much progress can be expected (no progress was achieved in NAFTA).

The need for an MAI arises because foreign investment has become an important part of the global economy. Today, the majority of international business is not done by traded goods, but through services and investments. Over 70 per cent of North Americans work in the service sector, with only 30 per cent in manufacturing. So the new agenda for international agreements is to negotiate rules for trade in services and investment.

Canada's outward stock of FDI is nearly 75 per cent in the US, with which it already has national treatment through the FTA and NAFTA. Thus, its exporting businesses would prefer an MAI with transparent rules.

Business opportunities in Canada

Although the Canadian economy began to slow down during the early 1990s, the country still offers excellent investment and trade opportunities for foreign investors. This is particularly true for US firms, thanks to the Free Trade Agreement of 1988 and its extension, the **North American Free Trade Agreement (NAFTA)**, which includes Mexico.[16]

North American Free Trade Agreement (NAFTA)
A regional free trade agreement between Canada, the US and Mexico

The **United States–Canada Free Trade Agreement (FTA)** is designed to eliminate tariffs and most other barriers to trade between the two countries.[17] Some specific provisions of the FTA are:

United States–Canada Free Trade Agreement (FTA)
A trade agreement that eliminates most trade restrictions (such as tariffs) between these two countries and extends national treatment to foreign investment

1. All tariffs on US and Canadian goods were to be eliminated by 1998.
2. Most import and export quotas were to be eliminated by 1998.
3. Use of product standards as a trade barrier is prohibited and national treatment of testing labs and certification bodies is established.
4. Many restrictions on agricultural products, wine and distilled spirits, auto parts, and energy goods have been sharply reduced, if not totally eliminated.
5. The size of the government procurement markets that will be open to suppliers from the other country is slightly increased.
6. Travel by business visitors, investors, traders, professionals, and executives transferred intracompany is facilitated.
7. The opportunity to make investments in each other's country is facilitated and encouraged through the adoption of national treatment.
8. A binational commission to resolve disagreements that may arise from the enforcement of the FTA has been established and dealt with some 20 cases in the first three years of the Agreement.[18]

Marketing in Canada

Companies doing business in Canada need to know distribution practices and advertising and promotion channels. In many cases these are similar to those in other countries, but there are some important differences.

Distribution practices Despite the country's vast size, sales to Canadian industries are characterized by short marketing channels with direct producer-to-user distribution. Many Canadian industries are dominated by a few large-scale enterprises that are highly concentrated geographically. It is not unusual for 90 per cent of prospective customers for an industrial product to be located in or near two or three cities.

The consumer goods market is more diffused than the industrial market, and the use of marketing intermediaries is often necessary. In many cases complete coverage of the consumer market requires representation in a number of commercial centers across the country. Firms having only one representative or distribution point typically choose Toronto. If the country is divided into two major markets, the other is often Calgary or Vancouver. If the market is divided into three areas, distributors are frequently put in Montreal, Ontario, and Vancouver.[19]

Direct selling is another growing area. This includes the sale of goods from manufacturing premises, by mail, through home delivery, through personal selling, and through other non-retail channels. Today direct selling accounts for over $3.5 billion annually in Canada.

Wholesale and retail trade are also important forms of distribution. Because of the wide dispersion of customers, wholesale trade is critical. However, retail trade is even more important and accounts for over $277 billion in sales annually.[20] Independent stores earn about 88 per cent of this, and general merchandisers, including department stores, make the other 12 per cent.[21] Quebec and Ontario account for about 61 per cent of all retail sales, and, in western Canada, British Columbia and Alberta make up approximately 24 per cent of the total.[22] Department stores and supermarkets constitute a large percentage of retail sales. However, as in the US, they are facing increased competition from discount food stores, showroom retailing, and other forms of self-service retailing. There are also specialized markets for recreation and leisure equipment and associated services. There is also a growing demand for consumer durables. These trends are likely to continue well into the millennium.

Advertising and promotion Media used for advertising in Canada include television, radio, newspapers, and magazines. Television and radio advertising are particularly popular because 97 per cent of all Canadian households have at least one television, and 99 per cent have at least one radio. Hundreds of private firms operate cable television and major broadcasting stations in metropolitan areas, and there are over 1,300 television stations and 550 cable television systems in the country, with over 50 per cent of the population hooked into a cable system. In addition, the Canadian Broadcasting Corporation (CBC) operates two national television networks, one in English and one in French. There are 1,400 licensed AM and FM radio stations.

Over 100 daily newspapers are published in Canada, and they are widely used by advertisers, as are trade magazines that are directed at specific industries such as computers, real estate, banking, and retailing. General interest Canadian magazines such as *Reader's Digest*, *L'actualité*, and *Quest* have raised their share of net advertising expenditure in Canadian periodicals to about 30 per cent, approaching the advertising of national newspapers. Two business newspapers, *The Financial Post* and *The Globe and Mail* (*Report on Business* section), also are widely read in the business and financial community. There are over 450 advertising agencies in Canada that can be of assistance in developing advertising and promotion campaigns.

Exporting

One of the most popular ways of doing business in Canada is through exports. As noted earlier, Canada is the US's largest foreign market. Every year Canadians buy as much US goods as do all the member nations of the EU combined.[23] In fact, over 20 per cent of all US exports go to Canada. In recent years the Canadian government has simplified the process for shipping goods into the country. This is particularly true for products coming from the US since duties have been greatly reduced or eliminated, thanks to the FTA and NAFTA.

Active learning check 

Review your answer to Active Learning Case question 4 and make any changes you like. Then compare your answer with the one below.

4. Will an FTAA lead to increased trade in the Americas; why or why not?

The FTAA will lead to an increase in trade in the Americas for three reasons. First, the elimination of all tariffs under the FTAA will encourage exports. Second, under the FTAA arrangements all countries are more likely to specialize in producing those goods and services for which they have a competitive advantage and, in turn, buy the others from their neighbor. Third, as the economies of the member countries grow, so will the amount of trade as each begins to adapt operations to the desires of the other and starts to tap this market further.

Franchising

Canada is the dominant foreign market for US franchisers. Currently there are over 300 US franchise firms operating approximately 10,000 franchise units in Canada. A recent report by *Entrepreneur* magazine rated over 1,100 US franchises. Of those rated in the top 10, eight indicated that they were seeking to establish franchises in Canada, so there is a great deal of opportunity for those who want to do business in Canada via the franchise route.

Additionally, in recent years Canadian banks have become more responsive to the needs of franchised operations. Canadian chartered banks now offer various loans and repayment plans for franchises. In some cases these financial institutions also offer payroll and cash management services. So there is considerable opportunity in international franchise operations in Canada.

MEXICO

Mexico, with a land area of approximately 760,000 square miles, is equal in size to almost 25 per cent of the contiguous US. It is the third largest nation in Latin America and has a population of over 95 million. The country is a federal democratic republic divided into 31 states and the Federal District (Mexico City). Although the country endured political turmoil early in this century, since World War II the government has been stable,[24] and during the presidencies of Carlos Salinas (1988–1994) and Ernest Zedillo (1994–2000) relations with the US have been particularly cordial.

Mexico's economy

The country's economy is currently in a state of flux, which has been brought on by new economic relations with the US. Today Mexico has the strongest economy in Latin America. One of the primary reasons has been the economic policies of Carlos Salinas, who, after becoming president in 1988, introduced liberalization rules regarding foreign investment and privatization. These changes have dramatically improved the economy. Gross domestic product growth in 1996 was 5.1 per cent, but inflation continued to remain in the range of 25 per cent. By 2000, gross domestic growth had decreased to 4.4 per cent, but inflation had also been reduced to 9 per cent. The country has also vigorously promoted exports, especially to the US, which now counts on Mexico for 25 per cent of all imported fruit and vegetables. The *maquiladora* industry (see Chapter 15) is another growing source of economic strength for the country.[25] At the same time Mexico has become a major region for international investment.

MNE investment

The climate for foreign investment in Mexico has grown increasingly favorable in recent years. Although there were strict controls on foreign investment during the 1970s, regulations introduced in 1989 reversed many of these restrictions. As a result, an increasing number of MNEs are investing in Mexico. Ford Motor invested $700 million in expansion of an automotive plant in Chihuahua; Nissan put $1 billion in a new assembly plant to produce cars for export to both the US and Japan; Volkswagen invested $950 million to expand its plant; McDonald's earmarked $500 million to open 250 new restaurants by the year 2000; Sears Roebuck put $150 million into new stores and malls throughout the country, in addition to renovating older units; Wal-Mart purchased Cifra, a successful Mexican retailer; and PepsiCo expanded its snack business by purchasing a majority stake in Gamesa, Mexico's largest cookie maker.

One of the major reasons for the increase in FDI is the privatization campaign that began in 1982 and which has picked up speed since then. By 2000, the number of state-owned enterprises had decreased to 200 from 1,000 prior to 1982.[26] While the government continues to play a major role in the economy, primarily through state-owned entities such as Pemex, the giant oil firm, there has been significant reduction in its ownership. These sales have been made to both foreign companies and Mexican investors.

Another reason has been the changes in investment laws that now permit foreigners to hold major equity positions. In the past, foreign ownership in auto parts companies had been limited to 40 per cent of equity, but a new decree now sharply reduces the number of firms that are subject to this law by creating exemptions based on percentages of export sales and sales to individuals. Today approximately 80 per cent of the economy is open to full foreign ownership.[27]

Labor

Labor is relatively plentiful and inexpensive. However, although there are numerous engineers, MNEs report a serious shortage of skilled labor and managerial personnel, particularly at the middle and upper levels of the organization. Worker absenteeism in recent years has declined, but turnover remains a serious problem, even in the *maquiladora* sector.

Approximately 40 per cent of the total work force is unionized. In industrial operations with more than 25 workers, about 80 per cent of the work force is unionized. Union control over the members has weakened in recent years, and this trend is likely to continue. However, strikes are not uncommon.

There is a three-tier minimum wage structure in Mexico, but increases have not kept up with the cost of living. Minimum wage in US dollars in Mexico City and surrounding towns in 2001 was approximately $4.60 per day, whereas it was $4.40 in many other large cities and $4.20 in the rest of the country.[28]

Government regulations require that at least 90 per cent of a firm's skilled and unskilled workers be Mexican nationals, and employers must favor Mexicans over foreigners and union personnel over non-union personnel. On the other hand, these regulations are unlikely to limit investment by MNEs since the government permits hiring exceptions.

Mexico and the North American Free Trade Agreement

In conjunction with their privatization policies, Presidents Salinas and Zedillo sought to motivate business through increased exposure to international competitive forces and access to the dynamic US market.[29] To this end, the government opened negotiations with the US and Canadian governments in Toronto on June 12, 1991 to create the North American Free Trade Agreement (NAFTA). This marked the first time that a less developed country entered into an agreement with two wealthy countries to create a free trade area. The NAFTA started in January, 1994 has had a major impact on Mexico's trade and investment.

Trade in several sectors has experienced considerable growth. In the textile and apparel sectors, quotas on Mexican products will be phased out and customs duties on all textile and apparel products will be completely eliminated over a 10-year period. For automotive products, Mexico immediately reduced its tariffs on cars and light trucks by 50 per cent and pledged to eliminate the remaining duties over 10 years. In agriculture, tariff restrictions were lifted on a broad range of goods when the Agreement went into effect on January 1, 1994.

The investment climate in Mexico has also been affected by the NAFTA. In the automotive sector, all investment restrictions are to be eliminated over a 10-year period. In transportation, Mexico allowed 49 per cent ownership of cars and trucking companies three years after the Agreement went into effect, 51 per cent after seven years, and 100 per cent after 10 years. Similar liberalization approaches are planned for the finance and insurance sectors.[30] All these changes will open up Mexico even more to FDI and in turn lead to the growth of the Mexican economy and two-way flows of trade and investment with the US in the future.

As with the United States–Canada FTA, binational panels will play an important role in resolving trade disputes. Under the NAFTA, panels will continue to contribute toward resolution of disputes in trade and now also investment matters. Where investments are concerned, complainants may also take their cases to binding investor–state arbitration.

Latin American Integration Association (LAIA)
A free trade group formed to reduce intraregional trade barriers and to promote regional economic cooperation. Argentina, Bolivia, Brazil, Chile, Colombia, Ecuador, Mexico, Paraguay, Peru, Uruguay, and Venezuela are all members

Regional trade agreements

Other developments involving Mexico as a leader in the movement toward free trade and privatization have included the efforts to create and sustain regional trade agreements based on the NAFTA. One of the major regional integration efforts has been the creation of the **Latin American Integration Association (LAIA)**, a free trade group that was formed in 1980 to reduce intraregional trade barriers and to promote regional economic cooperation. Argentina, Bolivia, Brazil, Chile, Colombia, Ecuador, Mexico, Paraguay, Peru,

Uruguay, and Venezuela are all members. The primary objective of LAIA is to create a Latin American common market. In recent years the association's slow process toward economic integration has led some members to create subregional groups. For example, in the southern cone, Argentina, Brazil, Paraguay, and Uruguay have established a common market called **Mercosur**, which was operational by 1996. In the north, Mexico, Colombia, and Venezuela have a similar agreement, and via NAFTA Mexico is likely to be a key bridge between Latin American countries and the US. The NAFTA has a clause permitting accession of other countries. A second major integration effort is the **Andean common market (Ancom)**, a subregional free trade compact that is designed to promote economic and social integration and cooperation.[31] Bolivia, Colombia, Ecuador, Peru, and Venezuela are all members.

Mercosur
A subregional free trade group formed to promote economic cooperation; the group consists of Argentina, Brazil, Paraguay, and Uruguay

Andean common market (Ancom)
A subregional free trade compact designed to promote economic and social integration and cooperation; Bolivia, Colombia, Ecuador, Peru, and Venezuela are all members

Enterprise for the Americas
An idea launched by President Bush; the aim of this effort is to create the free trade area from Alaska to Argentine Antarctica

Free Trade Area of the Americas (FTAA)
A regional trade agreement that is expected to succeed NAFTA and include 34 countries across North, Central, and South America

In 1990 President Bush launched his **Enterprise for the Americas**, which is aimed at creating an all-American free trade area from Alaska to Argentine Antarctica. The **Free Trade Area of the Americas (FTAA)** that is presently being negotiated by 34 countries would achieve the main objectives of continental integration.[32] If such an idea comes to fruition, it will eliminate the need for LAIA, Ancom, and similar Latin American trade agreements. The US is aware of the need for reducing, and then eliminating, trade barriers in the Americas if it hopes to establish a viable world market that can compete against the EU and the Pacific Rim. The idea is also appealing to Latin American countries that see the opportunities associated with linking into the North American diamond and profiting from the economic growth that it creates. This development will bring about a "Western hemisphere" trading bloc and may well become a reality by the early 21st century.

Doing business in Mexico

A number of strategic approaches are being used to conduct business in Mexico. (See the box "International Business Strategy in Action: Four common approaches in Mexico.") Two primary reasons for the success of these approaches are the high quality of the workforce and the dramatic improvement in the economy over the 1990s. MNEs operating in Mexico report that the quality of the workforce is excellent. For example, senior-level executives at firms such as Caterpillar, Ford, General Electric, IBM, and Procter & Gamble all report that their Mexican workforces produce high-quality output. Moreover, a Massachusetts Institute of Technology study has named Ford's Mercury Tracer plant in Hermosillo the highest-quality assembly plant in the world. The head of IBM Mexico has stated that, "for every dollar you pay a Mexican engineer, you get more from him or her than you'd get in other societies around the world".[33]

At the same time the market for goods and services is growing rapidly. Many MNEs admit that they are not in Mexico because of the low wage rates but because of rapidly growing demand. Despite a high inflation rate and loss of purchasing power, people want to buy consumer goods and to live more like their neighbors to the north. Mexicans are also expressing an interest in high-quality merchandise, resulting in US companies now reducing their reliance on agents and dealers and, instead, opening sales subsidiaries and warehouses to provide direct technical assistance. A good example is Compaq, which opened its first subsidiary in Mexico City in 1990 and was able to double personal computer sales the next year. With a burgeoning population of 99 million and an economy that is growing even faster, Mexico promises to be a major target area for MNEs during the millennium.[34] At the same time, these developments help Mexico to link itself to the triad via the US.

INTERNATIONAL BUSINESS STRATEGY *IN ACTION*

Four common approaches in Mexico

Doing business in Mexico can take a number of different forms. Four strategies have proven particularly profitable.

One is to establish a wholly-owned subsidiary. This can be an expensive strategy, but it gives the company total control and allows management to make decisions quickly and efficiently. Quite often a local manager runs the subsidiary and almost always the majority of the management team are locals. However, headquarters exercises key control.

A second approach is to become part of the *maquiladora* program. This strategy works best for firms aiming to export most of their output back to the US. The *maquiladora* arrangement allows manufacturing, assembly, and processing plants to import materials, components, and equipment duty free, complete the work with Mexican labor, and then ship the finished products back north. Under recent changes in the arrangement, if the company wants, it can sell up to one-third of the output in Mexico and still participate in the program.

A third approach is the so-called shelter program. Under this arrangement local contractors assume responsibility for all aspects of the manufacturing operation from site selection to recruitment of personnel to running the factory. After a predetermined time, however, the US company can buy out the shelter operator at a preset price and take over the business.

A fourth approach is a joint venture with a local partner. This combines a foreign company with financial and manufacturing know-how and a local partner who knows how to market the output. A number of US firms have opted for this approach, including Ford, DuPont, and General Electric (GE). In the latter case GE formed a joint venture with MABE, one of Mexico's largest appliance manufacturers. Since then the two have opened a gas range plant that now produces 800,000 units annually for the US, Canadian, and Mexican markets.

In most cases US MNEs will decide in advance which of these four strategies to implement. However, some firms have discovered that the need for such a decision is unanticipated. Take the example of Pace Foods, which went to Mexico City to film commercials for its Pace Picante Sauce. Since the crew did not want to carry back the jars of Pace's hot sauce that they used in the filming, they told a local store manager to keep the jars and to try to sell them. A few weeks later the company got a call from the manager. He had sold all 350 jars and wanted to know what he should do now. Today Pace has a thriving business selling products in Mexico.

Websites: ***www.ge.com***; ***www.ford.com***; ***www.pacefoods.com*** and ***www.dupont.com***.

Sources: Adapted from Nancy J. Perry, "What's Powering Mexico's Success," *Fortune*, February 10, 1992, pp. 109–115; Louis Uchitelle, "US Discounters Invade Mexico," *New York Times*, March 12, 1993, pp. C 1–C 2; Louis S. Richman, "How NAFTA Will Help America," *Fortune*, April 19, 1993, pp. 95–102; Joel Millman, "Nafta Motivates Asian Companies to Invest in Mexico," *Wall Street Journal*, August 14, 1998, p. A 13; Joel Millman, "High-Tech Jobs Transfer to Mexico With Surprising Speed," *Wall Street Journal*, April 9, 1998, p. A 18; Laurie P. Cohen, "With Help From INS, US Meatpacker Taps Mexican Work Force," *Wall Street Journal*, October 15, 1998, pp. A 1, 8.

Active learning check

Review your answer to Active Learning Case question 5 and make any changes you like. Then compare your answer with the one below.

5. Should environmental laws be included in the FTAA, and why or why not?

Whether environmental laws should become part of the FTAA is still up for debate. On one hand, there are issues of sovereignty. Should an international agreement set the standard for environmental laws or should the individual governments make their own laws to be responsive to their national needs? While an environmental chapter was included in NAFTA, there is a growing concern among developing countries that environmental laws would be used as a non-tariff barrier to trade, keeping out their goods from the rich US market.

The US and Canada are pressing for the inclusion of environmental standards in the prospective FTAA. Not surprisingly, the US and Canada advocate the use of clean technology while the developing countries may be better served by pollution vouchers or direct transfers of clean technology.

Mexico and the double diamond

In order to maintain its economic growth, Mexico must continue developing international competitive strength.[35] This is currently being done by linking to the US market.[36] In particular, MNEs must view this market not just as a source for export, but also as part of the home market (see Figure 15.7). Specifically, this requires:

1. developing innovative new products and services that simultaneously meet the needs of US and Mexican customers, recognizing that close relationships with demanding US customers should set the pace and style of product development;
2. drawing on the support industries and infrastructure of both the US and Mexican diamonds, realizing that the US diamond is more likely to possess deeper and more efficient markets for such industries; and
3. making free and full use of the physical and human resources in both countries.[37]

Mexico is doing this by relying heavily on a series of strategic clusters. The six major ones, in order of importance, are petroleum/chemicals, automotive, housing and household, materials and metals, food and beverage, and semiconductors and computers. The two that are most internationally competitive and provide the best insights into how the Mexican double diamond is used are the petroleum and automotive clusters.

Petroleum cluster Mexico's petroleum industry accounted for 10 per cent of all exports in 2000. The country has the second largest proven oil reserves after Venezuela and is the world's fifth largest producer. The largest firm is state-owned Petroleos Mexicanos (Pemex), which is the world's largest crude oil producer (does not include refining) and 81st largest firm. The company has a workforce of 135,000 employees and assets of nearly $60 billion, including pipelines, refineries, tankers, aircraft, and rail cars. This huge asset base helps to explain why Mexico is a net exporter of energy, principally oil, natural gas, hydraulic power, nuclear and geothermal power, and coal.

The country also has strong petroleum-related industries and infrastructure. At present there are 175 companies operating 490 basic and secondary petrochemical plants throughout the country and employing approximately 130,000 people.

Domestic demand of oil-related products in Mexico has been increasing sharply, forcing Pemex to become considerably more productive. The export market for this oil is expected to remain at current levels for the foreseeable future. The US will remain Mexico's largest customer as US conservation measures and depressed prices will continue to create demand for oil imports. Moreover, although energy was excluded from NAFTA, recent discussions have centered on US access to Mexican oil through imports and increased opportunities for US technologies in the energy sector. Major US companies such as Arco, Chevron, and Phillips are selling off some of their domestic properties and are looking for exploration opportunities outside the US, and Mexico is likely to prove a very attractive location. At present turnkey exploration contracts are being used to integrate US expertise and to improve Mexican drilling efficiency, thus reducing the cost of oil. This trend will make Mexico one of the lowest-cost producers in the world.

The commodity nature of the energy business provides little opportunity for Mexico to insulate itself from the cyclical changes of both pricing and demand in this cluster. The real opportunities for Mexico lie in trying to improve efficiencies through (1) liberalizing exploration programs by allowing more efficient foreign drilling contractors to carry out turnkey operations; (2) reducing the cost base by working with the unions to rationalize jobs that are not required; (3) using foreign technologies in areas where Mexican expertise is lacking; (4) allowing greater participation of foreign firms in producing petrochemicals to expand capacity and competitiveness of commodity products to meet domestic and export demand; (5) using foreign MNEs to bring in technology to produce advanced petrochemicals to be used in the US market; and (6) developing alternative, cleaner-burning fuels, such as natural gas and unleaded fuels, to reduce reliance on US imports and to comply with international environmental standards.

The potential of this cluster looks promising, even though in recent years Mexican proven reserves have fallen slightly and the international benchmark price for crude oil has dropped to the $16 to $30 per barrel range. The vast unexplored areas of Mexico provide long-term opportunities to continue a strong hydrocarbon-based cluster. Additionally, the proximity of the US, with its declining proven reserves and increased dependence on imports, will provide Mexico with an export base for improving economies of scale and generating funds for reinvestment in drilling and exploration activities. Thus Mexico's economic progress will be closely linked to the US diamond.

Automotive cluster The global auto industry is currently undergoing worldwide restructuring. In this process Mexico is emerging as a major car and truck producer. Since 1986 the industry has grown rapidly. In 2001 total unit production was 1.9 million units and exports to the US totaled 1.2 million.[38] Over the last decade the Big Three US auto makers have been expanding their capacities in Mexico while closing plants in the US and Canada. Today, Daimler Chrysler, Ford, and General Motors account for about 60 per cent of all light vehicle production. At the same time European and Japanese firms are investing in Mexico, in an effort to tap such benefits as low-cost labor, low capital cost, proximity to the largest auto market in the world, growth of domestic demand, and accessibility to related support industries.

Mexico has a strong, rich resource base supporting its automotive cluster. There is an abundance of young, skilled, adaptable labor. Foreign auto firms are finding that these workers are particularly effective after they have been given training in total quality management, just-in-time inventory, and related concepts. In addition, unions in Mexico are much more cooperative with management than their counterparts to the north. As a result, this resource base is now producing some of the highest quality cars and trucks in North America, and the Hermosillo plant is widely regarded as the number one auto factory on the continent.

There are also strong supporting industries and a well-developed infrastructure in the automotive cluster. The auto parts industry employs over 500,000 Mexican workers, a five-fold increase since 1990 and has revenues of $450 million.[39] Parts companies produce for both the domestic and export markets, and many are a result of foreign direct investment by US-based auto part firms. For example, General Motors has component plants in the country as well as financial participation with Mexican auto part companies. Ford Motor has similar arrangements, as do Volkswagen, Nissan, and a host of other foreign firms. In fact, between 1996 and 1998, 30 new auto parts companies have settled in Mexico. In one instance, the decision by Volkswagen to produce the VW Beetle fueled foreign investment in auto parts to meet the increasing demand.[40]

While the boom of foreign investment in auto parts initially displaced inefficient local parts producers, a handful of efficiently run local companies have emerged to become multinational producers. For instance, with an initial $30 million investment, Mexico's Nemak is opening a plant in the Czech Republic that will employ 200 people.

The primary customers for auto output in Mexico are in the local market. However, the percentage of this output that goes for export is increasing every year. In particular, with the signing of the NAFTA, Mexico's accessibility to the largest auto market in the world will increase sharply. This accessibility is especially critical to the country since US protectionism is now threatening to raise import barriers. At the same time Mexican acceptance of US cars manufactured in Mexico is at an all-time high. The same is true in the US, where the quality reputation of Mexican assembly plants is being felt at the dealer showroom.

The market potential of the automotive cluster is extremely high. There are some problems, however, that will have to be dealt with if the country is to continue increasing its competitiveness.[41] Foremost among these is the need for greater technology. One of the major reasons that Mexican autos are cost efficient is the lack of high automation and robotics. It is unlikely that this trend can continue. In addition, as more and more US and Canadian auto business is shifted to Mexico, it will put major pressure on the NAFTA to ensure that these two countries benefit handsomely from this strategy and that other foreign producers, such as the Japanese and Europeans, do not.

Overall, Mexico's economic future is closely linked to that of the US and North America. When analyzed in terms of the Porter diamond, some of the country's strategic clusters have already developed worldwide competitive strength. During the 1990s the petroleum and automotive clusters have proven to be highly competitive.

Mexico is likely to begin making major inroads into other areas such as semiconductors and computers. Motorola already has a semiconductor plant in Mexico and HP, IBM, Toshiba, Samsung, NEC, and Phillips, among others, produce computer hardware components in Mexican facilities. As in its automotive success, this is the result of favorable factor conditions, related and supporting industries, demand conditions, and the structure and rivalry of the firms. As a result, Mexico will find that it can link its diamond framework with that of the US and in the process become a worldwide competitor in still other areas. Porter's diamond framework will prove to be a useful paradigm.[42]

KEY POINTS

1. **Canada, with approximately 32 million people and a gross domestic product of about $775 billion annually, is the single largest trading partner of the US. There has been a move toward privatization in the past few years as well as toward deregulation. As in the US, the government attempts to promote competition, and the North American Free Trade Agreement (NAFTA) with Mexico has recognized the high degree of trade between the two countries.**
2. **Financial institutions are similar to those in the US, as are labor relations practices. However, a much larger percentage of Canadian employees are unionized, and the unions have been major opponents of the FTA and the subsequent NAFTA.**
3. **The NAFTA will eventually eliminate most trade barriers between the US and Canada. This should help to open up Canada to more economic development. At the same time the government welcomes foreign investment, and there are a wide variety of incentive programs that are designed to encourage such investments.**
4. **The approaches to doing business in Canada are similar to those in the US. However, there are some important regulatory differences. The chapter identified and discussed both.**
5. **Mexico has the strongest economy in Latin America and its close business ties to the US, as reflected by imports, exports, and US FDI, bode well for its future. The potential of the free trade agreement between the two countries and the growth of the *maquiladora* industry are helping Mexico to link its economy to that of the US. Mexico's petrochemical and automotive clusters are key industries in this linkage and are likely to become world-class competitors in their respective areas.**

KEY TERMS

- Competition Act
- Canada Labor Code
- Investment Canada Act (ICA)
- North American Free Trade Agreement (NAFTA)
- United States–Canada Free Trade Agreement (FTA)
- Latin American Integration Association (LAIA)
- Mercosur
- Andean common market (Ancom)
- Enterprise for the Americas
- Free Trade Area of the Americas (FTAA)

REVIEW AND DISCUSSION QUESTIONS

1 How high is the Canadian standard of living? Of what value is this information to a company that is interested in doing business in Canada?

2 Is the Competition Act of any concern to US firms, given that the FTA has eliminated most trade restrictions? Explain.

3 What do companies seeking to set up businesses in Canada need to know about labor relations in that country? Identify and discuss three areas of importance.

4 What are the most important provisions of the Free Trade Agreement and how do they affect US firms doing business in Canada?

5 Are there any restrictions on foreign investments in Canada? Identify and describe two of them.

6 What should a firm seeking to enter the Canadian market know about marketing practices there? Identify and describe three practices.

7 How good are franchise opportunities in Canada? Explain.

8 Why is Mexico doing so well economically? Identify two developments that have been particularly helpful in bringing this about.

9 What is the purpose of the LAIA? Of what value is the organization to its members?

10 How might the creation of an "Enterprise for the Americas" impact on the LAIA and Ancom? Give an example.

11 How is Mexico using its petroleum cluster to link itself to the North American triad?

12 How is Mexico using its automotive cluster to link itself to the North American triad?

13 Why are these linkages to the North American triad likely to be economically advantageous to Mexico? Cite two reasons.

REAL CASE

Bombardier's planes and trains

In 1942 the dreams of a budding young Quebec entrepreneur came true with the incorporation of L'Auto-Neige Bombardier, the world's first snowmobile manufacturer. Although the mechanic-turned-industrialist Joseph Armand Bombardier had great plans for his innovative transportation inventions, he could never have foreseen the course his company would take in the next 50 years.

Today Bombardier is one of the world's top manufacturers of transportation products with yearly revenues of over CDN $16.1 billion (US $10.9 billion) and 79,000 employees. Having begun with snowmobile production, Bombardier is now among the world leaders in commuter and general transportation trains, as well as transport vehicles for industrial and military use, sailboats, motorcycles, and, more recently, smaller aircraft. This extension into numerous other industries has transformed Bombardier from a once small-town Quebec company into a global market competitor and leader with 90 per cent of its total business now conducted outside Canada.

Bombardier's success is mostly due to the industrious and timely business instincts of company CEO Laurent Beaudoin, who in the past 30 years has followed a strategy of market entry and product improvement through acquisition, instead of relying strictly on R&D. As a result, the company has managed to produce the most technically advanced, innovative, and reliable products on the market, thereby gaining substantial market share in many industries, especially with its rubberwheeled subway car, sold to New York City in the 1980s.

This strategy has been exemplified with Bombardier's entry into the aerospace industry with the acquisition of Canadair in 1986, 12 years after diversifying into the transportation equipment business. The Canadair purchase brought the company a large pool of human resources and technical expertise which has been applied to develop such "in-house" products as the twin-engine Challenger Business Jet. As a result, Bombardier all of a sudden held lead positions in numerous niche markets which ensured ongoing relations with such manufacturing giants as Boeing and MacDonnell-Douglas. This acquisition quickly resulted in numerous contracts for CF-18 fighters from the Canadian government and contracts for Airbus components from both British Aerospace and France's Aerospatiale.

Further acquisition was a logical step for the company, and, by acquiring Northern Ireland's Short Brothers, Bombardier extended itself firmly into the European market as a supplier and manufacturer of aerospace technology. Then at the outset of the 1990s purchases of both Learjet out of Wichita, Kansas, and Boeing's deHavilland, propelled diversification into regional jets, and turboprop aircraft. Finally, production of the first-of-its-kind 50-passenger Canadair Regional Jet signified Bombardier's full-fledged entry into the airline industry. With already the bulk of its profit coming from this industry and the shared know-how, technology, resources, and markets of all of these companies pooled under one roof, Bombardier is ripe to become a major player in the aerospace industry through the millennium.

Websites: **www.bombardier.com**.

Sources: Rita Kolselka, "Let's Make a Deal," *Forbes*, April 27, 1992, pp. 62–63; Brenda Dalglish, "Tycoons in Progress," *Maclean's*, July 6, 1992, pp. 64–65; Christopher J. Chipello and G. Pierre Goad, "Bombardier, Bolstered by Acquisition, Enters New Phase," *Wall Street Journal*, September 17, 1992, p. B 4; Clyde H. Farnsworth, "Bombardier Snares DeHavilland," *New York Times*, January 26, 1992, p. 12; Clyde H. Farnsworth, "Bombardier Returns to Earth," *New York Times*, December 28, 1991, pp. L 33, L 35.

1. **How would you describe Bombardier's strategic approach to the aerospace industry and why?**
2. **The purchase of Canadair opened Bombardier up to a whole new market. Explain why the actions the company has taken since then have been wise business decisions.**
3. **Where do you foresee Bombardier in the future of the aerospace industry?**

REAL CASE

South of the border, Mexico way

Many opponents of NAFTA argued that the agreement would lead to the export of US jobs to Mexico, with a resulting decline in gross national product (GNP). Economists, however, reported that the agreement would help to save US jobs and GNP would rise by $30 billion annually once the treaty was fully implemented. Recent research also found that the first five years of NAFTA had improved growth and efficiency in all three members of NAFTA. Certainly, MNEs in the motor vehicle and parts industry and the telecommunications industry agreed with the economists and have already formulated strategies to address these impending changes.

The US motor vehicle and parts industry expects to see some jobs go to Mexico. Moreover, the export of vehicles from foreign-owned factories in Mexico doubled in the three years after NAFTA. However, prior to NAFTA, Mexican government regulations forced US auto makers to buy Mexican parts, which in many cases did not meet global standards. This led Mexican subsidiaries of US auto makers to run plants at less-than-maximum efficiency levels. The government also forced the Big Three car companies to export more than they imported into Mexico. NAFTA has allowed companies to act regionally instead of on a country-by-country basis and to reorganize production more efficiently across North America. In an unexpected surge of events, some of the manufacturing previously assigned to Mexico is being brought back into the US. For example, Ford relocated its production of Thunderbirds and Mercury Cougars from Cuautitlan to its assembly plant in Lorain, Ohio. At the same time US auto suppliers are doing better since the NAFTA requires 62.5 per cent of a vehicle's content to originate in North America. This means that foreign suppliers in Asia and Europe are losing out to regional, high quality firms such as TRW and Dana. So NAFTA is proving to be a boon to the US motor and auto parts industry.

Telecommunications is another industry where US firms are doing very well. Annual US telecommunications exports to Mexico are now in excess of $2.8 billion, and Telmex, the previously state-owned phone company, is 9.1 per cent owned by SBC. In 2001 Telmex had 24.2 million phones wired in an all-digital network, up from 12 million in 1993, and US companies are likely to supply much of this new equipment. At the same time some business customers in Mexico feel that it is taking too long for Telmex to provide them the service they need. So they are purchasing private networks that carry voice, data, and images by satellite. Scientific-Atlanta, a Georgia-based firm, is the market leader in this area and has been able to land a series of large contracts for installing communication systems, including those for Cifra, the country's largest retailer, and for the Mexican Navy. Other companies that are likely to benefit from the growing market include McCaw, Cantel, and Motorola. As a result, US telecommunications firms appear to have found a lucrative market just south of the border.

Websites: ***www.ford.com***; ***www.telmex.com.mx*** and ***www.motorola.com***.

Sources: Adapted from Louis S. Richman, "How NAFTA Will Help America," *Fortune*, April 19, 1993, pp. 95–102; Stephen Baker, Geri Smith and Elizabeth Weinger, "The Mexican Worker," *Business Week*, April 19, 1993, pp. 84–92; Geri Smith and Douglas Harbrecht, "The Moment of 'Truth' for Mexico," *Business Week*, June 28, 1993, pp. 44–45; Alan M. Rugman and John Kirton, "Multinational Enterprise Strategy and the NAFTA Trade and Environment Regime", *Journal of World Business*, vol. 33, no. 4 (December 1998), pp. 438–454; Alan M. Rugman, John Kirton and Julie Soloway, *Environmental Regulations and Corporate Strategy* (Oxford: Oxford University Press, 1999); ***www.ford.com; www.telmex.com.mx/***.

1. **Why is the NAFTA likely to be of benefit for US MNEs doing business in Mexico? Identify and describe one reason.**
2. **How might the NAFTA help the US to deal with its own unemployment problem?**
3. **Can linking its trade to the US market help Mexico's economic growth? Why or why not?**

ENDNOTES

1 Christopher J. Chipello and Roger Ricklefs, "Low Productivity Clouds Canada's Competitiveness, Living Standards," *Wall Street Journal*, February 9, 1999, p. A 19.

2 Tamsin Carlisle, "Calgary Becomes Outpost On High-Tech Frontier," *Wall Street Journal*, March 24, 1998, p. A 19.

3 US Department of Commerce, Bureau of Economic Analysis, *Survey of Current Business*, January 2002.

4 Also, see Rosanna Tamburri, "Canada Considers New Stand Against American Culture," *Wall Street Journal*, February 4, 1998, p. A 18; Roger Ricklefs, "Canada Fights to Fend Off American Tastes and Tunes," *Wall Street Journal*, September 24, 1998, pp. B 1, 8.

5 Barbara Wickens, "Getting the GST of It," *Maclean's*, September 10, 1990, pp. 40–43.

6 For more on the GST, see Joseph E. Payne, Jr, "Canada's New Goods and Services Tax Has Implications for US Exporters," *Business America*, August 13, 1990, p. 12.

7 See Rosanna Tamburri, "Canadians Clash Over Cost of Diversity," *Wall Street Journal*, April 1, 1998, p. A 15.

8 For additional insights into the role of Quebec in US–Canadian economic ties, see Thane Peterson and William J. Holstein, "How a Freer Quebec Could Reshape the Continent," *Business Week*, July 9, 1990, pp. 40–43.

9 For a contrast, see Christopher J. Chipello, "Francophones Struggle Outside Quebec," *Wall Street Journal*, February 26, 1998, p. A 12.

10 Government of Canada, Department of Finance, *Canada's Banks*, August 2001 (***www.fin.gc.ca/toce/2001/bank_e.html***).

11 See ***www.tse.com***.

12 Statistics Canada, *Perspectives on Labour and Income: Unionization–An Update*, 2000 and US Bureau of Labor Statistics, *Union Members Summary*, January 17, 2002.

13 E. Kaye Fulton and Nancy Wood, "A 'Reasonable Limit'," *Maclean's*, December 17, 1990, pp. 20–21.

14 Shona McKay, "Narrowing the Gap," *Maclean's*, January 8, 1990, pp. 31–32.

15 "Diageo Closes Seagram Transaction," Diageo Press Release, December 21, 2001.

16 Todd Mason, "Now Tariffs Can't Fall Fast Enough," *Business Week*, October 23, 1989, p. 80.

17 *Summary of the US–Canada Free Trade Agreement* (Washington DC: US Department of Commerce, International Trade Administration, 1988), p. 12.

18 Ibid., pp. 10–11.

19 *Marketing in Canada* (Washington DC: US Department of Commerce), International Marketing Information Series, Overseas Business Reports, OBR 88–05, May 1988, p. 8.

20 Statistics Canada, *Cansim Database*, Matrix: D657192.

21 Statistics Canada, *Cansim Database*, Matrix: D657192 and D657205.

22 Ibid.

23 *Marketing in Canada* (Washington DC: US Department of Commerce), International Marketing Information Series, Overseas Business Reports, OBR 88–05, May 1988, p. 8.

24 Also, see Stephen Baker, "Mexico: Can Zedillo Stem the Tide of Crisis?" *Business Week*, April 18, 1994, p. 60.

25 Also, see Bob Ortega, "Some Mexicans Charge North in NAFTA's Wake," *Wall Street Journal*, February 22, 1994, pp. B 1, B 5.

26 "Mexico Proves a Resilient, Robust Market for U.S. Exports," *AgExporter*, January 2002.

27 Ministry of Finance and Public Credit of Mexico, *Mexico's Bimonthly Economic News*, June 13, 2000.

28 "Mexico Approves Small Minimum Wage Increase," *Sign On San Diego*, December 27, 2001.

29 Len J. Trevino, "Strategic Responses of Mexican Managers to Economic Reform," *Business Horizons*, May/June 1998, pp. 73–80.

30 Keith Bradsher, "US Trade Official Talks Tougher on Pact," *New York Times*, March 17, 1993, pp. C 1, C 2.

31 Some of the material in this section can be found in "Latin American Introduction," *ILT Latin America*, July 1991, pp. 1–13.

32 For more on the FTAA, see ***www.ftaa-alca.org/***.

33 "The Business of the American Hemisphere," *Economist*, August 24, 1991, pp. 37–38.

34 Also, see Rick Wartzman, "In the Wake of Nafta, A Family Firm Sees Business Go South," *Wall Street Journal*, February 23, 1999, pp. A 1, 10.

35 Jonathan Friedland, "Mexico Is Hit Despite Belt-Tightening," *Wall Street Journal*, September 14, 1998, p. A 27.

36 Richard M. Hodgetts, "Porter's Diamond and Framework in a Mexican Context," *Management International Review*, vol. 33, Special Issue (1993), pp. 41–54.

37 J. R. D'Cruz and Alan M. Rugman, *New Concepts for Canadian Competitiveness* (Toronto: Kodak Canada, 1992).

38 "Ward's Reports Estimated Production," *PR Newswire*, December 27, 2001 and ITA, *U.S. Motor Vehicle Industry: Domestic and International Trade Quick Facts*, January 28, 2002.

39 Geri Smith and Elisabeth Malkin, "Mexico's Makeover," *Business Week*, December 21, 1998 and Elizabeth Malkin and Jonathan Wheatley, "Parts Shops Are Tailgating Carmakers to Latin America," *Business Week*, October 23, 2000.

40 Elizabeth Malkin and Jonathan Wheatley, "Parts Shops Are Tailgating Carmakers to Latin America," *Business Week*, October 23, 2000.

41 Elisabeth Malkin, "Holding Off Asia's Assault," *Business Week*, April 13, 1991, pp. 44–45.

42 Alan M. Rugman and Michael Gestrin, "The Strategic Response of Multinational Enterprises to NAFTA," *Columbia Journal of World Business*, vol. 28, no. 4 (1993), pp. 18–29.

ADDITIONAL BIBLIOGRAPHY

Averyt, William F. "Canadian and Japanese Foreign Investment Screening," *Columbia Journal of World Business*, vol. 21, no. 4 (Winter 1986).

Batres, Robertos E. "A Mexican View of the North American Free Trade Agreement," *Columbia Journal of World Business*, vol. 26, no. 2 (Summer 1991).

Beamish, Paul W., Craig, Ron and McLellan, Kerry. "The Performance Characteristics of Canadian Versus UK Exporters in Small and Medium Sized Firms," *Management International Review*, vol. 33, no. 2 (Second Quarter 1993).

Birkinshaw, Julian and Hood, Neil. "An Empirical Study of Development Process in Foreign Owned Subsidiaries in Canada and Scotland," *Management International Review*, vol. 37, no. 4 (1997).

Crookell, Harold. "Managing Canadian Subsidiaries in a Free Trade Environment," *Sloan Management Review*, vol. 29, no. 1 (Fall 1987).

Eden, Lorraine (ed.) *Multinationals in North America* (Calgary: University of Calgary Press, 1994).

Feinberg, Susan E. "Do World Product Mandates Really Matter?" *Journal of International Business Studies*, vol. 31, no. 1 (Spring 2000).

Finnerty, Joseph E., Owers, James and Creran, Francis J. "Foreign Exchange Forecasting and Leading Economic Indicators: The US–Canadian Experience," *Management International Review*, vol. 27, no. 2 (Second Quarter 1987).

Gillispie, Kate and Teegen, Hildy J. "Market Liberalization and International Alliance Formation: The Mexican Paradigm," *Columbia Journal of World Business*, vol. 30, no. 4 (Winter 1995).

Globerman, Steven and Walker, Michael (eds.) *Assessing NAFTA: A Trinational Analysis* (Vancouver BC: Fraser Institute, 1993).

Globerman, Steven and Shapiro, Daniel M. "The Impact of Government Policies on Foreign Direct Investment: The Canadian Experience," *Journal of International Business Studies*, vol. 30, no. 3 (Fall 1999).

Griffith, David A., Hu, Michael Y. and Ryans Jr, John K. "Process Standardization across Intra and Inter-Cultural Relationships," *Journal of International Business Studies*, vol. 31, no. 2 (Summer 2000).

Hecht, Laurence and Morici, Peter. "Managing Risks in Mexico," *Harvard Business Review*, vol. 71, no. 4 (July/August 1993).

Hodgetts, Richard. "Porters's Diamond Framework in a Mexican Context," *Management International Review*, vol. 33, no. 2 (Second Quarter 1993).

Hufbanes, Gary C. et al. *NAFTA and the Environment* (Washington, DC: Institute for International Economics, 2000).

Hufbauer, Gary Clyde and Schott, Jeffrey J. *North American Free Trade: Issues and Recommendations* (Washington DC: Institute for International Economics, 1992).

Hufbauer, Gary Clyde and Schott, Jeffrey J. *NAFTA: An Assessment* (Washington, DC: Institute for International Economics, 1993).

Hung, G. L. "Strategic Business Alliances Between Canada and the Newly Industrialized Countries of Pacific Asia," *Management International Review*, vol. 32, no. 4 (Fourth Quarter 1992).

Janisch, H. N. "Canadian Telecommunications in a Free Trade Era," *Columbia Journal of World Business*, vol. 24, no. 1 (Spring 1989).

Kamath, Shyam J. and Tilley, J. Roderick. "Canadian International Banking and the Debt Crisis," *Columbia Journal of World Business*, vol. 22, no. 4 (Winter 1987).

Kaynak, Erdener. "A Cross Regional Comparison of Export Performance of Firms in Two Canadian Regions," *Management International Review*, vol. 32, no. 2 (Second Quarter 1992).

Kirton, John and Maclaren, Virginia (eds). *Linking Trade, Environment and Social Cohesion* (Aldershot: Ashgate, 2002).

Martinez, Zaida L. and Ricks, David A. "Multinational Parent Companies' Influence over Human Resource Decisions of Affiliates: US Firms in Mexico," *Journal of International Business Studies*, vol. 20, no. 3 (Fall 1989).

Neale, Charles W., Shipley, David D. and Dodds, J. Colin. "The Countertrade Experience of British and Canadian Firms," *Management International Review*, vol. 31, no. 1 (First Quarter 1991).

Nichols, Nancy A. "The Monterrey Group: A Mexican Keiretsu," *Harvard Business Review*, vol. 71, no. 5 (September/October 1993).

Rugman, Alan M. *Multinationals in Canada: Theory, Performance and Economic Impact* (Boston MA: Martinus Nijhoff, 1980).

Rugman, Alan M. "The Role of Multinational Enterprises in US–Canadian Economic Relations," *Columbia Journal of World Business*, vol. 21, no. 2 (Summer 1986).

Rugman, Alan M. *Outward Bound: Canadian Direct Investment in the United States* (Toronto: Canadian–American Committee, and Prentice-Hall of Canada, 1987).

Rugman, Alan M. *Multinationals and Canada–United States Free Trade* (Columbia SC: University of South Carolina Press, 1990).

Rugman, Alan M. "A Canadian Perspective on NAFTA," *International Executive*, vol. 36, no. 1 (January/February 1994).

Rugman, Alan M. (ed.) *Foreign Investment and NAFTA* (Columbia SC: University of South Carolina Press, 1994).

Rugman, Alan M. and D'Cruz, Joseph R. "The 'Double Diamond' Model of International Competitiveness: The Canadian Experience," *Management International Review*, vol. 33, no. 2 (Second Quarter 1993).

Rugman, Alan M. and Gestrin, Michael. "The Investment Provisions of NAFTA," in Steven Globerman and Michael Walker (eds.), *Assessing NAFTA: A Trinational Analysis* (Vancouver BC: Fraser Institute, 1993).

Rugman, Alan M. and Gestrin, Michael. "The Strategic Response of Multinational Enterprises to NAFTA," *Columbia Journal of World Business*, vol. 28, no. 4 (Winter 1993).

Rugman, Alan M., Kirton, John and Soloway, Julie A. *Environmental Regulations and Corporate Strategy: A NAFTA Perspective* (Oxford: Oxford University Press, 1999).

Rugman, Alan M. and Verbeke, Alain. "Multinational Corporate Strategy and the Canada–US Free Trade Agreement," *Management International Review*, vol. 30, no. 3 (Third Quarter 1990).

Rugman, Alan M. and Verbeke, Alain (eds.) *Research in Global Strategic Management: Volume 1: International Business Research for the Twenty-First Century; Canada's New Research Agenda* (Greenwich CT: JAI Press, 1990).

Rugman, Alan M. and Verbeke, Alain. "Foreign Subsidiaries and Multinational Strategic Management: An Extension and Correction of Porter's Single Diamond Framework," *Management International Review*, vol. 33, no. 2 (Second Quarter 1993).

Sanderson, Susan Walsh and Hayes, Robert H. "Mexico – Opening Ahead of Eastern Europe," *Harvard Business Review*, vol. 68, no. 5 (September/October 1990).

Seringhaus, F. H. Rolf and Botschen, Guenther. "Cross-National Comparison of Export Promotion Services: The Views of Canadian and Austrian Companies," *Journal of International Business Studies*, vol. 22, no. 1 (First Quarter 1991).

Solocha, Andrew, Soskin, Mark D. and Kasoff, Mark J. "Determinants of Foreign Direct Investment: A Case of Canadian Direct Investment in the United States," *Management International Review*, vol. 30, no. 4 (Fourth Quarter 1990).

Spencer, William J. and Grindley, Peter. "SEMATECH After Five Years: High Technology Consortia and US Competitiveness," *California Management Review*, vol. 35, no. 4 (Summer 1993).

Ulgado, Francis M. "Location Characteristics of Manufacturing Investments in the US: A Comparison of American and Foreign-based Firms," *Management International Review*, vol. 36, no. 1 (1996).

Weintraub, Sydney. *NAFTA at Three* (Washington DC: Center for Strategies on International Studies, 1997).

Willard, Kristen L. "Do Taxes Level the Playing Field? How US Tax Policy Affects the Investment Decisions of Foreign Affiliates in the United States," *Columbia Journal of World Business*, vol. 29, no. 4 (Winter 1994).

Chapter 19

Non-Triad Nations

CONTENTS

OBJECTIVES OF THE CHAPTER

More than 100 nations in the world are not triad members. How do organizations in them conduct international business? In order to build a global operation from the base of a smaller country, there must be access to the markets of at least one of the triad blocs. This chapter develops a general framework on the need for such market access. It also examines a number of representative non-triad countries as examples of how these general principles apply to any non-triad country.

The specific objectives of this chapter are to:

1. *Discuss* why all firms in non-triad countries need market access to a triad bloc in order to build a global business.
2. *Explain* the general principles of triad market access and relate this to the international business needs of non-triad countries.
3. *Describe* the major steps being taken in non-triad countries to develop successful global industries, especially in terms of the double diamond framework.
4. *Relate* how well select non-triad nations are doing in their attempts to establish economic linkages to triad countries.

ACTIVE LEARNING CASE

Acer Taiwan goes international

Acer Taiwan is one of the largest PC manufacturers in the world. It has more than 80 branch offices worldwide, distribution networks in over 100 countries, and more than 20,000 employees. The company is the best known brand in Asia, and a large player in Latin America. In the US, where IBM, Compaq, and Dell dominate, Acer is a major competitor in the consumer electronics market. Not bad for a company no one knew just a few decades ago.

In 1976 CEO Stan Shin and some of his friends managed to pull together $25,000 and start Multitech. With seven employees, the company began developing small electronic products such as pocket calculators and games. Slowly the company began to grow by commercializing microprocessor technology and its applications. Its initial entrance into the PC market was as a supplier. Multitech began producing computers to be sold under other brand names. Then in 1986 the company launched its own brand name computer: Acer and it began to sell in Europe and in Japan. While the firm still supplies under other brand names, Acer has become one of the best-known PC brands in the world.

How did a small company from Taiwan gain market share in an industry dominated by well-established computer manufacturers? The answer is by niching. Shin explains this decision by noting, "It is better to be a big fish in a small pond than a small fish in a big pond." Small markets, especially in Asia, which were not yet captured by the likes of IBM and Compaq, were a driving force behind Acer's initial international success. Additionally, Shin decided to develop tailored PCs. Instead of a computer that could do everything, Acer would build task-specific computers at a low cost. By the 1990s, Acer had developed world-class computer technologies and introduced the world's first dual-Pentium PC in 1994.

Acer's distribution system is also a novelty. With the product life of computer components at about three months, exporting overseas becomes a problem, but Acer has manufacturing and assembling plants all over the world. The company distributes parts with long product lives by ship, while highly volatile products like semiprocessors, PCB, and memory are shipped by plane. This allows for just-in-time production that Shin compares to the distribution system of a fast-food chain with perishable and non-perishable ingredients.

The success of the company is also highly correlated with the management structure created by Shin. Unlike traditional Chinese businesses, where management is highly hierarchical and controlled by the owning family, Shin uses decentralized management. Autonomy is important. Managers are encouraged to think like owners, so as to take advantage of all profit opportunities. Additionally, Acer has gone public and employees have the option of buying shares at extremely low prices.

To succeed in the long term, the company has also built alliances. To enter the US, for example, Acer formed a joint venture with Texas Instruments. And to acquire needed technology the company bought a host of firms including Counterpoint Computers, Altos, and Kangaroo Computer. Acer has also entered into cross-licensing agreements with IBM and Intel. The company has recently decided to make e-business its core focus because it wants to be a leader in the knowledge economy with innovative marketing, services, and investment. In particular, Acer is changing its focus from that of a manufacturing company to that of a knowledge-based firm that can compete effectively in this rapidly changing, high-tech industry.

Websites: ***www.acer.com***; ***www.ibm.com***; ***www.compaq.com***; ***www.ti.com*** and ***www.dell.com***.

Sources: Adapted from Stefan Simmons, "Lessons from the Village Shop," *Spiegel*, November 4, 1997; Brian Dumaine, "Asia's Wealth Creators Confront a New Reality," *Fortune*, December 8, 1997; Catherine Shepherd and Alejandro Reyes, "Lords of High Tech," *Asiaweek*, November 7, 1997; Charles Goldsmith, "Russia's Plane Makers Reverse Free Fall," *Wall Street Journal*, June 17, 1997, p. A 14; ***www.acer.com.tw/***.

1. **What was the internationalization strategy of Acer and why was it successful?**
2. **Why did Acer form strategic alliances with IBM and Texas Instruments?**
3. **Why has Acer become a successful MNE whereas Russia has not developed a world-class computer firm?**

INTRODUCTION

Many countries are relatively small and depend on international trade and investment to maintain their economic growth. As seen in Chapters 3 and 15, countries that are not members of the triad must develop connections to these trading blocs if they hope to prosper internationally. A non-triad country that fails to do this will find itself uncompetitive and be forced to erect inefficient trade barriers or to see its industry overwhelmed by foreign imports. In this chapter select non-triad nations are considered, including Chile, Brazil, China, India, South Korea, Singapore, Australia, India, Russia, and Poland.

Although each country's performance reflects a unique response to a particular set of conditions, a number of common developments pervade the economies of these non-triad nations. Privatization,[1] the attracting of foreign investment, and strategies that are designed to help the country link to the triad are three of the most important. These are the reasons that they were chosen for consideration.

The focus of this textbook is the multinational enterprises (MNEs) that are responsible for the vast majority of international business activity. As explained earlier in Chapters 2 and 3, now 80 per cent of the world's largest MNEs come from the industrialized countries "triad" of North America, the EU and Japan. As Table 19.1 shows, 65.8 per cent of all the world's FDI is from such industrialized countries.

What, then, is the role of international business in smaller, non-triad nations? As Table 19.1 reveals, about one-third of all the foreign direct investment (FDI) stock is now in developing countries. In this chapter we shall look into the FDI and MNEs in some of the more important non-triad countries. These countries are Brazil, Chile in Latin America (Mexico was discussed in Chapter 15); China, Hong Kong, South Korea, Singapore, and Australia in Asia-Pacific and some emerging economies in Europe such as Russia and Poland. Earlier we discussed Anglogold (in Chapter 7) as a typical South African resource-based company. In fact, all of Africa accounts for only 2.3 per cent of the stock of FDI in the world, see Table 19.1.[2]

MARKET ACCESS TO THE TRIAD

International business operations in the 21st century are going to be even more challenging than in the past. One reason is the emergence of the three strong trade and investment blocs. These are complex arrangements with varying degrees of economic trade liberalization and protectionism that are inherent in their institutional and political structures. The triad represents both globalization and sovereignty dimensions. The EU is the most politically integrated, in terms of institutional structures, and the Japanese-based bloc is the least. The NAFTA is a free trade agreement, not a common market, but the NAFTA contains provisions for the accession of Latin American and Caribbean and Central American nations, and it may then evolve into stronger political linkages like the EU model.

To develop global industries, non-triad nations need both trade and investment from the triad nations and also access to the markets of at least one of the triads. This implies that the focus of business strategy for firms in a smaller, non-triad, nation should be to secure inward triad investment and market access for exports to a triad bloc. This can be done by direct business contact of a double diamond type, but it is helped and reinforced by formal linkages arranged by the governments. As demonstrated in the last chapter, both Canada and Mexico have already gone this route.

Table 19.1 **The world's stocks of inward FDI**

Country/Region	*1990 (billions of US $)*	*% of total*	*2000 (billions of US $)*	*% of total*
Industrialized countries	1,388.8	73.5	4,157.6	65.8
Developing countries	499.9	26.5	2,156.7	34.2
Africa (1)	48.6	2.6	148.0	2.3
of which				
South Africa	9.2	0.5	52.7	0.8
Nigeria	8.0	0.4	20.3	0.3
Latin America and the Caribbean	116.7	6.2	606.9	9.6
Brazil	37.1	2.0	197.7	3.1
Argentina	9.1	0.5	73.4	1.2
Chile	10.1	0.5	42.9	0.7
Mexico	22.4	1.2	91.2	1.4
Asia and the Pacific (2)	328.2	17.4	1,261.8	20.0
Saudi Arabia	22.5	1.2	28.8	0.5
China	24.7	1.3	346.7	5.5
Hong Kong, China	162.7	8.6	469.8	7.4
Indonesia	38.8	2.1	60.6	1.0
South Korea	5.2	0.3	42.3	0.7
Malaysia	10.3	0.5	54.3	0.9
Singapore	28.6	1.5	89.3	1.4
Developing Europe	4.1	0.2	136.2	2.2
Czech Republic	1.4	0.1	21.1	0.3
Poland	0.1	0.0	36.5	0.6
Hungary	0.6	0.0	19.9	0.3
Russia	—	—	19.2	0.3
Total	1,888.7	100.0	6,314.3	100.0

Notes:

(1) The *World Investment Report 2001* considers South Africa as a developed nation but in this table we have included it among developing countries.

(2) Middle Eastern countries are included in the Asia-Pacific category.

Source: United Nations, *World Investment Report 2001* (Geneva: United Nations Conference on Trade and Development, 2001).

In Chapter 2 we identified "clusters" of nations that are making such arrangements with triad blocs. In general, the NAFTA is the basis for a trading bloc of the Americas; the EU is the locus for Eastern European and African nations; Japan is the hub for many Asian businesses. Some smaller, non-triad nations may attempt to open the doors to two triad markets. For example, both South Korea and Taiwan have equal trade and investment with the US and Japan. Firms from these countries need two double diamonds. Australia still has a large amount of trade with Britain and the EU, but its trade with Japan and other Asian nations is increasing rapidly. Indeed, the geographical basis of the triad serves to reinforce the dependence of neighboring nations on their dominant regional economic partner. We begin our consideration by examining countries in Latin America, then move to Asia and finally to Russia and Eastern Europe.

Active learning check

Review your answer to Active Learning Case question 1 and make any changes you like. Then compare your answer with the one below.

1. What was the internationalization strategy of Acer and why was it successful?

Acer built up from its relatively small home base "diamond" in Taiwan and expanded production throughout South East Asia. It then undertook a "double diamond" strategy for accessing the triad markets of North America and Europe. It formed strategic alliances with the US and European MNEs and used these as a stepping-stone to FDI in these key triad markets. It also kept its production-based efficiencies of employee involvement in company growth and ongoing R&D to improve the quality of its products.

LATIN AMERICA

Latin America (see accompanying map) is a rapidly growing region and a destination of FDI. Mexico's linkage to the North American triad via the NAFTA was discussed in Chapter 15 and there the Mexico–US double diamond was explained. Mexico's experience will be extremely helpful to regional integration, and other Latin American countries will also be following this lead as in the Free Trade Agreement of the Americas (FTAA), which is presently being discussed. Chile and Brazil are relevant examples. (We do not have the space to report on other large Latin American economies such as Argentina, Colombia, and Venezuela.)

Chile

Chile has one of Latin America's strongest economies. The gross domestic product grew at a 4–5 per cent annual rate during most of the 1980s, unemployment remained fairly low, and purchasing power improved. Despite a slowdown in late 1999, Chile's economic picture improved in the 1990s, with growth averaging 5.8 per cent per year.[3]

The government has a positive attitude toward foreign investment. During the Pinochet administration (1974–1990) companies that had been nationalized were returned to the private sector. At the same time many state businesses were sold. These included the airline LAN-Chile, Entel (telecommunications), Enaex (explosives), CAP (steel), and Laboratorio Chile (pharmaceuticals). Privatization continued under the Lagos–Escobar governments.

MNE investment

FDI in Chile had been approximately $1.8 billion annually but saw a slowdown by the late 1990s. Most of these funds are from NAFTA and EU multinationals and are for mining and forestry projects. Table 19.2 shows flows and stock of FDI in Chile. The EU is the largest investor in Chile, accounting for 40.1 per cent of all flows in 2000 and 36.9 of the stock of FDI. Together, the NAFTA countries account for 46.5 per cent of the stock of FDI, with the US accounting for 27.3 per cent.

Most FDI stock is concentrated in select industries. Accounting for 36.4 per cent of all FDI stock, the largest recipient of FDI is the mining industry. The second largest beneficiary of FDI is the service industry with 22 per cent. Other significant investments have been made in manufacturing, transportations, telecommunications, and utilities. In recent years, and partly as a result of government investment in infrastructure, investment in electricity, gas, and water has outpaced investment in the mining industry.[4]

For example, Exxon Minerals is investing up to $1.2 billion over a 10-year period to expand its Los Bronces mine in the mountains near Santiago and to boost fine-copper output. Cominco Resources of Canada is developing the Quebrada Blanca copper deposit at a cost of $280 million. Foresta e Industrial Santa Fe, a joint venture involving Royal Dutch Shell (60 per cent), Scott Paper Worldwide (20 per cent), and Citicorp (20 per cent), is investing $350 million to build a plant that annually will produce 250,000 metric tons of eucalyptus pulp for export. PepsiCo is investing $100 million to purchase the country's largest bottler and to open up Pizza Hut and Kentucky Fried Chicken outlets in Santiago.

Table 19.2 FDI in Chile, 1991–2000

Country/period	*1991*	*% of total*	*2000*	*% of total*	*Stock of FDI (1)*	*% of total*
NAFTA	449,540	45.8	1,400,477	46.7	1,850,017	46.5
United States	350,524	35.7	734,016	24.5	1,084,540	27.3
Canada	92,016	9.4	664,662	22.2	756,678	19.0
Mexico	7,000	0.7	1,799	0.1	8,799	0.2
Latin America and the Caribbean	47,531	4.8	132,754	4.4	180,285	4.5
European Union	267,560	27.2	1,201,067	40.1	1,468,627	36.9
Japan	78,407	8.0	53,456	1.8	131,863	3.3
Triad (2)	696,491	70.9	1,988,539	66.3	2,685,030	67.5
Others	139,069	14.2	209,765	7.0	348,834	8.8
Total per period	982,107	100.0	2,997,519	100.0	3,979,626	100.0

Notes: Country amounts include investment transferred among them, the year they occur.

(1) Refers to the sum of all flows over the 1974–2001 period.
(2) Refers to the US, the EU, and Japan.

Source: Foreign Investment Committee, October 31, 2001.

Outokumpo Oy of Finland and the Luksic Group of Santiago and London are investing $60 million in the Lince copper mine in the Atacama desert to produce 20,000 metric tones of copper cathodes annually. Table 19.3 shows selected MNEs operating in Chile.

Local MNEs

Compared with other countries in the region, Chile is a relatively small country. For that reason, local companies tend to be smaller than in the large markets of Brazil and Mexico. Yet, the rapid growth of the country has trained a body of managers that are now able to compete nationally and have expanded their businesses internationally. In fact, Chile is proving to be a source of FDI to other Latin American countries.

Sixteen Chilean MNEs made the *Financial Times* Top 100 Latin American companies and two companies, Enersis and Copec, made it to the Top 25. (See Appendix 19A.) In addition, the state-owned copper company, Codelco, is a big exporter, and was discussed in a Chapter 3 Real Case. Enersis is the first private Latin American electricity company. Previously called Compañía Chilena Metropolitana de Distribución Eléctrica SA, Enersis was completely privatized in 1988. In the 1990s, the company began to expand its internal operations to water and through acquisitions, started to operate in Peru, Argentina, Brazil, and Colombia. In 1999, Endesa of Spain purchased a majority holding in Enersis. Another company, CMPC, is a forestry company that first began to operate internationally in collaboration with Procter & Gamble. Together, the companies produced disposable diapers and sanitary napkins in Chile, Argentina, Paraguay, Uruguay, and Bolivia. In subsequent years, CMPC acquired forestry operations in neighboring countries, as well as paper manufacturers.

Labor

In contrast to other Latin American countries, Chile has a highly educated population and a well-trained, skilled labor force. Unemployment in recent years has been in the 6–10 per cent range, with one of the biggest problems being underemployment in the middle class. Approximately 12 per cent of the labor force is unionized, and in recent years the unions have increased their power. New regulations, for example, permit indefinite work stoppages, provided that the majority of employees approve them. Minimum monthly salaries are fixed by law and adjusted periodically by the government.

Table 19.3 **Selected MNEs operating in Chile, by sector, 2001**

Sector	*MNEs*
Agribusiness	Nestlé (Switzerland) Unilever (UK–The Netherlands) Seagram Company (Canada) Frutesa (New Zealand) Parmalat (Italy) Arcor (Argentina) Danisco A/S (Denmark) Cilpac, Blue Fish (Luxembourg) Tiger Oats (South Africa)
Fishing and aquaculture	ASC Group (US) British Columbia Packers (Canada) Ergofinn Oy (Finland) Nippon Suisan Kaisha (Japan) Nutreco, Stolt Seafarm (The Netherlands) Pescanova (Spain)
Industry	Quebecor Printing (Canada); Coca-Cola, 3M, Procter & Gamble, Caterpillar, Eastman Kodak, General Electric, General Motors, Abbot Laboratories (US) L'Oreal (France) Sumitomo Corp., Komatsu (Japan) AGA AB (Sweden) Dyno Industries (Norway) Hoechst, Siemens, BASF (Germany) F.I.L.A. (Italy) Axol (Brazil) Imsatec, Milton (Mexico)
Information technology	Telefónica de España, Endesa (Spain) Telecom Italia, AT&T, IBM, Bellsouth, Microsoft, Motorola, Hewlett-Packard, Xerox, Delta Air Lines (US) National Grid (UK) SR Telecom (Canada) Voicenet (Australia) Ericsson (Sweden) Alcatel (Francia)
Electricity, gas, and water	Endesa, Aguas Barcelona, Iberdrola (Spain) Suez Lyonnaise des Eaux, TotalFinaElf (France) PSEG Global (US) Thames Water, Biwater (UK) Hydro-Québec, Sask Energy (Canada) Tractebel (Belgium) Repsol-YPF (Spain–Argentina) AGL (Australia)
Financial services	ABN Amro, ING (The Netherlands) BSCH, BBVA, Mapfre (Spain) Crédit Lyonnais, Caisse Nationale, UAP (France) Istituto San Paolo–IMI, Sudameris (Italy) National Bank of Canada, Scotiabank (Canada) Zurich (Switzerland) J. P. Morgan Chase, Citibank, BankBoston, Chubb, HSBC, MetLife (US) AMP (Australia) Bank of Tokyo-Mitsubishi (Japan) Deutsche Bank (Germany) Banco de la Nación Argentina (Argentina) Banco do Brasil (Brazil)
Mining	Homestake, BHP Billiton (Australia) Phelps Dodge, Cyprus, Exxon, Minnesota Mining (US) Outokumpu (Finland) Boliden (Sweden) Placer Dome, Teck, Barrick, Falconbridge, Noranda, PCS (Canada) Sumitomo (Japan) Rio Tinto, Anglo American (UK)

Source: Foreign Investment Committee, October 31, 2001.

Chile is likely to continue as a favorite investment area for MNEs because of its attractive economy. The gross domestic product in 2000 rose by 5.4 per cent and is expected to continue increasing at a rate of over 5 per cent per year. Multinationals are particularly motivated by the government's assurances that its economic approach will remain free-market driven. In linking itself to triad nations, the country relies heavily on such exports as copper, forestry products, and fruit.[5] The triad accounts for 56 per cent of all Chilean exports. Of this, the EU is the largest recipient with 25 per cent, followed by the US at 17 per cent, and Japan at 14 per cent. An additional 22 per cent of all exports are destined for other Latin American countries, notably Brazil and Argentina which together account for 9 per cent of all Chilean exports. Chile also relies heavily on most of these same countries for imports. The emphasis, however, is more on its Latin American neighbors, which account for 36 per cent of all Chilean imports. In other words, Chile needs four double diamonds, as its trade is pretty evenly split as follows: Chile–NAFTA; Chile–Mercosur; Chile–EU; and Chile–Asia.

The importance of FDI and trade for the Chilean economy provide an assurance that the government will continue to encourage foreign investment and to nurture a market-oriented economy as it works to link itself to all three triad members and with its neighboring Latin American countries.[6]

Brazil

In recent years the government of Brazil has launched sweeping economic liberalization and reform.[7] Most non-tariff import barriers have been removed and the country is speeding efforts toward trade integration, most notably with Argentina. Additionally, the government's attitude toward free enterprise has been stronger than that in most developing countries.

At the same time, however, the economy has been encountering a host of problems.[8] In particular, Brazil has been running a trade deficit and the 1999 decision to devalue the currency[9] produced many negative results including high interest rates and a slowing of economic growth. Firms such as Volkswagen, Fiat, Mercedes-Benz, and General Motors sharply cut back their auto production because of the difficulty of competing with a weakened currency.[10] In turn the country's problems had a negative impact on its Mercosur partners: Argentina, Paraguay, and Uruguay.[11]

By early 2001, Brazil seemed to be back on its feet. Economic growth was expected to reach 4.5 per cent for that year and real interest rates fell almost to single digits. However, a series of economic blows managed to significantly reduce Brazil's economic prospects. In 10 months, the Brazilian Real depreciated by 20 per cent and economic forecasts of growth were reduced to between 1 and 2 per cent. The country's energy crisis can be largely blamed for this. As the economy grew, energy supply was not able to keep up with growth in demand. Shortages in residential and business areas followed. With varying degrees of success, the government has been asking energy consumers to reduce consumption by nearly 30 per cent.

The US economic slowdown in 2001 also affected the Brazilian economy. Twenty-four per cent of all Brazilian exports and 23 per cent of its imports are with the US. Even more significant is the financial and economic crisis of Argentina, a neighbor and a major trade partner under the Mercosur agreement. In fact, Brazil's exports to Argentina fell by nearly 30 per cent between 1997 and 2000. Its imports also declined by 16 per cent.[12] Brazil is also burdened by a large foreign debt that amounts to 7 per cent of GDP.[13]

The importance of Latin America to the Brazilian economy cannot be overstated. In fact, 26 per cent of Brazil's exports are destined to other Latin American countries. The country's strategic position helps to explain why this is true. With 170.6 million people and situated in the center of South America, Brazil has been able to negotiate major FDI into the country. Foreign MNEs have preferred to settle operations in Brazil and export to neighboring countries rather than locate elsewhere in Latin America and have to face trade barriers in the continent's largest market. Perhaps the most notorious industry to have followed this pattern is the auto industry. Today, Brazil is the manufacturing hub for motor vehicles in South America.

MNE investment

There have been hundreds of new investments and expansions in Brazil in recent years. Mercedes-Benz has completed a five-year, $500 million investment in new lines of trucks and buses. Ferruzi of Italy spent $250 million to buy a large local cleaning products company. Michelin put $140 million into tire plant expansions. The Bank of Boston invested $75 million in computerization and telecommunications. Dell opened its first manufacturing plant in Brazil with an initial investment of over $100 million dollars. The plant is expected to become South America's manufacturing hub.[14] MNE-controlled firms dominate a number of manufacturing sectors, including automobiles, electrical and communications products, large computers, pharmaceuticals, and non-ferrous metals.

The government's privatization program, which was initiated in the early 1990s, has also been a source of FDI. Telebras, the state-owned telecommunications company, was privatized for $19 billion in 1998. The company was broken into 12 subsidiaries that were sold mostly to foreign MNEs, including Spain's Telefónica and MCI of the US. In the banking sector, Santander Central Hispano of Spain invested $3.6 billion for a controlling interest in Brazil's Banco do Estado de São Paolo in 2000 and ABN Amro invested 29.4 billion to purchase the state bank Paraiban in 2001. (See the Real Case: "Brazil: state-owned enterprises are privatized," in Chapter 14.)

Table 19.4 displays the source of Brazilian FDI. The EU is the largest investor in Brazil, accounting for 46.8 per cent of total stocks. The US is the second largest source of FDI at 24.2 per cent.

Local MNEs

The size of the economy, the amount of natural resources, and the government's protectionist industrial policy all contributed to the development of Brazil's MNEs. Today, 41 of Latin American's top 100 companies are Brazilian.[15]

Table 19.4 FDI in Brazil, 2000

Country/period	*FDI flows 2000*	*% of total*	*Stock of FDI 2000*	*% of total*
United States	5,398.7	18.1	35,388.7	24.2
Canada	192.8	0.6	2,920.5	2.0
Mercosur (1)	1,226.7	4.1	2,256.9	1.5
European Union (2)	19,542.0	65.4	68,483.2	46.8
Japan	384.7	1.3	4,129.6	2.8
Triad	25,325.5	84.8	108,001.4	73.9
Others	3,131.4	10.5	33,039.1	22.6
Total per period	29,876.4	100.0	146,217.9	100.0

Notes: Only FDI of over US $10 million is recorded.

(1) Mercosur refers to FDI from Argentina and Uruguay.

(2) Only includes Germany, France, Italy, the Netherlands, Belgium, Spain, Portugal, Sweden, Luxembourg, and the UK.

Source: Banco Central do Brasil.

Brazil's large oil reserves provided the necessary environment for the emergence of Petrobras, Brazil's largest oil company and the largest Latin American company with revenues of $25.5 billion. (See Appendix 19A.) Through international alliances, Braspetro, Petrobras' international branch, has secured participation in over 130 exploration contracts around the world. Utilities and telecommunication companies in Brazil are also among the largest in Latin America. These companies benefited from the large population base and the protectionism afforded by the government prior to privatization.

Brazil is one of the best-known examples of technology and skill transfers from MNEs to local producers. The enforcement of local content rules of up to 95 per cent during the late 1950s and early 1960s forced foreign MNEs to set up local operations and most importantly to hire and train Brazilian suppliers. The auto sector is the best example.[16] Skill transfers have made Brazil a major exporter of auto parts and have allowed the development of other industries. Founded in 1969, Embraer, Brazil's small plane manufacturer, benefited from both the supply of engineers and mechanics and the education that was made available to supply the requirements of foreign MNEs. Today, Embraer is the world's fourth largest civilian aircraft manufacturer.[17]

Labor

Multinationals report that the Brazilian labor force is quite good. However, many firms find that they have to offer remedial education as well as regular training because of the country's poor educational system. A shortage of managerial talent has increased the competition for hiring at the management level and thus has driven up salaries. However, labor costs are low in comparison with those of industrial nations.

The 1988 constitution gives workers freedom to strike, restricted only by requirements such as protection of essential services and minimum quorums for strike votes. Many trade unions are highly politicized and work stoppages have become common.

The government has been slow to reduce inflation, the deficit, and the size of the federal bureaucracy. Yet because of its huge market, the country continues to be of interest to MNEs. At the same time it is particularly interested in linking itself to both the US and the EU markets via increased trade.

ASIA AND THE PACIFIC

Pacific nations constitute a huge geographic area and, in some cases, a rapidly growing market.[18] This helps to explain why, despite the economic slowdown in Asia that began in the late 1990s, many foreign firms are targeting these markets. In 1999, inward flows of FDI to developing South East Asia were $96.1 billion.[19]

DuPont intends to invest $3 billion in Asia during the current decade. After only five years on-site, Apple Computer has established ties with over 100 Asian software developers, including a host of firms in Hong Kong that are providing programming for its product line. Colgate-Palmolive has moved into Thailand and taken 40 per cent of the shampoo market away from the Japanese while Pizza Hut and Kentucky Fried Chicken are signing up dozens of local franchisees in the region. Sheraton, Hyatt, and Holiday Inns are expanding into the area, and Citibank is offering a wide variety of services, including automated teller machines, credit cards, and home equity loans.[20]

In establishing successful operations, MNEs use guidelines that are similar to those employed in Japan. These include (1) have a local partner and get to know the individual,[21] (2) put a strong and enduring emphasis on the quality of output, (3) tailor output to the specific needs of the local market, (4) rely heavily on nationals to market the product, and (5) have a solid understanding of local service requirements.[22]

China

China (see accompanying map) has the largest population in the world, and in recent years the nation's economy has done much better than casual observers realize.[23] Exports have outpaced imports and inflation, which at the beginning of the 1990s stood at over 20 per cent, dropped to 10 per cent by 1999.[24] At the same time annual GDP growth slowed from its rapid 10 per cent annual rate in the mid-1990s, but still remained a healthy 7.5 per cent in 2001.[25] Today the country's GDP is approximately $4.5 trillion and GDP per capita is in the range of $3,600.[26]

At the same time the government has been moving toward privatization and encouraging greater entrepreneurial efforts.[27] The International Monetary Fund estimates that China's GDP is far greater than commonly believed. Today the country's economy is just slightly smaller than Japan's and approximately half that of the US. Clearly, China is a major economic power.[28] In November 2001, China was finally admitted to the World Trade Organization after 15 years trying to join. This should reinforce moves towards market liberalization.[29]

In particular, southern China is proving to be one of the world's booming economies, although this geographic region has begun to slow down somewhat in the last four years.[30]

Many companies, especially those in nearby Hong Kong, now have their production handled in provinces directly across from Hong Kong on the mainland because of the low wage rates in China. In addition, China is becoming a preferred area for investment, second only to the US[31] for annual inflows of FDI.

FDI and trade account for approximate 40 per cent of China's GDP.[32] Despite international enthusiasm at China's reforms, critics argue that change is not occurring fast enough. The largest Chinese banks are all burdened with non-performing debt, a legacy of supporting inefficient state-owned enterprises. China still has one of the most unreliable banking systems in the Asian region.

MNE investment

Multinationals have made a large number of investments in China. Occidental Petroleum has put over $180 million into a coal mining project. Motorola has invested $120 million to produce semiconductors and mobile phones, and General Motors has a $1.3 billion joint venture with a Shanghai automotive company to build Buick Century and Regal cars in China.[33] Dow Chemical has a $25 million joint venture in a polyurethane plant. H. J. Heinz has a majority interest in a $10 million baby-food plant. Procter & Gamble has put $10 million into a joint venture factory to produce laundry and personal care products, and Hewlett-Packard has a similar amount in an electronics joint venture. RJR Nabisco has a $9 million venture to manufacture Ritz crackers. Seagram has put up $6 million to make whiskey and wine products. Babcock and Wilcox have put $6 million into a joint venture boiler factory. Mitsubishi has invested $4.3 million in a venture to build elevators. Other firms on this growing list include Bell Telephone, DaimlerChrysler, General Bearing, Gillette, Lockheed, Pabst Brewing, Peugeot, Squibb, Volkswagen, and Xerox, to name but 10.

In 2000 alone, over 12,000 foreign companies set up wholly-owned subsidiaries in China for a total of US $53.6 billion in FDI. In the same year, the number of Chinese–foreign MNE joint ventures reached over 10,000.[34] There are a number of reasons that MNEs want to do business in China. One is the growing market for both industrial and consumer goods. A second is the rapid growth of the economy, which is increasing the country's purchasing power as well as the desire to modernize its roads, communications system, and other aspects of its infrastructure. At the same time MNEs must be cautious.[35] The Tiananmen Square massacre showed multinationals how quickly the government could change position and subsequently increase a firm's political risk.[36] Similarly, foreign investors are wary of the communist party's fall 2002 meeting in which a new set of leaders will be selected to run the country.[37]

Local MNEs

When the East China Trade Fair opened in 2001, it featured 100 international companies seeking to enter the Chinese market and 1,000 Chinese companies hoping to access markets abroad.[38] The rising demand from a growing middle class sector is not only attracting foreign MNEs but also fueling the growth of local companies, which are now seeking to expand internationally. One example is that of Legend, China's largest PC manufacturer with a 30 per cent market share. The company is also emerging as the Asia-Pacific market leader. Despite its dominant position, Legend must begin to prepare for more intense competition from foreign PC manufacturers eager to enter the lucrative Chinese market. US companies are already competing in China, but together they have less than 15 per cent of the market. Dell is one of the smallest competitors in the Chinese market, nonetheless, over the last few years, the company has grown considerably by tailoring its market strategy to the performance-seeking Chinese consumer. A Chinese buyer can now go to Dell's website and virtually build his or her own machine. Dell will then assemble it and ship it. To protect market share, local companies like Legend are going to have to learn to innovate, particularly in the area of marketing.

Though not included in Appendix 19B, Sinopec is China's largest oil company with revenues of over $45.3 billion in 2000. Petroleum companies in China are state-owned enterprises. Yet, Sinopec and PetroChina (the second largest oil company) are tasting the waters of privatization by offering minority ownership to foreign and domestic investors. For instance, in 2000 Sinopec raised $1 billion in international markets and in 2001 an additional $1.4 billion was raised in the Shanghai Stock Exchange.[39] Despite being the largest companies, Sinopec and PetroChina lag behind the smaller China National Petroleum Corporation (CNPC) in expanding their international presence. In 2002, CNPC purchased Repsol-YPF's operations in Indonesia for $585 million and, only a week later, two subsidiaries of CNPC purchased a 30 per cent share of two Azerbaijan onshore fields. For more on China, see the box "International Business Strategy in Action: Chinese multinational enterprises."

INTERNATIONAL BUSINESS STRATEGY *IN ACTION*

The Chinese multinational enterprises

Since Prime Minister Deng Xiaoping moved to reform China in 1978, the world's largest country in terms of population has been moving from closed central planning towards an open market economy. The Chinese government has introduced incentives for entrepreneurship, opened stock markets, and lured foreign investors. China's entry into the World Trade Organization in November 2001, a culminating point after nearly two decades of negotiations, officially ended the country's isolation. For the first time, however, the competitiveness of large Chinese companies will be tested against foreign companies.

Most large Chinese MNEs are also state-owned enterprises (SOEs) that were created during the communist period. SOEs employ approximately 44 per cent of the urban population in China and represent 70 per cent of the government's revenues, making them an important sector in the economy. The table below shows the 12 largest Chinese MNEs.

The largest SOEs are in the petroleum, energy, utilities, and banking sectors (see table). Many of these companies also do international business. Indeed, Sinochem, the country's largest trader of chemicals, generates 57 per cent of its revenue outside China. Even among smaller SOEs, such as Citic Pacific, foreign revenue can constitute upwards of 50 per cent of total revenue.

The Chinese government has placed SOEs in one of three categories depending on management skills and the nature of the industry in which they operate: (1) The most badly managed and least likely to succeed – by some accounts nearly half of SOEs fall

The largest Chinese MNEs, 2000

Rank	*MNE*	*Industry*	*Revenues $m*
1	Sinopec	Petroleum refining	45,346
2	State Power	Utilities: Gas and electric	42,549
3	China National Petroleum	Energy	41,684
4	Industrial & Commercial Bank of China	Banks: Commercial and savings	22,070
5	China Telecommunications	Telecommunications	20,813
6	Bank of China	Banks: Commercial and savings	19,496
7	Sinochem	Trading	18,036
8	China Mobile Communications	Telecommunications	15,045
9	China Construction Bank	Banks: Commercial and savings	12,616
10	Cofco	Trading	12,517
11	Agricultural Bank of China	Banks: Commercial and savings	11,662
12	Jardine Matheson	Food and drugstores	10,362

Sources: Fortune, *The Fortune Global 500*, 2001.

in this category; (2) those which could be restructured under better management; and (3) those with potential to become national drivers of the economy – these are estimated at 10 per cent of SOEs. Those SOEs in the first category will most likely be forced out of business as quickly as the government can find ways of employing the layoffs in the private sector. SOEs in the second category are being sold off in the hope that better management will make them more efficient. Approximately 1,000 SOEs were sold in the 1990s. The third category of SOEs are considered the government's jewels, and are to be polished to compete under international rules. These SOEs are expected to do for China what the *chaebols* and *keiretsus* did for South Korea and Japan.

The Chinese government has put these best performing companies on the path of liberalization. These SOEs now enjoy more autonomy from the central government and control over their suppliers. Foreign investors have also been allowed to hold minority stakes in these large SOEs. By measuring stock market confidence in its foreign listings, SOEs have begun to incorporate concepts of best practice. The government hopes that this will slowly change the mentality of SOEs to allow them to compete successfully with foreign MNEs.

The banking industry

At 40 per cent of GDP, China has a large savings rate. These resources, however, have often been used to fuel inefficient SOEs. Banking reform is therefore crucial to the development of a free market. There are four major banks in China: the Bank of China, the Agricultural Bank of China, the Industrial & Commercial Bank of China, and the China Construction Bank. Eighty per cent of these banks' loans are to SOEs, and capital allocation is often the result of connections, not reliability and profitability.

The Chinese government attempted to solve the problem by creating Asset Management Companies (AMCs), which were to take over the bank's bad loans while the large banks got a fresh slate. By 2000, however, there was little improvement and, of all loans by major banks, 65 per cent were held by SOEs and over 30 per cent were deemed bad loans.

One reason for this failure is the government's concern that large-scale bankruptcies will lead to a destabilization of the economy and huge unemployment. Banks, therefore, continue to be pressured into lending to underperforming SOEs. Overstaffing is a problem at all levels of SOEs, with analysts estimating that, even after large layoffs over the last few years, 30–50 per cent of SOEs employees are redundant. The Chinese government is raising capital in foreign markets to increase economic efficiency, but also to finance social programs for displaced workers, including unemployment benefits, pensions, and retraining. Retrained employees will be expected to join the growing private sector. If this is done carefully, the government hopes, social unrest will be avoided.

The banking industry must also walk a fine line. On the one hand, banks must cater to the needs of government and SOEs and, on the other, increase efficiency of funds to prepare for foreign competition. There are signs that the banks are doing just this; over the last few years, an increasing number of loans by large banks have been to consumers seeking mortgages.

Websites: ***www.sinopec.com.cn***; ***www.sp.com.cn***; ***www.cnpc.com.cn***; ***www.icbc.com.cn***; ***www.chinatelecom.com.cn***; ***www.bank-of-china.com***; ***www.sinochem.com***; ***www.chinamobile.com***; ***www.ccb.com.cn/***; ***www.cofco.com.cn***; ***www.abchina.com*** and ***www.jardines.com***.

Sources: United Nations, *World Investment Report 2000*; "Pump Action," *Economist*, June 21, 2001; "The Giant Stirs," *Economist*, April 5, 2001; "An Outbreak of Honesty," *Economist*, May 17, 2001; "The Longer March," *Economist*, September 28, 2000.

Labor

One of the primary reasons that China is becoming a focal point for multinational investment is its low labor costs. The average factory wage ($100 per month) is about 10 per cent of that in more industrialized Pacific Rim countries such as Taiwan. On the other hand, the country has come under severe criticism for using prison labor to manufacture goods for export. This has caused Congress to back curbs on the country's access to markets in the US. A number of changes are now taking place regarding the country's human rights program.[40] However, there is great skepticism in many quarters regarding China's willingness to make changes.[41]

Doing business

The business environment in China is different from that of many other Pacific Rim countries because of its communist government. In recent years the government has often changed its approach to dealing with MNEs, resulting in confusion regarding both rules of operation and assessment of risk.[42] In dealing with this environment, one of the first important steps is to find an appropriate domestic partner.[43] It is more common in China for multinationals to use intermediaries in the process than elsewhere in the Pacific Rim. Among other sources, the China International Trust and Investment Corporation and the Ministry of Foreign Trade and Economic Cooperation offer such assistance. It is important to note that the government has a priority list of desired investments. Ventures involving advanced technology, exports, or the generation of foreign exchange are given the highest priority.

In a joint venture the local partner is typically responsible for providing the land and buildings and for carrying out local marketing. The MNE is expected to contribute the equipment, technology, and capital and to be responsible for export marketing. In those cases where the multinational is manufacturing for sales in China, high quality products, excellent service, and good promotional efforts are critical to success. Researchers have found that outstanding service and effective promotion can often make up for some lack of quality. However, price reductions and special sales terms are unlikely to offset poor quality. Similarly, while customer relations are important, they are often not enough to make up for poor quality or poor service. The Chinese want to buy the best quality available.

Additionally, it is important to remember that China still has a predominantly planned economy. The government determines imports and exports, and these decisions can have strong consequences for MNEs doing business here. For example, China has been running a large trade surplus with the US in recent years, and there is every reason to believe that, unless this situation is corrected, the US government will limit Chinese imports. This could result in a backlash against US MNEs in China. In addition, the US administration is creating a new trade policy toward China and other South East Asian countries that will require more open markets. So there are important political/economic risks that must be weighed when planning a joint venture here.

Active learning check 

Review your answer to Active Learning Case question 2 and make any changes you like. Then compare your answer with the one below.

2. Why did Acer form strategic alliances with IBM and Texas Instruments?

Acer was not familiar with the North American market and it was a new boy on the computer block. So it formed strategic alliances, whenever possible, with the dominant US MNEs. In doing so, Acer learned about the US triad market and how to distribute its products there. Acer was then able to move ahead of these once dominant US firms once it combined its efficiency in production with its new market knowledge of the rich North American customers.

India

India (see map of South and East Asia above) encompasses an area of approximately 1.3 million square miles and has a population of over 1 billion. In 2000, the country's GDP was estimated at $2.2 trillion. Economic growth during the 1990s was relatively high, averaging 6 per cent, with the highest growth occurring in the services and manufacturing sectors, which grew at a rate of 7.8 and 7.5 per cent respectively. The mere size of the market and its potential for growth should be of interest to foreign MNEs; however, a high level of economic and political uncertainty has consistently seen FDI flows fall short of expectations. In fact, in 2000, India FDI flows were 5 per cent of those destined to China.[44]

Prior to 1990 the government had done little to promote multinational interest. Politics often prevailed over economic interests and many MNEs found their dealings with the government to be time-consuming and frustrating. For example, both IBM and Coca-Cola left India in the late 1970s rather than accede to the government's demand that they reduce their majority holdings to 40 per cent. And when PepsiCo sought permission to invest in India in 1986, the company's request had to be reviewed by 15 committees and was subjected to a host of parliamentary debates as well as to thousands of unfavorable newspaper articles. In recent years, however, the political climate has changed and the government is now trying very hard to attract foreign investment, although there are still many pitfalls facing investors.[45]

MNE investment

Since the early 1990s India has been the focus of new attention by MNEs. The primary reason is that there is now greater operating freedom for foreign investors than at any time since the country gained its independence in 1947. Total FDI stock in 1990 was less than $1 billion, but today it is more than $16.4 billion and is continuing to increase with US MNEs leading the way. Coca-Cola has returned and invested $20 million to set up a wholly-owned subsidiary. IBM is back and has joined a $20 million 50/50 joint venture with India's Tata group to make computers and to develop software. Mission Energy, a Los Angeles-based company, has signed a memorandum of understanding to build a $900 million power plant near Bombay. J. P. Morgan, the investment banking firm, has a 40 per cent equity interest in a joint venture to trade securities, to underwrite new stock issues, and to handle related financial activities in addition to managing the India Magnum Fund, which has an investment value of $400 million. General Electric has formed a $40 million joint venture to make refrigerators and washing machines. To date, Toyota has invested over $130 million in India and is considering a further investment of $400–450 million to develop an affordable car.[46] Other firms doing business in the country include Gillette, BMW, DuPont, General Motors, Fujitsu, Kellogg's, and Texas Instruments.

Potential and problems

One of the primary attractions of India is the large middle class. Estimates place this group at over 100 million, a sizable market with the potential to generate billions of dollars of sales for MNE investors. The lower middle class, estimated at 200 million, is another significant market niche. A second attraction is the government's recent efforts to make things easier for foreign investors. The government has now eased restrictions on the repatriation of dividends by foreign MNEs and has begun sharply to reduce tariffs on imported goods. One of the major reasons behind these policy changes is that India realizes that the vigorous growth of its economy depends heavily on foreign capital, and in the past the country has failed to exploit this avenue.[47]

At the same time MNEs remain cautious. If the government were to change its policies, as it has so often in the past, these firms could end up losing millions of dollars.[48] On the other hand, many countries in Asia are making giant economic strides, most notably China, and India does not want to fall behind. For this reason, the country is likely to keep its doors open to MNEs. At the same time the nation will have to continue pushing its exports and creating more market links to Japan and the triad nations. To the extent that it can maintain strong relations with MNEs, India's chances of doing this will increase.[49]

Local MNEs

Over the last few years India has become a hub of information technology. Some of this can be attributed to Azim Premji, India's most prominent IT entrepreneur and one of the world's richest men, who turned his father's vegetable oil business into an international

IT conglomerate. The Premji company, Wipro, is the second largest Indian company in terms of market capitalization. Half of its revenues comes from its international IT branch, Wipro Technologies, which offers consulting, R&D, and a global support service to large MNEs, including Nortel Networks and Cisco Systems. Wipro Infotech, which provides IT services in India, accounts for an additional third of revenues. The company's other products include foodstuff, toiletries, and lightbulbs.[50] Wipro is only one company in a growing software sector in India that today not only enjoys internal recognition but also the support system necessary at the government and the education level.

India also has extensive natural resources and it is not surprising that two of its largest companies in terms of market capitalization are in the oil and gas industry: Reliance Petroleum and Indian Oil Corporation. With $22 billion in revenues and a third of India's oil refining capacity, state-owned Indian Oil Corporation is among Fortune 500 largest corporations; however, its international operations are limited to overseas offices in Kuwait, Kuala Lumpur, Dubai, and Mauritius. India also has a thriving pharmaceutical sector.

South Korea

South Korea has experienced rapid economic growth over the last two decades. The free enterprise system is well entrenched and the private sector dominates business, although government influence is considerable. GDP grew by 8.6 per cent in 2000, but in 2001 growth fell to 2 per cent. Interest rates have been rising and bankruptcies are up sharply.[51]

MNE investment

Despite the same type of resistance to foreign firms that is present in Japan, multinationals continue to invest in South Korea. Some major investments in recent years have come in chemicals, electronics, and machinery. Glaxo, the British pharmaceutical firm, is working with Lucky, a local pharmaceutical manufacturer, to develop and market antibiotics. Clerical Medical International, a British insurance group, has a joint venture with Coryo, a Korean firm, to sell insurance in that country. BASF, the German chemical firm, has bought three Korean operations, and GE Capital has purchased a controlling interest in Korea First Bank.[52] Other major investors include BP Amoco, Corning Glass, General Motors, Hewlett-Packard, IBM, Monsanto, Philips, Siemens, and Unilever.

Some major advantages of doing business in South Korea include a growing economy and increasing disposable income. Some major disadvantages include the difficulty of breaking into the market and of developing alliances that can effectively compete with the local conglomerates.

Local MNEs

South Korea's MNEs are some of the largest in the developing world and include such household names as Samsung, Hyundai, and Daewoo. These large MNEs are family-run conglomerates in industries ranging from electronics to construction. Individual companies in these conglomerates have traditionally enjoyed benefits from other conglomerate partners, including banking concessions, coordinated lobbying to the government and interconglomerate loans. For more on *chaebols*, see the Real Case: "Korean *chaebols*" at the end of this chapter.

Labor

Labor unrest has been a problem, although this may be subsiding. MNEs face labor shortages, and there are basic labor laws that provide for minimum working conditions, collective bargaining, and labor arbitration disputes. In recent years labor unrest has pushed wages up dramatically, and fringe benefits add as much as 80 per cent to the basic cost of the wage package. This has resulted in an increase in the cost of exported goods and thus some firms have seen their overseas sales drop sharply.

At present Korean companies and their workers are trying to put aside their differences and to regain productivity ground that was lost in the late 1980s. Many firms are cutting executive jobs, streamlining operations, and emphasizing high-tech output. These efforts are designed to protect local markets and to generate exports. As a result, South Korea will continue to be a competitive market for MNEs, and the country is likely to continue linking strongly to the US and EU parts of the triad as well as to Japan.[53]

Singapore

Singapore has seen strong economic growth and in 2000 GDP growth was estimated at 9.9 per cent, but in 2001 the economy contracted by 2 per cent.[54] Some of this is the economic downturn in the US. At the same time the government has been encouraging foreign investment, and restrictions on equity, licensing, and joint ventures are negligible.

MNE investment

Singapore has been a major target for investment by MNEs in recent years, especially for US firms which have invested more over the last five years than either the Japanese or the Europeans. DuPont is spending $100 million to build a fiber plant, which is part of a $1.1 billion investment planned for the country. Texas Instruments is building a $185 million plant to upgrade its memory-chip assembly facility and testing center. Matsushita is investing $330 million in a factory to make high-precision automatic insertion equipment. Sony is putting $200 million in a cathode-ray tube manufacturing plant.

Labor

Productivity has been rising rapidly in Singapore, and this has put a strain on the country to recruit the needed personnel. Unemployment is extremely low and the tight market has been producing average wage increases of 7–8 per cent annually through most of the 1990s. Workers, however, became responsive to the Asian crisis of the late 1990s and took on a wage cut of 5 per cent and 8 per cent in the late 1990s. Most workers in industrial plants and offices are unionized, but there has been little labor unrest in recent years. There is talk of paying new hires a lower wage than those currently in the workforce, resulting in two-tiered compensation. The country is also looking to increase its manufacturing and research and development expertise, and to let others handle the low-skill work.

Singapore's geographic size and limited labor force require that the country pick the right business niches. High-tech manufacturing, transportation, and financial services are primary targets of interest, and MNEs in these areas are finding the government prepared to help create the necessary environment to attract their investment. This strategy should also be useful in ensuring Singapore's continued success among US and EU triad members.

Australia

Australia is the only continent occupied by one country. Australia has a two-party political system and a legal framework that was developed from British law. There are approximately 19 million people in the country. The economy is strongly based on private enterprise, and the government's stated industry goal is to encourage the development of internationally competitive manufacturing and service sectors. In particular, this is resulting in government action to upgrade industrial science and technology, to promote and encourage the processing of local resources, and to assist in the diffusion of new management and production techniques.

MNE investment

Australia has been working very hard to attract FDI. Manufacturing has been receiving the largest share of new investment, followed by finance and real estate. The Japanese and Americans have been the major investors in recent years. Mitsui and Nippon Shinpan have purchased the remaining 50 per cent of the Mirage Resort Trust, investing a total of $390 million in the process. Chevron, Shell, and BP Amoco have continued their $9 billion gas development on the North West Shelf. Mobil has purchased oil refining and marketing operations from another oil company. Coca-Cola has bought 59 per cent of a local soft-drink manufacturer for $500 million.

Most foreign investments are not subject to specific equity rules; they simply need to be approved on a case-by-case basis. However, foreign investment is prohibited in utilities, radio, television, daily newspapers, and some parts of the civil aviation industry. There are also specific regulations governing foreign participation in the development of natural resources such as oil, coal, gas, and uranium, and real estate investments are examined to ensure that they clearly benefit the national interest. In the case of acquisitions and takeovers there are a series of basic rules which must be followed, including full knowledge of who is making the acquisition and providing the shareholders with reasonable time to consider the offer.

Local MNEs

Australia has a number of successful MNEs; however, like other non-triad nations, it lacks the scale necessary to be competitive at an international level. For this reason, businesses depend on ties with triad members and neighboring economies. For example, Australia's largest company BHP Billiton, the largest exporter of energy and hard coking coal, has resource-extracting operations in Africa, Australia, and Latin America and a presence in the North American, European, and Asian markets. Brambles Groups is another Australia company that has expanded through international markets. The Groups' business includes equipment pooling systems, waste management services, information management, and shipping to industrial clients. Brambles Industrial Services operates in Australia, the EU, and North America.

Labor

The workforce consists of 8 million people, who, in contrast to some other Asian and Pacific countries, are educated and well trained. As a result, there is an abundance of professionally skilled people but a shortage of skilled manual laborers. The government has attempted to address this problem through an aggressive immigration program in which skilled workers are given priority. Average weekly earnings vary from state to state, but companies must pay men and women equal wages for the same work. Worker salaries generally have three components: a minimum wage, a margin for skill, and a market premium offered by the employer and established by collective bargaining. Many workers are unionized, but unions are organized according to job function or trade rather than according to industry. As a result, there may be as many as 10 unions in a particular company and the power of any one of them is small. Moreover, wage and labor conflicts are traditionally settled by an arbitrator so that the union has less chance of "flexing its muscle" than it does in many other countries.

Australia has strong trading ties to Japan, which in recent years has purchased about 25 per cent of all exports. The US and the EU together purchase a similar percentage, but this is slowly declining. So as the 21st century unwinds, Australia is fashioning increased ties to the Japanese segment of the triad and is likely to find its economic future closely intertwined with that of Pacific Rim countries, rather than with traditional Anglo nations.

INTERNATIONAL BUSINESS STRATEGY *IN ACTION*

Unilever in Asia and Latin America

The second largest consumer goods business in the world, Unilever employs 261,000 people worldwide. It has production plants in 70 countries and sells its products in 158 countries. With annual revenues of $44 billion, it is considered one of the world's 100 largest MNEs. Its products include food and home and personal care products. The company's success can be attributed to two things: its long history of global presence and its decision in the 1990s to restructure its operations to better suit emerging markets.

Unilever was founded in 1929 through the merger of Margarine Unie (Dutch) and Lever Brothers (UK). Lever Brothers already had operations in Africa and Asia, so that, when Unilever was created, it was already a multinational enterprise with 20 per cent of its profits originating outside Europe. By 1980, this number had doubled, mainly due to expansions in Africa, South America, and Asia.

Today, the company sees itself as a multicultural multinational with a global strategy. This strategy includes the development of its operations in five key selected regions: Southern South America, Central and Eastern Europe, India, China, and South East Asia. Unilever understands that it has an advantage in national responsiveness against its main competitors in many of these regions. It has been in South America since the company was founded, with operations in Chile (1928), Argentina (1928), and Brazil (1929). In 1927 it started operations in the Philippines, followed by Thailand in 1932 and India and Indonesia in 1933. The company started operations in China in the 1920s and when the government opened up in the 1980s Unilever was quick to sign joint ventures to re-enter the market. Today it has sales of $300 million in China.

Unilever's success in emerging markets is a result of its regional perspective. To sell to consumers from different cultures and economic means, it must comprehend their specific needs. The company recognizes this need for adapting to local tastes and is committed to ensuring that managers understand the special needs of their diverse customers. Differences in taste, culture, and income must all be taken into account. In India, one of their most profitable regions, future managers are required to live with a family in a remote village for six months. This is to remind them of who their customers are. In Brazil, the largest economy in South America, the company has developed a special cheap shampoo to cater to the poorest and the largest social group. Furthermore, the company hopes to increase the amount of local innovation in emerging markets and is expected to finish a program to institute innovation centres in key regions.

Emerging markets require a long-term approach. The majority of the world's growth potential is in these markets, but the short-term risks are high. Economic situations like the Argentinian crisis of 2001, the Asian crisis of 1998, and the Mexican peso devaluation of 1994 can cause large setbacks in the short run. A multinational can reduce risk by having operations in different areas of the world. Bad times in one region can be offset by good times in another region. Unilever's global presence certainly allows it to reduce risk in this way, but the company goes a step further. It produces a variety of products to cater to different income levels. In one country it may sell a cheap shampoo and an expensive shampoo. If the country goes into a recession, operations are shifted to produce more of the cheap shampoo, reducing the impact.

Website: ***www.unilever.com***.

Sources: Adapted from Deborah Orr, "A Giant Reawakens," *Forbes*, January 25, 1999, pp. 52–54; "Munching on Change – Unilever's Food Business," *Economist*, January 6, 1996, pp. 56–61; ***www.unilever.com***; Fortune, *The Global 500*, 2001; "Foreign Firms Weight Argentinean Fall-Out," *BBC.co.uk*, December 21, 2001.

EASTERN EUROPE

The difficulty of moving from a communist to a market system has plunged much of Eastern Europe into economic turmoil. National currencies such as the Russian ruble have lost much of their value, and because many administered prices have been eliminated, the purchasing power of the average citizen in Eastern Europe has declined. So too have the GNP and the industrial and agricultural outputs declined, while unemployment has risen. Simply put, the economic picture in this geographic region is bleak. The region needs triad-based investment and access to the rich markets of the triad countries for its exports.

The move toward a free-market economy carries with it a host of short-term problems. Yet, if these countries continue their efforts toward privatization, with the encouragement of foreign investment, they can turn the corner and begin developing more prosperous economies.[55] The major challenges that these countries must be prepared to face include (1) resisting the temptation to move back toward centralized planning in order to control current inflation and unemployment and (2) accepting the fact that the inflow of foreign capital, technology, and managerial expertise often brings with it social and political pressures to do things that up to now have been anathema, such as allowing foreign ownership and control of local operations. This is the type of environment in which the countries of Eastern Europe now find themselves. Because of its size and economic conditions, the country that faces the greatest challenge is Russia.

Russia

On December 8, 1991, the leaders of Russia, the Ukraine, and Byelorussia declared that the Soviet Union had ceased to exist and proclaimed a new "Commonwealth of Independent States".[56] The accompanying map shows Russia both before and after the breakup of the Soviet Union. Currently there are numerous changes being introduced as the Russian government works to right the nation's economic "ship". This will be a major challenge for a number of reasons, including the fact that the country faces far more problems than do most other Eastern European nations.

Price and economic reform

The Russians are currently undertaking price reform. In many areas administered prices and subsidies are being eliminated and free-market forces are taking over. These developments have had a major effect on the economy. During the first six months of 1991 GNP declined by 10 per cent, agricultural output went down by 11 per cent, and industrial output sank by 6 per cent. On the positive side, these developments were not unexpected, given the experiences of other countries that have moved from command to market economies. For example, Poland's industrial output declined by 29 per cent in the year following the transition to a free-market economy.

Since then, however, things have gone from bad to worse. By the end of the 1990s the economy was reeling.[57] Russia's foreign debt, which stood at around $115 billion in 1992, had risen to $145 billion by 1998.[58] In addition, annual debt payments were a whopping

Source: www.state.gov.

$17 billion and some analysts were predicting that the government would default on its foreign debt.

At the same time the Yeltsin government was having political problems and a majority of Russians wanted to see him resign before his term of office was up.[59] The International Monetary Fund has tried to help, and, despite initial opposition to reform, a deal was negotiated in 1998.[60] Since then, Russia's economy has recovered substantially. GDP growth in 2000 was estimated at 3.5 per cent.[61] One reason is the high price of oil, which has allowed the government to finance much needed infrastructure.

Privatization

Another major undertaking is the privatization of industry. There are thousands of state-owned factories in Russia and privatization is critical because without it the government is unlikely to stimulate a broad industrial recovery. Private ownership is the key to economic growth. However, progress in this area is difficult since management skills and capital are lacking.

Privatization is taking a number of different forms. One is that of turning 25–35 per cent of the state-run businesses over to the workers and managers, who then assume managerial responsibility and also set up a board of directors to oversee the operation. A second is to attract private investors both inside and outside the country.

Business dealings in Russia

Despite the economic turbulence, some MNEs are doing business in Russia and others have plans to do so. (Table 19.5 provides a list of major US firms in Russia.) For example, IBM is providing 40,000 personal computers for Russian schools; DaimlerChrysler has a contract for a $140 million plant to build buses; the Carroll Group of Britain is constructing a $250 million hotel/trade center; Alcatel, the giant French telecommunications company, has a $2.8 billion contract to supply advanced digital telephone switches; McDonald's constructed an office building in downtown Moscow and opened many additional restaurants throughout the country; and United Technologies is installing the first-ever data communications switching center to handle fax and electronic mail. But this FDI is still relatively small (on a triad perspective), and it will remain so until profits can be repatriated at a rate commensurate with the political risk in Russia.

US soft-drink companies provide other examples. In the mid-1990s, Coca-Cola opened its first production plant in Russia. This plant allowed Coca-Cola to stop relying on imports from Coke plants in Western Europe. PepsiCo agreed to spend more than

Table 19.5 Major US firms doing business in Russia

Abbott Laboratories	Cooper Industries	IBM	Polaroid
American Express	Corning*	Johnson & Johnson	Procter & Gamble
Andersen (Arthur)	CSX*	Lilly (Eli)	Radisson Hotels*
Archer-Daniels-Midland	Dow Chemical	Litton Industries	Ralston Purina
AT&T	Dresser Industries	McDermott*	RJR Nabisco Holdings
BankAmerica Corp.	DuPont	McDonald's*	Strauss (Levi)*
BP Amoco*	Emerson Electric	Minnesota Mining & Manufacturing	Texaco*
Cargill	Ernst & Young	Mobil*	Union Carbide
Caterpillar	Exxon*	Monsanto	United Telecomm.*
Chase Manhattan Corp.	FMC	Occidental Petroleum	Upjohn & Pharmacia
Chevron*	General Motors	PepsiCo	US West*
Coca-Cola	Hewlett-Packard	Pfizer	Xerox
Conoco*	Honeywell	Philip Morris	Young & Rubicam
Control Data			

* Established business in Russia after 1986.

$1 billion to increase to 50 the number of bottling plants in the Soviet Union, allowing it to produce 2 billion 8-ounce containers annually. The company also received government permission to introduce disposable, lightweight aluminum cans and plastic containers to replace the heavy 11½-ounce bottles that must be returned and which limit distribution to 20 kilometers around each bottling plant. In return for the soft-drink products PepsiCo took payment in the form of Stolichnaya vodka and received transfer titles to 10 Soviet-built ocean-going ships. This barter agreement is important to PepsiCo because the ruble is currently worthless in the international market. However, by selling vodka, the company can earn a substantial profit on its investment.

Another development is the rise in joint ventures. Bankers Trust, J. P. Morgan, Boeing, and Pennzoil also have joint ventures, and other firms such as Archer-Daniel-Midland, Dresser Industries, Eastman Kodak, General Electric, Johnson & Johnson, Pratt & Whitney, and RJR Nabisco are working on deals of their own.

Another interesting development is the increase in joint ventures between Russian businesses and foreign partners. Aeroflot, the giant Russian airline, has 42 joint ventures and is looking to establish even more as management seeks to make the company a major player in the international airline industry.

Active learning check

Review your answer to Active Learning Case question 3 and make any changes you like. Then compare your answer with the one below.

3. Why has Acer become a successful MNE whereas Russia has not developed a world-class computer firm?

Whereas Acer built its international success on the hardworking entrepreneurial capabilities of Taiwan, Russian businesses are still burdened by the legacy of communism and state control. The Russian people are just as hard working as the Chinese in Taiwan but the free-market system of Taiwan generates new businesses and rewards entrepreneurship. In contrast the old Soviet command economy system destroyed individual initiative, alienated workers from capital and prevented international expansion as Russia's large domestic organizations were economically inefficient.

Poland

Poland encompasses an area of approximately 121,000 square miles, and has a population of almost 40 million. The country's borders were reconfigured at the end of World War II, and in the decade that followed Poland was ruled by Stalinist communists. By the late 1950s, however, a more independent Polish Communist party began to emerge – collectivization of farms was ended and religious freedom was permitted. During the 1980s the powerful, non-communist labor unions wrested major concessions from the government, and, despite the use of martial law and the imprisonment of union leaders, at the end of the decade there were free elections and economic policies that were designed to privatize industry and to bring about free-market conditions. In the process the country encountered major price inflation.[62] By the mid-1990s, however, the GDP was growing at over 6 per cent per year as legislation to promote an open and liberal investment environment was beginning to generate results. The country slowed down by the late 1990s with growth falling to 4–5 per cent and, by 2001, the country's economy had slowed down even further to 1.5–2 per cent. The present economic problems are partly the result of external factors, such as the slowdown of its major partners, including Germany, but also of the inability of the government to speed up economic reform that threatened to put a stop to FDI.[63]

Business dealings in the country

A number of MNEs have invested in Poland and many others are looking to do so.[64] Between 1991 and 2000, FDI inflows totalled $39 billion.[65] Pilkington, the world-renowned glass manufacturer, has put $150 million into HSO Sandomierz, a local company in the same industry. Asea Brown Boveri has bought Zamech, a turbine manufacturer, for $50 million. One factor that lures investors is the low hourly wage in industries such as manufacturing. This makes Poland an attractive locale for manufacturers. Other investors are being lured by the opportunity to apply their technology and management expertise in improving Polish businesses and making them competitive in the local and regional markets. This is particularly important because of the major privatization effort that is now under way by the government. Although it will take years to privatize the economy totally, given that there are over 8,000 large state-owned enterprises, rapid strides have been made and free enterprise is beginning to take a strong foothold. The government is encouraging small business formation, and in 2000 the country had 2 million small and medium-sized enterprises.[66]

Like the other Eastern European countries examined in this section, Poland faces a myriad of economic challenges.[67] However, the nation's vigorous growth in the private sector and its determination to close the gap in living standards between itself and Western neighbors will continue to make the country attractive to MNEs during the millennium.

While we have only been able to consider some of the more important non-triad countries in this chapter, we have actually discussed most of the FDI and the large multinational enterprises. Some areas, such as Africa, have few multinational enterprises of any significance (other than a few resource-based firms like Anglogold – see Chapter 7). The focus of this book is upon the international business done by the world's largest 500 multinationals (which account for over 80 per cent of all the FDI and half of the world's trade). The activities of these large firms govern the nature of international business activity.

Based on an extension of Appendix 19A, the largest 100 Latin American companies come from: Brazil (41); Mexico (30); Chile (16); Argentina (9); Peru (2); and Venezuela (2). See Appendix 19D. Thus, by discussing Brazil, Mexico, and Chile in this book we have covered 87 per cent of the largest Latin American companies. Much the same is true for the Top 100 Asia-Pacific companies (from Appendix 19E) and for the Top 100 Eastern European countries (from Appendix 19F). There is no need to discuss all countries and all companies, just the significant ones. See Appendixes 19E, 19F, and 19G.

KEY POINTS

1. **Non-triad countries need investment from, and access to, a triad bloc in order to develop global industries. Current trends such as privatization and legislative changes that are designed to encourage foreign direct investment (FDI) are helping these countries to tap their economic potential. A number of factors will influence their success during this decade, including privatization, attraction of foreign capital, and intra-regional trade agreements that can be helpful in creating mini common markets. Additionally, each non-triad nation will continue trying to establish markets in triad countries.**
2. **Countries in Latin America are beginning to follow Mexico's lead and to link their economies more closely to triad nations. Chile and Brazil, for example, are now encouraging FDI and have privatized many state-owned businesses. As a result, their economies are beginning to improve.**

3. Asia has some of the fastest growing economies in the world. China has been doing extremely well in recent years, as labor costs are so low that more and more companies in the Asian region are transferring their manufacturing to China. The government, however, will have to take steps to deal with the country's large trade surpluses with triad countries such as the US. There is likely to be strong pressure for continued improvement in human rights or many industrialized countries will take trade action against China.
4. Other Asian countries that are of interest to MNEs include India, South Korea, and Singapore. India is now trying to attract foreign investment and the government's new policies are designed to make it easier for MNEs to set up operations there. The government is also interested in linking the country's trade to triad partners. Korea and Singapore have had strong economic growth in the past but are currently facing economic downturns. Both are looking to establish stronger ties to the EU and North American triads. Australia is following a slightly different strategy, becoming more economically intertwined with Asian countries like Japan and relying less on the triads of the EU and the US as their primary markets.
5. Russia is currently undergoing major economic changes. One way that the country is trying to improve its economy is through privatization. This development is taking a number of different forms, including turning control over to the workers and managers and entering into joint ventures with foreign MNEs. Poland has over 8,000 large state-owned businesses, and foreign investment banks and accounting firms are acting as advisors in helping to privatize them. At the same time many Poles have started their own businesses.

REVIEW AND DISCUSSION QUESTIONS

1. Why is it critical for Latin American countries such as Chile and Brazil to link with the triad, in most cases the US? Why do these countries not simply create their own economic union and compete directly with triad members?
2. How well has the Chinese economy done in recent years? What has helped to account for this? Cite and describe two factors.
3. China currently faces a number of problems that could lead to an economic slowdown. What are two of them? Identify and describe both.
4. Why does China want to link its trade to nations such as the US? Why not simply trade with Pacific Rim countries?
5. What guidelines must MNEs follow when doing business in China? Identify and briefly describe each.
6. Why is India now becoming a focal point of interest for multinationals? Identify and describe two reasons.
7. Why do South Korea and Singapore want to link their economies to those of Japan and other triad members? Based on what you have learned in other chapters, as well as in this one, explain the logic of this international business strategy.
8. How well has the Australian economy done in recent years? Why is it critical for Australia to link its economy with the triad? Which triad members would be of most value? Explain.
9. How is privatization taking place in Russia? Identify and describe two different approaches.
10. How successful has Russia been in attracting foreign investment? What accounts for this?
11. How well is privatization progressing in Poland? What are the major stumbling blocks?
12. Where has Poland had the greatest business success in the transition to a free-market economy? How likely is it that this development will continue? Explain.

REAL CASE

Korean *chaebols*

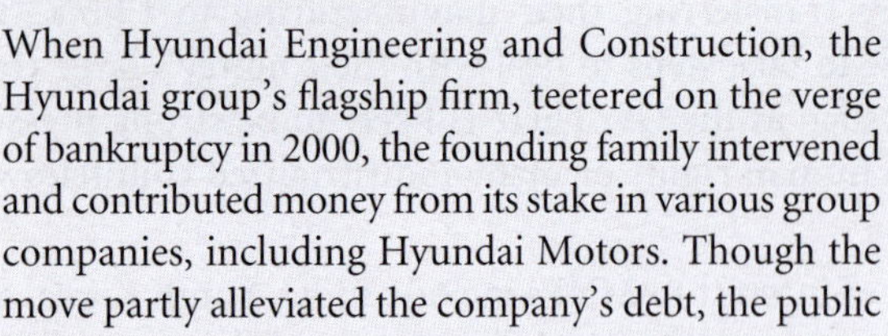

When Hyundai Engineering and Construction, the Hyundai group's flagship firm, teetered on the verge of bankruptcy in 2000, the founding family intervened and contributed money from its stake in various group companies, including Hyundai Motors. Though the move partly alleviated the company's debt, the public saw the move as the continuation of the cartel-like operations of South Korea's largest MNEs, the *chaebols*.

For over three decades, these family-run conglomerates were revered as South Korea's engines of growth. There is much merit to this. Between 1970 and 2000, South Korea's GDP grew by 750 per cent. Industrial production increased at an even higher rate and grew to account for 93 per cent of GDP in 2000. In South Korea's transition to industrialization, a transition that many other poor countries have tried to make with little success, *chaebols* played a mayor role.

The four largest *chaebols* are Hyundai, Samsung, LG International, and SK. Across the world, these companies have become household names producing everything from shipbuilding, auto manufacturing to electronics. For instance, Samsung Electronics is the largest South Korean company and the seventh largest electronics company in the world with revenues of nearly $38.5 billion. The Hyundai group's most profitable company, Hyundai Motors, is the 13th largest auto maker in the world. It is also the largest non-triad auto maker.

Chaebols had their origin on the vision of individuals. In 1938, Byung-Chull Lee founded Samsung and began exporting food to China and not long after that he opened a light manufacturing business. The 1970s saw Samsung enter into the chemical and heavy industries. In the 1980s, the company entered the aerospace and telecommunications industry. During this decade, Samsung also became a major world supplier of semiconductors.

In 1946 Chung Ju Yung, who worked as a delivery boy for a rice mill in the 1930s, purchased an auto repair shop that was the early foundation of the Hyundai group. In 1947 Hyundai Engineering and Construction was established to take advantage of reconstruction contracts at the end of World War II. By 1976, Hyundai brought its country into the auto business with the introduction of the Pony.

During the 1960s, *chaebols* prospered under a government fostered development plan. When Park Chung Hee became South Korea's president after a military coup d'état, he instituted an import-substitution strategy that favored large local producers and provided them with cheap credit, tax breaks, and other benefits. After Park Chung Hee's death, low-interest loans continued to be made available to *chaebols* because of ties with banks. Since banks could not let a borrower the size of *chaebols* fail, credit was made available regardless of profitability, depriving the non-*chaebol* businesses sector from needed credit.

In the 1990s, the *chaebols* took on debt to finance large expansion projects. The Asian financial crisis in 1997 reduced their revenues to such an extent that these companies could no longer pay their creditors. For a long time, *chaebols* managed to conceal their troubles by providing member companies with intra-conglomerate loans. In addition, foreign and domestic investors became increasingly aware of murky financial reporting practices. By the end of the crisis, Daewoo had become bankrupt.

In 1997, the IMF was called to bail out the South Korean economy after an unprecedented drop on the Korean won created a debt crisis. As part of the bailout, South Korea was to restructure its *chaebols*. Debt-to-equity ratios had to be reduced. Financial reporting had to become transparent. Most importantly, non-core businesses were to be spun off.

To oversee the transformation of the *chaebol* and, in turn, the Korean economy, the Financial Supervisory Commission (FSC) was established in 1998. Yet, only two years later, a senior officer of the FSC committed suicide amid allegations that FSC employees had been taking bribes from *chaebols*. Although *chaebols* have reduced their debt-to-equity ratios, unreliable financial reporting continues to occur. Most importantly, many *chaebols* continue to resist selling off their non-core businesses.

Websites: ***www.daewoo.com***; ***www.hmc.co.kr***; ***www.hyundai.com***; ***www.hyundai-motor.com***; ***www.samsung.com***; ***www.samsungelectronics.com***; ***www.samsung.co.kr***; ***www.lgikorea.com*** and ***www.sk.co.kr***.

Sources: Orla Ryan, "Collapse of the Korean Chaebol," *BBC.co.uk*, December 19, 2000; "Hyundai's New Rescue Plan," *BBC.co.uk*, November 20, 2000; Donald Macintyre, "Eulogy: 'He Was a Nation Builder'," *Asia Times*, March 23, 2001; Assif Shameen, "Reinventing Korea Inc." *Asiaweek.com*, September 20, 1996; ***www.samsung.com/***; Sohn Jie-Ae, "With IMF Bailout, South Korea Braces for Belt-tightening," *CNN.com*, November 22, 1997.

1. **Hyundai Motors is the largest non-triad auto maker. What type of obstacles does this create for Hyundai Motors that triad auto makers do not have?**
2. **Are Korean *chaebols* much the same as Japanese *keiretsus*? Why or why not?**
3. **Why and how did Korea restructure its *chaebols* after the Asian financial crisis?**

REAL CASE

Kiwifruit: a New Zealand success story

New Zealand farmers invented the name "Kiwifruit" in 1959 for their famous green version of the Chinese gooseberry, a fruit first developed by horticulturalist Hayward Wright. In the winter months for Europe and North America, New Zealand accounts for 70–80 per cent of world sales of Kiwifruit, although it only has a one-third annual share of the world market. Other large producers are Italy, France, Greece, and the US.

One of the advantages of improved sea transportation in refrigerated containers is that perishable fresh fruit can be produced in Southern hemisphere countries like New Zealand and Chile and marketed through the Northern hemisphere winter. Fruit is a low value, bulky product that can only be transported by ship in a cost-effective manner. This contra-seasonal production works both ways. New Zealand actually imports from California in its winter months. Chile competes with New Zealand for the winter contra-seasonal market.

In both New Zealand and Chile the many small fruit farmers face a problem in transporting and selling their products. One solution has been to form producers' cooperatives and export marketing boards. In 1988 the New Zealand Kiwifruit Marketing Board was formed to coordinate exports and in 1997 this was privatized to become Kiwifruit New Zealand (KNZ). This company launched a brand product "Zespri" to differentiate the high quality New Zealand product from competitors and to provide a better customer focus.

Kiwifruit is a specialty fruit in a niched world market with few rivals, so the major management issues are logistical ones of developing an effective internal supply chain plus reliable export marketing. In contrast, New Zealand also produces apples, pears, and other "pipfruit". These are now commodity products, with many large producers all over the world. Here New Zealand is an insignificant participant, with under 1 per cent of the world market and no power to manage industry pricing, as it can with Kiwifruit. For small, open, trading economies like New Zealand and Chile, market access to triad regions is essential to build a business, whether it be in a niche or in a commodity.

Website: **www.zespri.com**.

Sources: Trade New Zealand, *Monthly Export Statistics*, January 1999, ***www.tradenz.govt.nz/nz/stats/monthly/199901MKT.html***; *The Economy of New Zealand*, ***www.treasury.govt.nz/pubs/ nzdmo/ EFO_98***; *New Zealand ,Treasury's Assessment of the Impact of Asian Economies on the NZ Economy*, January, 1998, ***www. treasury.govt.nz/briefing.asia.html***; *External Sector*, ***www.treasury. govt.nz/pubs/ nzdmo/EFO_98***; *Key Facts and Figures about FDI in New Zealand*, ***www.oic.govt.nz/invest/brief/ appenda.html***.

1. **How does New Zealand gain access to large foreign markets?**
2. **What is the role of the KNZ?**
3. **What global strategy is being followed for Kiwifruit?**

ENDNOTES

1 Ravi Ramamurti, "Why Are Developing Countries Privatizing?" *Journal of International Business Studies*, vol. 23, no. 2 (Second Quarter 1992), pp. 225–249.

2 Even more telling, in 2000, the inflows of FDI to Africa have been less than 1 per cent of the world total, according to the United Nations, *World Investment Report 2001*, p. 19.

3 Instituto Nacional de Estadisticas, *Compendio Estadistico*, 2001.

4 Chile, Foreign Direct Investment Committee, *Statistics*, 2001.

5 Craig Torres, "Chilean Firms Suffer Pain of a Japanese Recession," *Wall Street Journal*, February 25, 1999, p. A 14.

6 See also "All Good Things Must Slow Down," *Economist*, March 7, 1998, pp. 35–36.

7 Seth Schiesel, "Brazil Sells Most of State Phone Utility," *New York Times*, July 30, 1998, pp. C 1, 5.

8 Peter Fritsch and Pamela Druckerman, "Brazil's Falling Currency Stirs Concern Over Its Ability to Keep Up with Debt," *Wall Street Journal*, January 28, 1999, pp. A 13, 15; Peter Fritsch, "Brazil's Currency Falls Further as Nerves Fray," *Wall Street Journal*, February 1, 1999, pp. A 15, 18.

9 Peter Fritsch and Michael M. Phillips, "Brazil's Devaluation Reignites Global Fears of Spreading Malaise," *Wall Street Journal*, January 14, 1999, pp. A 1, 8.

10 Craig Torres, "Brazilian Turmoil Threatens Argentine Car Exports," *Wall Street Journal*, February 1, 1999,

pp. A 15, 17; and Diana Jean Schemo, "Global Crisis Hits Brazil's Auto Industry," *Miami Herald*, September 29, 1998, p. 7 B.

11 "Brazil Rocks the Mercosur Boat," *Economist*, February 13, 1999, pp. 35–36.

12 Geoff Dyer, "Survey – Brazil: Shocks to the System," *FT.com*, July 20, 2001.

13 James C. Cooper and Kathleen Madigan, "Brazil: A Plunging Currency and a Trapped Economy," *Business Week*, October 22, 2001.

14 "Dell Dedicates First Latin American Manufacturing Plant and Customer Center in Rio Grande do Sul, Brazil", Dell Press Release, November 3, 1999.

15 "Top 100 Latin American Companies," *Financial Times*, 2001.

16 Helen Shapiro, "The Mechanics of Brazil's Auto Industry," *NACLA's Report on the Americas*, January/February 1996.

17 James Cox, "Canada, Brazil Duke it Out over Smaller Planes," *USA Today*, July 18, 2001.

18 See, for example, Earl F. Cheit, "A Declaration on Open Regionalism in the Pacific," *California Management Review*, Fall 1992, pp. 116–130.

19 United Nations, *World Investment Report 2000* (Geneva: United Nations Conference on Trade and Development, 2000).

20 Pete Engardio, "Motorola in China: A Great Leap Forward," *Business Week*, May 17, 1993.

21 In most cases the interface will be with male managers, but there is an increasing number of Asian businesswomen who manage large enterprises. For more on this, see Louis Kraar, "Iron Butterflies," *Fortune*, October 7, 1991, pp. 143–154.

22 For more on this, see Bernard P. Zwirn, "Operating a Manufacturing Plant in Indonesia," *The Investment Executive*, September/October 1991, pp. 37–39; and Joseph D. O'Brian, "Focusing on Quality in the Pacific Rim," *International Executive*, July/August 1991, pp. 21–24.

23 Joyce Barnathan et al., "China: Birth of a New Economy," *Business Week*, January 31, 1994, pp. 42–48.

24 *Wall Street Journal Almanac*, 1999, p. 399.

25 "China Just Misses GDP Goal, But Data Signal New Trouble," *Wall Street Journal*, December 31, 1998, p. A 6 and "SURVEY – CHINA: The 'Middle Kingdom' Takes World Stage," *FT.com*, October 8, 2001.

26 CIA, *World Factbook*, 2001.

27 Ian Johnson and Leslie Chang, "China Offers an Array of Reforms," *Wall Street Journal*, March 25, 1999, pp. A 18, 23.

28 Joyce Barnathan, Pete Engardio and Lynne Curry, "China: The Emerging Economic Powerhouse of the 21st Century," *Business Week*, May 17, 1993, pp. 54–68.

29 Frances Williams, "WTO Formally Approves China as a Member," *FT.com*, November 10, 2001.

30 Karby Leggett, "China's Economic Zones Losing Luster," *Wall Street Journal*, December 29, 1998, p. A 10.

31 "Investing in China Gains Favour," *BBC.co.uk*, February 14, 2001.

32 "SURVEY – CHINA: The 'Middle Kingdom' Takes World Stage," *FT.com*, October 8, 2001.

33 Kathy Chen and Hilary Stout, "Boeing, GM Obtain China Agreements," *Wall Street Journal*, March 25, 1997, pp. A 3, 4.

34 ***www.chinafdi.org.cn/.***

35 Joyce Barnathan, Michael Weiss and Dave Lindorff, "All the Tea in China Might Not Put Out this Fire," *Business Week*, January 17, 1994, p. 47.

36 Also, see "Colliding with China," *Economist*, March 12, 1994, p. 37.

37 "SURVEY – CHINA: The 'Middle Kingdom' Takes World Stage," *FT.com*, October 8, 2001.

38 "Chinese Exporters Seek New Openings," *BBC.co.uk*, March 1, 2001.

39 "Sinopec Shares Stall on Debut," *BBC.co.uk*, August 8, 2001.

40 Ian Johnson, "WTO Talks Between US, China Turn Serious," *Wall Street Journal*, March 5, 1999, pp. A 9, 11.

41 Richard Tomlinson, "China's Reform: Now Comes the Hard Part," *Fortune*, March 1, 1999, pp. 156–164.

42 Helene Cooper and Dean Takahashi, "GOP's China Bashing Finally Worries Business," *Wall Street Journal*, March 16, 1999, p. A 28; Jane Perlez, "Hopes For Improved Ties with China Fade," *New York Times*, February 12, 1999, p. A 6; Ian Johnson, "China Fosters Price-Fixing Cartels As Economy Crimps Firms' Profits," *Wall Street Journal*, December 3, 1998, p. A 17; Seth Faison, "China Applies Brakes on Move Toward Market Economy," *New York Times*, September 30, 1998, p. C 3; Ian Johnson, "China's Venture Ban Could Cost Foreign Firms," *Wall Street Journal*, September 23, 1998, pp. A 14, 17.

43 Michael Y. Hu, Chen Haiyang and Joseph C. Shieh, "Impact of US–China Joint Ventures on Stockholders: Wealth by Degree of International Involvement," *Management International Review*, vol. 32, no. 2, 1992, pp. 135–148.

44 "FDI Not Up to Expectations: Maran," *The Times of India*, August 10, 2001.

45 Manjeet Kripalani, "Investing in India Is Not for the Fainthearted," *Business Week*, August 11, 1997, pp. 46–47.

46 "Toyota Maps Out Long-term Gameplan for India," *Auto Asia Online*, November 28, 2001.

47 "Assocham Seeks Easy Norms for Foreign Investors," *The Times of India*, January 20, 2002.

48 Manjeet Kripalani, "Why India's Ruling Party is Flirting with Disaster," *Business Week*, August 10, 1998, p. 42.

49 Also see Jonathan Karp, "India Unveils Reform Plan for Telecom Industry," *Wall Street Journal*, March 29, 1999, p. A 19.

50 See ***www.wiproindia.com*** and ***www.wipro.com*** and "India's Software Giant Beats Forecasts," *BBC.co.uk*, October 18, 2001.

51 Moon Ihlwan, "It's Not Just the *Chaebol* that Are Squeezed," *Business Week*, February 16, 1998, p. 54.

52 Stephanie Strom, "Korea to Sell Control of Bank to US Investors," *New York Times*, January 31, 1999, pp. C 1, 3.

53 Stephanie Strom, "Korea Places 55 Companies On 'Death List,'" *New York Times*, June 19, 1998, pp. C 1–2; Louis Kraar, "Korea's Comeback . . . Don't Expect A Miracle," *Fortune*, May 25, 1998, pp. 120–126; Jane L. Lee, "Mobile-Phone Companies Target Korea," *Wall Street Journal*, November 9, 1998, p. 13 B.

54 John Thornhill, "Survey – Singapore: Big Progress as Advance Up Value-added Chain Continues," *FT.com*, April 11, 2001.

55 See Cacilie Rohwedder, "For Hugo Boss, 'It's Time to Leave Home'," *Wall Street Journal*, April 15, 1994, p. A 5.

56 Serge Schemann, "Declaring Death of Soviet Union, Russia and Two Republics Form New Commonwealth," *New York Times*, December 9, 1991, pp. 1, 4.

57 Michael R. Sesit, "Investors' Confidence in Russia Fades Further," *Wall Street Journal*, July 8, 1998, pp. A 11–12.

58 Timothy O'Brien, "Horrific Debt, Devastated Economy," *New York Times*, September 15, 1998, p. A 12.

59 Patricia Kranz et al., "Who Will Lead Russia?" *Business Week*, November 9, 1998, pp. 62–64.

60 "Russia's Crisis Isn't Over," *Economist*, June 27, 1998, pp. 49–50.

61 "IMF praises Russian reforms," *FT.com*, December 12, 2001.

62 *New York Times*, October 25, 1991, p. C 4.

63 "Poland's Economic Challenge," *BBC.co.uk*, September 24, 2001.

64 Also, see James B. Treece et al., "New Worlds to Conquer," *Business Week*, February 28, 1994, pp. 50–52.

65 "Poland's Economic Challenge," *BBC.co.uk*, September 24, 2001.

66 Breffni O'Rourke, "Poland/Hungary: Can Small Business Lead To Prosperity?" *Radio Free Europe*, March 28, 2000.

67 See "Solidarity v Solidarity," *Economist*, April 25, 1998, pp. 51–52.

ADDITIONAL BIBLIOGRAPHY

Ali, Abbas J. "Middle East Competitiveness in the 21st Century's Global Market," *Academy of Management Executive*, vol. 13, no. 1 (February 1999).

Barclay, Lou Anne, *Foreign Direct Investment in Emerging Economies: The Caribbean* (London: Routledge, 2000).

Beamish, Paul W. and Wang, Hui Y. "Investing in China via Joint Ventures," *Management International Review*, vol. 29, no. 1 (First Quarter 1989).

Bugajski, Janusz. "Eastern Europe in the Post-Communist Era," *Columbia Journal of World Business*, vol. 26, no. 1 (Spring 1991).

Capon, Noel, Christodoulou, Chris, Farley, John U. and Hulbert, James M. "A Comparative Analysis of the Strategy and Structure of United States and Australian Corporations," *Journal of International Business Studies*, vol. 18, no. 1 (Spring 1987).

Cartwright, Wayne R. "Multiple Linked 'Diamonds' and the International Competitiveness of Export-Dependent Industries: The New Zealand Experience," *Management International Review*, vol. 33, no. 2 (Second Quarter 1993).

Child, John, "China and International Business," in Alan M. Rugman and Thomas L. Brewer (eds.), *The Oxford Handbook of International Business* (New York: Oxford University Press, 2001).

Child, John and Tse, David K. "China's Transition and its Implications for International Business," *Journal of International Business Studies*, vol. 32, no. 1 (Spring 2001).

Clegg, Jeremy, Kamall, Syed and Leung, Mary. "European Multinational Activity in Telecommunications Services in the People's Republic of China: Firm Strategy and Government Policy," *Management International Review*, vol. 36, no. 1 (1996).

De Meyer, Arnoud, "Technology Transfer into China: Preparing for a New Era," *European Management Journal*, vol. 19, no. 2 (April 2001).

Feinberg, Susan E. and Majumdar, Sumit K. "Technology Spillovers from Foreign Direct Investment in the Indian Pharmaceutical Industry," *Journal of International Business Studies*, vol. 32, no. 3 (Fall 2001).

Geier, Philip H., Jr. "Doing Business in Brazil," *Columbia Journal of World Business*, vol. 31, no. 2 (Summer 1996).

Grosse, Robert, "International Business in Latin America," in Alan M. Rugman and Thomas L. Brewer (eds.), *The Oxford Handbook of International Business* (New York: Oxford University Press, 2001).

Hu, Michael Y., Haiyang, Chen and Shieh, Joseph C. "Impact of US–China Joint Ventures on Stockholders' Wealth by Degree of International Involvement," *Management International Review*, vol. 32, no. 2 (Second Quarter 1992).

Hung, C. L. "Strategic Business Alliances Between Canada and the Newly Industralized Countries of Pacific Asia," *Management International Review*, vol. 32, no. 4 (Fourth Quarter 1992).

Johnson, Simon and Loveman, Gary. "Starting Over: Poland After Communism," *Harvard Business Review*, vol. 73, no. 2 (March/April 1995).

Kao, John. "The Worldwide Web of Chinese Business," *Harvard Business Review*, vol. 71, no. 2 (March/April 1993).

Krawczyk, Marek and Lopez-Lopez, Jose A. "The Role of Government in Poland's Economic Transition: Ideas and Experience from the Recent Past," *Columbia Journal of World Business*, vol. 28, no. 1 (Spring 1993).

Lane, Henry W. and Beamish, Paul W. "Cross-Cultural Cooperative Behavior in Joint Ventures in LDCs," *Management International Review*, vol. 30, Special Issue (1990).

Lawrence, Paul and Vlachoutsicos, Charalambos. "Joint Ventures in Russia: Put the Locals in Charge," *Harvard Business Review*, vol. 71, no. 1 (January/February 1993).

Leung, Hing-Man. "The China–Hong Kong Connection: The Key to China's Open-Door Policy," *Journal of International Business Studies*, vol. 24, no. 1 (First Quarter 1993).

Luders, Rolf J. "The Success and Failure of State-Owned Enterprise Divestitures in a Developing Country: The Case of Chile," *Columbia Journal of World Business*, vol. 28, no. 1 (Spring 1993).

Luo, Yadong. "Strategic Traits of Foreign Direct Investment in China," *Management International Review*, vol. 38, no. 2 (Second Quarter 1998).

Luo, Yadong, Shenkar, Oded and Nyaw, Mee-Kau. "A Dual Parent Perspective on Control and Performance in International Joint Ventures: Lessons From a Developing Economy," *Journal of International Business Studies*, vol. 32, no. 1 (Spring 2001).

Meyer, Klaus E. "International Research in Transitional Economies," in Alan M. Rugman and Thomas L. Brewer (eds.), *The Oxford Handbook of International Business* (New York: Oxford University Press, 2001).

McCarthy, Daniel J. and Puffer, Sheila M. "Strategic Investment Flexibility for MNE Success in Russia: Evolving Beyond Entry Modes," *Journal of World Business*, vol. 32, no. 4 (Winter 1997).

Nigh, Douglas and Smith, Karen D. "The New US Joint Venture in the USSR: Assessment and Management of Political Risk," *Columbia Journal of World Business*, vol. 24, no. 2 (Summer 1989).

Olivier, Maurice J. "Eastern Europe: The Path to Success," *Columbia Journal of World Business*, vol. 26, no. 1 (Spring 1991).

Osland, Gregory. "MNC-Host Government Interaction: Government Pressures on MNCS in China," *European Management Journal*, vol. 16, no. 1 (February 1998).

Pan, Yigang and Tse, David. "The Hierarchical Model of Market Entry Modes," *Journal of International Business Studies*, vol. 31, no. 4 (Winter 2000).

Prahalad, C. K. and Lieberthal, Kenneth. "The End of Corporate Imperialism", *Harvard Business Review*, vol. 76, no. 4 (July–August 1998).

Puffer, Sheila M., McCarthy, Daniel J. and Naumov, Alexander I. "Russian Managers' Beliefs about Work: Beyond Stereotypes," *Journal of World Business*, vol. 32, no. 3 (Fall 1997).

Quelch, John A., Joachimsthaler, Erich and Nueño, Jose Luis. "After the Wall: Marketing Guidelines for Eastern Europe," *Sloan Management Review*, vol. 32, no. 2 (Winter 1991).

Ramamurti, Ravi. "Why are Developing Countries Privatizing?" *Journal of International Business Studies*, vol. 23, no. 2 (Second Quarter 1992).

Redding, Gordon. "The Smaller Economies of Asia and their Business Systems," in Alan M. Rugman and Thomas L. Brewer (eds.), *The Oxford Handbook of International Business* (New York: Oxford University Press, 2001).

Rondinelli, Dennis A. "Resolving US–China Trade Conflicts: Conditions for Trade and Investment Expansion in the 1990s," *Columbia Journal of World Business*, vol. 28, no. 2 (Summer 1993).

Rugman, Alan M. "Strategies for Canadian and Korean Multinational Enterprises," in Dalchoong Kim and Brian L. Evans (eds.), *Korea and Canada: New Frontiers in the Asia-Pacific Era* (Yonsei University: Seoul, Korea, 1989).

Schroath, Frederick W., Hu, Michael Y. and Chen, Haiyang. "Country-of-Origin Effects of Foreign Investments in the People's Republic of China," *Journal of International Business Studies*, vol. 24, no. 2 (Second Quarter 1993).

Siddharthan, N. S. and Safarian, A. E. "Transnational Corporations, Technology Transfer and Imports of Capital Goods: The Recent Indian Experience," *Transnational Corporations*, vol. 6, no. 1 (April 1997).

Stewart, Sally, Cheung, Michael Tow and Yeung, David W. K. "The South China Economic Community: The Latest Asian Newly Industrialized Economy Emerges," *Columbia Journal of World Business*, vol. 27, no. 2 (Summer 1992).

Tallman, Stephen B. and Shenkar, Oded. "International Cooperative Venture Strategies: Outward Investment and Small Firms from NICs," *Management International Review*, vol. 30, no. 4 (Fourth Quarter 1990).

Tatoglu, Ekrem and Glaister, Keith W. "Western MNCs' FDI in Turkey," *Management International Review*, vol. 38, no. 2 (1998).

Vasconcellos, Geraldo M. "Factors Affecting Foreign Direct Investment in the Brazilian Manufacturing Sector: 1955–1980," *Management International Review*, vol. 28, no. 4 (Fourth Quarter 1988).

Vernon-Wortzel, Heidi and Wortzel, Lawrence H. "Globalizing Strategies for Multinationals from Developing Countries," *Columbia Journal of World Business*, vol. 23, no. 1 (Spring 1988).

Von Glinow, Mary Ann and Clarke, Linda. "Vietnam: Tiger or Kitten," *Academy of Management Executive*, vol. 9, no. 4 (November 1995).

Welfens, Paul J. J. "Foreign Investment in the East European Transition," *Management International Review*, vol. 32, no. 3 (Third Quarter 1992).

Wells, Louis T., Jr. "Multinationals and Developing Countries," *Journal of International Business Studies*, vol. 29, no. 1 (First Quarter 1998).

Williams, Christopher. "New Rules for a New World: Privatization of the Czech Cement Industry," *Columbia Journal of World Business*, vol. 28, no. 1 (Spring 1993).

APPENDIXES TO CHAPTER 19

Appendix 19A The 25 largest Latin American MNEs, 2000

Rank	Company	Country	Sector	Revenues $m
1	Petrobras	Brazil	Oil and gas	25,459.0
2	Telecom Carso Global	Mexico	Telecommunications	12,919.3
3	Telefonos de Mexico	Mexico	Telecommunications	10,700.9
4	GCarso	Mexico	Holding Company	9,330.0
5	Wal-Mart de Mexico	Mexico	General merchandisers	7,725.2
6	Eletrobras	Brazil	Electricity	6,250.5
7	GSanborns (Com Car)	Mexico	Specialty retailers	5,707.3
8	Cemex	Mexico	Building materials	5,648.9
9	Vale Rio Doce	Brazil	Mining, crude oil production	4,875.7
10	Fomento Econ Mex UBD	Mexico	Beverages	4,748.6
11	Alfa	Mexico	Diversified	4,712.7
12	Enersis	Chile	Electricity	4,512.9
13	Telemar	Brazil	Telecommunications	4,156.2
14	Pao de Acucar	Brazil	Food and consumer goods	3,902.0
15	Light	Brazil	Electricity	3,856.2
16	Telesp Operac	Brazil	Telecommunications	3,738.2
17	GMexico	Mexico	Mining, crude oil production	3,621.4
18	Copec	Chile	Diversified	3,609.2
19	Embratel Part	Brazil	Telecommunications	3,433.8
20	Comercial Mexicana UBC	Mexico	Food and drugstores	3,302.4
21	Bimbo	Mexico	Food and consumer goods	3,288.4
22	Telecom Argentina	Argentina	Telecommunications	3,226.0
23	Savia	Mexico	Tobacco	3,220.6
24	Gmodelo	Mexico	Beverages	3,064.0
25	Gigante	Mexico	Food and drugstores	2,842.2

Note: Among the Top 100 largest Latin American companies listed in the *Financial Times* Top 100 Latin American companies, 16 had no information on revenue. Thus, this table lists the 25 top companies among the 83 for which revenue was available.

The *Financial Times* Top 100 ranks firms based on market capitalization.

Source: Adapted from *Financial Times*, The Top 100 Latin American Companies, 2001.

Appendix 19B The 25 largest Asia-Pacific MNEs, 2000

Rank	*Company*	*Country*	*Sector*	*Revenues $m*
1	Petrochina	Hong Kong	Oil and gas	29,236.00
2	Samsung Electronics*	South Korea	Electronics, electrical equipment	21,369.80
3	Coles Myer	Australia	Food and drug stores	13,286.90
4	Korea Electric Power*	South Korea	Electricity	12,887.50
5	News Corporation	Australia	Entertainment	12,338.50
6	BHP	Australia	Mining, crude oil production	11,823.40
7	Woolworths	Australia	Food and drug stores	11,006.40
8	Pohang Iron & Steel	South Korea	Metals	10,392.10
9	Jardine Matheson	Singapore	Food and drug stores	10,362.10
10	Telstra Corporation	Australia	Telecommunications	10,230.70
11	Korea Telecom*	South Korea	Telecommunications	9,618.50
12	China Mobile Hong Kong	Hong Kong	Telecommunications	7,851.00
13	Hutchison Whampoa	Hong Kong	Diversified	7,311.40
14	Rio Tinto*	Australia	Mining, crude oil production	6,128.80
15	Jardine Strategic	Singapore	Diversified	5,960.00
16	Singapore Airlines	Singapore	Aerospace	5,131.10
17	Cathay Pacific Airways	Hong Kong	Aerospace	4,426.60
18	Reliance Industries	India	Diversified	4,344.30
19	Oil & Natural Gas	India	Oil and gas	4,276.10
20	Nan Ya Plastics*	Taiwan	Plastics and electronics	4,042.60
21	Tenaga Nasional	Malaysia	Electricity	3,539.80
22	SK Telecom*	South Korea	Telecommunications	3,505.90
23	Li & Fung	Hong Kong	Diversified	3,204.60
24	CLP Holdings	Hong Kong	Electricity	3,135.10
25	China Unicom	Hong Kong	Telecommunications	2,862.40

* Refers to companies for which the latest revenue figures are from 1999.

Note: Among the Top 100 largest Asia-Pacific companies listed in the *Financial Times* Top 100 Asia-Pacific companies, 30 had no information on revenue. Thus, this table lists the 25 top companies among the 70 for which revenue was available. The *Financial Times* Top 100 ranks firms based on market capitalization.

Source: Adapted from *Financial Times*, The Top 100 Latin American Companies, 2001.

Appendix 19C The Top 25 largest Eastern European companies, 2000

Rank	*Company*	*Country*	*Sector*	*Revenues $m*
1	Gazprom*	Russia	Oil and gas	12,447.2
2	Lukoil*	Russia	Oil and gas	10,910.3
3	Unified Energy System*	Russia	Electricity	10,067.0
4	PKNorlen	Poland	Oil and gas	5,785.1
5	Oil Company YUKOS*	Russia	Oil and gas	4,087.6
6	Telecomunikacja Polska	Poland	Telecommunications	3,662.4
7	MOL	Hungary	Oil and gas	3,648.1
8	Surgutneftegaz*	Russia	Oil and gas	3,287.9
9	Norilsk Nickel*	Russia	Steel and other metals	2,718.1
10	Tatneft*	Russia	Oil and gas	2,075.9
11	Sibneft*	Russia	Oil and gas	1,746.5
12	MATAV	Hungary	Telecommunications	1,585.2
13	CEZ*	Czech Republic	Electricity	1,546.7
14	Severstal*	Russia	Steel and other metals	1,504.3
15	UNIPETROL*	Czech Republic	Oil and gas	1,502.8
16	Cesky Telecom*	Czech Republic	Telecommunications	1,499.3
17	KGHM Polska Miedz	Poland	Steel and other metals	1,148.7
18	Aeroflot-Russian Airlines*	Russia	Aerospace	1,136.0
19	Slovnaft*	Slovakia	Oil and gas	1,057.9
20	GAZ Auto Plant*	Russia	Automobiles and parts	988.1
21	Mercator Poslovni Sistem*	Slovenia	Food and drugstore	959.7
22	Rostelecom*	Russia	Telecommunications	933.5
23	Petrol*	Slovenia	Oil and gas	921.1
24	Mosenergo*	Russia	Electricity	918.6
25	Tiszai Vegyi Kombinat	Hungary	Pharmaceuticals	664.1

* Refers to companies for which the latest revenue figures are from 1999.

Note: Among the Top 100 largest Eastern European companies listed in the *Financial Times* Top 100 Eastern European companies, 17 had no information on revenue. Thus, this table lists the 25 top companies among the 83 for which revenue was available.

The *Financial Times* Top 100 ranks firms based on market capitalization.

Source: Adapted from *Financial Times*, The Top 100 Eastern European Companies, 2001.

Appendix 19D Distribution of the Top 100 Latin American companies, 2000

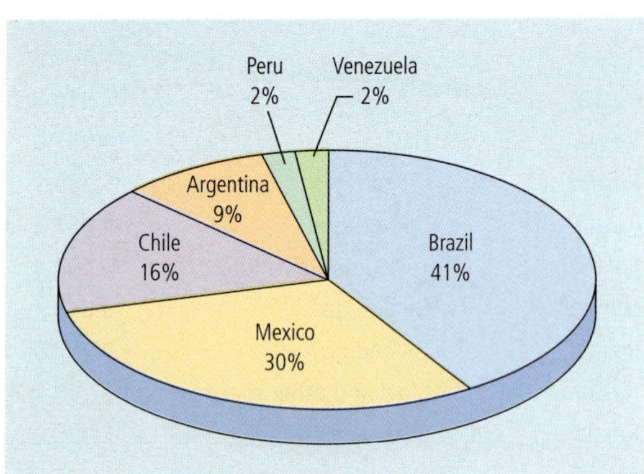

Note: Sorted by market capitalization.

Source: Adapted from *Financial Times*, The Top 100 Latin American Companies, 2001.

Appendix 19E Distribution of Top 100 Asia-Pacific companies, 2000

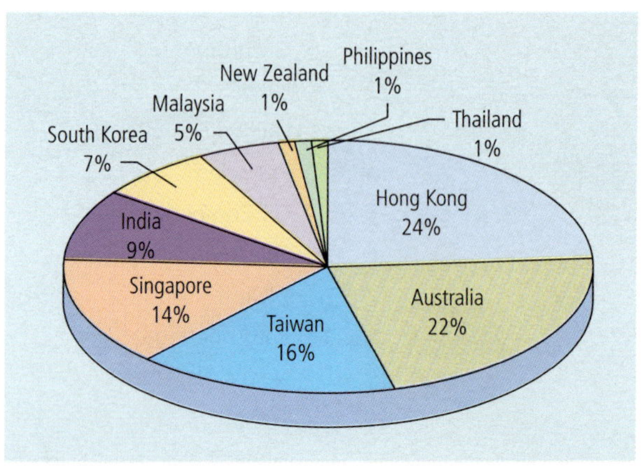

Note: Sorted by market capitalization.

Source: Adapted from *Financial Times*, The Top 100 Asia-Pacific companies, 2001.

Appendix 19F Distribution of the Top 100 Eastern European companies, 2000

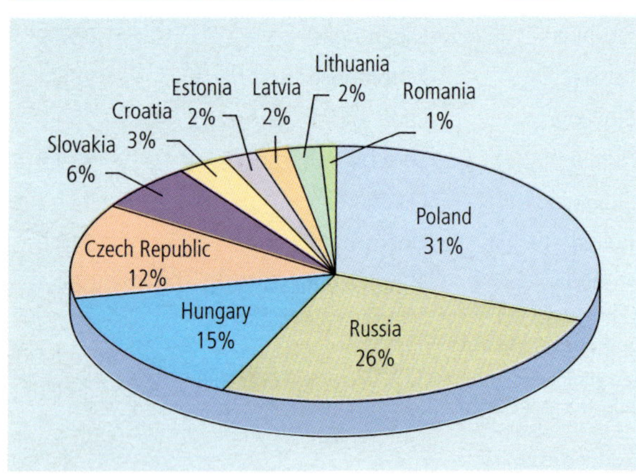

Note: Sorted by market capitalization.

Source: Adapted from *Financial Times*, The Top 100 Asia Pacific Companies, 2001.

Appendix 19G Distribution of Top 50 Middle Eastern companies, 2000

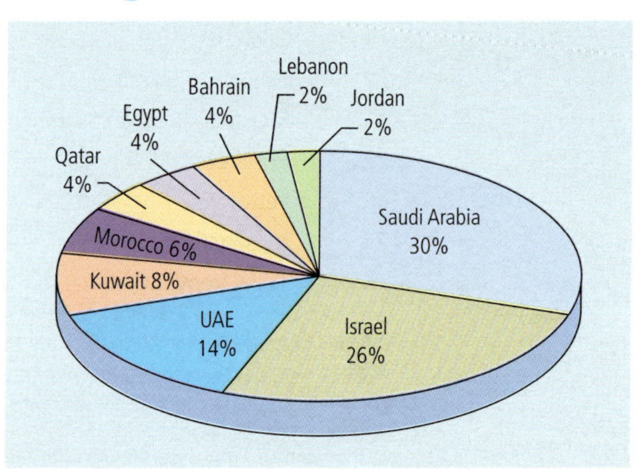

Note: Sorted by market capitalization.

Source: Adapted from *Financial Times*, The Top 100 Asia Pacific Companies, 2001.

PART FIVE

International Business Frameworks

Chapter 20

The Future Challenges of International Business

CONTENTS

OBJECTIVES OF THE CHAPTER

Over the course of this text we have seen how much the world of international business has changed in the last decade. In the next decade, there will be even more changes to the field of international business. This will affect both the country factors and the strategies of multinational firms. In this chapter we explore three useful frameworks to help analyze the future of international business. First, we link the country-specific advantages (CSAs) to the firm-specific advantages (FSAs) in a matrix. We relate this to examples of future changes in environmental CSAs and strategic FSAs. Second, we consider how multinational enterprises often serve as "flagship" firms at the hubs of business networks. Again we relate this to environmental and firm-level strategies and future trends. Third, we develop a framework to analyze trade and investment agreements. We incorporate a discussion of corporate ethics and the role of NGOs into this final framework.

The specific objectives of this chapter are to:

1. *Examine* how these changing developments will create both challenges and opportunities for MNEs over the next decade.
2. *Explain* why research will continue to be of critical importance to the field of international business.
3. *Examine* three frameworks in which MNEs can cope with their changing political and economic environments.
4. *Relate* the importance of the NGOs and ethical issues to the strategies of multinational enterprises.

ACTIVE LEARNING CASE

The environment, NGOs, and MNEs

What do BP, The Body Shop, Honda, Ford, and Royal Dutch/Shell have in common? They are ranked as the top five companies in the world "that best manage and effect environmental resources". Furthermore, these are the rankings exclusively of civil society activists and the media.

The table below reports the top 20 MNEs that are recognized as environmentally friendly by NGOs and the media.

In a separate ranking of business leaders it was again found that BP was number 1, followed (in order) by Royal Dutch/Shell, Toyota, Weyerhaeuser, and DuPont. In the business leader ranking Honda was at 14 and Ford at 16. This shows that there is a high correlation between the rankings by NGOs and media, on the one hand (groups usually critical of MNEs), and the CEOs who actually manage the MNEs. Most startling is that both surveys separately identified BP as the most "green" MNE.

BP is recognized for its success in aligning its business strategy and economic operations with the needs of the natural environment. The reasons:

1. BP makes exceptional efforts to replenish environmental resources.
2. BP develops alternative fuels and alternative energy.
3. BP communicates very well with stakeholders.

BP is the leading supplier of solar energy panels (already a $200 million business in 2000); it has made major expenditures on marine research and the environment; and it is now well "beyond petroleum". The NGOs recognize that the oil business damages the environment, but they credit BP with accepting this responsibility to reduce the adverse effects on resources. The CEO of BP, Lord Browne, is given credit for the success of BP as a green company.

Under Lord Browne, BP has pledged to reduce the level of its own greenhouse gas emissions by 10 per cent by 2010. It was close to the goal by early 2002. BP has also invested in research initiatives to reduce carbon in fuels and to power cars with hydrogen fuel cells. BP has been an active supporter of the Kyoto protocol, believes in sustainable development, and supports codes of conduct on human rights for oil and mining groups.

Media and NGOs: companies that best manage and effect environmental resources

Rank 2001	*Name*	*Country*	*Sector*
1	BP	UK	Energy/Chemicals
2	The Body Shop	UK	Retail
3	Honda	Japan	Engineering
4	Ford	US	Engineering
5	Royal Dutch/Shell	Netherlands/UK	Energy/Chemicals
6	Ben & Jerry's (Unilever)	Netherlands/UK	Food/Beverages
7	Vivendi Universal	France	Utilities and media/Leisure
8	Toyota	Japan	Engineering
9	Otto-Versand	Germany	Retail
10	Siemens	Germany	Electrical/Electronics
11	Patagonia	US	Retail
12	Procter & Gamble	US	Food/Beverages
13	Interface	US	Resources
14	McDonald's	US	Media/Leisure
15	General Motors	US	Engineering
16	Greenpeace	UK	
17	IKEA	Sweden	Retail
18	Co-operative Group	UK	Retail and finance
19	GlaxoSmithKline	UK	Health care
20	Microsoft	US	IT

Source: *Financial Times*, "Survey of the World's Most Respected Companies", December 12, 2001, p. VII, Supplement.

Other oil companies have also invested in being green; the best example is Royal Dutch/Shell, once targeted by Greenpeace over its inappropriate disposal plans for the Brent Spar North Seas oil rig. Now NGOs rank it number 5 and business executives number 2 in being an environmental leader. In contrast, Exxon Mobil is criticized by environmentalists for opposing the Kyoto protocol whereas it ranks 17 by business leaders for the Exxon Valdez oil disaster in Alaska.

Another odd result is that McDonald's ranks at 14 in the NGO and media list for its success in recycling its packaging and reducing waste. Yet McDonald's is a number one target by antiglobal activists and its restaurants have been destroyed from Seattle to London to Genoa. This would seem to indicate that the civil society has no consistent agenda; some NGOs are just antibusiness and will attack any MNEs whereas other NGOs believe in sustainable development and in working with MNEs to improve the natural environment. It also indicates that many MNEs are not the problem, but the solutions to environmental problems.

Websites: **www.bp.com**; **www.the-body-shop.com**; **www.honda.com**; **www.ford.com**; **www.shell.com**; **www.greenpeace.org**; **www.toyota.com**; **www.dupont.com**; **www.weyerhaeuser.com** and **www.mcdonalds.com**.

Source: *Financial Times*, "Survey of the World's Most Respected Companies," December 12, 2001, p. VII, Supplement.

1. **How have non-governmental organizations (NGOs) changed the external environment in which multinational enterprises operate? Why is BP the most successful multinational to respond to NGOs?**
2. **In terms of the CSA/FSA matrix where does BP appear and why?**
3. **As multinational enterprises operate across the world and NGOs operate globally, why are there no "global" or "international" environmental agreements to set rules for sustainable development?**

INTRODUCTION

Multinational enterprises (MNEs) are finding that one of the major challenges they face is to develop effective strategies for coping with changing environments. The international microcomputer chip industry is a good example. During the 1980s the Japanese dominated this industry, pushing out many US and European competitors to gain the majority of the world market. In the early 1990s US firms (most notably Intel) counterattacked and regained the lead. Strategic countermoves can cause successful firms to be dislodged by competitors.[1] But this is an ongoing process of triad-based attack and counterattack, and today's victor could be dislodged by the competition tomorrow. This process explains development in many industries, from autos to computers to real estate.[2] It also helps to explain why continual innovation and strategy modification are necessary for MNEs to retain their competitive advantage. In doing so, multinationals will be focusing increased attention on strategies that are designed to cope with changing environments.

DEVELOPING EFFECTIVE STRATEGIES

There are a number of ways that MNEs are supplementing or supplanting their old strategies in order to compete more effectively worldwide.[3] Two of the most recent developments include going where the action is and developing new business networks with governments, suppliers, customers, and competitors.

Going where the action is

One strategy that is proving increasingly important is the need to go international in order to keep up with the competition.[4] Successful multinationals have operations in the home countries of their major triad competitors. For example, IBM's strongest competitors are located in the US, Europe, and Japan. In turn the company has facilities in all three places, to monitor the competition as well as to conduct research. Moreover, the communication network among the company's facilities allows each to share information with the others and to provide assistance. This also helps the company to maintain a strong competitive posture.[5]

Another reason for locating near major competitors is that some markets develop faster than others and the experience and knowledge that is learned here can help in other markets. For example, in the US market IBM is now trying to develop a strategy of providing the best service in the industry. In the past the company had often referred service problems to its dealers. However, now the firm is attempting to address these issues directly, ensuring a higher level of service and taking back customers who were lured away by smaller firms with better service, support, and prices. If this strategy works well, the company is likely to use it in other worldwide locations where small firms have been gaining market share.[6]

Another important aspect of a location-focused strategy is that MNEs often establish a home base for each major product line, and a multiproduct-line company will have "centers for excellence" all over the world. These centers are responsible for providing global leadership for their respective product lines. For example, Asea Brown Boveri, a Swiss firm, uses Sweden as the home base for transmission equipment. Research, development, and production are centralized in that country. Nestlé, the giant food company, has the world headquarters for its confectionery business in Great Britain because this home base is more dynamic in terms of the marketing environment and the high per capita consumption of confectionery products. At the same time Nestlé has made its Italian company, Buitoni, the world center for pasta operations. Meanwhile, Siemens has designated the US as the world home base for medical electronics because this is where the market is most dynamic and will provide the company with the best chance of developing and maintaining state-of-the-art products.

It is also important to realize that the product line will dictate the degree of globalization. For example, food companies in Europe tend to be less international and more regional in focus. Local tastes vary widely and there are only modest gains to be achieved through large-scale operations, so European food companies tend to have an extensive local presence. The same is true for home appliances, which are often produced for regional markets. On the other hand, when European companies have become truly global, they have tended to focus on products that do not require high levels of integration on a worldwide basis.

So some companies have a need for global centers throughout the world, whereas others tend to stay in closer geographic proximity because of the nature of their product lines. Still others combine both of these approaches, as seen in the box "International Business Strategy in Action: 3M".

Active learning check

Review your answer to Active Learning Case question 1 and make any changes you like. Then compare your answer with the one below.

1. **How have non-governmental organizations (NGOs) changed the external environment in which multinational enterprises operate? Why is BP the most successful multinational to respond to NGOs?**

NGOs have captured public attention and won a lot of support in North America and Western Europe for their "green" and antiglobalization agendas. Multinational enterprises cannot afford to ignore NGOs, especially the US and EU MNEs whose home base "diamond" is threatened by NGOs who can influence government policy and regulation. BP has gained recognition as the most successful MNE because it had a responsible CEO who undertook a series of measures to make its operations more environmentally friendly.

INTERNATIONAL BUSINESS STRATEGY *IN ACTION*

3M

The 3M company is a major MNE that has over 50,000 products comprising everything from office supplies to construction and building maintenance to chemicals. It employs over 73,000 people and has operations in 60 countries. How does the firm manage such a large international operation? One way is by matching its global strategies with the needs of the local market. Some goods such as home videocassettes are standardized and are sold on the basis of price and quality. Culture and local usage are not important considerations. Other products are greatly influenced by local preferences or regulations; telecommunications is an example. Each country or region of the world has its own modifications for local application.

The company balances its global strategies and national responses on a region-by-region basis. For example, in Europe the company has set up a series of business centers to address local differences. The company also uses European management action teams (EMATs) to balance the needs of subsidiaries in responding to local expectations with the corporation's need for global direction. Today, 3M has 50 EMATs in Europe, each consisting of from 8 to 14 people, most of whom are marketing personnel. These groups are charged with bringing the firm's global plans to life by helping their execution at the local level. EMAT meetings, which usually occur quarterly, are designed to create action plans for the European subsidiaries. When the meetings are over, the members then return to their respective subsidiaries and begin executing the plans. In Asia the company uses a different approach, relying heavily on its Japanese operation to provide much of the needed direction to the subsidiaries. At the same time there are regional centers in Singapore and South Korea that help subsidiaries to address their local markets. In Latin America, meanwhile, 3M uses a macro approach, conducting business on a national rather than regional basis.

The company also carefully identifies those products that it will sell in each geographic area while following two basic strategies: (1) try to be the first in the market with new offerings because this strategy puts the competition at a disadvantage, and (2) grow new markets gradually by picking out those products that address the country's most pressing needs and focus exclusively on them. Commenting on its worldwide strategy, a company executive said:

> We don't believe in formulating a single global strategy for selling videocassettes in India and laser imagers in France and Post-it brand notes in Brazil. For each of 3M's 23 strategic business centers in each region the company's strategy is a blend of global, regional, and local companies and that will continue.

Websites: **www.3m.com**.

Sources: Adapted from Harry Mammerly, "Matching Global Strategies with National Responses," Journal of Business Strategy, March/April 1992, pp. 8–13; Kevin Kelly, "3M Run Scared? Forget About It," Business Week, September 16, 1991, pp. 59, 62; James Braham, "Engineering Your Way to the Top," Machine Design, August 22, 1991, pp. 65–68; **www.3m.com**; 3M, Annual Report, 1997 and 2000.

INTERNATIONAL BUSINESS RESEARCH FRAMEWORKS

No study of international business would be complete without paying attention to the role and importance of theoretical frameworks. Much of what has been discussed in this book is based on research findings. In many cases the data were drawn from government statistics, company records, and business reports on recent developments and strategies. In other cases the information was garnered from formal studies that examined managerial behaviors among senior managers. Collectively, research provides important input for building international business theories and for formulating and implementing future strategies. As a result, it is useful to both academicians and practitioners.

Unfortunately, research can be confusing and contradictory. For example, many studies are extremely limited in focus and thus cannot be generalized to a universal setting. Similarly, when research is broadly based, it is likely that the findings cannot be generalized to specific situations. The Porter diamond, for example, helps to explain how triad nations develop competitive advantage. However, its value to non-triad nations, as explained in Chapter 15, is limited and the findings must be revised and modified in order to apply them. Despite such shortcomings, however, international business research will continue to be of critical importance to the field. Such research will allow us to test theories and to refine their practical applications.

Theories of international business

A great many theories have relevance to the study of international business. In some cases these are first constructed and then tested. A good example is Adam Smith's theory of labour specialization. Smith presented this concept over 200 years ago in his *Wealth of Nations*, and in recent years learning curve analysts have confirmed these findings. Of course, not all theories have had to wait centuries before being proven. However, this example does illustrate that international business research can be advanced through the formulation of useful theories.[7]

In other cases theories are being tested for the purpose of reconfirming earlier findings. This is particularly important in learning how well a theory stands the test of time. A good example is the theory of lifetime employment in Japan. For many years theorists have argued that lifetime employment creates a highly motivated workforce and Western organizations would be wise to copy this approach. More recent research, however, reveals that lifetime employment is less useful as a motivator than as a control tool for ensuring worker loyalty and performance. In return for guaranteed employment, workers stay with the firm for their entire career, work hard, and are compliant with management's wishes. Even unions are employer-dominated and serve more to maintain harmony within the employee ranks than to represent the workers.

Based on an analysis of empirical data collected on this topic, two researchers recently concluded, "Lifetime employment is offered within a . . . context of loyalty and benevolence based on cultural values. Its impact, however, is to increase the control of Japanese employees by managers."[8] Moreover, these researchers found that lifetime employment was not widely used by firms in tight labor markets because it was not possible to control the workers, who could easily find jobs with other companies and who derived little motivation from such guarantees.

This type of research is also important because it generates new hypotheses for testing. For example, as workers in large companies with guaranteed lifetime employment near retirement (55 to 60 years of age), will management replace them with younger people who are not given such guarantees? As the competitive environment increases, will companies stop offering these guarantees because they reduce the firms' flexibility in responding to changing conditions? Will young workers entering the Japanese workforce during this decade be motivated by such guarantees, or will they turn them down because they are unwilling to commit their career to one firm in return for job security? These types of questions will be focal points for future international business research efforts, since changing economic, cultural, and social environments are creating new conditions in which MNEs must compete. Research can help to shed light on the effect of these changes.

Practical applications of the theory

Strategic fit
A strategic management concept which holds that an organization must align its resources in such a way as to mesh effectively with the environment

Research is also going to play an increasing role in helping to uncover how and why multinationals succeed. In particular, greater attention will be given to strategy research that is designed to explain why some firms do better than others and how these strategies are changing. For example, during the 1970s traditional international business strategy gave strong support to **strategic fit**, the notion that an organization must align its resources in such a way as to mesh with the environment. Auto firms had to design and build cars that were in demand, and this might mean a variety of models and accessories, depending on the number of markets being served. Similarly, electronics firms had to maintain state-of-the-art technology so as to meet consumer demand for new, high-quality, high-performance products. Today, however, successful multinationals realize that they must do much more than attempt to attain a strategic fit. The rapid pace of competitive change is requiring linkages between all segments of the business from manufacturing on down to point-of-purchase selling, and in every phase of operation there must be attention to value-added concepts.[9] So the basic strategic concepts of the past, once widely accepted, must be reconsidered and sometimes reformulated.

Other research areas likely to receive future attention will be cross-national collaborative research by individuals from two or more countries and joint efforts by international and non-international researchers. The world of international business is getting larger every day, and it is critical that research be designed not only to help explain what is happening and why it is occurring, but also to help predict future developments and thus better prepare students and practitioners for the international challenges of the 21st century.

A FRAMEWORK FOR GLOBAL STRATEGIES: THE CSA/FSA MATRIX

Firm-specific advantages (FSAs) Strengths or benefits specific to a firm and a result of contributions that can be made by its personnel, technology, and/or equipment

Country-specific advantages (CSAs) Strengths or benefits specific to a country that result from its competitive environment, labor force, geographic location, government policies, industrial clusters, etc

Much of the material in this book can be synthesized within a single analytical framework.[10] We will develop this here to help summarize our key points. There are two basic building blocks in an international business course, as illustrated in Figure 20.1.

First, there is a set of firm-specific factors that determine the competitive advantage of an organization. We call these **firm-specific advantages (FSAs)**. An FSA is defined as a unique capability proprietary to the organization. It may be built upon product or process technology, marketing or distributional skills.

Second, there are country factors. These, of course, are unique to an international business course. They can lead to **country-specific advantages (CSAs)**. The CSAs can be based on natural resource endowments (minerals, energy, forests) or on the labour force, and associated cultural factors.

In this book, Part One introduced a set of FSAs used by MNEs. Part Two was a survey of potential CSAs due to political, cultural, economic, and financial factors. Building upon the interaction of FSAs and CSAs, Part Three considered management strategies for MNE managers. Part Four then applied these strategies to the triad and smaller economies.

Managers of most MNEs use strategies that build upon the interactions of CSAs and FSAs. They do this so that they can be positioned in a unique strategic space. The CSAs

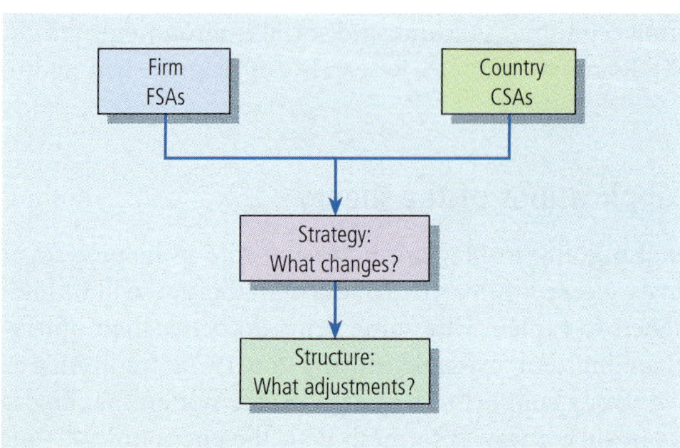

Figure 20.1 The basic components of international business

represent the natural factor endowments of a nation; they are based on the key variables in its aggregate production function. For example, CSAs can consist of the quantity, quality, and cost of the major factor endowment, namely resources.

In Porter (1990) terminology, the CSAs form the basis of the global platform from which the multinational firm derives a home-base "diamond" advantage in global competition. Tariff and non-tariff barriers to trade, and government regulation also influence CSAs. Building on these CSAs, the firm makes decisions about the efficient global configuration and coordination between segments of its value chain (operations, marketing, R&D, and logistics). The skill in making such decisions represents a strong, managerial firm-specific advantage (FSA).

The FSAs possessed by a firm are based ultimately on its internalization of an asset, such as production knowledge, managerial or marketing capabilities, over which the firm has proprietary control. FSAs are thus related to the firm's ability to coordinate the use of the advantage in production, marketing, or the customization of services.

The competitive advantage matrix

To help formulate the strategic options of the MNE, it is useful to identify the relative strengths and weaknesses of the CSAs and FSAs they possess. Figure 20.2, the competitive advantage matrix, provides a useful framework for discussion of these issues. It should be emphasized that the "strength" or "weakness" of FSAs and CSAs is a relative notion. It depends upon the relevant market and the CSAs and FSAs of potential competitors. A strong FSA implies that, under identical CSAs, a firm has a potential competitive advantage over its rivals.

Quadrants 1, 2, and 3 correspond broadly to the three generic strategies suggested by Porter (1980): cost leadership, differentiation, and focus. Quadrant 3 firms generally can follow any of the strategies. Firms in quadrant 4 are generally differentiated firms with strong FSAs in marketing and customization. These firms follow basically a differentiation strategy. In quadrant 4 the FSAs dominate, so in world markets the home-country CSAs are not essential in the long run. Quadrant 1 firms are generally resource-based and/or mature, globally oriented firms producing a commodity-type product. Given their late

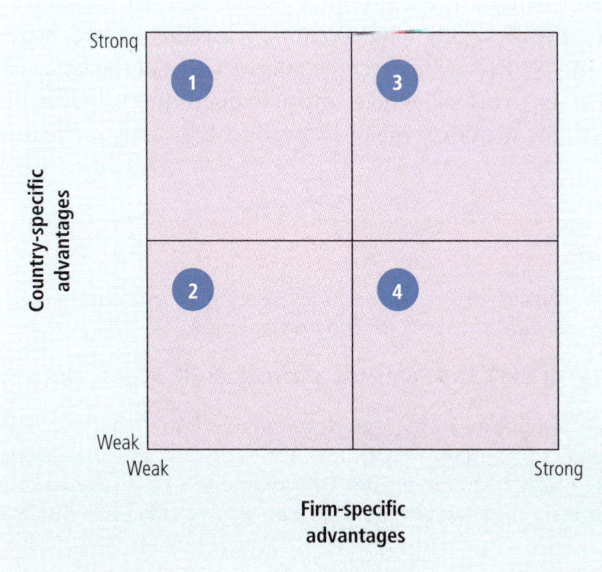

Figure 20.2
The competitive advantage matrix

stage in the product life cycle, production FSAs flowing from the possession of intangible skills are less important than the CSAs of location and energy costs, which are the main sources of the firm's competitive advantage. Thus these firms are following low cost and price competition strategies. Quadrant 2 firms represent inefficient, floundering firms with no consistent strategy, nor any intrinsic CSAs or FSAs. These firms are preparing to exit or to restructure. Quadrant 2 can also represent domestically based small and medium-sized firms with little global exposure.

In terms of business strategy, quadrants 3 and 2 are unambiguous in their implications. A quadrant 3 firm can benefit from strategies of both low cost and differentiation. Such a firm is constantly evaluating its production mix. As a product line matures and then declines it eventually graduates to quadrant 2. However, by adopting new product lines, developing dynamic organizational capabilities, and maintaining an effective strategy, the firm can maintain its overall position in quadrant 3. In quadrant 2 there is no alternative but to restructure or to eventually leave the market.

Quadrants 4 and 1 are credible positions for different types of firms. For instance, a quadrant 4 firm that has strong FSAs in marketing (customization) can operate globally without reliance on its home market CSA, or the CSAs of the host nation. For such a firm, quadrant 4 does not signal a CSA weakness; the CSA is not relevant. In contrast, quadrant 1 has mature multinationals or product lines determined more by CSAs than by FSAs. By improving potential FSAs in marketing or product innovation and increasing value added through vertical integration, the quadrant 1 firm can move to quadrant 3, where its profitability should be enhanced.

Although quadrants 1, 3, and 4 represent appropriate strategic positioning for some firms, there exists an asymmetry between quadrants 4 and 1. A quadrant 4 strategic choice may be a stable one for some firms; however, quadrant 1 firms should be able to aim for quadrant 3. The reason for this asymmetry is rooted in the fact that CSAs are for the most part exogenous to the firm, while FSAs are not. Even to the extent that CSAs can be influenced by government protection, there is always increased uncertainty associated with such strategies. For the firm in quadrant 4 already following an efficiency-based strategy there is no incentive, nor need, to move to quadrant 3.

It is useful to note the following two points. First, if the firm has a conglomerate structure it would be more useful to situate each division or product line individually, recognizing that different units of the diversified firm would use different generic strategies. Second, changes in the trading environment, such as the EU 1992 single market measures, or the EU 1999 single currency, or the United States–Canada Free Trade Agreement and NAFTA, will affect the relative CSAs of the firms. To the extent that CSAs are improved, the firms will tend to move to quadrant 3, and, to the extent that the CSAs are hampered, the firm or some of its product lines may move to exit, as in quadrant 2.

Active learning check

Review your answer to Active Learning Case question 2 and make any changes you like. Then compare your answer with the one below.

2. In terms of the CSA/FSA matrix where does BP appear and why?

BP is a quadrant 3 firm. Here it has developed a high managerial FSA in being responsive to stakeholders (including NGOs). It is also high CSA as it has access to UK oil resources in the North Sea. It builds on the UK "diamond" of oil-based resource CSAs. Without the NGO pressure, BP would most probably have stayed in quadrant 1, high CSAs and low FSAs.

DEVELOPING BUSINESS NETWORKS

In the future governments will become more selective in their approach to industrial policy, aware that in the past billions of dollars have been wasted by bureaucratic efforts to streamline and refocus economic efforts. This recent trend is likely to result in more government–business efforts. However, the success of international business firms will depend more heavily on the companies themselves than on the government. Some of these developments will include the forging of new business networks for competitive advantage and the development of new relationships with non-business sector groups.[11]

Forging new business networks

Increasingly, the relationship of successful MNEs with their suppliers, customers, and competitors is changing. New strategies based on trust and reciprocal support are replacing the old business–client relationship in which companies sought to dictate the terms and conditions of sales and services.

In the case of suppliers, the current trend is toward reducing this number to a small group of reliable, efficient, and highly responsive firms. These suppliers are then brought into a close working relationship with the MNE so that both sides understand the other's strategy and plans can be formulated for minimizing working problems. The multinational will detail its needs and the supplier will draw up plans that ensure timely, accurate delivery. Another trend is the increase in the amount of responsibility being given to suppliers. Previously they were charged only with manufacturing, assembly, and delivery. Now many MNEs use their network partners to develop new materials and components, to perform industrial engineering functions, and to assume liability for warranties.

Flagship firms
Multinational firms characterized by global competitiveness and international benchmarks

In the case of customers, network linkages now involve changing the focus of the relationship from one in which sales representatives would work directly with MNE purchasing agents to one in which sellers interact more directly with their customers. D'Cruz and Rugman have explained this idea in the case of **flagship firms**, characterized by global competitiveness and international benchmarks.[12] In the conventional system the flagship firm and its customers maintain an arm's length relationship. However, new relationships are now being forged in which there is a direct link between the flagship firm and its most important customers (see Figure 20.3, segments 1 and 2), whereas traditional relations are maintained with some distributors to serve the firm's less important customers. At the same time, network linkages are being developed with key distributors to serve other customers better. (Again see Figure 20.3, segments 3 and 4, etc.)

Network arrangements are also being created between international competitors in the form of joint ventures, technology transfers, and market sharing agreements such as a Japanese firm selling the product of a US firm in the Japanese market in return for a similar concession in the US. Mazda and Ford Motor are excellent examples.

These strategic relationships among suppliers, customers, and competitors are becoming integral parts of MNE strategies, as are linkages to non-business organizations such as unions with whom multinationals are now sharing their strategies in the hope of creating a working relationship that will save jobs and ensure company profitability. Partnerships are also being fostered with universities that can help to educate and train human resources, and research institutions that can provide scientific knowledge that is useful for helping organizations to develop and maintain worldwide competitiveness. Another group that is getting increased attention is government, since this institution can be particularly helpful in supporting legislation that will encourage the upgrading of the workforce, development of state-of-the-art technology and products, exports, and the building of world-class competitors. Figure 20.4 provides an illustration of the basic

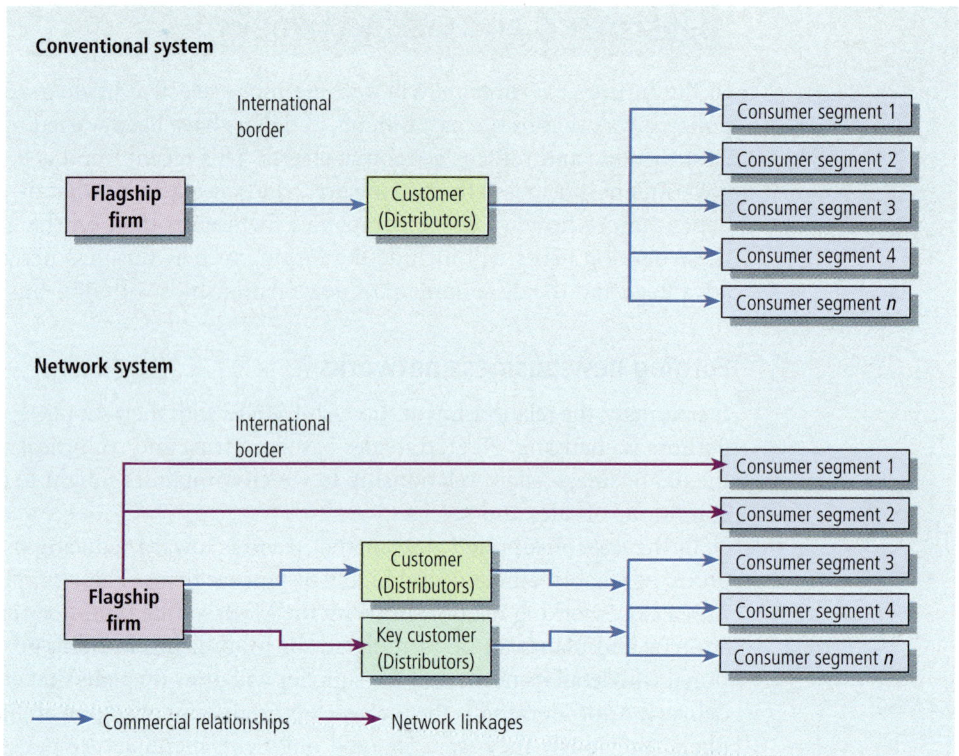

Figure 20.3 Network linkage and the changing shape of international distribution systems

Source: © Alan Rugman and Joseph R. D'Cruz, 2000. Reprinted from *Multinationals as Flagship Firms: Regional Business Networks* by Alan M. Rugman and Joseph R. D'Cruz (2000) by permission of Oxford University Press.

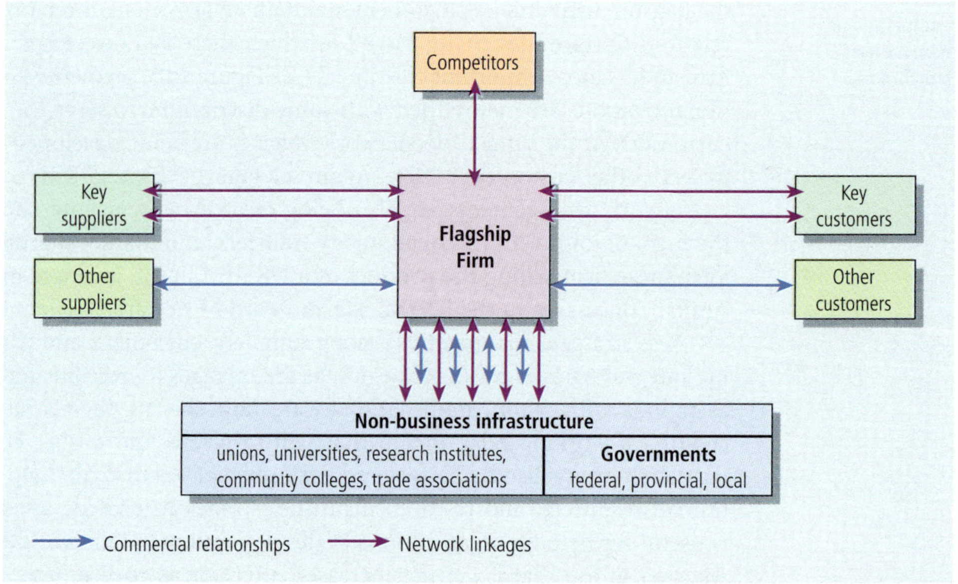

Figure 20.4 Network linkages for successful MNEs

Source: © Alan Rugman and Joseph R. D'Cruz, 2000. Reprinted from *Multinationals as Flagship Firms: Regional Business Networks* by Alan M. Rugman and Joseph R. D'Cruz (2000) by permission of Oxford University Press.

Five partners
A business network consisting of five partners organizations: the flagship firm (a multinational enterprise), key suppliers, key customers, key competitors, and the non-business infrastructure

structure of the **five partners** in an effective network. Notice how these relationships go beyond commercial transactions and involve network linkages to a wide variety of other groups. This is one of the waves of the future in international business.

COPING WITH CHANGING ENVIRONMENTS

The international environment of the future will continue to be one of rapid change, and MNEs will have to stay abreast of a number of developments. The political and economic environments will present the greatest challenges.

Political environment

As already seen, the political environment affects MNE activities in many ways. For example, all major triad groups have trade barriers that are designed to limit the sale of foreign goods in their countries. This in turn typically results in trade negotiations that are designed to open up these markets and/or to reduce trade deficits. Protectionism trends are particularly treacherous because they are psychological as well as legislative.[13] That is, even when trade barriers are lowered, there is a tendency for people to be protectionist and to "buy local".

Many managers say that they favor open markets, but, when questioned closely, they state strong support for protectionist strategies such as government assistance to domestic businesses and help for home-based firms that are seeking to go international.[14] In short, many businesspeople speak out for free trade but advocate policies that put foreign firms at a distinct disadvantage. The Japanese are some of the strongest supporters of free trade. However, research shows that these opinions are not translated into action. For example, Monroe shock absorbers hold 59 per cent of the US market and 28 per cent of the European market, yet the company (Tenneco Automotive) holds a scant 1 per cent of the Japanese market. Similarly, General Motors has approximately 35 per cent of the US market and 12 per cent of the European market, but it has less than three-tenths of 1 per cent of the Japanese market. Ford has similar statistics, holding 24 per cent of the US market and 11 per cent of the European market, but holds a mere one-tenth of 1 per cent of the Japanese market.

The ability of US firms to penetrate foreign markets will also be influenced by US government policies. The Clinton administration was more vigorous than its predecessor in pushing for open markets in Asia.[15] Its formulation of a US government trade policy toward Japan and South East Asia includes guidelines for negotiations for open markets in the region, coupled with US aid to US high-tech industries, among others. The administration's objective was to increase the market share of US firms in this geographic region as well as to reduce the large trade deficit that the US is running, most noticeably with Japan and China. The latter is likely to receive particular attention, given that in recent years China has sold far more to the US than it has purchased from them.

At the same time overseas companies are lobbying their governments to negotiate greater access to the US market. In Asia, for example, US air carriers such as United Airlines and Northwest Airlines can pick up passengers in one Asian locale and fly them to another locale. However, Asian airlines flying into the US are limited in terms of market access. As a result, most of Asia's large airlines have now banded together to insist that they be given the same rights in the US that US air carriers have in Asia. If they are

Table 20.1 The world's major trade agreements

EU (15)	*EFTA (4)*	*OPEC (11)*	*NAFTA (3)*	*CARICOM (14)*	*CACM (5)*	*Council of Arab Economic Unity (7)*	*ASEAN (10)*	*MERCOSUR (4)*	*Andean Group (5)*	*LAIA (12)*	*ECOWAS (15)*	*SADC (14)*
Austria	Iceland	Algeria	Canada	Antigua and Barbuda	Costa Rica	Egypt	Indonesia	Argentina	Bolivia	Argentina	Benin	Angola
Belgium	Liechtenstein	Indonesia	Mexico	Barbados	Guatemala	Iraq	Malaysia	Brazil	Colombia	Bolivia	Burkina Faso	Botswana
Denmark	Norway	Iran	United States	Belize	El Salvador	Jordan	Philippines	Paraguay	Ecuador	Brazil	Cape Verde	Dem. Rep. Congo
Finland	Switzerland	Iraq		Dominica	Honduras	Libya	Singapore	Uruguay	Peru	Chile	Côte d'Ivoire	Lesotho
France		Kuwait		Grenada	Nicaragua	Mauritania	Thailand		Venezuela	Colombia	Gambia	Malawi
Germany		Libya		Guyana		Syria	Brunei			Ecuador	Ghana	Mauritius
Greece		Nigeria		Haiti		Yemen	Vietnam			Mexico	Guinea	Mozambique
Ireland		Qatar		Jamaica			Cambodia			Paraguay	Guinea-Bissau	Namibia
Italy		Saudi Arabia		Montserrat			Laos			Peru	Liberia	Seychelles
Luxembourg		United Arab Emirates		St Kitts and Nevis			Myanmar			Uruguay	Mali	South Africa
Netherlands		Venezuela		Saint Lucia						Venezuela	Mauritania	Swaziland
Portugal				St Vincent and the Grenadines						Cuba	Niger	Tanzania
Spain				Surinam							Nigeria	Zambia
Sweden				Trinidad and Tobago							Senegal	Zimbabwe
United Kingdom											Sierra Leone	
											Togo	

Key: EU – European Union; EFTA – European Free Trade Agreement; OPEC – Organization of Petroleum Exporting Countries; NAFTA – North American Free Trade Agreement; CARICOM – Caribbean Community and Common Market; CACM – Central American Common Market; ASEAN – Association of South East Asian Nations; MERCOSUR – Mercado Comun del Sur; LAIA – Latin American Integration Association; ECOWAS – Economic Community of West African States; SADC – Southern African Development Community.

Sources: Adapted from ***http://europa.eu.int/abc-en.htm***; ***www.opec.org***; ***www.efta.int***; ***www.caricom.org/***; ***http://wellsfargo.com/inatl/wrldalmn/intro/other/***; ***www.sice.oas.org/***; ***www.aladi.org/***; ***www.sadc-usa.net/members/default.html***; ***www.imf.org/external/np/sec/decdo/ecowas.htm***.

successful, this will open new markets for such carriers as Japan Airlines, Singapore Airlines, Thai Airways, Cathay Pacific Airways of Hong Kong, and Qantas Airways of Australia.

A related issue is political risk. Many small countries are now embracing free-market concepts, privatizing state-owned businesses, encouraging foreign investment, and trying to get their economies moving. Will this trend continue? In some cases, such as Russia, the government has intervened and slowed down the move toward free markets in order to halt the short-term rapid inflation that accompanies such changes. This type of action is detrimental and merely increases the time needed to strengthen the economy. These changes also increase the risk to multinationals doing business there since any step back from the charted course toward free enterprise could herald the beginning of renewed state control. The US government and others are helping with financial and technical support. The goal of this aid is to ensure that the forces of democracy and free enterprise continue to progress. But the political climate in Russia and Eastern Europe remains uncertain.

Hong Kong also faces an uncertain political future. The former British colony was returned to China in 1997. The latter is now investing heavily in Hong Kong and has more total direct investment there than in any other country. At the same time two-thirds of foreign investment in China comes from Hong Kong Chinese. Yet relations between Hong Kong and China have sometimes been strained and have resulted in some Hong Kong firms diversifying their investments and moving funds to other geographic locales. Many Hong Kong businesspeople believe that relations with China will be worked out for the betterment of both sides. Certainly China needs Hong Kong and vice versa. Forty per cent of China's international trade passes through Hong Kong, and the latter provides China with a window to the West. At the same time China will eventually decide the political fate of Hong Kong. However, a great deal of concern continues to remain about what will happen over the next decade, thus increasing the political risk for MNEs doing business there.

Another region where political risk is being re-evaluated is Vietnam.[16] Relations between the US and Vietnam are now beginning to normalize, and the country is seeking business ties with US multinationals that can provide assistance in helping to rebuild the economy. President Clinton approved a renewal of lending to Vietnam by both the International Monetary Fund and the World Bank. These funds were necessary to allow critical highway and seaport projects to begin. At the same time, Vietnam has been trying to attract billions of dollars in manufacturing investment from European and Asian companies. Now that the US trade embargo has ended, Vietnam is also trying to lure US banks, aircraft, and power plant manufacturers to help in the rebuilding effort. One major reason that Vietnam is interested in rapprochement with the US is that it sees America as a counterbalance to Japan and the growing military might of China. As relations between the two countries continue to thaw, political risk will decline and Vietnam will become an increasingly popular area for investment opportunities.

The continuing development of free trade agreements will also work to lessen political risk. For example, the North American Free Trade Agreement (NAFTA) will bind Canada, the US, and Mexico together into an interdependent market in which each nation will profit by working harmoniously with the others.[17] The same is true for members of the EU as well as for other economic unions, from those being fostered in Latin America to those in Africa and the former Soviet Union. Firms doing business in these geographic areas will find that the greatest ongoing challenge is more likely to be economic than political. There will also be further consolidation of the world's trade agreements into a triad-based system (see Table 20.1).

Economic environment

The economic environment will be replete with opportunities for MNEs. (The box "International Business Strategy in Action: Volvo's success" provides one example.) US multinationals, for example, will continue to be a dominant force in the export market, as seen by the fact that the US again became the world's largest exporter in 1992. This is due, in no small part, to the growing competitiveness of US manufacturing and the fact that labour costs in the US have risen more slowly than in other major economies.[18] Part of this development is a result of cooperative agreements between US management and labour unions, a trend that now appears to be shaping labour relations in Germany, where manufacturing labor wages far outdistance those anywhere else in the world.[19]

Economic opportunity will also be provided by the growing trend of privatization. In Western Europe, for example, governments are now seeking to sell many of their state-owned businesses. The governments collectively hope to raise approximately $150 billion from these privatization efforts. In an effort to stimulate economic development, nations in newly emerging markets are also employing this strategy. In Mexico, for example, privatization is attracting both new businesses and investment in local enterprises such as Anheuser-Busch's purchase of 18 per cent ownership in Corona, the country's largest brewer. In Russia, Coca-Cola announced plans to invest more than $50 million over a three-year period to build a soft-drink production plant in St Petersburg. In China, a growing number of businesses are finding markets for their goods, as seen by such recent examples as AT&T's contract to provide over $1 billion worth of telecommunications equipment, Boeing's $800 million order for six 777 jets, General Electric's contract for $150 million

INTERNATIONAL BUSINESS STRATEGY *IN ACTION*

Volvo's success

Ford bought Volvo in 1999 as it was a successful, high-quality brand which added to Ford's portfolio of upmarket cars. Before the takeover, Volvo made 70 per cent of its cars in Sweden but had 90 per cent of its sales abroad. The firm had developed as a high-quality niche manufacturer of safe vehicles, competing against rivals such as Saab, BMW, Audi, and Mercedes.

The first Volvos produced in Gothenburg in 1927 were rugged cars designed to survive on the rough roads and in the winter cold of Sweden. This emphasis on durability has been transformed into a concern for passenger safety. Volvos are recognized as high-quality, well-built, and safe vehicles. Over the years Volvo has continuously invested in standard-setting safety improvements. These include side-collision protection, integrated child booster cushions, and the three-point passenger safety belt.

By the 1960s Volvos were out of favor as they were regarded as old fashioned, even if they were safe. So the top management team decided to change its design from "safe, but boxy" to "safe, but slinky". The Volvo management also took on board lean production techniques (with robots and total quality management) which led to more efficient manufacturing. In the 1970s Volvo greatly improved worker participation and in the 1980s it helped set industry standards in green environmentalism. The latter was partly achieved by greater recycling features in its vehicles. Volvo has also reduced pollution and has, for example, the lowest paint solvent emissions in the industry.

Despite mergers of large firms like Chrysler and Daimler-Benz, smaller vehicle producers like Volvo continue in global niche markets. Volvo is to be successful in a niche of high-end, safe, dependable, and well-engineered vehicles. Its brand name is still globally recognized and reinforced by Ford's advertising emphasizing safety features and durability. In 1999, when Ford bought Volvo cars, it left the high quality and safety brand positioning in place. But by 2002, Ford was now looking to use common platforms for its different brands. The challenge for Volvo is going to be to keep its niche market, while using up to 30 per cent of Ford's standardized components.

Websites: ***www.volvo.com***; ***www.daimlerchrysler.com*** and ***www.ford.com***.

Sources: Volvo Annual Report; ***www.volvo.com***; Alex Taylor III, "Volvo and Saab," *Fortune, July 21*, 1997; and Christine Tierney, "Will Volvo Become Just Another Ford?," *BW Online*, December 10, 2001; Christopher Brown-Humes, "Volvo exceeds earnings forecasts," *FT.com*, February 11, 2002.

of aircraft engines, and Motorola's order for $120 million of pagers, cellular phones, and semiconductors. Investor attention is also being directed to smaller countries such as Estonia, Latvia, and Lithuania. Although the total population of all three former Soviet republics is less than 8 million, these nations have natural resources such as oil shale, peat, timber, and amber, in addition to their warm-water ports on the Baltic Sea. The GDP per capita is in the neighborhood of $6,000 and the governments of these nations are trying to build bridges of free enterprise with the West. Similar opportunities are likely to evolve in other countries that currently are finding themselves falling further and further behind and will want to take action before the standard of living gap becomes any greater.

New goods and services will help to create new markets. An example is the tiny, portable personal computers (PCs) that are now entering the marketplace. These PCs are small, lightweight, and cost less than $800. The machines rely on superchips that provide the same power as that of many desktop models and are likely to revolutionize the PC market. These products also lend themselves to a globalization strategy since purchasers buy them based primarily on performance characteristics and not on cultural requirements. As a result, computer industry MNEs are likely to find the millennium offering both new opportunities and new challenges. The opportunities will come in the form of emerging markets since sharp declines in PC prices tend to increase demand sharply. The major challenge will come in the form of increased competition since PC technology tends to be easy to emulate, and so the barriers to entry for new firms are often quickly surmounted.

An accompanying development is the rise of the Internet as a source of competition. Today a growing number of MNEs are becoming electronic companies, or e-corporations for short.[20] The Internet is driving down costs and helping companies reach thousands of new potential customers worldwide.[21] As a result, MNEs are now throwing out their old business models and creating new ones that will help them do business electronically with customers who in the past were not accessible to them.[22] One of the keys to this new development is the rapid rise of both businesses and households with Internet access. As recently as 1998 approximately 25 per cent of households in Europe and 46 per cent of those in the US had personal computers. Moreover, 6 per cent of the European and 18 per cent of the American homes had Internet access.[23] In addition, 47 per cent of European and 61 per cent of American businesses had Internet access. As a result, e-commerce is now accounting for a growing percentage of GDP in these economies.[24]

Major MNEs that are finding themselves unable to compete in the ever-changing international arena are restructuring[25] and realigning markets. A good example is IBM; by 1993 it was cutting over 25,000 jobs annually and trying to stem its loss of revenues and profits. The company's poor performance in the microcomputer market and the stagnation of sales growth in the mainframe market called into question the viability of IBM in the 1990s. The decision to bring in a chief executive officer from outside the computer industry helped to highlight the fact that the firm believed that it needed fresh leadership, and recent results show that the company's decision was a good one, as IBM has now begun to increase its profitability. The firm is not alone. Most large computer MNEs are finding it difficult to maintain market share. This same situation exists in a host of other international industries, including (1) aircraft manufacturing, where Boeing is having to scurry to meet competition from Airbus; (2) autos, where Volkswagen, General Motors, and Ford are trying to stave off the onslaught of Japanese competition; and (3) household electronics, where such well-known manufacturers as Sony, Panasonic, and Goldstar are finding that the markets for products such as videocassette recorders are now becoming saturated and the key to the future will be new product development.

Exporting is likely to gain popularity, especially among multinationals with operations in the US. There are a number of reasons supporting this development. One is the low wage rates of the US vis-à-vis other industrialized countries, which help to create a competitive edge. A second is the major retooling that is occurring in many US firms, helping to dramatically improve the companies' efficiency. A third is the continuing effort of the US government to open up foreign markets for US goods and services.

New strategies, carefully crafted to the specific market, will offer increased opportunities for MNEs. In Japan, for example, the success of firms such as Toys "Я" Us, Spiegel, and Amway is a result of learning how to work within the system. As discussed in Chapter 17, in the Real Case, Toys "Я" Us set up its own retail stores by teaming up with the former director of McDonald's Japan for local knowledge and investment capital. It relentlessly pursued its objective of its discounted "category killer" toys despite vigorous opposition from small, local merchants who opposed letting Toys "Я" Us into the Japanese market. Thanks to its dogged determination, the company was eventually given permission to open a large retail store and today it has over 100 stores in Japan.[26] Spiegel, famous for its mail order business, formed a joint venture with Sumitomo Trading Company and introduced an upscale fashion catalog in Japan. The company directed its efforts at women from 20 to 40 years of age. Catalog selling proved so successful that by the mid-1990s the joint venture was generating annual sales of over $160 million. Amway decided to penetrate the Japanese market by sidestepping the complex, costly distribution system used by many retailers and by setting up its own distribution system. The company began hiring independent distributors who sell household goods through catalogs, mainly to neighbors, friends, and relatives. Today there are over 700,000 part-time and full-time people working for Amway, covering virtually every part of the Japanese market. These efforts, which are characterized by strategies that are designed to circumvent problems in the distribution system rather than trying to meet them head on, are typical of those strategies that will be used in Japan and other foreign locations during the years ahead.

Business-to-business (B2B)

An example of an ethnocentric MNE is Air Liquide, the French manufacturer of industrial and medical gases. At its Paris headquarters, the vice presidents for each geographic region are all French. All regional managers in foreign offices are French and have previously worked in Paris. This allows Air Liquide to have a standardized, "global" strategy that treats the world as one integrated market. This works as the nature of the industry is B2B. The main customers of Air Liquide are other large industrial manufacturers in oil, iron and steel, and other types of chemicals. These companies depend on the gases supplied by Air Liquide. It has flagship relationships with many of those manufacturers.

The main competitors of Air Liquide are the UK-based BOC Group and Linde AG. While Air Liquide is more concentrated in the core gas business, its competitors are more diversified into the gases needed for consumers, transportation, etc.

In general, the largest number of B2B relationships would be between ethnocentric partners. Then there are clear rules of the game – both partners are in mature, standardized industries with easy to maintain long-term relationships. So, B2B occurs in chemicals, autos and auto parts, oil, and other "commoditized" sectors.

TRADE AND INVESTMENT FRAMEWORKS

The tendency towards international trade liberalization has been exemplified by two recent developments, namely the North American Free Trade Agreement (NAFTA) of 1993 and the deeper integration of the European Union (EU). Both these regional triad agreements have developed from previous agreements. The principles of the 1989 United States–Canada Free Trade Agreement (FTA) are also the basis for NAFTA. Similarly, before 1995, the European Union was the European Community (EC). Albeit very

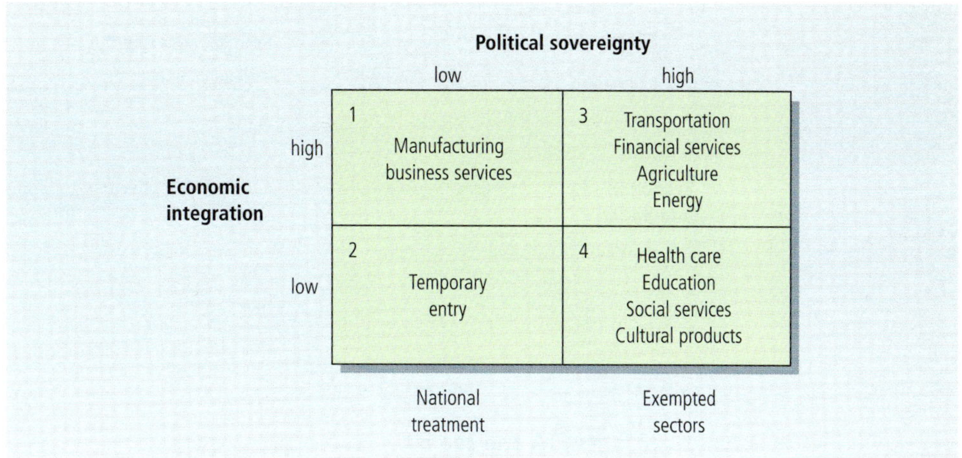

Figure 20.5 **Foreign direct investment, NAFTA and the EU**

different, in terms of goals and content, these two examples of trade and investment liberalization create a protected business environment for member countries, while in turn discriminating against third country businesses.[27]

From the Canadian and Mexico perspective, the main rationale for negotiating the FTA, and subsequently NAFTA, was to secure access to the US market for both exports and FDI. Mexico also sought to create a secure economy for inward flows of FDI. In contrast, the EU's predecessor, the EC, was considered by many observes to create a "Fortress Europe" at the expense of third country firms.[28]

Figure 20.5 classifies the different industries in the countries affected by trade liberalization in NAFTA. (It will also provide an initial framework for the EU.) The vertical axis denominates economic integration and the horizontal axis reflects the political sovereignty of nation states. The left side column therefore shows low political sovereignty in the form of national treatment. With national treatment, discrimination against foreign investors is not permitted; they are to be treated equally with domestic investors in the application of host country laws and regulations.

Quadrant 1 refers to business sectors where there is high economic integration and low political sovereignty. But not all aspects of "free trade" agreements are here. Quadrant 2 refers to business sectors with low economic integration and low political sovereignty. These are sectors that tend to be naturally local, such as labor. Quadrant 3 refers to business sectors with combined high levels of economic integration and political sovereignty. While national treatment refers to the obligation of member states to treat all businesses from other member countries as if they were domestic businesses, this does not always apply; there are exempted sectors. Sectors in quadrant 3 are exempted from national treatment despite the efficiencies that would result from the application of national treatment. The last matrix section, quadrant 4, refers to sectors that are typically local and are exempted from national treatment.

According to the NAFTA document, national treatment in quadrant 1 applies to sectors such as manufacturing and business service. In quadrant 2 are the temporary entry permits for business service professionals (such as consultants and engineers). Exempted sectors are in quadrants 3 and 4. Those with a high level of economic integration in quadrant 3 include transportation, financial services, energy, and agriculture. Those with low levels of economic integration in quadrant 4 are health care, education, social services, and cultural products.

This framework is also a model for the Free Trade Area of the Americas (FTAA), agreed to at Quebec City in 2001, with implementation expected at 2005. It is also the

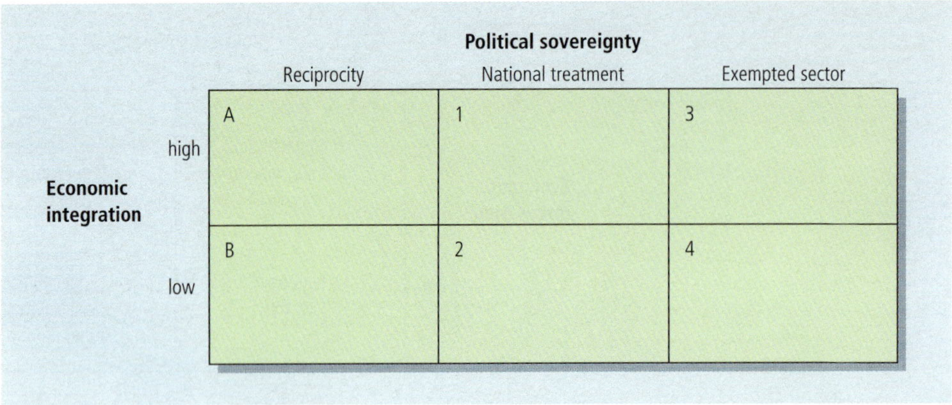

		Political sovereignty		
		Reciprocity	National treatment	Exempted sector
Economic integration	high	A	1	3
	low	B	2	4

Figure 20.6 **NAFTA and the EU**

model for the Asia-Pacific Economic Cooperation (APEC), although this will not be fully effective until 2015 and 2020.

Figure 20.6 shows the more complex EU matrix. The two extra quadrants in the extreme left column capture the concept of an even lower level of political sovereignty, reciprocity. The EU 1992 measures and subsequent "deepening" programs of political, social, and economic integration aim at quadrant A in everything but select sectors, such as culture. The manufacturing sector and business services are in quadrant A, which also includes banking and mutual funds, securities, insurance, transportation, broadcasting, tourism, and information services. In addition, there are harmonization laws regulating company behavior, including mergers and acquisitions, trademarks and copyrights, cross-border mergers, and accounting operations across borders. Another important objective of harmonization is the opening of public procurement. It is clear that such harmonization efforts place almost all economic sectors in quadrant A of Figure 20.6.[29] In conclusion, in contrast to NAFTA, the EU has a much deeper degree of economic, political, and social integration and a consequent loss of sovereignty for its member states.

Although both NAFTA and the EU can be analyzed in this way, many groups are opposed to such trade and investment liberalization. When they are opposed, they frequently cloak themselves in the guise of ethics, as we shall see in the box "International Business Strategy in Action: Is The Body Shop an ethical business?"

Active learning check

Review your answer to Active Learning Case question 3 and make any changes you like. Then compare your answer with the one below.

3. As multinational enterprises operate across the world and NGOs operate globally, why is there no "global" or "international" environmental agreement to set rules for sustainable development?

The reason that there is no effective international environmental agreement is that there is no single international institution that can enforce one. The WTO deals with trade matters, not environmental issues. The United Nations deals with human rights in a political but not economic context. Further, the MNEs really do not operate globally, but are mainly "triad" based. And here, the US and EU triad blocks are often at odds on environmental, trade, and investment policies. Paradoxically, the NGOs are criticizing MNES for something that they do not do: operate globally. The more responsible NGOs, who believe in sustainable development, should lobby the respective home-based triad authorities. This is where the power is – not with "global" governance. To ensure a safe environment, NGOs need to learn the realities of triad power.

INTERNATIONAL BUSINESS STRATEGY *IN ACTION*

Is The Body Shop an ethical business?

When it comes to the ethical company, The Body Shop is hailed as the prototype of the responsible firm. The company's website not only states the company's values but urges visitors to become active in the fight to end animal cruelty, to protect human rights, and to implement fair trade practices. Its founder, Anita Roddick, started the company in 1976 by opening a small store in Brighton, England, to support her family. In 1978, the opening of a small store in Brussels became its first overseas expansion. By the 1980s, the company was opening two stores per month. Today, The Body Shop has grown into a multinational enterprise with 1,840 stores in 50 countries around the world.

The company has a lengthy résumé of its social achievements. In the animal rights arena, The Body Shop joined the campaign for a ban on animal testing for cosmetic products. This was a major factor in the 1998 decision of the UK government to ban animal testing in the industry. On the environmental front, the company has publicly joined NGO causes. For example, in the 1980s, the company sponsored Greenpeace posters, joined the "Save the Whales Campaign", and started a signature petition to ask the Brazilian government to halt the burning of the Amazon forest. The company also brought attention to Shell's involvement in Nigeria. Shell's operations were blamed for severe environmental deterioration, prosecution of protestors, and bribery of state officials. More recently, the company has converted many of its operations into Ecotricity, or energy from renewal resources, and helped create an academy of business with an ethical curriculum in the University of Bath.

The company's image is tied to that of its founder. Anita Roddick has been an active participant on environmental rallies, fair trade missions and in lobbying governments. She has also defied the cosmetics industry's portrayal of women and urged women to accept cellulite and wrinkles as a natural part of their bodies. She has stated publicly that cosmetics claiming to solve these problems do not really work, an assertion that has created a backlash from competitors. Since the company went public in 1985, she has often found herself at odds with shareholders. In fact, in 1998 shareholders pressured her to step down from the CEO chair in favor of Patrick Gournay, who oversaw a major restructuring that saw 300 job cuts, the company's withdrawal from manufacturing, and a management hiring spree to revitalize the company. In 2000, Roddick announced that she would slowly retire from managing The Body Shop to concentrate on her activism. In 2002, she and her husband resigned as co-chairs but retained seats on the board of directors. Gournay also resigned and was replaced by CEO Peter Saunders.

Another signature of The Body Shop is the "Trade not Aid" slogan. Under it, the company has sought to advance the plight of indigenous communities in third world countries by promoting "Fair Trade". The goal is to support marginalized sectors of society to develop a livelihood within the context of sustainable development. Today, the company sources cocoa butter, babasu oil, massagers, among other ingredients and products, from Community Trade suppliers in 26 countries, including India, Honduras, Nepal, and Mexico. In 2000/2001, the company purchased £5 million in natural products through its Community Trade Program.

In the 1990s, the company suffered a severe blow to its reputation when *Business Ethics* published an article by Jon Entine claiming that the company was the opposite of what it represented itself to be. Entine accused the company of selling drugstore quality products at a large premium by marketing cosmetics with petrochemical ingredients as natural products. In addition, the author claimed the company misrepresented the amount of its donations to charity, did not adhere to its own principles of "Fair Trade", and had itself committed unnecessary environmental damage. For instance, Entine mentions an incident in which The Body Shop went back on a contract to purchase large amounts of shea butter from suppliers in Ghana. This left the suppliers with a lot of useless stock they could not sell anywhere else. There are also alleged incidents of the company forcing low margins on suppliers in third world countries. And, a franchisee in France claimed that The Body Shop dumped a load of plastic containers in a landfill.

A number of consumer groups, NGOs, and Internet websites have all jumped on the wagon. The website mcspotlight.com claims that The Body Shop sells products with ingredients that have been tested on animals, as long as the testing was not done for cosmetics, and that some of its products contain gelatin, an animal product. The same website claims that, in industrialized countries, The Body Shop pays its employees near minimum wages and is unwilling to recognize unions. The company is also accused of exaggerating the importance of its Community Trade Program and of using the Kayapo Indians of Brazil for promotions without compensating them.

The Body Shop has denied most allegations and threatened legal action to a number of news media but has only taken action against a few, including Channel 4 of England. For the company, which was built on the confidence of the "conscious customer", the consequences of this bad publicity could be devastating. Premium prices are, after all, what customers are willing to pay for that extra social responsibility.

Whether the allegations are true or not, The Body Shop can still claim to be a pioneer of corporate responsibility because it brought the issues to the table. Many companies have emulated its principles, including Boots of the UK, which has developed its own brand of environmentally friendly cosmetics to compete with The Body Shop.

Websites: **www.the-body-shop.com** and **www.greenpeace.org**.

Sources: "Body Shops Shares Slump," *BBC.co.uk*, January 12, 2001; "Body Shop Cuts Jobs," *BBC.co.uk*, May 6, 1999; "Roddick Quits to 'smash' WTO," *BBC.co.uk*, September 17, 2000; ***www.the-body-shop.com***; ***www.jonentine.com***; Jon Entine, "Shattered Image: Is the Body Shop Too Good to Be True?" *Business Ethics*, September/October 1994; Sharlene Buszka, "A Case of Greenwashing: The Body Shop," in *Proceedings of the Association of Management and the International Association of Management 15th Annual Conference, Organizational Management Division*, vol. 15, no. 1 (1997), pp. 199–294; ***www.mcspotlight.org/***; "Passion or Profit," *FT.com*, February 13, 2002; "Body Swap," *FT.com*, February 13, 2002; Alison Smith, "US Team Hopeful of Reviving Flagging Fortune," Financial Times, February 13, 2002, p. 20.

KEY POINTS

1. There will be an increase in the amount of international business research that is being conducted. This will come in the form of both theory testing and the practical application of information. Both academicians and practitioners will find this development helpful.
2. The key concepts in this book can be brought together in the framework of the CSA–FSA matrix. The multinational enterprises have firm-specific advantages (FSAs) that can be related to home and host country-specific advantages (CSAs).
3. Multinationals, as flagship firms, are beginning to develop new business network relationships with suppliers, competitors, governments, unions, universities, and a host of other external groups. This networking relationship is proving particularly helpful in increasing productivity, profitability, and overall competitiveness.
4. The two environments that will present the greatest challenges for MNEs in the future are the political and the economic. The rising tide of protectionism will require that multinationals deal astutely with foreign governments. They will also have to weigh carefully the political risk associated with investing in countries that are now beginning to shed their central planning systems and to move toward free enterprise economies.
5. The principle of national treatment reduces political sovereignty, although some sectors are exempted in NAFTA, the FTAA, and APEC. In contrast, the EU has deep integration across political and social areas, as well as economic.

KEY TERMS

- **country-specific advantages (CSAs)**
- **firm-specific advantages (FSAs)**
- **flagship firms**
- **five partners**
- **strategic fit**

REVIEW AND DISCUSSION QUESTIONS

1. Why is theory testing of value to the field of international business research? What can be learned from such information?
2. In addition to theory testing, how is international business research of value to both scholars and practitioners? In your answer, give an example of how each group can benefit from such research.
3. Why is the FSA/CSA framework a useful one for the analysis of the field of international business?
4. In what ways are MNEs developing new business networks? Give two examples and then explain why these developments are likely to help the companies maintain their competitive strengths.
5. How is the political environment likely to change during the future? Give one example and relate its significance for multinationals.
6. How is the economic environment likely to change in the future? Give one example and relate its significance for multinationals.
7. How does NAFTA differ from the EU?
8. Why are NGOs opposed to MNEs? What should MNEs do?

REAL CASE

Dell: B2C

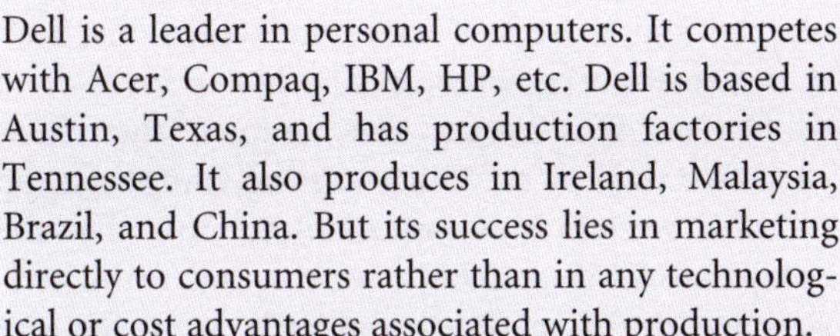

Dell is a leader in personal computers. It competes with Acer, Compaq, IBM, HP, etc. Dell is based in Austin, Texas, and has production factories in Tennessee. It also produces in Ireland, Malaysia, Brazil, and China. But its success lies in marketing directly to consumers rather than in any technological or cost advantages associated with production.

Dell introduced the Dell Direct model, a business-to-consumer (B2C) concept, which has now been copied by major competitors. By eliminating retailers, Dell can deal directly with individual customers, offering detailed and richly configured systems. There is consumer customization, plus services and support. This method saves on inventory and introduces new technology quickly. Dell became a market leader with the first B2C direct business model.

The computer industry is at a mature stage of manufacturing. This means that there is pressure either to be extremely cost competitive or to develop value-added services that build on the computer itself. The five major computer manufacturers have responded to these market changes in different ways. IBM invented the personal computer and was perhaps the first to move strongly towards customer service. In late 2002 Hewlett-Packard and Compaq were talking a merger to try to consolidate production but also to develop the service end. This left Apple and Dell as the firms driven by low cost and technology.

In China, where Dell is a very small competitor, the company has developed an innovative B2C concept that is allowing it to quickly increase its market share. PC manufacturers have been flocking to China because of expected growth of 20 per cent per year over the next few years. Dell entered the Chinese market in the 1990s, trailing behind IBM and Compaq. Yet, today, Dell is the largest foreign PC market player, after three local Chinese manufacturers. One way in which Dell was able to achieve this was by introducing the affordable Smart PC. Another has been to offer tailor-made PCs over the Internet. A Chinese customer virtually builds his or her desired computer and then Dell assembles and delivers it. Implementing B2C retailing has not been easy because Chinese people are not used to credit cards. To overcome this obstacle, the company has made deals with major banks to allow customers to go to a branch and make a payment that is then reported to Dell.

Throughout the world, Dell has tried to add service value in its B2C process. It has 80 Internet sites on which more than 65,000 institutional customers do business with Dell. Through ***www.dell.com*** customers can order, price, and configure products. Dell maintains after-sale service with customers. It also brings new technology quickly to the customer. In short, Dell's B2C system allows the MNE to engage in mass customization.

Websites: ***www.dell.com***; ***www.dell.com.cn***; ***www.hp.com***; ***www.hp.com.cn***; ***www.compaq.com***; ***www.compaq.com.cn***; ***www.ibm.com***; ***www.ibm.com.cn*** and ***www.acer.com***.

Sources: ***www.dell.com***; Bruce Einhorn, "Dell Takes a Different Tack in China," *BW Online*, December 3, 2001; Scott Morrison, "Stronger Consumer Demand for PCs Lifts Dell," *FT.com*, February 15, 2002.

1. **What is meant by B2C? How does Dell achieve B2C?**
2. **Why is Dell so successful in China?**
3. **Is B2C a viable strategy in the mature, competitive, computer industry of today?**

REAL CASE

Hewlett-Packard's environmental management policy

Today, like never before, MNEs have to be concerned about their public image. Consumers, employees, and shareholders all expect the corporation to behave responsibly and ethically towards the communities (or "stakeholders") with which they operate. Some companies have learned the hard way that they are accountable. For instance, Royal Dutch/Shell had to apologize to its shareholders when the company's environmental and human rights report card did not measure up to their expectations. By 2001, it ranked as the world's fifth best company, see the table in "Active Learning Case: The Environment, NGOs and MNEs" above. Today's MNEs are trying to get in line with the expectations of the stakeholders, and some companies, like BP, 3M, Kodak, and Hewlett-Packard, are outdoing themselves.

Hewlett-Packard's Environmental Management Policy (EMP) oversees the environmental quality of its products through their life cycle. The company's EMP is complemented with an Environmental Management System (EMS). Through its EMS, Hewlett-Packard audits its operations regularly with business managers being accountable to the CEO on their environmental standing. The system is based on the principles of total quality management. The quality of their products depends on their effect on the environment.

Environmental issues are an integral part of the planning and decision process. Hewlett-Packard designs and constructs its facilities to minimize waste generation, and to promote energy efficiency and ecosystem protection. It pursues a strategy of pollution prevention to reduce the generation of chemical and solid waste and proactively addresses contamination resulting from its operations. It also encourages suppliers to adopt similar environmental principles.

In 1992 the company began a product stewardship program. The program maintains the following guidelines: to design products and packaging to minimize the energy they consume, to use fewer raw materials, and to use more recycled material; to develop products that are easier to reuse or recycle; and to reduce waste and emissions from the manufacturing process. The first priority is to avoid hazardous wastes. The company then finds proactive ways of recycling, treating, and disposing of these wastes. It is important to note that the company's EMS and EMP were found to be consistent with international standards set in the ISO 14001.

In 2002, the proposed merger between Hewlett-Packard and Compaq overshadowed the excellent environmental performance of Hewlett-Packard. Perhaps this indicated that stakeholder ethics and environmental management are still secondary to the core strategy of a company. The Hewlett-Packard CEO, Ms Carley Fiorina, pushed for the merger with Compaq in order to create a more balanced overall business portfolio. This would give the new combined company a much more competitive position in servers and storage and improve its performance as a customer-based service/knowledge organization, rather than as a basic printer and imaging manufacturer. In early 2002, the stock market was not reacting well to the proposed merger, possibly because it perceived that the two company cultures were not all that complementary.

Websites: ***www.hp.com***.

Sources: Adapted from Alan M. Rugman and Alain Verbeke, "Six Cases of Corporate Strategic Responses to Environmental Regulations," *European Management Journal*, vol. 8, no. 4 (July 2000), pp. 377–385. Alan M. Rugman and Alain Verbeke, "Corporate Strategies and Environmental Regulations: An Organizing Framework," *Strategic Management Journal*, vol. 19, no. 4 (April 1998), pp. 363–376; ***www.hp.com/abouthp/envrnmnt/***; "Shellman Says Sorry (Cor Herkstroter)," *Economist*, May 10, 1997, p. 95; "Walters Hewlett's Counterplan," *Wall Street Journal*, 11 February 2002, p. 81.

1. How can environmental innovation allow a company to gain a first-mover advantage against its competitors?

2. Governments constantly update their environmental regulations. How does the amount of flexibility allowed to a company influence the kinds of environmental investments it makes?

3. What kind of problems might make it difficult for an MNE to coordinate environmental strategies in different countries?

ENDNOTES

1 See, for example, Dean Takahashi, "How the Competition Got Ahead of Intel in Making Cheap Chips," *Wall Street Journal*, February 12, 1998, pp. A 1, 11.

2 Jeanne B. Pinder, "Japan's New York Realty Investing Plunges," *New York Times*, March 19, 1993, p. C 10.

3 Shaker A. Zahra, "The Changing Rules of Global Competitiveness in the 21st Century," *Academy of Management Executive*, vol. 13, no. 1 (February 1999), pp. 36–42.

4 Also, see James B. Treece et al. "New Worlds to Conquer," *Business Week*, February 28, 1994, pp. 50–52.

5 Also see Howard Thomas, Timothy Pollock and Philip Gorman, "Global Strategic Analyses: Frameworks and Approaches," *Academy of Management Executive*, February 1999, pp. 70–82.

6 Also, see David Kirkpatrick, "Why the Internet Is Boosting IBM's Mainframe Sales," *Fortune*, January 11, 1999, pp. 148–149.

7 Otto Andersen, "On the Internationalization Process of Firms: A Critical Analysis," *Journal of International Business Studies*, vol. 24, no. 2 (Second Quarter 1993), pp. 209–231; and Sumantra Ghoshal and Nitin Nohria, "Horses for Courses: Organizational Forms for Multinational Corporations," *Sloan Management Review*, Winter 1993, pp. 23–35.

8 Jeremiah J. Sullivan and Richard B. Peterson, "A Test of Theories Underlying the Japanese Lifetime Employment System," *Journal of International Business Studies*, vol. 22, no. 1 (First Quarter 1991), p. 79.

9 Richard M. Hodgetts, "A Conversation with Michael E. Porter," *Organizational Dynamics*, Summer 1999, pp. 25–26.

10 Alan M. Rugman, *Inside the Multinationals: The Economics of Internal Markets* (New York: Columbia University Press, 1981); Alan M. Rugman (ed.), *International Business in Canada: Strategies for Management* (Toronto: Prentice-Hall Canada, 1989), Chapters 8, 13; Alan M. Rugman, *The Theory of Multinational Enterprises* (Cheltenham: Edward Elgar, 1996).

11 Joseph R. D'Cruz and Alan M. Rugman, *Multinationals as Flagship Firms: Regional Business Networks* (Oxford: Oxford University, 2000). This book is based on earlier work such as: Alan M. Rugman and Joseph R. D'Cruz, *New Compacts for Canadian Competitiveness* (Toronto: Kodak Canada, 1992), p. 31; and Joseph R. D'Cruz and Alan M. Rugman, "Business Networks for International Competitiveness," *Business Quarterly*, vol. 56, no. 4 (Spring 1992), pp. 101–107.

12 D'Cruz and Rugman (2000) n. 11 above.

13 For an example of this psychological reaction, see David E. Sanger, "64 per cent of Japanese Say US Relations Are 'Unfriendly,'" *New York Times*, July 6, 1993, pp. A 1, A 6.

14 For more on this, see Rosabeth Moss Kanter, "Transcending Business Boundaries: 12,000 World Managers View Change," *Harvard Business Review*, vol. 69, no. 3 (May/June 1991), pp. 151–164.

15 See, for example, Keith Bradsher, "US Upset with Japan on Chip Pact," *New York Times*, March 4, 1993, pp. C 1, C 2.

16 Mark Landler, "Back to Vietnam, This Time to Build," *New York Times*, September 13, 1998, Section 3, pp. 1, 11.

17 See "Mexico: A Market that Is Ready for Services," *New York Times*, July 21, 1993, pp. C 10–C 15; and Bob Graham, "Free Trade Means Fair Trade," *Miami Herald*, July 22, 1993, p. 21 A.

18 See, for example, John Templeman et al., "Germany Fights Back," *Business Week*, May 31, 1993, p. 48.

19 Brian Coleman, "German Union Sends a Warning with Series of Strikes for Pay Rise," *Wall Street Journal*, February 2, 1999, p. A 19.

20 Gary Hamel and Jeff Sampler, "The E-Corporation," *Fortune*, December 7, 1998, pp. 80–92.

21 R. Duane Ireland and Michael A. Hitt, "Achieving and Maintaining Strategic Competitiveness in the 21st Century: The Role of Strategic Leadership," *Academy of Management Executive*, February 1999, pp. 43–57.

22 Heather Green and Linda Himelstein, "Throw Out Your Old Business Model," *Business Week E-Biz*, March 22, 1999, pp. EB 22–23.

23 Thane Peterson and Stephen Baker, "A High-Tech Europe Is Finally in Sight," *Business Week*, August 31, 1998, p. 122.

24 Robert D. Hof, Gary McWilliams and Gabrielle Savers, "The 'Click Here' Economy," *Business Week*, June 22, 1998, pp. 122–128.

25 Claude H. Deutsch, "Digital Polish for Factory Floors," *New York Times*, March 22, 1999, pp. C 1, 7.

26 Debora L. Spar, *Ruling the Waves: Cycles of Discovery, Chaos and Wealth* (New York: Harcourt, 2001).

27 Alan M. Rugman and Alain Verbeke, "Corporate Strategy After the Free Trade Agreement and Europe 1992," in John Longair (ed.), *Proceedings: Regional Integration in the World Economy: Europe and North America* (Ottawa: Conference Board of Canada, March 1990).

28 See Gerard Curzon, "Ten Reasons to Fear Fortress Europe," Mimeo. Graduate Institute of International Studies, Geneva, 1989 and B. Burgenmeir and J. L. Mucchielii, *Multinational and Europe 1992* (London: Routledge, 1990) for an overview.

29 Rugman and Verbeke (1990) n. 27 above.

ADDITIONAL BIBLIOGRAPHY

Brewer, Thomas L. and Young, Stephen. *The Multilateral Investment System and Multinational Enterprise* (Oxford: Oxford University Press, 1998).

Clarkson, Max B. E. "A Stakeholder Framework for Analyzing and Evaluating Corporate Social Performance," *Academy of Management Review*, vol. 20, no. 1 (January 1995).

D'Cruz, Joseph R. and Rugman, Alan M. "Developing International Competitiveness: The Five Partners Model," *Business Quarterly* (Winter 1993).

D'Cruz, Joseph R. and Rugman, Alan M. "Business Network Theory and the Canadian Telecommunications Industry," *International Business Review*, vol. 3, no. 3 (1994).

Doyle, Frank P. "People-Power: The Global Human Resource Challenge for the '90s," *Columbia Journal of World Business*, vol. 25, nos. 1, 2 (Spring/Summer 1990).

Dunning, John H. *Multinational Enterprises and the Global Economy* (Reading, UK: Addison-Wesley, 1993).

Dunning, John H. *The Globalization of Business: The Challenge of the 1990s* (London and New York: Routledge, 1993).

Egelhoff, William G. "Information-Processing Theory and the Multinational Enterprise," *Journal of International Business*, vol. 22, no. 3 (Third Quarter 1991).

Emmerij, Louis. "Globalization, Regionalization and World Trade," *Columbia Journal of World Business*, vol. 27, no. 2 (Summer 1992).

Ghoshal, Sumantra and Bartlett, Christopher A. "The Multinational Corporation as an Interorganizational Network," *Academy of Management Review*, vol. 15, no. 4 (October 1990).

Guntz, Hugh P. and Jalland, R. Michael. "Managerial Careers and Business Strategies," *Academy of Management Review*, vol. 21, no. 3 (July 1996).

Kim, W. Chan and Mauborgne, Renee A. "Effectively Conceiving and Executing Multinationals' Worldwide Strategies," *Journal of International Business Studies*, vol. 24, no. 3 (Third Quarter 1993).

Kirton, John J., Daniels, Joseph P. and Freytag, Andreas (eds.) *Guiding Global Order: G8 Governance in the 21st Century* (Aldershot: Ashgate, 2001).

Kogut, Bruce. "Methodological Contributions in International Business Research and the Direction of Academic Research Activity", in Alan M. Rugman and Thomas Brewer (eds.) *The Oxford Handbook of International Business* (Oxford: Oxford University Press, 2001).

Martinez, Jon I. and Jarillo, J. Carlos. "Coordination Demands of International Strategies," *Journal of International Business Studies*, vol. 22, no. 3 (Third Quarter 1991).

Miller, Kent D. "Industry and Country Effects of Managers' Perceptions of Environmental Uncertainties," *Journal of International Business Studies*, vol. 24, no. 4 (Fourth Quarter 1993).

Morrison, Allen J. and Inkpen, Andrew C. "An Analysis of Significant Contributions to the International Business Literature," *Journal of International Business Studies*, vol. 22, no. 1 (First Quarter 1991).

Nehrt, Chad. "Maintaining a First Mover Advantage When Environmental Regulations Differ Between Countries," *Academy of Management Review*, vol. 23, no. 1 (January 1998).

Ohmae, Kenichi. "Managing in a Borderless World," *Harvard Business Review*, vol. 67, no. 3 (May/June 1989).

Rosenzweig, Philip M. and Singh, Jitendra V. "Organizational Environments and the Multinational Enterprise," *Academy of Management Review*, vol. 16, no. 2 (April 1991).

Rugman, Alan M. "Multinationals and Trade in Services: A Transaction Cost Approach," *Weltwirtschaftliches Archiv*, vol. 123, no. 4 (December 1987).

Rugman, Alan M. and D'Cruz, Joseph R. "A Theory of Business Networks," in Lorraine Eden (ed.), *Multinationals in North America* (Alberta: University of Calgary Press, 1993).

Rugman, Alan M., Kirton, John and Soloway, Julie. *Environmental Regulations and Corporate Strategy* (Oxford: Oxford University Press, 1999).

Rugman, Alan M. and Verbeke, Alain. *Research in Global Strategic Management: Volume 3: Corporate Response to Global Change* (Greenwich CT: JAI Press, 1992).

Rugman, Alan M. and Verbeke, Alain. *Research in Global Strategic Management: Volume 4: Beyond the Three Generics* (Greenwich CT: JAI Press, 1993).

Rugman, Alan M. and Verbeke, Alain. "Corporate Strategies and Environmental Regulations: An Organizing Framework," *Strategic Management Journal*, vol. 19, Special Issue (April 1998).

Rugman, Alan M. and Verbeke, Alain. "Six Cases of Corporate Strategic Response to Environmental Regulations", *European Management Journal*, vol. 18, no. 4 (August 2000), pp. 377–385.

Shan, Weijian. "Environmental Risks and Joint Venture Sharing Arrangements," *Journal of International Business Studies*, vol. 22, no. 4 (Fourth Quarter 1991).

Vandermerwe, Sandra and Oliff, Michael D. "Corporate Challenges for an Age of Reconsumption," *Columbia Journal of World Business*, vol. 26, no. 3 (Fall 1991).

Westcott, William F., II. "Environmental Technology Cooperation: A Quid Pro Quo for Transnational Corporations and Developing Countries," *Columbia Journal of World Business*, vol. 27, no. 3 (Fall/Winter 1992).

Wright, Richard W. *International Entrepreneurship: Globalization of Emerging Business: Volume 7: Research in Global Strategic Management* (Oxford: Elsevier/JAI Press, 1999).

Yip, George S. "Global Strategy . . . In a World of Nations?" *Sloan Management Review*, vol. 31, no. 1 (Fall 1989).

Zahra, Shaker A. "The Changing Rules of Global Competitiveness in the 21st Century," *Academy of Management Executive*, vol. 13, no. 1 (February 1999).

Glossary

Acceptance zone. An area within which a party is willing to negotiate.

Achievement culture. A culture in which people are accorded status based on how well they perform their jobs.

Achievement motivation. The desire to accomplish objectives and attain success.

Ad valorem duty. A tax which is based on a percentage of the value of imported goods.

Advertising. A non-personal form of promotion in which a firm attempts to persuade consumers of a particular point of view.

Aesthetics. The artistic tastes of a culture.

Andean common market (Ancom). A subregional free trade compact designed to promote economic and social integration and cooperation; Bolivia, Colombia, Ecuador, Peru, and Venezuela are all members.

Andean Pact. An economic union consisting of Bolivia, Colombia, Ecuador, Peru, and Venezuela.

Antidumping duties (AD). Import tariffs intended to protect domestic producers from foreign products sold at less than their cost of production or at lower prices than in their home market.

Arm's length price. The price a buyer will pay for merchandise in a market under conditions of perfect competition.

Ascription culture. A culture in which status is attributed based on who or what a person is.

Association of Southeast Asian Nations (ASEAN). An economic union founded in 1967 by Indonesia, Malaysia, the Philippines, Singapore, and Thailand; this economic bloc focuses not on reducing trade barriers among members but, rather, on promoting exports to other nations.

Attitude. A persistent tendency to feel and behave in a particular way toward some object.

Autonomous infrastructure. An infrastructure used by multinationals that compete in dissimilar national markets and do not share resources.

Backward integration. The ownership of equity assets used earlier in the production cycle, such as an auto firm that acquires a steel company.

Balance of payments (BOP). The record of all values of all transactions between a country's residents and the rest of the world.

Base salary. The amount of cash compensation that an individual receives in the home country.

Basic economic infrastructure. The primary economic industries, including transportation, communication, and energy.

Basic mission. The reason that a firm is in existence.

British Export Credits Guarantee Department (ECGD). A governmental agency that lends money for export financing of British equipment.

Business managers. Managers responsible for coordinating the efforts of people in a corporate organization; for example, in a matrix structure.

Canada Labor Code. A federal law that covers areas such as wages, employment practices, work safety, and conciliation of labor disputes.

Capital account items. A balance-of-payments account that involves transactions which involve claims in ownership.

Capital expenditures. Major projects in which the costs are to be allocated over a number of years.

Caribbean Basin Initiative. A trade agreement that eliminates tariffs on many imports to the US from the Caribbean and Central American regions.

Cartel. A group of firms that collectively agree to fix prices or quantities sold in an effort to control price.

Centrally determined economy. An economy in which goods and services are allocated based on a plan formulated by a committee that decides what is to be offered.

Civil society. A group of individuals, organizations, and institutions that act outside the government and the market to advance a diverse set interests.

Cluster analysis. A marketing approach to forecasting customer demand; it involves the grouping of data based on market area, customer, or similar variables.

Codetermination. A legal system that requires workers and their managers to discuss major strategic decisions before companies implement the decisions.

Collectivism. The tendency of people to belong to groups who look after each other in exchange for loyalty.

Common market. A form of economic integration characterized by the elimination of trade barriers among member nations, a common external trade policy, and mobility of factors of production among member countries.

Communication. The process of transferring meanings from sender to receiver.

Communism. A political system in which the government owns all property and makes all decisions regarding production and distribution of goods and services.

Comparative advertising. The comparing of similar products for the purpose of persuading customers to buy a particular one.

Competition Act. A Canadian federal law which regulates anticompetitive practices and prohibits actions that will substantially lessen or prevent competition; it is similar to US antitrust laws.

Competitive intelligence. The gathering of external information on competitors and the competitive environment as part of the decision-making process.

Competitive scope. The breadth of a firm's target market within an industry.

Compound duty. A tariff consisting of both a specific and an ad valorem duty.

Concurrent engineering. The process of having design, engineering, and manufacturing people working together to create a product, in contrast to working in a sequential manner.

Confucian work ethic. A belief that people should work hard at their tasks.

Consolidation. The combining of the major financial statements of subsidiaries into composite statements for the parent firm.

Container ships. Vessels used to carry standardized containers that can be simply loaded onto a carrier and then unloaded at their destination without any repackaging of the contents of the containers.

Contract management. A process by which an organization (such as the government) transfers operating responsibility of an industry without transferring the legal title and ownership.

Controlling. The process of determining that everything goes according to plan.

Coordinated infrastructure. An infrastructure used when there is a high degree of similarity among national markets, and business units share resources in an effort to help each other to increase overall sales.

Cost strategy. A strategy that relies on low price and is achieved through approaches such as vigorous pursuit of cost reductions and overhead control, avoidance of marginal customer accounts, and cost minimization in areas such as sales and advertising.

Cost-of-living allowance. A payment to compensate for differences in expenditures between the home country and the foreign location.

Council for Mutual Economic Assistance (Comecon). An economic union of communist countries led by the former USSR and including most Eastern bloc nations; today Comecon's role has been greatly diminished.

Council of Ministers. The major policy decision-making body of the EU; it consists of one minister from each of the 15 member states and is one of four major institutions of the EU.

Countertrade. Barter trade in which the exporting firm receives payment in products from the importing country.

Countervailing duties (CVD). Import tariffs intended to protect domestic producers from harmful subsidization by foreign governments.

Country-specific advantages (CSAs). Strengths or benefits specific to a country that result from its competitive environment, labor force, geographic location, government polices, industrial clusters, etc.

Court of Justice. A court that has one judge appointed from each EU member country; this court serves as the official interpreter of EU law.

Cross-cultural school of international selection. A school of thought which holds that the effectiveness of a particular managerial behavior is a function of the culture in which the behavior is performed.

Cross rate. An exchange rate computed from two other rates, such as the relationship between Swiss francs and German marks.

Cultural assimilator. A programmed learning technique designed to expose members of one culture to some of the basic concepts, attitudes, role perceptions, customs, and values of another culture.

Culture. The acquired knowledge that people use to interpret experience and to generate social behavior.

Currency diversification. The spreading of financial assets across several or more currencies.

Currency option. An instrument that gives the purchaser the right to buy or sell a specific amount of foreign currency at a predetermined rate within a specified time period.

Current account. A balance-of-payments account that consists of merchandise trade, services, and unrequited transfers.

Customs. Common or established practices.

Customs union. A form of economic integration in which all tariffs between member countries are eliminated and a common trade policy toward nonmember countries is established.

Decision making. The process of choosing from among alternatives.

Delayed differentiation. A strategy in which all products are manufactured in the same way for all countries or regions until as late in the assembly process as possible, at which time differentiation is used to introduce particular features or special components.

Demand-Flow™ Technology (DFT). A production process that is flexible to demand changes.

Democracy. A system of government in which the people, either directly or through their elected officials, decide what is to be done.

Development Bank of Japan (DBJ). A publicly funded financial institution with a mandate to advance business projects in accordance with the government's social and economic policies. (Previously known as the Japan Development Bank.)

Diet. The branch of the Japanese government in which legislative power is vested; it consists of a popularly elected House of Representatives and House of Councillors.

Differentiation strategy. A strategy directed toward creating something that is perceived as being unique.

Distribution. The course that goods take between production and the final consumer.

Divestiture. (Also see *Privatization.*) A process by which a government or business sells assets.

Dumping. The selling of imported goods at a price below cost or below that in the home country.

Economic exposure. The foreign exchange risk involved in pricing products, sourcing parts, or locating investments to develop a competitive position.

Economic integration. The establishment of transnational rules and regulations that enhance economic trade and cooperation among countries.

Economic union. A form of economic integration characterized by free movement of goods, services, and factors of production among member countries and full integration of economic policies.

Embargo. A quota set at zero, thus preventing the importation of those products that are involved.

Empowerment. The process of giving employees increased control over their work.

Emotional culture. A culture in which emotions are expressed openly and naturally.

Enterprise for the Americas. An idea launched by President Bush; the aim of this effort is to create the free trade area from Alaska to Argentine Antarctica.

Estimation by analogy. A method of forecasting market demand or market growth based on information generated in other countries, such as determining the number of refrigerators sold in the US as a percentage of new housing starts and using this statistic in planning for the manufacture of these products in other world markets.

Ethics. A set of moral principles and values that govern behavior.

Ethnocentric predisposition. The tendency of a manager or multinational company to rely on the values and interests of the parent company in formulating and implementing the strategic plan.

Ethnocentric solution. An approach to determining parent–subsidiary relations; it involves treating all foreign operations as if they were extensions of domestic operations.

Ethnocentrism. The belief that one's way of doing things is superior to that of others.

Eurobond. A financial instrument that is typically underwritten by a syndicate of banks from different countries and is sold in countries other than the one in which its currency is denominated.

Eurocurrency. Any currency banked outside its country of origin.

Eurodollars. Dollars banked outside the US.

European Bank for Reconstruction and Development. A bank created to promote democracy and free enterprise in Eastern Europe and to lend public and private money.

European Coal and Steel Community (ECSC). A community formed in 1952 by Belgium, France, Italy, Luxembourg, the Netherlands, and West Germany for the purpose of creating a common market that would revitalize the efficiency and competitiveness of the coal and steel industries in those countries.

European Commission. A 20-member group chosen by agreement of member governments of the EU; the Commission is the executive branch of the EU.

European Council. Composed of the heads of state of each EU member country as well as the president of the European Commission. Meetings of the Council take place at least twice a year and their purpose is to resolve major policy issues and to set policy direction.

European Free Trade Association. A free trade area currently consisting of Iceland, Liechtenstein, Norway, and Switzerland; past members included the UK (before it joined the EU).

European Monetary System (EMS). A system created by some major members of the EU which fixes their currency values in relation to each other (within a band) and floats them together against the rest of the world.

European Parliament. A group of 630 members elected directly by voters in each member country of the EU; the Parliament serves as a watchdog on EU expenditures.

European Research Cooperation Agency. A research and development alliance which emphasizes projects in the fields of energy, medicine, biotechnology, communications, information technology, transport, new materials, robotics, production automation, lasers, and the environment.

European Union (EU). A treaty based institutional framework that manages economic and political cooperation among its 15 member states: Austria, Belgium, Denmark, France, Finland, Germany, Greece, Ireland, Italy, Luxembourg, the Netherlands, Portugal, Spain, Sweden, and the UK.

Exchange controls. Controls that restrict the flow of currency.

Exchange rate. The amount of one currency that can be obtained for another currency.

Exchange risk. The probability that a company will be unable to adjust prices and costs to offset changes in the exchange rate.

Exchange risk adaptation. The use of hedging to provide protection against exchange rate fluctuations.

Exchange risk avoidance. The elimination of exchange risk by doing business locally.

Expatriates. Individuals who reside abroad but are citizens of the parent country of the multinational; they are citizens of the home, not of the host country.

Export tariff. A tax levied on goods sent out of a country.

Exports. Goods and services produced by a firm in one country and then sent to another country.

Expropriation. The governmental seizure of private businesses coupled with little, if any, compensation to their owners.

External economies of scale. Efficiencies brought about by access to cheaper capital, highly skilled labor, and superior technology.

Factor conditions. Land, labor, and capital.

Factor endowment theory. A trade theory which holds that nations will produce and export products that use large amounts of production factors that they have in abundance and will import products requiring a large amount of production factors that are scarce in their country.

FDI cluster. A group of developing countries usually located in the same geographic region as a triad member and having some form of economic link to this member.

Femininity. The degree to which the dominant values of a society are caring for others and the quality of life.

Financial infrastructure. The monetary system of a country; it consists of the nation's banking, insurance, and financial services.

Firm-specific advantages (FSAs). Strengths or benefits specific to a firm and a result of contributions that can be made by its personnel, technology, and/or equipment.

Fisher effect. An international finance theory which describes the relationship between inflation and interest rates and holds that, as inflation rises, so will the nominal interest rate.

Five partners. A business network consisting of five partner organizations: the flagship firm (a multinational enterprise), key suppliers, key customers, key competitors, and the non-business infrastructure.

Flagship firms. Multinational firms characterized by global competitiveness and international benchmarks.

Focus strategy. A strategy that concentrates on a particular buyer group and segments that niche based on product line or geographic market.

Foreign bond. A bond sold outside the borrower's country.

Foreign direct investment (FDI). Equity funds invested in other nations.

Foreign exchange. Any financial instrument that carries out payment from one currency to another.

Foreign exchange arbitrageurs. Individuals who simultaneously buy and sell currency in two or more foreign markets and profit from the exchange rate differences.

Foreign exchange brokers. Individuals who work in brokerage firms where they often deal in both spot rate and forward rate transactions.

Foreign exchange hedgers. Individuals who limit potential losses by locking in guaranteed foreign exchange positions.

Foreign exchange traders. Individuals who buy and sell foreign currency for their employer.

Foreign investment controls. Limits on foreign direct investment or the transfer or remittance of funds.

Foreign investment review agencies. Agencies which review foreign investments to ensure that they benefit the local economy.

Foreign Sales Corporation Act. Legislation designed to allow US exporters to establish overseas affiliates and not pay taxes on the affiliates' income until the earnings are remitted to the parent company.

Foreign trade zones. Areas where foreign goods may be held and processed and then re-exported without incurring customs duties (same as a free trade zone).

Forward exchange contract. A legally binding agreement between a firm and a bank that calls for the delivery of foreign currency at a specific exchange rate on a predetermined future date.

Forward integration. The purchase of assets or facilities that move the company closer to the customer such as a computer manufacturer that acquires a retail chain which specializes in computer products.

Forward rate. The rate quoted for the delivery of foreign currency at a predetermined future date such as 90 days from now.

Free trade area. An economic integration arrangement in which barriers to trade (such as tariffs) among member countries are removed.

Free Trade Area of the Americas (FTAA). A regional trade agreement that is expected to succeed NAFTA and include 34 countries across North, Central, and South America.

Free trade zone. A designated area where importers can defer payment of customs duty while further processing of products takes place (same as a foreign trade zone).

Fronting loan. A funds positioning strategy that involves having a third party manage the loan.

Funds positioning techniques. Strategies used to move monies from one multinational operation to another.

Gaijin. A Japanese word which means "outsider"; it is used to refer to foreigners doing business in Japan.

Gairojin. A Japanese person who leaves his or her company to work for a foreign firm.

General Agreement on Tariffs and Trade (GATT). A major trade organization that has been established to negotiate trade concessions among member countries.

Geocentric predisposition. The tendency of a multinational to construct its strategic plan with a global view of operations.

Geocentric solution. An approach to determining parent–subsidiary relations; it involves handling financial planning and controlling decisions on a global basis.

Global area structure. An organizational arrangement in which primary operational responsibility is delegated to area managers, each of whom is responsible for a specific geographic region.

Global functional structure. An organizational arrangement in which all areas of activity are built around the basic tasks of the enterprise.

Global product structure. An organizational arrangement in which domestic divisions are given worldwide responsibility for product groups.

Global sourcing. The use of suppliers anywhere in the world, chosen on the basis of their efficiency.

Globalization. The production and distribution of products and services of a homogeneous type and quality on a worldwide basis.

Hardship allowance. A special payment made to individuals posted to geographic areas regarded as less desirable.

Heckscher–Ohlin theory. A trade theory that extends the concept of comparative advantage by bringing into consideration the endowment and cost of factors of production and helps to explain why nations with relatively large labor forces will concentrate on producing labor-intensive goods, whereas countries with relatively more capital than labor will specialize in capital-intensive goods.

Hedge. A form of protection used against an adverse movement of an exchange rate.

Home country nationals. Citizens of the country where the multinational resides.

Horizontal integration. The purchase of firms in the same line of business such as a computer chip firm which acquires a competitor.

Host country nationals. Local people hired by a multinational.

Ideology. A set of integrated beliefs, theories, and doctrines that helps to direct the actions of a society.

Import tariff. A tax levied on goods shipped into a country.

Imports. Goods and services produced in one country and bought in another country.

Indigenization laws. Laws which require that nationals hold a majority interest in all enterprises.

Individualism. The tendency of people to look after themselves and their immediate family only.

Industrial democracy. The legally mandated right of employees to participate in significant management decisions.

Initial screening. The process of determining the basic need potential of the multinational's goods and services in foreign markets.

Integrative techniques. Strategies designed to help a multinational become a part of the host country's infrastructure.

Intermodal containers. Large metal boxes that fit on trucks, railroads, and airplanes and help to reduce handling cost and theft losses by placing the merchandise in an easy-to-move unit that is tightly sealed.

Internal economies of scale. Efficiencies brought about by lower production costs and other savings within a firm.

International Bank for Reconstruction and Development. (See World Bank.)

International business. The study of transactions taking place across national borders for the purpose of satisfying the needs of individuals and organizations.

International division structure. An organizational arrangement in which all international operations are centralized in one division.

International finance. An area of study concerned with the balance of payments (BOP) and the international monetary system.

International Fisher effect (IFE). An international finance theory which holds that the interest rate differential between two countries is an unbiased predictor of future changes in the spot exchange rate.

International human resource management (IHRM). The process of selecting, training, developing, and compensating personnel in overseas positions.

International joint venture (IJV). An agreement between two or more partners to own and control an overseas business.

International logistics. The designing and managing of a system to control the flow of materials and products throughout the organization.

International market assessment. An evaluation of the goods and services that the multinational can sell in the global marketplace.

International marketing. The process of identifying the goods and services that customers outside the home country want and then providing them at the right price and place.

International Monetary Fund (IMF). An agency that seeks to maintain balance-of-payments stability in the international financial system.

International monetary system. The multinational arrangement among the central banks of those countries that belong to the International Monetary Fund.

International product life cycle theory (IPLC). A theory of the stages of production of a product with new "know-how"; it is first produced by the parent firm, then by its foreign subsidiaries, and finally anywhere in the world where costs are the lowest; it helps to explain why a product that begins as a nation's export often ends up as an import.

International screening criteria. Factors used to identify individuals regarded as most suitable for overseas assignments.

International trade. The branch of economics concerned with the exchange of goods and services with foreign countries.

Internationalization. The process by which a company enters a foreign market.

Investment Canada Act (ICA). An act designed to create a welcome climate for foreign investment by significantly loosening previous restrictions.

Japan External Trade Organization (JETRO). A non-profit, government-supported organization dedicated to the promotion of mutually beneficial trade between Japan and other nations.

Just-in-time inventory. The delivery of parts and supplies just as they are needed.

***Kaizen*.** A Japanese term which means continuous improvement.

***Keiretsu*.** A Japanese term for a business group consisting of a host of companies and banks linked together through ownership and/or joint ventures.

Kinesics. A form of non-verbal communication which deals with conveying information through the use of body movement and facial expression.

Lag strategy. A hedging strategy that calls for delaying the receipt of foreign currency payment if this foreign currency is expected to strengthen, and delaying foreign currency payables when the local currency is expected to weaken.

Large Retail Store Law. A Japanese law that limits the size of retail stores and requires that local competitors approve the opening of any facility that is more than 500 square meters.

Latin American Integration Association (LAIA). A free trade group formed to reduce intraregional trade barriers and to promote regional economic cooperation. Argentina, Bolivia, Brazil, Chile, Colombia, Ecuador, Mexico, Paraguay, Peru, Uruguay, and Venezuela are all members.

Lead strategy. A hedging strategy that calls for collecting foreign currency receivables before they are due if the currency is expected to weaken, and paying foreign currency payables before they are due if the currency is expected to strengthen.

Leontief paradox. A finding by Wassily Leontief, a Nobel prize economist, which shows that the US, surprisingly, exports relatively more labor-intensive goods and imports capital-intensive goods.

License. A contractual arrangement in which one firm (the licensor) provides access to some of its patents, trademarks, or technology to another firm in exchange for a fee or royalty.

Licensee. A firm given access to some of the patents, trademarks, or technology of another firm in exchange for a fee or royalty.

Licensing agreement. An arrangement whereby one firm gives another firm the right to use certain assets such as trademarks, patents, or copyrights in exchange for a fee.

Licensor. A company that provides access to some of its patents, trademarks, or technology to another firm in exchange for a fee or royalty.

Lighter aboard ship (LASH) vessel. Barges stored on a ship and lowered at the point of destination.

Localization of production. The manufacturing of goods in the host market.

Localization of profits. The reinvestment of earnings in the local market.

London Inter-Bank Offered Rate (LIBOR). The interest rate banks charge one another on Eurocurrency loans.

Macro political risk. A risk that affects all foreign enterprises in the same way.

Managerial development. The process by which managers obtain the necessary skills, experience, and attitudes that they need to become or remain successful leaders.

Manners. Behaviors regarded as appropriate in a particular society.

Maquiladora industry. A free trade zone that has sprung up along the US–Mexican border for the purpose of producing goods and then shipping them between the two countries.

Maquiladoras. (Also see *Twin factories.*) Production operations set up on both sides of the US–Mexican border in a free trade zone for the purpose of shipping goods between the two countries.

Market coordination infrastructure. An infrastructure used by firms that compete in similar national markets but do little resource sharing among their businesses.

Market-driven economy. An economy in which goods and services are allocated on the basis of consumer demand.

Market growth. The annual increase in sales in a particular market.

Market indicators. Indicators used for measuring the relative market strengths of various geographic areas.

Market intensity. The richness of a market or the degree of purchasing power in one country as compared with others.

Market size. An economic screening consideration used in international marketing; it is the relative size of each market as a percentage of the total world market.

Masculinity. The degree to which the dominant values of a society are success, money, and material things.

Material culture. Culture which consists of objects that people make.

Material goods. Objects made by people.

Materials handling. The careful planning of when, where, and how much inventory will be available to ensure maximum production efficiency.

Matrix structure. An organizational arrangement that blends two organizational responsibilities such as functional and product structures or regional and product structures.

Mercantilism. A trade theory which holds that a government can improve the economic well-being of the country by encouraging exports and stifling imports.

Merchandise trade. A balance-of-payments account that reports imports of goods from foreign sources and exports of goods to foreign destinations.

Mercosur. A subregional free trade group formed to promote economic cooperation; the group consists of Argentina, Brazil, Paraguay, and Uruguay.

Micro political risk. A risk that affects selected sectors of the economy or specific foreign businesses.

Ministry of International Trade and Industry (MITI). A Japanese ministry charged with providing information about foreign markets and with encouraging investment in select industries and, in the process, helping to direct the economy.

Mixed economies. Economic systems characterized by a combination of market and centrally driven planning.

Mixed structure. A hybrid organization design that combines structural arrangements in a way that best meets the needs of the enterprise.

Modular integrated robotized system (MIRB). A software-based production process that relies entirely on robots.

Modular manufacturing. A manufacturing process that consists of modules that can be easily adapted to fit changing demand.

Monetary exchange rate. The price of one currency stated in terms of another currency.

Multilateral netting. The process of determining the net amount of money owed to subsidiaries through multilateral transactions.

Multinational enterprise (MNE). A company headquartered in one country but having operations in other countries.

National responsiveness. The ability of MNEs to understand different consumer tastes in segmented regional markets and to respond to different national standards and regulations imposed by autonomous governments and agencies.

Nationalization. A process by which the government takes control of business assets, sometimes with remuneration of the owners and other times without such remuneration.

Neutral culture. A culture in which emotions are held in check.

Nominal rate of interest. The interest rate charged to a borrower; it is called the "money" rate of interest to distinguish it from the "real" rate.

Non-governmental organizations (NGOs). Non-profit organizations that act to advance diverse social interests. (See also Civil Society.)

Non-tariff barriers. Rules, regulations, and bureaucratic red tape that delay or preclude the purchase of foreign goods.

North American Free Trade Agreement (NAFTA). A regional free trade agreement between Canada, the US, and Mexico.

Organization for European Economic Cooperation. A group established to administer the Marshall plan and to help with the reconstruction of Europe after World War II. It is the predecessor of the OECD.

Organization for Economic Cooperation and Development (OECD). A group of 30 relatively wealthy member countries that facilitates a forum for the discussion of economic, social, and governance issues across the world.

Overseas Private Investment Corporation (OPIC). An organization that provides insurance of US foreign investment against blocked funds, expropriation and war, and revolution and insurrection.

Particularism. The belief that circumstances dictate how ideas and practices should be applied and something cannot be done the same everywhere.

Personal selling. A direct form of promotion used to persuade customers of a particular point of view.

Political risk. The probability that political forces will negatively affect a multinational's profit or impede the attainment of other critical business objectives.

Political union. An economic union in which there is full economic integration, unification of economic policies, and a single government.

Polycentric predisposition. The tendency of a multinational to tailor its strategic plan to meet the needs of the local culture.

Polycentric solution. An approach to determining parent–subsidiary relations; it involves treating the MNE as a holding company and decentralizing decision making to the subsidiary levels.

Portfolio investment. The purchase of financial securities in other firms for the purpose of realizing a financial gain when these marketable assets are sold.

Power distance. A cultural dimension which measures the degree to which less powerful members of organizations and institutions accept the fact that power is not distributed equally.

Practical school of international selection. A school of thought which holds that leaders can be successful in any culture because effective managerial behavior is universal.

Privatization. The process of selling government assets to private buyers.

Process mapping. A flow charting of every step that goes into producing a product.

Product managers. Managers responsible for coordinating the efforts of their people in such a way as to ensure the profitability of a particular business or product line.

Production system. A group of related activities designed to create value.

Promotion. The process of stimulating demand for a company's goods and services.

Protective and defensive techniques. Strategies designed to discourage a host country from interfering in multinational operations.

Protestant work ethic. A belief which holds that people should work hard, be industrious, and save their money.

Proxemics. A form of non-verbal communication which deals with how people use physical space to convey messages.

Purchasing power parity (PPP) theory. An international finance theory which holds that the exchange rate between two currencies will be determined by the relative purchasing power of those currencies.

Quota. A quantity limit on imported goods.

Real interest rate. The difference between the nominal interest rate and the rate of inflation.

Regiocentric predisposition. The tendency of a multinational to use a strategy that addresses both local and regional needs.

Regional managers. In a geocentric matrix, managers charged with selling products in their geographic locale.

Regression analysis. A mathematical approach to forecasting which attempts to test the explanatory power of a set of independent variables.

Repatriation. The process of returning home at the end of an overseas assignment.

Repatriation agreement. An agreement which spells out how long a person will be posted overseas and sets forth the type of job that will be given to the person upon returning.

Resource managers. In a matrix structure, managers charged with providing people for operations.

Resource-sharing infrastructure. An infrastructure used by firms that compete in dissimilar national markets but share resources such as R&D efforts and manufacturing information.

Return on investment (ROI). A percentage determined by dividing net income before taxes by total assets.

***Ringsei*.** Decision making by consensus; this process is widely used in Japan.

Roll-on-roll-off (RORO) vessels. Ocean-going ferries that can carry trucks that drive onto built-in ramps and roll off at the point of debarkation.

Scenario analysis. The formulation and analysis of events that are likely to happen; this strategic planning tool is used to help firms deal with future events.

Secular totalitarianism. A system of government in which the military controls everything and makes decisions which it deems to be in the best interests of the country.

Shinto work ethic. A belief that people should work hard at their tasks.

Single European Act (SEA). An Act passed by the EU which contains many measures to further integrate the member states, along economic and political dimensions, and which allows the Council of Ministers to pass most proposals by a majority vote, in contrast to the unanimous vote that was needed previously.

Single European market (SEM). A market consisting of all members of the EU, bound together by a single currency, a special charter, complete harmonization of social and economic policies, and a common defense policy.

Small and medium-sized enterprises (SMEs). The definition of SMEs varies according to the nation. In the US, SMEs are companies with up to 500 employees. In the EU, SMEs have between 11 and 200 employees and sales of under US $40 billion. In Japan, SMEs in industry have up to 300 employees while those in wholesale and retail have up to 150 and 50 employees respectively. Developing countries use the World Bank benchmark of 11 to 150 employees and sales of under US $5 billion.

Social infrastructure. The societal underpinnings of an economy; they consist of the country's health, housing, and educational systems.

Special drawing right (SDR). A unit of value that has been created by the IMF to replace the dollar as a reserve asset.

Specific duty. A tariff based on the number of items being shipped into a country.

Speculator. In foreign exchange markets, a person who takes an open position.

Spot rate. The rate quoted for current foreign currency transactions.

Standardized training programs. Generic programs that can be used with managers anywhere in the world.

Strategic alliance. A business relationship in which two or more companies work together to achieve a collective advantage.

Strategic business units (SBUs). Operating units with their own strategic space; they produce and sell goods and services to a market segment and have a well-defined set of competitors.

Strategic cluster. A network of businesses and supporting activities located in a specific region, where flagship firms compete globally and supporting activities are home-based.

Strategic fit. A strategic management concept which holds that an organization must align its resources in such a way as to mesh effectively with the environment.

Strategic management. Managerial actions that include strategy formulation, strategy implementation, evaluation, and control, and encompass a wide range of activities, including environmental analysis of external and internal conditions and evaluation of organizational strengths and weaknesses.

Strategic alliance or partnership. An agreement between two or more competitive multinational enterprises for the purpose of serving a global market.

Strategic planning. The process of evaluating the enterprise's environment and its internal strengths and then identifying long- and short-range activities.

Strategy formulation. The process of evaluating the enterprise's environment and its internal strengths.

Strategy implementation. The process of attaining goals by using the organizational structure to properly execute the formulated strategy.

Tailor-made training programs. Programs designed to meet the specific needs of the participants, typically including a large amount of culturally based input.

Tariff. A tax on goods shipped internationally.

Tax havens. Low-tax countries that are hospitable to business.

Theocratic totalitarianism. A system of government in which a religious group exercises total power and represses or persecutes non-orthodox factions.

Theory of absolute advantage. A trade theory which holds that, by specializing in the production of goods which they can produce more efficiently than any others, nations can increase their economic well-being.

Theory of comparative advantage. A trade theory which holds that nations should produce those goods for which they have the greatest relative advantage.

Third country nationals. Citizens of countries other than the one in which the multinational is headquartered or the one in which they are assigned to work by the multinational.

Time-to-market accelerators. Factors that help reduce bottlenecks and errors and ensure product quality and performance.

Totalitarianism. A system of government in which one individual or party maintains complete control and either refuses to recognize other parties or suppresses them.

Trade adjustment assistance. Assistance offered by the US government to US businesses and individuals harmed by competition from imports.

Trade creation. A process in which members of an economic integration group begin to focus their efforts on those goods and services for which they have a comparative advantage and start trading more extensively with each other.

Training. The process of altering employee behavior and attitudes in a way that increases the probability of goal attainment.

Transaction exposure. The risk that a firm faces when paying bills or collecting receivables in the face of changing exchange rates.

Transfer price. An internal price set by a company in intrafirm trade such as the price at which one subsidiary will sell a product to another subsidiary.

Transit tariff. A tax levied on goods passing through a country.

Transition strategies. Strategies designed to help smooth the move from foreign to domestic assignments.

Translation. The process of restating foreign financial statements in the currency of the parent company.

Translation exposure. The foreign exchange risk that a firm faces when translating foreign currency financial statements into the reporting currency of the parent company.

Transnational network structure. An organization design which helps MNCs take advantage of global economics of scale while also being responsive to local customer demands.

Trend analysis. The estimation of future demand by either extrapolating the growth over the last 3 to 5 years and assuming that this trend will continue or by using some form of average growth rate over the recent past.

Triad. The three major trading and investment blocs in the international arena: the United States, the EU, and Japan.

Twin factories. (Also see *Maquiladoras.*) Production operations set up on both sides of the US–Mexican border for the purpose of shipping goods between the two countries.

Uncertainty avoidance. The extent to which people feel threatened by ambiguous situations and have created institutions and beliefs for minimizing or avoiding those uncertainties.

Unconventional cargo vessels. Vessels used for shipping oversized and unusual cargoes.

United States–Canada Free Trade Agreement (FTA). A trade agreement that eliminates most trade restrictions (such as tariffs) between these two countries and extends national treatment to foreign investment.

Universalism. The belief that ideas and practices can be applied everywhere in the world without modification.

Unrequited transfers. A balance-of-payments account that reports transactions which do not involve repayment or performance of any service.

Value chain. The way in which primary and support activities are combined in providing goods and services and increasing profit margins.

Values. Basic convictions that people have regarding what is right and wrong, good and bad, important and unimportant.

Vertical integration. The ownership of assets involved in producing a good or service and delivering it to the final customer.

Virtual integration. A networking strategy based on cooperation within and across company boundaries. Unlike vertical integration, virtual integration does not require common ownership of all parts of the production process.

Work councils. Groups that consist of both worker and manager representatives and are charged with dealing with matters such as improving company performance, working conditions, and job security.

Working capital. The difference between current assets and current liabilities.

World Bank. A multigovernment-owned bank created to promote development projects through the use of low-interest loans.

World Trade Organization (WTO). An international organization that deals with the rules of trade among member countries. One of its most important functions is to act as a dispute-settlement mechanism.

Indexes

SUBJECT INDEX

COMPANY INDEX

NAME INDEX

IMPORTANT: READ CAREFULLY

WARNING: BY OPENING THE PACKAGE YOU AGREE TO BE BOUND BY THE TERMS OF THE LICENCE AGREEMENT BELOW.

This is a legally binding agreement between You (the user or purchaser) and Pearson Education Limited. By retaining this licence, any software media or accompanying written materials or carrying out any of the permitted activities You agree to be bound by the terms of the licence agreement below.

If You do not agree to these terms then promptly return the entire publication (this licence and all software, written materials, packaging and any other components received with it) with Your sales receipt to Your supplier for a full refund.

SINGLE USER LICENCE AGREEMENT

❒ YOU ARE PERMITTED TO:

- Use (load into temporary memory or permanent storage) a single copy of the software on only one computer at a time. If this computer is linked to a network then the software may only be installed in a manner such that it is not accessible to other machines on the network.
- Make one copy of the software solely for backup purposes or copy it to a single hard disk, provided you keep the original solely for back up purposes.
- Transfer the software from one computer to another provided that you only use it on one computer at a time.

❒ YOU MAY NOT:

- Rent or lease the software or any part of the publication.
- Copy any part of the documentation, except where specifically indicated otherwise.
- Make copies of the software, other than for backup purposes.
- Reverse engineer, decompile or disassemble the software.
- Use the software on more than one computer at a time.
- Install the software on any networked computer in a way that could allow access to it from more than one machine on the network.
- Use the software in any way not specified above without the prior written consent of Pearson Education Limited.

ONE COPY ONLY

This licence is for a single user copy of the software

PEARSON EDUCATION LIMITED RESERVES THE RIGHT TO TERMINATE THIS LICENCE BY WRITTEN NOTICE AND TO TAKE ACTION TO RECOVER ANY DAMAGES SUFFERED BY PEARSON EDUCATION LIMITED IF YOU BREACH ANY PROVISION OF THIS AGREEMENT.

Pearson Education Limited owns the software You only own the disk on which the software is supplied.

LIMITED WARRANTY

Pearson Education Limited warrants that the diskette or CD rom on which the software is supplied are free from defects in materials and workmanship under normal use for ninety (90) days from the date You receive them. This warranty is limited to You and is not transferable. Pearson Education Limited does not warrant that the functions of the software meet Your requirements or that the media is compatible with any computer system on which it is used or that the operation of the software will be unlimited or error free.

You assume responsibility for selecting the software to achieve Your intended results and for the installation of, the use of and the results obtained from the software. The entire liability of Pearson Education Limited and its suppliers and your only remedy shall be replacement of the components that do not meet this warranty free of charge.

This limited warranty is void if any damage has resulted from accident, abuse, misapplication, service or modification by someone other than Pearson Education Limited. In no event shall Pearson Education Limited or its suppliers be liable for any damages whatsoever arising out of installation of the software, even if advised of the possibility of such damages. Pearson Education Limited will not be liable for any loss or damage of any nature suffered by any party as a result of reliance upon or reproduction of or any errors in the content of the publication.

Pearson Education Limited does not limit its liability for death or personal injury caused by its negligence.

This licence agreement shall be governed by and interpreted and construed in accordance with English law.